JET AIRLINERS OF THE WORLD
1949 - 2007

including military transport, reconnaissance and surveillance types and variants.

8th edition

Edited by Barrie Towey

in collaboration with Don Schofield and Terry Smith

An AIR-BRITAIN Publication

Published in the United Kingdom by
Air-Britain (Historians) Ltd

Registered Office: Victoria House,
Stanbridge Park, Staplefield Lane,
Staplefield, West Sussex RH17 6AS
http://www.air-britain.com

Sales Department: 41 Penshurst Road, Leigh,
Tonbridge, Kent TN11 8HL
e-mail: sales@air-britain.co.uk

Membership Enquiries: I Rose Cottages,
179 Penn Road, Hazlemere, Bucks HP15 7NE

ISBN 0 85130 348 X
EAN 9 780851 303482

Printed in the United Kingdom by
Bell & Bain Ltd, 303 Burnfield Road,
Thornliebank, Glasgow G46 7UQ

VOLUME 2
Front cover:
*Cathay Pacific Boeing 747-412BCF lifts off past the
control tower at London-Heathrow on 25 August 2007.
(Ian Schofield - www.iesphotography.co.uk)*

Back cover:
Top: *Fokker F.28 Fellowship 3000RC PK-HNK of Gatari
Air Service in open storage at Jakarta-Soekarno Hatta
International, 26 October 2006. (Ray Barber)*
Centre: *Ilyushin Il-76TD EX-054 of Reem Airlines on
take-off at Kandahar, 31 August 2005. (Pete Webber)*
Bottom: *USAF Lockheed C-141A Starlifter 63-8078
arriving at Mildenhall in 1980. (Keith Sowter)*

CONTENTS

BOEING 707/720 - Line No to C/n

line no	c/n	line no	c/n	line no	c/n	line no	c/n	line no	c/n
1	17586	76	17601	151	17622	226	18154	301	18392
2	17587	77	17652	152	17918	227	18068	302	18373
3	17588	78	17623	153	17919	228	18069	303	18461
4	17589	79	17676	154	17929	229	18334	304	18419
5	17590	80	17677	155	17930	230	18383	305	18405
6	17591	81	17614	156	18017	231	18355	306	18393
7	17628	82	17615	157	18018	232	18156	307	18451
8	17629	83	17602	158	18019	233	18157	308	18394
9	17630	84	17603	159	17920	234	18158	309	18395
10	17631	85	17907	160	17921	235	18159	310	18452
11	17632	86	17678	161	17922	236	18160	311	18396
12	17633	87	17692	162	17721	237	18384	312	18397
13	17592	88	17679	163	17711	238	18356	313	18400
14	17634	89	17680	164	17712	239	18161	314	18453
15	17635	90	17718	165	18020	240	18162	315	18401
16	17636	91	17604	166	18023	241	18163	316	18402
17	17637	92	17624	167	17923	242	18164	317	18403
18	17658	93	17616	168	17924	243	18420	318	18404
19	17659	94	17722	169	17713	244	18421	319	18454
20	17593	95	17908	170	17714	245	18086	320	18406
21	17660	96	17693	171	17715	246	18240	321	18379
22	17661	97	17694	172	18041	247	18241	322	18455
23	17662	98	17605	173	18021	248	18242	323	18407
24	17663	99	17625	174	18022	249	18087	324	18380
25	17609	100	17723	175	17716	250	18165	325	18456
26	17638	101	17704	176	17717	251	18166	326	18408
27	17664	102	17695	177	18024	252	18072	327	18457
28	17665	103	17681	178	18044	253	18073	328	18460
29	17696	104	17682	179	18045	254	18243	329	18458
30	17639	105	17724	180	18025	255	18244	330	18412
31	17640	106	17719	181	18026	256	18422	331	18409
32	17666	107	17606	182	18042	257	18378	332	18579
33	17925	108	17903	183	18046	258	18248	333	18462
34	17667	109	17909	184	18047	259	18074	334	18413
35	17703	110	17617	185	18048	260	18075	335	18459
36	17641	111	17618	186	18049	261	18076	336	18580
37	17610	112	17705	187	18064	262	18249	337	18588
38	17668	113	17706	188	18043	263	18250	338	18589
39	17697	114	17905	189	18027	264	18245	339	18590
40	17926	115	17720	190	18057	265	18077	340	18587
41	17642	116	17683	191	18050	266	18411	341	18591
42	17643	117	17684	192	18056	267	18078	342	18584
43	17669	118	17626	193	18028	268	18335	343	18585
44	17698	119	17904	194	18029	269	18246	344	18582
45	17691	120	18013	195	18030	270	18336	345	18586
46	17670	121	17607	196	18065	271	18372	346	18583
47	17927	122	17608	197	18061	272	18357	347	18581
48	17671	123	17685	198	18031	273	18251	348	18693
49	17611	124	17686	199	18032	274	18247	349	18707
50	17644	125	17687	200	18055	275	18414	350	18709
51	17645	126	17619	201	18067	276	18337	351	18687
52	17646	127	17707	202	18058	277	18385	352	18710
53	17647	128	17708	203	18059	278	18079	353	18694
54	17699	129	17906	204	18062	279	18376	354	18689
55	17672	130	17910	205	18070	280	18386	355	18738
56	17612	131	17911	206	18033	281	18424	356	18690
57	18012	132	17912	207	18034	282	18415	357	18691
58	17594	133	17627	208	18066	283	18374	358	18692
59	17700	134	17928	209	18083	284	18080	359	18685
60	17701	135	17688	210	18060	285	18377	360	18686
61	17595	136	17689	211	18351	286	18387	361	18688
62	17596	137	17690	212	18084	287	18338	362	18714
63	17648	138	17620	213	18063	288	18416	363	18463
64	17702	139	17621	214	18035	289	18423	364	18715
65	17613	140	18054	215	18036	290	18425	365	18716
66	17649	141	17913	216	18071	291	18388	366	18717
67	17650	142	17914	217	18085	292	18339	367	18746
68	17597	143	18014	218	18352	293	18375	368	18718
69	17673	144	17709	219	18353	294	18389	369	18747
70	17598	145	17710	220	18037	295	18417	370	18711
71	17599	146	17915	221	18167	296	18390	371	18765
72	17651	147	17916	222	18381	297	18081	372	18766
73	17674	148	17917	223	18382	298	18082	373	18712
74	17675	149	18015	224	18354	299	18391	374	18749
75	17600	150	18016	225	18155	300	18418	375	18708

BOEING 707/720 - Line No to C/n

line no	c/n	line no	c/n	line no	c/n	line no	c/n	line no	c/n
376	18767	452	18925	528	19238	604	19339	680	19569
377	18737	453	18964	529	19265	605	19278	681	19741
378	18713	454	18927	530	19215	606	19436	682	19341
379	18748	455	18916	531	19266	607	19227	683	19841
380	18745	456	18961	532	19321	608	19515	684	19695
381	18792	457	18928	533	19324	609	19442	685	19571
382	18763	458	18954	534	19433	610	19381	686	19587
383	18756	459	19004	535	19325	611	19443	687	19572
384	18793	460	18917	536	19291	612	19516	688	19696
385	18739	461	18929	537	19350	613	19213	689	19624
386	18825	462	18918	538	19133	614	19517	690	19633
387	18757	463	19034	539	19326	615	19438	691	19706
388	18740	464	18930	540	19411	616	19518	692	19588
389	18826	465	18978	541	19267	617	19295	693	19625
390	18818	466	18956	542	19239	618	19361	694	19697
391	18758	467	18955	543	19240	619	19519	695	19634
392	18759	468	18979	544	19268	620	19362	696	19736
393	18760	469	18980	545	19315	621	19439	697	19698
394	18790	470	19160	546	19293	622	19340	698	19789
395	18761	471	18941	547	19316	623	19363	699	19699
396	18762	472	18957	548	19441	624	19523	700	19869
397	18824	473	19002	549	19248	625	19286	701	19589
398	18819	474	19003	550	19294	626	19214	702	19870
399	18764	475	18958	551	19502	627	19382	703	19626
400	18913	476	18981	552	19351	628	19364	704	19573
401	18820	477	18932	553	19355	629	19435	705	19773
402	18873	478	18959	554	19440	630	19296	706	19635
403	18832	479	18986	555	19241	631	19365	707	19627
404	18808	480	19162	556	19416	632	19529	708	19774
405	18833	481	19161	557	19317	633	19366	709	19820
406	18834	482	18931	558	19216	634	19631	710	19574
407	18809	483	18982	559	19224	635	19530	711	19871
408	18835	484	18960	560	19292	636	19297	712	19842
409	18836	485	18983	561	19322	637	19367	713	19737
410	18827	486	18987	562	19327	638	19581	714	19575
411	18837	487	18984	563	19412	639	19582	715	19760
412	18838	488	19001	564	19217	640	19368	716	19628
413	18880	489	18988	565	19328	641	19383	717	19566
414	18831	490	19185	566	19434	642	19715	718	19821
415	18914	491	19186	567	19218	643	19664	719	19576
416	18890	492	18989	568	19225	644	19716	720	19567
417	18839	493	19187	569	19219	645	19498	721	20076
418	18840	494	19163	570	19269	646	19531	722	19577
419	18841	495	18948	571	19329	647	19384	723	19963
420	18882	496	18985	572	19270	648	19369	724	20087
421	18842	497	18949	573	19220	649	19632	725	19738
422	18883	498	19104	574	19271	650	19583	726	19822
423	18828	499	19105	575	19330	651	19370	727	20088
424	18915	500	19179	576	19352	652	19621	728	20077
425	18800	501	18962	577	19221	653	19371	729	19775
426	18884	502	19106	578	19272	654	19590	730	19986
427	18829	503	19354	579	19331	655	19372	732	19636
428	18889	504	18950	580	19273	656	19373	732	19776
429	18830	505	19164	581	19413	657	19809	733	19964
430	18886	506	19188	582	19417	658	19374	734	19965
431	18887	507	19107	583	19222	659	19767	735	19843
432	18885	508	19168	584	19521	660	19622	736	19988
433	18963	509	19284	585	19226	661	19376	737	19629
434	18938	510	19209	586	19332	662	19375	738	19866
435	18923	511	19108	587	19353	663	19584	739	20008
436	18881	512	19207	588	19212	664	19810	740	19777
437	18939	513	19177	589	19333	665	19723	741	20089
438	18810	514	19208	590	19275	666	19377	742	19872
439	18940	515	19210	591	19334	667	19724	743	19966
440	18921	516	19263	592	19276	668	19585	744	19844
441	18891	517	19178	593	19335	669	19568	745	19967
442	18977	518	19211	594	19274	670	19586	746	19630
443	18953	519	19235	595	19336	671	19623	747	19997
444	18922	520	19247	596	19522	672	19378	748	19996
445	18975	521	19236	597	19414	673	19693	749	20224
446	18926	522	19320	598	19223	674	19570	750	19998
447	19000	523	19237	599	19410	675	19705	751	19969
448	18924	524	19285	600	19337	676	19740	752	20016
449	18976	525	19380	601	19415	677	19379	753	20017
450	18991	526	19323	602	19338	678	19694	754	19961
451	18937	527	19264	603	19277	679	19840	755	19962

BOEING 707/720 - Line No to C/n

line no	c/n	line no	c/n	line no	c/n	line no	c/n
756	19999	832	20287	908	21123	984	23428
757	20225	833	20319	909	21208	985	23429
758	20084	834	20341	910	21124	986	23889
759	20000	835	20301	911	21228	987	23890
760	20085	836	20297	912	21125	988	23891
761	20018	837	20342	913	21209	989	23892
762	19916	838	20374	914	21126	990	23893
763	19917	839	20288	915	21127	991	23894
764	20086	840	20298	916	21250	992	24500
765	19739	841	20375	917	21128	993	24109
766	20058	842	20340	918	21129	994	24501
767	20019	843	20474	919	21261	995	24502
768	20020	844	20275	920	20637	996	24110
769	20021	845	20428	921	21434	997	24504
770	20035	846	20429	922	21367	998	24505
771	20056	847	20487	923	21334	999	24506
772	20059	848	20395	924	21435	1000	24115
773	20060	849	20488	925	21368	1001	24503
774	20022	850	20494	926	21436	1002	24507
775	20023	851	20456	927	21437	1003	24116
776	20024	852	20495	928	21396	1004	24111
777	20057	853	20457	929	21428	1005	24508
778	20036	854	20517	930	21551	1006	24117
779	20097	855	20522	931	21552	1007	24112
780	20025	856	20518	932	21553	1008	24509
781	20026	857	20514	933	21554	1009	24510
782	20027	858	20519	934	21555	1010	24113
783	20028	859	20515	935	21556	1011	24114
784	20061	860	20546	936	21475	1012	24499
785	20062	861	20547	937	21752		
786	20043	862	20630	938	21651		
787	19342	863	20629	939	21753		
788	20123	864	20669	940	21754		
789	20063	865	20760	941	21956		
790	20029	866	20741	942	21755		
791	20030	867	20761	943	21756		
792	20031	868	20762	944	21757		
793	20032	869	20714	945	22855		
794	19343	870	20715	946	22829		
795	20170	871	20763	947	22838		
796	20171	872	20718	948	22830		
797	20033	873	20719	949	22839		
798	20034	874	20720	950	22831		
799	20064	875	20721	951	22832		
800	20110	876	20830	952	22833		
801	19344	877	20722	953	22840		
802	20065	878	20803	954	22841		
803	20136	879	20723	955	22842		
804	20172	880	20716	956	22843		
805	20173	881	20831	957	22844		
806	20124	882	20717	958	22834		
807	20122	883	20804	959	22845		
808	20174	884	20805	960	22835		
809	19845	885	20897	961	22846		
810	20066	886	20832	962	22836		
811	20175	887	20898	963	22847		
812	20067	888	20919	964	22848		
813	20198	889	20889	965	22837		
814	20068	890	20833	966	22849		
815	20069	891	20890	967	22850		
816	20199	892	20891	968	22851		
817	20176	893	20920	969	22852		
818	20177	894	20834	970	22853		
819	20230	895	20835	971	22854		
820	20178	896	21049	972	23417		
821	20179	897	21070	973	23418		
822	20259	898	20615	974	23419		
823	20260	899	21092	975	23422		
824	20315	900	21096	976	23420		
825	20316	901	21046	977	23423		
826	20317	902	21047	978	23424		
827	20261	903	21081	979	23425		
828	20200	904	21185	980	23421		
829	20318	905	21103	981	23426		
830	20262	906	21104	982	23427		
831	20283	907	21207	983	23430		

BOEING 717 - Line No to C/n

line no	c/n	line no	c/n	line no	c/n
5001	55000	5076	55026	5151	55191
5002	55001	5077	55092	5152	55192
5003	55002	5078	55154	5153	55193
5004	55003	5079	55128	5154	55194
5005	55004	5080	55129	5155	55098
5006	55005	5081	55027	5156	55099
5007	55006	5082	55028		
5008	55007	5083	55093		
5009	55008	5084	55094		
5010	55009	5085	55152		
5011	55010	5086	55155		
5012	55011	5087	55095		
5013	55054	5088	55134		
5014	55055	5089	55130		
5015	55056	5090	55135		
5016	55053	5091	55029		
5017	55058	5092	55131		
5018	55012	5093	55096		
5019	55069	5094	55030		
5020	55057	5095	55097		
5021	55013	5096	55031		
5022	55070	5097	55032		
5023	55059	5098	55132		
5024	55071	5099	55033		
5025	55072	5100	55136		
5026	55060	5101	55034		
5027	55014	5102	55035		
5028	55073	5103	55137		
5029	55061	5104	55138		
5030	55074	5105	55139		
5031	55062	5106	55036		
5032	55075	5107	55140		
5033	55015	5108	55037		
5034	55063	5109	55038		
5035	55076	5110	55141		
5036	55016	5111	55039		
5037	55064	5112	55142		
5038	55077	5113	55040		
5039	55078	5114	55041		
5040	55017	5115	55042		
5041	55151	5116	55166		
5042	55079	5117	55167		
5043	55080	5118	55168		
5044	55018	5119	55169		
5045	55081	5120	55170		
5046	55082	5121	55171		
5047	55019	5122	55172		
5048	55065	5123	55173		
5049	55083	5124	55174		
5050	55121	5125	55175		
5051	55020	5126	55176		
5052	55084	5127	55177		
5053	55118	5128	55178		
5054	55066	5129	55179		
5055	55085	5130	55195		
5056	55086	5131	55043		
5057	55021	5132	55196		
5058	55022	5133	55180		
5059	55067	5134	55044		
5060	55087	5135	55181		
5061	55122	5136	55045		
5062	55023	5137	55046		
5063	55088	5138	55182		
5064	55123	5139	55047		
5065	55068	5140	55183		
5066	55024	5141	55048		
5067	55089	5142	55184		
5068	55090	5143	55049		
5069	55124	5144	55050		
5070	55125	5145	55185		
5071	55025	5146	55186		
5072	55153	5147	55187		
5073	55126	5148	55051		
5074	55127	5149	55190		
5075	55091	5150	55052		

BOEING 727 - Line No to C/n

line no	c/n	line no	c/n	line no	c/n	line no	c/n	line no	c/n
1	18293	76	18752	151	18900	226	18877	301	19135
2	18464	77	18315	152	18904	227	18863	302	19095
3	18294	78	18743	153	18901	228	19132	303	19166
4	18295	79	18270	154	18329	229	18970	303	19287
5	18296	80	18316	155	18283	230	18971	304	19249
6	18297	81	18742	156	18330	231	18864	305	19096
7	18298	82	18271	157	18893	232	18865	306	18952
8	18252	83	18753	158	18331	233	18996	307	19097
9	18299	84	18754	159	18910	234	18935	308	19173
10	18300	85	18811	160	18905	235	18997	309	19391
11	18253	86	18744	161	18284	236	18878	310	19113
12	18301	87	18755	162	18804	237	18951	311	19385
13	18254	88	18317	163	18919	238	18990	312	19114
14	18255	89	18272	164	18332	239	18998	313	19250
15	18426	90	18797	165	18791	240	18999	314	19136
16	18256	91	18273	166	18874	241	18866	315	19251
17	18257	92	18812	167	18911	242	18972	316	19137
18	18427	93	18798	168	18894	243	19127	317	19392
19	18302	94	18813	169	18912	244	18898	318	19098
20	18258	95	18318	170	18843	245	18973	319	19122
21	18428	96	18274	171	18844	246	19138	320	19169
22	18303	97	18441	172	18285	247	18867	321	19386
23	18304	98	18366	173	18895	248	18868	322	19099
24	18360	99	18794	174	18920	249	18936	323	19172
25	18259	100	18814	175	18845	250	19089	324	19100
26	18429	101	18275	176	18906	251	19180	325	19167
27	18305	102	18799	177	18848	252	18974	326	19174
28	18361	103	18276	178	18849	253	18869	327	19252
29	18260	104	18795	179	18805	254	18879	328	19115
30	18261	105	18442	180	18850	255	19139	329	19387
31	18430	106	18815	181	18851	256	18899	330	19116
32	18431	107	18277	182	18286	257	19005	331	19255
33	18362	108	18796	183	18846	258	18870	332	19170
34	18306	109	18367	184	18896	259	18871	333	19101
35	18363	110	18319	185	18933	260	19242	334	19123
36	18569	111	18443	186	18852	261	18872	335	19298
37	18364	112	18816	187	18847	262	19006	336	19102
38	18307	113	18278	188	18806	263	18945	337	19084
39	18570	114	18444	189	18853	264	19121	338	19244
40	18308	115	18445	190	18287	265	19181	339	19175
41	18262	116	18800	191	18854	266	19182	340	19388
42	18571	117	18368	192	18288	267	19183	341	19103
43	18432	118	18817	193	18807	268	19079	342	19245
44	18433	119	18320	194	18289	269	19007	343	19389
45	18263	120	18801	195	18855	270	19080	344	19299
46	18572	121	18279	196	19128	271	19109	345	19398
47	18309	122	18321	197	19129	272	19035	346	19300
48	18310	123	18446	198	18942	273	19243	347	19124
49	18573	124	18821	199	18856	274	18946	348	19318
50	18434	125	18369	200	18857	275	19081	349	19085
51	18435	126	18822	201	18290	276	19171	350	19390
52	18365	127	18447	202	18875	277	19090	351	19228
53	18264	128	18802	203	18943	278	19036	352	19301
54	18265	129	18280	204	18291	279	19082	353	19086
55	18311	130	18322	205	18965	280	19091	354	19302
56	18574	131	18448	206	18992	281	19083	355	19256
57	18575	132	18449	207	18858	282	19184	356	19356
58	18436	133	18908	208	18859	283	19110	357	19303
59	18437	134	18370	209	18944	284	19037	358	19428
60	18312	135	18823	210	18860	285	19038	359	19087
61	18266	136	18823	211	18897	286	18947	360	19357
62	18267	137	18803	212	18861	287	19304	361	19125
63	18576	138	18902	213	19130	288	19279	362	19429
64	18577	139	18324	214	18966	289	19134	363	19126
65	18438	140	18450	215	18993	290	19176	364	19008
66	18313	141	18325	216	18862	291	19092	365	19088
67	18439	142	18326	217	18876	292	19165	366	19430
68	18578	143	18281	218	19131	293	19093	367	19358
69	18440	144	18327	219	18994	294	19206	368	19359
70	18750	145	18371	220	18967	295	19094	369	19140
71	18268	146	18328	221	18995	296	19253	370	19141
72	18741	147	18903	222	18934	297	19111	371	19360
73	18314	148	18892	223	18968	298	19254	372	19431
74	18269	149	18282	224	18907	299	19112	373	19280
75	18751	150	18909	225	18969	300	19305	374	19009

BOEING 727 - Line No to C/n

line no	c/n	line no	c/n	line no	c/n	line no	c/n	line no	c/n
375	19427	451	19145	526	19992	601	19564	676	19914
376	19117	452	19146	527	19827	602	19490	677	19701
377	19620	453	19501	528	19558	603	19565	678	20004
378	19281	454	19534	529	19868	604	19873	679	20048
379	19118	455	19445	530	19459	605	20046	680	19702
380	19399	456	19535	531	19460	606	19473	681	19915
381	19432	457	19508	532	19812	607	19474	682	19861
382	19010	458	19233	533	19477	608	19798	683	19976
384	19404	459	19509	534	19874	609	19828	684	19703
385	19257	460	19527	535	19478	610	19689	685	19862
386	19191	461	19618	536	19728	611	19491	686	20078
387	19011	462	19818	537	19817	612	19799	687	20005
388	19192	463	19234	538	19461	613	20139	688	20006
389	19288	464	19450	539	19462	614	19899	689	19704
390	19229	465	19528	540	19690	615	19808	690	19977
391	19012	466	19520	541	19543	616	19800	691	19863
392	19193	467	19595	542	19839	617	19801	692	19978
393	19119	468	19717	543	19805	618	19900	693	20049
394	19194	469	19532	544	19479	619	20143	694	20050
395	19310	470	19619	545	19480	620	19901	695	20111
396	19120	471	19446	546	19826	621	19802	696	19864
397	19258	472	19147	547	19806	622	19902	697	19979
398	19405	473	19148	548	19481	623	19803	698	20180
399	19311	474	19718	549	19993	624	19804	699	20181
400	19400	475	19533	550	19559	625	20217	700	20112
401	19393	476	19665	551	19838	626	20042	701	20037
402	19230	477	19447	552	19463	627	19903	702	20182
403	19289	478	19719	553	19464	628	19854	703	19865
404	19231	479	19596	554	19465	629	19829	704	20075
405	19557	480	19666	555	19846	630	19890	705	20183
406	19195	481	19149	556	19685	631	19891	706	19980
407	19196	482	19720	557	19482	632	19855	707	20184
408	19259	483	19451	558	19483	633	19830	708	20051
409	19312	484	19662	559	19859	634	19987	709	20052
410	19197	485	19150	560	19484	635	19856	710	20185
411	19313	486	19833	561	19466	636	19831	711	20113
412	19260	487	19691	562	19544	637	19904	712	20114
413	19198	488	19683	563	19537	638	20140	713	20053
414	19199	488	19721	564	19545	639	19905	714	20161
415	19402	489	19834	565	19560	640	19892	715	20162
416	19200	491	19663	566	19467	641	19857	716	20038
417	19290	492	19452	567	19468	642	19832	717	20240
418	19394	493	19722	568	19469	643	19893	718	20054
419	19401	494	19836	569	19470	644	19906	719	20055
420	19503	495	19282	570	19686	645	19858	720	20039
421	19201	496	19448	571	19485	646	20243	721	20186
422	19261	497	19850	572	19546	647	19894	722	20187
423	19246	498	19692	573	19607	648	19970	723	20163
424	19202	499	19837	574	19561	649	20141	724	20164
425	19232	500	19449	575	19807	650	20244	725	20165
426	19262	501	19835	576	19562	651	19907	726	20241
427	19504	502	19283	577	19510	652	19492	727	20166
428	19524	503	19684	578	19486	653	19908	728	20167
429	19497	504	19151	579	19487	654	19994	729	20040
430	19406	505	19816	580	19538	655	19971	730	20188
431	19395	506	19453	581	19511	656	19909	731	20098
432	19505	507	19152	582	19512	657	19493	732	20041
433	19536	508	19153	583	19539	658	19895	733	20189
434	19203	509	19454	584	19540	659	19910	734	20099
435	19403	510	19851	585	19541	660	19968	735	20115
436	19204	511	19475	586	19542	661	19494	736	19981
437	19314	512	19154	587	19563	662	19972	737	19982
438	19205	513	19455	588	19488	663	20245	738	20190
439	19525	514	19867	589	19688	664	19495	739	20191
440	19142	515	19456	590	19471	665	19973	740	20168
441	19319	516	19819	591	19472	666	19995	741	19983
442	19526	517	19852	592	20044	667	19974	742	20144
443	19815	518	19457	593	19489	668	19911	743	20169
444	19499	519	19793	594	19813	669	19496	744	19984
445	19444	520	19811	595	19513	670	19912	745	19985
446	19143	521	19991	596	20045	671	20003	746	20289
447	19506	522	19853	597	19514	672	19913	747	20290
448	19500	523	19476	598	19797	673	19700	748	20279
449	19507	524	19597	599	19860	674	19975	749	20145
450	19144	525	19458	600	19814	675	20047	750	20263

BOEING 727 - Line No to C/n

line no	c/n	line no	c/n	line no	c/n	line no	c/n	line no	c/n
751	20146	826	20421	901	20618	976	20737	1051	20896
752	20192	827	20432	902	20619	977	20738	1052	20946
753	20291	828	20366	903	20620	978	20658	1053	20863
754	20292	829	20426	904	20621	979	20659	1054	20551
755	20193	830	20430	905	20595	980	20745	1055	20885
756	20264	831	20383	906	20552	981	20746	1056	20555
757	20293	832	20367	907	20548	982	20772	1057	20874
758	20265	833	20415	908	20596	983	20773	1058	20901
759	20294	834	20416	909	20597	984	20765	1059	20902
760	20266	835	20441	910	20598	985	20660	1060	20864
761	20248	836	20442	911	20599	986	20780	1061	20886
762	20267	837	20443	912	20600	987	20747	1062	20865
763	20249	838	20433	913	20601	988	20748	1063	20843
764	20268	839	20444	914	20602	989	20549	1064	20661
765	20201	840	20445	915	20603	990	20749	1065	20844
766	20228	841	20446	916	20604	991	20553	1066	20845
767	20147	842	20434	917	20634	992	20750	1067	20866
768	20278	843	20447	918	20635	993	20766	1068	20867
769	20148	844	20448	919	20636	994	20823	1069	20932
770	20149	845	20409	920	20637	995	20824	1070	20947
771	20150	846	20410	921	20605	996	20822	1071	20933
772	20295	847	20411	922	20673	997	20774	1072	20662
773	20151	848	20471	923	20674	998	20775	1073	20663
774	20202	849	20468	924	20675	999	20787	1074	20934
775	20152	850	20472	925	20676	1000	20751	1075	20955
776	20203	851	20431	926	20638	1001	20752	1076	20935
777	20296	852	20469	927	20639	1002	20757	1077	20974
778	20204	853	20470	928	20612	1003	20811	1078	20936
779	20153	854	20475	929	20613	1004	20812	1079	20664
780	20154	855	20473	930	20654	1005	20813	1080	20975
781	20250	856	20489	931	20678	1006	20814	1081	20950
782	20251	857	20476	932	20677	1007	20815	1082	21021
783	20252	858	20512	933	20622	1008	20816	1083	20978
784	20343	859	20460	934	20655	1009	20817	1084	20948
785	20232	860	20461	935	20640	1010	20818	1085	20980
786	20233	861	20513	936	20641	1011	20788	1086	20981
787	20435	862	20462	937	20606	1012	20753	1087	20982
788	20436	863	20490	938	20656	1013	20754	1088	20983
789	20302	864	20491	939	20623	1014	20755	1089	20903
790	20234	865	20466	940	20624	1015	20789	1090	20904
791	20306	866	20467	941	20625	1016	20837	1091	20905
792	20307	867	20509	942	20679	1017	20838	1092	20906
793	20303	868	20285	943	20607	1018	20819	1093	20918
794	20384	869	20533	944	20642	1019	20820	1094	21037
795	20308	870	20525	945	20705	1020	20875	1095	21018
796	20309	871	20526	946	20626	1021	20790	1096	20972
797	20327	872	20538	947	20627	1022	20791	1097	21019
798	20437	873	20539	948	20628	1023	20792	1098	20979
799	20438	874	20540	949	20706	1024	20868	1099	20973
800	20385	875	20286	950	20709	1025	20869	1100	21010
801	20386	876	20510	951	20643	1026	20876	1101	20951
802	20310	877	20545	952	20739	1027	20554	1102	21020
803	20422	878	20568	953	20707	1028	20756	1103	20937
804	20387	879	20569	954	20724	1029	20877	1104	21041
805	20388	880	20570	955	20729	1030	20550	1105	20938
806	20328	881	20572	956	20730	1031	20839	1106	21042
807	20463	882	20592	957	20731	1032	20870	1107	21068
808	20304	883	20593	958	20725	1033	20879	1108	21050
809	20464	884	20571	959	20644	1034	20878	1109	21051
810	20423	885	20594	960	20764	1035	20821	1110	21052
811	20392	886	20579	961	20645	1036	20840	1111	21053
812	20418	887	20560	962	20726	1037	20880	1112	20939
813	20393	888	20573	963	20732	1038	20860	1113	21043
814	20465	889	20580	964	20733	1039	20871	1114	21078
815	20419	890	20581	965	20734	1040	20872	1115	21060
816	20394	891	20608	966	20727	1041	20861	1116	21061
817	20424	892	20609	967	20646	1042	20862	1117	21055
818	20379	893	20610	968	20647	1043	20873	1118	21038
819	20420	894	20611	969	20728	1044	20930	1119	21039
820	20380	895	20648	970	20657	1045	20931	1120	20940
821	20370	896	20649	971	20743	1046	20899	1121	20984
822	20371	897	20614	972	20744	1047	20894	1122	21056
823	20381	898	20615	973	20735	1048	20945	1123	20985
824	20425	899	20616	974	20736	1049	20895	1124	21082
825	20382	900	20617	975	20710	1050	20900	1125	20986

BOEING 727 - Line No to C/n

line no	c/n	line no	c/n	line no	c/n	line no	c/n	line no	c/n
1126	20987	1201	21244	1276	21370	1351	21413	1426	21608
1127	21062	1202	21245	1277	21371	1352	21480	1427	21689
1128	20941	1203	21199	1278	21372	1353	21463	1428	21566
1129	21036	1204	21210	1279	21373	1354	21414	1429	21637
1130	20942	1205	21222	1280	21374	1355	21464	1430	21567
1131	21079	1206	21200	1281	21394	1356	21415	1431	21622
1132	21044	1207	21223	1282	21347	1357	21479	1432	21568
1133	21045	1208	21232	1283	21395	1358	21314	1433	21623
1134	21091	1209	21234	1284	21323	1359	21510	1434	21646
1135	21057	1210	21235	1285	21426	1360	21315	1435	21580
1136	21058	1211	21233	1286	21324	1361	21390	1436	21647
1137	21059	1212	21256	1287	21348	1362	21484	1437	21581
1138	21074	1213	21229	1288	21325	1363	21465	1438	21663
1139	21075	1214	21257	1289	21349	1364	21485	1439	21511
1140	21076	1215	21230	1290	21375	1365	21513	1440	21492
1141	20988	1216	21246	1291	21427	1366	21416	1441	21569
1142	21040	1217	21247	1292	21308	1367	21391	1442	21493
1143	21071	1218	21248	1293	21376	1368	21417	1443	21570
1144	20989	1219	21249	1294	21309	1369	21609	1444	21529
1145	21072	1220	21201	1295	21377	1370	21418	1445	21571
1146	21080	1221	21202	1296	21398	1371	21539	1446	21530
1147	21077	1222	21260	1297	21378	1372	21466	1447	21572
1148	21100	1223	21258	1298	21310	1373	21494	1448	21664
1149	20665	1224	21259	1299	21379	1374	21430	1449	21573
1150	21101	1225	21264	1300	21311	1375	21419	1450	21531
1151	20666	1226	21265	1301	21438	1376	21431	1451	21574
1152	21102	1227	21266	1302	21457	1377	21420	1452	21655
1153	20667	1228	21267	1303	21399	1378	21474	1453	21532
1154	20668	1229	21268	1304	21382	1379	21577	1454	21628
1155	21142	1230	21269	1305	21392	1380	21610	1455	21656
1156	21143	1231	21270	1306	21449	1381	21432	1456	21629
1157	21144	1232	21171	1307	21393	1382	21611	1457	21638
1158	21105	1233	21284	1308	21450	1383	21421	1458	21630
1159	21145	1234	21288	1309	21400	1384	21433	1459	21519
1160	21106	1235	21289	1310	21451	1385	21422	1460	21631
1161	21146	1236	21297	1311	21401	1386	21540	1461	21520
1162	21147	1237	21178	1312	21452	1387	21423	1462	21632
1163	21148	1238	21290	1313	21402	1388	21488	1463	21521
1164	21149	1239	21291	1314	21453	1389	21603	1464	21633
1165	21150	1240	21292	1315	21403	1390	21489	1465	21522
1166	21151	1241	21293	1316	21455	1391	21505	1466	21634
1167	21118	1242	21271	1317	21503	1392	21506	1467	21523
1168	21154	1243	21272	1318	21456	1393	21424	1468	21624
1169	21155	1244	21273	1319	21504	1394	21661	1469	21690
1170	21156	1245	21274	1320	21343	1395	21425	1470	21625
1171	21179	1246	21298	1321	21404	1396	21490	1471	21697
1172	21107	1247	21299	1322	21344	1397	21557	1472	21626
1173	21157	1248	21086	1323	21405	1398	21409	1473	21524
1174	21108	1249	21327	1324	21383	1399	21558	1474	21698
1175	21119	1250	21087	1325	21406	1400	21470	1475	21525
1176	21113	1251	21328	1326	21442	1401	21559	1476	21526
1177	21158	1252	21318	1327	21458	1402	21491	1477	21527
1178	21114	1253	21341	1328	21384	1403	21495	1478	21584
1179	21159	1254	21329	1329	21459	1404	21618	1479	21585
1180	21160	1255	21088	1330	21312	1405	21560	1480	21691
1181	21161	1256	21342	1331	21385	1406	21595	1481	21695
1182	21152	1257	21332	1332	21407	1407	21619	1482	21692
1183	21153	1258	21363	1333	21386	1408	21561	1483	21696
1184	20990	1259	21333	1334	21408	1409	21578	1484	21669
1185	20991	1260	21330	1335	21387	1410	21562	1485	21699
1186	21197	1261	21364	1336	21409	1411	21471	1486	21670
1187	20992	1262	21303	1337	21461	1412	21579	1487	21777
1188	21203	1263	21089	1338	21481	1413	21472	1488	21586
1189	20993	1264	21304	1339	21502	1414	21636	1489	21700
1190	20994	1265	21322	1340	21460	1415	21688	1490	21778
1191	21198	1266	21331	1341	21482	1416	21617	1491	21741
1192	20995	1267	21090	1342	21462	1417	21676	1492	21587
1193	20996	1268	21305	1343	21512	1418	21563	1493	21701
1194	21204	1269	21319	1344	21410	1419	21620	1494	21949
1195	20997	1270	21306	1345	21388	1420	21564	1495	21788
1196	21242	1271	21320	1346	21411	1421	21662	1496	21789
1197	21243	1272	21307	1347	21313	1422	21582	1497	21836
1198	21205	1273	21365	1348	21412	1423	21583	1498	21779
1199	21084	1274	21366	1349	21389	1424	21565	1499	21780
1200	21085	1275	21369	1350	21483	1425	21621	1500	21892

BOEING 727 - Line No to C/n

line no	c/n	line no	c/n	line no	c/n	line no	c/n	line no	c/n
1501	21781	1576	21985	1651	22005	1726	22491	1801	22765
1502	21945	1577	21998	1652	22359	1727	22608	1802	22982
1503	21893	1578	22035	1653	22011	1728	22413	1803	22623
1504	21946	1579	21950	1654	22344	1729	22492	1804	22992
1505	21894	1580	21986	1655	22012	1730	22532	1805	22825
1506	21947	1581	21999	1656	22076	1731	22609	1806	22983
1507	21895	1582	21987	1657	22362	1732	22603	1807	22770
1508	21930	1583	22000	1658	22432	1733	22574	1808	22993
1509	21826	1584	22019	1659	22013	1734	22548	1809	22263
1510	21948	1585	22001	1660	22068	1735	22163	1810	22998
1511	21896	1586	21988	1661	22069	1736	22533	1811	22999
1512	21842	1587	22108	1662	22372	1737	22549	1812	22606
1513	21897	1588	22079	1663	22014	1738	22534	1813	22984
1514	21742	1589	22109	1664	22373	1739	22550	1814	22702
1515	21898	1590	21989	1665	22085	1740	22448	1815	22968
1516	21953	1591	21823	1666	22015	1741	22493	1816	23014
1517	21899	1592	22020	1667	22385	1742	22459	1817	23052
1518	21844	1593	21913	1668	22433	1743	22164	1818	22924
1519	21900	1594	22081	1669	22386	1744	22551	1819	22925
1520	21978	1595	21824	1670	22360	1745	22350	1820	22926
1521	21901	1596	22036	1671	22434	1746	22460	1821	22927
1522	21702	1597	21914	1672	22387	1747	22476	1822	22928
1523	21671	1598	22080	1673	21345	1748	22414	1823	22929
1524	21902	1599	22152	1674	22435	1749	22494	1824	22930
1525	21954	1600	22037	1675	21346	1750	22461	1825	22931
1526	21903	1601	22153	1676	22409	1751	22462	1826	22932
1527	21849	1602	22045	1677	22436	1752	22167	1827	22933
1528	21904	1603	22082	1678	22410	1753	22641	1828	22934
1529	21845	1604	22046	1679	21600	1754	22676	1829	22935
1530	21905	1605	22083	1680	21951	1755	22463	1830	22936
1531	21931	1606	22047	1681	22393	1756	22449	1831	22937
1532	21854	1607	22156	1682	22437	1757	22661	1832	22938
1533	21958	1608	22048	1683	22424	1758	22464		
1534	21979	1609	21915	1684	22250	1759	22642		
1535	21855	1610	22049	1685	22438	1760	22450		
1536	21850	1611	21916	1686	22262	1761	22465		
1537	21856	1612	22038	1687	22251	1762	22643		
1538	21672	1613	22110	1688	22474	1763	22466		
1539	21857	1614	22039	1689	22439	1764	22535		
1540	21971	1615	22111	1690	22475	1765	22467		
1541	21673	1616	21917	1691	22394	1766	22468		
1542	21858	1617	22021	1692	22440	1767	22451		
1543	21674	1618	22112	1693	21952	1768	22644		
1544	21859	1619	22157	1694	21601	1769	22469		
1545	21837	1620	22053	1695	22441	1770	22168		
1546	21860	1621	22146	1696	22411	1771	22470		
1547	21838	1622	22295	1697	22252	1772	22452		
1548	21906	1623	22147	1698	22425	1773	22552		
1549	21846	1624	22073	1699	22345	1774	22536		
1550	21703	1625	21918	1700	22543	1775	22553		
1551	21851	1626	22040	1701	22269	1776	22662		
1552	21813	1627	22002	1702	22253	1777	22604		
1553	21852	1628	22041	1703	22544	1778	22663		
1554	21861	1629	22003	1704	22346	1779	22537		
1555	21675	1630	22042	1705	22391	1780	22664		
1556	21814	1631	22004	1706	22091	1781	22554		
1557	21847	1632	21919	1707	22392	1782	22538		
1558	21907	1633	22377	1708	22347	1783	22555		
1559	22043	1634	21920	1709	22270	1784	22687		
1560	21908	1635	22165	1710	22287	1785	22677		
1561	22044	1636	22006	1711	22374	1786	22665		
1562	21909	1637	21972	1712	22288	1787	22605		
1563	21967	1638	22084	1713	22271	1788	22763		
1564	22017	1639	21921	1714	22348	1789	22759		
1565	21968	1640	21853	1715	22430	1790	22666		
1566	22016	1641	22268	1716	22361	1791	22621		
1567	21969	1642	22158	1717	22162	1792	22622		
1568	22052	1643	22007	1718	22092	1793	22556		
1569	21983	1644	22078	1719	22289	1794	22539		
1570	21910	1645	22154	1720	22412	1795	22557		
1571	21996	1646	22008	1721	22490	1796	22540		
1572	21911	1647	22261	1722	22349	1797	22541		
1573	21997	1648	22155	1723	22375	1798	22558		
1574	21984	1649	22009	1724	22290	1799	22542		
1575	21912	1650	22010	1725	22166	1800	22559		

BOEING 737 - Line No to C/n

line no	c/n	line no	c/n	line no	c/n	line no	c/n	line no	c/n
1	19437	76	19070	151	19939	226	20397	301	20589
2	19013	77	19931	152	20209	227	20221	302	20582
3	19014	78	19682	153	19425	228	20281	303	20583
4	19015	79	19884	154	20129	229	20344	304	20590
5	19016	80	19713	155	19711	230	20254	305	20584
6	19039	81	19609	156	20130	231	20276	306	20585
7	19017	82	19707	157	19848	232	20334	307	20586
8	19040	83	19610	158	20299	233	20345	308	20587
9	19018	84	19847	159	20212	234	20255	309	20591
10	19019	85	19071	160	20213	235	20277	310	20631
11	19020	86	19072	161	20092	236	20403	311	20650
12	19041	87	19708	162	19712	237	20335	312	20671
13	19306	88	19714	163	20210	238	20256	313	20672
14	19042	89	19679	164	20300	239	20336	314	20680
15	19021	90	19073	165	20131	240	20222	315	20670
16	19758	91	19885	166	20236	241	20413	316	20632
17	19022	92	19611	167	20132	242	20205	317	20685
18	19043	93	19612	168	20226	243	20404	318	20633
19	19044	94	19680	169	20093	244	20414	319	20681
20	19307	95	19074	170	20074	245	20282	320	20711
21	19045	96	19742	171	19940	246	20453	321	20740
22	19046	97	19075	172	20214	247	20454	322	20758
23	19023	98	19028	173	20138	248	20405	323	20786
24	19047	99	19076	174	19941	249	20206	324	20777
25	19048	100	19920	175	19942	250	20329	325	20778
26	19024	101	19886	176	20133	251	20389	326	20686
27	19049	102	19594	177	20134	252	20223	327	20779
28	19050	103	19077	178	20227	253	20142	328	20776
29	19418	104	19613	179	19943	254	20455	329	20687
30	19051	105	19614	180	20155	255	20417	330	20688
31	19052	106	19078	181	20156	256	20440	331	20768
32	19025	107	19547	182	20094	257	20330	332	20759
33	19598	108	19029	183	19944	258	20346	333	20793
34	19053	109	19887	184	19768	259	20449	334	20689
35	19026	110	19408	185	19945	260	20331	335	20785
36	19054	111	19921	186	19946	261	20406	336	20690
37	19055	112	19888	187	19947	262	20450	337	20691
38	19709	113	19030	188	20095	263	20407	338	20806
39	19599	114	19548	189	20157	264	20368	339	20692
40	19308	115	19549	190	20096	265	20408	340	20693
41	19419	116	19550	191	19948	266	20451	341	20807
42	19056	117	19551	192	20158	267	20369	342	20808
43	19420	118	19031	193	20159	268	20496	343	20694
44	19600	119	19032	194	19769	269	20480	344	20917
45	19601	120	19033	195	20160	270	20452	345	20695
46	19602	121	19552	196	20194	271	20481	346	20794
47	19309	122	19553	197	19949	272	20482	347	20696
48	19057	123	19554	198	19950	273	20483	348	20795
49	19058	124	20070	199	20218	274	20257	349	20697
50	19059	125	19615	200	19951	275	20484	350	20698
51	19603	126	19616	201	19952	276	20258	351	20907
52	19027	127	19794	202	19953	277	20485	352	20908
53	19421	128	19409	203	19770	278	20458	353	20909
54	19710	129	19555	204	20231	279	20486	354	20836
55	19060	130	19556	205	20195	280	20506	355	20699
56	19604	131	20071	206	19954	281	20492	356	20882
57	19605	132	19617	207	20215	282	20507	357	20700
58	19061	133	19932	208	20219	283	20498	358	20910
59	19062	134	20125	209	20361	284	20499	359	20701
60	19929	135	19933	210	19955	285	20523	360	20911
61	19422	136	20072	211	19956	286	20500	361	20884
62	19063	137	19934	212	19771	287	20508	362	20702
63	19064	138	19935	213	20216	288	20521	363	20703
64	19606	139	19743	214	20229	289	20536	364	20967
65	19065	140	20126	215	20220	290	20544	365	20912
66	19930	141	20211	216	20362	291	20537	366	20883
67	19423	142	20073	217	19772	292	20561	367	20968
68	19681	143	20196	218	20363	293	20562	368	20892
69	19066	144	20127	219	20364	294	20574	369	20969
70	19607	145	20128	220	20365	295	20575	370	20922
71	19067	146	19936	221	20396	296	20563	371	20893
73	19426	147	19424	222	20242	297	20576	372	20926
73	19608	148	19937	223	20253	298	20577	373	20925
74	19068	149	20197	224	20280	299	20578	374	20960
75	19069	150	19938	225	20412	300	20588	375	20961

BOEING 737 - Line No to C/n

line no	c/n	line no	c/n	line no	c/n	line no	c/n	line no	c/n
376	20970	451	21192	526	21534	601	21981	676	22088
377	20957	452	21215	527	21546	602	21817	677	21803
378	21000	453	21193	528	21612	603	21928	678	22340
379	20964	454	21211	529	21596	604	21810	679	22281
380	20962	455	21194	530	21613	605	21822	680	22273
381	20965	456	21216	531	21653	606	21818	681	22282
382	20971	457	21195	532	21654	607	21973	682	22274
383	20963	458	21226	533	21616	608	21929	683	22301
384	21001	459	21212	534	21665	609	21811	684	22159
385	21002	460	21219	535	21645	610	21959	685	22267
386	20956	461	21236	536	21640	611	21812	686	21804
387	20966	462	21231	537	21641	612	21975	687	22275
388	20976	463	21224	538	21677	613	21970	688	22160
389	21003	464	21225	539	21639	614	22070	689	22283
390	21004	465	21196	540	21642	615	21974	690	22406
391	20958	466	21227	541	21693	616	22022	691	22338
392	21012	467	21275	542	21694	617	21840	692	22339
393	21013	468	21276	543	21535	618	21957	693	22030
394	21005	469	21277	544	21593	619	22074	694	22115
395	20959	470	21262	545	21477	620	22071	695	22343
396	20914	471	21280	546	21710	621	22057	696	22364
397	21014	472	21281	547	21666	622	22050	697	21805
398	21006	473	21285	548	21667	623	22072	698	22407
399	20913	474	21301	549	21685	624	22054	699	21806
400	21007	475	21302	550	21686	625	21976	700	22365
401	20915	476	21282	551	21719	626	21791	701	22116
402	21008	477	21283	552	21720	627	21819	702	22415
403	20916	478	21296	553	21721	628	21792	703	22117
404	21015	479	21278	554	21687	629	22058	704	22118
405	20943	480	21279	555	21747	630	22075	705	22408
406	21016	481	21294	556	21712	631	22059	706	22367
407	21063	482	21286	557	21736	632	22089	707	22368
408	20944	483	21317	558	21748	633	22055	708	22369
409	21064	484	21295	559	21732	634	22051	709	22416
410	21017	485	21360	560	21716	635	21793	710	21807
411	21011	486	21287	561	21739	636	22023	711	22602
412	21094	487	21335	562	21740	637	21809	712	21808
413	21066	488	21361	563	21774	638	22060	713	22383
414	21067	489	21336	564	21733	639	22061	714	22119
415	21069	490	21337	565	21714	640	22062	715	22120
416	21065	491	21500	566	21734	641	22024	716	22370
417	21009	492	21501	567	21723	642	21960	717	22371
418	21135	493	21355	568	21722	643	21794	718	22384
419	21073	494	21338	569	21749	644	22026	719	22356
420	21136	495	21339	570	21775	645	21795	720	22121
421	21137	496	21356	571	21763	646	22278	721	22122
422	21138	497	21357	572	21729	647	22025	722	22031
423	21117	498	21358	573	21711	648	21796	723	22399
424	21112	499	21340	574	21750	649	22113	724	22531
425	21115	500	21359	575	21751	650	22279	725	22357
426	21130	501	21443	576	21738	651	22018	726	22123
427	21116	502	21440	577	21776	652	22161	727	22124
428	21131	503	21496	578	21820	653	21797	728	22352
429	21169	504	21497	579	21715	654	22027	729	22395
430	21170	505	21498	580	21728	655	22056	730	22396
431	21176	506	21445	581	21717	656	22028	731	22353
432	21095	507	21397	582	21735	657	22114	732	22358
433	21177	508	21447	583	21766	658	21798	733	22398
434	21163	509	21448	584	21718	659	21955	734	22125
435	21164	510	21597	585	21767	660	21799	735	22126
436	21109	511	21362	586	21768	661	21800	736	22354
437	21139	512	21598	587	21769	662	22029	737	22397
438	21186	513	21499	588	21770	663	22148	738	22426
439	21172	514	21599	589	21815	664	22090	739	22284
440	21184	515	21467	590	21821	665	22276	740	22456
441	21165	516	21444	591	21478	666	22255	741	22355
442	21167	517	21528	592	21816	667	22086	742	22032
443	21187	518	21508	593	21839	668	22296	743	22033
444	21188	519	21476	594	21771	669	21801	744	22402
445	21166	520	21538	595	21765	670	21802	745	22127
446	21183	521	21509	596	21980	671	22280	746	22633
447	21173	522	21518	597	21926	672	22256	747	22473
448	21206	523	21544	598	21713	673	22087	748	22453
449	21214	524	21533	599	21790	674	22300	749	22575
450	21191	525	21545	600	21927	675	22277	750	22529

BOEING 737 - Line No to C/n

line no	c/n	line no	c/n	line no	c/n	line no	c/n	line no	c/n
751	22034	827	22674	901	22802	976	22887	1051	23103
752	22128	828	22585	902	22861	977	23036	1052	22942
753	22264	829	22586	903	22862	978	23045	1053	23160
754	22129	830	22737	904	22874	979	22888	1054	23135
755	22265	831	22652	905	22903	980	23059	1055	23161
756	22257	832	22653	906	22803	981	23046	1056	23162
757	22457	833	22601	907	22863	982	23037	1057	22956
758	22624	834	22738	908	22804	983	22889	1058	23163
759	22516	834	22807	909	22743	984	22961	1059	23148
760	22577	835	22587	910	22856	985	22779	1060	23164
761	22576	836	22588	911	22728	986	22890	1061	23184
762	22130	837	22445	912	22795	987	22962	1062	23104
763	22596	838	22143	913	22904	988	22891	1063	23251
764	22131	839	22675	914	22796	989	23065	1064	23165
765	22266	840	22634	915	22729	990	22892	1065	23185
766	22400	841	22730	916	22797	991	23073	1066	23186
767	22578	842	22629	917	22875	992	23066	1067	23166
768	22645	843	22589	918	22905	993	23074	1068	23105
769	22132	844	22739	919	22857	994	23075	1069	23060
770	22258	845	22752	920	22985	995	23076	1070	23187
771	22259	846	22657	921	22878	996	23077	1071	23188
772	22133	847	22632	922	22876	997	23114	1072	23189
773	22597	848	22637	923	22744	998	23115	1073	23152
774	22635	849	22660	924	22798	999	23116	1074	23167
775	22607	850	22761	925	22986	1000	23078	1076	23153
776	22625	851	22767	926	22879	1001	22950	1076	23218
777	22134	852	22760	927	22880	1002	23051	1077	23168
778	22646	853	22766	928	22994	1003	23079	1078	23154
779	22627	854	22590	929	22963	1004	23080	1079	23155
780	22401	855	22699	930	23000	1005	23081	1080	23061
781	22135	856	22762	931	22881	1006	23082	1081	23169
782	22443	857	22751	932	22799	1007	22951	1082	23156
783	22136	858	22638	933	22964	1008	23083	1083	23062
784	22260	859	22591	934	22882	1009	23084	1084	23220
785	22647	860	22630	935	22883	1010	23113	1085	23157
786	22341	861	22658	936	23001	1011	23085	1086	23170
787	22580	862	22654	937	23002	1012	23086	1087	23181
788	22137	863	22639	938	22806	1013	23087	1088	23171
789	22648	864	22731	939	23003	1014	23108	1089	23158
790	22138	865	22753	940	22866	1015	22952	1090	23219
791	22139	866	22771	941	23004	1016	23109	1091	23172
792	22598	867	22640	942	22965	1017	23110	1092	23063
793	22140	868	22777	943	23005	1018	23088	1093	23272
794	22667	869	22775	944	23006	1019	23089	1094	23252
795	22141	870	22754	945	22864	1020	23090	1095	23249
796	22581	871	22741	946	22966	1021	23091	1096	23253
797	22142	872	22655	947	22778	1022	22953	1097	23273
798	22285	873	22755	948	23007	1023	23092	1098	23173
799	22286	074	22659	949	23038	1024	23093	1099	23274
800	22444	875	22742	950	22979	1025	23121	1100	23288
801	22649	876	22656	951	23049	1026	23094	1101	22943
802	22626	877	22732	952	23008	1027	23095	1102	23225
803	22431	878	22826	953	22967	1028	23096	1103	23228
804	22504	879	22756	954	23039	1029	23097	1104	23174
805	22582	880	22877	955	23040	1030	22954	1105	23226
806	22650	881	22828	956	22884	1031	23098	1106	23182
807	22679	882	22827	957	23023	1032	23136	1107	23254
808	22636	883	22757	958	23009	1033	23117	1108	23183
809	22583	884	22772	959	23010	1034	23129	1109	23283
810	22342	885	22700	960	22865	1035	23099	1110	23175
811	22703	886	22701	961	22867	1036	23122	1111	23331
812	22733	887	22792	962	23041	1037	22940	1112	23229
813	22618	888	22906	963	22868	1038	23100	1113	23292
814	22599	889	22758	964	22869	1039	23131	1114	23294
815	22505	890	22859	965	23024	1040	23130	1115	23230
816	22600	891	22776	966	22885	1041	23101	1116	23295
817	22697	892	22793	967	23042	1042	23123	1117	23351
818	22734	893	22773	968	23053	1043	22955	1118	23332
819	22651	894	22631	969	23054	1044	23132	1119	23352
820	22628	895	22774	970	23055	1045	23102	1120	23320
821	22584	896	22736	971	23011	1046	23124	1121	23296
822	22620	897	22800	972	23043	1047	23159	1122	23297
823	22698	898	22873	973	23044	1048	22941	1123	23298
825	22735	899	22860	974	22886	1049	23133	1124	23257
826	22673	900	22801	975	23050	1050	23134	1125	23255

BOEING 737 - Line No to C/n

line no	c/n	line no	c/n	line no	c/n	line no	c/n	line no	c/n
1126	23258	1201	23335	1276	23571	1351	23342	1426	23793
1127	22957	1202	23373	1277	23485	1352	23488	1427	23384
1128	23256	1203	23475	1278	23525	1353	23684	1428	23555
1129	23353	1204	23374	1279	23656	1354	23669	1429	23798
1130	23354	1205	23290	1280	23657	1355	23515	1430	23771
1131	23355	1206	23495	1281	23658	1356	23489	1431	23750
1132	23259	1207	23375	1282	23526	1357	23685	1432	23772
1133	23356	1208	23234	1283	23625	1358	23578	1433	23871
1134	23329	1209	23401	1284	23626	1359	23734	1434	23808
1135	23349	1210	23315	1285	23527	1360	23738	1435	23556
1136	23330	1211	23291	1286	23486	1361	23603	1436	23635
1137	22958	1212	23316	1287	23597	1362	23379	1437	23557
1138	22944	1213	23176	1288	23538	1363	23747	1438	23636
1139	22945	1214	23235	1289	23598	1364	23670	1439	23833
1140	22959	1215	23406	1290	23528	1365	23717	1440	23385
1141	23357	1216	23177	1291	23512	1366	23380	1441	23773
1142	23358	1217	23496	1292	23659	1367	23550	1442	23594
1143	23386	1218	23440	1293	23529	1368	23579	1443	23774
1144	23359	1219	23236	1294	23660	1369	23604	1444	23827
1145	23310	1220	23441	1295	23539	1370	23671	1445	23811
1146	23260	1221	23317	1296	23572	1371	23605	1446	23828
1147	23360	1222	23237	1297	23530	1372	23826	1447	23872
1148	22946	1223	23464	1298	23573	1373	23580	1448	23588
1149	23311	1224	23302	1299	23519	1374	23787	1449	23558
1150	23361	1225	23477	1300	23642	1375	23766	1450	23595
1151	23443	1226	23465	1301	23535	1376	23581	1451	23559
1152	23362	1227	23497	1302	23627	1377	23343	1452	23699
1153	23363	1228	23455	1303	23540	1378	23344	1453	23849
1154	23444	1229	23336	1304	23628	1379	23606	1454	23834
1155	23445	1230	23456	1305	23714	1380	23551	1455	23778
1156	22947	1231	23337	1306	23487	1381	23748	1456	23914
1157	23261	1232	23338	1307	23531	1382	23552	1457	23779
1158	23364	1233	23498	1308	23376	1383	23582	1458	23809
1159	23365	1234	23318	1309	23541	1384	23414	1459	23780
1160	22948	1235	23299	1310	23715	1385	23583	1460	23829
1161	22949	1236	23466	1311	23629	1386	23786	1461	23700
1162	23312	1237	23303	1312	23630	1387	23607	1462	23830
1163	23387	1238	23457	1313	23677	1388	23707	1463	23560
1164	23231	1239	23442	1314	23661	1389	23749	1464	23701
1165	23446	1240	23451	1315	23643	1390	23490	1465	23835
1166	23396	1241	23481	1316	23662	1391	23491	1466	23589
1167	23447	1242	23499	1317	23542	1392	23789	1467	23970
1168	23440	1243	23500	1318	23505	1393	23788	1468	23590
1169	23232	1244	23458	1319	23795	1394	23381	1469	23739
1170	23345	1245	23467	1320	23377	1395	23708	1470	23672
1171	23415	1246	23522	1321	23716	1396	23584	1471	23831
1172	23346	1247	23459	1322	23644	1397	23792	1472	23591
1173	23347	1248	23510	1323	23663	1398	23689	1473	23832
1174	23366	1249	23506	1324	23599	1399	23608	1474	23810
1175	23416	1250	23319	1325	23543	1400	23690	1475	23702
1176	23404	1251	23478	1326	23664	1401	23912	1476	23592
1177	23313	1252	23507	1327	23513	1402	23718	1477	23740
1178	23405	1253	23460	1328	23574	1403	23609	1478	23593
1179	23314	1254	23601	1329	23520	1404	23585	1479	23673
1180	23367	1255	23339	1330	23665	1405	23678	1480	23703
1181	23368	1256	23503	1331	23514	1406	23553	1481	23674
1182	23289	1257	23516	1332	23666	1407	23691	1482	23971
1183	23333	1258	23569	1333	23575	1408	23554	1483	23675
1184	23449	1259	23479	1334	23667	1409	23800	1484	23752
1185	23334	1260	23653	1335	23544	1410	23382	1485	23947
1186	23470	1261	23517	1336	23712	1411	23586	1486	23791
1187	23388	1262	23468	1337	23631	1412	23775	1487	23886
1188	23369	1263	23570	1338	23576	1413	23587	1488	23704
1189	23471	1264	23483	1339	23378	1414	23847	1489	23873
1190	23370	1265	23518	1340	23577	1415	23679	1490	24208
1191	23371	1266	23469	1341	23713	1416	23797	1491	23948
1192	23372	1267	23504	1342	23521	1417	23776	1492	24209
1193	23397	1268	23511	1343	23545	1418	23848	1493	23949
1194	23472	1269	23596	1344	23632	1419	23777	1494	23781
1195	23411	1270	23484	1345	23733	1420	23796	1495	23874
1196	23450	1271	23523	1346	23668	1421	23633	1496	23782
1197	23473	1272	23524	1347	23602	1422	23790	1497	23705
1198	23412	1273	23654	1348	23340	1423	23634	1498	23741
1199	23474	1274	23655	1349	23546	1424	23794	1499	23706
1200	23233	1275	23537	1350	23341	1425	23383	1500	23875

BOEING 737 - Line No to C/n

line no	c/n	line no	c/n	line no	c/n	line no	c/n	line no	c/n
1501	23856	1576	24008	1651	23976	1726	24270	1801	24563
1502	23742	1577	24210	1652	24301	1727	24093	1802	24641
1503	23857	1578	24009	1653	24296	1728	24452	1803	24520
1504	23950	1579	23913	1654	24030	1729	24094	1804	24181
1505	23838	1580	23927	1655	23977	1730	24453	1805	24545
1506	24068	1581	24197	1656	24280	1731	24345	1806	24642
1507	23839	1582	23865	1657	24364	1732	23990	1807	24564
1508	23836	1583	23915	1658	24277	1733	24467	1808	24492
1509	23858	1584	23861	1659	23978	1734	24408	1809	24633
1510	23743	1585	24236	1660	24278	1735	24412	1810	24653
1511	23812	1586	23862	1661	23979	1736	24167	1811	24546
1512	23885	1587	23937	1662	24022	1737	24095	1812	24654
1513	23921	1588	24191	1663	24123	1738	24271	1813	24547
1514	23837	1589	23866	1664	24281	1739	24096	1814	24655
1515	24081	1590	24192	1665	24070	1740	24297	1815	24571
1516	23840	1591	24090	1666	24300	1741	24097	1816	24778
1517	24059	1592	24193	1667	23980	1742	24474	1817	24554
1518	23841	1593	24091	1668	24319	1743	24478	1818	24565
1519	24060	1594	24228	1669	24092	1744	24179	1819	24555
1520	23941	1595	24026	1670	24430	1745	24479	1820	24430
1521	23692	1596	23880	1671	24282	1746	23991	1821	24556
1522	23942	1597	24027	1672	24321	1747	24468	1822	24656
1523	24031	1598	24299	1673	24279	1748	24409	1823	24634
1524	24140	1599	24028	1674	23984	1749	24469	1824	24682
1525	23693	1600	24219	1675	24023	1750	24454	1825	24710
1526	24141	1601	24029	1676	23985	1751	24493	1826	24182
1527	23064	1602	24220	1677	24283	1752	24455	1827	24130
1528	23876	1603	23867	1678	23981	1753	24464	1828	24703
1529	23694	1604	24221	1679	24124	1754	24532	1829	24676
1530	24139	1605	24229	1680	24314	1755	24465	1830	24657
1531	23783	1606	24010	1681	24404	1756	24533	1831	24460
1532	23951	1607	24230	1682	24133	1757	24494	1832	24658
1533	23784	1608	24011	1683	24326	1758	24534	1833	24461
1534	23952	1609	24240	1684	23986	1759	24511	1834	24694
1535	23785	1610	23881	1685	24284	1760	24535	1835	24557
1536	23695	1611	24241	1686	24151	1761	24298	1836	24659
1537	23972	1612	24012	1688	24152	1762	24536	1837	24677
1538	23922	1613	24242	1689	24024	1763	24098	1838	24660
1539	23930	1614	24020	1689	24125	1764	23992	1839	24769
1540	23923	1615	24243	1690	24153	1765	24470	1840	24661
1541	24131	1616	23868	1691	24462	1766	24180	1841	24684
1542	23924	1617	24244	1692	24360	1767	24515	1842	24651
1543	23877	1618	24302	1693	24387	1768	24514	1843	24711
1544	23925	1619	24245	1694	24361	1769	24516	1844	24573
1545	23696	1620	24303	1695	24365	1770	24529	1845	24558
1546	23953	1621	23882	1696	24362	1771	24466	1846	24698
1547	23697	1622	24304	1697	24126	1772	24530	1847	24559
1548	23954	1623	24211	1698	23987	1773	24480	1848	24776
1549	23938	1624	24237	1699	24366	1774	24537	1849	24560
1550	23955	1625	24255	1700	24163	1775	24569	1850	24773
1551	23859	1626	24238	1701	24463	1776	24538	1851	24804
1552	23931	1627	24234	1702	24164	1777	24512	1852	24183
1553	23939	1628	24269	1703	24410	1778	24521	1853	24678
1554	23932	1629	24256	1704	24378	1778	24539	1854	24901
1555	24132	1630	24021	1705	24352	1779	24513	1855	24704
1556	24025	1631	23883	1706	24403	1780	24540	1856	24328
1557	23940	1632	24246	1707	24127	1781	24519	1857	24449
1558	23943	1633	24212	1708	24374	1782	24637	1858	24329
1559	23933	1634	24247	1709	24355	1783	24129	1859	24685
1560	23860	1635	24069	1710	24375	1784	24638	1860	24643
1561	23878	1636	24248	1711	24356	1785	24561	1861	24686
1562	23926	1637	24275	1712	24327	1786	24639	1862	24662
1563	23934	1638	24249	1713	24411	1787	24562	1863	24431
1564	23956	1639	23869	1714	23988	1789	24548	1864	24184
1565	24103	1640	24261	1715	24128	1790	24572	1865	24687
1566	23957	1641	24305	1716	23989	1791	24549	1866	24332
1567	23959	1642	24262	1717	24376	1792	24650	1867	24866
1568	23958	1643	23884	1718	24178	1793	24550	1868	24754
1569	23935	1644	24250	1719	24377	1794	24213	1869	24712
1570	24147	1645	24276	1720	24165	1795	24551	1870	24795
1571	23960	1646	24251	1721	24353	1796	24214	1871	24231
1572	24148	1647	23870	1722	24166	1797	24552	1872	24695
1573	23879	1648	24252	1723	24344	1798	24640	1873	24450
1574	24149	1649	24295	1724	24379	1799	24553	1874	24781
1575	23936	1650	24253	1725	24388	1800	24570	1875	24663

BOEING 737 - Line No to C/n

line no	c/n	line no	c/n	line no	c/n	line no	c/n	line no	c/n
1876	24688	1951	24936	2026	25024	2101	25291	2176	25177
1877	24664	1952	25003	2027	25089	2102	25242	2177	25425
1878	24805	1953	24789	2028	25065	2103	25250	2178	25407
1879	24432	1954	24933	2029	24188	2104	25226	2179	25387
1880	24807	1955	24790	2030	24910	2105	25251	2180	25229
1881	24433	1956	24934	2031	24939	2106	25247	2181	25388
1882	24785	1957	24701	2032	25063	2107	24751	2182	25416
1883	24689	1958	24816	2033	24911	2108	25227	2183	25408
1884	24413	1959	24435	2034	24940	2109	25313	2184	25423
1885	24690	1960	24696	2035	24274	2110	25381	2185	25428
1886	24699	1961	24928	2036	25052	2111	25218	2186	25419
1887	24796	1962	24921	2037	25070	2112	25400	2187	25263
1888	24808	1963	24692	2038	25066	2113	25321	2188	25839
1889	24665	1964	24922	2039	25071	2114	25160	2189	26642
1890	24811	1965	25004	2040	25090	2115	24709	2190	26643
1891	24666	1966	24926	2041	24826	2116	25270	2191	25230
1892	24812	1967	24817	2042	24941	2117	25271	2192	24986
1893	24667	1968	24927	2043	25147	2118	25272	2193	24963
1894	24825	1969	25038	2044	25062	2119	25382	2194	25264
1895	24414	1970	24919	2045	25056	2120	25248	2195	25371
1896	24834	1971	24705	2046	25057	2121	25318	2196	26428
1897	24679	1972	24693	2047	25124	2122	25309	2197	25840
1898	24786	1973	24902	2048	24942	2123	25256	2198	25744
1899	24830	1974	24818	2049	24943	2124	25314	2199	25178
1900	24787	1975	24968	2050	25115	2125	25050	2200	25424
1901	24683	1976	25005	2051	24944	2126	25310	2201	25180
1902	24857	1977	24970	2052	24913	2127	25051	2202	26564
1903	24858	1978	24903	2053	25069	2128	25311	2203	25181
1904	24691	1979	24819	2054	24914	2129	25166	2204	26565
1905	24668	1980	24979	2055	24915	2130	25361	2205	25179
1906	24841	1981	25006	2056	24189	2131	25267	2206	25743
1907	24669	1982	24980	2057	24707	2132	25355	2207	26429
1908	24842	1983	25007	2058	24190	2133	24961	2208	25231
1909	24670	1984	24791	2059	25125	2134	25319	2209	26525
1910	24862	1985	24820	2060	24232	2135	25307	2210	25168
1911	24856	1986	24996	2061	25116	2136	25320	2211	25182
1912	24434	1987	25008	2062	24813	2137	25303	2212	26645
1913	24671	1988	24904	2063	24945	2138	24646	2213	24648
1914	24863	1989	24989	2064	24912	2139	24962	2214	26646
1915	24672	1990	24997	2065	25118	2140	25360	2215	25429
1916	24750	1991	25015	2066	24916	2141	25357	2216	26430
1917	24652	1992	25020	2067	25401	2142	25362	2217	25729
1918	24664	1993	24821	2068	25159	2143	24647	2218	25183
1919	24859	1994	24702	2069	25119	2144	25304	2219	26526
1920	24673	1995	25021	2070	24946	2145	25249	2220	25185
1921	24788	1996	24706	2071	24917	2146	25383	2221	26279
1922	24831	1997	24822	2072	24645	2147	25305	2222	25841
1923	24272	1998	24436	2073	25254	2148	25348	2223	25594
1924	24700	1999	25009	2074	25150	2149	25384	2224	26566
1925	24828	2000	24823	2075	25255	2150	25175	2225	24649
1926	24869	2001	24905	2076	24708	2151	25358	2226	25161
1927	24680	2002	25078	2077	25148	2152	25385	2227	25184
1928	24674	2003	24897	2078	25153	2153	25138	2228	25842
1929	24681	2004	25016	2079	24898	2154	25386	2229	25789
1930	24717	2005	25017	2080	25154	2155	25176	2230	26648
1931	24873	2006	24824	2081	25149	2156	25349	2231	25232
1932	24185	2007	25039	2082	25215	2157	25317	2232	25737
1933	24815	2008	25010	2083	25134	2158	25359	2233	25595
1934	24186	2009	24906	2084	25216	2159	25402	2234	26440
1935	24935	2010	25022	2085	25048	2160	25417	2235	26850
1936	24874	2011	24937	2086	25243	2161	25412	2236	25186
1937	24718	2012	25011	2087	24918	2162	24437	2237	25169
1938	24644	2013	24907	2088	25262	2163	25418	2238	25188
1939	24878	2014	25032	2089	25172	2164	25414	2239	26280
1940	24187	2015	24908	2090	25210	2165	25419	2240	25189
1941	24770	2016	25079	2091	25049	2166	25364	2241	25162
1942	24888	2017	25040	2092	25219	2167	25350	2242	26431
1943	24877	2018	24273	2093	24899	2168	25174	2243	24827
1944	24892	2019	25084	2094	25217	2169	25352	2244	25843
1945	24881	2020	25023	2095	24900	2170	25228	2245	25790
1946	24893	2021	24909	2096	25290	2171	24438	2246	26649
1947	24889	2022	25037	2097	25173	2172	25426	2247	26432
1948	25001	2023	24938	2098	25244	2173	25167	2248	25187
1949	24959	2024	25041	2099	25206	2174	25430	2249	26437
1950	25002	2025	25033	2100	25239	2175	25415	2251	25233

BOEING 737 - Line No to C/n

line no	c/n	line no	c/n	line no	c/n	line no	c/n	line no	c/n
2251	26441	2326	26857	2401	27419	2476	25104	2551	25108
2252	27046	2327	26445	2402	26687	2477	26580	2552	26104
2253	26639	2328	27003	2403	27083	2478	25615	2553	26105
2254	25080	2329	26668	2404	26688	2479	26447	2554	25897
2255	25596	2330	26612	2405	25604	2480	26288	2555	27272
2256	25190	2331	25788	2406	27420	2481	26614	2556	27273
2257	26651	2332	26453	2407	27085	2482	26290	2557	26295
2258	25261	2333	25603	2408	26691	2483	26960	2558	25896
2259	26652	2334	25099	2409	25853	2484	26448	2559	27274
2260	25191	2335	25765	2410	27166	2485	26699	2560	26463
2261	25738	2336	26671	2411	25234	2486	26289	2561	25109
2262	25192	2337	26542	2412	26422	2487	26088	2562	25374
2263	25081	2338	26613	2413	26438	2488	25996	2563	26320
2264	25163	2339	26543	2414	25508	2489	25893	2564	26298
2265	24439	2340	26464	2415	27125	2490	26700	2565	27275
2266	25095	2341	25504	2416	26285	2491	26449	2566	27314
2267	26851	2342	25505	2417	25854	2492	27156	2567	27276
2268	24987	2343	26672	2418	26284	2493	27128	2568	27190
2269	25736	2344	27004	2419	27167	2494	26739	2569	24446
2270	24814	2345	26675	2420	25855	2495	27176	2570	26584
2271	25739	2346	25100	2421	26692	2496	26451	2571	27315
2272	26443	2347	27061	2422	25856	2497	26597	2572	27304
2273	26852	2348	25101	2423	26695	2498	26703	2573	27316
2274	26655	2349	26070	2424	26286	2499	25895	2574	27305
2275	26853	2350	25102	2425	26077	2500	26598	2575	27287
2276	26052	2351	25791	2426	27086	2501	26452	2576	27317
2277	26442	2352	26069	2427	26287	2502	27157	2577	27288
2278	25096	2353	25792	2428	25235	2503	26450	2578	26297
2279	26421	2354	27081	2429	26574	2504	26599	2579	26585
2280	25372	2355	26282	2430	26575	2505	25105	2580	26586
2281	27074	2356	27082	2431	26078	2506	25997	2581	26296
2282	26051	2357	27047	2432	27094	2507	26455	2582	27318
2283	26567	2358	26446	2433	26576	2508	26704	2583	27257
2284	26065	2359	27005	2434	25797	2509	26581	2584	26529
2285	26568	2360	25506	2435	27168	2510	25998	2585	27213
2286	25288	2361	26071	2436	27138	2511	26454	2586	25110
2287	26569	2362	26465	2437	27151	2512	26707	2587	27336
2288	25289	2363	24441	2438	27421	2513	26291	2588	26530
2289	26656	2364	26676	2439	25994	2514	25844	2589	27256
2290	25373	2365	26679	2440	26696	2515	26582	2590	27319
2291	26658	2366	26680	2441	27087	2516	27153	2591	27232
2292	26570	2367	27007	2442	26081	2517	26961	2592	27268
2293	26659	2368	26683	2443	25236	2518	25106	2593	27289
2294	26594	2369	26072	2444	26439	2519	26292	2594	27337
2295	26595	2370	27126	2445	26468	2520	26583	2595	27290
2296	26537	2371	24442	2446	25613	2521	26457	2596	27320
2297	26596	2372	26466	2447	25164	2522	25858	2597	27321
2298	26538	2373	25507	2448	27130	2523	27271	2598	25375
2299	25097	2374	26075	2449	27155	2524	27179	2599	25511
2300	26539	2375	26073	2450	27169	2525	26458	2600	27267
2301	26066	2376	26074	2451	25857	2526	25107	2601	27233
2302	25787	2377	27127	2452	25103	2527	26456	2602	26299
2303	26854	2378	26467	2453	26531	2528	27286	2603	27368
2304	26067	2379	25848	2454	24444	2529	27180	2604	26300
2305	26855	2380	26281	2455	25995	2530	26459	2605	25111
2306	26068	2381	25849	2456	26082	2531	25713	2606	27284
2307	26571	2382	25663	2457	27143	2532	25859	2607	27322
2308	26444	2383	26283	2458	27131	2533	26460	2608	27285
2309	26572	2384	27045	2459	26083	2534	26097	2609	27335
2310	25502	2385	25891	2460	26084	2535	25714	2610	26587
2311	27000	2386	25850	2461	25740	2536	26461	2611	26588
2312	26662	2387	25851	2462	27170	2537	25715	2612	26589
2313	25503	2388	26684	2463	25165	2538	26100	2613	26590
2314	25764	2389	27416	2464	25237	2539	24445	2614	25767
2315	26663	2390	25852	2465	27171	2540	25716	2615	27347
2316	27001	2391	27084	2466	24988	2541	26293	2616	27323
2317	26540	2392	27417	2467	25614	2542	26462	2617	26600
2318	26611	2393	25664	2468	26085	2543	25766	2618	26603
2319	26541	2394	27102	2469	26577	2544	26101	2619	27343
2320	25098	2395	27096	2470	26578	2545	25860	2620	26302
2321	26856	2396	25892	2471	27149	2546	25717	2621	27324
2322	26573	2397	27418	2472	26527	2547	27283	2622	27344
2323	27002	2398	24443	2473	26579	2548	25718	2623	26301
2324	24440	2399	27097	2474	26640	2549	25719	2624	27352
2325	26667	2400	27139	2475	26086	2550	26294	2625	27345

BOEING 737 - Line No to C/n

line no	c/n	line no	c/n	line no	c/n	line no	c/n	line no	c/n
2626	26601	2701	27912	2776	27540	2851	28556	2926	28902
2627	26602	2702	27695	2777	26340	2852	27673	2927	28903
2628	26591	2703	27454	2778	28157	2853	28462	2928	29056
2629	26592	2704	26313	2779	27932	2854	28200	2929	28866
2630	27325	2705	27905	2780	27933	2855	27680	2930	28719
2631	27361	2706	26315	2781	27934	2856	28721	2931	28400
2632	27353	2707	26314	2782	26334	2857	27632	2932	28401
2633	27326	2708	27381	2783	27432	2858	27628	2933	28904
2634	27327	2709	27455	2784	28083	2859	28657	2934	28905
2635	26303	2710	27523	2785	28151	2860	25776	2935	28906
2636	27346	2711	26316	2786	26333	2861	28470	2936	28564
2637	27354	2712	27532	2787	27701	2862	28557	2937	28727
2638	25112	2713	27953	2788	28084	2863	28746	2938	28728
2639	27362	2714	27954	2789	27702	2864	27469	2939	28758
2640	27328	2715	27955	2790	27935	2865	28658	2940	28664
2641	27329	2716	27956	2791	25772	2866	27631	2941	28973
2642	26593	2717	25377	2792	27626	2867	25795	2942	29057
2643	27378	2718	27916	2793	26335	2868	28722	2943	29032
2644	27379	2719	26317	2794	28038	2869	28329	2944	28565
2645	27380	2720	27424	2795	27703	2870	28330	2945	29068
2646	27355	2721	27635	2796	27704	2871	28331	2946	29058
2647	27374	2722	28085	2797	27705	2872	27434	2947	28995
2648	27330	2723	27430	2798	27706	2873	27910	2948	28670
2649	26304	2724	25768	2799	27707	2874	28752	2949	28731
2650	27372	2725	27533	2800	27627	2875	27435	2950	28729
2651	26305	2726	27534	2801	28271	2876	28558	2951	29069
2652	27331	2727	27522	2802	28334	2877	27674	2952	28730
2653	26306	2728	27535	2803	25794	2878	27633	2953	28832
2654	27356	2729	27917	2804	27914	2879	28867	2954	28053
2655	27375	2730	27425	2805	26336	2880	28659	2955	28671
2656	25113	2731	26318	2806	28198	2881	28868	2956	28907
2657	27383	2732	25378	2807	27936	2882	28559	2957	28720
2658	27373	2733	27678	2808	27937	2883	28660	2958	28908
2659	27332	2734	27679	2809	28332	2884	28747	2959	27458
2660	27333	2735	26323	2810	28333	2885	28471	2960	28909
2661	27334	2736	27900	2811	26337	2886	28723	2961	28548
2662	27181	2737	25769	2812	28087	2887	28869	2962	28703
2663	27182	2738	27521	2813	27708	2888	28560	2963	29033
2664	26307	2739	27426	2814	27709	2889	27634	2964	28566
2665	26308	2740	27926	2815	27433	2890	28668	2965	28052
2666	25114	2741	27927	2816	25771	2891	28885	2966	28732
2667	27689	2742	27928	2817	28128	2892	27717	2967	29059
2668	27690	2743	27901	2818	28158	2893	27718	2968	28704
2669	27526	2744	27929	2819	27710	2894	27719	2969	28733
2670	27830	2745	27696	2820	27711	2895	28753	2970	29087
2671	27395	2746	28081	2821	27712	2896	28561	2971	28567
2672	27527	2747	28082	2822	26338	2897	28669	2972	28910
2673	27384	2748	26319	2823	28129	2898	28606	2973	28911
2674	26309	2749	27456	2824	27966	2899	28870	2974	28734
2675	27528	2750	27457	2825	28130	2900	28871	2975	28873
2676	27191	2750	27697	2826	28199	2901	27720	2976	28672
2677	27831	2751	27431	2827	28489	2902	28886	2977	28701
2678	27519	2752	26605	2828	28131	2903	28887	2978	28702
2679	27452	2753	27930	2829	28152	2904	28537	2979	28060
2680	26310	2754	27931	2830	28490	2905	25773	2980	28912
2681	26311	2755	28033	2831	27463	2906	28898	2981	28759
2682	27903	2757	27698	2832	28491	2907	28097	2982	29099
2683	27529	2758	27699	2833	28881	2908	28562	2983	29108
2684	26604	2759	27700	2834	27629	2909	25774	2984	29100
2685	27306	2760	27924	2835	28554	2910	28661	2985	28913
2686	27530	2761	28034	2836	28389	2911	28831	2986	28914
2687	27453	2762	28035	2837	28492	2912	28899	2987	28568
2688	27833	2763	27925	2838	28493	2913	28900	2988	28738
2689	25376	2764	26321	2839	28494	2914	28662	2989	28760
2690	27907	2765	27462	2840	27713	2915	27721	2990	28888
2691	27904	2766	28036	2841	27714	2916	27722	2991	29122
2692	27834	2767	28037	2842	27715	2917	28398	2992	28742
2693	26312	2768	27518	2843	27716	2918	28399	2993	28915
2694	27826	2769	26325	2844	28549	2919	28972	2994	28916
2695	27691	2770	26322	2845	28882	2920	28726	2995	28673
2696	27692	2771	26339	2846	28555	2921	28563	2996	28569
2697	27693	2772	26324	2847	28550	2922	28663	2997	29107
2698	27906	2773	28150	2848	27630	2923	29055	2998	28996
2699	27694	2774	28156	2849	28469	2924	28901	2999	28201
2700	27531	2775	27520	2850	28461	2925	25775	3000	28889

BOEING 737 - Line No to C/n

line no	c/n	line no	c/n
3001	29109	3076	29235
3002	28990	3077	28928
3003	28740	3078	29207
3004	28472	3079	28741
3005	29116	3080	29412
3006	28890	3081	29208
3007	27459	3082	28872
3008	28997	3083	29073
3009	28202	3084	29333
3010	28570	3085	29485
3011	28761	3086	29074
3012	29072	3087	29209
3013	29140	3088	29486
3014	28473	3089	29334
3015	29034	3090	28586
3016	28054	3091	29210
3017	28991	3092	29266
3018	29201	3093	29267
3019	28917	3094	29335
3020	29326	3095	29750
3021	27460	3096	28475
3022	28571	3097	28590
3023	29327	3098	28895
3024	28055	3099	28896
3025	29202	3100	29407
3026	28918	3101	29075
3027	28891	3102	29336
3028	28474	3103	28476
3029	28735	3104	29408
3030	28992	3105	29130
3031	28572	3106	29915
3032	28736	3107	28594
3033	29000	3108	30102
3034	29088	3109	29794
3035	29141	3110	30161
3036	28892	3111	29864
3037	28737	3112	28596
3038	29270	3113	29337
3039	28893	3114	29338
3040	29001	3115	28599
3041	28573	3116	29795
3042	29318	3117	30333
3043	27660	3118	28602
3044	28994	3119	29339
3045	28919	3120	30334
3046	29035	3121	29340
3047	29405	3122	29487
3048	28920	3123	25606
3049	29203	3124	28606
3050	28894	3125	29341
3051	29204	3126	25607
3052	28921	3127	29342
3053	29410	3128	25608
3054	29315	3129	30335
3055	28922	3130	25609
3056	29205	3131	28477
3057	29189	3132	28478
3058	29206		
3059	29244		
3060	28923		
3061	29245		
3062	29331		
3063	28924		
3064	28739		
3065	29316		
3066	28925		
3067	29914		
3068	29234		
3069	28926		
3070	29264		
3071	29411		
3072	29332		
3073	29265		
3074	28927		
3075	28993		

BOEING 737NG - Line No to C/n

line no	c/n	line no	c/n	line no	c/n	line no	c/n	line no	c/n
1	27841	76	28775	151	28821	226	28221	301	30496
2	27842	77	28226	152	29044	227	28301	302	29106
3	27843	78	28214	153	28930	228	29771	303	30189
4	27835	79	28776	154	28582	229	29082	304	28942
5	28110	80	29765	155	29276	230	29091	305	29133
6	27836	81	28777	156	28787	231	29507	306	29799
7	27981	82	27853	157	29277	232	29490	307	29918
8	27982	83	29089	158	28976	233	28591	308	29776
9	27977	84	28778	159	28931	234	29200	309	29777
10	28004	85	28375	160	28218	235	29047	310	29498
11	28005	86	29084	161	28407	236	28982	311	30075
12	27837	87	29766	162	28932	237	29491	312	28579
13	28099	88	28781	163	28583	238	28826	313	29751
14	28209	89	28578	164	29036	239	29121	314	29959
15	27838	90	29085	165	28933	240	29508	315	28796
16	28100	91	28575	166	28822	241	29865	316	29515
17	28101	92	28289	167	29142	242	29772	317	28797
18	28102	93	28779	168	28934	243	28302	318	27863
19	28088	94	28780	169	29045	244	30070	319	27864
20	27839	95	29767	170	28584	245	28222	320	27865
21	28296	96	28878	171	28935	246	27990	321	28944
22	28210	97	28782	172	29278	247	28789	322	29516
23	28103	98	29076	173	28585	248	27991	323	29272
24	27840	99	29768	174	28823	249	29958	324	27866
25	28089	100	28290	175	29279	250	28381	325	28945
26	28006	101	29102	176	29624	251	30031	326	29039
27	28107	102	29769	177	29037	252	28376	327	29960
28	28108	103	28576	178	29444	253	28790	328	28943
29	28762	104	29077	179	30076	254	29509	329	28306
30	28297	105	28783	180	28824	255	28310	330	28307
31	28109	106	28070	181	29046	256	28382	331	29800
32	28763	107	28784	182	28936	257	28303	332	29517
33	28211	108	29086	183	28219	258	28592	333	28308
34	27844	109	29090	184	29503	259	29773	334	28946
35	28212	110	29190	185	28937	260	29902	335	30190
36	28068	111	29441	186	29445	261	29132	336	29791
37	28764	112	28291	187	29078	262	28788	337	29876
38	27845	113	28402	188	28825	263	29510	338	29798
39	28104	114	29770	189	29139	264	29625	339	29969
40	27978	115	29619	190	29504	265	29317	340	30265
41	28436	116	28292	191	28298	266	28383	341	29919
42	28069	117	28403	192	28587	267	29511	342	28947
43	28765	118	29620	193	28299	268	29496	343	29801
44	27979	119	28785	194	29079	269	29774	344	29518
45	27980	120	28293	195	28938	270	28304	345	29947
46	28766	121	27854	196	29505	271	29512	346	28799
47	28767	122	28216	197	29233	272	28223	347	29904
48	28768	123	29621	198	29131	273	28056	348	29149
49	28288	124	28577	199	27855	274	27859	349	29778
50	28213	125	28786	200	28073	275	29968	350	29752
51	28373	126	28581	201	27856	276	27860	351	30349
52	28769	127	29191	202	29120	277	28377	352	28948
53	27846	128	29622	203	28008	278	27861	353	29519
54	27847	129	29103	204	29957	279	29775	354	27867
55	28980	130	28404	205	28090	280	29268	355	29134
56	28770	131	29024	206	29135	281	28792	356	30327
57	28374	132	28405	207	29506	282	29497	357	27868
58	28771	133	28071	208	27857	283	28791	358	27869
59	27989	134	28929	209	28300	284	27862	359	29877
60	28981	135	28580	210	29916	285	28595	360	27870
61	27848	136	28007	211	29080	286	28941	361	30266
62	27849	137	28294	212	28220	287	28793	362	29920
63	28772	138	29043	213	27858	288	29048	363	29520
64	28750	139	29104	214	28939	289	29513	364	28800
65	28773	140	29912	215	29081	290	28305	365	30350
66	28105	141	28406	216	28497	291	28378	366	29802
67	28574	142	28217	217	29188	292	30074	367	29801
68	28106	143	29054	218	27983	293	29514	368	28309
69	28177	144	29275	219	28940	294	28984	369	28224
70	27851	145	29623	220	27984	295	29105	370	29779
71	27852	146	29273	221	28009	296	28794	371	28949
72	28437	147	28072	222	28178	297	29038	372	29905
73	29042	148	29913	223	28091	298	29917	373	29803
74	28774	149	28295	224	29329	299	29798	374	28802
75	28215	150	29251	225	29136	300	28795	375	28605

BOEING 737NG - Line No to C/n

line no	c/n	line no	c/n	line no	c/n	line no	c/n	line no	c/n
376	28950	451	30752	526	30137	601	27880	676	30513
377	30328	452	28227	527	29530	602	30789	677	29810
378	29521	453	29527	528	30593	603	27881	678	29983
379	29878	454	29780	529	28318	604	30773	679	30086
380	28803	455	28612	530	29858	605	30357	680	28234
381	30071	456	29749	531	30080	606	30576	681	30171
382	28311	457	30374	532	30542	607	30474	682	28013
383	29522	458	28314	533	28388	608	29533	683	30016
384	30329	459	30458	534	28619	609	27882	684	29971
385	29753	460	30230	535	30560	610	30202	685	30539
386	28804	461	29781	536	30543	611	28626	686	30610
387	29804	462	30077	537	29806	612	30083	687	30737
388	30049	463	28613	538	28231	613	30790	688	30006
389	30345	464	28315	539	29784	614	28322	689	30776
390	28499	465	29040	540	28536	615	30577	690	30182
391	28951	466	30072	541	29807	616	30598	691	30205
392	29083	467	28827	542	28620	617	30590	692	30611
393	30346	468	27874	543	29500	618	30578	693	30602
394	28952	469	30375	544	29785	619	30501	694	30381
395	28953	470	27985	545	30755	620	30591	695	30173
396	28010	471	29093	546	30138	621	30592	696	30195
397	29274	472	30344	547	28232	622	29981	697	28235
398	29523	473	29528	548	28319	623	30791	698	29811
399	28607	474	27986	549	30389	624	29534	699	29537
400	29848	475	29246	550	30167	625	28323	700	30166
401	30751	476	28316	551	28320	626	27883	701	30039
402	28805	477	28614	552	29595	627	30579	702	30183
403	28806	478	28229	553	29531	628	27884	703	30414
404	30191	479	29051	554	30772	629	30084	704	30087
405	29524	480	28535	555	30390	630	29597	705	29812
406	30162	481	30753	556	28623	631	30169	706	30612
407	28312	482	28615	557	29052	632	30378	707	30603
408	29866	483	28616	558	30460	633	30358	708	30802
409	28954	484	28228	559	30081	634	30467	709	30540
410	28608	485	30062	560	29921	635	30599	710	29893
411	28955	486	30192	561	29248	636	30413	711	32353
412	30347	487	30073	562	28622	637	30512	712	30799
413	28956	488	30078	563	29501	638	30537	713	30635
414	28500	489	29041	564	30561	639	29598	714	30355
415	30330	490	29782	565	28828	640	30203	715	30236
416	29849	491	30572	566	29786	641	30774	716	30738
417	28609	492	28983	567	30499	642	29972	717	30470
418	30348	493	29247	568	29980	643	27885	718	29816
419	27871	494	30459	569	30756	644	30580	719	30415
420	28384	495	27875	570	28621	645	29535	720	29538
421	28385	496	29979	571	29922	646	30601	721	30604
422	27872	497	29783	572	30159	647	30581	722	29926
423	30547	498	28379	573	28628	648	30101	723	30382
424	29049	499	27987	574	30497	649	30085	724	30778
425	29850	500	28317	575	29532	650	30582	725	32354
426	28386	501	28985	576	29923	651	30200	726	30088
427	29879	502	30465	577	28321	652	30204	727	29927
428	30139	503	29529	578	29924	653	29249	728	30356
429	30050	504	28617	579	30082	654	30170	729	30541
430	30163	505	30466	580	30587	655	30600	730	30237
431	28807	506	28230	581	30429	656	30583	731	30475
432	29269	507	29094	582	28829	657	30379	732	30800
433	28225	508	27988	583	29596	658	30736	733	30196
434	29525	509	30079	584	30377	659	30359	734	28635
435	28808	510	29499	585	28624	660	30584	735	29928
436	30051	511	29880	586	30782	661	30165	736	27886
437	27873	512	27876	587	30193	662	30538	737	27887
438	28809	513	30376	588	29925	663	29982	738	30829
439	30343	514	28618	589	30562	664	28630	739	28236
440	29526	515	30231	590	28625	665	30775	740	30271
441	28957	516	30754	591	30613	666	30194	741	29539
442	29961	517	30063	592	30588	667	30779	742	30781
443	28958	518	30536	593	30500	668	30468	743	30664
444	29050	519	28986	594	30160	669	28830	744	27888
445	29857	520	27877	595	30589	670	29808	745	30089
446	30373	521	27878	596	30017	671	29536	746	30007
447	28313	522	28387	597	30164	672	30235	747	30884
448	30544	523	27992	598	28233	673	30469	748	30605
449	28610	524	28380	599	27879	674	30380	749	30403
450	30498	525	29805	600	30168	675	29809	750	30487

BOEING 737NG - Line No to C/n

line no	c/n	line no	c/n	line no	c/n	line no	c/n	line no	c/n
751	30206	826	32627	901	32402	976	30477	1051	32773
752	30627	827	28442	902	30857	977	30098	1052	30128
753	29929	828	28643	903	29817	978	30185	1053	29630
754	30792	829	30807	904	32407	979	32916	1054	28245
755	30835	830	30618	905	30134	980	29836	1055	30514
756	28636	831	32373	906	31583	981	29602	1056	32732
757	29930	832	28240	907	29626	982	31589	1057	30822
758	30739	833	30392	908	30689	983	32574	1058	30245
759	30876	834	29543	909	30041	984	28243	1059	32609
760	30882	835	30404	910	29546	985	30032	1060	33036
761	30567	836	32451	911	30122	986	28654	1061	29935
762	29540	837	30093	912	32806	987	31590	1062	31592
763	30793	838	30015	913	30238	988	32970	1063	29552
764	30090	839	28644	914	29627	989	30744	1064	30246
765	28638	840	28645	915	30096	990	32453	1065	29789
766	28014	841	28241	916	31584	991	30620	1066	30247
767	28324	842	30488	917	30493	992	29549	1067	30881
768	30636	843	30273	918	32357	993	29822	1068	30135
769	28237	844	30878	919	30243	994	32583	1069	32597
770	30836	845	30274	920	30276	995	32625	1070	28327
771	29787	846	32374	921	30813	996	32971	1071	30899
772	28639	847	28239	922	30743	997	30478	1072	29097
773	29095	848	29984	923	30814	998	32578	1073	30407
774	30013	849	29344	924	29600	999	29987	1074	29631
775	28498	850	30569	925	30184	1000	29823	1075	33079
776	30740	851	32404	926	32807	1001	30099	1076	30281
777	30332	852	29985	927	30405	1002	32579	1077	31593
778	30416	853	32774	928	31585	1003	29629	1078	32733
779	32438	854	30803	929	30706	1004	30126	1079	31594
780	30606	855	30830	930	32403	1005	30727	1080	30641
781	30417	856	30619	931	30042	1006	30818	1081	28246
782	30877	857	30119	932	28650	1007	30785	1082	29989
783	30883	858	30638	933	32348	1008	30819	1083	29883
784	27889	859	32406	934	27895	1009	32581	1084	32360
785	28015	860	29544	935	30639	1010	30279	1085	30746
786	30494	861	32575	936	30571	1011	30629	1086	30632
787	32450	862	30855	937	29547	1012	31591	1087	32906
788	29541	863	30094	938	28652	1013	32582	1088	29790
789	30476	864	30742	939	31586	1014	28325	1089	33080
790	30806	865	30489	940	32805	1015	32600	1090	32734
791	29788	866	29599	941	30097	1016	30406	1091	28247
792	29250	867	30490	942	28242	1017	29824	1092	28012
793	30568	868	30207	943	30123	1018	30652	1093	29826
794	29096	869	32243	944	30239	1019	29550	1094	29884
795	28440	870	32375	945	27896	1020	29931	1095	28987
796	30794	871	30879	946	27897	1021	30127	1096	29553
797	30091	872	28651	947	30277	1022	30100	1097	30642
798	30197	873	30784	948	28653	1023	32722	1098	32361
799	28640	874	30419	949	30815	1024	32580	1099	31595
800	30637	875	32576	950	29821	1025	30280	1100	30420
801	30828	876	30495	951	30124	1026	29988	1101	29827
802	30014	877	30133	952	30816	1027	30745	1102	30901
803	27890	878	28647	953	32628	1028	32596	1103	29632
804	30783	879	30570	954	32440	1029	30820	1104	32735
805	30837	880	27892	955	32358	1030	29932	1105	29828
806	27891	881	27893	956	29818	1031	30821	1106	30643
807	32355	882	32777	957	31587	1032	30630	1107	30644
808	30628	883	29545	958	28244	1033	32601	1108	30622
809	28641	884	30120	959	29601	1034	30241	1109	29829
810	29813	885	27894	960	29819	1035	30640	1110	32610
811	29814	886	30095	961	32624	1036	28326	1111	33102
812	30617	887	28649	962	30125	1037	33010	1112	30129
813	28642	888	28648	963	30278	1038	29933	1113	32736
814	30391	889	32775	964	29628	1039	29825	1114	29830
815	30418	890	30242	965	28655	1040	32452	1115	30209
816	29502	891	29986	966	31588	1041	32359	1116	29098
817	28238	892	30491	967	29820	1042	29551	1117	32907
818	29542	893	30121	968	30817	1043	30880	1118	30248
819	32356	894	30492	969	32915	1044	32731	1119	29831
820	30118	895	32244	970	31632	1045	30101	1120	29885
821	29815	896	30208	971	29548	1046	32905	1121	33003
822	30092	897	31582	972	32599	1047	30631	1122	30646
823	30741	898	30675	973	32577	1048	30649	1123	28249
824	30272	899	32626	974	30240	1049	30897	1124	33361
825	30858	900	30275	975	30707	1050	29934	1125	32362

BOEING 737NG - Line No to C/n

line no	c/n	line no	c/n	line no	c/n	line no	c/n	line no	c/n
1126	28248	1201	32614	1276	29890	1351	33409	1426	33555
1127	32903	1202	32413	1277	30795	1352	33725	1427	32469
1128	30249	1203	28011	1278	33462	1353	29833	1428	33556
1129	30645	1204	33405	1279	32919	1354	33410	1429	32470
1130	32737	1205	32632	1280	30286	1355	32930	1430	32933
1131	30545	1206	33378	1281	32749	1356	29834	1431	32758
1132	29345	1207	32615	1282	30411	1357	32421	1432	33058
1133	29888	1208	29993	1283	28254	1358	29835	1433	32423
1134	33005	1209	32365	1284	28255	1359	33758	1434	32739
1135	32611	1210	32917	1285	32417	1360	29837	1435	30291
1136	30623	1211	33434	1286	32750	1361	33549	1436	30665
1137	33478	1212	32616	1287	32797	1362	32931	1437	28261
1138	30786	1213	32923	1288	30035	1363	32422	1438	33557
1139	32363	1214	32414	1289	32368	1364	33759	1439	33788
1140	32778	1215	33417	1290	32927	1365	32459	1440	31634
1141	33479	1216	33379	1291	33011	1366	33550	1441	33558
1142	28250	1217	33499	1292	33463	1367	33014	1442	33802
1143	30282	1218	30019	1293	32920	1368	33551	1443	33559
1144	33004	1219	33038	1294	29891	1369	29838	1444	32740
1145	30136	1220	30633	1295	30654	1370	32757	1445	32759
1146	30408	1221	30463	1296	30856	1371	33552	1446	33017
1147	32885	1222	32753	1297	33715	1372	33553	1447	33560
1148	30244	1223	33500	1298	28256	1373	33794	1448	30667
1149	30033	1224	30517	1299	33464	1374	29839	1449	30037
1150	30210	1225	32633	1300	32418	1375	33795	1450	32424
1151	32412	1226	33418	1301	33716	1376	33707	1451	30292
1152	30546	1227	33039	1302	32904	1377	33796	1452	29350
1153	29889	1228	30410	1303	33697	1378	28259	1453	32425
1154	33103	1229	30634	1304	30656	1379	33708	1454	30021
1155	32881	1230	32924	1305	29892	1380	33680	1455	29349
1156	30283	1231	33380	1306	33012	1381	33783	1456	31606
1157	33480	1232	33542	1307	30671	1382	30662	1457	33059
1158	30650	1233	30284	1308	30287	1383	32634	1458	32495
1159	30647	1234	30787	1309	33699	1384	33015	1459	33420
1160	33481	1235	32366	1310	33717	1385	32754	1460	30666
1161	30462	1236	29936	1311	33718	1386	30663	1461	29846
1162	29990	1237	30285	1312	33719	1387	33709	1462	33799
1163	32882	1238	29937	1313	32454	1388	29841	1463	33561
1164	30211	1239	32747	1314	30412	1389	33797	1464	32742
1165	30515	1240	29938	1315	28258	1390	31596	1465	32934
1166	32364	1241	30464	1316	33465	1391	33798	1466	33562
1167	32779	1242	32371	1317	33013	1392	32738	1467	32799
1168	30516	1243	29844	1318	29347	1393	33784	1468	33803
1169	32278	1244	33040	1319	30657	1394	28438	1469	30294
1170	32602	1245	33474	1320	29994	1395	32932	1470	32798
1171	30648	1246	33656	1321	32419	1396	32755	1471	29351
1172	33482	1247	28253	1322	30288	1397	33710	1472	32760
1173	30461	1248	30625	1323	32928	1398	33785	1473	33563
1174	32698	1249	33544	1324	33722	1399	30289	1474	32426
1175	30174	1250	32925	1325	30658	1400	28260	1475	31635
1176	32631	1251	33419	1326	30018	1401	29842	1476	29847
1177	33483	1252	33545	1327	32372	1402	30680	1477	29851
1178	32780	1253	32367	1328	32455	1403	33786	1478	32943
1179	32883	1254	33657	1329	30659	1404	30679	1479	30669
1180	33484	1255	32918	1330	30660	1405	33720	1480	32462
1181	32884	1256	33658	1331	33408	1406	30290	1481	30670
1182	30175	1257	33659	1332	29995	1407	32635	1482	30668
1183	33485	1258	29886	1333	32751	1408	33764	1483	33800
1184	32612	1259	29845	1334	33470	1409	33721	1484	32463
1185	30409	1260	32415	1335	33723	1410	30692	1485	33856
1186	30661	1261	28988	1336	30036	1411	31597	1486	33677
1187	32921	1262	29939	1337	33104	1412	33760	1487	32741
1188	29991	1263	29887	1338	29996	1413	32756	1488	33018
1189	33367	1264	29346	1339	32752	1414	30690	1489	32427
1190	29992	1265	29940	1340	33724	1415	29348	1490	33857
1191	32604	1266	32748	1341	32420	1416	29997	1491	29352
1192	33471	1267	30651	1342	32456	1417	29363	1492	32497
1193	30624	1268	32926	1343	33472	1418	33554	1493	32761
1194	30621	1269	33546	1344	33679	1419	28439	1494	29998
1195	28252	1270	32416	1345	30421	1420	33761	1495	32428
1196	33473	1271	33547	1346	33698	1421	33787	1496	30293
1197	32613	1272	32796	1347	33057	1422	30693	1497	30672
1198	33037	1273	30626	1348	32299	1423	31598	1498	32944
1199	32922	1274	33548	1349	29832	1424	28328	1499	32464
1200	28251	1275	30034	1350	33740	1425	31599	1500	30673

BOEING 737NG - Line No to C/n

line no	c/n	line no	c/n	line no	c/n	line no	c/n	line no	c/n
1501	32762	1576	33806	1651	29358	1726	33664	1801	32493
1502	33019	1577	32473	1652	33572	1727	33994	1802	34321
1503	32743	1578	33807	1653	33999	1728	33009	1803	34620
1504	33801	1579	33852	1654	29641	1729	30001	1804	32664
1505	33705	1580	33971	1655	33573	1730	33919	1805	32606
1506	31600	1581	29354	1656	32483	1731	34153	1806	34248
1507	32935	1582	34014	1657	33816	1732	30826	1807	33580
1508	29353	1583	33854	1658	33574	1733	34026	1808	34297
1509	31636	1584	32744	1659	29359	1734	34154	1809	33581
1510	32465	1585	34006	1660	33575	1735	32488	1810	33476
1511	30674	1586	29356	1661	33061	1736	33995	1811	33582
1512	29999	1587	33853	1662	32655	1737	34232	1812	34298
1513	32466	1588	33016	1663	29855	1738	30020	1813	34004
1514	32679	1589	33855	1664	30824	1739	34263	1814	32842
1515	32467	1590	33808	1665	32769	1740	33976	1815	34180
1516	33451	1591	32476	1666	32801	1741	32489	1816	34286
1517	32468	1592	33809	1667	33021	1742	33666	1817	34251
1518	33706	1593	32661	1668	34010	1743	33453	1818	34157
1519	33829	1594	34015	1669	30683	1744	32490	1819	33823
1520	30677	1595	33810	1670	33576	1745	29672	1820	34333
1521	33830	1596	33867	1671	32656	1746	34260	1821	34005
1522	32763	1597	33793	1672	33022	1747	34293	1822	32494
1523	33858	1598	33972	1673	30682	1748	34164	1823	29364
1524	33789	1599	32766	1674	34242	1749	34019	1824	33585
1525	33859	1600	30295	1675	34011	1750	33644	1825	34477
1526	32681	1601	30038	1676	34167	1751	34323	1826	33824
1527	33969	1602	32825	1677	33817	1752	33660	1827	32665
1528	33860	1603	32938	1678	34012	1753	33920	1828	34405
1529	33804	1604	33836	1679	29856	1754	32771	1829	34299
1530	33805	1605	33866	1680	33833	1755	33649	1830	34247
1531	32936	1606	33973	1681	32800	1756	32491	1831	34450
1532	33762	1607	32939	1682	33023	1757	33766	1832	32607
1533	33790	1608	32663	1683	32484	1758	34303	1833	32666
1534	33763	1609	29355	1684	34151	1759	34284	1834	33583
1535	32471	1610	33974	1685	33818	1760	33645	1835	32496
1536	30000	1611	33454	1686	29668	1761	34294	1836	33584
1537	33831	1612	33991	1687	32657	1762	34000	1837	34537
1538	33411	1613	33811	1688	33024	1763	34320	1838	33663
1539	33765	1614	33962	1689	30684	1764	33646	1839	33963
1540	33452	1615	33812	1690	34162	1765	34295	1840	34181
1541	33832	1616	32477	1691	33819	1766	32603	1841	29365
1542	31607	1617	33813	1692	29669	1767	34027	1842	34182
1543	33861	1618	33814	1693	30010	1768	34165	1843	34474
1544	33412	1619	30676	1694	29361	1769	34020	1844	33586
1545	32474	1620	30002	1695	32658	1770	33661	1845	33922
1546	33566	1621	33868	1696	33820	1771	34028	1846	34183
1547	33567	1622	33455	1697	34168	1772	34155	1847	33825
1548	33826	1623	32667	1698	33821	1773	34166	1848	34300
1549	32475	1624	32940	1699	34163	1774	34021	1849	34304
1550	33917	1625	33869	1700	29671	1775	33665	1850	33872
1551	33996	1626	32478	1701	34170	1776	34259	1851	34252
1552	33988	1627	32652	1702	30691	1777	34322	1852	34406
1553	32764	1628	32479	1703	34024	1778	33921	1853	34538
1554	32277	1629	32767	1704	30686	1779	34001	1854	34184
1555	33989	1630	29357	1705	32841	1780	34290	1855	32608
1556	33970	1631	33568	1706	33992	1781	33916	1856	34539
1557	33791	1632	30827	1707	33025	1782	33577	1857	34249
1558	33990	1633	32480	1708	32485	1783	34296	1858	32498
1559	33997	1634	33956	1709	32659	1784	34250	1859	34683
1560	33413	1635	33569	1710	32660	1785	34622	1860	34593
1561	33998	1636	32481	1711	29670	1786	34022	1861	34896
1562	33564	1637	33570	1712	33993	1787	34002	1862	34621
1563	33565	1638	32482	1713	29362	1788	32662	1863	30694
1564	29853	1639	33815	1714	34152	1789	30685	1864	33587
1565	28262	1640	30022	1715	33026	1790	33654	1865	34865
1566	32653	1641	32654	1716	33975	1791	34003	1866	34253
1567	31601	1642	33571	1717	34217	1792	33578	1867	34588
1568	29852	1643	29639	1718	33008	1793	34156	1868	34592
1569	32937	1644	29360	1719	32770	1794	33579	1869	33589
1570	32472	1645	30681	1720	34262	1795	34023	1870	34684
1571	33792	1646	33060	1721	32486	1796	32605	1871	33873
1572	33918	1647	30296	1722	33648	1797	34285	1872	29366
1573	34013	1648	32768	1723	32487	1798	33822	1873	34407
1574	32765	1649	29640	1724	34025	1799	32492	1874	34479
1575	33841	1650	29854	1725	32802	1800	34030	1875	34596

BOEING 737NG - Line No to C/n

line no	c/n	line no	c/n	line no	c/n	line no	c/n	line no	c/n
1876	32668	1951	32693	2026	35178	2102	35362	2176	35093
1877	34540	1952	32674	2027	34973	2103	33020	2177	36328
1878	33977	1953	30702	2028	34277	2104	34898	2178	35788
1879	32772	1954	34714	2029	35959	2105	35046	2179	33609
1880	34408	1955	35478	2030	34399	2106	34949	2180	33064
1881	32499	1956	34289	2031	35177	2107	35990	2181	36088
1882	34595	1957	33978	2032	35570	2108	36323	2182	32523
1883	33062	1958	34704	2033	32691	2109	33602	2183	33610
1884	34633	1959	32503	2034	33046	2110	34656	2184	34690
1885	33477	1960	32694	2035	31604	2111	35787	2185	30712
1886	33590	1961	30709	2036	34560	2112	33603	2186	32685
1887	34701	1962	34535	2037	35114	2113	35559	2187	34755
1888	32500	1963	33979	2038	32511	2114	32518	2188	30710
1889	32684	1964	30703	2039	34653	2115	35070	2189	33611
1890	33874	1965	32504	2040	32512	2116	34281	2190	33928
1891	30695	1966	35238	2041	34861	2117	32682	2191	35365
1892	30696	1967	33925	2042	35089	2118	36106	2192	35184
1893	32501	1968	33030	2043	34561	2119	35790	2193	32525
1894	33591	1969	32505	2044	34799	2120	33604	2194	35048
1895	32669	1970	32675	2045	35571	2121	34709	2195	35094
1896	29367	1971	33875	2046	34707	2122	35116	2196	36090
1897	34254	1972	34413	2047	35977	2122	35117	2197	35073
1898	32670	1973	34863	2048	32834	2123	33623	2198	33640
1899	34177	1974	32676	2049	32513	2124	33828	2199	32524
1900	34480	1975	34255	2050	35045	2125	34801	2200	35549
1901	34685	1976	33043	2051	35360	2126	35109	2201	35789
1902	33041	1977	34864	2052	34278	2127	35210	2202	30714
1903	34686	1978	34414	2053	34400	2128	34899	2203	29374
1904	33592	1979	33964	2054	35558	2129	33929	2204	32526
1905	32502	1980	35175	2055	32678	2130	35047	2205	30370
1906	34594	1981	35680	2056	34443	2131	29372	2206	33065
1907	34687	1982	32506	2057	33596	2132	36324	2207	33612
1908	34807	1983	33006	2058	33621	2133	32517	2208	34756
1909	34688	1984	32507	2059	32514	2134	35181	2209	34803
1910	29368	1985	30704	2060	33597	2135	35985	2210	30716
1911	30698	1986	33007	2061	34279	2136	32683	2211	36493
1912	34287	1987	33044	2062	32515	2137	29370	2212	35185
1913	33063	1988	34415	2063	33598	2138	35071	2213	33613
1914	33593	1989	32508	2064	29371	2139	32519	2214	33931
1915	30697	1990	34256	2065	32832	2140	33605	2215	34962
1916	34630	1991	33987	2066	35363	2141	34809	2216	34401
1917	34702	1992	33876	2067	35209	2142	36325	2217	35074
1918	33027	1993	34542	2068	36027	2143	33930	2218	32688
1919	32695	1994	31602	2069	34897	2144	34710	2219	33614
1920	34798	1995	34536	2070	35115	2145	33878	2220	30713
1921	34029	1996	34416	2071	33900	2146	35211	2221	35186
1922	32696	1997	33926	2072	35179	2147	35110	2222	33641
1923	33594	1998	34705	2073	35090	2148	36326	2223	35366
1924	34409	1999	33045	2074	34948	2149	34562	2224	32527
1925	32671	2000	32509	2075	34654	2150	35791	2225	35332
1926	33595	2001	30705	2076	32516	2151	35118	2226	35187
1927	34410	2002	32677	2077	35361	2152	35134	2227	35550
1928	34631	2003	34440	2078	33599	2153	32520	2228	30717
1929	34178	2004	35111	2079	35069	2154	36327	2229	32687
1930	34632	2005	34951	2080	33965	2155	35072	2230	30715
1931	34288	2006	34543	2082	33600	2156	35364	2231	29644
1932	32672	2007	34797	2083	33923	2157	33879	2232	33880
1933	30699	2008	34808	2084	35091	2158	33606	2233	36089
1934	33986	2009	34417	2085	34800	2159	30711	2234	33932
1935	34689	2010	35176	2086	33877	2160	35092	2235	30720
1936	33028	2011	35785	2087	30708	2161	32521	2236	35551
1937	34541	2012	34418	2088	33601	2162	35331	2237	35367
1938	33834	2013	34559	2089	32680	2163	33607	2238	32528
1939	29369	2014	34706	2090	35180	2164	35182	2239	34967
1940	33924	2015	34441	2091	34655	2165	34753	2240	34963
1941	34703	2016	35112	2092	35554	2166	35183	2241	34757
1942	30700	2017	31603	2093	35679	2167	34900	2242	35131
1943	32673	2018	35044	2094	34862	2168	33624	2243	34169
1944	34411	2019	34972	2095	35330	2169	33927	2244	32529
1945	33029	2020	34475	2096	34258	2170	34802	2245	33980
1946	30701	2021	34419	2097	34708	2171	29373	2246	34691
1947	33042	2022	35113	2098	35786	2172	34754	2247	29642
1948	34438	2023	34461	2099	35103	2173	33608	2248	36073
1949	34412	2024	34257	2100	34280	2174	32522	2249	34692
1950	34713	2025	32510	2101	33622	2175	32686	2250	32690

BOEING 737NG - Line No to C/n

line no	c/n	line no	c/n	line no	c/n	line no	c/n	line no	c/n
2251	30718	2326	29635	2401	34761	2476		2551	
2252	30687	2327	35121	2402	35381	2477	30734	2552	
2253	35333	2328	32535	2403	36483	2478		2553	
2254	32689	2329	35376	2404	34806	2479		2554	
2255	30721	2330	35749	2405	36756	2480		2555	
2256	36153	2331	32276	2406	35220	2481		2556	
2257	30719	2332	34964	2407	34268	2482		2557	
2258	36329	2333	35681	2408	33637	2483		2558	
2259	35188	2334	35503	2409	32541	2484		2559	
2260	34693	2335	34903	2410	33643	2485		2560	
2261	30722	2336	35096	2411	36077	2486		2561	
2262	32530	2337	32536	2412	34269	2487		2562	
2263	35552	2338	33982	2413	36613	2488		2563	
2264	35368	2339	36845	2414	29675	2489		2564	
2265	34968	2340	36714	2415	36078	2490		2565	
2266	34758	2341	34965	2416	33618	2491		2566	
2267	34901	2342	35218	2417	32542	2492		2567	
2268	33882	2343	35068	2418	35052	2493		2568	
2269	33981	2344	32537	2419	35077	2494		2569	
2270	34402	2345	35097	2420	34270	2495		2570	
2271	35049	2346	35378	2421	36114	2496		2571	
2272	35369	2347	34904	2422	35684	2497		2572	
2273	35119	2348	35122	2423	35067	2498		2573	
2274	32531	2349	35712	2424	35100	2499		2574	
2275	32692	2350	36611	2425	36118	2500		2575	
2276	35132	2351	35792	2426	34952	2501		2576	
2277	35212	2352	34760	2427	34762	2502		2577	
2278	33933	2353	36602	2428	35793	2503		2578	
2279	35553	2354	36633	2429	36190	2504		2579	
2280	30688	2355	29660	2430	36080	2505		2580	
2281	36441	2356	36603	2431	35078	2506		2581	
2282	29646	2357	36269	2432	29676	2507		2582	
2283	30723	2358	36146	2433	35747	2508		2583	
2284	32532	2359	35217	2434	35560	2509		2584	
2285	35710	2360	34805	2435	35700	2510		2585	
2286	30724	2361	35098	2436	35505	2511		2586	
2287	35075	2362	35768	2437	35713	2512		2587	
2288	30471	2363	36632	2438	32543	2513		2588	
2289	35334	2364	35051	2439	35099	2514		2589	
2290	35120	2365	35682	2440	36079	2515		2590	
2291	35372	2366	35504	2441	36484	2516		2591	
2292	30725	2367	34966	2442	36614	2517		2592	
2293	34969	2368	36046	2443	36082	2518		2593	
2294	32533	2369	35561	2444	35221	2519		2594	
2295	35095	2370	33883	2445	34271	2520		2595	
2296	33934	2371	35219	2446	35384	2521		2596	
2297	34804	2372	35380	2447	35053	2522		2597	
2298	30726	2373	29673	2448	36081	2523		2598	
2299	35370	2374	35123	2449	34272	2524		2599	
2300	35213	2375	33615	2450	35336	2525		2600	
2301	33881	2376	33616	2451	35135	2526		2601	
2302	35371	2377	33617	2452	30733	2527		2602	
2303	29643	2378	32539	2453	36191	2528		2603	
2304	36091	2379	34970	2454	35685	2529		2604	
2305	35050	2380	35076	2455	35717	2530		2605	
2306	35215	2381	36332	2456	35124	2531		2606	
2307	36528	2382	36075	2457	29685	2532		2607	
2308	35214	2383	32538	2458	35686	2533		2608	
2309	34902	2384	36076	2459	35101	2534		2609	
2310	35954	2385	35683	2460	32544	2535		2610	
2311	34267	2386	30728	2461	35714	2536		2611	
2312	36399	2387	36612	2462	32545	2537		2612	
2313	35133	2388	36847	2463	35222	2538		2613	
2314	35375	2389	33642	2464	34273	2539		2614	
2315	33935	2390	32540	2465	35136	2540		2615	
2316	35767	2391	36074	2466	34953	2541		2616	
2317	36330	2392	34905	2467	30360	2542		2617	
2318	32534	2393	35189	2468	34274	2543		2618	
2319	35711	2394	33888	2469	36615	2544		2619	
2320	34759	2395	35335	2470	36485	2545		2620	
2321	35216	2396	33619	2471	35102	2546		2621	
2322	36610	2397	33620	2472		2547		2622	
2323	35502	2398	36270	2473		2548		2623	
2324	36331	2399	30730	2474		2549		2624	
2325	36107	2400	34971	2475		2550		2625	

BOEING 747 - Line No to C/n

line no	c/n	line no	c/n	line no	c/n	line no	c/n	line no	c/n
1	20235	76	19957	151	20082	226	20802	301	21263
2	19639	77	20105	152	20398	227	20799	302	21239
3	19638	78	19678	153	20083	228	20800	303	21326
4	19637	79	20106	154	20237	229	20782	304	21300
5	19667	80	20080	155	20246	230	20783	305	21240
6	19640	81	19919	156	20399	231	20784	306	21441
7	19641	82	19897	157	20400	232	20684	307	21093
8	19668	83	19786	158	20238	233	20841	308	21321
9	19669	84	19744	159	20247	234	20923	309	21316
10	19642	85	20081	160	20239	235	20924	310	21352
11	19643	86	20107	161	20332	236	20881	311	21381
12	19746	87	20108	162	20011	237	20653	312	21439
13	19644	88	20356	163	20359	238	20842	313	21429
14	19645	89	19875	164	20274	239	20928	314	21354
15	19646	90	20109	165	20360	240	20888	315	21486
16	19647	91	19958	166	20333	241	20921	316	21353
17	19648	92	20401	167	20121	242	20826	317	21241
18	19649	93	19787	168	20373	243	21034	318	21446
19	19749	94	19898	169	20270	244	20927	319	21487
20	19670	95	20402	170	20427	245	20887	320	21380
21	19671	96	19922	171	20012	246	20952	321	21350
22	19750	97	19876	172	20271	247	20929	322	21454
23	19761	98	20320	173	20137	248	20953	323	21351
24	19650	99	19877	174	20376	249	21032	324	21468
25	19651	100	20207	175	19882	250	20977	325	21547
26	19652	101	19878	176	20377	251	21030	326	21516
27	19778	102	20321	177	20378	252	20954	327	21594
28	19672	103	20347	178	20501	253	21048	328	21536
29	19747	104	20013	179	20527	254	21033	329	21652
30	19653	105	20355	180	20503	255	21031	330	21473
31	19725	106	20348	181	20504	256	21035	331	21548
32	19654	107	19764	182	20505	257	20949	332	21541
33	19655	108	19745	183	20272	258	21120	333	21537
34	19656	109	19765	184	20273	259	21029	334	21576
35	19673	110	20349	185	20459	260	21054	335	21542
36	19729	111	19766	186	20559	261	21121	336	21549
37	19657	112	20116	187	20284	262	21097	337	21515
38	19674	113	20322	188	20558	263	21098	338	21615
39	19751	114	20120	189	20502	264	21099	339	21657
40	19779	115	20323	190	20520	265	21022	340	21507
41	19762	116	19823	191	20528	266	20827	341	21658
42	19733	117	20350	192	20529	267	21140	342	21588
43	19675	118	19923	193	19883	268	21023	343	21514
44	19748	119	20324	194	20556	269	21122	344	21550
45	19780	120	19731	195	20534	270	21024	345	21589
46	20100	121	20014	196	20530	271	21110	346	21604
47	19658	122	19824	197	20531	272	21190	347	21592
48	19763	123	20208	198	20557	273	21025	348	21590
49	19659	124	19959	199	20532	274	21189	349	21725
50	19660	125	20325	200	20541	275	20998	350	21591
51	19726	126	20117	201	20542	276	21111	351	21605
52	19753	127	20351	202	20682	277	21182	352	21643
53	19752	128	20493	203	20543	278	20999	353	21614
54	19727	129	20352	204	20683	279	21141	354	21650
55	19781	130	19960	205	19925	280	21132	355	21627
56	19730	131	20353	206	19926	281	21213	356	21644
57	20101	132	20372	207	19927	282	21133	357	21704
58	19734	133	20326	208	19928	283	21162	358	21575
59	20102	134	19732	209	20651	284	21174	359	21543
60	19754	135	20357	210	20708	285	21237	360	21606
61	19755	136	20390	211	20652	286	21026	361	21678
62	19782	137	19825	212	20704	287	21180	362	21737
63	19676	138	19924	213	20770	288	21134	363	21772
64	19735	139	19879	214	20767	289	21181	364	21731
65	20103	140	20135	215	20771	290	21175	365	21635
66	19756	141	20358	216	20742	291	21217	366	21773
67	19757	142	20354	217	20535	292	21238	367	21648
68	19918	143	20391	218	20712	293	21253	368	21517
69	20104	144	20015	219	20713	294	21220	369	21659
70	19661	145	19880	220	20809	295	21255	370	21745
71	19783	146	20305	221	20781	296	21251	371	21758
72	19896	147	20009	222	20810	297	21252	372	21730
73	19677	148	19881	223	20825	298	21254	373	21649
74	19784	149	20010	224	20798	299	21221	374	21705
75	19785	150	20269	225	20801	300	21218	375	21682

BOEING 747 - Line No to C/n

line no	c/n	line no	c/n	line no	c/n	line no	c/n	line no	c/n
376	21679	451	22239	526	22442	601	23150	676	23610
377	21706	452	22246	527	22723	602	23222	677	23799
378	21707	453	22291	528	22724	603	23032	678	23823
379	21708	454	22481	529	22503	604	23138	679	23824
380	21680	455	21933	530	22502	605	22487	680	23887
381	21759	456	22292	531	22530	606	23223	681	23721
382	21681	457	21940	532	22592	607	23151	682	23888
383	21825	458	22245	533	22510	608	23139	683	23813
384	21743	459	22247	534	22547	609	23033	684	23641
385	21746	460	22237	535	22678	610	23224	685	23825
386	21843	461	22248	536	22511	611	22489	686	23751
387	21683	462	22299	537	22672	612	23243	687	23864
388	21835	463	22272	538	22668	613	23300	688	23722
389	21660	464	22614	539	22380	614	23286	689	23919
390	21829	465	22234	540	22496	615	23221	690	23920
391	21684	466	22149	541	22709	616	23262	691	23969
392	21744	467	21934	542	22512	617	23287	692	23967
393	21922	468	22249	543	22616	618	23301	693	23968
394	21764	469	22107	544	22710	619	23263	694	24018
395	21923	470	21941	545	22545	620	23264	695	24019
396	21841	471	21942	546	22513	621	23244	696	23719
397	21848	472	22169	547	22745	622	23265	697	24088
398	21787	473	22302	548	22746	623	23350	698	24067
399	21935	474	22376	549	22669	624	23266	699	24071
400	21668	475	21943	550	22670	625	23348	700	23817
401	21936	476	22150	551	22747	626	23245	701	24106
402	21782	477	22293	552	22593	627	23394	702	24107
403	21726	478	22151	553	22740	628	23461	703	24108
404	21727	479	22337	554	22764	629	23395	704	24161
405	21785	480	22306	555	22748	630	23267	705	23814
406	21827	481	22294	556	22447	631	23268	706	24138
407	22064	482	22390	557	22749	632	23413	707	24162
408	21828	483	22615	558	22794	633	23393	708	23720
409	21977	484	22482	559	22711	634	23392	709	24215
410	22145	485	22427	560	22750	635	23389	710	24177
411	22065	486	22170	561	22768	636	23390	711	24159
412	21709	487	22297	562	22769	637	23409	712	24134
413	21786	488	22171	563	22725	638	23408	713	24194
414	21993	489	22478	564	22805	639	23407	714	24158
415	21961	490	22363	565	22366	640	23482	715	23818
416	21964	491	22379	566	22872	641	23480	716	24156
417	21783	492	22506	567	22858	642	23547	717	24061
418	22254	493	22429	568	22791	643	23269	718	24195
419	21937	494	22477	569	22939	644	23548	719	24160
420	21924	495	22303	570	22704	645	23270	720	24196
421	21832	496	22479	571	22989	646	23439	721	23819
422	21925	497	22507	572	22712	647	23476	722	24062
423	21833	498	22382	573	22870	648	23501	723	23816
424	21784	499	22508	574	22671	649	23502	724	24359
425	21834	500	22381	575	22969	650	23600	725	23999
426	22066	501	22483	576	22705	651	23549	726	23820
427	22067	502	22304	577	22970	652	23271	727	23908
428	21982	503	22428	578	22971	653	23410	728	23815
429	22077	504	22471	579	22990	654	23391	729	24198
430	21830	505	22495	580	23026	655	23637	730	23909
431	21994	506	22305	581	22991	656	23611	731	24354
432	22063	507	22484	582	23048	657	23508	732	24000
433	21932	508	22378	583	23027	658	23638	733	24322
434	21995	509	22454	584	23028	659	23534	734	23910
435	22105	510	21944	585	22995	660	23621	735	23982
436	21938	511	22594	586	22996	661	23676	736	24063
437	21991	512	22498	587	23056	662	23688	737	24001
438	21965	513	22485	588	23067	663	23509	738	24315
439	21962	514	22579	589	23068	664	23639	739	24199
440	21831	515	22455	590	23029	665	23622	740	24363
441	21963	516	22595	591	23071	666	23769	741	24154
442	22389	517	22499	592	23070	667	23698	742	23821
443	22106	518	22514	593	23030	668	23640	743	24346
444	22388	519	22446	594	23111	669	23652	744	23911
445	22298	520	22486	595	23112	670	23746	745	24405
446	21966	521	22515	596	23120	671	23709	746	24373
447	21992	522	22500	597	22472	672	23711	747	24285
448	22480	523	22722	598	23031	673	23736	748	24200
449	21939	524	22403	599	23149	674	23735	749	24286
450	22238	525	22501	600	23137	675	23737	750	24399

BOEING 747 - Line No to C/n

line no	c/n	line no	c/n	line no	c/n	line no	c/n	line no	c/n
751	24406	826	24887	901	25600	976	27141	1051	27898
752	24308	827	24976	902	26341	977	24313	1052	26560
753	24047	828	24058	903	25432	978	26352	1053	27899
754	24287	829	24447	904	25879	979	25645	1054	25883
755	24064	830	24621	905	26342	980	26353	1055	26397
756	24386	831	24227	906	25601	981	27134	1056	26552
757	24288	832	24920	907	26347	982	27142	1057	26398
758	24423	833	24993	908	25435	983	25778	1058	25434
759	24380	834	24925	909	25602	984	26880	1059	25813
760	24424	835	24974	910	26426	985	26473	1060	27436
761	24065	836	24969	911	25379	986	26394	1061	27595
762	24381	837	24895	912	25422	987	27078	1062	27915
763	24201	838	24975	913	25380	988	26474	1063	27965
764	24481	839	24731	914	25639	989	26881	1064	25783
765	24482	840	24998	915	26427	990	27137	1065	27503
766	24309	841	24629	916	25545	991	25647	1066	27442
767	24425	842	24630	917	24956	992	26374	1067	27662
768	24426	843	24990	918	26343	993	25869	1068	27663
769	24458	844	25213	919	25395	994	27154	1069	26553
770	24202	845	25045	920	25640	995	26638	1070	26554
771	24631	846	24966	921	25640	996	27163	1071	27723
772	24735	847	25046	922	26395	997	25701	1072	27071
773	24048	848	24967	923	26548	998	27173	1073	28096
774	24049	849	25082	924	25546	999	25702	1074	26562
775	24347	850	25086	925	25871	1000	27068	1075	26555
776	24568	851	25064	926	25880	1001	26609	1076	28092
777	24459	852	25068	927	25642	1002	25866	1077	28093
778	24310	853	25205	928	25641	1003	27164	1078	25809
779	24050	854	25087	929	26344	1004	27174	1079	25814
780	24427	855	24896	930	25872	1005	27261	1080	28086
781	24483	856	25047	931	26875	1006	25779	1081	26255
782	24517	857	25067	932	27042	1007	25870	1082	28022
783	24518	858	25126	933	25605	1008	25867	1083	26400
784	24051	859	25127	934	25628	1009	27165	1084	26556
785	24715	860	25128	935	26345	1010	27069	1085	26890
786	24740	861	25152	936	25547	1011	25704	1086	25784
787	24741	862	25074	937	25873	1012	27262	1087	26401
788	24850	863	25135	938	25413	1013	27072	1088	26892
789	24052	864	24155	939	26876	1014	27202	1089	28094
790	24053	865	25151	940	27066	1015	27178	1090	28195
791	24066	866	25158	941	26348	1016	26062	1091	27672
792	24348	867	25224	942	27062	1017	27043	1092	26402
793	24619	868	25075	943	26637	1018	25811	1093	28095
794	24054	869	24311	944	26877	1019	27177	1094	28263
795	24055	870	25207	945	27093	1020	27175	1095	26403
796	24761	871	25212	946	25777	1021	25882	1096	28367
797	24777	872	25238	947	27063	1022	25812	1097	26616
798	24784	873	25211	948	26349	1023	27217	1098	28335
799	24222	874	25275	949	25874	1024	26354	1099	28023
800	24223	875	25245	950	26615	1025	25703	1100	28194
801	24779	876	25260	951	26396	1026	26355	1101	26557
802	24056	877	24955	952	25646	1027	26055	1102	25817
803	24224	878	25266	953	27067	1028	24958	1103	28284
804	24225	879	25214	954	24312	1029	25705	1104	25818
805	24801	880	25405	955	27132	1030	26549	1105	28026
806	24382	881	25278	956	25629	1031	27099	1106	28285
807	24806	882	25279	957	25881	1032	26056	1107	26404
808	24836	883	25315	958	26393	1033	27230	1108	27478
809	24226	884	25302	959	27090	1034	27214	1109	28286
810	24837	885	25308	960	25630	1035	25780	1110	28287
811	24383	886	25171	961	26350	1036	26563	1111	27724
812	24833	887	25351	962	27133	1037	27341	1112	28459
813	24851	888	25356	963	26351	1038	27827	1113	26899
814	24960	889	25344	964	27091	1039	27828	1114	28709
815	24855	890	25366	965	25699	1040	26550	1115	25782
816	24730	891	25292	966	26878	1041	27044	1116	28700
817	24057	892	25452	967	27092	1042	26561	1117	28757
818	24576	893	26392	968	25632	1043	26326	1118	26405
819	24384	894	25544	969	26372	1044	25781	1119	28754
820	24385	895	25406	970	27117	1045	26551	1120	28715
821	24870	896	26373	971	24957	1046	27338	1121	26901
822	24879	897	26346	972	25643	1047	26610	1122	28339
823	24883	898	26425	973	26879	1048	27349	1123	26406
824	24885	899	25599	974	25700	1049	27070	1124	28716
825	24886	900	25427	975	25644	1050	27350	1125	25868

BOEING 747 - Line No to C/n

line no	c/n	line no	c/n	line no	c/n	line no	c/n	line no	c/n
1126	28717	1201	28811	1276	28029	1351	33748	1426	
1127	28196	1202	26362	1277	32340	1352	33749	1427	
1128	28755	1203	29730	1278	32370	1353	33734	1428	
1129	28848	1204	29263	1279	30608	1354	33735	1429	
1130	28426	1205	29493	1280	27646	1355	33739	1430	
1131	28551	1206	26477	1281	29733	1356	34150	1431	
1132	28710	1207	28812	1282	30805	1357	33736	1432	
1133	28282	1208	29899	1283	30811	1358	33737	1433	
1134	27725	1209	29166	1284	26412	1359	33733	1434	
1135	28849	1210	27603	1285	26559	1360	34016	1435	
1136	28711	1211	29167	1286	26413	1361	33097	1436	
1137	28712	1212	28859	1287	32745	1362	33738	1437	
1138	28340	1213	29256	1288	30765	1363	34017	1438	
1139	29053	1214	28706	1289	28025	1364	32902	1439	
1140	29061	1215	29328	1290	28433	1365	34301	1440	
1141	26902	1216	28342	1291	27073	1366	34235	1441	
1142	28283	1217	29257	1292	32445	1367	34239	1442	
1143	29101	1218	29168	1293	29871	1368	34302	1443	
1144	28850	1219	29906	1294	30766	1369	32901	1444	
1145	29030	1220	29258	1295	26414	1370	29907	1445	
1146	25820	1221	28813	1296	29900	1371	28434	1446	
1147	28427	1222	29731	1297	33001	1372	34265	1447	
1148	28851	1223	30267	1298	28030	1373	34240	1448	
1149	25821	1224	28032	1299	29872	1374	29902	1449	
1150	28428	1225	28460	1300	30767	1375	35526	1450	
1151	29111	1226	30268	1301	29901	1376	35170	1451	
1152	28435	1227	29259	1302	30455	1377	35207	1452	
1153	26359	1228	29375	1303	33002	1378	34018	1453	
1154	25810	1229	29071	1304	32837	1379	34266	1454	
1155	26407	1230	25564	1305	29170	1380	35171	1455	
1156	25819	1231	29732	1306	32803	1381	35232	1456	
1157	25822	1232	30269	1307	32838	1382	35233	1457	
1158	28959	1233	25565	1308	32909	1383	35172	1458	
1159	29112	1234	27650	1309	30609	1384	34283	1459	
1160	28552	1235	30400	1310	30812	1385	30771	1460	
1161	27602	1236	27100	1311	30401	1386	35234	1461	
1162	28468	1237	29868	1312	32804	1387	35173	1462	
1163	26408	1238	30201	1313	32910	1388	35667	1463	
1164	28705	1239	25566	1314	30768	1389	35235	1464	
1165	29252	1240	29260	1315	32866	1390	35804	1465	
1166	26360	1241	29950	1316	32809	1391	35169	1466	
1167	28960	1242	30558	1317	33096	1392	35208	1467	
1168	26900	1243	30158	1318	32867	1393	35662	1468	
1169	29253	1244	30559	1319	32840	1394	36132	1469	
1170	26409	1245	30023	1320	32911	1395	35420	1470	
1171	26903	1246	26416	1321	32912	1396	35669	1471	
1172	28852	1247	28432	1322	32897	1397	36133	1472	
1173	26558	1248	26411	1323	32808	1398		1473	
1174	28961	1249	30759	1324	33684	1399		1474	
1175	28756	1250	30322	1325	32868	1400		1475	
1176	29219	1251	30607	1326	33694	1401		1476	
1177	29406	1252	30760	1327	32869	1402		1477	
1178	28853	1253	27648	1328	33695	1403		1478	
1179	29254	1254	30761	1329	33515	1404		1479	
1180	26910	1255	30804	1330	32913	1405		1480	
1181	29070	1256	28027	1331	32914	1406		1481	
1182	28341	1257	30808	1332	33729	1407		1482	
1183	28854	1258	30454	1333	32898	1408		1483	
1184	29255	1259	30809	1334	33731	1409		1484	
1185	26906	1260	30810	1335	33770	1410		1485	
1186	29031	1261	29869	1336	32746	1411		1486	
1187	29119	1262	27645	1337	33771	1412		1487	
1188	26361	1263	30762	1338	33516	1413		1488	
1189	29729	1264	29870	1339	33732	1414		1489	
1190	28855	1265	28343	1340	33517	1415		1490	
1191	29492	1266	28031	1341	33696	1416		1491	
1192	29261	1267	30763	1342	32899	1417		1492	
1193	26908	1268	30885	1343	32871	1418		1493	
1194	28856	1269	30764	1344	32870	1419		1494	
1195	25823	1270	28028	1345	33827	1420		1495	
1196	28857	1271	32571	1346	30769	1421		1496	
1197	28810	1272	32337	1347	33945	1422		1497	
1198	28858	1273	32369	1348	30770	1423		1498	
1199	29262	1274	32338	1349	32900	1424		1499	
1200	25824	1275	32339	1350	33946	1425		1500	

BOEING 757 - Line No to C/n

line no	c/n	line no	c/n	line no	c/n	line no	c/n	line no	c/n
1	22212	76	23321	151	22690	226	24369	301	24473
2	22191	77	23398	152	23917	227	24451	302	24838
3	22192	78	23399	153	23929	228	24497	303	24583
4	22193	79	23322	154	23613	229	24389	304	24584
5	22194	80	23323	155	22691	230	24390	305	24839
6	22195	81	23400	156	23918	231	24471	306	24840
7	22196	82	23200	157	23614	232	24401	307	24860
8	22197	83	23201	158	23615	233	24402	308	24585
9	22172	84	22820	159	23762	234	24486	309	24586
10	22173	85	22821	160	24072	235	24472	310	24861
11	22174	86	23202	161	23983	236	24487	311	24871
12	22198	87	22822	162	24017	237	24456	312	24872
13	22175	88	23203	163	24118	238	24391	313	24890
14	22176	89	23492	164	23763	239	24392	314	24868
15	22780	90	23493	165	24135	240	24488	315	24587
16	22177	91	22823	166	24073	241	24622	316	24588
17	22199	92	22907	167	24119	242	24489	317	24589
18	22781	93	23533	168	24074	243	24490	318	23903
19	22960	94	23452	169	24136	244	24233	319	24891
20	22200	95	22908	170	24104	245	24491	320	24931
21	22201	96	23566	171	23760	246	24623	321	24590
22	22202	97	23567	172	24105	247	24624	322	23904
23	22178	98	23532	173	24176	248	24524	323	24882
24	22179	99	23568	174	24120	249	24527	324	24591
25	22180	100	23453	175	24101	250	24528	325	24884
26	22203	101	22909	176	23728	251	24625	326	23905
27	22204	102	23454	177	23761	252	24522	327	24592
28	22205	103	23686	178	24137	253	24525	328	24593
29	22181	104	23204	179	24102	254	24626	329	24932
30	22182	105	23205	180	24235	255	24566	330	23906
31	22206	106	23687	181	23729	256	24523	331	24977
32	22183	107	23206	182	23863	257	24567	332	24923
33	22184	108	23207	183	24121	258	24635	333	24924
34	22185	109	23208	184	23730	259	24636	334	23907
35	22207	110	23209	185	24254	260	24526	335	24972
36	23118	111	22910	186	23731	261	24393	336	24594
37	22808	112	22911	187	24122	262	24/14	337	24595
38	22208	113	22912	188	23845	263	24627	338	24978
39	22809	114	22612	189	23732	264	24394	339	24994
40	22209	115	22688	190	23846	265	24395	340	24971
41	22810	116	23651	191	23851	266	24396	341	24995
42	22210	117	22689	192	24263	267	24737	342	24991
43	22811	118	22913	193	23852	268	24543	343	24992
44	23125	119	23616	194	24264	269	24577	344	24596
45	23126	120	22914	195	23853	270	24743	345	24597
46	22812	121	23617	196	24265	271	24772	346	25018
47	23127	122	23618	197	23854	272	24771	347	25012
48	23128	123	23710	198	23993	273	24739	348	25014
49	22813	124	23619	199	23855	274	24738	349	25013
50	22186	125	23770	200	24330	275	24747	350	24598
51	23119	126	22915	201	23994	276	24578	351	24599
52	22187	127	23767	202	23995	277	24744	352	25019
53	23190	128	22916	203	24331	278	24794	353	25043
54	22188	129	22917	204	24260	279	24792	354	25034
55	23191	130	23822	205	23996	280	24544	355	25035
56	23293	131	23620	206	23997	281	24760	356	25036
57	23227	132	23895	207	23998	282	24758	357	24600
58	22189	133	22918	208	24367	283	24579	358	25053
59	23192	134	22919	209	24289	284	24763	359	25083
60	23193	135	22920	210	24266	285	24748	360	24601
61	22814	136	23842	211	24267	286	24419	361	25042
62	23194	137	23843	212	24290	287	24420	362	25054
63	22190	138	23612	213	24368	288	24774	363	25059
64	22815	139	23723	214	24268	289	24580	364	25060
65	22816	140	23844	215	24291	290	24780	365	24602
66	22817	141	23724	216	24216	291	24799	366	25072
67	23195	142	23850	217	24217	292	24793	367	25073
68	23196	143	23725	218	24370	293	24421	368	25085
69	23197	144	24014	219	24292	294	24422	369	25044
70	23198	145	23975	220	24293	295	24749	370	24603
71	22818	146	23928	221	24397	296	24581	371	25155
72	23199	147	23726	222	24218	297	24582	372	25129
73	22819	148	24015	223	24372	298	24809	373	25130
74	22211	149	23727	224	24398	299	24810	374	25133
75	22611	150	24016	225	24371	300	24845	375	24604

BOEING 757 - Line No to C/n

line no	c/n	line no	c/n	line no	c/n	line no	c/n	line no	c/n
376	25141	451	25300	526	26158	601	25806	676	26274
377	25142	452	26964	527	26693	602	27237	677	27055
378	24605	453	25592	528	25623	603	26243	678	27810
379	24606	454	26653	529	26053	604	27238	679	25473
380	25156	455	25981	530	25622	605	27201	680	27056
381	25157	456	25982	531	26694	606	27208	681	27811
382	25140	457	25621	532	26434	607	27244	682	27556
383	24607	458	25131	533	27103	608	26635	683	25474
384	24608	459	25301	534	27123	609	27259	684	27681
385	25222	460	25333	535	27104	610	25807	685	27513
386	25223	461	25884	536	25695	611	25494	686	27557
387	25220	462	26654	537	26435	612	26269	687	25475
388	25240	463	25334	538	26267	613	27260	688	26332
389	25258	464	25901	539	26697	614	27291	689	27589
390	24609	465	25983	540	27124	615	27269	690	27971
391	24610	466	25593	541	25624	616	26244	691	25476
392	25259	467	26657	542	26698	617	26245	692	27598
393	25252	468	25335	543	26701	618	27220	693	26482
394	25253	469	26660	544	27144	619	27292	694	27972
395	25281	470	25487	545	26634	620	26246	695	26483
396	25276	471	25488	546	27145	621	26975	696	27599
397	24611	472	26151	547	26054	622	27270	697	26484
398	24612	473	25336	548	25730	623	27293	698	27517
399	25324	474	25337	549	25626	624	27367	699	26485
400	25268	475	25898	550	26702	625	25467	700	26486
401	25698	476	25885	551	27146	626	27342	701	26487
402	24613	477	25457	552	27147	627	26976	702	27558
403	25325	478	26152	553	26239	628	25468	703	26488
404	24614	479	26661	554	25887	629	27294	704	26276
405	25322	480	25886	555	26160	630	27245	705	26489
406	25323	481	25458	556	26705	631	25469	706	27559
407	25369	482	26153	557	26161	632	27295	707	27057
408	25353	483	25338	558	26270	633	26977	708	28112
409	24615	484	25339	559	26706	634	25470	709	26490
410	24616	485	25459	560	27152	635	26980	710	26491
411	25370	486	26154	561	26240	636	25471	711	26492
412	25345	487	26664	562	25731	637	27296	712	27058
413	25367	488	26665	563	26709	638	27386	713	26493
414	25368	489	25460	564	27148	639	27351	714	26494
415	25331	490	26666	565	25899	640	27387	715	26495
416	25332	491	25340	566	25696	641	27297	716	26496
417	24617	492	26669	567	26710	642	27388	717	26330
418	25294	493	25461	568	25697	643	27246	718	28142
419	25436	494	26670	569	25462	644	27389	719	28143
420	25396	495	26155	570	26713	645	27298	720	27446
421	25397	496	26058	571	26717	646	27390	721	28160
422	25437	497	26673	572	26241	647	27303	722	27447
423	25295	498	26674	573	25463	648	27299	723	28161
424	24964	499	26677	574	25900	649	27735	724	28144
425	25296	500	26955	575	25888	650	27300	725	28336
426	25398	501	26678	576	27183	651	27736	726	28337
427	25399	502	26956	577	25464	652	27301	727	28145
428	25438	503	26156	578	26972	653	27302	728	25477
429	25977	504	25341	579	25465	654	27737	729	25478
430	25978	505	25489	580	26973	655	27805	730	25479
431	26641	506	26681	581	25466	656	27738	731	28338
432	25297	507	25342	582	26974	657	27806	732	28162
433	25298	508	26682	583	25889	658	26277	733	25480
433	25440	509	25343	584	27198	659	25472	734	25481
434	25277	510	25490	585	25890	660	27051	735	27973
435	26644	511	25491	586	27199	661	27052	736	27620
436	25299	512	26685	587	26436	662	27807	737	27974
437	25439	513	26686	588	27203	663	27234	738	27621
438	24965	514	26266	589	27200	664	27053	739	28463
439	25979	515	26689	590	26268	665	25808	740	28446
440	26962	516	26957	591	27204	666	27808	741	28163
441	25597	517	26965	592	26271	667	27588	742	28479
442	26647	518	26958	593	26242	668	27555	743	28165
444	26057	519	26633	594	26272	669	27511	744	27625
445	25598	520	26966	595	27258	670	27054	745	27622
446	25441	521	26433	596	27219	671	26278	746	28674
447	26650	522	26967	597	26273	672	26275	747	28665
448	25980	523	25493	598	27235	673	27809	748	27560
449	25620	524	26690	599	25495	674	27512	749	28164
450	26963	525	27122	600	27236	675	27739	750	28480

BOEING 757 - Line No to C/n

line no	c/n	line no	c/n	line no	c/n	line no	c/n
751	28666	826	29725	901	30340	976	32585
752	28718	827	29426	902	26253	977	32385
753	27561	828	29427	903	30351	978	32586
754	28168	829	29028	904	29610	979	32386
755	28265	830	29488	905	26254	980	32587
756	28166	831	29726	906	30178	981	32387
757	28169	832	29607	907	29378	982	26500
758	28481	833	29793	908	30234	983	32388
759	28266	834	29489	909	29018	984	32389
760	27624	835	29608	910	29611	985	32588
761	27562	836	29380	911	30352	986	32390
762	28667	837	29428	912	30179	987	26501
763	28267	838	29727	913	30353	988	32391
764	28173	839	29012	914	30396	989	32392
765	28268	840	29282	915	29019	990	32810
766	27563	841	28750	916	30423	991	32393
767	28269	842	29589	917	30397	992	32394
768	27564	843	29330	918	29020	993	32941
769	25482	844	28751	919	29379	994	32395
770	28482	845	29728	920	29306	995	32811
771	25483	846	29013	921	30422	996	32396
772	28172	847	29590	922	30394	997	32812
773	28707	848	29283	923	29021	998	31308
774	25484	849	29014	924	29307	999	32813
775	28167	850	28834	925	30043	1000	32397
776	25485	851	29284	926	29022	1001	32982
777	28483	852	29591	927	30395	1002	32398
778	25486	853	29592	928	30757	1003	32589
779	27975	854	28485	929	29023	1004	29434
780	28989	855	30030	930	30548	1005	32399
781	28966	856	29285	931	30735	1006	30046
782	28833	857	29377	932	30758	1007	32591
783	29025	858	28835	933	30354	1008	32592
784	29113	859	29436	934	30480	1009	32942
785	28708	860	26247	935	29308	1010	29382
786	27565	861	28836	936	29309	1011	33391
787	29026	862	29593	937	30481	1012	32400
788	28967	863	26248	938	29310	1013	33392
789	28748	864	29941	939	30482	1014	32981
790	27566	865	28174	940	29311	1015	32343
791	28968	866	29594	941	30483	1016	33393
792	27623	867	29942	942	30484	1017	32590
793	29114	868	29217	943	29312	1018	32593
794	28749	869	28486	944	30777	1019	32983
795	27567	870	29304	945	30886	1020	32984
796	28969	871	29943	946	30887	1021	32985
797	29215	872	29944	947	30824	1022	32987
798	29115	873	29945	948	30052	1023	32986
799	28970	874	29964	949	30405	1024	32988
800	27586	875	30060	950	32446	1025	32989
801	28170	876	29609	951	32447	1026	33098
802	28203	877	29946	952	30863	1027	32990
803	27587	878	28487	953	30486	1028	33099
804	29016	879	28844	954	30044	1029	33100
805	28171	880	30318	955	30838	1030	32991
806	28971	881	26249	956	30424	1031	33525
807	27172	882	28845	957	30045	1032	33526
808	27585	883	30319	958	29381	1033	32992
809	29281	884	28488	959	30839	1034	32993
810	29017	885	29911	960	32241	1035	32994
811	29216	886	30061	961	32341	1036	32995
812	29423	887	29970	962	32379	1037	32996
813	28842	888	30232	963	32242	1038	32814
814	27976	889	26250	964	32380	1039	32815
815	28843	890	30337	965	32381	1040	32816
816	29424	891	30338	966	32342	1041	33101
817	29425	892	30187	967	32448	1042	32817
818	29015	893	29385	968	26497	1043	32818
819	29442	894	29305	969	32382	1044	33959
820	29724	895	30233	970	32383	1045	33960
821	29443	896	30339	971	26498	1046	33961
822	29792	897	26251	972	32584	1047	34008
823	28846	898	30188	973	32384	1048	34009
824	29027	899	30229	974	32449	1049	33966
825	28484	900	26252	975	26499	1050	33967

BOEING 767 - Line No to C/n

line no	c/n	line no	c/n	line no	c/n	line no	c/n	line no	c/n
1	22233	76	22224	151	23276	226	24037	301	24727
2	21862	77	22225	152	23277	227	24038	302	24574
3	21863	78	22226	153	23278	228	24039	303	24742
4	21864	79	22981	154	23279	229	24142	304	24759
5	21865	80	23016	155	23744	230	24040	305	24728
6	22213	81	23057	156	23745	231	24146	306	24764
7	21866	82	23017	157	22326	232	24041	307	24762
8	22307	83	22227	158	23764	233	24143	308	24765
9	21867	84	23018	159	22327	234	24144	309	24846
10	21868	85	23019	160	22328	235	24042	310	24766
11	21869	86	22974	161	23803	236	24145	311	24575
12	22214	87	22523	162	23435	237	24043	312	24775
13	21870	88	22524	163	23436	238	24044	313	24800
14	22564	89	22975	164	22329	239	24150	314	24843
15	21871	90	23106	165	23765	240	24045	315	24847
16	22517	91	22525	166	22330	241	24046	316	24832
17	22215	92	22526	167	23433	242	24316	317	24802
18	22681	93	23107	168	22331	243	24239	318	24803
19	22308	94	22315	169	22332	244	24349	319	24853
20	21872	95	22316	170	23801	245	24350	320	24852
21	22565	96	23020	171	23434	246	24317	321	24835
22	22518	97	23178	172	23802	247	24407	322	24865
23	22309	98	23179	173	23897	248	24086	323	24767
24	22692	99	23180	174	23645	249	24087	324	24844
25	22310	100	22696	175	23898	250	24323	325	24848
26	22216	101	23058	176	23756	251	24257	326	24854
27	22217	102	22527	177	23757	252	24324	327	24782
28	22693	103	23021	178	23804	253	24157	328	24797
29	22566	104	23022	179	23758	254	24325	329	24783
30	22567	105	22528	180	23805	255	24258	330	24849
31	22218	106	23140	181	23806	256	24457	331	24798
32	22694	107	23072	182	23899	257	24318	332	24768
33	22568	108	23141	183	23896	258	24306	333	24867
34	22311	109	22317	184	23807	259	24307	334	24983
35	22695	110	23142	185	23759	260	24484	335	24340
36	22683	111	22318	186	23965	261	24733	336	24880
37	22219	112	22319	187	23916	262	24357	337	24477
38	22220	113	23250	188	23437	263	24358	338	24894
39	22569	114	23143	189	23438	264	24485	339	24984
40	22519	115	23144	190	23900	265	24333	340	24985
41	21873	116	23145	191	23966	266	24734	341	24341
42	21874	117	23212	192	23961	267	24495	341	25061
43	21875	118	23213	193	23962	268	24259	343	24929
44	22312	119	23304	194	22333	269	24400	344	24930
45	21876	120	23305	195	22334	270	24496	345	24981
46	21877	121	23146	196	22335	271	24351	346	25122
47	22520	122	23214	197	23901	272	24448	347	24973
48	21878	123	23147	198	22336	273	24475	348	24982
49	21879	124	23326	199	24002	274	24476	349	25143
50	21880	125	23306	200	24075	275	24541	350	25144
51	22785	126	23307	201	24076	276	24415	351	24947
52	22684	127	23308	202	24032	277	24498	352	25055
53	22221	128	22320	203	24077	278	24531	353	25123
54	22786	129	23309	204	24007	279	24428	354	24999
55	22921	130	22321	205	24033	280	24416	355	24745
56	22222	131	23280	206	24034	281	24334	356	25145
57	22922	132	23215	207	24078	282	24542	357	24952
58	22787	133	23402	208	23973	283	24628	358	24729
59	22923	134	23327	209	24079	284	24335	359	25088
60	22682	135	23281	210	24013	285	24632	360	25091
61	22788	136	23275	211	24035	286	24336	361	25120
62	22972	137	23403	212	24003	287	24713	362	25058
63	22570	138	23282	213	24082	288	24337	363	24342
64	22571	139	22322	214	23974	289	24752	364	24343
65	22572	140	22323	215	24083	290	24417	365	25203
66	22521	141	23494	216	24080	291	24753	366	25076
67	22789	142	23623	217	23902	292	24618	367	25092
68	22973	143	23431	218	24004	293	24338	368	25093
69	22790	144	23624	219	24084	294	24429	369	25094
70	22573	145	23432	220	24085	295	24755	370	25117
71	22980	146	22324	221	24036	296	24736	371	24875
72	22313	147	22325	222	24005	297	24716	372	25121
73	22314	148	23216	223	24006	298	24339	373	25139
74	22223	149	23328	224	23963	299	24757	374	25146
75	22522	150	23217	225	23964	300	24756	375	25225

BOEING 767 - Line No to C/n

line no	c/n	line no	c/n	line no	c/n	line no	c/n	line no	c/n
376	25204	451	25575	526	25831	601	27569	676	28452
377	25137	452	25389	527	27193	602	27597	677	28745
378	24746	453	25446	528	27205	603	27918	678	27748
379	25136	454	25533	529	25832	604	25587	679	28453
380	24948	455	26991	530	25877	605	27610	680	28838
381	25208	456	26388	531	27212	606	25588	681	27615
382	25209	457	25390	532	27194	607	28098	682	27749
383	25257	458	25618	533	27206	608	25834	683	28454
384	25221	459	26389	534	26259	609	27959	684	27944
385	25077	460	25391	535	27195	610	28039	685	28455
386	25000	461	25987	536	27059	611	28147	686	27685
387	25246	462	25392	537	26985	612	28111	687	27476
388	25193	463	25654	538	26234	613	28040	688	28553
389	25241	464	26204	539	25660	614	28041	689	28159
390	25269	465	25655	540	27060	615	28153	690	28456
391	25280	466	26987	541	27184	616	25761	691	28979
392	25306	467	27095	542	25170	617	27582	692	28132
393	25273	468	25393	543	25661	618	28016	693	29129
394	25194	469	25447	544	26237	619	27993	694	28206
395	25365	470	26992	545	27310	620	28148	695	28207
396	25274	471	26983	546	27309	621	26327	696	28457
397	25316	472	25394	547	27311	622	27759	697	28458
398	25444	473	25826	548	27312	623	28154	698	29227
399	25347	474	26205	549	25576	624	27760	699	29228
400	25312	475	27048	550	25577	625	27960	700	29429
401	25293	476	25828	551	25662	626	27761	701	29430
402	25363	477	25534	552	26260	627	28149	702	29230
403	25346	478	25876	553	26986	628	27740	703	29431
404	25195	479	27112	554	27313	629	28270	704	29231
405	24953	480	27113	555	26264	630	27762	705	28208
406	25354	481	25448	556	27339	631	27583	706	29689
407	25421	482	27049	557	27385	632	27741	707	29236
408	25411	483	25829	558	26913	633	27611	708	29232
409	25403	484	26256	559	26608	634	27763	709	29432
410	25409	485	27114	560	27376	635	28370	710	29117
411	25404	486	26847	561	27377	636	27764	711	29237
412	26544	487	26206	562	26988	637	26328	712	25756
413	24876	488	26257	563	27448	638	27742	713	29118
414	25530	489	25449	564	27449	639	25760	714	27616
415	26469	490	27140	565	27450	640	27743	715	29238
416	26470	491	25535	566	27451	641	26329	716	29239
417	25132	492	27110	567	27444	642	28017	717	29690
418	25442	493	27135	568	27392	643	28495	718	not
419	25443	494	27115	569	25878	644	28264		built
420	25283	495	25450	570	26265	645	25619	719	29691
421	25732	496	27111	571	27393	646	25990	720	29435
422	25196	497	27136	572	27394	647	27612	721	25991
423	25531	498	25451	573	27445	648	25733	722	27617
424	25264	499	25988	574	26915	649	28042	723	29692
425	25197	500	26995	575	26261	650	28392	724	27750
426	25864	501	26233	576	27961	651	27942	725	29693
427	25984	502	26235	577	27902	652	27613	726	27751
428	25985	503	26207	578	27908	653	28447	727	27618
429	25875	504	25536	579	27427	654	28448	728	27752
430	25865	505	26208	580	27239	655	27600	729	29229
431	25198	506	25989	581	27658	656	25763	730	27753
432	25616	507	27158	582	25758	657	28865	731	29867
433	25199	508	25583	583	26262	658	25762	732	27754
434	26063	509	26912	584	27468	659	28656	733	29137
435	25200	510	25656	585	27962	660	27744	734	28043
436	26236	511	26471	586	27428	661	27614	735	29694
437	25201	512	26996	587	27957	662	28724	736	29695
438	26064	513	27159	588	27391	663	26971	737	28883
439	25617	514	27160	589	27958	664	28449	738	28884
440	26238	515	25657	590	27240	665	28725	739	29603
441	25202	516	27050	591	27909	666	27745	740	29696
442	25532	517	25537	592	26263	667	27659	741	29617
443	25285	518	26984	593	27568	668	25759	742	30024
444	25286	519	25658	594	27241	669	27943	743	30008
445	26387	520	25659	595	27619	670	27746	744	29604
446	25986	521	27189	596	25585	671	28450	745	29697
447	25445	522	27254	597	25585	672	27758	746	30009
448	26417	523	25757	598	27242	673	28451	747	29383
449	25287	524	27192	599	25586	673	28837	748	29605
450	26200	525	27255	600	27243	674	27747	749	30180

694

BOEING 767 - Line No to C/n

line no	c/n	line no	c/n	line no	c/n	line no	c/n	line no	c/n
750	29698	825	30434	900	33083	975			
751	27584	826	29450	901	33424	976			
752	29606	827	30435	902	30847	977			
753	30198	828	30048	903	33685	978			
754	29898	829	30840	904	33469	979			
755	30199	830	29718	905	33493	980			
756	27755	831	29386	906	33084	981			
757	30025	832	30846	907	33085	982			
758	29703	833	30436	908	33086	983			
759	30331	834	30028	909	33425	984			
760	27756	835	30850	910	33087	985			
761	30107	836	30851	911	33494	986			
762	30301	837	30853	912	33686	987			
763	29240	838	30575	913	33088	988			
764	27757	839	30437	914	32980	989			
765	30112	840	29387	915	33495	990			
766	30026	841	30841	916	33089	991			
767	30109	842	29451	917	33496	992			
768	30341	843	30852	918	33767	993			
769	29713	844	30854	919	33497	994			
770	27941	845	30438	920	33506	995			
771	30108	846	32572	921	33845	996			
772	29863	847	32776	922	33768	997			
773	29705	848	32573	923	33840	998			
774	30342	849	27684	924	33507	999			
775	30110	850	28140	925	33846	1000			
776	30111	851	30439	927	33847				
777	30027	852	30029	928	33078				
778	29881	853	28141	928	33968				
779	29241	854	32843	929	33848				
780	27477	855	29714	930	33687				
781	30393	856	29715	931	33508				
782	29242	857	28139	932	33844				
783	29138	858	32844	933	33769				
784	29384	859	29452	934	34245				
785	29388	860	30842	935	33849				
786	30563	861	32954	937	33509				
787	30388	862	29453	937	34246				
788	30573	863	30115	938	33851				
789	30574	864	29454	939	33510				
790	30594	865	29716	940	34626				
791	29699	866	29455	941	33688				
792	29618	867	30843	942	33850				
793	27686	868	29456	943	33958				
794	30595	869	29457	944	34629				
795	30596	870	29390	945	34628				
796	30186	871	29717	946	35155				
797	30597	872	29458	947	35709				
798	30564	873	29459	948	34627				
799	29446	874	29719	949	35229				
800	29243	875	32886	950	35156				
801	29700	876	29460	951	35877				
802	30565	877	32972	952	33689				
803	29701	878	29461	953	35876				
804	29702	879	32887	954	35813				
805	29447	880	32888	955	35230				
806	30780	881	32973	956	35816				
807	29704	882	32974	957	35814				
808	30586	883	32975	958	35796				
809	29448	884	32976	959	35817				
810	29706	885	33404	960	35818				
811	30430	886	32977	961	35231				
812	30383	887	33421	962	36710				
813	29707	888	32978	963	34433				
814	29708	889	33047	964					
815	30431	890	33466	965					
816	29449	891	33048	966					
817	30566	892	33422	967					
818	29709	893	33049	968					
819	30432	894	33467	969					
820	29710	895	32979	970					
821	29711	896	33081	971					
822	28138	897	33423	972					
823	30433	898	33468	973					
824	29712	899	33082	974					

BOEING 777 - Line No to C/n

line no	c/n	line no	c/n	line no	c/n	line no	c/n	line no	c/n
1	27116	76	27491	151	28415	226	28518	301	30308
2	26936	77	27938	152	28393	227	29859	302	28279
3	26932	78	28410	153	28514	228	29964	303	30309
4	26929	79	27637	154	28354	229	29908	304	29213
5	26930	80	28424	155	28416	230	28361	305	28444
6	27105	81	27034	156	29150	231	28418	306	28364
7	26916	82	26942	157	29319	232	30213	307	30456
8	26917	83	28508	158	28394	233	29965	308	30310
9	26918	84	28411	159	27641	234	29860	309	28445
10	27106	85	28425	160	28274	235	29734	310	29214
11	26919	86	28509	161	27577	236	29966	311	30311
12	26921	87	28698	162	28371	237	28519	312	30312
13	26925	88	26935	163	28699	238	28397	313	30256
14	27265	89	27730	164	27608	239	28523	314	29011
15	27107	90	28510	165	27578	240	29157	315	30257
16	27027	91	27253	166	28355	241	29956	316	30796
17	27108	92	26943	167	27579	242	30302	317	30222
18	27266	93	26933	168	29153	243	29861	318	30551
19	27109	94	27507	169	27580	244	28531	319	30831
20	27357	95	27731	170	29151	245	29735	320	30614
21	27028	96	26934	171	29324	246	28676	321	30012
22	26947	97	26946	172	27939	247	27037	322	28681
23	27364	98	28344	173	29154	248	27510	323	28365
24	27358	99	28345	174	29271	249	29736	324	30797
25	27726	100	27732	175	28356	250	29211	325	30832
26	27365	101	28346	176	29325	251	29967	326	29395
27	26937	102	27506	177	27581	252	29953	327	30615
28	27263	103	28347	178	27948	253	29862	328	30258
29	27029	104	28275	179	29155	254	30214	329	29065
30	27247	105	26953	180	28515	255	28362	330	28521
31	27264	106	27604	181	28357	256	29062	331	28682
32	27727	107	27638	182	29320	257	29737	332	30259
33	27248	108	26927	183	29476	258	29008	333	30798
34	26940	109	28348	184	28516	259	30215	334	30313
35	26941	110	27605	185	29578	260	29212	335	30833
36	26944	111	27492	186	28358	261	29738	336	29066
37	27030	112	26931	187	29005	262	29063	337	28522
38	27031	113	27733	188	28517	263	29009	338	29746
39	27366	114	28349	189	29006	264	30216	339	30260
40	26945	115	28412	190	29579	265	30303	340	30223
41	27483	116	26924	191	28713	266	29586	341	30261
42	27249	117	28840	192	28534	267	29010	342	30314
43	26939	118	27505	193	29321	268	30304	343	30866
44	27728	119	28350	194	28359	269	30305	344	29747
45	27636	120	27950	195	27609	270	30003	345	30262
46	27359	121	27606	196	28395	271	30004	346	30316
47	27250	122	28511	197	29477	272	29588	347	30552
48	27360	123	26928	198	29580	273	28678	348	30867
49	27484	124	28351	199	29583	274	30005	349	29748
50	27032	125	28743	200	29478	275	30306	350	28524
51	27729	126	28512	201	29007	276	30250	351	28366
52	26938	127	27493	202	29951	277	30010	352	30553
53	27485	128	28413	203	29322	278	28277	353	28525
54	27251	129	29002	204	27508	279	28679	354	30263
55	27524	130	28841	205	28714	280	29744	355	28526
56	27486	131	27035	206	29323	281	30307	356	27949
57	26948	132	28273	207	29952	282	30217	357	30224
58	27487	133	29003	208	29581	283	30011	358	30264
59	27945	134	27639	209	29584	284	30457	359	28686
60	26950	135	27607	210	28675	285	30252	360	30868
61	27488	136	27504	211	29479	286	28278	361	30317
62	27946	137	29029	212	28396	287	30251	362	32629
63	27252	138	29004	213	27642	288	27952	363	32636
64	28408	139	26926	214	29156	289	30254	364	28528
65	27489	140	28414	215	29582	290	29745	365	28689
66	27525	141	27036	216	30212	291	30549	366	30869
67	28507	142	28272	217	29962	292	30253	367	28683
68	27651	143	28352	218	29585	293	30218	368	32630
69	26951	144	28513	219	28360	294	30550	369	30315
70	27490	145	28744	220	29480	295	30219	370	32306
71	28423	146	27640	221	29963	296	30220	371	32637
72	27652	147	28353	222	28416	297	30221	372	28527
73	26954	148	27947	223	29587	298	28363	373	28692
74	28409	149	28998	224	27509	299	30255	374	30870
75	27033	150	28999	225	29955	300	28680	375	30225

BOEING 777 - Line No to C/n

line no	c/n	line no	c/n	line no	c/n	line no	c/n	line no	c/n
376	32638	451	33370	526	29175	601	33778	676	36009
377	30554	452	33727	527	32433	602	34570	677	35576
378	30871	453	33503	528	34207	603	34571	678	35166
379	31477	454	33711	529	32648	604	34572	679	35244
380	30226	455	32783	530	32845	605	34379	680	36155
381	30555	456	33702	531	32640	606	32651	681	35575
382	32308	457	33712	532	32788	607	35960	682	34211
383	32309	458	27654	533	33396	608	32962	683	33753
384	30556	459	32781	534	29404	609	35295	684	34214
385	28684	460	27655	535	33862	610	36300	685	36156
386	29313	461	29397	536	32708	611	33779	686	36103
387	29743	462	33703	537	34376	612	33750	687	34567
388	30557	463	32782	538	34597	613	35296	688	
389	28529	464	33394	539	32707	614	36124	689	
390	28530	465	33713	540	32785	615	34573	690	
391	31679	466	32723	541	32717	616	32846	691	
392	32698	467	33775	542	32787	617	35547	692	
393	31478	468	28691	543	34598	618	34574	693	
394	28419	469	33776	544	34599	619	32729	694	
395	32305	470	33704	545	32853	620	35256	695	
396	32697	471	28533	546	34377	621	36301	696	
397	31680	472	32703	547	34600	622	33864	697	
398	30872	473	33777	548	34601	623	34575	698	
399	31479	474	29398	549	34481	624	32847	699	
400	28685	475	32894	550	29401	625	31687	700	
401	32310	476	32704	551	32709	626	35254	701	
402	29396	477	32784	552	34711	627	35157	702	
403	30859	478	32724	553	29171	628	32713	703	
404	28420	479	33681	554	32718	629	36302	704	
405	33169	480	32727	555	33539	630	32721	705	
406	30875	481	29174	556	34482	631	34894	706	
407	28532	482	33406	557	32649	632	32794	707	
408	29067	483	32895	558	32848	633	34209	708	
409	32334	484	32327	559	34712	634	33751	709	
410	32889	485	33372	560	32791	635	27653	710	
411	27951	486	33505	561	32720	636	32854	711	
412	32316	487	33373	562	32719	637	35158	712	
413	32855	488	28281	563	32646	638	35298	713	
414	32699	489	32896	564	32712	639	34895	714	
415	32335	490	32726	565	32960	640	35239	715	
416	28372	491	33504	566	33540	641	32714	716	
417	32890	492	32851	567	34244	642	35255	717	
418	28064	493	32705	568	32792	643	36308	718	
419	28520	494	32849	569	32710	644	34576	719	
420	32317	495	33407	570	32961	645	32963	720	
421	32856	496	28421	571	34892	646	30861	721	
422	32336	497	33714	572	32643	647	35678	722	
423	32430	498	28422	573	35676	648	36083	723	
424	32857	499	29399	574	33414	649	35242	724	
425	32858	500	32850	575	34378	650	35159	725	
426	32859	501	32711	576	33863	651	35243	726	
427	32891	502	32725	577	32434	652	36309	727	
428	33368	503	33374	578	34483	653	35160	728	
429	32431	504	33781	579	35677	654	35572	729	
430	30874	505	33375	580	33415	655	36084	730	
431	30873	506	32706	581	34565	656	36310	731	
432	28687	507	27657	582	32715	657	34210	732	
433	32879	508	32789	583	32435	658	33752	733	
434	32700	509	32647	584	34208	659	30860	734	
435	32892	510	32852	585	32730	660	35164	735	
436	28688	511	27038	586	34568	661	36154	736	
437	27656	512	32790	587	34566	662	35573	737	
438	32320	513	34243	588	34586	663	36303	738	
439	32860	514	33682	589	34893	664	33865	739	
440	27039	515	33376	590	34484	665	34590	740	
441	32318	516	33501	591	29403	666	35162	741	
442	27040	517	29402	592	33377	667	27041	742	
443	32701	518	32716	593	32650	668	36126	743	
444	32702	519	33782	594	32728	669	32795	744	
445	32880	520	34206	595	34587	670	35299	745	
446	32893	521	32432	596	34588	671	35297	746	
447	32321	522	33683	597	32645	672	34591	747	
448	33369	523	28276	598	32793	673	34577	748	
449	33371	524	32639	599	34589	674	34432	749	
450	33502	525	33395	600	34569	675	35163	750	

DOUGLAS DC-8 - Line No to C/n

line no	c/n	line no	c/n	line no	c/n	line no	c/n	line no	c/n
1	45252	75	45379	151	45628	226	45757	301	45890
2	45278	76	45387	152	45437	227	45758	302	45916
3	45279	77	45263	153	45636	228	45759	303	45896
4	45280	78	45418	154	45607	229	45803	304	45899
5	45253	79	45600	155	45608	230	45756	305	45891
6	45254	80	45569	156	45638	231	45751	306	45892
7	45255	81	45419	157	45637	232	45762	307	45909
8	45281	82	45429	158	45629	233	45752	308	45883
9	45442	83	45568	159	45630	234	45800	309	45904
10	45282	84	45604	160	45631	235	45801	310	45893
11	45283	85	45298	161	45634	236	45816	311	45910
12	45284	86	45264	162	45633	237	45761	312	45919
13	45285	87	45380	163	45635	238	45819	313	45897
14	45408	88	45596	164	45632	239	45807	314	45940
15	45286	89	45526	165	45641	240	45768	315	45912
16	45287	90	45388	166	45645	241	45763	316	45900
17	45288	91	45265	167	45646	242	45818	317	45941
18	45443	92	45299	168	45647	243	45808	318	45911
19	45409	94	45277	169	45648	244	45805	319	45920
20	45289	95	45605	170	45649	245	45806	320	45898
21	45410	96	45381	171	45659	246	45820	321	45948
22	45290	97	45597	172	45642	247	45802	322	45921
23	45411	98	45389	173	45643	248	45817	323	45926
24	45412	99	45430	174	45644	249	45815	324	45937
25	45413	100	45266	175	45640	250	45767	325	45913
26	45588	101	45300	176	45652	251	45764	326	45944
27	45589	102	45267	177	45650	252	45810	327	45927
28	45590	103	45431	178	45653	253	45859	328	45932
29	45591	104	45268	179	45654	254	45804	329	45949
30	45291	105	45432	180	45655	255	45821	330	45935
31	45444	106	45382	181	45658	256	45860	331	45938
32	45592	107	45601	182	45669	257	45850	332	45917
33	45593	108	45390	183	45661	258	45814	333	45925
34	45422	109	45269	184	45660	259	45862	334	45928
35	45594	110	45433	185	45667	260	45851	335	45922
36	45423	111	45565	186	45662	261	45861	336	45985
37	45424	112	45270	187	45668	262	45811	337	45945
38	45391	113	45421	188	45657	263	45852	338	45952
39	45595	114	45271	189	45663	264	45809	339	45946
40	45256	115	45606	190	45670	265	45765	340	45884
41	45425	116	45393	191	45656	266	45853	341	45947
42	45445	117	45566	192	45672	267	45824	342	45885
43	45292	118	45272	193	45673	268	45879	343	45970
44	45257	119	45609	194	45665	269	45856	344	45936
45	45392	120	45383	195	45684	270	45822	345	45982
46	45258	121	45273	196	45671	271	45857	346	45965
47	45293	122	45610	197	45676	272	45766	347	45960
48	45376	123	45613	198	45651	273	45877	348	45953
49	45426	124	45620	199	45677	274	45858	349	45942
50	45384	125	45304	200	45675	275	45880	350	45983
51	45294	126	45614	201	45674	276	45881	351	45939
52	45274	127	45611	202	45666	277	45812	352	45981
53	45377	128	45301	203	45679	278	45854	353	45918
53	45420	129	45305	204	45685	279	45823	354	45950
54	45416	130	45623	205	45688	280	45878	355	45963
55	45385	131	45615	206	45664	281	45855	356	45971
56	45427	132	45621	207	45692	282	45882	357	45972
57	45598	133	45302	208	45683	283	45886	358	45973
58	45259	134	45570	209	45691	284	45813	359	45943
59	45378	135	45612	210	45686	285	45848	360	45992
60	45602	136	45617	211	45687	286	45903	361	45961
61	45428	137	45622	212	45689	287	45887	362	45954
62	45386	138	45618	213	45680	288	45907	363	45979
63	45295	139	45624	214	45681	289	45849	364	45964
64	45275	140	45306	215	45769	290	45888	365	45955
65	45296	141	45303	216	45760	291	45889	366	45987
66	45260	142	45619	217	45750	292	45914	367	45929
67	45297	143	45626	218	45678	293	45901	368	45974
68	45261	144	45625	219	45690	294	45902	369	45975
69	45417	145	45627	220	45682	295	45915	370	45984
70	45262	146	45307	221	45693	296	45908	371	45989
71	45567	147	45616	222	45755	297	45894	372	45976
72	45276	148	45434	223	45753	298	45905	373	45977
73	45599	149	45435	224	45694	299	45895	374	45980
74	45603	150	45436	225	45754	300	45906	375	45990

DOUGLAS DC-8 - Line No to C/n

line no	c/n	line no	c/n	line no	c/n
376	45956	451	46076	526	46114
377	45999	452	46026	527	46137
378	45930	453	46054	528	46140
379	45986	454	46087	529	46155
380	45991	455	46067	530	46115
381	45978	456	46059	531	46135
382	45993	457	46063	532	46144
383	45923	458	46082	533	46141
384	45933	459	46064	534	46133
385	45967	460	46065	535	46132
386	46000	461	46028	536	46146
387	45994	462	46066	537	46139
388	45995	463	46068	538	46149
389	45968	464	46088	539	46150
390	45934	465	46069	540	46151
391	45931	466	46080	541	46157
392	45924	467	46070	542	46130
393	45966	468	46074	543	46158
394	46002	469	46071	544	46159
395	46001	470	46077	545	46160
396	45969	471	46081	546	46142
397	45996	472	46060	547	46143
398	45997	473	46084	548	46145
399	45998	474	46057	549	46147
400	46014	475	46078	550	46152
401	46003	476	46079	551	46153
402	45962	477	46072	552	46161
403	46004	478	46086	553	46148
404	46009	479	46049	554	46154
405	46015	480	46061	555	46162
406	46010	481	46085	556	46163
407	46023	482	46094		
408	46011	483	46103		
409	46016	484	46075		
410	46012	485	46073		
411	46019	486	46062		
412	46005	487	46110		
413	46006	488	46104		
414	45951	489	46101		
415	46020	490	46106		
416	45988	491	46111		
417	46022	492	46055		
418	46017	493	46109		
419	46037	494	46105		
420	46018	495	46056		
421	46042	496	46093		
422	46007	497	46095		
423	46008	498	46107		
424	46021	499	46096		
425	46029	500	46121		
426	46030	501	46089		
427	46013	502	46100		
428	46024	503	46097		
429	46038	504	46090		
430	46050	505	46092		
431	46033	506	46122		
432	46044	507	46099		
433	46058	508	46123		
434	46034	509	46136		
435	46031	510	46127		
436	46032	511	46124		
437	46027	512	46102		
438	46035	513	46134		
439	46041	514	46128		
440	46051	515	46125		
441	46045	516	46098		
442	46052	517	46131		
443	46043	518	46116		
444	46046	519	46091		
445	46036	520	46112		
446	46053	521	46113		
447	46047	522	46108		
448	46039	523	46129		
449	46040	524	46126		
450	46048	525	46117		

DOUGLAS DC-9/MD-80*/MD-90+ - Line No to C/n

line no	c/n	line no	c/n	line no	c/n	line no	c/n	line no	c/n
1	45695	76	45831	151	47005	226	47146	301	47254
2	45696	77	45708	152	47009	227	47141	302	47198
3	45697	78	45709	153	47100	228	47156	303	47189
4	45711	79	45826	154	47039	229	47132	304	47242
5	45698	80	45777	155	47081	230	47133	305	47221
6	45712	81	47004	156	47015	231	47159	306	47214
7	45714	82	45778	157	47029	232	47142	307	47208
8	45699	83	47000	158	47023	233	47135	308	47116
9	45713	84	45832	159	47024	234	47087	309	47250
10	45715	85	45834	160	47068	235	47106	310	47255
11	45700	86	47003	161	47073	236	47107	311	47193
12	45701	87	47007	162	47034	237	47093	312	47218
13	45716	88	47043	163	47079	238	47143	313	47215
14	45728	89	47056	164	47080	239	47144	314	47176
15	45702	90	45786	165	47044	240	47190	315	47216
16	45729	91	45845	166	47075	241	47160	316	47224
17	45718	92	45779	167	47110	242	45828	317	47225
18	45719	93	45780	168	47046	243	47136	318	47138
19	45725	94	47001	169	47139	244	47251	319	47117
20	45717	95	45835	170	47152	245	47204	320	47263
21	45703	96	45836	171	45788	246	47148	321	47199
22	45724	97	47010	172	47040	247	47145	322	47157
23	45842	98	47008	173	47016	248	47158	323	47178
24	45704	99	47006	174	47030	249	47161	324	47194
25	45735	100	47010	175	47069	250	47205	325	47219
26	45742	101	45781	176	47070	251	47108	326	47256
27	45720	102	47011	177	47083	252	47109	327	47209
28	45843	103	45837	178	47035	253	47123	328	47206
29	45743	104	45838	179	47084	254	47124	329	47264
30	45772	105	47002	180	47088	255	47162	330	47177
31	45744	106	47025	181	47082	256	47163	331	45869
32	45745	107	47053	182	47111	257	47248	332	45870
33	45844	108	47098	183	47047	258	47137	333	47226
34	45731	109	47060	184	47045	259	47164	334	47227
35	47048	110	47054	185	47153	260	47165	335	47179
36	45726	111	47063	186	47017	261	47115	336	45774
37	45730	112	45846	187	47031	262	47312	337	47279
38	45746	113	47019	188	47071	263	47172	338	47200
39	45773	114	45782	189	47089	264	45790	339	47265
40	45747	115	47012	190	47090	265	47166	340	47295
41	45732	116	45839	191	47095	266	47167	341	47210
42	47049	117	45840	192	47096	267	47181	342	47247
43	45727	118	47050	193	47097	268	47313	343	47291
44	45721	119	47026	194	47055	269	47065	344	45871
45	45736	120	47064	195	47101	270	47072	345	45872
46	45841	121	47037	196	47118	271	47182	346	47240
47	45748	122	47057	197	47099	272	47183	347	47273
48	45733	123	47058	198	47102	273	47173	348	47274
49	45737	124	45863	199	47112	274	47184	349	45791
50	45749	125	47059	200	47041	275	47185	350	45873
51	45797	126	47020	201	47154	276	47186	351	45874
52	45794	127	45787	202	47149	277	47121	352	47266
53	45705	128	45783	203	47018	278	47195	353	47289
54	45738	129	47013	204	47032	279	47314	354	47180
55	45722	130	45864	205	47103	280	47191	355	47228
56	45739	131	47051	206	47091	281	47241	356	47229
57	45770	132	47027	207	47061	282	47187	357	47211
58	45771	133	47021	208	47147	283	45867	358	47213
59	45798	134	47076	209	47120	284	47150	359	47286
60	45734	135	45827	210	47128	285	47151	360	47217
61	45706	136	47038	211	47130	286	47174	361	47267
62	45740	137	45865	212	47140	287	47192	362	47296
63	45723	138	45866	213	47113	288	47196	363	47275
64	45785	139	47085	214	47131	289	47197	364	47287
65	45795	140	45784	215	47134	290	45868	365	45875
66	45741	141	47014	216	47155	291	47188	366	45876
67	45825	142	47052	217	45789	292	47246	367	47290
68	45829	143	47067	218	47114	293	47207	368	47212
69	45799	144	47022	219	47086	294	47252	369	47288
70	45707	145	47028	220	47104	295	47253	370	47268
71	45775	146	47078	221	47105	296	47220	371	47269
72	45776	147	47033	222	47092	297	47249	372	45792
73	45833	148	47077	223	47062	298	47175	373	47276
74	45796	149	47094	224	47122	299	47222	374	47270
75	45830	150	47066	225	47129	300	47223	375	47036

DOUGLAS DC-9/MD-80*/MD-90+ - Line No to C/n

line no	c/n	line no	c/n	line no	c/n	line no	c/n	line no	c/n
376	47074	451	47237	526	47433	601	47494	676	47544
377	47297	452	47355	527	47488	602	47419	677	47511
378	47119	453	47352	528	47489	603	47526	678	47512
379	47277	454	47320	529	47369	604	47497	679	47513
380	47278	455	47321	530	47366	605	47479	680	47575
381	45793	456	47322	531	47375	606	47522	681	47564
382	47301	457	47407	532	47429	607	47480	682	47576
383	47292	458	47394	533	47411	608	47393	683	47569
384	47293	459	47201	534	47412	609	47430	684	47570
385	47317	460	47343	535	47450	610	47535	685	47562
386	47257	461	47332	536	47414	611	47468	686	47577
387	47258	462	47306	537	47434	612	47478	687	47563
388	47125	463	47307	538	47383	613	47477	688	47567
389	47271	464	47346	539	47367	614	47518	689	47568
390	47272	465	47238	540	47435	615	47519	690	47574
391	47327	466	47239	541	47436	616	47481	691	47566
392	47328	467	47408	542	47385	617	47528	692	47581
393	47309	468	47323	543	47384	618	47527	693	47579
394	45847	469	47324	544	47437	619	47514	694	47573
395	47230	470	47356	545	47438	620	47457	695	47571
396	47231	471	47353	546	47500	621	47466	696	47584
397	47283	472	47344	547	47451	622	47547	697	47583
398	47311	473	47171	548	47448	623	47550	698	47585
399	47298	474	47308	549	47459	624	47530	699	47588
400	47202	475	47360	550	47386	625	47529	700	47587
401	47203	476	47357	551	47370	626	47532	701	47582
402	47294	477	47358	552	47449	627	47460	702	47578
403	47340	478	47347	553	47487	628	47486	703	47590
404	47341	479	47382	554	47404	629	47521	704	47580
405	47126	480	47410	555	47395	630	47516	705	47593
406	47329	481	47333	556	47420	631	47525	706	47591
407	47330	482	47402	557	47396	632	47524	707	47586
408	47331	483	47354	558	47421	633	47548	708	47572
409	47259	484	47364	559	47492	634	47551	709	47595
410	47260	485	47345	560	47490	635	47520	710	47600
411	47261	486	47042	561	47446	636	47397	711	47589
412	47262	487	47405	562	47493	637	47539	712	47592
413	47284	488	47361	563	47447	638	47531	713	47597
414	47285	489	47389	564	47462	639	47549	714	47596
415	47337	490	47390	565	47453	640	47552	715	47601
416	47338	491	47391	566	47498	641	47533	716	47599
417	47127	492	47362	567	47454	642	47553	717	47594
418	47342	493	47334	568	47499	643	47509	718	47602
419	47348	494	47335	569	47476	644	47534	719	47598
420	47349	495	47359	570	47418	645	47510	720	47603
421	47299	496	47377	571	47501	646	47458	721	47607
422	47302	497	47409	572	47426	647	47467	722	47604
423	47168	498	47244	573	47427	648	47484	723	47609
424	47169	499	47406	574	47502	649	47463	724	47605
425	47170	500	47336	575	47464	650	47471	725	47610
426	47318	501	47439	576	47422	651	47504	726	47611
427	47281	502	47440	577	47443	652	47542	727	47606
428	47232	503	47441	578	47444	653	47475	728	47623
429	47233	504	47365	579	47455	654	47543	729	47621
430	47399	505	47368	580	47456	655	47546	730	47638
431	47350	506	47371	581	47423	656	47495	731	47637
432	47303	507	47403	582	47424	657	47556	732	47608
433	47315	508	47378	583	47517	658	47554	733	47624
434	47319	509	47379	584	47465	659	47536	734	47640
435	47234	510	47245	585	47445	660	47452	735	47639
436	47235	511	47415	586	47505	661	47557	736	47612
437	47339	512	47416	587	47503	662	47537	737	47625
438	47300	513	47372	588	47506	663	47461	738	47626
439	47316	514	47380	589	47425	664	47560	739	47627
440	47304	515	47325	590	47469	665	47538	740	47628
441	47305	516	47326	591	47470	666	47485	741	47649
442	47351	517	47376	592	47482	667	47555	742	47613
443	47400	518	47417	593	47523	668	47540	743	47631
444	47401	519	47381	594	47507	669	47428	744	47629
445	47363	520	47431	595	47508	670	47541	745	47630
446	47282	521	47413	596	47472	671	47545	746	47641
447	47392	522	47373	597	47280	672	47559	747	47614
448	47243	523	47374	598	47473	673	47496	748	47632
449	47310	524	47442	599	47491	674	47561	749	47642
450	47236	525	47432	600	47474	675	47565	750	47643

DOUGLAS DC-9/MD-80*/MD-90+ - Line No to C/n

line no	c/n	line no	c/n	line no	c/n	line no	c/n	line no	c/n
751	47615	826	47722	901	47788	976	48130	1051	49101*
752	47633	827	47736	902	47784	977	48046*	1052	48156
753	47622	828	47730	903	47796	978	48032*	1053	48094*
754	47635	829	47737	904	47785	979	48028*	1054	48157
755	47646	830	47738	905	47786	980	48134	1055	48095*
756	47634	831	47725	906	47789	981	48008*	1056	48158
757	47654	832	47716	907	47790	982	48137	1057	48096*
758	47636	833	47717	908	47791	983	48049*	1058	48159
759	47616	834	47718	909	48000*	984	48148	1059	48097*
760	47653	835	47740	910	47792	985	48009*	1060	48098*
761	47648	836	47741	911	47793	986	48053*	1061	49116*
762	47617	837	47744	912	47787	987	48135	1062	49110*
763	47655	838	47723	913	47797	988	48033*	1063	49117*
764	47618	839	47747	914	47798	989	48050*	1064	49111*
765	47668	840	47691	915	47794	990	48149	1065	49118*
766	47667	841	47703	916	47795	991	48058*	1066	49114*
767	47644	842	47705	917	48001*	992	48010*	1067	48099*
768	47619	843	47690	918	47799	993	48136	1068	49112*
769	47670	844	47711	919	48114	994	48011*	1069	49113*
770	47645	845	47719	920	48115	995	48018*	1070	49119*
771	47650	846	47720	921	48116	996	48054*	1071	49120*
772	47666	847	47721	922	48117	997	48012*	1072	49121*
773	47647	848	47727	923	48111	998	48047*	1073	49122*
774	47671	849	47726	924	48015*	999	48070*	1074	49125*
775	47664	850	47662	925	48103	1000	48013*	1075	49123*
776	47669	851	47663	926	48112	1001	48019*	1076	49102*
777	47620	852	47739	927	48100	1002	48038*	1077	49124*
778	47672	853	47724	928	48104	1003	48039*	1078	48021*
779	47673	854	47729	929	48105	1004	48071*	1079	48022*
780	47651	855	47748	930	48113	1005	48048*	1080	49126*
781	47680	856	47754	931	48101	1006	48040*	1081	48165
782	47675	857	47742	932	48102	1007	48055*	1082	49127*
783	47656	858	47728	933	48106	1008	48041*	1083	49103*
784	47681	859	47743	934	48123	1009	48042*	1084	48166
785	47676	860	47731	935	48121	1010	48043*	1085	49104*
786	47684	861	47732	936	48107	1011	48072*	1086	49149*
787	47657	862	47733	937	48108	1012	48056*	1087	49150*
788	47682	863	47745	938	48002*	1013	48014*	1088	49151*
789	47678	864	47746	939	48109	1014	48150	1089	49152*
790	47658	865	47749	940	48131	1015	48062*	1090	49138*
791	47677	866	47751	941	48016*	1016	48079*	1091	49139*
792	47683	867	47753	942	48118	1017	48151	1092	49140*
793	47674	868	47734	943	48119	1018	48073*	1093	49141*
794	47685	869	47735	944	48003*	1019	48066*	1094	49142*
795	47687	870	47750	945	48110	1020	48063*	1095	49143*
796	47665	871	47759	946	48034*	1021	48138	1096	49144*
797	47679	872	47752	947	48125	1022	48080*	1097	49145*
798	47652	873	47756	948	48024*	1023	48057*	1098	49166*
799	47688	874	47760	949	48120	1024	48139	1099	49167*
800	47686	875	47761	950	48004*	1025	49100*	1100	49168*
801	47699	876	47762	951	48126	1026	48074*	1101	49153*
802	47689	877	47757	952	48025*	1027	48140	1102	49154*
803	47692	878	47755	953	48029*	1028	48067*	1103	49155*
804	47693	879	47763	954	48124	1029	48086*	1104	49156*
805	47694	880	47758	955	48035*	1030	48141	1105	49157*
806	47695	881	47769	956	48132	1031	48068*	1106	49158*
807	47659	882	47764	957	48005*	1032	48069*	1107	49159*
808	47696	883	47771	958	48017*	1033	48142	1108	49160*
809	47698	884	47774	959	48133	1034	48092*	1109	49161*
810	47660	885	47767	960	48026*	1035	48087*	1110	49162*
811	47700	886	47766	961	48127	1036	48143	1111	49163*
812	47661	887	47768	962	48030*	1037	48088*	1112	49171*
813	47708	888	47775	963	48036*	1038	48089*	1113	49172*
814	47709	889	47776	964	48128	1039	48144	1114	49173*
815	47712	890	47772	965	48037*	1040	48090*	1115	49174*
816	47697	891	47773	966	48006*	1041	48091*	1116	49175*
817	47702	892	47770	967	48044*	1042	48145	1117	49165*
818	47710	893	47782	968	48129	1043	48083*	1118	49169*
819	47704	894	47780	969	48031*	1044	48146	1119	49170*
820	47713	895	47781	970	48045*	1045	48020*	1120	49176*
821	47706	896	47777	971	48007*	1046	48154	1121	49177*
822	47701	897	47778	972	48122	1047	48059*	1122	49178*
823	47707	898	47779	973	48027*	1048	48147	1123	49179*
824	47714	899	47783	974	48052*	1049	48093*	1124	49180*
825	47715	900	47765	975	48051*	1050	48155	1125	49181*

DOUGLAS DC-9/MD-80*/MD-90+ - Line No to C/n

line no	c/n	line no	c/n	line no	c/n	line no	c/n	line no	c/n
1126	49192*	1201	49373*	1276	49364*	1351	49489*	1426	49472*
1127	49193*	1202	49211*	1277	49365*	1352	49490*	1427	49473*
1128	49182*	1203	49233*	1278	49417*	1353	49438*	1428	49433*
1129	49183*	1204	49234*	1279	49393*	1354	49449*	1429	49662*
1130	49194*	1205	49379*	1280	49322*	1355	49537*	1430	49404*
1131	49184*	1206	49370*	1281	49323*	1356	49400*	1431	49474*
1132	49185*	1207	49371*	1282	49282*	1357	49401*	1432	49475*
1133	49186*	1208	49374*	1283	49423*	1358	49442*	1433	49542*
1134	49187*	1209	49284*	1284	49424*	1359	49461*	1434	49543*
1135	49115*	1210	49291*	1285	49394*	1360	49491*	1435	49602*
1136	49195*	1211	49292*	1286	49395*	1361	49492*	1436	49557*
1137	49196*	1212	49293*	1287	49386*	1362	49531*	1437	49663*
1138	49197*	1213	49294*	1288	49387*	1363	49504*	1438	49659*
1139	49222*	1214	49295*	1289	49324*	1364	49493*	1439	49476*
1140	49229*	1215	49296*	1290	49325*	1365	49538*	1440	49570*
1141	49230*	1216	49297*	1291	49443*	1366	49539*	1441	49477*
1142	49198*	1217	49298*	1292	49501*	1367	49567*	1442	49603*
1143	49199*	1218	49299*	1293	49478*	1368	49494*	1443	49544*
1144	49237*	1219	49300*	1294	49358*	1369	49580*	1444	49545*
1145	49245*	1220	49301*	1295	49326*	1370	49344*	1445	49660*
1146	49246*	1221	49302*	1296	49327*	1371	49345*	1446	49434*
1147	49200*	1222	49303*	1297	49479*	1372	49346*	1447	49546*
1148	49201*	1223	49304*	1298	49480*	1373	49347*	1448	49591*
1149	49249*	1224	49355*	1299	49283*	1374	49348*	1449	49508*
1150	49260*	1225	49380*	1300	49502*	1375	49349*	1450	49553*
1151	49247*	1226	49305*	1301	49328*	1376	49350*	1451	49558*
1152	49248*	1227	49306*	1302	49329*	1377	49431*	1452	49661*
1153	49261*	1228	49307*	1303	49436*	1378	49432*	1453	49670*
1154	49251*	1229	49308*	1304	49440*	1379	49554*	1454	49577*
1155	49253*	1230	49279*	1305	49396*	1380	49568*	1455	49578*
1156	49254*	1231	49381*	1306	49331*	1381	49505*	1456	49604*
1157	49255*	1232	49382*	1307	49332*	1382	49527*	1457	49585*
1158	49256*	1233	49212*	1308	49481*	1383	49528*	1458	49571*
1159	49262*	1234	49235*	1309	49482*	1384	49581*	1459	49657*
1160	49257*	1235	49236*	1310	49219*	1385	49351*	1460	49559*
1161	49258*	1236	49383*	1311	49333*	1386	49352*	1461	49658*
1162	49259*	1237	49384*	1312	49334*	1387	49353*	1462	49560*
1163	49263*	1238	49266*	1313	49448*	1388	49451*	1463	49671*
1164	49269*	1239	49267*	1314	49483*	1389	49452*	1464	49617*
1165	49270*	1240	49425*	1315	49484*	1390	49453*	1465	49579*
1166	49271*	1241	49428*	1316	49485*	1391	49454*	1466	49667*
1167	49272*	1242	49429*	1317	49486*	1392	49455*	1467	49668*
1168	49273*	1243	49213*	1318	49439*	1393	49456*	1468	49572*
1169	49252*	1244	49385*	1319	49220*	1394	49418*	1469	49573*
1170	49202*	1245	49214*	1320	49335*	1395	49540*	1470	49583*
1171	49264*	1246	49309*	1321	49336*	1396	49529*	1471	49584*
1172	49188*	1247	49310*	1323	49444*	1397	49530*	1472	49586*
1173	49189*	1248	49311*	1324	49450*	1398	49457*	1473	49644*
1174	49203*	1249	49312*	1325	49337*	1399	49426*	1474	49561*
1175	49286*	1250	49356*	1326	49388*	1400	49506*	1475	49562*
1176	49287*	1251	49357*	1327	49338*	1401	49427*	1476	49464*
1177	49231*	1252	49372*	1328	49339*	1402	49555*	1477	49462*
1178	49232*	1253	49215*	1329	49340*	1403	49419*	1478	49701*
1179	49204*	1254	49420*	1330	49221*	1404	49403*	1479	49702*
1180	49190*	1255	49313*	1331	49397*	1405	49569*	1480	49645*
1181	49277*	1256	49314*	1332	49398*	1406	49458*	1481	49646*
1182	49164*	1257	49315*	1332	49441*	1407	49459*	1482	49509*
1183	49278*	1258	49316*	1333	49389*	1408	49460*	1483	49619*
1184	49205*	1259	49317*	1334	49430*	1409	49468*	1484	49620*
1185	49265*	1260	49415*	1335	49487*	1410	49469*	1485	49563*
1186	49250*	1261	49402*	1336	49341*	1411	49582*	1486	49564*
1187	49288*	1262	49216*	1337	49342*	1412	49411*	1487	49707*
1188	49206*	1263	49421*	1338	49532*	1413	49574*	1488	49463*
1189	49207*	1264	49422*	1339	49343*	1414	49575*	1489	49703*
1190	49208*	1265	49318*	1340	49525*	1415	49556*	1490	49704*
1191	49209*	1266	49319*	1341	49533*	1416	49541*	1491	49705*
1192	49210*	1267	49320*	1342	49526*	1417	49470*	1492	49711*
1193	49289*	1268	49217*	1343	49399*	1418	49471*	1493	49669*
1194	49280*	1269	49390*	1344	49534*	1419	49634*	1494	49672*
1195	49290*	1270	49391*	1345	49437*	1420	49635*	1495	49621*
1196	49366*	1271	49416*	1346	49503*	1421	49642*	1496	49565*
1197	49367*	1272	49392*	1347	49535*	1422	49576*	1497	49566*
1198	49368*	1273	49321*	1348	49536*	1423	49643*	1498	49622*
1199	49369*	1274	49218*	1349	49359*	1424	49412*	1499	49623*
1200	49281*	1275	49363*	1350	49488*	1425	49507*	1500	49712*

DOUGLAS DC-9/MD-80*/MD-90+ - Line No to C/n

line no	c/n	line no	c/n	line no	c/n	line no	c/n	line no	c/n
1501	49605*	1576	49723*	1652	49799*	1726	49982*	1801	53021*
1502	49624*	1577	49825*	1653	49911*	1727	49466*	1802	53025*
1503	49625*	1578	49826*	1654	49827*	1728	49855*	1803	49999*
1504	49435*	1579	49844*	1655	49792*	1729	49916*	1804	53026*
1505	49592*	1580	49627*	1656	49793*	1730	49837*	1805	53027*
1506	49593*	1581	49846*	1657	49766*	1731	53052*	1806	53053*
1507	49594*	1582	49628*	1658	49519*	1732	49928*	1807	49851*
1508	49673*	1583	49629*	1659	49912*	1733	49838*	1808	53161*
1509	49595*	1584	49550*	1660	49800*	1734	49907*	1809	53022*
1510	49596*	1585	49847*	1661	49801*	1735	49917*	1810	53172*
1511	49597*	1586	49551*	1662	49802*	1736	53012*	1811	53173*
1512	49607*	1587	49767*	1663	49803*	1737	49970*	1812	53000*
1513	49598*	1588	49810*	1664	49878*	1738	53013*	1813	53028*
1514	49510*	1589	49514*	1665	49913*	1739	49839*	1814	53029*
1515	49599*	1590	49811*	1666	49879*	1740	53014*	1815	53001*
1516	49600*	1591	49630*	1667	49828*	1741	49929*	1816	53030*
1517	49609*	1592	49848*	1668	49968*	1742	49467*	1817	53149*
1518	49601*	1593	49812*	1669	49804*	1743	49918*	1818	53015*
1519	49613*	1594	49877*	1670	49779*	1744	49919*	1819	53031*
1520	49647*	1595	49768*	1671	49520*	1745	49840*	1820	53032*
1521	49648*	1596	49631*	1672	49805*	1746	49524*	1821	53023*
1522	49611*	1597	49552*	1673	49806*	1747	49983*	1822	53033*
1523	49713*	1598	49820*	1674	49780*	1748	49984*	1823	53214*
1524	49714*	1599	49813*	1675	49856*	1749	49908*	1824	53215*
1525	49405*	1600	49794*	1676	49880*	1750	49920*	1825	53024*
1526	49649*	1601	49854*	1677	49881*	1751	49841*	1826	53034*
1527	49650*	1602	49814*	1678	49785*	1752	49921*	1827	49612*
1528	49651*	1603	49632*	1678	49829*	1753	49922*	1828	53083*
1529	49652*	1604	49465*	1679	49882*	1754	49931*	1829	49807*
1530	49715*	1605	49815*	1680	49904*	1755	49971*	1830	53084*
1531	49716*	1606	49759*	1681	49413*	1756	49932*	1831	53150*
1532	49717*	1607	49733*	1682	49414*	1757	49972*	1832	53241*
1533	49718*	1608	49816*	1683	49883*	1758	49923*	1833	53242*
1534	49653*	1609	49515*	1684	49830*	1759	49924*	1834	53243*
1535	49654*	1610	49726*	1685	49884*	1760	49987*	1835	53002*
1536	49655*	1611	49618*	1686	49890*	1761	49889*	1836	49808*
1537	49511*	1612	49817*	1687	49857*	1762	49973*	1837	49933*
1538	49626*	1613	49818*	1688	49831*	1763	49842*	1838	49985*
1539	49822*	1614	49706*	1689	49885*	1764	49934*	1839	53085*
1540	49823*	1615	49821*	1690	49521*	1765	49900*	1840	53086*
1541	49587*	1616	49925*	1691	49886*	1766	49901*	1841	53087*
1542	49709*	1617	49641*	1692	49888*	1767	49905*	1842	49986*
1543	49615*	1618	49740*	1693	49914*	1768	49988*	1843	49809*
1544	49549*	1619	49734*	1694	49891*	1769	49989*	1844	53003*
1545	49656*	1620	49760*	1695	49892*	1770	49990*	1845	53257*
1546	49675*	1621	49727*	1696	49893*	1771	49843*	1846	53004*
1547	49710*	1622	49516*	1697	49894*	1772	49849*	1847	53198*
1548	49512*	1623	49761*	1698	49895*	1773	49935*	1848	53258*
1549	49724*	1624	49762*	1699	49887*	1774	49974*	1849	53259*
1550	49676*	1625	49909*	1700	49976*	1775	49975*	1850	53016*
1551	49677*	1626	49763*	1701	49977*	1776	53044*	1851	53063*
1552	49725*	1627	49784*	1702	49522*	1777	53045*	1852	53088*
1553	49728*	1628	49819*	1703	49832*	1778	49936*	1853	53089*
1554	49824*	1629	49741*	1704	53050*	1779	53018*	1854	53174*
1555	49678*	1630	49786*	1705	49610*	1780	49991*	1855	53005*
1556	49614*	1631	49764*	1706	49833*	1781	49992*	1856	53054*
1557	49679*	1632	49764*	1707	49896*	1782	49993*	1857	53055*
1558	49680*	1633	49517*	1708	49897*	1783	53019*	1858	53090*
1559	49769*	1634	49777*	1709	49898*	1784	49937*	1859	53266*
1560	49681*	1635	49735*	1710	49978*	1785	49938*	1860	53267*
1561	49708*	1636	49787*	1711	49979*	1786	49906*	1861	53268*
1562	49682*	1637	49788*	1712	49980*	1787	49939*	1862	53207*
1563	49683*	1638	49910*	1713	49796*	1788	49940*	1863	53091*
1564	49684*	1639	49795*	1714	49834*	1789	53020*	1864	53092*
1565	49730*	1640	49736*	1715	49926*	1790	49994*	1865	53208*
1566	49731*	1641	49737*	1716	49927*	1791	49995*	1866	53151*
1567	49732*	1642	49789*	1717	49835*	1792	49996*	1867	53209*
1568	49513*	1643	49790*	1718	53051*	1793	49941*	1868	53175*
1569	49606*	1644	49791*	1719	49969*	1794	53046*	1869	53006*
1570	49719*	1645	49765*	1720	49930*	1795	53115*	1870	53273*
1571	49720*	1646	49778*	1721	49836*	1796	53116*	1871	53210*
1572	49608*	1647	49518*	1722	49899*	1797	53017*	1872	53137*
1573	49845*	1648	49738*	1723	49915*	1798	49850*	1873	53274*
1574	49721*	1649	49739*	1724	49523*	1799	49942*	1874	53211*
1575	49722*	1650	49797*	1725	49981*	1800	49998*	1875	53152*

DOUGLAS DC-9/MD-80*/MD-90+ - Line No to C/n

line no	c/n	line no	c/n	line no	c/n	line no	c/n	line no	c/n
1876	53153*	1951	53117*	2026	53126*	2101	53466*	2176	53547*
1877	53212*	1952	53346*	2027	53415*	2102	53467*	2177	53528+
1878	53154*	1953	53336*	2028	53205*	2103	53227*	2178	53472*
1879	53213*	1954	53118*	2029	53416*	2104	53228*	2179	53358+
1880	53039*	1955	53362*	2030	53048*	2105	53229*	2180	53548*
1881	53039*	1956	53119*	2031	53049*	2106	53230*	2181	53570+
1882	53007*	1957	53061*	2032	53417*	2107	53231*	2182	53573+
1883	53155*	1958	53363*	2033	53418*	2108	53232*	2183	53473*
1884	53156*	1959	49852*	2034	53206*	2109	53452*	2184	53359+
1885	53157*	1960	53062*	2035		2110	53233*	2185	53549*
1886	53138*	1961	53364*	2036	53419*	2111	53234*	2186	53574+
1887	49943*	1962	53337*	2037	49967*	2112	53453*	2187	53550*
1888	49944*	1963	53370*	2038	49997*	2113	53235*	2188	
1889	49945*	1964	53120*	2039	49956*	2114	53468*	2189	53577*
1890	53193*	1965	53371*	2040	53297*	2115	53387+	2190	53360+
1891	53158*	1966	53284*	2041	53164*	2116	53469*	2191	53491+
1892	53159*	1967	53340*	2042	53165*	2117	53388+	2192	53562+
1893	53160*	1968	53199*	2043	53351*	2118	53187*	2193	53571+
1894	53057*	1969	53042*	2044	49965*	2119	53188*	2194	53543+
1895	53008*	1970	53372*	2045	53298*	2120	53353+	2195	53576+
1896	53275*	1971	53121*	2046	53446*	2121	53189*	2196	53563+
1897	53040*	1972	53176*	2047	49966*	2122	53389+	2197	53544+
1898	49946*	1973	53177*	2048	53216*	2123	53390+	2198	53582+
1899	53139*	1974	53303*	2049	49957*	2124	53479*	2199	53564+
1900	49947*	1975	53304*	2050	53420*	2125	53354+	2200	53583+
1901	53244*	1976	53074*	2051	53421*	2126	53391+	2201	53565*
1902	53247*	1977	53075*	2052	53166*	2127	53480*	2202	53361+
1903	53248*	1978	53245*	2053	53217*	2128	53485*	2203	53584+
1904	53249*	1979	53347*	2054	49958*	2129	53489+	2204	53581*
1905	49948*	1980	53378*	2055	49959*	2130	53486*	2205	53492+
1906	49949*	1981	49853*	2056	53167*	2131	53355+	2206	53566+
1907	53250*	1982	53043*	2057	53377*	2132	53487*	2207	53555+
1908	53064*	1983	53379*	2058	53422*	2133	53490+	2208	53591*
1909	53251*	1984	53122*	2059	53423*	2134	53488*	2209	53493+
1910	53252*	1985	53348*	2060	53218*	2135	53470*	2210	53556+
1911	53194*	1986	53380*	2061	53168*	2136	53392+	2211	53557+
1912	53311*	1987	53123*	2062	53219*	2137	53520*	2212	53558+
1913	49950*	1988	53076*	2063	53169*	2138	53457+	2213	53494+
1914	53312*	1989	53285*	2064	53447*	2139	53471*	2214	53602*
1915	49951*	1990	53409*	2065	53170*	2140	53458+	2215	53495+
1916	53009*	1991	53124*	2066	53093*	2141	53459+	2216	53496+
1917	53294*	1992	53410*	2067	53171*	2142	53460+	2217	53572+
1918	53246*	1993	53125*	2068	53182*	2143	53523+	2218	53603*
1919	53253*	1994	53178*	2069	53147*	2144	53551+	2219	53497+
1920	53254*	1995	53077*	2070		2145	53481*	2220	53529+
1921	53010*	1996	53078*	2071	53183*	2146	53524+	2221	53498+
1922	53295*	1997	53179*	2072	53148*	2147	53461+	2222	53530+
1923	53140*	1998	53365*	2073	53220*	2148	53190*	2223	53499+
1924	53313*	1999	53366*	2074	53448*	2149	53462+	2224	53585+
1925	53065*	2000	53286*	2075	53299*	2150	53525+	2225	53500+
1926	53338*	2001	53305*	2076	53300*	2151	53191*	2226	53501+
1927	53058*	2002	53180*	2077	53449*	2152	53542*	2227	53502+
1928	53339*	2003	53368*	2078	53450*	2153	53534+	2228	53531+
1929	53195*	2004	53079*	2079	53221*	2154	53393+	2229	53503+
1930	53196*	2005	53181*	2080	53222*	2155	53192*	2230	53504+
1931	53011*	2006	53287*	2081	53223*	2156	53394+	2231	53505+
1932	53255*	2007	53203*	2082	53301*	2157	53356+	2232	53506+
1933	53256*	2008		2083	53451*	2158	53535+	2233	53586+
1934	49952*	2009	53204*	2084	53224*	2159	53395+	2234	53592*
1935	53141*	2010	53162*	2085	53302*	2160	53536+	2235	53507+
1936	53341*	2011	53288*	2086	53225*	2161	53396+	2236	53559+
1937	53296*	2012	53289*	2087	53226*	2162	53537+	2237	53508+
1938	53066*	2013	53290*	2088	53184*	2163	53552+	2238	53578+
1939	53342*	2014	53306*	2089	53463*	2164	53357+	2239	53593*
1940	53197*	2015	53307*	2090	53185*	2165	53553+	2240	53587+
1941	53343*	2016	53047*	2091	53464*	2166	53554+	2241	53594+
1942	53059*	2017		2092	53186*	2167	53546*	2242	53579+
1943	53344*	2018	53367+	2093	53465*	2168	53538+	2243	53601+
1944	53060*	2019	53291*	2094	53382+	2169	53567+	2244	53595+
1945	53041*	2020	53292*	2095	53383+	2170	53526+	2245	53560+
1946	53314*	2021	53293*	2096	53384+	2171	53568+	2246	53580+
1947	53315*	2022	53308*	2097	53385+	2172	53539+	2247	53596+
1948	49902*	2023	53309*	2098	53352+	2173	53569+	2248	53588+
1949	49903*	2024	53310*	2099	53386+	2174	53561*	2249	53597*
1950	53345*	2025	53163*	2100	53381+	2175	53527+	2250	53509+

DOUGLAS DC-9/MD-80*/MD-90+ - Line No to C/n

line no	c/n
2251	53510+
2252	53598*
2253	53532+
2254	53599*
2255	53511+
2256	53512+
2257	53513+
2258	53533+
2259	53589+
2260	53514+
2261	53590+
2262	53515+
2263	53516+
2264	53611*
2265	53612*
2266	53613*
2267	53614*
2268	53615*
2269	53616*
2270	53617*
2271	53618*
2272	53619*
2273	53620*
2274	53621*
2275	53622*
2276	53623*
2277	53624*
2278	53625*
2279	53626*
2280	53627*
2281	53628*
2282	53629*
2283	53630*
2284	53631*
2285	53632*
2286	53633*
2287	53634*
2288	53517+
2289	53518+
2290	53519+
4001	60001+
4002	60002+

DOUGLAS DC-10/MD-11* - Line No to C/n

line no	c/n	line no	c/n	line no	c/n	line no	c/n	line no	c/n
1	46500	76	46615	154	46623	229	47889	305	47818
2	46501	77	46890	155	46624	230	46662	306	47823
3	46502	78	46907	156	46945	231	46957	307	46635
4	46600	79	46754	157	47907	232	46958	308	47824
5	46503	80	47969	158	46932	233	46872	309	46636
6	46601	81	46825	159	46933	234	46959	310	47825
7	46504	82	46553	160	46934	235	46956	311	48200
8	46602	83	46727	161	46767	236	46961	312	47813
9	46505	84	46554	162	46942	237	46960	313	47826
10	46603	85	46851	163	46943	238	46962	314	47819
11	46604	86	46616	164	46768	239	46964	315	47814
12	46506	87	46925	165	46713	240	46640	316	47816
13	46507	88	47862	166	47925	241	46969	317	47820
14	46700	89	46617	167	46714	242	46950	318	47832
15	46605	90	47886	168	46769	243	46968	319	47828
16	46701	91	46555	169	46625	244	46963	320	47821
17	46606	92	47800	170	47926	245	46965	321	47829
18	46702	93	46852	171	46868	246	46951	322	47833
19	46703	94	47863	172	46935	247	46947	323	47830
20	46508	95	46908	173	47807	248	46975	324	47834
21	46509	97	46755	174	46869	249	46948	325	47815
22	46510	98	47801	175	46770	250	46984	326	47835
23	46511	99	46926	176	46941	251	46977	327	47831
24	46512	100	46927	177	47808	252	46983	328	47837
25	46607	101	47802	178	47867	253	46986	329	47841
26	46608	102	46756	179	46949	254	46976	330	47836
27	46609	104	46928	180	46771	255	46987	331	47850
28	46750	105	46711	181	47956	256	46978	332	47842
29	46704	106	46712	182	46910	258	46971	333	48201
30	46513	107	46929	183	46580	259	46981	334	47851
31	46514	108	46757	184	46581	260	46990	335	47843
32	46610	109	46826	185	46952	261	46991	336	47844
33	46705	111	46758	186	47981	262	46966	337	47840
34	46900	112	46930	187	46582	263	46993	338	47838
35	46611	113	46759	188	46912	264	46985	339	47870
36	46751	114	46577	189	46911	265	46967	340	47852
37	46515	115	47906	190	47927	266	46590	341	46543
38	46706	116	47847	191	47809	267	46998	342	48252
39	46612	117	47921	192	47928	268	46540	343	47853
40	46901	118	46618	193	46854	269	46970	344	48260
41	46902	119	46619	194	47810	270	46996	345	48265
42	46613	120	46760	195	46914	271	46989	346	48258
43	46903	121	47864	196	47929	272	46973	347	48261
44	46904	122	47922	197	46557	273	46994	348	48266
45	46614	123	47923	198	46626	274	46974	349	47855
46	46550	124	46761	199	46915	275	46995	350	48283
47	46905	125	47887	200	47868	276	46972	351	48262
48	46516	126	46762	201	47957	277	46835	352	48285
49	46517	127	46891	202	46916	278	46988	353	48263
50	46906	128	46763	203	46939	279	47982	354	48277
51	46518	129	47924	204	46892	280	46836	355	48282
52	46519	130	46764	205	46627	281	46541	356	47845
53	46752	131	46578	206	46913	282	46837	357	48259
54	46520	132	46579	207	46628	283	46645	358	48275
55	46521	133	46944	208	46629	284	46685	359	48202
56	46522	134	46853	209	46630	285	46646	360	48203
57	46575	135	47865	210	46631	286	46686	361	48204
58	46523	136	47848	211	46917	287	46591	362	48276
59	47965	137	46931	212	46920	288	46997	363	48205
60	46551	138	46620	213	47849	289	46999	364	48288
61	46707	139	47803	214	46921	290	46982	365	48289
62	46708	140	46621	215	47908	291	47888	366	47856
63	46850	141	46940	216	46923	292	46583	367	47857
64	47966	142	47804	217	46870	293	46584	368	48292
65	46524	143	46765	218	46924	294	47827	369	48286
66	46753	144	46622	219	46871	295	46542	370	48296
67	47967	145	47805	220	46660	296	46632	371	48293
68	46709	146	46556	221	46922	297	46633	372	48294
69	47846	147	46936	222	46946	298	46634	373	48206
70	46710	148	47806	223	46918	299	46595	374	48295
71	46552	149	47866	224	46661	300	47817	375	48207
72	46525	150	47980	225	46953	301	46596	376	48208
73	46576	151	46766	226	46919	302	47811	377	48209
74	47968	152	46937	227	46954	303	47812	378	48210
75	47861	153	46938	228	46955	304	47822	379	48264

DOUGLAS DC-10/MD-11* - Line No to C/n

line no	c/n	line no	c/n	line no	c/n	line no	c/n
380	48211	455	48449*	530	48552*	605	48623*
381	48301	456	48407*	531	48553*	606	48757*
382	48212	457	48408*	532	48532*	607	48770*
383	48213	458	48443*	533	48538*	608	48753*
384	48214	459	48444*	534	48431*	609	48773*
385	48215	460	48445*	535	48554*	610	48774*
386	48216	461	48495*	536	48479*	611	48540*
387	48217	462	48505*	537	48596*	612	48564*
388	48218	463	48446*	538	48480*	613	48755*
389	48219	464	48447*	539	48519*	614	48634*
390	48220	465	48448*	540	48597*	615	48758*
391	48221	466	48416*	541	48520*	616	48775*
392	48222	467	48417*	542	48565*	617	48776*
393	48223	468	48426*	543	48566*	618	48777*
394	48224	469	48487*	544	48533*	619	48778*
395	48225	470	48459*	545	48549*	620	48779*
396	48226	471	48427*	546	48470*	621	48541*
397	48227	472	48452*	547	48406*	622	48624*
398	48228	473	48453*	548	48504*	623	48756*
399	48229	474	48428*	549	48602*	624	48780*
400	48230	475	48461*	550	48598*	625	48781*
401	48231	476	48434*	551	48603*	626	48782*
402	48232	477	48454*	552	48571*	627	48783*
403	48233	478	48435*	553	48604*	628	48784*
404	48234	479	48450*	554	48439*	629	48785*
405	48235	480	48472*	555	48605*	630	48786*
406	48236	481	48473*	556	48572*	631	48787*
407	48237	482	48481*	557	48555*	632	48788*
408	48238	483	48436*	558	48471*	633	48789*
409	48287	484	48484*	559	48573*	634	48790*
410	48239	485	48474*	560	48600*	635	48791*
411	48240	486	48499*	561	48556*	636	48792*
412	48291	487	48455*	562	48601*	637	48798*
413	48241	488	48413*	563	48633*	638	48794*
414	48242	489	48475*	564	48513*	639	48799*
415	48243	490	48409*	565	48581*	640	48801*
416	48297	491	48414*	566	48574*	641	48800*
417	48244	492	48489*	567	48630*	642	48802*
418	48245	493	48500*	568	48575*	643	48803*
419	48298	494	48456*	569	48557*	644	48804*
420	48246	495	48410*	570	48542*	645	48805*
421	48247	496	48496*	571	48539*	646	48806*
422	48299	497	48460*	572	48543*		
423	48248	498	48457*	573	48558*		
424	48249	499	48490*	574	48576*		
425	48250	500	48429*	575	48559*		
426	48251	501	48418*	576	48415*		
427	48303	502	40405*	577	48616*		
428	48304	503	48491*	578	48560*		
429	48305	504	48527*	579	48631*		
430	48306	505	48451*	580	48544*		
431	48307	506	48437*	581	48617*		
432	48308	507	48528*	582	48632*		
433	48300	508	48430*	583	48577*		
434	48267	509	48486*	584	48618*		
435	48290	510	48476*	585	48561*		
436	48315	511	48477*	586	48629*		
437	48316	512	48497*	587	48545*		
438	48319	513	48501*	588	48578*		
439	48309	514	48478*	589	48546*		
440	48311	515	48514*	590	48743*		
441	48310	516	48523*	591	48562*		
442	48312	517	48547*	592	48744*		
443	48313	518	48468*	593	48563*		
444	48314	519	48469*	594	48747*		
445	48317	520	48502*	595	48748*		
446	48318	521	48548*	596	48745*		
447	48401*	522	48498*	597	48746*		
448	48402*	523	48404*	598	48749*		
449	48458*	524	48405*	599	48579*		
450	48419*	525	48518*	600	48766*		
451	48420*	526	48550*	601	48768*		
452	48421*	527	48551*	602	48767*		
453	48411*	528	48503*	603	48769*		
454	48412*	529	48512*	604	48754*		

Master Index

Civil-registered commercial jet airliners are arranged in order of country registration prefix, registrations relating to each country being listed in alphabetical or numerical order as appropriate. The number sequence for Russia etc. is listed at the end of the civil index for convenience.

For each registration a three-, four- or five character abbreviation for each type of aircraft is given, see decode below, followed by the c/n (or s/n). To fit into the spaces in Soviet types has been removed, as have the common prefixes.

For ease of reference all aircraft flying with registration prefixes, whether operated in civilian or government role are included in the civil section of the master index. Aircraft flying with purely numerical identities, (except the former Soviet Union as mentioned above) or with recognised military alphabetical prefixes or with military call-signs are included in the military section, which is listed by country name.

All civil and military aircraft which are in current use are indicated in bold typeface; reserved marks are given in normal typeface.

As the purpose of this index is to enable the reader to locate the details in the main volume, the codes refer to the generic type and not the actual subtype, so, for example, all military variants of the 707 and the Boeing 720 are given the code "707" - the actual designation appears in the 707 listing

Codes used are:

Code	Type	Code	Type
1-11	British Aircraft Corporation BAC 1-11	CV880	Convair 880
146	British Aerospace 146	CV990	Convair 990
737NG	Boeing 737 New Generation	DC-8	Douglas DC-8
A300	Airbus A300	DC-9	Douglas DC-9
A310	Airbus A310	DC-10	Douglas DC-10
A318	Airbus A318	DO328	Fairchild Dornier 328Jet
A319	Airbus A319	E145	Embraer RJ-135, RJ-140, RJ-145 family
A320	Airbus A320	E170	Embraer 170
A321	Airbus A321	E190	Embraer 190
A330	Airbus A330	F.28	Fokker F.28
A340	Airbus A340	F.70	Fokker 70
A380	Airbus A380	F.100	Fokker 100
AN124	Antonov An-124	IL62	Ilyushin Il-62
AN148	Antonov An-148	IL76	Ilyushin Il-76
AN225	Antonov An-225	IL86	Ilyushin Il-86
AN7x	Antonov An-71, An-72, An-74 etc	IL96	Ilyushin Il-96
ASHT	Avro 706 Ashton (see Experimental)	KC135	Boeing KC-135
B707	Boeing 707/720 and variants	L1011	Lockheed L-1011 Tristar
B717	Boeing 717	MD11	McDonnell Douglas MD-11
B727	Boeing 727	MD80	McDonnell Douglas MD-80 family
B737	Boeing 737	MD90	McDonnell Douglas MD-90
B747	Boeing 747	MERC	Dassault Mercure
B757	Boeing 757	NIMROD	Hawker-Siddley HS.801 Nimrod
B767	Boeing 767	SE210	Sud Aviation SE.210 Caravelle
B777	Boeing 777	TRDNT	Hawker-Siddley HS.121 Trident
B787	Boeing 787	TU104	Tupolev Tu-104
BB152	VEB BB-152 (see Experimental)	TU110	Tupolev Tu-110
BE200	Beriev Be-200 (see Experimental)	TU124	Tupolev Tu-124
C-1	Kawasaki C-1	TU134	Tupolev Tu-134
C-5	Lockheed C-5 Galaxy	TU144	Tupolev Tu-144
C-14	Boeing C-14 (see Experimental)	TU154	Tupolev Tu-154
C-15	McDonnell Douglas C-15 (see Experimental)	TU204	Tupolev Tu-204
C-17	Boeing C-17 Globemaster II	TU214	Tupolev Tu-214
C-141	Lockheed C-141 Starlifter	TU334	Tupolev Tu-334 (see Experimental)
C102	Avro Canada C-102 Jetliner (see Experimental)	VC10	Vickers VC-10
CNCRD	BAC/Aerospatiale Concorde	VFW	VFW-Fokker VFW-614
COMET	de Havilland DH.106 Comet	Y-10	Shanghai Y-10 (see Experimental)
CRJ	Canadair RJ100/RJ200 Regional Jet	YAK40	Yakovlev Yak-40
CRJ700	Canadair RJ700 Regional Jet	YAK42	Yakovlev Yak-42
CRJ900	Canadair RJ900 Regional Jet		

CIVIL INDEX

Azerbaijan
(see also 4K-)

Reg	Type	c/n
AHY-78001	IL76	0083489683
AHY-78129	IL76	0083489683
AL-65708	TU134	63447
AL-65711	TU134	63498

Nicaragua
(see also YN-)

Reg	Type	c/n
AN-BBI	1-11	BAC.111
AN-BBS	1-11	050
AN-BHJ	1-11	BAC.206
AN-BHN	1-11	074
AN-BIA	CV880	22-00-39
AN-BIB	CV880	22-00-9
AN-BLW	CV880	22-00-4
AN-BLX	CV880	22-00-36
AN-BSQ	B727	18843

Pakistan

Reg	Type	c/n
AP-AMG	B707	18378
AP-AMH	B707	18379
AP-AMJ	B707	18380
AP-ATK	TRDNT	2130
AP-ATL	TRDNT	2131
AP-ATM	TRDNT	2132
AP-ATQ	B707	18745
AP-AUG	TRDNT	2133
AP-AUN	B707	19284
AP-AUO	B707	19284
AP-AUO	B707	19285
AP-AUP	B707	19286
AP-AVL	B707	19866
AP-AVZ	B707	20487
AP-AWA	B707	20488
AP-AWB	B707	20275
AP-AWD	B707	19716
AP-AWE	B707	19715
AP-AWU	B707	18991
AP-AWV	B707	19441
AP-AWY	B707	19866
AP-AWZ	B707	20275
AP-AXA	B707	19286
AP-AXC	DC-10	46931
AP-AXD	DC-10	46940
AP-AXE	DC-10	46935
AP-AXG	B707	20488
AP-AXK	B707	18590
AP-AXL	B707	18818
AP-AXM	B707	18749
AP-AXQ	B707	18062
AP-AYM	DC-10	47889
AP-AYV	B747	20928
AP-AYW	B747	21035
AP-AZP	B707	18250
AP-AZW	B707	19636
AP-BAA	B707	19635
AP-BAF	B707	18589
AP-BAK	B747	21825
AP-BAT	B747	22077
AP-BAX	A300	096
AP-BAY	A300	098
AP-BAZ	A300	099
AP-BBA	A300	114
AP-BBK	B707	19576
AP-BBL	DC-10	47868
AP-BBM	A300	064
AP-BBV	A300	144
AP-BCA	B737	23294
AP-BCB	B737	23295
AP-BCC	B737	23296
AP-BCD	B737	23297
AP-BCE	B737	23298
AP-BCF	B737	23299
AP-BCJ	A300	268
AP-BCL	B747	20929
AP-BCM	B747	20802
AP-BCN	B747	20801
AP-BCO	B747	20927
AP-BCP	A300	025
AP-BDZ	A310	585
AP-BEB	A310	587
AP-BEC	A310	590
AP-BEG	A310	653
AP-BEH	B737	25504
AP-BEL	A300	269
AP-BEP	B737	22278
AP-BEQ	A310	656
AP-BEU	A310	691
AP-BEV	B737	22667
AP-BEW	B737	23113
AP-BEY	A300	146
AP-BFC	1-11	BAC.401
AP-BFD	1-11	BAC.404
AP-BFE	1-11	BAC.406
AP-BFF	1-11	BAC.407
(AP-BFG)	A300	259
AP-BFL	A300	204
AP-BFT	B737	23298
AP-BFU	B747	23392
AP-BFV	B747	23534
AP-BFW	B747	23221
AP-BFX	B747	23709
AP-BFY	B747	23920
AP-BGG	B747	24215
AP-BGJ	B777	33775
AP-BGK	B777	33776
AP-BGL	B777	33777
AP-BGN	A310	676
AP-BGO	A310	678
AP-BGP	A310	682
AP-BGQ	A310	660
AP-BGR	A310	687
AP-BGS	A310	689
AP-BGU	A320	0394
AP-BGV	A320	0443
AP-BGW	A320	0760
AP-BGY	B777	33781
AP-BGZ	B777	33782
AP-BHA	B737	22645
AP-BHB	B737	22655
AP-BHC	B737	21509
AP-BHG	B737	21666
AP-BHU	B737	21819
AP-BHV	B777	33778
AP-BHW	B777	33779
AP-BHX	B777	35296
AP-BIC	B747	23501
AP-BID	B777	33780
AP-BJA	A321	1199
AP-BJB	A321	1218
AP-BJH	B737	22275
AP-BJI	B737	22444
AP-BRJ	A321	1008
(AP-GOP)	A310	473
AP-OOI	A310	473

Botswana

Reg	Type	c/n
A2-ABD	146	E1101
A2-ABF	146	E1160

Tonga

Reg	Type	c/n
(A3-RTA)	MD80	49673

Oman

Reg	Type	c/n
A40-	737NG	35272
A40-	737NG	35284
A40-	737NG	35287
(A40-)	A320	0542
(A40-)	A320	0543
A40-AA	A320	2566
A40-AB	VC10	820
A40-BA	737NG	29685
A40-BB	1-11	BAC.162
A40-BB	737NG	30721
A40-BC	B737	21355
A40-BD	B737	21356
A40-BE	B737	21357
A40-BF	B737	21358
A40-BG	B737	21359
A40-BH	B737	21612
A40-BI	B737	21677
A40-BJ	B737	21733
A40-BJ	737NG	34242
A40-BK	B737	21734
A40-BL	B727	22633
A40-BM	B737	22396
A40-BN	737NG	30652
A40-BO	737NG	33103
A40-BR	737NG	33104
A40-BS	737NG	30649
A40-BT	737NG	28250
A40-BU	1-11	BAC.157
A40-BX	1-11	BAC.121
A40-CF	B727	18369
A40-EA	A320	0313
A40-EB	A320	0325
A40-EC	A320	0345
A40-ED	A320	0375
A40-EE	A320	0419
A40-EF	A320	0421
A40-EG	A320	0438
A40-EH	A320	0445
A40-EI	A320	0459
A40-EJ	A320	0466
A40-EK	A320	0481
A40-EL	A320	0497
A40-EM	A320	0536
A40-EN	A320	0537
A40-EO	A320	0409
A40-EP	A320	0289
A40-ER	A320	0407
(A40-GE)	B767	24349
A40-GF	B767	23764
A40-GG	B767	24349
A40-GH	B767	24484
A40-GI	B767	24485
A40-GJ	B767	24495
A40-GK	B767	24496
A40-GL	B767	24983
A40-GM	B767	24984
A40-GN	B767	24985
A40-GO	B767	25241
A40-GP	B767	25269
A40-GR	B767	25354
A40-GS	B767	26236
A40-GT	B767	26238
A40-GU	B767	26233
A40-GV	B767	26235
A40-GW	B767	27254
A40-GX	B767	27255
A40-GY	B767	26234
A40-GZ	B767	26237
A40-HM	DC-8	46149
A40-HMQ	DC-8	46149
A40-KA	A330	276
A40-KB	A330	281
A40-KC	A330	286
A40-KD	A330	287
A40-KE	A330	334
A40-KF	A330	340
A40-LA	A340	036
A40-LB	A340	039
A40-LC	A340	040
A40-LD	A340	097
A40-LE	A340	103
A40-LF	A340	133
A40-LG	A340	212
A40-LH	A340	215
A40-LI	A340	554
A40-LJ	A340	282
A40-MA	A320	0230
A40-MB	A320	0225
A40-MC	A320	0289
A40-OA	A310	409
A40-OB	A310	410
A40-OC	A310	640
A40-OD	A310	642
A40-OMN	B747	32445
A40-PA	DC-8	45821
A40-SO	B747	21785
A40-SP	B747	21992
A40-TA	L1011	193U-1201
A40-TB	L1011	193U-1203
(A40-TC)	L1011	193U-1131
A40-TP	L1011	193E-1025
A40-TR	L1011	193E-1047
A40-TS	L1011	193P-1068
A40-TT	L1011	193U-1223
A40-TV	L1011	193A-1056
A40-TW	L1011	193U-1131
A40-TX	L1011	193U-1133
A40-TY	L1011	193U-1138
A40-TZ	L1011	193U-1140
A40-VC	VC10	806
A40-VG	VC10	809
A40-VI	VC10	811
A40-VK	VC10	813
A40-VL	VC10	814

Bhutan

Reg	Type	c/n
A5-RGD	146	E1095
A5-RGE	146	E1199
A5-RGF	A319	2306
A5-RGG	A319	2346

United Arab Emirates

Reg	Type	c/n
A6-	A300	157
A6-	A300	178
A6-	A300	196
A6-	CRJ9	15124
A6-	DC-8	46034
A6-	E145	14500973
A6-AAA	B737	21613
A6-AAM	A318	1593
A6-ABA	A320	2158
A6-ABB	A320	2166
A6-ABC	A320	2278
A6-ABD	A320	2349
A6-ABE	A320	2712
A6-ABF	A320	2764
A6-ABG	A320	2930
A6-ABH	A320	2964
A6-ABI	A320	3044
A6-ABJ	A320	3218
A6-ABX	A320	0371
A6-ABY	A320	0112
A6-AIN	737NG	29268
A6-AUH	737NG	29857
A6-AUH	737NG	33473
A6-AVA	B737	22650
A6-AVE	B737	22624
A6-AVF	B737	22625
A6-BSM	L1011	193G-1222
A6-DAS	737NG	29858
A6-DPA	B707	20123
A6-DPW	E145	14500955

Reg	Type	c/n	Reg	Type	c/n	Reg	Type	c/n	Reg	Type	c/n
A6-EAA	A330	348	A6-EKF	A300	608	A6-EYC	A340	117	A6-ZYB	B737	21928
A6-EAB	A330	365	A6-EKG	A310	545	A6-EYD	A330	658	A6-ZYC	B737	22679
A6-EAC	A330	372	A6-EKH	A310	600	A6-EYE	A330	688	A6-ZYD	B707	20718
A6-EAD	A330	382	A6-EKI	A310	588	A6-EYF	A330	717	A6-ZYI	A300	666
A6-EAE	A330	384	A6-EKJ	A310	597	A6-EYG	A330	724			
A6-EAF	A330	392	A6-EKK	A310	648	A6-EYH	A330	729			
A6-EAG	A330	396	A6-EKK	A310	658	A6-EYI	A330	730	Qatar		
A6-EAH	A330	409	A6-EKL	A310	667	A6-EYJ	A330	737			
A6-EAI	A330	437	A6-EKM	A300	701	A6-EYK	A330	788	A7-AAA	B707	21334
A6-EAJ	A330	451	A6-EKN	A310	573	A6-EYL	A330	809	A7-AAB	B727	21595
A6-EAK	A330	452	A6-EKO	A300	747	A6-EYM	A330	824	A7-AAC	B707	20375
A6-EAL	A330	462	A6-EKP	A310	695	A6-EYN	A330	832	A7-AAF	A310	473
A6-EAM	A330	491	A6-EKQ	A330	248	A6-EYO	A330	852	A7-AAG	A320	0927
A6-EAN	A330	494	A6-EKR	A330	251	A6-EYP	A330	854	A7-AAH	A340	528
A6-EAO	A330	509	A6-EKS	A330	283	A6-EYQ	A330	868	A7-ABA	A310	267
A6-EAP	A330	525	A6-EKT	A330	293	A6-EYV	A330	272	A7-ABB	A310	276
A6-EAQ	A330	518	A6-EKU	A330	295	A6-EYW	A330	339	A7-ABC	B727	21951
A6-EAR	A330	536	A6-EKV	A330	314	A6-EYX	A330	232	A7-ABD	B727	22982
A6-EAS	A330	455	A6-EKW	A330	316	A6-EYY	A330	238	A7-ABE	B727	22044
A6-EBA	B777	32706	A6-EKX	A330	326	A6-EYZ	B767	30341	A7-ABG	B727	22043
A6-EBB	B777	32789	A6-EKY	A330	328	A6-GDP	B747	21098	A7-ABK	B747	21604
A6-EBC	B777	32790	A6-EKZ	A330	345	(A6-GZA)	B707	18809	A7-ABL	B747	21605
A6-EBD	B777	33501	A6-EMA	B727	21951	(A6-GZB)	B747	21218	A7-ABM	B747	21786
A6-EBE	B777	32788	A6-EMB	B727	22982	A6-HEH	737NG	32825	A7-ABN	A300	664
A6-EBF	B777	32708	A6-EMC	B727	21852	(A6-HHK)	B737	21613	A7-ABO	A300	668
A6-EBG	B777	33862	A6-EMD	B777	27247	A6-HHM	B727	22982	A7-ABP	A300	630
A6-EBH	B777	32707	A6-EME	B777	27248	(A6-HHP)	B707	21049	A7-ABR	A320	0928
A6-EBI	B777	32785	A6-EMF	B777	27249	A6-HHR	B707	18016	A7-ABS	A320	0932
A6-EBJ	B777	32787	A6-EMG	B777	27252	A6-HLA	DC-8	46034	A7-ABT	A320	0943
A6-EBK	B777	34481	A6-EMH	B777	27251	A6-HLB	DC-8	46035	A7-ABU	A320	0977
A6-EBL	B777	32709	A6-EMI	B777	27250	A6-HMK	B737	23553	A7-ABV	A300	690
A6-EBM	B777	34482	A6-EMJ	B777	27253	A6-HPZ	B707	21049	A7-ABW	A300	688
A6-EBN	B777	32791	A6-EMK	B777	29324	A6-HRM	B747	26903	A7-ABX	A300	554
A6-EBO	B777	32792	A6-EML	B777	29325	A6-HRR	B727	21951	A7-ABY	A300	560
A6-EBP	B777	32710	A6-EMM	B777	29062	A6-HRS	737NG	29251	A7-ABZ	A319	1335
A6-EBQ	B777	33863	A6-EMN	B777	29063	A6-KTH	1-11	BAC.126	A7-ACA	A330	473
A6-EBR	B777	34483	A6-EMO	B777	28680	A6-KUA	A310	447	A7-ACB	A330	489
A6-EBS	B777	32715	A6-EMP	B777	29395	A6-KUB	A310	448	A7-ACC	A330	511
A6-EBT	B777	32730	A6-EMQ	B777	32697	A6-KUC	A310	472	A7-ACD	A330	521
A6-EBU	B777	34484	A6-EMR	B777	29396	A6-KUD	A310	481	A7-ACE	A330	571
A6-EBV	B777	32728	A6-EMS	B777	29067	A6-KUE	A310	475	A7-ACF	A330	638
A6-EBW	B777	32793	A6-EMT	B777	32699	A6-LIW	146	E1267	A7-ACG	A330	743
A6-EBX	B777	32729	A6-EMU	B777	29064	A6-LIW	737NG	29857	A7-ACH	A330	441
A6-EBY	B777	33864	A6-EMV	B777	28687	A6-MJD	A320	0345	A7-ACI	A330	746
A6-EBZ	B777	32713	A6-EMW	B777	32700	A6-MMM	B747	26906	A7-ACJ	A330	760
A6-ECA	B777	32794	A6-EMX	B777	32702	A6-MRM	737NG	32450	A7-ACK	A330	792
A6-ECB	B777	32714	A6-ERA	A340	457	A6-MRS	737NG	35238	A7-ACL	A330	820
A6-ECC	B777	33865	A6-ERB	A340	471	A6-NGA	B737	24234	A7-ACM	A330	849
A6-ECD	B777	32795	A6-ERC	A340	485	A6-NKL	E145	14500944	A7-ADA	A320	1566
A6-ECE	B777	35575	A6-ERD	A340	520	A6-PFD	A300	374	A7-ADB	A320	1648
A6-ECF	B777	35574	A6-ERE	A340	572	A6-PHA	B737	23444	A7-ADC	A320	1773
A6-ECG	B777	35579	A6-ERF	A340	394	A6-PHC	B737	23626	A7-ADD	A320	1895
A6-ECH	B777	35581	A6-ERG	A340	608	A6-PHD	B737	22395	A7-ADE	A320	1957
A6-ECI	B777	35580	A6-ERH	A340	611	A6-PHF	B737	21645	A7-ADF	A320	2097
A6-ECJ	B777	35583	A6-ERI	A340	685	A6-PHZ	B767	23280	A7-ADG	A320	2121
A6-EDA	A380	011	A6-ERJ	A340	694	A6-RAK	1-11	084	A7-ADH	A320	2138
A6-EDB	A380	013	A6-ERM	A340	236	A6-RCA	B727	21920	A7-ADI	A320	2161
A6-EDC	A380	016	A6-ERN	A340	166	A6-RCB	B727	21917	A7-ADJ	A320	2288
A6-EDD	A380	017	A6-ERO	A340	163	A6-RJE	146	E2299	A7-ADS	A321	1928
A6-EDE	A380	020	A6-ERP	A340	185	A6-RJK	146	E1267	A7-ADT	A321	2107
A6-EDF	A380	023	A6-ERQ	A340	190	A6-RJX	737NG	29865	A7-ADU	A320	3071
A6-EDG	A380	025	A6-ERR	A340	202	A6-RJY	737NG	29857	A7-AEA	A330	623
A6-EDH	A380	028	A6-ERS	A340	139	A6-RJZ	737NG	29269	A7-AEB	A330	637
A6-EDI	A380	030	A6-ERT	A340	149	A6-RKA	B757	29311	A7-AEC	A330	659
A6-EDJ	A380	042	A6-ESA	DC-9	48136	A6-RKT	1-11	BAC.126	A7-AED	A330	680
A6-EFA	A310	646	A6-ESH	A319	0910	A6-RSA	B727	22046	A7-AEE	A330	711
A6-EFB	A310	592	A6-ESH	B737	22628	A6-SAA	B727	22043	A7-AEF	A330	721
A6-EFC	A310	622	A6-ESJ	B737	22628	A6-SHA	DC-8	45429	A7-AEG	A330	734
A6-EGD	A320	0313	A6-ETA	B777	34597	A6-SHJ	1-11	075	A7-AEH	A330	789
A6-EHA	A340	748	A6-ETB	B777	34598	A6-SHK	146	E1091	A7-AEI	A330	813
A6-EHB	A340	757	A6-ETC	B777	34599	A6-SHZ	A300	354	A7-AEJ	A330	826
A6-EHC	A340	761	A6-ETD	B777	34600	A6-SIR	737NG	29269	A7-AFA	A300	630
A6-EHD	A340	783	A6-ETE	B777	34601	A6-SMM	B747	21963	A7-AFB	A300	614
A6-EHE	A340	829	A6-EWA	B777	35572	A6-SMR	B747	21961	A7-AFC	A300	611
A6-EHF	A340	837	A6-EWB	B777	35573	A6-SUL	B767	30341	A7-AFD	A300	613
A6-EH	A340	856	A6-EWC	B777	35576	A6-SUN	E145	14501001	A7-AFE	A310	667
A6-EH	A340	870	A6-EWD	B777	35577	A6-UAE	B707	18931	A7-AFL	A330	612
A6-EKA	A310	432	A6-EWE	B777	35582	A6-UAE	B747	28551	A7-AFM	A330	616
A6-EKB	A310	436	A6-EWF	B777	35578	(A6-XAI)	A300	354	A7-AFN	A330	463
A6-EKC	A300	505	A6-EWG	B777	35586	A6-YAS	B747	28961	A7-AFO	A330	504
A6-EKD	A300	558	A6-EYA	A330	361	A6-ZSN	B747	23610	A7-AFP	A330	684
A6-EKE	A300	563	A6-EYB	A330	259	A6-ZYA	B737	21926	A7-AGA	A340	740

Reg	Type	Serial	Reg	Type	Serial	Reg	Type	Serial	Reg	Type	Serial
A7-AGB	A340	715	250	TRDNT	2162	B-254	TRDNT	2164	B-1860	B747	19898
A7-AGC	A340	766	256	TRDNT	2131	B-256	TRDNT	2165	B-1861	B747	22298
A7-AGD	A340	798	2004	IL62	90504	B-258	TRDNT	2166	B-1862	B747	21300
A7-AHM	B747	21786	2020	IL62	21203	B-260	TRDNT	2167	B-1864	B747	21454
A7-AHN	A320	0758	2022	IL62	11005	B-261	TRDNT	2165	(B-1865)	B747	22299
A7-BAA	B777	36009	2024	IL62	11101	B-262	TRDNT	2168	B-1866	B747	21843
A7-BAB	B777	36103	2026	IL62	21201	B-263	TRDNT	2185	B-1868	B747	19896
A7-CJA	A319	1656	2028	IL62	21202	B-264	TRDNT	2169	B-1870	B737	20226
A7-CJB	A319	2341	2402	B707	20714	B-265	TRDNT	2186	B-1872	B737	20227
A7-HHH	A340	495	2404	B707	20715	B-266	TRDNT	2170	B-1874	B737	20277
A7-HHJ	A319	1335	2406	B707	20716	B-267	TRDNT	2187	B-1876	B737	23913
A7-HHK	A340	026	2408	B707	20717	B-268	TRDNT	2188	B-1878	B737	24197
A7-HHM	A330	605	2410	B707	20718	B-269	TRDNT	2327	B-1880	B747	22298
A7-HJJ	A330	487	2412	B707	20719	B-270	TRDNT	2328	(B-1882)	B747	22547
A7-	A321	3274	2414	B707	20720	B-271	TRDNT	2189	B-1885	B747	22299
			2416	B707	20721	B-272	TRDNT	2171	B-1886	B747	22446
			2418	B707	20722	B-274	TRDNT	2172	B-1888	B747	22447
Liberia			2420	B707	20723	B-276	TRDNT	2173	B-1894	B747	22299
			50050	TRDNT	2132	B-278	TRDNT	2174	B-2005	B777	27524
A8-AAA	L1011	193N-1101	50051	TRDNT	2130	B-280	TRDNT	2175	B-2016	IL86	51483210097
A8-AAB	L1011	193N-1093	50052	TRDNT	2171	B-282	TRDNT	2176	B-2018	IL86	51483210099
			50053	TRDNT	2189	B-284	TRDNT	2177	B-2019	IL86	51483210100
			50054	TRDNT	2186	B-286	TRDNT	2178	B-2020	IL62	21203
Bahrain			50055	TRDNT	2188	B-288	TRDNT	2179	B-2022	IL62	11005
			50056	TRDNT	2130	B-290	TRDNT	2180	B-2024	IL62	11101
A9C-	B727	22643	50056	TRDNT	2185	B-292	TRDNT	2181	B-2026	IL62	21201
A9C-BA	B727	21824	50057	TRDNT	2187	B-294	TRDNT	2182	B-2028	IL62	21202
A9C-EB	A320	0325	50058	TRDNT	2328	B-296	TRDNT	2183	B-2051	B777	27357
A9C-ED	A320	0375	50059	TRDNT	2327	B-298	TRDNT	2184	B-2052	B777	27358
A9C-EE	A320	0419	50152	TRDNT	2133	B-513L	B707	20718	B-2053	B777	27359
A9C-EI	A320	0459	50158	TRDNT	2174	B-540L	MD80	49517	B-2054	B777	27360
A9C-EJ	A320	0466	B-	737NG	30733	B-542L	MD80	49519	B-2056	B777	27525
A9C-EL	A320	0497	B-	737NG	35274	B-584L	146	E1035	B-2057	B777	27604
A9C-EN	A320	0537	B-	737NG	35276	B-585L	146	E1068	B-2058	B777	27605
A9C-EO	A320	0409	B-	737NG	35285	"B-603L"	A319	2172	B-2059	B777	29153
A9C-EP	A320	0289	B-	737NG	35793	B-604L	CRJ	7512	B-2060	B777	29154
A9C-ER	A320	0407	B-	A330	881	B-605L	B707	20722	B-2061	B777	29155
A9C-GI	B767	24485	B-	B747	29262	B-606L	TU154	88A-790	B-2062	B777	27606
A9C-GJ	B767	24496	B-	B747	30322	B-607L	TU154	88A-791	B-2063	B777	29156
A9C-GK	B767	24496	B-	B777	27606	B-608L	TU154	88A-783	B-2064	B777	29157
A9C-GS	B767	26236	B-	IL76	073409267	B-609L	TU154	89A-797	B-2065	B777	29744
A9C-GT	B767	26238	B-	737NG	35100	B-610L	B737	22802	B-2066	B777	29745
A9C-GU	B767	26233	(B-)	B737	21763	B-614L	B737	22803	B-2067	B777	29746
A9C-GV	B767	26235	(B-)	B737	22131	B-615L	B737	22804	B-2068	B777	29747
A9C-GY	B767	26234	(B-)	B737	22132	B-632L	146	E1076	B-2069	B777	29748
A9C-GZ	B767	26237	(B-)	B737	22133	B-633L	146	E1081	B-2070	B777	32703
A9C-KA	A330	276	(B-)	B737	22136	B-634L	146	E1083	B-2100	MD90	60001
A9C-KB	A330	281	(B-)	B737	24279	B-635L	146	E1085	B-2101	MD80	49140
A9C-KC	A330	286	(B-)	B737	25191	B-652L	A320	0533	B-2102	MD80	49141
A9C-KD	A330	287	(B-)	B737	26105	B-653L	A320	0548	B-2103	MD80	49355
A9C-KE	A330	334	(B-)	B757	28446	B-1008	CV880	22-00-44M	B-2103	MD90	60002
A9C-KF	A330	340	(B-)	D0328	3219	B-1018	B727	19175	B-2104	MD80	49425
A9C-LB	A340	039	(B-)	IL76	093420599	B-1775	146	E3161	B-2105	MD80	49428
A9C-LC	A340	040	B-0002	Y-10	0002	B-1776	146	E3174	B-2106	MD80	49415
A9C-LD	A340	097	B-150	MD11	48468	B-1777	146	E3205	B-2107	MD80	49501
A9C-LE	A340	103	B-151	MD11	48469	B-1778	146	E3209	B-2108	MD80	49502
A9C-LF	A340	133	B-152	MD11	48470	B-1781	146	E3202	B-2109	MD80	49503
A9C-LG	A340	212	B-153	MD11	48471	B-1800	A300	529	B-2110	B737	28055
A9C-LH	A340	215	B-160	B747	24308	B-1802	A300	533	B-2111	B737	29405
A9C-LI	A340	554	B-161	B747	24309	B-1804	A300	536	B-2112	B737	28599
A9C-LJ	A340	282	B-162	B747	24310	B-1806	A300	666	B-2113	B737	28602
A9C-BDF	146	E2390	B-163	B747	24311	B-1810	A300	179	B-2115	B737	28606
A9C-DHL	B757	24635	B-164	B747	24312	B-1812	A300	171	B-2117	B737	24961
A9C-HAK	B747	23610	B-165	B747	24313	B-1814	A300	578	B-2120	MD80	49504
(A9C-HH)	A340	046	B-180	B737	23795	(B-1814)	A300	529	B-2121	MD80	49505
A9C-HHH	B747	21649	B-182	B737	23796	B-1816	A300	580	B-2122	MD80	49506
A9C-HMH	B747	21649	(B-184)	B737	23913	(B-1818)	A300	536	B-2123	MD80	49507
A9C-HMK	B747	33684	(B-186)	B737	24197	B-1818	B727	19399	B-2124	MD80	49508
A9C-HWR	146	E2306	B-188	B727	19818	B-1820	B727	19520	B-2125	MD80	49509
(A9C-ISA)	B747	21649	B-190	A300	193	B-1822	B727	20111	B-2126	MD80	49510
A9C-MAN	E145	14500978	B-192	A300	197	B-1824	B707	20261	B-2127	MD80	49511
A9C-MTC	E145	14500975	B-194	A300	221	B-1826	B707	20262	B-2128	MD80	49512
			B-196	A300	232	B-1828	B707	18710	B-2129	MD80	49513
			B-198	B747	22390	B-1830	B707	19178	B-2130	MD80	49514
China & Taiwan			B-232	TRDNT	2130	B-1832	B707	18825	B-2131	MD80	49515
			B-240	TRDNT	2157	B-1834	B707	18887	B-2132	MD80	49516
232	TRDNT	2130	B-242	TRDNT	2158	B-1836	B767	22681	B-2133	MD80	49517
240	TRDNT	2157	B-244	TRDNT	2159	B-1838	B767	22682	B-2134	MD80	49518
242	TRDNT	2158	B-246	TRDNT	2160	B-1850	SE210	121	B-2135	MD80	49519
244	TRDNT	2159	B-248	TRDNT	2161	B-1852	SE210	122	B-2136	MD80	49520
246	TRDNT	2160	B-250	TRDNT	2162	B-1854	SE210	38	B-2137	MD80	49521
248	TRDNT	2161	B-252	TRDNT	2163	B-1856	SE210	170	B-2138	MD80	49522

Reg	Type	c/n	Reg	Type	c/n	Reg	Type	c/n	Reg	Type	c/n
B-2139	MD80	49523	B-2225	A319	1654	B-2328	A300	756	B-2408	B707	20717
B-2140	MD80	49524	B-2226	A319	1786	B-2329	A300	762	B-2409	B747	26560
B-2141	MD80	49849	B-2227	A319	1778	B-2330	A300	763	B-2410	A320	2437
B-2142	MD80	49850	B-2228	A320	1906	B-2331	A319	1285	B-2410	B707	20718
B-2143	MD80	49851	B-2229	A320	1911	B-2332	A319	1303	B-2411	A320	2451
B-2144	MD80	49852	B-2230	A320	1964	B-2333	A319	1377	B-2412	A320	2478
B-2145	MD80	49853	B-2231	F.100	11383	B-2334	A319	1386	B-2412	B707	20719
B-2146	MD80	53162	B-2232	F.100	11389	B-2335	A320	1312	B-2413	A320	2493
B-2147	MD80	53163	B-2233	F.100	11394	B-2336	A320	1330	B-2414	B707	20720
B-2148	MD80	53169	B-2234	F.100	11401	B-2337	A320	1357	B-2415	A320	2498
B-2149	MD80	53170	B-2235	F.100	11409	B-2338	A320	1361	B-2416	A320	0994
B-2150	MD80	53171	B-2236	F.100	11430	B-2339	A319	1753	B-2416	B707	20721
B-2151	MD80	49852	B-2237	F.100	11421	B-2340	A320	0540	B-2417	A321	2521
B-2152	MD80	53164	B-2238	F.100	11423	B-2341	A320	0551	B-2418	A321	2530
B-2153	737NG	28242	B-2239	F.100	11429	B-2342	A320	0556	B-2418	B707	20722
B-2155	737NG	28649	B-2240	F.100	11431	B-2343	A320	0696	B-2419	A321	2882
B-2156	737NG	28650	B-2250	MD90	53523	B-2345	A320	0698	B-2420	A321	2895
B-2157	737NG	32600	B-2251	MD90	53524	B-2346	A320	0704	B-2420	B707	20723
B-2158	737NG	32601	B-2252	MD90	53525	B-2347	A320	0705	B-2421	B747	35169
B-2159	737NG	32599	B-2253	MD90	53526	B-2348	A320	0709	B-2422	B707	19353
B-2160	737NG	28652	B-2254	MD90	53527	B-2348	A320	0912	B-2422	B747	35173
B-2161	737NG	28655	B-2255	MD90	53528	B-2349	A320	0710	B-2423	B707	19352
B-2162	737NG	30041	B-2256	MD90	53582	B-2350	A320	0712	B-2423	B747	35174
B-2163	737NG	30042	B-2257	MD90	53583	B-2351	A320	0718	B-2424	B707	19530
B-2165	B737	23499	B-2258	MD90	53584	B-2352	A320	0720	B-2425	B707	19964
B-2166	B737	23500	B-2259	MD90	53529	B-2353	A320	0722	B-2425	B747	35207
B-2167	737NG	30631	B-2260	MD90	53530	B-2354	A320	0707	B-2426	B707	19294
B-2168	737NG	30632	B-2261	MD90	53531	B-2355	A320	0724	B-2426	B747	35208
B-2169	737NG	32936	B-2262	MD90	53585	B-2356	A320	0665	B-2428	B747	28263
B-2170	MD11	48461	B-2263	MD90	53586	B-2357	A320	0754	B-2429	B747	28032
B-2171	MD11	48495	B-2264	MD90	53587	B-2358	A320	0838	B-2430	B747	27137
B-2172	MD11	48496	B-2265	MD90	53532	B-2359	A320	0854	B-2431	B747	30761
B-2173	MD11	48497	B-2266	MD90	53533	B-2360	A320	0772	B-2438	B747	21933
B-2174	MD11	48498	B-2267	MD90	53533	B-2361	A320	0799	B-2439	B747	35170
B-2175	MD11	48520	B-2268	MD90	53588	B-2362	A320	0828	B-2440	B747	19732
B-2177	MD11	48544	B-2269	MD90	53589	B-2363	A320	0883	B-2440	B747	35171
B-2178	MD11	48543	B-2270	MD90	53590	B-2364	A319	2499	B-2441	B747	35172
B-2201	A320	0914	B-2280	A321	1596	B-2365	A320	0849	B-2442	B747	21932
B-2201	TRDNT	2157	B-2281	A321	1614	B-2366	A320	0859	B-2443	B747	25881
B-2202	A320	0925	B-2282	A321	1776	B-2367	A320	0881	B-2444	B747	21933
B-2202	TRDNT	2158	B-2283	A321	1788	B-2368	A320	0895	B-2445	B747	25882
B-2203	A320	1005	B-2284	A321	1974	B-2369	A320	0900	(B-2446)	B747	21934
B-2203	TRDNT	2168	B-2285	A321	1995	B-2370	A321	0878	B-2446	B747	23071
B-2204	TRDNT	2175	B-2286	A321	0550	B-2371	A321	0915	B-2447	B747	25883
B-2205	A320	0984	B-2287	A321	2080	B-2372	A320	0897	B-2448	B747	23461
B-2205	TRDNT	2176	B-2288	A321	2067	B-2373	A320	0919	B-2450	B747	23746
B-2206	A320	0986	B-2289	A321	2309	B-2374	A320	2345	B-2452	B747	21934
B 2206	TRDNT	2101	B-2290	A321	2315	B-2375	A320	0909	B-2454	B747	22302
B-2207	A320	1028	B-2291	A321	2543	B-2376	A320	0876	B-2456	B747	24346
"B-2207"	TRDNT	2133	B-2292	A321	2549	B-2377	A320	0921	B-2458	B747	24347
B-2207	TRDNT	2182	B-2293	A321	0591	B-2378	A320	0939	B-2459	A320	0709
B-2208	A320	1070	B-2294	A319	2371	B-2379	A320	0967	B-2460	B747	24348
B-2208	TRDNT	2165	B-2295	A319	2408	B-2380	A340	129	B-2461	B747	32804
B-2209	A320	1030	B-2296	A319	2426	B-2381	A340	131	B-2462	B747	24960
B-2209	TRDNT	2164	B-2297	A319	2435	B-2382	A340	141	B-2464	B747	25879
B-2210	A320	1296	B-2298	A319	2534	B-2383	A340	161	B-2466	B747	25880
B-2210	TRDNT	2178	B-2299	A319	2597	B-2384	A340	182	B-2467	B747	28754
B-2211	A320	1041	B-2300	A319	2639	B-2385	A340	192	B-2468	B747	28755
B-2211	TRDNT	2180	B-2301	A310	311	B-2386	A340	199	B-2469	B747	28756
B-2212	A320	1316	B-2302	A310	320	B-2387	A340	201	B-2470	B747	29070
B-2212	TRDNT	2162	B-2303	A310	419	B-2388	A340	242	B-2471	B747	29071
B-2213	A320	1345	B-2304	A310	435	B-2389	A340	243	B-2472	B747	30158
B-2213	TRDNT	2173	B-2305	A310	440	B-2390	A340	264	B-2473	B747	32803
B-2214	A320	0548	B-2306	A300	521	B-2391	A320	0950	B-2475	B747	34239
B-2214	TRDNT	2163	B-2307	A300	525	B-2392	A320	0966	B-2476	B747	34240
B-2215	A319	1541	B-2308	A300	532	B-2393	A320	1035	B-2477	B747	24998
B-2215	TRDNT	2166	B-2309	A300	584	B-2395	A320	1039	B-2478	B747	25075
B-2216	A319	1551	B-2310	A300	603	B-2396	A320	1057	B-2490	B767	33047
B-2216	TRDNT	2177	B-2311	A300	688	B-2397	A320	1013	B-2491	B767	33048
B-2217	A319	1601	B-2312	A300	690	B-2398	A320	1108	B-2492	B767	33049
B-2217	TRDNT	2179	B-2315	A300	733	B-2399	A320	1093	B-2493	B767	28132
B-2218	TRDNT	2159	B-2316	A300	734	B-2400	A320	1072	B-2494	B767	30301
B-2219	A320	1532	B-2317	A300	741	B-2401	A320	0710	B-2495	B767	27909
B-2219	TRDNT	2160	B-2318	A300	707	B-2402	B707	20714	B-2496	B767	30301
B-2220	A320	1542	B-2319	A300	732	B-2403	A320	2275	B-2497	B767	27477
B-2220	TRDNT	2183	B-2320	A300	709	B-2404	A319	2454	B-2498	B767	27684
B-2221	A320	1639	B-2321	A300	713	B-2404	B707	20715	B-2499	B767	30597
B-2221	TRDNT	2184	B-2322	A300	715	B-2405	A320	2343	B-2500	B767	35155
B-2222	A319	1603	B-2323	A300	739	B-2406	A320	2354	B-2501	B737	22802
B-2223	A319	1679	B-2324	A300	725	B-2406	B707	20716	B-2501	SE210	108
B-2223	TRDNT	2161	B-2325	A300	746	B-2407	A320	2334	B-2502	737NG	30075
B-2224	A320	0533	B-2326	A300	754	B-2408	A320	2361			
			B-2327	A300	750						

Reg.	Type	C/n	Reg.	Type	C/n	Reg.	Type	C/n	Reg.	Type	C/n
B-2502	B737	22803	B-2574	B737	29407	B-2633	737NG	29190	B-2719	146	E3218
B-2503	737NG	30074	B-2575	B737	29408	(B-2635)	737NG	29086	B-2720	146	E3219
B-2503	B737	22804	B-2576	B737	29915	B-2635	737NG	29191	B-2751	YAK42	3116650
B-2503	SE210	110	B-2577	737NG	30168	B-2636	737NG	28574	B-2752	YAK42	4116664
B-2504	B737	23065	B-2578	B737	25603	B-2637	737NG	28576	B-2753	YAK42	4116677
B-2504	B737	28333	B-2579	B737	25505	B-2638	737NG	28220	B-2754	YAK42	3116579
B-2505	B737	23066	B-2580	B737	25080	B-2639	737NG	29912	B-2755	YAK42	2116644
B-2505	SE210	197	B-2581	B737	25081	B-2640	737NG	29913	B-2756	YAK42	4116669
B-2506	B737	23272	B-2582	B737	25895	B-2641	737NG	29876	B-2757	YAK42	3403018
B-2507	B737	23273	B-2583	B737	25897	B-2642	737NG	29877	B-2758	YAK42	4404018
B-2508	B737	23274	B-2584	B737	25891	B-2643	737NG	29878	B-2801	B757	24014
B-2509	737NG	30072	B-2585	B737	27045	B-2645	737NG	29879	B-2802	B757	24015
B-2509	B737	23188	B-2586	B737	27047	B-2646	737NG	28056	B-2803	B757	24016
B-2510	737NG	30071	B-2587	B737	25892	B-2647	737NG	29947	B-2804	B757	24330
B-2510	B737	23189	B-2588	B737	25893	B-2648	737NG	29880	B-2805	B757	24331
B-2511	737NG	30073	B-2589	B737	27127	B-2649	737NG	30159	B-2806	B757	24401
B-2511	B737	23443	B-2590	B737	27126	B-2650	737NG	30160	B-2807	B757	24402
B-2512	B737	23444	B-2591	B737	25792	B-2651	737NG	30474	B-2808	B757	24471
B-2514	B737	23445	B-2592	B737	27153	B-2652	737NG	30475	B-2809	B757	24472
B-2515	B737	23446	B-2593	B737	27155	B-2653	B737	24570	B-2810	B757	24473
B-2516	B737	23447	B-2594	B737	26853	B-2655	B737	26288	B-2811	B757	24714
B-2517	B737	23396	B-2595	B737	26072	B-2656	B737	26292	B-2812	B757	24758
B-2518	B737	23397	B-2596	B737	27151	B-2657	737NG	30517	B-2812	B757	32341
B-2519	B737	23448	B-2597	B737	27176	B-2658	737NG	30512	B-2813	B757	32342
B-2520	B737	23449	B-2598	B737	27128	B-2659	737NG	30513	B-2814	B757	32343
B-2521	B737	23450	B-2599	B737	25896	B-2660	737NG	30494	B-2815	B757	24774
B-2522	B737	23451	B-2600	B737	28554	B-2661	B737	26284	B-2816	B757	25083
B-2523	B737	24913	B-2601	B737	19936	B-2662	B737	24988	B-2817	B757	25258
B-2524	B737	24236	B-2601	TU154	85A-716	B-2663	737NG	28437	B-2818	B757	25259
B-2525	B737	24918	B-2602	B737	28573	B-2665	737NG	30495	B-2819	B757	25898
B-2526	B737	25172	B-2602	TU154	85A-717	B-2666	737NG	30169	B-2820	B757	25885
B-2527	B737	25173	B-2603	B737	19939	B-2667	737NG	30170	B-2821	B757	25886
B-2528	B737	25174	B-2603	TU154	85A-718	B-2668	737NG	30171	B-2822	B757	25884
B-2529	B737	22735	B-2604	B737	26333	B-2669	737NG	32722	B-2823	B757	25888
B-2529	B737	26297	B-2604	TU154	86A-724	B-2671	737NG	30514	B-2824	B757	25889
B-2530	B737	27046	B-2605	B737	19712	B-2672	737NG	30515	B-2825	B757	25890
B-2531	B737	23302	B-2605	B737	23811	B-2673	737NG	29888	B-2826	B757	26155
B-2532	B737	23303	B-2605	TU154	86A-725	B-2675	737NG	32885	B-2827	B757	26156
B-2533	B737	27138	B-2606	TU154	86A-728	B-2676	737NG	32602	B-2828	B757	25899
B-2534	B737	26070	B-2607	B737	20132	B-2677	737NG	32604	B-2829	B757	25900
B-2535	B737	25078	B-2607	TU154	86A-729	B-2678	737NG	32244	(B-2830)	B757	26160
B-2536	B737	25079	B-2608	B737	28662	B-2679	737NG	29893	B-2831	B757	26153
B-2537	B737	25089	B-2608	TU154	86A-734	B-2680	737NG	30282	B-2832	B757	25887
B-2538	B737	25090	B-2609	TU154	86A-735	B-2681	737NG	33037	B-2833	B757	27152
B-2539	B737	26068	B-2610	B737	28555	B-2682	737NG	33038	B-2834	B757	27183
B-2540	B737	27139	B-2610	TU154	86A-740	B-2683	737NG	28253	B-2835	B757	25598
B-2541	B737	24696	B-2611	B737	21518	B-2684	737NG	33039	B-2836	B757	27258
B-2542	B737	24897	B-2611	TU154	86A-726	B-2685	737NG	33040	B-2837	B757	27259
B-2543	B737	24898	B-2612	737NG	33411	B-2686	737NG	28251	B-2838	B757	27260
B-2544	B737	24899	B-2613	737NG	33412	B-2687	B737	28555	B-2839	B757	27269
B-2545	B737	24900	B-2613	B737	20134	B-2688	737NG	33471	B-2840	B757	27270
B-2546	B737	25175	D-2614	D737	20550	B-2689	737NG	33472	B-2841	B757	27367
B-2547	B737	25176	B-2614	TU154	86A-741	B-2690	737NG	29600	B-2842	B757	27342
D-2548	D737	25102	B-2615	B737	21687	B-2691	737NG	30628	D-2043	D757	27601
B-2549	B737	25183	B-2615	TU154	88A-783	B-2692	737NG	28241	B-2844	B757	27511
B-2550	B737	25188	B-2616	TU154	88A-790	B-2693	737NG	32921	B-2845	B757	27512
B-2551	B767	23307	B-2617	B737	20130	B-2694	737NG	32922	B-2848	B757	27513
B-2552	B767	23308	B-2617	TU154	88A-791	B-2695	737NG	32923	B-2849	B757	27517
B-2553	B767	23744	B-2618	TU154	89A-797	B-2696	737NG	32924	B-2850	B757	30338
B-2554	B767	23745	B-2619	TU154	89A-814	B-2697	737NG	32925	B-2851	B757	29215
B-2555	B767	24007	B-2620	737NG	32937	B-2698	737NG	32583	B-2852	B757	28833
B-2556	B767	24157	B-2620	TU154	89A-815	B-2699	737NG	32596	B-2853	B757	29216
B-2557	B767	25875	B-2621	B737	19014	B-2700	737NG	33413	B-2855	B757	29792
B-2558	B767	25876	B-2621	TU154	89A-823	B-2701	146	E1019	B-2856	B757	29793
B-2559	B767	25877	B-2622	737NG	32938	(B-2701)	B737	19936	B-2857	B757	33959
B-2560	B767	25878	B-2622	TU154	90A-846	B-2702	146	E1026	B-2858	B757	33960
B-2561	B767	25865	B-2623	B737	19017	B-2703	146	E1032	B-2859	B757	29217
B-2561	B767	30563	B-2623	TU154	90A-855	(B-2703)	B737	19939	B-2860	B757	29945
B-2562	B767	25864	B-2624	TU154	91A-886	B-2704	146	E1035	B-2861	B757	29946
B-2562	B767	30566	B-2625	B737	23794	B-2705	146	E1068	B-2862	B757	34008
B-2563	B767	27309	B-2625	TU154	91A-893	B-2706	146	E1071	B-2863	737NG	30673
B-2564	B767	25121	B-2626	TU154	91A-894	B-2707	146	E1076	B-2865	737NG	30679
B-2565	B767	26259	B-2627	B737	26315	B-2708	146	E1081	B-2866	B757	34009
B-2566	B767	25170	B-2627	TU154	92A-917	B-2709	146	E1083	B-2868	B757	32941
B-2566	B767	35156	B-2628	TU154	92A-922	B-2710	146	E1085	B-2869	B757	32942
B-2567	B767	27685	B-2629	TU154	92A-919	B-2711	146	E3207	B-2871	TU204	3664030
B-2568	B767	28148	B-2630	B737	26317	B-2712	146	E3212	B-2875	B757	33966
B-2569	B767	28149	B-2630	TU154	93A-954	B-2715	146	E3214	B-2876	B757	33967
B-2570	B767	27941	B-2631	737NG	28212	B-2716	146	E3215	B-2877	B737	29331
B-2571	B737	29410	B-2632	737NG	28216	B-2717	146	E3216	B-2878	B737	28760
B-2572	B737	29411				B-2718	146	E3222	B-2880	B757	33961
B-2573	B737	29412							B-2901	B737	26284

Reg	Type	C/n	Reg	Type	C/n	Reg	Type	C/n	Reg	Type	C/n
B-2902	B737	24988	B-2986	B737	29069	B-3973	DO328	3158	B-5033	737NG	30657
B-2903	B737	26292	B-2987	B737	28663	B-3975	DO328	3159	B-5034	737NG	30036
(B-2903)	B737	26288	B-2988	B737	29087	B-3976	DO328	3177	B-5035	B737	28672
B-2904	B737	26288	B-2989	B737	28758	B-3977	DO328	3182	B-5036	B737	28673
(B-2904)	B737	26292	B-2990	B737	25766	B-3978	DO328	3187	B-5037	737NG	29892
B-2905	B737	25506	B-2991	737NG	29085	B-3979	DO328	3191	B-5038	737NG	30656
B-2906	B737	25507	B-2992	737NG	29086	B-3982	DO328	3195	B-5039	737NG	28258
B-2907	B737	25508	B-2993	B737	28759	B-3983	DO328	3211	B-5040	737NG	32929
B-2908	B737	26854	B-2994	B737	25604	B-3985	DO328	3215	B-5041	737NG	32930
B-2909	B737	26082	B-2995	B737	29315	B-3986	DO328	3217	B-5042	737NG	32931
B-2910	B737	26083	B-2996	B737	29316	B-3987	DO328	3218	B-5043	737NG	33408
B-2911	B737	26084	B-2997	737NG	28223	B-4001	TU154	85A-711	B-5044	737NG	33409
B-2912	B737	26100	B-2998	737NG	29042	B-4002	TU154	85A-712	B-5045	737NG	33410
B-2913	737NG	30167	B-2999	737NG	29084	B-4003	TU154	85A-713	B-5046	B737	24276
B-2915	B737	26101	B-3000	B737	29326	B-4004	TU154	85A-714	B-5047	B737	24278
B-2916	737NG	32939	B-3001	CRJ	7565	B-4005	CRJ	7138	B-5048	737NG	33470
B-2917	737NG	32940	B-3005	CRJ	7435	B-4006	CRJ	7149	B-5049	737NG	28639
B-2918	B737	24986	B-3006	CRJ	7443	B-4007	CRJ	7180	B-5050	737NG	28643
B-2919	B737	24987	B-3007	CRJ	7498	B-4008	B737	23839	B-5053	B737	24378
B-2920	B737	27271	B-3008	CRJ	7512	B-4009	B737	23840	B-5054	737NG	29365
B-2921	B737	27286	B-3009	CRJ	7522	B-4010	CRJ	7189	B-5055	B737	24283
B-2922	B737	27272	B-3010	CRJ	7565	B-4011	CRJ	7193	B-5056	B737	23836
B-2923	B737	27275	B-3011	CRJ	7556	B-4012	YAK42	4914375	B-5057	B737	23837
B-2924	B737	27287	B-3012	CRJ	7557	B-4013	YAK42	49144..	B-5058	B737	23835
B-2925	B737	27288	B-3013	CRJ	7571	B-4014	TU154	90A-847	B-5059	B737	24362
B-2926	B737	27289	B-3015	CRJ	7167	B-4015	TU154	90A-856	B-5060	737NG	28582
B-2927	B737	27290	B-3016	CRJ	7614	B-4016	TU154	91A-872	B-5061	737NG	28583
B-2928	B737	26294	B-3017	CRJ	7142	B-4017	TU154	91A-873	B-5062	737NG	28585
B-2929	B737	27343	B-3018	CRJ	7453	B-4018	B737	25502	B-5063	737NG	30736
B-2930	B737	27273	B-3019	CRJ	7581	B-4019	B737	25503	B-5064	737NG	30737
B-2931	B737	27276	B-3020	CRJ	7459	B-4020	B737	28081	B-5065	B737	28664
B-2932	B737	25787	B-3021	CRJ	7596	B-4021	B737	28082	B-5066	B737	28761
B-2933	B737	25788	B-3040	E145	145317	B-4022	TU154	87A-765	B-5067	737NG	32932
B-2934	B737	27274	B-3041	E145	145349	B-4023	TU154	88A-770	B-5068	737NG	32933
B-2935	B737	27283	B-3042	E145	145352	B-4024	TU154	88A-789	B-5069	737NG	32934
B-2936	B737	27335	B-3043	E145	145377	B-4025	737NG	33470	B-5070	737NG	32935
B-2937	B737	26295	B-3045	E145	145470	B-4025	B767	30597	B-5071	B737	24277
B-2938	B737	26296	B-3049	E145	14500839	B-4026	737NG	33472	B-5072	B737	24279
B-2939	B737	27345	B-3050	E145	14500848	B-4027	TU154	92A-943	B-5073	737NG	30680
B-2940	B737	27346	B-3051	E145	14500898	B-4028	TU154	93A-967	B-5074	737NG	33008
B-2941	B737	27344	B-3052	E145	14500905	B-4029	TU154	93A-950	B-5075	737NG	30692
B-2942	B737	25997	B-3053	E145	14500882	B-4030	IL76	1013407233	B-5076	737NG	32739
B-2943	B737	25998	B-3055	E145	14500921	B-4031	IL76	1013408254	B-5077	737NG	32742
B-2945	B737	27362	B-3056	E145	14500928	B-4032	IL76	1013409289	B-5078	737NG	30690
B-2946	B737	27375	B-3057	E145	14500932	B-4033	IL76	1033416512	B-5079	737NG	30693
B-2947	B737	25511	B-3058	E145	14500958	B-4034	IL76	1033416524	B-5080	737NG	28614
B-2948	B737	27361	B-3059	E145	14500949	B-4035	IL76	1033416529	B-5081	737NG	30231
B-2949	B737	27372	B-3060	E145	145701	B-4036	IL76	1033417550	B-5082	737NG	30193
B-2950	B737	27374	B-3061	E145	145755	B-4037	IL76	1033417557	B-5083	737NG	28319
B-2951	B737	27373	B-3062	E145	145781	B-4038	IL76	1033417567	B-5084	737NG	33009
B-2952	B737	27519	B-3063	E145	14500804	B-4039	IL76	1043418576	B-5085	737NG	30691
B-2953	B737	27523	B-3065	E145	14500815	B-4040	IL76	1053419656	B-5086	737NG	32800
B-2954	B737	27518	B-3066	E145	14500823	B-4041	IL76	1053420663	B-5087	737NG	32802
B-2955	B737	27453	B-3070	CRJ	7647	B-4042	IL76	1063418587	B-5088	737NG	30666
B-2956	B737	27907	B-3071	CRJ	7684	B-4043	IL76	1063420671	B-5089	737NG	28320
B-2957	B737	27521	B-3072	CRJ	7697	B-4050	TU154	86A-730	B-5090	737NG	28321
B-2958	B737	27522	B-3073	CRJ	7217	B-4051	TU154	86A-741	B-5091	737NG	29091
B-2959	B737	27520	B-3075	CRJ	7226	B-4052	B737	24701	B-5092	737NG	29092
B-2960	B737	24332	B-3076	CRJ	7690	B-4053	B737	24702	B-5093	737NG	29357
B-2961	B737	28156	B-3077	CRJ	7690	B-4060	CRJ7	10164	B-5094	737NG	29358
B-2962	B737	28157	B-3078	CRJ	7704	B-4061	CRJ7	10183	B-5095	737NG	29361
B-2963	B737	26325	B-3079	CRJ7	10118	B-4062	CRJ7	10187	B-5096	737NG	29362
B-2965	B737	26334	B-3080	CRJ7	10120	B-4063	CRJ7	10204	B-5097	737NG	29364
B-2966	B737	27462	B-3873	DO328	3201	B-4064	CRJ7	10206	B-5098	B737	29140
B-2967	B737	26335	B-3892	DO328	3212	B-4071	CRJ	7639	B-5099	B737	29189
B-2968	B737	28158	(B-3893)	DO328	3219	B-4072	CRJ	7455	B-5100	737NG	30681
B-2969	B737	23866	B-3946	DO328	3202	B-4138	TU154	85A-712	B-5101	737NG	30682
B-2969	B737	30102	B-3947	DO328	3203	B-5001	B767	28264	B-5102	737NG	33644
B-2970	B737	26337	B-3948	DO328	3204	B-5018	B767	28207	B-5103	737NG	33645
B-2971	B737	25373	B-3949	DO328	3198	B-5020	737NG	32926	B-5105	737NG	33646
B-2972	B737	27463	B-3960	DO328	3123	B-5021	737NG	32927	B-5106	737NG	33648
B-2973	B737	26336	B-3961	DO328	3128	B-5022	737NG	32928	B-5107	737NG	34320
B-2975	B737	26338	B-3962	DO328	3138	B-5023	737NG	29890	B-5108	737NG	34321
B-2976	B737	29244	B-3963	DO328	3140	B-5024	B737	26321	B-5109	737NG	33649
B-2977	B737	28560	B-3965	DO328	3135	B-5025	737NG	30741	B-5110	737NG	29987
B-2978	B737	28561	B-3966	DO328	3144	B-5026	737NG	30742	B-5111	737NG	33660
B-2979	B737	28562	B-3967	DO328	3144	B-5027	737NG	29891	B-5112	737NG	34248
B-2980	B737	24300	B-3968	DO328	3148	B-5028	737NG	30034	B-5113	737NG	34250
B-2981	B737	28972	B-3970	DO328	3153	B-5029	737NG	30634	B-5115	737NG	29640
B-2982	B737	28657	B-3971	DO328	3154	B-5030	737NG	30651	B-5116	737NG	29672
B-2983	B737	28973	B-3972	DO328	3172	B-5031	737NG	28255	B-5117	737NG	33661
B-2985	B737	29068	B-3972	DO328	3175	B-5032	737NG	30035	B-5118	737NG	33664

Reg	Type	S/N	Reg	Type	S/N	Reg	Type	S/N	Reg	Type	S/N	Reg	Type	S/N
B-5119	737NG	33665	B-5217	737NG	34022	B-6007	A320	2056	B-6129	A330	791			
B-5120	737NG	32580	B-5218	737NG	34027	B-6008	A320	2049	B-6151	A319	1263			
B-5121	737NG	32609	B-5219	737NG	34028	B-6009	A320	2219	B-6152	A319	0946			
B-5122	737NG	32610	B-5220	737NG	34539	B-6010	A320	2221	B-6153	A319	2841			
B-5123	737NG	32611	B-5221	737NG	29366	B-6011	A320	2235	B-6155	A319	0949			
B-5125	737NG	32612	B-5222	737NG	29367	B-6012	A320	2239	B-6156	A319	2849			
B-5126	737NG	32613	B-5223	737NG	33044	B-6013	A320	2244	B-6157	A319	2891			
B-5127	737NG	32615	B-5225	737NG	33045	B-6014	A319	2525	B-6158	A319	2901			
B-5128	737NG	32882	B-5226	737NG	34540	B-6015	A320	2212	B-6159	A319	2905			
B-5129	737NG	32884	B-5227	737NG	34541	B-6016	A320	2155	B-6160	A319	2940			
B-5130	737NG	32801	B-5228	737NG	34542	B-6017	A320	2274	B-6161	A319	2948			
B-5131	737NG	30686	B-5229	737NG	34543	B-6018	A319	1971	B-6162	A319	2969			
B-5132	737NG	30685	B-5230	737NG	29371	B-6019	A319	1986	B-6163	A319	3024			
B-5133	737NG	34252	B-5231	737NG	33046	B-6020	A319	2004	B-6165	A319	2935			
B-5135	737NG	32603	B-5232	737NG	35360	B-6021	A319	2008	B-6167	A319	3168			
B-5136	737NG	32605	B-5233	737NG	35361	B-6022	A319	2000	B-6168	A319	3020			
B-5137	737NG	32606	B-5235	737NG	29370	B-6023	A319	2007	B-6169	A319	2985			
B-5138	737NG	32607	B-5236	737NG	35362	B-6024	A319	2015	B-6170	A319	2396			
B-5139	737NG	32608	B-5237	737NG	29372	B-6025	A320	0573	B-6171	A319	2431			
B-5140	737NG	30698	B-5238	737NG	35363	B-6026	A320	0582	B-6172	A319	3186			
B-5141	737NG	34030	B-5239	737NG	35364	B-6027	A320	1007	B-6173	A319	3114			
B-5142	737NG	30700	B-5240	737NG	35368	B-6028	A320	2171	B-6175	A319	3116			
B-5143	737NG	32691	B-5241	737NG	35372	B-6029	A320	2182	B-6176	A319	3124			
B-5145	737NG	33007	B-5242	737NG	36269	B-6030	A320	2199	B-6196	A319	2672			
B-5146	737NG	34253	B-5243	737NG	36270	B-6031	A319	2172	B-6197	A319	2684			
B-5147	737NG	30697	B-5248	737NG	30626	B-6032	A319	2202	B-6198	A319	2617			
B-5148	737NG	34254	B-5249	737NG	33011	B-6033	A319	2205	B-6199	A319	2644			
B-5149	737NG	30699	B-5250	737NG	35378	B-6034	A319	2237	B-6200	A319	2519			
B-5151	737NG	34255	B-5251	737NG	35384	B-6035	A319	2269	B-6201	A319	2541			
B-5152	737NG	34256	B-5300	737NG	35375	B-6036	A319	2285	B-6202	A319	2546			
B-5153	737NG	34029	B-5301	737NG	35048	B-6037	A319	2293	B-6203	A319	2554			
B-5155	737NG	30783	B-5302	737NG	35049	B-6038	A319	2298	B-6205	A319	2505			
B-5156	737NG	30786	B-5303	737NG	35050	B-6039	A319	2200	B-6206	A319	2574			
B-5157	737NG	30787	B-5305	737NG	35051	B-6040	A319	2203	B-6207	A319	2579			
B-5159	737NG	35044	B-5306	737NG	35052	B-6041	A319	2232	B-6208	A319	2555			
B-5160	737NG	35045	B-5307	737NG	35053	B-6042	A319	2273	B-6209	A319	2558			
B-5161	737NG	35046	B-5308	737NG	32687	B-6043	A319	2313	B-6210	A319	2557			
B-5162	737NG	35047	B-5309	737NG	32689	B-6044	A319	2532	B-6211	A319	2561			
B-5163	737NG	30708	B-5310	737NG	35376	B-6045	A319	2348	B-6212	A319	2581			
B-5165	737NG	30709	B-5311	737NG	29373	B-6046	A319	2545	B-6213	A319	2614			
B-5166	737NG	33006	B-5312	737NG	29374	B-6047	A319	2551	B-6215	A319	2611			
B-5167	737NG	34701	B-5313	737NG	30716	B-6048	A319	2559	B-6216	A319	2643			
B-5168	737NG	34702	B-5315	737NG	35767	B-6049	A320	0902	B-6217	A319	2693			
B-5169	737NG	34703	B-5316	737NG	35768	B-6050	A340	468	B-6218	A319	2757			
B-5170	737NG	34705	B-5317	737NG	32686	B-6051	A340	488	B-6219	A319	2667			
B-5171	737NG	34706	B-5318	737NG	30723	B-6052	A340	514	B-6220	A319	2815			
B-5172	737NG	30704	B-5319	737NG	35102	B-6053	A340	577	B-6221	A319	2746			
B-5173	737NG	30705	B-5320	737NG	30718	B-6054	A319	2510	B-6222	A319	2733			
B-5175	737NG	35209	B-5321	737NG	35073	B-6055	A340	586	B-6223	A319	2805			
B-5176	737NG	34258	B-5322	737NG	32688	B-6056	A330	649	B-6225	A319	2819			
B-5177	737NG	35210	B-5323	737NG	30725	B-6057	A330	652	B-6226	A319	2839			
B-5178	737NG	32682	B-5325	737NG	32692	B-6058	A330	656	B-6227	A319	2847			
B-5179	737NG	35211	B-5326	737NG	35214	B-6059	A330	664	B-6228	A319	2890			
R-5180	737NG	35089	R-5327	737NG	35219	R-6070	A330	750	R-6229	A319	2762			
B-5181	737NG	35090	B-5328	737NG	35221	B-6071	A330	756	B-6230	A319	2774			
B-5182	737NG	34708	B-5329	737NG	35222	B-6072	A330	759	B-6231	A319	2825			
B-5183	737NG	30711	B-5330	737NG	35212	B-6073	A330	780	B-6232	A319	2879			
B-5185	737NG	30715	B-5331	737NG	35075	B-6075	A330	785	B-6233	A319	2913			
B-5186	737NG	33020	B-5332	737NG	35095	B-6076	A330	797	B-6235	A319	3195			
B-5187	737NG	33828	B-5333	737NG	35096	B-6077	A330	818	B-6236	A319	3200			
B-5189	737NG	35365	B-5335	737NG	35097	B-6078	A330	840	B-6237	A319	3226			
B-5190	737NG	35366	B-5336	737NG	35098	B-6079	A330	810	B-6239	A319	3144			
B-5191	737NG	35367	B-5337	737NG	35747	B-6080	A330	815	B-6250	A320	1372			
B-5192	737NG	35369	B-5338	737NG	35749	B-6081	A330	839	B-6251	A320	2484			
B-5193	737NG	35370	B-5339	737NG	35380	B-6082	A330	821	B-6252	A320	2506			
B-5195	737NG	35371	B-5340	737NG	35381	B-6083	A330	830	B-6253	A320	2511			
B-5201	737NG	34023	B-5341	737NG	36483	B-6085	A330	836	B-6255	A320	2637			
B-5202	737NG	34537	B-5342	737NG	36484	B-6090	A330	860	B-6256	A320	0872			
B-5203	737NG	34538	B-5343	737NG	36485	B-6091	A330	867	B-6257	A320	0874			
(B-5204)	737NG	34539	B-5345	737NG	35215	B-6092	A330	873	B-6258	A320	0879			
B-5205	737NG	33654	B-5346	737NG	29673	B-6095	A330	851	B-6259	A320	2562			
B-5206	737NG	33666	B-5347	737NG	36190	B-6096	A330	862	B-6260	A320	2591			
B-5207	737NG	33663	B-5348	737NG	36191	B-6097	A330	866	B-6261	A320	2606			
B-5208	737NG	33041	B-5353	737NG	30728	B-6119	A330	713	B-6262	A320	2627			
B-5209	737NG	33042	B-5355	737NG	35104	B-6120	A330	720	B-6263	A320	2708			
B-5210	737NG	33043	B-5356	737NG	35385	B-6121	A330	728	B-6265	A321	2713			
B-5211	737NG	34019	B-6001	A320	1981	B-6122	A330	732	B-6266	A320	1751			
B-5212	737NG	34024	B-6002	A320	2022	B-6123	A330	735	B-6267	A321	2741			
B-5213	737NG	34020	B-6003	A320	2034	B-6125	A330	773	B-6269	A320	2743			
B-5214	737NG	34021	B-6004	A319	2508	B-6126	A330	777	B-6270	A321	2759			
B-5215	737NG	34025	B-6005	A320	2036	B-6127	A330	781	B-6271	A321	2767			
B-5216	737NG	34026	B-6006	A320	2068	B-6128	A330	782	B-6272	A320	2770			

Reg	Type	No.	Reg	Type	No.	Reg	Type	No.	Reg	Type	No.
B-6273	A321	2809	B-28005	MD80	53066	B-16707	B777	33751	B-18581	A300	193
B-6275	A320	2680	B-28015	MD80	53168	B-16708	B777	33752	B-18582	A300	197
B-6276	A320	2689	B-28025	MD80	53602	B-16709	B777	33753	B-18583	A300	221
B-6277	A320	2701	B-28035	MD80	53480	B-16710	B777	33754	B-18585	A300	232
B-6278	A320	2714	B-22306	A320	0441	B-16711	B777	33755	B-18601	737NG	28402
B-6279	A320	2772	B-22606	A321	0731	B-16801	B747	27965	B-18602	737NG	28403
B-6280	A320	1286	B-22307	A320	0347	B-16802	737NG	28236	B-18603	737NG	29103
B-6281	A320	2796	B-22607	A321	0746	B-16803	737NG	30664	B-18605	737NG	28404
B-6282	A320	2824	B-27007	B757	27204	B-16805	737NG	30636	B-18606	737NG	28405
B-6283	A320	2834	B-27017	B757	29610	B-16821	E190	19000087	B-18607	737NG	29104
B-6285	A321	1060	B-28007	MD80	49807	B-16822	E190	19000091	B-18608	737NG	28406
B-6286	A320	2909	B-28017	MD80	53166	B-16823	E190	19000099	B-18609	737NG	28407
B-6287	A320	2899	B-28027	MD80	53603	B-16901	MD90	53534	B-18610	737NG	29105
B-6288	A320	2855	B-22308	A320	0344	B-16902	MD90	53568	B-18611	737NG	29106
B-6289	A320	2861	(B-11150)	F.100	11290	B-17501	B757	25133	B-18612	737NG	30173
B-6290	A320	2877	(B-11152)	F.100	11296	B-17811	146	E3202	B-18615	737NG	30174
B-6291	A320	2915	B-12291	F.100	11500	B-17911	MD90	53535	B-18616	737NG	30175
B-6292	A320	2960	B-12292	F.100	11496	B-17912	MD90	53536	B-18617	737NG	29106
B-6293	A320	2986	B-12293	F.100	11517	B-17913	MD90	53537	B-18671	B737	28489
B-6295	A320	1500	B-12295	F.100	11527	B-17915	MD90	53538	B-18672	B737	28490
B-6296	A320	2973	B-12296	F.100	11505	B-17916	MD90	53539	B-18673	B737	28491
B-6297	A320	2980	B-12297	F.100	11461	B-17917	MD90	53572	B-18675	B737	28492
B-6298	A320	2975	B-15301	MD90	53567	B-17918	MD90	53571	B-18676	B737	28493
B-6300	A321	1293	B-16101	MD11	48542	B-17919	MD90	53569	B-18677	B737	28494
B-6301	A320	2939	B-16102	MD11	48543	B-17920	MD90	53574	B-18701	B747	30759
B-6302	A321	2936	B-16103	MD11	48415	B-17921	MD90	53554	B-18702	B747	30760
B-6303	A320	2950	(B-16105)	MD11	48544	B-17922	MD90	53601	B-18703	B747	30761
B-6305	A321	2971	B-16106	MD11	48545	B-17923	MD90	53534	B-18705	B747	30762
B-6306	A321	3067	B-16107	MD11	48484	B-17925	MD90	53568	B-18706	B747	30763
B-6307	A321	3075	B-16108	MD11	48778	B-17926	MD90	53567	B-18707	B747	30764
B-6308	A321	3112	B-16109	MD11	48779	B-18151	MD11	48470	B-18708	B747	30765
B-6309	A321	3014	B-16110	MD11	48786	B-18152	MD11	48471	B-18709	B747	30766
B-6310	A320	3023	B-16111	MD11	48787	B-18172	MD11	48469	B-18710	B747	30767
B-6311	A320	3027	B-16112	MD11	48789	B-18201	B747	28709	B-18711	B747	30768
B-6312	A320	3131	B-16113	MD11	48790	B-18202	B747	28710	B-18712	B747	33729
B-6313	A320	3132	B-16301	A330	530	B-18203	B747	28711	B-18715	B747	33731
B-6315	A320	3153	B-16302	A330	535	B-18205	B747	28712	B-18716	B747	33732
B-6316	A320	3206	B-16303	A330	555	B-18206	B747	29030	B-18717	B747	30769
B-6317	A321	3217	B-16305	A330	573	B-18207	B747	29219	B-18718	B747	30770
B-6319	A321	3241	B-16306	A330	587	B-18208	B747	29031	B-18719	B747	33739
B-6320	A320	1686	B-16307	A330	634	B-18209	B747	29906	B-18720	B747	33733
B-6321	A320	3210	B-16308	A330	655	B-18210	B747	33734	B-18721	B747	33738
B-6322	A320	3158	B-16309	A330	661	B-18211	B747	33735	B-18722	B747	34265
B-6323	A320	3167	B-16310	A330	678	B-18212	B747	33736	B-18723	B747	34266
B-6325	A320	3196	B-16311	A330	693	B-18215	B747	33737	B-18725	B747	30771
B-6328	A320	0978	B-16312	A330	755	B-18251	B747	27965	B-18751	B747	21454
B-6329	A321	3233	B-16401	B747	27062	B-18252	B747	21300	B-18752	B747	22299
B-6330	A321	3247	B-16402	B747	27063	B-18253	B747	22298	B-18753	B747	22446
B-6333	A320	3170	B-16403	B747	27141	B-18255	B747	21843	B-18755	B747	22447
B-6335	A320	3197	B-16405	B747	27142	B-18271	B747	24309	B-18771	B747	24308
B-6336	A320	3215	B-16406	B747	27898	B-18272	B747	24310	B-18801	A340	402
B-6337	A320	3221	B-16407	B747	27899	B-18273	B747	24311	B-18802	A340	406
B-6340	A320	3234	B-16408	B747	28092	B-18275	B747	24312	B-18803	A340	411
B-7692	CRJ	7228	B-16409	B747	28093	B-18301	A330	602	B-18805	A340	415
B-7693	CRJ	7239	B-16410	B747	29061	B-18302	A330	607	B-18806	A340	433
B-7698	CRJ	7247	B-16411	B747	29111	B-18303	A330	641	B-18807	A340	541
B-22310	A320	0791	B-16412	B747	29112	B-18305	A330	671	B-18851	A340	528
B-22301	A320	0332	B-16461	B747	27154	B-18306	A330	675	B-88888	MD80	53479
B-22311	A320	0822	B-16462	B747	27173	B-18307	A330	691	B-88889	MD80	53480
B-22311	A320	0872	B-16463	B747	27174	B-18308	A330	699	B-88898	MD80	53481
B-22601	A321	0538	B-16465	B747	26062	B-18309	A330	707	B-88899	MD80	53542
B-27001	B757	25044	B-16481	B747	30607	B-18310	A330	714	B-88988	MD80	53577
B-27011	B757	29607	B-16482	B747	30608	B-18311	A330	752	B-88989	MD80	53581
B-27021	B757	29611	B-16483	B747	30609	B-18312	A330	769			
B-27201	B757	24868	B-16601	B767	25076	B-18315	A330	823			
B-28001	MD80	53064	B-16603	B767	25117	B-18316	A330	838	China - Hong Kong		
B-28011	MD80	53118	B-16605	B767	26063	B-18317	A330	861	(see also VR-H)		
B-28021	MD80	53167	(B-16606)	B767	26064	B-18351	A330	725			
B-28031	MD80	49950	(B-16607)	B767	27192	B-18352	A330	805			
B-22302	A320	0369	(B-16608)	B767	27193	B-18501	A300	767	B-HIA	B747	21966
B-22602	A321	0555	(B-16609)	B767	27194	B-18502	A300	775	B-HIB	B747	22149
B-22603	A321	0602	B-16621	B767	27195	B-18503	A300	788	B-HIC	B747	22429
B-27013	B757	29608	B-16622	B767	27192	B-18505	A300	559	B-HID	B747	22530
B-28003	MD80	53065	B-16623	B767	27193	B-18551	A300	666	B-HIE	B747	22872
B-28013	MD80	53119	B-16625	B767	27194	B-18571	A300	529	B-HIF	B747	23048
B-28023	MD80	49952	B-16688	B767	25221	B-18572	A300	533	B-HIH	B747	23120
B-28033	MD80	53577	B-16701	B777	32639	B-18573	A300	536	B-HII	B747	23221
B-22305	A320	0478	B-16702	B777	32640	B-18575	A300	559	B-HIJ	B747	23392
B-22315	A320	0812	B-16703	B777	32643	B-18576	A300	743	B-HIK	B747	23534
B-22605	A321	0606	B-16705	B777	32645	B-18577	A300	677	B-HKD	B747	26548
B-27005	B757	27203	B-16706	B777	33750	B-18578	A300	625	B-HKE	B747	25127
B-27015	B757	29609				B-18579	A300	555	B-HKF	B747	25128
									B-HKG	B747	21746

Reg	Type	Serial
B-HKH	B747	24227
B-HKJ	B747	27133
B-HKS	B747	27070
B-HKT	B747	27132
B-HKU	B747	27069
B-HKV	B747	26552
B-HLA	A330	071
B-HLB	A330	083
B-HLC	A330	099
B-HLD	A330	102
B-HLE	A330	109
B-HLF	A330	113
B-HLG	A330	118
B-HLH	A330	121
B-HLI	A330	155
B-HLJ	A330	012
B-HLK	A330	017
B-HLL	A330	244
B-HLM	A330	386
B-HLN	A330	389
B-HLO	A330	393
B-HLP	A330	418
B-HLQ	A330	420
B-HLR	A330	421
B-HLS	A330	423
B-HLT	A330	439
B-HLU	A330	539
B-HLV	A330	548
B-HLW	A330	565
B-HMD	B747	22105
B-HME	B747	22106
B-HMF	B747	22107
B-HMX	A340	192
B-HMY	A340	199
B-HMZ	A340	201
B-HNA	B777	27265
B-HNB	B777	27266
B-HNC	B777	27263
B-HND	B777	27264
B-HNE	B777	27507
B-HNF	B777	27506
B-HNG	B777	27505
B-HNH	B777	27504
B-HNI	B777	27508
B-HNJ	B777	27509
B-HNK	B777	27510
B-HNL	B777	27116
B-HNM	B777	33702
B-HNN	B777	33703
B-HNO	B777	33704
B-HNP	B777	34243
B-HNQ	B777	34244
B-HOL	B747	23709
B-HOM	B747	23920
B-HON	B747	24215
B-HOO	B747	23814
B-HOP	B747	23815
B-HOR	B747	24631
B-HOS	B747	24850
B-HOT	B747	24851
B-HOU	B747	24925
B-HOV	B747	25082
B-HOW	B747	25211
B-HOX	B747	24955
B-HOY	B747	25351
B-HOZ	B747	25871
B-HQA	A340	436
B-HQB	A340	453
B-HQC	A340	475
B-HSD	A320	0756
B-HSE	A320	0784
B-HSF	A320	0816
B-HSG	A320	0812
B-HSH	A320	0877
B-HSI	A320	0930
B-HSJ	A320	1253
B-HSK	A320	1721
B-HSL	A320	2229
B-HSM	A320	2238
B-HSN	A320	2428
B-HTD	A321	0993
B-HTE	A321	1024

Reg	Type	Serial
B-HTF	A321	0633
B-HTG	A321	1695
B-HTH	A321	1984
B-HTI	A321	2021
B-HUA	B747	25872
B-HUB	B747	25873
B-HUD	B747	25874
B-HUE	B747	27117
B-HUF	B747	25869
B-HUG	B747	25870
B-HUH	B747	27175
B-HUI	B747	27230
B-HUJ	B747	27595
B-HUK	B747	27503
B-HUL	B747	30804
(B-HUM)	B747	32571
B-HUN	B747	30805
B-HUO	B747	32571
B-HUQ	B747	34150
B-HUR	B747	24976
B-HUS	B747	25152
B-HVX	B747	24568
B-HVY	B747	22306
B-HVZ	B747	23864
B-HWF	A330	654
B-HWG	A330	662
B-HWH	A330	692
B-HWI	A330	716
B-HWJ	A330	741
B-HWK	A330	786
B-HXA	A340	136
B-HXB	A340	137
B-HXC	A340	142
B-HXD	A340	147
B-HXE	A340	157
B-HXF	A340	160
B-HXG	A340	208
B-HXH	A340	218
B-HXI	A340	220
B-HXJ	A340	227
B-HXK	A340	228
B-HXL	A340	381
B-HXM	A340	123
B-HXN	A340	126
B-HXO	A340	128
B-HYA	A330	098
B-HYB	A330	106
B-HYC	A330	111
B-HYD	A330	132
B-HYE	A330	177
B-HYF	A330	234
B-HYG	A330	405
B-HYH	A330	407
B-HYI	A330	479
B-HYJ	A330	512
B-HYO	A320	0393
B-HYP	A320	0394
B-HYQ	A330	581
B-HYR	A320	0414
B-HYS	A320	0430
B-HYT	A320	0443
B-HYU	A320	0447
B-HYV	A320	0415
B-KAA	B747	23769
B-KAB	B747	23409
B-KAC	B747	23600
B-KAD	B747	24308
B-KAE	B747	25068
B-KAF	B747	26547
B-KAG	B747	27067
B-KBA	CRJ	7690
B-KBB	CRJ7	10052
B-KBE	737NG	32605
B-KBH	737NG	34707
B-KBI	737NG	34709
B-KBJ	CRJ	7565
B-KBK	737NG	35072
B-KBL	737NG	35074
B-KBM	737NG	35076
B-KBN	737NG	35077
B-KBO	737NG	35101
B-KBP	737NG	35105

Reg	Type	Serial
B-KPA	B777	36154
B-KPB	B777	35299
B-KPC	B777	34432
B-KPD	B777	36155
B-KPE	B777	36156
B-KPF	B777	36832
B-KPG	B777	35300
B-KPH	B777	35301
B-KXA	E170	17000081
B-KXB	E170	17000099
B-KXC	E170	17000111
B-KXD	E170	17000128
B-KXE	737NG	34710
B-KXF	737NG	34967
B-KXG	737NG	34968
B-KXH	737NG	34971
B-LAA	A330	669
B-LAB	A330	673
B-LAC	A330	679
B-LAD	A330	776
B-LAE	A330	850
B-LAF	A330	855
B-LDA	A300	855
B-LDB	A300	856
B-LDC	A300	857
B-LDD	A300	858
B-LDE	A300	859
B-LDF	A300	860
B-LDG	A300	870
B-LDH	A300	871
B-LFA	B747	24063
B-LFB	B747	24065
B-LFC	B747	29263
(B-LFZ)	B747	25703

China - Macau
(see also CS-M)

Reg	Type	Serial
B-MAA	A321	0550
B-MAB	A321	0557
B-MAD	A320	0573
B-MAE	A320	0582
B-MAF	A321	0620
B-MAG	A321	0631
B-MAH	A320	0805
B-MAJ	A321	0908
B-MAK	A319	1758
B-MAL	A319	1790
B-MAM	A319	1893
B-MAN	A319	1912
B-MAO	A319	1962
B-MAP	A321	1850
B-MAQ	A321	1926
B-MAR	A321	0597
B-MAS	A300	743
B-MAV	B767	24716
B-MAW	B767	24798

Mongolia
(see also MT-/JU-)

Reg	Type	Serial
BNMAU-8556	TU154	82A-564

Canada
(see also CF-)

Reg	Type	Serial
C-FACA	B727	22052
C-FACJ	B727	21979
C-FACK	B727	21056
C-FACM	B727	22759
C-FACN	B727	22540
C-FACP	B727	22072
C-FACR	B727	21055
C-FACW	B727	18974
C-FACW	B727	19405
C-FACW	B727	21366
C-FACX	B727	19500
C-FAIF	F.28	11032
C-FANA	F.28	11075

Reg	Type	Serial
C-FAWH	CRJ7	10148
C-FAWJ	737NG	35502
C-FAWJ	B737	21770
C-FBAB	146	E2090
C-FBAE	146	E2092
C-FBAF	146	E2096
C-FBAO	146	E2111
C-FBAV	146	E2121
(C-FBCA)	B747	24896
C-FBCA	B747	25422
C-FBEF	B767	24323
C-FBEG	B767	24324
C-FBEM	B767	24325
C-FBFI	CRJ	7950
C-FBJZ	CRJ9	15037
C-FBKA	CRJ7	10003
C-FBKT	DC-9	47186
C-FBKV	B737	22754
C-FBLQ	CRJ7	10150
C-FBNI	CRJ7	10164
C-FBQO	CRJ	7958
C-FBQS	CRJ7	10155
C-FBUS	A330	095
C-FBWG	B727	19719
C-FBWJ	737NG	32767
C-FBWX	B727	18286
C-FBWY	B727	19085
C-FCAB	B767	24082
C-FCAE	B767	24083
C-FCAF	B767	24084
C-FCAG	B767	24085
C-FCAJ	B767	24086
C-FCAU	B767	24087
C-FCAV	B737	22906
C-FCEU	CRJ	7973
C-FCFR	B737	26684
C-FCGF	B737	26680
C-FCGG	B737	26683
C-FCGS	B737	26691
C-FCGX	CRJ	7963
C-FCHO	CRJ7	10165
C-FCID	CRJ	7975
C-FCJF	B727	22011
C-FCJI	B727	22435
C-FCJP	B727	22012
C-FCJU	B727	22759
C-FCJZ	CRJ9	15040
C-FCLV	CRJ	7966
C-FCMV	DC-8	46038
C-FCNN	CRJ	7981
C-FCPB	B737	19884
(C-FCPB)	DC-10	47966
C-FCPC	B737	19885
(C-FCPC)	DC 10	47968
C-FCPD	B737	19886
(C-FCPD)	DC-10	47969
C-FCPE	B737	19887
C-FCPF	DC-8	45620
C-FCPG	B737	23173
C-FCPG	DC-8	45623
C-FCPH	DC-8	45621
C-FCPI	B737	23174
C-FCPI	DC-8	45661
C-FCPJ	B737	23175
C-FCPJ	DC-8	45661
C-FCPK	B737	23176
C-FCPL	B737	23177
C-FCPL	DC-8	46095
C-FCPM	B737	22761
C-FCPM	DC-8	45809
C-FCPN	B737	22762
C-FCPO	DC-8	45926
C-FCPP	DC-8	45927
C-FCPQ	DC-8	45928
C-FCPS	DC-8	45928
C-FCPU	B737	19888
C-FCPV	B737	20196
C-FCPZ	B737	20197
C-FCQX	CRJ7	10183
C-FCRA	B747	24895
C-FCRA	CRJ7	10183
C-FCRA	DC-10	46931

Reg	Type	Serial	Reg	Type	Serial	Reg	Type	Serial	Reg	Type	Serial
C-FCRB	DC-10	46940	C-FEZT	CRJ	8038	**C-FHNW**	**E190**	**19000077**	C-FLCX	CRJ9	15086
C-FCRB	F.28	11107	C-FEZX	CRJ	8040	C-FHNX	146	E2066	C-FLEU	B757	29941
C-FCRC	F.28	11044	C-FFAB	CRJ	8042	**C-FHNX**	**E190**	**19000083**	C-FLGD	CRJ7	10260
C-FCRD	B747	20927	**C-FFAL**	**B737**	**21711**	**C-FHNY**	**E190**	**19000085**	C-FLGI	CRJ7	15087
C-FCRD	DC-10	47889	**C-FFAN**	**B707**	**19789**	**C-FHON**	**E190**	**19000097**	**C-FLHJ**	**B727**	**21455**
C-FCRE	B747	20929	**C-FFAN**	**B757**	**28674**	**C-FHOS**	**E190**	**19000101**	C-FLHP	CRJ	7016
C-FCRE	CRJ7	10181	C-FFCR	F.28	11095	**C-FHOY**	**E190**	**19000105**	**C-FLHQ**	**CRJ**	**7086**
C-FCRE	CRJ7	10186	C-FFHA	CRJ	8043	C-FHRH	CRJ9	15058	**C-FLHR**	**B727**	**21524**
C-FCRE	DC-10	47868	C-FFHW	CRJ	8044	C-FHRK	CRJ9	15059	C-FLHX	CRJ	7021
C-FCRF	CRJ7	10187	**C-FFJA**	**CRJ**	**7985**	**C-FHTO**	**CRJ**	**8054**	C-FLHZ	CRJ	7025
C-FCRI	F.28	11043	C-FFKC	F.28	11025	C-FHUC	CRJ7	10248	C-FLIB	CRJ	7113
C-FCRJ	**CRJ**	**7001**	C-FFKD	DC-8	45854	C-FHWD	A310	441	C-FLIX	CRJ9	15090
C-FCRJ	CRJ7	10004	C-FFOY	CRJ	8046	C-FIBQ	CRJ7	10251	**C-FLJZ**	**CRJ9**	**15045**
C-FCRJ	CRJ7	10173	(C-FFQI)	DC-8	45855	C-FICA	A300	023	**C-FLKA**	**CRJ**	**8067**
C-FCRK	F.28	11087	C-FFRZ	DC-8	45685	C-FICB	A300	078	C-FLMJ	CRJ9	15106
C-FCRM	F.28	11035	C-FFSB	DC-8	45935	C-FICB	F.100	11248	C-FLMK	CRJ9	15111
C-FCRN	DC-8	45752	C-FFUN	B747	20305	C-FICI	A300	173	C-FLMN	CRJ9	15113
C-FCRP	F.28	11037	C-FFVE	CRJ	8048	C-FICL	F.100	11263	C-FLMQ	CRJ9	15115
C-FCRU	F.28	11032	C-FFVJ	CRJ	8050	C-FICO	F.100	11249	C-FLMS	CRJ9	15117
C-FCRW	F.28	11029	C-FFVX	CRJ7	10220	C-FICP	B737	22025	C-FLNS	CRJ	7004
C-FCRX	CRJ	7984	**C-FFWI**	**A320**	**0149**	C-FICP	F.100	11259	**C-FLOA**	**CRJ**	**8068**
C-FCRZ	F.28	11061	**C-FFWJ**	**A320**	**0150**	C-FICQ	F.100	11260	C-FLOK	B757	25054
C-FCWJ	B737	22703	**C-FFWM**	**A320**	**0154**	C-FICW	F.100	11247	C-FLSF	A320	0279
C-FCWW	DC-8	45762	**C-FFWN**	**A320**	**0159**	C-FICY	F.100	11246	C-FLSI	A320	0283
C-FCXB	L1011	193N-1083	**C-FFYG**	**E170**	**17000116**	C-FIFA	B727	20381	**C-FLSS**	**A320**	**0284**
C-FCXJ	L1011	193N-1102	**C-FFYJ**	**E190**	**19000013**	C-FIIW	CRJ9	15063	**C-FLSU**	**A320**	**0309**
C-FCZD	CRJ	7989	**C-FFYM**	**E190**	**19000015**	C-FIIY	CRJ9	15064	**C-FLWE**	**E190**	**19000092**
C-FDAT	**A310**	**658**	**C-FFYT**	**E190**	**19000018**	C-FIIZ	CRJ9	15065	**C-FLWH**	**E190**	**19000094**
C-FDCA	**A320**	**0232**	C-FGAX	CRJ	8053	**C-FIJA**	**CRJ**	**7987**	C-FLWJ	B737	23148
C-FDCD	B737	26688	C-FGCJ	B737	22352	C-FIPX	CRJ	7036	**C-FLWK**	**E190**	**19000096**
C-FDCH	**B737**	**26700**	C-FGEL	CRJ	8055	**C-FITL**	**B777**	**35256**	C-FM	CRJ	7305
C-FDCU	**B737**	**26739**	C-FGEP	CRJ	8058	**C-FITU**	**B777**	**35254**	C-FM	CRJ	8012
C-FDCZ	**B737**	**26707**	C-FGHQ	B737	23811	**C-FITW**	**B777**	**35298**	C-FM	CRJ	8013
C-FDJA	**CRJ**	**7979**	C-FGHT	B737	24059	**C-FIUA**	**B777**	**35239**	C-FMCF	B757	24369
C-FDJC	B747	20208	C-FGHZ	B747	27827	**C-FIUF**	**B777**	**35243**	C-FMCJ	B737	22398
C-FDJZ	**CRJ9**	**15041**	C-FGKZ	CRJ	8047	**C-FIUJ**	**B777**	**35244**	**C-FMCY**	**CRJ**	**7064**
C-FDKH	CRJ	8008	**C-FGLW**	**E190**	**19000022**	**C-FIUL**	**B777**	**35255**	C-FMDO	CRJ	7006
C-FDQP	CRJ	8005	**C-FGLX**	**E190**	**19000024**	**C-FIUR**	**B777**	**35242**	**C-FMEA**	**B727**	**21329**
C-FDQQ	**A320**	**0059**	**C-FGLY**	**E190**	**19000028**	**C-FIUV**	**B777**	**35248**	**C-FMEE**	**B727**	**21330**
C-FDQV	**A320**	**0068**	**C-FGMF**	**E190**	**19000019**	**C-FIUW**	**B777**	**35249**	**C-FMEI**	**B727**	**21327**
C-FDRH	**A320**	**0073**	C-FGNB	CRJ9	15054	**C-FIVK**	**B777**	**35245**	C-FMEP	CRJ9	15114
C-FDRK	**A320**	**0084**	C-FGND	CRJ9	15055	**C-FIVP**	**B777**	**35250**	**C-FMEQ**	**A320**	**0302**
C-FDRO	**A340**	**048**	**C-FGQR**	**CRJ**	**8051**	**C-FIVM**	**B777**	**35251**	C-FMES	A320	0305
C-FDRP	**A320**	**0122**	**C-FGQS**	**CRJ**	**8052**	**C-FIWJ**	**737NG**	**30712**	**C-FMEY**	**B727**	**21328**
C-FDSN	**A320**	**0126**	C-FGRE	CRJ7	10229	C-FIWJ	B737	21955	**C-FMGV**	**CRJ**	**8069**
C-FDST	**A320**	**0127**	C-FGTV	CRJ	8060	**C-FIWS**	**737NG**	**32404**	**C-FMGW**	**CRJ**	**8070**
C-FDSU	**A320**	**0141**	C-FGWD	A310	438	C-FIWW	DC-8	45820	C-FMHJ	CRJ7	10261
C-FDWK	CRJ	7144	**C-FGWJ**	**737NG**	**32764**	C-FJBK	CRJ	8063	C-FMJK	A320	0342
C-FDWO	CRJ	7164	C-FGWJ	B737	20196	**C-FJCJ**	**B737**	**21667**	C-FMKF	B727	21523
C-FDWW	DC-8	45856	C-FGYE	CRJ	8061	**C-FJFC**	**CRJ7**	**10002**	C-FMKT	CRJ	7122
C-FECJ	B737	21975	**C-FGYL**	**A320**	**0254**	C-FJGI	CRJ	7010	C-FMKU	CRJ	7229
C-FEHG	CRJ7	10202	**C-FGYS**	**A320**	**0255**	C-FJGK	CRJ	7023	C-FMKV	CRJ	7007
C-FEHT	CRJ7	10204	C-FHAA	146	E2138	**C-FJJZ**	**CRJ9**	**15043**	C-FMKV	CRJ	7008
C-FEHU	CRJ7	10206	C-FHAA	DC-8	45961	**C-FJLB**	**B737**	**22273**	C-FMKV	CRJ	7039
C-FEHV	CRJ	8022	C-FHAB	DC-8	45658	C-FJLT	B737	20206	C-FMKV	CRJ	7069
C-FEIQ	**E170**	**17000083**	C-FHAP	146	E2136	C-FJRI	F.28	11103	C-FMKV	CRJ	7194
C-FEIX	**E170**	**17000085**	C-FHAV	146	E2012	C-FJRN	CRJ	8065	C-FMKV	CRJ	7224
C-FEJA	**CRJ**	**7983**	C-FHAX	146	E2014	C-FJTE	CRJ9	15079	C-FMKV	CRJ	7254
C-FEJB	**E170**	**17000086**	C-FHAZ	146	E2016	C-FJTF	CRJ9	15071	C-FMKV	CRJ	7284
C-FEJC	**E170**	**17000089**	C-FHCJ	B737	21666	C-FJTJ	CRJ9	15074	C-FMKV	CRJ	7314
C-FEJD	**E170**	**17000090**	C-FHCN	CRJ	8057	C-FJTQ	CRJ9	15062	C-FMKV	CRJ	7344
C-FEJF	**E170**	**17000091**	C-FHCP	B737	22024	C-FJVR	CRJ9	15083	C-FMKV	CRJ	7374
C-FEJL	**E170**	**17000095**	C-FHCW	CRJ	8064	C-FJVT	CRJ9	15073	C-FMKV	CRJ	7404
C-FEJP	**E170**	**17000096**	C-FHFP	F.28	11016	**C-FJWS**	**737NG**	**28651**	C-FMKV	CRJ	7434
C-FEJY	**E170**	**17000097**	**C-FHGE**	**B737**	**23970**	C-FKAJ	A320	0333	C-FMKV	CRJ	7464
C-FEKD	**E170**	**17000101**	C-FHGK	CRJ	8049	C-FKCK	A320	0265	C-FMKV	CRJ	7494
C-FEKH	**E170**	**17000102**	**C-FHIQ**	**E190**	**19000031**	**C-FKCO**	**A320**	**0277**	C-FMKV	CRJ	7524
C-FEKI	**E170**	**17000103**	**C-FHIS**	**E190**	**19000036**	**C-FKCR**	**A320**	**0290**	C-FMKV	CRJ	7554
C-FEKJ	**E170**	**17000105**	**C-FHIU**	**E190**	**19000037**	C-FKFO	B727	18971	C-FMKV	CRJ	7584
C-FEKS	**E170**	**17000110**	**C-FHJJ**	**E190**	**19000041**	**C-FKJZ**	**CRJ9**	**15044**	C-FMKV	CRJ	7614
C-FEPL	B737	20396	**C-FHJT**	**E190**	**19000043**	C-FKLI	MD80	49941	C-FMKV	CRJ	7644
C-FEPO	B737	20300	**C-FHJU**	**E190**	**19000044**	C-FKLO	MD80	53464	C-FMKV	CRJ	7674
C-FEPP	B737	20681	**C-FHKA**	**E190**	**19000046**	C-FKLT	MD80	53463	C-FMKV	CRJ	7704
C-FEPR	B737	20397	**C-FHKE**	**E190**	**19000048**	C-FKLY	MD80	53465	C-FMKV	CRJ	7734
C-FEPU	B737	20776	**C-FHKI**	**E190**	**19000052**	C-FKLZ	MD80	53466	C-FMKV	CRJ	7764
C-FETB	B707	18024	**C-FHKP**	**E190**	**19000055**	C-FKOJ	A320	0330	C-FMKV	CRJ	7794
C-FETZ	CRJ	8031	**C-FHKS**	**E190**	**19000064**	C-FKPO	A320	0311	C-FMKV	CRJ	7824
C-FEUP	CRJ7	10202	**C-FHLH**	**E190**	**19000068**	C-FKPS	A320	0310	C-FMKV	CRJ	7854
C-FEVZ	CRJ7	10214	C-FHMG	CRJ7	10247	**C-FKPT**	**A320**	**0324**	C-FMKV	CRJ	7884
C-FEWJ	**737NG**	**32769**	C-FHNL	E190	19000070	C-FKWJ	B737	21811	C-FMKV	CRJ	7914
C-FEXN	146	E2020	**C-FHNP**	**E190**	**19000071**	**C-FKWS**	**737NG**	**30134**	C-FMKV	CRJ	7944
C-FEXV	CRJ	8034	C-FHNV	E190	19000075	**C-FLBV**	**CRJ**	**8066**	C-FMKV	CRJ	7974

Reg			Reg			Reg			Reg		
C-FMKV	CRJ	8004	C-FMLB	CRJ	7647	C-FMLQ	CRJ	7290	C-FMLT	CRJ	7772
C-FMKV	CRJ	8073	C-FMLB	CRJ	7677	C-FMLQ	CRJ	7320	C-FMLT	CRJ	7802
C-FMKW	CRJ	7009	C-FMLB	CRJ	7707	C-FMLQ	CRJ	7380	C-FMLT	CRJ	7832
C-FMKW	CRJ	7040	C-FMLB	CRJ	7737	C-FMLQ	CRJ	7410	C-FMLT	CRJ	7862
C-FMKW	CRJ	7070	C-FMLB	CRJ	7767	C-FMLQ	CRJ	7440	C-FMLT	CRJ	7892
C-FMKW	CRJ	7195	C-FMLB	CRJ	7797	C-FMLQ	CRJ	7470	C-FMLT	CRJ	7922
C-FMKW	CRJ	7225	C-FMLB	CRJ	7827	C-FMLQ	CRJ	7500	C-FMLT	CRJ	7952
C-FMKW	CRJ	7255	C-FMLB	CRJ	7857	C-FMLQ	CRJ	7530	C-FMLT	CRJ	7982
C-FMKW	CRJ	7285	C-FMLB	CRJ	7887	C-FMLQ	CRJ	7560	C-FMLT	CRJ	8021
C-FMKW	CRJ	7315	C-FMLB	CRJ	7917	C-FMLQ	CRJ	7590	C-FMLU	CRJ	7018
C-FMKW	CRJ	7375	C-FMLB	CRJ	7947	C-FMLQ	CRJ	7620	C-FMLU	CRJ	7048
C-FMKW	CRJ	7405	C-FMLB	CRJ	7977	C-FMLQ	CRJ	7650	C-FMLU	CRJ	7078
C-FMKW	CRJ	7435	C-FMLB	CRJ	8016	C-FMLQ	CRJ	7680	C-FMLU	CRJ	7088
C-FMKW	CRJ	7465	C-FMLB	CRJ	8076	C-FMLQ	CRJ	7710	C-FMLU	CRJ	7093
C-FMKW	CRJ	7495	C-FMLF	CRJ	7013	C-FMLQ	CRJ	7740	C-FMLU	CRJ	7108
C-FMKW	CRJ	7525	C-FMLF	CRJ	7043	C-FMLQ	CRJ	7770	C-FMLU	CRJ	7123
C-FMKW	CRJ	7555	C-FMLF	CRJ	7073	C-FMLQ	CRJ	7800	C-FMLU	CRJ	7168
C-FMKW	CRJ	7585	C-FMLF	CRJ	7228	C-FMLQ	CRJ	7830	C-FMLU	CRJ	7214
C-FMKW	CRJ	7615	C-FMLF	CRJ	7258	C-FMLQ	CRJ	7860	C-FMLU	CRJ	7244
C-FMKW	CRJ	7645	C-FMLF	CRJ	7288	C-FMLQ	CRJ	7890	C-FMLU	CRJ	7263
C-FMKW	CRJ	7675	C-FMLF	CRJ	7318	C-FMLQ	CRJ	7920	C-FMLU	CRJ	7274
C-FMKW	CRJ	7705	C-FMLF	CRJ	7348	C-FMLQ	CRJ	7950	C-FMLU	CRJ	7304
C-FMKW	CRJ	7735	C-FMLF	CRJ	7378	C-FMLQ	CRJ	7980	C-FMLU	CRJ	7364
C-FMKW	CRJ	7765	C-FMLF	CRJ	7408	C-FMLQ	CRJ	8049	C-FMLU	CRJ	7394
C-FMKW	CRJ	7795	C-FMLF	CRJ	7438	C-FMLS	CRJ	7016	C-FMLU	CRJ	7424
C-FMKW	CRJ	7825	C-FMLF	CRJ	7468	C-FMLS	CRJ	7046	C-FMLU	CRJ	7454
C-FMKW	CRJ	7855	C-FMLF	CRJ	7498	C-FMLS	CRJ	7076	C-FMLU	CRJ	7484
C-FMKW	CRJ	7885	C-FMLF	CRJ	7528	C-FMLS	CRJ	7231	C-FMLU	CRJ	7514
C-FMKW	CRJ	7915	C-FMLF	CRJ	7588	C-FMLS	CRJ	7261	C-FMLU	CRJ	7544
C-FMKW	CRJ	7945	C-FMLF	CRJ	7618	C-FMLS	CRJ	7291	C-FMLU	CRJ	7574
C-FMKW	CRJ	7975	C-FMLF	CRJ	7648	C-FMLS	CRJ	7321	C-FMLU	CRJ	7604
C-FMKW	CRJ	8074	C-FMLF	CRJ	7678	C-FMLS	CRJ	7351	C-FMLU	CRJ	7634
C-FMKZ	CRJ	7011	C-FMLF	CRJ	7708	C-FMLS	CRJ	7381	C-FMLU	CRJ	7664
C-FMKZ	CRJ	7041	C-FMLF	CRJ	7738	C-FMLS	CRJ	7411	C-FMLU	CRJ	7694
C-FMKZ	CRJ	7071	C-FMLF	CRJ	7768	C-FMLS	CRJ	7441	C-FMLU	CRJ	7724
C-FMKZ	CRJ	7196	C-FMLF	CRJ	7798	C-FMLS	CRJ	7471	C-FMLU	CRJ	7754
C-FMKZ	CRJ	7226	C-FMLF	CRJ	7828	C-FMLS	CRJ	7501	C-FMLU	CRJ	7784
C-FMKZ	CRJ	7256	C-FMLF	CRJ	7858	C-FMLS	CRJ	7531	C-FMLU	CRJ	7814
C-FMKZ	CRJ	7286	C-FMLF	CRJ	7888	C-FMLS	CRJ	7561	C-FMLU	CRJ	7844
C-FMKZ	CRJ	7316	C-FMLF	CRJ	7918	C-FMLS	CRJ	7621	C-FMLU	CRJ	7874
C-FMKZ	CRJ	7376	C-FMLF	CRJ	7948	C-FMLS	CRJ	7651	C-FMLU	CRJ	7904
C-FMKZ	CRJ	7406	C-FMLF	CRJ	7978	C-FMLS	CRJ	7681	C-FMLU	CRJ	7934
C-FMKZ	CRJ	7436	C-FMLF	CRJ	8047	C-FMLS	CRJ	7711	C-FMLU	CRJ	7964
C-FMKZ	CRJ	7466	C-FMLF	CRJ	8077	C-FMLS	CRJ	7741	C-FMLU	CRJ	8033
C-FMKZ	CRJ	7496	C-FMLI	CRJ	7014	C-FMLS	CRJ	7771	C-FMLV	CRJ	7019
C-FMKZ	CRJ	7526	C-FMLI	CRJ	7044	C-FMLS	CRJ	7801	C-FMLV	CRJ	7049
C-FMKZ	CRJ	7556	C-FMLI	CRJ	7074	C-FMLS	CRJ	7831	C-FMLV	CRJ	7079
C-FMKZ	CRJ	7586	C-FMLI	CRJ	7199	C-FMLS	CRJ	7861	C-FMLV	CRJ	7094
C-FMKZ	CRJ	7616	C-FMLI	CRJ	7259	C-FMLS	CRJ	7891	C-FMLV	CRJ	7109
C-FMKZ	CRJ	7646	C-FMLI	CRJ	7289	C-FMLS	CRJ	7921	C-FMLV	CRJ	7139
C-FMKZ	CRJ	7676	C-FMLI	CRJ	7319	C-FMLS	CRJ	7951	C-FMLV	CRJ	7233
C-FMKZ	CRJ	7706	C-FMLI	CRJ	7349	C-FMLS	CRJ	7981	C-FMLV	CRJ	7293
C-FMKZ	CRJ	7736	C-FMLI	CRJ	7379	C-FMLS	CRJ	8011	C-FMLV	CRJ	7323
C FMKZ	CRJ	7766	C-FMLI	CRJ	7409	C-FMLS	CRJ	8019	C-FMLV	CRJ	7353
C-FMKZ	CRJ	7796	C-FMLI	CRJ	7431	C-FMLS	CRJ	8020	C-FMLV	CRJ	7383
C-FMKZ	CRJ	7826	C-FMLI	CRJ	7469	C-FMLT	CRJ	7017	C-FMLV	CRJ	7413
C-FMKZ	CRJ	7856	C-FMLI	CRJ	7499	C-FMLT	CRJ	7047	C-FMLV	CRJ	7443
C-FMKZ	CRJ	7886	C-FMLI	CRJ	7529	C-FMLT	CRJ	7077	C-FMLV	CRJ	7473
C-FMKZ	CRJ	7916	C-FMLI	CRJ	7559	C-FMLT	CRJ	7092	C-FMLV	CRJ	7503
C-FMKZ	CRJ	7946	C-FMLI	CRJ	7589	C-FMLT	CRJ	7137	C-FMLV	CRJ	7533
C-FMKZ	CRJ	7976	C-FMLI	CRJ	7619	C-FMLT	CRJ	7152	C-FMLV	CRJ	7563
C-FMKZ	CRJ	8015	C-FMLI	CRJ	7649	C-FMLT	CRJ	7167	C-FMLV	CRJ	7593
C-FMKZ	CRJ	8045	C-FMLI	CRJ	7679	C-FMLT	CRJ	7182	C-FMLV	CRJ	7623
C-FMKZ	CRJ	8075	C-FMLI	CRJ	7709	C-FMLT	CRJ	7202	C-FMLV	CRJ	7653
C-FMLB	CRJ	7012	C-FMLI	CRJ	7739	C-FMLT	CRJ	7232	C-FMLV	CRJ	7683
C-FMLB	CRJ	7042	C-FMLI	CRJ	7769	C-FMLT	CRJ	7262	C-FMLV	CRJ	7713
C-FMLB	CRJ	7072	C-FMLI	CRJ	7799	C-FMLT	CRJ	7292	C-FMLV	CRJ	7743
C-FMLB	CRJ	7197	C-FMLI	CRJ	7829	C-FMLT	CRJ	7322	C-FMLV	CRJ	7773
C-FMLB	CRJ	7203	C-FMLI	CRJ	7859	C-FMLT	CRJ	7352	C-FMLV	CRJ	7803
C-FMLB	CRJ	7257	C-FMLI	CRJ	7889	C-FMLT	CRJ	7382	C-FMLV	CRJ	7833
C-FMLB	CRJ	7287	C-FMLI	CRJ	7919	C-FMLT	CRJ	7412	C-FMLV	CRJ	7863
C-FMLB	CRJ	7317	C-FMLI	CRJ	7949	C-FMLT	CRJ	7442	C-FMLV	CRJ	7893
C-FMLB	CRJ	7347	C-FMLI	CRJ	7979	C-FMLT	CRJ	7472	C-FMLV	CRJ	7923
C-FMLB	CRJ	7377	C-FMLI	CRJ	8009	C-FMLT	CRJ	7502	C-FMLV	CRJ	7953
C-FMLB	CRJ	7407	C-FMLI	CRJ	8048	C-FMLT	CRJ	7532	C-FMLV	CRJ	7983
C-FMLB	CRJ	7437	C-FMLQ	CRJ	7013	C-FMLT	CRJ	7562	C-FMLV	CRJ	8022
C-FMLB	CRJ	7467	C-FMLQ	CRJ	7015	C-FMLT	CRJ	7592	C-FMLW	CRJ	7504
C-FMLB	CRJ	7497	C-FMLQ	CRJ	7045	C-FMLT	CRJ	7622	C-FMLZ	CRJ	7227
C-FMLB	CRJ	7527	C-FMLQ	CRJ	7075	C-FMLT	CRJ	7652	C-FMMB	CRJ	7020
C-FMLB	CRJ	7557	C-FMLQ	CRJ	7200	C-FMLT	CRJ	7682	C-FMMB	CRJ	7050
C-FMLB	CRJ	7587	C-FMLQ	CRJ	7230	C-FMLT	CRJ	7712	C-FMMB	CRJ	7080
C-FMLB	CRJ	7617	C-FMLQ	CRJ	7260	C-FMLT	CRJ	7742	C-FMMB	CRJ	7110

C-FMMB	CRJ	7125	C-FMMN	CRJ	7458	C-FMMT	CRJ	7834	C-FMMY	CRJ	7147			
C-FMMB	CRJ	7155	C-FMMN	CRJ	7488	C-FMMT	CRJ	7864	C-FMMY	CRJ	7162			
C-FMMB	CRJ	7185	C-FMMN	CRJ	7518	C-FMMT	CRJ	7894	C-FMMY	CRJ	7177			
C-FMMB	CRJ	7216	C-FMMN	CRJ	7548	C-FMMT	CRJ	7924	C-FMMY	CRJ	7192			
C-FMMB	CRJ	7246	C-FMMN	CRJ	7578	C-FMMT	CRJ	7954	C-FMMY	CRJ	7222			
C-FMMB	CRJ	7276	C-FMMN	CRJ	7608	C-FMMT	CRJ	7984	C-FMMY	CRJ	7312			
C-FMMB	CRJ	7306	C-FMMN	CRJ	7638	C-FMMV	CRJ	7400	C-FMMY	CRJ	7342			
C-FMMB	CRJ	7366	C-FMMN	CRJ	7668	C-FMMW	CRJ	7025	"C-FMMY"	CRJ	7371			
"C-FMMB"	CRJ	7373	C-FMMN	CRJ	7698	C-FMMW	CRJ	7055	C-FMMY	CRJ	7372			
C-FMMB	CRJ	7396	C-FMMN	CRJ	7728	C-FMMW	CRJ	7085	C-FMMY	CRJ	7402			
C-FMMB	CRJ	7426	C-FMMN	CRJ	7758	C-FMMW	CRJ	7130	C-FMMY	CRJ	7432			
C-FMMB	CRJ	7456	C-FMMN	CRJ	7788	C-FMMW	CRJ	7145	C-FMMY	CRJ	7462			
C-FMMB	CRJ	7486	C-FMMN	CRJ	7818	C-FMMW	CRJ	7220	C-FMMY	CRJ	7492			
C-FMMB	CRJ	7516	C-FMMN	CRJ	7848	C-FMMW	CRJ	7250	C-FMMY	CRJ	7522			
C-FMMB	CRJ	7546	C-FMMN	CRJ	7878	C-FMMW	CRJ	7280	C-FMMY	CRJ	7552			
C-FMMB	CRJ	7576	C-FMMN	CRJ	7908	C-FMMW	CRJ	7310	C-FMMY	CRJ	7582			
C-FMMB	CRJ	7606	C-FMMN	CRJ	7938	C-FMMW	CRJ	7340	C-FMMY	CRJ	7612			
C-FMMB	CRJ	7636	C-FMMN	CRJ	7968	C-FMMW	CRJ	7370	C-FMMY	CRJ	7642			
C-FMMB	CRJ	7666	C-FMMN	CRJ	8007	C-FMMW	CRJ	7430	C-FMMY	CRJ	7672			
C-FMMB	CRJ	7696	C-FMMQ	CRJ	7023	C-FMMW	CRJ	7460	C-FMMY	CRJ	7702			
C-FMMB	CRJ	7726	C-FMMQ	CRJ	7053	C-FMMW	CRJ	7490	C-FMMY	CRJ	7732			
C-FMMB	CRJ	7756	C-FMMQ	CRJ	7113	C-FMMW	CRJ	7520	C-FMMY	CRJ	7762			
C-FMMB	CRJ	7786	C-FMMQ	CRJ	7128	C-FMMW	CRJ	7550	C-FMMY	CRJ	7792			
C-FMMB	CRJ	7816	C-FMMQ	CRJ	7143	C-FMMW	CRJ	7580	C-FMMY	CRJ	7822			
C-FMMB	CRJ	7846	C-FMMQ	CRJ	7158	C-FMMW	CRJ	7610	C-FMMY	CRJ	7852			
C-FMMB	CRJ	7876	C-FMMQ	CRJ	7173	C-FMMW	CRJ	7640	C-FMMY	CRJ	7882			
C-FMMB	CRJ	7906	C-FMMQ	CRJ	7188	C-FMMW	CRJ	7670	C-FMMY	CRJ	7912			
C-FMMB	CRJ	7936	C-FMMQ	CRJ	7219	C-FMMW	CRJ	7700	C-FMMY	CRJ	7942			
C-FMMB	CRJ	7966	C-FMMQ	CRJ	7249	C-FMMW	CRJ	7730	C-FMMY	CRJ	7972			
C-FMMB	CRJ	8005	C-FMMQ	CRJ	7279	C-FMMW	CRJ	7760	C-FMMY	CRJ	8002			
C-FMMB	CRJ	8065	C-FMMQ	CRJ	7309	C-FMMW	CRJ	7790	C-FMMY	CRJ	8041			
C-FMML	CRJ	7021	C-FMMQ	CRJ	7339	C-FMMW	CRJ	7820	C-FMNB	CRJ	7028			
C-FMML	CRJ	7051	C-FMMQ	CRJ	7369	C-FMMW	CRJ	7850	C-FMNB	CRJ	7058			
C-FMML	CRJ	7081	C-FMMQ	CRJ	7399	C-FMMW	CRJ	7880	C-FMNB	CRJ	7103			
C-FMML	CRJ	7111	C-FMMQ	CRJ	7429	C-FMMW	CRJ	7910	C-FMNB	CRJ	7133			
C-FMML	CRJ	7126	C-FMMQ	CRJ	7459	C-FMMW	CRJ	7940	C-FMNB	CRJ	7148			
C-FMML	CRJ	7141	C-FMMQ	CRJ	7489	C-FMMW	CRJ	7970	C-FMNB	CRJ	7223			
C-FMML	CRJ	7171	C-FMMQ	CRJ	7519	C-FMMW	CRJ	8000	C-FMNB	CRJ	7313			
C-FMML	CRJ	7186	C-FMMQ	CRJ	7549	C-FMMW	CRJ	8039	C-FMNB	CRJ	7373			
C-FMML	CRJ	7217	C-FMMQ	CRJ	7579	C-FMMW	CRJ	8069	C-FMNB	CRJ	7403			
C-FMML	CRJ	7247	C-FMMQ	CRJ	7609	C-FMMX	CRJ	7026	C-FMNB	CRJ	7433			
C-FMML	CRJ	7277	C-FMMQ	CRJ	7639	C-FMMX	CRJ	7056	C-FMNB	CRJ	7463			
C-FMML	CRJ	7307	C-FMMQ	CRJ	7669	C-FMMX	CRJ	7086	C-FMNB	CRJ	7493			
C-FMML	CRJ	7337	C-FMMQ	CRJ	7699	C-FMMX	CRJ	7101	C-FMNB	CRJ	7523			
C-FMML	CRJ	7367	C-FMMQ	CRJ	7729	C-FMMX	CRJ	7116	C-FMNB	CRJ	7553			
C-FMML	CRJ	7397	C-FMMQ	CRJ	7759	C-FMMX	CRJ	7131	C-FMNB	CRJ	7583			
C-FMML	CRJ	7427	C-FMMQ	CRJ	7789	C-FMMX	CRJ	7146	C-FMNB	CRJ	7613			
C-FMML	CRJ	7457	C-FMMQ	CRJ	7819	C-FMMX	CRJ	7161	C-FMNB	CRJ	7643			
C-FMML	CRJ	7487	C-FMMQ	CRJ	7849	C-FMMX	CRJ	7176	C-FMNB	CRJ	7673			
C-FMML	CRJ	7517	C-FMMQ	CRJ	7879	C-FMMX	CRJ	7191	C-FMNB	CRJ	7703			
C-FMML	CRJ	7547	C-FMMQ	CRJ	7909	C-FMMX	CRJ	7221	C-FMNB	CRJ	7733			
C-FMML	CRJ	7577	C-FMMQ	CRJ	7939	C-FMMX	CRJ	7237	C-FMNB	CRJ	7763			
C-FMML	CRJ	7607	C-FMMQ	CRJ	7969	C-FMMX	CRJ	7251	C-FMNB	CRJ	7793			
C-FMML	CRJ	7637	C-FMMQ	CRJ	8008	C-FMMX	CRJ	7281	C-FMNB	CRJ	7853			
C-FMML	CRJ	7667	C-FMMT	CRJ	7024	C-FMMX	CRJ	7311	C-FMNB	CRJ	7883			
C-FMML	CRJ	7697	C-FMMT	CRJ	7054	C-FMMX	CRJ	7341	C-FMNB	CRJ	7913			
C-FMML	CRJ	7727	C-FMMT	CRJ	7084	C-FMMX	CRJ	7371	C-FMNB	CRJ	7943			
C-FMML	CRJ	7757	C-FMMT	CRJ	7114	C-FMMX	CRJ	7401	C-FMNB	CRJ	7973			
C-FMML	CRJ	7787	C-FMMT	CRJ	7129	C-FMMX	CRJ	7439	C-FMNB	CRJ	8003			
C-FMML	CRJ	7817	C-FMMT	CRJ	7144	C-FMMX	CRJ	7461	C-FMND	CRJ	7029			
C-FMML	CRJ	7847	C-FMMT	CRJ	7159	C-FMMX	CRJ	7491	C-FMND	CRJ	7059			
C-FMML	CRJ	7877	C-FMMT	CRJ	7174	C-FMMX	CRJ	7521	C-FMND	CRJ	7119			
C-FMML	CRJ	7907	C-FMMT	CRJ	7175	C-FMMX	CRJ	7551	C-FMND	CRJ	7134			
C-FMML	CRJ	7937	C-FMMT	CRJ	7204	C-FMMX	CRJ	7611	C-FMND	CRJ	7149			
C-FMML	CRJ	7967	C-FMMT	CRJ	7234	C-FMMX	CRJ	7641	C-FMND	CRJ	7164			
C-FMML	CRJ	8006	C-FMMT	CRJ	7264	C-FMMX	CRJ	7671	C-FMND	CRJ	7179			
C-FMML	CRJ	8036	C-FMMT	CRJ	7294	C-FMMX	CRJ	7701	C-FMND	CRJ	7212			
C-FMMN	CRJ	7022	C-FMMT	CRJ	7324	C-FMMX	CRJ	7731	C-FMND	CRJ	7242			
C-FMMN	CRJ	7052	C-FMMT	CRJ	7354	C-FMMX	CRJ	7761	C-FMND	CRJ	7272			
C-FMMN	CRJ	7127	C-FMMT	CRJ	7384	C-FMMX	CRJ	7791	C-FMND	CRJ	7283			
C-FMMN	CRJ	7142	C-FMMT	CRJ	7414	C-FMMX	CRJ	7821	C-FMND	CRJ	7302			
C-FMMN	CRJ	7157	C-FMMT	CRJ	7444	C-FMMX	CRJ	7851	C-FMND	CRJ	7332			
C-FMMN	CRJ	7172	C-FMMT	CRJ	7474	C-FMMX	CRJ	7911	C-FMND	CRJ	7362			
C-FMMN	CRJ	7187	C-FMMT	CRJ	7534	C-FMMX	CRJ	7941	C-FMND	CRJ	7392			
C-FMMN	CRJ	7218	C-FMMT	CRJ	7564	C-FMMX	CRJ	7971	C-FMND	CRJ	7422			
C-FMMN	CRJ	7248	C-FMMT	CRJ	7594	C-FMMX	CRJ	8001	C-FMND	CRJ	7452			
C-FMMN	CRJ	7278	C-FMMT	CRJ	7654	C-FMMX	CRJ	8070	C-FMND	CRJ	7482			
C-FMMN	CRJ	7308	C-FMMT	CRJ	7684	C-FMMY	CRJ	7027	C-FMND	CRJ	7512			
C-FMMN	CRJ	7338	C-FMMT	CRJ	7714	C-FMMY	CRJ	7057	C-FMND	CRJ	7542			
C-FMMN	CRJ	7368	C-FMMT	CRJ	7744	C-FMMY	CRJ	7102	C-FMND	CRJ	7572			
C-FMMN	CRJ	7398	C-FMMT	CRJ	7774	C-FMMY	CRJ	7117	C-FMND	CRJ	7602			
C-FMMN	CRJ	7428	C-FMMT	CRJ	7804	C-FMMY	CRJ	7132	C-FMND	CRJ	7632			

Reg	Type	No.	Reg	Type	No.	Reg	Type	No.	Reg	Type	No.
C-FMND	CRJ	7662	C-FMNW	CRJ	7062	C-FMNY	CRJ	7868	C-FMOW	CRJ	7570
C-FMND	CRJ	7692	C-FMNW	CRJ	7099	C-FMNY	CRJ	7898	C-FMOW	CRJ	7600
C-FMND	CRJ	7722	C-FMNW	CRJ	7236	C-FMNY	CRJ	7928	C-FMOW	CRJ	7630
C-FMND	CRJ	7752	C-FMNW	CRJ	7266	C-FMNY	CRJ	7958	C-FMOW	CRJ	7660
C-FMND	CRJ	7782	C-FMNW	CRJ	7296	C-FMNY	CRJ	7988	C-FMOW	CRJ	7690
C-FMND	CRJ	7812	C-FMNW	CRJ	7326	C-FMNY	CRJ	8018	C-FMOW	CRJ	7720
C-FMND	CRJ	7842	C-FMNW	CRJ	7356	C-FMNY	CRJ	8027	C-FMOW	CRJ	7750
C-FMND	CRJ	7872	C-FMNW	CRJ	7386	C-FMNZ	CRJ	7569	C-FMOW	CRJ	7780
C-FMND	CRJ	7932	C-FMNW	CRJ	7416	C-FMOI	CRJ	7035	C-FMOW	CRJ	7810
C-FMND	CRJ	7962	C-FMNW	CRJ	7446	C-FMOI	CRJ	7065	C-FMOW	CRJ	7840
C-FMNH	CRJ	7030	C-FMNW	CRJ	7476	C-FMOI	CRJ	7154	C-FMOW	CRJ	7870
C-FMNH	CRJ	7060	C-FMNW	CRJ	7506	C-FMOI	CRJ	7184	C-FMOW	CRJ	7900
C-FMNH	CRJ	7090	C-FMNW	CRJ	7536	C-FMOI	CRJ	7215	C-FMOW	CRJ	7930
C-FMNH	CRJ	7105	C-FMNW	CRJ	7566	C-FMOI	CRJ	7245	C-FMOW	CRJ	7960
C-FMNH	CRJ	7135	C-FMNW	CRJ	7596	C-FMOI	CRJ	7275	C-FMOW	CRJ	7990
C-FMNH	CRJ	7150	C-FMNW	CRJ	7656	C-FMOI	CRJ	7335	C-FMOW	CRJ	8029
C-FMNH	CRJ	7165	C-FMNW	CRJ	7686	C-FMOI	CRJ	7365	C-FMST	A320	0350
C-FMNH	CRJ	7205	C-FMNW	CRJ	7716	C-FMOI	CRJ	7395	C-FMSV	A320	0359
C-FMNH	CRJ	7235	C-FMNW	CRJ	7746	C-FMOI	CRJ	7425	C-FMSX	A320	0378
C-FMNH	CRJ	7265	C-FMNW	CRJ	7776	C-FMOI	CRJ	7455	C-FMSY	A320	0384
C-FMNH	CRJ	7295	C-FMNW	CRJ	7806	C-FMOI	CRJ	7485	C-FMUQ	CRJ	7009
C-FMNH	CRJ	7325	C-FMNW	CRJ	7836	C-FMOI	CRJ	7515	C-FMUR	CRJ	7019
C-FMNH	CRJ	7355	C-FMNW	CRJ	7866	C-FMOI	CRJ	7545	C-FMUV	CRJ	7073
C-FMNH	CRJ	7385	C-FMNW	CRJ	7896	C-FMOI	CRJ	7575	C-FMVS	CRJ	8071
C-FMNH	CRJ	7415	C-FMNW	CRJ	7926	C-FMOI	CRJ	7605	C-FMWJ	737NG	32771
C-FMNH	CRJ	7445	C-FMNW	CRJ	7956	C-FMOI	CRJ	7635	C-FMWP	B767	25583
C-FMNH	CRJ	7475	C-FMNW	CRJ	7986	C-FMOI	CRJ	7665	C-FMWQ	B767	25584
C-FMNH	CRJ	7505	C-FMNW	CRJ	8025	C-FMOI	CRJ	7695	C-FMWU	B767	25585
C-FMNH	CRJ	7535	C-FMNX	CRJ	7033	C-FMOI	CRJ	7725	C-FMWV	B767	25586
C-FMNH	CRJ	7565	C-FMNX	CRJ	7064	C-FMOI	CRJ	7755	C-FMWY	B767	25587
C-FMNH	CRJ	7595	C-FMNX	CRJ	7169	C-FMOI	CRJ	7785	C-FMXC	B767	25588
C-FMNH	CRJ	7655	C-FMNX	CRJ	7207	C-FMOI	CRJ	7815	C-FMYV	E190	19000108
C-FMNH	CRJ	7685	C-FMNX	CRJ	7267	C-FMOI	CRJ	7845	C-FMZB	E190	19000111
C-FMNH	CRJ	7715	C-FMNX	CRJ	7297	C-FMOI	CRJ	7875	C-FMZD	E190	190001..
C-FMNH	CRJ	7745	C-FMNX	CRJ	7327	C-FMOI	CRJ	7905	C-FMZR	E190	190001..
C-FMNH	CRJ	7775	C-FMNX	CRJ	7357	C-FMOI	CRJ	7935	C-FMZU	E190	190001..
C-FMNH	CRJ	7805	C-FMNX	CRJ	7387	C-FMOI	CRJ	7965	C-FMZW	E190	190001..
C-FMNH	CRJ	7835	C-FMNX	CRJ	7417	C-FMOI	CRJ	8034	(C-FNAA)	DC-8	45902
C-FMNH	CRJ	7865	C-FMNX	CRJ	7447	C-FMOL	CRJ	7036	C-FNAB	B737	19847
C-FMNH	CRJ	7895	C-FMNX	CRJ	7477	C-FMOL	CRJ	7066	C-FNAH	B737	19848
C-FMNH	CRJ	7925	C-FMNX	CRJ	7507	C-FMOS	CRJ	7037	C-FNAI	E190	190001..
C-FMNH	CRJ	7955	C-FMNX	CRJ	7537	C-FMOS	CRJ	7067	C-FNAJ	B737	22354
C-FMNH	CRJ	7985	C-FMNX	CRJ	7567	C-FMOS	CRJ	7163	C-FNAJ	E190	190001..
C-FMNH	CRJ	8024	C-FMNX	CRJ	7597	C-FMOS	CRJ	7239	C-FNAN	E190	190001..
C-FMNH	CRJ	8054	C-FMNX	CRJ	7657	C-FMOS	CRJ	7269	C-FNAP	B737	20496
C-FMNO	CRJ	7363	C-FMNX	CRJ	7687	C-FMOS	CRJ	7299	C-FNAP	E190	190001..
C-FMNQ	CRJ	7031	C-FMNX	CRJ	7717	C-FMOS	CRJ	7329	C-FNAQ	B737	20455
C-FMNQ	CRJ	7061	C-FMNX	CRJ	7747	C-FMOS	CRJ	7359	C-FNAQ	E190	190001..
C-FMNQ	CRJ	7083	C-FMNX	CRJ	7777	C-FMOS	CRJ	7389	C-FNAW	B737	20521
C-FMNQ	CRJ	7091	C-FMNX	CRJ	7807	C-FMOS	CRJ	7419	C-FNAW	E190	190001..
C-FMNQ	CRJ	7106	C-FMNX	CRJ	7837	C-FMOS	CRJ	7449	C-FNAX	B737	21815
C-FMNQ	CRJ	7121	C-FMNX	CRJ	7867	C-FMOS	CRJ	7479	C-FNAX	E190	190001..
C-FMNQ	CRJ	7136	C-FMNX	CRJ	7897	C-FMOS	CRJ	7509	C-FNBC	B757	24260
C-FMNQ	CRJ	7151	C-FMNX	CRJ	7927	C-FMOS	CRJ	7539	C-FNII	CRJ	8072
C-FMNQ	CRJ	7181	C-FMNX	CRJ	7957	C-FMOS	CRJ	7599	C-FNJW	CRJ	7363
C-FMNQ	CRJ	7213	C-FMNX	CRJ	7987	C-FMOS	CRJ	7659	C-FNJZ	CRJ9	15046
C-FMNQ	CRJ	7243	C-FMNX	CRJ	8017	C-FMOS	CRJ	7689	C-FNKC	CRJ	7379
C-FMNQ	CRJ	7273	C-FMNX	CRJ	8026	C-FMOS	CRJ	7719	C-FNMY	CRJ	7282
C-FMNQ	CRJ	7303	C-FMNX	CRJ	8057	C-FMOS	CRJ	7749	C-FNNA	A320	0426
C-FMNQ	CRJ	7333	C-FMNY	CRJ	7034	C-FMOS	CRJ	7779	C-FNND	B777	35246
C-FMNQ	CRJ	7393	C-FMNY	CRJ	7063	C-FMOS	CRJ	7809	C-FNNH	B777	35247
C-FMNQ	CRJ	7423	C-FMNY	CRJ	7208	C-FMOS	CRJ	7839	C-FNRJ	CRJ	7002
C-FMNQ	CRJ	7453	C-FMNY	CRJ	7238	C-FMOS	CRJ	7869	C-FNUI	CRJ9	15126
C-FMNQ	CRJ	7483	C-FMNY	CRJ	7268	C-FMOS	CRJ	7899	C-FNVK	B737	23130
C-FMNQ	CRJ	7513	C-FMNY	CRJ	7298	C-FMOS	CRJ	7929	(C-FNVT)	A320	0397
C-FMNQ	CRJ	7543	C-FMNY	CRJ	7328	C-FMOS	CRJ	7959	C-FNVT	B737	21011
C-FMNQ	CRJ	7573	C-FMNY	CRJ	7358	C-FMOS	CRJ	7989	C-FNVU	A320	0403
C-FMNQ	CRJ	7603	C-FMNY	CRJ	7388	C-FMOS	CRJ	8028	C-FNVV	A320	0404
C-FMNQ	CRJ	7633	C-FMNY	CRJ	7448	C-FMOW	CRJ	7038	C-FNWB	CRJ9	15131
C-FMNQ	CRJ	7663	C-FMNY	CRJ	7478	C-FMOW	CRJ	7068	C-FNWD	A310	444
C-FMNQ	CRJ	7693	C-FMNY	CRJ	7508	C-FMOW	CRJ	7210	C-FNXA	B747	20493
C-FMNQ	CRJ	7723	C-FMNY	CRJ	7538	C-FMOW	CRJ	7240	C-FNXP	B747	21162
C-FMNQ	CRJ	7753	C-FMNY	CRJ	7568	C-FMOW	CRJ	7270	C-FNXY	B757	25593
C-FMNQ	CRJ	7783	C-FMNY	CRJ	7598	C-FMOW	CRJ	7300	C-FNZE	DC-8	45985
C-FMNQ	CRJ	7813	C-FMNY	CRJ	7628	C-FMOW	CRJ	7330	C-FOAA	B757	23767
C-FMNQ	CRJ	7843	C-FMNY	CRJ	7658	C-FMOW	CRJ	7360	C-FOBH	B757	29944
C-FMNQ	CRJ	7873	C-FMNY	CRJ	7688	C-FMOW	CRJ	7390	C-FOBI	CRJ	8077
C-FMNQ	CRJ	7903	C-FMNY	CRJ	7718	C-FMOW	CRJ	7420	C-FOCA	B767	24575
C-FMNQ	CRJ	7933	C-FMNY	CRJ	7748	C-FMOW	CRJ	7450	C-FOCR	F.28	11063
C-FMNQ	CRJ	7963	C-FMNY	CRJ	7778	C-FMOW	CRJ	7480	C-FOFO	CRJ9	15134
C-FMNQ	CRJ	8032	C-FMNY	CRJ	7808	C-FMOW	CRJ	7510	C-FOFW	CRJ	8073
C-FMNW	CRJ	7032	C-FMNY	CRJ	7838	C-FMOW	CRJ	7540	C-FOJZ	A320	1965

Reg	Type	c/n	Reg	Type	c/n	Reg	Type	c/n	Reg	Type	c/n
C-FOMN	CRJ	8074	C-FSXX	CRJ	7471	C-FTMJ	DC-9	47348	C-FVNC	B737	24344
C-FONF	F.28	11060	C-FTAE	737NG	30637	C-FTMK	DC-9	47349	C-FVND	B737	24545
C-FONG	F.28	11070	C-FTAH	737NG	29351	C-FTML	DC-9	47350	(C-FVNF)	B737	24682
C-FOOA	B757	23767	C-FTAN	B737	20206	C-FTMM	DC-9	47611	C-FVNM	B767	22681
C-FOOB	B757	23822	C-FTAO	B737	20205	C-FTMO	DC-9	47353	C-FVZA	CRJ	7361
C-FOOE	B757	24369	C-FTAR	F.28	11047	C-FTMP	DC-9	47354	C-FWAD	737NG	32753
C-FOOG	B757	24292	C-FTAS	F.28	11098	C-FTMQ	DC-9	47422	C-FWAF	737NG	32747
C-FOOH	B757	24293	C-FTAV	F.28	11033	C-FTMR	DC-9	47423	C-FWAI	737NG	33656
C-FOON	B757	28161	C-FTAV	F.28	11106	C-FTMS	DC-9	47424	C-FWAO	737NG	33657
C-FOVM	CRJ9	15139	C-FTAY	F.28	11084	C-FTMT	DC-9	47546	C-FWAQ	737NG	32748
C-FOWE	CRJ9	15124	C-FTCA	B767	24307	C-FTMU	DC-9	47554	C-FWBG	737NG	32749
C-FOWF	CRJ9	15140	C-FTDA	A320	0795	C-FTMV	DC-9	47557	C-FWBL	737NG	32750
C-FOXW	CRJ	8075	C-FTDD	A320	0371	C-FTMW	DC-9	47560	C-FWBW	737NG	33697
C-FOYA	CRJ	8076	C-FTDF	A320	0437	C-FTMX	DC-9	47485	C-FWBX	737NG	32751
C-FPCA	B767	24306	C-FTDI	A320	0446	C-FTMY	DC-9	47592	C-FWCC	737NG	32752
C-FPCR	F.28	11096	C-FTDQ	A320	1686	C-FTMZ	DC-9	47632	C-FWCN	737NG	33698
C-FPDN	A320	0341	C-FTDU	A320	0379	C-FTNA	L1011	193M-1019	C-FWCR	L1011	193P-1099
(C-FPEP)	B757	25268	C-FTDV	B757	24017	C-FTNB	L1011	193A-1010	C-FWDX	A310	425
C-FPKF	B727	21524	C-FTDW	737NG	34704	C-FTNB	L1011	193M-1023	C-FWJB	CRJ	7087
C-FPQO	CRJ9	15120	C-FTDW	A320	0389	C-FTNC	L1011	193E-1023	C-FWJF	CRJ	7095
C-FPUN	CRJ9	15122	C-FTIH	DC-8	45933	C-FTND	L1011	193E-1025	C-FWJI	CRJ	7096
C-FPWB	B737	20785	C-FTII	DC-8	45934	C-FTNE	L1011	193E-1027	C-FWJS	CRJ	7097
C-FPWC	B737	20142	C-FTIK	DC-8	46033	C-FTNF	L1011	193E-1047	C-FWJT	CRJ	7098
C-FPWD	A320	0231	C-FTIL	DC-8	46034	C-FTNG	L1011	193E-1048	C-FWOQ	A320	0437
C-FPWD	B737	19742	C-FTIM	DC-8	46035	C-FTNH	L1011	193E-1049	C-FWOR	A320	0467
C-FPWD	B737	22761	C-FTIN	DC-8	46036	C-FTNI	L1011	193E-1058	C-FWRN	CRJ	7089
C-FPWD	B737	23495	C-FTIO	DC-8	46076	C-FTNJ	L1011	193E-1067	C-FWRR	CRJ	7107
C-FPWE	A320	0175	C-FTIP	DC-8	46100	C-FTNK	L1011	193E-1069	C-FWRS	CRJ	7112
C-FPWE	B737	19743	C-FTIQ	DC-8	46123	C-FTNL	L1011	193E-1073	C-FWRT	CRJ	7118
C-FPWE	B737	22762	C-FTIR	DC-8	46124	C-FTNP	A340	093	C-FWSC	CRJ	7120
C-FPWE	B737	23497	C-FTIS	DC-8	46125	C-FTNQ	A340	088	C-FWSF	737NG	32758
C-FPWJ	B707	18746	C-FTIU	DC-8	46113	C-FTOA	B747	20013	C-FWSO	737NG	32759
C-FPWM	B737	19921	C-FTIV	DC-8	46126	C-FTOB	B747	20014	C-FWSV	737NG	32760
C-FPWP	B737	20588	C-FTIX	DC-8	46115	C-FTOC	B747	20015	C-FWSX	737NG	32761
C-FPWV	B707	17696	C-FTJH	737NG	29642	C-FTOD	B747	20767	C-FWSY	737NG	32762
C-FPWW	B737	20670	C-FTJJ	DC-8	45612	C-FTOE	B747	20881	C-FWTF	A319	1963
C-FPXB	B727	19174	C-FTJL	DC-8	45640	(C-FTOF)	B747	20977	C-FWXI	B707	18021
C-FPXD	B727	19859	C-FTJO	A320	0183	C-FTOR	DC-9	47013	C-FWXL	B707	18027
C-FQBN	1-11	BAC.110	C-FTJO	DC-8	45655	C-FTOT	DC-9	47015	C-FXCA	B767	24574
C-FQBO	1-11	BAC.112	C-FTJP	A320	0233	C-FTOU	DC-9	47152	C-FXCA	B767	25864
C-FQBR	1-11	094	C-FTJP	DC-8	45679	C-FTSI	L1011	193K-1032	C-FXCD	A320	2018
C-FQCR	F.28	11036	C-FTJQ	A320	0242	C-FTSW	L1011	193H-1246	C-FXCE	B747	21316
C-FQPL	DC-8	45974	C-FTJQ	DC-8	45686	C-FTWJ	737NG	30713	C-FXFB	CRJ	7100
C-FQPM	DC-8	45941	C-FTJR	A320	0248	C-FTWJ	B737	21767	C-FXMY	CRJ	7124
(C-FR.X)	L1011	193P-1154	C-FTJS	A320	0253	C-FUAC	B727	22012	C-FXOC	B757	24017
C-FRAA	A320	1411	C-FTJS	DC-8	45861	C-FUBG	B757	29942	C-FXOD	B757	24235
C-FRAE	A330	143	C-FTJT	DC-8	45890	C-FUCL	B767	22682	C-FXOF	B757	24544
C-FRAP	A330	087	C-FTJU	DC-8	45891	(C-FUCN)	B767	22681	C-FXOK	B757	24924
C-FRAR	A320	0447	C-FTJV	DC-8	45892	C-FUFA	B727	20941	C-FXOO	B757	25621
C-FRAV	A330	171	C-FTJW	DC-8	45893	C-FUJZ	CRJ9	15048	C-FXPI	CRJ	7104
C-FRCA	B747	20801	C-FTJX	DC-8	45963	C-FUWS	737NG	32765	C-FXPQ	CRJ	7115
C-FRCB	B747	20802	C-FTJY	DC-8	45964	C-FVAZ	CRJ	7241	C-FXTA	F.28	11064
C-FRIA	CRJ	7045	C-FTJZ	CRJ9	15047	C-FVAZ	CRJ	7271	C-FXWJ	737NG	32768
C-FRIB	CRJ	7047	C-FTJZ	DC-8	45980	C-FVAZ	CRJ	7301	C-FYIY	A319	0634
C-FRID	CRJ	7049	C-FTLH	DC-9	45845	C-FVAZ	CRJ	7331	C-FYJB	A319	0639
C-FRIL	CRJ	7051	C-FTLI	DC-9	45846	C-FVAZ	CRJ	7391	C-FYJD	A319	0649
C-FRJX	CRJ7	10001	C-FTLJ	DC-9	47019	C-FVAZ	CRJ	7421	C-FYJE	A319	0656
C-FRJX	CRJ9	15991	C-FTLK	DC-9	47020	C-FVAZ	CRJ	7451	C-FYJG	A319	0670
C-FRKQ	CRJ	7032	C-FTLL	DC-9	47021	C-FVAZ	CRJ	7481	C-FYJH	A319	0672
C-FRSA	CRJ	7033	C-FTLM	DC-9	47022	C-FVAZ	CRJ	7511	C-FYJI	A319	0682
C-FRST	B727	19169	C-FTLN	DC-9	47023	C-FVAZ	CRJ	7541	C-FYJP	A319	0688
C-FRYA	MD80	53488	C-FTLO	DC-9	47024	C-FVAZ	CRJ	7571	C-FYKC	A319	0691
C-FRYG	B737	21721	C-FTLP	DC-9	47068	C-FVAZ	CRJ	7601	C-FYKR	A319	0693
C-FRYH	B737	21816	C-FTLQ	DC-9	47069	C-FVAZ	CRJ	7631	C-FYKW	A319	0695
C-FRYH	B757	23822	C-FTLR	DC-9	47070	C-FVAZ	CRJ	7661	C-FYKX	A340	150
C-FRYH	MD80	53520	C-FTLS	DC-9	47071	C-FVAZ	CRJ	7691	C-FYKZ	A340	154
C-FRYL	B737	21970	C-FTLT	DC-9	47195	C-FVAZ	CRJ	7721	C-FYLC	A340	167
C-FRYL	B757	24017	C-FTLU	DC-9	47196	C-FVAZ	CRJ	7751	C-FYLD	A340	170
C-FRYS	B727	21349	C-FTLW	DC-9	47198	C-FVAZ	CRJ	7781	C-FYLG	A340	175
C-FSDZ	CRJ	7787	C-FTLX	DC-9	47199	C-FVAZ	CRJ	7811	C-FYLU	A340	179
C-FSJF	CRJ	7054	C-FTLY	DC-9	47200	C-FVAZ	CRJ	7841	C-FYNS	A319	0572
(C-FSJJ)	CRJ	7057	C-FTLZ	DC-9	47265	C-FVAZ	CRJ	7871	C-FYXI	L1011	193B-1107
C-FSJJ	CRJ	7058	C-FTMA	DC-9	47266	C-FVAZ	CRJ	7901	C-FZAL	CRJ	7147
(C-FSJU)	CRJ	7058	C-FTMB	DC-9	47289	C-FVAZ	CRJ	7931	C-FZAN	CRJ	7153
C-FSJU	CRJ	7060	C-FTMC	DC-9	47290	C-FVAZ	CRJ	7961	C-FZAQ	CRJ	7155
(C-FSKE)	CRJ	7064	C-FTMD	DC-9	47292	C-FVCJ	B737	22353	C-FZAT	CRJ	7138
C-FSKE	CRJ	7065	C-FTME	DC-9	47293	C-FVHC	B737	20588	C-FZAZ	A320	2003
(C-FSKI)	CRJ	7067	C-FTMF	DC-9	47294	C-FVHG	B737	20670	C-FZCR	F.28	11054
C-FSKI	CRJ	7068	C-FTMG	DC-9	47340	C-FVKM	CRJ	7074	C-FZIS	CRJ	7149
(C-FSKM)	CRJ	7068	C-FTMH	DC-9	47341	C-FVKN	CRJ	7078	C-FZJA	CRJ	7988
C-FSKM	CRJ	7071	C-FTMI	DC-9	47342	C-FVKR	CRJ	7083	C-FZKS	CRJ	7140
C-FSWD	A310	418				C-FVMD	CRJ	7082	C-FZQR	CRJ	7746

Reg	Type	No.	Reg	Type	No.	Reg	Type	No.	Reg	Type	No.
C-FZQS	A320	2145	C-GAGX	B727	19191	C-GCIS	B747	20376	C-GFIO	CRJ	7526
C-FZSC	CRJ	7156	C-GAGY	B727	19192	C-GCIT	A310	455	C-GFJZ	CRJ9	15050
C-FZSI	CRJ	7160	C-GAGZ	B727	19195	C-GCIV	A310	451	C-GFKE	F.28	11040
C-FZSY	CRJ	7422	C-GAHB	B737	26538	C-GCJB	B727	21855	C-GFKQ	CRJ	7343
C-FZSZ	CRJ	7405	C-GAIG	B737	21928	C-GCJD	B727	21988	C-GFKR	CRJ	7350
C-FZTH	CRJ	7401	C-GAIK	CRJ	7170	C-GCJN	B727	21451	C-GFLG	B707	19416
C-FZTT	CRJ	7372	C-GANX	B757	22176	C-GCJQ	B727	22437	C-GFPW	B737	21294
C-FZTU	CRJ	7336	C-GAPW	B737	20922	C-GCJY	B727	22460	C-GFRB	B727	19120
C-FZTW	CRJ	7361	C-GAPY	A319	0728	C-GCJZ	B727	21854	C-GFUR	A330	344
C-FZTY	CRJ	7367	C-GAQL	A319	0732	C-GCNO	B727	23790	C-GFVM	CRJ	7387
C-FZTZ	CRJ	7357	C-GAQX	A319	0736	C-GCPA	B727	21055	C-GGAB	B707	19629
C-FZUB	A320	1940	C-GAQZ	A319	0740	C-GCPB	B727	21056	C-GGBI	B767	26608
C-FZUG	A319	0697	C-GARG	A319	0742	C-GCPC	DC-10	46540	C-GGBJ	B767	26389
C-FZUH	A319	0711	C-GARJ	A319	0752	C-GCPD	DC-10	46541	C-GGBK	B767	25221
C-FZUJ	A319	0719	C-GARO	A319	0757	C-GCPE	DC-10	46542	C-GGBL	L1011	193E-1058
C-FZUK	CRJ	7481	C-GATH	L1011	293F-1235	C-GCPF	DC-10	46543	C-GGBQ	L1011	193E-1069
C-FZUL	A319	0721	C-GATM	CRJ	7180	C-GCPG	DC-10	48285	C-GGFJ	B767	24952
(C-FZVF)	A321	1794	C-GATM	L1011	293F-1236	C-GCPH	DC-10	48288	C-GGJA	CRJ	8002
C-FZVM	CRJ7	10047	C-GATY	CRJ	7189	C-GCPI	DC-10	48296	C-GGKD	CRJ	7394
(C-FZWD)	A310	502	C-GAUB	B767	22517	C-GCPJ	DC-10	46991	C-GGKF	B727	21523
C-FZWS	737NG	32731	C-GAUE	B767	22518	C-GCPM	B737	21716	C-GGKF	CRJ	7391
C-FZWS	CRJ	7166	C-GAUG	CRJ	7161	C-GCPN	B737	21717	C-GGKI	CRJ	7393
C-FZYP	B707	20043	C-GAUH	B767	22519	C-GCPO	B737	21718	C-GGKY	CRJ	7395
C-FZYS	CRJ7	10085	C-GAUN	B767	22520	C-GCPP	B737	22255	C-GGMX	B767	24947
C-FZZE	CRJ7	10087	C-GAUP	B767	22521	C-GCPQ	B737	22256	C-GGOF	B737	20563
C-FZZO	CRJ	7036	C-GAUS	B767	22522	(C-GCPR)	B737	22257	C-GGOH	B767	26200
C-FZZO	CRJ	7753	C-GAUU	B767	22523	C-GCPS	B737	22257	C-GGPW	B737	21639
C-G	CRJ9	15066	C-GAUW	B767	22524	(C-GCPS)	B737	22258	C-GGTS	A330	250
C-G	CRJ9	15068	C-GAUY	B767	22525	C-GCPT	B737	22258	C-GGWA	A330	205
C-G	CRJ9	15075	C-GAVA	B767	22526	C-GCPU	B737	22259	C-GGWB	A330	211
C-G	CRJ9	15076	C-GAVC	B767	22527	C-GCPV	B737	22260	C-GGWC	A330	272
C-G	CRJ9	15077	C-GAVF	B767	22528	C-GCPW	B737	20959	C-GGWD	A330	339
C-GAAA	B727	20932	C-GAVO	CRJ	7178	C-GCPX	B737	22341	C-GGWJ	737NG	35503
C-GAAB	B727	20933	C-GAWB	B757	24367	C-GCPY	B737	22342	C-GGWJ	B737	21500
C-GAAC	B727	20934	C-GBBS	L1011	193B-1108	C-GCPZ	B737	22658	C-GHCE	CRJ7	10006
C-GAAD	B727	20935	C-GBBY	CRJ	7139	C-GCRA	CRJ7	10005	C-GHCF	CRJ7	10007
C-GAAD	B727	20937	C-GBFF	CRJ	7190	C-GCRD	F.28	11097	C-GHCO	CRJ7	10008
C-GAAE	B727	20936	C-GBFR	CRJ	7193	C-GCRN	F.28	11051	C-GHCS	CRJ7	10009
C-GAAF	B727	20937	C-GBGL	B737	24970	C-GCSW	CRJ	7039	C-GHCV	CRJ7	10010
C-GAAG	B727	20938	C-GBHM	A319	0769	C-GCWD	A310	447	C-GHCZ	CRJ7	10011
C-GAAH	B727	20939	C-GBHN	A319	0773	C-GCWJ	737NG	33970	C-GHDM	CRJ	7430
C-GAAI	B727	20940	C-GBHO	A319	0779	C-GCWJ	B737	21739	C-GHKR	A330	400
C-GAAJ	B727	20941	C-GBHR	A319	0785	(C-GCWW)	B727	22439	C-GHKW	A330	408
C-GAAK	B727	20942	C-GBHY	A319	0800	C-GDBX	737NG	33699	C-GHKX	A330	412
C-GAAL	B727	21100	C-GBHZ	A319	0813	C-GDCC	B767	20681	C-GHLA	B767	26387
C-GAAM	B727	21101	C-GBIA	A319	0817	C-GDDM	CRJ	7249	C-GHLK	B767	26388
C-GAAN	B727	21102	C-GBIJ	A319	0829	C-GDDO	CRJ	7252	C-GHLM	A330	419
C-GAAO	B727	21624	C-GBIK	A319	0831	C-GDJZ	CRJ9	15049	C-GHLQ	B767	30846
C-GAAP	B727	21625	C-GBIM	A319	0840	C-GDNH	CRJ9	15002	C-GHLT	B767	30850
C-GAAQ	B727	21626	C-GBIN	A319	0845	C-GDPA	B737	22056	C-GHLU	B767	30851
C-GAAR	B727	21671	C-GBIP	A319	0546	(C-GDPG)	B737	22793	C-GHLV	B767	30852
C-GAAS	B727	21672	C-GBIW	B737	28549	C-GDPW	B737	21116	C-GHML	B767	24948
C-GAAT	B727	21673	C-GBIX	B737	28550	C-GDSJ	B727	21525	C-GHOZ	B767	24087
C-GAAU	B727	21674	C-GBLX	CRJ	7201	C-GDSP	B767	24142	C-GHPA	B767	25000
C-GAAV	B727	21675	C-GBMF	CRJ	7198	C-GDSS	B767	24143	C-GHPD	B767	24999
C-GAAW	B727	22035	C-GBNO	CRJ	7206	C-GDSU	B767	24144	C-GHPF	B767	26206
C-GAAX	B727	22036	C-GBNW	CRJ	7209	C-GDSY	B767	24145	C-GHPH	B767	26207
C-GAAY	B727	22037	C-GBNX	CRJ	7224	C-GDUZ	B767	25347	C-GHRG	A320	1942
C-GAAZ	B727	22038	C-GBOD	B757	24235	C-GDVV	A340	257	C-GHRR	CRJ	7432
(C-GABE)	B727	22345	C-GBOD	CRJ	7227	C-GDVW	A340	273	C-GHTK	CRJ	7442
(C-GABF)	B727	22346	C-GBPW	B737	20958	C-GDVZ	A340	278	C-GHUT	CRJ	7455
(C-GABG)	B727	22347	C-GBQM	A340	216	C-GDWD	A310	448	C-GHWC	B727	19195
(C-GABH)	B727	22348	C-GBQQ	DC-10	46916	C-GDYX	CRJ	7089	C-GHWD	CRJ	7466
(C-GABI)	B727	22349	C-GBQS	B737	21231	C-GEIM	B737	22355	C-GHZV	CRJ7	10012
(C-GABJ)	B727	22350	(C-GBQU)	B737	22276	C-GEMV	DC-8	46032	C-GHZV	CRJ7	10042
C-GACC	B727	20550	C-GBWA	B727	19890	C-GENL	B737	22148	C-GHZV	CRJ7	10072
C-GACG	B727	22011	C-GBWD	A310	446	C-GEOQ	B767	30112	C-GHZY	CRJ7	10013
C-GACG	B727	22460	C-GBWH	B727	19814	C-GEOU	B767	30108	C-GHZY	CRJ7	10043
C-GACU	B727	20152	C-GBWO	DC-9	47639	C-GEPA	B737	20976	C-GHZY	CRJ7	10073
C-GAEG	A319	2113	C-GBWS	737NG	34288	C-GEPB	B737	21112	C-GHZZ	CRJ7	10044
C-GAGA	B747	20977	C-GBWS	B727	18867	C-GEPM	B737	22395	C-GHZZ	CRJ7	10074
C-GAGB	B747	21627	C-GBZB	B727	21671	C-GEPW	B737	21115	C-GIAB	CRJ7	10020
C-GAGC	B747	21354	C-GBZR	B767	25404	C-GEWJ	737NG	35571	C-GIAD	CRJ7	10045
C-GAGF	L1011	193H-1202	C-GCAU	B737	22640	C-GEWJ	B737	22055	C-GIAD	CRJ7	10075
C-GAGG	L1011	193H-1206	(C-GCAW)	B767	25865	C-GFAF	A330	277	C-GIAE	CRJ7	10016
C-GAGH	L1011	193H-1207	C-GCBS	CRJ	7226	C-GFAH	A330	279	C-GIAE	CRJ7	10046
C-GAGI	L1011	193H-1209	C-GCDG	B737	20776	C-GFAJ	A330	284	C-GIAE	CRJ7	10076
C-GAGJ	L1011	193H-1216	C-GCGB	CRJ	7137	C-GFAT	A310	545	C-GIAH	CRJ7	10017
C-GAGK	L1011	193H-1218	C-GCGF	CRJ	7139	C-GFAX	CRJ	7748	C-GIAH	CRJ7	10047
C-GAGL	B747	24998	C-GCIH	B747	21162	C-GFCN	CRJ	7320	C-GIAH	CRJ7	10077
C-GAGM	B747	25074	C-GCIL	A310	439	C-GFCP	B737	22659	C-GIAI	CRJ7	10048
C-GAGN	B747	25075	C-GCIO	A310	449	C-GFHX	DC-10	46990	C-GIAI	CRJ7	10050

Reg	Type	Ser	Reg	Type	Ser	Reg	Type	Ser	Reg	Type	Ser
C-GIAJ	CRJ7	10019	C-GIUF	A321	1638	Č-GKEP	CRJ	7303	C-GMWJ	737NG	35985
C-GIAJ	CRJ7	10049	C-GIWD	A310	472	C-GKER	CRJ	7368	C-GMWJ	B737	21771
C-GIAJ	CRJ7	10079	C-GIXF	CRJ	7496	C-GKEU	CRJ	7376	C-GMWW	B747	24883
C-GIAJ	CRJ7	10097	C-GIXG	CRJ	7529	C-GKEW	CRJ	7385	C-GMXB	DC-8	45943
C-GIAO	CRJ7	10080	C-GIZD	CRJ	7504	C-GKEZ	CRJ	7327	C-GMXD	DC-8	45912
C-GIAO	CRJ9	15084	C-GIZF	CRJ	7513	C-GKFA	B727	19806	C-GMXL	DC-8	45981
C-GIAP	CRJ7	10021	C-GIZG	CRJ7	10024	C-GKFB	B727	19358	C-GMXP	DC-8	45804
C-GIAP	CRJ7	10051	C-GIZJ	A300	138	C-GKFC	B727	18897	C-GMXQ	DC-8	45982
C-GIAP	CRJ7	10081	C-GIZL	A300	192	C-GKFH	B727	20153	C-GMXR	DC-8	45925
C-GIAP	CRJ7	10141	C-GIZN	A300	212	C-GKFN	B727	19359	C-GMXY	DC-8	45920
C-GIAP	CRJ9	15088	C-GJAO	CRJ	7503	C-GKFP	B727	19205	C-GMYC	B757	23917
C-GIAR	CRJ7	10022	C-GJAZ	CRJ9	15036	C-GKFR	CRJ	7330	C-GMYD	B757	24254
C-GIAR	CRJ7	10052	C-GJCP	B737	22728	C-GKFT	B727	19807	C-GMYE	B757	32449
C-GIAR	CRJ7	10082	C-GJDX	CRJ	7521	C-GKFV	B727	19173	C-GMYH	B757	25053
C-GIAR	CRJ7	10172	C-GJEX	CRJ7	10025	C-GKFW	B727	19805	C-GNAU	B737	21817
C-GIAU	CRJ7	10053	C-GJEZ	CRJ7	10016	C-GKFZ	B727	19204	C-GNCR	F.28	11034
C-GIAU	CRJ7	10083	C-GJFG	CRJ	7548	C-GKGC	CRJ	7334	C-GNDA	DC-8	45902
C-GIAU	CRJ7	10143	C-GJFH	CRJ	7550	C-GKIT	CRJ	7309	C-GNDC	B737	21728
C-GIAV	CRJ7	10084	C-GJFR	CRJ	7547	C-GKKF	B727	21043	C-GNDD	B737	21112
C-GIAW	CRJ7	10055	C-GJHK	CRJ	7555	C-GKLC	MD80	53468	C-GNDE	DC-8	45618
C-GIAW	CRJ7	10115	C-GJHL	CRJ	7558	C-GKLE	MD80	49943	C-GNDF	DC-8	45619
C-GIAX	CRJ7	10026	C-GJIZ	CRJ	7563	C-GKLJ	MD80	53467	C-GNDG	B737	21719
C-GIAX	CRJ7	10056	C-GJJC	B767	27206	C-GKLK	MD80	53124	C-GNDG	B737	22054
C-GIAZ	CRJ7	10027	C-GJJC	CRJ	7531	C-GKLN	MD80	53486	C-GNDL	B737	21186
C-GIAZ	CRJ7	10054	C-GJJG	CRJ	7538	C-GKLQ	MD80	53487	C-GNDM	B737	22074
C-GIAZ	CRJ7	10057	C-GJJH	CRJ	7539	C-GKLR	MD80	53469	C-GNDR	B737	22075
C-GIBG	CRJ7	10028	C-GJJP	CRJ	7553	C-GKMV	MD80	49793	(C-GNDS)	B737	20345
C-GIBG	CRJ7	10058	C-GJKF	B727	21042	C-GKNW	A319	1805	C-GNDS	B737	21518
C-GIBH	CRJ7	10029	C-GJLH	CRJ	7546	C-GKOB	A319	1853	C-GNDU	B737	22877
C-GIBH	CRJ7	10059	C-GJLI	CRJ	7549	C-GKOC	A319	1886	C-GNDW	B737	21694
C-GIBH	CRJ7	10088	C-GJLK	CRJ	7551	C-GKOD	A320	1864	C-GNDX	B737	20911
C-GIBI	CRJ7	10030	C-GJLL	CRJ	7552	C-GKOE	A320	1874	C-GNJA	CRJ	8004
C-GIBI	CRJ7	10089	C-GJLN	B737	19594	C-GKOH	A321	0674	C-GNJZ	CRJ9	15052
C-GIBJ	CRJ7	10031	C-GJLQ	CRJ	7559	C-GKOI	A321	0675	C-GNKF	B727	20839
C-GIBJ	CRJ7	10060	C-GJLZ	CRJ7	10103	C-GKOJ	A321	0684	C-GNLN	B737	23050
C-GIBK	CRJ7	10061	C-GJOT	CRJ	7575	C-GKOL	A340	445	C-GNPW	B737	22159
C-GIBL	CRJ7	10032	C-GJPW	B737	21713	C-GKOM	A340	464	C-GNVC	CRJ	7519
C-GIBL	CRJ7	10062	C-GJQZ	CRJ	7591	C-GKPW	B737	21819	C-GNVX	146	E1010
C-GIBL	CRJ7	10091	C-GJSZ	CRJ	7588	C-GKTS	A330	111	C-GNVY	146	E1011
C-GIBN	CRJ7	10033	C-GJTA	A319	1673	C-GKWD	A310	481	C-GNWD	B737	19743
C-GIBN	CRJ7	10063	C-GJTC	A319	1668	C-GKWJ	737NG	34151	C-GNWI	B737	21066
C-GIBO	CRJ7	10064	C-GJUI	CRJ7	10018	(C-GKYB)	A319	1612	C-GNWM	B737	21067
C-GIBQ	CRJ7	10035	C-GJUK	A319	1598	C-GKZA	A319	1598	C-GNXB	B757	24772
C-GIBQ	CRJ7	10065	C-GJUL	A320	0427	C-GKZA	F.100	11403	C-GNXC	B757	24260
C-GIBR	CRJ7	10036	C-GJUM	A320	0579	C-GKZB	F.100	11352	C-GNXH	B747	20402
C-GIBR	CRJ7	10066	C-GJUP	A320	0645	(C-GKZC)	A319	1625	C-GNXI	B757	24367
C-GIBT	CRJ7	10037	C-GJUQ	A320	0671	C-GKZC	F.100	11340	C-GNXN	B757	22206
C-GIBT	CRJ7	10067	C-GJUU	A320	0409	C-GKZD	F.100	11395	C-GNXU	B757	24543
C-GIBT	CRJ7	10138	C-GJVI	CRJ	7584	C-GKZE	F.100	11359	C-GOAF	737NG	29883
C-GICB	CRJ7	10038	C-GJVS	A319	1718	C-GKZF	F.100	11361	C-GOEV	B757	29943
C-GICB	CRJ7	10068	C-GJVT	A320	1719	C-GKZG	F.100	11428	C-GOFA	B727	18815
C-GICD	A300	100	C-GJVX	A321	1726	C-GKZH	F.100	11360	C-GOJA	CRJ	8009
C-GICL	CRJ7	10039	C-GJVY	A319	1742	C-GKZJ	F.100	11396	C-GOJZ	CRJ9	15053
C-GICL	CRJ7	10069	C-GJWD	A310	475	C-GKZK	F.100	11369	C-GOKF	B727	20162
C-GICL	CRJ7	10099	C-GJWD	A321	1748	C-GKZL	F.100	11368	C-GOOG	B757	24292
C-GICL	CRJ9	15085	C-GJWE	A319	1756	C-GKZM	F.100	11408	C-GOOZ	B757	25593
C-GICN	CRJ7	10040	C-GJWF	A319	1765	C-GKZP	F.100	11406	C-GOPW	B737	22160
C-GICN	CRJ7	10070	C-GJWI	A321	1772	C-GKZS	F.100	11367	C-GPAT	A310	597
C-GICP	CRJ7	10041	C-GJWN	A321	1783	C-GKZU	F.100	11404	C-GPBJ	146	E1063
C-GICP	CRJ7	10071	C-GJWO	A321	1811	C-GKZV	F.100	11397	C-GPNL	F.100	11301
C-GICR	A300	183	C-GJWS	737NG	34152	C-GKZW	F.100	11437	C-GPPW	B737	22264
C-GIDJ	CRJ	7478	C-GJYV	CRJ	7622	C-GKZX	F.100	11434	C-GPTS	A330	480
C-GIES	L1011	193L-1064	C-GJYW	CRJ	7625	C-GLAT	A310	588	C-GPWA	B767	22683
C-GIFE	L1011	193L-1079	C-GJYX	CRJ	7629	C-GLBW	737NG	30671	C-GPWB	B767	22684
C-GIGH	CRJ	7486	C-GJZA	CRJ	7500	C-GLCA	B767	25120	C-GPWC	B737	22416
C-GIGJ	CRJ7	10086	C-GJZB	CRJ	7740	C-GLCR	F.28	11105	(C-GPWD)	A310	504
C-GIHG	CRJ	7494	C-GJZD	CRJ	7544	C-GLIV	CRJ	7316	C-GPWG	A320	0174
C-GIHJ	CRJ	7493	C-GJZF	CRJ	7545	C-GLJZ	CRJ9	15051	C-GPWG	B737	23498
C-GIKF	B727	20772	C-GJZF	CRJ	7624	C-GLKF	B727	21118	C-GPWS	737NG	34284
C-GIPW	B737	21712	C-GJZG	CRJ	7561	C-GLMC	B767	27205	C-GPZA	CRJ	7862
C-GIQL	CRJ	7514	C-GJZJ	CRJ	7553	C-GLPW	B737	22086	C-GQBA	B737	22072
C-GISU	CRJ7	10023	C-GJZL	CRJ	7572	C-GLSJ	B727	20738	C-GQBA	DC-8	46155
C-GISW	CRJ7	10014	C-GJZN	CRJ	7520	(C-GLUS)	B727	20014	C-GQBB	B737	22276
C-GISZ	CRJ7	10015	C-GJZZ	CRJ	7978	C-GLWD	A310	482	C-GQBC	B737	19426
C-GITP	A319	1562	C-GKAK	CRJ	7639	C-GLWS	737NG	32581	C-GQBD	B737	19594
C-GITR	A319	1577	C-GKCO	CRJ7	10040	C-GMCP	B727	22864	C-GQBE	B737	18970
C-GITS	A330	271	C-GKCP	B737	22729	C-GMJA	CRJ	8003	(C-GQBE)	B737	22398
C-GITT	A319	1630	C-GKCR	F.28	11101	C-GMKF	B727	21119	C-GQBF	DC-8	46116
C-GITU	A321	1602	C-GKDI	CRJ	7617	C-GMPG	A320	0428	C-GQBG	B707	17647
C-GITY	A321	1611	C-GKEJ	CRJ	7269	C-GMPW	B737	22087	C-GQBG	DC-8	45860
C-GIUB	A321	1623	C-GKEK	CRJ	7270	C-GMSJ	B727	21266	C-GQBH	B707	17650
C-GIUE	A321	1632	C-GKEM	CRJ	7277	C-GMSX	B727	21673	C-GQBH	B737	22516

Reg	Type	c/n	Reg	Type	c/n	Reg	Type	c/n	Reg	Type	c/n
C-GQBJ	B737	22277	C-GTIZ	F.28	11099	C-GWJO	737NG	33969	C-GZQK	CRJ9	15011
C-GQBP	1-11	BAC.122	C-GTJA	CRJ	7966	C-GWJO	B737	20299	C-GZQL	CRJ9	15012
C-GQBQ	B737	22070	C-GTKF	B727	21580	C-GWJT	B737	21262	C-GZQM	CRJ9	15013
C-GQBR	F.28	11012	C-GTPW	B737	22807	C-GWJU	737NG	34289	C-GZQO	CRJ9	15014
C-GQBS	B737	21231	C-GTSB	L1011	193T-1122	C-GWJU	B737	21117	C-GZQP	CRJ9	15015
C-GQBS	F.28	11013	C-GTSD	A310	547	C-GWKF	B727	21270	C-GZQQ	CRJ9	15016
C-GQBT	B737	21719	C-GTSE	B757	25488	(C-GWPW)	B737	22056	C-GZQR	CRJ9	15017
C-GQBV	1-11	BAC.123	C-GTSF	A310	472	C-GWPW	B737	23283	C-GZQT	CRJ9	15069
(C-GQBV)	B737	22277	C-GTSF	B757	25491	(C-GWSA)	737NG	32767	C-GZQV	CRJ9	15070
C-GQCA	A320	0210	C-GTSH	A310	599	C-GWSA	737NG	34153	C-GZSQ	CRJ	7717
C-GQCA	B737	22415	C-GTSI	A310	595	C-GWSB	737NG	34285	C-GZSQ	CRJ	7866
C-GQCP	B737	22865	C-GTSJ	B757	24772	C-GWSE	737NG	33379	C-GZUC	CRJ7	10078
C-GQDT	B737	21719	C-GTSK	B757	24367	C-GWSH	737NG	29886	C-GZUC	CRJ7	10129
C-GQJA	CRJ	7963	C-GTSK	L1011	193E-1021	C-GWSI	737NG	34286	C-GZUD	CRJ7	10079
C-GQKF	B727	21265	C-GTSN	B757	24543	C-GWSJ	737NG	34621	C-GZUJ	CRJ	7881
C-GQPW	B737	22265	C-GTSP	L1011	293B-1242	C-GWSK	737NG	34287	C-GZUM	B767	27135
C-GQWJ	737NG	35505	C-GTSQ	L1011	293B-1243	C-GWSL	737NG	34633	C-GZUR	CRJ	7732
C-GQWJ	B737	21769	C-GTSR	B757	26330	(C-GWWJ)	737NG	35505	(C-GZWS)	737NG	32768
C-GRCP	B737	21397	C-GTSR	L1011	293B-1239	C-GWWW	CRJ	8057	C-GZWS	737NG	32770
C-GRJJ	CRJ	7004	C-GTSU	B757	25268	C-GXBB	A320	0389			
C-GRJN	CRJ	7005	C-GTSV	B757	24260	C-GXCP	B737	22640			
C-GRJO	CRJ	7006	C-GTSV	B757	25622	C-GXFA	B727	20938	Chile		
C-GRJW	CRJ	7010	C-GTSX	A310	527	C-GXJA	CRJ	8017			
C-GRMU	B727	21055	C-GTSX	L1011	193N-1094	C-GXKF	B727	21663	CC-	A320	3280
C-GRNH	CRJ9	15001	C-GTSY	A310	447	C-GXPW	B737	20521	(CC-)	B707	20547
C-GRNT	146	E2140	C-GTSY	L1011	193A-1037	C-GXRA	B727	21516	(CC-)	B727	20217
C-GRNU	146	E2139	C-GTSZ	L1011	193P-1103	C-GXRB	DC-10	46976	(CC-)	B737	21665
C-GRNV	146	E2133	C-GTUK	B737	23049	C-GXRC	DC-10	46978	(CC-)	B767	24948
C-GRNX	146	E2130	C-GTUU	F.28	11006	C-GXRD	B747	21517	CC-BIN	B737	22703
C-GRNY	146	E2115	C-GTWS	737NG	32883	C-GXTU	CRJ	7789	CC-CAF	B707	19435
C-GRNZ	146	E2106	C-GUBA	B757	32446	C-GXWJ	737NG	35570	CC-CAG	B727	19811
C-GRPW	B737	22266	C-GUEW	A320	1961	C-GXWJ	B737	21766	CC-CAL	B727	22433
C-GRWS	737NG	32881	C-GUJA	CRJ	8011	C-GYCR	F.28	11050	CC-CAL	B737	23635
(C-GRWW)	DC-8	45820	C-GUJC	B727	21979	C-GYFA	B727	21234	CC-CAN	B727	19527
C-GRYA	A310	448	C-GUPW	B737	22873	C-GYKF	B727	20551	CC-CAP	B737	22027
C-GRYC	B727	21055	C-GUWJ	B737	20807	C-GYNA	B727	22039	CC-CAQ	B727	19812
C-GRYD	A310	435	C-GUWJ	B737	21694	C-GYNB	B727	22040	CC-CAR	DC-8	45976
C-GRYI	A310	432	C-GUWS	737NG	33378	C-GYNC	B727	22041	CC-CAS	B737	19945
C-GRYK	B757	25593	C-GVAT	A310	485	C-GYND	B727	22042	CC-CAX	B737	45970
C-GRYN	B707	19623	C-GVCH	B727	18853	C-GYNE	B727	22345	CC-CBJ	B767	27613
C-GRYO	B707	18746	C-GVFA	B727	20475	C-GYNF	B727	22346	CC-CCE	B707	18748
C-GRYO	B727	20710	C-GVJB	B737	20365	C-GYNG	B727	22347	CC-CCG	B707	18462
C-GRYO	B757	24118	C-GVJC	B737	19598	C-GYNH	B727	22348	CC-CCK	B707	19443
C-GRYP	B727	20766	C-GVKI	A330	357	C-GYNI	B727	22349	CC-CCO	SE210	140
C-GRYQ	B727	22574	C-GVNY	A320	0279	C-GYNJ	B727	22350	CC-CCP	SE210	164
C-GRYR	B727	21056	C-GVPW	B737	22874	C-GYNK	B727	22621	CC-CCQ	SE210	160
C-GRYU	B757	24235	C-GVRD	B737	20956	C-GYNL	B727	22622	CC-CCX	B707	18584
C-GRYU	L1011	193B-1221	C-GVRE	B737	22396	C-GYNM	B727	22623	CC-CCZ	B767	24849
C-GRYV	A310	440	C-GVRJ	CRJ	7003	C-GYNR	F.100	11265	CC-CDB	B737	22120
C-GRYY	A320	0189	C-GVWJ	737NG	36421	(C-GYPW)	B737	23707	CC-CDE	B737	22744
C-GRYY	B737	22275	C-GVWJ	B737	20563	C-GYVM	CRJ	7785	CC-CDG	B737	23024
C-GRYZ	B727	20550	C-GVWJ	B737	21768	C-GYWJ	737NG	32772	CC-CDH	B737	22121
C-GRYZ	B757	24119	C-GVXA	A320	0397	C-GYXS	CRJ	7761	CC-CDH	B767	24716
C-GSAT	A310	600	C-GVXB	A320	0409	C-GYYA	CRJ	7772	CC-CDI	B707	19517
C-GSCA	B767	25121	C-GVXC	A320	0427	C-GZCD	A320	0379	CC-CDJ	B767	24762
C-GSHI	B727	20055	C-GVXD	A320	0579	C-GZFC	CRJ	7796	CC-CDL	B737	22122
C-GSPW	B737	22618	C-GVXE	A320	0645	C-GZFH	CRJ	7802	CC-CDL	B767	24947
C-GSUW	CRJ	8047	C-GVXF	A320	0671	C-GZGP	CRJ	7813	CC-CDM	B767	26261
C-GSWJ	B737	21593	C-GVXH	A320	0132	C-GZGX	CRJ	7489	CC-CDN	B707	18747
C-GSWQ	DC-8	45387	C-GWAZ	737NG	32763	C-GZIA	A340	395	CC-CDP	B767	27597
C-GSWX	DC-8	45388	C-GWBF	737NG	32757	C-GZJA	CRJ	8018	CC-CDS	DC-8	45996
C-GTAH	F.28	11082	C-GWBJ	737NG	32754	C-GZJA	CRJ7	10091	CC-CDU	DC-8	45997
C-GTAI	B707	19434	C-GWBL	737NG	34154	C-GZJY	CRJ	7690	CC-CDX	B767	23280
C-GTAJ	B737	24344	C-GWBN	737NG	34155	C-GZJZ	CRJ	7700	CC-CEA	B707	18926
C-GTAN	F.28	11163	C-GWBT	737NG	32755	C-GZKA	CRJ	7704	CC-CEA	B737	22743
C-GTAQ	B737	20956	C-GWBX	737NG	34156	C-GZKC	CRJ	7705	CC-CEB	B707	19000
C-GTAR	B737	20223	C-GWCM	737NG	32756	C-GZKD	CRJ	7706	CC-CEB	B767	26327
C-GTBB	B757	32447	C-GWCN	737NG	34157	C-GZLM	CRJ	7846	CC-CEE	B737	22407
C-GTDB	A320	0525	C-GWCQ	737NG	35111	C-GZMM	B767	27136	CC-CEF	B767	24973
C-GTDC	A320	0496	C-GWCT	737NG	35112	C-GZNA	B767	27957	CC-CEI	B707	20021
C-GTDG	A320	1571	C-GWCY	737NG	35113	C-GZNC	B767	26263	CC-CEI	B737	20219
C-GTDH	A320	1605	C-GWEN	E190	19000010	C-GZNF	CRJ	7851	CC-CEJ	146	E2059
C-GTDK	A320	0338	C-GWGP	B727	19404	(C-GZPW)	B737	23708	CC-CEJ	B707	19693
C-GTDL	A320	0476	C-GWGT	B727	19405	C-GZQA	CRJ9	15003	CC-CEK	B707	19374
C-GTDL	B757	24543	C-GWGV	B727	19406	C-GZQB	CRJ9	15004	CC-CEK	B767	26329
C-GTDM	A320	0429	C-GWJE	737NG	35078	C-GZQC	CRJ9	15005	CC-CEL	B767	26204
C-GTDO	A320	0230	C-GWJE	B737	20588	C-GZQE	CRJ9	15006	CC-CEN	146	E2064
C-GTDP	A320	1780	C-GWJF	737NG	32766	C-GZQF	CRJ9	15007	CC-CEN	B767	26265
C-GTDS	A319	1901	C-GWJG	737NG	35504	C-GZQG	CRJ9	15008	CC-CER	B707	18711
C-GTDT	A319	1884	C-GWJG	B737	20670	C-GZQI	CRJ9	15009	CC-CET	146	E2061
C-GTDX	A319	1846	C-GWJK	B737	19743	C-GZQJ	CRJ9	15010	CC-CEU	B767	25403
C-GTEO	F.28	11991	C-GWJK	B737	21206				CC-CEX	B767	24716

Reg	Type	Serial
CC-CEY	B767	24762
CC-CEY	B767	24947
CC-CFD	B727	19813
CC-CFD	B737	22761
CC-CFE	B727	19814
CC-CFG	B727	18796
CC-CGD	B727	19532
CC-CGM	B707	17928
CC-CGM	B737	22256
CC-CGN	B767	26544
CC-CHC	B727	19251
CC-CHJ	B737	22602
CC-CHK	B737	22589
CC-CHR	B737	21792
CC-CHS	B737	21802
CC-CHU	B737	21927
(CC-CIJ)	B737	21003
CC-CIM	B737	22340
CC-CIO	B767	25132
CC-CIW	B727	18323
CC-CIY	B737	22792
CC-CJK	B737	22856
CC-CJM	B737	20212
CC-CJM	B727	22857
CC-CJN	B737	20214
CC-CJN	DC-10	46712
CC-CJO	B737	19059
CC-CJO	B737	19616
(CC-CJP)	B737	19712
CC-CJP	B737	22762
CC-CJP	B767	24150
CC-CJQ	B737	20215
CC-CJR	B767	24448
CC-CJS	DC-10	46954
CC-CJT	DC-10	46950
CC-CJU	B767	23623
CC-CJV	B767	23624
CC-CJW	B737	22397
CC-CJZ	B737	20913
CC-CLB	B727	19196
CC-CLD	B737	21960
(CC-CLE)	B737	19606
CC-CLF	B737	19609
CC-CLJ	B727	18428
CC-CLZ	B727	18445
CC-CLZ	B767	24762
CC-CML	B767	28206
CC-COC	A320	1304
CC-COD	A320	1332
CC-COE	A320	1351
CC-COF	A320	1355
CC-COG	A320	1491
CC-COH	A320	1512
CC-COI	A320	1526
CC-COK	A320	1548
CC-COL	A320	1568
CC-COM	A320	1626
CC-COO	A320	1854
CC-COP	A320	1858
CC-COQ	A320	1877
CC-COT	A320	1903
CC-COU	A319	2089
CC-COX	A319	2096
CC-COY	A319	2295
CC-COZ	A319	2304
CC-CPE	A319	2321
CC-CPF	A319	2572
CC-CPI	A319	2585
CC-CPJ	A319	2845
CC-CPL	A319	2858
CC-CPM	A319	2864
CC-CPO	A319	2872
CC-CPQ	A319	2886
CC-CPV	B727	22433
CC-CPX	A319	2887
CC-CQA	A340	359
CC-CQC	A340	363
CC-CQE	A340	429
CC-CQF	A340	442
CC-CQG	A340	167
CC-CQK	A319	2892
CC-CQL	A319	2894

Reg	Type	Serial
CC-CQQ	B737	22115
CC-CQR	B737	22128
CC-CQS	B737	22127
CC-CQT	B737	22124
CC-CQU	B737	22126
(CC-CRA)	B737	22113
CC-CRG	B767	25865
CC-CRH	B767	25864
CC-CRI	B737	19616
CC-CRP	B737	22134
CC-CRQ	B737	22135
CC-CRR	B737	22114
CC-CRS	B737	22139
CC-CRT	B767	27615
CC-CSD	B737	20417
CC-CSF	B737	19945
CC-CSH	B737	20632
CC-CSI	B737	20633
CC-CSK	B727	21690
CC-CSK	B737	20562
CC-CSL	B737	20223
CC-CSP	B737	20808
CC-CSW	B727	21655
CC-CSW	B737	23002
CC-CTB	B737	23481
(CC-CTD)	B737	20586
CC-CTD	B737	23117
CC-CTH	B737	22636
CC-CTI	B737	22516
CC-CTJ	B737	22276
CC-CTK	B737	22402
(CC-CTM)	B737	20582
(CC-CTM)	B737	20583
(CC-CTO)	B727	21861
(CC-CTO)	B737	20583
CC-CTO	B737	20586
CC-CTU	B737	20582
(CC-CTW)	B727	21861
CC-CTW	B737	22697
CC-CTX	B737	22698
CC-CUE	B707	20069
CC-CVA	A318	3001
CC-CVA	B737	19424
CC-CVB	A318	3030
CC-CVB	B737	20221
CC-CVC	B737	21596
CC-CVD	B737	21840
CC-CVF	A318	3062
CC-CVG	B737	22743
CC-CVH	A318	3214
CC-CVH	B737	23024
CC-CVI	B737	22367
CC-CVJ	B737	22736
CC-CVN	A318	3216
CC-CWF	B767	34626
CC-CWG	B767	34629
CC-CWH	B767	34628
CC-CWN	B767	35229
CC-CWV	B767	35230
CC-CWY	B767	35231
CC-CXC	B767	36710
CC-CYA	B707	19530
CC-CYB	B707	20022
CC-CYC	B737	21131
CC-CYD	B737	21219
CC-CYE	B737	23787
CC-CYF	1-11	033
CC-CYG	B757	25044
CC-CYH	B757	25131
CC-CYI	1-11	035
CC-CYJ	B737	25373
CC-CYK	B737	21445
(CC-CYK)	B737	26293
CC-CYL	1-11	040
CC-CYM	1-11	039
CC-CYN	B737	21231
CC-CYO	B707	19374
CC-CYP	B737	22632
CC-CYQ	DC-8	45810
CC-CYR	B737	20195
CC-CYS	B737	21184
CC-CYT	B737	21112

Reg	Type	Serial
CC-CYV	B737	23148
CC-CYW	B737	20913
CC-CZB	A320	0990
CC-CZF	L1011	193E-1058
CC-CZK	B737	21804
CC-CZL	B737	21808
CC-CZM	B737	22027
CC-CZN	B737	22029
CC-CZO	B737	22030
CC-CZP	B737	22031
CC-CZR	L1011	193E-1069
CC-CZS	L1011	193E-1058
CC-CZT	B767	29228
CC-CZU	B767	29229
CC-CZW	B767	29227
CC-CZX	B767	29881
CC-CZY	B767	30780
CC-CZZ	B767	25756
CC-PBZ	B707	19374
CC-PFL	B727	22433

Russia

Reg	Type	Serial
CCCP-L5400	TU104	unknown
CCCP-L5411	TU104	1881301
"CCCP-L5412"	TU104	021905
CCCP-L5412	TU104	5350001
"CCCP-L5412"	TU104	921102
CCCP-L5413	TU104	6350002
CCCP-L5414	TU104	6350101
CCCP-L5415	TU104	6350102
CCCP-L5416	TU104	6350103
CCCP-L5417	TU104	6350105
CCCP-L5418	TU104	6350201
CCCP-L5419	TU104	66600101
CCCP-L5420	TU104	66600102
CCCP-L5421	TU104	66600201
CCCP-L5422	TU104	66600202
CCCP-L5423	TU104	66600203
CCCP-L5424	TU104	76600301
CCCP-L5425	TU104	76600303
CCCP-L5426	TU104	76600402
CCCP-L5427	TU104	76600401
CCCP-L5428	TU104	76600403
CCCP-L5429	TU104	76600501
CCCP-L5430	TU104	76600502
CCCP-L5431	TU104	76600603
CCCP-L5432	TU104	86600701
CCCP-L5433	TU104	86600702
CCCP-L5434	TU104	7350202
CCCP-L5435	TU104	7350501
CCCP-L5436	TU104	7350502
CCCP-L5437	TU104	7350203
CCCP-L5438	TU104	7350204
CCCP-L5439	TU104	7350205
CCCP-L5440	TU104	7350301
CCCP-L5441	TU104	7350302
CCCP-L5442	TU104	7350303
CCCP-L5443	TU104	7350304
CCCP-L5444	TU104	8350305
CCCP-L5445	TU104	8350401
CCCP-L5453	TU104	86600703
CCCP-L5457	TU104	96601801
CCCP-L5458	TU104	86600801
CCCP-L5511	TU110	?
CCCP-L5512	TU110	?
CCCP-L5513	TU110	?
CCCP-L5600	TU110	?
CCCP-1967	YAK40	97.0100
CCCP-1974	YAK42	?
CCCP-1975	YAK42	?
CCCP-1976	YAK42	?
CCCP-1977	YAK42	?
CCCP-06146	IL76	0013434018
CCCP-06153	IL62	30002
CCCP-06156	IL62	30001
CCCP-06170	IL62	40004
CCCP-06176	IL62	30003
CCCP-06185	TU124	1350304
CCCP-06188	IL76	093421635
CCCP-06195	TU104	021502

Reg	Type	Serial
CCCP-06300	IL62	40005
CCCP-10985	YAK42	?
CCCP-11363	IL76	1023411363
CCCP-19661	YAK40	019
(CCCP-19671)	YAK40	97.0100
CCCP-19672	YAK40	97.0200
CCCP-19673	YAK40	97.0300
CCCP-19674	YAK40	97.0400
CCCP-19675	YAK40	9820500
CCCP-19676	YAK40	9820600
CCCP-19681	YAK40	9820700
CCCP-19774	AN7x	004
CCCP-19793	AN7x	003
CCCP-19795	AN7x	005
CCCP-21500	YAK40	9741356
CCCP-21501	YAK40	9741756
CCCP-21502	YAK40	9831858
CCCP-21504	YAK40	9831758
CCCP-21505	YAK40	9830159
CCCP-21506	YAK40	9840259
CCCP-36580	TU110	?
CCCP-36582	TU110	?
CCCP-42300	YAK42	11820101
CCCP-42302	YAK42	427401004
CCCP-42303	YAK42	.
CCCP-42304	YAK42	11820201
CCCP-42305	YAK42	118..01202?
CCCP-42306	YAK42	11840202
CCCP-42307	YAK42	11..0302
CCCP-42308	YAK42	11040303
CCCP-42309	YAK42	01005
CCCP-42310	YAK42	11040403
CCCP-42311	YAK42	11940103
CCCP-42312	YAK42	11940203
CCCP-42313	YAK42	11030503
CCCP-42314	YAK42	22204245134
CCCP-42316	YAK42	2202030
CCCP-42317	YAK42	2202039
CCCP-42318	TU104	5350001
CCCP-42318	YAK42	3402051
CCCP-42319	TU104	6350002
CCCP-42319	YAK42	3402062
(CCCP-42320)	TU104	6350101
CCCP-42320	YAK42	1302075
(CCCP-42321)	TU104	6350102
CCCP-42321	YAK42	3402088
CCCP-42322	TU104	6350103
CCCP-42322	YAK42	3402108
(CCCP-42323)	TU104	6350105
CCCP-42323	YAK42	3402116
CCCP-42324	TU104	6350201
CCCP-42324	YAK42	1402125
(CCCP-42325)	TU104	66600101
CCCP-42325	YAK42	4402148
CCCP-42326	TU104	66600102
CCCP-42326	YAK42	4402154
CCCP-42327	TU104	66600201
CCCP-42327	YAK42	4402161
CCCP-42328	TU104	66600202
CCCP-42328	YAK42	1505058
CCCP-42329	TU104	66600203
CCCP-42329	YAK42	2505093
CCCP-42330	TU104	76600301
CCCP-42330	YAK42	2505122
CCCP-42331	TU104	76600303
CCCP-42331	YAK42	4505128
CCCP-42332	TU104	76600402
CCCP-42332	YAK42	4505135
CCCP-42333	TU104	76600401
CCCP-42333	YAK42	2606156
CCCP-42334	TU104	76600403
CCCP-42334	YAK42	2606164
CCCP-42335	TU104	76600501
CCCP-42335	YAK42	2606204
CCCP-42336	TU104	76600502
CCCP-42336	YAK42	2606220
CCCP-42337	TU104	76600603
CCCP-42337	YAK42	3606235
CCCP-42338	TU104	86600701
CCCP-42338	YAK42	3606256
CCCP-42339	TU104	86600702
CCCP-42339	YAK42	4606267

```
CCCP-42340 TU104 7350202      CCCP-42381 YAK42 2014576      CCCP-42440 TU104 920902      CCCP-42536 YAK42 22204251823
CCCP-42340 YAK42 4606270      CCCP-42382 TU104 8350602      CCCP-42441 TU104 920903      CCCP-42537 YAK42 22204254019
CCCP-42341 TU104 7350501      CCCP-42382 YAK42 2016196      CCCP-42442 TU104 920904      CCCP-42538 YAK42 11130404
CCCP-42341 YAK42 1706292      CCCP-42383 TU104 8350603      CCCP-42443 TU104 920905?     CCCP-42539 YAK42 11140504
CCCP-42342 TU104 7350502      CCCP-42383 YAK42 2016201      CCCP-42444 TU104 921001      CCCP-42540 YAK42 11140604
CCCP-42342 YAK42 1706302      CCCP-42384 TU104 8350604      CCCP-42445 TU104 921002      CCCP-42541 YAK42 11140704
CCCP-42343 TU104 7350203      CCCP-42384 YAK42 3016230      CCCP-42446 TU104 921003      CCCP-42542 YAK42 11140804
CCCP-42343 YAK42 1708285      CCCP-42385 TU104 8350605      CCCP-42447 TU104 921004      CCCP-42543 YAK42 11250904
CCCP-42344 TU104 7350204      CCCP-42385 YAK42 3016309      CCCP-42448 TU104 921005      CCCP-42544 YAK42 11151004
CCCP-42344 YAK42 2708295      CCCP-42386 TU104 8350701      CCCP-42449 TU104 921101      CCCP-42549 YAK42 11040105
CCCP-42345 TU104 7350205      CCCP-42386 YAK42 4016310      CCCP-42450 TU104 921102      CCCP-42550 YAK42 11140205
CCCP-42345 YAK42 2708304      CCCP-42387 TU104 8350702      CCCP-42451 TU104 96601603     CCCP-42551 YAK42 11140305
CCCP-42346 TU104 8350402      CCCP-42387 YAK42 4016436      CCCP-42452 TU104 96601701     CCCP-42644 YAK42 4914090
CCCP-42346 YAK42 3708311      CCCP-42388 TU104 8350703      CCCP-42453 TU104 96601702     CCCP-45000 TU124 0000
CCCP-42347 TU104 7350301      CCCP-42388 YAK42 4016510      CCCP-42454 TU104 96601703     CCCP-45001 TU124 0350001
CCCP-42347 YAK42 3711322      CCCP-42389 TU104 8350704      CCCP-42455 TU104 9350904      CCCP-45002 TU124 0350101
CCCP-42348 TU104 7350302      CCCP-42389 YAK42 4016542      CCCP-42456 TU104 9350905      CCCP-45003 TU124 0350102?
CCCP-42348 YAK42 3711342      CCCP-42390 TU104 8350705      CCCP-42457 TU104 96601801     CCCP-45004 TU124 0350201
(CCCP-42349)TU104 7350303     CCCP-42390 YAK42 4016557      CCCP-42458 TU104 96601802     CCCP-45005 TU124 0350202
CCCP-42349 YAK42 .7113..      CCCP-42391 TU104 9350801      CCCP-42459 TU104 06601901     CCCP-45006 TU124 1350301
CCCP-42350 TU104 7350304      CCCP-42392 TU104 9350802      CCCP-42460 TU104 06601902     CCCP-45007 TU124 1350302
CCCP-42350 YAK42 4711372      CCCP-42393 TU104 9350803      CCCP-42461 TU104 06601903     CCCP-45008 TU124 1350303
CCCP-42351 TU104 8350305      CCCP-42394 TU104 9350804      CCCP-42462 TU104 06602001     CCCP-45009 TU124 1350304
CCCP-42351 YAK42 1811379      CCCP-42395 TU104 9350805      CCCP-42463 TU104 06602002     CCCP-45010 TU124 1350305
CCCP-42352 TU104 8350401      CCCP-42396 TU104 9350901      CCCP-42464 TU104 06602003     CCCP-45011 TU124 1350401
CCCP-42352 YAK42 1811395      CCCP-42397 TU104 9350902      CCCP-42465 TU104 021103      CCCP-45012 TU124 1350402
CCCP-42353 TU104 86600703     CCCP-42398 TU104 9350903      CCCP-42466 TU104 021104      CCCP-45013 TU124 1350403
CCCP-42353 YAK42 4711396      CCCP-42399 TU104 820101       CCCP-42467 TU104 021105      CCCP-45014 TU124 1350404
CCCP-42354 TU104 86600801     CCCP-42400 TU104 820102       CCCP-42468 TU104 021201      CCCP-45015 TU124 1350405
CCCP-42354 YAK42 4711397      CCCP-42401 TU104 820103       CCCP-42469 TU104 021202      CCCP-45016 TU124 1350501
CCCP-42355 YAK42 4711399      CCCP-42401 YAK42 1116567      CCCP-42470 TU104 021203      CCCP-45017 TU124 1350502
CCCP-42356 TU104 86600802     CCCP-42402 TU104 820104       CCCP-42471 TU104 021204      "CCCP-45017"TU124 7350610
CCCP-42356 YAK42 2811400      CCCP-42402 YAK42 2116583      CCCP-42472 TU104 021205      CCCP-45018 TU124 2350503
CCCP-42357 TU104 86600803     CCCP-42403 TU104 820105       CCCP-42473 TU104 021301      CCCP-45019 TU124 2350504
CCCP-42357 YAK42 2811408      CCCP-42403 YAK42 2116588      CCCP-42474 TU104 021302      CCCP-45020 TU124 2350505
CCCP-42358 TU104 86600901     CCCP-42404 TU104 820201       CCCP-42475 TU104 021303      CCCP-45021 TU124 2350701
CCCP-42358 YAK42 2811413      CCCP-42404 YAK42 2116617      CCCP-42476 TU104 021304      CCCP-45022 TU124 2350702
CCCP-42359 TU104 86600902     CCCP-42405 TU104 820202       CCCP-42477 TU104 021305      CCCP-45023 TU124 2350703
CCCP-42359 YAK42 3811417      CCCP-42405 YAK42 3116624      CCCP-42478 TU104 021401      CCCP-45024 TU124 2350704
CCCP-42360 TU104 86600903     CCCP-42406 TU104 820203       CCCP-42479 TU104 021402      CCCP-45025 TU124 2350705
CCCP-42360 YAK42 3811421      CCCP-42406 YAK42 4116683      CCCP-42480 TU104 021403      CCCP-45026 TU124 2350801
CCCP-42361 TU104 86601001     CCCP-42407 TU104 820204       CCCP-42481 TU104 021404      CCCP-45027 TU124 2350802
CCCP-42361 YAK42 3811427      CCCP-42407 YAK42 4116690      CCCP-42482 TU104 021405      CCCP-45028 TU124 2350803
CCCP-42362 TU104 86601002     CCCP-42408 TU104 820205       CCCP-42483 TU104 021501      CCCP-45029 TU124 2350804
CCCP-42362 YAK42 4811431      CCCP-42408 YAK42 4116698      CCCP-42485 TU104 021503      CCCP-45030 TU124 2350805
CCCP-42363 TU104 86601003     CCCP-42409 TU104 820301       CCCP-42486 TU104 021504      CCCP-45031 TU124 2350901
CCCP-42363 YAK42 4811438      CCCP-42409 YAK42 1216709      CCCP-42487 TU104 021505      CCCP-45032 TU124 2350902
CCCP-42364 TU104 86601101     CCCP-42410 TU104 820302       CCCP-42488 TU104 021601      CCCP-45033 TU124 2350903
CCCP-42364 YAK42 4811442      CCCP-42410 YAK42 1219029      CCCP-42489 TU104 021602      CCCP-45034 TU124 2350904
CCCP-42365 TU104 86601102     CCCP-42411 TU104 820303       CCCP-42490 TU104 021603      CCCP-45035 TU124 2350905
CCCP-42365 YAK42 4811447      CCCP-42411 YAK42 1219043      CCCP-42491 TU104 021604      CCCP-45036 TU124 2351001
CCCP-42366 TU104 86601103     CCCP-42412 TU104 820304       CCCP-42492 TU104 021605      CCCP-45037 TU124 2351002
CCCP-42366 YAK42 4814047      CCCP-42412 YAK42 2219055      CCCP-42493 TU104 021701      CCCP-45038 TU124 3351003
CCCP-42367 TU104 86601201     CCCP-42413 TU104 820305       CCCP-42494 TU104 021702      CCCP-45039 TU124 3351004?
CCCP-42367 YAK42 1914133      CCCP-42414 TU104 820401       CCCP-42495 TU104 021703      CCCP-45040 TU124 3351005
CCCP-42368 TU104 86601202     CCCP-42415 TU104 920402       CCCP-42496 TU104 021704      CCCP-45041 TU124 3351101
CCCP-42368 YAK42 2914166      CCCP-42415 YAK42 2219089      CCCP-42497 TU104 021705      CCCP-45042 TU124 3351102
CCCP-42369 TU104 86601203     CCCP-42416 TU104 920403       CCCP-42498 TU104 021801      CCCP-45043 TU124 3351103
CCCP-42369 YAK42 2914190      CCCP-42416 YAK42 3219102      CCCP-42499 TU104 021802      CCCP-45044 TU124 3351104
CCCP-42370 TU104 86601301     CCCP-42417 TU104 920404       CCCP-42500 TU104 021803      CCCP-45045 TU124 3351105
CCCP-42370 YAK42 2914203      CCCP-42418 TU104 920405       CCCP-42501 TU104 021804      CCCP-45046 TU124 3351201
CCCP-42371 TU104 96601401     CCCP-42419 TU104 920501       CCCP-42502 TU104 021805      CCCP-45047 TU124 3351202
CCCP-42371 YAK42 2914225      CCCP-42420 TU104 920502       CCCP-42503 TU104 021901      CCCP-45048 TU124 3351203
CCCP-42372 TU104 96601402     CCCP-42421 TU104 920503       CCCP-42504 TU104 021902      CCCP-45049 TU124 3351204
CCCP-42372 YAK42 3914266      CCCP-42422 TU104 920504       CCCP-42505 TU104 021903      CCCP-45050 TU124 3351205?
CCCP-42373 TU104 96601403     CCCP-42423 TU104 920505       CCCP-42506 TU104 021904      CCCP-45051 TU124 3351301
CCCP-42373 YAK42 3914323      CCCP-42424 TU104 920601       CCCP-42507 TU104 021905      CCCP-45052 TU124 3351302
CCCP-42374 TU104 96601501     CCCP-42425 TU104 920602       CCCP-42508 TU104 022001      CCCP-45053 TU124 4351303
CCCP-42374 YAK42 3914340      CCCP-42426 TU104 920603       CCCP-42520 YAK42 ?           CCCP-45054 TU124 4351304
CCCP-42375 TU104 96601502     CCCP-42427 TU104 920604       CCCP-42523 YAK42 22204249136 CCCP-45055 TU124 4351305
CCCP-42375 YAK42 4914410      CCCP-42428 TU104 920605       CCCP-42524 YAK42 11030603    CCCP-45056 TU124 4351401
CCCP-42376 TU104 96601503     CCCP-42429 TU104 920701       CCCP-42525 YAK42 11040703    CCCP-45057 TU124 4351402
CCCP-42376 YAK42 4914477      CCCP-42430 TU104 920702       CCCP-42526 YAK42 11040803    CCCP-45058 TU124 4351403
CCCP-42377 TU104 96601601     CCCP-42431 TU104 920703       CCCP-42527 YAK42 11040903    CCCP-45059 TU124 4351404
CCCP-42377 YAK42 1014479      CCCP-42432 TU104 920704       CCCP-42528 YAK42 11041003    CCCP-45060 TU124 4351405
CCCP-42378 TU104 96601602     CCCP-42433 TU104 920705       CCCP-42529 YAK42 11040104    CCCP-45061 TU124 4351406
CCCP-42378 YAK42 1014494      CCCP-42434 TU104 920801       CCCP-42530 YAK42 11120204    CCCP-45062 TU124 4351407
CCCP-42379 TU104 8350403      CCCP-42435 TU104 920802       CCCP-42531 YAK42 11130304    CCCP-45063 TU124 4351408
CCCP-42379 YAK42 1014542      CCCP-42436 TU104 920803       CCCP-42532 YAK42 22204249191 CCCP-45064 TU124 4351409
CCCP-42380 TU104 8350404      CCCP-42437 TU104 920804       CCCP-42533 YAK42 22204249244 CCCP-45065 TU124 4351410
CCCP-42380 YAK42 2014549      CCCP-42438 TU104 920805       CCCP-42534 YAK42 22204251128 CCCP-45066 TU124 4351501
CCCP-42381 TU104 8350601      CCCP-42439 TU104 920901       CCCP-42535 YAK42 22204251536 CCCP-45067 TU124 4351502
```

```
CCCP-45068 TU124 4351506      CCCP-65012 TU134 46175        CCCP-65094 TU134 83.60255     CCCP-65607 TU134 6350104
CCCP-45069 TU124 4351507      CCCP-65013 TU134 46180        CCCP-65095 TU134 60256        CCCP-65608 TU134 38040
CCCP-45070 TU124 4351509      CCCP-65014 TU134 46200        CCCP-65096 TU134 60257        CCCP-65608 TU134 6350105
CCCP-45071 TU124 4351510      CCCP-65015 TU134 48325        CCCP-65097 TU134 60540        CCCP-65609 TU134 46155
CCCP-45072 TU124 5351604      CCCP-65016 TU134 48340        CCCP-65098 TU134 73550815     CCCP-65609 TU134 7350201
CCCP-45073 TU124 5351605      CCCP-65017 TU134 48360        CCCP-65099 TU134 63700        CCCP-65610 TU134 40150
CCCP-45074 TU124 5351606      CCCP-65018 TU134 48365        CCCP-65100 TU134 60258        CCCP-65610 TU134 7350202
CCCP-45075 TU134 0000         CCCP-65019 TU134 48375        CCCP-65101 TU134 60260        CCCP-65611 TU134 3351903
CCCP-45076 TU124 0350001      CCCP-65020 TU134 48380        CCCP-65102 TU134 60267        CCCP-65611 TU134 7350204
CCCP-45076 TU124 0001         CCCP-65021 TU134 48390        CCCP-65103 TU134 60297        CCCP-65612 TU134 3352102
CCCP-45077 TU124 5351608      CCCP-65022 TU134 48395        CCCP-65104 TU134 60301        CCCP-65612 TU134 7350205
CCCP-45078 TU124 5351701      CCCP-65023 TU134 48415        CCCP-65105 TU134 60308        CCCP-65613 TU134 3352106
CCCP-45079 TU124 5351702      CCCP-65024 TU134 48420        CCCP-65106 TU134 60315        CCCP-65613 TU134 8350403
CCCP-45080 TU124 5351703      CCCP-65025 TU134 48450        CCCP-65107 TU134 60328        CCCP-65614 TU134 4352207
CCCP-45081 TU124 5351704      CCCP-65026 TU134 48470        CCCP-65108 TU134 60332        CCCP-65614 TU134 7350302
CCCP-45082 TU124 5351705      CCCP-65027 TU134 48485        CCCP-65109 TU134 60339        CCCP-65615 TU134 4352205
CCCP-45083 TU124 5351706      CCCP-65028 TU134 48490        CCCP-65110 TU134 60343        CCCP-65615 TU134 7350303
CCCP-45084 TU124 5351709      CCCP-65029 TU134 48500        CCCP-65111 TU134 60346        CCCP-65616 TU134 4352206
CCCP-45085 TU124 5351710      CCCP-65030 TU134 48520        CCCP-65112 TU134 60350        CCCP-65616 TU134 7350304
CCCP-45086 TU124 5351801      CCCP-65031 TU134 48530        CCCP-65113 TU134 60380        CCCP-65617 TU134 08068
CCCP-45087 TU124 5351802      CCCP-65032 TU134 48535        CCCP-65114 TU134 60395        CCCP-65617 TU134 8350305
CCCP-45088 TU124 5351803      CCCP-65033 TU134 48540        CCCP-65115 TU134 60405        CCCP-65618 TU134 12095
CCCP-45089 TU124 5351804      CCCP-65034 TU134 63.48565     CCCP-65116 TU134 60420        CCCP-65618 TU134 7350301
CCCP-45090 TU124 5351805      CCCP-65035 TU134 48590        CCCP-65117 TU134 60450        CCCP-65619 TU134 31218
CCCP-45091 TU124 5351806      CCCP-65036 TU134 63.48700     CCCP-65118 TU134 60462        CCCP-65619 TU134 8350401
CCCP-45092 TU124 5351807      CCCP-65037 TU134 48850        CCCP-65119 TU134 60475        CCCP-65620 TU134 35180
CCCP-45093 TU124 5351810      CCCP-65038 TU134 48950        CCCP-65120 TU134 60482        CCCP-65620 TU134 8350402
CCCP-45094 TU124 6351904      CCCP-65039 TU134 49080        CCCP-65121 TU134 60505        CCCP-65621 TU134 48320
CCCP-45095 TU124 8350706      CCCP-65040 TU134 63.49100     CCCP-65122 TU134 60518        CCCP-65621 TU134 8350404
CCCP-45097 TU124 4351503      CCCP-65041 TU134 49200        CCCP-65123 TU134 60525        CCCP-65622 TU134 60495
CCCP-45098 TU124 5351607      CCCP-65042 TU134 49350        CCCP-65124 TU134 60560        CCCP-65622 TU134 8350504
CCCP-45099 TU124 1350303      CCCP-65043 TU134 49400        CCCP-65125 TU134 60575        CCCP-65623 TU134 73.49985
CCCP-45135 TU124 8350707      CCCP-65044 TU134 49450        CCCP-65126 TU134 60588        CCCP-65623 TU134 8350505
CCCP-45146 TU124 4351601      CCCP-65045 TU134 49500        CCCP-65127 TU134 60627        CCCP-65624 TU134 8350601
CCCP-45158 TU124 4351602      CCCP-65046 TU134 49550        CCCP-65128 TU134 60628        CCCP-65625 TU134 83507037
CCCP-45173 TU124 4351603      CCCP-65047 TU134 49600        CCCP-65129 TU134 60630        CCCP-65626 TU134 9350704
CCCP-45199 TU124 5351707      CCCP-65048 TU134 49750        CCCP-65130 TU134 60635        CCCP-65627 TU134 9350803
CCCP-48019 AN225 19530503763  CCCP-65049 TU134 49755        CCCP-65131 TU134 60637        CCCP-65628 TU134 9350809
CCCP-48094 AN225 19530501001? CCCP-65050 TU134 49756        CCCP-65132 TU134 60639        CCCP-65629 TU134 9350810
CCCP-48095 TU124 1350304      CCCP-65051 TU134 49758        CCCP-65133 TU134 60645        CCCP-65630 TU134 9350901
CCCP-48110 YAK40 9230623      CCCP-65052 TU134 49825        CCCP-65134 TU134 60647        CCCP-65631 TU134 9350902
CCCP-48111 YAK40 9211420      CCCP-65053 TU134 49838        CCCP-65135 TU134 60648        CCCP-65632 TU134 9350903
CCCP-48112 YAK40 9211520      CCCP-65054 TU134 49840        CCCP-65136 TU134 60885        CCCP-65633 TU134 9350907
CCCP-58642 AN7x 47010947      CCCP-65055 TU134 49856        CCCP-65137 TU134 60890        CCCP-65634 TU134 9350908
CCCP-63757 TU134 63757        CCCP-65056 TU134 49860        CCCP-65138 TU134 60907        CCCP-65635 TU134 9350909
CCCP-63769 TU134 63769        CCCP-65057 TU134 49865        CCCP-65139 TU134 60915        CCCP-65636 TU134 9350910
CCCP-63775 TU134 63775        CCCP-65058 TU134 49868        CCCP-65140 TU134 60932        CCCP-65637 TU134 9350911
CCCP-63780 TU134 63780        CCCP-65059 TU134 49870        CCCP-65141 TU134 60945        CCCP-65638 TU134 9350915
CCCP-63791 TU134 13.63761     CCCP-65060 TU134 49872        CCCP-65142 TU134 60955        CCCP-65639 TU134 9350917
CCCP-63820 TU134 63820        CCCP-65061 TU134 49874        CCCP-65143 TU134 60967        CCCP-65640 TU134 0350919
CCCP-63832 TU134 63832        CCCP-65062 TU134 49875        CCCP-65144 TU134 60977        CCCP-65641 TU134 0350920
CCCP-63950 TU134 63950?       CCCP-65063 TU134 49880        CCCP-65145 TU134 60985        CCCP-65642 TU134 0350926
CCCP-63955 TU134 63955        CCCP-65064 TU134 49886        CCCP-65146 TU134 61000        CCCP-65643 TU134 0350927
CCCP-63957 TU134 63957        CCCP-65065 TU134 49890        CCCP-65147 TU134 61012        CCCP-65644 TU134 0350928
CCCP-63960 TU134 63960        CCCP-65066 TU134 49898        CCCP-65148 TU134 61025        CCCP-65645 TU134 0351005
CCCP-63961 TU134 63961        CCCP-65067 TU134 49905        CCCP-65149 TU134 61033        CCCP-65646 TU134 9351001
CCCP-63975 TU134 63975        CCCP-65068 TU134 49907        CCCP-65550 TU134 66200        CCCP-65647 TU134 0351002
CCCP-63976 TU134 63976        CCCP-65069 TU134 49908        CCCP-65551 TU134 66212        CCCP-65648 TU134 0351003
CCCP-63979 TU134 63979        CCCP-65070 TU134 49912        CCCP-65552 TU134 66270        CCCP-65649 TU134 0351004
CCCP-63982 TU134 63982        CCCP-65071 TU134 49915        CCCP-65553 TU134 66300        CCCP-65650 TU134 0351006
CCCP-64001 TU204 ..64001      CCCP-65072 TU134 49972        CCCP-65554 TU134 66320        CCCP-65651 TU134 0351007
CCCP-64003 TU204 ..64003      CCCP-65073 TU134 49980        CCCP-65555 TU134 66350        CCCP-65652 TU134 0351008
CCCP-64004 TU204 1164004      CCCP-65074 TU134 49987        CCCP-65556 TU134 66372        CCCP-65653 TU134 0351009
CCCP-64006 TU204 3164006      CCCP-65075 TU134 49998        CCCP-65557 TU134 66380        CCCP-65654 TU134 0351010
CCCP-64073 TU134 64073        CCCP-65076 TU134 60001        CCCP-65559 TU134 73.49909     CCCP-65655 TU134 9351101
CCCP-64451 TU134 66550        CCCP-65077 TU134 60028        CCCP-65560 TU134 60321        CCCP-65656 TU134 0351102
CCCP-64452 TU134 5351708      CCCP-65078 TU134 60043        CCCP-65561 TU134 2350208      CCCP-65657 TU134 0351103
CCCP-64454 TU134 66140        CCCP-65079 TU134 60054        CCCP-65562 TU134 2350204      CCCP-65658 TU134 0351104
CCCP-64585 TU134 64585        CCCP-65080 TU134 60065        CCCP-65563 TU134 60035        CCCP-65659 TU134 0351105
CCCP-64728 TU134 64728        CCCP-65081 TU134 60076        CCCP-65564 TU134 63165        CCCP-65660 TU134 0351106
CCCP-65000 TU134 42230        CCCP-65082 TU134 60081        CCCP-65565 TU134 63998        CCCP-65661 TU134 0351107
CCCP-65001 TU134 42235        CCCP-65083 TU134 60090        CCCP-65600 TU134 5350002      CCCP-65662 TU134 1351108
CCCP-65002 TU134 44020        CCCP-65084 TU134 60115        CCCP-65601 TU134 6350003      CCCP-65663 TU134 0351109
CCCP-65003 TU134 44040        CCCP-65085 TU134 60123        CCCP-65602 TU134 6350004      CCCP-65664 TU134 1351210
CCCP-65004 TU134 44060        CCCP-65086 TU134 60130        CCCP-65603 TU134 6350005      CCCP-65665 TU134 1351201
CCCP-65005 TU134 44065        CCCP-65087 TU134 60155        CCCP-65604 TU134 62561        CCCP-65666 TU134 1351202
CCCP-65006 TU134 44080        CCCP-65088 TU134 60172        CCCP-65604 TU134 6350101      CCCP-65667 TU134 1351207
CCCP-65007 TU134 46100        CCCP-65089 TU134 60180        CCCP-65605 TU134 09070        CCCP-65668 TU134 1351306
CCCP-65008 TU134 46105        CCCP-65090 TU134 83.60185     CCCP-65605 TU134 6350102      CCCP-65669 TU134 9350916
CCCP-65009 TU134 46120        CCCP-65091 TU134 60195        CCCP-65606 TU134 46300        CCCP-65670 TU134 0351110
CCCP-65010 TU134 46130        CCCP-65092 TU134 60206        CCCP-65606 TU134 6350103      CCCP-65671 TU134 1351208
CCCP-65011 TU134 46140        CCCP-65093 TU134 60215        CCCP-65607 TU134 48560        CCCP-65672 TU134 9350701
```

CCCP-65673 TU134 9350705	CCCP-65757 TU134 62215	CCCP-65839 TU134 18117	CCCP-65924 TU134 9350806
CCCP-65674 TU134 8350502	CCCP-65758 TU134 62230	CCCP-65840 TU134 18118	CCCP-65926 TU134 66101
CCCP-65675 TU134 2351705	CCCP-65759 TU134 62239	CCCP-65841 TU134 18120	CCCP-65927 TU134 66198
CCCP-65676 TU134 1351502	CCCP-65760 TU134 62187	CCCP-65842 TU134 18121	CCCP-65928 TU134 66491
CCCP-65679 TU134 23249	CCCP-65761 TU134 62244	CCCP-65843 TU134 18123	CCCP-65929 TU134 66495
CCCP-65680 TU134 49020	CCCP-65762 TU134 62279	CCCP-65844 TU134 18125	CCCP-65930 TU134 66500
CCCP-65681 TU134 49760	CCCP-65763 TU134 62299	CCCP-65845 TU134 23131	CCCP-65931 TU134 66185
CCCP-65682 TU134 62120	CCCP-65764 TU134 62305	CCCP-65846 TU134 23132	CCCP-65932 TU134 66405
CCCP-65683 TU134 62199	CCCP-65765 TU134 62315	CCCP-65847 TU134 23135	CCCP-65933 TU134 8350602
CCCP-65684 TU134 62205	CCCP-65766 TU134 62327	CCCP-65848 TU134 23136	CCCP-65934 TU134 66143
CCCP-65685 TU134 62375	CCCP-65767 TU134 62335	CCCP-65849 TU134 23138	CCCP-65935 TU134 66180
CCCP-65686 TU134 62390	CCCP-65768 TU134 62350	CCCP-65850 TU134 23240	CCCP-65950 TU134 2351702
CCCP-65687 TU134 62400	CCCP-65769 TU134 62415	CCCP-65851 TU134 23241	CCCP-65951 TU134 2351703
CCCP-65688 TU134 62575	CCCP-65770 TU134 62430	CCCP-65852 TU134 23244	CCCP-65952 TU134 2351704
CCCP-65689 TU134 62655	CCCP-65771 TU134 62445	CCCP-65853 TU134 23245	CCCP-65953 TU134 2351706
CCCP-65690 TU134 62805	CCCP-65772 TU134 62472	CCCP-65854 TU134 23248	CCCP-65954 TU134 2351707
CCCP-65691 TU134 63195	CCCP-65773 TU134 62495	CCCP-65855 TU134 23252	CCCP-65955 TU134 2351708
CCCP-65692 TU134 63215	CCCP-65774 TU134 62519	CCCP-65856 TU134 23253	CCCP-65956 TU134 2351709
CCCP-65693 TU134 63221	CCCP-65775 TU134 62530	CCCP-65857 TU134 23255	CCCP-65957 TU134 2351802
CCCP-65694 TU134 63235	CCCP-65776 TU134 62545	CCCP-65858 TU134 23256	CCCP-65958 TU134 3351804
CCCP-65695 TU134 63285	CCCP-65777 TU134 62552	CCCP-65859 TU134 23264	CCCP-65959 TU134 3351805
CCCP-65696 TU134 63295	CCCP-65778 TU134 62590	CCCP-65860 TU134 28265	CCCP-65960 TU134 3351806
CCCP-65697 TU134 63307	CCCP-65779 TU134 62602	CCCP-65862 TU134 28269	CCCP-65961 TU134 3351807
CCCP-65698 TU134 63325	CCCP-65780 TU134 62622	CCCP-65862 TU134 28270	CCCP-65962 TU134 3351901
CCCP-65699 TU134 63333	CCCP-65781 TU134 62645	CCCP-65863 TU134 28283	CCCP-65963 TU134 0350921
CCCP-65700 TU134 63340	CCCP-65782 TU134 62672	CCCP-65864 TU134 28284	CCCP-65965 TU134 2351803
CCCP-65701 TU134 63365	CCCP-65783 TU134 62708	CCCP-65865 TU134 28286	CCCP-65966 TU134 3351902
CCCP-65702 TU134 63375	CCCP-65784 TU134 62715	CCCP-65866 TU134 28292	CCCP-65967 TU134 3351905
CCCP-65703 TU134 63383	CCCP-65785 TU134 62750	CCCP-65867 TU134 28296	CCCP-65968 TU134 3351907
CCCP-65704 TU134 63410	CCCP-65786 TU134 62775	CCCP-65868 TU134 28305	CCCP-65969 TU134 3351909
CCCP-65705 TU134 63415	CCCP-65787 TU134 62798	CCCP-65869 TU134 28306	CCCP-65970 TU134 3351910
CCCP-65706 TU134 63425	CCCP-65788 TU134 62835	CCCP-65870 TU134 28310	CCCP-65971 TU134 3352001
CCCP-65707 TU134 63435	CCCP-65789 TU134 62850	CCCP-65871 TU134 28311	CCCP-65972 TU134 3352002
CCCP-65708 TU134 63447	CCCP-65790 TU134 63100	CCCP-65872 TU134 29312	CCCP-65973 TU134 3352003
CCCP-65709 TU134 63484	CCCP-65791 TU134 63110	CCCP-65873 TU134 29314	CCCP-65974 TU134 3352004
CCCP-65710 TU134 63490	CCCP-65792 TU134 63121	CCCP-65874 TU134 29315	CCCP-65975 TU134 3352006
CCCP-65711 TU134 63498	CCCP-65793 TU134 63128	CCCP-65875 TU134 29317	CCCP-65976 TU134 3352007
CCCP-65712 TU134 63515	CCCP-65794 TU134 63135	CCCP-65876 TU134 31220	CCCP-65977 TU134 63245
CCCP-65713 TU134 63520	CCCP-65795 TU134 63145	CCCP-65877 TU134 31250	CCCP-65978 TU134 63245
CCCP-65714 TU134 63527	CCCP-65796 TU134 63150	CCCP-65878 TU134 31260	CCCP-65979 TU134 63158
CCCP-65715 TU134 63536	CCCP-65797 TU134 63173	CCCP-65879 TU134 31265	CCCP-65980 TU134 63207
CCCP-65716 TU134 63595	CCCP-65798 TU134 63179	CCCP-65880 TU134 35200	CCCP-65981 TU134 63250
CCCP-65717 TU134 63657	CCCP-65799 TU134 63187	CCCP-65881 TU134 35220	CCCP-65982 TU134 63315
CCCP-65718 TU134 63668	CCCP-65800 TU134 3352009	CCCP-65882 TU134 35270	CCCP-65983 TU134 63350
CCCP-65719 TU134 63637	CCCP-65801 TU134 3352010	CCCP-65883 TU134 35300	CCCP-65984 TU134 63468
CCCP-65720 TU134 62820	CCCP-65802 TU134 3352101	CCCP-65884 TU134 36150	CCCP-65985 TU134 63468
CCCP-65721 TU134 66130	CCCP-65803 TU134 3352103	CCCP-65885 TU134 36160	CCCP-65986 TU134 63475
CCCP-65722 TU134 66420	CCCP-65804 TU134 3352104	CCCP-65886 TU134 36165	CCCP-65987 TU134 63550
CCCP-65723 TU134 66440	CCCP-65805 TU134 3352105	CCCP-65887 TU134 36170	CCCP-65988 TU134 63550
CCCP-65724 TU134 66445	CCCP-65806 TU134 3352107	CCCP-65888 TU134 36175	CCCP-65989 TU134 63605
CCCP-65725 TU134 66472	CCCP-65807 TU134 3352108	CCCP-65889 TU134 38010	CCCP-65990 TU134 63610
CCCP-65726 TU134 63720	CCCP-65808 TU134 3352109	CCCP-65890 TU134 38020	CCCP-65991 TU134 63845
CCCP-65727 TU134 1351307	CCCP-65809 TU134 3352110	CCCP-65891 TU134 38030	CCCP-65992 TU134 63850
CCCP-65728 TU134 1361308	CCCP-65810 TU134 3352201	CCCP-65892 TU134 38050	CCCP-65993 TU134 63860
CCCP-65729 TU134 1351309	CCCP-65811 TU134 3352202	CCCP-65893 TU134 5340120	CCCP-65994 TU134 66207
CCCP-65730 TU134 1351310	CCCP-65812 TU134 3352203	CCCP-65894 TU134 40130	CCCP-65995 TU134 66400
CCCP-65731 TU134 1351401	CCCP-65813 TU134 3352204	CCCP-65895 TU134 40140	CCCP-65996 TU134 63825
CCCP-65732 TU134 1351402	CCCP-65814 TU134 4352208	CCCP-65896 TU134 42200	CCCP-68001 TU144 0000
CCCP-65733 TU134 1351403	CCCP-65815 TU134 4352209	CCCP-65897 TU134 42210	CCCP-68012 AN124 19530501001?
CCCP-65734 TU134 1351404	CCCP-65816 TU134 4352210	CCCP-65898 TU134 42220	CCCP-68021 AN124 19530501002?
CCCP-65735 TU134 1351405	CCCP-65817 TU134 4352301	CCCP-65899 TU134 42225	CCCP-68034 AN124 19530501003?
CCCP-65736 TU134 2351501	CCCP-65818 TU134 4352302	CCCP-65900 TU134 63684	CCCP-69313 TU134 60321
CCCP-65737 TU134 2351506	CCCP-65819 TU134 4352304	CCCP-65901 TU134 63731	CCCP-71052 AN7x 72080775
CCCP-65738 TU134 2351507	CCCP-65820 TU134 08056	CCCP-65902 TU134 63742	CCCP-72000 AN7x 005
CCCP-65739 TU134 2351509	CCCP-65821 TU134 08060	CCCP-65903 TU134 63750	CCCP-72003 AN7x 003
CCCP-65740 TU134 2351510	CCCP-65822 TU134 09071	CCCP-65904 TU134 63953	CCCP-72004 AN7x 004
CCCP-65741 TU134 2351601	CCCP-65823 TU134 09073	CCCP-65905 TU134 63965	CCCP-72900 AN7x 72020337
CCCP-65742 TU134 2351604	CCCP-65824 TU134 09074	CCCP-65906 TU134 66175	CCCP-72901 AN7x 72020358
CCCP-65743 TU134 2351605	CCCP-65825 TU134 09078	CCCP-65907 TU134 63996	CCCP-72902 AN7x 72020362
CCCP-65744 TU134 2351606	CCCP-65826 TU134 12083	CCCP-65908 TU134 63870	CCCP-72903 AN7x 72020385
CCCP-65745 TU134 2351607	CCCP-65827 TU134 12084	CCCP-65910 TU134 63969	CCCP-72904 AN7x 72030425
CCCP-65746 TU134 2351608	CCCP-65828 TU134 12086	CCCP-65911 TU134 63972	CCCP-72905 AN7x 72030430
CCCP-65747 TU134 2351609	CCCP-65829 TU134 12087	CCCP-65912 TU134 63985	CCCP-72906 AN7x 72030447
CCCP-65748 TU134 2351610	CCCP-65830 TU134 12093	CCCP-65914 TU134 66109	CCCP-72907 AN7x 72020375
CCCP-65749 TU134 2351701	CCCP-65831 TU134 17102	CCCP-65915 TU134 66120	CCCP-72908 AN7x 76094880
CCCP-65750 TU134 61042	CCCP-65832 TU134 17106	CCCP-65916 TU134 66152	CCCP-72909 AN7x 72040509
CCCP-65751 TU134 61066	CCCP-65833 TU134 17107	CCCP-65917 TU134 63991	CCCP-72910 AN7x 72040455
CCCP-65752 TU134 61079	CCCP-65834 TU134 17109	CCCP-65918 TU134 63995	CCCP-72913 AN7x 72030477
CCCP-65753 TU134 61099	CCCP-65835 TU134 17112	CCCP-65919 TU134 66168	CCCP-72914 AN7x 72030479
CCCP-65754 TU134 62154	CCCP-65836 TU134 17113	CCCP-65921 TU134 63997	CCCP-72915 AN7x 72040520
CCCP-65755 TU134 62165	CCCP-65837 TU134 17114	CCCP-65922 TU134 9350805	CCCP-72916 AN7x 72040525
CCCP-65756 TU134 62179	CCCP-65838 TU134 18116	CCCP-65923 TU134 9350804	CCCP-72917 AN7x 72040530

Reg.	Type	Serial	Reg.	Type	Serial	Reg.	Type	Serial	Reg.	Type	Serial
CCCP-72918	AN7x	72040548	CCCP-76457	IL76	093421621	CCCP-76540	IL76	0033442238	CCCP-76623	IL76	0053457705
CCCP-72919	AN7x	72040565	CCCP-76458	IL76	0013430888	CCCP-76541	IL76	0033442241	CCCP-76624	IL76	0053457710
CCCP-72920	AN7x	72040570	CCCP-76459	IL76	0013430890	CCCP-76542	IL76	0033443249	CCCP-76625	IL76	0053457713
CCCP-72921	AN7x	72040581	CCCP-76460	IL76	0013431928	CCCP-76543	IL76	0033443255	CCCP-76626	IL76	0053457720
CCCP-72922	AN7x	72040560	CCCP-76461	IL76	0013431935	CCCP-76544	IL76	0033443262	CCCP-76627	IL76	0053458733
CCCP-72923	AN7x	72060590	CCCP-76462	IL76	0013432955	CCCP-76545	IL76	0033443266	CCCP-76628	IL76	0053458741
CCCP-72925	AN7x	72040563	CCCP-76463	IL76	0013432960	CCCP-76546	IL76	0033443272	CCCP-76629	IL76	0053458745
CCCP-72926	AN7x	72060620	CCCP-76464	IL76	0023437090	CCCP-76547	IL76	0033443273	CCCP-76630	IL76	0053458749
CCCP-72927	AN7x	72060625	CCCP-76465	IL76	0023438101	CCCP-76548	IL76	0033443278	CCCP-76631	IL76	0053458756
CCCP-72928	AN7x	72060640	CCCP-76466	IL76	0023440153	CCCP-76549	IL76	0033444283	CCCP-76632	IL76	0053459757
CCCP-72929	AN7x	72060653	CCCP-76467	IL76	0023440157	CCCP-76550	IL76	0033445306	CCCP-76633	IL76	0053459764
CCCP-72930	AN7x	72070678	CCCP-76468	IL76	0023441195	CCCP-76551	IL76	0033445309	CCCP-76634	IL76	0053459770
CCCP-72931	AN7x	72070695	CCCP-76469	IL76	0033444286	CCCP-76552	IL76	0033445313	CCCP-76635	IL76	0053459775
CCCP-72934	AN7x	72080777	CCCP-76470	IL76	0033444291	CCCP-76553	IL76	0033445318	CCCP-76636	IL76	0053459781
CCCP-72935	AN7x	72080778	CCCP-76471	IL76	0033446345	CCCP-76554	IL76	0033445324	CCCP-76637	IL76	0053460797
CCCP-72936	AN7x	72060642?	CCCP-76472	IL76	0033446350	CCCP-76555	IL76	0033446325	CCCP-76638	IL76	0053460802
CCCP-72937	AN7x	72070688	CCCP-76473	IL76	0033448404	CCCP-76556	IL76	0033445294	CCCP-76639	IL76	0053460805
CCCP-72938	AN7x	72070693	CCCP-76474	IL76	0033448407	CCCP-76557	IL76	0033446329	CCCP-76640	IL76	0053460811
CCCP-72939	AN7x	72080780	CCCP-76475	IL76	0043451523	CCCP-76558	IL76	0033446333	CCCP-76641	IL76	0053460813
CCCP-72940	AN7x	72080781	CCCP-76476	IL76	0043451528	CCCP-76559	IL76	0033446340	CCCP-76642	IL76	0053460820
CCCP-72941	AN7x	72080783	CCCP-76477	IL76	0043453575	CCCP-76560	IL76	0033446341	CCCP-76643	IL76	0053460822
CCCP-72942	AN7x	72080786	CCCP-76478	IL76	0053459788	CCCP-76561	IL76	0033447364	CCCP-76644	IL76	0053460827
CCCP-72943	AN7x	72080787	CCCP-76479	IL76	0053460790	CCCP-76562	IL76	0033447365	CCCP-76645	IL76	0053461834
CCCP-72944	AN7x	72090796	CCCP-76481	IL76	0053460795	CCCP-76563	IL76	0033447372	CCCP-76646	IL76	0053461837
CCCP-72945	AN7x	72090799	CCCP-76482	IL76	0053460832	CCCP-76564	IL76	0033448373	CCCP-76647	IL76	0053461843
CCCP-72946	AN7x	72090801	CCCP-76483	IL76	0063468042	CCCP-76565	IL76	0033448382	CCCP-76648	IL76	0053461848
CCCP-72947	AN7x	72090803	CCCP-76484	IL76	0063469081	CCCP-76566	IL76	0033448385	CCCP-76649	IL76	0053462864
CCCP-72948	AN7x	72091815	CCCP-76485	IL76	0063470088	CCCP-76567	IL76	0033448390	CCCP-76650	IL76	0053462865
CCCP-72949	AN7x	72091818	CCCP-76486	IL76	0073476281	CCCP-76568	IL76	0033448420	CCCP-76651	IL76	0053462872
CCCP-72950	AN7x	72091819	CCCP-76487	IL76	0073479367	CCCP-76569	IL76	0033448421	CCCP-76652	IL76	0053462873
CCCP-72951	AN7x	72090809	CCCP-76488	IL76	0073479371	CCCP-76570	IL76	0033448427	CCCP-76653	IL76	0053462879
CCCP-72953	**AN7x**	**72080793**	CCCP-76489	IL76	0083485554	CCCP-76571	IL76	0033448429	CCCP-76654	IL76	0053462884
CCCP-72955	AN7x	72090807	CCCP-76491	IL76	093421630	CCCP-76572	IL76	0033449434	CCCP-76655	IL76	0053463885
CCCP-72956	**AN7x**	**72092853**	CCCP-76492	IL76	0043452549	CCCP-76573	IL76	0033449437	CCCP-76656	IL76	0053463891
CCCP-72957	AN7x	72092856	CCCP-76492	IL76	093418548	CCCP-76574	IL76	0033449441	CCCP-76657	IL76	0053463896
CCCP-72958	AN7x	72092841	CCCP-76493	IL76	0043453900	CCCP-76575	IL76	0033449445	CCCP-76658	IL76	0053463902
CCCP-72959	AN7x	72092858	CCCP-76494	IL76	0063465956	CCCP-76576	IL76	0043449449	CCCP-76659	IL76	0053463908
CCCP-72960	AN7x	72093865	CCCP-76495	IL76	073410292	CCCP-76577	IL76	0043449462	CCCP-76660	IL76	0053463910
CCCP-72961	AN7x	72093866	CCCP-76496	IL76	073410301	CCCP-76578	IL76	0043449468	CCCP-76661	IL76	0053463913
CCCP-72962	AN7x	72091831	CCCP-76497	IL76	073410320	CCCP-76579	IL76	0043449471	CCCP-76662	IL76	0053464919
CCCP-72963	AN7x	72092845	CCCP-76498	IL76	0023442218	CCCP-76580	IL76	0043450476	CCCP-76663	IL76	0053464922
CCCP-72964	AN7x	72093860	CCCP-76499	IL76	0023441186	CCCP-76581	IL76	0043450484	CCCP-76664	IL76	0053464926
CCCP-72965	AN7x	72093863	CCCP-76500	IL76	033401016	CCCP-76582	IL76	0043450487	CCCP-76665	IL76	0053464930
CCCP-72966	AN7x	72092847	CCCP-76501	IL76	033401019	CCCP-76583	IL76	0043450491	CCCP-76666	IL76	0053464934
CCCP-72967	AN7x	72091837	CCCP-76502	IL76	063407206	CCCP-76584	IL76	0043450493	CCCP-76667	IL76	0053465941
CCCP-72970	AN7x	76093870	CCCP-76503	IL76	063408209	CCCP-76585	IL76	0043451503	CCCP-76668	IL76	0053465946
CCCP-72972	AN7x	72094883	CCCP-76504	IL76	073411328	CCCP-76586	IL76	0043451508	CCCP-76669	IL76	0053465949
CCCP-72974	AN7x	72094878	CCCP-76505	IL76	073411331	CCCP-76587	IL76	0043451517	CCCP-76670	IL76	0053465958
CCCP-72975	AN7x	72094888	CCCP-76506	IL76	073411334	CCCP-76588	IL76	0043451530	CCCP-76671	IL76	0063465963
CCCP-72976	AN7x	72094884	CCCP-76507	IL76	073411338	CCCP-76589	IL76	0043452534	CCCP-76672	IL76	0063466981
CCCP-72980	AN7x	72095909	CCCP-76508	IL76	083413412	CCCP-76590	IL76	0043452544	CCCP-76673	IL76	0063466988
CCCP-72984	AN7x	76096926	CCCP-76509	IL76	083413415	CCCP-76591	IL76	0043452546	CCCP-76674	IL76	0063466989
CCCP-74000	AN7x	47060649	CCCP-76510	IL76	083414432	CCCP-76592	IL76	0043452555	CCCP-76675	IL76	0063466998
CCCP-74001	AN7x	47070655	CCCP-76511	IL76	083414444	CCCP-76593	IL76	0043453562	CCCP-76676	IL76	0063467003
CCCP-74002	AN7x	47070682	CCCP-76512	IL76	083414447	CCCP-76594	IL76	0043453568	CCCP-76677	IL76	0063467005
CCCP-74003	AN7x	47070690	CCCP-76513	IL76	084514451	CCCP-76595	IL76	0043453571	CCCP-76678	IL76	0063467011
CCCP-74004	AN7x	47094890	CCCP-76514	IL76	083415453	CCCP-76596	IL76	0043453583	CCCP-76679	IL76	0063467014?
CCCP-74005	AN7x	47094892	CCCP-76515	IL76	093417526	CCCP-76597	IL76	0043453585	CCCP-76680	IL76	0063467020
CCCP-74006	AN7x	47095896	CCCP-76516	IL76	093418556	CCCP-76598	IL76	0043453591	CCCP-76681	IL76	0063467021
CCCP-74007	AN7x	47095903	CCCP-76517	IL76	093418560	CCCP-76599	IL76	0043453593	CCCP-76682	IL76	0063467027
CCCP-74008	AN7x	47095900	CCCP-76518	IL76	093420594	CCCP-76600	IL76	0043454602	CCCP-76683	IL76	0063468029
CCCP-74010	AN7x	47030450	CCCP-76519	IL76	093420599	CCCP-76601	IL76	0043454606	CCCP-76684	IL76	0063468036
CCCP-74025	AN7x	47095905	CCCP-76520	IL76	093420605	CCCP-76602	IL76	0043454611	CCCP-76685	IL76	0063468037?
CCCP-74026	AN7x	47096919	CCCP-76521	IL76	0003423699	CCCP-76603	IL76	0043454623	CCCP-76686	IL76	0063468045
CCCP-76401	IL76	1023412399	CCCP-76522	IL76	0003424707	CCCP-76604	IL76	0043454625	CCCP-76687	IL76	0063469051
CCCP-76403	IL76	1023412414	CCCP-76523	IL76	0003425732	CCCP-76605	IL76	0043454631	CCCP-76688	IL76	0063469062
CCCP-76423	IL76	0053457720	CCCP-76524	IL76	0003425746	CCCP-76606	IL76	0043454633	CCCP-76689	IL76	0063469066
CCCP-76425	IL76	1003405167	CCCP-76525	IL76	0003427787	CCCP-76607	IL76	0043453559	CCCP-76690	IL76	0063469080
CCCP-76426	IL76	1013405184	CCCP-76526	IL76	0003427792	CCCP-76609	IL76	0043453597	CCCP-76691	IL76	0063470089
CCCP-76434	IL76	1023412395	CCCP-76527	IL76	0003427796	CCCP-76610	IL76	0043454640	CCCP-76692	IL76	0063470096
CCCP-76435	IL76	1023413428	CCCP-76528	IL76	073410293	CCCP-76611	IL76	0043455653	CCCP-76693	IL76	0063470100
CCCP-76437	IL76	0083484527	CCCP-76529	IL76	073410308	CCCP-76612	IL76	0043455660	CCCP-76694	IL76	0063470107
CCCP-76442	IL76	1023414450	CCCP-76530	IL76	0023441180	CCCP-76613	IL76	0043455664	CCCP-76695	IL76	0063470112
CCCP-76443	IL76	0043452534	CCCP-76531	IL76	0023441181	CCCP-76614	IL76	0043455665	CCCP-76696	IL76	0063470113
CCCP-76447	IL76	1023412389	CCCP-76532	IL76	0023441201	CCCP-76615	IL76	0043455672	CCCP-76697	IL76	0063470118
CCCP-76450	IL76	0053463900	CCCP-76533	IL76	0023442205	CCCP-76616	IL76	0043455676	CCCP-76698	IL76	0063471123
CCCP-76451	IL76	0053464938	CCCP-76534	IL76	0023442210	CCCP-76617	IL76	0043455677	CCCP-76699	IL76	0063471131
CCCP-76452	IL76	0053465965	CCCP-76535	IL76	0023442213	CCCP-76618	IL76	0043455682	CCCP-76700	IL76	0063471134
CCCP-76453	IL76	0063469074	CCCP-76536	IL76	0023442221	CCCP-76619	IL76	0043455686	CCCP-76701	IL76	0063471139
CCCP-76454	IL76	0063469074	CCCP-76537	IL76	0033442225	CCCP-76620	IL76	0043456692	CCCP-76702	IL76	0063471142
CCCP-76455	IL76	0073471125	CCCP-76538	IL76	0023442231	CCCP-76621	IL76	0043456695?	CCCP-76703	IL76	0063471147
CCCP-76456	IL76	0073474208	CCCP-76539	IL76	0033442234	CCCP-76622	IL76	0053457702	CCCP-76704	IL76	0063471150

CCCP-76705 IL76 0063472158	CCCP-76787 IL76 0093495854	CCCP-78752 IL76 0083483519	CCCP-78835 IL76 1003402033
CCCP-76706 IL76 0083472163	CCCP-76788 IL76 0013433996	CCCP-78753 IL76 0083484522	CCCP-78836 IL76 0003499986
CCCP-76707 IL76 0063472166	CCCP-76789 IL76 0013433999	CCCP-78754 IL76 0083484527	CCCP-78838 IL76 1003402044
CCCP-76708 IL76 0063473171	CCCP-76790 IL76 0093496903	CCCP-78755 IL76 0083484531	CCCP-78839 IL76 1003402047
CCCP-76709 IL76 0063473173	CCCP-76791 IL76 0093497936	CCCP-78756 IL76 0083484536	CCCP-78840 IL76 1003403056
CCCP-76710 IL76 0063473182	CCCP-76792 IL76 0093497942	CCCP-78757 IL76 0083484547	CCCP-78842 IL76 1003403069
CCCP-76711 IL76 0063473187	CCCP-76793 IL76 0093498951	CCCP-78758 IL76 0083484551	CCCP-78843 IL76 1003403082
CCCP-76712 IL76 0063473190	CCCP-76794 IL76 0093498954	CCCP-78759 IL76 0083485558	CCCP-78844 IL76 1003403092
CCCP-76713 IL76 0063474193	CCCP-76795 IL76 0093498962	CCCP-78760 IL76 0083485566	CCCP-78845 IL76 1003403095
CCCP-76714 IL76 0063474198	CCCP-76796 IL76 1003499994	CCCP-78761 IL76 0083486570	CCCP-78846 IL76 1003403115
CCCP-76715 IL76 0073479394	CCCP-76797 IL76 1003403052	CCCP-78762 IL76 0083486574	CCCP-78847 IL76 1003404132
CCCP-76716 IL76 0073474211	CCCP-76798 IL76 1003403063	CCCP-78763 IL76 0083486582	CCCP-78848 IL76 1013405159
CCCP-76717 IL76 0073474216	CCCP-76799 IL76 1003403075	CCCP-78764 IL76 0083486586	CCCP-78849 IL76 1013405192
CCCP-76718 IL76 0073474219	CCCP-76800 IL76 0093493810	CCCP-78765 IL76 0083486590	CCCP-78850 IL76 1013405196
CCCP-76719 IL76 0073474226	CCCP-76801 IL76 0093495866	CCCP-78766 IL76 0083486595	CCCP-78851 IL76 1013406204
CCCP-76720 IL76 0073475229	CCCP-76802 IL76 0093495874	CCCP-78767 IL76 0083487598	CCCP-78852 IL76 1013407212
CCCP-76721 IL76 0073475239	CCCP-76803 IL76 0093497927	CCCP-78768 IL76 0083487603	CCCP-78853 IL76 1013407215
CCCP-76722 IL76 0073475242	CCCP-76804 IL76 0093497931	CCCP-78769 IL76 0083487607	CCCP-78854 IL76 1013407220
CCCP-76723 IL76 0073475245	CCCP-76805 IL76 1003403109	CCCP-78770 IL76 0083487617	CCCP-82002 AN124 19530501003?
CCCP-76724 IL76 0073475250	CCCP-76806 IL76 1003403121	CCCP-78771 IL76 0083487622	CCCP-82005 AN124 977305451600
CCCP-76725 IL76 0073475253	CCCP-76807 IL76 1013405176	CCCP-78772 IL76 0083487627	CCCP-82006 AN124 19530501004
CCCP-76726 IL76 0073475261	CCCP-76808 IL76 1013405177	CCCP-78773 IL76 0083488638	CCCP-82007 AN124 19530501005
CCCP-76727 IL76 0073475268	CCCP-76809 IL76 1013408252	CCCP-78774 IL76 0083488643	CCCP-82008 AN124 19530501006
CCCP-76728 IL76 0073475270	CCCP-76810 IL76 1013409282	CCCP-78775 IL76 0083489647	CCCP-82009 AN124 19530501007
CCCP-76729 IL76 0073476275	CCCP-76811 IL76 1013407223	CCCP-78776 IL76 0083489652	CCCP-82010 AN124 977305361601
CCCP-76730 IL76 0073476277	CCCP-76812 IL76 1013407230	CCCP-78777 IL76 0083489654	CCCP-82011 AN124 977305461602
CCCP-76731 IL76 0073476290	CCCP-76813 IL76 1013408246	CCCP-78778 IL76 0083489659	CCCP-82012 AN124 977305273202
CCCP-76732 IL76 0073476296	CCCP-76814 IL76 1013408269	CCCP-78779 IL76 0083489662	CCCP-82013 AN124 977305373203
CCCP-76733 IL76 0073476304	CCCP-76815 IL76 1013409310	CCCP-78780 IL76 0083489666	CCCP-82014 AN124 977305473203
CCCP-76734 IL76 0073476312	CCCP-76816 IL76 1023410336	CCCP-78781 IL76 0083489670	CCCP-82020 AN124 19530502001
CCCP-76735 IL76 0073476314	CCCP-76817 IL76 1023412387	CCCP-78782 IL76 0083489678	CCCP-82021 AN124 19530502002
CCCP-76736 IL76 0073476317	CCCP-76818 IL76 1013408264	CCCP-78783 IL76 0083489683	CCCP-82022 AN124 19530502003
CCCP-76737 IL76 0073477323	CCCP-76819 IL76 1013409274	CCCP-78784 IL76 0083489687	CCCP-82023 AN124 19530502012
CCCP-76738 IL76 0073477326	CCCP-76820 IL76 1013409295	CCCP-78785 IL76 0083489691	CCCP-82024 AN124 19530502033
CCCP-76739 IL76 0073477332	CCCP-76821 IL76 0023441200	CCCP-78786 IL76 0083490693	CCCP-82025 AN124 19530502106
CCCP-76740 IL76 0073477335	CCCP-76822 IL76 0093499982	CCCP-78787 IL76 0083490698	CCCP-82027 AN124 19530502288
CCCP-76741 IL76 0073478337	CCCP-76823 IL76 0023441189	CCCP-78788 IL76 0083490703	CCCP-82028 AN124 19530502599
CCCP-76742 IL76 0073478346	CCCP-76824 IL76 1023410327	CCCP-78789 IL76 0083490706	CCCP-82029 AN124 19530502630
CCCP-76743 IL76 0073478349	CCCP-76825 IL76 1003404136	CCCP-78790 IL76 0083490712	CCCP-82031 AN124 977305473204
CCCP-76744 IL76 0073478359	CCCP-76826 IL76 1003404143	CCCP-78791 IL76 0093490714	CCCP-82032 AN124 977305183204
CCCP-76745 IL76 0073479362	CCCP-76827 IL76 1003404151	CCCP-78792 IL76 0093490718	CCCP-82033 AN124 977305283205
CCCP-76746 IL76 0073479374	CCCP-76828 IL76 1003405164	CCCP-78793 IL76 0093490721	CCCP-82034 AN124 977305383205
CCCP-76747 IL76 0073479381	CCCP-76829 IL76 1003405172	CCCP-78794 IL76 0093490726	CCCP-82035 AN124 977305483206
CCCP-76748 IL76 0073479386	CCCP-76830 IL76 1023410348	CCCP-78795 IL76 0093491729	CCCP-82036 AN124 977305483206
CCCP-76749 IL76 0073479392	CCCP-76831 IL76 1013409287	CCCP-78796 IL76 0093491735	CCCP-82037 AN124 977305295507
CCCP-76750 IL76 0083485561	CCCP-76832 IL76 1023410360	CCCP-78797 IL76 0093491742	CCCP-82038 AN124 977305495507
CCCP-76751 IL76 0083487610	CCCP-76834 IL76 1023409319	CCCP-78798 IL76 0093491747	CCCP-82039 AN124 977305205508
CCCP-76752 IL76 0093498967	CCCP-76835 IL76 1013408244	CCCP-78799 IL76 0093491754	CCCP-82040 AN124 977305305508
CCCP-76753 IL76 0083481461	CCCP-76836 IL76 1013409305	CCCP-78800 IL76 0093491758	CCCP-82041 AN124 977305405508
CCCP-76754 IL76 093421637	CCCP-76837 IL76 1023409316	CCCP-78801 IL76 0093492763	CCCP-82042 AN124 977305405509
CCCP-76755 IL76 0013433984	CCCP-76838 IL76 1023411370	CCCP-78802 IL76 0093492771	CCCP-82043 AN124 977305415510
CCCP-76756 IL76 0013428839	CCCP-76839 IL76 1023411375	CCCP-78803 IL76 0093492774	CCCP-82044 AN124 977305415510
CCCP-76757 IL76 0013433990	CCCP-76844 IL76 1033416525	CCCP-78804 IL76 0093492778	CCCP-82045 AN124 977305225511
CCCP-76758 IL76 0073474203	CCCP-77101 TU144 011	CCCP-78805 IL76 0093492783	CCCP-82060 AN225 19530503763
CCCP-76759 IL76 093418543	CCCP-77102 TU144 012	CCCP-78806 IL76 0093492786	CCCP-82066 AN124 19530502761
CCCP-76760 IL76 0073479400	CCCP-77103 TU144 021	CCCP-78807 IL76 0093493791	CCCP-82067 AN124 977305225511
CCCP-76761 IL76 0073479401	(CCCP-77104) TU144 022	CCCP-78808 IL76 0093493794	CCCP-82069 AN124 977305..5912
CCCP-76762 IL76 0073480406	CCCP-77105 TU144 031	CCCP-78809 IL76 0093493807	CCCP-83944 AN7x 004
CCCP-76763 IL76 0073480413	CCCP-77106 TU144 10041	CCCP-78810 IL76 0093493814	CCCP-83961 TU124 4351505
CCCP-76764 IL76 0073480424	CCCP-77107 TU144 051	CCCP-78811 IL76 0093494823	CCCP-83963 TU124 4351508
CCCP-76765 IL76 0073481426	CCCP-77108 TU144 042	CCCP-78812 IL76 0093494826	CCCP-85000 TU154 67-KH1
CCCP-76766 IL76 0083481431	CCCP-77109 TU144 10052	CCCP-78813 IL76 0093494830	CCCP-85001 TU154 69M001
CCCP-76767 IL76 0073481436	CCCP-77110 TU144 10061	CCCP-78814 IL76 0093494838	CCCP-85002 TU154 ..M002
CCCP-76768 IL76 0073481448	CCCP-77111 TU144 10062	CCCP-78815 IL76 0093494842	CCCP-85003 TU154 ..M003
CCCP-76769 IL76 0073481452	CCCP-77112 TU144 10071	CCCP-78816 IL76 0093495846	CCCP-85004 TU154 ..M004
CCCP-76770 IL76 0073481456	CCCP-77113 TU144 081	CCCP-78817 IL76 0093495851	CCCP-85005 TU154 ..M005
CCCP-76771 IL76 0083482466	CCCP-77114 TU144 100802	CCCP-78818 IL76 0093495858	CCCP-85006 TU154 70M006
CCCP-76772 IL76 0083482472	CCCP-77115 TU144 091	CCCP-78819 IL76 0093495883	CCCP-85007 TU154 70M007
CCCP-76773 IL76 0083482473	CCCP-77116 TU144 092	CCCP-78820 IL76 0093496907	CCCP-85008 TU154 70M008
CCCP-76774 IL76 0083482478	CCCP-77144 TU144 022	CCCP-78821 IL76 0093496914	CCCP-85009 TU154 70M009
CCCP-76775 IL76 0083481440	CCCP-78015 AN7x 01	CCCP-78822 IL76 0093495880	CCCP-85010 TU154 70M010
CCCP-76776 IL76 0083482486	CCCP-78033 AN7x 003	CCCP-78823 IL76 1003496918	CCCP-85011 TU154 71A-011
CCCP-76777 IL76 0083482490	CCCP-78036 AN7x 03	CCCP-78824 IL76 1003499991	CCCP-85012 TU154 71A-012
CCCP-76778 IL76 0083483502	CCCP-78306 AN7x 72010930	CCCP-78825 IL76 1013495871	CCCP-85013 TU154 71A-013
CCCP-76779 IL76 0083483505	CCCP-78357 AN7x 72010935	CCCP-78826 IL76 1003499991	CCCP-85014 TU154 71A-014
CCCP-76780 IL76 0013430901	CCCP-78407 AN7x 47010940	CCCP-78827 IL76 1003499997	CCCP-85015 TU154 71A-015
CCCP-76781 IL76 0023439133	CCCP-78731 IL76 0013428831	CCCP-78828 IL76 1003401004	CCCP-85016 TU154 71A-016
CCCP-76782 IL76 0093498971	CCCP-78734 IL76 1013409303	CCCP-78829 IL76 1013401006	CCCP-85017 TU154 71A-017
CCCP-76783 IL76 0093498974	CCCP-78736 IL76 1013408257	CCCP-78831 IL76 1003401010	CCCP-85018 TU154 71A-018
CCCP-76784 IL76 0093494835	CCCP-78738 IL76 0033442247	CCCP-78833 IL76 1003401017	CCCP-85019 TU154 71A-019
CCCP-76785 IL76 0093495863	CCCP-78750 IL76 0083483510	CCCP-78833 IL76 1003401025	CCCP-85020 TU154 71A-020
CCCP-76786 IL76 0093496923	CCCP-78751 IL76 0083483513	CCCP-78834 IL76 1003401032	

CCCP-85021 TU154 71A-021
CCCP-85022 TU154 71A-022
CCCP-85023 TU154 72A-023
CCCP-85024 TU154 72A-024
CCCP-85025 TU154 72A-025
CCCP-85028 TU154 72A-028
CCCP-85029 TU154 72A-029
CCCP-85030 TU154 72A-030
CCCP-85031 TU154 72A-031
CCCP-85032 TU154 72A-032
CCCP-85033 TU154 72A-033
CCCP-85034 TU154 72A-034
CCCP-85035 TU154 72A-035
CCCP-85037 TU154 73A-037
CCCP-85038 TU154 73A-038
CCCP-85039 TU154 73A-039
CCCP-85040 TU154 73A-040
CCCP-85041 TU154 73A-041
CCCP-85042 TU154 73A-042
CCCP-85043 TU154 73A-043
CCCP-85044 TU154 73A-044
CCCP-85049 TU154 73A-049
CCCP-85050 TU154 73A-050
CCCP-85051 TU154 73A-051
CCCP-85052 TU154 73A-052
CCCP-85053 TU154 74A-053
CCCP-85054 TU154 74A-054
CCCP-85055 TU154 74A-055
CCCP-85056 TU154 74A-056
CCCP-85057 TU154 74A-057
CCCP-85059 TU154 74A-059
CCCP-85060 TU154 74A-060
CCCP-85061 TU154 74A-061
CCCP-85062 TU154 74A-062
CCCP-85063 TU154 74A-063
CCCP-85064 TU154 74A-064
CCCP-85065 TU154 74A-065
CCCP-85066 TU154 74A-066
CCCP-85067 TU154 74A-067
CCCP-85068 TU154 74A-068
CCCP-85069 TU154 74A-069
CCCP-85070 TU154 74A-070
CCCP-85071 TU154 74A-071
CCCP-85072 TU154 74A-072
CCCP-85074 TU154 74A-074
CCCP-85075 TU154 74A-075
CCCP-85076 TU154 74A-076
CCCP-05070 TU154 74A 078
CCCP-85079 TU154 74A-079
CCCP-85080 TU154 74A-080
CCCP-85081 TU154 74A-081
CCCP-85082 TU154 74A-082
CCCP-85083 TU154 74A-083
CCCP-85084 TU154 74A-084
CCCP-85085 TU154 74A-085
CCCP-85086 TU154 74A-086
CCCP-85087 TU154 74A-087
CCCP-85088 TU154 74A-088
CCCP-85089 TU154 74A-089
CCCP-85090 TU154 75A-090
CCCP-85091 TU154 75A-091
CCCP-85092 TU154 75A-092
CCCP-85093 TU154 75A-093
CCCP-85094 TU154 75A-094
CCCP-85096 TU154 75A-096
CCCP-85097 TU154 75A-097
CCCP-85098 TU154 75A-098
CCCP-85099 TU154 75A-099
CCCP-85100 TU154 75A-100
CCCP-85101 TU154 75A-101
CCCP-85102 TU154 75A-102
CCCP-85103 TU154 75A-103
CCCP-85104 TU154 75A-104
CCCP-85105 TU154 75A-105
CCCP-85106 TU154 75A-106
CCCP-85107 TU154 75A-107
CCCP-85108 TU154 75A-108
CCCP-85109 TU154 75A-109
CCCP-85110 TU154 75A-110
CCCP-85111 TU154 75A-111
CCCP-85112 TU154 75A-112
CCCP-85113 TU154 75A-113

CCCP-85114 TU154 75A-114
CCCP-85115 TU154 75A-115
CCCP-85116 TU154 75A-116
CCCP-85117 TU154 75A-117
CCCP-85118 TU154 75A-118
CCCP-85119 TU154 75A-119
CCCP-85120 TU154 75A-120
CCCP-85121 TU154 75A-121
CCCP-85122 TU154 75A-122
CCCP-85123 TU154 75A-123
CCCP-85124 TU154 75A-124
CCCP-85125 TU154 75A-125
CCCP-85130 TU154 75A-130
CCCP-85131 TU154 75A-131
CCCP-85132 TU154 76A-132
CCCP-85133 TU154 78A-133
CCCP-85134 TU154 75A-134
CCCP-85135 TU154 76A-135
CCCP-85136 TU154 76A-136
CCCP-85137 TU154 76A-137
CCCP-85138 TU154 76A-138
CCCP-85139 TU154 76A-139
CCCP-85140 TU154 76A-140
CCCP-85141 TU154 76A-141
CCCP-85142 TU154 76A-142
CCCP-85145 TU154 76A-145
CCCP-85146 TU154 76A-146
CCCP-85147 TU154 76A-147
CCCP-85148 TU154 76A-148
CCCP-85149 TU154 76A-149
CCCP-85150 TU154 76A-150
CCCP-85151 TU154 76A-151
CCCP-85152 TU154 76A-152
CCCP-85153 TU154 76A-153
CCCP-85154 TU154 76A-154
CCCP-85155 TU154 76A-155
CCCP-85156 TU154 76A-156
CCCP-85157 TU154 76A-157
CCCP-85158 TU154 76A-158
CCCP-85160 TU154 76A-160
CCCP-85162 TU154 76A-162
CCCP-85163 TU154 76A-163
CCCP-85164 TU154 76A-164
CCCP-85165 TU154 76A-165
CCCP-85166 TU154 76A-166
CCCP-85167 TU154 76A-167
CCCP-85168 TU154 76A-168
CCCP-85169 TU154 76A-169
CCCP-85170 TU154 76A-170
CCCP-85171 TU154 76A-171
CCCP-85172 TU154 76A-172
CCCP-85173 TU154 76A-173
CCCP-85174 TU154 76A-174
CCCP-85176 TU154 76A-176
CCCP-85177 TU154 76A-177
CCCP-85178 TU154 76A-178
CCCP-85179 TU154 76A-179
CCCP-85180 TU154 76A-180
CCCP-85181 TU154 76A-181
CCCP-85182 TU154 76A-182
CCCP-85183 TU154 76A-183
CCCP-85184 TU154 76A-184
CCCP-85185 TU154 76A-185
CCCP-85186 TU154 76A-186
CCCP-85187 TU154 76A-187
CCCP-85188 TU154 76A-188
CCCP-85189 TU154 76A-189
CCCP-85190 TU154 76A-190
CCCP-85192 TU154 77A-192
CCCP-85193 TU154 77A-193
CCCP-85194 TU154 77A-194
CCCP-85195 TU154 77A-195
CCCP-85196 TU154 77A-196
CCCP-85197 TU154 77A-197
CCCP-85198 TU154 77A-198
CCCP-85199 TU154 77A-199
CCCP-85200 TU154 77A-200
CCCP-85201 TU154 77A-201
CCCP-85202 TU154 77A-202
CCCP-85203 TU154 77A-203
CCCP-85204 TU154 77A-204
CCCP-85205 TU154 77A-205

CCCP-85206 TU154 77A-206
CCCP-85207 TU154 77A-207
CCCP-85210 TU154 77A-210
CCCP-85211 TU154 77A-211
CCCP-85212 TU154 77A-212
CCCP-85213 TU154 77A-213
CCCP-85214 TU154 77A-214
CCCP-85215 TU154 77A-215
CCCP-85216 TU154 77A-216
CCCP-85217 TU154 77A-217
CCCP-85218 TU154 77A-218
CCCP-85219 TU154 77A-219
CCCP-85220 TU154 77A-220
CCCP-85221 TU154 77A-221
CCCP-85222 TU154 77A-222
CCCP-85223 TU154 77A-223
CCCP-85226 TU154 77A-226
CCCP-85227 TU154 77A-227
CCCP-85228 TU154 77A-228
CCCP-85229 TU154 77A-229
CCCP-85230 TU154 77A-230
CCCP-85231 TU154 77A-231
CCCP-85232 TU154 77A-232
CCCP-85233 TU154 77A-233
CCCP-85234 TU154 77A-234
CCCP-85235 TU154 77A-235
CCCP-85236 TU154 77A-236
CCCP-85237 TU154 77A-237
CCCP-85238 TU154 77A-238
CCCP-85240 TU154 77A-240
CCCP-85241 TU154 77A-241
CCCP-85242 TU154 77A-242
CCCP-85243 TU154 77A-243
CCCP-85244 TU154 77A-244
CCCP-85245 TU154 77A-245
CCCP-85246 TU154 77A-246
CCCP-85247 TU154 77A-247
CCCP-85248 TU154 77A-248
CCCP-85249 TU154 77A-249
CCCP-85250 TU154 77A-250
CCCP-85251 TU154 77A-251
CCCP-85252 TU154 77A-252
CCCP-85253 TU154 78A-253
CCCP-85254 TU154 78A-254
CCCP-85255 TU154 78A-255
CCCP-85256 TU154 78A-256
CCCP-85257 TU154 78A-257
CCCP-85259 TU154 78A-259
CCCP-85260 TU154 78A-260
CCCP-85261 TU154 78A-261
CCCP-85263 TU154 78A-263
CCCP-85264 TU154 78A-264
CCCP-85265 TU154 78A-265
CCCP-85266 TU154 78A-266
CCCP-85267 TU154 78A-267
CCCP-85268 TU154 78A-268
CCCP-85269 TU154 78A-269
CCCP-85271 TU154 78A-271
CCCP-85272 TU154 78A-272
CCCP-85273 TU154 78A-273
CCCP-85274 TU154 78A-274
CCCP-85275 TU154 78A-275
CCCP-85276 TU154 78A-276
CCCP-85278 TU154 ?
CCCP-85279 TU154 78A-279
CCCP-85280 TU154 78A-280
CCCP-85281 TU154 78A-281
CCCP-85282 TU154 78A-282
CCCP-85283 TU154 78A-283
CCCP-85284 TU154 78A-284
CCCP-85285 TU154 78A-285
CCCP-85286 TU154 78A-286
CCCP-85287 TU154 78A-287
CCCP-85288 TU154 78A-288
CCCP-85289 TU154 78A-289
CCCP-85290 TU154 78A-290
CCCP-85291 TU154 78A-291
CCCP-85292 TU154 78A-292
CCCP-85293 TU154 78A-293
CCCP-85294 TU154 78A-294
CCCP-85295 TU154 78A-295
CCCP-85296 TU154 78A-296

CCCP-85297 TU154 78A-297
CCCP-85298 TU154 78A-298
CCCP-85299 TU154 78A-299
CCCP-85300 TU154 78A-300
CCCP-85301 TU154 78A-301
CCCP-85302 TU154 78A-302
CCCP-85303 TU154 78A-303
CCCP-85304 TU154 78A-304
CCCP-85305 TU154 78A-305
CCCP-85306 TU154 78A-306
CCCP-85307 TU154 78A-307
CCCP-85308 TU154 78A-308
CCCP-85309 TU154 78A-309
CCCP-85310 TU154 78A-310
CCCP-85311 TU154 78A-311
CCCP-85312 TU154 78A-312
CCCP-85313 TU154 78A-313
CCCP-85314 TU154 78A-314
CCCP-85315 TU154 78A-315
CCCP-85316 TU154 78A-316
CCCP-85317 TU154 78A-317
CCCP-85318 TU154 79A-318
CCCP-85319 TU154 79A-319
CCCP-85321 TU154 79A-321
CCCP-85322 TU154 79A-322
CCCP-85323 TU154 79A-323
CCCP-85324 TU154 79A-324
CCCP-85327 TU154 79A-327
CCCP-85328 TU154 79A-328
CCCP-85329 TU154 79A-329
CCCP-85330 TU154 79A-330
CCCP-85331 TU154 79A-331
CCCP-85332 TU154 79A-332
CCCP-85333 TU154 79A-333
CCCP-85334 TU154 79A-334
CCCP-85335 TU154 79A-335
CCCP-85336 TU154 79A-336
CCCP-85337 TU154 79A-337
CCCP-85338 TU154 79A-338
CCCP-85339 TU154 79A-339
CCCP-85340 TU154 79A-340
CCCP-85341 TU154 79A-341
CCCP-85343 TU154 79A-343
CCCP-85344 TU154 79A-344
CCCP-85345 TU154 79A-345
CCCP-85346 TU154 79A-346
CCCP-85347 TU154 79A-347
CCCP-85348 TU154 79A-348
CCCP-85349 TU154 79A-349
CCCP-85350 TU154 79A-350
CCCP-85351 TU154 79A-351
CCCP-85352 TU154 79A-352
CCCP-85353 TU154 79A-353
CCCP-85354 TU154 79A-354
CCCP-85355 TU154 79A-355
CCCP-85356 TU154 79A-356
CCCP-85357 TU154 79A-357
CCCP-85358 TU154 79A-358
CCCP-85359 TU154 79A-359
CCCP-85360 TU154 79A-360
CCCP-85361 TU154 79A-361
CCCP-85362 TU154 79A-362
CCCP-85363 TU154 79A-363
CCCP-85364 TU154 79A-364
CCCP-85365 TU154 79A-365
CCCP-85366 TU154 79A-366
CCCP-85367 TU154 79A-367
CCCP-85368 TU154 79A-368
CCCP-85369 TU154 79A-369
CCCP-85370 TU154 79A-370
CCCP-85371 TU154 79A-371
CCCP-85372 TU154 79A-372
CCCP-85373 TU154 79A-373
CCCP-85374 TU154 79A-374
CCCP-85375 TU154 79A-375
CCCP-85376 TU154 79A-376
CCCP-85377 TU154 79A-377
CCCP-85378 TU154 79A-378
CCCP-85379 TU154 79A-379
CCCP-85380 TU154 79A-380
CCCP-85381 TU154 79A-381
CCCP-85382 TU154 79A-382

CCCP-85383 TU154 79A-383	CCCP-85471 TU154 81A-471	CCCP-85559 TU154 82A-559	CCCP-85647 TU154 88A-785
CCCP-85384 TU154 79A-384	CCCP-85472 TU154 81A-472	CCCP-85560 TU154 82A-560	CCCP-85648 TU154 88A-786
CCCP-85385 TU154 79A-385	CCCP-85475 TU154 81A-475	CCCP-85561 TU154 82A-561	CCCP-85649 TU154 88A-787
CCCP-85386 TU154 79A-386	CCCP-85476 TU154 81A-476	CCCP-85562 TU154 82A-562	CCCP-85650 TU154 88A-788
CCCP-85387 TU154 79A-387	CCCP-85477 TU154 81A-477	CCCP-85563 TU154 82A-563	CCCP-85651 TU154 88A-793
CCCP-85388 TU154 79A-388	CCCP-85478 TU154 81A-478	CCCP-85564 TU154 82A-564	CCCP-85652 TU154 88A-794
CCCP-85389 TU154 80A-389	CCCP-85479 TU154 81A-479	CCCP-85565 TU154 82A-565	CCCP-85653 TU154 88A-795
CCCP-85390 TU154 80A-390	CCCP-85480 TU154 81A-480	CCCP-85566 TU154 82A-566	CCCP-85654 TU154 88A-796
CCCP-85391 TU154 80A-391	CCCP-85481 TU154 81A-481	CCCP-85567 TU154 83A-567	CCCP-85655 TU154 89A-798
CCCP-85392 TU154 80A-392	CCCP-85482 TU154 81A-482	CCCP-85568 TU154 83A-568	CCCP-85656 TU154 89A-801
CCCP-85393 TU154 80A-393	CCCP-85485 TU154 81A-485	CCCP-85570 TU154 83A-570	CCCP-85657 TU154 89A-802
CCCP-85394 TU154 80A-394	CCCP-85486 TU154 81A-486	CCCP-85571 TU154 83A-571	CCCP-85658 TU154 89A-808
CCCP-85395 TU154 80A-395	CCCP-85487 TU154 81A-487	CCCP-85572 TU154 83A-572	CCCP-85659 TU154 89A-809
CCCP-85396 TU154 80A-396	CCCP-85488 TU154 81A-488	CCCP-85574 TU154 83A-574	CCCP-85660 TU154 89A-810
CCCP-85397 TU154 80A-397	CCCP-85489 TU154 81A-489	CCCP-85575 TU154 83A-575	CCCP-85661 TU154 89A-811
CCCP-85398 TU154 80A-398	CCCP-85490 TU154 81A-490	CCCP-85577 TU154 83A-577	CCCP-85662 TU154 89A-816
CCCP-85399 TU154 80A-399	CCCP-85491 TU154 81A-491	CCCP-85578 TU154 83A-578	CCCP-85663 TU154 89A-817
CCCP-85400 TU154 80A-400	CCCP-85492 TU154 81A-492	CCCP-85579 TU154 83A-579	CCCP-85664 TU154 89A-818
CCCP-85401 TU154 80A-401	CCCP-85494 TU154 81A-494	CCCP-85580 TU154 83A-580	CCCP-85665 TU154 89A-819
CCCP-85402 TU154 80A-402	CCCP-85495 TU154 81A-495	CCCP-85581 TU154 83A-581	CCCP-85666 TU154 89A-820
CCCP-85403 TU154 80A-403	CCCP-85496 TU154 81A-496	CCCP-85582 TU154 83A-582	CCCP-85667 TU154 89A-825
CCCP-85404 TU154 80A-404	CCCP-85497 TU154 81A-497	CCCP-85583 TU154 83A-583	CCCP-85668 TU154 89A-826
CCCP-85405 TU154 80A-405	CCCP-85498 TU154 81A-498	CCCP-85584 TU154 83A-584	CCCP-85669 TU154 89A-827
CCCP-85406 TU154 80A-406	CCCP-85499 TU154 81A-499	CCCP-85585 TU154 83A-585	CCCP-85670 TU154 89A-828
CCCP-85407 TU154 80A-407	CCCP-85500 TU154 81A-500	CCCP-85586 TU154 83A-586	CCCP-85671 TU154 89A-829
CCCP-85409 TU154 80A-409	CCCP-85502 TU154 81A-502	CCCP-85587 TU154 83A-587	CCCP-85672 TU154 89A-830
CCCP-85410 TU154 80A-410	CCCP-85503 TU154 81A-503	CCCP-85588 TU154 83A-588	CCCP-85673 TU154 90A-833
CCCP-85411 TU154 80A-411	CCCP-85504 TU154 81A-504	CCCP-85589 TU154 83A-589	CCCP-85674 TU154 90A-834
CCCP-85412 TU154 80A-412	CCCP-85505 TU154 81A-505	CCCP-85590 TU154 83A-590	CCCP-85675 TU154 90A-835
CCCP-85413 TU154 80A-413	CCCP-85506 TU154 81A-506	CCCP-85591 TU154 83A-591	CCCP-85676 TU154 90A-836
CCCP-85414 TU154 80A-414	CCCP-85507 TU154 81A-507	CCCP-85592 TU154 83A-592	CCCP-85677 TU154 90A-839
CCCP-85416 TU154 80A-416	CCCP-85508 TU154 81A-508	CCCP-85593 TU154 83A-593	CCCP-85678 TU154 90A-841
CCCP-85417 TU154 80A-417	CCCP-85509 TU154 81A-509	CCCP-85594 TU154 83A-594	CCCP-85679 TU154 90A-842
CCCP-85418 TU154 80A-418	CCCP-85510 TU154 82A-510	CCCP-85595 TU154 83A-595	CCCP-85680 TU154 90A-843
CCCP-85419 TU154 80A-419	CCCP-85511 TU154 81A-511	CCCP-85596 TU154 84A-596	CCCP-85681 TU154 90A-848
CCCP-85421 TU154 80A-421	CCCP-85512 TU154 81A-512	CCCP-85597 TU154 84A-597	CCCP-85682 TU154 90A-849
CCCP-85423 TU154 80A-423	CCCP-85513 TU154 81A-513	CCCP-85598 TU154 84A-598	CCCP-85683 TU154 90A-850
CCCP-85424 TU154 80A-424	CCCP-85514 TU154 81A-514	CCCP-85600 TU154 84A-600	CCCP-85684 TU154 90A-851
CCCP-85425 TU154 80A-425	CCCP-85515 TU154 81A-515	CCCP-85602 TU154 84A-602	CCCP-85685 TU154 90A-853
CCCP-85426 TU154 81A-426	CCCP-85516 TU154 81A-516	CCCP-85603 TU154 84A-603	CCCP-85686 TU154 90A-854
CCCP-85427 TU154 80A-427	**CCCP-85517 TU154 ?**	CCCP-85604 TU154 84A-604	CCCP-85687 TU154 90A-857
CCCP-85429 TU154 80A-429	CCCP-85518 TU154 81A-518	CCCP-85605 TU154 84A-605	CCCP-85688 TU154 90A-859
CCCP-85430 TU154 80A-430	CCCP-85519 TU154 81A-519	CCCP-85606 TU154 84A-701	CCCP-85689 TU154 90A-860
CCCP-85431 TU154 80A-431	CCCP-85520 TU154 81A-520	CCCP-85607 TU154 84A-702	CCCP-85690 TU154 90A-861
CCCP-85432 TU154 80A-432	CCCP-85521 TU154 81A-521	CCCP-85608 TU154 84A-703	CCCP-85691 TU154 90A-864
CCCP-85433 TU154 80A-433	CCCP-85522 TU154 81A-522	**CCCP-85609 TU154 84A-704**	CCCP-85692 TU154 90A-865
CCCP-85434 TU154 80A-434	CCCP-85523 TU154 81A-523	CCCP-85610 TU154 84A-705	CCCP-85693 TU154 91A-866
CCCP-85435 TU154 80A-435	CCCP-85524 TU154 82A-524	CCCP-85612 TU154 85A-721	CCCP-85694 TU154 91A-867
CCCP-85436 TU154 80A-436	CCCP-85525 TU154 82A-525	CCCP-85613 TU154 85A-722	CCCP-85695 TU154 91A-868
CCCP-85437 TU154 80A-437	CCCP-85526 TU154 82A-526	CCCP-85614 TU154 86A-723	CCCP-85696 TU154 91A-869
CCCP-85438 TU154 80A-438	CCCP-85527 TU154 82A-527	CCCP-85615 TU154 86A-731	CCCP-85697 TU154 91A-870
CCCP-85439 TU154 80A-439	CCCP-85528 TU154 82A-528	CCCP-85616 TU154 86A-732	CCCP-85698 TU154 91A-871
CCCP-85440 TU154 80A-440	CCCP-85529 TU154 82A-529	CCCP-85617 TU154 86A-736	CCCP-85699 TU154 91A-874
CCCP-85441 TU154 80A-441	CCCP-85530 TU154 82A-530	CCCP-85618 TU154 86A-737	CCCP 85700 TU154 91A-075
CCCP-85442 TU154 80A-442	CCCP-85531 TU154 82A-531	CCCP-85619 TU154 86A-738	CCCP-85701 TU154 69M001
CCCP-85443 TU154 80A-443	CCCP-85532 TU154 82A-532	CCCP-85620 TU154 86A-739	CCCP-85701 TU154 91A-876
CCCP-85444 TU154 80A-444	CCCP-85533 TU154 82A-533	CCCP-85621 TU154 86A-742	CCCP-85702 TU154 ..M002
CCCP-85445 TU154 80A-445	CCCP-85534 TU154 82A-534	CCCP-85622 TU154 87A-746	CCCP-85702 TU154 91A-877
CCCP-85446 TU154 80A-446	CCCP-85535 TU154 82A-535	CCCP-85623 TU154 87A-749	CCCP-85703 TU154 ..M003
CCCP-85448 TU154 80A-448	CCCP-85536 TU154 82A-536	CCCP-85624 TU154 87A-750	CCCP-85703 TU154 91A-878
CCCP-85449 TU154 80A-449	CCCP-85537 TU154 82A-537	CCCP-85625 TU154 87A-752	CCCP-85704 TU154 ..M004
CCCP-85450 TU154 80A-450	CCCP-85538 TU154 82A-538	CCCP-85626 TU154 87A-753	CCCP-85704 TU154 91A-879
CCCP-85451 TU154 80A-451	CCCP-85539 TU154 82A-539	CCCP-85627 TU154 87A-756	CCCP-85705 TU154 91A-880
CCCP-85452 TU154 80A-452	CCCP-85540 TU154 82A-540	CCCP-85628 TU154 87A-757	CCCP-85706 TU154 91A-881
CCCP-85453 TU154 80A-453	**CCCP-85541 TU154 ?**	CCCP-85629 TU154 87A-758	CCCP-85707 TU154 91A-882
CCCP-85454 TU154 80A-454	CCCP-85542 TU154 82A-542	CCCP-85630 TU154 87A-759	CCCP-85708 TU154 91A-883
CCCP-85455 TU154 80A-455	CCCP-85543 TU154 82A-543	CCCP-85631 TU154 87A-760	CCCP-85709 TU154 91A-884
CCCP-85456 TU154 80A-456	CCCP-85544 TU154 82A-544	CCCP-85632 TU154 87A-761	CCCP-85710 TU154 91A-885
CCCP-85457 TU154 80A-457	CCCP-85545 TU154 82A-545	CCCP-85633 TU154 87A-762	CCCP-85711 TU154 91A-887
CCCP-85458 TU154 80A-458	CCCP-85546 TU154 82A-546	CCCP-85634 TU154 87A-763	CCCP-85712 TU154 91A-888
CCCP-85459 TU154 80A-459	CCCP-85547 TU154 82A-547	CCCP-85635 TU154 87A-764	CCCP-85713 TU154 91A-889
CCCP-85460 TU154 80A-460	CCCP-85548 TU154 82A-548	CCCP-85636 TU154 87A-766	CCCP-85714 TU154 91A-890
CCCP-85461 TU154 80A-461	CCCP-85549 TU154 82A-549	CCCP-85637 TU154 87A-767	CCCP-85715 TU154 91A-891
CCCP-85462 TU154 80A-462	CCCP-85550 TU154 82A-550	CCCP-85638 TU154 87A-768	CCCP-85716 TU154 91A-892
CCCP-85463 TU154 80A-463	CCCP-85551 TU154 82A-551	CCCP-85639 TU154 88A-771	CCCP-85717 TU154 91A-897
CCCP-85464 TU154 80A-464	CCCP-85552 TU154 82A-552	CCCP-85640 TU154 88A-772	CCCP-85718 TU154 91A-900
CCCP-85465 TU154 80A-465	CCCP-85553 TU154 82A-553	CCCP-85641 TU154 88A-773	CCCP-85719 TU154 91A-901
CCCP-85466 TU154 80A-466	CCCP-85554 TU154 82A-554	CCCP-85642 TU154 88A-778	(CCCP-85720)TU154 85A-720
CCCP-85467 TU154 81A-467	CCCP-85555 TU154 82A-555	CCCP-85643 TU154 88A-779	CCCP-85720 TU154 91A-902
CCCP-85468 TU154 81A-468	CCCP-85556 TU154 82A-556	CCCP-85644 TU154 88A-780	CCCP-85721 TU154 91A-903
CCCP-85469 TU154 81A-469	CCCP-85557 TU154 82A-557	CCCP-85645 TU154 88A-782	CCCP-85722 TU154 91A-904
CCCP-85470 TU154 81A-470	CCCP-85558 TU154 82A-558	CCCP-85646 TU154 88A-784	CCCP-85723 TU154 91A-905

CCCP-85724 TU154 91A-906	CCCP-86059 IL86 51483203026	ČCCP-86461 IL62 3624711	CCCP-86552 IL62 2052345
CCCP-85725 TU154 91A-907	CCCP-86060 IL86 51483203027	CCCP-86462 IL62 3624623	CCCP-86553 IL62 3052657
CCCP-85727 TU154 92A-909	CCCP-86061 IL86 51483203028	CCCP-86463 IL62 4624434	CCCP-86554 IL62 4053514
CCCP-85728 TU154 92A-910	CCCP-86062 IL86 51483203029	CCCP-86464 IL62 4624151	CCCP-86555 IL62 4547315
CCCP-85729 TU154 92A-911	CCCP-86063 IL86 51483203030	CCCP-86465 IL62 4625315	CCCP-86556 IL62 31401
CCCP-85730 TU154 92A-912	CCCP-86064 IL86 51483204031	CCCP-86466 IL62 2749316	CCCP-86557 IL62 2725456
CCCP-85731 TU154 92A-913	CCCP-86065 IL86 51483204032	CCCP-86467 IL62 3749733	CCCP-86558 IL62 1052128
CCCP-85732 TU154 92A-914	CCCP-86066 IL86 51483204033	CCCP-86468 IL62 4749857	CCCP-86559 IL62 2153258
CCCP-85733 TU154 92A-915	CCCP-86067 IL86 51483204034	CCCP-86469 IL62 1725121	CCCP-86560 IL62 2153347
CCCP-85735 TU154 92A-917	CCCP-86068 IL86 51483204035	CCCP-86470 IL62 1725234	CCCP-86561 IL62 4154842
CCCP-85736 TU154 92A-918	CCCP-86069 IL86 51483204036	CCCP-86471 IL62 2725345	CCCP-86562 IL62 4831517
CCCP-85737 TU154 92A-920	CCCP-86070 IL86 51483204037	CCCP-86472 IL62 2726517	CCCP-86563 IL62 3036931
CCCP-85738 TU154 92A-921	CCCP-86071 IL86 51483204038	CCCP-86473 IL62 3726841	CCCP-86564 IL62 4934734
CCCP-85739 TU154 92A-925	CCCP-86072 IL86 51483204039	CCCP-86474 IL62 3726952	CCCP-86565 IL62 2546812
CCCP-85740 TU154 91A-895	CCCP-86073 IL86 51483204040	CCCP-86475 IL62 3727213	CCCP-86572 IL62 3154624
CCCP-85741 TU154 91A-896	CCCP-86074 IL86 51483205041	CCCP-86476 IL62 4728229	CCCP-86573 IL62 4140536
CCCP-85742 TU154 79A-320	CCCP-86075 IL86 51483205044	CCCP-86477 IL62 4727435	CCCP-86574 IL62 3344833
CCCP-85743 TU154 92A-926	CCCP-86076 IL86 51483205045	CCCP-86478 IL62 4727657	CCCP-86575 IL62 1647928
CCCP-85744 TU154 92A-927	CCCP-86077 IL86 51483205047	CCCP-86479 IL62 4728118	CCCP-86576 IL62 4546257
(CCCP-85765)TU154 87A-765	CCCP-86078 IL86 51483205049	CCCP-86480 IL62 2828354	CCCP-86577 IL62 2748552
(CCCP-85789)TU154 88A-789	CCCP-86079 IL86 51483205050	CCCP-86481 IL62 2829415	CCCP-86578 IL62 1951525
CCCP-85846 TU154 90A-846	CCCP-86080 IL86 51483206051	CCCP-86482 IL62 2829526	CCCP-86579 IL62 2951636
(CCCP-85898)TU154 91A-898	CCCP-86081 IL86 51483206052	CCCP-86483 IL62 2829637	CCCP-86580 IL62 2343554
(CCCP-85899)TU154 91A-899	CCCP-86082 IL86 51483206053	CCCP-86484 IL62 4727324	CCCP-86581 IL62 2932526
CCCP-86000 IL86 0101?	CCCP-86083 IL86 51483206054	CCCP-86485 IL62 3830912	CCCP-86582 IL62 3036253
CCCP-86001 IL86 0102?	CCCP-86084 IL86 51483206055	CCCP-86486 IL62 3830123	CCCP-86600 IL76 033401022
CCCP-86002 IL86 0103	CCCP-86085 IL86 51483206056	CCCP-86487 IL62 3830234	CCCP-86601 IL76 033402026
CCCP-86003 IL86 51483200001	CCCP-86086 IL86 51483206057	CCCP-86488 IL62 4830345	CCCP-86602 IL76 033402031
CCCP-86004 IL86 51483200002	CCCP-86087 IL86 51483206058	CCCP-86489 IL62 4830456	CCCP-86603 IL76 043402035
CCCP-86005 IL86 51483200003	CCCP-86088 IL86 51483206059	CCCP-86490 IL62 4831739	CCCP-86604 IL76 043402039
CCCP-86006 IL86 51483200004	CCCP-86089 IL86 51483206060	CCCP-86491 IL62 1931142	CCCP-86605 IL62 41701
CCCP-86007 IL86 51483200005	CCCP-86090 IL86 51483207061	CCCP-86492 IL62 4140324	CCCP-86606 IL62 41702
CCCP-86008 IL86 51483200006	CCCP-86091 IL86 51483207062	CCCP-86493 IL62 4140748	CCCP-86607 IL62 41703
CCCP-86009 IL86 51483200007	CCCP-86092 IL86 51483207063	CCCP-86494 IL62 4140859	CCCP-86608 IL62 41704
CCCP-86010 IL86 51483201008	CCCP-86093 IL86 51483207064	CCCP-86495 IL62 2726628	CCCP-86609 IL62 41705
CCCP-86011 IL86 51483201009	CCCP-86094 IL86 51483207065	CCCP-86496 IL62 3829859	CCCP-86610 IL62 41801
CCCP-86012 IL86 51483201010	CCCP-86095 IL86 51483207066	CCCP-86497 IL62 1931253	CCCP-86611 IL62 41803
CCCP-86013 IL86 51483201011	CCCP-86096 IL86 51483207067	CCCP-86498 IL62 1932314	CCCP-86612 IL62 41804
CCCP-86014 IL86 51483202012	CCCP-86097 IL86 51483207068	CCCP-86499 IL62 2932637	CCCP-86613 IL62 51901
CCCP-86015 IL86 51483202013	CCCP-86101 IL86 51483207069	CCCP-86500 IL62 2932859	CCCP-86614 IL62 51903
CCCP-86016 IL86 51483202014	CCCP-86102 IL86 51483207070	CCCP-86501 IL62 3933121	CCCP-86615 IL62 51904
CCCP-86017 IL86 51483202015	CCCP-86103 IL86 51483208071	CCCP-86502 IL62 3933345	CCCP-86616 IL62 51905
CCCP-86018 IL86 51483202016	CCCP-86104 IL86 51483208072	CCCP-86503 IL62 4934512	CCCP-86617 IL62 2520314
CCCP-86020 IL76 083413403	CCCP-86105 IL86 51483208073	CCCP-86504 IL62 4934623	CCCP-86618 IL62 3520422
CCCP-86021 IL76 083413405	CCCP-86106 IL86 51483208074	CCCP-86505 IL62 4934847	CCCP-86619 IL62 3520233
CCCP-86022 IL76 083413417	CCCP-86107 IL86 51483208075	CCCP-86506 IL62 1035234	CCCP-86620 IL62 3520345
CCCP-86023 IL76 083413422	CCCP-86108 IL86 51483208076	CCCP-86507 IL62 2035546	CCCP-86621 IL62 3520556
CCCP-86024 IL76 083414425	CCCP-86109 IL86 51483208077	CCCP-86508 IL62 2036718	CCCP-86622 IL62 4521617
CCCP-86025 IL76 083414433	CLCP-86110 IL86 51483200070	CCCP-86509 IL62 2036829	CCCP-86623 IL62 4521728
CCCP-86026 IL76 083414439	CCCP-86111 IL86 51483208079	CCCP-86510 IL62 1035213	CCCP-86624 IL62 4521839
CCCP-86027 IL76 083415459	CCCP-86112 IL86 51483208080	CCCP-86511 IL62 3036142	CCCP-86625 IL76 063405130
CCCP-86028 IL76 083415464	CCCP-86113 IL86 51483209081	CCCP-86512 IL62 3037314	CCCP-86626 IL76 063405135
CCCP-86029 IL76 083415465	CCCP-86114 IL86 51483209082	CCCP-86513 IL62 4037536	CCCP-86627 IL76 063405137
CCCP-86030 IL76 093415475	CCCP-86115 IL86 51483209083	CCCP-86514 IL62 4037647	CCCP-86628 IL76 063405144
CCCP-86031 IL76 093415477	CCCP-86116 IL86 51483209084	CCCP-86515 IL62 2138657	CCCP-86629 IL76 063406148
CCCP-86032 IL76 093415482	CCCP-86117 IL86 51483209085	CCCP-86516 IL62 2139524	CCCP-86630 IL76 063406149
CCCP-86033 IL76 093416488	CCCP-86118 IL86 51483209086	CCCP-86517 IL62 3139732	CCCP-86631 IL76 063407202
CCCP-86034 IL76 093416489	CCCP-86119 IL86 51483209087	CCCP-86518 IL62 3139956	CCCP-86632 IL76 073409251
CCCP-86035 IL76 093416494	CCCP-86120 IL86 51483209088	CCCP-86519 IL62 4140212	CCCP-86633 IL76 073409256
CCCP-86036 IL76 093416500?	CCCP-86121 IL86 51483209089	CCCP-86520 IL62 1241314	CCCP-86634 IL76 063408214
CCCP-86037 IL76 093417511	CCCP-86122 IL86 51483209090	CCCP-86521 IL62 1241425	CCCP-86635 IL76 063408217
CCCP-86038 IL76 093417514	CCCP-86123 IL86 51483210091	CCCP-86522 IL62 2241536	CCCP-86636 IL76 063408222
CCCP-86039 IL76 093417518	CCCP-86124 IL86 51483210092	CCCP-86523 IL62 2241647	CCCP-86637 IL76 063409228
CCCP-86040 IL76 093417521	CCCP-86132 IL62 1034152	CCCP-86524 IL62 3242321	CCCP-86638 IL76 073409232
CCCP-86041 IL76 093417532	CCCP-86133 IL62 1138234	CCCP-86525 IL62 4851612	CCCP-86639 IL76 073409235
CCCP-86042 IL76 093417535	CCCP-86134 IL62 1138546	CCCP-86526 IL62 2951447	CCCP-86640 IL76 073409237
CCCP-86043 IL76 093418539	CCCP-86135 IL62 1748445	CCCP-86527 IL62 4037758	CCCP-86641 IL76 073409243
CCCP-86044 IL76 093418552	CCCP-86146 IL86 51483205042	CCCP-86528 IL62 4038111	CCCP-86642 IL76 073409248
CCCP-86045 IL76 093418564	CCCP-86147 IL86 51483205043	CCCP-86529 IL62 4038625	CCCP-86643 IL76 043402041
CCCP-86046 IL76 093418565	CCCP-86148 IL86 51483205046	CCCP-86530 IL62 3242543	CCCP-86644 IL76 043402046
CCCP-86047 IL76 093418572	CCCP-86149 IL86 51483205048	CCCP-86531 IL62 4242654	CCCP-86645 IL76 043402049
CCCP-86048 IL76 093419573	CCCP-86450 IL62 4521941	CCCP-86532 IL62 4243111	CCCP-86646 IL76 043402053
CCCP-86049 IL76 093419580	CCCP-86451 IL62 4521152	CCCP-86533 IL62 1343123	CCCP-86647 IL76 043402060
CCCP-86050 IL86 51483202017	CCCP-86452 IL62 1622212	CCCP-86534 IL62 1343332	CCCP-86648 IL62 00605
CCCP-86051 IL86 51483202018	CCCP-86453 IL62 1622323	CCCP-86535 IL62 2444555	CCCP-86649 IL62 00703
CCCP-86052 IL86 51483202019	CCCP-86454 IL62 1622434	CCCP-86536 IL62 4445948	CCCP-86650 IL62 00705
CCCP-86053 IL86 51483202020	CCCP-86455 IL62 2622656	CCCP-86537 IL62 3546733	CCCP-86651 IL62 00801
CCCP-86054 IL86 51483203021	CCCP-86456 IL62 2623717	CCCP-86538 IL62 2241758	CCCP-86652 IL62 00802
CCCP-86055 IL86 51483203022	CCCP-86457 IL62 2623822	CCCP-86539 IL62 2344615	CCCP-86653 IL62 00803
CCCP-86056 IL86 51483203023	CCCP-86458 IL62 3623834	CCCP-86540 IL62 3546548	CCCP-86654 IL62 00804
CCCP-86057 IL86 51483203024	CCCP-86459 IL62 3623945	CCCP-86541 IL62 3951359	CCCP-86655 IL62 00805
CCCP-86058 IL86 51483203025	CCCP-86460 IL62 3623856	CCCP-86542 IL62 3952714	CCCP-86656 IL62 00901

CCCP-86657 IL62 10904	CCCP-86740 IL76 083412358	CCCP-86878 IL76 0013430875	CCCP-87232 YAK40 9531742
CCCP-86659 IL62 31404	CCCP-86741 IL76 083412361	CCCP-86879 IL76 0013430893	CCCP-87233 YAK40 9531842
CCCP-86661 IL62 50101	CCCP-86742 IL76 083412366	CCCP-86880 IL76 0013430897	CCCP-87234 YAK40 9531942
CCCP-86662 IL62 50102	CCCP-86743 IL76 083412369	CCCP-86881 IL76 0013431906	CCCP-87235 YAK40 9530143
CCCP-86663 IL62 60103	CCCP-86744 IL76 083412376	CCCP-86882 IL76 0013431917	CCCP-87236 YAK40 9530243
CCCP-86664 IL62 60104	CCCP-86745 IL76 063407162	CCCP-86883 IL76 0013431921	CCCP-87237 YAK40 9530343
CCCP-86665 IL62 60105	CCCP-86746 IL76 063407165	CCCP-86884 IL76 0013431932	CCCP-87238 YAK40 9530543
CCCP-86666 IL62 60201	CCCP-86747 IL76 063407170	CCCP-86885 IL76 0013431939	CCCP-87239 YAK40 9530643
CCCP-86667 IL62 60202	CCCP-86748 IL76 063407175	CCCP-86886 IL76 0013431943	CCCP-87240 YAK40 9530743
CCCP-86668 IL62 70203	CCCP-86749 IL76 063407179	CCCP-86887 IL76 0013431945	CCCP-87241 YAK40 9530943
CCCP-86669 IL62 70204	CCCP-86805 IL76 053403073	CCCP-86888 IL76 0013432966	CCCP-87242 YAK40 9531043
CCCP-86670 IL62 70205	CCCP-86806 IL76 053403078	CCCP-86889 IL76 0013434009	CCCP-87243 YAK40 9531143
CCCP-86671 IL62 70301	CCCP-86807 IL76 053404083	CCCP-86890 IL76 0013434013	CCCP-87244 YAK40 9531243
CCCP-86672 IL62 70302	CCCP-86808 IL76 053404085	CCCP-86891 IL76 093421628	CCCP-87245 YAK40 9531343
CCCP-86673 IL62 3154416	CCCP-86809 IL76 053404091	CCCP-86892 IL76 0013432969	CCCP-87246 YAK40 9541443
CCCP-86673 IL62 70303	CCCP-86810 IL76 053404094	CCCP-86893 IL76 0013432975	CCCP-87247 YAK40 9531543
CCCP-86674 IL62 80304	CCCP-86811 IL76 053404098	CCCP-86894 IL76 0013432977	CCCP-87248 YAK40 9540144
CCCP-86675 IL62 80305	CCCP-86812 IL76 053404103	CCCP-86895 IL76 0013433985	CCCP-87249 YAK40 9530244
CCCP-86676 IL62 80401	CCCP-86813 IL76 053404105	CCCP-86896 IL76 0013434018	CCCP-87250 YAK40 9310726
CCCP-86677 IL62 80402	CCCP-86814 IL76 053405110	CCCP-86897 IL76 0013434023	CCCP-87251 YAK40 9310826
CCCP-86678 IL62 80403	CCCP-86815 IL76 063407183	CCCP-86898 IL76 0023435028	CCCP-87252 YAK40 9310926
CCCP-86679 IL62 80404	CCCP-86816 IL76 063407185	CCCP-86899 IL76 0023435030	CCCP-87253 YAK40 9321026
CCCP-86680 IL62 80405	CCCP-86817 IL76 063407191	CCCP-86900 IL76 0023435034	CCCP-87254 YAK40 9311126
CCCP-86681 IL62 90501	CCCP-86818 IL76 063407194	CCCP-86901 IL76 0023436038	CCCP-87255 YAK40 9311226
CCCP-86682 IL62 90502	CCCP-86819 IL76 063407199	CCCP-86902 IL76 0023436043	CCCP-87256 YAK40 9311326
CCCP-86683 IL62 90503	CCCP-86821 IL76 053405114	CCCP-86903 IL76 0023436048	CCCP-87257 YAK40 9311426
CCCP-86684 IL62 90504	CCCP-86822 IL76 053405117	CCCP-86904 IL76 0023436050	CCCP-87258 YAK40 9311526
CCCP-86685 IL62 90505	CCCP-86823 IL76 053405124	CCCP-86905 IL76 0023436054	CCCP-87259 YAK40 9311626
CCCP-86686 IL62 90601	CCCP-86824 IL76 053405128	CCCP-86906 IL76 0023436064	CCCP-87260 YAK40 9311126A
CCCP-86687 IL62 90604	CCCP-86825 IL76 093419581	CCCP-86907 IL76 0023436065	CCCP-87261 YAK40 9311726
CCCP-86688 IL62 10905	CCCP-86826 IL76 093419588	CCCP-86908 IL76 0023437070	CCCP-87262 YAK40 9321826
CCCP-86689 IL62 11001	CCCP-86827 IL76 093419589	CCCP-86909 IL76 0023437076	CCCP-87263 YAK40 9311926
CCCP-86690 IL62 11002	CCCP-86828 IL76 093420604	CCCP-86910 IL76 0023437077	CCCP-87264 YAK40 9312026
CCCP-86691 IL62 11003	CCCP-86829 IL76 0003427798	CCCP-86911 IL76 0023437093	CCCP-87265 YAK40 9310127
CCCP-86692 IL62 11102	CCCP-86830 IL76 093421626	CCCP-86912 IL76 0023437099?	CCCP-87266 YAK40 9310227
CCCP-86693 IL62 11103	CCCP-86831 IL76 093421642	CCCP-86913 IL76 0023438108	CCCP-87267 YAK40 9310327
CCCP-86694 IL62 11104	CCCP-86832 IL76 0003421646	CCCP-86914 IL76 0023438111	CCCP-87268 YAK40 9310427
CCCP-86695 IL62 21204	CCCP-86833 IL76 0003422650	CCCP-86915 IL76 0023438116	CCCP-87269 YAK40 9310527
CCCP-86696 IL62 21205	CCCP-86834 IL76 0003422655	CCCP-86916 IL76 0023438120	CCCP-87270 YAK40 9310627
CCCP-86697 IL62 21301	CCCP-86835 IL76 0003422658	CCCP-86917 IL76 0023438122	CCCP-87271 YAK40 9310727
CCCP-86698 IL62 21303	CCCP-86836 IL76 0003422661	CCCP-86918 IL76 0023438127	CCCP-87272 YAK40 9330827
CCCP-86699 IL62 21304	CCCP-86837 IL76 0003423668	CCCP-86919 IL76 0023438129	CCCP-87273 YAK40 9310927
CCCP-86700 IL62 31503	CCCP-86838 IL76 0003423669	CCCP-86920 IL76 0023440152	CCCP-87274 YAK40 9311027
CCCP-86701 IL62 31504	CCCP-86839 IL76 0003423684	CCCP-86921 IL76 0023440161	CCCP-87275 YAK40 9311127
CCCP-86702 IL62 31505	CCCP-86840 IL76 0003423688	CCCP-86922 IL76 0023440168	CCCP-87276 YAK40 9311227
CCCP-86703 IL62 31601	CCCP-86841 IL76 0003423690	CCCP-86923 IL76 0023441169	CCCP-87277 YAK40 9311327
CCCP-86704 IL62 41603	CCCP-86842 IL76 0003423694	CCCP-86924 IL76 0023441174	CCCP-87278 YAK40 9311427
CCCP-86705 IL62 41605	CCCP-86843 IL76 0003423701	CCCP-86925 IL76 0093492766	CCCP-87279 YAK40 9321527
CCCP-86706 IL62 21105	CCCP-86844 IL76 0003424711	CCCP-86925 IL76 093421621	CCCP-87280 YAK40 9322025
CCCP-86707 IL62 41604	CCCP-86845 IL76 0003426762	CCCP-86926 IL76 0013430901	CCCP-87281 YAK40 9311627
CCCP-86708 IL62 41802	CCCP-86846 IL76 0003426765	CCCP-86927 IL76 0023439133	CCCP-87282 YAK40 9321727
CCCP-86709 IL62 ..62204	CCCP-86847 IL76 0003426769	CCCP-87200 YAK40 9811956	CCCP-87283 YAK40 9311827
CCCP-86710 IL62 2647646	CCCP-86848 IL76 0003426776	CCCP-87201 YAK40 9741256	CCCP-87284 YAK40 9311927
CCCP-86711 IL62 4648414	CCCP-86849 IL76 0003426779	CCCP-87202 YAK40 9812056	CCCP-87285 YAK40 9322027
CCCP 86711 IL76 01-03	CCCP-86850 IL76 0003427782	CCCP-87203 YAK40 9741456	CCCP-87286 YAK40 9310128
CCCP-86712 IL62 4648339	CCCP-86851 IL76 0003424715	CCCP-87204 YAK40 9810157	CCCP-87287 YAK40 9320228
CCCP-86712 IL76 01-01	**CCCP-86852 IL76 0003424719**	CCCP-87205 YAK40 9810257	CCCP-87288 YAK40 9320328
CCCP-86713 IL76 043403061	CCCP-86853 IL76 0003424723	CCCP-87206 YAK40 9810357	CCCP-87289 YAK40 9320428
CCCP-86714 IL76 053403067	CCCP-86854 IL76 0003425728	CCCP-87207 YAK40 9810457	CCCP-87290 YAK40 9320528
CCCP-86715 IL76 053403072	CCCP-86855 IL76 0003425734	CCCP-87208 YAK40 9810557	CCCP-87291 YAK40 9320628
CCCP-86716 IL76 063406156	CCCP-86856 IL76 0003425740	CCCP-87209 YAK40 9810657	CCCP-87292 YAK40 9320728
CCCP-86717 IL76 063406160	CCCP-86857 IL76 0003425744	CCCP-87210 YAK40 9810757	CCCP-87293 YAK40 9320828
CCCP-86718 IL76 073409259	CCCP-86858 IL76 0003426751	CCCP-87211 YAK40 9440737	CCCP-87294 YAK40 9320928
CCCP-86719 IL76 073409263	CCCP-86859 IL76 0003426755	CCCP-87212 YAK40 9431536	CCCP-87295 YAK40 9321228
CCCP-86720 IL76 073409267	CCCP-86860 IL76 0003426759	CCCP-87213 YAK40 9641050	CCCP-87296 YAK40 9321328
CCCP-86721 IL76 073410271	CCCP-86861 IL76 0003427804	CCCP-87214 YAK40 9640851	CCCP-87297 YAK40 9321428
CCCP-86722 IL76 073410276	CCCP-86862 IL76 0003427806	CCCP-87215 YAK40 9510540	CCCP-87298 YAK40 9321325
CCCP-86723 IL76 073410279	CCCP-86863 IL76 0003428809	CCCP-87216 YAK40 9510440	CCCP-87299 YAK40 9341528
CCCP-86724 IL76 073410284	CCCP-86864 IL76 0003428816	CCCP-87217 YAK40 9510340	CCCP-87300 YAK40 9321628
CCCP-86725 IL76 073410285	CCCP-86865 IL76 0003428817	CCCP-87218 YAK40 9440937	CCCP-87301 YAK40 9321728
CCCP-86726 IL76 083412380	CCCP-86866 IL76 0003428821	CCCP-87219 YAK40 9932059	CCCP-87302 YAK40 9321828
CCCP-86727 IL76 083413383	CCCP-86867 IL76 0013428825	CCCP-87221 YAK40 9831958	CCCP-87303 YAK40 9321958
CCCP-86728 IL76 073410322	CCCP-86868 IL76 0013428833	CCCP-87222 YAK40 9832058	CCCP-87304 YAK40 9322028
CCCP-86729 IL76 073410300	CCCP-86869 IL76 0013428844	CCCP-87223 YAK40 9840359	CCCP-87305 YAK40 9320129
CCCP-86731 IL76 083413391	CCCP-86870 IL76 0013429847	CCCP-87224 YAK40 9841459	CCCP-87306 YAK40 9320229
CCCP-86732 IL76 083413388?	CCCP-86871 IL76 0013434002	CCCP-87225 YAK40 9841359	CCCP-87307 YAK40 9320329
CCCP-86733 IL76 083413396	CCCP-86872 IL76 0013434008	CCCP-87226 YAK40 9841259	CCCP-87308 YAK40 9320429
CCCP-86734 IL76 083413397	CCCP-86873 IL76 0013429850	CCCP-87227 YAK40 9841559	CCCP-87309 YAK40 9320529
CCCP-86736 IL76 083411342	CCCP-86874 IL76 0013429853	CCCP-87228 YAK40 9841659	CCCP-87310 YAK40 9321327A
CCCP-86737 IL76 083411347	CCCP-86875 IL76 0013429859	CCCP-87229 YAK40 9841759	CCCP-87311 YAK40 9320629
CCCP-86738 IL76 083411352	CCCP-86876 IL76 0013429861	CCCP-87230 YAK40 9541542	CCCP-87312 YAK40 9320729
CCCP-86739 IL76 08341.354	CCCP-86877 IL76 0013429867	CCCP-87231 YAK40 9531642	CCCP-87313 YAK40 9330829

CCCP-87314 YAK40 9330929	CCCP-87396 YAK40 9410833	CCCP-87478 YAK40 9440638	CCCP-87560 YAK40 9211121
CCCP-87315 YAK40 9331429	CCCP-87397 YAK40 9410933	CCCP-87479 YAK40 9441838	CCCP-87561 YAK40 9211221
CCCP-87316 YAK40 9331529	CCCP-87398 YAK40 9411033	CCCP-87480 YAK40 9441938	CCCP-87562 YAK40 9211321
CCCP-87317 YAK40 9331629	CCCP-87399 YAK40 9411133	CCCP-87481 YAK40 9440938	CCCP-87563 YAK40 9211421
CCCP-87318 YAK40 9331729	CCCP-87400 YAK40 9421233	CCCP-87482 YAK40 9441038	CCCP-87564 YAK40 9211621
CCCP-87319 YAK40 9331829	CCCP-87401 YAK40 9411333	CCCP-87483 YAK40 9441138	CCCP-87565 YAK40 9211721
CCCP-87320 YAK40 9331929	CCCP-87402 YAK40 9411433	CCCP-87484 YAK40 9441238	CCCP-87566 YAK40 9211821
CCCP-87321 YAK40 9332029	CCCP-87403 YAK40 9411533	CCCP-87485 YAK40 9441338	CCCP-87567 YAK40 9211921
CCCP-87322 YAK40 9330130	CCCP-87404 YAK40 9411633	CCCP-87486 YAK40 9441438	CCCP-87568 YAK40 9222021
CCCP-87323 YAK40 9330230	CCCP-87405 YAK40 9421733	CCCP-87487 YAK40 9441538	CCCP-87569 YAK40 9220222
CCCP-87324 YAK40 9330330	CCCP-87406 YAK40 9421833	CCCP-87488 YAK40 9441638	CCCP-87570 YAK40 9220322
CCCP-87325 YAK40 9330430	CCCP-87407 YAK40 9421933	CCCP-87489 YAK40 9512038	CCCP-87571 YAK40 9221521
CCCP-87326 YAK40 9330530	CCCP-87408 YAK40 9422033	CCCP-87490 YAK40 9110117	CCCP-87572 YAK40 9220422
CCCP-87327 YAK40 9330630	CCCP-87409 YAK40 9420134	CCCP-87491 YAK40 9621647	CCCP-87573 YAK40 9220522
CCCP-87328 YAK40 9330730	CCCP-87410 YAK40 9420234	CCCP-87492 YAK40 9541545	CCCP-87574 YAK40 9220622
CCCP-87329 YAK40 9330830	CCCP-87411 YAK40 9420334	CCCP-87493 YAK40 9611645	CCCP-87575 YAK40 9220722
CCCP-87330 YAK40 9510139	CCCP-87412 YAK40 9420434	CCCP-87494 YAK40 9541745	CCCP-87576 YAK40 9220822
CCCP-87331 YAK40 9510239	CCCP-87413 YAK40 9420534	CCCP-87495 YAK40 9541845	CCCP-87577 YAK40 9220922
CCCP-87332 YAK40 9510339	CCCP-87414 YAK40 9420634	CCCP-87496 YAK40 9541945	CCCP-87578 YAK40 9221022
CCCP-87333 YAK40 9510439	CCCP-87415 YAK40 9420734	CCCP-87497 YAK40 9542045	CCCP-87579 YAK40 9221122
CCCP-87334 YAK40 9510738	CCCP-87416 YAK40 9420834	CCCP-87498 YAK40 9540146	CCCP-87580 YAK40 9221222
CCCP-87335 YAK40 9510838	CCCP-87417 YAK40 9420934	CCCP-87499 YAK40 9610246	CCCP-87581 YAK40 9221322
CCCP-87336 YAK40 9510539	CCCP-87418 YAK40 9421034	CCCP-87500 YAK40 9511939	CCCP-87582 YAK40 9221422
CCCP-87337 YAK40 9510639	CCCP-87419 YAK40 9421134	CCCP-87501 YAK40 9512039	CCCP-87583 YAK40 9221522
CCCP-87338 YAK40 9510739	CCCP-87420 YAK40 9421234	CCCP-87502 YAK40 9510140	CCCP-87584 YAK40 9221622
CCCP-87339 YAK40 9510839	CCCP-87421 YAK40 9421734	CCCP-87503 YAK40 9520240	CCCP-87585 YAK40 9221722
CCCP-87340 YAK40 9510939	CCCP-87422 YAK40 9421834	CCCP-87504 YAK40 9510640	CCCP-87586 YAK40 9221822
CCCP-87341 YAK40 9521039	CCCP-87423 YAK40 9421934	CCCP-87505 YAK40 9510740	CCCP-87587 YAK40 9221922
CCCP-87342 YAK40 9511139	CCCP-87424 YAK40 9422034	CCCP-87506 YAK40 9520840	CCCP-87588 YAK40 9222022
CCCP-87343 YAK40 9511239	CCCP-87425 YAK40 9420135	CCCP-87507 YAK40 9520940	CCCP-87589 YAK40 9220123
CCCP-87344 YAK40 9511339	CCCP-87426 YAK40 9420235	CCCP-87508 YAK40 9521040	CCCP-87590 YAK40 9110416
CCCP-87345 YAK40 9511439	CCCP-87427 YAK40 9420335	CCCP-87509 YAK40 9521140	CCCP-87591 YAK40 9110516
CCCP-87346 YAK40 9511539	CCCP-87428 YAK40 9420435	CCCP-87510 YAK40 9521240	CCCP-87592 YAK40 9110616
CCCP-87347 YAK40 9511639	CCCP-87429 YAK40 9420535	CCCP-87511 YAK40 9521340	CCCP-87593 YAK40 9110716
CCCP-87348 YAK40 9511739	CCCP-87430 YAK40 9420635	CCCP-87512 YAK40 9521440	CCCP-87594 YAK40 9110816
CCCP-87349 YAK40 9511839	CCCP-87431 YAK40 9420735	CCCP-87513 YAK40 9521540	CCCP-87595 YAK40 9110916
CCCP-87350 YAK40 9331930	CCCP-87432 YAK40 9420835	CCCP-87514 YAK40 9521640	CCCP-87596 YAK40 9111016
CCCP-87351 YAK40 9412030	CCCP-87433 YAK40 9420935	CCCP-87515 YAK40 9521740	CCCP-87597 YAK40 9110117
CCCP-87352 YAK40 9330131	CCCP-87434 YAK40 9421035	CCCP-87516 YAK40 9521840	CCCP-87598 YAK40 9110217
CCCP-87353 YAK40 9330231	CCCP-87435 YAK40 9431135	CCCP-87517 YAK40 9521940	CCCP-87599 YAK40 9110317
CCCP-87354 YAK40 9330331	CCCP-87436 YAK40 9431235	CCCP-87518 YAK40 9522040	CCCP-87600 YAK40 9120917
CCCP-87355 YAK40 9340431	CCCP-87437 YAK40 9431335	CCCP-87519 YAK40 9520141	CCCP-87601 YAK40 9121017
CCCP-87356 YAK40 9340531	CCCP-87438 YAK40 9431435	CCCP-87520 YAK40 9520241	CCCP-87602 YAK40 9120118
CCCP-87357 YAK40 9340631	CCCP-87439 YAK40 9431535	CCCP-87521 YAK40 9520341	CCCP-87603 YAK40 9120218
CCCP-87358 YAK40 9340731	CCCP-87440 YAK40 9431635	CCCP-87522 YAK40 9520441	CCCP-87604 YAK40 9120318
CCCP-87359 YAK40 9340831	CCCP-87441 YAK40 9431735	CCCP-87523 YAK40 9530541	CCCP-87605 YAK40 9120418
CCCP-87360 YAK40 9340931	CCCP-87442 YAK40 9431835	CCCP-87524 YAK40 9520641	CCCP-87606 YAK40 9120518
CCCP-87361 YAK40 9341031	CCCP-87443 YAK40 9432035	CCCP-87525 YAK40 9520741	CCCP-87607 YAK40 9120618
CCCP-87362 YAK40 9341131	CCCP-87444 YAK40 9430136	CCCP-87526 YAK40 9520841	CCCP-87608 YAK40 9120718
CCCP-87363 YAK40 9341231	CCCP-87445 YAK40 9430236	CCCP-87527 YAK40 9520941	CCCP-87609 YAK40 9120818
CCCP-87364 YAK40 9341331	CCCP-87446 YAK40 9430336	CCCP-87528 YAK40 9521041	CCCP-87610 YAK40 9120918
CCCP-87365 YAK40 9341531	CCCP-87447 YAK40 9430436	CCCP-87529 YAK40 9521141	CCCP-87611 YAK40 9121018
CCCP-87366 YAK40 9341631	CCCP-87448 YAK40 9430536	CCCP-87530 YAK40 9521241	CCCP-87612 YAK40 9121118
CCCP-87367 YAK40 9341731	CCCP-87449 YAK40 9430636	CCCP-87531 YAK40 9521341	CCCP-87613 YAK40 9131218
CCCP-87368 YAK40 9341831	CCCP-87450 YAK40 9430736	CCCP-87532 YAK40 9521641	CCCP-87614 YAK40 9131318
CCCP-87369 YAK40 9341931	CCCP-87451 YAK40 9430836	CCCP-87533 YAK40 9541741	CCCP-87615 YAK40 9131618
CCCP-87370 YAK40 9342031	CCCP-87452 YAK40 9430936	CCCP-87534 YAK40 9521841	CCCP-87616 YAK40 9131718
CCCP-87371 YAK40 9340232	CCCP-87453 YAK40 9431036	CCCP-87535 YAK40 9521941	CCCP-87617 YAK40 9131818
CCCP-87372 YAK40 9340332	CCCP-87454 YAK40 9431136	CCCP-87536 YAK40 9522041	CCCP-87618 YAK40 9131918
CCCP-87373 YAK40 9410732	CCCP-87455 YAK40 9431236	CCCP-87537 YAK40 9520242	CCCP-87619 YAK40 9132018
CCCP-87374 YAK40 9410832	CCCP-87456 YAK40 9431336	CCCP-87538 YAK40 9530342	CCCP-87620 YAK40 9130119
CCCP-87375 YAK40 9410932	CCCP-87457 YAK40 9431636	CCCP-87539 YAK40 9530442	CCCP-87621 YAK40 9130219
CCCP-87376 YAK40 9411032	CCCP-87458 YAK40 9431736	CCCP-87540 YAK40 9530542	CCCP-87622 YAK40 9130319
CCCP-87377 YAK40 9411132	CCCP-87459 YAK40 9431836	CCCP-87541 YAK40 9530642	CCCP-87623 YAK40 9130419
CCCP-87378 YAK40 9411425	CCCP-87460 YAK40 9431936	CCCP-87542 YAK40 9530742	CCCP-87624 YAK40 9130519
CCCP-87379 YAK40 9411030A	CCCP-87461 YAK40 9432036	CCCP-87543 YAK40 9530842	CCCP-87625 YAK40 9130619
CCCP-87380 YAK40 9421225	CCCP-87462 YAK40 9430137	CCCP-87544 YAK40 9530942	CCCP-87626 YAK40 9130719
CCCP-87381 YAK40 9411232	CCCP-87463 YAK40 9430237	CCCP-87545 YAK40 9531042	CCCP-87627 YAK40 9130819
CCCP-87382 YAK40 9411332	CCCP-87464 YAK40 9430337	CCCP-87546 YAK40 9531142	CCCP-87628 YAK40 9130919
CCCP-87383 YAK40 9411432	CCCP-87465 YAK40 9430437	CCCP-87547 YAK40 9531242	CCCP-87629 YAK40 9131019
CCCP-87384 YAK40 9411532	CCCP-87466 YAK40 9430537	CCCP-87548 YAK40 9531342	CCCP-87630 YAK40 9131119
CCCP-87385 YAK40 9411632	CCCP-87467 YAK40 9440637	CCCP-87549 YAK40 9531442	CCCP-87631 YAK40 9131219
CCCP-87386 YAK40 9411732	CCCP-87468 YAK40 9441337	CCCP-87550 YAK40 9210121	CCCP-87632 YAK40 9131319
CCCP-87387 YAK40 9411832	CCCP-87469 YAK40 9441437	CCCP-87551 YAK40 9210221	CCCP-87633 YAK40 9131419
CCCP-87388 YAK40 9412032	CCCP-87470 YAK40 9441537	CCCP-87552 YAK40 9210321	CCCP-87634 YAK40 9131519
CCCP-87389 YAK40 9410133	CCCP-87471 YAK40 9441637	CCCP-87553 YAK40 9210421	CCCP-87635 YAK40 9141619
CCCP-87390 YAK40 9410233	CCCP-87472 YAK40 9441737	CCCP-87554 YAK40 9210521	CCCP-87636 YAK40 9141719
CCCP-87391 YAK40 9410333	CCCP-87473 YAK40 9441837	CCCP-87555 YAK40 9210621	CCCP-87637 YAK40 9141819
CCCP-87392 YAK40 9410433	CCCP-87474 YAK40 9441937	CCCP-87556 YAK40 9210721	CCCP-87638 YAK40 9141919
CCCP-87393 YAK40 9410533	CCCP-87475 YAK40 9442037	CCCP-87557 YAK40 9210821	CCCP-87639 YAK40 9142019
CCCP-87394 YAK40 9410633	CCCP-87476 YAK40 9440438	CCCP-87558 YAK40 9210921	CCCP-87640 YAK40 9140120
CCCP-87395 YAK40 9410733	CCCP-87477 YAK40 9440538	CCCP-87559 YAK40 9211021	CCCP-87641 YAK40 9140220

737

CCCP-87642 YAK40 9140320	CCCP-87724 YAK40 9940908	CCCP-87804 YAK40 9231023	CCCP-87931 YAK40 9740256
CCCP-87643 YAK40 9140420	CCCP-87725 YAK40 9941008	CCCP-87805 YAK40 9231123	CCCP-87932 YAK40 9740356
CCCP-87644 YAK40 9140520	CCCP-87726 YAK40 9940109	CCCP-87806 YAK40 9231223	CCCP-87933 YAK40 9740456
CCCP-87645 YAK40 9140620	CCCP-87727 YAK40 9940209	CCCP-87807 YAK40 9231723	CCCP-87934 YAK40 9740556
CCCP-87646 YAK40 9140720	CCCP-87728 YAK40 9940309	CCCP-87808 YAK40 9231823	CCCP-87935 YAK40 9811856
CCCP-87647 YAK40 9140820	(CCCP-87729) YAK40 9020409	CCCP-87809 YAK40 9231923	CCCP-87936 YAK40 9740756
CCCP-87648 YAK40 9140920	CCCP-87730 YAK40 9940509	CCCP-87810 YAK40 9232023	CCCP-87937 YAK40 9740856
CCCP-87649 YAK40 9141020	CCCP-87731 YAK40 9019701	CCCP-87811 YAK40 9230124	CCCP-87938 YAK40 9710153
CCCP-87650 YAK40 9141120	CCCP-87731 YAK40 9940609	CCCP-87812 YAK40 9230424	CCCP-87939 YAK40 9640352
CCCP-87651 YAK40 9141220	CCCP-87732 YAK40 9019801	CCCP-87813 YAK40 9230324	CCCP-87940 YAK40 9540445
CCCP-87652 YAK40 9141320	CCCP-87732 YAK40 9940709	CCCP-87814 YAK40 9230524	CCCP-87941 YAK40 9540545
CCCP-87653 YAK40 9211620	CCCP-87733 YAK40 9940809	CCCP-87815 YAK40 9230624	CCCP-87942 YAK40 9610645
CCCP-87654 YAK40 9211720	CCCP-87734 YAK40 9940909	CCCP-87816 YAK40 9230724	CCCP-87943 YAK40 9540745
CCCP-87655 YAK40 9211820	CCCP-87735 YAK40 9011009	CCCP-87817 YAK40 9230824	CCCP-87944 YAK40 9540845
CCCP-87656 YAK40 9211920	CCCP-87736 YAK40 9010110	CCCP-87818 YAK40 9230924	CCCP-87945 YAK40 9610945
CCCP-87657 YAK40 9020409	CCCP-87737 YAK40 9010210	CCCP-87819 YAK40 9230122	CCCP-87946 YAK40 9611045
CCCP-87658 YAK40 9240225	CCCP-87738 YAK40 9010310	CCCP-87819 YAK40 9231024	CCCP-87947 YAK40 9621145
CCCP-87659 YAK40 9240325	CCCP-87739 YAK40 9010410	CCCP-87820 YAK40 9231224	CCCP-87948 YAK40 9621245
CCCP-87660 YAK40 9240425	CCCP-87740 YAK40 9010510	CCCP-87821 YAK40 9241324	CCCP-87949 YAK40 9621345
CCCP-87661 YAK40 9240525	CCCP-87741 YAK40 9010610	CCCP-87822 YAK40 9241424	CCCP-87950 YAK40 9810857
CCCP-87662 YAK40 9240625	CCCP-87742 YAK40 9010710	CCCP-87823 YAK40 9241524	CCCP-87951 YAK40 9810957
CCCP-87663 YAK40 9240725	CCCP-87743 YAK40 9010810	CCCP-87824 YAK40 9241624	CCCP-87952 YAK40 9811057
CCCP-87664 YAK40 9240825	CCCP-87744 YAK40 9010910	CCCP-87825 YAK40 9241724	CCCP-87953 YAK40 9811157
CCCP-87665 YAK40 9240925	CCCP-87745 YAK40 9011010	CCCP-87826 YAK40 9241824	CCCP-87954 YAK40 9811357
CCCP-87666 YAK40 9241025	CCCP-87746 YAK40 9010111	CCCP-87827 YAK40 9241924	CCCP-87955 YAK40 9811457
CCCP-87667 YAK40 9241525	CCCP-87747 YAK40 9020211	CCCP-87828 YAK40 9242024	CCCP-87956 YAK40 9821757
CCCP-87668 YAK40 9021460	CCCP-87748 YAK40 9020311	CCCP-87829 YAK40 9240125	CCCP-87957 YAK40 9821857
CCCP-87669 YAK40 9021760	CCCP-87749 YAK40 9020411	CCCP-87830 YAK40 9241625	CCCP-87958 YAK40 9821957
CCCP-87669 YAK40 9330827	CCCP-87750 YAK40 9020511	CCCP-87831 YAK40 9241725	CCCP-87959 YAK40 9822057
CCCP-87671 YAK40 9820600	CCCP-87751 YAK40 9020611	CCCP-87832 YAK40 9241825	CCCP-87960 YAK40 9820358
CCCP-87672 YAK40 9820700	CCCP-87752 YAK40 9020711	CCCP-87833 YAK40 9241925	CCCP-87961 YAK40 9820458
CCCP-87673 YAK40 9820800	CCCP-87753 YAK40 9020811	CCCP-87834 YAK40 9241125	CCCP-87962 YAK40 9820558
CCCP-87674 YAK40 9820900	CCCP-87754 YAK40 9020911	CCCP-87835 YAK40 9240126	CCCP-87963 YAK40 9831058
CCCP-87675 YAK40 9831100	CCCP-87755 YAK40 9021011	CCCP-87836 YAK40 9240226	CCCP-87964 YAK40 9820758
CCCP-87676 YAK40 9831200	CCCP-87756 YAK40 9030112	CCCP-87837 YAK40 9240326	CCCP-87965 YAK40 9820858
CCCP-87677 YAK40 9840101	CCCP-87757 YAK40 9020212	CCCP-87838 YAK40 9240426	CCCP-87966 YAK40 9820958
CCCP-87678 YAK40 9840201	CCCP-87758 YAK40 9020312	CCCP-87839 YAK40 9240526	CCCP-87967 YAK40 9831158
CCCP-87679 YAK40 9840301	CCCP-87759 YAK40 9030412	CCCP-87840 YAK40 9240626	CCCP-87968 YAK40 9841258
CCCP-87680 YAK40 9840401	CCCP-87760 YAK40 9030512	CCCP-87841 YAK40 9330930	CCCP-87969 YAK40 9831358
CCCP-87681 YAK40 9840501	CCCP-87761 YAK40 9030612	CCCP-87842 YAK40 9331030	CCCP-87970 YAK40 9831458
CCCP-87682 YAK40 9840202	CCCP-87762 YAK40 9030712	CCCP-87843 YAK40 9331130	CCCP-87971 YAK40 9831558
CCCP-87683 YAK40 9840302	CCCP-87763 YAK40 9030012	CCCP-87844 YAK40 9331330	CCCP-87972 YAK40 9921658
CCCP-87684 YAK40 9840402	CCCP-87764 YAK40 9030912	CCCP-87845 YAK40 9331430	CCCP-87973 YAK40 9041860
CCCP-87685 YAK40 9840502	CCCP-87765 YAK40 9031012	CCCP-87846 YAK40 9331530	CCCP-87974 YAK40 9041960
CCCP-87686 YAK40 9840103	CCCP-87766 YAK40 9030113	CCCP-87847 YAK40 9331630	CCCP-87980 YAK40 9530344
CCCP-87687 YAK40 9840102?	CCCP-87767 YAK40 9030213	CCCP-87848 YAK40 9331730	CCCP-87981 YAK40 9540444
CCCP-87688 YAK40 9910303	CCCP-87768 YAK40 9030313	CCCP-87849 YAK40 9331830	CCCP-87982 YAK40 9540544
CCCP-87689 YAK40 9910403	CCCP-87769 YAK40 9030413	CCCP-87850 YAK40 9441738	CCCP-87983 YAK40 9540644
CCCP-87690 YAK40 9910503	CCCP-87770 YAK40 9030513	CCCP-87883 YAK40 ?	CCCP-87984 YAK40 9540744
CCCP-87691 YAK40 9910104	CCCP-87771 YAK40 9030613	CCCP-87891 YAK40 ?	CCCP-87985 YAK40 9540844
CCCP-87692 YAK40 9910204	CCCP-87772 YAK40 9030713	CCCP-87893 YAK40 ?	CCCP-87986 YAK40 9540944
CCCP-87693 YAK40 9910304	CCCP-87773 YAK40 9080813	CCCP-87900 YAK40 9720254	CCCP-87987 YAK40 9541144
CCCP-87694 YAK40 9910404	CCCP-87774 YAK40 9030913	CCCP-87901 YAK40 9720354	CCCP-87988 YAK40 9541244
CCCP 87695 YAK40 9910504	CCCP-87775 YAK40 9031013	CCCP-07902 YAK40 9720454	CCCP-87989 YAK40 9541344
CCCP-87696 YAK40 9910105	CCCP-87776 YAK40 9040114	CCCP-87903 YAK40 9720654	CCCP-87990 YAK40 9541444
CCCP-87697 YAK40 9910205	CCCP-87777 YAK40 9040214	CCCP-87904 YAK40 9720854	CCCP-87991 YAK40 9541544
CCCP-87698 YAK40 9920305	CCCP-87778 YAK40 9040314	CCCP-87905 YAK40 9730954	CCCP-87992 YAK40 9541644
CCCP-87699 YAK40 9920405	CCCP-87779 YAK40 9040414	CCCP-87906 YAK40 9731054	CCCP-87993 YAK40 9541744
CCCP-87700 YAK40 9920505	CCCP-87780 YAK40 9040514	CCCP-87907 YAK40 9731254	CCCP-87994 YAK40 9541844
CCCP-87701 YAK40 9920106	CCCP-87781 YAK40 9040614	CCCP-87908 YAK40 9721354	CCCP-87995 YAK40 9541944
CCCP-87702 YAK40 9920206	CCCP-87782 YAK40 9040714	CCCP-87909 YAK40 9721454	CCCP-87996 YAK40 9542044
CCCP-87703 YAK40 9920306	CCCP-87783 YAK40 9040814	CCCP-87910 YAK40 9731654	CCCP-87997 YAK40 9540145
CCCP-87704 YAK40 9920406	CCCP-87784 YAK40 9040914	CCCP-87911 YAK40 9731854	CCCP-87998 YAK40 9540245
CCCP-87705 YAK40 9920506	CCCP-87785 YAK40 9041014	CCCP-87912 YAK40 9732054	CCCP-87999 YAK40 9540345
CCCP-87706 YAK40 9920107	CCCP-87786 YAK40 9040115	CCCP-87913 YAK40 9730255	CCCP-88150 YAK40 9610346
CCCP-87707 YAK40 9930207	CCCP-87787 YAK40 9040215	CCCP-87914 YAK40 9730355	CCCP-88151 YAK40 9610546
CCCP-87708 YAK40 9930307	CCCP-87788 YAK40 9040315	CCCP-87915 YAK40 9730455	CCCP-88152 YAK40 9610646
CCCP-87709 YAK40 9930407	CCCP-87789 YAK40 9040415	CCCP-87916 YAK40 9730655	CCCP-88153 YAK40 9610746
CCCP-87710 YAK40 9940507	CCCP-87790 YAK40 9110515	CCCP-87917 YAK40 9730755	CCCP-88154 YAK40 9610846
CCCP-87711 YAK40 9930607	CCCP-87791 YAK40 9910203	CCCP-87918 YAK40 9730855	CCCP-88155 YAK40 9610946
CCCP-87712 YAK40 9930707	CCCP-87792 YAK40 97.0400	CCCP-87919 YAK40 9730955	CCCP-88156 YAK40 9611046
CCCP-87713 YAK40 9930807	CCCP-87793 YAK40 9110615	CCCP-87920 YAK40 9731055	CCCP-88157 YAK40 9611146
CCCP-87714 YAK40 9930907	CCCP-87794 YAK40 9110715	CCCP-87921 YAK40 9731155	CCCP-88158 YAK40 9611246
CCCP-87715 YAK40 9931007	CCCP-87795 YAK40 9110815	CCCP-87922 YAK40 9731355	CCCP-88159 YAK40 9611346
CCCP-87716 YAK40 9930108	CCCP-87796 YAK40 9110915	CCCP-87923 YAK40 9741455	CCCP-88160 YAK40 9611455
CCCP-87717 YAK40 9930208	CCCP-87797 YAK40 9110116	CCCP-87924 YAK40 9731555	CCCP-88161 YAK40 9611546
CCCP-87718 YAK40 9930308	CCCP-87798 YAK40 9110216	CCCP-87925 YAK40 9731655	CCCP-88162 YAK40 9611646
CCCP-87719 YAK40 9940408	CCCP-87799 YAK40 9040316	CCCP-87926 YAK40 9741755	CCCP-88163 YAK40 9611746
CCCP-87720 YAK40 9940508	CCCP-87800 YAK40 9220223	CCCP-87927 YAK40 9741855	CCCP-88164 YAK40 9611846
CCCP-87721 YAK40 9940608	CCCP-87801 YAK40 9220423	CCCP-87928 YAK40 9741955	CCCP-88165 YAK40 9611946
CCCP-87722 YAK40 9940708	CCCP-87802 YAK40 9230523	CCCP-87929 YAK40 9742055	CCCP-88166 YAK40 9612046
CCCP-87723 YAK40 9940808	CCCP-87803 YAK40 9230923	CCCP-87930 YAK40 9740156	CCCP-88167 YAK40 9610147

Registration	Type	c/n
CCCP-88168	YAK40	9610647
CCCP-88169	YAK40	9610747
CCCP-88170	YAK40	9620847
CCCP-88171	YAK40	9620947
CCCP-88172	YAK40	9631047
CCCP-88173	YAK40	9621147
CCCP-88174	YAK40	9621247
CCCP-88175	YAK40	9621347
CCCP-88176	YAK40	9621447
CCCP-88177	YAK40	9621747
CCCP-88178	YAK40	9621847
CCCP-88179	YAK40	9621947
CCCP-88180	YAK40	9622047
CCCP-88181	YAK40	9620148
CCCP-88182	YAK40	9620248
CCCP-88183	YAK40	9620348
CCCP-88184	YAK40	9620448
CCCP-88185	YAK40	9620548
CCCP-88186	YAK40	9620648
CCCP-88187	YAK40	9620748
CCCP-88188	YAK40	9620848
CCCP-88189	YAK40	9620948
CCCP-88190	YAK40	9621048
CCCP-88191	YAK40	9621148
CCCP-88192	YAK40	9621248
CCCP-88193	YAK40	9621348
CCCP-88194	YAK40	9621448
CCCP-88195	YAK40	9631548
CCCP-88196	YAK40	9631648
CCCP-88197	YAK40	9631948
CCCP-88198	YAK40	9632048
CCCP-88199	YAK40	9630249
CCCP-88200	YAK40	9630149
CCCP-88201	YAK40	9630349
CCCP-88202	YAK40	9630449
CCCP-88203	YAK40	9630549
CCCP-88204	YAK40	9630649
CCCP-88205	YAK40	9630749
CCCP-88206	YAK40	9630949
CCCP-88207	YAK40	9631149
CCCP-88208	YAK40	9631349
CCCP-88209	YAK40	9710353
CCCP-88210	YAK40	9631649
CCCP-88211	YAK40	9631749
CCCP-88212	YAK40	9631849
CCCP-88213	YAK40	9631949
CCCP-88214	YAK40	9632049
CCCP-88215	YAK40	9630150
CCCP-88216	YAK40	9630250
CCCP-88217	YAK40	9630350
CCCP-88218	YAK40	9630450
CCCP-88219	YAK40	9630550
CCCP-88220	YAK40	9630650
CCCP-88221	YAK40	9630750
CCCP-88222	YAK40	9630850
CCCP-88223	YAK40	9640950
CCCP-88224	YAK40	9641150
CCCP-88225	YAK40	9641250
CCCP-88226	YAK40	9641350
CCCP-88227	YAK40	9641550
CCCP-88228	YAK40	9641750
CCCP-88229	YAK40	9641850
CCCP-88230	YAK40	9641950
CCCP-88231	YAK40	9642050
CCCP-88232	YAK40	9640151
CCCP-88233	YAK40	9640251
CCCP-88234	YAK40	9640351
CCCP-88235	YAK40	9640451
CCCP-88236	YAK40	9640551
CCCP-88237	YAK40	9640751
CCCP-88238	YAK40	9640951
CCCP-88239	YAK40	9641051
CCCP-88240	YAK40	9641151
CCCP-88241	YAK40	9641351
CCCP-88242	YAK40	9641551
CCCP-88243	YAK40	9641651
CCCP-88244	YAK40	9641751
CCCP-88245	YAK40	9641851
CCCP-88246	YAK40	9641951
CCCP-88247	YAK40	9642051
CCCP-88248	YAK40	9640152
CCCP-88249	YAK40	9640252
CCCP-88250	YAK40	9710452
CCCP-88251	YAK40	9710552
CCCP-88252	YAK40	9710652
CCCP-88253	YAK40	9710852
CCCP-88254	YAK40	9710952
CCCP-88255	YAK40	9711052
CCCP-88256	YAK40	9711152
CCCP-88257	YAK40	9711252
CCCP-88258	YAK40	9711352
CCCP-88259	YAK40	9711452
CCCP-88260	YAK40	9711552
CCCP-88261	YAK40	9711652
CCCP-88262	YAK40	9711752
CCCP-88263	YAK40	9711852
CCCP-88264	YAK40	9711952
CCCP-88265	YAK40	9722052
CCCP-88266	YAK40	9710453
CCCP-88267	YAK40	9720553
CCCP-88268	YAK40	9720653
CCCP-88269	YAK40	9720753
CCCP-88270	YAK40	9720853
CCCP-88271	YAK40	9720953
CCCP-88272	YAK40	9721053
CCCP-88273	YAK40	9721153
CCCP-88274	YAK40	9721253
CCCP-88275	YAK40	9721353
CCCP-88276	YAK40	9721453
CCCP-88277	YAK40	9721953
CCCP-88278	YAK40	9722053
CCCP-88279	YAK40	9720154
CCCP-88280	YAK40	9820658
CCCP-88287	YAK40	9940360
CCCP-88290	YAK40	9840459
CCCP-93929	TU134	1351206
CCCP-93930	TU134	1351203
CCCP-96000	IL96	0101
CCCP-96001	IL96	0103
CCCP-96002	IL96	74393201001
CCCP-96005	IL96	74393201002
CCCP-96006	IL96	74393201003
CCCP-98102	YAK40	9720554
CCCP-98106	YAK40	9740656
CCCP-98109	YAK40	9740956
CCCP-98110	YAK40	9741556
CCCP-98111	YAK40	9741656
CCCP-98113	YAK40	9710253
CCCP-98114	YAK40	9631549

Canada
(see also C-)

Registration	Type	c/n
CF-ASF	B737	20221
CF-CPB	B737	19884
CF-CPC	B737	19885
CF-CPD	B737	19886
CF-CPE	B737	19887
CF-CPF	DC-8	45620
CF-CPG	DC-8	45623
CF-CPH	DC-8	45621
CF-CPI	DC-8	45622
CF-CPJ	DC-8	45661
CF-CPK	B727	20328
CF-CPK	DC-8	45761
CF-CPL	DC-8	46095
CF-CPM	DC-8	45809
CF-CPN	B727	20327
CF-CPN	DC-8	45252
CF-CPO	DC-8	45926
CF-CPP	DC-8	45927
CF-CPQ	DC-8	45928
CF-CPS	DC-8	45929
CF-CPT	DC-8	45858
CF-CPU	B737	19888
CF-CPV	B737	20196
CF-CPZ	B737	20197
CF-CUM	COMET	06013
CF-CUN	COMET	06014
CF-CUR	B727	20512
CF-CUS	B727	20513
CF-DJC	B747	20208
CF-EJD-X	C102	?
CF-EPL	B737	20396
CF-EPO	B737	20300
CF-EPP	B737	20681
CF-EPR	B737	20397
CF-EPU	B737	20776
CF-FAN	B707	19789
CF-FUN	B727	19242
(CF-FUN)	B747	20208
CF-FUN	B747	20305
CF-NAB	B737	19847
(CF-NAD)	B737	19848
(CF-NAD)	B737	20521
CF-NAH	B737	19848
CF-NAI	B737	19945
CF-NAP	B737	19946
CF-NAP	B737	20496
CF-NAQ	B737	20455
CF-NAW	B737	20521
CF-PWC	B737	20142
CF-PWD	B737	19742
CF-PWE	B737	19743
CF-PWJ	B707	18746
CF-PWM	B737	19921
CF-PWP	B737	20588
CF-PWV	B707	17696
CF-PWW	B707	17700
CF-PWW	B737	20670
CF-PWZ	B737	18826
CF-PXB	B727	19174
(CF-QBG)	B707	20043
CF-QBN	1-11	BAC.110
CF-QBO	1-11	BAC.112
CF-QBR	1-11	094
CF-SVR	COMET	06018
CF-TAI	B707	19410
CF-TAN	B737	20206
CF-TAO	B737	20205
CF-TAR	B737	20223
CF-TAV	F.28	11033
CF-TAY	F.28	11038
CF-TIH	DC-8	45933
CF-TII	DC-8	45934
CF-TIJ	DC-8	45962
CF-TIK	DC-8	46033
CF-TIL	DC-8	46034
CF-TIM	DC-8	46035
CF-TIN	DC-8	46036
CF-TIO	DC-8	46076
CF-TIP	DC-8	46100
CF-TIQ	DC-8	46123
CF-TIQ	DC-8	46124
CF-TIR	DC-8	46124
CF-TIS	DC-8	46125
(CF-TIT)	DC-8	46113
CF-TIU	DC-8	46113
(CF-TIU)	DC-8	46126
(CF-TIV)	DC-8	46114
CF-TIV	DC-8	46126
CF-TIW	DC-8	46114
(CF-TIW)	DC-8	46115
CF-TIX	DC-8	46115
CF-TJA	DC-8	45442
CF-TJB	DC-8	45443
CF-TJC	DC-8	45444
CF-TJD	DC-8	45445
CF-TJE	DC-8	45565
CF-TJF	DC-8	45566
CF-TJG	DC-8	45609
CF-TJH	DC-8	45610
CF-TJI	DC-8	45611
CF-TJJ	DC-8	45612
CF-TJK	DC-8	45638
CF-TJL	DC-8	45640
CF-TJM	DC-8	45653
CF-TJN	DC-8	45654
CF-TJO	DC-8	45655
CF-TJP	DC-8	45679
CF-TJQ	DC-8	45686
CF-TJR	DC-8	45860
CF-TJS	DC-8	45861
CF-TJT	DC-8	45890
CF-TJU	DC-8	45891
CF-TJV	DC-8	45892
CF-TJW	DC-8	45893
CF-TJX	DC-8	45963
CF-TJY	DC-8	45964
CF-TJZ	DC-8	45980
CF-TLB	DC-9	45711
CF-TLC	DC-9	45712
CF-TLD	DC-9	45713
CF-TLE	DC-9	45725
CF-TLF	DC-9	45726
CF-TLG	DC-9	45727
CF-TLH	DC-9	45845
CF-TLI	DC-9	45846
CF-TLJ	DC-9	47019
CF-TLK	DC-9	47020
CF-TLL	DC-9	47021
CF-TLM	DC-9	47022
CF-TLN	DC-9	47023
CF-TLO	DC-9	47024
CF-TLP	DC-9	47068
CF-TLQ	DC-9	47069
CF-TLR	DC-9	47070
CF-TLS	DC-9	47071
CF-TLT	DC-9	47195
CF-TLU	DC-9	47196
CF-TLV	DC-9	47197
CF-TLW	DC-9	47198
CF-TLX	DC-9	47199
CF-TLY	DC-9	47200
CF-TLZ	DC-9	47265
CF-TMA	DC-9	47266
CF-TMB	DC-9	47289
CF-TMC	DC-9	47290
CF-TMD	DC-9	47292
CF-TME	DC-9	47293
CF-TMF	DC-9	47294
CF-TMG	DC-9	47340
CF-TMH	DC-9	47341
CF-TMI	DC-9	47342
CF-TMJ	DC-9	47348
CF-TMK	DC-9	47349
CF-TML	DC-9	47350
CF-TMM	DC-9	47351
CF-TMN	DC-9	47041
CF-TMN	DC-9	47352
CF-TMO	DC-9	47353
CF-TMP	DC-9	47354
CF-TMQ	DC-9	47422
CF-TMR	DC-9	47423
CF-TMS	DC-9	47424
CF-TMT	DC-9	47546
CF-TMU	DC-9	47554
CF-TMV	DC-9	47557
CF-TMW	DC-9	47560
CF-TMX	DC-9	47485
CF-TMY	DC-9	47592
CF-TMZ	DC-9	47598
CF-TNA	L1011	193M-1019
CF-TNB	L1011	193E-1021
CF-TNC	L1011	193M-1023
CF-TND	L1011	193E-1025
CF-TNE	L1011	193E-1027
CF-TNF	L1011	193E-1047
CF-TNG	L1011	193E-1048
CF-TNH	L1011	193E-1049
CF-TNI	L1011	193E-1058
CF-TOA	B747	20013
CF-TOB	B747	20014
CF-TOC	B747	20015
CF-TOD	B747	20767
CF-TOE	B747	20881
CF-TON	DC-9	45826
CF-TOO	DC-9	47010
CF-TOP	DC-9	47011
CF-TOQ	DC-9	47012
CF-TOR	DC-9	47013
CF-TOS	DC-9	47014
CF-TOT	DC-9	47015
CF-TOU	DC-9	47152
CF-ZYP	B707	20043

Morocco

CNA-NR	B707	21956
CNA-NS	B707	18334
CN-ANS	B707	18334
CN-CCC	B707	21956
CN-CCF	B727	20304
CN-CCG	B727	20471
CN-CCH	B727	20705
CN-CCT	SE210	254
CN-CCV	SE210	32
CN-CCW	B727	21068
CN-CCX	SE210	57
CN-CCY	SE210	154
CN-CCZ	SE210	195
CN-RDA	B737	24356
CN-RDB	B737	23771
CN-REB	B737	24511
CN-RGA	**B747**	**25629**
(CN-RLF)	E145	145376
(CN-RLG)	E145	145431
CN-RMA	B707	18375
CN-RMB	B707	19773
CN-RMC	B707	19774
CN-RMD	B707	17619
CN-RME	**B747**	**21615**
CN-RMF	**B737**	**24807**
CN-RMG	**B737**	**24808**
CN-RMH	B737	22632
CN-RMI	B737	21214
CN-RMJ	B737	21215
CN-RMK	B737	21216
CN-RML	B737	21112
CN-RML	B737	22767
CN-RMM	B737	23049
CN-RMN	B737	23050
CN-RMO	B727	21297
CN-RMP	B727	21298
CN-RMQ	B727	21299
CN-RMR	B727	22377
CN-RMS	B747	21253
CN-RMT	**B757**	**23686**
CN-RMU	B737	24922
CN-RMV	**B737**	**25317**
CN-RMW	**B737**	**25364**
CN-RMX	B737	22632
CN-RMX	**B737**	**26526**
CN-RMY	**B737**	**26525**
CN-RMZ	**B757**	**23687**
CN-RNA	**B737**	**26531**
CN-RNB	**B737**	**26527**
CN-RNC	**B737**	**26529**
CN-RND	**B737**	**26530**
(CN-RNE)	B737	27678
CN-RNF	B737	27678
(CN-RNF)	B737	27679
CN-RNG	**B737**	**27679**
CN-RNH	**B737**	**27680**
CN-RNJ	**737NG**	**28980**
CN-RNK	**737NG**	**28981**
CN-RNL	**737NG**	**28982**
CN-RNM	**737NG**	**28984**
CN-RNN	737NG	28592
CN-RNO	737NG	28595
CN-RNP	**737NG**	**28983**
CN-RNQ	**737NG**	**28985**
CN-RNR	**737NG**	**28986**
CN-RNS	**B767**	**30115**
CN-RNT	**B767**	**30843**
CN-RNU	**737NG**	**28987**
CN-RNV	**737NG**	**28988**
CN-RNW	**737NG**	**33057**
CN-RNX	**A321**	**2064**
CN-RNY	**A321**	**2076**
CN-RNZ	**737NG**	**33058**
CN-ROA	**737NG**	**33059**
CN-ROB	**737NG**	**33060**
CN-ROC	**737NG**	**33061**
CN-ROD	**737NG**	**33062**
CN-ROE	**737NG**	**33063**
CN-ROF	**A321**	**2726**
CN-ROG	**B767**	**27212**

CN-ROH	**737NG**	**33978**
CN-ROJ	**737NG**	**33979**
CN-ROK	**737NG**	**33064**
CN-ROL	**737NG**	**33065**
CN-ROM	**A321**	**3070**
CN-RON	**B737**	**24652**
CN-ROP	**737NG**	**33066**
CN-RPA	**B737**	**24750**
CN-RPB	**B737**	**24751**
CN-RYM	B747	21439

Bolivia

CP-	**B727**	**22449**
CP-1070	B727	19860
CP-1223	B727	18795
CP-1276	**B727**	**21082**
CP-1339	B727	20512
CP-1365	B707	18692
CP-1366	**B727**	**21494**
CP-1367	**B727**	**21495**
CP-1698	B707	19586
CP-1741	B727	22770
CP-2217	DC-8	45668
CP-2232	A310	562
CP-2247	146	E1104
CP-2249	146	E1017
CP-2254	146	E2058
CP-2260	146	E2060
CP-2273	A310	475
CP-2274	B727	19132
CP-2277	B727	19429
CP-2278	B727	18437
CP-2294	B727	22079
CP-2307	A310	661
CP-2313	B737	28389
CP-2320	B727	18445
CP-2322	B727	18428
CP-2323	B727	22605
CP-2324	**B727**	**21823**
(CP-2338)	A310	562
CP-2365	B727	22538
CP-2370	B727	18449
CP-2377	B727	20044
CP-2385	B727	22542
CP-2389	B727	21655
CP-2391	B737	24366
CP-2422	**B727**	**21617**
CP-2423	**B727**	**21638**
CP-2424	**B727**	**22156**
CP-2425	B767	23764
CP-2426	B767	24349
CP-2427	B727	22164
CP-2428	B727	21502
CP-2429	**B727**	**22475**
CP-2431	B727	22411
CP-2438	**B737**	**21815**
CP-2447	B727	22409
CP-2455	**B727**	**22606**
CP-2462	**B727**	**22158**
CP-2463	**B727**	**22463**
CP-2464	**B727**	**22464**
CP-2476	**B737**	**21771**
(CP-2480)	B747	23150
CP-2484	B737	21768
CP-2486	**B737**	**21769**
CP-2489	**DC-10**	**46903**
CP-861	B727	20279

Mozambique
(see also C9-)

CR-BAA	B737	20280
CR-BAB	B737	20281
CR-BAC	B737	20536
CR-BAD	B737	20786
(CR-LOR)	B737	21172
(CR-LOS)	B737	21173

Portugal

CS-DGI	B707	20514
CS-DGJ	B707	20515
CS-TBA	B707	18961
CS-TBB	B707	18962
CS-TBC	B707	19740
CS-TBD	B707	19969
CS-TBE	B707	20136
CS-TBF	B707	20297
CS-TBG	B707	20298
CS-TBH	B707	19415
CS-TBI	B707	19767
CS-TBJ	B707	19179
CS-TBK	B727	19404
CS-TBL	B727	19405
CS-TBM	B727	19406
CS-TBN	B727	19597
CS-TBO	B727	19968
CS-TBP	B727	20489
CS-TBQ	B727	19665
CS-TBR	B727	20972
CS-TBS	B727	20973
CS-TBT	B707	20514
CS-TBU	B707	20515
CS-TBV	B727	19618
CS-TBW	B727	21949
CS-TBX	B727	21950
CS-TBY	B727	22430
CS-TCA	SE210	117
CS-TCB	SE210	125
CS-TCC	SE210	137
CS-TCH	B727	20866
CS-TCI	B727	20867
CS-TCJ	B727	21018
CS-TDI	**A310**	**573**
CS-TEA	L1011	293B-1239
CS-TEB	**L1011**	**293B-1240**
CS-TEC	L1011	293B-1241
CS-TED	L1011	293B-1242
CS-TEE	L1011	293B-1243
CS-TEF	L1011	193H-1246
CS-TEG	L1011	293A-1248
CS-TEH	**A310**	**483**
CS-TEI	**A310**	**495**
CS-TEJ	**A310**	**494**
CS-TEK	B737	23041
CS-TEL	B737	23042
CS-TEM	B737	23043
CS-TEN	B737	23044
CS-TEO	B737	23045
CS-TEP	B737	23046
CS-TEQ	B737	23051
CS-TER	B737	22636
CS-TES	B737	22637
CS-TFT	B737	22115
CS-TEU	B737	22416
CS-TEV	B737	22402
CS-TEW	**A310**	**541**
CS-TEX	**A310**	**565**
CS-TEY	A310	573
CS-TEZ	A310	472
CS-TFK	**B757**	**23983**
CS-TGP	B737	24131
CS-TGQ	B737	28570
CS-TGR	B737	24902
CS-TGU	**A310**	**571**
CS-TGV	**A310**	**651**
CS-TGW	B737	23981
CS-TGZ	B737	28491
CS-TIA	B737	24364
CS-TIB	B737	24365
CS-TIC	B737	24366
CS-TID	B737	24449
CS-TIE	B737	24450
CS-TIF	B737	24212
CS-TIG	B737	24213
CS-TIH	B737	24214
CS-TII	B737	24986
CS-TIJ	B737	24987
CS-TIK	B737	25161
CS-TIL	B737	25162
(CS-TIM)	B737	24988
CS-TIN	B737	23827
CS-TIO	B737	23830

CS-TIR	B737	23411
CS-TIS	B737	23024
CS-TJA	B747	20501
CS-TJB	B747	20502
CS-TJC	B747	20928
CS-TJD	B747	21035
CS-TJE	**A321**	**1307**
CS-TJF	**A321**	**1399**
CS-TJG	**A321**	**1713**
CS-TKA	B727	20765
CS-TKB	B727	20764
CS-TKC	B737	23830
CS-TKD	B737	23827
CS-TKE	B737	24905
CS-TKF	B737	27284
CS-TKG	B737	27285
CS-TKI	**A310**	**448**
CS-TKJ	**A320**	**0795**
CS-TKK	**A320**	**2390**
CS-TKL	**A320**	**2425**
CS-TKM	**A310**	**661**
CS-TKN	**A310**	**624**
CS-TLI	B737	23830
CS-TLL	B737	24213
CS-TLM	B767	25535
CS-TLO	**B767**	**24318**
CS-TLQ	**B767**	**26205**
CS-TLX	**B757**	**24176**
CS-TMA	B737	22640
CS-TMB	B737	23023
CS-TMC	B737	23024
CS-TMD	B737	22599
CS-TME	B737	22600
CS-TMP	**L1011**	**293A-1248**
CS-TMR	L1011	293B-1241
CS-TMT	**A330**	**096**
(CS-TMT)	A330	441
CS-TMW	**A320**	**1667**
CS-TMX	**L1011**	**193H-1206**
CS-TMZ	B737	23827
CS-TNA	**A320**	**0185**
CS-TNB	**A320**	**0191**
CS-TNC	**A320**	**0234**
CS-TND	A320	0235
CS-TNE	**A320**	**0395**
CS-TNF	A320	0407
CS-TNG	**A320**	**0945**
CS-TNH	**A320**	**0960**
CS-TNI	**A320**	**0982**
CS-TNJ	**A320**	**1181**
CS-TNK	**A320**	**1206**
CS-TNL	**A320**	**1231**
CS-TNM	**A320**	**1799**
CS-TNN	**A320**	**1816**
CS-TNO	**A320**	**0234**
CS TNP	**A320**	**2178**
CS-TOA	**A340**	**041**
CS-TOB	**A340**	**044**
CS-TOC	**A340**	**079**
CS-TOD	**A340**	**091**
CS-TOE	**A330**	**305**
CS-TOF	**A330**	**308**
CS-TOG	**A330**	**312**
CS-TOH	**A330**	**181**
CS-TOI	**A330**	**195**
CS-TOJ	**A330**	**223**
CS-TOK	**A330**	**317**
CS-TOL	**A330**	**877**
CS-TOM	**A330**	**899**
CS-TON	**A330**	**904**
CS-TOO	**A330**	**914**
CS-TOP	**A330**	**930**
CS-TPA	**F.100**	**11257**
CS-TPB	**F.100**	**11262**
CS-TPC	**F.100**	**11287**
CS-TPD	**F.100**	**11317**
CS-TPE	**F.100**	**11342**
CS-TPF	**F.100**	**11258**
CS-TPG	**E145**	**145014**
CS-TPH	**E145**	**145017**
CS-TPI	**E145**	**145031**
CS-TPJ	**E145**	**145036**
CS-TPK	**E145**	**145041**
CS-TPL	**E145**	**145051**
CS-TPM	**E145**	**145095**

Reg	Type	c/n
CS-TPN	**E145**	**145099**
CS-TQA	A320	1439
CS-TQB	A320	1450
CS-TQC	A319	1494
CS-TQD	**A320**	**0870**
CS-TQE	A320	0221
CS-TQF	A330	087
CS-TQG	A320	0022
CS-TQH	A320	0023
CS-TRA	**A330**	**461**
CS-TTA	**A319**	**0750**
(CS-TTA)	L1011	293B-1239
CS-TTB	**A319**	**0755**
CS-TTC	**A319**	**0763**
CS-TTD	**A319**	**0790**
CS-TTE	**A319**	**0821**
CS-TTF	**A319**	**0837**
CS-TTG	**A319**	**0906**
CS-TTH	**A319**	**0917**
CS-TTI	**A319**	**0933**
CS-TTJ	**A319**	**0979**
CS-TTK	**A319**	**1034**
CS-TTL	**A319**	**1100**
CS-TTM	**A319**	**1106**
CS-TTN	**A319**	**1120**
CS-TTO	**A319**	**1127**
CS-TTP	**A319**	**1165**
CS-TTQ	**A319**	**0629**

Macau
(see also B-M)

Reg	Type	c/n
CS-MAA	A321	0550
CS-MAB	A321	0557
CS-MAD	A320	0573
CS-MAE	A320	0582
CS-MAF	A321	0620
CS-MAG	A321	0631
CS-MAH	A320	0805
CS-MAJ	A321	0908

Cuba

Reg	Type	c/n
(CU-)	B707	17903
(CU-)	B707	17904
CU-T994	IL62	11001
CU-C1222	TU154	80A-447
CU-C1250	IL76	0043454615
CU-C1271	IL76	0053459767
CU-C1419	IL76	0043454615
CU-C1700	**TU204**	**..64036**
CU-C1701	**TU204**	**..64035**
CU-T1200	DC-8	45638
CU-T1201	DC-8	45611
CU-T1202	YAK40	9631449
CU-T1203	YAK40	9641450
CU-T1204	YAK40	9641650
CU-T1207	YAK40	9541445
CU-T1208	IL62	3726739
CU-T1209	IL62	1828132
CU-T1210	DC-8	45612
CU-T1211	YAK40	9731554
CU-T1212	YAK40	9731754
CU-T1213	YAK40	9731954
CU-T1215	IL62	1828243
CU-T1216	IL62	3829748
CU-T1217	IL62	3933232
CU-T1218	IL62	2035657
CU-T1219	YAK40	9840959
CU-T1220	YAK40	9841059
CU-T1221	YAK40	9841159
CU-T1222	TU154	80A-447
CU-T1224	TU154	81A-493
CU-T1225	IL62	3139845
CU-T1226	IL62	3242219
CU-T1227	TU154	82A-541
CU-T1232	**YAK40**	**9011060**
CU-T1242	YAK42	2014549
CU-T1243	YAK42	1303016
CU-T1245	YAK42	4934512
CU-T1246	**YAK42**	**4711397**
CU-T1247	**YAK42**	**4309017**
CU-T1248	IL62	?
CU-T1249	**YAK42**	**4116677**
CU-T1250	**IL96**	**74393202015**
CU-T1251	**IL96**	**74393202016**
CU-T1252	IL62	2343341
CU-T1253	TU154	83A-576
CU-T1254	**IL96**	**74393202017**
CU-T1255	**YAK42**	**4116664**
CU-T1256	TU154	84A-599
CU-T1258	IL76	0043454615
CU-T1259	IL62	3445111
CU-T1264	TU154	85A-720
CU-T1265	TU154	87A-751
CU-T1271	IL76	0053459767
CU-T1272	**YAK42**	**4811442**
CU-T1273	YAK42	3914340
CU-T1274	YAK42	2606204
CU-T1275	TU154	88A-777
CU-T1276	TU154	85A-719
CU-T1277	YAK42	3016238
CU-T1278	YAK42	3016269
CU-T1279	**YAK42**	**4914057**
CU-T1280	**IL62**	**3749648**
CU-T1281	IL62	3850453
CU-T1282	**IL62**	**2052436**
CU-T1283	**IL62**	**4053823**
CU-T1284	**IL62**	**4053732**
CU-T1285	YAK42	4914068
CU-T1298	**YAK40**	**9011160**
CU-T1438	YAK40	?
CU-T1440	**YAK40**	**9631249**
CU-T1441	YAK40	9631049
CU-T1442	**YAK40**	**9541445**
CU-T1443	**YAK40**	**9710752**
CU-T1448	YAK40	9011160
CU-T1449	YAK40	9021260
CU-T1450	YAK40	9021360
CU-T1534	YAK40	9731754
CU-T1535	YAK40	?
CU-T1537	**YAK40**	**9021360**
CU-T1538	**YAK40**	**9021260**

Uruguay

Reg	Type	c/n
CX-BHM	B737	20299
CX-BJV	B707	19212
CX-BKA	B727	19793
CX-BKB	B727	19010
CX-BLN	DC-8	45804
(CX-RML)	B707	17605
CX-BNT	B727	19314
CX-BNU	B707	19239
CX-BOH	B707	19240
CX-BON	**B737**	**22737**
CX-BOO	**B737**	**22738**
CX-BOP	**B737**	**22739**
(CX-BOU)	DC-8	45989
CX-BPL	B707	19435
CX-BPQ	B707	18716
CX-BPZ	B707	19210
CX-BPZ	DC-8	46097
CX-BQG	B707	18829
CX-BQN	DC-8	45925
CX-BQN-F	DC-8	45925
CX-BSB	B707	18766
CX-BSI	B707	20315
CX-FAT	B737	21518
CX-PUA	**B737**	**24700**
CX-PUB	**B767**	**28495**
CX-PUD	**B757**	**24291**
CX-PUE	737NG	32362
CX-UAA	F.100	11383
CX-UAB	F.100	11389
CX-VVT	B737	21130

Nauru

Reg	Type	c/n
C2-RN1	F.28	11041
C2-RN10	B737	26960
C2-RN11	B737	26961
C2-RN2	F.28	11056
C2-RN3	B737	21073
C2-RN4	B727	20370
C2-RN5	B727	19252
C2-RN6	B737	21616
C2-RN7	B727	20278
C2-RN8	B737	22070
C2-RN9	B737	22072

Gambia

Reg	Type	c/n
C5-ABM	B727	21781
(C5-ACE)	F.28	11027
C5-ADA	B727	19970
C5-ADD	F.28	11003
C5-ADE	F.28	11004
C5-ADF	F.28	11052
C5-AEA	DC-9	47401
C5-AMM	B707	20176
C5-BIN	B707	20172
C5-DMB	B727	20411
C5-DSZ	B727	20470
C5-EUN	**B737**	**22798**
C5-FBS	B747	19875
C5-GAE	**B727**	**19124**
C5-GAL	B727	22043
C5-GNM	**IL62**	**3036142**
C5-GOA	B707	20177
C5-GOB	B707	19335
C5-GOC	B707	18839
C5-IFY	**B737**	**22797**
C5-JDZ	**DC-9**	**48145**
C5-LKI	1-11	BAC.158
C5-LPS	**DC-9**	**48146**
C5-MBM	**B707**	**19966**
C5-NYA	**B737**	**22799**
C5-OAA	B747	21439
C5-OBJ	**B737**	**22795**
C5-OUK	**B737**	**22796**
C5-OUS	**F.28**	**11052**
C5-RTG	**IL62**	**1356234**
C5-SBM	**B727**	**21609**
C5-SMM	B727	19973
C5-WAL	L1011	193B-1066
C5-ZNA	**B737**	**22806**

Bahamas

Reg	Type	c/n
(C6-BDF)	B707	18085
C6-BDG	B707	18084
C6-BDJ	1-11	089
C6-BDN	1-11	062
C6-BDP	1-11	063
C6-BDZ	B737	21231
C6-BEC	B737	20413
C6-BEH	B727	22531
C6-BEI	B737	20128
C6-BEK	B737	20956
C6-BEQ	B737	21279
C6-BES	B737	19921
C6-BEX	B737	21528
C6-BFB	B737	20221
C6-BFC	B737	21278
C6-BFJ	B737	20211
C6-BFM	**B737**	**22596**
C6-BFW	**B737**	**22601**
C6-BGK	**B737**	**22086**
C6-BGL	**B737**	**22087**
C6-TTB	737NG	29749

Mozambique
(see also CR-)

Reg	Type	c/n
(C9-)	B767	26471
C9-ARF	B707	17593
C9-ARG	B707	18013
C9-BAA	B737	20280
C9-BAB	B737	20281
C9-BAC	B737	20536
C9-BAD	B737	20786
C9-BAE	IL62	3344724
C9-BAF	B767	26471
C9-BAG	**B737**	**23677**
C9-BAH	B737	21808
C9-BAI	**B737**	**23405**
C9-BAJ	**B737**	**23464**
C9-BAK	**B737**	**23404**
C9-BAL	**B737**	**21808**
C9-BAM	**B737**	**21733**
C9-BAN	**B737**	**23283**
C9-CAA	TU134	63457

Germany

Reg	Type	c/n
D-		**737NG 35277**
(D-)	DC-8	45879
D-AAAI	**E145**	**14500991**
D-AACI	A319	1157
D-AAMS	A320	0437
D-AASL	B737	24637
D-AAST	SE210	230
D-ABAA		**737NG 30271**
D-ABAA		737NG 30637
D-ABAB		**737NG 30277**
D-ABAB	B737	24769
D-ABAC		**737NG 30501**
D-ABAC	B737	24687
D-ABAD		**737NG 30876**
D-ABAD	B737	25178
D-ABAE		**737NG 30877**
D-ABAE	B737	27171
D-ABAF		**737NG 30878**
D-ABAF	B737	26081
D-ABAF	SE210	21
D-ABAF	SE210	263
D-ABAG		**737NG 30879**
D-ABAG	B737	27213
D-ABAH	B737	27826
D-ABAI	B737	28038
D-ABAJ	B737	25180
D-ABAK	B737	28271
D-ABAK	SE210	232
D-ABAL	B737	28334
D-ABAM	B737	28867
(D-ABAM)	F.28	11030
D-ABAM	SE210	214
D-ABAN		**737NG 28068**
D-ABAN	F.28	11029
D-ABAO		**737NG 28069**
D-ABAP		**737NG 28070**
D-ABAP	SE210	235
D-ABAQ		**737NG 28071**
D-ABAQ	F.28	11004
D-ABAR		**737NG 28072**
D-ABAS		**737NG 28073**
(D-ABAS)	F.28	11031
(D-ABAS)	F.28	11048
D-ABAT		**737NG 29120**
D-ABAU		**737NG 29121**
D-ABAV		**737NG 30498**
D-ABAV	SE210	243
D-ABAW		**737NG 30062**
D-ABAW	SE210	239
D-ABAX		**737NG 30063**
D-ABAX	F.28	11006
D-ABAY		**737NG 30499**
D-ABAZ		**737NG 30500**
D-ABBA		**737NG 30570**
D-ABBB		**737NG 32624**
D-ABBC		**737NG 32625**
D-ABBD		**737NG 30880**
D-ABBE		**737NG 30881**
D-ABBE	B737	20253
D-ABBF		**737NG 32917**
D-ABBG		**737NG 32918**
D-ABBH		**737NG 32919**
D-ABBI		**737NG 32920**
D-ABBI	B727	19793
D-ABBJ		**737NG 30286**
D-ABBK		**737NG 33013**
D-ABBL		**737NG 28821**
D-ABBM		**737NG 28823**
D-ABBN		**737NG 30293**
D-ABBO		**737NG 30827**
D-ABBP		**737NG 29641**
D-ABBQ		**737NG 28608**
D-ABBR		**737NG 28825**
D-ABBS		**737NG 28654**
D-ABBT		**737NG 32582**
D-ABBU		**737NG 30627**

Reg	Type	Ser	Reg	Type	Ser	Reg	Type	Ser	Reg	Type	Ser
D-ABBV	**737NG**	**30629**	D-ABFI	B727	20525	**D-ABIC**	**B737**	**24817**	D-ABKM	B727	21442
D-ABBW	**737NG**	**30642**	D-ABFK	B727	22119	D-ABID	B727	18362	D-ABKN	B727	21618
D-ABBX	**737NG**	**34969**	D-ABFL	B737	22120	**D-ABID**	**B737**	**24818**	D-ABKP	B727	21619
D-ABBY	**737NG**	**34970**	D-ABFM	B737	22121	D-ABIE	B727	19012	D-ABKQ	B727	21620
D-ABBZ	**737NG**	**30478**	D-ABFN	B737	22122	**D-ABIE**	**B737**	**24819**	D-ABKR	B727	21621
D-ABCC	B737	25262	D-ABFP	B737	22123	D-ABIF	B727	18363	D-ABKS	B727	21622
"D-ABCE"	B707	17587	D-ABFR	B737	22124	**D-ABIF**	**B737**	**24820**	D-ABKT	B727	21623
D-ABCE	B737	20254	D-ABFS	B737	22125	D-ABIG	B727	18364	**D-ABLA**	**737NG**	**36114**
"D-ABCE"	B737	22114	D-ABFS	B757	24738	D-ABIH	B727	18365	D-ABLA	A320	1081
D-ABCI	B727	20430	(D-ABFT)	B737	22126	**D-ABIH**	**B737**	**24821**	D-ABLB	A320	1370
D-ABDA	**A320**	**2539**	D-ABFT	B737	22402	D-ABII	B727	19310	(D-ABLC)	A321	1012
D-ABDB	**A320**	**2619**	D-ABFU	B737	22126	**D-ABII**	**B737**	**24822**	D-ABLI	B727	20674
D-ABDC	**A320**	**2654**	(D-ABFU)	B737	22127	D-ABIJ	B727	19314	D-ABMA	B737	23153
D-ABDD	**A320**	**2685**	D-ABFW	B737	22127	**D-ABIJ**	**B737**	**25041**	D-ABMB	B737	23154
D-ABDD	B737	24813	(D-ABFW)	B737	22128	D-ABIK	B727	18366	D-ABMC	B737	23155
D-ABDE	**A320**	**2696**	D-ABFX	B737	22128	**D-ABIK**	**B737**	**24823**	D-ABMD	B737	23156
D-ABDE	B737	20255	(D-ABFX)	B737	22129	D-ABIL	B727	18367	D-ABME	B737	23157
D-ABDF	**A320**	**2820**	D-ABFY	B737	22129	**D-ABIL**	**B737**	**24824**	D-ABMF	B737	23158
D-ABDF	B737	24571	D-ABFY	B737	22130	D-ABIM	B727	18368	D-ABMI	B727	20675
D-ABDG	**A320**	**2835**	(D-ABFY)	B737	22130	**D-ABIM**	**B737**	**24937**	D-ABNA	B757	24737
D-ABDH	A320	2846	D-ABFZ	B737	22130	D-ABIN	B727	18369	D-ABNB	B757	24738
D-ABDI	**A320**	**2853**	(D-ABFZ)	B737	22131	**D-ABIN**	**B737**	**24938**	D-ABNC	B757	24747
D-ABDI	B727	20431	**D-ABGA**	**A319**	**2383**	D-ABIO	B727	19311	D-ABND	B757	24748
D-ABDI	B737	27337	**D-ABGB**	**A319**	**2467**	**D-ABIO**	**B737**	**24939**	D-ABNE	B757	24749
D-ABDJ	**A320**	**2865**	**D-ABGC**	**A319**	**2468**	D-ABIP	B727	18370	D-ABNF	B757	25140
D-ABDK	**A320**	**2968**	**D-ABGD**	**A319**	**2335**	**D-ABIP**	**B737**	**24940**	D-ABNH	B757	25436
D-ABDL	**A320**	**2991**	**D-ABGE**	**A319**	**3139**	D-ABIQ	B727	18371	D-ABNI	B727	20676
D-ABDM	**A320**	**3006**	D-ABGE	B737	20257	D-ABIR	B727	18933	D-ABNI	B757	25437
D-ABDN	**A320**	**3021**	**D-ABGF**	**A319**	**3188**	**D-ABIR**	**B737**	**24941**	D-ABNK	B757	25438
D-ABDO	**A320**	**3055**	**D-ABGG**	**A319**	**3202**	D-ABIS	B727	18934	D-ABNL	B757	25439
D-ABDP	**A320**	**3093**	**D-ABGH**	**A319**	**3245**	**D-ABIS**	**B737**	**24942**	D-ABNM	B757	25440
D-ABDQ	**A320**	**3121**	D-ABGI	B727	20526	D-ABIT	B727	18935	D-ABNN	B757	25441
D-ABDR	**A320**	**3242**	D-ABGM	A340	212	**D-ABIT**	**B737**	**24943**	D-ABNO	B757	25901
D-ABDS	**A320**	**3289**	D-ABHA	B737	22131	D-ABIU	B727	19312	D-ABNP	B757	26433
D-ABDX	B737	28659	(D-ABHA)	B737	22132	**D-ABIU**	**B737**	**24944**	D-ABNR	B757	26434
D-ABEA	B737	19013	D-ABHB	B737	22132	D-ABIV	B727	18936	D-ABNS	B757	26435
D-ABEA	**B737**	**24565**	(D-ABHB)	B737	22133	D-ABIW	B727	19008	D-ABNT	B757	26436
D-ABEB	B737	19014	D-ABHC	B737	22133	**D-ABIW**	**B737**	**24945**	D-ABNX	B757	24838
D-ABEB	**B737**	**25148**	(D-ABHC)	B737	22134	D-ABIX	B727	19009	D-ABNY	B757	22781
D-ABEC	B737	19015	(D-ABHD)	B737	22134	**D-ABIX**	**B737**	**24946**	D-ABNZ	B757	22960
D-ABEC	**B737**	**25149**	(D-ABHD)	B737	22135	D-ABIY	B727	19313	**D-ABOA**	**B757**	**29016**
D-ABED	**B737**	**25215**	D-ABHD	B737	22635	**D-ABIY**	**B737**	**25243**	D-ABOB	B707	17718
D-ABEE	**B737**	**25216**	D-ABHE	B737	20258	D-ABIZ	B727	19010	**D-ABOB**	**B757**	**29017**
D-ABEF	B737	19017	D-ABHF	B737	22134	**D-ABIZ**	**B737**	**25244**	**D-ABOC**	**B757**	**29015**
D-ABEF	**B737**	**25217**	(D-ABHF)	B737	22135	**D-ABJA**	**B737**	**25270**	D-ABOC	B707	17719
D-ABEH	B737	19019	(D-ABHF)	B737	22136	**D-ABJB**	**B737**	**25271**	D-ABOD	B707	17720
D-ABEH	**B737**	**25242**	D-ABHH	1-11	084	**D-ABJC**	**B737**	**25272**	**D-ABOE**	**B757**	**29012**
D-ABEI	B737	19020	D-ABHH	B737	22135	**D-ABJD**	**B737**	**25309**	D-ABOF	B707	17721
D-ABEI	**B737**	**25359**	(D-ABHH)	B737	22136	**D-ABJE**	**B737**	**25310**	**D-ABOF**	**B757**	**29013**
D-ABEK	B737	19021	(D-ABHH)	B737	22137	**D-ABJF**	**B737**	**25311**	D-ABOG	B707	18056
D-ABEK	**B737**	**25414**	D-ABHI	B727	20560	**D-ABJH**	**B737**	**25357**	**D-ABOG**	**B757**	**29014**
D-ABEL	B737	19022	D-ABHK	B737	22136	**D-ABJI**	**B737**	**25358**	D-ABOH	B707	18057
D-ABEL	**B737**	**25415**	(D-ABHK)	B737	22137	(D-ABJK)	B737	25359	**D-ABOH**	**B757**	**30030**
D-ABEM	B737	19023	(D-ABHK)	B737	22138	(D-ABJL)	B737	25414	**D-ABOI**	**B767**	**29010**
D-ABEM	**B737**	**25416**	D-ABHL	B737	22137	(D-ABJM)	B737	25415	**D-ABOJ**	**B757**	**29019**
D-ABEN	B737	19024	(D-ABHL)	B737	22138	(D-ABJN)	B737	25416	D-ABOK	B707	18058
D-ABEN	**B737**	**26428**	(D-ABHL)	B737	22139	D-ABJW	B757	24748	**D-ABOK**	**B757**	**29020**
D-ABEO	B737	19025	D-ABHM	B737	22138	**D-ABKA**	**737NG**	**29329**	D-ABOL	B707	18059
D-ABEO	**B737**	**26429**	(D-ABHM)	B737	22139	D-ABKA	B727	20899	**D-ABOL**	**B757**	**29021**
D-ABEP	B737	19026	(D-ABHM)	B737	22140	D-ABKA	B737	27000	D-ABOM	B707	18060
D-ABEP	**B737**	**26430**	D-ABHN	B737	22139	**D-ABKB**	**737NG**	**28577**	**D-ABOM**	**B757**	**29022**
D-ABEQ	B737	19027	(D-ABHN)	B737	22140	D-ABKB	B727	20900	D-ABON	B707	18248
D-ABER	B737	19028	(D-ABHN)	B737	22141	D-ABKB	B737	27001	**D-ABON**	**B757**	**29023**
D-ABER	**B737**	**26431**	D-ABHP	B737	22140	D-ABKC	B727	20901	D-ABOP	B707	18249
D-ABES	B737	19029	(D-ABHP)	B737	22141	D-ABKC	B737	27002	D-ABOQ	B707	18250
D-ABES	**B737**	**26432**	(D-ABHP)	B737	22142	D-ABKD	B727	20902	D-ABOR	B707	18251
D-ABET	B737	19030	D-ABHR	B737	22141	D-ABKD	B737	27003	D-ABOS	B707	18462
D-ABET	**B737**	**27903**	(D-ABHR)	B737	22142	D-ABKE	B727	20903	D-ABOT	B707	18463
D-ABEU	B737	19031	(D-ABHR)	B737	22143	(D-ABKE)	B737	27004	D-ABOV	B707	18462
D-ABEU	**B737**	**27904**	D-ABHS	B737	22142	D-ABKF	B727	20904	D-ABOX	B707	18819
D-ABEV	B737	19032	(D-ABHS)	B737	22143	D-ABKF	B737	27004	D-ABPI	B727	20677
D-ABEW	B737	19033	(D-ABHT)	B737	22634	(D-ABKF)	B737	27005	D-ABQI	B727	20757
D-ABEW	**B737**	**27905**	D-ABHT	B737	22636	D-ABKG	B727	20905	D-ABRI	B727	20788
D-ABEY	B737	19794	D-ABHU	B737	22143	D-ABKH	B727	20906	D-ABSG	B757	24747
D-ABFA	B737	22114	(D-ABHU)	B737	22635	(D-ABKH)	B737	27007	D-ABSI	B727	20789
D-ABFB	B737	22113	D-ABHW	B737	22634	D-ABKI	B727	20673	**D-ABTA**	**B747**	**24285**
D-ABFC	B737	22115	(D-ABHW)	B737	22636	D-ABKJ	B727	20918	**D-ABTB**	**B747**	**24286**
D-ABFD	B737	22116	D-ABHX	B737	22637	D-ABKK	B727	21113	**D-ABTC**	**B747**	**24287**
D-ABFE	B737	20256	D-ABIA	B737	19011	(D-ABKK)	B737	27004	**D-ABTD**	**B747**	**24715**
D-ABFF	B737	22117	**D-ABIA**	**B737**	**24815**	D-ABKK	B737	27005	**D-ABTE**	**B747**	**24966**
D-ABFH	A300	755	D-ABIB	B727	18360	D-ABKL	B727	21114	**D-ABTF**	**B747**	**24967**
D-ABFH	B737	22118	**D-ABIB**	**B737**	**24816**	D-ABKL	B737	27007	**D-ABTH**	**B747**	**25047**
			D-ABIC	B727	18361						

Reg	Type	Serial	Reg	Type	Serial	Reg	Type	Serial	Reg	Type	Serial
D-ABTI	B727	20790	D-ABXK	B737	23530	D-ACJE	CRJ	7165	D-ACRN	CRJ	7486
D-ABTK	B747	29871	D-ABXL	B737	23531	D-ACJF	CRJ	7200	D-ACRO	CRJ	7494
D-ABTL	B747	29872	D-ABXM	B737	23871	D-ACJG	CRJ	7220	D-ACRP	CRJ	7625
D-ABTM	B747	33430	D-ABXN	B737	23872	D-ACJH	CRJ	7266	D-ACRQ	CRJ	7629
D-ABTN	B747	33431	D-ABXO	B737	23873	D-ACJI	CRJ	7282	D-ACSB	CRJ7	10028
D-ABTO	B747	33432	D-ABXP	B737	23874	D-ACJJ	CRJ	7298	D-ACSC	CRJ7	10039
D-ABTP	B747	33433	D-ABXR	B737	23875	(D-ACJK)	CRJ	7378	D-ACVK	SE210	176
D-ABUA	B707	18937	D-ABXS	B737	24280	D-ACJZ	CRJ	7036	D-ADAC	A310	313
(D-ABUA)	B767	26983	D-ABXT	B737	24281	D-ACKA	CRJ9	15072	D-ADAM	VFW	G-017
D-ABUA	B767	26991	D-ABXU	B737	24282	D-ACKB	CRJ9	15073	D-ADAO	DC-10	47921
D-ABUB	B707	18923	D-ABXW	B737	24561	D-ACKC	CRJ9	15078	D-ADAP	B707	17697
(D-ABUB)	B767	26984	D-ABXX	B737	24562	D-ACKD	CRJ9	15080	D-ADAQ	B707	17701
D-ABUB	B767	26987	D-ABXY	B737	24563	D-ACKE	CRJ9	15081	D-ADBA	B737	26441
(D-ABUB)	B767	26992	D-ABXZ	B737	24564	D-ACKF	CRJ9	15083	D-ADBB	B737	26440
D-ABUC	B707	18926	D-ABYA	B747	19746	D-ACKG	CRJ9	15084	D-ADBC	B737	26442
D-ABUC	B767	26992	D-ABYB	B747	19747	D-ACKH	CRJ9	15085	D-ADBD	B737	27061
D-ABUD	B707	18927	D-ABYC	B747	19748	D-ACKI	CRJ9	15088	D-ADBE	B737	24569
D-ABUD	B767	26983	D-ABYD	B747	20372	D-ACKJ	CRJ9	15089	D-ADBG	B737	25125
D-ABUE	B707	18932	D-ABYE	B747	20373	D-ACKK	CRJ9	15094	D-ADBH	B737	27336
D-ABUE	B767	26984	D-ABYF	B747	20493	D-ACKL	CRJ9	15095	D-ADBJ	B737	27833
D-ABUF	B707	18928	D-ABYG	B747	20527	D-ACLA	CRJ	7004	D-ADBK	B737	29055
D-ABUF	B767	26985	D-ABYJ	B747	21220	D-ACLB	CRJ	7005	D-ADBL	B737	29056
D-ABUG	B707	18929	D-ABYK	B747	21221	D-ACLC	CRJ	7006	D-ADBM	B737	29057
D-ABUH	B707	18930	(D-ABYL)	B727	20675	D-ACLD	CRJ	7009	D-ADBN	B737	29058
D-ABUH	B767	26986	D-ABYL	B747	21380	D-ACLE	CRJ	7010	D-ADBO	B737	29059
D-ABUI	B707	19317	(D-ABYM)	B727	20676	D-ACLF	CRJ	7015	D-ADBO	DC-10	47922
D-ABUI	B767	26988	D-ABYM	B747	21588	(D-ACLG)	CRJ	7007	D-ADBP	B737	29060
D-ABUJ	B707	20123	(D-ABYN)	B727	20677	D-ACLG	CRJ	7016	D-ADBQ	B737	29099
D-ABUK	B707	18931	D-ABYN	B747	21589	D-ACLH	CRJ	7007	D-ADBR	B737	29100
D-ABUL	B707	19315	D-ABYO	B747	21592	(D-ACLH)	CRJ	7016	D-ADBS	B737	29116
D-ABUM	B707	19316	D-ABYP	B747	21590	D-ACLI	CRJ	7019	D-ADBT	B737	29264
D-ABUO	B707	20124	D-ABYQ	B747	21591	D-ACLJ	CRJ	7021	D-ADBU	B737	29265
D-ABUV	B767	29867	D-ABYR	B747	21643	D-ACLK	CRJ	7023	D-ADBV	B737	29266
D-ABUW	B767	30331	D-ABYS	B747	21644	D-ACLL	CRJ	7024	D-ADBW	B737	29267
D-ABUX	B767	25137	D-ABYT	B747	22363	D-ACLM	CRJ	7025	(D-ADCA)	A320	0573
D-ABUY	B707	20395	D-ABYU	B747	22668	D-ACLN	CRJ	7039	D-ADCO	DC-10	47923
D-ABUY	B767	25208	D-ABYW	B747	22669	D-ACLO	CRJ	7041	(D-ADDA)	B737	22070
D-ABUZ	B767	25209	D-ABYX	B747	22670	D-ACLP	CRJ	7064	D-ADDO	DC-10	47924
D-ABVA	B747	23816	D-ABYY	B747	22671	D-ACLQ	CRJ	7073	D-ADEI	146	E2086
D-ABVB	B747	23817	D-ABYZ	B747	23286	D-ACLR	CRJ	7086	D-ADFA	F.100	11307
D-ABVC	B747	24288	D-ABZA	B747	23287	D-ACLS	CRJ	7090	D-ADFB	F.100	11311
D-ABVD	B747	24740	D-ABZB	B747	23348	D-ACLT	CRJ	7093	D-ADFC	F.100	11315
D-ABVE	B747	24741	D-ABZC	B747	23393	D-ACLU	CRJ	7104	D-ADFD	F.100	11344
D-ABVF	B747	24761	D-ABZD	B747	23407	D-ACLV	CRJ	7113	D-ADFE	F.100	11363
(D-ABVG)	B747	29872	D-ABZE	B747	23509	D-ACLW	CRJ	7114	D-ADFO	DC-10	47925
D-ABVH	B747	25045	D-ABZF	B747	23621	D-ACLX	CRJ	7036	D-ADGO	DC-10	47926
D-ABVI	B727	20791	D-ABZH	B747	23622	D-ACLY	CRJ	7119	D-ADHO	DC-10	47927
(D-ABVI)	B747	29871	D-ABZI	B747	24138	D-ACLZ	CRJ	7121	D-ADIA	B737	30333
D-ABVK	B747	25046	D-ABZL	73/NG	32915	"D-ACME"	AJ40	001	D-ADIB	B737	30334
D-ABVL	B747	26425	D-ACAF	A320	0444	D-ACPA	CRJ7	10012	D-ADIC	B737	30335
(D-ABVM)	B747	26426	D-ACBA	B737	24652	D-ACPB	CRJ7	10013	D-ADID	B737	23773
D-ABVM	B747	29101	D-ACBB	B737	24828	D-ACPC	CRJ7	10014	D-ADIE	B737	23774
D-ABVN	B747	26427	D-ACBC	B737	24273	D-ACPD	CRJ7	10015	D-ADIF	B737	25125
D-ABVO	B747	28086	D-ACBG	E145	14501016	D-ACPE	CRJ7	10027	D-ADIG	B737	26441
D-ABVP	B747	28284	(D-ACCA)	DC-8	45667	D-ACPF	CRJ7	10030	D-ADIH	B737	23921
D-ABVR	B747	28285	(D-ACCB)	DC-8	45684	D-ACPG	CRJ7	10034	(D-ADIH)	B737	24221
D-ABVS	B747	28286	D-ACEB	DC-9	47218	D-ACPH	CRJ7	10043	D-ADII	B737	23775
D-ABVT	B747	28287	D-ACEC	DC-9	47219	D-ACPI	CRJ7	10046	D-ADIK	B737	24365
D-ABVU	B747	29492	D-ACFA	146	E2200	D-ACPJ	CRJ7	10040	D-ADIM	DC-8	45416
D-ABVW	B747	29493	D-ACHA	CRJ	7378	D-ACPK	CRJ7	10063	D-ADIR	DC-8	45526
D-ABVX	B747	29868	D-ACHB	CRJ	7391	D-ACPL	CRJ7	10076	D-ADIS	DC-9	47459
D-ABVY	B747	29869	D-ACHC	CRJ	7394	D-ACPM	CRJ7	10080	D-ADIT	DC-9	47450
D-ABVZ	B747	29870	D-ACHD	CRJ	7403	D-ACPN	CRJ7	10083	D-ADIU	DC-9	47457
(D-ABWA)	B737	19679	D-ACHE	CRJ	7407	D-ACPO	CRJ7	10085	D-ADIX	DC-8	46137
D-ABWA	B737	23833	D-ACHF	CRJ	7431	D-ACPP	CRJ7	10086	D-ADIY	DC-8	46143
(D-ABWB)	B737	19680	D-ACHG	CRJ	7439	D-ACPQ	CRJ7	10091	D-ADIZ	DC-8	46145
D-ABWB	B737	23834	D-ACHH	CRJ	7449	D-ACPR	CRJ7	10098	D-ADJO	DC-10	47928
D-ABWC	B737	23835	D-ACHI	CRJ	7464	D-ACPS	CRJ7	10100	D-ADKO	DC-10	47929
D-ABWD	B737	23836	D-ACHK	CRJ	7499	D-ACPT	CRJ7	10103	D-ADLO	DC-10	46917
D-ABWE	B737	23837	(D-ACIM)	CRJ	7413	D-ACRA	CRJ	7567	D-ADLY	CRJ	7351
D-ABWF	B737	24283	D-ACIN	B737	24825	D-ACRB	CRJ	7570	D-ADMO	DC-10	46965
D-ABWH	B737	24284	(D-ACIN)	CRJ	7419	D-ACRC	CRJ	7573	D-ADNA	A319	1053
D-ABWI	B727	20792	D-ACIP	B707	18162	D-ACRD	CRJ	7583	D-ADPO	DC-10	46595
D-ABWS	B737	23811	D-ACIQ	B707	18163	D-ACRE	CRJ	7607	D-ADQO	DC-10	46596
D-ABXA	B737	23522	D-ACIR	B707	18240	D-ACRF	CRJ	7619	(D-ADSL)	A320	0168
D-ABXB	B737	23523	D-ACIR	E145	145230	D-ACRG	CRJ	7630	D-ADSO	DC-10	48252
D-ABXC	B737	23524	D-ACIS	B707	18242	D-ACRH	CRJ	7738	D-ADUA	DC-8	46003
D-ABXD	B737	23525	D-ACIT	B707	18244	D-ACRI	CRJ	7862	D-ADUC	DC-8	46106
D-ABXE	B737	23526	D-ACJA	CRJ	7122	D-ACRJ	CRJ	7864	D-ADUE	DC-8	46044
D-ABXF	B737	23527	D-ACJB	CRJ	7128	D-ACRK	CRJ	7901	D-ADUI	DC-8	45991
D-ABXH	B737	23528	D-ACJC	CRJ	7130	D-ACRL	CRJ	7902	D-ADUO	DC-8	46047
D-ABXI	B737	23529	D-ACJD	CRJ	7135	D-ACRM	CRJ	7478	D-AERA	L1011	193R-1033

Registration	Type	Serial
D-AERB	MD11	48484
D-AERC	L1011	193A-1085
D-AERD	A330	143
D-AERE	L1011	193L-1120
D-AERF	A330	082
D-AERG	A330	072
D-AERH	A330	087
D-AERI	L1011	193L-1114
D-AERJ	A330	095
D-AERK	**A330**	**120**
D-AERL	L1011	193J-1196
D-AERM	L1011	193A-1153
D-AERN	L1011	193A-1158
D-AERO	L1011	193A-1008
D-AERP	L1011	193A-1152
D-AERQ	**A330**	**127**
D-AERS	**A330**	**171**
D-AERT	L1011	193J-1183
D-AERU	L1011	193L-1125
D-AERV	L1011	193Y-1195
D-AERW	MD11	48485
D-AERX	MD11	48486
D-AERY	L1011	193A-1008
D-AERZ	MD11	48538
D-AEWA	**146**	**E3163**
D-AEWB	**146**	**E3183**
D-AEWD	**146**	**E2069**
D-AEWE	**146**	**E2077**
D-AEWF	**146**	**E2184**
D-AEWL	**146**	**E3123**
D-AEWM	**146**	**E3125**
D-AEWN	146	E3158
D-AEWO	**146**	**E3162**
D-AEWP	**146**	**E3165**
D-AEWQ	**146**	**E3203**
D-AFGK	B727	19314
"D-AFHG"	B707	17720
D-AFRO	A320	0230
(D-AFRO)	A320	0437
"D-AFSG"	TU154	73A-046
D-AFTI	A320	0338
(D-AFWA)	1-11	BAC.161
(D-AFWB)	1-11	094
(D-AFWC)	1-11	091
D-AGAB	F.28	11046
D-AGAC	F.28	11050
D-AGAD	F.28	11051
D-AGAE	F.28	11052
D-AGBM	A340	185
D-AGEA	**B737**	**23951**
D-AGEA	B737	23970
D-AGEB	B737	23971
D-AGEB	**B737**	**24320**
D-AGEC	B737	23972
(D-AGCD)	B737	24237
D-AGED	B737	24269
D-AGEE	**B737**	**24238**
(D-AGEF)	B737	24269
D-AGEF	B737	25069
D-AGEG	**B737**	**24237**
D-AGEH	B737	23717
D-AGEI	B737	24220
D-AGEJ	**B737**	**24221**
D-AGEK	**B737**	**25015**
D-AGEL	**737NG**	**28110**
D-AGEM	737NG	28099
D-AGEN	**737NG**	**28100**
D-AGEO	737NG	28101
D-AGEP	**737NG**	**28102**
D-AGEQ	**737NG**	**28103**
D-AGER	**737NG**	**28107**
D-AGES	**737NG**	**28108**
D-AGET	**737NG**	**28109**
D-AGEU	**737NG**	**28104**
D-AGEV	737NG	28105
D-AGEW	737NG	28106
D-AGEX	B737	23708
D-AGEY	737NG	29076
D-AGEZ	737NG	29077
(D-AGMB)	E145	145607
D-AGMR	**B737**	**27007**
D-AGPA	**F.100**	**11276**
D-AGPB	**F.100**	**11278**
D-AGPC	**F.100**	**11280**
D-AGPD	**F.100**	**11281**
D-AGPE	**F.100**	**11300**
D-AGPF	F.100	11303
D-AGPG	**F.100**	**11306**
D-AGPH	**F.100**	**11308**
D-AGPI	F.100	11310
D-AGPJ	**F.100**	**11312**
D-AGPK	**F.100**	**11313**
D-AGPL	**F.100**	**11314**
D-AGPM	F.100	11331
D-AGPN	F.100	11333
D-AGPO	**F.100**	**11334**
D-AGPP	F.100	11337
D-AGPQ	**F.100**	**11338**
D-AGPR	**F.100**	**11391**
D-AGPS	**F.100**	**11399**
D-AGWA	**A319**	**2813**
D-AGWA	MD80	49845
D-AGWB	**A319**	**2833**
D-AGWB	MD80	49846
D-AGWC	**A319**	**2976**
D-AGWC	MD80	49847
D-AGWD	**A319**	**3011**
D-AGWD	MD80	49848
D-AGWE	**A319**	**3128**
D-AGWE	MD80	49788
D-AGWF	**A319**	**3172**
D-AGWF	MD80	49793
D-AGWG	**A319**	**3193**
D-AGYA	B767	28039
D-AGYC	B767	28041
D-AGYE	B767	28979
D-AGYF	B767	28208
D-AGYH	B767	28883
D-AHFA	**737NG**	**27981**
D-AHFB	**737NG**	**27982**
D-AHFC	**737NG**	**27977**
D-AHFD	**737NG**	**27978**
D-AHFE	**737NG**	**27979**
D-AHFF	**737NG**	**27980**
D-AHFG	**737NG**	**27989**
D-AHFH	**737NG**	**27983**
D-AHFI	**737NG**	**27984**
D-AHFJ	**737NG**	**27990**
D-AHFK	**737NG**	**27991**
D-AHFL	**737NG**	**27985**
D-AHFM	**737NG**	**27986**
D-AHFN	**737NG**	**28228**
D-AHFO	**737NG**	**27987**
D-AHFP	**737NG**	**27988**
D-AHFQ	**737NG**	**27992**
D-AHFR	**737NG**	**30593**
D-AHFS	737NG	28623
D-AHFT	**737NG**	**30413**
D-AHFU	**737NG**	**30414**
D-AHFV	**737NG**	**30415**
D-AHFW	**737NG**	**30882**
D-AHFX	**737NG**	**30416**
D-AHFY	**737NG**	**30417**
D-AHFZ	**737NG**	**30883**
D-AHIA	**737NG**	**29082**
D-AHIB	**737NG**	**29083**
D-AHIC	**737NG**	**30617**
D-AHID	**737NG**	**29080**
D-AHIE	**737NG**	**29081**
D-AHIF	**737NG**	**29079**
D-AHIG	**B737**	**23827**
D-AHLA	A300	064
D-AHLA	A310	520
(D-AHLA)	B737	24776
D-AHLA	F.28	11027
D-AHLB	A300	083
D-AHLB	A310	528
(D-AHLB)	B737	24926
D-AHLB	F.28	11031
D-AHLC	A300	017
D-AHLC	A310	620
(D-AHLC)	B737	24927
D-AHLC	F.28	11034
D-AHLD	B737	22596
D-AHLD	**B737**	**24926**
(D-AHLD)	F.28	11032
(D-AHLD)	SE210	238
D-AHLE	B737	22597
D-AHLE	B737	24776
D-AHLF	B737	22598
D-AHLF	B737	24927
D-AHLG	B737	22599
D-AHLG	**B737**	**24776**
D-AHLG	B737	26316
(D-AHLG)	B737	27074
D-AHLH	737NG	30783
D-AHLH	B737	22600
D-AHLI	B737	22601
D-AHLI	B737	25037
D-AHLJ	A300	169
D-AHLJ	B737	24125
D-AHLK	A300	174
D-AHLK	B737	24126
D-AHLL	B727	18823
D-AHLL	B737	24127
D-AHLM	B727	18919
D-AHLM	B737	27102
D-AHLN	B727	18952
D-AHLN	B737	25062
D-AHLO	B727	19401
D-AHLO	B737	24128
D-AHLP	**737NG**	**32905**
D-AHLP	B727	18990
D-AHLP	B737	24129
D-AHLQ	**737NG**	**32906**
D-AHLQ	B727	19282
D-AHLQ	B737	24130
D-AHLR	**737NG**	**32907**
D-AHLR	B727	19138
D-AHLR	B737	24901
D-AHLS	B727	19139
D-AHLS	B737	27074
D-AHLT	B727	21851
D-AHLT	B737	27830
D-AHLU	B727	21852
D-AHLU	B737	27831
D-AHLV	A310	430
D-AHLV	B727	21853
D-AHLW	A310	427
D-AHLX	A310	487
D-AHLZ	A300	025
D-AHLZ	A310	468
D-AHOI	**146**	**E3187**
D-AHSH	B737	24659
D-AHXA	**737NG**	**30714**
D-AHXB	**737NG**	**30717**
D-AHXC	**737NG**	**34693**
D-AHXD	**737NG**	**30726**
D-AHXE	**737NG**	**35135**
D-AHXF	**737NG**	**35136**
D-AIAA	**A300**	**021**
D-AIAB	**A300**	**022**
D-AIAC	**A300**	**026**
D-AIAD	**A300**	**048**
D-AIAE	**A300**	**052**
(D-AIAF)	A300	057
D-AIAF	**A300**	**132**
D-AIAH	**A300**	**380**
D-AIAI	**A300**	**391**
D-AIAK	**A300**	**401**
D-AIAL	**A300**	**405**
D-AIAM	**A300**	**408**
D-AIAN	**A300**	**411**
D-AIAP	**A300**	**414**
D-AIAR	**A300**	**546**
D-AIAS	**A300**	**553**
D-AIAT	**A300**	**618**
D-AIAU	**A300**	**623**
D-AIAW	**A300**	**764**
D-AIAX	**A300**	**773**
D-AIAY	**A300**	**608**
D-AIAZ	**A300**	**701**
D-AIBA	**A300**	**053**
D-AIBA	A340	008
D-AIBB	**A300**	**057**
D-AIBB	A340	009
D-AIBC	A300	075
D-AIBC	A340	011
D-AIBD	A300	076
D-AIBD	A340	018
D-AIBE	A340	019
D-AIBF	A300	077
D-AIBF	A340	006
D-AIBH	A340	021
D-AICA	A310	191
D-AICA	**A320**	**0774**
D-AICA	E145	145564
D-AICB	A310	201
D-AICB	A320	0793
D-AICC	A310	230
D-AICC	**A320**	**0809**
D-AICD	A310	233
D-AICD	**A320**	**0884**
D-AICE	**A320**	**0894**
D-AICF	A310	237
D-AICF	**A320**	**0905**
D-AICG	**A320**	**0957**
D-AICH	A310	254
D-AICH	**A320**	**0971**
D-AICI	**A320**	**1381**
D-AICJ	**A320**	**1402**
D-AICK	A310	257
D-AICK	**A320**	**1416**
D-AICL	A310	273
D-AICL	**A320**	**1437**
D-AICM	A310	356
D-AICM	**A320**	**1929**
D-AICN	A310	359
D-AICN	**A320**	**1968**
D-AICP	A310	360
D-AICR	A310	397
D-AICS	A310	400
D-AICY	A319	2263
D-AICY	A319	2650
D-AICY	A319	3085
D-AIDA	A310	434
D-AIDB	A310	484
D-AIDC	A310	485
D-AIDD	A310	488
D-AIDE	A310	522
D-AIDF	A310	524
D-AIDH	A310	527
D-AIDI	A310	523
D-AIDK	A310	526
D-AIDL	A310	547
D-AIDM	A310	595
D-AIDN	A310	599
D-AIDR	A319	2949
D-ATFA	**A318**	**3100**
D-AIEL	**A340**	**016**
D-AIFA	**A340**	**352**
D-AIFB	**A340**	**355**
D-AIFC	**A340**	**379**
D-AIFD	**A340**	**390**
D-AIFE	**A340**	**434**
D-AIFF	**A340**	**447**
D-AIFL	**A340**	**236**
D-AIFR	A319	2840
D-AIFR	**A319**	**3073**
D-AIGA	**A340**	**020**
D-AIGB	**A340**	**024**
D-AIGC	**A340**	**027**
D-AIGD	**A340**	**028**
(D-AIGF)	A340	032
D-AIGF	**A340**	**035**
(D-AIGH)	A340	033
D-AIGH	**A340**	**052**
(D-AIGI)	A340	034
D-AIGI	**A340**	**053**
(D-AIGK)	A340	036
D-AIGK	**A340**	**056**
D-AIGL	**A340**	**135**
D-AIGM	**A340**	**158**
D-AIGN	**A340**	**213**
D-AIGO	**A340**	**233**
D-AIGP	**A340**	**252**
D-AIGR	**A340**	**274**

Reg	Type	No.	Reg	Type	No.	Reg	Type	No.	Reg	Type	No.
D-AIGS	A340	297	D-AIMM	A319	2837	D-AKFX	A320	0142	D-ALLD	MD80	49402
D-AIGT	A340	304	D-AIPA	A320	0069	D-AKFY	A320	0157	D-ALLE	MD80	49449
D-AIGU	A340	321	D-AIPB	A320	0070	D-AKNF	A319	0646	(D-ALLF)	A320	0245
D-AIGV	A340	325	D-AIPC	A320	0071	D-AKNG	A319	0654	D-ALLF	MD80	49602
D-AIGW	A340	327	D-AIPD	A320	0072	D-AKNH	A319	0794	(D-ALLG)	A320	0300
D-AIGX	A340	354	D-AIPE	A320	0078	D-AKNI	A319	1016	D-ALLG	MD80	49670
D-AIGY	A340	335	D-AIPF	A320	0083	D-AKNJ	A319	1172	D-ALLH	MD80	49671
D-AIGZ	A340	347	D-AIPH	A320	0086	D-AKNK	A319	1077	D-ALLI	1-11	BAC.116
D-AIHA	A340	482	D-AIPK	A320	0093	(D-AKNK)	A319	1466	D-ALLI	MD80	49767
D-AIHB	A340	517	D-AIPL	A320	0094	D-AKNL	A319	1084	D-ALLJ	MD80	49768
D-AIHC	A340	523	D-AIPM	A320	0104	D-AKNM	A319	1089	D-ALLK	MD80	49769
D-AIHD	A340	537	D-AIPN	A320	0105	D-AKNN	A319	1136	D-ALLL	MD80	49854
D-AIHE	A340	540	D-AIPP	A320	0110	D-AKNO	A319	1147	D-ALLM	MD80	49856
D-AIHF	A340	543	D-AIPR	A320	0111	D-AKNP	A319	1155	D-ALLN	MD80	49857
D-AIHH	A340	566	D-AIPS	A320	0116	D-AKNQ	A319	1170	D-ALLO	MD80	53012
D-AIHI	A340	569	D-AIPT	A320	0117	D-AKNR	A319	1209	D-ALLP	MD80	53013
D-AIHK	A340	580	D-AIPU	A320	0135	D-AKNS	A319	1277	D-ALLQ	MD80	53014
D-AIHL	A340	583	D-AIPW	A320	0137	D-AKNT	A319	2607	D-ALLR	MD80	53015
D-AIHM	A340	762	D-AIPX	A320	0147	D-AKNU	A319	2628	D-ALLS	MD80	49379
D-AIHN	A340	763	D-AIPY	A320	0161	D-AKNV	A319	2632	(D-ALLS)	MD80	53016
D-AIHO	A340	767	D-AIPZ	A320	0162	D-AKNX	A320	0525	D-ALLT	MD80	49440
D-AIHP	A340	771	D-AIQA	A320	0172	D-AKNY	A320	0579	(D-ALLT)	MD80	53063
D-AIHQ	A340	790	D-AIQB	A320	0200	D-AKNZ	A320	0645	D-ALLU	MD80	49619
D-AIHR	A340	794	D-AIQC	A320	0201	D-AKPV	A321	0956	D-ALLV	MD80	49620
D-AIHS	A340	812	D-AIQD	A320	0202	D-ALAA	A320	0565	D-ALLW	MD80	49792
D-AIHT	A340	846	D-AIQE	A320	0209	D-ALAB	A320	0575	D-ALOA	146	E2066
D-AIHU	A340	848	D-AIQF	A320	0216	D-ALAC	A320	0580	D-ALPA	A330	403
D-AIHV	A340	897	D-AIQH	A320	0217	D-ALAD	A320	0661	D-ALPB	A330	432
D-AIJA	A318	1599	D-AIQK	A320	0218	D-ALAE	A320	0659	D-ALPC	A330	444
D-AIJA	A318	2910	D-AIQL	A320	0267	D-ALAF	A320	0667	D-ALPD	A330	454
D-AIJO	A319	1608	D-AIQM	A320	0268	D-ALAG	A321	0787	D-ALPE	A330	469
D-AIJO	A319	1908	D-AIQN	A320	0269	D-ALAH	A321	0792	D-ALPF	A330	476
D-AIJO	A319	2192	D-AIQP	A320	0346	D-ALAI	A321	0954	D-ALPG	A330	493
D-AIJO	A319	2675	D-AIQR	A320	0382	D-ALAJ	A320	0990	D-ALPH	A330	739
D-AIJW	A310	501	D-AIQS	A320	0401	D-ALAK	A321	1004	D-ALPI	A330	828
(D-AIKA)	A319	1212	D-AIQT	A320	1337	D-ALAL	A321	1195	D-ALSA	A321	1629
D-AIKA	A330	570	D-AIQU	A320	1365	D-ALAL	B707	17638	D-ALSB	A321	1994
D-AIKB	A330	576	D-AIQW	A320	1367	D-ALAM	A321	1199	D-ALSC	A321	2005
D-AIKC	A330	579	D-AIRA	A321	0458	D-ALAM	B707	17637	D-ALSD	A321	1607
D-AIKD	A330	629	D-AIRB	A321	0468	D-ALAN	A321	1218	D-ALTA	A320	0530
D-AIKE	A330	636	D-AIRC	A321	0473	D-ALAO	A321	1408	D-ALTB	A320	1385
D-AIKF	A330	642	D-AIRD	A321	0474	D-ALAP	A321	1421	D-ALTC	A320	1441
D-AIKG	A330	645	D-AIRE	A321	0484	D-ALAQ	1-11	BAC.229	D-ALTD	A320	1493
D-AIKH	A330	648	D-AIRF	A321	0493	D-ALAQ	A321	1438	D-ALTE	A320	1504
D-AIKI	A330	687	D-AIRH	A321	0412	D-ALAR	1-11	BAC.207	D-ALTE	CRJ7	10217
D-AIKJ	A330	701	D-AIRK	A321	0502	D-ALAR	A320	1459	D-ALTF	A320	1553
D-AIKK	A330	896	D-AIRL	A321	0505	D-ALAS	1-11	BAC.208	D-ALTG	A320	1762
D-AIKL	A330	905	D-AIRM	A321	0518	D-ALAS	A321	1487	D-ALTH	A320	1797
D-AIKM	A330	913	D-AIRN	A321	0560	D-ALAT	1-11	BAC.187	D-ALTI	A320	1806
D-AILA	A319	0609	D-AIRO	A321	0563	D-ALAT	A320	1996	D-ALTJ	A320	1838
D-AILB	A319	0610	D-AIRP	A321	0564	D-ALAU	A320	1935	D-ALTK	A320	1931
D-AILC	A319	0616	D-AIRR	A321	0567	D-ALCA	MD11	48781	D-ALTL	A320	2009
D-AILD	A319	0623	D-AIRS	A321	0595	D-ALCB	MD11	48782	D-AMAJ	146	E2028
D-AILE	A319	0627	D-AIRT	A321	0652	D-ALCC	MD11	48783	D-AMAM	1-11	BAC.229
D-AILF	A319	0636	D-AIRU	A321	0692	D-ALCD	MD11	48784	D-AMAP	A300	009
D-AILH	A319	0641	D-AIRW	A321	0699	D-ALCE	MD11	48785	D-AMAS	1-11	BAC.187
D-AILI	A319	0651	D-AIRX	A321	0887	D-ALCF	MD11	48798	D-AMAT	1-11	BAC.235
D-AILK	A319	0679	D-AIRY		0901	D-ALCG	MD11	48799	D-AMAX	A300	012
D-AILL	A319	0689	D-AISB	A321	1080	D-ALCH	MD11	48801	D-AMAY	A300	020
D-AILM	A319	0694	D-AISC	A321	1161	D-ALCI	MD11	48800	D-AMAZ	A300	025
D-AILN	A319	0700	D-AISD	A321	1188	D-ALCJ	MD11	48802	D-AMGL	146	E2055
D-AILP	A319	0717	D-AISE	A321	1214	D-ALCK	MD11	48803	D-AMIE	1-11	BAC.190
D-AILR	A319	0723	D-AISF	A321	1260	D-ALCL	MD11	48804	D-AMOR	1-11	BAC.197
D-AILS	A319	0729	(D-AISF)	A321	1273	D-ALCM	MD11	48805	D-AMOR	DC-9	45787
D-AILT	A319	0738	D-AISG	A321	1273	D-ALCN	MD11	48806	D-AMTA		1602
D-AILU	A319	0744	D-AISH	A321	3265	D-ALCO	MD11	48413	D-AMTB	A321	1623
D-AILW	A319	0853	D-AISI	A321	3339	D-ALCP	MD11	48414	D-AMTC	A321	1632
D-AILX	A319	0860	D-AISJ	A321	3360	D-ALCQ	MD11	48431	D-AMTD	A321	1638
D-AILY	1-11	BAC.163	D-AISK	A321	3387	D-ALCR	MD11	48581	D-AMTH	A321	0761
D-AILY	A319	0875	D-AISL	A321	3434	D-ALCS	MD11	48630	D-AMUB	B757	23119
D-AIMA	A380	038	D-AISY	1-11	BAC.158	D-ALEX	A320	0857	D-AMUC	1-11	BAC.227
D-AIMA	A330	305	D-AITA	A300	134	D-ALFA	1-11	BAC.234	D-AMUC	B757	23651
D-AIMB	A380	041	D-AITB	A300	151	D-ALIA	E170	17000006	D-AMUG	B757	29488
D-AIMB	A330	308	"D-AIWY"	A340	151	D-ALIE	E170	17000059	D-AMUH	B757	29489
D-AIMC	A380	044	D-AIZV	A321	0520	D-ALIF	737NG	32655	D-AMUI	B757	28112
D-AIMC	A330	312	D-AJAA	B727	18951	D-ALIG	737NG	32658	D-AMUJ	B767	28111
D-AIMD	A330	322	(D-AJAA)	B737	22025	D-ALIT	CRJ	7309	D-AMUK	B757	22689
D-AIME	A330	324	D-AJET	146	E2201	D-ALIV	CRJ	7316	D-AMUL	B757	25597
D-AIMF	A340	047	D-AJGP	A340	190	D-ALLA	DC-9	47673	D-AMUM	B757	24451
D-AIMG	A340	051	D-AJWF	A319	1002	D-ALLB	DC-9	47680	D-AMUN	B767	24259
D-AIMM	A319	1703	D-AKEN	CRJ	7489	D-ALLC	DC-9	47672	D-AMUO	B767	29435
D-AIMM	A319	2592	D-AKFW	A320	0140	D-ALLD	DC-9	47639	D-AMUP	B767	25531

Reg	Type	S/N	Reg	Type	S/N	Reg	Type	S/N	Reg	Type	S/N
D-AMUQ	B757	26278	(D-AOUP)	B737	22070	D-ATUI	737NG	30287	D-AVW.	A319	3253
D-AMUR	1-11	BAC.195	D-APAA	A319	1947	D-ATUI	737NG	34690	D-AVWA	A319	1062
(D-AMUR)	1-11	BAC.197	D-APAB	A319	1955	D-ATUJ	737NG	32904	D-AVWA	A319	1131
D-AMUR	B757	23118	D-APAC	A319	1727	D-ATWO	E145	14501010	D-AVWA	A319	1261
D-AMUR	B767	24257	D-APAD	A319	1880	D-AUAA	A318	1660	D-AVWA	A319	1373
D-AMUS	B757	23119	D-APOL	A310	447	D-AUAA	A318	2317	D-AVWA	A319	1444
D-AMUS	B767	24258	D-APOM	A310	448	D-AUAA	A318	2523	D-AVWA	A319	1569
D-AMUT	B757	23651	D-APON	A310	472	D-AUAA	A318	2686	D-AVWA	A319	1668
D-AMUU	B757	22688	D-APOO	A310	475	D-AUAA	A318	2910	D-AVWA	A319	1839
D-AMUV	B757	23928	D-APOP	A310	481	D-AUAA	A318	3110	D-AVWA	A319	2002
D-AMUW	B757	23929	D-APOQ	A310	475	D-AUAB	A318	1991	D-AVWA	A319	2122
D-AMUX	B757	23983	D-AQUA	146	E3118	D-AUAB	A318	2218	D-AVWA	A319	2295
D-AMUY	B757	24176	D-ARAT	A300	102	D-AUAB	A318	2544	D-AVWA	A319	2406
D-AMUZ	B757	24497	D-ARFA	A321	1218	D-AUAB	A318	2750	D-AVWA	A319	2487
D-ANDA	A319	1102	D-ARFB	A321	1199	D-AUAB	A318	2918	D-AVWB	A319	1064
D-ANDE	A319	1283	D-ARFC	A320	0580	D-AUAB	A318	3092	D-AVWB	A319	1267
(D-ANDI)	1-11	BAC.158	D-ARFD	A320	2108	D-AUAC	A318	2017	D-AVWB	A319	1375
D-ANDI	A319	1305	D-ARFE	A320	0575	D-AUAC	A318	2276	D-AVWB	A319	1445
D-ANDY	1-11	BAC.127	D-ARFF	A320	2128	D-AUAC	A318	2552	D-AVWB	A319	1768
D-ANDY	A300	758	D-ARFO	B747	32445	D-AUAC	A318	2931	D-AVWB	A319	1886
(D-ANDY)	A320	0428	(D-ARJA)	CRJ	7004	D-AUAC	A318	3163	D-AVWB	A319	2004
D-ANIK	CRJ	7032	(D-ARJB)	CRJ	7005	D-AUAD	A318	2035	D-AVWB	A319	2124
D-ANIM	CRJ	7036	(D-ARJC)	CRJ	7006	D-AUAD	A318	2328	D-AVWB	A319	2296
D-ANJA	A321	0519	(D-ARJD)	CRJ	7013	D-AUAD	A318	2575	D-AVWB	A319	2408
D-ANNA	A320	0916	(D-ARJE)	CRJ	7014	D-AUAD	A318	2951	D-AVWB	A319	2499
D-ANNB	A320	1240	(D-ARJF)	CRJ	7015	D-AUAD	A318	3214	D-AVWB	A319	2628
D-ANNC	A320	1257	(D-ARJG)	CRJ	7023	D-AUAE	A318	2051	D-AVWB	A319	2748
D-ANND	A320	1546	(D-ARJH)	CRJ	7024	D-AUAE	A318	2333	D-AVWB	A319	2860
D-ANNE	A320	0530	(D-ARJI)	CRJ	7025	D-AUAE	A318	2582	D-AVWB	A319	3011
(D-ANNE)	A320	0659	(D-ARJJ)	CRJ	7028	D-AUAE	A318	2955	D-AVWB	A319	3168
D-ANNE	A320	1557	(D-ARJK)	CRJ	7034	D-AUAE	A318	3216	D-AVWC	A319	1069
D-ANNF	A320	1650	(D-ARJL)	CRJ	7037	D-AUAF	A318	2059	D-AVWC	A319	1135
D-ANNG	A320	1464	(D-ARJM)	CRJ	7038	D-AUAF	A318	2344	D-AVWC	A319	1271
D-ANNH	A320	1835	D-ARND	A330	308	D-AUAF	A318	2601	D-AVWC	A319	1386
(D-ANNI)	A320	0902	D-ARNO	A330	312	D-AUAF	A318	2967	D-AVWC	A319	1524
D-ANNO	1-11	BAC.160	D-ARTN	E145	14500941	D-AUAF	A318	3220	D-AVWC	A319	1612
(D-ANOR)	1-11	BAC.197	D-ASAA	A300	121	D-AUAG	A318	2071	D-AVWC	A319	1770
D-ANTJ	146	E2100	D-ASAB	A300	042	D-AUAG	A318	2350	D-AVWC	A319	1923
D-ANUE	1-11	BAC.238	D-ASAD	A300	152	D-AUAG	A318	2972	D-AVWC	A319	2047
D-ANYL	SE210	247	D-ASAD	A310	542	D-AUAG	A318	3225	D-AVWC	A319	2228
D-AOAA	A310	498	D-ASAE	A300	134	D-AUAH	A318	1599	D-AVWC	A319	2355
D-AOAB	A310	499	D-ASAF	A300	073	D-AUAH	A318	2081	D-AVWC	A319	2436
D-AOAC	A310	503	D-ASAG	A300	196	D-AUAH	A318	2358	D-AVWC	A319	2510
D-AOAD	IL62	3036931	D-ASAH	A300	218	D-AUAI	A318	2100	D-AVWC	A319	2720
D-AOAE	IL62	4831517	D-ASAI	A300	208	D-AUAI	A318	2367	D-AVWC	A319	2864
D-AOAF	IL62	4934734	(D-ASAJ)	A300	255	D-AUAI	A318	3001	D-AVWC	A319	3026
D-AOAG	IL62	4140536	D-ASAK	A310	278	D-AUAJ	A318	2109	D-AVWC	A319	3195
D-AOAH	IL62	3344833	D-ASAL	A310	267	D-AUAJ	A318	2377	D-AVWD	A319	1068
D-AOAI	IL62	2546812	D-ASAX	VFW	G-015	D-AUAJ	A318	3009	D-AVWD	A319	1159
D-AOAJ	IL62	1647928	D-ASAY	A300	116	D-AUAJ	A318	3238	D-AVWD	A319	1287
D-AOAK	IL62	4546257	D-ASAZ	A300	117	D-AUAK	A318	2394	D-AVWD	A319	1358
D-AOAL	IL62	2748552	D-ASBA	CRJ	7990	D-AUAK	A318	3030	D-AVWD	A319	1449
D-AOAM	IL62	1951525	D-ASDB	VFW	G-019	D-AUAL	A318	3038	D-AVWD	A319	1570
D-AOAN	IL62	2951636	D-ASFB	A340	204	D-AUAM	A318	3062	D-AVWD	A319	16/1
D-AOBA	TU134	3351903	D-ASIA	A340	117	D-AUAN	A318	3100	D-AVWD	A319	1801
(D-AOBB)	TU134	1351304	D-ASIB	A340	163	(D-AUKT)	A320	0429	D-AVWD	A319	1955
D-AOBC	TU134	3352102	D-ASIC	A340	166	D-AUKT	A320	0476	D-AVWD	A319	2086
D-AOBD	TU134	3352106	D-ASID	A340	202	D-AV	A321	3274	D-AVWD	A319	2230
D-AOBE	TU134	4352205	D-ASIH	A340	528	D-AV	A321	3339	D-AVWD	A319	2335
D-AOBF	TU134	4352206	D-ASIJ	A340	215	D-AV	A321	3360	D-AVWD	A319	2427
D-AOBG	TU134	4352207	D-ASIL	A340	282	D-AV	A321	3387	D-AVWD	A319	2501
D-AOBH	TU134	08068	D-ASIM	A340	139	D-AV	A321	3434	D-AVWD	A319	2631
D-AOBI	TU134	09070	D-ASIN	A340	149	D-AVIP	A319	2507	D-AVWD	A319	2751
D-AOBJ	TU134	12095	D-ASKH	737NG	29082	D-AVIP	A319	2706	D-AVWD	A319	2866
D-AOBK	TU134	31218	D-ASQA	A310	363	D-AVRA	146	E2256	D-AVWD	A319	3028
D-AOBL	TU134	48320	D-ASRA	A310	399	D-AVRB	146	E2253	D-AVWD	A319	3243
D-AOBM	TU134	60495	D-ASRB	A310	412	D-AVRC	146	E2251	D-AVWE	A319	1066
D-AOBN	TU134	35180	D-ASSE	A321	0633	D-AVRD	146	E2257	D-AVWE	A319	1157
D-AOBO	TU134	38040	D-ASSR	A320	0429	D-AVRE	146	E2261	D-AVWE	A319	1377
D-AOBP	TU134	40150	(D-ASSR)	A320	0476	D-AVRF	146	E2269	D-AVWE	A319	1453
D-AOBQ	TU134	46155	D-ASSY	A321	0666	D-AVRG	146	E2266	D-AVWE	A319	1573
D-AOBR	TU134	46300	D-ATRA	A320	0659	D-AVRH	146	E2268	D-AVWE	A319	1673
(D-AOBS)	TU134	48560	D-ATUA	737NG	30465	D-AVRI	146	E2270	D-AVWE	A319	1803
(D-AOEB)	B757	24122	D-ATUA	737NG	34691	D-AVRJ	146	E2277	D-AVWE	A319	1934
(D-AOFM)	A320	0774	D-ATUB	737NG	30466	D-AVRK	146	E2278	D-AVWE	A319	2262
(D-AOFN)	A320	0793	D-ATUB	737NG	34692	D-AVRL	146	E2285	D-AVWE	A319	2370
(D-AOFP)	A320	0809	D-ATUC	737NG	34684	D-AVRM	146	E2288	D-AVWE	A319	2454
(D-AOFQ)	A320	0884	D-ATUD	737NG	34685	D-AVRN	146	E2293	D-AVWE	A319	2525
(D-AOFR)	A320	0894	D-ATUE	737NG	34686	D-AVRO	146	E2246	D-AVWE	A319	2632
(D-AOFS)	A320	0905	D-ATUF	737NG	34687	D-AVRP	146	E2303	D-AVWE	A319	2723
D-AONE	E145	14500988	D-ATUG	737NG	34688	D-AVRQ	146	E2304	D-AVWE	A319	2894
D-AORX	A320	0429	D-ATUH	737NG	34689	D-AVRR	146	E2317	D-AVWE	A319	3059

D-AVWE	A319	3245	D-AVWK	A319	2527	D-ÄVWP	A319	2644	D-AVWV	A319	2803
D-AVWF	A319	1071	D-AVWK	A319	2639	D-AVWP	A319	2771	D-AVWV	A319	2938
D-AVWF	A319	1172	D-AVWK	A319	2763	D-AVWP	A319	2901	D-AVWV	A319	3116
D-AVWF	A319	1291	D-AVWK	A319	2873	D-AVWP	A319	3065	D-AVWW	A319	1167
D-AVWF	A319	1360	D-AVWK	A319	3041	D-AVWQ	A319	1098	D-AVWW	A319	1323
D-AVWF	A319	1456	D-AVWK	A319	3204	D-AVWQ	A319	1170	D-AVWW	A319	1600
D-AVWF	A319	1574	D-AVWL	A319	1086	D-AVWQ	A319	1321	D-AVWW	A319	1740
D-AVWF	A319	1677	D-AVWL	A319	1160	D-AVWQ	A319	1397	D-AVWW	A319	1846
D-AVWF	A319	1805	D-AVWL	A319	1289	D-AVWQ	A319	1576	D-AVWW	A319	2023
D-AVWF	A319	1936	D-AVWL	A319	1364	D-AVWQ	A319	1727	D-AVWW	A319	2172
D-AVWF	A319	2050	D-AVWL	A319	1547	D-AVWQ	A319	2113	D-AVWW	A319	2268
D-AVWF	A319	2181	D-AVWL	A319	1685	D-AVWQ	A319	2264	D-AVWW	A319	2382
D-AVWF	A319	2298	D-AVWL	A319	1820	D-AVWQ	A319	2373	D-AVWW	A319	2465
D-AVWG	A319	1073	D-AVWL	A319	1959	D-AVWQ	A319	2446	D-AVWW	A319	2545
D-AVWG	A319	1142	D-AVWL	A319	2089	D-AVWQ	A319	2514	D-AVWW	A319	2664
D-AVWG	A319	1313	D-AVWL	A319	2237	D-AVWQ	A319	2646	D-AVWW	A319	2805
D-AVWG	A319	1378	D-AVWL	A319	2371	D-AVWQ	A319	2795	D-AVWW	A319	2940
D-AVWG	A319	1527	D-AVWL	A319	2448	D-AVWQ	A319	2905	D-AVWW	A319	3118
D-AVWG	A319	1616	D-AVWL	A319	2532	D-AVWQ	A319	3077	D-AVWX	A319	1305
D-AVWG	A319	1709	D-AVWL	A319	2641	D-AVWR	A319	1106	D-AVWX	A319	1601
D-AVWG	A319	1808	D-AVWL	A319	2765	D-AVWR	A319	1180	D-AVWX	A319	1742
D-AVWG	A319	1938	D-AVWL	A319	2876	D-AVWR	A319	1275	D-AVWX	A319	1851
D-AVWG	A319	2339	D-AVWL	A319	3043	D-AVWR	A319	1577	D-AVWX	A319	2026
D-AVWG	A319	2429	D-AVWL	A319	3209	D-AVWR	A319	1729	D-AVWX	A319	2186
D-AVWG	A319	2505	D-AVWM	A319	1088	D-AVWR	A319	1831	D-AVWX	A319	2269
D-AVWG	A319	2634	D-AVWM	A319	1301	D-AVWR	A319	2012	D-AVWX	A319	2433
D-AVWG	A319	2754	D-AVWM	A319	1369	D-AVWR	A319	2129	D-AVWX	A319	2546
D-AVWG	A319	2870	D-AVWM	A319	1549	D-AVWR	A319	2265	D-AVWX	A319	2666
D-AVWG	A319	3032	D-AVWM	A319	1688	D-AVWR	A319	2375	D-AVWX	A319	2815
D-AVWG	A319	3200	D-AVWM	A319	1824	D-AVWS	A319	1107	D-AVWX	A319	2942
"D-AVWG"	A321	1161	D-AVWM	A319	2007	D-AVWS	A319	1197	D-AVWX	A319	3122
D-AVWH	A319	1074	D-AVWM	A319	2126	D-AVWS	A319	1319	D-AVWY	A319	1309
D-AVWH	A319	1145	D-AVWM	A319	2302	D-AVWS	A319	1579	D-AVWY	A319	1603
D-AVWH	A319	1315	D-AVWM	A319	2414	D-AVWS	A319	1731	D-AVWY	A319	1743
D-AVWH	A319	1380	D-AVWM	A319	2492	D-AVWS	A319	1833	D-AVWY	A319	1853
D-AVWH	A319	1529	D-AVWM	A319	2567	D-AVWS	A319	2013	D-AVWY	A319	2271
D-AVWH	A319	1618	D-AVWM	A319	2684	D-AVWS	A319	2131	D-AVWZ	A319	1745
D-AVWH	A319	1810	D-AVWM	A319	2813	D-AVWS	A319	2266	D-AVWZ	A319	1912
D-AVWH	A319	1943	D-AVWM	A319	2935	D-AVWS	A319	2378	D-AVWZ	A319	2028
D-AVWH	A319	2103	D-AVWM	A319	3090	D-AVWS	A319	2444	D-AVWZ	A319	2119
D-AVWH	A319	2300	D-AVWN	A319	1102	D-AVWS	A319	2516	D-AVWZ	A319	2273
D-AVWH	A319	2412	D-AVWN	A319	1176	D-AVWT	A319	1111	D-AVWZ	A319	2440
D-AVWH	A319	2490	D-AVWN	A319	1303	D-AVWT	A319	1201	D-AVWZ	A319	2773
D-AVWH	A319	2636	D-AVWN	A319	1382	D-AVWT	A319	1324	D-AVWZ	A319	2913
D-AVWH	A319	2757	D-AVWN	A319	1551	D-AVWT	A319	1581	D-AVWZ	A319	3096
D-AVWH	A319	2897	D-AVWN	A319	1714	D-AVWT	A319	1733	D-AVXA	A319	2568
D-AVWH	A319	3061	D-AVWN	A319	1826	D-AVWT	A319	1841	D-AVXA	A319	2690
D-AVWII	**A319**	**3248**	D-AVWN	A319	2008	D-AVWT	A319	2015	D-AVXA	A319	2818
D-AVWI	A319	1077	D-AVWN	A319	2127	D-AVWT	A319	2170	D-AVXA	A319	2946
D-AVWI	A319	1147	D-AVWN	A319	2304	D-AVWT	A319	2362	D-AVXA	A319	3124
D-AVWI	A319	1243	D-AVWN	A319	2416	D-AVWT	A319	2442	D-AVXA	A321	1442
D-AVWI	A319	1354	D-AVWN	A319	2507	D-AVWT	A319	2518	D-AVXA	A321	1720
D-AVWI	A319	1541	D-AVWN	A319	2790	D-AVWT	A319	2648	D-AVXA	A321	1928
D-AVWI	A319	1679	D-AVWN	A319	2898	D-AVWT	A319	2797	D-AVXA	A321	2472
D-AVWI	A319	1815	D-AVWN	A319	3094	D-AVWT	A319	2907	"D-AVXB"	A319	2192
D-AVWI	A319	1947	D-AVWO	A319	1103	D-AVWT	A319	3069	D-AVXB	A319	2570
D-AVWI	A319	2087	D-AVWO	A319	1191	D-AVWU	A319	1113	D-AVXB	A319	2691
D-AVWI	A319	2232	D-AVWO	A319	1265	D-AVWU	A319	1164	D-AVXB	A319	2819
D-AVWJ	A319	1078	D-AVWO	A319	1371	D-AVWU	A319	1295	D-AVXB	A319	2948
D-AVWJ	A319	1149	D-AVWO	A319	1552	D-AVWU	A319	1594	D-AVXB	A319	3128
D-AVWJ	A319	1277	D-AVWO	A319	1828	D-AVWU	A319	1737	D-AVXB	A321	1447
D-AVWJ	A319	1362	D-AVWO	A319	2010	D-AVWU	A319	1863	D-AVXB	A321	1724
D-AVWJ	A319	1543	D-AVWO	A319	2184	D-AVWU	A319	1962	D-AVXB	A321	1932
D-AVWJ	A319	1683	D-AVWO	A319	2346	D-AVWU	A319	2091	D-AVXB	A321	2105
D-AVWJ	A319	2263	D-AVWO	A319	2431	D-AVWU	A319	2241	D-AVXB	A321	2476
D-AVWJ	A319	2452	D-AVWO	A319	2508	D-AVWU	A319	2379	D-AVXC	A319	2572
D-AVWJ	A319	2528	D-AVWO	A319	2643	D-AVWU	A319	2464	D-AVXC	A319	2693
D-AVWJ	A319	2638	D-AVWO	A319	2769	D-AVWU	A319	2555	D-AVXC	A319	2821
D-AVWJ	A319	2762	D-AVWO	A319	2878	D-AVWU	A319	2660	D-AVXC	A319	2949
D-AVWJ	A319	2872	D-AVWO	A319	3045	D-AVWU	A319	2801	D-AVXC	A319	3133
D-AVWJ	A319	3036	**D-AVWO**	**A319**	**3250**	D-AVWV	A319	1116	D-AVXC	A321	1451
D-AVWJ	A319	3202	D-AVWP	A319	1109	D-AVWV	A319	1165	D-AVXC	A321	1726
D-AVWK	A319	1084	D-AVWP	A319	1178	D-AVWV	A319	1297	D-AVXC	A321	1941
D-AVWK	A319	1151	D-AVWP	A319	1269	D-AVWV	A319	1598	D-AVXC	A321	2480
D-AVWK	A319	1317	D-AVWP	A319	1384	D-AVWV	A319	1738	D-AVXD	A319	2574
D-AVWK	A319	1545	D-AVWP	A319	1575	D-AVWV	A319	1844	D-AVXD	A319	2694
D-AVWK	A319	1684	D-AVWP	A319	1722	D-AVWV	A319	2019	D-AVXD	A319	2825
D-AVWK	A319	1819	D-AVWP	A319	1908	D-AVWV	A319	2243	D-AVXD	A319	2978
D-AVWK	A319	1952	D-AVWP	A319	2240	D-AVWV	A319	2380	D-AVXD	A319	3169
D-AVWK	A319	2236	D-AVWP	A319	2438	D-AVWV	A319	2463	D-AVXD	A321	1455
D-AVWK	A319	2341	D-AVWP	A319	2512	D-AVWV	A319	2541	D-AVXD	A321	1734
D-AVWK	A319	2450				D-AVWV	A319	2662	D-AVXD	A321	1946

Reg	Type	MSN	Reg	Type	MSN	Reg	Type	MSN	Reg	Type	MSN
D-AVXD	A321	2107	D-AVYA	A319	0717	D-AVYD	A319	2277	D-AVYH	A319	2245
D-AVXD	A321	2488	D-AVYA	A319	0767	D-AVYD	A319	2385	D-AVYH	A319	2348
D-AVXE	A319	2578	D-AVYA	A319	0845	D-AVYE	A319	0608	D-AVYH	A319	2435
D-AVXE	A319	2697	D-AVYA	A319	0929	D-AVYE	A319	0670	D-AVYH	A319	2469
D-AVXE	A319	2827	D-AVYA	A319	1010	D-AVYE	A319	0728	D-AVYH	A319	2550
D-AVXE	A319	2954	D-AVYA	A319	1122	D-AVYE	A319	0800	D-AVYH	A319	2669
D-AVXE	A319	3134	D-AVYA	A319	1203	D-AVYE	A319	0882	D-AVYH	A319	2779
D-AVXE	A321	1458	D-AVYA	A319	1311	D-AVYE	A319	0948	D-AVYH	A319	2889
D-AVXE	A321	1748	D-AVYA	A319	1401	D-AVYE	A319	1025	D-AVYH	A319	3078
D-AVXE	A321	1950	D-AVYA	A319	1490	D-AVYE	A319	1090	D-AVYH	A319	3271
D-AVXF	A319	2579	D-AVYA	A319	1582	D-AVYE	A319	1212	D-AVYI	A319	0616
D-AVXF	A319	2698	D-AVYA	A319	1643	D-AVYE	A319	1423	D-AVYI	A319	0686
D-AVXF	A319	2829	D-AVYA	A319	1746	D-AVYE	A319	1513	D-AVYI	A319	0744
D-AVXF	A319	2979	D-AVYA	A319	1855	D-AVYE	A319	1698	D-AVYI	A319	0831
D-AVXF	A319	3171	D-AVYA	A319	1963	D-AVYE	A319	1778	D-AVYI	A319	0904
D-AVXF	A321	1953	D-AVYA	A319	2052	D-AVYE	A319	2093	D-AVYI	A319	0976
D-AVXF	A321	2110	D-AVYA	A319	2188	D-AVYE	A319	2200	D-AVYI	A319	1120
D-AVXG	A319	2581	D-AVYA	A319	2306	D-AVYE	A319	2308	D-AVYI	A319	1209
D-AVXG	A319	2727	D-AVYA	A319	2383	D-AVYF	A319	0609	D-AVYI	A319	1283
D-AVXG	A319	2847	D-AVYA	A319	2466	D-AVYF	A319	0672	D-AVYI	A319	1389
D-AVXG	A319	2981	D-AVYA	A319	2547	D-AVYF	A319	0729	D-AVYI	A319	1460
D-AVXG	A319	3172	D-AVYA	A319	2650	D-AVYF	A319	0804	D-AVYI	A319	1556
D-AVXG	A321	1972	D-AVYA	A319	3102	D-AVYF	A319	0885	D-AVYI	A319	2095
D-AVXG	A321	2115	D-AVYB	A319	0588	D-AVYF	A319	0952	D-AVYI	A319	2222
D-AVXH	A319	2585	D-AVYB	A319	0646	D-AVYF	A319	1031	D-AVYI	A319	2313
D-AVXH	A319	2700	D-AVYB	A319	0713	D-AVYF	A319	1216	D-AVYI	A319	2418
D-AVXH	A319	2831	D-AVYB	A319	0769	D-AVYF	A319	1325	D-AVYI	A319	2485
D-AVXH	A319	2959	D-AVYB	A319	0847	D-AVYF	A319	1415	D-AVYI	A319	2617
D-AVXH	A319	3137	D-AVYB	A319	0910	D-AVYF	A319	1505	D-AVYI	A319	2709
D-AVXH	A321	1988	D-AVYB	A319	1205	D-AVYF	A319	1589	D-AVYI	A319	2839
D-AVXI	A319	2586	D-AVYB	A319	1263	D-AVYF	A319	1758	D-AVYI	A319	2961
D-AVXI	A319	2702	D-AVYB	A319	1404	D-AVYF	A319	1872	D-AVYI	A319	3104
D-AVXI	A319	2833	D-AVYB	A319	1494	D-AVYF	A319	1982	D-AVYI	A319	3276
D-AVXI	A319	2983	D-AVYB	A319	1627	D-AVYF	A319	2066	D-AVYJ	A319	0618
D-AVXI	A319	3175	D-AVYB	A319	1750	D-AVYF	A319	2202	D-AVYJ	A319	0688
D-AVXI	A321	2005	D-AVYB	A319	1866	D-AVYF	A319	2279	D-AVYJ	A319	0755
D-AVXJ	A319	2588	D-AVYB	A319	1976	D-AVYF	A319	2387	D-AVYJ	A319	0833
D-AVXJ	A319	2704	D-AVYB	A319	2053	D-AVYF	A319	2467	D-AVYJ	A319	0917
D-AVXJ	A319	2849	D-AVYB	A319	2192	D-AVYF	A319	2548	D-AVYJ	A319	1002
D-AVXJ	A319	2985	D-AVYB	A319	2706	D-AVYF	A319	2652	D-AVYJ	A319	1232
D-AVXJ	A319	3176	D-AVYB	A319	2858	D-AVYF	A319	2774	D-AVYJ	A319	1328
D-AVXJ	A321	2021	D-AVYB	A319	3003	D-AVYF	A319	2887	D-AVYJ	A319	1391
D-AVXK	A319	2592	D-AVYB	A319	3181	D-AVYF	A319	3046	D-AVYJ	A319	1463
D-AVXK	A319	2729	D-AVYC	A319	0600	D-AVYF	A319	3184	D-AVYJ	A319	1479
D-AVXK	A319	2850	D-AVYC	A319	0660	D-AVYG	A319	0610	D-AVYJ	A319	1558
D-AVXK	A319	2997	D-AVYC	A319	0727	D-AVYG	A319	0679	D-AVYJ	A319	1640
D-AVXK	A319	3179	D-AVYC	A319	0790	D-AVYG	A319	0736	D-AVYJ	A319	1753
D-AVXL	A319	2593	D-AVYC	A319	0875	D-AVYG	A319	0813	D-AVYJ	A319	1893
D-AVXL	A319	2733	D-AVYC	A319	0944	D-AVYG	A319	0890	D-AVYJ	A319	1986
D-AVXL	A319	2852	D-AVYC	A319	1029	D-AVYG	A319	0949	D-AVYJ	A319	2069
D-AVXL	A319	3017	D-AVYC	A319	1089	D-AVYG	A319	1033	D-AVYJ	A319	2205
D-AVXL	A319	3255	D-AVYC	A319	1092	D-AVYG	A319	1222	D-AVYJ	A319	2318
D-AVXM	A319	2595	D-AVYC	A319	1211	D-AVYG	A319	1326	D-AVYJ	A319	2389
D-AVXM	A319	2735	D-AVYC	A319	1281	D-AVYG	A319	1300	D-AVYJ	A319	2470
D-AVXM	A319	2854	D-AVYC	A319	1406	D-AVYG	A319	1477	D-AVYJ	A319	2551
D-AVXM	A319	3019	D-AVYC	A319	1498	D-AVYG	A319	1699	D-AVYJ	A319	2655
D-AVXN	A319	2597	D-AVYC	A319	1583	D-AVYG	A319	1779	D-AVYJ	A319	2780
D-AVXN	A319	2738	D-AVYC	A319	1645	D-AVYG	A319	1916	D-AVYJ	A319	2890
D-AVXN	A319	2879	D-AVYC	A319	1756	D-AVYG	A319	2030	D-AVYJ	A319	3053
D-AVXN	A319	3020	D-AVYC	A319	1870	D-AVYG	A319	2203	D-AVYJ	A319	3226
D-AVXN	A319	3255	D-AVYC	A319	1971	D-AVYG	A319	2311	D-AVYK	A319	0572
D-AVXO	A319	2603	D-AVYC	A319	2057	D-AVYG	A319	2468	D-AVYK	A319	0621
D-AVXO	A319	2739	D-AVYC	A319	2196	D-AVYG	A319	2556	D-AVYK	A319	0773
D-AVXO	A319	2884	D-AVYC	A319	2629	D-AVYG	A319	2667	D-AVYK	A319	0850
D-AVXO	A319	3139	D-AVYD	A319	0598	D-AVYG	A319	2777	D-AVYK	A319	0931
D-AVXP	A319	2605	D-AVYD	A319	0647	D-AVYG	A319	2888	D-AVYK	A319	1016
D-AVXP	A319	2742	D-AVYD	A319	0723	D-AVYG	A319	3049	D-AVYK	A319	1082
D-AVXP	A319	2886	D-AVYD	A319	0794	D-AVYG	A319	3186	D-AVYK	A319	1225
D-AVXP	A319	3073	D-AVYD	A319	0880	D-AVYH	A319	0612	D-AVYK	A319	1335
D-AVXQ	A319	2607	D-AVYD	A319	0946	D-AVYH	A319	0682	D-AVYK	A319	1560
D-AVXQ	A319	2744	D-AVYD	A319	1022	D-AVYH	A319	0740	D-AVYK	A319	1647
D-AVXQ	A319	2921	D-AVYD	A319	1182	D-AVYH	A319	0829	D-AVYK	A319	1781
D-AVXQ	A319	3142	D-AVYD	A319	1410	D-AVYH	A319	0896	D-AVYK	A319	1897
D-AVXR	A319	2611	D-AVYD	A319	1501	D-AVYH	A319	0965	D-AVYK	A319	2032
D-AVXR	A319	2836	D-AVYD	A319	1585	D-AVYH	A319	1040	D-AVYK	A319	2120
D-AVXR	A319	3024	D-AVYD	A319	1630	D-AVYH	A319	1127	D-AVYK	A319	2258
D-AVXS	A319	2614	D-AVYD	A319	1693	D-AVYH	A319	1223	D-AVYK	A319	2281
D-AVXS	A319	2837	D-AVYD	A319	1774	D-AVYH	A319	1329	D-AVYK	A319	2392
D-AVXT	A319	2615	D-AVYD	A319	1890	D-AVYH	A319	1429	D-AVYK	A319	2471
D-AVXT	A319	3144	D-AVYD	A319	1980	D-AVYH	A319	1634	D-AVYK	A319	2557
D-AVYA	A319	0578	D-AVYD	A319	2062	D-AVYH	A319	1752	D-AVYK	A319	2672
D-AVYA	A319	0644	D-AVYD	A319	2198	D-AVYH	A319	1875	D-AVYK	A319	2806

D-AVYK	A319	2923	D-AVYO	A319	2214	D-AVYS	A319	2659	D-AVYW	A319	1352
D-AVYK	A319	3082	D-AVYO	A319	2321	D-AVYS	A319	2784	D-AVYW	A319	1488
D-AVYL	A319	0623	D-AVYO	A319	2421	D-AVYS	A319	2891	D-AVYW	A319	1590
D-AVYL	A319	0689	D-AVYO	A319	2495	D-AVYS	A319	3054	D-AVYW	A319	1662
D-AVYL	A319	0748	D-AVYO	A319	2561	D-AVYS	A319	3193	D-AVYW	A319	1795
D-AVYL	A319	0837	D-AVYO	A319	2673	D-AVYT	A319	0637	D-AVYX	A319	0654
D-AVYL	A319	0913	D-AVYO	A319	2782	D-AVYT	A319	0697	D-AVYX	A319	0721
D-AVYL	A319	1034	D-AVYP	A319	0634	D-AVYT	A319	0779	D-AVYX	A319	0732
D-AVYL	A319	1091	D-AVYP	A319	0691	D-AVYT	A319	0862	D-AVYX	A319	0798
D-AVYL	A319	1228	D-AVYP	A319	0752	D-AVYT	A319	0972	D-AVYX	A319	0873
D-AVYL	A319	1336	D-AVYP	A319	0858	D-AVYT	A319	1048	D-AVYX	A319	1020
D-AVYL	A319	1414	D-AVYP	A319	0933	D-AVYT	A319	1115	D-AVYX	A319	1100
D-AVYL	A319	1759	D-AVYP	A319	1000	D-AVYT	A319	1193	D-AVYX	A319	1169
D-AVYL	A319	1876	D-AVYP	A319	1058	D-AVYT	A319	1285	D-AVYX	A319	1395
D-AVYL	A319	1990	D-AVYP	A319	1140	D-AVYT	A319	1392	D-AVYX	A319	1507
D-AVYL	A319	2072	D-AVYP	A319	1239	D-AVYT	A319	1565	D-AVYX	A319	1592
D-AVYL	A319	2209	D-AVYP	A319	1342	D-AVYT	A319	1656	D-AVYX	A319	1664
D-AVYL	A319	2319	D-AVYP	A319	1440	D-AVYT	A319	2039	D-AVYX	A319	1796
D-AVYL	A319	2420	D-AVYP	A319	1537	D-AVYT	A319	2194	D-AVYX	A319	2260
D-AVYL	A319	2494	D-AVYP	A319	1649	D-AVYT	A319	2326	D-AVYX	A319	2369
D-AVYL	A319	2618	D-AVYP	A319	1786	D-AVYT	A319	2424	D-AVYX	A319	2456
D-AVYL	A319	2746	D-AVYP	A319	1901	D-AVYT	A319	2497	D-AVYX	A319	2519
D-AVYL	A319	2857	D-AVYP	A319	2033	D-AVYT	A319	2622	D-AVYX	A319	2624
D-AVYL	A319	3007	D-AVYP	A319	2174	D-AVYT	A319	2715	D-AVYX	A319	2716
D-AVYL	A319	3188	D-AVYP	A319	2283	D-AVYT	A319	2843	D-AVYX	A319	2845
D-AVYM	A319	0742	D-AVYP	A319	2396	D-AVYT	A319	2969	D-AVYX	A319	2976
D-AVYM	A319	0817	D-AVYP	A319	2473	D-AVYT	A319	3114	D-AVYX	A319	3165
D-AVYM	A319	0889	D-AVYP	A319	2558	D-AVYU	A319	0639	D-AVYY	A319	0651
D-AVYM	A319	0979	D-AVYP	A319	2675	D-AVYU	A319	0700	D-AVYY	A319	0721
D-AVYM	A319	1055	D-AVYP	A319	2811	D-AVYU	A319	0785	D-AVYY	A319	0783
D-AVYM	A319	1136	D-AVYP	A319	2925	D-AVYU	A319	0867	D-AVYY	A319	0871
D-AVYM	A319	1230	D-AVYP	A319	3084	D-AVYU	A319	0989	D-AVYY	A319	1043
D-AVYM	A319	1338	D-AVYQ	A319	0625	D-AVYU	A319	1049	D-AVYY	A319	1154
D-AVYM	A319	1420	D-AVYQ	A319	0693	D-AVYU	A319	1118	D-AVYY	A319	1510
D-AVYM	A319	1515	D-AVYQ	A319	0757	D-AVYU	A319	1186	D-AVYY	A319	1608
D-AVYM	A319	1604	D-AVYQ	A319	0840	D-AVYU	A319	1279	D-AVYY	A319	2101
D-AVYM	A319	1761	D-AVYQ	A319	0922	D-AVYU	A319	1393	D-AVYY	A319	2293
D-AVYM	A319	1880	D-AVYQ	A319	1018	D-AVYU	A319	1466	D-AVYY	A319	2404
D-AVYM	A319	2074	D-AVYQ	A319	1095	D-AVYU	A319	1483	D-AVYY	A319	2483
D-AVYM	A319	2213	D-AVYQ	A319	1190	D-AVYU	A319	1567	D-AVYY	A319	2565
D-AVYM	A319	2353	D-AVYQ	A319	1254	D-AVYU	A319	1659	D-AVYY	A319	2681
D-AVYM	A319	2460	D-AVYQ	A319	1344	D-AVYU	A319	1766	D-AVYY	A319	2788
D-AVYM	A319	2534	D-AVYQ	A319	1468	D-AVYU	A319	1884	D-AVYY	A319	2893
D-AVYM	A319	2621	D-AVYQ	A319	1706	D-AVYU	A319	2037	D-AVYY	A319	3088
D-AVYM	A319	2711	D-AVYQ	A319	1837	D-AVYU	A319	2043	D-AVYZ	A319	0656
D-AVYM	A319	2841	D-AVYQ	A319	1999	D-AVYU	A319	2179	D-AVYZ	A319	0734
D-AVYM	A319	2963	D-AVYQ	A319	2251	D-AVYU	A319	2287	D-AVYZ	A319	0825
D-AVYM	A319	3108	D-AVYR	A319	0629	D-AVYU	A319	2400	D-AVYZ	A319	0898
D-AVYN	A319	0738	D-AVYR	A319	0694	D-AVYU	A319	2477	D-AVYZ	A319	1046
D-AVYN	A319	0821	D-AVYR	A319	0759	D-AVYU	A319	2559	D-AVYZ	A319	1129
D-AVYN	A319	0906	D-AVYR	A319	0843	D-AVYU	A319	2677	D-AVYZ	A319	1256
D-AVYN	A319	0980	D-AVYR	A319	0924	D-AVYU	A319	2812	D-AVYZ	A319	1522
D-AVYN	A319	1053	D-AVYR	A319	1019	D-AVYU	A319	2929	D-AVYZ	A319	1625
D-AVYN	A319	1245	D-AVYR	A319	1096	D-AVYU	A319	3085	D-AVYZ	A319	1800
D-AVYN	A319	1331	D-AVYR	A319	1184	D-AVYV	A319	0546	D-AVYZ	A319	2000
D-AVYN	A319	1426	D-AVYR	A319	1258	D-AVYV	A319	0641	D-AVYZ	A319	2083
D-AVYN	A319	1520	D-AVYR	A319	1346	D-AVYV	A319	0711	D-AVYZ	A319	2224
D-AVYN	A319	1606	D-AVYR	A319	1471	D-AVYV	A319	0893	D-AVYZ	A319	2332
D-AVYN	A319	1703	D-AVYR	A319	1562	D-AVYV	A319	0997	D-AVYZ	A319	2360
D-AVYN	A319	2096	D-AVYR	A319	1653	D-AVYV	A319	1051	D-AVYZ	A319	2426
D-AVYN	A319	2249	D-AVYR	A319	1790	D-AVYV	A319	1124	D-AVYZ	A319	2503
D-AVYN	A319	2365	D-AVYR	A319	2253	D-AVYV	A319	1247	D-AVYZ	A319	2625
D-AVYN	A319	2458	D-AVYS	A319	0636	D-AVYV	A319	1350	D-AVYZ	A319	2718
D-AVYN	A319	2538	D-AVYS	A319	0695	D-AVYV	A319	1485	**D-AVZ.**	**A321**	**3251**
D-AVYN	A319	2657	D-AVYS	A319	0763	D-AVYV	A319	2098	**D-AVZ.**	**A321**	**3294**
D-AVYO	A319	0627	D-AVYS	A319	0860	D-AVYV	A319	2289	D-AVZA	A321	0412
D-AVYO	A319	0690	D-AVYS	A319	0938	D-AVYV	A319	2402	D-AVZA	A321	0529
D-AVYO	A319	0750	D-AVYS	A319	1036	D-AVYV	A319	2481	D-AVZA	A321	0602
D-AVYO	A319	0853	D-AVYS	A319	1097	D-AVYV	A319	2560	D-AVZA	A321	0725
D-AVYO	A319	0985	D-AVYS	A319	1155	D-AVYV	A319	2679	D-AVZA	A321	0841
D-AVYO	A319	1056	D-AVYS	A319	1252	D-AVYV	A319	2786	D-AVZA	A321	0974
D-AVYO	A319	1139	D-AVYS	A319	1348	D-AVYV	A319	2892	D-AVZA	A321	1042
D-AVYO	A319	1157	D-AVYS	A319	1474	D-AVYV	A319	3057	D-AVZA	A321	1218
D-AVYO	A319	1236	D-AVYS	A319	1563	D-AVYV	A319	3231	D-AVZA	A321	1356
D-AVYO	A319	1340	D-AVYS	A319	1654	D-AVYW	A319	0649	D-AVZA	A321	1428
D-AVYO	A319	1434	D-AVYS	A319	1791	D-AVYW	A319	0719	D-AVZA	A321	1511
D-AVYO	A319	1534	D-AVYS	A319	1925	D-AVYW	A319	0788	D-AVZA	A321	1614
D-AVYO	A319	1622	D-AVYS	A319	2176	D-AVYW	A319	0869	D-AVZA	A321	1695
D-AVYO	A319	1765	D-AVYS	A319	2285	D-AVYW	A319	0998	D-AVZA	A321	1772
D-AVYO	A319	1882	D-AVYS	A319	2398	D-AVYW	A319	1038	D-AVZA	A321	1878
D-AVYO	A319	1997	D-AVYS	A319	2474	D-AVYW	A319	1126	D-AVZA	A321	2041
D-AVYO	A319	2078	D-AVYS	A319	2554	D-AVYW	A319	1249	D-AVZA	A321	2270

Reg	Type	c/n	Reg	Type	c/n	Reg	Type	c/n	Reg	Type	c/n
D-AVZA	A321	2756	D-AVZE	A321	3112	D-AVZJ	A321	3067	D-AVZP	A321	0959
D-AVZA	A321	2895	D-AVZF	A321	0484	D-AVZJ	A321	3241	D-AVZP	A321	1080
D-AVZA	A321	3070	D-AVZF	A321	0544	D-AVZK	A319	2406	D-AVZP	A321	1299
D-AVZA	A321	3212	D-AVZF	A321	0631	D-AVZK	A321	0498	D-AVZP	A321	1658
D-AVZB	A321	0434	D-AVZF	A321	0775	D-AVZK	A321	0560	D-AVZP	A321	1905
D-AVZB	A321	0532	D-AVZF	A321	0878	D-AVZK	A321	0663	D-AVZP	A321	2067
D-AVZB	A321	0604	D-AVZF	A321	0993	D-AVZK	A321	0781	D-AVZP	A321	2323
D-AVZB	A321	0680	D-AVZF	A321	1153	D-AVZK	A321	0901	D-AVZP	A321	2799
D-AVZB	A321	0864	D-AVZF	A321	1250	D-AVZK	A321	1008	D-AVZP	A321	2996
D-AVZB	A321	0983	D-AVZF	A321	1412	D-AVZK	A321	1195	D-AVZQ	A321	0515
D-AVZB	A321	1023	D-AVZF	A321	1476	D-AVZK	A321	1293	D-AVZQ	A321	0570
D-AVZB	A321	1094	D-AVZF	A321	1517	D-AVZK	A321	1436	D-AVZQ	A321	0684
D-AVZB	A321	1219	D-AVZF	A321	1632	D-AVZK	A321	1587	D-AVZQ	A321	0806
D-AVZB	A321	1333	D-AVZF	A321	1794	D-AVZK	A321	1711	D-AVZQ	A321	0926
D-AVZB	A321	1431	D-AVZF	A321	2543	D-AVZK	A321	1817	D-AVZQ	A321	1021
D-AVZB	A321	1536	D-AVZF	A321	2707	D-AVZK	A321	1970	D-AVZQ	A321	1204
D-AVZB	A321	1619	D-AVZF	A321	3222	D-AVZK	A321	2211	D-AVZQ	A321	1487
D-AVZB	A321	1763	D-AVZG	A321	0385	D-AVZK	A321	2410	D-AVZQ	A321	1651
D-AVZB	A321	2117	D-AVZG	A321	0488	D-AVZK	A321	2590	D-AVZQ	A321	1921
D-AVZB	A321	2290	D-AVZG	A321	0550	D-AVZK	A321	2741	D-AVZQ	A321	2324
D-AVZB	A321	2462	D-AVZG	A321	0731	D-AVZK	A321	3247	D-AVZQ	A321	2916
D-AVZB	A321	2563	D-AVZG	A321	0852	D-AVZL	A321	0502	D-AVZQ	A321	3098
D-AVZB	A321	2730	D-AVZG	A321	0995	D-AVZL	A321	0564	**D-AVZQ**	**A321**	**3267**
D-AVZB	A321	2862	D-AVZG	A321	1161	D-AVZL	A321	0664	D-AVZR	A321	0516
D-AVZB	A321	3075	D-AVZG	A321	1241	D-AVZL	A321	0787	D-AVZR	A321	0576
D-AVZB	A321	3262	D-AVZG	A321	1417	D-AVZL	A321	0908	D-AVZR	A321	0687
D-AVZC	A321	0473	D-AVZG	A321	1554	D-AVZL	A321	1027	D-AVZR	A321	0811
D-AVZC	A321	0535	D-AVZG	A321	1636	D-AVZL	A321	1238	D-AVZR	A321	0935
D-AVZC	A321	0606	D-AVZG	A321	1798	D-AVZL	A321	1438	D-AVZR	A321	1207
D-AVZC	A321	0848	D-AVZG	A321	1960	D-AVZL	A321	1596	D-AVZR	A321	1492
D-AVZC	A321	0987	D-AVZG	A321	2247	D-AVZL	A321	1638	D-AVZR	A321	1843
D-AVZC	A321	1060	D-AVZG	A321	3229	D-AVZL	A321	2267	D-AVZR	A321	1994
D-AVZC	A321	1220	D-AVZH	A321	0493	D-AVZL	A321	2599	D-AVZR	A321	2220
D-AVZC	A321	1366	D-AVZH	A321	0552	D-AVZL	A321	2759	D-AVZR	A321	2330
D-AVZC	A321	1433	D-AVZH	A321	0642	D-AVZL	A321	2912	D-AVZR	A321	2919
D-AVZC	A321	1539	D-AVZH	A321	0746	D-AVZL	A321	3081	D-AVZR	A321	3120
D-AVZC	A321	1629	D-AVZH	A321	0855	D-AVZL	A321	3265	D-AVZS	A321	0517
D-AVZC	A321	1776	D-AVZH	A321	1012	D-AVZM	A321	0505	D-AVZS	A321	0581
D-AVZC	A321	1887	D-AVZH	A321	1174	D-AVZM	A321	0567	D-AVZS	A321	0675
D-AVZC	A321	2045	D-AVZH	A321	1421	D-AVZM	A321	0666	D-AVZS	A321	0810
D-AVZC	A321	2303	D-AVZH	A321	1519	D-AVZM	A321	0792	D-AVZS	A321	0940
D-AVZC	A321	2521	D-AVZH	A321	1707	D-AVZM	A321	0915	D-AVZS	A321	1214
D-AVZC	A321	2653	D-AVZH	A321	1807	D-AVZM	A321	1017	D-AVZS	A321	1496
D-AVZC	A321	2809	D-AVZH	A321	1966	D-AVZM	A321	1199	D-AVZS	A321	1713
D-AVZC	A321	2927	D-AVZH	A321	2060	D-AVZM	A321	1307	D-AVZS	A321	1926
D-AVZC	A321	3106	D-AVZH	A321	2255	D-AVZM	A321	1462	D-AVZS	A321	2076
D-AVZC	A321	3290	D-AVZH	A321	3233	D-AVZM	A321	1602	D-AVZS	A321	2337
"D-AVZD"	A319	1159	D-AVZI	A321	0494	D-AVZM	A321	2315	D-AVZS	A321	2933
D-AVZD	A321	0364	D-AVZI	A321	0555	D-AVZM	A321	2610	D-AVZS	A321	3126
D-AVZD	A321	0474	D-AVZI	A321	0652	D-AVZM	A321	2767	D-AVZT	A321	0518
D-AVZD	A321	0538	D-AVZI	A321	0777	D-AVZM	A321	2971	D-AVZT	A321	0583
D-AVZD	A321	0614	D-AVZI	A321	0887	D-AVZN	A321	0509	D-AVZT	A321	0692
D-AVZD	A321	0954	D-AVZI	A321	1004	D-AVZN	A321	0563	D-AVZT	A321	0815
D-AVZD	A321	1024	D-AVZI	A321	1185	D-AVZN	A321	0668	D-AVZT	A321	0941
D-AVZD	A321	1133	D-AVZI	A321	1260	D-AVZN	A321	0796	D-AVZT	A321	1227
D-AVZD	A321	1233	D-AVZI	A321	1399	D-AVZN	A321	0920	D-AVZT	A321	1499
D-AVZD	A321	1403	D-AVZI	A321	1481	D-AVZN	A321	1015	D-AVZT	A321	1716
D-AVZD	A321	1701	D-AVZI	A321	1572	D-AVZN	A321	1202	D-AVZT	A321	2342
D-AVZD	A321	1783	D-AVZI	A321	1666	D-AVZN	A321	1465	D-AVZT	A321	2936
D-AVZD	A321	2190	D-AVZI	A321	1811	D-AVZN	A321	1607	D-AVZT	A321	3130
D-AVZD	A321	2309	D-AVZI	A321	1967	D-AVZN	A321	1642	D-AVZU	A321	0519
D-AVZD	A321	2530	D-AVZI	A321	2208	D-AVZN	A321	1836	D-AVZU	A321	0586
D-AVZD	A321	2682	D-AVZI	A321	2381	D-AVZN	A321	1974	D-AVZU	A321	0819
D-AVZD	A321	2903	D-AVZI	A321	2549	D-AVZN	A321	2216	D-AVZU	A321	0961
D-AVZD	A321	3051	D-AVZI	A321	2713	D-AVZN	A321	2793	D-AVZU	A321	1273
D-AVZD	A321	3217	D-AVZI	A321	2868	D-AVZN	A321	2974	D-AVZU	A321	1503
D-AVZE	A321	0477	D-AVZI	A321	3005	D-AVZO	A321	0513	D-AVZU	A321	1670
D-AVZE	A321	0541	D-AVZI	A321	3235	D-AVZO	A321	0677	D-AVZU	A321	1848
D-AVZE	A321	0620	D-AVZJ	A321	0495	D-AVZO	A321	0802	D-AVZU	A321	1977
D-AVZE	A321	0771	D-AVZJ	A321	0557	D-AVZO	A321	0956	D-AVZU	A321	2226
D-AVZE	A321	0991	D-AVZJ	A321	0633	D-AVZO	A321	1045	D-AVZU	A321	2351
D-AVZE	A321	1144	D-AVZJ	A321	0761	D-AVZO	A321	1276	D-AVZU	A321	2957
D-AVZE	A321	1408	D-AVZJ	A321	0891	D-AVZO	A321	1472	D-AVZU	A321	3146
D-AVZE	A321	1704	D-AVZJ	A321	1006	D-AVZO	A321	1611	D-AVZV	A321	0591
D-AVZE	A321	1788	D-AVZJ	A321	1188	D-AVZO	A321	1881	D-AVZV	A321	1525
D-AVZE	A321	1956	D-AVZJ	A321	1425	D-AVZO	A321	2064	D-AVZV	A321	1675
D-AVZE	A321	2055	D-AVZJ	A321	1521	D-AVZO	A321	2320	D-AVZV	A321	1978
D-AVZE	A321	2305	D-AVZJ	A321	1623	D-AVZO	A321	2726	D-AVZV	A321	2234
D-AVZE	A321	2536	D-AVZJ	A321	2261	**D-AVZO**	**A321**	**3249**	D-AVZV	A321	2357
D-AVZE	A321	2687	D-AVZJ	A321	2553	D-AVZP	A321	0514	D-AVZV	A321	2999
D-AVZE	A321	2823	D-AVZJ	A321	2736	D-AVZP	A321	0674	D-AVZV	A321	3254
D-AVZE	A321	2965	D-AVZJ	A321	2882	D-AVZP	A321	0808	D-AVZW	A321	0521

Reg	Type	Serial
D-AVZW	A321	0593
D-AVZW	A321	0765
D-AVZW	A321	0963
D-AVZW	A321	1531
D-AVZW	A321	1681
D-AVZW	A321	2080
D-AVZW	A321	2363
D-AVZW	A321	3013
D-AVZW	A321	3191
D-AVZX	A321	0522
D-AVZX	A321	0595
D-AVZX	A321	0715
D-AVZX	A321	0823
D-AVZX	A321	0968
D-AVZX	A321	1690
D-AVZX	A321	1850
D-AVZX	A321	1984
D-AVZX	A321	3015
D-AVZX	A321	3198
D-AVZY	A321	0524
D-AVZY	A321	0597
D-AVZY	A321	0699
D-AVZY	A321	0827
D-AVZY	A321	0970
D-AVZY	A321	1691
D-AVZY	A321	1859
D-AVZY	A321	3022
D-AVZY	A321	3207
D-AVZZ	A321	0526
D-AVZZ	A321	0599
D-AVZZ	A321	0835
D-AVZZ	A321	1869
D-AVZZ	A321	1995
D-AVZZ	A321	3034
D-AWBA	**146**	**E3134**
D-AWDL	**146**	**E1011**
D-AWFR	A319	0910
D-AWOH	737NG	29083
D-AWOR	A319	1795
D-AWUE	**146**	**E2050**
D-AWWW	A320	0478
D-AXDB	VFW	G-018
D-AXEL	A330	305
D-AXLA	**A320**	**2500**
D-AXLB	**A320**	**1860**
D-AXLC	**A320**	**1564**
D-AXLD	**737NG**	**35093**
D-AXLE	**737NG**	**30724**
D-AXXL	737NG	30076
D-AYAA	B737	27826
D-AYAB	B737	28038
D-AYAC	B737	28867
D-AYDB	VFW	G-014
D-AYYA	A319	3114
D-AYYB	A319	3116
D-AYYC	A319	3124
D-AZUR	146	E2060
D-B	D0328	3199
(D-BAAB)	D0328	3147
D-BABA	D0328	3120
D-BABA	VFW	G-01
D-BABB	VFW	G-2
D-BABC	VFW	G-3
D-BABD	VFW	G-4
D-BABE	VFW	G-5
D-BABF	VFW	G-6
D-BABG	VFW	G-7
D-BABH	VFW	G-8
D-BABI	VFW	G-9
D-BABJ	VFW	G-10
D-BABK	VFW	G-011
"D-BABK"	VFW	G-015
D-BABL	VFW	G-012
D-BABM	VFW	G-013
D-BABN	VFW	G-015
D-BABO	VFW	G-016
D-BABP	VFW	G-017
D-BADA	**D0328**	**3224**
D-BADC	**D0328**	**3216**
D-BALI	D0328	3111
D-BALL	D0328	3105
D-BALU	D0328	3108

Reg	Type	Serial
(D-BAUU)	D0328	3201
(D-BBUU)	D0328	3206
(D-BCUU)	D0328	3207
D-BDMO	D0328	3200
(D-BDUU)	D0328	3210
D-BDX.	D0328	3164
D-BDX.	D0328	3178
D-BDX.	D0328	3179
D-BDX.	D0328	3180
D-BDX.	D0328	3181
D-BDX.	D0328	3182
D-BDX.	D0328	3183
D-BDX.	D0328	3184
D-BDX.	D0328	3186
D-BDX.	D0328	3187
D-BDX.	D0328	3188
D-BDX.	D0328	3189
D-BDX.	D0328	3190
D-BDX.	D0328	3191
D-BDX.	D0328	3192
D-BDX.	D0328	3193
D-BDX.	D0328	3196
D-BDX.	D0328	3209
D-BDX.	D0328	3213
D-BDXA	D0328	3114
D-BDXA	D0328	3150
D-BDXA	D0328	3197
D-BDXB	D0328	3118
D-BDXB	D0328	3144
D-BDXB	D0328	3224
D-BDXC	D0328	3120
D-BDXC	D0328	3146
D-BDXC	D0328	3169
D-BDXC	D0328	3214
D-BDXC	D0328	3220
D-BDXD	D0328	3122
D-BDXD	D0328	3216
D-BDXE	D0328	3121
D-BDXE	D0328	3148
D-BDXE	D0328	3171
D-BDXE	D0328	3207
D-BDXF	D0328	3125
D-BDXF	D0328	3160
D-BDXF	D0328	3212
D-BDXG	D0328	3126
D-BDXG	D0328	3162
D-BDXH	D0328	3127
D-BDXH	D0328	3163
D-BDXH	D0328	3173
D-BDXH	D0328	3174
D-BDXH	D0328	3217
D-BDXI	D0328	3121
D-BDXI	D0328	3124
D-BDXI	D0328	3176
D-BDXI	D0328	3208
D-BDXJ	D0328	3123
D-BDXJ	D0328	3155
D-BDXJ	D0328	3172
D-BDXJ	D0328	3194
D-BDXJ	D0328	3195
D-BDXK	D0328	3128
D-BDXK	D0328	3156
D-BDXK	D0328	3175
D-BDXK	D0328	3211
D-BDXL	D0328	3129
D-BDXL	D0328	3157
D-BDXL	D0328	3198
D-BDXM	D0328	3116
D-BDXM	D0328	3130
D-BDXM	D0328	3199
D-BDXN	D0328	3131
D-BDXN	D0328	3153
D-BDXN	D0328	3200
D-BDXO	D0328	3133
D-BDXO	D0328	3137
D-BDXO	D0328	3152
D-BDXO	D0328	3201
D-BDXP	D0328	3134
D-BDXP	D0328	3154
D-BDXP	D0328	3203
D-BDXQ	D0328	3135
D-BDXQ	D0328	3158

Reg	Type	Serial
D-BDXQ	D0328	3185
D-BDXQ	D0328	3194
D-BDXQ	D0328	3210
D-BDXR	D0328	3136
D-BDXR	D0328	3218
D-BDXR	D0328	3219
D-BDXS	D0328	3137
D-BDXS	D0328	3142
D-BDXS	D0328	3161
D-BDXT	D0328	3138
D-BDXT	D0328	3151
D-BDXT	D0328	3204
D-BDXU	D0328	3145
D-BDXU	D0328	3159
D-BDXU	D0328	3202
D-BDXU	D0328	3219
D-BDXV	D0328	3147
D-BDXV	D0328	3165
D-BDXV	D0328	3167
D-BDXV	D0328	3215
D-BDXW	D0328	3140
D-BDXW	D0328	3166
D-BDXW	D0328	3168
D-BDXX	D0328	3141
D-BDXX	D0328	3143
D-BDXX	D0328	3205
D-BDXY	D0328	3149
D-BDXY	D0328	3177
D-BDXY	D0328	3206
D-BDXZ	D0328	3139
D-BDXZ	D0328	3170
D-BEJR	D0328	3102
D-BEOL	D0328	3197
D-BEUU	D0328	3211
D-BGAB	D0328	3134
(D-BGAD)	D0328	3136
D-BGAE	D0328	3146
(D-BGAF)	D0328	3137
D-BGAG	D0328	3133
D-BGAL	**D0328**	**3131**
D-BGAQ	**D0328**	**3130**
D-BGAR	D0328	3152
D-BGAS	D0328	3139
(D-BGUU)	D0328	3212
D-BHUU	D0328	3215
D-BIRD	**D0328**	**3180**
D-BIUU	D0328	3216
D-BJET	D0328	3002
D DJET	**D0328**	**3207**
D-BJUU	D0328	3217
D-BKUU	D0328	3218
(D-BMAA)	D0328	3134
(D-BMAA)	D0328	3141
(D-BMAB)	D0328	3151
(D-BMAC)	D0328	3158
(D-BMAD)	D0328	3159
(D-BMAE)	D0328	3173
(D-BMAF)	D0328	3178
(D-BMAF)	D0328	3184
(D-BMAG)	D0328	3192
(D-BMAH)	D0328	3200
(D-BMAI)	D0328	3204
(D-BMAJ)	D0328	3212
(D-BMUU)	D0328	3219
D-BMYD	D0328	3121
D-BOBA	YAK40	9211420
D-BOBB	YAK40	9211520
D-BOBC	YAK40	9230122
D-BOBD	YAK40	9230323
D-BOBE	YAK40	9230623
(D-BSUN)	D0328	3210
D-BWAL	D0328	3099
D-BXXX	D0328	3203
D-BYYY	D0328	3204
D-CATI	D0328	3002
D-COBA	YAK40	9211420
D-COBB	YAK40	9211520
D-COBC	YAK40	9230122
D-COBD	YAK40	9230323
D-COBE	YAK40	9230623
D-WWBB	A320	2571

East Germany

Reg	Type	Serial
DDR-ABA	A310	498
DDR-ABB	A310	499
DDR-ABC	A310	503
DDR-SCB	TU134	8350503
DDR-SCE	TU134	9350904
DDR-SCF	TU134	9350905
DDR-SCG	TU134	9350912
DDR-SCH	TU134	9350906
DDR-SCI	TU134	3351903
DDR-SCK	TU134	1351304
DDR-SCL	TU134	1351305
DDR-SCN	TU134	3352102
DDR-SCO	TU134	3352106
DDR-SCP	TU134	4352205
DDR-SCR	TU134	4352206
DDR-SCS	TU134	4352207
DDR-SCT	TU134	08068
DDR-SCU	TU134	09070
DDR-SCV	TU134	12095
DDR-SCW	TU134	31218
DDR-SCX	TU134	48320
DDR-SCY	TU134	60495
DDR-SCZ	TU134	9350913
DDR-SDC	TU134	35180
DDR-SDE	TU134	38040
DDR-SDF	TU134	40150
DDR-SDG	TU134	46155
DDR-SDH	TU134	46300
DDR-SDI	TU134	48560
DDR-SDK	TU134	49900
DDR-SDL	TU134	60108
DDR-SDM	TU134	60435
DDR-SDN	TU134	60612
DDR-SDO	TU134	62259
DDR-SDP	TU134	63260
DDR-SDR	TU134	63967
(DDR-SDS)	TU134	63952
DDR-SDT	TU134	63998
DDR-SDU	TU134	66135
DDR-SEB	IL62	00704
DDR-SEC	IL62	10903
DDR-SEF	IL62	31402
DDR-SEG	IL62	31403
DDR-SEH	IL62	31405
DDR-SEI	IL62	3036931
DDR-SEK	IL62	4831517
DDR-SEL	IL62	4934734
DDR-SEM	IL62	4140536
DDR-SEN	IL62	3242432
DDR-SEO	IL62	3344833
DDR-SEP	IL62	4445827
DDR-SER	IL62	2546812
DDR-SES	IL62	1647928
DDR-SET	IL62	4546257
DDR-SEU	IL62	2748552
DDR-SEV	IL62	3749224
DDR-SEW	IL62	2850324
DDR-SEY	IL62	1951525
DDR-SEZ	IL62	2951636
DDR-SFA	TU154	89A-799
DDR-SFB	TU154	89A-813
(DDR-SZA)	A310	498
(DDR-SZB)	A310	499
(DDR-SZC)	A310	503

East Germany

Reg	Type	Serial
DM-SCA	BB152	008
DM-SCA	TU134	8350502
DM-SCB	BB152	009
DM-SCB	TU134	8350503
DM-SCD	TU134	9350702
DM-SCE	TU134	9350904
DM-SCF	TU134	9350905
DM-SCG	TU134	9350912
DM-SCH	TU134	9350906
DM-SCI	TU134	3351903
DM-SCK	TU134	1351304
DM-SCL	TU134	1351305

Reg	Type	C/N
DM-SCM	TU134	3351904
DM-SCN	TU134	3352102
DM-SCO	TU134	3352106
DM-SCP	TU134	4352205
DM-SCR	TU134	4352206
DM-SCS	TU134	4352207
DM-SCT	TU134	08068
DM-SCU	TU134	09070
DM-SCV	TU134	12095
DM-SCW	TU134	31218
DM-SCX	TU134	48320
DM-SCY	TU134	60495
DM-SCZ	TU134	9350913
DM-SDA	TU124	4351508
DM-SDB	TU124	5351508
DM-SDE	TU134	38040
DM-SDF	TU134	40150
DM-SDG	TU134	46155
DM-SDH	TU134	46300
DM-SDI	TU134	48560
DM-SDK	TU134	49900
DM-SDL	TU134	60108
DM-SDM	TU134	60435
DM-SDN	TU134	60612
DM-SDO	TU134	62259
DM-SDP	TU134	63260
DM-SEA	IL62	00702
DM-SEB	IL62	00704
DM-SEC	IL62	10903
DM-SEF	IL62	31402
DM-SEG	IL62	31403
DM-SEH	IL62	31405
DM-SEI	IL62	3036931
DM-SEK	IL62	4831517
DM-SEL	IL62	4934734
DM-ZYA	BB152	V1
DM-ZYB	BB152	V4
DM-ZYC	BB152	V5

Fiji

Reg	Type	C/N
DQ-FBQ	1-11	BAC.245
DQ-FBV	1-11	BAC.250
DQ-FCR	1-11	BAC.116
DQ-FDM	B737	22679
DQ-FJA	B767	23058
DQ-FJB	B737	26067
DQ-FJC	**B767**	**26260**
DQ-FJD	B737	27285
DQ-FJE	B747	22614
DQ-FJF	**737NG**	**28878**
DQ-FJG	**737NG**	**29968**
DQ-FJH	**737NG**	**29969**
DQ-FJI	B747	22145
DQ-FJK	**B747**	**24064**
DQ-FJL	**B747**	**24062**

Angola

Reg	Type	C/N
D2-	B727	19405
D2-	**DC-9**	**47110**
D2-EAG	**YAK40**	**9230122**
D2-ECC	**TU134**	**49830**
D2-ERI	**B727**	**19813**
D2-ERJ	**DC-9**	**47765**
D2-ERL	**DC-9**	**47788**
D2-ESU	**B727**	**19431**
D2-EVD	**B727**	**19403**
D2-EVG	**B727**	**19402**
D2-EVW	**737NG**	**35954**
D2-FAS	B727	20773
D2-FAT	B727	19497
D2-FAV	B707	18717
D2-FBB	B727	19100
D2-FCI	B727	18429
D2-FCJ	B727	18435
D2-FCK	B727	18892
D2-FCL	B727	19867
D2-FCM	IL76	0063470107
D2-FCN	IL76	0053462872

Reg	Type	C/N
D2-FCO	IL76	0043454615
D2-FCP	**B727**	**20370**
D2-FDI	IL76	?
D2-FDX	**IL76**	**063407170**
D2-FDZ	**B707**	**19415**
D2-FEE	YAK40	?
D2-FEM	IL76	0063469062
D2-FEP	**AN7x**	**72070688**
D2-FER	**YAK40**	**9541844**
D2-FES	YAK40	?
D2-FEW	IL76	0073475239
D2-FFA	B727	19100
D2-FFB	B727	19206
D2-FLY	B727	19833
D2-FLZ	B727	19839
D2-FOO	B727	18426
D2-FSA	**B727**	**19987**
D2-MAN	**B707**	**20025**
D2-MAQ	AN7x	72093876
D2-MAS	**YAK40**	**9820558**
D2-MAY	B707	19374
D2-MBF	AN7x	47060649
D2-MBF	**AN7x**	**?**
D2-TAA	B737	21172
D2-TAB	B737	21173
D2-TAC	B707	18975
D2-TAD	B707	19355
D2-TAG	B707	18583
D2-TAH	B737	21723
(D2-TAL)	B707	19965
(D2-TAM)	B707	19963
D2-TBC	B737	21173
D2-TBD	B737	21723
D2-TBF	**737NG**	**34559**
D2-TBG	**737NG**	**34560**
D2-TBH	**737NG**	**34561**
D2-TBI	B737	19681
D2-TBJ	**737NG**	**34562**
D2-TBN	B737	22775
D2-TBO	**B737**	**22776**
D2-TBP	B737	23220
D2-TBT	B737	21278
D2-TBU	B737	21279
D2-TBV	B737	22626
D2-TBX	**B737**	**23351**
D2-TEA	**B747**	**23410**
D2-TEB	**B747**	**23751**
D2-TEC	B747	22971
D2-TED	**B777**	**34565**
D2-TEE	**B777**	**34566**
D2-TEF	**B777**	**34567**
D2-TIF	IL62	4648525
D2-TIG	IL62	4750919
D2-TJA	B727	19813
D2-TJB	B727	19005
D2-TJC	B727	19180
D2-TOB	B707	18975
D2-TOC	B707	19355
D2-TOG	B707	18583
D2-TOI	B707	18975
D2-TOJ	B707	19355
D2-TOK	B707	19869
D2-TOL	B707	19963
D2-TOM	B707	19965
D2-TON	B707	19871
D2-TOP	B707	20136
D2-TOR	B707	18748
D2-TOU	B707	18973
D2-TOV	B707	18881
D2-TPR	**B707**	**20715**
D2-TYA	YAK40	9721553
D2-TYB	YAK40	9721653
D2-TYC	YAK40	9721753
D2-TYD	YAK40	9721853

Cape Verde Islands

Reg	Type	C/N
D4-CBG	**B757**	**27599**
D4-CBN	B737	26333
D4-CBP	**B757**	**30045**

Comoros

Reg	Type	C/N
(D6-)	B737	20574
(D6-)	B737	20578
D6-CAJ	B737	22581
D6-OZX	B747	22302
(D6-QZA)	B747	22302

Spain

Reg	Type	C/N
(EC-)	A320	2248
EC-	**A320**	**3293**
EC-	**A340**	**088**
EC-101	MD80	49574
EC-102	MD80	49575
EC-113	MD80	49631
EC-116	B757	23119
EC-117	A310	638
EC-117	B737	23506
EC-117	B757	22176
EC-129	B737	23331
EC-135	B737	23636
EC-135	B737	23750
EC-136	B737	23808
EC-136	B747	24071
EC-138	B737	23941
EC-147	MD80	49577
EC-148	MD80	49579
EC-149	MD80	49621
EC-150	MD80	49672
EC-151	B737	23922
EC-152	B737	23923
EC-153	B737	23766
EC-154	A340	125
EC-155	A340	134
EC-155	B737	23787
EC-156	A340	145
EC-157	A340	146
EC-157	B757	24119
EC-159	B737	24131
EC-159	MD80	49710
EC-160	B737	24132
EC-163	MD80	49668
EC-166	MD80	49791
EC-167	B737	23752
EC-178	MD80	49624
EC-179	MD80	49622
EC-188	B737	24211
EC-189	B737	24299
EC-190	MD80	49642
EC-198	146	E2102
EC-202	B757	24120
EC-203	B757	24122
EC-204	B737	24256
EC-204	B757	24118
EC-206	MD80	49622
EC-211	B757	22781
EC-213	B737	23064
EC-214	DC-8	45905
EC-215	MD80	49627
EC-216	MD80	49630
EC-217	DC-8	46023
EC-223	MD80	49626
EC-230	DC-8	45921
"EC-231"	146	E2112
EC-238	B737	24376
EC-239	B737	23979
EC-244	B737	24462
EC-245	B737	24463
EC-245	YAK40	49398
EC-246	DC-9	47656
EC-247	B757	24289
EC-248	B757	24290
EC-251	B737	23981
EC-255	B737	23684
EC-256	B757	23651
EC-257	MD80	49642
EC-260	MD80	49628
EC-261	MD80	49631
EC-262	B737	25071
EC-265	B757	22185

Reg	Type	C/N
EC-269	MD80	49629
EC-273	A300	076
EC-274	A300	077
EC-276	B737	23787
EC-276	B767	24457
EC-277	B737	23788
EC-278	B757	24398
EC-279	B737	23809
EC-279	MD80	49624
EC-281	146	E2089
EC-287	B747	20137
EC-288	DC-8	45895
EC-289	MD80	49668
EC-290	MD80	49827
EC-291	MD80	49578
EC-291	MD80	49828
EC-292	MD80	49829
EC-293	MD80	49830
EC-294	MD80	49831
EC-295	MD80	49832
EC-296	MD80	49833
EC-297	MD80	49834
EC-298	MD80	49835
EC-299	MD80	49836
EC-300	MD80	49837
EC-301	MD80	49838
EC-302	MD80	49839
EC-303	MD80	49840
EC-304	MD80	49841
EC-305	MD80	49842
EC-306	MD80	49843
EC-307	MD80	49790
EC-308	B737	24345
EC-308	B737	24690
EC-309	B737	24124
EC-311	A310	440
EC-321	B757	22176
EC-323	MD80	49642
EC-326	B727	20606
EC-327	B727	20607
EC-328	B727	20593
EC-330	**A330**	**747**
EC-348	B737	25180
EC-348	MD80	49574
EC-349	B757	24397
EC-350	B757	24119
EC-355	B737	23712
EC-356	B737	23332
EC-356	B737	23748
EC-375	B737	23810
EC-376	B737	23826
EC-377	B737	23747
EC-382	MD80	49622
EC-389	MD80	49396
EC-390	B757	22689
EC-390	MD80	49578
EC-39G	A310	472
EC-401	B737	24545
EC-402	B737	24685
EC-403	B737	24689
EC-420	B757	26239
EC-421	B757	26240
EC-421	MD80	49661
EC-422	B757	26241
EC-429	B737	23713
EC-432	B757	24772
EC-438	MD80	49663
EC-439	MD80	53050
EC-440	MD80	49708
EC-440	MD80	53051
EC-446	B757	24792
EC-451	B757	22176
EC-457	B737	25858
EC-463	MD80	49577
EC-479	MD80	49398
EC-479	MD80	49621
EC-485	MD80	49622
EC-487	MD80	49672
EC-489	DC-9	47061
EC-490	B757	24793
EC-495	MD80	48022
EC-516	B757	24120

Reg	Type	c/n
EC-520	B737	26293
EC-524	MD80	49628
EC-525	MD80	49629
EC-529	DC-8	45945
EC-531	MD80	49620
EC-542	B737	24256
EC-544	B757	24121
EC-546	MD80	49791
EC-546	MD80	49826
EC-547	B737	26301
EC-547	B767	24999
EC-548	B767	25000
EC-575	A320	0134
EC-576	A320	0136
EC-577	A320	0143
EC-578	A320	0146
EC-579	A320	0158
EC-580	A320	0173
EC-581	A320	0176
EC-582	A320	0177
EC-583	A320	0199
EC-584	A320	0207
EC-585	A320	0223
EC-586	A320	0224
EC-587	A320	0240
EC-588	A320	0241
EC-589	A320	0246
EC-591	B737	23752
EC-591	MD80	49574
EC-592	B737	24131
EC-592	MD80	49938
EC-593	B737	24132
EC-594	B737	24299
EC-597	B757	24398
EC-597	B757	25597
EC-603	B737	24690
EC-607	MD80	49708
EC-608	B757	26242
EC-609	B757	26243
EC-610	B757	26244
EC-611	B757	26245
EC-612	B757	26246
EC-615	146	E2117
EC-616	B757	26240
EC-618	B757	26241
EC-622	DC-9	45695
EC-633	MD80	53207
EC-634	MD80	53208
EC-635	B737	23495
EC-635	MD80	53209
FC-636	MD80	53210
EC-637	MD80	53211
EC-638	MD80	49630
EC-638	MD80	53212
EC-639	MD80	53213
EC-640	A310	638
EC-642	MD80	49619
EC-642	MD80	49779
EC-644	B737	24706
EC-645	B737	24707
EC-646	MD80	49627
EC-655	B737	24124
EC-667	B737	23747
EC-667	B757	25053
(EC-668)	B757	25054
EC-669	B757	24794
EC-703	B737	25159
EC-704	B737	25256
EC-705	B737	25263
EC-706	B737	25264
EC-711	B737	24059
EC-712	146	E3154
EC-714	MD80	49401
EC-719	146	E3154
EC-733	MD80	49792
EC-737	B737	24682
EC-738	B737	24688
EC-742	MD80	49790
EC-744	B757	24122
EC-749	MD80	49401
EC-751	MD80	53193
EC-752	MD80	53194
EC-753	MD80	53195
EC-754	MD80	53196
EC-755	MD80	53197
EC-765	B747	20137
EC-772	B737	24686
EC-781	B737	23749
EC-782	B737	23707
EC-783	B737	23331
EC-784	B737	23332
EC-786	B757	24792
EC-793	MD80	48022
EC-796	B737	26315
EC-797	B737	26317
EC-798	B737	26322
EC-799	B737	27626
EC-805	MD80	49626
EC-807	146	E3165
EC-807	MD80	49642
EC-835	MD80	49709
EC-839	146	E3169
EC-843	B757	22185
EC-847	B757	23227
EC-850	B737	24906
EC-851	B737	24912
EC-876	146	E3163
EC-880	A320	0264
EC-881	A320	0266
EC-882	A320	0274
EC-883	A320	0303
EC-884	A320	0312
EC-885	A320	0323
EC-886	A320	0356
EC-892	DC-8	46105
EC-893	MD80	49900
EC-894	MD80	53165
EC-896	B757	22688
EC-897	B737	24462
EC-897	B757	25597
EC-898	B737	23923
EC-898	MD80	49668
EC-899	146	E3187
EC-936	B737	25180
EC-945	MD80	53303
EC-946	MD80	53304
EC-963	DC-8	46069
EC-964	MD80	53305
EC-965	MD80	53306
EC-966	MD80	53307
EC-969	146	E1007
EC-970	B737	25743
EC-971	146	E1015
EC-987	MD80	53308
EC-988	MD80	53309
EC-989	MD80	53310
EC-991	B737	25190
EC-994	MD80	49144
EC-996	B737	24569
EC-997	B737	25116
(EC-)	A310	475
EC-ARA	DC-8	45617
EC-ARB	DC-8	45618
EC-ARC	DC-8	45619
EC-ARI	SE210	107
EC-ARJ	SE210	108
EC-ARK	SE210	109
EC-ARL	SE210	110
EC-ASN	DC-8	45659
EC-ATP	DC-8	45658
EC-ATV	SE210	163
EC-ATX	SE210	165
EC-AUM	DC-8	45657
EC-AVY	SE210	173
EC-AVZ	SE210	159
"EC-AXN"	A310	492
EC-AXU	SE210	138
EC-AYD	SE210	197
EC-AYE	SE210	198
EC-BAV	DC-8	45814
(EC-BAX)	DC-9	45797
(EC-BAY)	DC-9	45798
(EC-BAZ)	DC-9	45799
EC-BBR	SE210	171
EC-BDC	SE210	176
EC-BDD	SE210	202
EC-BIA	SE210	226
EC-BIB	SE210	223
EC-BIC	SE210	225
EC-BID	SE210	228
EC-BIE	SE210	230
EC-BIF	SE210	232
EC-BIG	DC-9	47037
EC-BIH	DC-9	47076
EC-BII	DC-9	47077
EC-BIJ	DC-9	47079
EC-BIK	DC-9	47080
EC-BIL	DC-9	47084
EC-BIM	DC-9	47088
EC-BIN	DC-9	47089
EC-BIO	DC-9	47090
EC-BIP	DC-9	47091
EC-BIQ	DC-9	47092
EC-BIR	DC-9	47093
EC-BIS	DC-9	47312
EC-BIT	DC-9	47313
EC-BIU	DC-9	47314
EC-BJC	CV990	30-10-22
EC-BJD	CV990	30-10-23
EC-BMV	DC-8	45965
EC-BMX	DC-8	45930
EC-BMY	DC-8	45931
EC-BMZ	DC-8	45988
EC-BNM	CV990	30-10-32
EC-BPF	DC-9	47364
EC-BPG	DC-9	47365
EC-BPH	DC-9	47368
EC-BQA	CV990	30-10-36
EC-BQF	1-11	BAC.161
EC-BQQ	CV990	30-10-34
EC-BQS	DC-8	46079
EC-BQT	DC-9	47446
EC-BQU	DC-9	47447
EC-BQV	DC-9	47453
EC-BQX	DC-9	47454
EC-BQY	DC-9	47455
EC-BQZ	DC-9	47456
EC-BRJ	SE210	250
EC-BRO	B747	19957
EC-BRP	B747	19958
EC-BRQ	B747	20137
EC-BRX	SE210	261
EC-BRY	SE210	264
EC-BSD	DC-8	46116
EC-BSE	DC-8	46155
EC-BTE	CV990	30-10-21
EC-BVA	F.28	11017
EC-BVB	F.28	11019
EC-BVC	F.28	11023
EC-BXI	CV990	30-10-35
EC-BXR	DC-8	45422
EC-BYD	DC-9	47522
EC-BYE	DC-9	47504
EC-BYF	DC-9	47542
EC-BYG	DC-9	47543
EC-BYH	DC-9	47556
EC-BYI	DC-9	47452
EC-BYJ	DC-9	47461
EC-BYK	DC-9	47428
EC-BYL	DC-9	47545
EC-BYM	DC-9	47496
EC-BYN	DC-9	47565
EC-BZO	CV990	30-10-30
EC-BZP	CV990	30-10-18
EC-BZQ	DC-8	45426
EC-BZR	CV990	30-10-25
EC-CAD	DC-8	45423
EC-CAE	SE210	176
EC-CAI	B727	20592
EC-CAJ	B727	20593
EC-CAK	B727	20594
EC-CAM	DC-8	45427
EC-CBA	B727	20595
EC-CBB	B727	20596
EC-CBC	B727	20597
EC-CBD	B727	20598
EC-CBE	B727	20599
EC-CBF	B727	20600
EC-CBG	B727	20601
EC-CBH	B727	20602
EC-CBI	B727	20603
EC-CBJ	B727	20604
EC-CBK	B727	20605
EC-CBL	B727	20606
EC-CBM	B727	20607
EC-CBN	DC-10	46925
EC-CBO	DC-10	46926
EC-CBP	DC-10	46927
EC-CCF	DC-8	45897
EC-CCG	DC-8	45898
EC-CCN	DC-8	45569
EC-CDA	DC-8	45429
EC-CDB	DC-8	45424
EC-CDC	DC-8	45567
EC-CEZ	DC-10	47980
EC-CFA	B727	20811
EC-CFB	B727	20812
EC-CFC	B727	20813
EC-CFD	B727	20814
EC-CFE	B727	20815
EC-CFF	B727	20816
EC-CFG	B727	20817
EC-CFH	B727	20818
EC-CFI	B727	20819
EC-CFJ	B727	20820
EC-CFK	B727	20821
EC-CGN	DC-9	47637
EC-CGO	DC-9	47640
EC-CGP	DC-9	47642
EC-CGQ	DC-9	47643
EC-CGR	DC-9	47644
EC-CGS	DC-9	47645
EC-CGY	DC-9	45696
EC-CGZ	DC-9	45699
EC-CID	B727	20974
EC-CIE	B727	20975
EC-CIZ	SE210	247
EC-CLB	DC-10	47981
EC-CLD	DC-9	47675
EC-CLE	DC-9	47678
EC-CMS	SE210	238
EC-CMT	DC-8	45568
EC-CNF	CV990	30-10-8
EC-CNG	CV990	30-10-7
EC-CNH	CV990	30-10-17
EC-CNJ	CV990	30-10-14
EC-CPI	SE210	236
EC-CQM	DC-8	45668
EC-CSJ	DC-10	46922
EC-CSK	DC-10	46953
EC-CTR	DC-9	47702
EC-CTS	DC-9	47704
EC-CTT	DC-9	47706
EC-CTU	DC-9	47707
EC-CUM	SE210	212
EC-CUS	DC-8	45265
EC-CYI	SE210	263
EC-CZE	DC-8	45913
EC-DBE	DC-8	45824
EC-DCC	B727	21609
EC-DCD	B727	21610
EC-DCE	B727	21611
EC-DCN	SE210	199
EC-DDU	B727	21777
EC-DDV	B727	21778
EC-DDX	B727	21779
EC-DDY	B727	21780
EC-DDZ	B727	21781
EC-DEA	DC-10	47982
EC-DEG	DC-10	46962
EC-DEM	DC-8	45856
EC-DFP	SE210	257
EC-DGB	DC-9	48103
EC-DGC	DC-9	48104
EC-DGD	DC-9	48105
EC-DGE	DC-9	48106
EC-DHZ	DC-10	47834
EC-DIA	B747	22238

Reg	Type	MSN	Reg	Type	MSN	Reg	Type	MSN	Reg	Type	MSN
EC-DIB	B747	22239	EC-EKT	MD80	49642	EC-FEO	A320	0177	**EC-FTR**	**B757**	**26239**
EC-DIH	DC-8	45753	EC-ELA	MD80	24120	EC-FEP	MD80	49792	**EC-FTS**	**MD80**	**49621**
EC-DIR	DC-9	45698	EC-ELJ	B737	24299	EC-FEQ	MD80	49401	EC-FTT	MD80	49622
EC-DKH	DC-8	45412	EC-ELM	DC-8	45905	EC-FER	B737	24299	EC-FTU	MD80	49672
EC-DLC	B747	22454	EC-ELS	B757	24122	EC-FET	B737	24132	EC-FUA	B757	26240
EC-DLD	B747	22455	**EC-ELT**	**146**	**E2102**	**EC-FEY**	**MD80**	**53208**	EC-FUB	B757	26241
EC-DLE	A300	130	EC-ELV	B737	23064	**EC-FEZ**	**MD80**	**53207**	EC-FUT	B737	26293
EC-DLF	A300	133	EC-ELY	B737	24211	**EC-FFA**	**MD80**	**53209**	EC-FVA	DC-8	45945
EC-DLG	A300	135	EC-EMA	B757	24118	EC-FFB	B737	23752	EC-FVB	MD80	49628
EC-DLH	A300	136	EC-EMD	DC-8	46023	EC-FFC	B737	24131	EC-FVC	MD80	49629
EC-DNP	B747	22764	EC-EMG	MD80	49626	**EC-FFH**	**MD80**	**53211**	EC-FVJ	B737	24256
EC-DNQ	A300	156	EC-EMI	B737	23979	**EC-FFI**	**MD80**	**53210**	EC-FVR	MD80	49574
EC-DNR	A300	170	EC-EMT	MD80	49642	EC-FFK	B757	24122	EC-FVT	B737	23495
(EC-DNS)	A300	171	EC-EMU	B757	24290	EC-FFN	B737	25159	EC-FVV	MD80	49708
(EC-DNT)	A300	179	EC-EMV	B757	24289	EC-FFY	146	E3154	EC-FVX	MD80	49791
EC-DQP	DC-9	45792	EC-EMX	DC-8	45921	EC-FGG	B737	24059	**EC-FVY**	**146**	**E2117**
EC-DQQ	DC-9	47531	EC-EMY	B737	23981	**EC-FGH**	**A320**	**0223**	**EC-FXA**	**MD80**	**49938**
EC-DQT	DC-9	47613	EC-ENQ	B757	23651	**EC-FGM**	**MD80**	**53193**	EC-FXB	A310	638
EC-DSF	DC-10	46992	EC-ENS	B737	24462	EC-FGQ	MD80	48022	EC-FXI	MD80	49630
EC-DSV	DC-9	47458	EC-ENT	B737	24463	**EC-FGR**	**A320**	**0224**	EC-FXJ	B737	25858
EC-DTI	DC-9	47639	EC-ENZ	DC-9	47656	EC-FGT	146	E3165	EC-FXP	B737	24706
EC-DTR	B737	22597	EC-EOK	B757	22185	EC-FGU	A320	0199	EC-FXQ	B737	24707
EC-DUB	B737	22598	EC-EOL	B757	24398	**EC-FGV**	**A320**	**0207**	EC-FXU	B757	26240
EC-DUG	DC-10	46576	EC-EOM	MD80	49628	EC-FHA	B767	25000	EC-FXV	B757	26241
EC-DUL	B737	22369	EC-EON	A300	076	**EC-FHD**	**MD80**	**53212**	EC-FXX	MD80	49779
EC-DVB	DC-8	46037	EC-EOO	A300	077	**EC-FHG**	**MD80**	**53194**	EC-FXY	MD80	49627
EC-DVC	DC-8	46016	EC-EOY	MD80	49629	**EC-FHK**	**MD80**	**53213**	EC-FYE	B737	23747
EC-DVE	B737	22639	EC-EOZ	MD80	49627	EC-FHR	B737	25256	EC-FYF	B737	26301
EC-DVN	B737	22296	EC-EPA	146	E2089	EC-FHU	146	E3169	EC-FYG	B737	24124
EC-DXE	B747	20014	EC-EPL	MD80	49630	EC-FIA	A320	0240	EC-FYJ	B757	26242
EC-DXK	B737	22638	EC-EPM	MD80	49631	EC-FIC	A320	0241	EC-FYK	B757	26243
EC-DXV	B737	22407	EC-EPN	B737	24345	**EC-FIG**	**MD80**	**53195**	EC-FYL	B757	26244
EC-DYA	DC-8	45885	EC-EQI	DC-8	45895	**EC-FIH**	**MD80**	**53196**	EC-FYM	B757	26245
EC-DYB	DC-8	46011	EC-ESC	B757	24397	EC-FIU	146	E3163	EC-FYN	B757	26246
EC-DYY	DC-8	45888	EC-ESJ	MD80	49790	EC-FIX	MD80	49396	EC-FZC	MD80	49790
EC-DYZ	B737	22703	EC-EST	B737	23332	EC-FIY	B757	22688	**EC-FZE**	**146**	**E2105**
EC-DZA	DC-8	46032	EC-ETB	B737	24545	**EC-FJE**	**MD80**	**53197**	EC-FZQ	MD80	49401
EC-DZB	B737	20218	EC-ETZ	B757	22689	EC-FJQ	MD80	49900	EC-FZT	B737	24688
EC-DZC	DC-8	46015	EC-EUC	MD80	49829	EC-FJR	B737	24462	EC-FZX	B737	24682
EC-DZH	B737	20336	EC-EUD	MD80	49828	EC-FJZ	B737	23923	EC-FZZ	B737	24682
EC-EAK	B737	23535	EC-EUE	MD80	49827	EC-FKC	B737	23332	(EC-G..)	A321	0808
EC-EAM	DC-8	45908	EC-EUF	MD80	49663	EC-FKD	A320	0264	(EC-G..)	A321	0823
EC-EAZ	DC-10	46727	EC-EUL	MD80	49830	EC-FKF	146	E3187	EC-GAG	B747	20137
EC-EBX	B737	23747	EC-EUZ	MD80	53050	EC-FKH	A320	0246	EC-GAP	B737	26315
EC-EBY	B737	23748	EC-EVB	MD80	49831	EC-FKI	B737	23707	**EC-GAT**	**MD80**	**49709**
EC-EBZ	B737	23712	EC-EVC	B757	24792	EC-FKJ	B737	24749	EC-GAZ	MD80	24906
EC-ECA	B737	23713	EC-EVD	B757	24772	EC-FKS	B737	23331	**EC-GBA**	**MD80**	**49626**
EC-ECM	B737	23787	EC-EVE	B737	24685	EC-FLD	B737	25180	EC-GBN	B737	24912
EC-ECN	MD80	49401	EC-EVU	MD80	53051	EC-FLF	B737	25263	EC-GBU	B737	26317
EC-ECO	MD80	49442	EC-EVY	MD80	49661	EC-FLG	B737	25264	EC-GBV	MD80	49668
EC-ECQ	B737	23788	EC-EXF	MD80	49832	EC-FLK	MD80	53304	EC-GBX	B757	25597
EC-ECR	B737	23749	**EC-EXG**	**MD80**	**49833**	**EC-FLN**	**MD80**	**53303**	EC-GBY	MD80	49642
EC-ECS	B737	23707	EC-EXH	B757	24121	**EC-FLP**	**A320**	**0266**	EC-GCA	B757	22185
EC-ECU	DC-9	47201	EC-EXM	MD80	49835	**EC-FLQ**	**A320**	**0274**	EC-GCB	B757	23227
EC-EDM	B737	23388	EC-EXN	MD80	49836	EC-FLY	B757	25597	EC-GCI	B727	20598
EC-EEG	B737	20910	EC-EXR	MD80	49834	EC-FMJ	B737	25190	EC-GCJ	B727	20602
EC-EEK	B747	24071	**EC-EXT**	**MD80**	**49837**	EC-FML	A320	0303	EC-GCK	B727	20603
EC-EFJ	MD80	49575	EC-EXX	MD80	49398	EC-FMN	A320	0312	EC-GCL	B727	20604
EC-EFK	MD80	49576	EC-EXY	B737	24689	EC-FMO	MD80	49144	EC-GCM	B727	20606
(EC-EFL)	MD80	49642	**EC-EYB**	**MD80**	**49838**	EC-FMP	B737	25743	**EC-GCV**	**MD80**	**53165**
EC-EFU	MD80	49574	EC-EYP	MD80	48022	EC-FMQ	B757	24792	EC-GCY	DC-8	46105
EC-EFX	B757	23118	EC-EYS	DC-9	47061	EC-FMS	B737	24569	EC-GEE	DC-8	46069
EC-EGH	B757	23119	**EC-EYX**	**MD80**	**49839**	EC-FMY	MD80	49631	EC-GEO	146	E1007
EC-EGI	B757	22176	**EC-EYY**	**MD80**	**49840**	**EC-FND**	**MD80**	**53305**	EC-GEP	146	E1015
EC-EGQ	B737	23506	**EC-EYZ**	**MD80**	**49841**	EC-FNI	A310	638	EC-GEQ	B737	23750
EC-EHA	B737	23331	**EC-EZA**	**MD80**	**49842**	**EC-FNR**	**A320**	**0323**	EC-GEU	B737	23808
EC-EHJ	B737	23636	EC-EZR	MD80	49826	EC-FNU	MD80	49622	EC-GFE	B737	25116
EC-EHM	B737	23766	**EC-EZS**	**MD80**	**49843**	**EC-FOF**	**MD80**	**53307**	EC-GFJ	MD80	49710
EC-EHT	MD80	49577	EC-EZU	MD80	49620	**EC-FOG**	**MD80**	**53306**	EC-GFU	B737	24256
EC-EHX	B737	23752	EC-FAS	A320	0134	**EC-FOZ**	**MD80**	**53308**	EC-GGE	B737	26322
EC-EHY	B757	24119	EC-FBP	B737	24690	**EC-FPD**	**MD80**	**53309**	EC-GGO	B737	24376
EC-EHZ	B737	23922	EC-FBQ	A320	0136	**EC-FPJ**	**MD80**	**53310**	EC-GGS	A340	125
EC-EIA	B737	23923	EC-FBR	A320	0146	EC-FQB	B737	23684	**EC-GGV**	**MD80**	**49791**
EC-EID	B737	23941	EC-FBS	A320	0143	EC-FQP	B737	23809	EC-GGZ	B737	27626
EC-EIG	MD80	49579	**EC-FCB**	**A320**	**0158**	**EC-FQY**	**A320**	**0356**	EC-GHD	B737	25071
EC-EII	B737	24131	EC-FCQ	DC-9	45695	EC-FRP	B737	23748	**EC-GHE**	**MD80**	**49398**
EC-EIK	MD80	49668	EC-FCU	B767	24999	EC-FRZ	B737	23747	EC-GHF	B737	24124
EC-EIR	B737	24132	**EC-FDA**	**A320**	**0176**	EC-FSA	B737	23826	EC-GHH	MD80	49578
EC-EJQ	MD80	49672	**EC-FDB**	**A320**	**0173**	EC-FSC	B737	23810	EC-GHJ	MD80	49642
EC-EJU	MD80	49621	EC-FEB	MD80	49619	EC-FSY	MD80	49577	EC-GHK	B737	24690
EC-EJZ	MD80	49622	EC-FEE	B757	25053	EC-FSZ	MD80	49578	EC-GHM	B767	24457
EC-EKM	MD80	49624	EC-FEF	B757	24794	EC-FTL	B757	22176	EC-GHT	B737	25180

Reg	Type	Serial
EC-GHX	A340	134
EC-GIL	A310	472
EC-GJT	A340	145
EC-GKF	MD80	49389
EC-GKG	MD80	49706
EC-GKL	B727	21851
EC-GKM	A320	0280
EC-GKS	MD80	49708
EC-GLE	A340	146
EC-GLT	A320	0314
EC-GMU	A310	451
EC-GMY	B737	28658
EC-GNB	A320	0308
EC-GNC	B737	24124
EC-GNG	DC-10	46953
EC-GNU	B737	28660
EC-GNY	MD80	49396
EC-GNZ	B737	28659
EC-GOA	B737	25116
EC-GOB	B737	25180
EC-GOJ	B767	23072
EC-GOM	MD80	49579
EC-GOT	A310	455
EC-GOU	MD80	53198
EC-GPB	A340	193
EC-GPI	B737	28661
EC-GQG	MD80	49577
EC-GQK	A340	197
EC-GQO	146	E2086
EC-GQP	146	E2100
EC-GQZ	MD80	49579
EC-GRE	A320	0134
EC-GRF	A320	0136
EC-GRG	A320	0143
EC-GRH	A320	0146
EC-GRI	A320	0177
EC-GRJ	A320	0246
EC-GRK	MD80	49827
EC-GRL	MD80	49828
EC-GRM	MD80	49829
EC-GRN	MD80	49830
EC-GRO	MD80	49831
EC-GRX	B737	24123
EC-GSU	B767	26206
EC-GSX	B727	20594
EC-GSY	B727	20597
EC-GSZ	B727	20599
EC-GTA	B727	20605
EC-GTB	DC-10	46556
EC-GTC	DC-10	46972
EC-GTD	DC-10	46982
EC-GTG	CRJ	7020
EC-GTI	B767	26207
EC-GTO	MD80	49570
EC-GUG	B737	25116
EC-GUI	B737	24690
EC-GUO	B737	26285
EC-GUP	A340	217
EC-GUQ	A340	221
EC-GUR	A320	0308
EC-GVB	B737	24689
EC-GVI	MD80	49936
EC-GVO	MD80	49642
EC-GXR	B737	24685
EC-GXU	MD80	49622
EC-GYI	CRJ	7249
EC-GYK	B737	24688
EC-GZA	CRJ	7249
EC-GZD	A320	0879
EC-GZE	A320	0888
EC-GZI	E145	145098
EC-GZU	E145	145106
EC-GZY	B757	26247
EC-GZZ	B757	26248
EC-HAA	B757	26249
EC-HAB	A320	0994
EC-HAC	A321	1021
EC-HAD	A320	0992
EC-HAE	A321	1027
EC-HAF	A320	1047
EC-HAG	A320	1059
EC-HAH	B727	21084
EC-HAL	A310	594
EC-HAN	B737	25740
EC-HBH	B727	20661
EC-HBL	737NG	28381
EC-HBM	737NG	28382
EC-HBN	737NG	28383
EC-HBP	MD80	49629
EC-HBR	B727	20662
EC-HBT	B737	24545
EC-HBZ	B737	25180
EC-HCN	B737	24682
EC-HCP	B737	24124
EC-HCR	A320	0225
EC-HDG	B757	24794
EC-HDH	146	E2056
EC-HDK	A320	1067
EC-HDL	A320	1063
EC-HDM	B757	26250
EC-HDN	A320	1087
EC-HDO	A320	1099
EC-HDP	A320	1101
EC-HDQ	A340	302
EC-HDR	B757	26251
EC-HDS	B757	26252
EC-HDT	A320	1119
EC-HDU	B757	26253
EC-HDV	B757	26254
EC-HEK	CRJ	7320
EC-HFB	A310	542
EC-HFP	MD80	53148
EC-HFQ	A310	492
EC-HFS	MD80	49517
EC-HFT	MD80	49521
EC-HGA	MD80	53052
EC-HGJ	MD80	49519
EC-HGO	737NG	28384
EC-HGP	737NG	28385
EC-HGQ	737NG	28386
EC-HGR	A319	1154
EC-HGS	A319	1180
EC-HGT	A319	1247
EC-HGU	A340	318
EC-HGV	A340	329
EC-HGX	A340	332
EC-HGY	A320	1200
EC-HGZ	A320	1208
EC-HHA	A320	1221
EC-HHB	A320	1229
EC-HHC	A320	1255
EC-HHF	MD80	49509
EC-HHG	737NG	28608
EC-HHH	737NG	28610
EC-HHI	CRJ	7343
EC-HHP	MD80	49501
EC-HHU	B727	22644
EC-HHV	CRJ	7350
EC-HIF	A310	624
EC-HIG	B727	22641
EC-HIP	B757	29306
EC-HIQ	B757	29307
EC-HIR	B757	29308
EC-HIS	B757	29309
EC-HIT	B757	29310
EC-HIU	B757	29311
EC-HIV	B757	29312
EC-HIX	B757	30052
EC-HJB	MD80	49507
EC-HJH	146	E2112
EC-HJJ	737NG	28617
EC-HJP	737NG	28535
EC-HJQ	737NG	28387
EC-HJV	B727	20895
EC-HKI	A320	1262
EC-HKJ	A320	1278
EC-HKK	A320	1288
EC-HKL	A320	1292
EC-HKM	A320	1318
EC-HKN	A320	1347
EC-HKO	A319	1362
EC-HKP	MD80	49624
EC-HKQ	737NG	28388
EC-HKR	737NG	28536
EC-HKS	B767	27686
EC-HLA	A310	489
EC-HLM	B737	24211
EC-HLN	737NG	28619
EC-HLP	B727	20896
EC-HME	B737	24124
EC-HMI	MD80	49403
EC-HMJ	737NG	28621
EC-HMK	737NG	28624
EC-HNB	B737	26280
EC-HNC	MD80	49620
EC-HND	A300	101
EC-HNO	B737	24214
EC-HNY	B717	55059
EC-HNZ	B717	55060
EC-HOA	B717	55061
EC-HOV	MD80	49416
EC-HPM	A321	1276
EC-HPR	CRJ	7430
EC-HPU	B767	30048
EC-HQF	A340	378
EC-HQG	A320	1379
EC-HQH	A340	387
EC-HQI	A320	1396
EC-HQJ	A320	1430
EC-HQK	A320	1454
EC-HQL	A320	1461
EC-HQM	A320	1484
EC-HQN	A340	414
EC-HQT	A300	124
EC-HQV	B757	23118
EC-HQX	B757	23651
EC-HQZ	A321	1333
EC-HRB	B757	23119
EC-HRG	A321	1366
EC-HRP	A320	1349
EC-HSE	A320	1229
EC-HSF	A320	1255
EC-HSH	CRJ	7466
EC-HSV	B767	29387
EC-HTA	A320	1516
EC-HTB	A320	1530
EC-HTC	A320	1540
EC-HTD	A320	1550
EC-HTE	A321	1554
EC-HTF	A321	1572
EC-HTZ	CRJ	7493
EC-HUH	A321	1021
EC-HUI	A321	1027
EC-HUJ	A320	1292
EC-HUK	A320	1318
EC-HUL	A320	1347
EC-HUT	B757	24121
EC-HUZ	B717	55066
EC-HVB	A310	443
EC-HVD	B747	22454
EC-HVG	B767	29867
EC-HVX	MD80	49572
EC-HVY	B737	24690
EC-HVZ	A300	227
EC-HXA	A320	1497
EC-HXM	CRJ	7514
EC-HXT	B737	24769
EC-HYC	A320	1262
EC-HYD	A320	1288
EC-HYG	CRJ	7529
EC-HZR	CRJ	7547
EC-HZS	737NG	30276
EC-HZU	A320	1578
EC-I	737NG	30281
EC-IAA	CRJ	7563
EC-IAF	B747	22455
EC-IAG	A320	1597
EC-IAZ	A340	1631
EC-IBM	CRJ	7591
EC-ICD	737NG	30785
EC-ICF	A340	459
EC-ICK	A320	1657
EC-ICL	A320	1682
EC-ICN	A320	1717
EC-ICQ	A320	0199
EC-ICR	A320	0240
EC-ICS	A320	0241
EC-ICT	A320	0264
EC-ICU	A320	0303
EC-ICV	A320	0312
EC-IDA	737NG	32773
EC-IDB	A330	461
EC-IDC	CRJ	7622
EC-IDF	A340	474
EC-IDQ	B727	19489
EC-IEF	A320	1655
EC-IEG	A320	1674
EC-IEI	A320	1694
EC-IEJ	A320	1749
EC-IEN	737NG	28592
EC-IEP	A320	1775
EC-IEQ	A320	1767
EC-IEZ	B737	23628
EC-IFC	B727	22643
EC-IFN	B737	24124
EC-IFV	B737	23626
EC-IGC	B757	24747
EC-IGK	A321	1572
EC-IGO	CRJ	7661
EC-IGZ	DC-8	46133
EC-IHI	B737	25134
EC-IHV	A310	640
EC-IIG	A321	1554
EC-IIH	A340	483
EC-III	737NG	30284
EC-IIR	E145	145540
EC-IIZ	A320	1862
EC-IJE	CRJ	7700
EC-IJF	CRJ	7705
EC-IJH	A330	072
EC-IJN	A321	1836
EC-IJS	CRJ	7706
EC-IJU	A321	1843
EC-IKZ	CRJ	7732
EC-ILF	CRJ	7746
EC-ILG	A321	1233
EC-ILH	A320	1914
EC-ILO	A321	1681
EC-ILP	A321	1716
EC-ILQ	A320	1736
EC-ILR	A320	1793
EC-ILS	A320	1809
EC-ILX	737NG	28618
EC-IMA	A321	1219
EC-IMB	A320	1933
EC-IMU	A320	1130
EC-IMY	B727	21293
EC-INB	A321	1946
EC-IND	737NG	28305
EC-INF	CRJ	7785
EC-ING	737NG	28306
EC-INM	A320	1979
EC-INO	A340	431
EC-INP	737NG	32903
EC-INQ	B737	25169
EC-INT	737NG	28304
EC-INZ	A320	2011
EC-IOB	A340	440
EC-IOH	A320	1998
EC-IOO	B747	24106
EC-IOR	B737	24449
EC-IOU	B737	24689
EC-IPF	B737	24125
EC-IPI	A320	2027
EC-IPN	B747	21938
EC-IPS	B737	23827
EC-IPT	A310	642
EC-IPV	F.100	11451
EC-IQA	B767	27310
EC-IQR	A340	460
EC-IRA	B737	24692
EC-IRI	CRJ	7851
EC-ISE	737NG	30290
EC-ISI	A320	2123
EC-ISL	737NG	32740
EC-ISN	737NG	30291
EC-ISY	B757	26241
EC-ITN	A321	2115

Reg	Type	C/n
EC-ITU	CRJ	7866
EC-IUA	B747	23509
EC-IUC	737NG	28612
EC-IVE	B727	20994
EC-IVF	B727	20905
EC-IVG	A320	2168
EC-IVH	CRJ	7915
EC-IVO	F.100	11452
EC-IVR	B737	24352
EC-IVV	737NG	28323
EC-IXD	A321	2220
EC-IXE	737NG	30468
EC-IXO	737NG	30467
EC-IXY	A321	1006
EC-IYB	A330	205
EC-IYG	A320	2210
EC-IYI	737NG	30194
EC-IYN	A330	211
EC-IYS	B737	24690
EC-IZD	A320	2207
EC-IZG	B737	27213
EC-IZH	A320	2225
EC-IZK	A320	2223
EC-IZL	B747	22592
EC-IZM	B737	24027
EC-IZP	CRJ	7950
EC-IZR	A320	2242
EC-IZX	A340	601
EC-IZY	A340	604
EC-JAB	A320	2227
EC-JAP	737NG	33971
EC-JAZ	A319	2264
EC-JBA	A340	606
EC-JBJ	737NG	33972
EC-JBK	737NG	33973
EC-JBL	737NG	33974
EC-JCG	CRJ	7973
EC-JCL	CRJ	7975
EC-JCM	CRJ	7981
EC-JCO	CRJ	7984
EC-JCY	A340	617
EC-JCZ	A340	619
EC-JDH	B747	21726
EC-JDK	A320	1769
EC-JDL	A319	2365
EC-JDM	A321	2357
EC-JDN	F.100	11322
EC-JDO	A320	2114
"EC-JDR"	A320	2347
EC-JDR	A321	2488
EC-JDU	737NG	32655
EC-JEE	CRJ	7989
EC-JEF	CRJ	8008
EC-JEI	A319	2311
EC-JEJ	A321	2381
EC-JEN	CRJ	7958
EC-JEX	737NG	32669
EC-JFB	737NG	32658
EC-JFF	A320	2388
EC-JFG	A320	2143
EC-JFH	A320	2104
EC-JFP	A320	2391
EC-JFR	B747	22272
EC-JFX	A340	672
EC-JGE	737NG	29671
EC-JGM	A320	2407
EC-JGS	A321	2472
EC-JGU	A340	031
EC-JHC	B727	21619
EC-JHD	B747	23676
EC-JHJ	A320	1775
EC-JHK	737NG	33975
EC-JHL	737NG	33976
EC-JHO	A300	095
EC-JHP	A330	670
EC-JHU	B727	21442
EC-JHV	737NG	30826
EC-JHX	B737	24166
EC-JIB	A320	0496
EC-JIS	A340	007
EC-JIU	A320	1597
EC-JJD	A320	2479
EC-JJG	B747	22593
EC-JJJ	B767	27428
EC-JJM	F.100	11497
EC-JJS	MD80	49793
EC-JJV	B737	23626
EC-JJZ	B737	24672
EC-JKC	MD80	53351
EC-JKZ	737NG	34251
EC-JLE	A340	702
EC-JLI	A321	2563
EC-JMB	A320	2540
EC-JMF	A330	054
(EC-JMG)	A321	2270
EC-JMR	A321	2599
EC-JNA	A320	2596
EC-JNB	CRJ9	15057
EC-JNC	A320	2589
EC-JND	A320	1657
EC-JNF	737NG	33977
EC-JNI	A321	2270
EC-JNQ	A340	727
EC-JNT	A320	2623
EC-JNU	B737	26285
EC-JNX	CRJ	8058
EC-JOD	CRJ	8061
EC-JOH	A340	731
EC-JOI	MD80	53446
EC-JOM	F.100	11498
EC-JOY	CRJ	8064
EC-JOZ	B767	24150
EC-JPF	A330	733
EC-JPL	A320	2678
EC-JPU	A340	744
EC-JQA	B737	23870
EC-JQG	A330	745
EC-JQP	A320	2745
EC-JQQ	A330	749
EC-JQT	A319	2396
EC-JQU	A319	2431
EC-JQV	MD80	49526
EC-JQX	B737	23774
EC-JQZ	A321	2736
EC-JRC	A320	0438
EC-JRE	A321	2756
EC-JRI	A320	2761
EC-JRL	737NG	30568
EC-JRR	MD80	49612
EC-JRT	B757	24772
EC-JRV	F.100	11491
EC-JRX	A320	0580
EC-JSB	A320	2776
EC-JSJ	B737	24126
EC-JSK	A320	2807
EC-JSL	B737	23628
EC-JSS	B737	24128
EC-JST	A320	1767
EC-JSU	MD80	49610
EC-JSY	A320	2785
EC-JTA	A320	0445
EC-JTB	A330	082
EC-JTK	MD80	53348
EC-JTN	B757	25597
EC-JTQ	A320	2794
EC-JTR	A320	2798
EC-JTS	CRJ9	15071
EC-JTT	CRJ9	15074
EC-JTU	CRJ9	15079
EC-JTV	A340	24027
EC-JUC	B737	24672
EC-JUF	MD80	53168
EC-JUG	MD80	49847
EC-JUV	B737	23741
EC-JVE	A319	2843
EC-JVJ	146	E3195
EC-JVO	146	E3179
EC-JVV	MD80	49906
EC-JXA	A320	2870
EC-JXD	B737	23633
EC-JXJ	A319	2889
EC-JXV	A319	2897
EC-JXZ	CRJ9	15087
EC-JYA	CRJ9	15090
EC-JYB	E145	145155
EC-JYD	MD80	49605
EC-JYV	CRJ9	15106
EC-JYX	A320	2962
EC-JZI	A320	2988
EC-JZL	A330	814
EC-JZM	A321	2996
EC-JZQ	A320	0992
EC-JZS	CRJ9	15111
EC-JZT	CRJ9	15113
EC-JZU	CRJ9	15115
EC-JZV	CRJ9	15117
EC-JZX	B717	55065
EC-K..	A320	3246
EC-KAJ	A340	015
EC-KAX	A320	3040
EC-KAZ	MD80	49614
EC-KBA	MD80	53052
EC-KBI	E145	145362
EC-KBJ	A319	3054
EC-KBM	A320	0426
EC-KBO	B737	23870
EC-KBQ	A320	1657
EC-KBU	A320	1413
EC-KBV	737NG	33980
EC-KBX	A319	3078
EC-KCF	A340	013
EC-KCG	737NG	33981
EC-KCL	A340	005
EC-KCP	A330	833
EC-KCU	A320	3109
EC-KCX	MD80	49619
EC-KCZ	MD80	49609
EC-KDD	A320	1767
EC-KDF	A330	822
EC-KDG	A320	3095
EC-KDH	A320	3083
EC-KDI	A319	3102
EC-KDJ	B737	23743
EC-KDT	A320	3145
EC-KDX	A320	3151
EC-KDY	B737	23811
EC-KDZ	B737	27826
EC-KEC	A320	1183
EC-KEN	A320	1597
EC-KEO	737NG	33982
EC-KEP	B747	23652
EC-KET	MD80	49608
EC-KEV	A319	3169
EC-KEZ	A320	3152
EC-KFB	737NG	28591
EC-KFI	A320	3174
EC-KFM	A320	0088
EC-KFQ	E145	14500995
EC-KFR	B717	55056
EC-KFT	A320	3179
EC-KGM	B737	24494
EC-KHA	MD80	49611
EC-KHI	B737	24026
EC-KHJ	A320	2347
EC-KHM	A319	3209
EC-KHN	A320	3203
EC-KHT	E145	14500863
EC-KHX	B717	55053
EC-KID	A320	0087
EC-KIK	A320	0662
EC-KIL	A330	205
EC-KIM	A330	211
EC-KIN	737NG	28628
EC-KJC	A319	3255
EC-KJD	A320	3237
EC-KJE	MD80	49606
EC-KJG	A320	0342
EC-KJI	MD80	49836
EC-KJL	A310	501

Ireland

Reg	Type	C/n
EI-ALA	B707	18041
EI-ALB	B707	18042
EI-ALC	B707	18043
EI-AMW	B707	18737
EI-ANE	1-11	049
EI-ANF	1-11	050
EI-ANG	1-11	051
EI-ANH	1-11	052
EI-ANO	B707	18880
EI-ANV	B707	19001
EI-APG	B707	19410
(EI-APP)	B737	19424
(EI-APS)	B737	19425
EI-ASA	B737	19424
EI-ASB	B737	19425
EI-ASC	B737	20218
EI-ASD	B737	20219
EI-ASE	B737	20220
EI-ASF	B737	20221
EI-ASG	B737	20222
EI-ASH	B737	20223
EI-ASI	B747	19744
EI-ASJ	B747	19745
EI-ASK	B737	19947
EI-ASL	B737	21011
EI-ASM	B707	19263
EI-ASN	B707	18976
EI-ASO	B707	19354
EI-ATR	SE210	110
EI-AVY	SE210	108
EI-BCC	B737	21131
EI-BCR	B737	20276
EI-BDY	B737	21112
(EI-BEA)	B737	21112
EI-BEB	B737	21714
EI-BEC	B737	21715
EI-BED	B747	19748
EI-BEE	B737	20413
EI-BEF	B737	20449
EI-BER	B707	19212
EI-BFC	B737	20336
EI-BFN	B707	17719
EI-BFU	B707	17929
EI-BII	B737	21279
EI-BJE	B737	19742
EI-BJP	B737	19743
EI-BKQ	B707	18832
EI-BLC	B707	19964
(EI-BMB)	B737	22071
EI-BMY	B737	21278
EI-BNA	DC-8	45989
EI-BNS	B737	20521
EI-BOC	B737	20455
(EI-BOG)	B737	22071
EI-BOJ	B737	22071
EI-BOM	B737	22368
EI-BON	B737	22369
EI-BOS	B747	19898
EI-BOU	B747	20013
EI-BPG	DC-8	45897
EI-BPH	B747	20013
EI-BPR	B737	21775
EI-BPV	B737	22024
EI-BPW	B737	21776
EI-BPY	B737	21774
EI-BRA	B727	20580
EI-BRB	B737	22279
EI-BRD	B727	20580
EI-BRF	B727	20710
EI-BRN	B737	22529
EI-BRR	B747	20014
EI-BRZ	B737	22703
EI-BSS	1-11	BAC.402
EI-BSY	1-11	BAC.266
EI-BSZ	1-11	BAC.272
EI-BTA	MD80	49391
EI-BTB	MD80	49392
EI-BTC	MD80	49393
EI-BTD	MD80	49394
EI-BTF	B737	23684
EI-BTG	DC-8	46001
EI-BTI	MD80	49398
EI-BTL	MD80	49399
EI-BTM	B737	23826
EI-BTN	L1011	193C-1046

Reg	Type	Ser	Reg	Type	Ser	Reg	Type	Ser	Reg	Type	Ser
EI-BTQ	B747	21650	EI-BZX	DC-9	47059	EI-CGY	DC-8	45976	**EI-CNR**	**MD80**	**53199**
EI-BTR	B737	21735	EI-BZY	DC-9	47085	EI-CGZ	B737	21685	EI-CNS	B767	27600
EI-BTS	B747	22381	EI-BZZ	DC-9	47122	EI-CHA	B737	23747	EI-CNT	B737	22115
EI-BTT	B737	23921	(EI-B..)	B737	22396	EI-CHB	B737	21206	EI-CNV	B737	22128
EI-BTU	MD80	49619	(EI-CAG)	B767	25421	EI-CHC	B737	21686	EI-CNW	B737	22133
EI-BTV	MD80	49620	EI-CAI	B747	20108	EI-CHD	B737	23176	EI-CNX	B737	22127
EI-BTW	B737	21960	EI-CAK	DC-8	46121	EI-CHE	B737	23826	EI-CNY	B737	22113
EI-BTX	MD80	49660	EI-CAL	B767	24952	**EI-CHH**	**B737**	**23177**	EI-CNZ	B737	22126
(EI-BTY)	MD80	49661	EI-CAM	B767	24953	EI-CHQ	B737	23173	EI-COA	B737	22637
EI-BTY	MD80	49667	EI-CAS	1-11	BAC.406	EI-CHU	B737	23175	EI-COB	B737	22124
EI-BTZ	B737	22576	(EI-CAV)	DC-8	46121	EI-CIB	1-11	BAC.191	EI-COF	146	E1006
EI-BUD	B737	23809	EI-CBA	DC-9	47123	EI-CIC	1-11	BAC.177	**EI-COH**	**B737**	**27001**
EI-BUE	B737	23810	EI-CBB	DC-9	45785	EI-CID	1-11	BAC.174	**EI-COI**	**B737**	**27002**
EI-BUI	B727	19249	EI-CBE	MD80	49398	EI-CIE	1-11	BAC.176	**EI-COJ**	**B737**	**27005**
(EI-BUO)	1-11	BAC.255	EI-CBG	DC-9	47742	**EI-CIW**	**MD80**	**49785**	**EI-COK**	**B737**	**27003**
EI-BUP	B727	18877	EI-CBH	DC-9	47796	EI-CIX	B737	24911	EI-COL	L1011	193B-1036
(EI-BUQ)	1-11	BAC.406	EI-CBI	DC-9	48122	EI-CIY	B767	25208	EI-CON	B737	22396
(EI-BVD)	B707	18873	EI-CBL	B737	20957	EI-CJA	B767	26387	EI-COQ	146	E1254
EI-BVG	1-11	BAC.255	EI-CBM	L1011	193P-1068	EI-CJB	B767	26388	EI-COU	DC-8	24690
EI-BVH	1-11	BAC.407	EI-CBN	MD80	49401	EI-CJC	B737	22640	(EI-COW)	L1011	193A-1158
EI-BVI	1-11	BAC.256	EI-CBO	MD80	49442	EI-CJD	B737	22966	EI-COX	B737	22123
EI-BVO	B727	20381	EI-CBP	B737	24905	EI-CJE	B737	22639	EI-CPA	MD80	49936
EI-BWA	DC-9	47656	**EI-CBQ**	**B737**	**24907**	EI-CJF	B737	22967	EI-CPB	MD80	49940
EI-BWB	MD80	49661	**EI-CBR**	**MD80**	**49939**	EI-CJG	B737	22058	**EI-CPC**	**A321**	**0815**
EI-BWC	B737	23024	**EI-CBS**	**MD80**	**49942**	EI-CJH	B737	22057	**EI-CPD**	**A321**	**0841**
EI-BWC	MD80	49668	EI-CBT	B737	24692	EI-CJI	B737	22875	**EI-CPE**	**A321**	**0926**
EI-BWD	MD80	49575	(EI-CBU)	MD80	49673	EI-CJK	A300	020	**EI-CPF**	**A321**	**0991**
EI-BWE	MD80	49661	EI-CBW	A300	269	EI-CJP	146	E1160	**EI-CPG**	**A321**	**1023**
EI-BWF	B747	21575	EI-CBX	MD80	49943	EI-CJW	B737	21355	**EI-CPH**	**A321**	**1094**
EI-BWG	DC-8	46099	**EI-CBY**	**MD80**	**49944**	EI-CJX	B757	26160	EI-CPJ	146	E1258
EI-BWI	1-11	007	**EI-CBZ**	**MD80**	**49945**	EI-CJY	B757	26161	EI-CPK	146	E1260
EI-BWJ	1-11	009	**EI-CCC**	**MD80**	**49946**	EI-CKB	MD80	49400	EI-CPL	146	E1267
EI-BWK	1-11	011	**EI-CCE**	**MD80**	**49947**	EI-CKD	B767	26205	EI-CPU	B737	27004
EI-BWL	1-11	012	EI-CCU	1-11	BAC.237	EI-CKE	B767	26208	EI-CPV	B767	25132
EI-BWM	1-11	013	(EI-CCV)	1-11	BAC.201	EI-CKK	B737	21612	EI-CPY	146	E1003
EI-BWN	1-11	020	EI-CCW	1-11	BAC.186	EI-CKL	B737	21356	(EI-CPZ)	737NG	28575
EI-BWO	1-11	041	EI-CCX	1-11	BAC.211	**EI-CKM**	**MD80**	**49792**	(EI-CRA)	737NG	28578
EI-BWP	1-11	043	EI-CDA	B737	24878	EI-CKP	B737	22296	EI-CRC	B737	24124
EI-BWQ	1-11	057	EI-CDB	B737	24919	EI-CKQ	B737	22906	**EI-CRD**	**B767**	**26259**
EI-BWR	1-11	061	EI-CDC	B737	24968	EI-CKR	B737	22025	**EI-CRE**	**MD80**	**49854**
EI-BWS	1-11	085	**EI-CDD**	**B737**	**24989**	EI-CKS	B737	22023	**EI-CRF**	**B767**	**25170**
EI-BWT	1-11	BAC.127	**EI-CDE**	**B737**	**25115**	EI-CKV	B737	23747	**EI-CRH**	**MD80**	**49935**
EI-BWY	B737	22744	**EI-CDF**	**B737**	**25737**	EI-CKW	B737	21677	**EI-CRJ**	**MD80**	**53013**
EI-BWZ	B737	23023	**EI-CDG**	**B737**	**25738**	EI-CLG	146	E3131	**EI-CRK**	**A330**	**070**
(EI-BX.)	B737	23066	**EI-CDH**	**B737**	**25739**	(EI-CLG)	146	E3155	**EI-CRL**	**B767**	**30008**
EI-BXA	B737	24474	EI-CDI	MD11	48499	EI-CLH	146	E3146	**EI-CRM**	**B767**	**30009**
EI-BXB	B737	24521	EI-CDJ	MD11	48500	EI-CLI	146	E3159	EI-CRN	B737	23008
EI-BXC	B737	24773	EI-CDK	MD11	48501	EI-CLJ	146	E3155	**EI-CRO**	**B767**	**29383**
EI-BXD	B737	24866	(EI-CDL)	MD11	48502	EI-CLK	B737	21733	EI-CRP	737NG	29078
EI-BXE	B737	24878	(EI-CDM)	MD11	48503	EI-CLM	B757	24367	EI-CRQ	737NG	29080
EI-BXF	B737	24919	(EI-CDN)	MD11	48504	EI-CLN	B737	21443	EI-CRS	B777	29908
EI-BXG	B737	24968	EI-CDO	1-11	BAC.201	EI-CLO	B737	21444	EI-CRT	B777	28676
EI-BXH	B737	24989	EI-CDS	B737	26287	EI-CLP	B757	25620	**EI-CRW**	**MD80**	**49951**
EI-BXI	B737	25052	EI-CDT	B737	25165	EI-CLR	B767	25411	**EI-CRZ**	**B737**	**26322**
(EI-BXJ)	B737	25115	**EI-CDY**	**MD80**	**49948**	EI-CLS	B767	26262	**EI-CSA**	**737NG**	**29916**
EI-BXK	B737	25736	(EI-CEA)	B767	25411	EI-CLU	B767	26274	**EI-CSB**	**737NG**	**29917**
(EI-BXM)	B737	23065	EI-CEB	A300	240	EI-CLV	B757	26275	**EI-CSC**	**737NG**	**29918**
EI-BXV	B737	20492	EI-CEE	B737	23923	**EI-CLW**	**B737**	**25187**	**EI-CSD**	**737NG**	**29919**
EI-BXW	B737	22743	EI-CEH	MD80	49950	EI-CLY	146	E3149	**EI-CSE**	**737NG**	**29920**
EI-BXY	B737	22278	EI-CEK	MD80	49631	**EI-CLZ**	**B737**	**25179**	**EI-CSF**	**737NG**	**29921**
EI-BZA	B747	22496	EI-CEM	B767	25421	EI-CMA	B757	25054	**EI-CSG**	**737NG**	**29922**
EI-BZB	A300	083	EI-CEO	B747	21730	EI-CMD	B767	27392	**EI-CSH**	**737NG**	**29923**
EI-BZD	DC-10	46976	**EI-CEP**	**MD80**	**53122**	EI-CME	B767	27393	**EI-CSI**	**737NG**	**29924**
EI-BZE	B737	24464	**EI-CEQ**	**MD80**	**53123**	EI-CMH	B767	27568	**EI-CSJ**	**737NG**	**29925**
EI-BZF	B737	24465	**EI-CER**	**MD80**	**53123**	EI-CMM	MD80	49937	EI-CSK	146	E2062
EI-BZG	B737	24466	EI-CEU	B737	24345	EI-CMO	B737	23866	EI-CSL	146	E2074
EI-BZH	B737	24546	EI-CEV	B737	23979	EI-CMP	DC-9	47089	**EI-CSM**	**737NG**	**29926**
EI-BZI	B737	24547	EI-CEW	B737	23981	EI-CMQ	B767	27993	**EI-CSN**	**737NG**	**29927**
EI-BZJ	B737	24677	**EI-CEY**	**B757**	**26152**	**EI-CMS**	**146**	**E2044**	**EI-CSO**	**737NG**	**29928**
EI-BZK	B737	24678	**EI-CEZ**	**B757**	**26154**	**EI-CMY**	**146**	**E2039**	**EI-CSP**	**737NG**	**29929**
EI-BZL	B737	24680	EI-CFQ	B737	24255	(EI-CMZ)	146	E2046	**EI-CSQ**	**737NG**	**29930**
EI-BZM	B737	24681	EI-CFR	B767	25865	EI-CMZ	MD80	49390	**EI-CSR**	**737NG**	**29931**
EI-BZN	B737	24770	(EI-CFS)	B737	26065	**EI-CNB**	**146**	**E2046**	**EI-CSS**	**737NG**	**29932**
EI-BZO	B737	23922	(EI-CFT)	B737	25288	EI-CNE	B737	25116	**EI-CST**	**737NG**	**29933**
EI-BZP	B737	23923	(EI-CFU)	B737	25289	EI-CNF	B757	25180	**EI-CSU**	**B737**	**27626**
EI-BZQ	B737	24462	**EI-CFZ**	**MD80**	**53120**	EI-CNI	146	E2299	**EI-CSV**	**737NG**	**29934**
EI-BZR	B737	24463	EI-CGA	MD80	49668	EI-CNJ	146	E2300	**EI-CSW**	**737NG**	**29935**
EI-BZS	B737	23747	EI-CGI	MD80	49624	EI-CNK	146	E2306	**EI-CSY**	**737NG**	**32778**
EI-BZT	B737	23748	EI-CGO	DC-8	45924	EI-CNN	L1011	193K-1024	**EI-CSZ**	**737NG**	**32779**
EI-BZU	DC-8	45994	EI-CGR	MD80	49642	EI-CNO	MD80	49672	**EI-CTA**	**737NG**	**32780**
EI-BZV	MD80	49784	EI-CGS	MD80	49626	EI-CNP	B737	21192	**EI-CTA**	**737NG**	**29936**
EI-BZW	DC-9	47126	(EI-CGX)	B737	23177	**EI-CNQ**	**146**	**E2031**	**EI-CTB**	**737NG**	**29937**

Registration	Type	c/n
EI-CTD	A320	0085
EI-CTE	MD80	49517
EI-CTF	MD80	49521
EI-CTJ	MD80	53147
EI-CTM	146	E3129
EI-CTN	146	E3169
EI-CTO	146	E3193
EI-CTP	MD80	49509
EI-CTQ	MD80	49519
EI-CTV	MD80	49501
EI-CTW	B767	30342
EI-CTX	B737	23006
EI-CTY	146	E2072
EI-CUA	B737	24901
EI-CUC	A320	1152
EI-CUD	B737	26298
EI-CUF	MD80	49507
EI-CUK	A320	1198
EI-CUL	B737	28559
EI-CUM	A320	0542
EI-CUN	B737	27074
EI-CUO	146	E1223
EI-CUQ	A320	1259
EI-CVA	A320	1242
EI-CVB	A320	1394
EI-CVC	A320	1443
EI-CVD	A320	1467
(EI-CVG)	B747	30885
(EI-CVH)	B747	32337
(EI-CVI)	B747	32338
(EI-CVJ)	B747	32339
(EI-CVK)	B747	32340
EI-CVN	B737	24684
EI-CVO	B737	25594
EI-CVP	B737	26081
EI-CWA	146	E2022
EI-CWA	146	E2058
EI-CWB	146	E2051
EI-CWC	146	E2053
EI-CWD	146	E2108
EI-CWE	B737	24232
EI-CWF	B737	24814
EI-CWJ	B717	55068
EI-CWK	B717	55152
EI-CWM	B717	55134
EI-CWN	B717	55135
EI-CWT	A320	1413
EI-CWU	A320	1439
EI-CWV	A320	1450
EI-CWW	B737	24906
EI-CWX	B737	24912
EI-CWY	A319	1429
EI-CWZ	A319	1494
EI-CXA	A319	1612
EI-CXB	B767	24484
EI-CXD	737NG	29885
EI-CXE	737NG	32737
EI-CXF	A330	358
EI-CXG	A330	364
EI-CXH	B737	24070
EI-CXI	B737	28661
EI-CXJ	B737	25164
EI-CXK	B737	25596
EI-CXL	B737	28723
EI-CXM	B737	26302
EI-CXN	B737	23772
EI-CXO	B767	28111
EI-CXP	737NG	30467
EI-CXR	B737	24355
EI-CXT	737NG	30468
(EI-CXT)	737NG	32364
EI-CXU	737NG	28323
EI-CXV	737NG	32364
EI-CXW	737NG	30194
EI-CXZ	B767	24973
EI-CZB	B757	25597
EI-CZD	B767	23623
EI-CZE	A319	1184
EI-CZF	A319	1160
EI-CZG	B737	25740
EI-CZH	B767	29435
EI-CZK	B737	24519
EI-CZO	146	E2024
EI-CZR	A330	290
EI-CZS	A330	296
EI-CZT	A330	300
EI-CZV	A320	0553
EI-CZW	A320	0559
EI-DAA	A330	397
EI-DAC	737NG	29938
EI-DAD	737NG	33544
EI-DAE	737NG	33545
EI-DAF	737NG	29939
EI-DAH	737NG	33546
EI-DAI	737NG	33547
EI-DAJ	737NG	33548
EI-DAK	737NG	33717
EI-DAL	737NG	33718
EI-DAM	737NG	33719
EI-DAN	737NG	33549
EI-DAO	737NG	33550
EI-DAP	737NG	33551
EI-DAQ	737NG	33552
EI-DAR	737NG	33553
EI-DAT	737NG	33554
EI-DAV	737NG	33555
EI-DAW	737NG	33556
EI-DAX	737NG	33557
EI-DAY	737NG	33558
EI-DAZ	737NG	33559
EI-DBC	A320	1787
EI-DBD	A320	1975
EI-DBE	F.100	11329
EI-DBF	B767	24745
EI-DBG	B767	24746
EI-DBK	B777	32783
EI-DBL	B777	32781
EI-DBM	B777	32782
EI-DBP	B767	26389
EI-DBR	F.100	11323
EI-DBS	A321	1202
EI-DBU	B767	25077
EI-DBW	B767	23899
EI-DBY	146	E2012
EI-DBZ	146	E2014
EI-DCB	737NG	33560
EI-DCC	737NG	33561
EI-DCD	737NG	33562
EI-DCE	737NG	33563
EI-DCF	737NG	33804
EI-DCG	737NG	33805
EI-DCH	737NG	33566
EI-DCI	737NG	33567
EI-DCJ	737NG	33564
EI-DCK	737NG	33565
EI-DCL	737NG	33806
EI-DCM	737NG	33807
EI-DCN	737NG	33808
EI-DCO	737NG	33809
EI-DCP	737NG	33810
EI-DCR	737NG	33811
EI-DCS	737NG	33812
EI-DCT	737NG	33813
EI-DCV	737NG	33814
EI-DCW	737NG	33568
EI-DCX	737NG	33569
EI-DCY	737NG	33570
EI-DCZ	737NG	33815
EI-DDE	146	E2060
EI-DDF	146	E2047
EI-DDH	B777	32784
EI-DDK	B737	24165
EI-DDS	A321	1451
EI-DDT	B737	29073
EI-DDU	A330	463
EI-DDV	A330	504
EI-DDW	B767	26608
EI-DDY	B737	24904
EI-DEA	A320	2191
EI-DEB	A320	2206
EI-DEC	A320	2217
EI-DEE	A320	2250
EI-DEF	A320	2256
EI-DEG	A320	2272
EI-DEH	A320	2294
EI-DEI	A320	2374
EI-DEJ	A320	2364
EI-DEK	A320	2399
EI-DEL	A320	2409
EI-DEM	A320	2411
EI-DEN	A320	2432
EI-DEO	A320	2486
EI-DEP	A320	2542
EI-DER	A320	2583
EI-DES	A320	2635
EI-DET	A320	2810
EI-DEV	146	E3123
EI-DEW	146	E3142
EI-DEX	146	E3157
EI-DEY	A319	1102
EI-DEZ	A319	1283
EI-DFA	A319	1305
EI-DFB	F.100	11290
EI-DFC	F.100	11296
EI-DFD	B737	24163
EI-DFE	B737	24164
EI-DFF	B737	24167
EI-DFG	E170	17000008
EI-DFH	E170	17000009
EI-DFI	E170	17000010
EI-DFJ	E170	17000011
EI-DFK	E170	17000032
EI-DFL	E170	17000036
EI-DFN	A320	0204
EI-DFO	A320	0371
EI-DFP	A319	1048
EI-DFS	B767	25346
EI-DFT	A320	1635
EI-DFU	A320	1892
EI-DFW	A320	0839
EI-DFZ	F.100	11265
EI-DGB	A320	1902
EI-DGC	A320	1834
EI-DGD	B737	27000
(EI-DGE)	F.100	11351
EI-DGF	A320	0892
EI-DGL	B737	27171
EI-DGM	B737	26437
EI-DGN	B737	25429
EI-DGU	A300	557
EI-DGZ	737NG	28624
EI-DHA	737NG	33571
EI-DHB	737NG	33572
EI-DHC	737NG	33573
EI-DHD	737NG	33816
EI-DHE	737NG	33574
EI-DHF	737NG	33575
EI-DHG	737NG	33576
EI-DHH	737NG	33817
EI-DHI	737NG	33818
EI-DHJ	737NG	33819
EI-DHL	A300	274
EI-DHM	737NG	33821
EI-DHN	737NG	33577
EI-DHO	737NG	33578
EI-DHP	737NG	33579
EI-DHR	737NG	33822
EI-DHS	737NG	33580
EI-DHT	737NG	33581
EI-DHV	737NG	33582
EI-DHW	737NG	33823
EI-DHX	737NG	33585
EI-DHY	737NG	33824
EI-DHZ	737NG	33583
EI-DIG	A320	1597
EI-DIH	A320	1657
EI-DIJ	A320	0391
EI-DIL	737NG	32663
EI-DIM	737NG	29639
EI-DIN	737NG	29668
EI-DIP	A330	339
EI-DIR	A330	272
EI-DIS	737NG	28610
EI-DIT	737NG	28621
EI-DIU	A320	0990
EI-DIV	A320	1856
EI-DIW	A320	1909
EI-DIX	A320	1996
EI-DJH	A320	0814
EI-DJI	A320	1757
EI-DJJ	146	E2040
EI-DJK	B737	24365
EI-DJN	A300	529
EI-DJR	B737	23927
EI-DJS	B737	23926
EI-DJT	737NG	28592
EI-DJU	737NG	28619
EI-DKD	737NG	28617
EI-DKF	A320	1213
EI-DKG	A320	1390
EI-DKH	E145	145155
EI-DKL	B757	28482
EI-DKP	737NG	32578
EI-DKR	737NG	32579
EI-DKS	A320	1372
EI-DKV	B737	24272
EI-DKX	737NG	32577
EI-DLA	DC-10	46958
EI-DLB	737NG	33584
EI-DLC	737NG	33586
EI-DLD	737NG	33825
EI-DLE	737NG	33587
EI-DLF	737NG	33588
EI-DLG	737NG	33589
EI-DLH	737NG	33590
EI-DLI	737NG	33591
EI-DLJ	737NG	34177
EI-DLK	737NG	33592
EI-DLL	737NG	33593
EI-DLM	737NG	33594
EI-DLN	737NG	33595
EI-DLO	737NG	34178
EI-DLR	737NG	33596
EI-DLS	737NG	33621
EI-DLT	737NG	33597
EI-DLV	737NG	33598
EI-DLW	737NG	33599
EI-DLX	737NG	33600
EI-DLY	737NG	33601
EI-DLZ	737NG	33622
EI-DME	737NG	32738
EI-DMF	737NG	32614
EI-DMF	737NG	32616
EI-DMH	B767	23106
EI-DMJ	B767	27958
EI-DMK	146	E2022
EI-DMM	B737	24092
EI-DMN	B737	23411
EI-DMO	A300	533
EI-DMP	B737	24448
EI-DMR	B737	25851
EI-DMV	E145	145165
EI-DMW	E145	145227
EI-DMX	737NG	34297
EI-DMY	737NG	34298
EI-DMZ	737NG	29671
EI-DNA	B757	28483
EI-DNB	737NG	34299
EI-DNC	737NG	34300
EI-DND	737NG	28612
EI-DNH	B737	25614
EI-DNJ	146	E2136
EI-DNK	A320	0305
EI-DNM	B737	24166
EI-DNP	A320	0421
EI-DNS	B737	23771
EI-DNT	B737	24356
EI-DNX	B737	29055
EI-DNY	B737	23360
EI-DNZ	B737	23363
EI-DOD	A320	0444
EI-DOE	A320	0215
EI-DOF	B767	27610
EI-DOH	B737	29056
EI-DOM	B737	24011
EI-DON	B737	23812

Reg	Type	S/N		Reg	Type	S/N		Reg	Type	S/N		Reg	Type	S/N
EI-DOO	B737	23971		EI-DVP	CRJ9	15116		EI-RJE	146	E2335		EK-32007	A320	0726
EI-DOP	A320	0816		EI-DVR	CRJ9	15118		EI-RJF	146	E2337		EK-32008	A320	0229
EI-DOR	B737	24689		EI-DVS	CRJ9	15119		EI-RJG	146	E2344		(EK-32009)	A320	0142
EI-DOS	B737	28881		EI-DVT	CRJ9	15123		EI-RJH	146	E2345		EK-32009	A320	0547
EI-DOT	CRJ9	15066		EI-DVU	A319	0660		EI-RJI	146	E2346		EK-32010	A320	0632
EI-DOU	CRJ9	15068		EI-DVV	E170	17000154		EI-RJJ	146	E2347		EK-32011	A319	2277
EI-DOV	B737	27632		EI-DVW	E170	17000153		EI-RJK	146	E2348		EK-32012	A319	2362
EI-DOZ	A320	0279		EI-DVY	B737	29059		EI-RJL	146	E2349		EK-32075	A320	0575
EI-DPA	737NG	33602		EI-DWA	737NG	33617		EI-RJM	146	E2350		EK-42342	YAK42	1706302
EI-DPB	737NG	33603		EI-DWB	737NG	36075		EI-RJN	146	E2351		EK-42345	YAK42	2708304
EI-DPC	737NG	33604		EI-DWC	737NG	36076		EI-RJO	146	E2352		EK-42362	YAK42	4811431
EI-DPD	737NG	33623		EI-DWD	737NG	33642		EI-RJP	146	E2363		EK-42417	YAK42	3219110
EI-DPE	737NG	33605		EI-DWE	737NG	36074		EI-RJR	146	E2364		EK-65044	TU134	49450
EI-DPF	737NG	33606		EI-DWF	737NG	33619		EI-RJS	146	E2365		EK-65072	TU134	49972
EI-DPG	737NG	33607		EI-DWG	737NG	33620		EI-RJT	146	E2366		EK-65575	TU134	62305
EI-DPH	737NG	33624		EI-DWH	737NG	33637		EI-RJU	146	E2367		EK-65650	TU134	0351006
EI-DPI	737NG	33608		EI-DWI	737NG	33643		EI-RJV	146	E2370		EK-65731?	TU134	1351401
EI-DPJ	737NG	33609		EI-DWJ	737NG	36077		EI-RJW	146	E2371		EK-65822	TU134	09071
EI-DPK	737NG	33610		EI-DWK	737NG	36078		EI-RJX	146	E2372		EK-65831	TU134	17102
EI-DPL	737NG	33611		EI-DWL	737NG	33618		EI-SAF	A300	220		EK-65848	TU134	23136
EI-DPM	737NG	33640		EI-DWM	737NG	36080		(EI-SAI)	B747	21962		EK-65884	TU134	36150
EI-DPN	737NG	35549		EI-DWO	737NG	36079		EI-SHN	A330	054		EK-65975	TU134	3352006
EI-DPO	737NG	33612		EI-DWP	737NG	36082		EI-SKY	B727	20571		EK-72101	AN7x	72040548
EI-DPP	737NG	33613		EI-DWR	737NG	36081		EI-TAA	A320	0912		EK-72102	AN7x	?
EI-DPR	737NG	33614		EI-DWS	737NG	33625		EI-TAB	A320	1624		EK-72902	AN7x	72020362
EI-DPS	737NG	33641		EI-DWT	737NG	33626		EI-TAC	A320	1676		EK-72903	AN7x	72020385
EI-DPT	737NG	35550		EI-DWV	737NG	33627		EI-TAD	A320	1334		EK-74045	AN7x	47098966
EI-DPV	737NG	35551		EI-DWW	737NG	33629		EI-TAE	A320	0874		EK-74701	B747	21352
EI-DPW	737NG	35552		EI-DWX	737NG	33630		EI-TAF	A320	1374		EK-74702	B747	21054
EI-DPX	737NG	35553		EI-DWY	737NG	33638		EI-TAG	A320	2791		EK-74713	B747	23413
EI-DPY	737NG	33615		EI-DWZ	737NG	33628		EI-TAI	A320	0916		EK-74763	B747	24363
EI-DPZ	737NG	33616		EI-DXB	B737	29060		EI-TBG	L1011	193B-1030		EK-74774	B747	26474
EI-DRA	737NG	35114		EI-DXC	B737	26300		EI-TLA	DC-8	45973		EK-74779	B747	26879
EI-DRB	737NG	35115		EI-DXG	B737	25376		EI-TLB	A300	012		EK-74780	B747	23480
EI-DRC	737NG	35116		EI-DXO	B737	27826		EI-TLC	DC-8	45995		EK-74783	B747	24383
EI-DRD	737NG	35117		EI-EAA	A300	150		EI-TLD	DC-8	45812		EK-76400	IL76	1023413438
EI-DRE	737NG	35787		EI-EAB	A300	199		EI-TLE	A320	0429		EK-76445	IL76	1023410330
EI-DRG	A320	0338		EI-EAC	A300	250		EI-TLF	A320	0476		EK-76446	IL76	1023412418
EI-DRI	CRJ9	15076		EI-EAD	A300	289		EI-TLG	A320	0428		EK-76705	IL76	0063472158
EI-DRJ	CRJ9	15077		EI-EAE	A300	095		EI-TLH	A320	0247		EK-76707	IL76	073410292
EI-DRK	CRJ9	15075		EI-EAT	A300	116		EI-TLI	A320	0405		EK-76717	IL76	0073474216
EI-DRR	B737	23181		EI-EWR	A330	330		EI-TLJ	A320	0257		EK-76727	IL76	0073475268
EI-DRS	B737	28599		EI-EWW	B727	21269		EI-TLK	A300	161		EK-85162	TU154	76A-162
EI-DRY	B737	28602		EI-GAA	B767	23179		EI-TLL	A300	158		EK-85166	TU154	76A-166
EI-DRZ	B737	28606		EI-GBA	B767	23180		EI-TLM	A300	046		EK-85196	TU154	77A-196
EI-DSA	A320	2869		EI-GXA	E145	145588		EI-TLN	A300	047		EK-85200	TU154	77A-200
EI-DSB	A320	2932		EI-GXB	E145	145601		EI-TLO	A320	0758		EK-85210	TU154	77A-210
EI-DSC	A320	2995		EI-HCA	B727	20382		EI-TLP	A320	0760		EK-85279	TU154	78A-279
EI-DSD	A320	3076		EI-HCB	B727	19492		EI-TLQ	A300	131		EK-85403	TU154	80A-403
EI-DSE	A320	3079		EI-HCC	B727	19480		EI-TLR	A320	0414		EK-85442	TU154	80A-442
EI-DSF	A320	3080		EI-HCD	B727	20185		EI-TLS	A320	0430		EK-85536	TU154	82A-536
EI-DSG	A320	3115		EI-HCI	B727	20183		EI-TLS	A320	0430		EK-85566	TU154	82A-566
EI-DSH	A320	3178		EI-IGA	B757	24748		EI-TLT	A320	0415		EK-85607	TU154	84A-702
EI-DSI	A320	3213		EI-IGB	B757	24738		EI-TNT	B727	20725		EK-85803	TU154	89A-822
EI-DSJ	A320	3295		(EI-IGL)	B737	23636		EI-TVA	B737	28489		EK-86111	IL86	51483209085
EI-DTP	B737	23182		EI-JET	146	E2073		EI-TVB	B737	28493		EK-86118	IL86	51483209086
EI-DTU	B737	25175		EI-JFK	A330	086		EI-TVC	B737	24688		EK-86724	IL76	073410284
EI-DTV	B737	25183		EI-LAX	A330	269		EI-TVN	B737	28586		EK-86817	IL76	063407191
EI-DTW	B737	25188		EI-LCH	B727	20466		EI-TVO	B737	28333		EK-87316	YAK40	9331529
EI-DTX	B737	28052		(EI-LCY)	E145	145376		EI-TVP	B737	25041		EK-87359	YAK40	9340831
EI-DTY	B737	25017		EI-LTA	B757	27598		EI-TVQ	B737	28568		EK-87356	YAK40	9522041
EI-DUA	B757	26247		EI-LTE	A321	1775		EI-TVR	B737	28571		EK-87662	YAK40	9240625
EI-DUB	A330	055		EI-LTO	B757	30232		EI-TVS	B737	28670		EK-87908	YAK40	9721354
EI-DUC	B757	26248		EI-LTU	B757	30233		EI-UPA	MD11	48426		EK-87937	YAK40	9740856
EI-DUD	B757	26249		EI-LTY	B757	30735		EI-UPE	MD11	48427		EK-88157	YAK40	9611146
EI-DUE	B757	26250		EI-LVB	A321	1970		EI-UPI	MD11	48428		EK-88167	YAK40	9610147
EI-DUK	CRJ9	15104		EI-LVD	A321	0792		EI-UPO	MD11	48429		EK-88171	YAK40	9620947
EI-DUM	CRJ9	15103		EI-MON	B757	26151		EI-UPU	MD11	48430		EK-88199	YAK40	9630249
EI-DUO	A330	841		(EI-NYC)	A330	070		(EI-USA)	A330	059		EK-88250	YAK40	9710452
EI-DUS	B737	24021		EI-ORD	A330	059		EI-VIR	A320	0449		EK-88252	YAK40	9710652
EI-DUU	CRJ9	15102		EI-ORK	E145	145431						EK-88256	YAK40	9711152
EI-DUX	CRJ9	15110		EI-OZA	A300	148						EK-88262	YAK40	9711752
EI-DUY	CRJ9	15112		EI-OZB	A300	184		Armenia				EK-88272	YAK40	9721053
EI-DUZ	A330	847		EI-OZC	A300	189						EK-A001	B737	26855
EI-DVA	B737	25159		EI-PAK	B727	21245		EK-	B747	22711				
EI-DVB	A330	082		EI-PAM	B737	24069		EK-	DC-8	45953				
EI-DVC	B737	25426		EI-PAR	B737	24300		EK-10151	DC-10	48258		Liberia		
EI-DVD	A319	0647		EI-PAT	146	E2030		EK-30039	A300	239				
EI-DVE	A320	3129		EI-RJA	146	E2329		EK-30044	A300	244		(EL-...)	B727	18877
EI-DVF	A320	3136		EI-RJB	146	E2330		EK-30060	A300	160		EL-AAG	SE210	254
EI-DVG	A320	3318		EI-RJC	146	E2333		EK-31088	A310	488		EL-AAS	SE210	154
EI-DVH	A320	3345		EI-RJD	146	E2334		EK-32001	A320	0397		EL-ACP	B707	20547

Reg.	Type	c/n	Reg.	Type	c/n	Reg.	Type	c/n	Reg.	Type	c/n
EL-AIL	B737	21538	EP-ALI	IL76	1003499994	EP-IAH	B747	21218	EP-LAM	YAK42	1304016
EL-AIW	SE210	106	EP-ALJ	IL76	0013434018	EP-IAM	B747	21759	EP-LAN	YAK42	1303016
(EL-AIY)	B707	19377	EP-ALK	IL76	0053465941	EP-IBA	A300	723	EP-LAO	TU154	90A-841
EL-AIY	B707	19986	EP-AMU	B727	19011	EP-IBB	A300	727	EP-LAP	TU154	90A-842
EL-AIY	B727	18892	EP-AMV	B727	19314	EP-IBC	A300	632	EP-LAQ	TU154	90A-850
EL-AIZ	B727	18895	EP-AMW	B727	19314	EP-IBD	A300	696	EP-LAS	TU154	90A-841
EL-AJA	B707	19377	EP-ARG	TU154	91A-899	EP-IBK	A310	671	EP-LAT	TU154	90A-842
EL-AJB	B707	19210	EP-ARH	TU154	91A-904	EP-IBL	A310	436	EP-LAU	TU154	90A-848
EL-AJC	B707	17721	EP-ARI	TU154	?	EP-IBM	A310	338	EP-LAV	TU154	91A-879
EL-AJK	DC-8	46012	EP-ASA	B727	22081	EP-IBN	A310	375	EP-LAX	TU154	92A-913
EL-AJO	DC-8	45683	EP-ASB	B727	22082	EP-IBO	A310	379	EP-LAZ	TU154	93A-976
EL-AJQ	DC-8	45686	EP-ASC	B727	22084	EP-IBP	A310	370	EP-LBA	YAK40	9641250
EL-AJQ	DC-8	45858	EP-ASD	B727	22085	EP-IBQ	A310	389	EP-LBB	YAK40	9610246
EL-AJR	B707	19247	EP-ASE	F.28	11135	EP-IBR	A300	061	EP-LBC	TU154	86A-744
EL-AJS	B707	18873	EP-ASF	F.28	11144	EP-IBS	A300	080	EP-LBD	TU154	86A-743
EL-AJT	B707	18891	EP-ASG	F.100	11438	EP-IBT	A300	185	EP-LBE	TU154	85A-706
EL-AJU	B707	19315	EP-ASH	F.100	11439	EP-IBU	A300	186	EP-LBF	TU154	?
EL-AJV	B707	17635	EP-ASI	F.100	11519	EP-IBV	A300	187	EP-LBG	TU154	85A-706
EL-AJW	B707	17631	EP-ASJ	F.100	11378	EP-IBX	A310	390	EP-LBH	TU154	92A-913
EL-AKA	B707	19335	EP-ASK	F.100	11388	EP-IBZ	A300	226	EP-LBI	TU154	85A-707
EL-AKB	B707	20035	EP-ASL	F.100	11432	EP-ICA	B747	21487	EP-LBJ	YAK40	9642051
EL-AKC	B707	20177	EP-ASM	F.100	11433	EP-ICB	B747	21507	EP-LBK	YAK40	9620947
EL-AKD	B707	18030	EP-ASO	F.100	11454	EP-ICC	B747	21514	EP-LBL	TU154	87A-754
EL-AKE	B727	18877	EP-ASP	F.100	11504	EP-IDA	F.100	11292	EP-LBM	TU154	95A-1007
EL-AKF	B707	18839	EP-ASQ	F.100	11513	(EP-IDB)	F.100	11267	EP-LBN	TU154	85A-717
EL-AKF	B707	18922	EP-ASR	F.100	11522	EP-IDB	F.100	11299	EP-LBR	TU154	90A-838
EL-AKG	L1011	193P-1068	EP-AST	F.100	11523	EP-IDC	F.100	11267	EP-LBS	TU154	91A-901
EL-AKH	B707	19296	EP-AUA?	B747	22670	(EP-IDC)	F.100	11299	EP-LBT	YAK42	2914166
EL-AKI	B707	18925	EP-BOJ	TU154	91A-904	(EP-IDD)	F.100	11287	EP-LBX	TU154	87A-763
EL-AKJ	B707	19375	EP-BOM	TU154	91A-891	EP-IDD	F.100	11294	EP-LCD	TU154	89A-825
EL-AKK	B707	20177	EP-BON	TU154	92A-929	(EP-IDE)	F.100	11294	EP-MAB	TU154	91A-870
EL-AKL	B707	18922	EP-BOS	YAK42	?	(EP-IDE)	F.100	11298	EP-MAC	TU154	90A-857
EL-AKS	B707	20029	EP-CFA	IL76	0093490718	EP-IDF	F.100	11298	EP-MAE	TU154	91A-867
EL-ALA	AN7x	?	EP-CFB	IL76	0093495854	EP-IDG	F.100	11302	EP-MAF	TU154	91A-891
EL-ALD	1-11	011	EP-CFC	IL76	0063466981	(EP-IDH)	F.100	11304	EP-MAG	TU154	92A-929
EL-ALG	B707	20547	EP-CFD	F.100	11442	(EP-IDI)	F.100	11305	EP-MAH	IL76	1023409321
EL-ALI	B707	18689	EP-CFE	F.100	11422	(EP-IDJ)	F.100	11309	EP-MAI	TU154	91A-880
EL-ALJ	B707	18689	EP-CFH	F.100	11443	EP-IDK	F.100	11317	EP-MAJ	TU154	85A-719
EL-ALL	AN7x	72080789	EP-CFI	F.100	11511	(EP-IDL)	F.100	11319	EP-MAK	TU154	91A-884
EL-ALM	IL62	4648414	EP-CFJ	F.100	11516	(EP-IDN)	F.100	11322	EP-MAL	TU154	92A-915
EL-ALX	AN7x	72095909	EP-CFK	F.100	11518	EP-IGA	B737	20892	EP-MAM	TU154	90A-836
EL-ALZ	IL62	3052657	EP-CFL	F.100	11343	EP-IGD	B737	20893	EP-MAN	TU154	93A-961
EL-AMH	IL76	073411334	EP-CFM	F.100	11394	EP-IHK	TU154	?	EP-MAP	TU154	92A-923
FL-AWY	SE210	264	EP-CFN	F.100	11423	EP-IRA	B727	19171	EP-MAQ	TU154	91A-870
EL-CAR	YAK40	9412030	EP-CFO	F.100	11389	EP-IRB	B727	19172	EP-MAR	TU154	92A-932
EL-GNU	B707	19582	EP-CPA	YAK42	3219102	EP-IRC	B727	19816	EP-MAS	TU154	91A-866
EL-GOL	B727	18253	EP-CPB	YAK42	1219029	EP-IRD	B727	19817	EP-MAT	TU154	92A-934
EL-GPX	B727	19129	EP-CPC	YAK42	1401018	EP-IRF	B737	20498	EP-MAU	TU154	91A-904
EL-GPX	B727	20424	EP-CPE	YAK42	3219102	EP-IRG	B737	20499	EP-MAV	TU154	92A-929
EL-JNS	B707	18689	EP-CPF	YAK42	?	EP-IRH	B737	20500	EP-MAX	TU154	91A-891
EL-KRU	DC-8	45821	EP-CPG	TU154	87A-748	EP-IRI	B737	20740	EP-MAZ	TU154	90A-857
EL-LAT	B707	19350	EP-CPH	TU154	91A-897	EP-IRJ	B707	18958	EP-MBA	TU154	90A-860
EL-LIB	1-11	BAC.111	EP-CPI	YAK40	9831158	EP-IRK	B707	19267	EP-MBB	TU154	89A-821
EL-LIC	A300	031	EP-CPK	YAK42	4914477	EP-IRL	B707	20287	EP-MBC	TU154	90A-841
EL-OSZ	SE210	254	EP-CPL	TU154	93A-974	EP-IRM	B707	20288	EP-MBE	TU154	92A-932
EL-RDS	B707	19519	EP-CPM	TU154	87A-763	EP-IRN	B707	20741	EP-MBF	TU154	92A-934
EL-RDT	IL76	053403072	EP-CPN	TU154	91A-898	EP-IRP	B727	20945	EP-MBG	TU154	90A-858
EL-RDX	IL76	043402039	EP-CPO	TU154	91A-899	EP-IRR	B727	20946	EP-MBH	TU154	91A-880
EL-SKD	B707	18586	EP-CPR	YAK42	1219029	EP-IRS	B727	20947	EP-MBJ	TU154	93A-960
EL-TBA	B707	20283	EP-CPS	TU154	93A-957	EP-IRT	B727	21078	EP-MBK	TU154	89A-802
EL-WAM	B707	19335	EP-DAZ	YAK40	9740856	EP-IRU	B727	21079	EP-MBL	TU154	89A-799
EL-WNA	SE210	240	EP-DMS	YAK40	9522041	EP-ITA	TU154	91A-902	EP-MBM	TU154	92A-931
EL-WTA	IL76	1033415504	EP-EAA	TU154	91A-897	EP-ITB	TU154	91A-880	EP-MBN	TU154	92A-940
(EL-WTZ)	B707	19292	EP-EAB	TU154	90A-864	EP-ITC	TU154	91A-874	EP-MBO	TU154	93A-982
EL-WVD	DC-8	45885	EP-EAC	TU154	89A-814	EP-ITD	TU154	91A-903	EP-MBP	TU154	89A-800
EL-ZGS	B707	20261	EP-EAD	TU154	92A-930	EP-ITF	TU154	90A-860	EP-MBQ	TU154	92A-931
			EP-EAG	TU154	90A-864	EP-ITG	TU154	91A-866	EP-MBR	TU154	93A-975
			EP-EAJ	TU154	89A-821	EP-ITI	TU154	92A-939	EP-MBS	TU154	91A-871
Iran			EP-EAK	YAK40	9831058	EP-ITJ	TU154	91A-883	EP-MBT	TU154	92A-930
			EP-EAL	YAK40	9510340	EP-ITK	TU154	91A-877	EP-MBU	TU154	90A-855
EP-	A310	480	EP-EAM	YAK40	9731355	EP-ITL	TU154	89A-810	EP-MBV	TU154	91A-877
(EP-)	F.100	11431	EP-EAN	TU154	89A-800	EP-ITM	TU154	91A-884	EP-MBZ	TU154	91A-902
EP-AGA	B737	21317	EP-EKA	TU154	92A-912	EP-ITN	TU154	92A-942	EP-MCE	TU154	89A-799
EP-AGB	A321	1202	EP-EKB	TU154	93A-946	EP-ITS	TU154	90A-859	EP-MCF	TU154	88A-788
EP-ALA	IL76	0053460795	EP-GDS	B727	19557	EP-ITU	TU154	91A-867	EP-MCG	TU154	91A-883
EP-ALB	IL76	0023437076	EP-HIM	B707	21396	EP-ITV	TU154	89A-810	EP-MCH	TU154	91A-879
EP-ALC	IL76	0023442218	EP-IAA	B747	20998	EP-JAY	IL76	1013409297	EP-MCI	TU154	91A-892
EP-ALD	IL76	1023408265	EP-IAB	B747	20999	EP-JAZ	TU154	91A-898	EP-MCL	TU154	91A-880
EP-ALE	IL76	0043453575	EP-IAC	B747	21093	EP-LAD	TU154	92A-929	EP-MDA	A300	299
EP-ALF	IL76	0033448407	EP-IAD	B747	21758	EP-LAE	YAK42	1304016	EP-MDB	A300	302
EP-ALG	IL76	0033448404	EP-IAG	B747	21217	EP-LAH	YAK42	1303016	EP-MHB	TU154	91A-907
						EP-LAI	TU154	91A-891	EP-MHD	TU154	92A-936

Reg	Type	C/n
EP-MHE	**A300**	**035**
EP-MHF	**A300**	**055**
EP-MHG	**A300**	**204**
EP-MHH	A310	586
EP-MHI	A310	537
EP-MHJ	**A320**	**0857**
EP-MHK	**A320**	**0530**
EP-MHL	**A300**	**175**
EP-MHQ	TU154	93A-946
EP-MHR	TU154	92A-928
EP-MHS	TU154	89A-821
EP-MHT	TU154	93A-960
EP-MHU	YAK40	?
EP-MHV	TU154	92A-932
EP-MHX	TU154	92A-939
EP-MHZ	TU154	91A-890
EP-MKA	IL76	0033446345
EP-MRP	B727	19557
EP-NHA	B707	21123
EP-NHD	B747	19669
EP-NHJ	B747	19667
EP-NHK	B747	19668
EP-NHL	B707	18958
EP-NHN	B747	21486
EP-NHP	**B747**	**20082**
EP-NHR	B747	20081
EP-NHS	B747	20080
EP-NHT	B747	19678
EP-NHV	B747	19667
EP-NHW	B707	20834
EP-NHY	B707	21396
EP-PAS	F.28	11027
EP-PAT	**F.28**	**11164**
EP-PAU	F.28	11166
EP-PAV	F.28	11070
EP-PAX	F.28	11102
EP-PAZ	**F.28**	**11104**
EP-PBA	F.28	11052
EP-PBB	F.28	11093
EP-PBF	F.28	11003
EP-PBG	F.28	11092
EP-PBI	F.28	11135
EP-PBI	F.28	11144
EP-PCB	**IL76**	**1023409321**
EP-PCC	IL76	1013409297
EP-PLN	B727	18363
EP-QFA	**YAK42**	**2007018**
EP-QFB	**YAK42**	**2003019**
EP-RAB	IL76	0053465941
EP-RAJ	IL76	0033447365
EP-RAM	IL76	0083485554
EP-SAF	YAK42	2014576
EP-SAG	YAK42	4814047
EP-SFA	IL76	0093495854
EP-SFB	IL76	1023411378
EP-SHA	**B747**	**21507**
EP-SHB	B747	21486
EP-SHC	B747	20080
EP-SHD	**B747**	**20081**
EP-SHE	B707	21127
EP-SHE	B707	21128
EP-SHG	B707	20830
EP-SHG	B707	21125
EP-SHH	**B747**	**21487**
EP-SHJ	B707	21127
EP-SHK	**B707**	**21128**
EP-SHP	B707	20835
EP-SHP	**B707**	**21123**
EP-SHP	B727	18363
EP-SHU	**B707**	**21126**
EP-SHV	**B707**	**21125**
EP-TAK	YAK42	11030603
EP-TAV?	YAK42	2914166
EP-TPD	IL76	0083485558
EP-TPF	IL76	0013428831
EP-TPO	IL76	063407191
(EP-TPU)	IL76	0083487598
EP-TPU	**IL76**	**0093497936**
EP-TPV	**IL76**	**0043451523**
EP-TPW	IL76	0083487627
EP-TPX	IL76	0083484551
EP-TPY	IL76	0083482490

Reg	Type	C/n
EP-TPZ		
EP-TQA	YAK40	9340831
EP-TQC	IL76	0023437076
EP-TQD	TU154	86A-725
EP-TQE	TU154	92A-940
EP-TQF	YAK40	9831058
EP-TQG	YAK40	9240625
EP-TQH	YAK40	9510340
EP-TQI	IL76	1023409321
EP-TQJ	IL76	1013409297
EP-TQM	TU154	91A-906
EP-TQP	YAK40	9740856
EP-TQR	YAK40	9631648
EP-TQS	YAK40	9522041
EP-TQU	YAK40	9630249
EP-TUA	YAK40	9421035
EP-TUB	TU154	93A-955
EP-TUE	TU154	90A-865
EP-TUF	YAK40	9421035
EP-YAA	YAK42	2219055
EP-YAB	YAK42	2219066
EP-YAC	YAK42	4116698
EP-YAD	YAK42	?
EP-YAE	YAK42	1014543
EP-YAF	YAK42	3811421

Moldova

Reg	Type	C/n
ER-AAZ	TU134	62390
ER-ACA	AN7x	72094889
ER-ACF	AN7x	72094888
ER-ACG	IL76	1013405184
ER-ACN	AN7x	47095898
ER-AEJ	**AN7x**	**72094889**
ER-AEN	AN7x	47095898
ER-AEO	AN7x	47060649
ER-AER	AN7x	72094888
ER-AFZ	**AN7x**	**72070698**
ER-AVD	AN7x	72080786
ER-AVE	**AN7x**	**72080780**
ER-AVG	**AN7x**	**72095909**
ER-AWF	**AN7x**	**72070696**
ER-AWQ	AN7x	72070688
ER-AWS	AN7x	72093876
ER-AXT	**A320**	**0249**
ER-AXV	**A320**	**0622**
ER-AXW	A320	0662
ER-FZA	**F.100**	**11395**
ER-IAS	**IL76**	**1013406204**
ER-IAT	**IL76**	**0003425746**
ER-IAU	**IL76**	**0013432955**
ER-IBB	IL76	0063471147
ER-IBC	**IL76**	**0023442218**
ER-IBC	IL76	0083489683
ER-IBD	**IL76**	**073411338**
ER-IBE	IL76	0043454615
ER-IBF	**IL76**	**073410300**
ER-IBG	**IL76**	**093418548**
ER-IBH	**IL76**	**073411331**
ER-IBK	**IL76**	**0053460790**
ER-IBL	IL76	0053463908
ER-IBM	IL76	0063466981
ER-IBN	**IL76**	**0033448390**
ER-IBO	IL76	0043452546
ER-IBP	**IL76**	**093418556**
ER-IBR	IL76	0043454623
ER-IBS	IL76	0053460827
ER-IBT	IL76	0033447364
ER-IBV	**IL76**	**0003423699**
ER-IBW	IL76	093418543
ER-IBY	**IL76**	**0053460832**
ER-JGA	YAK40	9521640
ER-JGD	YAK40	9421334
ER-JGE	YAK40	9810757
ER-TAG	TU154	91A-895
ER-TAI	TU154	82A-546
ER-TCF	TU134	62390
ER-TCH	TU134	63.48565
ER-YCA	YAK42	4306017
ER-YCB	YAK42	4304017
ER-YCC	YAK42	3016309

Reg	Type	C/n
ER-YCD	YAK42	11040105
ER-YCE	YAK42	2007018
ER-YCF	YAK42	2003019
ER-YGA	YAK40	9540444
ER-YGB	YAK40	9820558
ER-YGC	YAK40	9411333
ER-YGD	**YAK40**	**9831458**
ER-YGR	YAK40	9521640
ER-42409	YAK42	1216709
ER-65036	TU134	63.48700
ER-65050	TU134	49756
ER-65051	TU134	49758
ER-65071	TU134	49915
ER-65094	TU134	83.60255
ER-65140	**TU134**	**60932**
ER-65686	TU134	62390
ER-65707	TU134	63435
ER-65736	TU134	2351501
ER-65741	TU134	2351601
ER-65791	TU134	63110
ER-65897	TU134	42210
ER-72932	AN7x	72070696
ER-72933	AN7x	72070698
ER-72975	AN7x	72094888
ER-72977	AN7x	72094889
ER-85044	TU154	73A-044
ER-85090	TU154	75A-090
ER-85285	TU154	78A-285
ER-85324	TU154	79A-324
ER-85332	TU154	79A-332
ER-85384	TU154	79A-384
ER-85405	TU154	80A-405
ER-85565	TU154	82A-565
ER-87230	YAK40	9541542
ER-87359	YAK40	9340831
ER-88202	YAK40	9630449

Estonia

Reg	Type	C/n
ES-AAE	TU134	48395
ES-AAF	TU134	63.48565
ES-AAG	TU134	49907
ES-AAH	TU134	35270
ES-AAI	TU134	60350
ES-AAJ	TU134	60627
ES-AAK	TU134	60977
ES-AAL	TU134	62350
ES-AAM	TU134	60380
ES-AAN	TU134	60560
ES-AAO	TU134	62239
ES-AAP	TU134	38020
ES-AAR	YAK40	9510439
ES-AAS	YAK40	9632049
ES-AAT	YAK40	9511639
ES-AAU	YAK40	9411333
ES-ABC	**B737**	**26324**
ES-ABD	**B737**	**26323**
ES-ABE	B737	28083
ES-ABF	B737	24778
ES-ABG	B737	25790
ES-ABH	**B737**	**29074**
ES-ABI	B737	29234
ES-ABJ	**B737**	**28873**
ES-ABK	**B737**	**28572**
ES-ABL	**B737**	**28997**
ES-LAI	TU154	91A-895
ES-LTA	TU154	60195
ES-LTC	TU154	91A-896
ES-LTP	TU154	92A-909
ES-LTR	TU154	91A-896
ES-NIT	IL76	1013409274
ES-NOB	**AN7x**	**72070695**
ES-NOC	AN7x	72010952
ES-NOE	AN7x	47097932
ES-NOG	AN7x	72080786
ES-NOI	**AN7x**	**72096914**
ES-NOK	AN7x	72080780
ES-NOL	**AN7x**	**72080789**
ES-NOP	AN7x	72010905

Ethiopia

Reg	Type	C/n
(ET-AAG)	B707	18165
ET-AAG	B707	18454
(ET-AAH)	B707	18166
ET-AAH	B707	18455
ET-ABP	B707	18977
ET-ACD	B707	19736
ET-ACQ	B707	19820
ET-AFA	B707	18418
ET-AFB	B707	18419
ET-AFK	B707	18417
ET-AHK	B727	22759
ET-AHL	B727	21978
ET-AHM	B727	21979
ET-AIE	B767	23106
ET-AIF	**B767**	**23107**
ET-AIV	B707	19531
ET-AIZ	B767	23916
ET-AJA	B737	23914
ET-AJB	**B737**	**23915**
ET-AJS	**B757**	**24845**
ET-AJU	B727	21851
ET-AJX	**B757**	**25014**
ET-AJZ	B707	19433
ET-AKC	**B757**	**25353**
ET-AKE	**B757**	**26057**
ET-AKF	**B757**	**26058**
ET-AKW	B767	25346
(ET-ALB)	A340	036
ET-ALC	**B767**	**28043**
ET-ALE	B737	23446
ET-ALH	**B767**	**30565**
ET-ALJ	**B767**	**33767**
ET-ALK	**737NG**	**33764**
ET-ALL	**B767**	**30564**
ET-ALM	**737NG**	**33765**
ET-ALN	**737NG**	**33766**
ET-ALO	**B767**	**33768**
ET-ALP	**B767**	**33769**
ET-ALQ	**737NG**	**33420**
ET-ALU	**737NG**	**32741**
ET-ALY	**B757**	**28480**
ET-ALZ	**B757**	**30319**
ET-AME	**B767**	**27611**
ET-AMF	**B767**	**30563**
ET-AMG	**B767**	**30566**
ET-AMK	**B757**	**32449**

Belarus

Reg	Type	C/n
EW-001PA	**737NG**	**33079**
EW-004DE	IL76	?
EW-100PJ	**CRJ**	**7309**
EW-101PJ	**CRJ**	**7316**
EW-239TH	**IL76**	**0053464934**
EW-240TH	**IL76**	**0063465956**
EW-241TH	**IL76**	**1023412414**
EW-242TH	**IL76**	**1033414480**
EW-243TH	**IL76**	**0043450493**
EW-244TH	**IL76**	**1023410344**
EW-250PA	**B757**	**26319**
EW-251PA	**B737**	**27634**
EW-258TH	**IL76**	**0063470088**
EW-63955	TU134	63955
EW-65049	TU134	49755
EW-65082	TU134	60081
EW-65085	**TU134**	**60123**
EW-65106	**TU134**	**60315**
EW-65108	TU134	60332
EW-65133	**TU134**	**60645**
EW-65145	**TU134**	**60985**
EW-65149	**TU134**	**61033**
EW-65565	TU134	09070
EW-65605	TU134	09070
EW-65614	TU134	7350302
EW-65663	TU134	0351109
EW-65664	TU134	1351210
EW-65676	TU134	1351502
EW-65754	**TU134**	**62154**
EW-65772	**TU134**	**62472**
EW-65803	TU134	3352103

Reg	Type	Serial
EW-65821	TU134	08060
EW-65832	TU134	17106
EW-65861	TU134	1351407
EW-65861	TU134	28269
EW-65892	TU134	38050
EW-65942	TU134	17103
EW-65943	TU134	63580
EW-65944	TU134	12096
EW-65957	TU134	2351802
EW-65974	TU134	3352004
EW-76446	IL76	1023412418
EW-76709	IL76	0063473173
EW-76710	IL76	0063473182
EW-76711	IL76	0063473187
EW-76712	IL76	0063473190
EW-76734	IL76	0073476312
EW-76735	IL76	0073476314
EW-76737	IL76	0073477323
EW-76778	IL76	0083483502
EW-76836	IL76	1013409305
EW-76837	IL76	1023409316
EW-78761	IL76	0083486570
EW-78763	IL76	0083486582
EW-78765	IL76	0083486590
EW-78769	IL76	0083487607
EW-78779	IL76	0083489662
EW-78787	IL76	0083490698
EW-78792	IL76	0093490718
EW-78793	IL76	0093490721
EW-78799	IL76	0093491754
EW-78801	IL76	0093492763
EW-78802	IL76	0093492771
EW-78808	IL76	0093493794
EW-78819	IL76	0093495883
EW-78826	IL76	1003499991
EW-78827	IL76	1003499997
EW-78828	IL76	1003401004
EW-78836	IL76	0003499986
EW-78839	IL76	1003402047
EW-78843	IL76	1003403082
EW-78848	IL76	1013405159
EW-78849	IL76	1013405192
EW-85122	TU154	75A-122
EW-85217	TU154	77A-217
EW-85260	TU154	78A-260
EW-85331	TU154	79A-331
EW-85339	TU154	79A-339
EW-85352	TU154	79A-352
EW-85372	TU154	79A-372
EW-85411	TU154	80A-411
EW-85419	TU154	80A-419
EW-85465	TU154	80A-465
EW-85486	TU154	81A-486
EW-85509	TU154	81A-509
EW-85538	TU154	82A-538
EW-85545	TU154	82A-545
EW-85580	TU154	83A-580
EW-85501	TU154	03A-501
EW-85582	TU154	83A-582
EW-85583	TU154	83A-583
EW-85591	TU154	83A-591
EW-85593	TU154	83A-593
EW-85703	TU154	91A-878
EW-85706	TU154	91A-881
EW-85724	TU154	91A-906
EW-85725	TU154	91A-907
EW-85741	TU154	91A-896
EW-85748	TU154	92A-924
EW-85757	TU154	92A-939
EW-85760	TU154	92A-942
EW-85815	TU154	95A-1010
EW-86062	IL86	51483203029
EW-87320	YAK40	9331929
EW-87330	YAK40	9510139
EW-87419	YAK40	9421134
EW-87577	YAK40	9220922
EW-87657	YAK40	9020409
EW-87658	YAK40	9240225
EW-87669	YAK40	9021760
"EW-87775"	YAK40	9031013
EW-88161	YAK40	9611546
EW-88187	YAK40	9620748
EW-88202	YAK40	9630449

Kyrgyzstan

Reg	Type	Serial
EX-	B737	23516
EX-	B737	23517
EX-00002	TU154	91A-904
EX-006	B737	21960
EX-007	YAK40	9640152
EX-009	B737	22088
EX-012	B737	21645
EX-015	B737	21819
EX-017	TU154	81A-478
EX-020	TU134	61042
EX-027	B737	23444
EX-032	IL76	073411331
EX-033	IL76	0033446325
EX-035	IL76	0093498962
EX-036	IL76	0093495863
EX-037	B737	22075
EX-039	IL76	0003427796
EX-040	B737	21509
EX-043	IL76	0043451509
EX-044	L1011	193C-1245
EX-046	IL76	0013428831
EX-047	B737	22074
EX-048	B737	22395
EX-049	IL76	083415453
EX-050	B737	21139
EX-054	IL76	1033414480
EX-056	L1011	193C-1237
EX-058	L1011	193C-1228
EX-061	B737	21927
EX-062	IL76	0013430890
EX-064	IL76	0063465956
EX-065	IL76	0053460832
EX-066	IL76	0053464934
EX-067	B767	23280
EX-069	IL76	0013432955
EX-070	IL76	0033447364
EX-071	IL76	0043452546
EX-075	IL76	0053463908
EX-076	B737	20882
EX-077	B737	21277
EX-079	B737	21275
EX-080	B737	21276
EX-081	B737	21283
EX-086	1-11	BAC.253
EX-087	TU154	87A-751
EX-088	L1011	193G-1179
EX-089	L1011	193B-1221
EX-090	IL76	?
EX-093	IL76	1013407212
EX-093	IL76	?
EX-098	IL76	?
EX-100	IL76	1023413438
EX-102	L1011	193U-1201
EX-103	1-11	BAC.403
EX-105	IL76	1003405167
EX-108	IL76	1013405177
EX-109	IL76	1023410355
EX-110	B737	21362
EX-112	YAK40	?
EX-121	B737	20577
EX-212	B737	22632
EX-214	B737	21960
EX-301	A310	524
EX-311	B737	21276
EX-411	IL76	1023411384
EX-436	IL76	1023411368
EX-450	B737	20450
EX-451	B737	20451
EX-452	B737	20452
EX-632	B737	22632
EX-736	B737	23517
EX-777	B737	21654
EX-832	IL76	1023410360
EX-901	YAK40	9411030A
EX-62100	IL62	51902
EX-65111	TU134	60346
EX-65119	TU134	60475
EX-65125	TU134	60575
EX-65778	TU134	62590
EX-65779	TU134	62602
EX-65789	TU134	62850
EX-76815	IL76	1013409310
EX-78130	IL76	0043454611
EX-85021	TU154	71A-021
EX-85252	TU154	77A-252
EX-85257	TU154	78A-257
EX-85259	TU154	78A-259
EX-85294	TU154	78A-294
EX-85313	TU154	78A-313
EX-85369	TU154	79A-369
EX-85444	TU154	80A-444
EX-85491	TU154	81A-491
EX-85497	TU154	81A-497
EX-85519	TU154	81A-519
EX-85590	TU154	83A-590
EX-85718	TU154	91A-900
EX-85754	TU154	92A-936
EX-85762	TU154	92A-945
EX-86911	IL76	0023437093
EX-86916	IL76	0023438120
EX-86917	IL76	0023438122
EX-86919	IL76	0023438129
EX-87228	YAK40	9841659
EX-87250	YAK40	9310726
EX-87259	YAK40	9311626
EX-87275	YAK40	9311127
EX-87293	YAK40	9320828
EX-87331	YAK40	9510239
EX-87354	YAK40	9330331
EX-87366	YAK40	9341631
EX-87379	YAK40	9411030A
EX-87412	YAK40	9420434
EX-87426	YAK40	9420235
EX-87442	YAK40	9431935
EX-87445	YAK40	9430236
EX-87470	YAK40	9441537
EX-87529	YAK40	9521141
EX-87538	YAK40	9530342
EX-87555	YAK40	9210621
EX-87561	YAK40	9211221
EX-87571	YAK40	9221521
EX-87589	YAK40	9220123
EX-87631	YAK40	9131219
EX-87632	YAK40	9131319
EX-87640	YAK40	9140120
EX-87643?	YAK40	9541643
EX-87664	YAK40	9240825
EX-87801	YAK40	9511639
EX-87802	YAK40	9411333
EX-87820	YAK40	9231224
EX-87836	YAK40	9240226
EX-88207	YAK40	9631149
EX-88270	YAK40	9720853

Tajikistan

Reg	Type	Serial
EY-1251	YAK40	9641251
EY-65003	TU134	44040
EY-65022	TU134	48395
EY-65730	TU134	1351310
EY-65763	TU134	62299
EY-65778	TU134	62590
EY-65787	TU134	62835
EY-65814	TU134	4352208
EY-65820	TU134	08056
EY-65835	TU134	17112
EY-65875	TU134	29317
EY-65876	TU134	31220
EY-85247	TU154	77A-247
EY-85251	TU154	77A-251
EY-85281	TU154	78A-281
EY-85385	TU154	79A-385
EY-85406	TU154	80A-406
EY-85440	TU154	80A-440
EY-85446	TU154	80A-466
EY-85469	TU154	81A-469
EY-85475	TU154	81A-475
EY-85487	TU154	81A-487
EY-85511	TU154	81A-511
EY-85651	TU154	88A-793
EY-85691	TU154	90A-864
EY-85692	TU154	90A-865
EY-85717	TU154	91A-897
EY-87214	YAK40	9640851
EY-87217	YAK40	9510340
EY-87310	YAK40	9321327A
EY-87356	YAK40	9340531
EY-87434	YAK40	9421035
EY-87446	YAK40	9430336
EY-87461	YAK40	9432036
EY-87522	YAK40	9520441
EY-87835	YAK40	9240126
EY-87922	YAK40	9731355
EY-87963	YAK40	9831058
EY-87965	YAK40	9340532
EY-87967	YAK40	9831158
EY-88196	YAK40	9631648
EY-88207	YAK40	9631149
EY-88267	YAK40	9720553

Turkmenistan

Reg	Type	Serial
EZ-42404	YAK42	2116617
EZ-85241	TU154	77A-241
EZ-85246	TU154	77A-246
EZ-85250	TU154	77A-250
EZ-85345	TU154	79A-345
EZ-85383	TU154	79A-383
EZ-85394	TU154	80A-394
EZ-85410	TU154	80A-410
EZ-85492	TU154	81A-492
EZ-85507	TU154	81A-507
EZ-85532	TU154	82A-532
EZ-85549	TU154	82A-549
EZ-85560	TU154	82A-560
EZ-87338	YAK40	9510739
EZ-87387	YAK40	9411832
EZ-87409	YAK40	9420134
EZ-87427	YAK40	9420335
EZ-87531	YAK40	9521341
EZ-87548	YAK40	9531342
EZ-87668	YAK40	9021460
EZ-88169	YAK40	9610747
EZ-88178	YAK40	9621847
EZ-88230	YAK40	9641950
EZ-A001	B737	26855
EZ-A002	B737	25994
EZ-A003	B737	25995
EZ-A004	737NG	36088
EZ-A005	737NG	36089
EZ-A010	B757	25345
EZ-A011	B757	28336
EZ-A012	B757	28337
EZ-A014	B757	30863
EZ-A101	B717	55153
EZ-A102	B717	55154
EZ-A103	B717	55155
EZ-A104	B717	55195
EZ-A105	B717	55196
EZ-A106	B717	55186
EZ-A107	B717	55187
EZ-A700	B767	33968
EZ-F421	IL76	1023498978
EZ-F422	IL76	1023410348
EZ-F423	IL76	1033418608
EZ-F424	IL76	1033418592
EZ-F425	IL76	1023410336
EZ-F426	IL76	1033418609
EZ-F427	IL76	1033418620
EZ-F428	IL76	1043418624
EZ-J672	YAK42	1316562
EZ-J673	YAK42	1316574
EZ-J674	YAK42	1319020

Eritrea

Reg	Type	Serial
E3-AAO	B767	24541
E3-AAQ	B767	23309
E3-NAS	B737	21960

France

Reg	Type	c/n
F-	737NG	35279
(F-BDHC)	A300	008
F-BGNX	COMET	06020
F-BGNY	COMET	06021
F-BGNZ	COMET	06022
F-BGSA	COMET	06015
F-BGSB	COMET	06016
F-BGSC	COMET	06019
F-BHHH	SE210	01
F-BHHI	SE210	02
F-BHOR	SE210	11
F-BHRA	SE210	1
F-BHRB	SE210	2
F-BHRC	SE210	5
F-BHRD	SE210	8
F-BHRE	SE210	9
F-BHRF	SE210	12
F-BHRG	SE210	13
F-BHRH	SE210	16
F-BHRI	SE210	17
F-BHRJ	SE210	23
F-BHRK	SE210	26
F-BHRL	SE210	31
F-BHRM	SE210	37
F-BHRN	SE210	39
F-BHRO	SE210	41
F-BHRP	SE210	45
F-BHRQ	SE210	46
F-BHRR	SE210	50
F-BHRS	SE210	54
F-BHRT	SE210	55
F-BHRU	SE210	58
F-BHRV	SE210	59
F-BHRX	SE210	60
F-BHRY	SE210	61
F-BHRZ	SE210	52
F-BHSA	B707	17613
F-BHSB	B707	17614
F-BHSC	B707	17615
F-BHSD	B707	17616
F-BHSE	B707	17617
F-BHSF	B707	17618
F-BHSG	B707	17619
F-BHSH	B707	17620
F-BHSI	B707	17621
F-BHSJ	B707	17622
F-BHSK	B707	17918
F-BHSL	B707	17919
F-BHSM	B707	17920
F-BHSN	B707	17921
F-BHSO	B707	17922
F-BHSP	B707	17923
F-BHSQ	B707	17924
F-BHSR	B707	18245
F-BHSS	B707	18246
F-BHST	B707	18247
F-BHSU	B707	18375
F-BHSV	B707	18456
F-BHSX	B707	18457
F-BHSY	B707	18458
F-BHSZ	B707	18459
F-BIUY	DC-8	45569
F-BIUZ	DC-8	45570
F-BJAK	SE210	219
F-BJAO	SE210	42
F-BJAP	SE210	62
F-BJAQ	SE210	19
F-BJAU	SE210	70
F-BJCB	DC-8	45671
F-BJCM	B707	19986
F-BJEN	SE210	185
F-BJGY	SE210	255
F-BJLA	DC-8	45567
F-BJLB	DC-8	45568
F-BJSO	SE210	143
F-BJTA	SE210	53
F-BJTB	SE210	68
F-BJTC	SE210	83
F-BJTD	SE210	162
F-BJTD	SE210	84

Reg	Type	c/n
F-BJTE	SE210	111
F-BJTF	SE210	113
F-BJTG	SE210	115
F-BJTH	SE210	124
F-BJTI	SE210	105
F-BJTJ	SE210	119
F-BJTK	SE210	141
F-BJTL	SE210	142
F-BJTM	SE210	144
F-BJTN	SE210	145
F-BJTO	SE210	148
F-BJTP	SE210	152
F-BJTQ	SE210	177
F-BJTR	SE210	22
F-BJTS	SE210	27
F-BJTU	SE210	189
F-BJUV	DC-8	45627
F-BKGZ	SE210	83
F-BLCA	B707	18685
F-BLCB	B707	18686
F-BLCC	B707	18881
F-BLCD	B707	18941
F-BLCE	B707	19291
F-BLCF	B707	19292
F-BLCG	B707	19521
F-BLCH	B707	19522
F-BLCI	B707	19723
F-BLCJ	B707	19724
F-BLCK	B707	19916
F-BLCL	B707	19917
F-BLCZ	SE210	51
F-BLHY	SE210	158
F-BLKF	SE210	42
F-BLKI	SE210	136
F-BLKJ	SE210	169
F-BLKS	SE210	176
F-BLKX	DC-8	45820
F-BLLB	B707	18686
F-BLLC	DC-8	45604
(F-BMKO)	B707	19351
F-BMKS	SE210	181
F-BNFE	SE210	200
F-BNGE	SE210	10
F-BNKA	SE210	206
F-BNKB	SE210	208
F-BNKC	SE210	217
F-BNKD	SE210	220
F-BNKE	SE210	224
F-BNKF	SE210	227
F-BNKG	SE210	229
F-BNKH	SE210	248
F-BNKI	SE210	214
(F-BNKI)	SE210	241
F-BNKJ	SE210	252
F-BNKK	SE210	256
F-BNKL	SE210	260
F-BNLD	DC-8	45819
F-BNLE	DC-8	45917
F-BNOG	SE210	269
F-BNOH	SE210	269
F-BNRA	SE210	201
F-BNRB	SE210	222
F-BOEE	SE210	212
F-BOHA	SE210	242
F-BOHB	SE210	244
F-BOHC	SE210	245
F-BOJA	B727	19543
F-BOJB	B727	19544
F-BOJC	B727	19545
F-BOJD	B727	19546
F-BOJE	B727	19861
F-BOJF	B727	19862
F-BOLF	DC-8	45918
F-BOLG	DC-8	45987
F-BOLH	DC-8	46028
F-BOLI	DC-8	45754
F-BOLJ	DC-8	45927
F-BOLK	DC-8	45803
F-BOLL	DC-8	46096
F-BOLM	DC-8	46058
(F-BOLN)	DC-8	45692
(F-BOLN)	DC-8	45862

Reg	Type	c/n
F-BPJG	B727	19863
F-BPJH	B727	19864
F-BPJI	B727	19865
F-BPJJ	B727	20075
F-BPJK	B727	20202
F-BPJL	B727	20203
F-BPJM	B727	20204
F-BPJN	B727	20409
F-BPJO	B727	20410
F-BPJP	B727	20411
F-BPJQ	B727	20470
F-BPJR	B727	20538
F-BPJS	B727	20539
F-BPJT	B727	20540
F-BPJU	B727	19683
F-BPJV	B727	19684
F-BPVA	B747	19749
F-BPVB	B747	19750
F-BPVC	B747	19751
F-BPVD	B747	19752
F-BPVE	B747	20355
F-BPVF	B747	20376
F-BPVG	B747	20377
F-BPVH	B747	20378
(F-BPVI)	B747	20541
F-BPVJ	B747	20541
(F-BPVJ)	B747	20542
F-BPVK	B747	20543
F-BPVL	B747	20798
F-BPVM	B747	20799
F-BPVN	B747	20800
F-BPVO	B747	20887
F-BPVP	B747	20954
F-BPVQ	B747	21141
F-BPVR	B747	21255
F-BPVS	B747	21326
F-BPVT	B747	21429
F-BPVU	B747	21537
F-BPVX	B747	21576
F-BPVY	B747	21731
F-BPVY	B747	21745
F-BPVZ	B747	21787
F-BRGU	SE210	237
F-BRGX	SE210	234
F-BRIM	SE210	193
F-BRUJ	SE210	209
F-BSEL	SE210	167
F-BSGT	B707	18837
F-BSGZ	SE210	83
F-BSRD	SE210	38
F-BSRR	SE210	21
F-BSRY	SE210	258
(F-BTDA)	DC-10	46850
(F-BTDB)	DC-10	46850
F-BTDC	DC-10	46851
(F-BTDC)	DC-10	46852
(F-BTDD)	DC-10	46852
(F-BTDD)	DC-10	46853
F-BTDD	DC-10	46963
F-BTDE	DC-10	46853
F-BTDF	DC-10	46852
(F-BTDF)	DC-10	46854
F-BTDG	B747	22514
F-BTDH	B747	22515
F-BTDL	SE210	136
F-BTMD	MERC	02
F-BTMD	MERC	11
F-BTOA	SE210	274
F-BTOB	SE210	277
F-BTOC	SE210	278
F-BTOD	SE210	279
F-BTOE	SE210	280
F-BTON	SE210	97
F-BTSC	CNCRD	203
F-BTSD	CNCRD	213
F-BTTA	MERC	1
F-BTTB	MERC	2
F-BTTC	MERC	3
F-BTTD	MERC	4
F-BTTE	MERC	5
F-BTTF	MERC	6

Reg	Type	c/n
F-BTTG	MERC	7
F-BTTH	MERC	8
F-BTTI	MERC	9
F-BTTJ	MERC	10
(F-BTTX)	MERC	11
F-BUAD	A300	003
F-BUAE	A300	004
F-BUAF	A300	008
F-BUAG	A300	015
F-BUAH	A300	027
F-BUAI	A300	062
F-BUAJ	A300	097
F-BUAK	A300	112
F-BUAL	A300	029
F-BUAM	A300	021
F-BUAN	A300	132
F-BUAO	A300	048
F-BUAP	A300	052
F-BUAQ	A300	057
F-BUAR	A300	020
F-BUFC	SE210	161
F-BUFF	SE210	101
F-BUFH	SE210	123
F-BUFM	SE210	209
F-BUOE	SE210	170
F-BUOR	DC-8	45862
F-BUTE	F.28	11031
F-BUTI	F.28	11034
F-BUZC	SE210	94
F-BUZJ	B707	17658
F-BVFA	CNCRD	205
F-BVFB	CNCRD	207
F-BVFC	CNCRD	209
F-BVFD	CNCRD	211
F-BVFF	CNCRD	215
F-BVGA	A300	005
F-BVGB	A300	006
F-BVGC	A300	007
F-BVGD	A300	010
F-BVGE	A300	011
F-BVGF	A300	013
F-BVGG	A300	019
F-BVGH	A300	023
F-BVGI	A300	045
F-BVGJ	A300	047
F-BVGK	A300	070
F-BVGL	A300	074
F-BVGM	A300	078
F-BVGN	A300	100
F-BVGO	A300	129
F-BVGP	A300	145
F-BVGQ	A300	146
F-BVGR	A300	175
F-BVGS	A300	178
F-BVGT	A300	183
F-BVPU	SE210	196
F-BVPY	SE210	271
F-BVPZ	SE210	218
F-BVSF	SE210	241
(F-BVTB)	SE210	270
F-BXOO	SE210	76
F-BYAI	SE210	139
F-BYAT	SE210	205
F-BYAU	SE210	192
F-BYCA	SE210	66
F-BYCB	SE210	175
F-BYCD	SE210	67
F-BYCN	B707	19370
F-BYCO	B707	19373
F-BYCP	B707	19377
F-BYCY	SE210	233
F-BYFM	DC-8	45664
F-GAPA	SE210	99
F-GATG	VFW	G-5
F-GATH	VFW	G-013
F-GATI	VFW	G-015
(F-GATN)	B747	21515
F-GATO	DC-8	46106
F-GATP	SE210	259
F-GATZ	SE210	175
F-GBBR	F.28	11051
F-GBBS	F.28	11050

Reg	Type	No	Reg	Type	No	Reg	Type	No	Reg	Type	No
F-GBBT	F.28	11052	F-GCLL	B737	19064	**F-GFKR**	**A320**	**0186**	F-GHGI	B767	27135
F-GBBX	F.28	11027	F-GCMV	B727	22608	**F-GFKS**	**A320**	**0187**	F-GHGJ	B767	27136
F-GBEA	A300	050	F-GCMX	B727	22609	**F-GFKT**	**A320**	**0188**	F-GHGK	B767	27212
F-GBEB	A300	102	F-GCSL	B737	19066	**F-GFKU**	**A320**	**0226**	(F-GHGL)	B767	27427
F-GBEC	A300	104	F-GCVI	SE210	272	**F-GFKV**	**A320**	**0227**	(F-GHGM)	A310	545
F-GBMI	SE210	19	F-GCVJ	SE210	275	**F-GFKX**	**A320**	**0228**	(F-GHGO)	B767	27428
F-GBMJ	SE210	149	F-GCVK	SE210	276	**F-GFKY**	**A320**	**0285**	F-GHHO	MD80	49985
F-GBMK	SE210	180	F-GCVL	SE210	273	**F-GFKZ**	**A320**	**0286**	F-GHHP	MD80	49986
F-GBNA	A300	065	F-GCVM	SE210	270	F-GFLV	B737	22597	F-GHKM	SE210	262
F-GBNB	A300	066	F-GDFC	F.28	11133	F-GFLX	B737	22598	(F-GHKN)	SE210	257
F-GBNC	A300	067	F-GDFD	F.28	11135	F-GFNU	B737	24256	F-GHKN	SE210	265
F-GBND	A300	068	F-GDFY	SE210	182	F-GFUA	B737	23635	(F-GHKO)	SE210	212
F-GBNE	A300	086	F-GDFZ	SE210	211	F-GFUB	B737	24025	F-GHKP	SE210	268
F-GBNF	A300	087	F-GDJK	DC-10	47849	F-GFUC	B737	24026	F-GHML	B737	19424
F-GBNG	A300	091	F-GDJM	DC-8	45960	F-GFUD	B737	24027	F-GHMU	SE210	249
F-GBNH	A300	092	F-GDJU	SE210	183	**F-GFUE**	**B737**	**24387**	F-GHOI	DC-10	46870
F-GBNI	A300	049	F-GDPM	DC-8	45662	**F-GFUF**	**B737**	**24388**	(F-GHOJ)	DC-10	46854
F-GBNI	A300	204	F-GDPS	DC-8	45981	F-GFUG	B737	24750	F-GHOL	B737	24825
F-GBNJ	A300	051	F-GDRM	DC-8	46063	F-GFUH	B737	24751	F-GHPC	B747	20137
F-GBNJ	A300	207	F-GDSK	F.28	11179	F-GFUI	B737	24023	F-GHPN	DC-10	46554
F-GBNK	A300	108	F-GDUA	B747	22870	(F-GFUI)	B737	24789	**F-GHQA**	**A320**	**0033**
F-GBNL	A300	118	(F-GDUE)	B747	23413	F-GFUJ	B737	25118	**F-GHQB**	**A320**	**0036**
F-GBNM	A300	119	F-GDUS	F.28	11053	F-GFUK	B747	21251	**F-GHQC**	**A320**	**0044**
F-GBNN	A300	120	(F-GDUT)	B747	22870	F-GFUU	MD80	49826	**F-GHQD**	**A320**	**0108**
F-GBNO	A300	124	F-GDUT	F.28	11091	F-GFVI	B737	20256	**F-GHQE**	**A320**	**0115**
F-GBNP	A300	152	F-GDUU	F.28	11108	F-GFVJ	B737	20254	**F-GHQF**	**A320**	**0130**
F-GBNQ	A300	153	F-GDUV	F.28	11109	(F-GFVK)	B737	19847	**F-GHQG**	**A320**	**0155**
F-GBNR	A300	154	F-GDUX	F.28	11110	F-GFVK	B737	19848	**F-GHQH**	**A320**	**0156**
F-GBNS	A300	155	F-GDUY	F.28	11142	(F-GFVR)	B737	19848	**F-GHQI**	**A320**	**0184**
F-GBNT	A300	158	F-GDUZ	F.28	11144	F-GFVR	B737	21538	**F-GHQJ**	**A320**	**0214**
F-GBNU	A300	161	F-GDVA	A300	261	F-GFYL	B737	20205	**F-GHQK**	**A320**	**0236**
F-GBNV	A300	211	F-GDVB	A300	271	F-GFZB	MD80	49707	**F-GHQL**	**A320**	**0239**
F-GBNX	A300	216	F-GDVC	A300	274	**F-GGEA**	**A320**	**0010**	**F-GHQM**	**A320**	**0237**
F-GBNY	A300	220	F-GECK	F.28	11004	**F-GGEB**	**A320**	**0012**	(F-GHQN)	A320	0258
F-GBNZ	A300	259	F-GELP	SE210	187	**F-GGEC**	**A320**	**0013**	**F-GHQO**	**A320**	**0278**
F-GBOX	B747	21835	F-GELQ	SE210	169	F-GGED	A320	0015	**F-GHQP**	**A320**	**0337**
F-GBYA	B737	23000	F-GEMA	A310	316	**F-GGEE**	**A320**	**0016**	**F-GHQQ**	**A320**	**0352**
F-GBYB	B737	23001	F-GEMB	A310	326	**F-GGEF**	**A320**	**0004**	**F-GHQR**	**A320**	**0377**
F-GBYC	B737	23002	F-GEMC	A310	335	(F-GGEF)	A320	0033	F-GHUC	A310	418
F-GBYD	B737	23003	F-GEMD	A310	355	**F-GGEG**	**A320**	**0003**	F-GHUD	A310	444
F-GBYE	B737	23004	F-GEME	A310	369	(F-GGEG)	A320	0036	F-GHUL	B737	24826
F-GBYF	B737	23005	F-GEMF	A310	172	(F-GGEH)	A320	0044	F-GHVM	B737	24026
F-GBYG	B737	23006	F-GEMG	A310	454	F-GGFI	B737	20138	F-GHVN	B737	25138
F-GBYH	B737	23007	F-GFMN	A310	502	F-GGFJ	B737	20218	F-GHVO	B737	24025
F-GBYI	B737	23008	F-GEMO	A310	504	F-GGGR	B727	20822	(F-GHXH)	B737	22453
F-GBYJ	B737	23009	F-GEMP	A310	550	F-GGKC	F.28	11073	**F-GHXK**	**B737**	**21599**
F-GBYK	B737	23010	F-GEMQ	A310	551	F-GGKD	SE210	255	**F-GHXL**	**B737**	**21775**
F-GBYL	B737	23011	F-GEPC	SE210	184	(F-GGLC)	DC-8	46110	F-GHXM	B737	24788
F-GBYM	B737	23349	(F-GEQL)	SE210	199	F-GGMA	MD80	49399	F-GHXN	B737	24877
F-GBYN	B737	23503	(F-GEQM)	SE210	236	F-GGMB	MD80	49617	F-GHYM	A310	571
F-GBYO	B737	23504	F-GESM	DC-8	46091	F-GGMC	MD80	49709	F-GIAH	F.28	11012
F-GBYP	B737	23792	F-GETA	B747	23413	F-GGMD	MD80	49618	F-GIAI	F.28	11013
F-GBYQ	B737	23793	F-GETB	B747	23480	(F-GGME)	MD80	49793	F-GIAJ	F.28	11070
(F-GBYR)	B737	25118	F-GETM	DC-8	46038	F-GGME	MD80	49855	F-GIAK	F.28	11104
F-GCBA	B747	21982	**F-GEXA**	**B747**	**24154**	F-GGMF	MD80	53463	F-GIDM	F.100	11273
F-GCBB	B747	22272	**F-GEXB**	**B747**	**24155**	F-GGML	B737	24785	F-GIDN	F.100	11272
F-GCBC	B747	22447	F-GEXI	B737	22406	F-GGMZ	DC-10	46990	F-GIDO	F.100	11271
F-QCBD	**B747**	**22428**	F-GEXJ	B737	22760	F-GGPA	B737	19847	F-GIDP	F.100	11270
F-GCBE	B747	22678	F-GEXT	F.28	11060	(F-GGPB)	B737	19848	F-GIDQ	F.100	11269
F-GCBF	B747	22794	F-GEXU	F.28	11070	F-GGPB	B737	20389	F-GIDT	F.100	11268
F-GCBG	**B747**	**22939**	F-GEXX	F.28	11102	F-GGPC	B737	20282	F-GIJS	A300	017
F-GCBH	**B747**	**23611**	F-GFBA	SE210	243	F-GGTP	B737	20196	F-GIJT	A300	009
F-GCBI	B747	23676	(F-GFBH)	SE210	199	F-GGVP	B737	20043	F-GIJU	A300	012
F-GCBJ	B747	24067	(F-GFBI)	SE210	236	F-GGVQ	B737	20944	F-GIMG	F.28	11003
F-GCBK	B747	24158	F-GFCN	DC-8	46159	F-GGZA	B737	20836	F-GIMH	F.28	11003
F-GCBL	**B747**	**24735**	**F-GFKA**	**A320**	**0005**	F-GHBM	B747	20120	F-GIMJ	B747	19658
F-GCBM	**B747**	**24879**	**F-GFKB**	**A320**	**0007**	F-GHEB	MD80	49822	F-GINL	B737	24827
F-GCBN	B747	25266	F-GFKC	A320	0009	F-GHEC	MD80	49662	F-GIOA	F.100	11261
F-GCDA	B727	22081	**F-GFKD**	**A320**	**0014**	F-GHED	MD80	49576	F-GIOB	F.100	11307
F-GCDB	B727	22082	**F-GFKE**	**A320**	**0019**	F-GHEF	A300	555	F-GIOC	F.100	11311
F-GCDC	B727	22083	**F-GFKF**	**A320**	**0020**	F-GHEG	A300	559	F-GIOD	F.100	11315
F-GCDD	B727	22084	**F-GFKG**	**A320**	**0021**	F-GHEH	MD80	49663	F-GIOE	F.100	11344
F-GCDE	B727	22085	**F-GFKH**	**A320**	**0061**	F-GHEI	MD80	49968	F-GIOF	F.100	11363
F-GCDF	B727	22287	**F-GFKI**	**A320**	**0062**	(F-GHEJ)	A300	555	**F-GIOG**	**F.100**	**11364**
F-GCDG	B727	22288	**F-GFKJ**	**A320**	**0063**	F-GHEJ	A310	535	(F-GIOH)	F.100	11364
F-GCDH	B727	22289	**F-GFKK**	**A320**	**0100**	F-GHEK	MD80	49823	F-GIOH	F.100	11424
F-GCDI	B727	22290	**F-GFKL**	**A320**	**0101**	F-GHFT	B707	19587	(F-GIOI)	F.100	11424
F-GCGQ	B727	20609	**F-GFKM**	**A320**	**0102**	F-GHGD	B767	24832	F-GIOI	F.100	11433
F-GCGR	B737	21278	**F-GFKN**	**A320**	**0128**	F-GHGE	B767	24854	(F-GIOJ)	F.100	11433
F-GCGS	B737	21279	**F-GFKO**	**A320**	**0129**	F-GHGF	B767	24745	F-GIOJ	F.100	11454
F-GCJL	B737	19067	**F-GFKP**	**A320**	**0133**	F-GHGG	B767	24746	(F-GIOK)	F.100	11454
F-GCJT	SE210	249	**F-GFKQ**	**A320**	**0002**	F-GHGH	B767	25077	F-GIOK	F.100	11455

Registration	Type	c/n
(F-GIOL)	F.100	11455
F-GIOV	F.100	11248
F-GIOX	F.100	11249
F-GISA	B747	25238
F-GISB	B747	25302
F-GISC	B747	25599
F-GISD	B747	25628
F-GISE	B747	25630
F-GISF	B747	24801
F-GITA	B747	24969
F-GITB	B747	24990
F-GITC	B747	25344
F-GITD	B747	25600
F-GITE	B747	25601
F-GITF	B747	25602
(F-GITG)	B747	25629
F-GITH	B747	32868
F-GITI	B747	32869
F-GITJ	B747	32871
(F-GIUA)	B747	25632
F-GIUA	B747	32866
F-GIUB	B747	33096
F-GIUC	B747	32867
F-GIUD	B747	32870
F-GIUE	B747	33097
F-GIUF	B747	35233
(F-GIVJ)	B707	19789
F-GIXA	B737	20836
F-GIXB	B737	24789
F-GIXC	B737	25124
F-GIXD	B737	25744
F-GIXE	B737	26850
F-GIXF	B737	26851
F-GIXG	B737	24364
F-GIXH	B737	23788
F-GIXI	B737	23809
F-GIXJ	B737	23685
F-GIXK	B737	24028
F-GIXL	B737	23810
F-GIXM	B737	25159
F-GIXO	B737	24132
F-GIXP	B737	24021
F-GIXR	B737	27125
F-GIXS	B737	27347
F-GIXT	B737	28898
(F-GIYJ)	DC-8	45819
(F-GIZP)	MD80	48051
(F-GIZQ)	MD80	48058
F-GJAO	F.100	11327
F-GJDL	B737	20440
F-GJDM	SE210	188
F-GJDY	A320	0653
(F-GJEY)	A310	594
F-GJEZ	A310	638
(F-GJHN)	MD80	48051
(F-GJHO)	MD80	48058
F-GJHQ	MD80	49668
(F-GJJG)	A300	069
F-GJKQ	A310	571
F-GJKR	A310	651
F-GJKS	A310	651
(F-GJKT)	A310	671
F-GJKW	A310	652
F-GJNA	B737	25206
F-GJNB	B737	25227
F-GJNC	B737	25228
F-GJND	B737	25229
F-GJNE	B737	25230
F-GJNF	B737	25231
F-GJNG	B737	25232
F-GJNH	B737	25233
F-GJNI	B737	25234
F-GJNJ	B737	25235
F-GJNK	B737	25236
(F-GJNL)	B737	25237
F-GJNL	B737	26448
F-GJNM	B737	25237
F-GJNN	B737	27304
F-GJNO	B737	27305
F-GJNP	B737	27356
(F-GJNP)	B737	27424
F-GJNQ	B737	26445
F-GJNR	B737	26446
(F-GJNR)	B737	27426
F-GJNS	B737	29073
F-GJNT	B737	29074
F-GJNU	B737	29075
F-GJNV	B737	26287
F-GJNX	B737	26454
F-GJNY	B737	26456
F-GJNZ	B737	26450
F-GJSV	A330	171
F-GJUA	B737	25165
F-GJVA	A320	0144
F-GJVB	A320	0145
F-GJVC	A320	0204
F-GJVD	A320	0211
F-GJVE	A320	0215
F-GJVF	A320	0244
F-GJVG	A320	0270
F-GJVU	A320	0436
F-GJVV	A320	0525
F-GJVW	A320	0491
F-GJVX	A320	0420
F-GJVY	A320	0436
F-GJVZ	A320	0085
F-GKAU	B767	25535
F-GKCI	A320	0132
(F-GKCI)	B707	20546
(F-GKCS)	B707	20085
(F-GKCT)	B707	20084
F-GKDY	B727	22438
F-GKDZ	B727	22441
F-GKHD	F.100	11381
F-GKHE	F.100	11386
F-GKLJ	B747	19660
F-GKLX	F.100	11328
(F-GKLX)	F.100	11375
F-GKLY	F.100	11332
(F-GKMR)	DC-10	46872
(F-GKMR)	MD11	48481
(F-GKMS)	DC-10	46954
F-GKMY	DC-10	47815
(F-GKPZ)	B727	21988
F-GKTA	B737	24413
F-GKTB	B737	24414
F-GKTD	A310	552
F-GKTE	A310	562
(F-GKTE)	B737	24021
(F-GKTF)	B737	24376
F-GKTK	B737	21011
F-GKXA	A320	0287
F-GKXB	A320	0235
F-GKXC	A320	1502
F-GKXD	A320	1873
F-GKXE	A320	1879
F-GKXF	A320	1885
F-GKXG	A320	1894
F-GKXH	A320	1924
F-GKXI	A320	1949
F-GKXJ	A320	1900
F-GKXK	A320	2140
F-GKXL	A320	2705
F-GKXM	A320	2721
F-GKXN	A320	3008
F-GKZL	MD80	49402
(F-GKZS)	DC-10	48252
F-GLGE	A320	0348
F-GLGG	A320	0203
F-GLGH	A320	0220
F-GLGI	A320	0221
F-GLGJ	A320	0222
F-GLGM	A320	0131
F-GLGN	A320	0132
F-GLIJ	CRJ	7081
F-GLIK	CRJ	7084
F-GLIR	F.100	11509
F-GLIS	F.70	11540
F-GLIT	F.70	11541
F-GLIU	F.70	11543
F-GLIV	F.70	11556
F-GLIX	F.70	11558
F-GLIY	CRJ	7053
F-GLIZ	CRJ	7057
F-GLLD	B737	23926
F-GLLE	B737	23927
F-GLMX	DC-10	47814
F-GLNA	B747	20399
F-GLNI	146	E2188
F-GLOC	A300	017
F-GLOV	B767	28039
(F-GLTB)	B737	24688
F-GLTF	B737	23684
F-GLTG	B737	28491
F-GLTM	B737	25070
F-GLTT	B737	23921
F-GLXF	B737	22657
F-GLXG	B737	21736
F-GLXH	B737	20544
F-GLXI	B737	26066
(F-GLXJ)	B737	23811
F-GLXJ	B737	25177
F-GLXK	B737	23979
(F-GLXO)	B737	25159
F-GLYS	DC-10	46872
F-GLZA	A340	005
F-GLZB	A340	007
F-GLZC	A340	029
F-GLZD	A340	031
F-GLZE	A340	038
F-GLZF	A340	043
F-GLZG	A340	049
F-GLZH	A340	078
F-GLZI	A340	084
(F-GLZJ)	A340	114
F-GLZJ	A340	186
F-GLZK	A340	207
(F-GLZL)	A340	168
F-GLZL	A340	210
(F-GLZM)	A340	174
F-GLZM	A340	237
(F-GLZN)	A340	186
F-GLZN	A340	245
F-GLZO	A340	246
F-GLZP	A340	260
F-GLZQ	A340	289
F-GLZR	A340	307
F-GLZS	A340	310
F-GLZT	A340	319
F-GLZU	A340	377
F-GMAI	A320	0258
F-GMBR	B737	24314
F-GMCD	MD80	49642
F-GMDA	A330	030
F-GMDB	A330	037
F-GMDC	A330	045
F-GMDD	A330	059
F-GMDE	A330	086
F-GMFM	DC-8	46099
F-GMJD	B737	22599
F-GMJO	B737	23980
F-GMLI	MD80	53014
F-GMLK	MD80	49672
F-GMMP	146	E2176
F-GMOL	F.28	11003
F-GMPG	F.100	11362
F-GMPP	MD80	49668
F-GMTM	B737	25070
F-GMZA	A321	0498
F-GMZB	A321	0509
F-GMZC	A321	0521
F-GMZD	A321	0529
F-GMZE	A321	0544
(F-GNAN)	F.100	11387
F-GNAO	B737	25168
F-GNAO	F.100	11476
F-GNBB	DC-10	46981
F-GNDC	DC-10	47849
F-GNEM	DC-10	46892
F-GNEU	F.100	11265
F-GNFC	B737	26315
F-GNFD	B737	26317
F-GNFH	B737	25162
F-GNFM	DC-8	45945
F-GNFS	B737	23981
F-GNFT	B737	23921
F-GNFU	B737	24256
F-GNIA	A340	010
F-GNIB	A340	014
F-GNIC	A340	022
F-GNID	A340	047
F-GNIE	A340	051
F-GNIF	A340	168
F-GNIG	A340	174
F-GNIH	A340	373
F-GNII	A340	399
(F-GNJQ)	B737	27425
F-GNLG	F.100	11363
F-GNLH	F.100	11311
F-GNLI	F.100	11315
F-GNLJ	F.100	11344
F-GNLK	F.100	11307
F-GNME	CRJ	7020
F-GNMN	CRJ	7003
(F-GNTA)	E145	145004
(F-GNTB)	E145	145007
F-GNZB	F.28	11073
(F-GNZI)	E145	145098
F-GOAA	A300	203
F-GOAF	B737	19847
(F-GOBR)	B727	20601
F-GOCJ	A310	217
F-GOFS	B767	26257
F-GOHA	E145	145169
F-GOHB	E145	145198
F-GOHC	E145	145243
F-GOHD	E145	145252
F-GOHE	E145	145335
F-GOHF	E145	145347
F-GOMA	146	E2211
F-GOZA	A300	148
F-GOZB	A300	184
F-GOZC	A300	189
F-GPAN	B747	21515
F-GPDJ	A310	162
F-GPJM	B747	20427
F-GPMA	A319	0598
F-GPMB	A319	0600
F-GPMC	A319	0608
F-GPMD	A319	0618
F-GPME	A319	0625
F-GPMF	A319	0637
F-GPMG	A319	0644
F-GPMH	A319	0647
F-GPMI	A319	0660
(F-GPMJ)	A319	0938
(F-GPMK)	A319	0985
F-GPNK	F.100	11324
F-GPNL	F.100	11325
F-GPPP	A320	0575
F-GPTA	CRJ	7039
F-GPTB	CRJ	7177
F-GPTC	CRJ	7182
F-GPTD	CRJ	7184
F-GPTE	CRJ	7183
F-GPTF	CRJ	7197
F-GPTG	CRJ	7223
F-GPTH	CRJ	7309
F-GPTI	CRJ	7316
(F-GPTJ)	CRJ	7322
F-GPTJ	CRJ	7323
F-GPTK	CRJ	7332
F-GPTM	CRJ	7020
F-GPVA	DC-10	47956
F-GPVB	DC-10	47957
F-GPVC	DC-10	48265
F-GPVD	DC-10	47865
F-GPVE	DC-10	46981
F-GPVV	B747	21576
F-GPXA	F.100	11487
F-GPXB	F.100	11492
F-GPXC	F.100	11493
F-GPXD	F.100	11494
F-GPXE	F.100	11495
F-GPXF	F.100	11330
F-GPXG	F.100	11387
F-GPXH	F.100	11476

Reg	Type	Serial	Reg	Type	Serial	Reg	Type	Serial	Reg	Type	Serial
F-GPXI	F.100	11503	F-GRMI	MD80	53488	F-GSPR	B777	28683	F-GUBD	E145	145333
F-GPXJ	F.100	11323	F-GRMJ	MD80	53520	F-GSPS	B777	32306	F-GUBE	E145	145668
F-GPXK	F.100	11329	F-GRML	MD80	49628	F-GSPT	B777	32308	F-GUBF	E145	145669
F-GPXL	F.100	11290	(F-GRMR)	DC-10	46854	F-GSPU	B777	32309	F-GUBG	E145	14500890
F-GPXM	F.100	11296	F-GRMV	F.100	11422	F-GSPV	B777	28684	F-GUEA	E145	145342
F-GPYP	CRJ	7126	F-GRNA	737NG	28823	(F-GSPX)	B777	32305	F-GUFD	E145	145197
F-GPYQ	CRJ	7144	F-GRNB	737NG	28824	F-GSPX	B777	32698	F-GUGA	A318	2035
F-GPYR	CRJ	7164	F-GRNC	737NG	28821	F-GSPY	B777	32305	F-GUGB	A318	2059
F-GPYZ	CRJ	7041	F-GRND	737NG	28827	F-GSPZ	B777	32310	F-GUGC	A318	2071
F-GPZA	MD80	49943	F-GRNE	737NG	30568	F-GSQA	B777	32723	F-GUGD	A318	2081
F-GPZC	MD80	48019	F-GRNF	B737	23774	F-GSQB	B777	32724	F-GUGE	A318	2100
F-GPZD	MD80	48059	F-GRNG	B757	30548	F-GSQC	B777	32727	F-GUGF	A318	2109
F-GPZE	MD80	49115	F-GRNG	B767	24798	F-GSQD	B777	32726	F-GUGG	A318	2317
F-GPZF	MD80	49164	F-GRNH	B737	24706	F-GSQE	B777	32851	F-GUGH	A318	2344
F-GQQJ	B737	24686	F-GRNI	B757	30886	F-GSQF	B777	32849	F-GUGI	A318	2350
F-GRFA	B737	28672	F-GRNJ	B757	30887	F-GSQG	B777	32850	F-GUGJ	A318	2582
F-GRFB	B737	28673	F-GRNS	A310	432	F-GSQH	B777	32711	F-GUGK	A318	2601
F-GRFC	B737	28569	F-GRNV	B737	24356	F-GSQI	B777	32725	F-GUGL	A318	2686
F-GRGA	E145	145008	F-GRNX	B737	25262	F-GSQJ	B777	32852	F-GUGM	A318	2750
F-GRGB	E145	145010	F-GRNZ	B737	27003	F-GSQK	B777	32845	F-GUGN	A318	2918
F-GRGC	E145	145012	F-GRSA	B737	25011	F-GSQL	B777	32853	F-GUGO	A318	2951
F-GRGD	E145	145043	F-GRSB	B737	25663	F-GSQM	B777	32848	F-GUGP	A318	2967
F-GRGE	E145	145047	F-GRSC	B737	25664	F-GSQN	B777	32960	F-GUGQ	A318	2972
F-GRGF	E145	145050	F-GRSD	A320	0653	F-GSQO	B777	32961	F-GUGR	A318	3009
F-GRGG	E145	145118	F-GRSE	A320	0657	F-GSQP	B777	35676	F-GUJA	E145	145407
F-GRGH	E145	145120	F-GRSG	A320	0737	F-GSQR	B777	35677	F-GUMA	E145	145405
F-GRGI	E145	145152	F-GRSH	A320	0749	F-GSQS	B777	32962	F-GUOA	B777	32967
F-GRGJ	E145	145297	F-GRSI	A320	0973	F-GSQT	B777	32846	F-GUPT	E145	145294
F-GRGK	E145	145324	F-GRSN	A320	1692	F-GSQU	B777	32847	F-GUYH	B737	23771
F-GRGL	E145	145375	F-GRSQ	A330	501	F-GSQV	B777	32854	F-GVAC	B737	20907
F-GRGM	E145	145418	F-GRXA	A319	1640	F-GSQX	B777	32963	(F-GVBG)	A319	1256
F-GRGP	E145	145188	F-GRXB	A319	1645	F-GSQY	B777	35678	F-GVGS	E145	145385
F-GRGQ	E145	145233	F-GRXC	A319	1677	F-GSTA	A300	655	F-GVHD	E145	145178
F-GRGR	E145	145236	F-GRXD	A319	1699	F-GSTB	A300	751	F-GVTH	DC-9	47308
F-GRHA	A319	0938	F-GRXE	A319	1733	F-GSTC	A300	765	F-GVVV	A300	069
F-GRHB	A319	0985	F-GRXF	A319	1938	F-GSTD	A300	776	F-GXAG	A319	2296
F-GRHC	A319	0998	F-GRXG	A319	2213	F-GSTF	A300	796	F-GXAH	A319	1846
F-GRHD	A319	1000	F-GRXH	A319	2228	F-GSTG	F.100	11443	F-GXFA	A319	1485
F-GRHE	A319	1020	F-GRXI	A319	2279	F-GSUN	B747	23030	F-GXFB	A319	1556
F-GRHF	A319	1025	F-GRXJ	A319	2456	F-GSVU	A319	1256	F-GYAI	A320	0293
F-GRHG	A319	1036	F-GRXK	A319	2716	F-GTAA	A321	0674	F-GYAJ	A321	2707
F-GRHH	A319	1151	F-GRXL	A319	2938	F-GTAB	A321	0675	F-GYAL	B737	19074
F-GRHI	A319	1169	F-GRXM	A319	2961	F-GTAC	A321	0684	F-GYAM	B737	24652
F-GRHJ	A319	1176	F-GRXN	A319	3065	F-GTAD	A321	0777	F-GYAN	A321	0535
F-GRHK	A319	1190	(F-GRYS)	E145	145789	F-GTAE	A321	0796	F-GYAO	A321	0642
F-GRHL	A319	1201	F-GRZA	CRJ7	10006	F-GTAF	A321	0761	F-GYAP	A321	0517
F-GRHM	A319	1216	F-GRZB	CRJ7	10007	F-GTAG	A321	0956	F-GYAQ	A321	0827
F-GRHN	A319	1267	F-GRZC	CRJ7	10008	F-GTAH	A321	1133	F-GYAR	A321	0891
F-GRHO	A319	1271	F-GRZD	CRJ7	10016	F-GTAI	A321	1299	F-GYAS	A319	1999
F-GRHP	A319	1344	F-GRZE	CRJ7	10032	F-GTAJ	A321	1476	F-GYAZ	A321	0519
F-GRHQ	A319	1404	F-GRZF	CRJ7	10036	F-GTAK	A321	1658	F-GYFK	A320	0533
F-GRHR	A319	1415	F-GRZG	CRJ7	10037	F-GTAL	A321	1691	F-GYFL	A320	0548
F-GRHS	A319	1444	F-GRZH	CRJ7	10089	F-GTAM	A321	1859	F-GYFM	A319	1068
F-GRHT	A319	1449	F-GRZI	CRJ7	10093	F-GTAN	A321	3051	(F-GYFN)	A319	1086
F-GRHU	A319	1471	F-GRZJ	CRJ7	10096	F-GTAO	A321	3098	F-GYJM	A319	1145
F-GRHV	A319	1505	F-GRZK	CRJ7	10198	(F-GTBC)	A300	203	F-GYPE	E145	145492
F-GRHX	A319	1524	F-GRZL	CRJ7	10245	(F-GTBD)	F.100	11265	(F-GYYY)	A310	363
F-GRHY	A319	1616	F-GRZM	CRJ7	10263	F-GTCA	B737	20196	F-GYYY	A310	486
F-GRHZ	A319	1622	F-GRZN	CRJ7	10264	(F-GTCB)	B727	21851	F-GZCA	A330	422
F-GRJA	CRJ	7070	F-GRZO	CRJ7	10265	(F-GTCC)	A300	219	F-GZCB	A330	443
F-GRJB	CRJ	7076	F-GSEA	B747	23032	(F-GTDC)	A300	125	F-GZCC	A330	448
F-GRJC	CRJ	7085	F-GSEU	A330	635	F-GTDF	DC-10	46854	F-GZCD	A330	458
F-GRJD	CRJ	7088	F-GSEX	B747	23028	F-GTDG	DC-10	46997	F-GZCE	A330	465
F-GRJE	CRJ	7106	(F-GSKA)	DC-10	47843	F-GTDH	DC-10	46851	F-GZCF	A330	481
F-GRJF	CRJ	7108	F-GSKY	B747	23244	F-GTDI	DC-10	46890	F-GZCG	A330	498
F-GRJG	CRJ	7143	F-GSPA	B777	29002	(F-GTIA)	A310	488	F-GZCH	A330	500
F-GRJH	CRJ	7162	F-GSPB	B777	29003	F-GTIB	B757	25131	F-GZCI	A330	502
F-GRJI	CRJ	7147	F-GSPC	B777	29004	F-GTID	B757	26270	F-GZCJ	A330	503
F-GRJJ	CRJ	7190	F-GSPD	B777	29005	F-GTLY	DC-10	46954	F-GZCK	A330	516
F-GRJK	CRJ	7219	F-GSPE	B777	29006	F-GTLZ	DC-10	46869	F-GZCL	A330	519
F-GRJL	CRJ	7221	F-GSPF	B777	29007	(F-GTNT)	146	E2089	F-GZCM	A330	567
F-GRJM	CRJ	7222	F-GSPG	B777	27609	F-GTNT	146	E2117	F-GZCN	A330	584
F-GRJN	CRJ	7262	F-GSPH	B777	28675	F-GTNU	146	E2112	F-GZCO	A330	657
F-GRJO	CRJ	7296	F-GSPI	B777	29008	F-GTOM	B747	21253	F-GZCP	A330	660
F-GRJP	CRJ	7301	F-GSPJ	B777	29009	F-GTUA	A340	367	F-GZHA	737NG	34901
F-GRJQ	CRJ	7321	F-GSPK	B777	29010	F-GTUB	A340	374	F-GZHB	737NG	34902
F-GRJR	CRJ	7375	F-GSPL	B777	30457	F-GTUI	B747	26875	F-GZHN	737NG	29445
F-GRJS	CRJ	7377	F-GSPM	B777	30456	F-GUAA	A321	0808	F-GZHV	737NG	29444
F-GRJT	CRJ	7389	F-GSPN	B777	29011	F-GUAM	E145	145266	F-GZNA	B777	35297
F-GRMC	MD80	53466	F-GSPO	B777	30614	F-GUBA	E145	145398	F-GZTA	B737	29333
F-GRMG	MD80	53464	F-GSPP	B777	30615	F-GUBB	E145	145419	F-GZTB	B737	29336
F-GRMH	MD80	53465	F-GSPQ	B777	28682	F-GUBC	E145	145556	F-GZZZ	A320	0030

Registration	Type	Serial
F-HALP	F.100	11470
F-HAVN	B757	25140
F-HAXY	B757	26635
F-HBAB	A321	0823
F-HBAC	A320	0888
F-HBAD	A320	0561
F-HBAE	A320	0558
F-HBAF	A321	1006
F-HBIL	A330	320
F-HBLA	E190	19000051
F-HBLB	E190	19000060
F-HBLC	E190	19000080
F-HBLD	E190	19000113
F-HBPE	E145	145106
F-HCAI	A321	1451
F-HCAT	A330	285
(F-HCCC)	B747	24383
F-HCEL	A340	081
F-HDDD	A300	625
F-HEEE	A300	555
F-HJAC	B747	23243
F-HKIS	B747	25380
F-HLOV	B747	25379
F-HPJA	A380	033
F-HPJB	A380	040
F-HSEA	B747	26877
F-HSEX	B747	26878
F-HSUN	B747	26880

France - d'Outremer

Registration	Type	Serial
F-O...	B777	35782
F-O...	B777	35783
F-OBNG	SE210	18
F-OBNH	SE210	20
F-OBNI	SE210	28
F-OBNJ	SE210	51
F-OBNK	SE210	73
F-OBNL	SE210	75
F-OCAZ	A300	001
F-OCHS	B737	23810
F-OCKH	SE210	263
F-OCPJ	SE210	258
(F-ODCX)	A300	003
F-ODCY	A300	009
F-ODGX	B737	24094
F-ODHC	A300	008
F-ODHY	A300	049
F-ODHZ	A300	051
F-ODJG	B747	21468
F-ODJU	A300	029
F-ODLX	DC-10	46872
F-ODLY	DC-10	46954
F-ODLZ	DC-10	46869
(F-ODOV)	DC-10	47849
F-ODRD	A300	022
F-ODRE	A300	026
F-ODRF	A300	048
F-ODRG	A300	052
(F-ODRM)	A300	354
F-ODRM	A300	374
(F-ODSU)	B737	24021
F-ODSV	A310	473
F-ODSX	A300	530
F-ODTK	A300	252
F-ODTN	MD80	49791
F-ODVD	A310	421
F-ODVE	A310	422
F-ODVF	A310	445
F-ODVG	A310	490
F-ODVH	A310	491
F-ODVI	A310	531
F-ODZB	F.28	11073
F-ODZJ	B737	24877
F-ODZY	B737	27452
F-ODZZ	B737	28898
F-OFDF	A330	253
F-OFLY	E170	17000017
F-OFRG	F.100	11475
F-OGIV	B707	18837
F-OGIW	B707	18840
F-OGJD	SE210	136
F-OGJE	SE210	167
F-OGQA	F.100	11272
F-OGQB	F.100	11273
F-OGQC	DC-10	47886
F-OGQI	F.100	11268
F-OGQN	A310	418
(F-OGQO)	A310	444
F-OGQQ	A310	592
F-OGQR	A310	593
F-OGQS	A310	596
F-OGQT	A310	622
F-OGQU	A310	646
F-OGQY	A310	574
F-OGQZ	A310	576
F-OGRT	B737	25138
(F-OGRT)	B737	26854
F-OGSD	B737	24789
F-OGSS	B737	25124
F-OGSX	B737	24364
F-OGSY	B737	23809
F-OGTA	A300	126
F-OGTB	A300	117
F-OGTC	A300	121
F-OGTG	B747	25629
F-OGYA	A320	0087
F-OGYB	A320	0088
F-OGYC	A320	0123
F-OGYC	A320	0569
F-OGYD	A320	0181
F-OGYE	A320	0182
F-OGYF	A320	0195
F-OGYM	A310	457
F-OGYN	A310	458
F-OGYO	A310	568
F-OGYP	A310	442
F-OGYP	A310	452
F-OGYQ	A310	453
F-OGYR	A310	456
F-OGYS	A310	467
F-OGYT	A310	660
F-OGYU	A310	687
F-OGYV	A310	689
F-OGYW	A310	276
F-OGYX	A310	278
(F-OHCN)	F.28	11149
(F-OHCO)	F.28	11159
F-OHCX	A320	0709
F-OHCY	A320	0710
F-OHFR	A320	0189
F-OHFT	A320	0343
F-OHFU	A320	0190
F-OHFX	A320	0235
F-OHGA	A320	0478
F-OHGB	A320	0289
F-OHGC	A320	0407
F-OHGI	B737	23543
F-OHGJ	B737	23546
F-OHGU	A321	0675
F-OHGV	A320	2649
F-OHGX	A320	2953
F-OHJM	D0328	3129
F-OHJV	A319	1048
F-OHJX	A319	1086
F-OHJY	A319	1124
F-OHJZ	A320	1054
F-OHKA	B737	22074
F-OHLE	A300	031
(F-OHLF)	A300	069
F-OHLH	A310	447
F-OHLI	A310	481
(F-OHLJ)	A300	125
(F-OHLK)	A300	203
(F-OHLL)	A300	219
F-OHLN	A300	747
F-OHLO	A320	0760
F-OHLP	A340	014
F-OHLQ	A340	022
F-OHMA	A320	0368
F-OHMB	A320	0376
F-OHMC	A320	0386
F-OHMD	A320	0433
F-OHME	A320	0252
F-OHMF	A320	0259
F-OHMG	A320	0260
F-OHMH	A320	0261
F-OHMI	A320	0275
F-OHMJ	A320	0276
F-OHMK	A320	0296
F-OHML	A320	0320
F-OHMM	A320	0321
F-OHMN	A320	0353
F-OHMO	A320	0640
F-OHMP	A321	0663
F-OHMQ	A321	0668
F-OHMR	A320	0676
F-OHOA	B727	22083
F-OHPA	A300	234
F-OHPB	A300	235
F-OHPC	A300	304
F-OHPD	A300	305
F-OHPE	A310	267
F-OHPF	A340	063
F-OHPG	A340	074
F-OHPH	A310	267
F-OHPH	A340	080
F-OHPI	A340	085
F-OHPJ	A340	173
F-OHPK	A340	176
F-OHPL	A340	187
F-OHPM	A340	196
F-OHPN	A300	208
F-OHPO	A300	210
F-OHPP	A310	278
F-OHPP	A310	331
F-OHPQ	A310	318
F-OHPR	A310	702
F-OHPS	A310	704
F-OHPT	A310	526
F-OHPU	A310	439
F-OHPV	A310	449
F-OHPX	A310	672
F-OHPY	A310	452
F-OHPZ	A340	036
F-OHRC	A321	0855
F-OHSD	A330	507
F-OHSE	A330	510
F-OHXA	F.100	11477
F-OHZA	A320	0706
F-OHZB	A320	0708
F-OHZM	A330	183
F-OHZN	A330	184
F-OHZO	A330	188
F-OHZP	A330	191
F-OHZQ	A330	189
F-OHZR	A330	198
F-OHZS	A330	200
F-OHZT	A330	203
(F-OIBB)	A320	0397
F-OIHA	A300	530
F-OIHB	A300	505
(F-OIHR)	A310	650
F-OIHS	A310	674
F-OIJE	E145	145360
F-OIJF	E145	145362
(F-OIKH)	E145	145098
F-OITN	A340	031
F-OIVU	A321	1017
(F-OJAC)	B747	23243
(F-OJAF)	A310	638
F-OJGF	A340	385
F-OJHH	A310	586
F-OJHI	A310	537
(F-OJKH)	E145	145098
F-OJSB	A320	2152
F-OJSE	A330	510
(F-OJTN)	A340	031
F-OJTN	A320	395
F-OKAI	A320	0258
F-OKBB	DC-10	46981
F-OKRM	A320	0615
(F-OKRM)	A320	2108
(F-OKRN)	A320	2128
F-OLGA	F.100	11290
F-OLGB	F.100	11296
F-OLLA	F.100	11461
F-OLLB	F.100	11326
F-OLLC	F.100	11265
F-OLLD	F.100	11322
F-OLLE	F.100	11350
F-OLLF	F.100	11527
(F-OLLG)	F.100	11320
F-OLLH	F.100	11505
F-OLLI	F.100	11517
F-OLLJ	F.100	11351
F-OLLL	F.100	11264
F-OLLM	F.100	11301
(F-OLLN)	F.100	11341
F-OLLP	F.100	11470
F-OLLQ	F.100	11472
F-OLLR	F.100	11473
F-OLOV	A340	668
F-OMAY	B777	29402
F-OMEA	A330	527
F-OMEB	A330	529
F-OMEC	A330	532
(F-OMOJ)	B727	22081
(F-OMOK)	B727	22082
(F-OMOL)	B727	22084
(F-OMOM)	B727	22085
F-OMSA	A330	054
F-ONAS	A319	2440
F-OORG	F.100	11444
F-OOUA	A319	0588
F-OPAR	B777	29908
F-OPTP	A330	240
F-ORLY	A330	758
F-ORME	A321	1878
F-ORMF	A321	1953
F-ORMG	A321	1956
F-ORMH	A321	1967
F-ORMI	A321	1977
F-ORMJ	A321	2055
F-ORUN	B777	28676
F-OSEA	A340	438
F-OSUN	A340	446

France - Military Call signs

Registration	Type	Serial
F-RAJA	A340	075
F-RAJB/081	A340	081

France - Test Marks

Registration	Type	Serial
F-W	SE210	188
F-W	SE210	190
F-W	SE210	191
F-W	SE210	202
F-W	SE210	205
F-W	SE210	207
F-W	SE210	210
F-W	SE210	211
F-W	SE210	213
F-W	SE210	214
F-W	SE210	216
F-W	SE210	218
F-W	SE210	225
F-W	SE210	226
F-W	SE210	228
F-W	SE210	230
F-W	SE210	232
F-W	SE210	233
F-W	SE210	236
F-W	SE210	241
F-W	SE210	246
F-W	SE210	250
F-W	SE210	251
F-W	SE210	253
F-W	SE210	254
F-W	SE210	255
F-W	SE210	257
F-W	SE210	259
F-W	SE210	261
F-W	SE210	262
F-W	SE210	264

Reg	Type	C/n	Reg	Type	C/n	Reg	Type	C/n	Reg	Type	C/n
F-W	SE210	267	F-WIHD	A320	1054	F-WJAM	SE210	102	F-WJAQ	SE210	191
F-W	SE210	271	F-WIHE	A319	1048	F-WJAM	SE210	107	F-WJAQ	SE210	204
F-W	SE210	272	F-WIHF	A319	1086	F-WJAM	SE210	109	F-WJAQ	SE210	223
F-W	SE210	273	F-WIHG	A319	1124	F-WJAM	SE210	110	F-WJAQ	SE210	42
F-W	SE210	276	F-WIHL	A330	230	F-WJAM	SE210	116	F-WJAU	SE210	70
F-WALP	F.100	11470	F-WIHM	A330	322	F-WJAM	SE210	125	F-WJKS	A310	652
F-WAST	A300	655	F-WIHP	A310	672	F-WJAM	SE210	138	F-WJSO	SE210	143
F-WAXY	B757	26635	F-WIHR	A310	695	F-WJAM	SE210	156	F-WJTA	SE210	53
F-WAYB	A310	276	F-WIHS	A310	492	F-WJAM	SE210	159	F-WJTB	SE210	68
F-WBAB	A321	0823	F-WIHT	A310	404	F-WJAM	SE210	164	F-WJTC	SE210	83
F-WBNG	SE210	18	F-WIHX	A320	0344	F-WJAM	SE210	185	F-WJTD	SE210	84
F-WBNH	SE210	20	F-WIHY	A300	265	F-WJAM	SE210	194	F-WJTE	SE210	111
F-WBNI	SE210	28	F-WIHZ	A300	249	F-WJAM	SE210	198	F-WJTF	SE210	113
F-WBNJ	SE210	51	F-WIQH	A310	598	F-WJAM	SE210	200	F-WJTG	SE210	115
F-WBNK	SE210	73	F-WIXM	B737	25159	F-WJAM	SE210	221	F-WJTH	SE210	124
F-WCPJ	SE210	258	F-WJAK	SE210	101	F-WJAM	SE210	235	F-WJTI	SE210	105
F-WEMP	A310	550	F-WJAK	SE210	108	F-WJAM	SE210	24	F-WJTJ	SE210	119
F-WEMQ	A310	551	F-WJAK	SE210	120	F-WJAM	SE210	243	F-WJTK	SE210	141
F-WFRG	F.100	11475	F-WJAK	SE210	122	F-WJAM	SE210	247	F-WJTL	SE210	142
F-WFYL	B737	20205	F-WJAK	SE210	129	F-WJAM	SE210	33	F-WJTM	SE210	144
F-WFYZ	A321	0555	F-WJAK	SE210	131	F-WJAM	SE210	42	F-WJTN	SE210	145
F-WGTP	B737	20196	F-WJAK	SE210	135	F-WJAM	SE210	57	F-WJTO	SE210	148
F-WGYM	A310	267	F-WJAK	SE210	138	F-WJAM	SE210	6	F-WJTP	SE210	152
F-WGYN	A310	276	F-WJAK	SE210	15	F-WJAM	SE210	66	F-WJTQ	SE210	177
F-WGYN	A310	458	F-WJAK	SE210	151	F-WJAM	SE210	80	F-WKCI	A320	0132
F-WGYO	A310	276	F-WJAK	SE210	162	F-WJAM	SE210	87	F-WKIS	B747	25380
F-WGYO	A310	568	F-WJAK	SE210	171	F-WJAM	SE210	90	F-WKPZ	B727	21988
F-WGYP	A310	278	F-WJAK	SE210	172	F-WJAM	SE210	92	F-WKRB	YAK40	?
F-WGYQ	A310	318	F-WJAK	SE210	19	F-WJAM	SE210	98	F-WLGA	A300	009
F-WGYR	A310	288	F-WJAK	SE210	192	F-WJAN	CNCRD	215	F-WLGA	A300	032
F-WGYR	A310	331	F-WJAK	SE210	195	F-WJAN	SE210	10	F-WLGA	A300	035
F-WGYT	A310	331	F-WJAK	SE210	21	F-WJAN	SE210	103	F-WLGA	SE210	134
F-WGYU	A320	0344	F-WJAK	SE210	219	F-WJAN	SE210	117	F-WLGA	SE210	139
F-WGYW	A310	432	F-WJAK	SE210	249	F-WJAN	SE210	123	F-WLGA	SE210	155
F-WGYX	A310	278	F-WJAK	SE210	263	F-WJAN	SE210	146	F-WLGA	SE210	166
F-WGYY	A321	0606	F-WJAK	SE210	266	F-WJAN	SE210	147	F-WLGA	SE210	168
F-WGYZ	A321	0538	F-WJAK	SE210	269	F-WJAN	SE210	157	F-WLGA	SE210	180
F-WGYZ	A321	0602	F-WJAK	SE210	3	F-WJAN	SE210	160	F-WLGA	SE210	197
"F-WGYZ"	A321	0606	F-WJAK	SE210	30	F-WJAN	SE210	170	F-WLGA	SE210	199
F-WHHH	SE210	01	F-WJAK	SE210	38	F-WJAN	SE210	174	F-WLGA	SE210	21
F-WHHI	SE210	02	F-WJAK	SE210	48	F-WJAN	SE210	193	F-WLGA	SE210	265
F-WHPF	A340	063	F-WJAK	SE210	64	F-WJAN	SE210	209	F-WLGA	SE210	78
F-WHPG	A340	074	F-WJAK	SE210	67	F-WJAN	SE210	25	F-WLGB	A300	014
F-WHPH	A310	267	F-WJAK	SE210	71	F-WJAN	SE210	263	F-WLGB	A300	016
F-WHPI	A300	530	F-WJAK	SE210	86	F-WJAN	SE210	268	F-WLGB	A300	017
F-WHPJ	A300	208	F-WJAK	SE210	91	F-WJAN	SE210	34	(F-WLGB)	A300	020
F-WHPK	A300	210	F-WJAK	SE210	93	F-WJAN	SE210	43	F-WLGB	A300	027
F-WHPR	A300	198	F-WJAK	SE210	97	F-WJAN	SE210	56	F-WLGB	A300	034
F-WHPS	A300	238	F-WJAL	SE210	106	F-WJAN	SE210	69	(F-WLGB)	A300	036
F-WHPT	A310	526	F-WJAL	SE210	114	F-WJAN	SE210	74	F-WLGB	A300	039
F-WHPU	A310	439	F-WJAL	SE210	127	F-WJAN	SE210	82	F-WLGB	A300	046
F-WHPV	A310	449	F-WJAL	SE210	132	F-WJAN	SE210	85	F-WLGB	SE210	128
F-WHPX	A300	195	F-WJAL	SE210	137	F-WJAN	SE210	88	F-WLGB	SE210	165
F-WHPY	A300	247	F-WJAL	SE210	153	F-WJAN	SE210	95	F-WLGB	SE210	183
F-WHPZ	A340	036	F-WJAL	SE210	154	F-WJAN	SE210	99	F-WLGB	SE210	187
F-WHRA	SE210	1	F-WJAL	SE210	161	F-WJAO	SE210	100	F-WLGB	SE210	231
F-WHRB	SE210	2	F-WJAL	SE210	173	F-WJAO	SE210	104	F-WLGB	SE210	238
F-WHRC	SE210	5	F-WJAL	SE210	175	F-WJAO	SE210	112	F-WLGB	SE210	259
F-WHRD	SE210	8	F-WJAL	SE210	179	F-WJAO	SE210	118	F-WLGC	A300	012
F-WHRE	SE210	9	F-WJAL	SE210	182	F-WJAO	SE210	121	F-WLGC	A300	015
F-WHRF	SE210	12	F-WJAL	SE210	186	F-WJAO	SE210	35	F-WLGC	A300	027
F-WHRG	SE210	13	F-WJAL	SE210	196	F-WJAO	SE210	44	F-WLGC	A300	031
F-WHRH	SE210	16	F-WJAL	SE210	203	F-WJAO	SE210	63	F-WLGC	SE210	130
F-WHRI	SE210	17	F-WJAL	SE210	215	F-WJAO	SE210	7	F-WLGC	SE210	143
F-WHRJ	SE210	23	F-WJAL	SE210	22	F-WJAO	SE210	76	F-WLGC	SE210	162
F-WHRK	SE210	26	F-WJAL	SE210	234	F-WJAO	SE210	96	F-WLGC	SE210	163
F-WHRL	SE210	31	F-WJAL	SE210	270	F-WJAP	SE210	11	F-WLGC	SE210	178
F-WHRM	SE210	37	F-WJAL	SE210	275	F-WJAP	SE210	27	F-WLGC	SE210	184
F-WHRN	SE210	39	F-WJAL	SE210	32	F-WJAP	SE210	29	F-WLGC	SE210	189
F-WHRO	SE210	41	F-WJAL	SE210	38	F-WJAP	SE210	36	F-WLGC	SE210	237
F-WHRP	SE210	45	F-WJAL	SE210	4	F-WJAP	SE210	47	F-WLGC	SE210	239
F-WHRQ	SE210	46	F-WJAL	SE210	40	F-WJAP	SE210	62	F-WLHY	SE210	158
F-WHRR	SE210	50	F-WJAL	SE210	49	F-WJAP	SE210	94	F-WLKF	SE210	42
F-WHRS	SE210	54	F-WJAL	SE210	65	F-WJAQ	SE210	126	F-WLKI	SE210	136
F-WHRT	SE210	55	F-WJAL	SE210	72	F-WJAQ	SE210	133	F-WLKJ	SE210	169
F-WHRU	SE210	58	F-WJAL	SE210	77	F-WJAQ	SE210	14	F-WLKS	SE210	176
F-WHRX	SE210	60	F-WJAL	SE210	78	F-WJAQ	SE210	140	F-WLLD	F.100	11322
F-WHRY	SE210	61	F-WJAL	SE210	79	F-WJAQ	SE210	149	F-WLLE	F.100	11350
F-WHRZ	SE210	52	F-WJAL	SE210	81	F-WJAQ	SE210	150	F-WLLF	F.100	11527
F-WHXA	F.100	11477	F-WJAL	SE210	89	F-WJAQ	SE210	167	F-WLLH	F.100	11505
F-WIHB	A300	505	F-WJAL?	SE210	240	F-WJAQ	SE210	181	F-WLLL	F.100	11264
F-WIHC	A320	0344	F-WJAM	CNCRD	213	F-WJAQ	SE210	19	F-WLLM	F.100	11301

Reg	Type	No	Reg	Type	No	Reg	Type	No	Reg	Type	No
F-WLOV	B747	25379	F-WQHS	A310	594	F-WSEX	B747	23028	F-WWAD	A300	608
F-WMLK	MD80	49672	F-WQHX	A310	475	F-WSEX	B747	26878	F-WWAD	A300	627
F-WMSA	A330	054	F-WQIC	A310	418	F-WSTB	A300	751	F-WWAD	A300	670
F-WNBB	DC-10	46981	(F-WQIP)	A300	147	F-WSTC	A300	765	F-WWAD	A300	709
F-WNDA	A300	021	(F-WQJA)	F.100	11321	F-WSTD	A300	776	F-WWAD	A300	736
F-WNDA	A300	025	F-WQJJ	F.100	11387	F-WSTF	A300	796	F-WWAD	A300	753
F-WNDA	A300	045	F-WQJK	F.100	11476	F-WSTG	F.100	11443	F-WWAD	A300	791
F-WNDB	A300	008	F-WQJR	A300	105	F-WSUN	B747	26880	F-WWAD	A300	811
F-WNDB	A300	026	F-WQJS	F.100	11329	F-WTCC	MERC	01	F-WWAD	A300	827
F-WNDB	A300	030	F-WQJX	F.100	11330	F-WTMD	MERC	02	F-WWAD	A310	316
F-WNDB	A300	048	F-WQKB	A310	535	F-WTMD	MERC	11	F-WWAE	A300	361
F-WNDB	A300	050	F-WQKR	A310	651	F-WTOA	SE210	274	F-WWAE	A300	466
F-WNDC	A300	022	(F-WQKU)	A300	069	F-WTOB	SE210	277	F-WWAE	A300	518
F-WNDC	A300	028	F-WQLD	A310	409	F-WTOC	SE210	278	F-WWAE	A300	572
F-WNDC	A300	033	F-WQLE	A310	410	F-WTOD	SE210	279	F-WWAE	A300	609
F-WNDC	A300	052	F-WQOH	A300	235	F-WTOE	SE210	280	F-WWAE	A300	628
F-WNDD	A300	024	F-WQOY	A300	304	**F-WTSA**	**CNCRD**	**02**	F-WWAE	A300	675
F-WNDD	A300	029	F-WQPG	F.100	11475	**F-WTSB**	**CNCRD**	**201**	F-WWAE	A300	711
F-WNKA	SE210	206	F-WQPK	F.100	11477	F-WTSC	CNCRD	203	F-WWAE	A300	734
F-WNKB	SE210	208	F-WQPL	F.28	11187	**F-WTSS**	**CNCRD**	**001**	F-WWAE	A300	752
F-WNKC	SE210	217	F-WQQE	A319	1102	F-WTTA	MERC	1	F-WWAE	A300	774
F-WNKD	SE210	220	F-WQQF	A319	1283	F-WTVH	DC-9	47308	F-WWAE	A300	788
F-WNKE	SE210	224	F-WQQG	A319	1305	F-WUAB	A300	004	F-WWAE	A300	812
F-WNKF	SE210	227	F-WQQJ	B737	24686	F-WUAB	A300	238	F-WWAE	A300	828
F-WNKG	SE210	229	F-WQQM	A330	205	F-WUAC	A300	002	F-WWAE	A300	866
F-WNKH	SE210	248	F-WQQN	A330	211	F-WUAD	A300	003	F-WWAF	A300	365
F-WNKJ	SE210	252	F-WQQO	A330	339	F-WUAT	A300	036	F-WWAF	A300	469
F-WNKK	SE210	256	F-WQQU	A321	0535	F-WUAT	A300	043	F-WWAF	A300	521
F-WNKL	SE210	260	F-WQQV	A321	0642	F-WUAU	A300	037	F-WWAF	A300	575
F-WNRA	SE210	201	F-WQQZ	A319	1364	F-WUAU	A300	042	F-WWAF	A300	610
F-WNRB	SE210	222	F-WQRF	A340	022	F-WUAV	A300	038	F-WWAF	A300	629
F-WOEE	SE210	212	F-WQRG	A340	014	F-WUAV	A300	049	F-WWAF	A300	677
F-WOHA	SE210	242	F-WQRH	A340	047	F-WUAX	A300	040	F-WWAF	A300	713
F-WOHB	SE210	244	F-WQRI	A340	051	F-WUAX	A300	044	F-WWAF	A300	737
F-WOHC	SE210	245	F-WQRR	A319	1068	F-WUAX	A300	047	F-WWAF	A300	757
F-WORG	F.100	11444	F-WQRS	A321	1012	F-WUAY	A300	031	F-WWAF	A300	771
F-WQAD	B737	25168	F-WQRT	A319	1145	F-WUAZ	A300	041	F-WWAF	A300	792
F-WQAE	B737	24345	F-WQRU	A319	1336	F-WVGA	A300	005	F-WWAF	A300	813
F-WQAV	A310	636	F-WQRV	A319	1388	F-WVGB	A300	006	F-WWAF	A300	836
F-WQAX	A320	0347	F-WQRZ	A319	1494	F-WVGC	A300	007	F-WWAF	A300	849
F-WQAY	A320	0354	F-WQSD	A320	0615	F-WVGH	A300	023	F-WWAF	A300	867
F-WQAZ	A320	0357	F-WQSE	A320	0662	F-WVRG	DC-9	47308	F-WWAG	A300	138
F-WQBA	A320	0411	F-WQSF	A320	0632	F-WW	A320	3256	F-WWAG	A300	368
F-WQBB	A320	0424	F-WQSG	A320	0622	F-WW	A320	3264	F-WWAG	A300	577
F-WQBC	A320	0441	F-WQSM	A320	0326	F-WW	A320	3278	F-WWAG	A300	611
F-WQBD	A320	0373	F-WQSN	A320	0478	F-WW	A320	3299	F-WWAG	A300	632
F-WQBP	F.100	11252	F-WQSO	A320	0344	F-WW	A320	3313	F-WWAG	A300	685
F-WQCK	B727	22608	F-WQSS	A321	1202	F-WW	A320	3318	F-WWAG	A300	721
F-WQCQ	A310	446	F-WQST	A321	0792	F-WW	A320	3325	F-WWAG	A300	740
F-WQCT	SE210	240	F-WQSY	A320	0533	F-WW	A320	3345	F-WWAG	A300	759
F-WQCU	SE210	261	F-WQSZ	A320	0548	F-WW	A330	899	F-WWAG	A300	793
F-WQCV	SE210	264	F-WQTA	A310	492	F-WW	A340	897	F-WWAG	A300	814
F-WQFL	F.100	11251	F-WQTB	A310	404	F-WWAA	A300	380	F-WWAG	A300	829
F-WQFM	1-11	BAC.111	F-WQTC	A310	678	F-WWAA	A300	470	F-WWAG	A300	850
F-WQFN	MD80	49628	F-WQTD	A300	559	F-WWAA	A300	516	F-WWAG	A300	868
F-WQFO	A300	199	F-WQTE	A310	300	F-WWAA	A300	563	F-WWAH	A300	371
F-WQFO	MD80	49629	F-WQTF	A310	682	F-WWAA	A300	606	F-WWAH	A300	471
F-WQFP	F.100	11256	F-WQTG	A310	676	F-WWAA	A300	621	F-WWAH	A300	532
F-WQFR	A300	116	F-WQTH	A310	686	F-WWAA	A300	746	F-WWAH	A300	578
F-WQFX	A300	435	F-WQTI	A320	1834	F-WWAA	A300	768	F-WWAH	A300	612
(F-WQFY)	A310	440	F-WQTJ	A320	1892	F-WWAA	A300	783	F-WWAH	A300	633
F-WQGD	B737	25663	F-WQTK	A320	1902	F-WWAA	A300	825	F-WWAH	A300	688
F-WQGH	A300	437	F-WQTL	A300	557	F-WWAB	A300	388	F-WWAH	A300	722
F-WQGL	A321	0731	F-WQTN	A340	031	F-WWAB	A300	536	F-WWAH	A300	743
F-WQGM	A321	0746	F-WQTO	A310	667	F-WWAB	A300	566	F-WWAH	A300	763
F-WQGP	A300	555	F-WQUE	B737	24356	F-WWAB	A300	607	F-WWAH	A300	794
F-WQGQ	A300	062	F-WQUG	F.100	11290	F-WWAB	A300	631	F-WWAH	A300	815
F-WQGS	A300	027	F-WQUN	A320	0739	F-WWAB	A300	681	F-WWAH	A300	862
F-WQGT	A300	150	F-WQUO	A320	0743	F-WWAB	A300	719	F-WWAI	A300	377
F-WQGX	F.100	11517	F-WQUR	A320	1132	F-WWAB	A300	739	F-WWAI	A320	0001
F-WQGY	F.100	11512	F-WQUS	A320	1179	F-WWAB	A300	756	F-WWAI	A330	195
F-WQGZ	F.100	11527	F-WQUT	A320	1244	F-WWAB	A300	787	**F-WWAI**	**A340**	**001**
F-WQHD	A320	0709	F-WQUU	A320	1308	F-WWAB	A300	803	F-WWAI	A340	394
F-WQHE	A320	0710	F-WQUV	A320	1162	F-WWAB	A300	810	F-WWAJ	A300	374
F-WQHE	F.100	11244	F-WQUX	A320	1322	F-WWAB	A300	826	F-WWAJ	A300	477
F-WQHG	F.100	11250	F-WQVC	A310	412	F-WWAC	A300	462	F-WWAJ	A300	525
F-WQHI	A300	017	F-WQVP	F.100	11445	F-WWAC	A300	512	F-WWAJ	A300	579
F-WQHJ	A300	102	F-WQVS	A320	0575	F-WWAD	A300	463	F-WWAJ	A300	616
F-WQHK	F.100	11254	F-WQVS	F.100	11395	F-WWAD	A300	517	F-WWAJ	A300	657
F-WQHN	A310	638	F-WQVS	F.100	11445	F-WWAD	A300	569	F-WWAJ	A300	683
F-WQHP	B737	25664	F-WQVU	A320	1259				F-WWAJ	A300	728
F-WQHQ	A300	052	F-WSEA	B747	26877				F-WWAJ	A300	742

Reg	Type	No	Reg	Type	No	Reg	Type	No	Reg	Type	No
F-WWAJ	A300	764	F-WWAP	A300	601	F-WWAX	A300	459	F-WWBD	A310	394
F-WWAJ	A300	799	F-WWAP	A300	635	F-WWAX	A300	513	F-WWBD	A319	2265
F-WWAJ	A300	816	F-WWAP	A300	690	F-WWAX	A300	553	F-WWBD	A320	0252
F-WWAJ	A300	830	F-WWAP	A300	726	F-WWAX	A300	604	F-WWBD	A320	0317
F-WWAJ	A300	851	F-WWAP	A300	745	F-WWAX	A300	637	F-WWBD	A320	0401
F-WWAJ	A300	870	F-WWAP	A300	772	F-WWAX	A300	715	F-WWBD	A320	0469
F-WWAK	A300	384	F-WWAP	A300	806	F-WWAX	A300	738	F-WWBD	A320	0589
F-WWAK	A300	474	F-WWAP	A300	834	F-WWAX	A300	755	F-WWBD	A320	0669
F-WWAK	A300	529	F-WWAP	A300	856	F-WWAX	A300	807	F-WWBD	A320	0818
F-WWAK	A300	580	F-WWAP	A300	874	F-WWAX	A300	847	F-WWBD	A320	0955
F-WWAK	A300	617	F-WWAQ	A300	408	F-WWAX	A300	864	F-WWBD	A320	1065
F-WWAK	A300	659	F-WWAQ	A300	507	F-WWAY	A300	460	F-WWBD	A320	1217
F-WWAK	A300	696	F-WWAQ	A300	557	F-WWAY	A300	514	F-WWBD	A320	1349
F-WWAK	A300	731	F-WWAQ	A300	625	F-WWAY	A300	556	F-WWBD	A320	1509
F-WWAK	A300	744	F-WWAQ	A300	673	F-WWAY	A300	605	F-WWBD	A320	1682
F-WWAK	A300	761	F-WWAQ	A300	724	F-WWAY	A300	666	F-WWBD	A320	1719
F-WWAK	A300	800	F-WWAQ	A300	770	F-WWAY	A300	717	F-WWBD	A320	1832
F-WWAK	A300	837	F-WWAQ	A300	777	F-WWAY	A300	741	F-WWBD	A320	2099
F-WWAK	A300	852	F-WWAQ	A300	786	F-WWAY	A300	754	F-WWBD	A320	2163
F-WWAK	A300	871	F-WWAQ	A300	797	F-WWAY	A300	782	F-WWBD	A320	2573
F-WWAL	A300	391	F-WWAQ	A300	821	F-WWAY	A300	824	F-WWBD	A320	2714
F-WWAL	A300	464	F-WWAQ	A300	835	F-WWAZ	A300	461	F-WWBD	A320	2832
F-WWAL	A300	530	F-WWAQ	A300	857	F-WWAZ	A300	515	F-WWBD	A320	2977
F-WWAL	A300	581	F-WWAQ	A300	875	F-WWAZ	A300	560	F-WWBD	A320	3121
F-WWAL	A300	630	F-WWAR	A300	411	F-WWAZ	A300	614	F-WWBD	A320	3228
F-WWAL	A300	679	F-WWAR	A300	508	F-WWAZ	A300	668	F-WWBE	A310	397
F-WWAL	A300	723	F-WWAR	A300	558	F-WWAZ	A300	727	F-WWBE	A320	0253
F-WWAL	A300	760	F-WWAR	A300	626	F-WWAZ	A300	762	F-WWBE	A320	0590
F-WWAL	A300	767	F-WWAR	A300	692	F-WWAZ	A300	779	F-WWBE	A320	0671
F-WWAL	A300	784	F-WWAR	A300	725	F-WWAZ	A300	789	F-WWBE	A320	0839
F-WWAL	A300	801	F-WWAR	A300	758	F-WWAZ	A300	848	F-WWBE	A320	0957
F-WWAL	A300	817	F-WWAR	A300	805	F-WWAZ	A300	865	F-WWBE	A320	1213
F-WWAL	A300	838	F-WWAR	A300	839	F-WWB.	A320	3257	F-WWBE	A320	1355
F-WWAL	A300	853	F-WWAR	A300	858	F-WWBA	A310	375	F-WWBE	A320	1512
F-WWAL	A300	872	F-WWAR	A300	876	**F-WWBA**	**A320**	**0001**	F-WWBE	A320	1689
F-WWAM	A300	395	F-WWAS	A300	414	F-WWBA	A320	0927	F-WWBE	A320	1827
F-WWAM	A300	465	F-WWAS	A300	509	F-WWBA	A320	1280	F-WWBE	A320	1979
F-WWAM	A300	533	F-WWAS	A300	559	F-WWBA	A320	1432	F-WWBE	A320	2104
F-WWAM	A300	582	F-WWAS	A300	822	F-WWBA	A340	004	F-WWBE	A320	2250
F-WWAM	A300	618	F-WWAS	A300	840	F-WWBB	A310	379	F-WWBE	A320	2423
F-WWAM	A300	641	F-WWAS	A300	859	F-WWBB	A320	0250	F-WWBE	A320	2596
F-WWAM	A300	699	F-WWAS	A300	877	F-WWBB	A320	0315	F-WWBE	A320	2732
F-WWAM	A300	729	F-WWAS	A319	0572	F-WWBB	A320	0394	F-WWBE	A320	2869
F-WWAM	A300	748	F-WWAS	A340	002	F-WWBB	A320	0466	F-WWBE	A320	3004
F-WWAM	A300	769	F-WWAT	A300	417	F-WWBB	A320	0587	F-WWBE	A320	3123
F-WWAM	A300	802	F-WWAT	A300	540	F-WWBB	A320	0665	F-WWBE	A320	3230
F-WWAM	A300	818	F-WWAT	A300	602	F-WWBB	A320	0838	F-WWBE	A340	006
F-WWAM	A300	831	F-WWAT	A300	623	F-WWBB	A320	1061	F-WWBF	A310	400
F-WWAM	A300	854	F-WWAT	A300	662	F-WWBB	A320	1353	F-WWBF	A319	1880
F-WWAN	A300	192	F-WWAT	A300	705	F-WWBB	A320	1508	F-WWBF	A320	0254
F-WWAN	A300	398	F-WWAT	A300	732	F-WWBB	A320	1812	F-WWBF	A320	0318
F-WWAN	A300	479	F-WWAT	A300	747	F-WWBB	A320	2001	F-WWBF	A320	0383
F-WWAN	A300	561	F-WWAT	A300	775	F-WWBB	A320	2136	F-WWBF	A320	0452
F-WWAN	A300	613	F-WWAT	A300	808	F-WWBB	A320	2252	F-WWBF	A320	0592
F-WWAN	A300	643	F-WWAT	A300	841	F-WWBB	A320	2422	F-WWBF	A320	0673
F-WWAN	A300	701	F-WWAT	A300	860	F-WWBB	A320	2712	F-WWBF	A320	0842
F-WWAN	A300	735	F-WWAT	A300	878	F-WWBB	A320	2865	F-WWBF	A320	0962
F-WWAN	A300	749	F-WWAU	A300	420	F-WWBB	A320	3002	F-WWBF	A320	1067
F-WWAN	A300	781	F-WWAU	A300	510	F-WWBB	A320	3117	F-WWBF	A320	1221
F-WWAN	A300	803	F-WWAU	A300	554	F-WWBB	A320	3218	F-WWBF	A320	1357
F-WWAN	A300	819	F-WWAU	A300	584	F-WWBC	A310	386	F-WWBF	A320	1514
F-WWAN	A300	832	F-WWAU	A300	619	F-WWBC	A320	0251	F-WWBF	A320	1680
F-WWAN	A300	855	F-WWAU	A300	664	F-WWBC	A320	0316	F-WWBF	A320	1834
F-WWAN	A300	869	F-WWAU	A300	707	F-WWBC	A320	0467	F-WWBF	A320	2212
F-WWAO	A300	247	F-WWAU	A300	733	F-WWBC	A320	0534	F-WWBF	A320	2376
F-WWAO	A300	401	F-WWAU	A300	750	F-WWBC	A320	0667	F-WWBF	A320	2569
F-WWAO	A300	505	F-WWAU	A300	780	F-WWBC	A320	0756	F-WWBF	A320	2734
F-WWAO	A300	543	F-WWAU	A300	809	F-WWBC	A320	0872	F-WWBF	A320	2871
F-WWAO	A300	583	F-WWAU	A300	845	F-WWBC	A320	0899	F-WWBF	A320	3006
F-WWAO	A300	615	F-WWAU	A300	861	F-WWBC	A320	0990	F-WWBF	A320	3125
F-WWAO	A300	645	F-WWAV	A300	423	F-WWBC	A320	1141	F-WWBF	A320	3232
F-WWAO	A300	703	F-WWAV	A300	511	F-WWBC	A320	1294	F-WWBG	A310	389
F-WWAO	A300	766	F-WWAV	A300	555	F-WWBC	A320	1435	F-WWBG	A319	2581
F-WWAO	A300	773	F-WWAV	A300	603	F-WWBC	A320	1561	F-WWBG	A320	0255
F-WWAO	A300	785	F-WWAV	A300	639	F-WWBC	A320	1809	F-WWBG	A320	0319
F-WWAO	A300	804	F-WWAV	A300	694	F-WWBC	A320	2345	F-WWBG	A320	0384
F-WWAO	A300	820	F-WWAV	A300	730	F-WWBC	A320	2594	F-WWBG	A320	0453
F-WWAO	A300	833	F-WWAV	A300	778	F-WWBC	A320	2731	F-WWBG	A320	0594
F-WWAO	A300	873	F-WWAV	A300	790	F-WWBC	A320	2867	F-WWBG	A320	0676
F-WWAP	A300	405	F-WWAV	A300	823	F-WWBC	A320	3000	F-WWBG	A320	0844
F-WWAP	A300	506	F-WWAV	A300	846	F-WWBC	A320	3119	F-WWBG	A320	1143
F-WWAP	A300	546	F-WWAV	A300	863	F-WWBC	A320	3227	F-WWBG	A320	1296

F-WWBG	A320	1437	F-WWBK	A320	0259	F-WWBO	A320	0504	F-WWBR	A320	2883
F-WWBG	A320	1566	F-WWBK	A320	0321	F-WWBO	A320	0859	F-WWBR	A320	3018
F-WWBG	A320	2046	F-WWBK	A320	0396	F-WWBO	A320	0969	F-WWBR	A320	3148
F-WWBG	A320	2210	F-WWBK	A320	0455	F-WWBO	A320	1119	F-WWBS	A320	0281
F-WWBG	A320	2347	F-WWBK	A320	0603	F-WWBO	A320	1288	F-WWBS	A320	0347
F-WWBG	A320	2502	F-WWBK	A320	0741	F-WWBO	A320	1424	F-WWBS	A320	0432
F-WWBG	A320	2717	F-WWBK	A320	0854	F-WWBO	A320	1578	F-WWBS	A320	0491
F-WWBG	A321	1675	F-WWBK	A320	0966	F-WWBO	A320	1749	F-WWBS	A320	0617
F-WWBH	A310	390	F-WWBK	A320	1114	F-WWBO	A320	1877	F-WWBS	A320	0737
F-WWBH	A320	0256	F-WWBK	A320	1284	F-WWBO	A320	2009	F-WWBS	A320	0866
F-WWBH	A320	0357	F-WWBK	A320	1422	F-WWBO	A320	2134	F-WWBS	A320	0992
F-WWBH	A320	0430	F-WWBK	A320	1580	F-WWBO	A320	2282	F-WWBS	A320	1152
F-WWBH	A320	0486	F-WWBK	A320	1732	F-WWBO	A320	2439	F-WWBS	A320	1308
F-WWBH	A320	0596	F-WWBK	A320	1898	F-WWBO	A320	2602	F-WWBS	A320	1443
F-WWBH	A320	0681	F-WWBK	A320	2058	F-WWBO	A320	2745	F-WWBS	A320	1591
F-WWBH	A320	0846	F-WWBK	A320	2161	F-WWBO	A320	2880	F-WWBS	A320	1744
F-WWBH	A320	0960	F-WWBK	A320	2256	F-WWBO	A320	3014	F-WWBS	A320	1888
F-WWBH	A320	1070	F-WWBK	A320	2432	F-WWBO	A320	3221	F-WWBS	A320	2016
F-WWBH	A320	1224	F-WWBK	A320	2600	F-WWBP	A320	0272	F-WWBS	A320	2141
F-WWBH	A320	1359	F-WWBK	A320	2743	F-WWBP	A320	0339	F-WWBS	A320	2288
F-WWBH	A320	1553	F-WWBK	A320	2877	F-WWBP	A320	0416	F-WWBS	A320	2445
F-WWBH	A320	1723	F-WWBK	A320	3012	F-WWBP	A320	0475	F-WWBS	A320	2608
F-WWBH	A320	1835	F-WWBK	A320	3131	F-WWBP	A320	0611	F-WWBS	A320	2764
F-WWBH	A320	2088	F-WWBK	A320	3239	F-WWBP	A320	0726	F-WWBS	A320	2885
F-WWBH	A320	2217	F-WWBL	A310	430	F-WWBP	A320	0861	F-WWBS	A320	3021
F-WWBH	A320	2425	F-WWBL	A320	0260	F-WWBP	A320	1150	F-WWBS	A320	3149
F-WWBH	A320	2580	F-WWBL	A320	0322	F-WWBP	A320	1300	F-WWBS	A320	3266
F-WWBH	A320	2737	F-WWBL	A320	0415	F-WWBP	A320	1555	F-WWBT	A320	0283
F-WWBH	A320	2874	F-WWBL	A320	1063	F-WWBP	A320	1725	F-WWBT	A320	0348
F-WWBH	A320	3008	F-WWBM	A310	468	F-WWBP	A320	1842	F-WWBT	A320	0507
F-WWBH	A320	3127	F-WWBM	A320	0261	F-WWBP	A320	2092	F-WWBT	A320	0619
F-WWBH	A320	3234	F-WWBM	A320	0323	F-WWBP	A320	2206	F-WWBT	A320	0698
F-WWBI	A310	415	F-WWBM	A320	0397	F-WWBP	A320	2349	F-WWBT	A320	0820
F-WWBI	A320	0257	F-WWBM	A320	0470	F-WWBP	A320	2506	F-WWBT	A320	0951
F-WWBI	A320	0320	F-WWBM	A320	0605	F-WWBP	A320	2668	F-WWBT	A320	1121
F-WWBI	A320	0386	F-WWBM	A320	0722	F-WWBP	A320	2834	F-WWBT	A320	1292
F-WWBI	A320	0551	F-WWBM	A320	0856	F-WWBP	A320	2980	F-WWBT	A320	1446
F-WWBI	A320	0632	F-WWBM	A320	0994	F-WWBP	A320	3132	F-WWBT	A320	1593
F-WWBI	A320	0718	F-WWBM	A320	1146	F-WWBP	A320	3242	F-WWBT	A320	1694
F-WWBI	A320	0849	F-WWBM	A320	1298	F-WWBQ	A320	0271	F-WWBT	A320	1895
F-WWBI	A320	0958	F-WWBM	A320	1439	F-WWBQ	A320	0340	F-WWBT	A320	2014
F-WWBI	A320	1072	F-WWBM	A320	1571	F-WWBQ	A320	0431	F-WWBT	A320	2165
F-WWBI	A320	1278	F-WWBM	A320	1735	F-WWBQ	A320	0506	F-WWBT	A320	2291
F-WWBI	A320	1418	F-WWBM	A320	1838	F-WWBQ	A320	0613	F-WWBT	A320	3029
F-WWBI	A320	1568	F-WWBM	A320	2090	F-WWBQ	A320	0730	F-WWBT	A320	3150
F-WWBI	A320	1728	F-WWBM	A320	2162	F-WWBQ	A320	0863	F-WWBT	A320	3246
F-WWBI	A320	1871	F-WWBM	A320	2361	F-WWBQ	A320	1148	F-WWBT	A340	371
F-WWBI	A320	1975	F-WWBM	A320	2504	F-WWBQ	A320	1302	F-WWBU	A320	0284
F-WWBI	A320	2138	F-WWBM	A320	2663	F-WWBQ	A320	1441	F-WWBU	A320	0349
F-WWBI	A320	2259	F-WWBM	A320	2792	F-WWBQ	A320	1588	F-WWBU	A320	0426
F-WWBI	A320	2428	F-WWBM	A320	2958	F-WWBQ	A320	1739	F-WWBU	A320	0492
F-WWBI	A320	2576	F-WWBM	A320	3027	F-WWBQ	A320	1883	F-WWBU	A320	0622
F-WWBI	A320	3025	F-WWBM	A320	3145	F-WWBQ	A320	1973	F-WWBU	A320	0720
F-WWBI	A320	3143	F-WWBM	A320	3240	F-WWBQ	A320	2102	F-WWBU	A320	0868
F-WWBI	A320	3236	F-WWBN	A310	486	F-WWBQ	A320	2284	F-WWBU	A320	1210
F-WWBI	A321	2682	F-WWBN	A319	2192	F-WWBQ	A320	2441	F-WWBU	A320	1361
F-WWBJ	A310	419	F-WWBN	A320	0264	F-WWBQ	A320	2604	F-WWBU	A320	1595
F-WWBJ	A319	2007	F-WWBN	A320	0334	F-WWBQ	A320	2747	F-WWBU	A320	1741
F-WWBJ	A320	0258	F-WWBN	A320	0402	F-WWBQ	A320	2881	F-WWBU	A320	1892
F-WWBJ	A320	0333	F-WWBN	A320	0536	F-WWBQ	A320	3016	F-WWBU	A320	2297
F-WWBJ	A320	0373	F-WWBN	A320	0607	F-WWBQ	A320	3147	F-WWBU	A320	2447
F-WWBJ	A320	0395	F-WWBN	A320	0724	F-WWBQ	A320	3244	F-WWBU	A320	2609
F-WWBJ	A320	0454	F-WWBN	A320	0857	F-WWBR	A320	0274	F-WWBU	A320	2785
F-WWBJ	A320	0601	F-WWBN	A320	0967	F-WWBR	A320	0341	F-WWBU	A320	2930
F-WWBJ	A320	0678	F-WWBN	A320	1117	F-WWBR	A320	0417	F-WWBU	A320	3031
F-WWBJ	A320	0851	F-WWBN	A320	1286	F-WWBR	A320	0476	F-WWBU	A320	3151
F-WWBJ	A320	0964	F-WWBN	A320	1427	F-WWBR	A320	0615	**F-WWBU**	**A320**	**3268**
F-WWBJ	A320	1112	F-WWBN	A320	1584	F-WWBR	A320	0733	F-WWBU	A321	1928
F-WWBJ	A320	1282	F-WWBN	A320	1760	F-WWBR	A320	0865	F-WWBV	A320	0288
F-WWBJ	A320	1419	F-WWBN	A320	1874	F-WWBR	A320	0973	F-WWBV	A320	0387
F-WWBJ	A320	1564	F-WWBN	A320	2003	F-WWBR	A320	1123	F-WWBV	A320	0443
F-WWBJ	A320	1730	F-WWBN	A320	2137	F-WWBR	A320	1290	F-WWBV	A320	0496
F-WWBJ	A320	1992	F-WWBN	A320	2520	F-WWBR	A320	1430	F-WWBV	A320	0624
F-WWBJ	A320	2215	F-WWBN	A320	2665	F-WWBR	A320	1586	F-WWBV	A320	0735
F-WWBJ	A320	2430	F-WWBN	A320	2794	F-WWBR	A320	1762	F-WWBV	A320	0874
F-WWBJ	A320	2598	F-WWBN	A320	2960	F-WWBR	A320	1891	F-WWBV	A320	0996
F-WWBJ	A320	2740	F-WWBN	A320	3086	F-WWBR	A320	2011	F-WWBV	A320	1156
F-WWBJ	A320	2875	F-WWBN	A320	3219	F-WWBR	A320	2140	F-WWBV	A320	1304
F-WWBJ	A320	3010	F-WWBO	A310	487	F-WWBR	A320	2286	F-WWBV	A320	1448
F-WWBJ	A320	3129	F-WWBO	A320	0266	F-WWBR	A320	2443	F-WWBV	A320	1605
F-WWBJ	A320	3237	F-WWBO	A320	0335	F-WWBR	A320	2606	F-WWBV	A320	1767
F-WWBK	A310	427	F-WWBO	A320	0403	F-WWBR	A320	2761	F-WWBV	A320	1889

Reg.	Type	No.	Reg.	Type	No.	Reg.	Type	No.	Reg.	Type	No.
F-WWBV	A320	2018	F-WWCB	A310	700	F-WWCI	A340	431	F-WWCQ	A310	539
F-WWBV	A320	2143	F-WWCB	A340	371	F-WWCI	A340	547	F-WWCQ	A310	594
F-WWBV	A320	2299	F-WWCB	A340	569	F-WWCI	A340	639	F-WWCQ	A310	647
F-WWBV	A320	2612	F-WWCB	A340	672	F-WWCI	A340	762	F-WWCQ	A340	475
F-WWBV	A320	2787	F-WWCB	A340	764	F-WWCI	A340	848	F-WWCQ	A340	583
F-WWBV	A320	2947	F-WWCB	A340	837	F-WWCJ	A310	413	F-WWCQ	A340	706
F-WWBV	A320	3087	F-WWCC	A310	399	F-WWCJ	A310	452	F-WWCQ	A340	771
F-WWBX	A320	0289	F-WWCC	A310	434	F-WWCJ	A310	485	F-WWCR	A310	428
F-WWBX	A320	0363	F-WWCC	A310	473	F-WWCJ	A310	522	F-WWCR	A310	444
F-WWBX	A320	0478	F-WWCC	A310	526	F-WWCJ	A310	576	F-WWCR	A310	482
F-WWBX	A320	0537	F-WWCC	A310	565	F-WWCJ	A310	654	F-WWCR	A310	541
F-WWBX	A320	0626	F-WWCC	A310	620	F-WWCJ	A310	684	F-WWCR	A310	595
F-WWBX	A320	0739	F-WWCC	A310	651	F-WWCJ	A340	436	F-WWCR	A310	648
F-WWBX	A320	0870	F-WWCC	A310	669	F-WWCJ	A340	566	F-WWCR	A340	517
F-WWBX	A320	1310	F-WWCC	A340	376	F-WWCJ	A340	677	F-WWCR	A340	586
F-WWBX	A320	1450	F-WWCD	A310	404	F-WWCJ	A340	763	F-WWCR	A340	715
F-WWBX	A320	1676	F-WWCD	A310	435	F-WWCJ	A340	856	F-WWCS	A310	429
F-WWBX	A320	1922	F-WWCD	A310	457	"F-WWCJY"	A340	856	F-WWCS	A310	443
F-WWBX	A320	2094	F-WWCD	A310	502	F-WWCK	A310	416	F-WWCS	A310	483
F-WWBX	A320	2191	F-WWCD	A310	527	F-WWCK	A310	453	F-WWCS	A310	542
F-WWBX	A320	2294	F-WWCD	A310	622	F-WWCK	A310	489	F-WWCS	A310	596
F-WWBX	A320	2449	F-WWCD	A310	672	F-WWCK	A310	523	F-WWCS	A340	482
F-WWBX	A320	2637	F-WWCD	A310	691	F-WWCK	A310	586	F-WWCS	A340	601
F-WWBX	A320	2789	F-WWCD	A340	383	F-WWCK	A310	638	F-WWCS	A340	723
F-WWBX	A320	2932	F-WWCE	A310	409	F-WWCK	A310	663	F-WWCS	A340	779
F-WWBX	A320	3033	F-WWCE	A310	438	F-WWCK	A310	697	F-WWCT	A310	431
F-WWBX	A320	3152	F-WWCE	A310	488	F-WWCK	A340	391	F-WWCT	A310	476
F-WWBX	**A320**	**3270**	F-WWCE	A310	528	F-WWCK	A340	575	F-WWCT	A310	499
F-WWBY	A320	0097	F-WWCE	A310	568	F-WWCK	A340	681	F-WWCT	A310	587
F-WWBY	A320	0290	F-WWCE	A310	624	F-WWCK	A340	765	F-WWCT	A310	646
F-WWBY	A320	0360	F-WWCE	A310	661	F-WWCK	A340	870	F-WWCT	A310	680
F-WWBY	A320	0444	F-WWCE	A310	687	F-WWCL	A310	418	F-WWCT	A340	488
F-WWBY	A320	0508	F-WWCE	A340	410	F-WWCL	A310	475	F-WWCU	A310	432
F-WWBY	A320	0628	F-WWCE	A340	543	F-WWCL	A310	503	F-WWCU	A310	455
F-WWBY	A320	0822	F-WWCE	A340	622	F-WWCL	A310	544	F-WWCU	A310	498
F-WWBY	A320	0971	F-WWCE	A340	731	F-WWCL	A310	640	F-WWCU	A310	547
F-WWBY	A320	1158	F-WWCE	A340	790	F-WWCL	A310	665	F-WWCU	A310	597
F-WWBY	A320	1306	F-WWCF	A310	410	F-WWCL	A310	704	F-WWCU	A310	678
F-WWBY	A320	1452	F-WWCF	A310	440	F-WWCL	A340	440	F-WWCU	A340	514
F-WWBY	A320	1597	F-WWCF	A310	458	F-WWCL	A340	617	F-WWCV	A310	436
F-WWBY	A320	1896	F-WWCF	A310	504	F-WWCL	A340	736	F-WWCV	A310	456
F-WWBY	A320	2006	F-WWCF	A310	570	F-WWCL	A340	798	F-WWCV	A310	496
F-WWBY	A320	2144	F-WWCF	A310	634	F-WWCM	A310	424	F-WWCV	A310	548
F-WWBY	A320	2235	F-WWCF	A310	660	F-WWCM	A310	446	F-WWCV	A310	598
F-WWBY	A320	2640	F-WWCF	A310	698	F-WWCM	A310	494	F-WWCV	A310	649
F-WWBY	A320	2791	F-WWCF	A340	416	F-WWCM	A310	534	F-WWCV	A340	523
F-WWBY	A320	2956	F-WWCF	A340	540	F-WWCM	A310	588	F-WWCV	A340	606
F-WWBY	A320	3089	F-WWCF	A340	626	F-WWCM	A310	671	F-WWCV	A340	727
F-WWBY	A320	3224	F-WWCF	A340	744	F-WWCM	A310	706	F-WWCV	A340	804
F-WWBZ	A320	0291	F-WWCF	A340	794	F-WWCM	A340	449	F-WWCW	A310	589
F-WWBZ	A320	0365	F-WWCG	A310	406	F-WWCM	A340	577	F-WWCX	A310	433
F-WWBZ	A320	0445	F-WWCG	A310	449	F-WWCM	A340	702	F-WWCX	A310	478
F-WWBZ	A320	0510	F-WWCG	A310	467	F-WWCM	A340	766	F-WWCX	A310	500
F-WWBZ	A320	0630	F-WWCG	A310	519	F-WWCN	A310	421	F-WWCX	A310	549
F-WWBZ	A320	0824	F-WWCG	A310	573	F-WWCN	A310	447	F-WWCX	A310	590
F-WWBZ	A320	0999	F-WWCG	A310	636	F-WWCN	A310	493	F-WWCX	A310	642
F-WWBZ	A320	1162	F-WWCG	A310	689	F-WWCN	A310	535	F-WWCX	A310	686
F-WWBZ	A320	1312	F-WWCG	A310	702	F-WWCN	A310	592	F-WWCX	A340	531
F-WWBZ	A320	1454	F-WWCG	A340	417	F-WWCN	A310	682	F-WWCX	A340	710
F-WWBZ	A320	1609	F-WWCG	A340	557	F-WWCN	A340	453	F-WWCX	A340	812
F-WWBZ	A320	1764	F-WWCG	A340	630	F-WWCN	A340	580	F-WWCY	A310	437
F-WWBZ	A320	1857	F-WWCG	A340	753	F-WWCN	A340	689	F-WWCY	A310	451
F-WWBZ	A320	2020	F-WWCG	A340	829	F-WWCN	A340	767	F-WWCY	A310	545
F-WWBZ	A320	2142	F-WWCH	A310	407	F-WWCO	A310	422	F-WWCY	A310	658
F-WWBZ	A320	2292	F-WWCH	A310	450	F-WWCO	A310	448	F-WWCY	A340	534
F-WWBZ	A320	2642	F-WWCH	A310	497	F-WWCO	A310	495	F-WWCZ	A310	442
F-WWBZ	A320	2896	F-WWCH	A310	585	F-WWCO	A310	537	F-WWCZ	A310	480
F-WWBZ	A320	3023	F-WWCH	A310	591	F-WWCO	A310	589	F-WWCZ	A310	552
F-WWBZ	A320	3153	F-WWCH	A310	652	F-WWCO	A310	644	F-WWCZ	A310	599
F-WWBZ	A320	3272	F-WWCH	A310	674	F-WWCO	A310	695	F-WWCZ	A310	653
F-WWCA	A310	378	F-WWCH	A340	426	F-WWCO	A340	460	F-WWCZ	A310	667
F-WWCA	A310	524	F-WWCH	A340	604	F-WWCP	A310	425	F-WWCZ	A340	537
F-WWCA	A310	562	F-WWCH	A340	719	F-WWCP	A310	492	F-WWCZ	A340	615
F-WWCA	A340	005	F-WWCH	A340	768	F-WWCP	A310	538	F-WWCZ	A340	787
F-WWCA	**A340**	**360**	F-WWCH	A340	846	F-WWCP	A310	593	F-WWDA	A318	1939
F-WWCB	A310	392	F-WWCI	A310	412	F-WWCP	A310	676	F-WWDA	A318	3001
F-WWCB	A310	472	F-WWCI	A310	439	F-WWCP	A340	468	F-WWDA	A320	0002
F-WWCB	A310	501	F-WWCI	A310	472	F-WWCP	A340	619	F-WWDA	A320	2168
F-WWCB	A310	564	F-WWCI	A310	484	F-WWCP	A340	740	F-WWDA	A320	2242
F-WWCB	A310	600	F-WWCI	A310	520	F-WWCQ	A310	426	F-WWDA	A320	2405
F-WWCB	A310	656	F-WWCI	A310	574	F-WWCQ	A310	441	F-WWDA	A320	2670
			F-WWCI	A310	650	F-WWCQ	A310	481	F-WWDA	A320	2820
			F-WWCI	A310	693						

F-WWDA	A320	2964	F-WWDE	A320	0245	F-WWDG	A320	2766	F-WWDJ	A320	2962
F-WWDA	A340	003	F-WWDE	A320	0305	F-WWDG	A320	2911	F-WWDK	A320	0009
F-WWDB	A319	0546	F-WWDE	A320	0373	F-WWDG	A320	3037	F-WWDK	A320	0032
F-WWDB	A320	0003	F-WWDE	A320	0436	F-WWDG	A320	3177	F-WWDK	A320	0092
F-WWDB	A320	0103	F-WWDE	A320	0523	F-WWDH	A319	1897	F-WWDK	A320	0144
F-WWDB	A320	0135	F-WWDE	A320	0638	F-WWDH	A320	0018	F-WWDK	A320	0206
F-WWDB	A320	0182	F-WWDE	A320	0762	F-WWDH	A320	0091	F-WWDK	A320	0247
F-WWDB	A320	0185	F-WWDE	A320	0884	F-WWDH	A320	0141	F-WWDK	A320	0326
F-WWDB	A320	0342	"F-WWDE"	A320	0886	F-WWDH	A320	0191	F-WWDK	A320	0405
F-WWDB	A320	0406	F-WWDE	A320	0981	F-WWDH	A320	0343	F-WWDK	A320	0459
F-WWDB	A320	0456	F-WWDE	A320	1105	F-WWDH	A320	0407	F-WWDK	A320	0540
F-WWDB	A320	0659	F-WWDE	A320	1264	F-WWDH	A320	0479	F-WWDK	A320	0661
F-WWDB	A320	0881	F-WWDE	A320	1457	F-WWDH	A320	0571	F-WWDK	A320	0772
F-WWDB	A320	0977	F-WWDE	A320	1610	F-WWDH	A320	0768	F-WWDK	A320	0897
F-WWDB	A320	1101	F-WWDE	A320	1751	F-WWDH	A320	0886	F-WWDK	A320	1003
F-WWDB	A320	1215	F-WWDE	A320	1847	F-WWDH	A320	1001	F-WWDK	A320	1099
F-WWDB	A320	1262	F-WWDE	A320	1945	F-WWDH	A320	1108	F-WWDK	A320	1163
F-WWDB	A320	1402	F-WWDE	A320	2063	F-WWDH	A320	1268	F-WWDK	A320	1318
F-WWDB	A320	1548	F-WWDE	A320	2157	F-WWDH	A320	1405	F-WWDK	A320	1467
F-WWDB	A320	1715	F-WWDE	A320	2257	F-WWDH	A320	1559	F-WWDK	A320	1621
F-WWDB	A320	1968	F-WWDE	A320	2409	F-WWDH	A320	1754	F-WWDK	A320	1769
F-WWDB	A320	2132	F-WWDE	A320	2583	F-WWDH	A320	1854	F-WWDK	A320	1906
F-WWDB	A320	2185	F-WWDE	A320	2752	F-WWDH	A320	2197	F-WWDK	A320	2024
F-WWDB	A320	2391	F-WWDE	A320	2900	F-WWDH	A320	2413	F-WWDK	A320	2130
F-WWDB	A320	2577	F-WWDE	A320	3035	F-WWDH	A320	2584	F-WWDK	A320	2187
F-WWDB	A320	2749	F-WWDE	A320	3154	F-WWDH	A320	2753	F-WWDK	A320	2314
F-WWDB	A320	2899	**F-WWDE**	**A320**	**3275**	F-WWDH	A320	2902	F-WWDK	A320	2457
F-WWDC	A310	567	F-WWDF	A319	0767	F-WWDH	A320	3039	F-WWDK	A320	2619
F-WWDC	A320	0004	F-WWDF	A320	0011	F-WWDH	A320	3155	F-WWDK	A320	2768
F-WWDC	A320	0073	F-WWDF	A320	0029	F-WWDI	A320	0005	F-WWDK	A320	2914
F-WWDC	A320	0136	F-WWDF	A320	0085	F-WWDI	A320	0030	F-WWDK	A320	3040
F-WWDC	A320	0189	F-WWDF	A320	0139	F-WWDI	A320	0059	F-WWDK	A320	3156
F-WWDC	A320	0238	F-WWDF	A320	0197	F-WWDI	A320	0142	F-WWDL	A320	0010
F-WWDC	A320	0324	F-WWDF	A320	0234	F-WWDI	A320	0199	F-WWDL	A320	0034
F-WWDC	A320	0388	F-WWDF	A320	0350	F-WWDI	A320	0230	F-WWDL	A320	0099
F-WWDC	A320	0433	F-WWDF	A320	0404	F-WWDI	A320	0262	F-WWDL	A320	0145
F-WWDC	A320	0511	F-WWDF	A320	0497	F-WWDI	A320	0325	F-WWDL	A320	0201
F-WWDC	A320	0568	F-WWDF	A320	0558	F-WWDI	A320	0389	F-WWDL	A320	0243
F-WWDC	A320	0758	F-WWDF	A320	0640	F-WWDI	A320	0527	F-WWDL	A320	0308
F-WWDC	A320	0883	F-WWDF	A320	0764	F-WWDI	A320	0643	F-WWDL	A320	0390
F-WWDC	A320	0978	F-WWDF	A320	0892	F-WWDI	A320	0712	F-WWDL	A320	0528
F-WWDC	A320	1104	F-WWDF	A320	0982	F-WWDI	A320	0799	F-WWDL	A320	0645
F-WWDC	A320	1266	F-WWDF	A320	1137	F-WWDI	A320	0894	F-WWDL	A320	0701
F-WWDC	A320	1407	F-WWDF	A320	1270	F-WWDI	A320	0984	F-WWDL	A320	0784
F-WWDC	A320	1550	F-WWDF	A320	1409	F-WWDI	A320	1110	F-WWDL	A320	0899
F-WWDC	A320	1717	F-WWDF	A320	1557	F-WWDI	A320	1272	F-WWDL	A320	1005
F-WWDC	A320	1840	F-WWDF	A320	1721	F-WWDI	A320	1413	F-WWDL	A320	1168
F-WWDC	A320	1944	F-WWDF	A320	1849	F-WWDI	A320	1613	F-WWDL	A320	1332
F-WWDC	A320	2061	F-WWDF	A320	1948	F-WWDI	A320	1747	F-WWDL	A320	1469
F-WWDC	A320	2156	F-WWDF	A320	2075	F-WWDI	A320	1856	F-WWDL	A320	1626
F-WWDC	A320	2254	F-WWDF	A320	2158	F-WWDI	A320	2146	F-WWDL	A320	1776
F-WWDC	A320	2407	F-WWDF	A320	2301	F-WWDI	A320	2204	F-WWDL	A320	1903
F-WWDC	A320	2564	F-WWDF	A320	2451	F-WWDI	A320	2364	F-WWDL	A320	1981
F-WWDC	A320	2719	F-WWDF	A320	2671	F-WWDI	A320	2696	F-WWDL	A320	2189
F-WWDC	A320	2822	F-WWDF	A320	2824	F-WWDI	A320	2826	F-WWDL	A320	2275
F-WWDC	A320	2966	F-WWDF	A320	2968	F-WWDI	A320	2970	F-WWDL	A320	2434
F-WWDD	A320	0006	F-WWDF	A320	3136	F-WWDI	A320	3138	F-WWDL	A320	2587
F-WWDD	A320	0027	F-WWDF	A321	2553	F-WWDJ	A318	3100	F-WWDL	A320	2755
F-WWDD	A320	0040	F-WWDG	A320	0017	F-WWDJ	A320	0007	F-WWDL	A320	3135
F-WWDD	A320	0137	F-WWDG	A320	0046	F-WWDJ	A320	0031	F-WWDL	A320	3286
F-WWDD	A320	0190	F-WWDG	A320	0105	F-WWDJ	A320	0086	F-WWDM	A320	0012
F-WWDD	A320	0241	F-WWDG	A320	0140	F-WWDJ	A320	0143	F-WWDM	A320	0039
F-WWDD	A320	0300	F-WWDG	A320	0198	F-WWDJ	A320	0200	F-WWDM	A320	0087
F-WWDD	A320	0366	F-WWDG	A320	0306	F-WWDJ	A320	0242	F-WWDM	A320	0146
F-WWDD	A320	0435	F-WWDG	A320	0367	F-WWDJ	A320	0307	F-WWDM	A320	0202
F-WWDD	A320	0512	F-WWDG	A320	0418	F-WWDJ	A320	0374	F-WWDM	A320	0235
F-WWDD	A320	0635	F-WWDG	A320	0457	F-WWDJ	A320	0446	F-WWDM	A320	0351
F-WWDD	A320	0760	F-WWDG	A320	0569	F-WWDJ	A320	0487	F-WWDM	A320	0437
F-WWDD	A320	0879	F-WWDG	A320	0766	F-WWDJ	A320	0573	F-WWDM	A320	0489
F-WWDD	A320	1026	F-WWDG	A320	0888	F-WWDJ	A320	0770	F-WWDM	A320	0561
F-WWDD	A320	1461	F-WWDG	A320	1028	F-WWDJ	A320	0895	F-WWDM	A320	0662
F-WWDD	A320	1617	F-WWDG	A320	1166	F-WWDJ	A320	0986	F-WWDM	A320	0776
F-WWDD	A320	1771	F-WWDG	A320	1316	F-WWDJ	A320	1138	F-WWDM	A320	0900
F-WWDD	A320	1904	F-WWDG	A320	1464	F-WWDJ	A320	1314	F-WWDM	A320	1007
F-WWDD	A321	1094	F-WWDG	A320	1620	F-WWDJ	A320	1736	F-WWDM	A320	1171
F-WWDD	A321	1188	F-WWDG	A320	1773	F-WWDJ	A320	1920	F-WWDM	A320	1334
F-WWDD	**A380**	**004**	F-WWDG	A320	1902	F-WWDJ	A320	2070	F-WWDM	A320	1484
F-WWDE	A320	0008	F-WWDG	A320	2022	F-WWDJ	A320	2173	F-WWDM	A320	1637
F-WWDE	A320	0028	F-WWDG	A320	2171	F-WWDJ	A320	2312	F-WWDM	A320	1777
F-WWDE	A320	0083	F-WWDG	A320	2238	F-WWDJ	A320	2455	F-WWDM	A320	1861
F-WWDE	A320	0138	F-WWDG	A320	2411	F-WWDJ	A320	2616	F-WWDM	A320	1983
F-WWDE	A320	0196	F-WWDG	A320	2566	F-WWDJ	A320	2817	F-WWDM	A320	2108

Reg	Type	No.	Reg	Type	No.	Reg	Type	No.	Reg	Type	No.
F-WWDM	A320	2278	F-WWDP	A320	1473	F-WWDS	A320	1322	F-WWDV	A320	0797
F-WWDM	A320	2459	F-WWDP	A320	1631	F-WWDS	A320	1478	F-WWDV	A320	0914
F-WWDM	A320	2620	F-WWDP	A320	1785	F-WWDS	A320	1646	F-WWDV	A320	1032
F-WWDM	A320	2770	F-WWDP	A320	1910	F-WWDS	A320	1784	F-WWDV	A320	1189
F-WWDM	A320	2915	F-WWDP	A320	2027	F-WWDS	A320	1909	F-WWDV	A320	1330
F-WWDM	A320	3042	F-WWDP	A320	2038	F-WWDS	A320	2147	F-WWDV	A320	1486
F-WWDM	A320	3157	F-WWDP	A320	2154	F-WWDS	A320	2207	F-WWDV	A320	1650
F-WWDM	A320	3280	F-WWDP	A320	2239	F-WWDS	A320	2310	F-WWDV	A320	1797
F-WWDN	A320	0013	F-WWDP	A320	2415	F-WWDS	A320	2475	F-WWDV	A320	1873
F-WWDN	A320	0037	F-WWDP	A320	2589	F-WWDS	A320	2626	F-WWDV	A320	1894
F-WWDN	A320	0088	F-WWDP	A320	2758	F-WWDS	A320	2775	F-WWDV	A320	2079
F-WWDN	A320	0147	F-WWDP	A320	2904	F-WWDS	A320	2922	F-WWDV	A320	2175
F-WWDN	A320	0203	F-WWDP	A320	3044	F-WWDS	A320	3050	F-WWDV	A320	2322
F-WWDN	A320	0292	F-WWDP	A320	3158	F-WWDS	A320	3178	F-WWDV	A320	2478
F-WWDN	A320	0361	F-WWDQ	A320	0016	F-WWDS	A320	3289	F-WWDV	A320	2627
F-WWDN	A320	0408	F-WWDQ	A320	0052	F-WWDS	A321	0855	F-WWDV	A320	2776
F-WWDN	A320	0460	F-WWDQ	A320	0093	F-WWDT	A320	0024	F-WWDV	A320	2924
F-WWDN	A320	0574	F-WWDQ	A320	0150	F-WWDT	A320	0042	F-WWDV	A320	3056
F-WWDN	A320	0774	F-WWDQ	A320	0207	F-WWDT	A320	0089	F-WWDV	A320	3183
F-WWDN	A320	0902	F-WWDQ	A320	0263	F-WWDT	A320	0152	F-WWDX	A320	0035
F-WWDN	A320	1009	F-WWDQ	A320	0327	F-WWDT	A320	0208	F-WWDX	A320	0090
F-WWDN	A320	1173	F-WWDQ	A320	0398	F-WWDT	A320	0248	F-WWDX	A320	0153
F-WWDN	A320	1339	F-WWDQ	A320	0462	F-WWDT	A320	0303	F-WWDX	A320	0218
F-WWDN	A320	1489	F-WWDQ	A320	0562	F-WWDT	A320	0375	F-WWDX	A320	0277
F-WWDN	A320	1644	F-WWDQ	A320	0683	F-WWDT	A320	0438	F-WWDX	A320	0346
F-WWDN	A320	1780	F-WWDQ	A320	0780	F-WWDT	A320	0490	F-WWDX	A320	0411
F-WWDN	A320	1907	F-WWDQ	A320	0907	F-WWDT	A320	0577	F-WWDX	A320	0464
F-WWDN	A320	1989	F-WWDQ	A320	1014	F-WWDT	A320	0789	F-WWDX	A320	0582
F-WWDN	A320	2146	F-WWDQ	A320	1179	F-WWDT	A320	0911	F-WWDX	A320	0795
F-WWDN	A320	2219	F-WWDQ	A320	1343	F-WWDT	A320	1183	F-WWDX	A320	0916
F-WWDN	A320	2366	F-WWDQ	A320	1475	F-WWDT	A320	1320	F-WWDX	A320	1035
F-WWDN	A320	2522	F-WWDQ	A320	1633	F-WWDT	A320	1480	F-WWDX	A320	1192
F-WWDN	A320	2699	F-WWDQ	A320	1860	F-WWDT	A320	1635	F-WWDX	A320	1345
F-WWDN	A320	2828	F-WWDQ	A320	2112	F-WWDT	A320	1787	F-WWDX	A320	1491
F-WWDN	A320	2973	F-WWDQ	A320	2169	F-WWDT	A320	1911	F-WWDX	A320	1652
F-WWDN	A320	3140	F-WWDQ	A320	2372	F-WWDT	A320	2031	F-WWDX	A320	1792
F-WWDN	A320	3261	F-WWDQ	A320	2526	F-WWDT	A320	2128	F-WWDX	A320	1879
F-WWDO	A320	0014	F-WWDQ	A320	2725	F-WWDT	A320	2280	F-WWDX	A320	2029
F-WWDO	A320	0043	F-WWDQ	A320	2906	F-WWDT	A320	2417	F-WWDX	A320	2133
F-WWDO	A320	0068	F-WWDQ	A320	3047	F-WWDT	A320	2591	F-WWDX	A320	2199
F-WWDO	A320	0148	F-WWDQ	A320	3159	F-WWDT	A320	2760	F-WWDX	A320	2327
F-WWDO	A320	0205	F-WWDQ	A320	3284	F-WWDT	A320	2908	F-WWDX	A320	2489
F-WWDO	A320	0249	F-WWDR	A320	0022	F-WWDT	A320	3052	F-WWDX	A320	2630
F-WWDO	A320	0314	F-WWDR	A320	0050	F-WWDT	A320	3180	F-WWDX	A320	2778
F-WWDO	A320	0391	F-WWDR	A320	0094	F-WWDT	A320	3291	F-WWDX	A320	2926
F-WWDO	A320	0447	F-WWDR	A320	0151	F-WWDT	A321	0908	F-WWDX	A320	3058
F-WWDO	A320	0499	F-WWDR	A320	0216	F-WWDU	A320	0025	F-WWDX	A320	3185
F-WWDO	A320	0575	F-WWDR	A320	0265	F-WWDU	A320	0048	F-WWDY	A320	0045
F-WWDO	A320	0778	F-WWDR	A320	0328	F-WWDU	A320	0096	F-WWDY	A320	0098
F-WWDO	A320	0903	F-WWDR	A320	0392	F-WWDU	A320	0163	F-WWDY	A320	0154
F-WWDO	A320	1011	F-WWDR	A320	0448	F-WWDU	A320	0279	F-WWDY	A320	0209
F-WWDO	A320	1175	F-WWDR	A320	0565	F-WWDU	A320	0345	F-WWDY	A320	0267
F-WWDO	A320	1337	F-WWDR	A320	0685	F-WWDU	A320	0409	F-WWDY	A320	0329
F-WWDO	A320	1470	F-WWDR	A320	0791	F-WWDU	A320	0480	F-WWDY	A320	0379
F-WWDO	A320	1628	F-WWDR	A320	0953	F-WWDU	A320	0579	F-WWDY	A320	0531
F-WWDO	A320	1702	F-WWDR	A320	1274	F-WWDU	A320	0793	F-WWDY	A320	0704
F-WWDO	A320	1899	F-WWDR	A320	1411	F-WWDU	A320	0912	F-WWDY	A320	0801
F-WWDO	A320	1993	F-WWDR	A320	1615	F-WWDU	A320	1030	F-WWDY	A320	0921
F-WWDO	A320	2139	F-WWDR	A320	1845	F-WWDU	A320	1187	F-WWDY	A320	1037
F-WWDO	A320	2223	F-WWDR	A320	1964	F-WWDU	A320	1327	F-WWDY	A320	1194
F-WWDO	A320	2368	F-WWDR	A320	2106	F-WWDU	A320	1482	F-WWDY	A320	1347
F-WWDO	A320	2524	F-WWDR	A320	2166	F-WWDU	A320	1648	F-WWDY	A320	1493
F-WWDO	A320	2724	F-WWDR	A320	2316	F-WWDU	A320	1789	F-WWDY	A320	1655
F-WWDO	A320	2830	F-WWDR	A320	2461	F-WWDU	A320	1914	F-WWDY	A320	1858
F-WWDO	A320	2975	F-WWDR	A320	2623	F-WWDU	A320	2042	F-WWDY	A320	1965
F-WWDO	A320	3141	F-WWDR	A320	2772	F-WWDU	A320	2155	F-WWDY	A320	2116
F-WWDO	**A320**	**3263**	F-WWDR	A320	2917	F-WWDU	A320	2374	F-WWDY	A320	2180
F-WWDP	A320	0015	F-WWDR	A320	3048	F-WWDU	A320	2728	F-WWDY	A320	2325
F-WWDP	A320	0047	F-WWDR	A320	3160	F-WWDU	A320	2909	F-WWDY	A320	2491
F-WWDP	A320	0084	F-WWDS	A320	0023	F-WWDU	A320	3055	F-WWDY	A320	2633
F-WWDP	A320	0149	F-WWDS	A320	0041	F-WWDU	A320	3182	F-WWDY	A320	2781
F-WWDP	A320	0195	F-WWDS	A320	0095	F-WWDU	A320	3293	F-WWDY	A320	2920
F-WWDP	A320	0419	F-WWDS	A320	0162	F-WWDV	A320	0026	F-WWDY	A320	3060
F-WWDP	A320	0461	F-WWDS	A320	0197	F-WWDV	A320	0053	F-WWDY	A320	3187
F-WWDP	A320	0530	F-WWDS	A320	0217	F-WWDV	A320	0097	F-WWDZ	A320	0038
F-WWDP	A320	0648	F-WWDS	A320	0273	F-WWDV	A320	0165	F-WWDZ	A320	0160
F-WWDP	A320	0702	F-WWDS	A320	0344	F-WWDV	A320	0231	F-WWDZ	A320	0219
F-WWDP	A320	0786	F-WWDS	A320	0650	F-WWDV	A320	0280	F-WWDZ	A320	0293
F-WWDP	A320	0905	F-WWDS	A320	0703	F-WWDV	A320	0353	F-WWDZ	A320	0354
F-WWDP	A320	1013	F-WWDS	A320	0782	F-WWDV	A320	0410	F-WWDZ	A320	0500
F-WWDP	A320	1177	F-WWDS	A320	0909	F-WWDV	A320	0463	F-WWDZ	A320	0584
F-WWDP	A320	1341	F-WWDS	A320	1181	F-WWDV	A320	0580	F-WWDZ	A320	0803

F-WWDZ	A320	0923	F-WWID	A320	2529	F-WWIG	A320	3203	F-WWIK	A320	0172
F-WWDZ	A320	1039	F-WWID	A320	2674	F-WWIH	A320	0054	F-WWIK	A320	0221
F-WWDZ	A320	1196	F-WWID	A320	2838	F-WWIH	A320	0113	F-WWIK	A320	0310
F-WWDZ	A320	1416	F-WWID	A320	2982	F-WWIH	A320	0169	F-WWIK	A320	0376
F-WWDZ	A320	1639	F-WWID	A320	3097	F-WWIH	A320	0296	F-WWIK	A320	0525
F-WWDZ	A320	1755	F-WWID	A320	3201	F-WWIH	A320	0356	F-WWIK	A320	0655
F-WWDZ	A320	1862	F-WWID	A321	0434	F-WWIH	A320	0427	F-WWIK	A320	0749
F-WWDZ	A320	1969	F-WWID	A321	1276	F-WWIH	A320	0542	F-WWIK	A320	0928
F-WWDZ	A320	2114	F-WWIE	A320	0060	F-WWIH	A320	0747	F-WWIK	A320	1076
F-WWDZ	A320	2193	F-WWIE	A320	0111	F-WWIH	A320	0877	F-WWIK	A320	1237
F-WWDZ	A320	2329	F-WWIE	A320	0164	F-WWIH	A320	0988	F-WWIK	A320	1372
F-WWDZ	A320	2493	F-WWIE	A320	0167	F-WWIH	A320	1125	F-WWIK	A320	1516
F-WWDZ	A320	2635	F-WWIE	A320	0295	F-WWIH	A320	1229	F-WWIK	A320	1672
F-WWDZ	A320	2783	F-WWIE	A320	0355	F-WWIH	A320	1367	F-WWIK	A320	1865
F-WWDZ	A320	2928	F-WWIE	A320	0420	F-WWIH	A320	1504	F-WWIK	A320	2118
F-WWDZ	A320	2941	F-WWIE	A320	0481	F-WWIH	A320	1661	F-WWIK	A320	2248
F-WWDZ	A320	3063	F-WWIE	A320	0553	F-WWIH	A320	1802	F-WWIK	A320	2676
F-WWDZ	A320	3189	F-WWIE	A320	0809	F-WWIH	A320	1931	F-WWIK	A320	2848
F-WWEA	**A380**	**009**	F-WWIE	A320	0930	F-WWIH	A320	2048	F-WWIK	A320	2989
F-WWFT	A320	0001	F-WWIE	A320	1047	F-WWIH	A320	2148	F-WWIK	A320	3107
F-WWHB	A320	0430	F-WWIE	A320	1198	F-WWIH	A320	2231	F-WWIK	A320	3210
F-WWIA	A318	1599	F-WWIE	A320	1363	F-WWIH	A320	2388	F-WWIL	A320	0065
F-WWIA	A320	0049	F-WWIE	A320	1500	F-WWIH	A320	2531	F-WWIL	A320	0117
F-WWIA	A320	0106	F-WWIE	A320	1663	F-WWIH	A320	2692	F-WWIL	A320	0173
F-WWIA	A320	0161	F-WWIE	A320	1864	F-WWIH	A320	2844	F-WWIL	A320	0222
F-WWIA	A320	0223	F-WWIE	A320	2123	F-WWIH	A320	2987	F-WWIL	A320	0311
F-WWIA	A320	0282	F-WWIE	A320	2229	F-WWIH	A320	3103	F-WWIL	A320	0369
F-WWIA	A321	0364	F-WWIE	A320	2384	F-WWIH	A320	3205	F-WWIL	A320	0428
F-WWIA	A321	1517	F-WWIE	A320	2515	F-WWII	A319	1303	F-WWIL	A320	0556
F-WWIB	A318	1660	F-WWIE	A320	2688	F-WWII	A320	0069	F-WWIL	A320	0705
F-WWIB	A318	2910	F-WWIE	A320	2840	F-WWII	A320	0114	F-WWIL	A320	0826
F-WWIB	A320	0051	F-WWIE	A320	2984	F-WWII	A320	0170	F-WWIL	A320	1050
F-WWIB	A320	0107	F-WWIE	A320	3099	F-WWII	A320	0246	F-WWIL	A320	1206
F-WWIB	A320	0157	F-WWIE	A320	3196	F-WWII	A320	0331	F-WWIL	A320	1370
F-WWIB	A320	0213	F-WWIE	A321	0412	F-WWII	A320	0450	F-WWIL	A320	1523
F-WWIB	A320	0268	F-WWIF	A319	0913	F-WWII	A320	0545	F-WWIL	A320	1674
F-WWIB	A320	0330	F-WWIF	A319	1256	F-WWII	A320	0696	F-WWIL	A320	1867
F-WWIB	A320	2272	F-WWIF	A320	0057	F-WWII	A320	0814	F-WWIL	A320	1954
F-WWIB	A320	2401	F-WWIF	A320	0112	F-WWII	A320	0934	F-WWIL	A320	2068
F-WWIB	A320	2533	F-WWIF	A320	0168	F-WWII	A320	1044	F-WWIL	A320	2177
F-WWIB	A320	2685	F-WWIF	A320	0304	F-WWII	A320	1200	F-WWIL	A320	2352
F-WWIB	A320	2835	F-WWIF	A320	0368	F-WWII	A320	1506	F-WWIL	A320	2498
F-WWIB	A321	0385	F-WWIF	A320	0533	F-WWII	A320	1667	F-WWIL	A320	2649
F-WWIC	A319	0910	F-WWIF	A320	0653	F-WWII	A320	1804	F-WWIL	A320	2802
F-WWIC	A320	0056	F-WWIF	A320	0743	F-WWII	A320	1933	F-WWIL	A320	2950
F-WWIC	A320	0109	F-WWIF	A320	0876	F-WWII	A320	2049	F-WWIL	A320	3079
F-WWIC	A320	0158	F-WWIF	A320	1678	F-WWII	A320	2150	F-WWIL	A320	3166
F-WWIC	A320	0210	F-WWIF	A320	1799	F-WWII	A320	2233	F-WWIM	A320	0055
F-WWIC	A320	0269	F-WWIF	A320	1915	F-WWII	A320	2390	F-WWIM	A320	0118
F-WWIC	A320	0332	F-WWIF	A320	2034	F-WWII	A320	2535	F-WWIM	A320	0174
F-WWIC	A320	0907	F-WWIF	A320	2164	F-WWII	A320	2695	F-WWIM	A320	0224
F-WWIC	A320	0919	F-WWIF	A320	2331	F-WWII	A320	2846	F-WWIM	A320	0276
F-WWIC	A320	1351	F-WWIF	A320	2496	F-WWII	A320	2988	F-WWIM	A320	0338
F-WWIC	A320	1495	F-WWIF	A320	2647	F-WWII	A320	3105	F-WWIM	A320	0413
F-WWIC	A320	1927	F-WWIF	A320	2798	F-WWII	A320	3206	F-WWIM	A320	0465
F-WWIC	A320	2044	F-WWIF	A320	3066	F-WWIJ	A319	1742	F-WWIM	A320	0706
F-WWIC	A320	2159	F-WWIF	A320	3162	F-WWIJ	A320	0070	F-WWIM	A320	0828
F-WWIC	A320	2307	F-WWIG	A320	0066	F-WWIJ	A320	0119	F-WWIM	A320	1052
F-WWIC	A320	2453	F-WWIG	A320	0104	F-WWIJ	A320	0171	F-WWIM	A320	1208
F-WWIC	A320	2645	F-WWIG	A320	0159	F-WWIJ	A320	0220	F-WWIM	A320	1374
F-WWIC	A320	2796	F-WWIG	A320	0212	F-WWIJ	A320	0309	F-WWIM	A320	1526
F-WWIC	A320	2934	F-WWIG	A320	0275	F-WWIJ	A320	0381	F-WWIM	A320	1687
F-WWIC	A320	3064	F-WWIG	A320	0336	F-WWIJ	A320	0439	F-WWIM	A320	1793
F-WWIC	A320	3161	F-WWIG	A320	0399	F-WWIJ	A320	0548	F-WWIM	A320	1996
F-WWIC	A320	3273	F-WWIG	A320	0449	F-WWIJ	A320	0918	F-WWIM	A320	2334
F-WWID	A319	1073	F-WWIG	A320	0554	F-WWIJ	A320	1128	F-WWIM	A320	2479
F-WWID	A319	1908	F-WWIG	A320	0812	F-WWIJ	A320	1231	F-WWIM	A320	2651
F-WWID	A320	0058	F-WWIG	A320	0932	F-WWIJ	A320	1368	F-WWIM	A320	2804
F-WWID	A320	0110	F-WWIG	A320	1075	F-WWIJ	A320	1518	F-WWIM	A320	2943
F-WWID	A320	0166	F-WWIG	A320	1226	F-WWIJ	A320	1669	F-WWIM	A320	3071
F-WWID	A320	0294	F-WWIG	A320	1365	F-WWIJ	A320	1806	F-WWIM	A320	3167
F-WWID	A320	0805	F-WWIG	A320	1502	F-WWIJ	A320	1935	F-WWIN	A320	0067
F-WWID	A320	0925	F-WWIG	A320	1665	F-WWIJ	A320	2274	F-WWIN	A320	0120
F-WWID	A320	1041	F-WWIG	A320	1957	F-WWIJ	A320	2403	F-WWIN	A320	0175
F-WWID	A320	1497	F-WWIG	A320	2084	F-WWIJ	A320	2537	F-WWIN	A320	0229
F-WWID	A320	1657	F-WWIG	A320	2227	F-WWIJ	A320	2800	F-WWIN	A320	0362
F-WWID	A320	1816	F-WWIG	A320	2386	F-WWIJ	A320	2937	F-WWIN	A320	0451
F-WWID	A320	1929	F-WWIG	A320	2517	F-WWIJ	A320	3068	F-WWIN	A320	0501
F-WWID	A320	2040	F-WWIG	A320	2689	F-WWIJ	A320	3164	F-WWIN	A320	0566
F-WWID	A320	2149	F-WWIG	A320	2842	F-WWIJ	A321	0633	F-WWIN	A320	0707
F-WWID	A320	2225	F-WWIG	A320	2986	F-WWIK	A320	0064	F-WWIN	A320	0830
F-WWID	A320	2419	F-WWIG	A320	3101	F-WWIK	A320	0116	F-WWIN	A320	1054

F-WWIN	A320	1235	F-WWIQ	A320	2356	F-WWIT	A320	3093	F-WWIY	A320	0754
F-WWIN	A320	1376	F-WWIQ	A320	2509	F-WWIT	A320	3192	F-WWIY	A320	0947
F-WWIN	A320	1528	F-WWIQ	A320	2678	F-WWIU	A320	0078	F-WWIY	A320	1087
F-WWIN	A320	1692	F-WWIQ	A320	2851	F-WWIU	A320	0126	F-WWIY	A320	1257
F-WWIN	A320	1818	F-WWIQ	A320	2990	F-WWIU	A320	0181	F-WWIY	A320	1398
F-WWIN	A320	2085	F-WWIQ	A320	3091	F-WWIU	A320	0414	F-WWIY	A320	1546
F-WWIN	A320	2160	F-WWIQ	A320	3190	F-WWIU	A320	0472	F-WWIY	A320	1712
F-WWIN	A320	2336	F-WWIQ	A321	0458	F-WWIU	A320	0547	F-WWIY	A320	1814
F-WWIN	A320	2482	F-WWIR	A320	0075	F-WWIU	A320	0658	F-WWIY	A320	1942
F-WWIN	A320	2654	F-WWIR	A320	0123	F-WWIU	A320	0751	F-WWIY	A320	2077
F-WWIN	A320	2807	F-WWIR	A320	0393	F-WWIU	A320	0942	F-WWIY	A320	2167
F-WWIN	A320	2944	F-WWIR	A320	0471	F-WWIU	A320	1083	F-WWIY	A320	2340
F-WWIN	A320	3072	F-WWIR	A320	0657	F-WWIU	A320	1253	F-WWIY	A320	2513
F-WWIN	A320	3170	F-WWIR	A320	0745	F-WWIU	A320	1390	F-WWIY	A320	2680
F-WWIO	A320	0071	F-WWIR	A320	0836	F-WWIU	A320	1540	F-WWIY	A320	2861
F-WWIO	A320	0121	F-WWIR	A320	0975	F-WWIU	A320	1705	F-WWIY	A320	2995
F-WWIO	A320	0176	F-WWIR	A320	1130	F-WWIU	A320	1829	F-WWIY	A320	3095
F-WWIO	A320	0225	F-WWIR	A320	1246	F-WWIU	A320	2082	**F-WWIY**	**A320**	**3199**
F-WWIO	A320	0297	F-WWIR	A320	1459	F-WWIU	A320	2221	F-WWIZ	A320	0082
F-WWIO	A320	0358	F-WWIR	A320	1641	F-WWIU	A320	2397	F-WWIZ	A320	0134
F-WWIO	A320	0421	F-WWIR	A320	1757	F-WWIU	A320	2542	F-WWIZ	A320	0194
F-WWIO	A320	0482	F-WWIR	A320	1917	F-WWIU	A320	2708	F-WWIZ	A320	0313
F-WWIO	A320	0708	F-WWIR	A320	1987	F-WWIU	A320	2859	F-WWIZ	A320	0382
F-WWIO	A320	0832	F-WWIR	A320	2056	F-WWIU	A320	2994	F-WWIZ	A320	0429
F-WWIO	A320	1057	F-WWIR	A320	2151	F-WWIU	A320	3113	F-WWIZ	A320	0485
F-WWIO	A320	1234	F-WWIR	A320	2244	F-WWIU	A320	3213	F-WWIZ	A320	0716
F-WWIO	A320	1379	F-WWIR	A320	2393	F-WWIV	A320	0079	F-WWIZ	A320	0950
F-WWIO	A320	1530	F-WWIR	A320	2539	F-WWIV	A320	0127	F-WWIZ	A320	1093
F-WWIO	A320	1696	F-WWIR	A320	2701	F-WWIV	A320	0182	F-WWIZ	A320	1259
F-WWIO	A320	1821	F-WWIR	A320	2853	F-WWIV	A320	0424	F-WWIZ	A320	1400
F-WWIO	A320	1937	F-WWIR	A320	2991	F-WWIV	A320	0503	F-WWIZ	A320	1624
F-WWIO	A320	2073	F-WWIR	A320	3109	F-WWIV	A320	0585	F-WWIZ	A320	1913
F-WWIO	A320	2182	F-WWIR	A320	3211	F-WWIV	A320	0659	F-WWIZ	A320	2036
F-WWIO	A320	2338	F-WWIS	A320	0076	F-WWIV	A320	0753	F-WWIZ	A320	2195
F-WWIO	A320	2484	F-WWIS	A320	0124	F-WWIV	A320	0943	F-WWIZ	A320	2399
F-WWIO	A320	2656	F-WWIS	A320	0179	F-WWIV	A320	1134	F-WWIZ	A320	2562
F-WWIO	A320	2808	F-WWIS	A320	0312	F-WWIV	A320	1251	F-WWIZ	A320	2710
F-WWIO	A320	2939	F-WWIS	A320	0380	F-WWIV	A320	1394	F-WWIZ	A320	2863
F-WWIO	A320	3074	F-WWIS	A320	0441	F-WWIV	A320	1542	F-WWIZ	A320	2998
F-WWIO	A320	3173	F-WWIS	A320	0937	F-WWIV	A320	1708	F-WWIZ	A320	3115
F-WWIP	A320	0072	F-WWIS	A320	1132	F-WWIV	A320	1998	F-WWIZ	A320	3215
F-WWIP	A320	0122	F-WWIS	A320	1248	F-WWIV	A320	2135	F-WWJA	A340	008
F-WWIP	A320	0177	F-WWIS	A320	1387	F-WWIV	A320	2343	F-WWJA	A340	040
F-WWIP	A320	0240	F-WWIS	A320	1535	F-WWIV	A320	2486	F-WWJA	A340	089
F-WWIP	A320	0298	F-WWIS	A320	1700	F-WWIV	A320	2661	F-WWJA	A340	091
F-WWIP	A320	0370	F-WWIS	A320	1918	F-WWIV	A320	2814	F-WWJA	A340	139
F-WWIP	A320	0422	F-WWIS	A320	2054	F-WWIV	A320	2952	F-WWJA	A340	164
F-WWIP	A320	0559	F-WWIS	A320	2153	F-WWIV	A320	3080	F-WWJA	A340	221
F-WWIP	A320	0709	F-WWIS	A320	2246	F-WWIV	A320	3194	F-WWJA	A340	446
F-WWIP	A320	0834	F-WWIS	A320	2395	F-WWIX	A319	2237	F-WWJB	A340	009
F-WWIP	A320	1059	F-WWIS	A320	2540	F-WWIX	A320	0080	F-WWJB	A340	041
F-WWIP	A320	1240	F-WWIS	A320	2703	F-WWIX	A320	0131	F-WWJB	A340	125
F-WWIP	A320	1381	F-WWIS	A320	2855	F-WWIX	A320	0183	F-WWJB	A340	176
F-WWIP	A320	1532	F-WWIS	A320	2992	F-WWIX	A320	0193	F-WWJB	A340	204
F-WWIP	A320	1686	F-WWIS	A320	3111	F-WWIX	A320	0301	F-WWJB	A340	292
F-WWIP	A320	1823	F-WWIS	A320	3208	F-WWIX	A320	0372	F-WWJB	A340	381
F-WWIP	A320	1940	F-WWIS	A321	0468	F-WWIX	A320	0425	F-WWJB	A340	447
F-WWIP	A320	2097	F-WWIT	A320	0077	F-WWIX	A320	0539	F-WWJB	A340	646
F-WWIP	A320	2178	F-WWIT	A320	0125	F-WWIX	A320	0714	**F-WWJB**	**A380**	**007**
F-WWIP	A320	2354	F-WWIT	A320	0180	F-WWIX	A320	0945	F-WWJC	A340	010
F-WWIP	A320	2500	F-WWIT	A320	0359	F-WWIX	A320	1085	F-WWJC	A340	046
F-WWIP	A320	2658	F-WWIT	A320	0400	F-WWIX	A320	1255	F-WWJC	A340	080
F-WWIP	A320	2810	F-WWIT	A320	0423	F-WWIX	A320	1396	F-WWJC	A340	141
F-WWIP	A320	2945	F-WWIT	A320	0483	F-WWIX	A320	1544	F-WWJC	A340	169
F-WWIP	A320	3076	F-WWIT	A320	0549	F-WWIX	A320	1710	F-WWJC	A340	208
F-WWIP	A320	3174	F-WWIT	A320	0710	F-WWIX	A320	1825	F-WWJC	A340	239
F-WWIQ	A320	0074	F-WWIT	A320	0816	F-WWIX	A320	1961	F-WWJC	A340	385
F-WWIQ	A320	0178	F-WWIT	A320	0936	F-WWIX	A320	2125	F-WWJC	A340	528
F-WWIQ	A320	0233	F-WWIT	A320	1081	F-WWIX	A320	2437	F-WWJC	A340	651
F-WWIQ	A320	0299	F-WWIT	A320	1242	F-WWIX	A320	2613	F-WWJD	A340	011
F-WWIQ	A320	0371	F-WWIT	A320	1385	F-WWIX	A320	2816	F-WWJD	A340	048
F-WWIQ	A320	0440	F-WWIT	A320	1538	F-WWIX	A320	2953	F-WWJD	A340	093
F-WWIQ	A320	0939	F-WWIT	A320	1702	F-WWIX	A320	3083	F-WWJD	A340	146
F-WWIQ	A320	1079	F-WWIT	A320	1852	F-WWIX	A320	3197	F-WWJD	A340	178
F-WWIQ	A320	1244	F-WWIT	A320	1958	F-WWIY	A320	0081	F-WWJD	A340	242
F-WWIQ	A320	1383	F-WWIT	A320	2121	F-WWIY	A320	0132	F-WWJD	A340	387
F-WWIQ	A320	1533	F-WWIT	A320	2201	F-WWIY	A320	0192	F-WWJD	A340	450
F-WWIQ	A320	1697	F-WWIT	A320	2359	F-WWIY	A320	0232	F-WWJD	A340	668
F-WWIQ	A320	1868	F-WWIT	A320	2511	F-WWIY	A320	0302	F-WWJE	A340	013
F-WWIQ	A320	1951	F-WWIT	A320	2683	F-WWIY	A320	0378	F-WWJE	A340	058
F-WWIQ	A320	2065	F-WWIT	A320	2856	F-WWIY	A320	0442	F-WWJE	A340	101
F-WWIQ	A320	2183	F-WWIT	A320	2993	F-WWIY	A320	0543	F-WWJE	A340	142

F-WWJE	A340	175	F-WWJO	A340	131	F-WWJY	A340	442	F-WWKH	A330	095
F-WWJE	A340	243	F-WWJO	A340	160	F-WWJY	A340	590	F-WWKH	A330	138
F-WWJE	A340	390	F-WWJO	A340	187	F-WWJZ	A340	039	F-WWKH	A330	200
F-WWJE	A340	467	F-WWJO	A340	220	F-WWJZ	A340	090	F-WWKH	A330	247
"F-WWJE"	A340	779	F-WWJO	A340	327	F-WWJZ	A340	128	F-WWKH	A330	283
F-WWJE	A340	793	F-WWJO	A340	415	F-WWJZ	A340	167	F-WWKH	A330	370
F-WWJF	A340	014	F-WWJO	A340	429	F-WWJZ	A340	225	F-WWKH	A330	455
F-WWJF	A340	057	F-WWJO	A340	554	F-WWJZ	A340	363	F-WWKI	A330	050
F-WWJF	A340	094	F-WWJP	A340	025	F-WWJZ	A340	643	F-WWKI	A330	106
F-WWJF	A340	145	F-WWJP	A340	085	F-WWKA	A330	012	F-WWKI	A330	172
F-WWJF	A340	170	F-WWJP	A340	133	F-WWKA	A330	181	F-WWKI	A330	203
F-WWJF	A340	395	F-WWJP	A340	194	F-WWKA	A330	357	F-WWKI	A330	249
F-WWJF	A340	470	F-WWJP	A340	236	F-WWKA	A330	699	F-WWKI	A330	281
F-WWJF	A340	800	F-WWJP	A340	270	F-WWKA	A330	750	F-WWKI	A330	375
F-WWJG	A340	015	F-WWJP	A340	329	F-WWKA	A330	820	F-WWKI	A330	456
F-WWJG	A340	076	F-WWJP	A340	424	**F-WWKA**	**A330**	**874**	F-WWKI	A330	493
F-WWJG	A340	103	F-WWJP	A340	559	F-WWKB	A330	017	F-WWKI	A330	498
F-WWJG	A340	147	F-WWJQ	A340	026	F-WWKB	A330	195	F-WWKI	A330	649
F-WWJG	A340	173	F-WWJQ	A340	052	F-WWKB	A330	255	F-WWKI	A330	707
F-WWJG	A340	217	F-WWJQ	A340	129	F-WWKB	A330	285	F-WWKI	A330	776
F-WWJG	A340	268	F-WWJQ	A340	161	F-WWKB	A330	365	F-WWKI	A330	828
F-WWJG	A340	402	F-WWJQ	A340	201	F-WWKB	A330	700	F-WWKI	A330	881
F-WWJG	A340	474	F-WWJQ	A340	331	F-WWKB	A330	751	F-WWKJ	A330	054
F-WWJG	A340	835	F-WWJQ	A340	561	F-WWKB	A330	821	F-WWKJ	A330	066
(F-WWJH)	A330	458	F-WWJR	A340	027	F-WWKD	A330	030	F-WWKJ	A330	119
F-WWJH	A340	016	F-WWJR	A340	075	F-WWKD	A330	082	F-WWKJ	A330	195
F-WWJI	A340	018	F-WWJR	A340	134	F-WWKD	A330	109	F-WWKJ	A330	315
F-WWJI	A340	061	F-WWJR	A340	163	F-WWKD	A330	148	F-WWKJ	A330	396
F-WWJI	A340	114	F-WWJR	A340	193	F-WWKD	A330	224	F-WWKJ	A330	494
F-WWJI	A340	154	F-WWJR	A340	332	F-WWKD	A330	276	F-WWKJ	A330	502
F-WWJI	A340	196	F-WWJR	A340	430	F-WWKD	A330	362	F-WWKJ	A330	721
F-WWJI	A340	228	F-WWJR	A340	562	F-WWKD	A340	444	F-WWKJ	A330	822
F-WWJI	A340	274	F-WWJS	A340	028	F-WWKD	A330	484	F-WWKJ	A330	882
F-WWJI	A340	378	F-WWJS	A340	079	F-WWKD	A330	578	F-WWKK	A330	121
F-WWJI	A340	483	F-WWJS	A340	135	F-WWKD	A330	644	F-WWKK	A330	162
F-WWJI	A340	844	F-WWJS	A340	166	F-WWKD	A330	701	F-WWKK	A330	205
F-WWJJ	A340	019	F-WWJS	A340	202	F-WWKD	A330	770	F-WWKK	A330	250
F-WWJJ	A340	053	F-WWJS	A340	257	F-WWKD	A330	824	F-WWKK	A330	288
F-WWJJ	A340	104	F-WWJS	A340	335	F-WWKD	A330	887	F-WWKK	A330	397
F-WWJJ	A340	149	F-WWJS	A340	433	F-WWKE	A330	037	F-WWKK	A330	462
F-WWJJ	A340	233	F-WWJS	A340	544	F-WWKE	A330	083	F-WWKK	A330	496
F-WWJJ	A340	280	F-WWJT	A340	032	F-WWKE	A330	110	F-WWKK	A330	581
F-WWJJ	A340	379	F-WWJT	A340	097	F-WWKE	A330	153	F-WWKK	A330	650
F-WWJJ	A340	538	F-WWJT	A340	150	F-WWKE	A330	272	F-WWKK	A330	709
F-WWJK	A340	020	F-WWJT	A340	218	F-WWKE	A330	364	F-WWKK	A330	777
F-WWJK	A340	056	F-WWJT	A340	273	F-WWKE	A330	451	F-WWKK	A330	830
F-WWJK	A340	123	F-WWJT	A340	347	F-WWKE	A330	551	F-WWKK	A330	883
F-WWJK	A340	156	F-WWJT	A340	434	F-WWKE	A330	645	F-WWKL	A330	068
F-WWJK	A340	185	F-WWJT	A340	582	F-WWKE	A330	703	F-WWKL	A330	111
F-WWJK	A340	216	F-WWJU	A340	033	F-WWKE	A330	772	F-WWKL	A330	165
F-WWJK	A340	297	F-WWJU	A340	180	F-WWKE	A330	825	F-WWKL	A330	211
F-WWJK	A340	406	F-WWJU	A340	192	F-WWKE	A330	876	F-WWKL	A330	248
F-WWJK	A340	541	F-WWJU	A340	212	F-WWKF	A330	087	"F-WWKL"	A330	251
F-WWJL	A340	021	F-WWJU	A340	263	F-WWKF	A330	118	F-WWKL	A330	286
F-WWJL	A340	074	F-WWJU	A340	302	F-WWKF	A330	155	F-WWKL	A330	398
F-WWJL	A340	126	F-WWJU	A340	352	F-WWKF	A330	234	F-WWKL	A330	461
F-WWJL	A340	157	F-WWJU	A340	435	F-WWKF	A330	241	F-WWKL	A330	504
F-WWJL	A340	197	F-WWJU	A340	459	F-WWKF	A330	275	F-WWKL	A330	587
F-WWJL	A340	227	F-WWJV	A340	035	F-WWKF	A330	368	F-WWKL	A330	652
F-WWJL	A340	318	F-WWJV	A340	088	F-WWKF	A330	452	F-WWKL	A330	708
F-WWJL	A340	411	F-WWJV	A340	136	F-WWKF	A330	490	F-WWKL	A330	778
F-WWJL	A340	545	F-WWJV	A340	159	F-WWKF	A330	571	F-WWKL	A330	831
F-WWJM	A340	022	F-WWJV	A340	215	F-WWKF	A330	647	F-WWKM	A330	069
F-WWJM	A340	063	F-WWJV	A340	278	F-WWKF	A330	704	F-WWKM	A330	112
F-WWJM	A340	117	F-WWJV	A340	354	F-WWKF	A330	773	F-WWKM	A330	171
F-WWJM	A340	182	F-WWJV	A340	438	F-WWKF	A330	826	F-WWKM	A330	206
F-WWJM	A340	213	F-WWJV	A340	585	F-WWKG	A330	098	F-WWKM	A330	253
F-WWJM	A340	252	F-WWJX	A340	036	F-WWKG	A330	122	F-WWKM	A330	287
F-WWJM	A340	321	F-WWJX	A340	089	F-WWKG	A330	144	F-WWKM	A330	400
F-WWJM	A340	413	F-WWJX	A340	137	F-WWKG	A330	184	F-WWKM	A330	465
F-WWJM	A340	546	F-WWJX	A340	152	F-WWKG	A330	244	F-WWKM	A330	508
F-WWJN	A340	023	F-WWJX	A340	190	F-WWKG	A330	266	F-WWKM	A330	588
F-WWJN	A340	044	F-WWJX	A340	282	F-WWKG	A330	369	F-WWKM	A330	663
F-WWJN	A340	115	F-WWJX	A340	355	F-WWKG	A330	454	F-WWKM	A330	722
F-WWJN	A340	158	F-WWJX	A340	598	F-WWKG	A330	501	F-WWKM	A330	788
F-WWJN	A340	199	F-WWJY	A340	034	F-WWKG	A330	579	F-WWKM	A330	847
F-WWJN	A340	235	F-WWJY	A340	151	F-WWKG	A330	648	F-WWKN	A330	073
F-WWJN	A340	325	F-WWJY	A340	179	F-WWKG	A330	705	F-WWKN	A330	120
F-WWJN	A340	414	F-WWJY	A340	214	F-WWKG	A330	774	F-WWKN	A330	209
F-WWJN	A340	556	F-WWJY	A340	264	F-WWKG	A330	827	F-WWKN	A330	256
F-WWJO	A340	024	F-WWJY	A340	304	F-WWKG	A330	879	F-WWKN	A330	323
F-WWJO	A340	081	F-WWJY	A340	359	F-WWKH	A330	042	F-WWKN	A330	401

Reg	Type	No	Reg	Type	No	Reg	Type	No	Reg	Type	No
F-WWKN	A330	463	F-WWKT	A330	230	**F-WWSY**	**A380**	**027**	F-WWYF	A330	629
F-WWKN	A330	576	F-WWKT	A330	254	**F-WWSZ**	**A380**	**028**	F-WWYF	A330	683
F-WWKN	A330	618	F-WWKT	A330	333	F-WWTA	A319	0578	F-WWYF	A330	742
F-WWKN	A330	671	F-WWKT	A330	409	F-WWTA	A340	360	F-WWYF	A330	810
F-WWKN	A330	724	F-WWKT	A330	476	F-WWTE	A340	394	F-WWYF	A330	859
F-WWKN	A330	789	F-WWKT	A330	518	F-WWTG	A340	478	F-WWYG	A330	349
F-WWKN	A330	832	F-WWKT	A330	616	F-WWTG	A340	886	F-WWYG	A330	432
F-WWKO	A330	077	F-WWKT	A330	674	F-WWTH	A340	445	F-WWYG	A330	539
F-WWKO	A330	127	F-WWKT	A330	732	F-WWTH	A340	894	F-WWYG	A330	631
F-WWKO	A330	177	F-WWKT	A330	796	F-WWTI	A340	457	F-WWYG	A330	684
F-WWKO	A330	219	F-WWKT	A330	852	F-WWTJ	A340	464	F-WWYG	A330	745
F-WWKO	A330	251	F-WWKU	A330	071	F-WWTK	A340	471	F-WWYG	A330	805
F-WWKO	A330	277	F-WWKU	A330	140	F-WWTL	A340	485	F-WWYG	A330	862
F-WWKO	A330	296	F-WWKU	A330	231	F-WWTM	A340	560	F-WWYH	A330	303
F-WWKO	A330	403	F-WWKU	A330	265	F-WWTN	A340	624	F-WWYH	A330	351
F-WWKO	A330	469	F-WWKU	A330	334	F-WWTO	A340	628	F-WWYH	A330	427
F-WWKO	A330	505	F-WWKU	A330	412	F-WWTP	A340	492	F-WWYH	A330	542
F-WWKO	A330	591	F-WWKU	A330	479	F-WWTP	A340	685	F-WWYH	A330	632
F-WWKO	A330	665	F-WWKU	A330	521	F-WWTQ	A340	495	F-WWYH	A330	686
F-WWKO	A330	725	F-WWKU	A330	614	F-WWTQ	A340	694	F-WWYH	A330	746
F-WWKO	A330	791	F-WWKU	A330	670	F-WWTR	A340	499	F-WWYH	A330	811
F-WWKO	A330	833	F-WWKU	A330	733	F-WWTR	A340	698	**F-WWYH**	**A330**	**863**
F-WWKP	A330	055	F-WWKU	A330	797	F-WWTS	A340	520	F-WWYI	A330	305
F-WWKP	A330	096	**F-WWKU**	**A330**	**871**	F-WWTS	A340	748	F-WWYI	A330	345
F-WWKP	A330	183	F-WWKV	A330	070	F-WWTU	A340	563	F-WWYI	A330	437
F-WWKP	A330	222	F-WWKV	A330	107	F-WWTU	A340	757	F-WWYI	A330	548
F-WWKP	A330	259	F-WWKV	A330	232	F-WWTV	A340	572	F-WWYI	A330	633
F-WWKP	A330	338	F-WWKV	A330	269	F-WWTV	A340	761	F-WWYI	A330	687
F-WWKP	A330	404	F-WWKV	A330	330	F-WWTX	A340	608	F-WWYI	A330	747
F-WWKP	A330	466	F-WWKV	A330	418	F-WWTX	A340	775	F-WWYI	A330	813
F-WWKP	A330	550	F-WWKV	A330	480	F-WWTY	A340	611	F-WWYJ	A330	294
F-WWKP	A330	593	F-WWKV	A330	525	F-WWTY	A340	783	F-WWYJ	A330	356
F-WWKP	A330	664	F-WWKV	A330	642	"F-WWXM"	A320	2721	F-WWYJ	A330	439
F-WWKP	A330	726	F-WWKV	A330	690	"F-WWXX"	A320	0886	F-WWYJ	A330	549
F-WWKP	A330	792	F-WWKV	A330	743	"F-WWXY"	A330	843	F-WWYJ	A330	634
F-WWKP	A330	849	F-WWKV	A330	799	F-WWYA	A330	284	F-WWYJ	A330	688
F-WWKP	A330	877	F-WWKV	A330	873	F-WWYA	A330	343	F-WWYJ	A330	749
F-WWKQ	A330	060	F-WWKX	A330	067	F-WWYA	A330	419	F-WWYJ	A330	814
F-WWKQ	A330	099	F-WWKY	A330	072	F-WWYA	A330	530	F-WWYJ	A330	865
F-WWKQ	A330	132	F-WWKY	A330	143	F-WWYA	A330	620	F-WWYK	A330	284
F-WWKQ	A330	188	F-WWKY	A330	153	F-WWYA	A330	676	F-WWYK	A330	308
F-WWKQ	A330	223	F-WWKY	A330	238	F-WWYA	A330	735	F-WWYK	A330	348
F-WWKQ	A330	258	F-WWKY	A330	271	F-WWYA	A330	861	F-WWYK	A330	441
F-WWKQ	A330	290	F-WWKY	A330	336	F-WWYB	A330	279	F-WWYK	A330	600
F-WWKQ	A330	405	F-WWKY	A330	526	F-WWYB	A330	342	F-WWYK	A330	653
F-WWKQ	A330	472	F-WWKZ	A330	100	F-WWYB	A330	420	F-WWYK	A330	711
F-WWKQ	A330	552	F-WWKZ	A330	240	F-WWYB	A330	529	F-WWYK	A330	759
F-WWKQ	A330	597	F-WWKZ	A330	267	F-WWYB	A330	621	F-WWYK	A330	836
F-WWKQ	A330	666	F-WWKZ	A330	337	F-WWYB	A330	678	F-WWYL	A330	306
F-WWKQ	A330	728	F-WWKZ	A330	527	F-WWYB	A330	737	F-WWYL	A330	380
F-WWKQ	A330	850	F-WWKZ	A330	612	F-WWYB	A330	809	F-WWYL	A330	486
F-WWKR	A330	062	F-WWKZ	A330	673	F-WWYC	A330	300	F-WWYL	A330	555
F-WWKR	A330	102	F-WWKZ	A330	752	F-WWYC	A330	344	F-WWYL	A330	636
F-WWKR	A330	191	F-WWKZ	A330	834	F-WWYC	A330	421	F-WWYL	A330	691
F-WWKR	A330	226	F-WWLE	A330	181	F-WWYC	A330	532	F-WWYL	A330	754
F-WWKR	A330	261	"F-WWLI"	A320	1206	F-WWYC	A330	623	F-WWYL	A330	815
F-WWKR	A330	293	F-WWLJ	F.100	11351	F-WWYC	A330	679	F-WWYL	A330	866
F-WWKR	A330	407	**F-WWOW**	**A380**	**001**	F-WWYC	A330	738	F-WWYM	A310	571
F-WWKR	A330	473	F-WWQL	A330	272	F-WWYC	A330	801	F-WWYM	A330	309
F-WWKR	A330	511	F-WWSA	A380	003	F-WWYC	A330	855	F-WWYM	A330	361
F-WWKR	A330	595	F-WWSB	A380	005	F-WWYD	A330	299	F-WWYM	A330	487
F-WWKR	A330	667	F-WWSC	A380	006	F-WWYD	A330	341	F-WWYM	A330	602
F-WWKR	A330	729	F-WWSD	A380	007	F-WWYD	A330	423	F-WWYM	A330	654
F-WWKR	A330	795	F-WWSE	A380	008	F-WWYD	A330	533	F-WWYM	A330	712
F-WWKR	A330	851	(F-WWSF)	A380	009	F-WWYD	A330	625	F-WWYM	A330	780
F-WWKS	A330	064	F-WWSF	A380	010	F-WWYD	A330	680	F-WWYM	A330	838
F-WWKS	A330	113	F-WWSH	A380	011	F-WWYD	A330	739	F-WWYN	A330	311
F-WWKS	A330	189	F-WWSI	A380	012	F-WWYD	A330	802	F-WWYN	A330	353
F-WWKS	A330	229	F-WWSJ	A380	013	F-WWYD	A330	857	F-WWYN	A330	489
F-WWKS	A330	262	F-WWSK	A380	014	F-WWYE	A330	301	F-WWYN	A330	603
F-WWKS	A330	291	F-WWSL	A380	015	F-WWYE	A330	346	F-WWYN	A330	658
F-WWKS	A330	408	F-WWSM	A380	016	F-WWYE	A330	425	F-WWYN	A330	717
F-WWKS	A330	477	F-WWSN	A380	017	F-WWYE	A330	535	F-WWYN	A330	806
F-WWKS	A330	553	**F-WWSO**	**A380**	**018**	F-WWYE	A330	627	F-WWYN	A330	860
F-WWKS	A330	610	**F-WWSP**	**A380**	**019**	F-WWYE	A330	682	F-WWYO	A330	312
F-WWKS	A330	669	**F-WWSQ**	**A380**	**021**	F-WWYE	A330	741	F-WWYO	A330	358
F-WWKS	A330	730	F-WWSS	A380	020	F-WWYE	A330	803	F-WWYO	A330	491
F-WWKS	A330	823	**F-WWSS**	**A380**	**022**	F-WWYE	A330	858	F-WWYO	A330	558
F-WWKS	A330	885	F-WWST	A380	023	F-WWYF	A330	295	F-WWYO	A330	635
F-WWKT	A330	065	**F-WWSU**	**A380**	**024**	F-WWYF	A330	350	F-WWYO	A330	692
F-WWKT	A330	116	**F-WWSV**	**A380**	**025**	F-WWYF	A330	428	F-WWYO	A330	760
F-WWKT	A330	198	**F-WWSX**	**A380**	**026**	F-WWYF	A330	536	F-WWYO	A330	839

Reg	Type	No	Reg	Type	No	Reg	Type	No	Reg	Type	No
F-WWYP	A330	313	F-WWZI	A320	0194	F-WZEL	A310	264	F-WZMD	A300	150
F-WWYP	A330	497	**F-WXXL**	**A380**	**002**	F-WZEL	A310	318	F-WZMD	A300	187
F-WWYP	A330	573	F-WZEA	A300	051	F-WZEL	A310	345	F-WZMD	A300	232
F-WWYP	A330	637	F-WZEA	A300	068	F-WZEM	A300	064	F-WZMD	A300	304
F-WWYP	A330	693	F-WZEA	A300	101	F-WZEM	A300	095	F-WZME	A300	151
F-WWYP	A330	755	F-WZEA	A300	135	F-WZEM	A300	109	F-WZME	A300	188
F-WWYP	A330	817	F-WZEA	A310	224	F-WZEM	A300	132	F-WZME	A300	226
F-WWYP	A330	867	F-WZEA	A310	283	F-WZEM	A310	267	F-WZME	A300	277
F-WWYQ	A330	317	F-WZEA	A310	329	F-WZEM	A310	309	F-WZMF	A300	156
F-WWYQ	A330	372	F-WZEB	A300	052	F-WZEM	A310	346	F-WZMF	A300	199
F-WWYQ	A330	522	F-WZEB	A300	069	F-WZEM	A310	364	F-WZMF	A300	234
F-WWYQ	A330	564	F-WZEB	A300	110	F-WZEN	A300	065	F-WZMG	A300	157
F-WWYQ	A330	638	F-WZEB	A300	133	F-WZEN	A300	079	F-WZMG	A300	189
F-WWYQ	A330	695	F-WZEB	A310	230	F-WZEN	A300	114	F-WZMG	A300	235
F-WWYQ	A330	756	F-WZEB	A310	285	F-WZEN	A300	136	F-WZMH	A300	159
F-WWYQ	A330	818	F-WZEC	A300	055	F-WZEN	A310	270	F-WZMH	A300	209
F-WWYQ	A330	868	F-WZEC	A300	071	F-WZEN	A310	372	F-WZMH	A300	262
F-WWYR	A330	314	F-WZEC	A300	085	F-WZEO	A300	066	F-WZMI	A300	160
F-WWYR	A330	382	F-WZEC	A300	103	F-WZEO	A300	080	F-WZMI	A300	190
F-WWYR	A330	512	F-WZEC	A300	126	F-WZEO	A300	125	F-WZMI	A300	236
F-WWYR	A330	565	F-WZEC	A310	233	F-WZEO	A310	273	F-WZMJ	A300	026
F-WWYR	A330	640	F-WZEC	A310	288	F-WZEO	A310	331	F-WZMJ	A300	163
F-WWYR	A330	657	F-WZED	A300	054	F-WZEO	A310	347	F-WZMJ	A300	202
F-WWYR	A330	696	F-WZED	A300	072	F-WZEO	A310	352	F-WZMJ	A300	243
F-WWYR	A330	758	F-WZED	A300	088	F-WZEP	A300	067	F-WZMK	A300	164
F-WWYR	A330	819	F-WZED	A300	105	F-WZEP	A300	081	F-WZMK	A300	210
F-WWYR	A330	869	F-WZED	A300	127	F-WZEP	A300	096	F-WZML	A300	165
F-WWYS	A330	316	F-WZED	A300	143	F-WZEP	A300	115	F-WZML	A300	192
F-WWYS	A330	384	F-WZED	A310	237	F-WZEP	A300	137	F-WZML	A300	239
F-WWYS	A330	507	F-WZED	A310	291	F-WZEP	A300	197	F-WZML	A300	282
F-WWYS	A330	568	F-WZED	A310	360	F-WZEP	A310	276	F-WZMM	A300	166
F-WWYS	A330	641	F-WZEE	A300	053	F-WZEP	A310	313	F-WZMM	A300	193
F-WWYS	A330	697	F-WZEE	A300	073	F-WZEP	A310	349	F-WZMM	A300	240
F-WWYS	A330	769	F-WZEE	A300	106	F-WZEP	A310	367	F-WZMM	A300	289
F-WWYS	A330	840	F-WZEE	A300	128	F-WZEQ	A300	031	F-WZMN	A300	167
F-WWYT	A330	322	F-WZEE	A310	241	F-WZEQ	A300	082	F-WZMN	A300	200
F-WWYT	A330	386	F-WZEE	A310	293	F-WZEQ	A300	138	F-WZMN	A300	238
F-WWYT	A330	510	F-WZEF	A300	056	F-WZEQ	A300	198	F-WZMO	A300	168
F-WWYT	A330	655	F-WZEF	A300	089	F-WZER	A300	046	F-WZMO	A300	203
F-WWYT	A330	713	F-WZEF	A300	140	F-WZER	A300	098	F-WZMO	A300	265
F-WWYT	A330	781	F-WZEF	A310	248	F-WZER	A300	117	F-WZMP	A300	169
F-WWYT	A330	841	F-WZEF	A310	295	F-WZER	A300	194	F-WZMP	A300	205
F-WWYU	A330	324	F-WZEF	A310	339	F-WZER	A310	278	F-WZMP	A300	247
F-WWYU	A330	388	F-WZEF	A310	362	F-WZER	A310	320	F-WZMQ	A300	170
F-WWYU	A330	506	F-WZEG	A300	057	F-WZES	A300	049	F-WZMQ	A300	208
F-WWYU	A330	574	F-WZEG	A300	075	F-WZES	A300	083	F-WZMR	A300	171
F-WWYU	A330	675	F-WZEG	A300	090	F-WZES	A300	116	F-WZMS	A300	173
F-WWYU	A330	734	F-WZEG	A300	144	F-WZES	A300	139	F-WZMS	A300	212
F-WWYU	A330	807	F-WZEG	A310	245	F-WZES	A300	195	F-WZMS	A300	244
F-WWYU	A330	853	F-WZEG	A310	300	F-WZET	A300	050	F WZMS	A300	292
F-WWYV	A330	326	F-WZEG	A310	333	F-WZET	A300	084	F-WZMT	A300	174
F-WWYV	A330	389	F-WZEH	A300	058	F-WZET	A300	099	F-WZMT	A300	213
F-WWYV	A330	513	F-WZEH	A300	122	F-WZET	A300	123	F-WZMT	A300	249
F-WWYV	A330	570	F-WZEH	A300	141	F-WZET	A300	142	F-WZMU	A300	176
F-WWYV	A330	656	F-WZEH	A310	251	F-WZET	A300	196	F-WZMU	A300	214
F-WWYV	A330	714	F-WZEH	A310	297	F-WZET	A310	281	F-WZMU	A300	250
F-WWYV	A330	782	F-WZEH	A310	340	F-WZET	A310	338	F-WZMV	A300	177
F-WWYV	A330	842	F-WZEI	A300	059	F-WZLH	A310	162	F-WZMV	A300	219
F-WWYX	A330	328	F-WZEI	A300	076	F-WZLH	A310	350	F-WZMV	A300	268
F-WWYX	A330	392	F-WZEI	A300	093	F-WZLH	A310	370	F-WZMV	A300	305
F-WWYX	A330	509	F-WZEI	A300	111	F-WZLI	A310	172	F-WZMW	A300	179
F-WWYX	A330	605	F-WZEI	A300	130	F-WZLJ	A310	191	F-WZMX	A300	180
F-WWYX	A330	659	F-WZEI	A310	254	F-WZLJ	A310	353	F-WZMX	A300	221
F-WWYX	A330	716	F-WZEI	A310	303	F-WZLK	A310	201	F-WZMX	A300	253
F-WWYX	A330	784	F-WZEI	A310	342	F-WZLK	A310	356	F-WZMX	A300	299
F-WWYX	A330	843	F-WZEI	A310	363	F-WZLL	A310	217	F-WZMY	A300	181
F-WWYY	A330	340	F-WZEJ	A300	060	F-WZLL	A310	357	F-WZMY	A300	215
F-WWYY	A330	393	F-WZEJ	A300	077	F-WZLR	A300	252	F-WZMY	A300	255
F-WWYY	A330	515	F-WZEJ	A300	094	F-WZLS	A300	284	F-WZMY	A300	302
F-WWYY	A330	607	F-WZEJ	A300	113	F-WZLS	A310	359	F-WZMZ	A300	182
F-WWYY	A330	661	F-WZEJ	A300	134	F-WZMA	A300	147	F-WZMZ	A300	218
F-WWYY	A330	718	F-WZEJ	A310	257	F-WZMA	A300	184	F-WZXP	A300	282
F-WWYY	A330	785	F-WZEJ	A310	311	F-WZMA	A300	222	F-WZYA	A300	294
F-WWYY	A330	854	F-WZEK	A300	046	F-WZMA	A300	256	F-WZYA	A300	354
F-WWYZ	A330	339	F-WZEK	A300	061	F-WZMB	A300	022	F-WZYB	A300	301
F-WWYZ	A330	366	F-WZEK	A300	121	F-WZMB	A300	148	F-WZYB	A300	351
F-WWYZ	A330	524	F-WZEK	A310	260	F-WZMB	A300	185	F-WZYC	A300	307
F-WWYZ	A330	609	F-WZEK	A310	306	F-WZMB	A300	225	F-WZYC	A300	358
F-WWYZ	A330	662	F-WZEK	A310	343	F-WZMB	A300	269	F-WZYD	A300	312
F-WWYZ	A330	720	F-WZEL	A300	063	F-WZMC	A300	149	F-WZYE	A300	317
F-WWYZ	A330	786	F-WZEL	A300	107	F-WZMC	A300	186	F-WZYF	A300	321
F-WWYZ	A330	845	F-WZEL	A300	131	F-WZMC	A300	227	F-WZYG	A300	327

F-WZYH	A300	332	G-5-103	146	E2103	G-6-183	146	E3183	G-6-272	146	E3272
F-WZYI	A300	336	G-5-104	146	E1104	G-6-184	146	E2184	G-6-273	146	E2273
F-WZYJ	A300	341	G-5-105	146	E2105	G-6-185	146	E3185	G-6-274	146	E3274
F-WZYK	A300	344	G-5-106	146	E2106	G-6-186	146	E3186	G-6-275	146	E2275
F-WZYL	A300	348	G-5-107	146	E2107	G-6-187	146	E3187	G-6-276	146	E3276
F-ZVMT	DC-8	46043	G-5-108	146	E2108	G-6-189	146	E3189	G-6-277	146	E2277
F-ZWMT	DC-8	45570	G-5-110	146	E2110	G-6-190	146	E3190	G-6-278	146	E2278
			G-5-111	146	E2111	G-6-191	146	E3191	G-6-279	146	E2279
			G-5-112	146	E2112	G-6-192	146	E2192	G-6-280	146	E3280
United Kingdom			G-5-115	146	E2115	G-6-193	146	E3193	G-6-281	146	E3281
			G-5-116	146	E2116	G-6-194	146	E3194	G-6-282	146	E3282
(G-1-1)	VC10	829	G-5-120	146	E3120	G-6-195	146	E3195	G-6-283	146	E3283
G-3-163	146	E3163	G-5-122	146	E3122	G-6-196	146	E2196	G-6-284	146	E3284
G-5-001	146	E2052	G-5-123	146	E3123	G-6-197	146	E3197	G-6-285	146	E2285
G-5-002	146	E2049	G-5-124	146	E1124	G-6-200	146	E2200	G-6-286	146	E3286
G-5-003	146	E2051	G-5-125	146	E3125	G-6-201	146	E2201	G-6-287	146	E2287
G-5-004	146	E2050	G-5-127	146	E2127	G-6-202	146	E3202	G-6-288	146	E2288
G-5-005	146	E1002	G-5-129	146	E3129	G-6-203	146	E3203	G-6-289	146	E2289
G-5-005	146	E1005	G-5-130	146	E2130	G-6-204	146	E2204	G-6-290	146	E2290
G-5-01	146	E1015	G-5-132	146	E3132	G-6-205	146	E3205	G-6-291	146	E3291
G-5-019	146	E1019	G-5-133	146	E2133	G-6-206	146	E3206	G-6-292	146	E2292
G-5-02	146	E1005	G-5-134	146	E3134	G-6-207	146	E3207	G-6-293	146	E2293
G-5-02	146	E1017	G-5-135	146	E2135	G-6-208	146	E2208	G-6-294	146	E2294
G-5-02	146	E1021	G-5-136	146	E2136	G-6-209	146	E3209	G-6-295	146	E2295
G-5-026	146	E1026	G-5-137	146	E3137	G-6-210	146	E2210	G-6-296	146	E2296
G-5-03	146	E1029	G-5-138	146	E2138	G-6-211	146	E2211	G-6-297	146	E2297
G-5-032	146	E1032	G-5-139	146	E2139	G-6-212	146	E3128	G-6-298	146	E3298
G-5-035	146	E1035	G-5-14	146	E1003	G-6-212	146	E3212	G-6-299	146	E2299
G-5-04	146	E1004	G-5-141	146	E3141	G-6-213	146	E3213	G-6-300	146	E2300
G-5-053	146	E2053	G-5-142	146	E3142	G-6-214	146	E3214	G-6-301	146	E3301
G-5-054	146	E2054	G-5-143	146	E3143	G-6-215	146	E3215	G-6-302	146	E2302
G-5-055	146	E2055	G-5-145	146	E3145	G-6-216	146	E3216	G-6-303	146	E2303
G-5-056	146	E2056	G-5-146	146	E1002	G-6-217	146	E3217	G-6-304	146	E2304
G-5-057	146	E2057	G-5-146	146	E2008	G-6-218	146	E3218	G-6-305	146	E2305
G-5-058	146	E2058	G-5-147	146	E3147	G-6-219	146	E3219	G-6-306	146	E2306
G-5-059	146	E2059	G-5-159	146	E3159	G-6-220	146	E2220	G-6-307	146	E2307
G-5-060	146	E2060	G-5-2	COMET	06002	G-6-222	146	E3222	G-6-308	146	E3308
G-5-061	146	E2061	G-5-23	COMET	06022	G-6-223	146	E1223	G-6-309	146	E2309
G-5-062	146	E2062	G-5-300	146	E3001	G-6-224	146	E1224	G-6-310	146	E2310
G-5-063	146	E1063	G-5-507	146	E1021	G-6-225	146	E1225	G-6-311	146	E2311
G-5-064	146	E2064	G-5-512	146	E1010	G-6-227	146	E2227	G-6-312	146	E2312
G-5-065	146	E2065	G-5-513	146	E1011	G-6-228	146	E1228	G-6-313	146	E2313
G-5-066	146	E2066	G-5-517	146	E2050	G-6-230	146	E1230	G-6-314	146	E2314
G-5-067	146	E2067	G-5-523	146	E1019	G-6-231	146	E2231	G-6-315	146	E3315
G-5-068	146	E1068	G-5-537	146	E1004	G-6-232	146	E3232	G-6-316	146	E2316
G-5-069	146	E2069	G-6-002	146	E1002	G-6-233	146	E2233	G-6-317	146	E2317
G-5-070	146	E2070	G-6-009	146	E1009	G-6-234	146	E3234	G-6-318	146	E2318
G-5-071	146	E1071	G-6-013	146	E1013	G-6-235	146	E2235	G-6-319	146	E2319
G-5-072	146	E2072	G-6-018	146	E2018	G-6-236	146	E3236	G-6-320	146	E3320
G-5-073	146	E2073	G-6-021	146	E1021	G-6-237	146	E3237	G-6-321	146	E2321
G-5-074	146	E2074	G-6-029	146	E1029	G-6-238	146	E3238	G-6-322	146	E3322
G-5-075	146	E2075	G-6-118	146	E3118	G-6-239	146	E2239	G-6-323	146	E2323
G-5-076	146	E1076	G-6-124	146	E1124	G-6-240	146	E3240	G-6-324	146	E3324
G-5-077	146	E2077	G-6-144	146	E1144	G-6-241	146	E3241	G-6-325	146	E2325
G-5-078	146	E2078	G-6-146	146	E3146	G-6-242	146	E3242	G-6-326	146	E2326
G-5-079	146	E2079	G-6-147	146	E3147	G-6-243	146	E3243	G-6-327	146	E3327
G-5-080	146	E2080	G-6-148	146	E2148	G-6-244	146	E3244	G-6-329	146	E2329
G-5-081	146	E1081	G-6-152	146	E1152	G-6-245	146	E3245	G-6-330	146	E2330
G-5-082	146	E2082	G-6-154	146	E3154	G-6-246	146	E2246	G-6-332	146	E3332
G-5-083	146	E1083	G-6-155	146	E3155	G-6-247	146	E3247	G-6-333	146	E2333
G-5-084	146	E2084	G-6-157	146	E3157	G-6-248	146	E3248	G-6-334	146	E2334
G-5-085	146	E1085	G-6-158	146	E3158	G-6-249	146	E1249	G-6-335	146	E2335
G-5-086	146	E2086	G-6-159	146	E3159	G-6-250	146	E3250	G-6-336	146	E3336
G-5-087	146	E2087	G-6-160	146	E1160	G-6-251	146	E2251	G-6-337	146	E2337
G-5-088	146	E2088	G-6-161	146	E3161	G-6-252	146	E1252	G-6-338	146	E3338
G-5-089	146	E2089	G-6-162	146	E3162	G-6-253	146	E2253	G-6-339	146	E3339
G-5-090	146	E2090	G-6-163	146	E3163	G-6-255	146	E3255	G-6-340	146	E3340
G-5-091	146	E1091	G-6-164	146	E2164	G-6-256	146	E2256	G-6-341	146	E3341
G-5-092	146	E2092	G-6-165	146	E3165	G-6-257	146	E2257	G-6-342	146	E3342
G-5-093	146	E2093	G-6-166	146	E3166	G-6-258	146	E1258	G-6-343	146	E3343
G-5-094	146	E2094	G-6-167	146	E2167	G-6-259	146	E3259	G-6-344	146	E2344
G-5-095	146	E1095	G-6-169	146	E3169	G-6-260	146	E1260	G-6-345	146	E2345
G-5-096	146	E2096	G-6-171	146	E3171	G-6-261	146	E2261	G-6-346	146	E2346
G-5-097	146	E2097	G-6-172	146	E2172	G-6-262	146	E3262	G-6-347	146	E2347
G-5-098	146	E2098	G-6-173	146	E3173	G-6-263	146	E3263	G-6-348	146	E2348
G-5-099	146	E2099	G-6-174	146	E3174	G-6-264	146	E3264	G-6-349	146	E2349
G-5-1	COMET	06001	G-6-175	146	E3175	G-6-265	146	E3265	G-6-350	146	E2350
G-5-1	COMET	6476	G-6-177	146	E3177	G-6-266	146	E2266	G-6-351	146	E2351
G-5-1	NIMR	6476	G-6-178	146	E2178	G-6-267	146	E1267	G-6-352	146	E2352
G-5-100	146	E2100	G-6-179	146	E3179	G-6-268	146	E2268	G-6-353	146	E2353
G-5-101	146	E1101	G-6-180	146	E2180	G-6-270	146	E2270	G-6-355	146	E3355
G-5-102	146	E2102	G-6-181	146	E3181	G-6-271	146	E2271	G-6-356	146	E3356

Reg	Type	No	Reg	Type	No	Reg	Type	No	Reg	Type	No
G-6-357	146	E3357	G-ALYS	COMET	06005	G̃-ÀPFO	B707	17716	G-ARWD	B707	18372
G-6-358	146	E3358	G-ALYT	COMET	06006	G-APFP	B707	17717	G-ARWE	B707	18373
G-6-359	146	E3359	(G-ALYT)	COMET	06007	G-APMA	COMET	6421	G-ASDZ	COMET	6457
G-6-360	146	E3360	G-ALYU	COMET	06007	G-APMB	COMET	6422	G-ASGA	VC10	851
G-6-361	146	E3361	(G-ALYU)	COMET	06008	G-APMC	COMET	6423	G-ASGB	VC10	852
G-6-362	146	E3362	G-ALYV	COMET	06008	(G-APMD)	COMET	6424	**G-ASGC**	**VC10**	**853**
G-6-363	146	E2363	(G-ALYV)	COMET	06009	G-APMD	COMET	6435	G-ASGD	VC10	854
G-6-364	146	E2364	G-ALYW	COMET	06009	(G-APME)	COMET	6425	G-ASGE	VC10	855
G-6-365	146	E2365	(G-ALYW)	COMET	06010	G-APME	COMET	6436	G-ASGF	VC10	856
G-6-366	146	E2366	G-ALYX	COMET	06010	G-APMF	COMET	6426	G-ASGG	VC10	857
G-6-367	146	E2367	(G-ALYX)	COMET	06011	(G-APMG)	COMET	6440	G-ASGH	VC10	858
G-6-370	146	E2370	G-ALYY	COMET	06011	(G-APMG)	COMET	6442	G-ASGI	VC10	859
G-6-371	146	E2371	(G-ALYY)	COMET	06012	G-APYC	COMET	6437	G-ASGJ	VC10	860
G-6-372	146	E2372	G-ALYZ	COMET	06012	G-APYD	COMET	6438	G-ASGK	VC10	861
G-6-373	146	E3373	(G-ALZA)	COMET	06013	G-APZM	COMET	6440	G-ASGL	VC10	862
G-6-374	146	E3374	(G-ALZB)	COMET	06014	G-ARBB	COMET	6443	G-ASGM	VC10	863
G-6-375	146	E3375	(G-ALZC)	COMET	06015	G-ARCO	COMET	6449	G-ASGN	VC10	864
G-6-377	146	E3377	(G-ALZD)	COMET	06016	G-ARCP	COMET	6451	G-ASGO	VC10	865
G-6-379	146	E3379	G-ALZK	COMET	06002	G-ARDI	COMET	6447	G-ASGP	VC10	866
G-6-380	146	E3380	G-AMXA	COMET	06023	(G-AREI)	COMET	6453	G-ASGR	VC10	867
G-6-383	146	E2383	G-AMXB	COMET	06024	G-ARGM	COMET	6453	G-ASHG	1-11	004
G-6-385	146	E2385	G-AMXC	COMET	06025	(G-ARJC)	COMET	6452	G-ASIW	VC10	819
G-6-388	146	E2388	G-AMXD	COMET	06026	(G-ARJD)	COMET	6455	G-ASIX	VC10	820
G-6-389	146	E2389	(G-AMXE)	COMET	06027	G-ARJE	COMET	6456	G-ASJA	1-11	005
G-6-390	146	E2390	(G-AMXF)	COMET	06028	(G-ARJF)	COMET	6459	G-ASJB	1-11	006
G-6-391	146	E2391	(G-AMXG)	COMET	06029	(G-ARJH)	COMET	6446	G-ASJC	1-11	007
G-6-392	146	E2392	(G-AMXH)	COMET	06030	G-ARJK	COMET	6452	G-ASJD	1-11	008
G-11-111	146	E2111	(G-AMXI)	COMET	06031	G-ARJL	COMET	6455	G-ASJE	1-11	009
G-11-115	146	E2115	(G-AMXJ)	COMET	06032	G-ARJM	COMET	6456	G-ASJF	1-11	010
G-11-121	146	E2121	G-AMXK	COMET	06033	G-ARJN	COMET	6459	G-ASJG	1-11	011
G-11-127	146	E2127	(G-AMXL)	COMET	06034	G-AROV	COMET	6460	G-ASJH	1-11	012
G-11-128	146	E3128	G-ANAV	COMET	06013	G-ARPA	TRDNT	2101	G-ASJI	1-11	013
G-11-131	146	E3131	G-ANLO	COMET	06100	G-ARPB	TRDNT	2102	G-ASJJ	1-11	014
G-11-134	146	E3134	(G-AODF)	COMET	6409	G-ARPC	TRDNT	2103	G-ASTJ	1-11	085
G-11-137	146	E3137	G-AOJT	COMET	06020	G-ARPD	TRDNT	2104	G-ASUF	1-11	015
G-11-140	146	E2140	G-AOJU	COMET	06021	G-ARPE	TRDNT	2105	(G-ASVT)	1-11	BAC.095
G-11-144	146	E1144	G-AOVU	COMET	6424	G-ARPF	TRDNT	2106	G-ASWU	TRDNT	2114
G-11-147	146	E3147	G-AOVV	COMET	6425	G-ARPG	TRDNT	2107	G-ASWV	TRDNT	2118
G-11-149	146	E2149	G-APAS	COMET	06022	G-ARPH	TRDNT	2108	G-ASYD	1-11	053
G-11-156	146	E2156	G-APDA	COMET	6401	G-ARPI	TRDNT	2109	G-ASYE	1-11	054
G-16-1	1-11	094	G-APDB	COMET	6403	G-ARPJ	TRDNT	2110	G-ASZF	B707	18924
G-16-10	1-11	BAC.196	G-APDC	COMET	6404	G-ARPK	TRDNT	2111	G-ASZG	B707	18925
G-16-11	1-11	BAC.197	G-APDD	COMET	6405	G-ARPL	TRDNT	2112	G-ATDJ	VC10	825
G-16-12	1-11	BAC.198	G-APDE	COMET	6406	G-ARPM	TRDNT	2113	G-ATNA	TRDNT	2130
G-16-13	1-11	BAC.212	G-APDF	COMET	6407	(G-ARPN)	TRDNT	2114	G-ATPH	1-11	BAC.110
G-16-14	1-11	BAC.157	(G-APDG)	COMET	6408	G-ARPN	TRDNT	2115	G-ATPI	1-11	BAC.112
G-16-15	1-11	BAC.236	(G-APDG)	COMET	6412	(G-ARPO)	TRDNT	2115	G-ATPJ	1-11	033
G-16-16	1-11	BAC.241	G-APDG	COMET	6427	G-ARPO	TRDNT	2116	G-ATPK	1-11	034
G-16-17	1-11	BAC.239	G-APDH	COMET	6409	(G-ARPP)	TRDNT	2117	G-ATPL	1-11	035
G-16-19	1-11	066	(G-APDH)	COMET	6413	(G-ARPP)	TRDNT	2117	G-ATTP	1-11	039
G-16-2	1-11	BAC.118	(G-APDI)	COMET	6410	(G-ARPR)	TRDNT	2117	G-ATVH	1-11	040
G-16-22	1-11	BAC.230	(G-APDI)	COMET	6414	G-ARPR	TRDNT	2119	G-ATVU	1-11	074
G-16-23	1-11	BAC.199	G-APDI	COMET	6428	(G-ARPS)	TRDNT	2118	G-ATWV	B707	19498
G-16-24	1-11	BAC.166	(G-APDJ)	COMET	6411	G-ARPS	TRDNT	2120	G-ATZC	B707	19416
G-16-25	1-11	BAC.260	(G-APDJ)	COMET	6415	(G-ARPT)	TRDNT	2119	G-ATZD	B707	19590
G-16-3	1-11	BAC.127	G-APDJ	COMET	6429	G-ARPT	TRDNT	2121	G-AVBW	1-11	BAC.107
G-16-32	1-11	BAC.131	G-APDK	COMET	6412	(G-ARPU)	TRDNT	2120	G-AVBX	1-11	BAC.109
G-16-4	1-11	BAC.130	(G-APDK)	COMET	6416	G-ARPU	TRDNT	2122	G-AVBY	1-11	BAC.113
G-16-5	1-11	BAC.121	G-APDL	COMET	6413	(G-ARPW)	TRDNT	2121	G-AVEJ	1-11	094
G-16-6	1-11	BAC.162	(G-APDL)	COMET	6418	G-ARPW	TRDNT	2123	G-AVFA	TRDNT	2140
G-16-7	1-11	BAC.192	G-APDM	COMET	6414	(G-ARPX)	TRDNT	2122	G-AVFB	TRDNT	2141
G-16-8	1-11	BAC.193	(G-APDM)	COMET	6420	G-ARPX	TRDNT	2124	G-AVFC	TRDNT	2142
G-16-9	1-11	BAC.194	G-APDN	COMET	6415	(G-ARPY)	TRDNT	2123	G-AVFD	TRDNT	2143
G-41-174	B707	17593	(G-APDN)	COMET	6424	G-ARPY	TRDNT	2126	G-AVFE	TRDNT	2144
G-41-274	B707	17603	G-APDO	COMET	6416	(G-ARPZ)	TRDNT	2124	G-AVFF	TRDNT	2145
G-41-3-72	B707	18084	G-APDP	COMET	6417	G-ARPZ	TRDNT	2128	G-AVFG	TRDNT	2146
G-41-372	B707	18085	G-APDR	COMET	6418	G-ARRA	B707	18411	G-AVFH	TRDNT	2147
G-52-1	1-11	005	G-APDS	COMET	6419	G-ARRB	B707	18412	G-AVFI	TRDNT	2148
G-52-19	L1011	293A-1249	G-APDT	COMET	6420	G-ARRC	B707	18413	G-AVFJ	TRDNT	2149
(G-)	B737	25594	G-APFB	B707	17703	G-ARTA	VC10	803	G-AVFK	TRDNT	2151
(G-)	B737	25595	G-APFC	B707	17704	G-ARVA	VC10	804	G-AVFL	TRDNT	2152
(G-)	B757	25597	G-APFD	B707	17705	G-ARVB	VC10	805	G-AVFM	TRDNT	2153
(G-)	B757	25598	G-APFE	B707	17706	G-ARVC	VC10	806	G-AVFN	TRDNT	2153
(G-AJJV)	ASHT	1395	G-APFF	B707	17707	G-ARVE	VC10	807	(G-AVFO)	TRDNT	2154
(G-AJJW)	ASHT	1396	G-APFG	B707	17708	**G-ARVF**	**VC10**	**808**	G-AVFO	TRDNT	2156
(G-AJJX)	ASHT	1397	G-APFH	B707	17709	G-ARVG	VC10	809	G-AVGP	1-11	BAC.114
(G-AJJY)	ASHT	1398	G-APFI	B707	17710	G-ARVH	VC10	810	G-AVKA	B707	19415
(G-AJJZ)	ASHT	1399	G-APFJ	B707	17711	G-ARVI	VC10	811	G-AVMH	1-11	BAC.136
(G-AJKA)	ASHT	1400	G-APFK	B707	17712	G-ARVJ	VC10	812	G-AVMI	1-11	BAC.137
G-ALVG	COMET	06001	G-APFL	B707	17713	G-ARVK	VC10	813	G-AVMJ	1-11	BAC.138
G-ALYP	COMET	06003	G-APFM	B707	17714	G-ARVL	VC10	814	G-AVMK	1-11	BAC.139
G-ALYR	COMET	06004	G-APFN	B707	17715	**G-ARVM**	**VC10**	**815**	G-AVML	1-11	BAC.140

Reg	Type	C/n	Reg	Type	C/n	Reg	Type	C/n	Reg	Type	C/n
G-AVMM	1-11	BAC.141	G-AWZS	TRDNT	2319	G-AZNZ	B737	19074	G-BCXR	1-11	BAC.198
G-AVMN	1-11	BAC.142	G-AWZT	TRDNT	2320	(G-AZOI)	B707	17602	G-BDAE	1-11	BAC.203
G-AVMO	1-11	BAC.143	G-AWZU	TRDNT	2321	G-AZPE	1-11	BAC.208	G-BDAN	B727	19279
G-AVMP	1-11	BAC.144	G-AWZV	TRDNT	2322	G-AZPW	B707	20275	G-BDAS	1-11	BAC.202
G-AVMR	1-11	BAC.145	G-AWZW	TRDNT	2323	G-AZPY	1-11	BAC.187	G-BDAT	1-11	BAC.232
G-AVMS	1-11	BAC.146	G-AWZX	TRDNT	2324	G-AZPZ	1-11	BAC.229	G-BDCN	B707	18975
G-AVMT	1-11	BAC.147	(G-AWZY)	TRDNT	2325	G-AZRO	B707	20488	G-BDCW	L1011	193U-1131
G-AVMU	1-11	BAC.148	G-AWZZ	TRDNT	2326	G-AZTG	B707	17600	G-BDCX	L1011	193U-1133
G-AVMV	1-11	BAC.149	G-AXBB	1-11	BAC.162	G-AZUK	1-11	BAC.241	G-BDCY	L1011	193U-1138
G-AVMW	1-11	BAC.150	G-AXCK	1-11	090	G-AZWA	B707	17605	G-BDCZ	L1011	193U-1140
G-AVMX	1-11	BAC.151	G-AXCP	1-11	087	G-AZXM	TRDNT	2154	G-BDDE	DC-8	45684
G-AVMY	1-11	BAC.152	**G-AXDN**	CNCRD	13522/01	G-AZZC	DC-10	46905	G-BDEA	B707	19296
G-AVMZ	1-11	BAC.153	G-AXGW	B707	20374	G-AZZD	DC-10	46906	G-BDHA	DC-8	45667
G-AVOE	1-11	BAC.129	G-AXGX	B707	20375	G-BAAA	L1011	193K-1024	G-BDIF	COMET	6463
G-AVOF	1-11	BAC.131	G-AXJK	1-11	BAC.191	G-BAAB	L1011	193K-1032	G-BDIT	COMET	6467
G-AVPB	B707	19843	G-AXJL	1-11	BAC.209	G-BABP	TRDNT	2163	G-BDIU	COMET	6468
G-AVRL	B737	19709	G-AXJM	1-11	BAC.214	G-BABR	TRDNT	2164	G-BDIV	COMET	6469
G-AVRM	B737	19710	G-AXLL	1-11	BAC.193	G-BABS	TRDNT	2165	G-BDIW	COMET	6470
G-AVRN	B737	19711	G-AXLM	1-11	BAC.199	G-BABT	TRDNT	2166	G-BDIX	COMET	6471
G-AVRO	B737	19712	G-AXLN	1-11	BAC.211	G-BABU	TRDNT	2167	G-BDKE	B707	19623
G-AVTF	1-11	BAC.122	G-AXLR	VC10	829	G-BABV	TRDNT	2168	G-BDLM	B707	19629
G-AVTW	B707	19767	G-AXMF	1-11	BAC.200	G-BADP	B737	20632	G-BDPV	B747	21213
(G-AVYA)	TRDNT	2135	G-AXMG	1-11	BAC.201	G-BADR	B737	20633	G-BDPZ	B747	19745
G-AVYB	TRDNT	2136	G-AXMH	1-11	BAC.202	G-BAEF	B727	18879	G-BDSJ	B707	19630
G-AVYC	TRDNT	2137	G-AXMI	1-11	BAC.203	G-BAEL	B707	17602	G-BDXA	B747	21238
G-AVYD	TRDNT	2138	G-AXMJ	1-11	BAC.204	G-BAFZ	B727	18877	G-BDXB	B747	21239
G-AVYE	TRDNT	2139	G-AXMK	1-11	BAC.205	G-BAJF	TRDNT	2169	G-BDXC	B747	21240
G-AVYZ	1-11	BAC.133	G-AXML	1-11	BAC.206	G-BAJG	TRDNT	2170	G-BDXD	B747	21241
G-AVZZ	B707	17699	G-AXMU	1-11	BAC.157	G-BAJH	TRDNT	2171	G-BDXE	B747	21350
G-AWBL	1-11	BAC.132	G-AXNA	B737	20282	G-BAJI	TRDNT	2172	G-BDXF	B747	21351
G-AWDF	1-11	BAC.134	G-AXNB	B737	20389	G-BAJJ	TRDNT	2173	G-BDXG	B747	21536
G-AWDG	B707	17702	G-AXNC	B737	20417	G-BAJK	TRDNT	2174	G-BDXH	B747	21635
G-AWEJ	1-11	BAC.115	G-AXOX	1-11	BAC.121	G-BAJL	TRDNT	2327	G-BDXI	B747	21830
G-AWGG	1-11	BAC.116	G-AXPH	1-11	BAC.194	G-BAJM	TRDNT	2328	G-BDXJ	B747	21831
G-AWHU	B707	19821	G-AXRS	B707	19664	G-BAJW	B727	18878	G-BDXK	B747	22303
G-AWKJ	1-11	BAC.128	G-AXSY	1-11	BAC.195	G-BAWP	B707	19354	(G-BDXK)	B747	22306
G-AWNA	B747	19761	G-AXVO	1-11	BAC.197	G-BAZG	B737	20806	G-BDXL	B747	22304
G-AWNB	B747	19762	G-AXXY	B707	20456	G-BAZH	B737	20807	G-BDXL	B747	22305
G-AWNC	B747	19763	G-AXXZ	B707	20457	G-BAZI	B737	20808	(G-BDXM)	B747	22305
G-AWND	B747	19764	G-AXYD	1-11	BAC.210	G-BBAE	L1011	193N-1083	G-BDXM	B747	23711
G-AWNE	B747	19765	G-AYAG	B707	18085	(G-BBAF)	L1011	193C-1096	G-BDXN	B747	22442
G-AWNF	B747	19766	G-AYBJ	B707	17597	G-BBAF	L1011	193N-1093	G-BDXN	B747	23735
G-AWNG	B747	20269	G-AYEX	B707	19417	G-BBAG	L1011	193N-1094	G-BDXO	B747	23799
G-AWNH	B747	20270	G-AYHM	1-11	BAC.161	(G-BBAG)	L1011	193N-1101	**G-BDXP**	B747	24088
G-AWNI	B747	20271	G-AYKN	1-11	BAC.215	G-BBAH	L1011	193N-1101	G-BEAF	B707	18591
G-AWNJ	B747	20272	G-AYLT	B707	20517	(G-BBAH)	L1011	193P-1103	G-BEAK	L1011	193N-1132
G-AWNK	B747	20273	G-AYOP	1-11	BAC.233	(G-BBAI)	L1011	193B-1107	G-BEAL	L1011	193N-1145
G-AWNL	B747	20284	G-AYOR	1-11	BAC.232	G-BBAI	L1011	193N-1102	G-BEAM	L1011	193N-1146
G-AWNM	B747	20708	G-AYOS	1-11	BAC.213	G-BBAJ	L1011	193N-1106	G-BEBL	DC-10	46949
G-AWNN	B747	20809	G-AYRZ	B707	18084	(G-BBAJ)	L1011	193P-1117	G-BEBM	DC-10	46921
G-AWNO	B747	20810	(G-AYSC)	1-11	BAC.235	**G-BBDG**	CNCRD	13523/202	G-BEBP	B707	18579
G-AWNP	B747	20952	G-AYSI	B707	18707	G-BBME	1-11	066	G-BECG	B737	21335
G-AWSY	B737	20236	G-AYSL	B707	17599	G-BBMF	1-11	074	G-BECH	B737	21336
G-AWTK	B707	18975	G-AYUW	B707	18239	G-BBMG	1-11	BAC.115	G-BEEX	1-11	BAC.115
G-AWWD	B707	19355	G-AYVE	B707	18083	G-BBPU	B747	20953	G-BEEY	COMET	6462
G-AWWX	1-11	BAC.184	G-AYVF	TRDNT	2325	G-BBSZ	DC-10	46727	G-BEEZ	COMET	6466
G-AWWY	1-11	BAC.185	G-AYVG	B707	17598	G-BBUU	COMET	6451	G-BEGZ	B707	19620
G-AWWZ	1-11	BAC.186	G-AYVS	COMET	6474	G-BBVS	TRDNT	2175	G-BEJM	1-11	BAC.118
G-AWXJ	1-11	BAC.166	G-AYWB	1-11	BAC.237	G-BBVT	TRDNT	2176	G-BEJW	1-11	BAC.154
G-AWYR	1-11	BAC.174	G-AYWX	COMET	6465	G-BBVU	TRDNT	2177	G-BEKA	1-11	BAC.230
G-AWYS	1-11	BAC.175	G-AYXB	1-11	BAC.192	G-BBVV	TRDNT	2178	G-BELO	DC-10	46501
G-AWYT	1-11	BAC.176	G-AYXR	B707	17608	G-BBVW	TRDNT	2179	G-BETJ	DC-8	45379
G-AWYU	1-11	BAC.177	G-AYZZ	B707	20089	G-BBVX	TRDNT	2180	G-BEVN	B707	19271
G-AWYV	1-11	BAC.178	(G-AZDG)	1-11	BAC.127	G-BBVY	TRDNT	2181	G-BEZT	B707	18765
G-AWYZ	TRDNT	2301	G-AZEB	1-11	BAC.188	G-BBVZ	TRDNT	2182	G-BFBS	B707	18693
G-AWZA	TRDNT	2302	G-AZEC	1-11	BAC.189	G-BBWA	TRDNT	2183	G-BFBZ	B707	18585
G-AWZB	TRDNT	2303	G-AZED	1-11	BAC.127	G-BBWB	TRDNT	2184	G-BFCA	L1011	193V-1157
G-AWZC	TRDNT	2304	G-AZFB	B707	18381	G-BBWD	TRDNT	2185	G-BFCB	L1011	193V-1159
G-AWZD	TRDNT	2305	G-AZFT	TRDNT	2157	G-BBWE	TRDNT	2186	G-BFCC	L1011	193V-1164
G-AWZE	TRDNT	2306	G-AZFU	TRDNT	2158	G-BBWF	TRDNT	2187	G-BFCD	L1011	193V-1165
G-AWZF	TRDNT	2307	G-AZFV	TRDNT	2159	G-BBWG	TRDNT	2188	G-BFCE	L1011	193V-1168
G-AWZG	TRDNT	2308	G-AZFW	TRDNT	2160	G-BBWH	TRDNT	2189	G-BFCF	L1011	193V-1174
G-AWZH	TRDNT	2309	G-AZFX	TRDNT	2161	G-BBZG	B707	18792	G-BFEO	B707	18691
G-AWZI	TRDNT	2310	G-AZFY	TRDNT	2162	G-BCAL	B707	19297	G-BFGI	DC-10	46590
G-AWZJ	TRDNT	2311	G-AZIY	COMET	6434	G-BCBA	B707	18014	G-BFGM	B727	19249
G-AWZK	TRDNT	2312	G-AZJM	B707	18886	G-BCBB	B707	18013	G-BFGN	B727	19251
G-AWZL	TRDNT	2313	G-AZKM	B707	18382	G-BCCV	1-11	BAC.198	G-BFHW	DC-8	45879
G-AWZM	TRDNT	2314	(G-AZLW)	COMET	6432	G-BCDA	B727	19281	G-BFIH	DC-9	47048
G-AWZN	TRDNT	2315	G-AZMF	1-11	BAC.240	G-BCLZ	B707	18710	G-BFKW	CNCRD	214
G-AWZO	TRDNT	2316	G-AZMI	1-11	066	G-BCRS	B707	17603	G-BFKX	CNCRD	216
G-AWZP	TRDNT	2317	G-AZND	TRDNT	2134	G-BCWA	1-11	BAC.205	G-BFLD	B707	19625
G-AWZR	TRDNT	2318	G-AZNX	B707	18383	G-BCWG	1-11	BAC.204	G-BFLE	B707	19293

Reg	Type	C/N	Reg	Type	C/N	Reg	Type	C/N	Reg	Type	C/N
G-BFMC	1-11	BAC.160	G-BHWE	B737	22364	G-BJXN	B747	20527	G-BMEC	B737	21776
G-BFMI	B707	17632	G-BHWF	B737	22365	G-BJYL	1-11	BAC.208	G-BMFM	146	E2042
G-BFVA	B737	21693	G-BIAD	146	E1001	G-BJYM	1-11	BAC.242	G-BMGS	B747	20121
G-BFVB	B737	21694	(G-BIAE)	146	E1002	G-BJZD	DC-10	46970	G-BMHG	B737	21774
G-BFWN	1-11	BAC.261	(G-BIAF)	146	E1003	G-BJZE	DC-10	46973	G-BMJE	B707	18954
G-BFZF	B707	18718	(G-BIAG)	146	E1004	G-BJZV	B737	22277	G-BMLP	B727	20710
G-BGAT	DC-10	46591	(G-BIAJ)	146	E1005	G-BJZW	B737	22516	(G-BMMP)	B737	22633
G-BGBB	L1011	193Y-1178	G-BIAS	DC-8	45816	G-BKAG	B727	21055	G-BMMZ	B737	20544
G-BGBC	L1011	193N-1182	G-BICV	B737	21528	G-BKAP	B737	21685	G-BMNA	A300	169
G-BGCT	B707	18054	G-BIII	1-11	BAC.128	G-BKAU	1-11	BAC.107	G-BMNB	A300	009
G-BGDA	B737	21790	G-BIKA	B757	22172	G-BKAV	1-11	BAC.109	G-BMNC	A300	012
G-BGDB	B737	21791	G-BIKB	B757	22173	G-BKAW	1-11	BAC.113	G-BMON	B737	22416
G-BGDC	B737	21792	**G-BIKC**	**B757**	**22174**	G-BKAX	1-11	BAC.133	G-BMOR	B737	21775
G-BGDD	B737	21793	G-BIKD	B757	22175	G-BKBT	B737	20943	G-BMRA	B757	23710
G-BGDE	B737	21794	(G-BIKF)	B757	22176	G-BKCG	B727	20328	G-BMRB	B757	23975
G-BGDF	B737	21795	**G-BIKF**	**B757**	**22177**	(G-BKGU)	B737	22966	**G-BMRC**	**B757**	**24072**
G-BGDG	B737	21796	(G-BIKG)	B757	22177	(G-BKGV)	B737	22967	**G-BMRD**	**B757**	**24073**
G-BGDH	B737	21797	**G-BIKG**	**B757**	**22178**	G-BKHE	B737	22966	**G-BMRE**	**B757**	**24074**
G-BGDI	B737	21798	(G-BIKH)	B757	22178	G-BKHF	B737	22967	**G-BMRF**	**B757**	**24101**
G-BGDJ	B737	21799	G-BIKH	B757	22179	G-BKHO	B737	22979	G-BMRG	B757	24102
G-BGDK	B737	21800	(G-BIKI)	B757	22179	G-BKHT	146	E1007	**G-BMRH**	**B757**	**24266**
G-BGDL	B737	21801	**G-BIKI**	**B757**	**22180**	G-BKMN	146	E1006	G-BMRI	B757	24267
G-BGDN	B737	21802	(G-BIKJ)	B757	22180	G-BKMS	B737	22453	**G-BMRJ**	**B757**	**24268**
G-BGDO	B737	21803	**G-BIKJ**	**B757**	**22181**	G-BKNG	B727	21056	G-BMSM	B737	22279
G-BGDP	B737	21804	(G-BIKK)	B757	22181	G-BKNH	B737	21820	(G-BMSR)	B737	22660
G-BGDR	B737	21805	**G-BIKK**	**B757**	**22182**	G-BKPW	B767	22980	G-BMTE	B737	23712
G-BGDS	B737	21806	(G-BIKL)	B757	22182	G-BKRM	B757	22176	G-BMTF	B737	23713
G-BGDT	B737	21807	G-BIKL	B757	22183	G-BKRO	B737	21278	G-BMTG	B737	23733
G-BGDU	B737	21808	(G-BIKM)	B757	22183	G-BKVZ	B767	22981	G-BMTH	B737	23734
(G-BGFA)	B707	17721	**G-BIKM**	**B757**	**22184**	G-BKWT	A310	295	G-BMUE	B727	18951
(G-BGFB)	B707	18056	(G-BIKN)	B757	22184	G-BKWU	A310	306	G-BMWD	DC-9	47570
G-BGFS	B737	21359	**G-BIKN**	**B757**	**22186**	G-BKXZ	146	E1010	(G-BMXE)	146	E2058
(G-BGIR)	B707	19270	(G-BIKO)	B757	22185	G-BKYA	B737	23159	(G-BMXK)	B747	21517
G-BGIS	B707	18717	**G-BIKO**	**B757**	**22187**	G-BKYB	B737	23160	G-BMYE	146	E2008
G-BGJE	B737	22026	(G-BIKP)	B757	22186	G-BKYC	B737	23161	G-BMYT	B727	18802
G-BGJF	B737	22027	**G-BIKP**	**B757**	**22188**	G-BKYD	B737	23162	G-BMZK	A300	076
G-BGJG	B737	22028	(G-BIKR)	B757	22187	G-BKYE	B737	23163	G-BMZL	A300	077
G-BGJH	B737	22029	G-BIKR	B757	22189	G-BKYF	B737	23164	G-BMZU	B727	18365
G-BGJI	B737	22030	(G-BIKS)	B757	22188	G-BKYG	B737	23165	G-BNAX	B767	23057
G-BGJJ	B737	22031	**G-BIKS**	**B757**	**22190**	G-BKYH	B737	23166	G-BNCT	B737	23766
G-BGJK	B737	22032	(G-BIKT)	B757	22189	G-BKYI	B737	23167	G-BNCW	B767	23807
G-BGJL	B737	22033	G-BIKT	B757	23398	G-BKYJ	B737	23168	(G-BNDR)	146	E2062
G-BGJM	B737	22034	(G-BIKU)	B757	22190	G-BKYK	B737	23169	(G-BNEP)	B757	22185
G-BGKE	1-11	BAC.263	**G-BIKU**	**B757**	**23399**	G-BKYL	B737	23170	G-BNFF	DC-9	47192
G-BGKF	1-11	BAC.264	**G-BIKV**	**B757**	**23400**	G-BKYM	B737	23171	(G-BNFG)	146	E2067
G-BGKG	1-11	BAC.265	G-BIKW	B757	23492	G-BKYN	B737	23172	(G-BNGG)	1-11	BAC.267
G-BGNW	B737	21131	G-BIKX	B757	23493	G-BKYO	B737	23225	G-BNGH	B707	18718
(G-BGRU)	B737	22057	G-BIKY	B757	23533	G-BKYP	B737	23226	G-BNGK	B737	22406
(G-BGRV)	B737	22058	**G-BIKZ**	**B757**	**23532**	G-BLDE	B737	22876	G-BNGL	B737	23924
(G-BGRW)	B737	22059	(G-BILB)	A300	127	G-BLDH	1-11	BAC.262	G-BNGM	B737	23925
G-BGTU	1-11	BAC.108	(G-BILC)	A300	131	G-BLEA	B737	21397	(G-BNHG)	B757	23227
G-BGTV	B737	22024	(G-BILD)	A300	144	(G-BLFP)	DC-10	48266	G-BNIA	B737	22737
G-BGTW	B737	22023	(G-BILE)	A300	177	(G-BLFR)	DC-10	47863	G-BNIH	1-11	BAC.406
G-BGTY	B737	21960	(G-BILF)	A300	180	(G-BLFS)	DC-10	47864	G-BNJI	146	E2072
(G-BGWP)	DC-9	45712	(G-BILG)	A300	190	G-BLHD	1-11	BAC.260	G-BNKJ	146	E2069
G-BGXE	DC-10	47811	(G-BILH)	A300	229	G-BLKB	B737	23060	G-BNKK	146	E2070
G-BGXF	DC-10	47812	(G-BILI)	A300	238	G-BLKC	B737	23061	**G-BNLA**	**B747**	**23908**
G-BGXG	DC-10	47813	(G-BILJ)	A300	282	G-BLKD	B737	23062	**G-BNLB**	**B747**	**23909**
G-BGXH	DC-10	47814	(G-BILK)	A300	305	G-BLKE	B737	23063	**G-BNLC**	**B747**	**23910**
G-BGXI	DC-10	47815	G-BIMA	A300	127	G-BLKV	B737	23072	**G-BNLD**	**B747**	**23911**
G-BGYJ	B737	22057	G-BIMB	A300	131	G-BLKW	B767	23250	**G-BNLE**	**B747**	**24047**
G-BGYK	B737	22058	G-BIMC	A300	144	(G-BLPS)	A310	370	**G-BNLF**	**B747**	**24048**
G-BGYL	B737	22059	(G-BIMD)	A300	177	**G-BLRA**	**146**	**E1017**	**G-BNLG**	**B747**	**24049**
G-BHBL	L1011	193C-1193	G-BIME	A300	180	G-BLUS	L1011	293C-1235	**G-BNLH**	**B747**	**24050**
G-BHBM	L1011	193N-1198	(G-BIMF)	A300	190	G-BLUT	L1011	293F-1236	**G-BNLI**	**B747**	**24051**
G-BHBN	L1011	193N-1204	G-BIMG	A300	229	G-BLVE	B747	21097	**G-BNLJ**	**B747**	**24052**
G-BHBO	L1011	193N-1205	(G-BIMH)	A300	238	G-BLVF	B747	21098	**G-BNLK**	**B747**	**24053**
G-BHBP	L1011	193N-1211	(G-BIMI)	A300	282	G-BLVH	B757	23227	**G-BNLL**	**B747**	**24054**
G-BHBR	L1011	193N-1212	(G-BIMJ)	A300	305	(G-BLVO)	1-11	041	**G-BNLM**	**B747**	**24055**
G-BHCL	B737	21955	G-BIUR	B727	19619	(G-BLVP)	1-11	043	**G-BNLN**	**B747**	**24056**
G-BHDH	DC-10	47816	G-BJBJ	B737	22632	(G-BLYX)	146	E2038	**G-BNLO**	**B747**	**24057**
G-BHDI	DC-10	47831	G-BJCT	B737	22638	G-BMAA	DC-9	47048	**G-BNLP**	**B747**	**24058**
G-BHDJ	DC-10	47840	G-BJCU	B737	22639	G-BMAB	DC-9	45738	**G-BNLR**	**B747**	**24447**
G-BHGE	B707	18421	G-BJCV	B737	22640	G-BMAC	DC-9	45739	**G-BNLS**	**B747**	**24629**
G-BHNE	B727	21676	G-BJFH	B737	22278	G-BMAG	DC-9	45719	**G-BNLT**	**B747**	**24630**
G-BHNF	B727	21438	G-BJMV	1-11	BAC.244	G-BMAH	DC-9	45712	**G-BNLU**	**B747**	**25406**
G-BHOX	B707	17640	G-BJRT	1-11	BAC.234	G-BMAI	DC-9	45713	**G-BNLV**	**B747**	**25427**
G-BHOY	B707	17651	G-BJRU	1-11	BAC.238	G-BMAK	DC-9	47430	**G-BNLW**	**B747**	**25432**
G-BHVG	B737	22395	G-BJSO	B737	22071	G-BMAM	DC-9	47468	**G-BNLX**	**B747**	**25435**
G-BHVH	B737	22396	G-BJXJ	B737	22657	G-BMAN	1-11	BAC.131	(G-BNLY)	B747	25434
G-BHVI	B737	22397	G-BJXL	B737	22054	G-BMAZ	B707	19270	(G-BNLY)	B747	25811
G-BHVT	B727	21349	G-BJXM	B737	22055	G-BMDF	B737	22875	**G-BNLY**	**B747**	**27090**

Reg	Type	c/n	Reg	Type	c/n	Reg	Type	c/n	Reg	Type	c/n
(G-BNLZ)	B747	25435	(G-BOZC)	B737	24220	(G=BSSG)	146	E2172	**G-BVKD**	**B737**	**26421**
(G-BNLZ)	B747	25812	(G-BOZD)	B737	24221	**G-BSST**	**CNCRD**	**13520/002**	**G-BVLJ**	**146**	**E1160**
G-BNLZ	**B747**	**27091**	G-BPAT	B707	19367	G-BSTA	146	E1002	G-BVMP	146	E2210
G-BNND	146	E2074	G-BPBS	146	E2117	(G-BSUA)	B757	24291	G-BVMS	146	E2227
G-BNNI	B727	20950	G-BPBT	146	E2119	(G-BSUB)	B757	24137	G-BVMT	146	E2220
G-BNNJ	B737	24068	G-BPEA	B737	24370	G-BSUY	146	E3182	G-BVNM	B737	24163
G-BNNK	B737	24069	G-BPEB	B757	24371	(G-BSXJ)	1-11	063	G-BVNN	B737	24164
G-BNNL	B737	24070	**G-BPEC**	**B757**	**24882**	(G-BSXK)	1-11	089	G-BVNO	B737	24167
G-BNPA	B737	23811	**G-BPED**	**B757**	**25059**	G-BSXL	146	E3186	G-BVPE	146	E3213
G-BNPB	B737	24059	**G-BPEE**	**B757**	**25060**	(G-BSXU)	1-11	093	G-BVRJ	146	E1254
G-BNPC	B737	24060	G-BPEF	B757	24120	(G-BSXV)	1-11	BAC.106	G-BVSA	146	E3159
G-BNPJ	146	E2078	G-BPEH	B757	24121	G-BSXZ	146	E3174	G-BVTE	F.70	11538
G-BNRT	B737	23064	**G-BPEI**	**B757**	**25806**	G-BSYN	1-11	BAC.186	G-BVTF	F.70	11539
G-BNSA	MD80	49643	**G-BPEJ**	**B757**	**25807**	G-BSYR	146	E3181	G-BVTG	F.70	11551
G-BNSB	MD80	49658	**G-BPEK**	**B757**	**25808**	G-BSYS	146	E3183	(G-BVTH)	F.70	11577
G-BNSD	B757	24118	G-BPFV	B767	24457	G-BSYT	146	E3187	G-BVUW	146	E1035
G-BNSE	B757	24121	G-BPGW	B757	22185	G-BSZA	B707	18586	G-BVUX	146	E1068
G-BNSF	B757	24122	G-BPKA	B737	24163	G-BSZE	A300	192	G-BVUY	146	E1071
G-BNUA	146	E2086	G-BPKB	B737	24164	G-BSZZ	146	E2180	(G-BVWD)	146	E2253
G-BNWA	**B767**	**24333**	G-BPKC	B737	24165	G-BTAC	DC-8	45768	G-BVYA	A320	0354
G-BNWB	**B767**	**24334**	G-BPKD	B737	24166	G-BTCP	146	E2178	G-BVYB	A320	0357
G-BNWC	**B767**	**24335**	G-BPKE	B737	24167	G-BTDO	146	E2188	G-BVYC	A320	0411
G-BNWD	**B767**	**24336**	G-BPLA	B737	22906	G-BTEB	B737	21736	G-BVYS	146	E3259
G-BNWE	B767	24337	G-BPND	B727	21021	G-BTEC	B737	20908	**G-BVZE**	**B737**	**26422**
G-BNWF	B767	24338	G-BPNP	146	E1002	G-BTED	B737	20909	G-BVZF	B737	25038
G-BNWG	B767	24339	G-BPNS	B727	20550	G-BTEJ	B757	25085	**G-BVZG**	**B737**	**25160**
G-BNWH	**B767**	**24340**	**G-BPNT**	**146**	**E3126**	G-BTHT	146	E3194	**G-BVZH**	**B737**	**25166**
G-BNWI	**B767**	**24341**	G-BPNX	1-11	BAC.110	G-BTIA	146	E2148	**G-BVZI**	**B737**	**25167**
G-BNWJ	B767	24342	G-BPNY	B727	20675	G-BTJG	146	E3163	G-BVZU	A320	0280
G-BNWK	B767	24343	(G-BPNY)	B737	22161	G-BTJT	146	E3128	G-BWCP	A320	0189
G-BNWL	B757	25203	G-BPNZ	B737	24332	G-BTKC	146	E2184	G-BWES	1-11	BAC.259
G-BNWM	**B767**	**25204**	G-BPSC	MD80	49823	G-BTLD	146	E3198	G-BWIN	DC-10	46936
G-BNWN	**B767**	**25444**	G-BPSD	MD80	49826	G-BTMI	146	E3193	G-BWJA	B737	24462
G-BNWO	**B767**	**25442**	G-BPSN	B757	24119	G-BTNU	146	E3155	(G-BWKH)	1-11	BAC.226
G-BNWP	B767	25443	(G-BPUV)	146	E2133	G-BTTP	146	E3203	(G-BWKI)	F.70	11578
G-BNWR	**B767**	**25732**	G-BRAB	146	E3131	G-BTUY	146	E3202	G-BWKN	A320	0190
G-BNWS	**B767**	**25826**	G-BRDR	B707	18688	G-BTVO	146	E3205	G-BWKO	A320	0343
G-BNWT	**B767**	**25828**	G-BRGK	146	E3150	G-BTVT	146	E2200	G-BWKY	146	E2277
G-BNWU	**B767**	**25829**	G-BRGM	146	E3151	G-BTXN	146	E3129	G-BWLG	146	E2176
G-BNWV	**B767**	**27140**	**G-BRIF**	**B767**	**24736**	G-BTYO	146	E1104	**G-BXAR**	**146**	**E3298**
G-BNWW	**B767**	**25831**	G-BRIG	B767	24757	G-BTZF	B737	22967	**G-BXAS**	**146**	**E3301**
G-BNWX	**B767**	**25832**	G-BRJD	B757	24397	**G-BTZN**	**146**	**E3149**	G-BXAT	A320	0436
G-BNWY	**B767**	**25834**	G-BRJE	B757	24398	G-BUDX	B757	25592	G-BXAW	A321	0666
G-BNWZ	**B767**	**25733**	G-BRJF	B757	24772	G-BUDZ	B757	25593	G-BXEU	146	E3308
G-BNXP	B737	23787	G-BRJG	B757	24771	G-BUFI	146	E1229	**G-BXKA**	**A320**	**0714**
G-BNXW	B737	23827	G-BRJH	B757	24794	G-BUHB	146	E3183	G-BXKB	A320	0716
G-BNYC	146	E2089	G-BRJI	B757	24792	G-BUHC	146	E3193	**G-BXKC**	**A320**	**0730**
G-BNYS	**B767**	**24013**	G-BRJJ	B757	24793	(G-BUHI)	B737	26284	**G-BXKD**	**A320**	**0735**
G-BNYT	B737	21112	G-BRJP	B737	22660	G-BUHJ	B737	25164	G-BXNF	F.100	11316
G-BNZT	B737	22703	G-BRJS	146	E1104	G-BUHK	B737	26289	G-BXNP	F.100	0775
(G-BNZU)	B737	21775	G-BRKF	B737	24795	G-BUHL	B737	25134	G-BXOL	B757	24528
G-BOAA	**CNCRD**	**206**	G-BRKG	B737	24796	G-BUHV	146	E3207	G-BXOP	B767	25221
G-BOAB	**CNCRD**	**208**	(G-BRLM)	146	E1144	G-BUHW	146	E3217	G-BXRE	F.28	11187
G-BOAC	**CNCRD**	**204**	G-BRLN	146	E1152	**G-BUSB**	**A320**	**0006**	G-BXRU	A300	031
G-BOAD	**CNCRD**	**210**	G-BRNG	146	E2077	**G-BUSC**	**A320**	**0008**	G-BXRW	A320	0308
G-BOAE	**CNCRD**	**212**	G-BROC	B737	24573	(G-BUSD)	A320	0011	(G-BXRX)	A320	0314
G-BOAF	**CNCRD**	**216**	G-BRPW	146	E3153	**G-BUSE**	**A320**	**0017**	G-BXTA	A320	0764
G-BOAG	**CNCRD**	**214**	(G-BRSA)	A320	0006	G-BUSF	A320	0018	G-BXWE	F.100	11327
G-BOEA	146	E1095	(G-BRSB)	A320	0008	**G-BUSG**	**A320**	**0039**	G-BXWF	F.100	11328
G-BOHC	B757	24120	G-BRUC	146	E1009	**G-BUSH**	**A320**	**0042**	**G-BYAA**	**B767**	**25058**
G-BOHK	146	E2100	G-BRXI	146	E3154	**G-BUSI**	**A320**	**0103**	**G-BYAB**	**B767**	**25139**
G-BOJJ	146	E3146	G-BRXJ	B737	23830	**G-BUSJ**	**A320**	**0109**	G-BYAC	B767	26962
G-BOKV	B727	20739	G-BRXT	146	E2115	**G-BUSK**	**A320**	**0120**	**G-BYAD**	**B757**	**26963**
G-BOKZ	146	E2102	G-BSGI	146	E3168	G-BUSL	B737	24096	**G-BYAE**	**B757**	**26964**
G-BOLM	B737	23942	G-BSKY	DC-8	45858	G-BUSM	B737	24097	**G-BYAF**	**B757**	**26266**
G-BOMA	146	E1091	G-BSLP	146	E1144	G-BVAE	146	E2239	G-BYAG	B757	26965
G-BOMI	146	E2105	(G-BSLS)	146	E3155	G-BVBY	B737	25844	**G-BYAH**	**B757**	**26966**
G-BOMJ	146	E2109	G-BSLZ	146	E3166	G-BVBZ	B737	25858	**G-BYAI**	**B757**	**26967**
G-BOMK	146	E2112	G-BSMR	146	E3158	G-BVCD	146	E2211	**G-BYAJ**	**B757**	**25623**
G-BONM	B737	22738	(G-BSNA)	B757	25053	G-BVCE	146	E3209	**G-BYAK**	**B757**	**26267**
G-BOPB	**B767**	**24239**	(G-BSNB)	B757	25054	G-BVFV	146	E2073	**G-BYAL**	**B757**	**25626**
G-BOPJ	B737	24123	(G-BSNC)	B757	25133	G-BVHA	B737	25859	G-BYAM	B757	23895
G-BOPK	B737	24124	G-BSNR	146	E3165	G-BVHB	B737	25860	**G-BYAN**	**B757**	**27219**
G-BOSA	B737	20808	G-BSNS	146	E3169	G-BVJA	F.100	11489	**G-BYAO**	**B757**	**27235**
G-BOSL	B737	22161	G-BSNV	B737	25168	G-BVJB	F.100	11488	**G-BYAP**	**B757**	**27236**
G-BOWR	B737	23401	G-BSNW	B737	25169	G-BVJC	F.100	11497	**G-BYAR**	**B757**	**27237**
G-BOWW	146	E3120	G-BSOC	146	E3161	G-BVJD	F.100	11503	**G-BYAS**	**B757**	**27238**
G-BOXD	146	E2113	G-BSOH	146	E2170	G-BVJV	A320	0437	**G-BYAT**	**B757**	**27208**
G-BOXE	146	E2114	(G-BSRA)	B737	25116	G-BVJW	A320	0467	**G-BYAU**	**B757**	**27220**
G-BOYN	B737	23788	(G-BSRB)	B737	25134	G-BVKA	B737	24694	**G-BYAW**	**B757**	**27234**
G-BOZA	B737	23718	G-BSRU	146	E2018	**G-BVKB**	**B737**	**27268**	**G-BYAX**	**B757**	**28834**
G-BOZB	B737	24219	G-BSRV	146	E2020	G-BVKC	B737	24695	**G-BYAY**	**B757**	**28836**

Reg	Type	Ser	Reg	Type	Ser	Reg	Type	Ser	Reg	Type	Ser
G-BYDA	DC-10	46990	G-CDNB	146	E1230	G-CEPJ	MD80	53170	G-CSJS	A330	309
G-BYDH	A300	210	G-CDNC	146	E1252	G-CEPK	MD80	53171	G-CSVS	B757	25620
G-BYDN	F.100	11329	G-CDOE	146	E1224	G-CEXC	A300	124	G-CTLA	A321	1887
G-BYDO	F.100	11323	G-CDOF	146	E1225	G-CEXH	A300	117	G-CVYD	A320	0393
G-BYDP	F.100	11321	G-CDPF	146	E3132	G-CEXI	A300	121	G-CVYE	A320	0394
G-BYFS	A320	0230	G-CDPT	B767	29388	G-CEXJ	A300	147	G-CVYG	A320	0443
G-BYGA	B747	28855	G-CDRA	737NG	28304	G-CEXK	A300	105	(G-DAAE)	B767	26204
G-BYGB	B747	28856	G-CDRB	737NG	28305	G-CFAA	146	E3373	G-DACR	A320	0349
G-BYGC	B747	25823	G-CDRK	146	E3265	G-CFAB	146	E3377	(G-DAIO)	MD80	49400
G-BYGD	B747	28857	G-CDUI	146	E3264	G-CFAC	146	E3379	G-DAJB	B757	23770
G-BYGE	B747	28858	G-CDUO	B757	24792	G-CFAD	146	E3380	G-DAJC	B767	27206
G-BYGF	B747	25824	G-CDUP	B757	24793	G-CFAE	146	E3381	G-DBAF	1-11	011
G-BYGG	B747	28859	G-CDXH	146	E3237	G-CFAF	146	E3382	G-DBCA	A319	2098
G-BYNB	737NG	30466	G-CDYK	146	E2329	G-CFAH	146	E3384	G-DBCB	A319	2188
(G-BYNC)	737NG	28231	G-CDZL	737NG	30465	(G-CHGN)	B707	18718	G-DBCC	A319	2194
G-BYNC	737NG	30465	G-CDZM	737NG	30466	G-CHSR	146	E2088	G-DBCD	A319	2389
G-BYRI	B737	20910	G-CDZN	737NG	32903	G-CITB	B747	22579	G-DBCE	A319	2429
G-BYTH	A320	0429	(G-CDZP)	146	E2346	G-CIVA	B747	27092	G-DBCF	A319	2466
G-BYYF	B737	21738	G-CEAA	A300	062	G-CIVB	B747	25811	G-DBCG	A319	2694
G-BYYK	B737	20916	G-CEAB	A300	027	G-CIVC	B747	25812	G-DBCH	A319	2697
G-BYYS	A300	069	G-CEAC	B737	20911	G-CIVD	B747	27349	G-DBCI	A319	2720
G-BYZJ	B737	24962	G-CEAD	B737	21137	G-CIVE	B747	27350	G-DBCJ	A319	2981
G-BYZN	B737	21139	G-CEAE	B737	20912	G-CIVF	B747	25434	G-DBCK	A319	3049
G-BZAT	146	E3320	G-CEAF	B737	20910	G-CIVG	B747	25813	G-DBLA	B767	26063
G-BZAU	146	E3328	G-CEAG	B737	21136	G-CIVH	B747	25809	G-DCAC	MD80	49935
G-BZAV	146	E3331	G-CEAH	B737	21135	G-CIVI	B747	25814	G-DCIO	DC-10	48277
G-BZAW	146	E3354	G-CEAI	B737	21176	G-CIVJ	B747	25817	G-DDDV	B737	22633
G-BZAX	146	E3356	G-CEAJ	B737	21177	G-CIVK	B747	25818	G-DEBA	146	E2028
G-BZAY	146	E3368	G-CEAP	L1011	193N-1145	G-CIVL	B747	27478	G-DEBC	146	E2024
G-BZAZ	146	E3369	G-CEBN	146	E3238	G-CIVM	B747	28700	G-DEBD	146	E2034
G-BZBA	146	E2028	G-CEBR	146	E2130	G-CIVN	B747	25821	G-DEBE	146	E2022
G-BZBB	146	E2034	G-CEBS	146	E2330	G-CIVN	B747	28848	G-DEBF	146	E2023
"G-BZBO"	B747	19745	G-CEBU	146	E2335	G-CIVO	B747	25810	G-DEBG	146	E2040
G-BZFA	146	E1223	G-CECU	B767	21864	G-CIVO	B747	28849	G-DEBH	146	E2045
G-BZHA	B767	29230	G-CEFD	B747	24363	(G-CIVP)	B747	25819	G-DEBJ	146	E1004
G-BZHB	B767	29231	G-CEFE	B747	24383	G-CIVP	B747	28850	G-DEBK	146	E2012
G-BZHC	B767	29232	G-CEFF	B747	26879	G-CIVR	B747	25820	G-DEBL	146	E2014
G-BZKP	B737	20915	G-CEFG	B767	26264	G-CIVR	B747	25822	G-DEBM	146	E2016
G-BZTB	A310	424	G-CEFL	146	E2334	G-CIVS	B747	28851	G-DEBN	146	E1015
G-BZWP	146	E2054	G-CEFN	146	E2337	G-CIVT	B747	25821	G-DEBZ	B737	24059
G-BZZA	B737	26441	G-CEFW	146	E3243	G-CIVU	B747	25810	(G-DEFE)	146	E2022
G-BZZB	B737	25125	G-CEHA	146	E2333	G-CIVV	B747	25819	G-DEFK	146	E2012
G-BZZE	B737	26310	G-CEHB	146	E2344	G-CIVW	B747	25822	G-DEFL	146	E2014
G-BZZF	B737	26311	G-CEIC	146	E2345	G-CIVX	B747	28852	G-DEFM	146	E2016
G-BZZG	B737	26312	G-CEIF	146	E2347	G-CIVY	B747	28853	G-DEVR	MD80	49941
G-BZZH	B737	26313	G-CEIH	146	E3232	G-CIVZ	B747	28854	G-DFUB	B737	22415
G-BZZI	B737	26314	G-CEIJ	146	E2204	G-CJAB	DO328	3200	G-DGDP	B737	22762
G-BZZJ	B737	26321	G-CEJM	B757	26276	(G-CJIG)	B757	23227	G-DHJH	A321	1238
G-CBAE	146	E2057	G-CEJO	737NG	29643	G-CJMB	CRJ	8055	G-DHJZ	A320	1965
G-CBFL	146	E2055	G-CEJP	737NG	29646	G-CLHA	146	E2024	G-DHRG	A320	1942
G-CBIA	1 11	DAC.166	G-CELA	B737	23663	G-CLHB	146	E2036	G-DHSW	B737	23495
G-CBMF	146	E2387	G-CELB	B737	23664	G-CLHC	146	E2088	G-DIAR	B737	23811
G-CBMG	146	E2393	G-CELC	B737	23831	G-CLHD	146	E2023	G-DIMB	B767	28865
G-CBMH	146	E2394	G-CELD	B737	23832	G-CLHE	146	E2045	G-DJAR	A320	0164
G-CBOH	A319	1068	G-CELE	B737	24029	G-CLHX	146	E2270	G-DJOS	1-11	BAC.237
G-CBOI	A321	1012	G-CELF	B737	24302	G-CMMP	B737	24220	G-DLCH	737NG	30040
G-CBOJ	A319	1145	G-CELG	B737	24303	G-CMMR	B737	24303	G-DMCA	DC-10	48266
G-CBSY	A319	1388	G-CELH	B737	23525	G-CNMF	146	E2079	G-DOCA	B737	25267
G-CBTP	A319	1336	G-CELI	B737	23526	G-COES	MD80	49937	G-DOCB	B737	25304
G-CBVJ	B737	22802	G-CELJ	B737	23529	G-COEZ	A320	0179	G-DOCC	B737	25305
G-CBXY	146	E1124	G-CELK	B737	23530	G-COLB	B737	26283	G-DOCD	B737	25349
G-CCJC	146	E2060	G-CELO	B737	24028	G-COLC	B737	26286	G-DOCE	B737	25350
G-CCJP	146	E2066	G-CELP	B737	23522	G-COLE	B737	24962	G-DOCF	B737	25407
G-CCKA	A319	2037	G-CELR	B737	23523	G-CPDA	COMET	6473	G-DOCG	B737	25408
G-CCKB	A319	2043	G-CELS	B737	23660	G-CPEL	B757	24398	G-DOCH	B737	25428
G-CCKC	A319	2050	G-CELU	B737	24962	G-CPEM	B757	28665	G-DOCI	B737	25839
G-CCKD	A319	2053	G-CELV	B737	23661	G-CPEN	B757	28666	G-DOCJ	B737	25840
G-CCKE	A319	2062	G-CELW	B737	23659	G-CPEO	B757	28667	G-DOCK	B737	25841
G-CCLD	E145	145169	G-CELX	B737	23654	G-CPEP	B757	25268	G-DOCL	B737	25842
G-CCLN	146	E1085	G-CELY	B737	23662	G-CPER	B757	29113	G-DOCM	B737	25843
G-CCMA	B747	22872	G-CELZ	B737	23658	G-CPES	B757	29114	G-DOCN	B737	25848
(G-CCMB)	B737	23048	G-CEMK	B767	21865	G-CPET	B757	29115	G-DOCO	B737	25849
G-CCMY	B757	24528	G-CEOD	B767	30586	G-CPEU	B757	29941	G-DOCP	B737	25850
G-CCTB	146	E3234	G-CEPA	MD80	49425	(G-CPEV)	B757	29942	G-DOCR	B737	25851
G-CCXY	146	E1083	G-CEPB	MD80	49428	G-CPEV	B757	29943	G-DOCS	B737	25852
G-CCYH	E145	145070	G-CEPC	MD80	49502	(G-CPEW)	B757	29943	G-DOCT	B737	25853
G-CDCN	146	E3236	G-CEPD	MD80	49505	(G-CPEX)	B757	29944	G-DOCU	B737	25854
G-CDEG	737NG	33022	G-CEPE	MD80	49510	(G-CPEY)	B757	29945	G-DOCV	B737	25855
G-CDFS	E145	145431	G-CEPF	MD80	49510	(G-CPEZ)	B757	29946	G-DOCW	B737	25856
G-CDKD	737NG	28302	G-CEPG	MD80	49512	G-CROS	146	E2226	G-DOCX	B737	25857
G-CDKT	737NG	28303	G-CEPH	MD80	53162	G-CRPH	A320	0424	G-DOCY	B737	25844
(G-CDMR)	B757	23452	G-CEPI	MD80	53169	G-CSJH	146	E2094	G-DOCZ	B737	25858

Reg	Type	Serial	Reg	Type	Serial	Reg	Type	Serial	Reg	Type	Serial
G-DPSP	DC-10	46646	G-EUPJ	A319	1232	G-EZBG	A319	2946	G-EZJP	737NG	32412
G-DRJC	B757	23895	G-EUPK	A319	1236	G-EZBH	A319	2959	G-EZJR	737NG	32413
G-DRVE	A320	0221	G-EUPL	A319	1239	G-EZBI	A319	3003	G-EZJS	737NG	32414
G-DUOA	CRJ7	10028	G-EUPM	A319	1258	G-EZBJ	A319	3036	G-EZJT	737NG	32415
G-DUOB	CRJ7	10029	G-EUPN	A319	1261	G-EZBK	A319	3041	G-EZJU	737NG	32416
G-DUOC	CRJ7	10039	G-EUPO	A319	1279	G-EZBL	A319	3053	G-EZJV	737NG	32417
G-DUOD	CRJ7	10048	G-EUPP	A319	1295	G-EZBM	A319	3059	G-EZJW	737NG	32418
G-DUOE	CRJ7	10052	G-EUPR	A319	1329	G-EZBN	A319	3061	G-EZJX	737NG	32419
G-DUOF	CRJ	7226	G-EUPS	A319	1338	G-EZBO	A319	3082	G-EZJY	737NG	32420
G-DUOG	CRJ	7247	G-EUPT	A319	1380	G-EZBP	A319	3084	G-EZJZ	737NG	32421
G-DUOH	CRJ	7248	G-EUPU	A319	1384	G-EZBR	A319	3088	G-EZKA	737NG	32422
G-DWHH	B737	22761	G-EUPV	A319	1423	G-EZBS	A319	2387	G-EZKB	737NG	32423
G-ECAL	146	E2058	G-EUPW	A319	1440	G-EZBT	A319	3090	G-EZKC	737NG	32424
G-ECAS	B737	28554	G-EUPX	A319	1445	G-EZBU	A319	3118	G-EZKD	737NG	32425
G-EEWM	146	E3179	G-EUPY	A319	1466	G-EZBV	A319	3122	G-EZKE	737NG	32426
G-EEWR	146	E3195	G-EUPZ	A319	1510	G-EZBW	A319	3134	G-EZKF	737NG	32427
G-EFPA	A321	1960	G-EURP	B737	24237	G-EZBX	A319	3137	G-EZKG	737NG	32428
G-EJAR	A319	2412	G-EURR	B737	23717	G-EZBY	A319	3176	G-EZMH	A319	2053
G-EJJB	A319	2380	G-EUUA	A320	1661	G-EZBZ	A319	3184	G-EZMK	A319	2370
G-EKPT	1-11	BAC.211	G-EUUB	A320	1689	G-EZDC	A319	2043	G-EZMS	A319	2378
G-ELDG	DC-9	47484	G-EUUC	A320	1696	G-EZEA	A319	2119	G-EZNC	A319	2050
G-ELDH	DC-9	47555	G-EUUD	A320	1760	G-EZEB	A319	2120	G-EZNM	A319	2402
G-ELDI	DC-9	47559	G-EUUE	A320	1782	G-EZEC	A319	2129	G-EZPG	A319	2385
G-ELNX	CRJ	7508	G-EUUF	A320	1814	G-EZED	A319	2170	G-EZSM	A319	2062
G-EMBA	E145	145016	G-EUUG	A320	1829	G-EZEF	A319	2176	(G-EZXA)	A319	2370
G-EMBB	E145	145021	G-EUUH	A320	1665	G-EZEG	A319	2181	(G-EZXB)	A319	2378
G-EMBC	E145	145024	G-EUUI	A320	1871	G-EZEH	A319	2184	(G-EZXC)	A319	2380
G-EMBD	E145	145039	G-EUUJ	A320	1883	G-EZEI	A319	2196	(G-EZXD)	A319	2385
G-EMBE	E145	145042	G-EUUK	A320	1899	G-EZEJ	A319	2214	(G-EZXE)	A319	2387
G-EMBF	E145	145088	G-EUUL	A320	1708	G-EZEK	A319	2224	(G-EZXF)	A319	2398
G-EMBG	E145	145094	G-EUUM	A320	1907	G-EZEM	A319	2230	G-EZYA	B737	23498
G-EMBH	E145	145107	G-EUUN	A320	1910	G-EZEN	A319	2245	G-EZYB	B737	24020
G-EMBI	E145	145126	G-EUUO	A320	1958	G-EZEO	A319	2249	(G-EZYC)	B737	23708
G-EMBJ	E145	145134	G-EUUP	A320	2038	G-EZEP	A319	2251	G-EZYC	B737	24462
G-EMBK	E145	145167	G-EUUR	A320	2040	G-EZES	A319	2265	G-EZYD	B737	24022
G-EMBL	E145	145177	G-EUUS	A320	3301	G-EZET	A319	2271	G-EZYE	B737	24068
G-EMBM	E145	145196	G-EUUT	A320	3314	G-EZEU	A319	2283	G-EZYF	B737	23708
G-EMBN	E145	145201	G-EUUU	A320	3351	G-EZEV	A319	2289	G-EZYG	B737	29331
G-EMBO	E145	145219	G-EUUV	A320	3368	G-EZEW	A319	2300	G-EZYH	B737	29332
G-EMBP	E145	145300	(G-EUWA)	A321	2305	G-EZEX	A319	2319	G-EZYI	B737	29333
G-EMBS	E145	145357	G-EUXC	A321	2305	G-EZEY	A319	2353	G-EZYJ	B737	29334
G-EMBT	E145	145404	G-EUXD	A321	2320	G-EZEZ	A319	2360	G-EZYK	B737	29335
G-EMBU	E145	145458	G-EUXE	A321	2323	G-EZIA	A319	2420	G-EZYL	B737	29336
G-EMBV	E145	145482	G-EUXF	A321	2324	G-FZIB	A319	2427	G-EZYM	B737	29337
G-EMBW	E145	145546	G-EUXG	A321	2351	G-EZIC	A319	2436	G-EZYN	B737	29338
G-EMBX	E145	145573	G-EUXH	A321	2363	G-EZID	A319	2442	G-EZYO	B737	29339
G-EMBY	E145	145617	G-EUXI	A321	2536	G-EZIE	A319	2446	G-EZYP	B737	29340
G-EOCO	B707	19294	G-EUXJ	A321	3081	G-EZIF	A319	2450	G-EZYR	B737	29341
G-EOMA	A330	265	G-EUXK	A321	3235	G-EZIG	A319	2460	G-EZYS	B737	29342
G-EPFR	A320	0437	G-EUXL	A321	3254	G-EZIH	A319	2463	G-EZYT	B737	26307
G-ERAA	A320	1411	G-EUXM	A321	3290	G-EZII	A319	2471	G-FBEA	E190	19000029
G-ERJA	E145	145229	G-EXPM	1-11	BAC.124	G-EZIJ	A319	2477	G-FBEB	E190	19000057
G-ERJB	E145	145237	G-EZAA	A319	2677	G-EZIK	A319	2481	G-FBEC	E190	19000069
G-ERJC	E145	145253	G-EZAB	A319	2681	G-EZIL	A319	2492	G-FBED	E190	19000084
G-ERJD	E145	145290	G-EZAC	A319	2691	G-EZIM	A319	2495	G-FBEE	E190	19000093
G-ERJE	E145	145315	G-EZAD	A319	2702	G-EZIN	A319	2503	G-FBEF	E190	19000104
G-ERJF	E145	145325	G-EZAE	A319	2709	G-EZIO	A319	2512	G-FCLA	B757	27621
G-ERJG	E145	145394	G-EZAF	A319	2715	G-EZIP	A319	2514	G-FCLB	B757	28164
(G-ESYA)	737NG	32422	G-EZAG	A319	2727	G-EZIR	A319	2527	G-FCLC	B757	28166
(G-ESYB)	737NG	32423	G-EZAH	A319	2729	G-EZIS	A319	2528	G-FCLD	B757	28718
(G-ESYC)	737NG	32424	G-EZAI	A319	2735	G-EZIT	A319	2538	G-FCLE	B757	28171
(G-ESYD)	737NG	32425	G-EZAJ	A319	2742	G-EZIU	A319	2548	G-FCLF	B757	28835
(G-ESYE)	737NG	32426	G-EZAK	A319	2744	G-EZIV	A319	2565	G-FCLG	B757	24367
(G-ESYF)	737NG	32427	G-EZAL	A319	2754	G-EZIW	A319	2578	G-FCLH	B757	26274
(G-ESYG)	737NG	32428	G-EZAM	A319	2037	G-EZIX	A319	2605	G-FCLI	B757	26275
G-EUOA	A319	1513	G-EZAN	A319	2765	G-EZIY	A319	2636	G-FCLJ	B757	26160
G-EUOB	A319	1529	G-EZAO	A319	2769	G-EZIZ	A319	2646	G-FCLK	B757	26161
G-EUOC	A319	1537	G-EZAP	A319	2777	G-EZJA	737NG	30235	G-FDZA	737NG	35134
G-EUOD	A319	1558	G-EZAS	A319	2779	G-EZJB	737NG	30236	G-FDZB	737NG	35131
G-EUOE	A319	1574	G-EZAT	A319	2782	G-EZJC	737NG	30237	G-FDZD	737NG	35132
G-EUOF	A319	1590	G-EZAU	A319	2795	G-EZJD	737NG	30242	G-FHAJ	A320	0444
G-EUOG	A319	1594	G-EZAV	A319	2803	G-EZJE	737NG	30238	G-FIGP	B737	22875
G-EUOH	A319	1604	G-EZAW	A319	2812	G-EZJF	737NG	30243	(G-FIOA)	F.100	11330
G-EUOI	A319	1606	G-EZAX	A319	2818	G-EZJG	737NG	30239	(G-FIOB)	F.100	11274
G-EUPA	A319	1082	G-EZAY	A319	2827	G-EZJH	737NG	30240	(G-FIOC)	F.100	11275
G-EUPB	A319	1115	G-EZAZ	A319	2829	G-EZJI	737NG	30241	(G-FIOD)	F.100	11277
G-EUPC	A319	1118	G-EZBA	A319	2860	G-EZJJ	737NG	30245	(G-FIOE)	F.100	11279
G-EUPD	A319	1142	G-EZBB	A319	2854	G-EZJK	737NG	30246	G-FIOO	F.100	11316
G-EUPE	A319	1193	G-EZBC	A319	2866	G-EZJL	737NG	30247	G-FIOR	F.100	11318
G-EUPF	A319	1197	G-EZBD	A319	2873	G-EZJM	737NG	30248	G-FIOS	F.100	11321
G-EUPG	A319	1222	G-EZBE	A319	2884	G-EZJN	737NG	30249	(G-FIOT)	F.100	11323
G-EUPH	A319	1225	G-EZBF	A319	2923	G-EZJO	737NG	30244	(G-FIOU)	F.100	11324

Registration	Type	Serial
(G-FIOV)	F.100	11325
(G-FIOW)	F.100	11326
(G-FIOX)	F.100	11327
(G-FIOY)	F.100	11328
(G-FIOZ)	F.100	11329
G-FJEA	B757	24636
G-FJEB	B757	24290
G-FJEC	B767	23624
G-FLRU	1-11	BAC.201
G-FLTA	146	E2048
G-FLTB	146	E2024
G-FLTC	146	E3205
G-FLTD	146	E2042
G-FLTK	MD80	49966
G-FLTL	MD80	49790
G-FLTM	MD80	53052
G-FMAH	F.100	11286
G-FTDF	A320	0437
G-GAFX	B747	20827
G-GBTA	B737	25859
G-GBTB	B737	25860
G-GCAL	DC-10	46501
G-GFAL	DC-10	46970
G-GFFA	B737	25038
G-GFFB	B737	25789
G-GFFC	B737	24272
G-GFFD	B737	26419
G-GFFE	B737	27424
G-GFFF	B737	24754
G-GFFG	B737	24650
G-GFFH	B737	27354
G-GFFI	B737	27425
G-GFFJ	B737	27355
G-GLYN	B747	21516
G-GMJM	MD80	49951
G-GNTZ	146	E2036
G-GOKT	DC-10	47838
G-GPAA	B737	22368
G-GPAB	B737	22071
G-GPFI	B737	20907
G-GSKY	DC-10	46973
G-GSPN	B737	29267
G-GSSA	B747	29256
G-GSSB	B747	29252
(G-GSSB)	B747	29255
G-GSSC	B747	29255
G-GTDK	A320	0338
G-GTDL	A320	0476
G-HAGT	A320	0294
G-HBAP	A320	0294
G-HCRP	MD80	49996
G-HEVY	B707	19350
G-HIHO	B747	20108
G-HKIT	1-11	BAC.196
G-HLAA	A300	047
G-HLAB	A300	045
G-HLAC	A300	074
G-HLAD	A300	131
G-HMCC	A319	2398
"G-HMCL"	A319	2398
G-HUGE	B747	21252
G-HWPB	146	E2018
G-IBTW	B737	21960
G-IBTX	B737	21736
G-IBTY	B737	22703
G-IBTZ	B737	22576
G-IEAA	B737	24098
G-IEAB	B757	24636
G-IEAC	B757	25620
G-IEAD	B757	24771
G-IEAE	B737	24795
G-IEAF	A320	0362
G-IEAG	A320	0363
G-IGOA	B737	24678
G-IGOB	B737	28660
G-IGOC	B737	24546
(G-IGOD)	B737	24219
G-IGOE	B737	24547
G-IGOF	B737	24698
G-IGOG	B737	23927
G-IGOH	B737	23926
G-IGOI	B737	24092
G-IGOJ	B737	28872
G-IGOK	B737	28594
G-IGOL	B737	28596
G-IGOM	B737	28599
G-IGOO	B737	28557
G-IGOP	B737	28602
G-IGOR	B737	28606
G-IGOS	B737	27336
G-IGOT	B737	24571
G-IGOU	B737	27337
G-IGOV	B737	25017
G-IGOW	B737	23923
G-IGOX	B737	24219
G-IGOY	B737	28570
G-IGOZ	B737	24699
G-IIIH	1-11	BAC.200
G-ILFC	B737	22161
G-INTL	B747	20826
(G-INTL)	B747	21841
G-IOII	L1011	193T-1118
G-IOIT	L1011	193N-1145
G-IRJX	146	E3378
G-ISEE	146	E2208
G-JALC	B757	22194
G-JANM	A320	0301
G-JAYV	146	E2269
G-JCWW	F.28	11135
G-JDFW	A320	0299
G-JEAJ	146	E2099
G-JEAK	146	E2103
G-JEAL	146	E3129
G-JEAM	146	E3128
G-JEAO	146	E1010
G-JEAR	146	E2018
G-JEAS	146	E2020
G-JEAT	146	E1071
G-JEAU	146	E1035
G-JEAV	146	E2064
G-JEAW	146	E2059
G-JEAX	146	E2136
G-JEAY	146	E2138
G-JEBA	146	E3181
G-JEBB	146	E3185
G-JEBC	146	E3189
G-JEBD	146	E3191
G-JEBE	146	E3206
G-JEBF	146	E3202
G-JEBG	146	E3209
G-JEBH	146	E3205
G-JEBU	146	E3234
G-JEBV	146	E3236
G-JECA	CRJ	7345
G-JECB	CRJ	7393
G-JECC	CRJ	7434
G-JECD	CRJ	7469
(G-JKID)	B737	26303
G-JMAA	B757	32241
G-JMAB	B757	32242
G-JMCD	B757	30757
G-JMCE	B757	30758
G-JMCF	B757	24369
G-JMCG	B757	26278
G-JOEE	A321	2060
G-JOEM	A320	0449
(G-JOEM)	B757	25054
G-JSJX	A321	0808
G-JSMC	MD80	49941
(G-JTWF)	B737	28558
G-KILO	B747	22306
G-KKAZ	A320	2003
G-KKUH	B737	24300
G-KMAM	A320	0301
G-KROO	1-11	BAC.125
G-LCRC	B757	24636
G-LFJB	737NG	29051
G-LGTE	B737	24908
G-LGTF	B737	24450
G-LGTG	B737	24470
G-LGTH	B737	23924
G-LGTI	B737	23925
(G-LOGI)	MD80	49398
G-LSAA	B757	24122
G-LSAB	B757	24136
G-LSAC	B757	25488
G-LSAD	B757	24397
G-LSAE	B757	24135
G-LSAF	B757	22689
G-LSAG	B757	24014
G-LSAH	B757	24015
G-LSAI	B757	24016
G-LUXE	146	E3001
G-LYON	DC-10	47818
G-MAAH	1-11	BAC.259
G-MABH	F.100	11291
G-MABR	146	E1015
G-MAJS	A300	604
(G-MALE)	A320	0422
G-MAMH	F.100	11293
G-MANS	146	E2088
G-MARA	A321	0983
G-MCEA	B757	22200
G-MCKE	B757	24368
G-MDBD	A330	266
(G-MDII)	MD11	48411
G-MEDA	A320	0480
G-MEDB	A320	0376
G-MEDD	A320	0386
G-MEDE	A320	1194
G-MEDF	A321	1690
G-MEDG	A321	1711
G-MEDH	A320	1922
G-MEDJ	A321	2190
G-MEDK	A320	2441
G-MEDL	A321	2653
G-MEDM	A321	2799
G-MGYB	E145	14500972
G-MIDA	A321	0806
G-MIDC	A321	0835
G-MIDE	A321	0864
"G-MIDE"	A321	0968
G-MIDF	A321	0810
G-MIDH	A321	0968
G-MIDI	A321	0974
G-MIDJ	A321	1045
G-MIDK	A321	1153
G-MIDL	A321	1174
G-MIDM	A321	1207
G-MIDO	A320	1987
G-MIDP	A320	1732
G-MIDR	A320	1697
G-MIDS	A320	1424
G-MIDT	A320	1418
G-MIDU	A320	1407
G-MIDV	A320	1383
G-MIDW	A320	1183
G-MIDX	A320	1177
G-MIDY	A320	1014
G-MIDZ	A320	0934
G-MIMA	146	E2079
G-MKAA	B747	22169
G-MKBA	B747	22481
G-MKDA	B747	22486
G-MLJL	A330	254
G-MOJO	A330	301
G-MONB	B757	22780
G-MONC	B757	22781
G-MOND	B757	22960
G-MONE	B757	23293
G-MONF	B737	23497
G-MONG	B737	23498
G-MONH	B737	23685
G-MONJ	B757	24104
G-MONK	B757	24105
G-MONL	B737	24255
G-MONM	B737	24256
G-MONN	B737	24029
G-MONP	B737	24028
G-MONR	A300	540
G-MONS	A300	556
(G-MONT)	A300	604
G-MONT	B737	24026
(G-MONU)	A300	605
G-MONU	B737	24025
G-MONV	B737	25033
G-MONW	A320	0391
G-MONX	A320	0392
G-MONY	A320	0279
G-MONZ	A320	0446
G-MPCD	A320	0379
G-MRJK	A320	1081
G-MRSG	CRJ7	10052
G-MRSH	CRJ7	10048
G-MRSI	CRJ7	10039
G-MRSJ	CRJ7	10029
G-MRSK	CRJ7	10028
G-MSJF	737NG	30710
G-MSKA	B737	24859
G-MSKB	B737	24928
G-MSKC	B737	25066
G-MSKD	B737	24778
G-MSKE	B737	28084
G-MSKK	CRJ	7226
G-MSKL	CRJ	7247
G-MSKM	CRJ	7248
G-MSKN	CRJ	7283
G-MSKO	CRJ	7299
G-MSKP	CRJ	7329
G-MSKR	CRJ	7373
G-MSKS	CRJ	7386
G-MSKT	CRJ	7436
G-MSKU	CRJ	7442
G-MULL	DC-10	47888
G-N81AC	CNCRD	204
G-N94AA	CNCRD	206
G-N94AB	CNCRD	208
G-N94AD	CNCRD	210
G-N94AE	CNCRD	212
G-N94AF	CNCRD	216
G-NAFH	B737	23788
G-NBAA	146	E2386
G-NIGB	B747	21517
G-NIII	1-11	BAC.128
G-NIKO	A321	1250
G-NIUK	DC-10	46932
(G-NJIA)	146	E3161
G-NJIB	146	E3174
G-NJIC	146	E3202
G-NJID	146	E3205
G-NJIE	146	E3209
G-NMAK	A319	2550
G-NROA	B727	21056
G-OABA	B737	24097
G-OABD	B737	24570
G-OABE	B737	24545
G-OABF	B737	24688
G-OABL	B737	24096
G-OAHF	B757	24136
G-OAHI	B757	24137
G-OAHK	B757	24291
G-OAJF	146	E3118
G-OALA	A320	0247
G-OAMS	B737	28548
G-OAVB	B757	24289
G-OBAF	146	E1004
G-OBBJ	737NG	32777
"G-OBHF"	1-11	BAC.203
G-OBMA	B737	23831
G-OBMB	B737	23832
G-OBMC	B737	24030
G-OBMD	B737	24092
G-OBME	B737	23867
G-OBMF	B737	23868
G-OBMG	B737	23870
G-OBMH	B737	24460
(G-OBMI)	B737	24461
G-OBMJ	B737	24461
G-OBMK	B737	25596
G-OBML	B737	24300
G-OBMM	B737	25177
G-OBMN	B737	24123
G-OBMO	B737	26280
G-OBMP	B737	24963
G-OBMR	B737	25185
G-OBMX	B737	25065
G-OBMY	B737	26419
G-OBMZ	B737	24754

Reg	Type	Ser	Reg	Type	Ser	Reg	Type	Ser	Reg	Type	Ser
G-OBOZ	B757	24971	G-OOAB	A320	0292	G-OZBN	A321	1153	G-SWJW	A300	302
G-OBWA	1-11	BAC.232	(G-OOAB)	B737	24688	G-OZBO	A321	1207	G-SYLJ	E145	14500937
G-OBWB	1-11	BAC.202	G-OOAC	A320	0327	G-OZRH	146	E2047	G-TAOS	DC-10	47832
G-OBWC	1-11	BAC.230	G-OOAD	A320	0336	G-PATA	MD80	49398	G-TARO	1-11	BAC.272
G-OBWD	1-11	BAC.203	G-OOAE	A321	0852	G-PATB	MD80	49400	G-TBAE	146	E2018
G-OBWE	1-11	BAC.242	G-OOAF	A321	0677	G-PATC	MD80	49662	G-TBIC	146	E2025
(G-OBWF)	1-11	BAC.210	G-OOAH	A321	0781	G-PATD	MD80	49663	G-TCBA	B757	28203
(G-OBWG)	1-11	BAC.184	G-OOAI	A321	1006	G-PATE	B737	24093	G-TCKE	A320	1968
(G-OBWH)	1-11	BAC.208	G-OOAJ	A321	1017	G-PIDS	B757	22195	G-TCXA	A330	795
(G-OBWI)	1-11	BAC.205	G-OOAL	B767	29617	G-PJLO	B767	26064	G-TDTW	DC-10	46983
(G-OBWJ)	1-11	BAC.244	G-OOAM	B767	29618	G-PKBD	DC-9	47666	(G-TDTW)	DC-10	47833
(G-OBWK)	1-11	BAC.198	G-OOAN	B767	26256	G-PKBE	DC-9	47523	G-TEAA	B737	24462
G-OBWS	B757	24528	G-OOAO	B767	26257	G-PKBM	DC-9	47648	G-TEAB	B737	23923
G-OBWW	B737	23923	G-OOAP	A320	1306	G-POWC	B737	25402	(G-TEAD)	B737	23636
G-OBWX	B737	24255	G-OOAR	A320	1320	G-PRCS	146	E2176	G-THOA	B737	24859
G-OBWY	B737	24059	G-OOAS	A320	1571	G-PRIN	146	E2148	G-THOB	B737	24928
G-OBWZ	B737	24699	G-OOAT	A320	1605	(G-PRMJ)	DC-10	46983	G-THOC	B737	24694
G-OBYA	B767	28039	G-OOAU	A320	1637	G-PROC	B737	23256	G-THOD	B737	24695
G-OBYB	B767	28040	G-OOAV	A321	1720	G-PROK	B737	23506	G-THOE	B737	26313
G-OBYC	B767	28041	G-OOAW	A320	1777	G-RAES	B777	27491	G-THOF	B737	26314
G-OBYD	B767	28042	G-OOAX	A320	2180	G-RDVE	A320	0163	G-THOG	B737	29057
G-OBYE	B767	28979	G-OOBA	B757	32446	G-REUB	E145	145505	G-THOH	B737	29058
G-OBYF	B767	28208	G-OOBB	B757	32447	G-RJER	MD80	49949	G-THOI	B737	29327
G-OBYG	B767	29137	G-OOBC	B757	33098	G-RJET	146	E1199	G-THOJ	B737	28659
G-OBYH	B767	28883	G-OOBD	B757	33099	G-RJGR	B757	22197	G-THOK	B737	28660
G-OBYI	B767	29138	G-OOBE	B757	33100	G-RJXA	E145	145136	G-THOL	B737	28594
G-OBYJ	B767	29384	G-OOBF	B757	33101	G-RJXB	E145	145142	G-THON	B737	28596
G-OCHA	B737	24068	G-OOBG	B757	29942	G-RJXC	E145	145153	G-THOO	B737	29335
G-OCLH	146	E2268	G-OOBH	B757	29944	G-RJXD	E145	145207	G-THOP	B737	28740
G-OCNW	1-11	012	G-OOBI	B757	27146	G-RJXE	E145	145245	G-TICL	A320	0169
(G-ODAN)	146	E1006	G-OOBJ	B757	27147	G-RJXF	E145	145280	G-TJAA	B707	17903
G-ODMW	737NG	29052	G-OOBK	B767	27392	G-RJXG	E145	145390	G-TJAB	B707	17640
G-ODSK	B737	28537	G-OOBL	B767	27393	G-RJXH	E145	145442	G-TJAC	B707	17651
G-ODUS	B737	28659	G-OOBM	B767	27568	G-RJXI	E145	145454	G-TJPM	146	E3150
G-OEXC	A320	0349	G-OOOA	B757	23767	G-RJXJ	E145	145473	G-TKYO	B747	21939
G-OFMC	146	E3264	G-OOOB	B757	23822	G-RJXK	E145	145494	G-TMDP	A320	0168
G-OFOA	146	E1006	G-OOOC	B757	24017	G-RJXL	E145	145376	G-TNTA	146	E2056
G-OFOM	146	E1144	G-OOOD	B757	24235	G-RJXM	E145	145216	G-TNTB	146	E2067
G-OFRA	B737	29327	G-OOOG	B757	24292	G-RJXN	E145	145336	G-TNTD	146	E2109
G-OGBA	B737	25596	G-OOOH	B757	24293	G-RJXO	E145	145339	G-TNTE	146	E3153
G-OGBB	B737	29108	G-OOOI	B757	24289	G-RLGG	E145	14500967	G-TNTF	146	E3154
G-OGBC	B737	29109	G-OOOJ	B757	24290	G-RRAZ	E145	14500954	G-TNTG	146	E3182
G-OGBD	B737	27833	G-OOOK	B757	25054	G-RRJE	A320	0222	G-TNTH	146	E2089
G-OGBE	B737	27834	G-OOOM	B757	22612	G-RUBN	E145	14500954	G-TNTI	A300	155
G-OGVA	B737	24024	G-OOOS	B757	24397	G-SAAW	737NG	32841	G-TNTJ	146	E2100
G-OHAJ	B737	29141	G-OOOT	B757	24793	G-SAIL	B707	18690	G-TNTK	146	E3186
(G-OHAP)	146	E2008	G-OOOU	B757	25240	G-SATR	B767	24457	G-TNTL	146	E3168
G-OHAP	146	E2061	G-OOOV	B757	22211	G-SBEA	B737	21694	G-TNTM	146	E3166
G-OIII	146	E3221	G-OOOW	B757	22211	G-SBEB	B737	20807	G-TNTO	146	E2117
G-OINV	146	E3171	G-OOOX	B757	26158	G-SCHH	146	E1003	G-TNTP	146	E2105
G-OITA	B767	27376	G-OOOY	B757	28203	(G-SCHH)	146	E1004	G-TNTR	146	E3151
G-OITB	B767	27377	G-OOOZ	B757	25593	G-SCHH	146	E1005	G-TNTS	A300	124
G-OITC	B767	27468	G-OPJB	B757	24924	G-SCSR	A320	0299	G-TOMO	1-11	BAC.267
G-OITF	B767	27908	G-OPMN	B727	21578	G-SCUH	B737	23254	G-TONW	MD80	49952
G-OITG	B767	27918	G-OPSA	146	E1002	G-SEFC	737NG	30687	C TOYA	B737	26310
G-OITL	B767	28147	G-ORJX	146	E2376	G-SFBH	B737	28723	G-TOYB	B737	26311
"G-OJAB"	DO328	3200	G-OSAS	146	E2204	G-SIRA	E145	14500832	G-TOYC	B737	26312
G-OJEG	A321	1015	G-OSKI	146	E2018	G-SJET	B767	23624	G-TOYD	B737	26307
G-OJET	146	E1004	G-OSLA	B737	22576	G-SJMC	B767	27205	G-TOYE	B737	27455
G-OJIB	B757	24292	G-OSLH	737NG	30283	G-SLVR	B767	24757	G-TOYF	B737	28557
G-OJMB	A330	427	G-OSUN	146	E2020	G-SMAN	A330	261	G-TOYG	B737	28872
G-OJMC	A330	456	G-OTDA	B737	29266	G-SMDB	B737	28557	G-TOYH	B737	28570
G-OJMR	A300	605	(G-OTNT)	146	E2056	G-SMTJ	A321	1972	G-TOYJ	B737	28332
G-OJSW	737NG	28218	G-OUTA	B737	23635	(G-SPAN)	B737	29267	G-TOYK	B737	28870
G-OJTW	B737	28558	G-OUZO	A320	0449	G-SRJG	B737	24771	G-TPTT	A320	0348
G-OKDN	737NG	28226	G-OWLD	146	E2031	G-SSAS	A320	0230	G-TRAD	B707	18717
G-OKJN	B727	21453	G-OXLA	737NG	30619	G-SSCH	146	E1003	G-TREN	B737	24796
G-OKJW	737NG	30637	G-OXLB	737NG	30806	G-SSHH	146	E1002	G-TTIA	A321	1428
(G-OLAN)	MD11	48412	G-OXLC	737NG	33029	G-SSSH	146	E1001	G-TTIB	A321	1433
G-OLCA	146	E2099	G-OZBA	A320	0422	G-STRA	B737	24059	G-TTIC	A321	1869
G-OLCB	146	E2103	G-OZBB	A320	0389	G-STRB	B737	24255	G-TTID	A321	2462
G-OLHB	146	E2020	G-OZBC	A321	0633	G-STRC	737NG	30736	G-TTIE	A321	2682
G-OLXX	146	E1228	G-OZBD	A321	1202	G-STRD	737NG	30737	G-TTIF	A321	3106
G-OMAK	A319	0913	G-OZBE	A321	1707	G-STRE	B737	28572	G-TTMC	A300	299
G-OMUC	B737	29405	G-OZBF	A321	1763	G-STRF	737NG	29885	G-TTOA	A320	1215
G-OMYA	A320	0716	G-OZBG	A321	1941	G-STRH	737NG	32737	G-TTOB	A320	1687
(G-OMYA)	A321	2117	G-OZBH	A321	2105	G-STRI	B737	25011	G-TTOC	A320	1715
G-OMYJ	A321	0677	G-OZBI	A321	2234	G-STRJ	B737	25119	G-TTOD	A320	1723
G-OMYT	A330	301	G-OZBJ	A320	0446	G-STRZ	B757	27622	G-TTOE	A320	1754
G-ONJC	E145	14500961	G-OZBK	A320	1370	G-SUEE	A320	0363	G-TTOF	A320	1918
G-OOAA	A320	0291	G-OZBL	A321	0864	G-SUEW	A320	1961	G-TTOG	A320	1969
(G-OOAA)	B737	24686	G-OZBM	A321	1045	G-SURE	1-11	BAC.129	G-TTOH	A320	1993

Reg	Type	Serial
G-TTOI	A320	2137
G-TTOJ	A320	2157
G-TTPT	MD80	49940
G-UKAC	146	E3142
G-UKAG	146	E3162
G-UKFA	F.100	11246
G-UKFB	F.100	11247
G-UKFC	F.100	11263
G-UKFD	F.100	11259
G-UKFE	F.100	11260
G-UKFF	F.100	11274
G-UKFG	F.100	11275
G-UKFH	F.100	11277
G-UKFI	F.100	11279
G-UKFJ	F.100	11248
G-UKFK	F.100	11249
G-UKFL	F.100	11268
G-UKFM	F.100	11269
G-UKFN	F.100	11270
G-UKFO	F.100	11271
G-UKFP	F.100	11272
G-UKFR	F.100	11273
G-UKHP	146	E3123
G-UKID	146	E3157
G-UKJF	146	E1011
G-UKLA	B737'	23865
G-UKLB	B737	24344
G-UKLC	B737	24231
G-UKLD	B737	24232
G-UKLE	B737	24468
G-UKLF	B737	24813
G-UKLG	B737	24814
G-UKLH	B767	26256
G-UKLI	B767	26257
G-UKLJ	A320	0190
G-UKLK	A320	0343
G-UKLL	A320	0189
G-UKLN	146	E2069
G-UKLO	A321	0677
G-UKPC	146	E1010
G-UKRC	146	E3158
G-UKRH	146	E2077
G-UKSC	146	E3125
G-UKZM	B767	27686
(G-UNIA)	A330	320
(G-UNIB)	A330	330
G-UNID	A321	0677
G-UNIE	A321	0781
(G-UNIF)	A321	0862
(G-UNIG)	A321	1006
(G-UNIH)	A321	1017
G-VAEL	A340	015
G-VAIR	A340	164
G-VAST	B747	28757
G-VATH	A321	1219
G-VATL	A340	376
G-VBEE	B747	22723
G-VBIG	B747	26255
G-VBLU	A340	723
G-VBUG	A340	804
G-VBUS	A340	013
G-VCAT	B747	22872
G-VCED	A320	0193
G-VEIL	A340	575
G-VELD	A340	214
G-VFAB	B747	24958
G-VFAR	A340	225
G-VFIT	A340	753
G-VFIZ	A340	764
G-VFLY	A340	058
G-VFOX	A340	449
G-VGAL	B747	32337
G-VGAS	A340	639
G-VGIN	B747	19732
G-VGOA	A340	371
(G-VHIP)	A340	723
G-VHOL	A340	002
G-VHOT	B747	26326
G-VIBE	B747	22791
G-VIIA	B777	27483
G-VIIB	B777	27484
G-VIIC	B777	27485
G-VIID	B777	27486
G-VIIE	B777	27487
G-VIIF	B777	27488
G-VIIG	B777	27489
G-VIIH	B777	27490
G-VIIJ	B777	27492
G-VIIK	B777	28840
G-VIIL	B777	27493
G-VIIM	B777	28841
G-VIIN	B777	29319
G-VIIO	B777	29320
G-VIIP	B777	29321
G-VIIR	B777	29322
G-VIIS	B777	29323
G-VIIT	B777	29962
G-VIIU	B777	29963
G-VIIV	B777	29964
G-VIIW	B777	29965
G-VIIX	B777	29966
G-VIIY	B777	29967
G-VIRG	B747	21189
G-VJFK	B747	20842
G-VKID	A320	1130
G-VKIS	A321	1233
G-VKNA	B757	25240
G-VKNB	B757	22211
G-VKNC	B757	22611
G-VKND	B757	22612
G-VKNG	B767	23765
G-VKNH	B767	26204
G-VKNI	B767	24358
G-VLAX	B747	20921
G-VLIP	B747	32338
G-VMED	A320	0978
G-VMEG	A340	391
G-VMIA	B747	20108
G-VNAP	A340	622
G-VOGE	A340	416
G-VOLH	A321	0823
G-VOYG	B747	20121
(G-VPOW)	A340	225
G-VPUF	B747	22725
G-VRED	A340	768
G-VRGN	B747	21949
G-VROC	B747	32746
G-VROM	B747	32339
G-VROS	B747	30885
G-VROY	B747	32340
G-VRUM	B747	23048
G-VSEA	A340	003
(G-VSEE)	A320	0449
G-VSHY	A340	383
G-VSKY	A340	016
G-VSSH	A340	615
G-VSSS	B747	22724
G-VSUN	A340	114
G-VTAN	A320	0764
G-VTOP	B747	28194
G-VWEB	A340	787
G-VWIN	A340	736
G-VWKD	A340	706
G-VWOW	B747	32745
G-VXLG	B747	29406
G-VYOU	A340	765
G-VZZZ	B747	22722
G-WAUS	146	E2008
G-WCCI	E145	145505
G-WGEL	B737	22161
G-WIND	B707	18689
G-WISC	146	E2008
G-WJAN	B757	28674
G-WLAD	1-11	BAC.112
G-WLCY	146	E2030
G-WWBB	A330	404
G-WWBD	A330	401
G-WWBM	A330	398
G-WWJC	F.28	11133
G-XAIR	146	E2235
G-XARJ	146	E2233
G-XBHX	B737	28572
G-XIAN	146	E1019
G-XLAA	737NG	28226
G-XLAB	737NG	28218
G-XLAC	737NG	29051
G-XLAD	737NG	29052
G-XLAE	737NG	30637
G-XLAF	737NG	29883
G-XLAG	737NG	33003
G-XLAH	737NG	29351
G-XLAI	737NG	30702
G-XLAJ	737NG	30703
G-XLAK	737NG	35092
G-XLAL	737NG	35093
G-XLAN	737NG	32685
G-XLAO	737NG	32690
G-XMAN	B737	28573
G-YIAN	E145	14500863
G-YJBM	A320	0362
G-YLBM	A320	1954
(G-YLBM)	DC-10	47833
G-YMMA	B777	30302
G-YMMB	B777	30303
G-YMMC	B777	30304
G-YMMD	B777	30305
G-YMME	B777	30306
G-YMMF	B777	30307
G-YMMG	B777	30308
G-YMMH	B777	30309
G-YMMI	B777	30310
G-YMMJ	B777	30311
G-YMMK	B777	30312
G-YMML	B777	30313
G-YMMM	B777	30314
G-YMMN	B777	30316
G-YMMO	B777	30317
G-YMMP	B777	30315
G-YMRU	1-11	BAC.110
G-ZAPK	146	E2148
G-ZAPL	146	E2030
G-ZAPM	B737	27285
G-ZAPN	146	E2119
G-ZAPO	146	E2176
G-ZAPR	146	E2114
G-ZAPU	B757	26151
G-ZAPV	B737	24546
G-ZAPW	B737	24219
G-ZAPX	B757	29309
G-ZAPZ	B737	25401
G-ZZZA	B777	27105
G-ZZZB	B777	27106
G-ZZZC	B777	27107
G-ZZZD	B777	27108
G-ZZZE	B777	27109
(G-ZZZF)	B777	27483
(G-ZZZG)	B777	27484
(G-ZZZH)	B777	27485
(G-ZZZI)	B777	27486
(G-ZZZJ)	B777	27487
(G-ZZZK)	B777	27488
(G-ZZZL)	B777	27489
(G-ZZZM)	B777	27490
(G-ZZZN)	B777	27491
(G-ZZZP)	B777	27492

Georgia
(see also 4L-)

Reg	Type	Serial
GR-85547	TU154	82A-547

Hungary

Reg	Type	Serial
HA-924	TU134	0350924
HA-925	TU134	0350925
HA-LBA	TU134	8350604
HA-LBC	TU134	8350605
HA-LBD	TU134	9350801
HA-LBE	TU134	9350802
HA-LBF	TU134	0350923
HA-LBG	TU134	0350924
HA-LBH	TU134	0350925
HA-LBI	TU134	1351301
HA-LBK	TU134	1351302
HA-LBL	TU134	38050
HA-LBM	TU134	12096
HA-LBN	TU134	12096
HA-LBO	TU134	17103
HA-LBP	A320	1635
HA-LBP	TU134	63560
HA-LBR	TU134	63580
HA-LBS	TU134	09074
HA-LBT	TU134	60343
HA-LBU	TU134	60450
HA-LCA	TU154	73A-045
HA-LCB	TU154	73A-046
HA-LCE	TU154	73A-047
HA-LCF	TU154	75A-126
HA-LCG	TU154	75A-127
HA-LCH	TU154	75A-128
HA-LCI	TU154	74A-053
HA-LCK	TU154	74A-054
HA-LCL	TU154	73A-051
HA-LCM	TU154	79A-325
HA-LCN	TU154	79A-326
HA-LCO	TU154	81A-473
HA-LCP	TU154	81A-474
HA-LCR	TU154	82A-543
HA-LCS	TU154	82A-530
HA-LCT	TU154	82A-542
HA-LCU	TU154	82A-531
HA-LCV	TU154	82A-544
HA-LCX	TU154	88A-788
HA-LCY	TU154	?
(HA-LCZ)	TU154	79A-384
HA-LEA	B737	21735
HA-LEB	B737	22090
HA-LEC	B737	22979
HA-LED	B737	24909
HA-LEF	B737	24914
HA-LEG	B737	24916
HA-LEH	B737	22453
HA-LEI	B737	22803
HA-LEJ	B737	26303
HA-LEK	B737	23404
HA-LEM	B737	22804
HA-LEN	B737	26069
HA-LEO	B737	26071
HA-LEP	B737	24776
HA-LER	B737	24926
HA-LES	B737	24676
HA-LET	B737	24910
HA-LEU	B737	25190
HA-LEV	B737	24904
HA-LEX	B737	24902
HA-LEY	B737	24682
HA-LEZ	B737	26290
HA-LGA	TU154	88A-775
HA-LGB	TU154	91A-905
HA-LGC	TU154	89A-806
HA-LGD	TU154	92A-925
HA-LHA	B767	27048
HA-LHB	B767	27049
HA-LHC	B767	25864
HA-LHC	B767	28884
HA-LHD	B767	24484
HA-LIA	IL62	4933456
(HA-LIB)	TU154	76A-132
(HA-LIC)	TU154	76A-145
HA-LJA	YAK40	9510340
HA-LJB	YAK40	9640851
HA-LJC	YAK40	9440937
HA-LJD	YAK40	9240225
HA-LJE	YAK40	9321928
HA-LJF	YAK40	9541542
HA-LJG	YAK40	9521640
(HA-LJG)	YAK42	2014576
HA-LKA	B737	24911
HA-LKB	737NG	30294
HA-LKM	737NG	34758
HA-LKO	B737	25185
HA-LKP	B737	25289
HA-LKR	B737	29332
HA-LKS	B737	29334
HA-LKT	B737	29335
HA-LKU	B737	29336

Reg	Type	Serial
HA-LKV	B737	29333
HA-LMA	**F.70**	**11564**
HA-LMB	**F.70**	**11565**
HA-LMC	**F.70**	**11569**
HA-LMD	F.70	11563
HA-LME	**F.70**	**11575**
HA-LMF	**F.70**	**11571**
HA-LNA	**CRJ**	**7676**
HA-LNB	**CRJ**	**7686**
HA-LNC	**CRJ**	**7784**
HA-LND	**CRJ**	**7807**
HA-LNX	CRJ	7032
HA-LOA	**737NG**	**28254**
HA-LOB	**737NG**	**29346**
HA-LOC	**737NG**	**32797**
HA-LOD	**737NG**	**28259**
HA-LOE	**737NG**	**28260**
HA-LOF	**737NG**	**29348**
HA-LOG	**737NG**	**28261**
HA-LOH	**737NG**	**30667**
HA-LOI	**737NG**	**29350**
HA-LOJ	**737NG**	**29349**
HA-LOK	**737NG**	**30669**
HA-LOL	**737NG**	**29352**
HA-LOM	**737NG**	**30672**
HA-LON	**737NG**	**29353**
HA-LOP	**737NG**	**29354**
HA-LOR	**737NG**	**29355**
HA-LOS	**737NG**	**29359**
(HA-LOT)	737NG	30684
HA-LOU	**737NG**	**30684**
HA-LPA	**A320**	**0839**
HA-LPC	**A320**	**0892**
HA-LPD	**A320**	**1902**
HA-LPE	**A320**	**1892**
HA-LPF	**A320**	**1834**
HA-LPG	A320	2571
HA-LPH	**A320**	**2688**
HA-LPI	**A320**	**2752**
HA-LPJ	**A320**	**3127**
HA-LPK	**A320**	**3143**
HA-LPL	**A320**	**3166**
HA-LPM	**A320**	**3177**
HA-LRA	YAK40	9440837
HA-TAB	146	E2105
HA-TCA	IL76	1013409303
HA-TCB	IL76	1013408257
HA-TCD	IL76	0063471123
HA-TCE	IL76	0063472166
HA-TCF	IL76	0073476275
HA-TCG	**IL76**	**0023436048**
HA-TCH	IL76	0083483513
HA-TCI	IL76	073410300
HA-TCJ	IL76	0083484527
HA-TCK	IL76	1023409280
HA-YLR	YAK40	9541044
HA-YSA	TU134	12096
HA-YSB	TU134	17103

Switzerland

Reg	Type	Serial
(HB-)	F.100	11483
(HB-)	F.100	11499
HB-AAS	F.28	11110
HB-AEU	**DO328**	**3199**
(HB-I..)	A320	1162
(HB-I..)	A320	1179
HB-IAA	DC-9	45702
HB-IBF	DC-8	46141
HB-ICA	CV990	30-10-7
HB-ICB	CV990	30-10-11
HB-ICC	CV990	30-10-12
HB-ICD	CV990	30-10-15
HB-ICE	CV990	30-10-14
HB-ICF	CV990	30-10-6
HB-ICG	CV990	30-10-17
HB-ICH	DC-8	46067
HB-ICI	SE210	250
HB-ICJ	SE210	169
HB-ICK	SE210	200
HB-ICL	CV880	22-00-43M

Reg	Type	Serial
HB-ICM	CV880	22-00-45M
HB-ICN	SE210	253
HB-ICO	SE210	255
HB-ICP	SE210	234
HB-ICQ	SE210	222
HB-ICR	SE210	119
HB-ICS	SE210	121
HB-ICT	SE210	122
HB-ICU	SE210	123
HB-ICV	SE210	147
HB-ICW	SE210	33
HB-ICX	SE210	38
HB-ICY	SE210	43
HB-ICZ	SE210	48
HB-IDA	DC-8	45416
HB-IDB	DC-8	45417
HB-IDC	DC-8	45526
"HB-IDD"	B707	18457
HB-IDD	DC-8	45656
HB-IDE	DC-8	45919
HB-IDF	DC-8	45920
HB-IDG	DC-8	45925
HB-IDH	DC-8	45984
HB-IDI	DC-8	46077
HB-IDJ	**CRJ**	**7136**
HB-IDK	DC-8	46078
HB-IDL	DC-8	46134
HB-IDM	DC-8	46001
HB-IDN	DC-9	47465
HB-IDO	DC-9	47480
HB-IDP	DC-9	47523
HB-IDR	DC-9	47535
HB-IDS	DC-8	45968
HB-IDT	DC-9	47711
HB-IDU	DC-8	45817
(HB-IDV)	DC-9	47114
HB-IDV	DC-9	47116
HB-IDW	DC-9	47115
HB-IDX	DC-9	47117
HB-IDY	DC-9	47395
HB-IDZ	DC-8	46074
HB-IEE	**B757**	**24527**
HB-IEF	DC-9	45702
HB-IEG	B707	17671
HB-IEH	B737	22431
HB-IEI	B707	19521
HB-IFA	DC-9	45731
HB-IFB	DC-9	45732
HB-IFC	DC-9	45785
HB-IFD	DC-9	45786
HB-IFE	DC-9	45787
HB-IFF	DC-9	45788
HB-IFG	DC-9	45789
HB-IFH	DC-9	45790
HB-IFI	DC-9	45791
HB-IFK	DC-9	45792
HB-IFL	DC-9	45793
HB-IFM	DC-9	45847
HB-IFN	DC-9	47094
HB-IFO	DC-9	47110
HB-IFP	DC-9	47111
HB-IFR	DC-9	47112
HB-IFS	DC-9	47113
HB-IFT	DC-9	47281
HB-IFU	DC-9	47282
HB-IFV	DC-9	47383
HB-IFW	DC-9	47384
HB-IFX	DC-9	47218
HB-IFY	DC-9	47219
HB-IFZ	DC-9	47479
HB-IGA	B747	20116
HB-IGB	B747	20117
HB-IGC	B747	22704
HB-IGD	B747	22705
HB-IGE	B747	22995
HB-IGF	B747	22996
HB-IGG	B747	23751
HB-IGH	DC-8	46067
(HB-IGI)	DC-10	46577
(HB-IGL)	DC-10	46579
"HB-IGL"	F.100	11460
(HB-IGM)	DC-10	46580

Reg	Type	Serial
HB-IGZ	A320	1125
HB-IHA	DC-10	46575
HB-IHB	DC-10	46576
HB-IHC	DC-10	46577
HB-IHD	DC-10	46578
HB-IHE	DC-10	46579
HB-IHF	DC-10	46580
HB-IHG	DC-10	46581
HB-IHH	DC-10	46582
HB-IHI	DC-10	46969
HB-IHK	DC-10	46998
HB-IHL	DC-10	46583
HB-IHM	DC-10	46584
HB-IHN	DC-10	48292
HB-IHO	DC-10	48293
HB-IHP	DC-10	46868
HB-IHR	**B757**	**29379**
HB-IHS	**B757**	**30394**
HB-IHT	B767	26387
HB-IHU	B757	24527
HB-IHU	B767	26388
HB-IHV	B767	30564
HB-IHW	B767	30565
HB-IHX	**A320**	**0942**
HB-IHY	**A320**	**0947**
HB-IHZ	**A320**	**1026**
HB-IIA	B737	24023
HB-IIB	B737	24024
HB-IIC	B737	25016
HB-IID	B737	24255
HB-IIE	B737	26307
HB-IIF	B737	26333
HB-IIG	B737	28200
HB-IIH	737NG	28209
HB-III	737NG	28210
HB-III	B737	29338
HB-IIJ	B737	29342
HB-IIK	B737	29337
HB-IIL	B737	28333
HB-IIN	B737	27924
HB-IIO	737NG	29865
HB-IIP	73/NG	29866
HB-IIQ	**737NG**	**30752**
HB-IIR	**737NG**	**30295**
HB-IIT	B737	29339
HB-IIX	B767	23326
HB-IJA	A320	0533
HB-IJB	**A320**	**0545**
HB-IJC	A320	0548
HB-IJD	A320	0553
HB-IJE	A320	0559
HB-IJF	**A320**	**0562**
HB-IJG	A320	0566
HB-IJH	**A320**	**0574**
HB-IJI	**A320**	**0577**
HB-IJJ	**A320**	**0585**
HB-IJK	**A320**	**0596**
HB-IJL	**A320**	**0603**
HB-IJM	**A320**	**0635**
HB-IJN	**A320**	**0643**
HB-IJO	**A320**	**0673**
HB-IJP	**A320**	**0681**
HB-IJQ	**A320**	**0701**
HB-IJR	**A320**	**0703**
HB-IJS	**A320**	**0782**
HB-IJT	A320	0870
(HB-IJU)	A320	1132
HB-IJU	**A320**	**1951**
HB-IJV	**A320**	**2024**
HB-IJW	**A320**	**2134**
HB-IJZ	**A320**	**0211**
HB-IKB	DC-9	47430
HB-IKC	DC-9	47468
HB-IKD	SE210	249
HB-IKF	DC-9	47714
HB-IKG	DC-9	47715
HB-IKH	DC-9	47713
HB-IKK	MD80	49247
HB-IKL	MD80	49248
HB-IKM	MD80	49935
HB-IKN	MD80	49951
HB-IKP	MD80	49629

Reg	Type	Serial
(HB-INA)	MD80	48000
HB-INA	MD80	49100
(HB-INB)	MD80	48001
HB-INB	MD80	49101
HB-INC	MD80	48002
HB-IND	MD80	48003
HB-INE	MD80	48004
HB-INF	MD80	48005
HB-ING	MD80	48006
HB-INH	MD80	48007
HB-INI	MD80	48008
HB-INK	MD80	48009
HB-INL	MD80	48010
HB-INM	MD80	48011
HB-INN	MD80	48012
HB-INO	MD80	48013
HB-INP	MD80	48014
HB-INR	MD80	49277
HB-INS	MD80	49356
HB-INT	MD80	49357
HB-INU	MD80	49358
HB-INV	MD80	49359
HB-INW	MD80	49569
HB-INX	MD80	49570
HB-INY	MD80	49571
HB-INZ	MD80	49572
HB-IOA	A321	0517
HB-IOB	A321	0519
HB-IOC	**A321**	**0520**
HB-IOD	**A321**	**0522**
HB-IOE	A321	0535
HB-IOF	**A321**	**0541**
HB-IOG	A321	0642
HB-IOH	**A321**	**0664**
HB-IOI	A321	0827
HB-IOJ	A321	0891
HB-IOK	**A321**	**0987**
HB-IOL	**A321**	**1144**
HB-IPA	A310	224
HB-IPB	A310	251
HB-IPC	A310	217
HB-IPD	A310	260
HB-IPE	A310	162
(HB-IPF)	A310	172
HB-IPF	A310	399
HB-IPG	A310	404
HB-IPH	A310	409
HB-IPI	A310	410
HB-IPK	A310	412
HB-IPL	A310	640
HB-IPM	A310	642
HB-IPN	A310	672
HB-IPO	A319	2592
HB-IPP	**A318**	**2910**
HB-IPR	**A319**	**1018**
HB-IPS	**A319**	**0734**
HB-IPT	**A319**	**0727**
HB-IPU	**A319**	**0713**
HB-IPV	**A319**	**0578**
HB-IPW	A319	0588
HB-IPX	**A319**	**0612**
HB-IPY	**A319**	**0621**
HB-IPZ	A319	0629
HB-IQA	**A330**	**229**
HB-IQB	A330	240
HB-IQC	**A330**	**249**
HB-IQD	A330	253
HB-IQE	A330	255
HB-IQF	A330	262
HB-IQG	**A330**	**275**
HB-IQH	**A330**	**288**
HB-IQI	**A330**	**291**
HB-IQJ	**A330**	**294**
HB-IQK	**A330**	**299**
HB-IQL	A330	305
HB-IQM	A330	308
HB-IQN	A330	312
HB-IQO	**A330**	**343**
HB-IQP	**A330**	**366**
HB-IQQ	**A330**	**322**
HB-IQR	**A330**	**324**
HB-IQZ	**A330**	**369**

HB-ISE	B767	27600	
HB-ISG	737NG	32915	
HB-ISK	DC-9	47654	
HB-ISL	DC-9	47655	
HB-ISM	DC-9	47656	
HB-ISN	DC-9	47657	
HB-ISO	DC-9	47658	
HB-ISP	DC-9	47659	
HB-ISR	DC-9	47660	
HB-ISS	DC-9	47661	
HB-IST	DC-9	47662	
HB-ISU	DC-9	47663	
HB-ISV	DC-9	47783	
HB-ISW	DC-9	47784	
HB-ISX	MD80	49844	
HB-ISZ	MD80	49930	
HB-ITK	1-11	BAC.166	
HB-ITL	1-11	BAC.212	
HB-IUA	MD80	49585	
HB-IUB	MD80	49586	
HB-IUC	MD80	49587	
HB-IUD	MD80	49641	
HB-IUG	MD80	53149	
HB-IUH	MD80	53150	
HB-IUI	MD80	49710	
HB-IUK	MD80	49398	
HB-IUL	MD80	49442	
HB-IUM	MD80	49847	
HB-IUN	MD80	49769	
HB-IUO	MD80	49857	
HB-IUP	MD80	49856	
HB-IVA	F.100	11244	
HB-IVB	F.100	11250	
HB-IVC	F.100	11251	
HB-IVD	F.100	11252	
HB-IVE	F.100	11253	
HB-IVF	F.100	11254	
HB-IVG	F.100	11255	
HB-IVH	F.100	11256	
(HB-IVI)	F.100	11292	
HB-IVI	F.100	11381	
(HB-IVK)	F.100	11299	
HB-IVK	F.100	11386	
HB-IVU	CRJ	7176	
HB-IWA	MD11	48443	
HB-IWB	MD11	48444	
HB-IWC	MD11	48445	
HB-IWD	MD11	4044C	
HB-IWE	MD11	48447	
HB-IWF	MD11	48448	
HB-IWG	MD11	48452	
HB-IWH	MD11	48453	
HB-IWI	MD11	48454	
HB-IWK	MD11	48455	
HB-IWL	MD11	48456	
HB-IWM	MD11	48457	
HB-IWN	MD11	48539	
HB-IWO	MD11	48540	
(HB-IWP)	MD11	48541	
HB-IWP	MD11	48634	
HB-IWQ	MD11	48541	
HB-IWR	MD11	48484	
HB-IWS	MD11	48485	
HB-IWT	MD11	48486	
HB-IWU	MD11	48538	
HB-IWX	E145	14500841	
HB-IXB	146	E2036	
HB-IXC	146	E2072	
HB-IXD	146	E2073	
HB-IXF	146	E2226	
HB-IXG	146	E2231	
HB-IXH	146	E2233	
HB-IXK	146	E2235	
HB-IXM	146	E3291	
HB-IXN	146	E3286	
HB-IXO	146	E3284	
HB-IXP	146	E3283	
HB-IXQ	146	E3282	
HB-IXR	146	E3281	
HB-IXS	146	E3280	
HB-IXT	146	E3259	
HB-IXU	146	E3276	
HB-IXV	146	E3274	
HB-IXW	146	E3272	
HB-IXX	146	E3262	
HB-IXY	146	E3163	
HB-IXZ	146	E3118	
HB-IYQ	146	E3384	
HB-IYR	146	E3382	
HB-IYS	146	E3381	
HB-IYT	146	E3380	
HB-IYU	146	E3379	
HB-IYV	146	E3377	
HB-IYW	146	E3359	
HB-IYX	146	E3357	
HB-IYY	146	E3339	
HB-IYZ	146	E3338	
HB-JAA	E145	145232	
HB-JAB	E145	145240	
HB-JAC	E145	145255	
HB-JAD	E145	145269	
HB-JAE	E145	145281	
HB-JAF	E145	145313	
HB-JAG	E145	145321	
HB-JAH	E145	145341	
HB-JAI	E145	145351	
HB-JAJ	E145	145382	
HB-JAK	E145	145387	
HB-JAL	E145	145400	
HB-JAM	E145	145420	
HB-JAN	E145	145434	
HB-JAO	E145	145456	
HB-JAP	E145	145475	
HB-JAQ	E145	145498	
HB-JAR	E145	145510	
HB-JAS	E145	145559	
HB-JAT	E145	145564	
HB-JAU	E145	145570	
HB-JAV	E145	145574	
HB-JAW	E145	145580	
HB-JAX	E145	145588	
HB-JAY	E145	145601	
HB-JEA	E145	145555	
HB-JED	E145	145644	
(HB-JEF)	E145	145789	
HB-JEL	E145	14500933	
HB-JEO	E145	14500802	
HB-JGV	737NG	30330	
HB-JGZ	E145	14501003	
HB-JIA	MD90	53552	
HB-JIB	MD90	53553	
HB-JIC	MD90	53576	
HB-JID	MD90	53460	
HB-JIE	MD90	53461	
HB-JIF	MD90	53462	
HB-JJA	737NG	34303	
HB-JJG	B767	30393	
HB-JMA	A340	538	
HB-JMB	A340	545	
HB-JMC	A340	546	
HB-JMD	A340	556	
HB-JME	A340	559	
HB-JMF	A340	561	
HB-JMG	A340	562	
HB-JMH	A340	585	
HB-JMI	A340	598	
HB-JMJ	A340	150	
HB-JMK	A340	169	
HB-JML	A340	263	
HB-JMM	A340	154	
HB-JVA	F.100	11460	
HB-JVB	F.100	11491	
HB-JVC	F.100	11501	
HB-JVD	F.100	11498	
HB-JVE	F.100	11459	
HB-JVF	F.100	11466	
HB-JVG	F.100	11478	
HB-JZA	A319	2037	
HB-JZB	A319	2043	
HB-JZC	A319	2050	
HB-JZD	A319	2053	
HB-JZE	A319	2062	
HB-JZF	A319	2184	
HB-JZG	A319	2196	
HB-JZH	A319	2230	
HB-JZI	A319	2245	
HB-JZJ	A319	2265	
HB-JZK	A319	2319	
HB-JZL	A319	2353	
HB-JZM	A319	2370	
HB-JZN	A319	2387	
HB-JZO	A319	2398	
HB-JZP	A319	2427	
HB-JZQ	A319	2450	

Ecuador

(HC-)	B727	20880	
HC-ALT	COMET	6428	
HC-AZO	B707	18033	
HC-AZP	B707	18036	
HC-AZQ	B707	18037	
HC-BAD	SE210	35	
HC-BAE	SE210	40	
HC-BAI	SE210	82	
HC-BAJ	SE210	117	
HC-BAT	SE210	125	
HC-BCT	B707	19265	
HC-BDP	B707	18033	
HC-BDS	SE210	146	
HC-BEI	DC-8	45606	
HC-BFC	B707	19277	
HC-BFM	SE210	156	
HC-BFN	SE210	166	
HC-BGP	B707	19273	
HC-BHM	B727	22078	
HC-BHY	B707	20033	
HC-BIB	B727	20513	
HC-BIC	B727	2032B	
HC-BIG	B737	22607	
HC-BJL	B727	19596	
HC-BJT	DC-8	45858	
HC-BKN	DC-8	45754	
HC-BKO	DC-10	46575	
HC-BLE	B727	19691	
HC-BLF	B727	19692	
(HC-BLM)	DC-8	45640	
HC-BLU	DC-8	45668	
HC-BLV	B727	20328	
HC-BLY	B707	18709	
HC-BMC	DC-8	45640	
HC-BMD	F.28	11220	
HC-BPL	B727	18753	
HC-BPV	DC-8	45651	
HC-BQH	DC-8	45860	
HC-BRA	A310	574	
HC-BRB	A310	576	
HC-BRF	B727	19388	
(HC-BRG)	B727	20268	
HC-BRG	B727	20973	
HC-BRI	B727	20560	
HC-BRP	A310	598	
HC-BSC	B727	20788	
HC-BSF	A310	661	
HC-BSP	B727	19393	
HC-BSU	B727	21622	
HC-BTB	B707	18937	
HC-BTI	B737	21130	
HC-BTV	A320	0405	
HC-BUH	A320	0425	
HC-BUJ	A320	0527	
HC-BUM	A320	0530	
HC-BVM	B727	21502	
HC-BVT	B727	22603	
HC-BVU	B727	21322	
HC-BVY	B727	21505	
HC-BXU	B727	21689	
HC-BZR	B727	21618	
HC-BZS	B727	21620	
HC-BZU	F.28	11112	
HC-CDA	F.28	11230	
HC-CDG	F.28	11240	
HC-CDJ	B727	21246	
HC-CDT	F.28	11222	
HC-CDW	F.28	11224	
HC-CDY	A320	2014	
HC-CDZ	A320	2044	
HC-CED	B737	22887	
HC-CEH	F.28	11228	
HC-CEQ	B737	23848	
HC-CER	B737	23847	
HC-CET	F.28	11159	
HC-CEX	E170	17000087	
HC-CEY	E170	17000092	
HC-CEZ	E190	19000027	
(HC-CFB)	F.28	11226	
HC-CFD	B737	21801	
HC-CFG	B737	21770	
HC-CFH	B737	22979	
HC-CFL	B737	22026	
HC-CFM	B737	22589	
HC-CFO	B737	22703	
HC-CFR	B737	22581	

Haiti

HH-JEC	B727	18743	
HH-JJD	B727	19393	
HH-PRI	B727	18742	
HH-RDD	YAK40	?	
HH-SMA	CV880	22-00-17	

Dominican Republic

HI-	146	E2082	
(HI-148)	1-11	BAC.114	
HI-177	DC-9	47500	
HI-212	B727	20426	
HI-212CT	B727	20426	
HI-242	B727	21036	
HI-242CT	B727	21036	
HI-312	B727	19505	
HI-312CT	B727	19505	
HI-372	B707	17915	
HI-384	B707	17610	
HI-384HA	B707	17610	
HI-401	B707	18049	
HI-413	DC-8	45387	
HI-415	B707	18072	
HI-426	DC-8	45667	
HI-426CA	DC-8	45667	
HI-426CT	DC-8	45667	
HI-427	DC-8	45684	
HI-435	DC-8	45416	
HI-442	B707	19767	
HI-442CT	B707	19767	
HI-452	B727	21021	
HI-452	DC-8	45410	
HI-459	DC-8	45640	
HI-472	B747	20104	
HI-499	SE210	154	
HI-573CA	DC-8	45765	
HI-576CT	DC-8	46110	
HI-588CA	DC-8	45685	
HI-588CT	DC-8	45685	
HI-595CA	DC-8	45410	
HI-596CA	B707	18716	
HI-606CA	B727	20267	
HI-612CA	B727	20302	
HI-616CA	B727	20726	
HI-617CA	B727	20726	
HI-629CA	B727	22441	
HI-630CA	B727	19991	
HI-637CA	B727	20267	
HI-656CA	B727	19970	
HI-659	A310	594	
HI-659CA	A310	594	
HI-660CA	B767	23280	
HI-756CA	B747	20009	
HI-764CA	B737	19955	
HI-777CA	B737	22754	

Colombia

Registration	Type	Serial
(HK)	B727	19868
HK-	B727	19915
HK-	**B727**	**21108**
HK-676	B707	18059
HK-677	B707	18057
HK-723	B707	18061
HK-724	B707	18086
HK-725	B707	18087
HK-726	B707	18831
HK-727	**B727**	**19127**
HK-749	B707	18248
HK-1271	**B727**	**19524**
HK-1272	B727	19525
HK-1273	**B727**	**19526**
HK-1337	B727	19303
HK-1400	B727	19662
HK-1400X	B727	19662
HK-1401	B727	19663
HK-1401X	B727	19663
HK-1402	B707	19741
HK-1403	B737	19679
HK-1404	B737	19680
HK-1410	B707	20340
HK-1709X	SE210	133
HK-1716	B727	18999
HK-1717	B727	18993
HK-1718	B707	18714
HK-1718X	B707	18714
HK-1773	B707	17671
HK-1778	SE210	140
HK-1779	SE210	164
HK-1780	SE210	160
HK-1802	B707	17638
HK-1802X	B707	17638
HK-1803	B727	19035
HK-1804	B727	19037
HK-1810	SE210	165
HK-1810X	SE210	165
HK-1811	SE210	138
HK-1811X	SE210	138
HK-1812	SE210	109
HK-1812X	SE210	109
HK-1818	B707	17637
HK-1818X	B707	17637
HK-1849	B707	18766
HK-1854	DC-8	45636
HK-1854X	DC-8	45636
HK-1855X	DC-8	45665
HK-1942	B707	17643
HK-1942X	B707	17643
HK-1973	B707	18023
HK-1974	B707	18028
HK-2000	B747	19734
HK-2000X	B747	19734
HK-2015	B707	19361
HK-2016	B707	19276
HK-2057	A300	029
HK-2057X	A300	029
HK-2070	B707	19266
HK-2070X	B707	19266
HK-2151X	B727	21343
HK-2152X	B727	21344
HK-2212	SE210	131
HK-2212X	SE210	131
HK-2287X	SE210	168
HK-2300	B747	21730
HK-2380	DC-8	45879
HK-2400X	B747	19735
HK-2401X	B707	18707
HK-2402	SE210	161
HK-2402X	SE210	161
HK-2410	B707	17605
HK-2410X	B707	17605
HK-2420X	B727	18874
HK-2421X	B727	18875
HK-2422X	B727	18876
HK-2473	B707	19375
HK-2473X	B707	19375
HK-2474	B727	19099
(HK-2474)	B727	22474
HK-2475	B727	19094
(HK-2475)	B727	22475
HK-2476	B727	19102
(HK-2476)	B727	22476
HK-2477X	B707	17602
HK-2541	B727	18281
HK-2558	B707	18060
HK-2558X	B707	18060
HK-2559	B727	18994
HK-2560X	B727	18996
HK-2587X	DC-8	45635
HK-2597X	SE210	136
HK-2598X	SE210	167
HK-2600	B707	18886
HK-2600X	B707	18886
HK-2604	B727	18287
HK-2604X	B727	18287
HK-2605X	B727	20217
HK-2606	B707	18709
HK-2606X	B707	18709
HK-2632X	DC-8	45768
HK-2637	B727	19815
HK-2667X	DC-8	45651
HK-2705	B727	18282
HK-2705X	B727	18282
HK-2717	B727	18252
HK-2717X	B727	18252
HK-2744X	B727	18266
HK-2833	B727	18321
HK-2833X	B727	18321
HK-2842	B707	19575
HK-2845	B727	19005
HK-2846X	B727	19007
HK-2850	SE210	261
HK-2850X	SE210	261
HK-2860X	SE210	223
HK-2864X	DC-9	45721
HK-2865X	DC-9	45722
HK-2900	B747	19733
HK-2910	B747	21381
HK-2910X	B747	21381
HK-2957	B727	18896
HK-2957X	B727	18896
HK-2960	B727	19249
HK-2960X	B727	19249
HK-2980X	B747	21730
HK-3030X	B707	18808
HK-3125X	DC-8	45809
HK-3126X	F.28	11085
HK-3133X	B727	18895
HK-3151	B727	19122
HK-3151X	B727	19122
HK-3155X	DC-9	45843
HK-3168X	B727	18858
HK-3178X	DC-8	45416
HK-3201X	B727	18877
HK-3203	B727	18845
HK-3203X	B727	18845
HK-3212X	B727	18846
HK-3229X	B727	18814
HK-3232X	B707	18717
HK-3246X	B727	19280
HK-3270X	B727	18877
HK-3288X	SE210	215
HK-3325X	SE210	219
HK-3333X	B707	18714
HK-3355X	B707	18886
HK-3384X	B727	18879
HK-3396X	B727	18997
HK-3421X	B727	20432
HK-3442X	B727	18742
HK-3458X	B727	18877
HK-3480X	B727	20739
HK-3483X	B727	19499
HK-3486X	DC-9	47125
HK-3490X	DC-8	46041
HK-3564X	DC-9	47127
HK-3588X	B727	18743
HK-3599X	B727	18879
HK-3604X	B707	19352
HK-3605X	B727	20434
HK-3606X	B727	20433
HK-3612X	B727	19281
HK-3618X	B727	22702
HK-3651X	B727	18743
HK-3667X	B727	19430
HK-3676X	SE210	232
HK-3710X	DC-9	45780
HK-3720X	DC-9	45783
HK-3738X	B727	21997
HK-3739X	B727	20418
HK-3745	B727	20420
HK-3745X	B727	20420
HK-3746X	DC-8	45632
HK-3752X	DC-9	45781
HK-3753X	DC-8	45765
HK-3756X	SE210	259
HK-3770X	B727	19242
HK-3771X	B727	19595
HK-3771X	B727	20422
HK-3785X	DC-8	46066
HK-3786X	DC-8	45849
HK-3795X	DC-9	45776
HK-3798X	B727	18969
HK-3803X	B727	19122
HK-3805	SE210	257
HK-3805X	SE210	257
HK-3806	SE210	262
HK-3806X	SE210	262
HK-3808X	AN7x	72094889
HK-3809X	AN7x	47095903
HK-3810X	AN7x	47096919
HK-3814X	**B727**	**18270**
HK-3816X	DC-8	45685
HK-3827X	DC-9	47048
HK-3830X	DC-9	45715
HK-3832X	DC-9	45735
HK-3833X	DC-9	45716
HK-3834X	B727	22759
HK-3835X	SE210	182
HK-3836	SE210	211
HK-3836X	SE210	211
HK-3837X	SE210	250
"HK-3837Z"	SE210	250
HK-3839X	DC-9	45742
HK-3840X	B727	18879
HK-3841X	B727	19281
HK-3842X	DC-8	45985
HK-3845X	B727	19534
HK-3855	SE210	265
HK-3855X	SE210	265
"HK-3857X"	SE210	232
HK-3857X	SE210	265
HK-3858X	SE210	212
HK-3859X	DC-9	45843
HK-3867X	DC-9	45735
HK-3869	SE210	268
HK-3869X	SE210	232
HK-3870X	B727	20422
HK-3871X	B727	19973
HK-3872X	B727	20303
HK-3891X	DC-9	45776
HK-3905X	DC-9	47399
HK-3906X	DC-9	47401
HK-3913X	SE210	255
HK-3914X	SE210	188
HK-3926X	DC-9	47231
HK-3927X	DC-9	47519
HK-3928X	DC-9	47311
HK-3932X	SE210	201
HK-3933X	B727	19165
HK-3939X	SE210	255
HK-3940X	SE210	188
HK-3947X	SE210	188
HK-3948X	SE210	255
HK-3955X	SE210	189
HK-3958	DC-9	45738
HK-3958X	DC-9	45738
HK-3962X	SE210	184
(HK-3962X)	SE210	189
HK-3963	DC-9	47437
HK-3963X	DC-9	47437
HK-3964X	DC-9	47434
HK-3973X	B727	19838
HK-3977X	B727	20548
HK-3979X	DC-8	45882
HK-3984X	DC-8	45862
HK-3985X	B727	20465
HK-3998X	B727	20620
HK-4010X	B727	21267
HK-4047X	B727	21458
HK-4056X	DC-9	45712
HK-4084X	DC-9	47330
HK-4137X	MD80	53190
HK-4154	**B727**	**18804**
HK-4154X	B727	18804
HK-4155X	DC-9	47524
HK-4165X	MD80	53093
HK-4176	DC-8	45945
HK-4176X	DC-8	45945
HK-4184X	MD80	53183
HK-4216	**B737**	**20253**
HK-4230X	DC-9	47526
HK-4237X	**MD80**	**48008**
HK-4238X	**MD80**	**48009**
HK-4245	**DC-9**	**47012**
HK-4245X	DC-9	47012
HK-4246X	DC-9	47062
HK-4253	**B737**	**21109**
HK-4255X	**MD80**	**48004**
HK-4259X	**MD80**	**48005**
HK-4261	**B727**	**21156**
HK-4261X	B727	21156
HK-4262	**B727**	**21427**
HK-4265X	**MD80**	**48002**
HK-4270X	DC-9	45841
HK-4271X	DC-9	45842
HK-4277	DC-8	45976
HK-4277X	DC-8	45976
HK-4294X	DC-8	46040
HK-4302	**MD80**	**48027**
HK-4302X	MD80	48027
HK-4305	**MD80**	**49237**
HK-4305X	MD80	49237
HK-4310X	DC-9	47133
HK-4315	**MD80**	**49968**
HK-4315X	MD80	49968
HK-4328	**B737**	**22148**
HK-4354	**B727**	**22608**
HK-4354X	B727	22608
HK-4374X	MD80	49484
HK-4386X	**B727**	**19968**
HK-4395	**MD80**	**53230**
HK-4396X	MD80	53231
HK-4399X	**MD80**	**53232**
HK-4401	**B727**	**22609**
HK-4401X	B727	22609
HK-4407	B727	19011
HK-4408	**MD80**	**53124**
HK-4410	**MD80**	**49937**
HK-4413	**MD80**	**53245**
HK-4419X	**F.100**	**11457**
HK-4420X	**F.100**	**11482**
HK-4430X	**F.100**	**11465**
HK-4431X	**F.100**	**11506**
HK-4437X	**F.100**	**11469**
HK-4438X	**F.100**	**11514**
HK-4443X	**F.100**	**11479**
HK-4444X	**F.100**	**11458**
HK-4445X	**F.100**	**11449**
HK-4451	F.100	11464
HK-4451X	F.100	11464
HK-4454X	**E190**	**19000061**
HK-4455X	**E190**	**19000063**
HK-4455X	**E190**	**19000076**
HK-4456X	**E190**	**19000074**
HK-4506	**E190**	**19000110**

South Korea

Registration	Type	C/n
(HL)	A321	0855
(HL)	A330	195
(HL)	B737	25773
(HL)	B737	25775
HL7200	B767	27212
HL7201	DC-9	45827
HL7203	MD80	53147
HL7204	MD80	53148
HL7205	DC-9	45787
HL7206	F.100	11378
HL7207	F.100	11387
HL7208	F.100	11388
HL7209	F.100	11432
HL7210	F.100	11438
HL7211	F.100	11439
HL7212	F.100	11476
HL7213	F.100	11504
HL7214	F.100	11513
HL7215	F.100	11519
HL7216	F.100	11522
HL7217	F.100	11523
HL7218	A300	014
HL7219	A300	016
HL7220	A300	018
HL7221	A300	024
HL7223	A300	028
HL7224	A300	030
HL7225	MD80	53467
HL7227	B737	25764
HL7228	B737	25765
HL7229	B737	24805
HL7230	B737	24778
HL7231	B737	25766
HL7232	B737	25767
HL7233	B737	25768
HL7235	B737	26308
HL7236	MD80	53468
HL7237	MD80	53469
HL7238	A300	031
HL7239	A300	627
HL7240	A300	631
HL7241	A300	662
HL7242	A300	685
HL7243	A300	692
HL7244	A300	722
HL7245	A300	731
HL7246	A300	081
HL7247	B767	25757
HL7248	B767	25758
HL7249	B767	26265
HL7250	B737	25769
HL7251	B737	23869
HL7252	B737	23976
HL7253	B737	23977
HL7254	B737	23978
HL7255	B737	23980
HL7256	B737	24314
HL7257	B737	24469
HL7258	B737	24493
HL7259	B737	24494
HL7260	B737	24520
HL7261	B737	24786
HL7262	B737	24787
HL7263	B767	24797
HL7264	B767	24798
HL7265	F.28	11203
HL7266	B737	25347
HL7267	B767	25404
HL7268	B767	25132
HL7269	B767	26206
HL7270	F.28	11219
HL7271	MD80	49785
HL7272	MD80	49373
HL7273	MD80	49374
HL7274	MD80	49787
HL7275	MD80	49416
HL7276	MD80	49417
HL7278	A300	277
HL7279	A300	292
HL7280	A300	361
HL7281	A300	365
HL7282	MD80	49418
HL7283	MD80	49419
HL7284	F.28	11223
HL7285	F.28	11221
HL7286	B767	26207
HL7287	A300	358
HL7288	A300	477
HL7289	A300	479
HL7290	A300	388
HL7291	A300	417
HL7292	A300	543
HL7293	A300	554
HL7294	A300	560
HL7295	A300	582
HL7296	A300	583
HL7297	A300	609
HL7298	A300	614
HL7299	A300	717
HL7307	B727	18875
HL7308	B727	18874
HL7309	B727	18876
HL7315	DC-10	46934
HL7316	DC-10	46912
HL7317	DC-10	46915
HL7328	DC-10	47887
HL7329	DC-10	48316
HL7336	B727	18321
HL7337	B727	18323
HL7339	DC-10	46960
HL7348	B727	20435
HL7349	B727	20468
HL7350	B727	20469
HL7351	B727	20572
HL7352	B727	20573
HL7353	B727	20728
HL7354	B727	21455
HL7355	B727	20466
HL7356	B727	21456
HL7357	B727	21474
HL7366	B727	20725
HL7367	B727	20571
HL7371	MD11	48407
HL7372	MD11	48408
HL7373	MD11	48409
HL7374	MD11	48410
HL7375	MD11	48523
HL7400	B747	26414
HL7401	B747	22245
HL7402	B707	18160
HL7402	B747	26407
HL7403	B707	18164
HL7403	B747	26408
HL7404	B747	26409
HL7405	B747	24195
HL7406	B707	20522
HL7407	B747	24198
HL7408	B747	24196
HL7409	B747	24199
HL7410	B747	20770
HL7411	B747	20771
HL7412	B707	19715
HL7412	B747	24200
HL7413	B747	25405
HL7414	B747	25452
HL7415	B747	25777
HL7416	B747	25778
HL7417	B747	25779
HL7418	B747	25780
HL7419	B747	25781
HL7420	B747	25783
HL7421	B747	25794
HL7422	B747	28367
HL7423	B747	25782
HL7424	B747	22169
HL7424	B747	28551
HL7425	B707	19716
HL7426	B747	27603
HL7427	B707	19372
HL7428	B747	28552
HL7429	B707	19363
HL7430	B707	18337
HL7431	B707	19369
HL7432	B707	19626
HL7433	B707	19628
HL7434	B747	32809
HL7435	B707	19366
HL7436	B747	29170
HL7437	B747	32808
HL7438	B747	33515
HL7439	B747	33516
HL7440	A330	676
HL7440	B747	20372
HL7441	B747	20373
HL7441	B747	33518
HL7442	B747	20559
HL7443	B747	21772
HL7445	B747	21773
HL7447	B747	20493
HL7448	B747	26416
HL7449	B747	26411
HL7451	B747	22480
HL7452	B747	22481
HL7453	B747	21938
HL7454	B747	22482
HL7456	B747	22483
HL7457	B747	22484
HL7458	B747	22485
HL7459	B747	22486
HL7460	B747	26404
HL7461	B747	26405
HL7462	B747	26406
HL7463	B747	20770
HL7464	B747	20771
HL7465	B747	26412
(HL7466)	B747	22487
HL7466	B747	26413
(HL7467)	B747	22489
HL7467	B747	27073
HL7468	B747	22487
HL7469	B747	22489
HL7470	B747	24194
HL7471	B747	20652
HL7472	B747	26403
HL7473	B747	28335
HL7474	B747	22169
HL7475	B747	24195
HL7476	B747	24196
HL7477	B747	24198
HL7478	B747	24199
HL7479	B747	24200
HL7480	B747	24619
HL7481	B747	24621
HL7482	B747	25205
HL7483	B747	25275
HL7484	B747	26392
HL7485	B747	26395
HL7486	B747	26396
HL7487	B747	26393
HL7488	B747	26394
HL7489	B747	27072
HL7490	B747	27177
HL7491	B747	27341
HL7492	B747	26397
HL7493	B747	26398
HL7494	B747	27662
HL7495	B747	28096
HL7496	B747	26400
HL7497	B747	26401
HL7498	B747	26402
HL7499	B747	33517
(HL75..)	B767	25756
HL7500	B777	28685
HL7505	B777	27394
HL7506	B767	25760
HL7507	B767	25761
HL7508	B737	25772
HL7509	B737	28198
HL7510	B737	25771
HL7511	B737	27630
HL7512	B737	27632
HL7513	B737	25776
HL7514	B767	25763
HL7515	B767	25762
HL7516	B767	25759
HL7517	B737	25774
HL7518	B737	28053
HL7519	A300	611
HL7520	A300	613
HL7521	A300	657
HL7523	A300	659
HL7524	A330	206
HL7525	A330	219
HL7526	B777	27947
HL7527	B737	26299
(HL7527)	B737	29122
HL7528	B767	29129
HL7529	A300	477
HL7530	B777	27945
HL7531	B777	27946
HL7532	B777	28371
HL7533	B777	27948
HL7534	B777	27950
HL7535	A300	479
HL7536	A300	543
HL7537	A300	554
HL7538	A330	222
HL7539	A330	226
HL7540	A330	241
HL7541	MD80	49373
HL7542	MD80	49374
HL7543	MD80	49416
HL7544	MD80	49417
HL7545	MD80	49418
HL7546	MD80	49419
HL7547	MD80	53147
HL7548	MD80	53148
HL7549	A321	1293
HL7550	A330	162
HL7551	A330	172
HL7552	A330	206
HL7552	A330	258
HL7553	A330	267
HL7554	A330	256
HL7555	737NG	30230
HL7556	737NG	28615
HL7557	737NG	28622
HL7558	737NG	28625
HL7559	737NG	28626
HL7560	737NG	29981
HL7561	737NG	29982
HL7562	737NG	29983
HL7563	737NG	28636
HL7564	737NG	28638
HL7565	737NG	29984
HL7566	737NG	29905
HL7567	737NG	28647
HL7568	737NG	29986
HL7569	737NG	29987
HL7570	MD80	53485
HL7571	MD80	53486
HL7572	MD80	53487
HL7573	B777	27952
HL7574	B777	28444
HL7575	B777	28445
HL7580	A300	756
HL7581	A300	762
HL7582	A300	530
HL7583	A300	750
HL7584	A330	338
HL7585	A330	350
HL7586	A330	351
HL7587	A330	356
HL7588	A321	0771
HL7589	A321	0855
HL7590	A321	1060
HL7591	B737	26291
HL7592	B737	26320
HL7593	B737	28492
HL7594	A321	1356
HL7595	B767	30840
HL7596	B777	28681
HL7597	B777	28686
HL7598	B777	27949
HL7599	737NG	29988
HL7600	B747	33945

Reg	Type	c/n
HL7601	B747	33946
HL7602	B747	34301
HL7603	B747	34302
HL7604	B747	29907
HL7605	B747	35526
HL7606	B747	24199
HL7607	B747	24198
HL7700	B777	30859
HL7701	A330	425
HL7702	A330	428
HL7703	A321	1511
HL7704	737NG	29989
HL7705	737NG	29990
HL7706	737NG	29991
HL7707	737NG	29992
HL7708	737NG	29993
HL7709	A330	484
HL7710	A330	490
HL7711	A321	1636
HL7712	A321	1670
HL7713	A321	1734
HL7714	B777	27951
HL7715	B777	28372
HL7716	737NG	29994
HL7717	737NG	29995
HL7718	737NG	29996
HL7719	737NG	29997
HL7720	A330	550
HL7721	B777	33727
HL7722	A321	2041
HL7723	A321	2045
HL7724	737NG	29998
HL7725	737NG	29999
HL7726	737NG	30001
HL7727	737NG	30000
HL7728	737NG	30002
HL7729	A321	2110
HL7730	A321	2226
HL7731	A321	2247
HL7732	B777	29174
HL7733	B777	34206
HL7734	B777	34207
HL7735	A321	2290
HL7736	A330	640
HL7737	A320	2397
HL7738	A320	2459
HL7739	B777	29175
HL7741	A330	708
HL7742	B777	29171
HL7743	B777	34208
HL7744	A320	2808
HL7745	A320	2840
HL7746	A330	772
HL7747	A330	803
HL7750	B777	34209
HL7751	B777	34210
HL7752	B777	34211
HL7753	A320	2943
HL7754	A330	845
HL7755	B777	30861
HL7756	B777	30860
HL7757	737NG	35790
HL7758	737NG	35791
HL7761	A321	1227
HL7762	A320	3244
HL7764	B777	34214
HL7765	B777	34212
HL7766	B777	34213
HL7770	737NG	32807

Panama

Reg	Type	c/n
(HP-)	B727	20465
HP-	DC-8	45988
(HP-)	DC-8	46162
(HP-)	DC-10	46714
HP-500A	B727	18894
HP-505	DC-9	45786
HP-619	B727	18920
HP-619API	B727	18920
HP-620	B727	18951

Reg	Type	c/n
HP-661	B727	19280
HP-679	B707	18080
HP-685	B707	18044
HP-756	B707	17591
HP-760	B707	17589
HP-768	DC-8	45806
"HP-780"	B707	17587
HP-791WAP	DC-8	46150
HP-792	B707	17589
HP-793	B707	17589
HP-794	B707	17591
HP-807	B707	17590
HP-807	DC-8	45660
HP-821	CV880	22-00-41
HP-826	DC-8	45298
HP-855	B707	17928
HP-873	B737	19768
HP-873CMP	B737	19768
HP-876	CV880	22-00-52
(HP-876P)	CV880	22-00-52
HP-927	DC-8	45804
HP-950	DC-8	45678
HP-1001	B727	19815
HP-1027	B707	18709
HP-1028	B707	19575
HP-1028	B737	19771
HP-1048	DC-8	45259
HP-1063	B727	19110
HP-1088	DC-8	45817
HP-1134	B737	20253
HP-1134CMP	B737	20253
HP-1163CMP	B737	21693
HP-1166TCA	DC-8	45272
HP-1169TLN	DC-8	45992
HP-1178TLN	B727	19393
HP-1179TLN	B727	18742
HP-1195CMP	B737	20806
HP-1205CMP	B737	22059
HP-1216CMP	B737	20588
HP-1218CMP	B737	20670
HP-1229PFC	B727	18429
HP-1234CMP	B737	22660
HP-1235CTH	B707	19210
HP-1245	B737	22620
HP-1245CMP	B737	22620
HP-1255CMP	B737	21359
HP-1261PVI	B727	18965
HP-1288CMP	B737	22088
HP-1297CMP	B737	21645
HP-1299PFC	B727	18435
HP-1310DAE	B727	20894
HP-1311CMP	B737	21109
HP-1322CMP	B737	22667
HP-1323CMP	B737	23113
HP-1339CMP	B737	21677
HP-1340CMP	B737	21612
HP-1369CMP	737NG	29047
HP-1370CMP	737NG	29048
HP-1371CMP	737NG	30049
HP-1372CMP	737NG	28607
HP-1373CMP	737NG	30458
HP-1374CMP	737NG	30459
HP-1375CMP	737NG	30460
HP-1376CMP	737NG	30497
HP-1377CMP	737NG	30462
HP-1378CMP	737NG	30461
HP-1379CMP	737NG	30463
HP-1380CMP	737NG	30464
HP-1388ALV	DC-9	47694
HP-1389ALV	DC-9	47695
HP-1408PVI	B737	20253
HP-1510DAE	B727	20709
HP-1520CMP	737NG	33707
HP-1521CMP	737NG	33708
HP-1522CMP	737NG	33709
HP-1523CMP	737NG	33710
HP-1524CMP	737NG	33705
HP-1525CMP	737NG	33706
HP-1526CMP	737NG	34006
HP-1527CMP	737NG	30676
HP-1528CMP	737NG	29360
HP-1529CMP	737NG	29670

Reg	Type	c/n
HP-1530CMP	737NG	34535
HP-1531CMP	737NG	34536
HP-1532CMP	737NG	35068
HP-1533CMP	737NG	35067
HP-1540CMP	E190	19000012
HP-1555	B727	20780
HP-1556CMP	E190	19000016
HP-1557CMP	E190	19000034
HP-1558CMP	E190	19000038
HP-1559CMP	E190	19000053
HP-1560CMP	E190	19000056
HP-1561CMP	E190	19000089
HP-1562CMP	E190	19000095
HP-1563CMP	E190	19000098
HP-1564CMP	E190	19000100
HP-1585PVI	B727	20662
HP-1610DAE	B727	20780
HP-1710DAE	B727	22424

Honduras
(see also VP-H)

Reg	Type	c/n
HR-ALZ	B727	18879
HR-AMA	B707	19964
HR-AMC	L1011	193B-1029
HR-AME	B707	18922
HR-AMF	B707	20316
HR-AMG	B707	19335
HR-AMH	B727	18849
HR-AMI	B727	19182
HR-AMN	B707	20315
HR-AMO	1-11	086
HR-AMP	B707	20172
HR-AMQ	B707	20176
HR-AMR	B727	19836
HR-AMU	DC-8	45882
HR-AMV	B707	18839
HR-AMW	B707	20177
HR-AMX	B707	18716
HR-AMZ	B707	18766
HR-ANG	B707	19210
(HR-ANU)	B707	18766
HR-ASC	YAK40	9332029
HR-ATM	B737	23039
HR-ATN	B737	23040
HR-ATR	B737	21641
HR-ATS	1-11	BAC.260
HR-ATS	B737	21747
HR-ATX	B737	21545
HR-AUB	B737	21747
HR-AUI	B737	21544
"HR-DPD"	A310	431
HR-SHA	B737	20957
HR-SHD	B737	20222
HR-SHE	B727	18823
HR-SHF	B727	18919
HR-SHG	B737	19921
HR-SHH	B737	20956
HR-SHI	B737	20956
HR-SHJ	B737	20492
HR-SHK	B737	24691
HR-SHL	B737	24683
(HR-SHM)	B737	24692
HR-SHO	B737	20299
HR-SHP	B737	20582
HR-SHQ	B737	21359
HR-SHU	B737	20128
HR-TNR	B737	20299
HR-TNS	B737	20223
(HR-)	B727	21246
(HR-)	B737	22340

Thailand

Reg	Type	c/n
(HS-)	B737	20300
HS-AAI	B737	23510
HS-AAJ	B737	23511
HS-AAK	B737	23236
HS-AAL	B737	23235
HS-AAM	B737	23233

Reg	Type	c/n
HS-AAN	B737	23234
HS-AAO	B737	23365
HS-AAP	B737	23367
HS-AAQ	B737	23368
HS-AAS	B737	23357
HS-AAT	B737	25071
HS-AAU	B737	23378
HS-AAV	B737	22951
HS-ABB	A320	3299
HS-AEF	B737	23259
HS-AKO	B737	20507
HS-AKU	B737	23115
HS-ARR	B737	23358
HS-AXA	L1011	193C-1147
HS-AXE	L1011	193C-1097
HS-AXF	L1011	193A-1012
HS-AXJ	B747	21659
(HS-BBA)	B707	17593
(HS-BBB)	B707	17603
HS-BTA	B757	23651
HS-CMV	B737	27906
HS-DDH	B737	27191
HS-DDJ	B737	27352
HS-DDK	B737	25594
HS-HRH	B737	24866
HS-KAA	B757	25131
HS-KAK	B757	26244
HS-LTA	L1011	193A-1043
HS-LTB	L1011	193A-1055
HS-OGA	B757	22688
HS-OGB	B757	23983
HS-OMA	MD80	49439
HS-OMB	MD80	49441
HS-OMC	MD80	49479
HS-OMD	MD80	49485
HS-OME	MD80	49182
HS-OMG	MD80	49183
HS-OMH	MD80	53050
HS-OMI	MD80	49464
HS-OTA	B757	24368
HS-OTB	B757	22185
HS-PBA	F.28	11123
HS-PBC	F.28	11120
HS-PBD	F.28	11116
HS-PBE	E145	145597
HS-PBF	E145	145607
HS-PBH	B767	24798
HS-PGO	B717	55067
HS-PGP	B717	55064
HS-PGQ	B717	55081
HS-PGR	B717	55074
HS-PGS	A319	3142
HS-PGU	A320	2254
HS-PGV	A320	2310
HS-PGW	A320	2509
HS-PTA	B727	21246
HS-PTD	B727	20448
HS-RTA	B737	27906
HS-SCH	B727	21700
HS-SCJ	B727	21392
HS-SEB	L1011	193A-1012
HS-SEC	L1011	193N-1212
HS-SSA	B767	21871
HS-SSB	B767	21872
HS-TAA	A300	368
HS-TAB	A300	371
HS-TAC	A300	377
HS-TAD	A300	384
HS-TAE	A300	395
HS-TAF	A300	398
(HS-TAG)	A300	417
HS-TAG	A300	464
HS-TAH	A300	518
HS-TAK	A300	566
HS-TAL	A300	569
HS-TAM	A300	577
HS-TAN	A300	628
HS-TAO	A300	629
HS-TAP	A300	635
HS-TAR	A300	681
HS-TAS	A300	705
HS-TAT	A300	782

Reg	Type	c/n
HS-TAW	A300	784
HS-TAX	A300	033
HS-TAX	A300	785
HS-TAY	A300	065
HS-TAY	A300	786
HS-TAZ	A300	066
HS-TAZ	A300	787
HS-TBA	B737	21440
HS-TBB	B737	21810
HS-TBC	B737	22267
HS-TBD	B737	22667
HS-TBE	B737	23113
HS-TBJ	146	E3191
HS-TBK	146	E3128
HS-TBK	146	E3185
HS-TBL	146	E3131
HS-TBL	146	E3181
HS-TBM	146	E3129
HS-TBM	146	E3206
HS-TBN	146	E3149
HS-TBO	146	E1104
HS-TBO	146	E3189
HS-TBQ	146	E2074
(HS-TCA)	A340	624
HS-TDA	B737	24830
HS-TDB	B737	24831
HS-TDC	B737	25321
HS-TDD	B737	26611
HS-TDE	B737	26612
HS-TDF	B737	26613
HS-TDG	B737	26614
HS-TDH	B737	28703
HS-TDJ	B737	28704
HS-TDK	B737	28701
HS-TDL	B737	28702
(HS-TEA)	A330	042
HS-TEA	A330	050
HS-TEB	A330	060
HS-TEC	A330	062
HS-TED	A330	064
HS-TEE	A330	065
HS-TEF	A330	066
HS-TEG	A330	112
HS-TEH	A330	122
HS-TEJ	A330	209
HS-TEK	A330	224
HS-TEL	A330	231
HS-TEM	A330	346
HS-TFS	B707	19372
(HS-TFS)	B707	19519
HS-TFS	B737	21440
HS-TGA	B747	21782
HS-TGA	B747	32369
HS-TGA	DC-10	46851
HS-TGB	B747	21783
HS-TGB	B747	32370
HS-TGB	DC-10	46892
HS-TGC	B747	21784
HS-TGC	DC-10	46952
(HS-TGD)	B747	22472
HS-TGD	B747	23721
HS-TGD	DC-10	46959
HS-TGE	B747	23722
HS-TGE	CV990	30-10-17
HS-TGE	DC-10	46961
HS-TGF	B747	22337
HS-TGF	B747	33770
HS-TGF	DC-8	45949
HS-TGF	SE210	56
HS-TGG	B747	22471
HS-TGG	B747	33771
HS-TGG	DC-8	45952
HS-TGG	SE210	49
HS-TGH	A300	033
HS-TGH	B747	24458
HS-TGH	SE210	29
HS-TGI	SE210	25
HS-TGJ	B747	24459
HS-TGK	A300	035
HS-TGK	B747	24993
HS-TGK	SE210	34
HS-TGL	A300	054
HS-TGL	B747	25366
HS-TGL	SE210	30
HS-TGM	A300	055
HS-TGM	B747	27093
HS-TGM	DC-9	47395
HS-TGN	A300	071
HS-TGN	B747	26615
HS-TGN	DC-9	47396
HS-TGO	A300	072
HS-TGO	B747	26609
HS-TGO	DC-8	45386
HS-TGP	A300	084
HS-TGP	B747	26610
HS-TGP	DC-8	45390
HS-TGQ	B737	24480
HS-TGQ	DC-8	45922
HS-TGQ	DC-8	46129
HS-TGQ	DC-8	46150
HS-TGR	A300	085
HS-TGR	B747	27723
HS-TGR	DC-8	45389
HS-TGS	B747	22472
HS-TGS	DC-8	45385
HS-TGS	DC-8	46150
HS-TGT	A300	141
HS-TGT	B747	26616
HS-TGT	DC-8	45384
HS-TGU	DC-8	45526
HS-TGW	A300	149
HS-TGW	B747	27724
HS-TGW	DC-8	45416
HS-TGX	A300	249
HS-TGX	B747	27725
HS-TGX	DC-8	45923
HS-TGY	A300	265
HS-TGY	B747	28705
HS-TGY	DC-8	46054
HS-TGZ	B747	28706
HS-TGZ	DC-8	45924
HS-TGZ	DC-8	46129
HS-THH	A300	033
HS-THK	A300	035
HS-THL	A300	054
HS-THM	A300	055
HS-THN	A300	071
HS-THO	A300	072
HS-THP	A300	084
HS-THR	A300	085
HS-THT	A300	141
HS-THW	A300	149
HS-THX	A300	249
HS-THY	A300	265
HS-TIA	A310	415
HS-TIC	A310	424
HS-TID	A310	438
HS-TIF	A310	441
HS-TJA	B777	27726
HS-TJB	B777	27727
HS-TJC	B777	27728
HS-TJD	B777	27729
HS-TJE	B777	27730
HS-TJF	B777	27731
HS-TJG	B777	27732
HS-TJH	B777	27733
HS-TJR	B777	34586
HS-TJS	B777	34587
HS-TJT	B777	34588
HS-TJU	B777	34589
HS-TJV	B777	34590
HS-TJW	B777	34591
HS-TKA	B777	29150
HS-TKB	B777	29151
HS-TKC	B777	29211
HS-TKD	B777	29212
HS-TKE	B777	29213
HS-TKF	B777	29214
HS-TLA	A340	624
HS-TLB	A340	628
HS-TLC	A340	698
HS-TLD	A340	775
HS-TMA	DC-10	48267
HS-TMB	DC-10	48290
HS-TMC	DC-10	46959
HS-TMC	DC-10	48319
HS-TMD	DC-10	46961
HS-TMD	MD11	48416
HS-TME	MD11	48417
HS-TMF	MD11	48418
HS-TMG	MD11	48451
HS-TNA	A340	677
HS-TNB	A340	681
HS-TNC	A340	689
HS-TND	A340	710
HS-TNE	A340	719
HS-TSA	B747	23056
HS-TSB	B747	23245
HS-TYQ	A310	591
HS-TYR	A319	1908
HS-TYS	737NG	35478
HS-UTA	L1011	193C-1225
HS-UTB	B747	20529
HS-UTC	B747	21658
HS-UTD	B747	21029
HS-UTE	L1011	193C-1199
(HS-UTF)	L1011	193C-1213
HS-UTG	L1011	193C-1226
HS-UTH	B747	20532
HS-UTI	B747	21031
HS-UTJ	B747	21678
HS-UTK	B747	23137
HS-UTL	B747	22489
HS-UTM	B747	23637
HS-UTO	B747	23639
HS-UTP	B747	20530
HS-UTQ	B747	23390
HS-VAA	B747	21848
HS-VAB	B747	23033
HS-VAC	B747	23056
HS-VAK	B747	22249
HS-VAN	B747	23245
HS-VAO	B747	22246
HS-VAU	B747	22247
HS-VAV	B747	21659
HS-VGA	B707	17666
HS-VGB	B747	19744
HS-VGC	B707	17663
HS-VGD	A300	008
HS-VGE	DC-10	47887
(HS-VGF)	A300	009
HS-VGF	B747	19745
HS-VGG	B747	20399
HS-VKK	B737	23131
HS-VKU	B737	20506

Saudi Arabia

Reg	Type	c/n
HZ-	737NG	32971
HZ-101	737NG	32451
HZ-101	737NG	32805
HZ-102	737NG	32451
HZ-122	B727	20533
HZ-123	B707	17696
HZ-124	A340	004
HZ-AB1	1-11	BAC.158
HZ-AB1	L1011	193H-1247
HZ-AB3	B727	22362
HZ-ABM2	1-11	060
HZ-ACA	B707	18165
HZ-ACB	B707	18166
HZ-ACC	B707	19809
HZ-ACD	B707	19810
HZ-ACE	B707	18582
HZ-ACF	B707	18583
HZ-ACG	B707	21103
HZ-ACH	B707	21104
HZ-ACI	B707	21261
HZ-ACJ	B707	21367
HZ-ACK	B707	21368
HZ-AEA	DC-9	47000
HZ-AEA	E170	17000108
HZ-AEB	DC-9	47001
HZ-AEB	E170	17000114
HZ-AEC	DC-9	47002
HZ-AEC	E170	17000118
HZ-AED	E170	17000119
HZ-AEE	E170	17000121
HZ-AEF	E170	17000123
HZ-AEG	E170	17000124
HZ-AEH	E170	17000135
HZ-AEI	E170	17000142
HZ-AEJ	E170	17000145
HZ-AEK	E170	17000149
HZ-AEL	E170	17000152
HZ-AEM	E170	17000155
HZ-AEN	E170	17000158
HZ-AEO	E170	17000161
HZ-AFA1	MD11	48533
HZ-AGA	B737	20574
HZ-AGB	B737	20575
HZ-AGC	B737	20576
HZ-AGD	B737	20577
HZ-AGE	B737	20578
HZ-AGF	B737	20882
HZ-AGG	B737	20883
HZ-AGH	B737	21275
HZ-AGI	B737	21276
HZ-AGJ	B737	21277
HZ-AGK	B737	21280
HZ-AGL	B737	21281
HZ-AGM	B737	21282
HZ-AGN	B737	21283
HZ-AGO	B737	21360
HZ-AGP	B737	21361
HZ-AGQ	B737	21362
HZ-AGR	B737	21653
HZ-AGS	B737	21654
HZ-AGT	B737	22050
HZ-AHA	L1011	193U-1110
HZ-AHB	L1011	193U-1116
HZ-AHC	L1011	193U-1137
HZ-AHD	L1011	193U-1144
HZ-AHE	L1011	193B-1124
HZ-AHF	L1011	193B-1130
HZ-AHG	L1011	193U-1148
HZ-AHH	L1011	193U-1149
HZ-AHI	L1011	193S-1160
HZ-AHJ	L1011	193S-1161
HZ-AHK	L1011	193S-1169
HZ-AHL	L1011	193S-1170
HZ-AHM	L1011	193S-1171
HZ-AHN	L1011	193S-1175
HZ-AHO	L1011	193S-1187
HZ-AHP	L1011	193S-1190
HZ-AHQ	L1011	193S-1192
HZ-AHR	L1011	193U-1214
HZ-AIA	B747	22498
HZ-AIB	B747	22499
HZ-AIC	B747	22500
HZ-AID	B747	22501
HZ-AIE	B747	22502
HZ-AIF	B747	22503
HZ-AIG	B747	22747
HZ-AIH	B747	22748
HZ-AII	B747	22749
HZ-AIJ	B747	22750
HZ-AIK	B747	23262
HZ-AIL	B747	23263
HZ-AIM	B747	23264
HZ-AIN	B747	23265
HZ-AIO	B747	23266
HZ-AIP	B747	23267
HZ-AIQ	B747	23268
HZ-AIR	B747	23269
HZ-AIS	B747	23270
HZ-AIT	B747	23271
HZ-AIU	B747	24359
HZ-AIV	B747	28339
HZ-AIW	B747	28340
HZ-AIX	B747	28341
HZ-AIY	B747	28342
HZ-AIZ	B747	28343
HZ-AJA	A300	284
HZ-AJB	A300	294
HZ-AJC	A300	301
HZ-AJD	A300	307

Reg	Type	Serial
HZ-AJE	A300	312
HZ-AJF	A300	317
HZ-AJG	A300	321
HZ-AJH	A300	336
HZ-AJI	A300	341
HZ-AJJ	A300	348
HZ-AJK	A300	351
HZ-AKA	B777	28344
HZ-AKB	B777	28345
HZ-AKC	B777	28346
HZ-AKD	B777	28347
HZ-AKE	B777	28348
HZ-AKF	B777	28349
HZ-AKG	B777	28350
HZ-AKH	B777	28351
HZ-AKI	B777	28352
HZ-AKJ	B777	28353
HZ-AKK	B777	28354
HZ-AKL	B777	28355
HZ-AKM	B777	28356
HZ-AKN	B777	28357
HZ-AKO	B777	28358
HZ-AKP	B777	28359
HZ-AKQ	B777	28360
HZ-AKR	B777	28361
HZ-AKS	B777	28362
HZ-AKT	B777	28363
HZ-AKU	B777	28364
HZ-AKV	B777	28365
HZ-AKW	B777	28366
HZ-AMB	1-11	069
HZ-AMH	1-11	BAC.158
HZ-AMH	1-11	BAC.183
HZ-AMH	B727	19620
HZ-AMK	1-11	054
HZ-ANA	MD11	48773
HZ-ANB	MD11	48775
HZ-ANC	MD11	48776
HZ-AND	MD11	48777
HZ-AP2	MD90	53517
HZ-AP3	MD90	53518
HZ-AP4	MD90	53519
HZ-AP7	MD90	53517
HZ-APA	MD90	53491
HZ-APB	MD90	53492
HZ-APC	MD90	53493
HZ-APD	MD90	53494
HZ-APE	MD90	53495
HZ-APF	MD90	53496
HZ-APG	MD90	53497
HZ-APH	MD90	53498
HZ-API	MD90	53499
HZ-APJ	MD90	53500
HZ-APK	MD90	53501
HZ-APL	MD90	53502
HZ-APM	MD90	53503
HZ-APN	MD90	53504
HZ-APO	MD90	53505
HZ-APP	MD90	53506
HZ-APQ	MD90	53507
HZ-APR	MD90	53508
HZ-APS	MD90	53509
HZ-APT	MD90	53510
HZ-APU	MD90	53511
HZ-APV	MD90	53512
HZ-APW	MD90	53513
HZ-APX	MD90	53514
HZ-APY	MD90	53515
HZ-APZ	MD90	53516
HZ-BBK	B737	25016
HZ-BL1	1-11	080
HZ-CJB	B737	24680
HZ-DA5	B727	21460
HZ-DAT	B707	17644
HZ-DG1	B727	19124
(HZ-DG5)	737NG	30547
HZ-DMO	B737	24681
HZ-DRW	B737	25138
HZ-GP2	1-11	060
(HZ-GP2)	B727	20228
HZ-GRP	1-11	060
HZ-GRP	1-11	067

Reg	Type	Serial
HZ-GRP	B727	20228
HZ-HE4	B727	19987
HZ-HM1	B707	21081
HZ-HM1	B747	21652
HZ-HM1	B747	28343
HZ-HM11	DC-8	46084
HZ-HM1B	B747	21652
HZ-HM2	B707	21081
HZ-HM3	B707	21368
HZ-HM4	B737	22050
(HZ-HM5)	B707	21104
HZ-HM5	L1011	193G-1250
HZ-HM6	L1011	293A-1249
HZ-HM7	MD11	48532
HZ-HM8	MD11	48533
HZ-HMED	B757	25495
HZ-HMIA	B747	23070
HZ-HMS	A340	204
HZ-HR1	1-11	081
HZ-HR1	B727	21853
HZ-HR3	B727	22968
HZ-JAM	1-11	BAC.111
HZ-KA1	B707	18451
(HZ-KA1)	B707	18740
HZ-KA4	B707	18453
HZ-KA7	1-11	BAC.260
HZ-KB1	1-11	BAC.158
HZ-MAA	1-11	060
HZ-MAJ	1-11	088
HZ-MAM	1-11	BAC.259
HZ-MBA	B727	19006
(HZ-MD1)	MD90	53491
(HZ-MD10)	MD90	53500
(HZ-MD11)	MD90	53501
(HZ-MD12)	MD90	53502
(HZ-MD13)	MD90	53503
(HZ-MD14)	MD90	53504
(HZ-MD15)	MD90	53505
(HZ-MD16)	MD90	53506
(HZ-MD17)	MD90	53507
(HZ-MD18)	MD90	53508
(HZ-MD19)	MD90	53509
(HZ-MD2)	MD90	53492
(HZ-MD20)	MD90	53510
(HZ-MD21)	MD90	53511
(HZ-MD22)	MD90	53512
(HZ-MD23)	MD90	53513
(HZ-MD24)	MD90	53514
(HZ-MD25)	MD90	53515
(HZ-MD26)	MD90	53516
(HZ-MD27)	MD90	53517
(HZ-MD28)	MD90	53518
(HZ-MD29)	MD90	53519
(HZ-MD3)	MD90	53493
(HZ-MD4)	MD90	53494
(HZ-MD5)	MD90	53495
(HZ-MD6)	MD90	53496
(HZ-MD7)	MD90	53497
(HZ-MD8)	MD90	53498
(HZ-MD9)	MD90	53499
HZ-MF1	1-11	BAC.158
HZ-MF1	737NG	33405
HZ-MF2	737NG	33499
HZ-MFA	1-11	080
HZ-MIS	B737	22600
HZ-MO1	1-11	BAC.135
HZ-MS11	DC-8	46084
HZ-NAA	B707	18451
HZ-NAS	A319	0913
HZ-NB2	1-11	064
HZ-NB3	1-11	060
(HZ-ND1)	1-11	BAC.183
HZ-NIR	1-11	088
HZ-NMA	B737	28563
HZ-NSA	A310	431
HZ-OCV	B727	19006
HZ-RH1	1-11	060
HZ-RH3	B727	22968
HZ-SAK1	B707	18586
(HZ-SIR)	B737	22601
HZ-SKI	B727	21460
HZ-SNA	B727	20896

Reg	Type	Serial
HZ-SNB	B727	21084
HZ-SNC	B727	20905
HZ-SND	B727	20994
(HZ-SNE)	B727	22644
(HZ-SNF)	B727	22643
HZ-TA1	1-11	078
HZ-TA1	B727	18365
HZ-TAA	737NG	29188
HZ-TAS	B707	18338
HZ-TBA	B737	23468
HZ-TFA	B727	19006
HZ-WBT	B727	19252
HZ-WBT2	B727	19252
HZ-WBT3	B767	27255
HZ-WBT4	A340	151
"HZ-WBT6"	B747	25880
HZ-WBT6	B767	27255
HZ-WBT7	B747	25880
(HZ-WBT8)	A321	0956
HZ-XY7	A320	2165

Solomon Islands

Reg	Type	Serial
H4-PAE	B727	21455
H4-SAL	B737	22395
H4-SOL	B737	25163

Italy

Reg	Type	Serial
(I-)	B737	19594
I-ACLG	D0328	3133
I-ACLH	D0328	3152
I-ADJA	CRJ	7478
I-ADJB	CRJ	7486
I-ADJC	CRJ	7494
I-ADJD	CRJ	7625
I-ADJE	CRJ	7629
I-ADJF	146	E3193
I-ADJG	146	E3169
I-ADJH	146	E3129
I-ADJI	146	E3149
I-ADJJ	146	E3155
I-AFTY	B767	25208
I-AEJA	B757	25133
I-AEJB	B767	24358
I-AEJC	B767	24357
(I-AEJD)	B767	26387
(I-AEJE)	B767	26388
I-AFRA	MD80	49834
I-AIGA	B757	24748
I-AIGB	B757	24738
I-AIGC	B757	24747
I-AIGG	B767	28041
I-AIGL	B737	23636
I-AIGM	B737	24299
I-AIMQ	B767	27993
"I-AIRH"	D0328	3199
I-AIRJ	D0328	3186
I-AIRX	D0328	3142
I-ALEC	DC-8	45682
I-ALPK	F.100	11244
I-ALPL	F.100	11250
I-ALPQ	F.100	11246
I-ALPS	F.100	11254
I-ALPW	F.100	11255
I-ALPX	F.100	11251
I-ALPX	F.100	11470
I-ALPZ	F.100	11252
I-ATIA	DC-9	47431
I-ATIE	DC-9	47436
I-ATIH	DC-9	47553
I-ATIJ	DC-9	47544
I-ATIK	DC-9	47477
I-ATIO	DC-9	47437
I-ATIQ	DC-9	47591
I-ATIU	DC-9	47438
I-ATIW	DC-9	47533
I-ATIX	DC-9	47474
I-ATIY	DC-9	47575
I-ATJA	DC-9	47641

Reg	Type	Serial
I-ATJB	DC-9	47653
I-ATJC	DC-9	47667
I-ATSC	146	E3146
I-ATSD	146	E3159
I-BIKA	A320	0951
I-BIKB	A320	1226
I-BIKC	A320	1448
I-BIKD	A320	1457
I-BIKE	A320	0999
I-BIKF	A320	1473
I-BIKG	A320	1480
I-BIKI	A320	1138
I-BIKL	A320	1489
I-BIKO	A320	1168
I-BIKU	A320	1217
I-BIMA	A319	1722
I-BIMB	A319	2033
I-BIMC	A319	2057
I-BIMD	A319	2074
I-BIME	A319	1740
I-BIMF	A319	2083
I-BIMG	A319	2086
I-BIMH	A319	2101
I-BIMI	A319	1745
I-BIMJ	A319	1779
I-BIML	A319	2127
I-BIMO	A319	1770
I-BIXA	A321	0477
I-BIXB	A321	0524
I-BIXC	A321	0526
I-BIXD	A321	0532
I-BIXE	A321	0488
I-BIXF	A321	0515
I-BIXG	A321	0516
I-BIXH	A321	0940
I-BIXI	A321	0494
I-BIXJ	A321	0959
I-BIXK	A321	1220
I-BIXL	A321	0513
I-BIXM	A321	0514
I-BIXN	A321	0576
I-BIXO	A321	0495
I-BIXP	A321	0583
I-BIXQ	A321	0586
I-BIXR	A321	0593
I-BIXS	A321	0599
I-BIXT	A321	0765
I-BIXU	A321	0434
I-BIXV	A321	0819
I-BIXZ	A321	0848
(I-BPAB)	B767	28111
(I-BPAC)	B737	25147
(I-BPAD)	B767	29435
I-BRJF	B757	24772
I-BUSB	A300	101
I-BUSC	A300	106
I BUSD	A300	107
I-BUSF	A300	123
I-BUSG	A300	139
I-BUSH	A300	140
I-BUSJ	A300	142
I-BUSL	A300	173
I-BUSM	A300	049
I-BUSN	A300	051
I-BUSP	A300	067
I-BUSQ	A300	118
I-BUSR	A300	120
I-BUST	A300	068
I-CGIA	DC-10	47843
I-CLBA	146	E2300
I-DABA	SE210	71
I-DABE	SE210	72
I-DABF	SE210	179
I-DABG	SE210	205
I-DABI	SE210	74
I-DABL	SE210	132
I-DABM	SE210	143
I-DABP	SE210	192
I-DABR	SE210	81
I-DABS	SE210	106
I-DABT	SE210	85
I-DABU	SE210	77

Reg	Type	c/n	Reg	Type	c/n	Reg	Type	c/n	Reg	Type	c/n
I-DABV	SE210	146	I-DAWO	MD80	49195	I-DIKT	DC-9	47230	I-DYNA	DC-10	47861
I-DABW	SE210	150	I-DAWP	MD80	49206	(I-DIKT)	DC-9	47283	I-DYNB	DC-10	47866
I-DABZ	SE210	82	I-DAWQ	MD80	49207	I-DIKU	DC-9	47101	I-DYNC	DC-10	47867
I-DACM	MD80	49971	I-DAWR	MD80	49208	I-DIKV	DC-9	47231	I-DYND	DC-10	47868
I-DACN	MD80	49972	I-DAWS	MD80	49209	(I-DIKV)	DC-9	47311	I-DYNE	DC-10	47862
I-DACP	MD80	49973	I-DAWT	MD80	49210	(I-DIKW)	DC-9	47230	I-DYNI	DC-10	47863
I-DACQ	MD80	49974	I-DAWU	MD80	49196	I-DIKW	DC-9	47283	I-DYNO	DC-10	47864
I-DACR	MD80	49975	I-DAWV	MD80	49211	I-DIKY	DC-9	47232	I-DYNU	DC-10	47865
I-DACS	MD80	53053	I-DAWW	MD80	49212	(I-DIKZ)	DC-9	47231	I-ECJA	A319	2440
I-DACT	MD80	53054	I-DAWY	MD80	49213	I-DIKZ	DC-9	47311	I-EEZA	A330	358
I-DACU	MD80	53055	I-DAWZ	MD80	49214	I-DIRA	B727	21264	I-EEZB	A330	364
I-DACV	MD80	53056	I-DAXA	SE210	35	I-DIRB	B727	21268	I-EEZC	A320	1852
I-DACW	MD80	53057	I-DAXE	SE210	36	I-DIRC	B727	21269	I-EEZD	A320	1920
I-DACX	MD80	53060	I-DAXI	SE210	40	I-DIRD	B727	21661	I-EEZE	A320	1937
I-DACY	MD80	53059	(I-DAXJ)	SE210	44	I-DIRE	B727	21265	I-EEZF	A320	1983
I-DACZ	MD80	53058	I-DAXO	SE210	44	I-DIRF	B727	21662	I-EEZG	A320	2001
I-DAND	MD80	53061	I-DAXT	SE210	80	I-DIRG	B727	21663	I-EEZH	A320	0737
I-DANF	MD80	53062	I-DAXU	SE210	79	I-DIRI	B727	21265	I-EEZI	A320	0749
I-DANG	MD80	53176	I-DEIB	B767	27376	I-DIRJ	B727	21270	I-EEZJ	A320	665
I-DANH	MD80	53177	I-DEIC	B767	27377	I-DIRL	B727	21664	I-EEZK	A320	1125
I-DANL	MD80	53178	I-DEID	B767	27468	I-DIRM	B727	22052	I-EEZL	A330	802
I-DANM	MD80	53179	I-DEIF	B767	27908	I-DIRN	B727	22053	(I-EEZM)	A330	822
I-DANP	MD80	53180	I-DEIG	B767	27918	I-DIRO	B727	21266	(I-ELGF)	F.100	11253
I-DANQ	MD80	53181	I-DEIL	B767	28147	I-DIRP	B727	22165	(I-ELGF)	F.100	11332
I-DANR	MD80	53203	I-DEMA	B747	19729	I-DIRQ	B727	22166	(I-EMCX)	E170	17000008
I-DANU	MD80	53204	I-DEMB	B747	20520	I-DIRR	B727	22167	(I-EMMX)	E170	17000011
I-DANV	MD80	53205	I-DEMC	B747	22506	I-DIRS	B727	22168	(I-EMRX)	E170	17000010
I-DANW	MD80	53206	I-DEMD	B747	22507	I-DIRT	B727	22702	(I-EMSX)	E170	17000009
I-DATA	MD80	53216	I-DEME	B747	19730	I-DIRU	B727	21267	I-EXMA	E145	145250
I-DATB	MD80	53221	I-DEMF	B747	22508	I-DISA	B777	32855	I-EXMB	E145	145330
I-DATC	MD80	53222	I-DEMG	B747	22510	I-DISB	B777	32859	I-EXMC	E145	145436
I-DATD	MD80	53223	I-DEML	B747	22511	I-DISD	B777	32860	I-EXMD	E145	145445
I-DATE	MD80	53217	I-DEMN	B747	22512	I-DISE	B777	32856	I-EXME	E145	145282
I-DATF	MD80	53224	I-DEMO	B747	19731	I-DISO	B777	32857	I-EXMF	E145	145641
I-DATG	MD80	53225	I-DEMP	B747	22513	I-DISU	B777	32858	I-EXMG	E145	145652
I-DATH	MD80	53226	I-DEMR	B747	22545	I-DIWA	DC-8	45598	I-EXMH	E145	145665
I-DATI	MD80	53218	I-DEMS	B747	22969	I-DIWB	DC-8	45625	I-EXMI	E145	145286
I-DATJ	MD80	53227	I-DEMT	B747	23300	I-DIWC	DC-8	45960	I-EXML	E145	145709
I-DATK	MD80	53228	I-DEMU	B747	19732	I-DIWD	DC-8	45631	I-EXMM	E145	145738
I-DATL	MD80	53229	I-DEMV	B747	23301	I-DIWE	DC-8	45599	I-EXMN	E145	145750
I-DATM	MD80	53230	I-DEMW	B747	23476	I-DIWF	DC-8	45630	I-EXMO	E145	145299
I-DATN	MD80	53231	I-DEMX	B747	23286	I-DIWG	DC-8	45660	I-EXMU	E145	145316
I-DATO	MD80	53219	I-DEMY	B747	21589	I-DIWH	DC-8	46132	I-FASI	146	E1260
I-DATP	MD80	53232	I-DIBA	DC-9	47038	I-DIWI	DC-8	45600	I-FLRA	146	E2204
I-DATQ	MD80	53233	I-DIBC	DC-9	47233	I-DIWJ	DC-8	45986	I-FLRE	146	E2210
I-DATR	MD80	53234	I-DIBD	DC-9	47234	I-DIWK	DC-8	46082	I-FLRI	146	E2220
I-DATS	MD80	53235	I-DIBE	DC-9	47046	I-DIWL	DC-8	45682	I-FLRO	146	E2227
I-DATU	MD80	53220	I-DIBI	DC-9	47129	I-DIWM	DC-8	45755	I-FLRU	146	E2204
I-DAVA	MD80	49215	I-DIBJ	DC-9	47235	I-DIWN	DC-8	45909	I-FLRV	146	E2184
I-DAVB	MD80	49216	I-DIBK	DC-9	47355	I-DIWO	DC-8	45601	I-FLRW	146	E2178
I-DAVC	MD80	49217	I-DIBL	DC-9	47101	I-DIWP	DC-8	45636	I-FLRX	146	E2170
I-DAVD	MD80	49218	I-DIBM	DC-9	47223	I-DIWQ	DC-8	45961	(I-FLRZ)	146	E2200
I-DAVF	MD80	49219	I-DIBN	DC-9	47339	I-DIWR	DC-8	45637	I-FLYY	DC-9	47754
I-DAVG	MD80	49220	I-DIBO	DC-9	47237	I-DIWS	DC-8	45665	I-FLYZ	DC-9	47697
I-DAVH	MD80	49221	I-DIBP	DC-9	47222	I-DIWT	DC-8	45666	I-GISA	SE210	21
I-DAVI	MD80	49430	I-DIBQ	DC-9	47236	I-DIWU	DC-8	45624	I-GISE	SE210	208
I-DAVJ	MD80	49431	I-DIBR	DC-9	47038	I-DIWV	DC-8	45910	I-GISI	SE210	188
I-DAVK	MD80	49432	I-DIBS	DC-9	47039	I-DIWW	DC-8	46098	I-GISO	SE210	187
I-DAVL	MD80	49433	I-DIBT	DC-9	47046	I-DIWX	DC-8	46142	I-GISU	SE210	169
I-DAVM	MD80	49434	I-DIBU	DC-9	47047	I-DIWY	DC-8	46027	I-JAKA	YAK40	9020409
I-DAVN	MD80	49435	I-DIBV	DC-9	47101	I-DIWZ	DC-8	46026	I-JAKE	YAK40	9141418
I-DAVP	MD80	49549	I-DIBW	DC-9	47129	I-DIZA	DC-9	47238	I-JAKI	YAK40	9141518
I-DAVR	MD80	49550	I-DIBX	DC-9	47283	I-DIZB	DC-9	47434	I-JAKO	YAK40	9230122
I-DAVS	MD80	49551	I-DIBY	DC-9	47223	I-DIZC	DC-9	47435	I-JETA	B737	21839
I-DAVT	MD80	49552	I-DIBZ	DC-9	47222	I-DIZE	DC-9	47239	(I-JETB)	B737	23008
I-DAVU	MD80	49794	I-DIKA	DC-9	47038	I-DIZE	DC-9	47502	I-JETC	B737	23153
I-DAVV	MD80	49795	I-DIKB	DC-9	47118	(I-DIZF)	DC-9	47436	I-JETD	B737	23158
I-DAVW	MD80	49796	I-DIKC	DC-9	47128	I-DIZF	DC-9	47519	I-LAUD	B767	25273
I-DAVX	MD80	49969	I-DIKD	DC-9	47129	(I-DIZG)	DC-9	47437	I-LINB	A320	0363
I-DAVZ	MD80	49970	I-DIKE	DC-9	47039	(I-DIZI)	DC-9	47431	I-LINF	A320	0393
I-DAWA	MD80	49192	I-DIKF	DC-9	47220	I-DIZI	DC-9	47432	I-LING	A320	0414
I-DAWB	MD80	49197	I-DIKG	DC-9	47221	(I-DIZL)	DC-9	47438	I-LINH	A320	0163
I-DAWC	MD80	49198	I-DIKI	DC-9	47046	I-DIZO	DC-9	47518	I-LIVA	A321	1950
I-DAWD	MD80	49199	I-DIKJ	DC-9	47222	I-DIZU	DC-9	47433	I-LIVB	A321	1970
I-DAWE	MD80	49193	I-DIKL	DC-9	47223	I-DUPA	MD11	48426	I-LIVC	A321	1202
I-DAWF	MD80	49200	I-DIKM	DC-9	47224	I-DUPB	MD11	48431	I-LIVD	A321	0792
I-DAWG	MD80	49201	I-DIKN	DC-9	47225	I-DUPC	MD11	48581	I-LIVL	A330	627
I-DAWH	MD80	49202	I-DIKO	DC-9	47047	I-DUPD	MD11	48630	I-LIVM	A330	551
I-DAWI	MD80	49194	I-DIKP	DC-9	47226	I-DUPE	MD11	48427	I-LIVN	A330	597
I-DAWJ	MD80	49203	I-DIKQ	DC-9	47227	I-DUPI	MD11	48428	I-LLAG	B767	25137
I-DAWL	MD80	49204	I-DIKR	DC-9	47228	I-DUPO	MD11	48429	I-MSAA	146	E2109
I-DAWM	MD80	49205	I-DIKS	DC-9	47229	I-DUPU	MD11	48430	I-NEOS	737NG	32733

I-NEOT	737NG	33004	I-RIZY	DC-9	47232	JA016D	A300	838	JA312J	737NG	35341
I-NEOU	737NG	29887	I-SARJ	DC-9	45702	(JA01A3)	737NG	33916	JA313J	737NG	35342
I-NEOX	737NG	33677	I-SARV	DC-9	45706	JA01AN	737NG	33916	JA314J	737NG	35343
I-OCEU	B747	22668	I-SARW	DC-9	47430	JA01G	A300	533	JA315J	737NG	35344
I-OECA	B747	21592	I-SARZ	DC-9	47468	JA01HD	B767	28159	JA316J	737NG	35345
I-PEIY	B767	25208	I-SAVA	B707	17664	JA01KZ	B747	34016	JA317J	737NG	35346
I-PEKA	A320	1132	I-SMEA	DC-9	47713	(JA01LQ)	B767	30847	JA318J	737NG	35347
I-PEKB	A320	1162	I-SMEB	MD80	53064	JA01MC	A320	2620	JA319J	737NG	35348
I-PEKC	A320	1179	I-SMEC	MD80	49808	JA01RJ	CRJ	7052	JA320J	737NG	35349
I-PEKD	A320	1244	I-SMED	MD80	53182	(JA02A3)	737NG	33872	JA321J	737NG	35350
I-PEKE	A320	1308	I-SMEE	DC-9	47656	JA02AN	737NG	33872	JA322J	737NG	35351
I-PEKF	A320	1322	I-SMEI	DC-9	47714	JA02GX	A300	872	JA323J	737NG	35352
I-PEKG	A320	1132	I-SMEJ	DC-9	47657	JA02KZ	B747	34017	JA324J	737NG	35353
I-PEKH	A320	1162	I-SMEL	MD80	49247	JA02MC	A320	2658	JA325J	737NG	35354
I-PEKI	A320	1179	I-SMEM	MD80	49248	JA02RJ	CRJ	7033	JA326J	737NG	35355
I-PEKL	A320	1244	I-SMEO	DC-9	47655	(JA02RJ)	CRJ	7059	JA327J	737NG	35356
I-PEKM	A321	1451	I-SMEP	MD80	49740	JA03AN	737NG	33873	JA328J	737NG	35357
I-PEKN	A321	1607	I-SMER	MD80	49901	JA03KZ	B747	34018	JA329J	737NG	35358
I-PEKO	A320	1152	I-SMES	MD80	49902	JA03MC	A320	2695	JA330J	737NG	35359
I-PEKP	A320	1198	I-SMET	MD80	49531	JA03RJ	CRJ	7624	JA351K	B737	25189
I-PEKQ	A320	1757	I-SMEU	DC-9	47715	JA04AN	737NG	33874	JA352K	B737	26097
I-PEKR	A320	0446	I-SMEV	MD80	49669	JA04KZ	B747	34283	JA353K	B737	26104
I-PEKS	A320	1856	I-SMEZ	MD80	49903	JA04MC	A320	3025	JA354K	B737	26105
I-PEKT	A320	1909	(I-STAE)	SE210	93	JA04RJ	CRJ	7798	JA355K	B737	28083
I-PEKU	A320	0990	I-TEAA	B737	24020	JA05AN	737NG	33875	JA356K	B737	28131
I-PEKV	A320	1996	(I-TEAB)	A310	588	JA05KZ	B747	36132	JA357K	B737	28128
I-PEKW	A320	0814	I-TEAE	B737	24022	JA06AN	737NG	33876	JA359K	B737	28130
I-PEKZ	A320	1162	I-TEAI	B737	25015	JA06KZ	B747	36133	JA368K	B737	24545
I-PIMQ	B767	27993	I-TERB	146	E2012	JA07AN	737NG	33900	JA391K	B737	28550
I-REJA	F.70	11563	I-TERK	146	E2066	JA08AN	737NG	33877	JA392K	B737	28550
(I-REJB)	F.70	11571	I-TERV	146	E2014	JA09AN	737NG	33878	JA401A	B747	28282
(I-REJC)	F.70	11579	I-TIAN	DC-9	47010	JA101A	A321	0802	JA401J	B747	33748
(I-REJD)	F.70	11581	I-TIAP	F.28	11009	JA102A	A321	0811	JA402A	B747	28283
I-REJE	F.70	11573	I-TIAR	DC-9	47015	JA103A	A321	0963	JA402J	B747	33749
I-REJI	F.70	11574	I-TIBB	F.28	11010	JA104A	A321	1008	JA403A	B747	29262
I-REJO	F.70	11570	I-TIDA	F.28	11014	JA105A	A321	1042	JA404A	B747	29263
I-REJU	F.70	11575	I-TIDB	F.28	11006	JA106A	A321	1204	JA405A	B747	30322
I-RIBC	DC-9	47233	I-TIDE	F.28	11015	JA107A	A321	1227	JA601A	B767	27943
I-RIBD	DC-9	47234	I-TIDI	F.28	11991	JA10AN	737NG	33879	JA601F	B767	33404
I-RIBJ	DC-9	47235	(I-TIDO)	F.28	11037	JA11AN	737NG	33882	JA601J	B767	32886
I-RIBN	DC-9	47339	I-TIDU	F.28	11004	JA12AN	737NG	33881	JA602A	B767	27944
I-RIBQ	DC-9	47236	I-TIGA	DC-9	45728	JA13AN	737NG	33880	JA602F	B767	33509
I-RIFB	DC-9	47432	I-TIGB	DC-9	47002	JA14AN	737NG	33883	JA602J	B767	32887
I-RIFC	DC-9	47233	I-TIGE	DC-9	45717	JA15AN	737NG	33888	JA603A	B767	32972
I-RIFD	DC-9	47234	I-TIGI	DC-9	45724	JA16AN	737NG	33889	JA603F	B767	33510
I-RIFE	DC-9	47518	I-TIGU	DC-9	45718	JA17AN	737NG	33884	JA603J	B767	32888
I-RIFG	DC-9	47225	I-TNTC	146	E2078	JA201A	A320	1973	JA604A	B767	32973
I-RIFH	DC-9	47128	I-TPGS	146	E2109	JA201J	CRJ	7452	JA604F	B767	35709
I-RIFJ	DC-9	47235	(I-VAFE)	F.28	11994	JA202A	A320	2054	JA604J	B767	33493
I-RIFL	DC-9	47435	(I-VAGA)	F.28	11032	JA202J	CRJ	7484	JA605A	B767	32974
I-RIFM	DC-9	47544	I-VEIY	B767	25208	JA203A	A320	2061	JA605J	B767	33494
I-RIFP	DC-9	47438	I-VIMQ	B767	27993	JA203J	CRJ	7626	JA606A	B767	32975
I-RIFS	DC-9	47229	I-VLEA	A320	1125	JA204A	A320	2998	JA606J	B767	33495
I-RIFT	DC-9	47591	(I-VLEB)	B767	27600	JA204J	CRJ	7643	JA607A	B767	32976
I-RIFU	DC-9	47433	I-VLEC	A330	205	JA205A	A320	3099	JA607J	B767	33496
I-RIFV	DC-9	47533	I-VLED	A330	211	JA205J	CRJ	7767	JA608A	B767	32977
I-RIFW	DC-9	47575	I-VLEE	A330	272	JA206A	A320	3147	JA608J	B767	33497
I-RIFY	DC-9	47232	I-VLEF	A330	339	JA206J	CRJ	7834	JA609A	B767	32978
I-RIFZ	DC-9	47436	I-VLEG	A330	463	JA207A	A320	3148	JA609J	B767	33845
I-RIKS	DC-9	47229	I-VLEH	A330	504	JA207J	CRJ	8050	JA610A	B767	32979
I-RIKT	DC-9	47230	I-VLEO	A320	1125	JA208A	A320	3189	JA610J	B767	33846
I-RIKV	DC-9	47231	I-WEBA	A320	3138	JA208JA	CRJ	8059	JA611A	B767	32980
I-RIKZ	DC-9	47311	I-WEBB	A320	3161	JA209J	CRJ	8062	JA611J	B767	33847
I-RIZA	DC-9	47238				JA300K	B737	27434	JA612A	B767	33506
I-RIZB	DC-9	47432				JA301J	737NG	35330	JA612J	B767	33848
I-RIZC	DC-9	47435	Japan			JA301K	B737	27435	JA613A	B767	33507
I-RIZF	DC-9	47519				JA302K	737NG	35331	JA613J	B767	33849
I-RIZG	DC-9	47225	JA001D	MD90	53555	JA302K	B737	28990	JA614A	B767	33508
I-RIZH	DC-9	47128	JA002D	MD90	53556	JA303J	737NG	35332	JA614J	B767	33851
I-RIZJ	DC-9	47434	JA003D	MD90	53557	JA303K	B737	28991	JA615A	B767	33850
I-RIZK	DC-9	47436	JA004D	MD90	53558	JA304J	737NG	35333	JA615J	B767	35877
I-RIZL	DC-9	47437	JA005D	MD90	53559	JA304K	B737	28992	JA616A	B767	35876
I-RIZN	DC-9	47653	JA006D	MD90	53560	JA305J	737NG	35334	JA616J	B767	35813
I-RIZP	DC-9	47438	JA007D	B777	27639	JA305K	B737	28993	JA617J	B767	35814
I-RIZQ	DC-9	47518	(JA007D)	MD80	53561	JA306J	737NG	35335	JA618J	B767	35815
I-RIZR	DC-9	47544	JA008D	B777	27640	JA306K	B737	29794	JA631J	B767	35816
I-RIZS	DC-9	47553	JA009D	B777	27641	JA307J	737NG	35336	JA632J	B767	35811
I-RIZT	DC-9	47591	JA010D	B777	27642	JA307K	B737	29795	JA633J	B767	35818
I-RIZU	DC-9	47433	JA011D	A300	783	JA308J	737NG	35337	JA701A	B777	27938
I-RIZV	DC-9	47533	JA012D	A300	797	JA309J	737NG	35338	JA701J	B777	32889
I-RIZW	DC-9	47575	JA014D	A300	836	JA310J	737NG	35339	JA702A	B777	27033
I-RIZX	DC-9	47237	JA015D	A300	837	JA311J	737NG	35340	JA702J	B777	32890

JA703A	B777	27034	JA8006	DC-8	45626	JA8087	B747	26346	(JA8164)	B747	23068
JA703J	B777	32891	JA8007	DC-8	45647	JA8088	B747	26341	JA8164	B747	23150
JA704A	B777	27035	JA8008	DC-8	45420	JA8089	B747	26342	JA8165	B747	21743
JA704J	B777	32892	JA8009	DC-8	45662	JA8090	B747	26347	JA8166	B747	23151
JA705A	B777	29029	JA8010	DC-8	45651	JA8091	B747	24730	JA8167	B747	23138
JA705J	B777	32893	JA8011	DC-8	45664	JA8092	B747	24731	JA8168	B747	23139
JA706A	B777	27036	JA8012	DC-8	45680	JA8094	B747	24801	JA8169	B747	23389
JA706J	B777	33394	JA8013	DC-8	45681	JA8095	B747	24833	JA8170	B747	23390
JA707A	B777	27037	JA8014	DC-8	45678	JA8096	B747	24920	JA8171	B747	23391
JA707J	B777	32894	JA8015	DC-8	45763	JA8097	B747	25135	JA8172	B747	23350
JA708A	B777	28277	JA8016	DC-8	45764	JA8098	B747	25207	JA8173	B747	23482
JA708J	B777	32895	JA8017	DC-8	45854	JA8099	B747	25292	JA8174	B747	23501
JA709A	B777	28278	JA8018	DC-8	45882	JA8101	B747	19725	JA8175	B747	23502
JA709J	B777	32896	JA8019	DC-8	45916	JA8102	B747	19726	JA8176	B747	23637
JA710A	B777	28279	JA8020	MD90	53360	JA8103	B747	19727	JA8177	B747	23638
JA710J	B777	33395	JA8021	CV880	22-7-5-57	JA8104	B747	19823	JA8178	B747	23639
JA711A	B777	33406	JA8022	CV880	22-7-6-58	JA8105	B747	19824	JA8179	B747	23640
JA711J	B777	33396	JA8023	CV880	22-7-7-59	JA8106	B747	19825	JA8180	B747	23641
JA712A	B777	33407	JA8024	CV880	22-7-8-60	JA8107	B747	20332	JA8181	B747	23698
JA713A	B777	32647	JA8025	CV880	22-7-9-61	JA8108	B747	20333	JA8182	B747	23813
JA714A	B777	28276	JA8026	CV880	22-00-46M	JA8109	B747	20503	JA8183	B747	23967
JA715A	B777	32646	JA8027	CV880	22-00-48M	JA8110	B747	20504	JA8184	B747	23968
JA716A	B777	33414	JA8028	CV880	22-00-49M	JA8111	B747	20505	JA8185	B747	23969
JA717A	B777	33415	JA8029	MD90	53361	JA8112	B747	20528	JA8186	B747	24018
JA731A	B777	28281	JA8030	CV880	22-00-45M	JA8113	B747	20529	JA8187	B747	24019
JA731J	B777	32430	JA8031	DC-8	45953	JA8114	B747	20530	JA8188	B747	23919
JA732A	B777	27038	JA8032	DC-8	45954	JA8115	B747	20531	JA8189	B747	24156
JA732J	B777	32431	JA8033	DC-8	45955	JA8116	B747	20532	JA8190	B747	24399
JA733A	B777	32648	JA8034	DC-8	45956	JA8117	B747	20781	JA8191	B747	24576
JA733J	B777	32432	JA8035	DC-8	46023	JA8118	B747	20782	JA8192	B747	22579
JA734A	B777	32649	JA8036	DC-8	46022	JA8119	B747	20783	JA8193	B747	21940
JA734J	B777	32433	JA8037	DC-8	46024	JA811J	B747	22989	JA8194	B747	25171
JA735A	B777	34892	JA8038	DC-8	46031	JA8120	B747	20784	JA8195	B737	27433
JA735J	B777	32434	JA8039	DC-8	46032	JA8121	B747	20923	JA8196	B737	27966
JA736A	B777	34893	JA8040	DC-8	46057	JA8122	B747	20924	JA8197	B777	27027
JA736J	B777	32435	JA8041	DC-8	46099	JA8123	B747	21034	JA8198	B777	27028
JA737A	B737	29000	JA8042	DC-8	46127	(JA8124)	B747	21030	JA8199	B777	27029
JA737B	B737	29001	JA8043	DC-8	46128	JA8124	B747	21032	JA821J	B787	34841
JA737C	B737	27086	JA8044	DC-8	46139	JA8125	B747	21030	JA822J	B787	34842
JA737D	B737	27168	JA8045	DC-8	46157	(JA8125)	B747	21032	JA8231	B767	23212
JA737E	B737	26069	JA8046	DC-8	46158	JA8126	B747	21033	JA8232	B767	23213
JA737F	B737	28492	JA8047	DC-8	46159	JA8127	B747	21031	JA8233	B767	23214
JA737H	737NG	34247	JA8048	DC-8	46160	JA8128	B747	21029	JA8234	B767	23216
JA737J	B777	36126	JA8049	DC-8	45887	JA8129	B747	21678	JA8235	B767	23217
JA737K	737NG	34249	JA8050	DC-8	45848	JA812J	B747	23067	JA8236	B767	23215
JA737L	737NG	32694	JA8051	DC-8	46152	JA8130	B747	21679	JA8237	A300	256
JA737M	737NG	32683	JA8052	DC-8	46153	JA8131	B747	21680	JA8238	B767	23140
JA737N	737NG	36845	JA8053	DC-8	46161	JA8132	B747	21681	JA8239	B767	23141
JA737P	737NG	29681	JA8054	DC-8	46148	JA8133	B747	21604	JA823J	B787	34846
JA737V	B737	29201	JA8055	DC-8	46154	JA8134	B747	21605	JA8240	B767	23142
JA737W	B737	29202	JA8056	DC-8	46162	JA8135	B747	21606	JA8241	B767	23143
JA738J	B777	32436	JA8057	DC-8	45982	JA813G	B747	21922	JA8242	B767	23144
JA739J	B777	32437	(JA8057)	DC-8	46164	JA8137	B747	21923	JA8243	B767	23145
JA751A	B777	28272	JA8058	DC-8	45942	JA8138	B747	21924	JA8244	B767	23146
JA751J	B777	27654	JA8059	DC-8	45943	JA8139	B747	21925	JA8245	B767	23147
JA752A	B777	28274	JA8060	DC-8	45888	JA813J	B747	23068	JA824J	B787	34847
JA752J	B777	27655	JA8061	DC-8	45889	JA8140	B747	22064	JA8250	B737	23481
JA753A	B777	28273	JA8062	MD90	53352	JA8141	B747	22065	JA8251	B767	23431
JA754A	B777	27939	JA8063	MD90	53353	JA8142	B747	22066	JA8252	B767	23432
JA756A	B777	27039	JA8064	MD90	53354	JA8143	B747	22067	JA8253	B767	23645
JA757A	B777	27040	JA8065	MD90	53355	JA8144	B747	22063	JA8254	B767	23433
JA767A	B767	27616	JA8066	MD90	53356	JA8145	B747	22291	JA8255	B767	23434
JA767B	B767	27617	JA8067	DC-8	45992	JA8146	B747	22292	JA8256	B767	23756
JA767C	B767	29390	JA8068	DC-8	45983	JA8147	B747	22293	JA8257	B767	23757
JA767D	B767	30847	JA8069	MD90	53357	JA8148	B747	22294	JA8258	B767	23758
JA767E	B767	27427	JA8070	MD90	53358	JA8149	B747	22478	JA8259	B767	23759
JA767F	B767	30840	JA8071	B747	24423	JA8150	B747	22479	JA825J	B787	34849
JA771J	B777	27656	JA8072	B747	24424	JA8151	B747	22477	JA8260	MD80	49461
JA772J	B777	27657	JA8073	B747	24425	JA8152	B747	22594	JA8261	MD80	49462
JA773J	B777	27653	JA8074	B747	24426	JA8153	B747	22595	JA8262	MD80	49463
JA777A	B777	32650	JA8075	B747	24427	JA8154	B747	22745	JA8263	A300	151
JA778A	B777	32651	JA8076	B747	24777	JA8155	B747	22746	JA8264	B767	23965
JA779A	B777	34894	JA8077	B747	24784	JA8156	B747	22709	JA8265	B767	23961
JA780A	B777	34895	JA8078	B747	24870	JA8157	B747	22710	JA8266	B767	23966
JA781A	B777	27041	JA8079	B747	24885	JA8158	B747	22711	JA8267	B767	23962
JA782A	B777	33416	JA8080	B747	24886	JA8159	B747	22712	JA8268	B767	23963
JA783A	B777	27940	JA8081	B747	25064	JA8160	B747	21744	JA8269	B767	23964
JA8001	DC-8	45418	JA8082	B747	25212	(JA8160)	B747	22989	JA826J	B787	34850
JA8002	DC-8	45419	JA8083	B747	25213	JA8161	B747	22990	JA8271	B767	24002
JA8003	DC-8	45420	JA8084	B747	25214	JA8162	B747	22991	JA8272	B767	24003
JA8004	MD90	53359	JA8085	B747	25260	(JA8163)	B747	23067	JA8273	B767	24004
JA8005	DC-8	45421	JA8086	B747	25308	JA8163	B747	23149	JA8274	B767	24005

Reg	Type	S/N	Reg	Type	S/N	Reg	Type	S/N	Reg	Type	S/N
JA8275	B767	24006	JA8350	B727	20876	JA8442	DC-9	47762	JA852J	B787	34832
JA8276	A300	169	JA8351	B727	20877	JA8443	B737	21476	JA8530	DC-10	46920
JA8277	A300	174	JA8352	B727	20878	JA8444	B737	21477	JA8531	DC-10	46923
JA8278	MD80	49464	JA8353	B727	21455	JA8445	B737	21478	JA8532	DC-10	46660
JA8279	MD80	49465	JA8354	B727	21456	JA8448	DC-9	47767	JA8533	DC-10	46661
JA827J	B787	34853	JA8355	B727	21474	JA8449	DC-9	47768	JA8534	DC-10	46913
JA8280	MD80	49466	JA8356	B767	25136	JA8450	DC-9	47780	JA8535	DC-10	46662
JA8281	MD80	49467	JA8357	B767	25293	JA8451	DC-9	47781	JA8536	DC-10	46966
JA8282	B737	24103	JA8358	B767	25616	JA8452	B737	21766	JA8537	DC-10	46967
JA8285	B767	24350	JA8359	B767	25617	JA8453	B737	21767	JA8538	DC-10	46974
JA8286	B767	24400	JA8360	B767	25055	JA8454	B737	21768	JA8539	DC-10	47822
JA8287	B767	24351	JA8362	B767	24632	JA8455	B737	21769	JA853J	B787	34833
JA8288	B767	24415	JA8363	B767	24756	JA8456	B737	21770	JA8540	DC-10	47823
JA8289	B767	24416	JA8364	B767	24782	JA8457	B737	21771	JA8541	DC-10	47824
JA828J	B787	34854	JA8365	B767	24783	JA8458	MD80	48029	JA8542	DC-10	47825
JA8290	B767	24417	JA8366	B737	23469	JA8459	MD80	48030	JA8543	DC-10	47826
JA8291	B767	24755	JA8368	B767	24880	JA8460	MD80	48031	JA8544	DC-10	47852
JA8292	A300	110	JA8369	A300	239	JA8461	MD80	48032	JA8545	DC-10	47853
JA8293	A300	194	JA8370	MD80	53039	JA8462	MD80	48033	JA8546	DC-10	47855
JA8294	MD80	49820	JA8371	MD80	53040	JA8464	A300	082	JA8547	DC-10	47856
JA8295	MD80	49821	JA8372	MD80	53041	JA8465	A300	089	JA8548	DC-10	47857
JA8296	MD80	49907	JA8373	MD80	53042	JA8466	A300	090	JA8549	DC-10	48301
JA8297	MD80	49908	JA8374	MD80	53043	JA8467	B737	22367	JA854J	B787	34834
JA8299	B767	24498	JA8375	A300	602	JA8468	MD80	48070	JA8550	DC-10	48315
JA829J	B787	34855	JA8376	A300	617	JA8469	MD80	48071	JA8551	DC-10	48316
JA8300	A320	0549	JA8377	A300	621	JA8470	MD80	48072	JA8552	MD80	53297
JA8301	B727	18821	JA8381	A320	0138	JA8471	A300	160	JA8553	MD80	53298
JA8302	B727	18822	JA8382	A320	0139	JA8472	A300	163	JA8554	MD80	53299
JA8303	B727	18823	JA8383	A320	0148	JA8473	A300	176	JA8555	MD80	53300
JA8304	A320	0531	JA8384	A320	0151	JA8475	B737	22736	JA8556	MD80	53301
JA8305	B727	18919	JA8385	A320	0167	JA8476	A300	209	JA8557	MD80	53302
JA8306	B727	18920	JA8386	A320	0170	JA8477	A300	244	JA8558	A300	637
JA8307	B727	18874	JA8387	A320	0196	JA8478	A300	253	JA8559	A300	641
JA8308	B727	18875	JA8388	A320	0212	JA8479	B767	22785	JA855A	B777	28275
JA8309	B727	18876	JA8389	A320	0219	JA8480	B767	22786	JA855J	B787	34835
JA830J	B787	34856	JA8390	A320	0245	JA8481	B767	22787	JA8560	A300	178
JA8310	B727	18877	JA8391	A320	0300	JA8482	B767	22788	JA8561	A300	670
JA8311	B727	18878	JA8392	A320	0328	JA8483	B767	22789	JA8562	A300	679
JA8312	B727	18879	JA8393	A320	0365	JA8484	B767	22790	JA8563	A300	683
JA8313	A320	0534	JA8394	A320	0383	JA8485	B767	23016	JA8564	A300	703
JA8314	B727	19138	JA8395	A320	0413	JA8486	B767	23017	JA8565	A300	711
JA8315	B727	19139	JA8396	A320	0482	JA8487	B767	23018	JA8566	A300	730
JA8316	B727	18951	JA8397	B767	27311	JA8488	B767	23019	JA8567	B767	25656
JA8317	B727	18952	JA8398	B767	27312	JA8489	B767	23020	JA8568	B767	25657
JA8318	B727	19279	JA8399	B767	27313	JA8490	B767	23021	JA8569	B767	27050
JA8319	B727	19280	JA8400	A320	0554	JA8491	B767	23022	JA856J	B787	34836
JA831J	B787	34857	JA8401	B737	20226	JA8492	B737	23117	JA8573	A300	737
JA8320	B727	19281	JA8402	B737	20227	JA8496	MD80	49280	JA8574	A300	740
JA8321	B727	19557	JA8403	B737	20276	JA8497	MD80	49281	JA8577	B737	23467
JA8322	B767	25618	JA8404	B737	27381	JA8498	MD80	49282	JA8578	B767	25658
JA8323	B767	25654	JA8405	B737	20277	JA8499	MD80	49283	JA8579	B767	25659
JA8324	B767	25655	JA8406	B737	20413	JA8500	B737	27431	JA857J	B787	34837
JA8325	B727	19282	JA8407	B737	20414	JA8501	L1011	193P-1053	JA8580	MD11	48571
JA8326	B727	19283	JA8408	B737	20449	JA8502	L1011	193P-1061	JA8581	MD11	48572
JA8327	B727	20078	JA8409	B737	20450	JA8503	L1011	193P-1062	JA8582	MD11	48573
JA8328	B727	20435	JA8410	B737	20451	JA8504	B737	27432	JA8583	MD11	48574
JA8329	B727	20436	JA8411	B737	20452	JA8505	L1011	193P 1060	JA8584	MD11	48575
JA832J	B787	34859	JA8412	B737	20506	JA8506	L1011	193P-1070	JA8585	MD11	48576
JA8330	B727	20468	JA8413	B737	20507	JA8507	L1011	193P-1082	JA8586	MD11	48577
JA8331	B727	20469	JA8414	B737	20508	JA8508	L1011	193P-1099	JA8587	MD11	48578
JA8332	B727	20466	JA8415	B737	20561	JA8509	L1011	193P-1100	JA8588	MD11	48579
JA8333	B727	20467	JA8416	B737	20562	JA8510	L1011	193P-1103	JA8589	MD11	48774
JA8334	B727	20509	JA8417	B737	20563	JA8511	L1011	193P-1105	JA858J	B787	34838
JA8335	B727	20285	(JA8419)	B737	24103	JA8512	L1011	193P-1112	JA8595	B737	28461
(JA8335)	B727	20510	JA8419	B737	27430	JA8513	L1011	193P-1113	JA8596	B737	28462
JA8336	B727	20286	JA8423	DC-9	47603	JA8514	L1011	193P-1117	JA8597	B737	27660
JA8337	B727	20510	JA8424	DC-9	47604	JA8515	L1011	193P-1119	JA859J	B787	34839
JA8338	B727	20568	JA8425	DC-9	47605	JA8516	L1011	193P-1127	JA8609	A320	0501
JA8339	B727	20569	JA8426	DC-9	47606	JA8517	L1011	193P-1128	JA860J	B787	34840
JA833J	B787	34860	JA8427	DC-9	47608	JA8518	L1011	193P-1129	JA861J	B787	34843
JA8340	B727	20570	JA8428	DC-9	47612	JA8519	L1011	193P-1134	JA862J	B787	34844
JA8341	B727	20571	JA8429	DC-9	47613	JA851J	B787	34831	JA863J	B787	34845
JA8342	B767	27445	JA8430	DC-9	47614	JA8520	L1011	193P-1154	JA864J	B787	34848
JA8343	B727	20572	JA8432	DC-9	47615	JA8521	L1011	193P-1155	JA8654	A320	0507
JA8343	B727	20573	JA8433	DC-9	47616	JA8522	L1011	193P-1156	JA8657	A300	753
JA8344	B727	20573	JA8434	DC-9	47617	JA8523	B737	26603	JA8659	A300	770
JA8345	B727	20724	JA8435	DC-9	47618	JA8524	B737	26604	JA865J	B787	34851
JA8346	B727	20725	JA8436	DC-9	47619	JA8525	B737	26605	JA8664	B767	27339
JA8347	B727	20726	JA8437	DC-9	47620	JA8526	B737	26606	JA8669	B767	27444
JA8348	B727	20727	JA8439	DC-9	47759	JA8527	A300	724	JA866J	B787	34852
JA8349	B727	20728	JA8440	DC-9	47760	JA8528	B737	23464	JA8670	B767	25660
			JA8441	DC-9	47761	JA8529	A300	729	JA8674	B767	25661

Reg	Type	c/n
JA8677	B767	25662
JA867J	B787	34858
JA8901	B747	26343
JA8902	B747	26344
JA8903	B747	26345
JA8904	B747	26348
JA8905	B747	26349
JA8906	B747	26350
JA8907	B747	26351
JA8908	B747	26352
JA8909	B747	26353
JA8910	B747	26354
JA8911	B747	26355
JA8912	B747	27099
JA8913	B747	26359
(JA8913)	B747	27827
JA8914	B747	26360
(JA8914)	B747	27828
JA8915	B747	26361
JA8916	B747	26362
JA8917	B747	29899
JA8918	B747	27650
JA8919	B747	27100
JA8920	B747	27648
JA8921	B747	27645
JA8922	B747	27646
JA8930	B737	27102
JA8931	B737	25247
JA8932	B737	25248
JA8933	B737	25226
JA8934	B737	27830
JA8937	B747	22477
JA8938	B737	29485
JA8939	B737	29486
JA8940	B737	29487
JA8941	B777	28393
JA8942	B777	28394
JA8943	B777	28395
JA8944	B777	28396
JA8945	B777	28397
JA8946	A320	0669
JA8947	A320	0685
JA8953	B737	24129
JA8954	B737	24130
JA8955	B747	25639
JA8956	B747	25640
JA8957	B747	25641
JA8958	B747	25641
JA8959	B747	25646
JA8960	B747	25643
JA0961	B747	25644
JA8962	B747	25645
JA8963	B747	25647
JA8964	B747	27163
JA8965	B747	27436
JA8966	B747	27442
JA8967	B777	27030
JA8968	B777	27031
JA8969	B777	27032
JA8970	B767	25619
JA8971	B767	27942
JA8975	B767	27658
JA8976	B767	27659
JA8977	B777	27636
JA8978	B777	27637
JA8979	B777	27638
JA8980	B767	28837
JA8981	B777	27364
JA8982	B777	27365
JA8983	B777	27366
JA8984	B777	27651
JA8985	B777	27652
JA8986	B767	28838
JA8987	B767	28553
JA8988	B767	29863
JA8991	B737	27916
JA8992	B737	27917
JA8993	B737	28087
JA8994	B737	28097
JA8995	B737	28831
JA8996	B737	28832
JA8997	A320	0658
JA8998	B737	28994
JA8999	B737	29864
JA98AD	B767	27476
JQ8501	C-1	8501

Mongolia
(see also MT-)

Reg	Type	c/n
JU-1036	B727	20572
JU-1037	B727	20573
JU-1054	B727	20435
(JU-1069)	A310	526
JU-8428	F.100	11428

Jordan
(see also 4YB-)

Reg	Type	c/n
(JY-)	B727	21483
JY-	B737	23065
JY-	B787	35214
JY-	B787	35312
JY-	E190	19000107
JY-ABH	A340	009
JY-ACS	SE210	199
JY-ACT	SE210	200
JY-ADG	SE210	236
JY-ADO	B707	20494
JY-ADP	B707	20495
JY-ADR	B727	20885
JY-ADS	B707	18250
JY-ADT	B707	18251
JY-ADU	B727	20886
JY-ADV	B727	21021
JY-AEB	B707	18948
JY-AEC	B707	18949
JY-AED	B707	18716
JY-AEE	B707	18767
JY-AES	B707	20017
JY-AFA	B747	21251
JY-AFB	B747	21252
JY-AFD	B707	20283
JY-AFR	B707	19706
JY-AFS	B747	22579
JY-AFT	B727	22268
JY-AFU	B727	22269
JY-AFV	B727	22270
JY-AFW	B727	22271
JY-AGA	L1011	293A-1217
JY-AGB	L1011	293A-1219
JY-AGC	L1011	293A-1220
JY-AGD	L1011	293A-1229
JY-AGE	L1011	293A-1238
JY-AGF	L1011	193J-1196
JY-AGH	L1011	293A-1249
JY-AGI	L1011	193H-1246
JY-AGJ	L1011	293A-1248
JY-AGK	A310	573
JY-AGL	A310	661
JY-AGM	A310	491
JY-AGN	A310	531
JY-AGP	A310	416
JY-AGS	A310	598
JY-AGT	A310	663
JY-AGU	A310	295
JY-AGV	A310	306
JY-AHS	B727	18934
JY-AIA	A340	038
JY-AIB	A340	043
JY-AIC	A340	014
JY-AID	A340	022
JY-AJK	B707	18948
JY-AJL	B707	19353
JY-AJM	B707	19590
JY-AJN	B707	20720
JY-AJO	B707	20723
JY-AUA	B727	22670
JY-AUB	B747	23622
JY-AYA	A320	0087
JY-AYB	A320	0088
JY-AYD	A320	2598
JY-AYF	A320	2692
JY-AYG	A321	2730
JY-AYH	A321	2793
JY-AYI	A320	0569
JY-CAB	B707	18716
JY-CAC	B707	20890
JY-CAD	A310	421
(JY-CAE)	A310	422
(JY-CAS)	A320	0569
JY-EMA	E190	19000107
JY-EME	E190	19000050
JY-EMF	E190	19000067
JY-EMG	E190	19000088
JY-GAX	A300	601
JY-GAZ	A300	616
JY-HKJ	L1011	193H-1247
JY-HMH	B727	18934
JY-HNH	B727	22362
JY-HS1	B727	20228
JY-HS2	B727	21010
JY-JA1	B737	26438
JY-JAA	B707	20022
JY-JAB	B737	23630
JY-JAD	B737	24662
JY-JAE	B727	21846
JY-JAF	B737	23130
JY-JAH	A310	481
JY-JAR	A320	0234
JY-JAV	A310	357
JY-JIA	IL76	0023437093
JY-JIB	IL76	?
JY-JIB	IL76	1023413438
JY-JOE	L1011	293B-1243
JY-JRF	B767	22526
JY-SGI	L1011	193C-1234

Djibouti

Reg	Type	c/n
J2-KAD	B727	19135
J2-KAF	B727	20893
J2-KBA	B727	19394
J2-KBG	B727	20470
J2-KBH	B727	20411
J2-KCB	B747	21352
J2-KCC	B737	20576
J2-KCD	B727	21054
J2-KCE	B737	21360
J2-KCG	DC-10	48258
J2-KCM	B727	22274
J2-KCN	B767	22526
J2-KCV	B747	21938
J2-KFC	B727	21090
J2-LBB	B747	21352
J2-SHB	B737	22354
J2-SHF	B747	21300
J2-SRH	B737	21280
J2-SRS	B737	21361

St. Lucia

Reg	Type	c/n
J6-SLF	B707	18689
J6-SLR	B707	18716

St. Vincent & Grenadines

Reg	Type	c/n
J8-VBA	146	E1068
J8-VBB	146	E1071
J8-VBC	146	E1035

Norway

Reg	Type	c/n
LN-AEO	B747	20121
(LN-AEQ)	B737	23923
LN-AET	B747	20120
LN-ALN	DC-10	46554
LN-BRA	B737	24270
LN-BRB	B737	24271
LN-BRC	B737	24650
LN-BRD	B737	24651
LN-BRE	B737	24643
LN-BRF	B737	24652
LN-BRG	B737	24272
LN-BRH	B737	24828
LN-BRI	B737	24644
LN-BRJ	B737	24273
LN-BRK	B737	24274
LN-BRL	B737	22277
LN-BRM	B737	24645
LN-BRN	B737	24646
LN-BRO	B737	24647
LN-BRP	B737	25303
LN-BRQ	B737	25348
LN-BRR	B737	24648
LN-BRS	B737	24649
LN-BRT	B737	25789
LN-BRU	B737	25790
LN-BRV	B737	25791
LN-BRW	B737	25792
LN-BRX	B737	25797
LN-BRY	B737	27155
LN-BRZ	B737	27153
(LN-BSC)	SE210	169
LN-BSE	SE210	259
(LN-BUA)	B737	25794
LN-BUA	B737	26297
LN-BUB	B737	24703
LN-BUC	B737	26304
LN-BUD	B737	25794
LN-BUE	B737	27627
LN-BUF	B737	25795
LN-BUG	B737	27631
LN-HLB	F.28	11031
LN-KKB	B737	27457
LN-KKC	B737	25615
LN-KKD	B737	29339
LN-KKE	B737	27285
LN-KKF	B737	24326
LN-KKG	B737	24327
LN-KKH	B737	24328
LN-KKI	B737	24329
LN-KKJ	B737	28564
LN-KKL	B737	28671
LN-KKM	B737	24676
(LN-KKM)	B737	25790
LN-KKN	B737	24910
LN-KKO	B737	24909
LN-KKP	B737	25040
LN-KKQ	B737	28658
LN-KKR	B737	24256
LN-KK3	B737	24094
(LN-KKT)	B737	25614
LN-KKT	B737	27336
LN-KKU	B737	27337
LN-KKV	B737	25613
LN-KKW	B737	24213
LN-KKX	B737	29072
LN-KKY	B737	29245
LN-KKZ	B737	27458
LN-KLH	SE210	3
LN-KLI	SE210	7
(LN-KLJ)	SE210	24
LN-KLN	SE210	209
LN-KLP	SE210	24
LN-KLR	SE210	30
(LN-LMA)	CV990	30-10-6
LN-MOA	DC-8	45385
LN-MOC	DC-8	46150
LN-MOF	DC-8	46097
LN-MOG	DC-8	46102
LN-MOH	DC-8	45767
LN-MOO	DC-8	45822
LN-MOT	DC-8	45388
LN-MOU	DC-8	45923
LN-MOW	DC-8	46131
LN-MOY	DC-8	46054
LN-MTC	B737	20453
LN-MTD	B737	20454
LN-NOR	B737	23827
LN-NOS	B737	23830
LN-NPB	B737	21763

Reg	Type	c/n
LN-PIP	DC-8	45256
LN-RCA	A300	079
LN-RCB	B767	24357
LN-RCC	B767	24728
(LN-RCD)	B767	24729
LN-RCD	B767	24847
LN-RCE	B767	24846
LN-RCF	B767	24849
LN-RCG	B767	24475
LN-RCH	B767	24318
LN-RCI	B767	24476
LN-RCK	B767	24729
LN-RCL	B767	25365
LN-RCM	B767	26544
LN-RCN	737NG	28318
LN-RCO	737NG	28319
LN-RCP	737NG	28320
LN-RCR	737NG	28321
LN-RCS	737NG	30193
LN-RCT	737NG	30189
LN-RCU	737NG	30190
LN-RCW	737NG	28308
LN-RCX	737NG	30196
LN-RCY	737NG	28324
LN-RCZ	737NG	30197
(LN-RDY)	B767	24848
LN-REF	A330	568
LN-RKA	DC-10	46868
LN-RKB	DC-10	46871
LN-RKC	DC-10	47814
LN-RKD	DC-10	46961
LN-RKF	A340	413
(LN-RKG)	A321	1817
LN-RKG	A340	424
LN-RKH	A330	497
LN-RKI	A321	1817
LN-RKK	A319	3231
LN-RKK	A321	1848
(LN-RKL)	A319	3292
LN-RLA	DC-9	47599
LN-RLB	DC-9	47497
LN-RLC	DC-9	47179
LN-RLD	DC-9	47396
LN-RLE	MD80	49382
LN-RLF	MD80	49383
LN-RLG	MD80	49423
LN-RLH	DC-9	47748
(LN-RLI)	MD80	49554
LN-RLJ	DC-9	47287
LN-RLK	DC-9	47116
LN-RLL	DC-9	47301
LN-RLM	DC-9	47304
LN-RLN	DC-9	47630
LN-RLO	DC-9	47307
LN-RLP	DC-9	47778
LN-RLR	DC-9	47396
LN-RLR	MD80	49437
LN-RLS	DC-9	47111
LN-RLS	DC-9	47623
LN-RLT	DC-9	47626
LN-RLU	DC-9	47511
(LN-RLV)	MD80	49557
LN-RLW	DC-9	47414
LN-RLX	DC-9	47513
LN-RLZ	DC-9	47634
LN-RMA	MD80	49554
LN-RMB	MD80	49557
LN-RMC	DC-9	47655
LN-RMD	MD80	49555
LN-RMF	MD80	49556
LN-RMG	MD80	49611
LN-RMH	MD80	49612
LN-RMJ	MD80	49912
LN-RMK	MD80	49610
LN-RML	MD80	53002
LN-RMM	MD80	53005
LN-RMN	MD80	53295
LN-RMO	MD80	53315
LN-RMP	MD80	53337
LN-RMR	MD80	53365
LN-RMS	MD80	53368
LN-RMT	MD80	53001
LN-RMU	MD80	53340
LN-RMX	MD80	49585
LN-RMY	MD80	49586
LN-RNA	B747	21381
(LN-RNB)	B747	22496
LN-RNN	737NG	28315
LN-RNO	737NG	28316
LN-ROA	MD90	53459
LN-ROB	MD90	53462
LN-ROM	MD80	53008
LN-RON	MD80	53347
LN-ROO	MD80	53366
LN-ROP	MD80	49384
LN-ROR	MD80	49385
LN-ROS	MD80	49421
LN-ROT	MD80	49422
LN-ROU	MD80	49424
LN-ROW	MD80	49438
LN-ROX	MD80	49603
LN-ROY	MD80	49615
LN-ROZ	MD80	49608
LN-RPA	737NG	28290
LN-RPB	737NG	28294
(LN-RPC)	737NG	28300
LN-RPC	737NG	28322
(LN-RPD)	737NG	28301
LN-RPD	737NG	28323
LN-RPE	737NG	28306
LN-RPF	737NG	28307
LN-RPG	737NG	28310
LN-RPH	737NG	28605
(LN-RPJ)	737NG	28315
LN-RPJ	737NG	30192
(LN-RPK)	737NG	28316
LN-RPK	737NG	28317
(LN-RPL)	737NG	28321
(LN-RPL)	737NG	28322
LN-RPL	737NG	30469
(LN-RPM)	737NG	28323
(LN-RPM)	737NG	30193
LN-RPM	737NG	30195
(LN-RPN)	737NG	30469
LN-RPN	737NG	30470
(LN-RPO)	737NG	30195
(LN-RPO)	737NG	30196
LN-RPO	737NG	30467
LN-RPP	737NG	30194
LN-RPR	737NG	30468
LN-RPS	737NG	28298
LN-RPT	737NG	28299
LN-RPU	737NG	28312
LN-RPW	737NG	28289
LN-RPX	737NG	28291
LN-RPY	737NG	28292
LN-RPZ	737NG	28293
LN-RRA	737NG	30471
LN-RRB	737NG	32276
LN-RRK	737NG	32278
LN-RRL	737NG	28328
LN-RRM	737NG	28314
LN-RRN	737NG	30191
LN-RRO	737NG	28288
LN-RRP	737NG	28311
LN-RRR	737NG	28309
LN-RRS	737NG	28325
LN-RRT	737NG	28326
LN-RRU	737NG	28327
LN-RRW	737NG	32277
LN-RRX	737NG	28296
LN-RRY	737NG	28297
LN-RRZ	737NG	28295
(LN-RTB)	DC-9	47111
(LN-SUA)	737NG	28211
LN-SUA	B737	20458
LN-SUA	B737	23464
(LN-SUB)	737NG	28099
LN-SUB	B737	21765
(LN-SUC)	737NG	29090
LN-SUC	F.28	11009
LN-SUD	B737	20711
LN-SUG	B737	20412
LN-SUH	B737	21219
LN-SUI	B737	21184
LN-SUJ	B737	23468
LN-SUK	B737	21729
LN-SUM	B737	21445
LN-SUM	F.28	11003
LN-SUM	F.28	11032
LN-SUN	F.28	11012
LN-SUO	F.28	11013
LN-SUP	B737	19409
LN-SUQ	B737	23467
(LN-SUR)	B737	23469
LN-SUS	B737	19408
LN-SUT	B737	22022
LN-SUU	B737	23465
LN-SUV	B737	23469
LN-SUV	B767	23057
LN-SUW	B767	23058
LN-SUX	F.28	11010
LN-SUY	F.28	11011
LN-SUZ	B737	23466
(LN-TEC)	SE210	263
LN-TUA	737NG	28211
LN-TUB	737NG	29089
LN-TUC	737NG	29090
LN-TUD	737NG	28217
LN-TUE	737NG	29091
LN-TUF	737NG	28222
LN-TUG	737NG	29092
LN-TUH	737NG	29093
LN-TUI	737NG	29094
LN-TUJ	737NG	29095
LN-TUK	737NG	29096
LN-TUL	737NG	29097
LN-TUM	737NG	29098
LN-TUU	B707	18041
LN-TUV	B707	18043
LN-TUW	B707	18158
LN-TUX	B737	25165

Argentina

Reg	Type	c/n
LV-AGC	B737	21005
LV-AHN	COMET	6408
LV-AHO	COMET	6410
LV-AHP	COMET	6411
LV-AHR	COMET	6430
LV-AHS	COMET	6432
LV-AHU	COMET	6434
LV-AHV	B737	21017
LV-AIB	COMET	6460
LV-AIV	A310	640
LV-AIX	B767	26205
LV-ALJ	B747	25422
LV-ARF	MD80	49252
LV-AXF	B747	24895
LV-AYD	MD80	53015
LV-AYE	B737	26456
LV-AYI	B737	25234
LV-AZF	B747	23048
LV-AZL	A310	686
LV-AZU	B737	25235
LV-BAR	B737	26450
LV-BAT	B737	27356
LV-BAX	B737	26448
LV-BAY	MD80	49284
LV-BBI	B737	22114
LV-BBM	B737	22135
LV-BBN	B737	26454
LV-BBO	B737	22139
LV-BBU	B747	24883
LV-BBW	B737	24897
LV-BBZ	B737	23811
LV-BCB	B737	22121
LV-BCD	B737	22122
LV-BDD	B737	24899
LV-BDE	MD80	49943
LV-BDO	MD80	49941
LV-BDV	B737	24900
LV-BEG	MD80	49630
LV-BEO	B737	25176
LV-BEP	MD80	49127
LV-BET	A320	1854
LV-BFD	B767	26265
LV-BFO	A320	1877
LV-BFU	B767	27615
(LV-BFV)	B767	24849
LV-BFY	A320	1858
LV-BGI	A320	1903
LV-BGV	MD80	49904
LV-BGZ	MD80	49906
LV-BHF	MD80	49508
LV-BHH	MD80	49741
LV-BHN	MD80	53190
LV-BIF	B737	23608
LV-BIH	B737	24786
LV-BIM	B737	25425
LV-BIX	B737	24788
LV-HGX	SE210	19
LV-HGY	SE210	127
LV-HGZ	SE210	149
LV-III	SE210	180
LV-ISA	B707	19238
LV-ISB	B707	19239
LV-ISC	B707	19240
LV-ISD	B707	19241
LV-IZR	1-11	BAC.122
LV-IZS	1-11	BAC.123
LV-JGP	B707	19962
LV-JGR	B707	19961
LV-JGX	1-11	BAC.117
LV-JGY	1-11	BAC.155
LV-JMW	B737	20403
LV-JMX	B737	20404
LV-JMY	B737	20405
LV-JMZ	B737	20406
LV-JND	B737	20407
LV-JNE	B737	20408
LV-JNR	1-11	BAC.192
LV-JNS	1-11	BAC.194
LV-JNT	1-11	BAC.196
LV-JNU	1-11	BAC.185
LV-JTD	B737	20523
LV-JTO	B737	20537
LV-LEB	B737	20768
LV-LGO	B707	20076
LV-LGP	B707	20077
LV-LHT	1-11	BAC.185
LV-LIU	B737	20964
LV-LIV	B737	20965
LV-LIW	B737	20966
LV-LOA	F.28	11085
LV-LOB	F.28	11086
LV-LOC	F.28	11083
LV-LOX	1-11	BAC.212
LV-LRG	B747	19896
LV-LRG	F.28	11046
LV-LTP	DC-8	45255
LV-LZD	R747	21189
LV-LZN	F.28	11048
LV-MCD	B727	21457
LV-MDB	B737	20836
LV-MEX	1-11	BAC.200
LV-MIM	B727	21688
LV-MIN	B727	21689
LV-MIO	B727	21690
LV-MLO	B747	21725
LV-MLP	B747	21726
LV-MLR	B747	21727
LV-MRZ	1-11	BAC.206
LV-MSG	B707	18591
LV-MZD	F.28	11127
LV-MZE	B707	19297
LV-MZM	1-11	BAC.187
LV-OAX	1-11	BAC.197
LV-OAY	1-11	BAC.227
LV-ODY	B727	21823
LV-OEP	B747	22297
LV-OHV	B747	21786
LV-OLN	B727	22603
LV-OLO	B727	22604
LV-OLP	B727	22605
LV-OLR	B727	22606
LV-OOZ	B747	22592

Reg	Type	S/N	Reg	Type	S/N	Reg	Type	S/N	Reg	Type	S/N
LV-OPA	B747	22593	LV-WMH	B757	26332	**LV-ZYI**	**B737**	**23010**	LX-LGX	B747	21133
LV-PBJ	SE210	180	LV-WNA	B737	22368	LV-ZYJ	B737	22744	**LX-LGX**	**E145**	**145147**
LV-PEW	1-11	BAC.187	LV-WNB	B737	22369	**LV-ZYN**	**B737**	**21794**	LX-LGY	B747	21263
LV-PFR	1-11	BAC.197	LV-WPA	B737	23065	LV-ZYV	B767	28206	LX-LGY	E145	145242
LV-PHT	B737	22278	LV-WPF	CRJ	7115	LV-ZYX	B737	20913	**LX-LGZ**	**E145**	**145258**
LV-PID	1-11	BAC.122	LV-WPY	MD80	48024	**LV-ZYY**	**B737**	**21799**	LX-LTM	B747	21132
LV-PIF	1-11	BAC.123	LV-WRO	B737	20521	LV-ZZA	B737	21219	(LX-LTM)	B747	21263
LV-PIG	737NG	28224	LV-WRZ	B737	20389	LV-ZZC	B737	21112	LX-MAM	1-11	BAC.259
LV-PIJ	B737	23349	LV-WSB	CRJ	7154	**LV-ZZD**	**B737**	**23011**	LX-MCV	B747	20106
LV-PIM	B737	23002	LV-WSH	B737	20282	**LV-ZZI**	**B737**	**23166**	**LX-MCV**	**B747**	**29729**
LV-PIP	B737	23504	LV-WSU	B737	21496	(LV-)	B737	20330	LX-MJM	B727	21853
LV-PIS	B737	23009	LV-WSY	B737	20562	(LV-)	B737	20331	LX-MMM	B727	21853
LV-PIU	B737	23503	LV-WSZ	B737	21192	(LV-)	B737	21645	LX-NCV	B747	20103
LV-PIV	B737	23003	LV-WSZ	DC-9	47140	(LV-)	B737	22088	LX-NCV	B747	20108
LV-PIX	B737	23793	LV-WTG	B737	21498				**LX-NCV**	**B747**	**29730**
LV-PJC	B737	23010	LV-WTH	DC-9	45839				LX-OCV	B747	21575
LV-PJH	MD80	49252	LV-WTS	B757	25131	Luxembourg			**LX-OCV**	**B747**	**29731**
LV-PJJ	MD80	49284	**LV-WTX**	**B737**	**20561**				LX-OOO	B737	21839
LV-PKA	1-11	BAC.155	LV-WTY	MD80	48011	LX-ACO	B747	21253	**LX-PCV**	**B747**	**29732**
LV-PKB	1-11	BAC.117	LV-WXB	CRJ	7175	LX-ACV	B747	21964	**LX-RCV**	**B747**	**30400**
LV-PLM	COMET	6408	LV-WXL	B707	19590	LX-ACV	DC-8	45989	LX-SAL	B747	20116
LV-PLO	COMET	6410	LV-WXT	CRJ	7041	LX-BCV	B747	22403	**LX-SCV**	**B747**	**29733**
LV-PLP	COMET	6411	LV-WYI	B737	21196	LX-BCV	DC-8	46002	(LX-TAM)	DC-8	46002
LV-PMD	B737	20282	LV-WYT	B747	20009	LX-BJV	B707	19212	LX-TAP	B747	22169
LV-PMI	B737	20561	LV-WZC	F.28	11017	LX-DCV	B747	20887	**LX-TCV**	**B747**	**30401**
LV-PMJ	MD80	48011	LV-WZU	CRJ	7160	LX-DCV	B747	21650	LX-TLA	DC-8	45960
LV-PMR	CRJ	7175	LV-YAB	DC-9	47313	LX-ECV	B747	21965	LX-TLB	DC-8	45925
LV-PMW	B737	21196	LV-YBS	B737	21193	LX-ECV	B747	22390	LX-TLC	DC-8	45920
LV-PNG	DC-9	47313	LV-YEB	B737	21733	LX-FAA	MD80	48051	LX-TLD	DC-10	47831
LV-PNI	B737	21193	LV-YGB	B737	22633	LX-FAB	MD80	48058	LX-TLE	DC-10	46949
LV-PNO	B737	21335	LV-YIB	B737	21335	LX-FCV	B707	18925	LX-TXA	A310	594
LV-PNP	DC-9	47614	LV-YLA	CRJ	7039	LX-FCV	B707	19212	**LX-UCV**	**B747**	**33827**
LV-PNS	B737	21336	LV-YNA	DC-9	47614	LX-FCV	B747	19658	**LX-VCV**	**B747**	**34235**
LV-PNT	CRJ	7039	LV-YOA	DC-9	47606	**LX-FCV**	**B747**	**25866**	**LX-WCV**	**B747**	**35804**
LV-PNU	DC-9	47606	LV-YPA	DC-9	47613	LX-GCV	B747	25867	LX-ZCV	B747	21252
LV-PNV	DC-9	47613	LV-YPC	B747	21938	LX-GCV	DC-8	45640			
LV-PNZ	737NG	28577	LV-YSB	B747	20116	LX-GJC	CRJ	7176	Lithuania		
LV-POF	737NG	28219	LV-YSY	B737	21335	**LX-GVV**	**737NG**	**30791**			
LV-POY	COMET	6430	LV-YXB	B737	21335	**LX-ICV**	**B747**	**25632**	LY-AAA	YAK40	9720154
LV-POZ	COMET	6432	LV-YYC	737NG	28210	LX-IDB	DC-8	45417	LY-AAB	YAK40	9520940
LV-PPA	COMET	6434	LV-YZA	B737	21336	LX-III	DC-8	45659	**LY-AAC**	**YAK40**	**9530344**
LV-PRQ	B737	20523	**LV-ZEC**	**B737**	**21796**	LX-IRA	B727	22081	LY-AAD	YAK40	9412032
LV-PRR	SE210	19	**LV-ZIE**	**B737**	**21798**	LX-IRB	B727	22082	LY-AAM	YAK42	3606235
LV-PSW	1-11	BAC.185	LV-ZON	737NG	28219	LX-IRC	B727	22084	LY-AAN	YAK42	3606256
LV-PTS	COMET	6460	(LV-ZOO)	B737	23171	LX-IRD	B727	22085	LY-AAO	YAK42	4606267
LV-PVT	SE210	127	**LV-ZPJ**	**A340**	**074**	LX-KCV	B747	20102	LY-AAP	YAK42	1706302
LV-PVU	SE210	149	LV-ZPL	B767	28206	**LX-KCV**	**B747**	**25868**	LY-AAQ	YAK42	2708295
LV-RAO	B737	22296	**LV-ZPO**	**A340**	**063**	LX-LCV	B747	20105	LY-AAR	YAK42	2708304
LV-RBH	B737	22296	**LV-ZPX**	**A340**	**080**	**LX-LCV**	**B747**	**29053**	LY-AAS	YAK42	1811395
LV-RCS	F.28	11074	**LV-ZRA**	**A340**	**085**	LX-LGE	SE210	234	LY-AAT	YAK42	4711397
LV-RNA	F.28	11145	LV-ZRC	737NG	29904	LX-LGF	B737	25429	LY-AAU	YAK42	4711397
LV-VAG	**MD80**	**53117**	LV-ZRD	B737	21192	LX-LGF	SE210	166	LY-AAV	YAK42	4711399
LV-VBX	**MD80**	**53047**	LV-ZRE	B737	23168	LX-LGG	B737	26437	LY-AAW	YAK42	3811417
LV-VBY	MD80	53048	LV-ZRM	737NG	28224	LX-LGG	SE210	156	LY-AAX	YAK42	4811431
LV-VBZ	**MD80**	**53049**	**LV-ZRO**	**B737**	**23164**	LX-LGH	B737	21443	LY-AAY	YAK40	9720753
LV-VCB	MD80	53351	LV-ZRP	737NG	29905	LX-LGI	B737	21444	LY-AAZ	YAK40	9641851
LV-VCS	F.28	11018	LV-ZSD	B737	23171	**LX-LGI**	**E145**	**145369**	LY-ABA	TU134	3352003
LV-VFJ	B727	20593	LV-ZSJ	737NG	28609	**LX-LGJ**	**E145**	**145395**	LY-ABB	TU134	48415
LV-VFL	B727	20606	LV-ZSN	737NG	30635	**LX-LGK**	**E145**	**14500886**	LY-ABC	TU134	63.49100
LV-VFM	B727	20607	LV-ZSS	DC-9	48123	**LX-LGL**	**E145**	**14500893**	LY-ABD	TU134	60054
LV-VGB	MD80	53446	LV-ZSU	MD80	48020	LX-LGN	B737	20907	LY-ABE	TU134	60076
LV-VGC	**MD80**	**53447**	**LV-ZSW**	**B737**	**23170**	LX-LGN	B737	25065	LY-ABF	TU134	60172
LV-VGF	B737	20913	LV-ZTB	CRJ	7137	LX-LGO	B737	26438	LY-ABG	TU134	60195
LV-VGF	B737	21138	LV-ZTC	CRJ	7139	LX-LGP	A300	269	LY-ABH	TU134	60308
LV-WAW	DC-9	47260	LV-ZTD	B737	23225	(LX-LGP)	A300	299	LY-ABI	TU134	60628
LV-WAX	DC-9	47262	**LV-ZTE**	**B737**	**23349**	**LX-LGP**	**B737**	**26439**	(LY-ABK)	SE210	262
LV-WBO	B737	20330	LV-ZTG	B737	23169	**LX-LGQ**	**737NG**	**33802**	(LY-ABL)	B737	22453
LV-WDS	B737	20169	LV-ZTI	B737	23002	**LX-LGR**	**737NG**	**33803**	**LY-AGP**	**B737**	**23808**
LV-WEG	DC-9	47446	LV-ZTJ	B737	23172	LX-LGR	B707	18891	**LY-AGQ**	**B737**	**26339**
LV-WEH	DC-9	47447	**LV-ZTT**	**B737**	**21806**	LX-LGR	B737	27424	LY-AGT	TU204	1364024
LV-WFC	B727	20678	LV-ZTX	B737	23504	**LX-LGS**	**737NG**	**33956**	**LY-AGZ**	**B737**	**26340**
LV-WFN	MD80	48025	**LV-ZTY**	**B737**	**23159**	LX-LGS	B707	20283	**LY-AQU**	**B737**	**24667**
LV-WFT	DC-9	47365	**LV-ZXB**	**B737**	**23009**	LX-LGS	B737	27425	**LY-AQV**	**B737**	**25069**
LV-WFX	B737	21357	LV-ZXC	737NG	30635	LX-LGT	B707	19706	LY-ARZ	YAK40	9641851
LV-WGM	**MD80**	**49784**	**LV-ZXC**	**B737**	**23160**	LX-LGT	E145	145076	LY-ASK	TU134	60054
LV-WGN	**MD80**	**49934**	LV-ZXE	DC-9	48124	LX-LGU	B707	19133	**LY-AZW**	**B737**	**27629**
LV-WGU	DC-9	47454	**LV-ZXH**	**B737**	**23503**	**LX-LGU**	**E145**	**145084**	LY-AZX	B737	28052
LV-WGX	B737	21358	**LV-ZXP**	**B737**	**23003**	LX-LGV	B707	18737	**LY-AZY**	**B737**	**26287**
LV-WHL	DC-9	47368	LV-ZXS	B737	20211	LX-LGV	E145	145129	LY-BAG	B737	24449
LV-WIS	DC-9	47312	**LV-ZXU**	**B737**	**23226**	LX-LGW	B707	17930	LY-BFV	B737	26419
LV-WJH	DC-9	47079	LV-ZXV	B737	23793	**LX-LGW**	**E145**	**145135**	**LY-BSD**	**B737**	**22701**
LV-WJS	B737	22278	**LV-ZYG**	**B737**	**21795**				LY-BSG	B737	22793

Reg	Type	c/n
LY-CXC	YAK42	?
LY-GBA	B737	22034
LY-GPA	B737	22453
"LY-IZR"	1-11	BAC.122
LY-LAU	**TU154**	**?**
LY-LJT	YAK42	?
LY-SKA	**B737**	**23972**
LY-SKA	YAK42	?
LY-SKB	YAK42	4811431
LY-SKC	YAK42	3016269
LY-SKD	YAK42	3914323
LY-SKW	**B737**	**25162**

Bulgaria

Reg	Type	c/n
LZ-	**A300**	**154**
(LZ-...)	A300	075
(LZ-...)	B707	20069
LZ-ABA	A320	0257
LZ-ABB	A320	0271
LZ-ABC	A320	0308
LZ-ABD	A320	0314
LZ-ACS	TU134	1351303
LZ-BHA	A320	0029
LZ-BHB	**A320**	**0294**
LZ-BHC	**A320**	**0349**
LZ-BHD	**A320**	**0221**
LZ-BHE	**A320**	**0305**
LZ-BOA	B737	24881
LZ-BOB	B737	24921
LZ-BOC	B737	25425
LZ-BOD	B737	23749
LZ-BOE	B737	23923
LZ-BOF	B737	25017
LZ-BOG	B737	23529
LZ-BOH	B737	23530
LZ-BOI	B737	25311
LZ-BOJ	B737	23718
LZ-BOK	B737	24023
LZ-BOL	B737	24024
LZ-BOM	B737	29059
LZ-BON	B737	29060
LZ-BOO	**B737**	**26852**
LZ-BOP	**B737**	**26704**
LZ-BOQ	**B737**	**26687**
LZ-BOR	**B737**	**25165**
LZ-BOT	**B737**	**24665**
LZ-BOU	**B737**	**23717**
LZ-BOV	**B737**	**23833**
LZ-BOW	**B737**	**23834**
LZ-BTA	TU154	72A-026
LZ-BTB	TU154	72A-027
LZ-BTC	TU154	73A-036
LZ-BTD	TU154	74A-058
LZ-BTE	TU154	74A-073
LZ-BTF	TU154	74A-077
LZ BTG	TU154	75A-095
LZ-BTH	TU154	87A-754
LZ-BTI	TU154	85A-706
LZ-BTJ	TU154	78A-270
LZ-BTK	TU154	76A-144
LZ-BTL	TU154	73A-051
LZ-BTL	TU154	77A-208
LZ-BTM	TU154	73A-052
LZ-BTM	TU154	77A-209
LZ-BTN	TU154	74A-054
LZ-BTN	TU154	90A-832
LZ-BTO	TU154	78A-258
LZ-BTP	TU154	78A-278
LZ-BTQ	TU154	86A-743
LZ-BTR	TU154	73A-051
LZ-BTR	TU154	79A-320
LZ-BTR	TU154	87A-760
LZ-BTS	TU154	80A-422
LZ-BTT	TU154	81A-483
LZ-BTU	TU154	81A-484
LZ-BTV	TU154	82A-569
LZ-BTW	TU154	85A-707
LZ-BTX	TU154	86A-744
LZ-BTY	TU154	89A-800
LZ-BTZ	**TU154**	**88A-781**

Reg	Type	c/n
LZ-CBD	**YAK40**	**9621547**
LZ-DOA	YAK40	9341431
LZ-DOB	YAK40	9340432
LZ-DOC	YAK40	9340532
LZ-DOD	YAK40	9340632
LZ-DOE	YAK40	9521441
LZ-DOF	YAK40	9521541
LZ-DOK	YAK40	9620247
LZ-DOL	YAK40	9620347
LZ-DOM	YAK40	9620447
LZ-DON	YAK40	9620547
LZ-DOR	YAK40	9231623
LZ-DOS	YAK40	9231423
LZ-FEB	B707	19584
LZ-HBA	**146**	**E2072**
LZ-HBB	**146**	**E2073**
LZ-HBC	**146**	**E2093**
LZ-HBD	**146**	**E3141**
LZ-HBE	**146**	**E3131**
LZ-HBF	**146**	**E3159**
LZ-HBG	**146**	**E3146**
LZ-HBZ	**146**	**E2103**
LZ-HMF	TU154	88A-777
LZ-HMH	TU154	87A-754
LZ-HMI	**TU154**	**85A-706**
LZ-HMN	TU154	90A-832
LZ-HMP	TU154	86A-733
LZ-HMQ	**TU154**	**86A-743**
LZ-HMR	TU154	87A-751
LZ-HMS	TU154	
LZ-HMW	**TU154**	**85A-707**
LZ-HMY	TU154	91A-875
LZ-HVA	**B737**	**26066**
LZ-HVB	**B737**	**24834**
LZ-INK	IL76	0093494835
LZ-JXA	A310	378
LZ-JXB	A310	419
LZ-JXC	A310	573
LZ-LCA	**TU154**	**89A-829**
LZ-LCB	TU154	93A-975
LZ-LCC	TU154	92A-921
LZ-LCD	**TU154**	**?**
LZ-LCE	TU154	90A-843
LZ-LCI	TU154	88A-788
LZ-LCO	TU154	91A-871
LZ-LCQ	**TU154**	**89A-802**
LZ-LCS	TU154	86A-727
LZ-LCT	**TU154**	**85A-717**
LZ-LCU	**TU154**	**90A-843**
LZ-LCV	**TU154**	**86A-733**
LZ-LCX	TU154	86A-744
LZ-LDA	**MD80**	**49572**
LZ-LDC	**MD80**	**49217**
LZ-LDD	**MD80**	**49218**
LZ-LDF	**MD80**	**49219**
LZ-LDG	**MD80**	**53149**
LZ-LDH	**MD80**	**53150**
LZ-LDK	**MD80**	**49432**
(LZ-LDL)	MD80	49433
LZ-LDR	**MD80**	**49227**
LZ-LDV	**MD80**	**49569**
LZ-LDX	**MD80**	**49844**
LZ-LDY	**MD80**	**49213**
LZ-LDZ	**MD80**	**49930**
LZ-LTA	TU154	92A-927
LZ-LTB	TU154	79A-365
LZ-LTC	TU154	93A-974
LZ-LTD	TU154	89A-802
LZ-LTE	TU154	90A-848
LZ-LTF	TU154	88A-794
LZ-LTG	TU154	92A-927
LZ-LTK	TU154	89A-810
LZ-LTO	TU154	91A-871
LZ-LTP	TU154	90A-860
LZ-LTR	TU154	90A-843
LZ-LTV	TU154	91A-895
LZ-LTX	TU154	86A-744
LZ-MDA	**A320**	**2732**
LZ-MDB	**A320**	**3125**
LZ-MDM	**A320**	**2804**
LZ-MDT	**A320**	**2108**
LZ-MIG	TU154	90A-840
LZ-MIK	TU154	90A-844

Reg	Type	c/n
LZ-MIL	TU154	90A-845
LZ-MIR	TU154	90A-852
LZ-MIS	TU154	90A-863
LZ-MIV	TU154	92A-920
LZ-MNA	TU154	92A-908
LZ-MNM	AN7x	47098946
"LZ-PTC"	L1011	193A-1152
LZ-PVA	B707	18937
LZ-PVB	B707	19570
LZ-TIM	**146**	**E1258**
LZ-TPC	L1011	193A-1152
LZ-TUA	TU134	8350405
LZ-TUB	TU134	8350501
LZ-TUC	TU134	9350807
LZ-TUD	TU134	9350808
LZ-TUE	TU134	9350914
LZ-TUF	TU134	0350918
LZ-TUG	TU134	73.49858
LZ-TUH	TU134	73.60142
LZ-TUJ	**TU134**	**49913**
LZ-TUK	TU134	1351209
LZ-TUL	TU134	4352303
LZ-TUM	TU134	3351906
LZ-TUN	TU134	4352307
LZ-TUO	TU134	0350922
LZ-TUP	TU134	1351303
LZ-TUR	TU134	4352308
LZ-TUS	TU134	60642
LZ-TUT	TU134	63987
LZ-TUU	TU134	1351409
LZ-TUV	TU134	1351408
LZ-TUZ	TU134	1351503
LZ-WZA	**A320**	**2571**
LZ-ZXY	DC-9	47605

Isle of Man

Reg	Type	c/n
M-YNJC	**E145**	**14500961**

Mongolia
(see also JU-)

Reg	Type	c/n
MPR-85644	TU154	88A-780
MT-1036	B727	20572
MT-1037	B727	20573
(MT-1044)	B757	26153
MT-1054	B727	20435

NASA

Reg	Type	c/n
NASA515	**B737**	**19437**
NASA711	**CV990**	**30-10-1**
NASA930	**KC135**	**17969**
NASA931	**KC135**	**18615**

United States of America

Reg		Type	c/n
N		**737NG**	**35278**
N		737NG	35717
(N	)	A320	0291
(N	)	A320	0292
(N	UA)	A320	0874
(N	)	B707	17610
(N	)	B707	20720
(N	)	B707	20723
(N	)	B727	20203
N		**B737**	**22353**
(N	)	B747	22380
N		B747	22672
N		B747	27827
(N	)	B757	22181
N		B757	23917
(N	)	B757	24072
(N	)	B757	24073
(N	)	B757	24074
N		B757	24254
(N	)	B757	24838
N		**E170**	**17000184**

Reg	Type	c/n
N	**E190**	**19000112**
N	**F.100**	**11352**
N1CC	1-11	18998
N1JR	1-11	055
N1PC	B737	21613
N1R	B707	18022
N1RL	**CRJ7**	**10004**
N1RN	CV880	22-7-5-57
N2CC	B727	19006
N2H	DC-9	45731
N2NF	B707	19375
N3E	1-11	068
N3H	MD80	49670
(N4..TA)	A320	0897
N4AS	737NG	29233
N5JY	B737	22255
N5LC	1-11	015
N5LC	1-11	073
N5LG	1-11	015
N5NE	DC-9	45706
(N5WM)	B737	22050
N5WM	B737	22629
N8LG	1-11	015
N9DC	DC-9	45695
N9KR	DC-9	45775
N9MD	DC-9	47696
N9WP	1-11	078
N10DC	DC-10	46500
N10DC	DC-10	46501
N10DC	DC-8	45610
N10HM	1-11	080
N10MB	DC-10	47907
N10SV	**E145**	**14500974**
N10VG	B707	18156
N10XY	B727	19254
"NO11JS"	B707	18044
N11AB	B737	24769
N11AZ	B737	20590
N11FQ	MD80	49759
N11RV	B707	17606
N12CZ	1-11	056
N12FQ	MD80	49766
N12SN	MD80	49968
N13FE	DC-9	45706
N14AZ	B707	19498
N14GA	B727	21246
N15DF	B727	20710
N15NP	DC-9	45702
N15VG	B707	18163
N15WF	MD11	48486
N15YC	**C-15**	**?**
N17MK	1-11	054
N17VK	1-11	055
N18AZ	B707	18748
N18G	B727	18935
N18HD	1-11	068
N18HH	1-11	068
N18HH	B727	18936
N18KM	B707	18519
N18NC	737NG	30070
N19B	DC-10	46661
N19B	DC-10	46662
N19B	DC-10	46934
N19B	DC-10	47840
N19B	DC-10	48258
N19B	DC-8	45927
N19B	DC-8	45929
N19B	DC-9	45722
N19B	DC-9	47702
N19B	MD80	48087
N19B	MD80	49252
N19B	MD80	49380
N19B	MD80	49403
N19B	MD80	49603
N19B	MD80	49605
N19B	MD80	49643
N19B	MD80	49968
N19B	MD80	53193
N20SW	B737	20369
N20SW	B737	21337
N20UA	DC-8	45890

Reg	Type	C/n	Reg	Type	C/n	Reg	Type	C/n	Reg	Type	C/n
N21AZ	B707	18747	N40AS	1-11	061	N57AJ	DC-8	45619	N73SW	B737	22673
N21CX	**DC-8**	**45955**	N40KA	DC-10	46727	N57FB	DC-8	45669	N73TH	B737	21729
N21FE	B727	21102	N40SH	DC-9	45775	N57JE	B737	20693	N74PW	B737	21339
N21KR	737NG	29139	(N41AF)	B737	19955	N57SW	B737	21722	N74SW	B737	22674
N21SW	B737	20345	**N41CX**	**DC-8**	**46129**	N58AD	B737	22058	N74WF	MD11	48452
N21UA	DC-8	45891	(N41UA)	DC-8	45675	N58AF	B737	22371	N75AA	L1011	193U-1201
N21UC	B727	18990	**N41XA**	**B737**	**24573**	(N58AJ)	B727	19464	N75AF	DC-9	47012
N22RB	1-11	080	N41XS	DC-9	47646	N58AW	B757	25345	N75PW	B737	22632
N22SW	B737	20336	N42	CV880	22-7-3-55	N58RD	B707	18694	N76GW	1-11	065
N22UA	DC-8	45892	N42AF	B737	19770	N58RD	CV880	22-00-48M	N76HN	146	E1076
N23	B707	18066	N42UA	DC-8	45676	N59AJ	DC-8	45272	N77	B727	18360
N23SW	B737	20346	**N42XA**	**B737**	**25729**	N59AW	B757	25493	N77AZ	B727	19813
N23SW	B737	21338	N43AE	F.28	11016	N59RD	B707	17905	N77CS	1-11	054
N23UA	DC-8	45893	N43UA	DC-8	45677	N59SW	B737	21811	N77NG	B737	24377
"N24-952"	B767	24952	**N43XA**	**B737**	**24796**	N59T	DC-9	47041	N77QS	1-11	054
N24AZ	B737	20591	N44MD	B727	19318	N60AF	DC-9	47011	N78	B727	18362
N24SW	B737	20925	(N44Q)	B727	18366	N60AJ	DC-8	45618	N78GF	IL76	0083485558
N24UA	DC-8	45963	N44R	1-11	BAC.120	N60FM	B727	19535	N78XS	DC-9	47778
N25AB	B737	24687	N44R	B727	18366	N60FM	DC-9	45731	N79SL	DC-9	47011
N25AS	DC-9	45725	N44UA	DC-8	45800	**N60GH**	**CRJ**	**7274**	N79XS	DC-9	47779
N25AZ	**B727**	**18370**	(N45AF)	B737	22054	N60NA	DC-10	46700	N80AF	B737	20223
N25SW	B737	20095	**N45NA**	**DC-9**	**47410**	N60SR	CRJ	7089	(N80AF)	B737	22697
N25UA	DC-8	46127	N45RT	B707	18961	N60SW	B737	21812	**N80AG**	**MD80**	**53581**
(N25WA)	B747	20305	N45SB	SE210	19	N61AF	B737	19552	N80AZ	B707	18748
N26ND	B757	26241	N45UA	DC-8	45801	N61CX	DC-8	46142	N80CC	B737	21957
N26SW	B737	21117	N46	B727	18360	(N61FB)	DC-8	46159	N80GM	1-11	BAC.126
N26UA	DC-8	45887	N46AF	B737	19768	N61MJ	737NG	30754	N80ME	DC-9	45795
N27	B727	19176	(N46AF)	B737	22055	N61NA	DC-10	46701	N80NA	DC-10	46711
N27KA	B727	18859	N46D	B707	18739	N61SW	B737	21970	N80SW	B737	22675
N27SW	B737	21262	N46RT	B707	18962	N61TA	B707	17651	N80UA	MD80	48022
N27UA	DC-8	45942	(N46SB)	SE210	149	N62AF	B737	19556	N81AC	CNCRD	204
N27W	F.28	11016	N46UA	DC-8	45802	N62NA	DC-10	46702	N81AF	B737	22697
N28AT	B757	24121	N47AF	B737	19771	N62SW	B737	22060	(N81AF)	B737	22698
N28JS	B707	18044	N47UA	DC-8	45964	N62TA	B707	17640	N81HN	146	E1081
N28KA	B727	18320	N47XS	DC-9	47747	**N62TY**	**A319**	**1625**	N81NA	DC-10	46712
(N28SW)	B737	21337	N48AF	B737	19772	N62WH	1-11	078	(N81R)	B707	18022
N28SW	B737	21339	N48CA	DC-8	45422	N63AF	B737	19553	N81SW	B737	22730
N28UA	DC-8	46031	N48UA	DC-8	45980	N63NA	DC-10	46703	N82AF	B737	22698
N29	DC-9	45732	N48WF	MD11	48538	N63SW	B737	22061	(N82AF)	B737	22699
N29AF	DC-9	45826	N48XS	DC-9	47748	N64AF	B737	19549	N82MV	MD80	49826
N29AZ	B707	19517	(N49SB)	SE210	180	N64NA	DC-10	46706	N82NA	DC-10	46713
N29KA	B727	18803	N49UA	DC-8	45886	N64RD	DC-8	46017	N82SW	B737	22731
N29LR	DC-9	47519	N50AF	DC-9	47010	**N64SW**	**B737**	**22062**	N82TF	B707	18922
(N29SW)	B737	21338	N50SW	B737	21447	N65AF	DC-9	47152	N83AF	B737	22699
N29SW	B737	21340	**N50TC**	**737NG**	**29024**	N65NA	DC-10	46707	(N83AF)	B737	22700
N29UA	**DC-8**	**46159**	N50UA	DC-8	45884	N65SS	DC-10	46541	N83HN	146	E1083
N30AU	B737	22407	N50XS	DC-9	47750	(N65SW)	B737	22356	N83MV	MD80	49823
N30GA	B727	20448	N51AF	B737	22529	N66AF	DC-9	47152	N83NA	DC-10	46714
N30KA	B727	18857	N51CX	DC-8	46027	N66NA	DC-10	46708	N83SW	B737	22732
N30MP	B727	18998	N51FB	DC-8	45935	N66XS	DC-9	47766	N83XA	737NG	30703
(N30SW)	B737	21339	N513W	D737	21448	**N667R**	**737NG**	**29233**	N84AF	B737	22700
N30UA	DC-8	45888	N51UA	DC-8	46032	N67AB	B737	23496	(N84AF)	B737	22701
N31AU	B737	22397	N52AF	B737	22368	N67AF	B737	19554	N84NA	DC-10	47837
N31CX	DC-8	45911	N52AW	B757	25489	N67AW	B767	25533	N84WA	B757	25493
N31EK	DC-8	46052	N52SW	B737	21533	**N67JR**	**B727**	**18936**	N85AF	B737	22701
(N31EV)	L1011	193B-1031	N52UA	DC-10	46905	N67NA	DC-10	46709	N85AS	DC-9	45711
N31KA	B727	18856	N53AF	B737	22054	N67SW	B737	22356	(N85NA)	DC-10	46954
(N31SW)	B737	21340	N53AF	DC-8	45637	(N67SW)	B737	22357	N85SW	B737	22826
N31TR	**B727**	**21948**	N53AW	B757	25490	N68AF	B737	19058	(N86AF)	B737	22800
N31UA	DC-9	45720	N53CA	DC-8	45377	N68NA	DC-10	46710	N86SW	B737	22827
N32UA	DC-9	47462	N53FA	DC-8	45666	N68SW	B737	22358	(N87AF)	B737	22801
N33AW	B737	25402	N53KM	DC-8	45604	(N68SW)	B737	22358	N87BL	1-11	BAC.120
N33UA	DC-9	47191	**N53NA**	**E145**	**145770**	N69AF	B737	19059	N87MD	MD80	49388
N33UT	B727	18936	N53SW	B737	21534	N69HM	1-11	061	N87SW	B737	22903
N34AW	B737	25426	N54AF	B737	22055	N69NA	DC-10	46942	N87WA	B737	20794
N34XS	DC-9	47634	N54AN	A330	054	N70AF	DC-9	47014	(N88AF)	B737	22802
N35LX	**B737**	**23528**	N54CP	CV880	22-00-46M	N70NA	146	E1063	N88AM	B757	24772
N35UA	DC-9	47192	N54FA	DC-8	45637	N70NA	DC-10	46943	N88CH	CV880	22-7-6-58
N36KA	B727	18850	**N54SW**	**B737**	**21535**	N70PA	B727	19402	N88NB	1-11	005
N36UA	DC-8	46022	N54UA	DC-9	47697	**N71CX**	**DC-8**	**45961**	N88TF	B707	18964
N37KA	B727	18858	N55AJ	B727	18951	N71MA	1-11	BAC.111	**N88WR**	**737NG**	**29441**
N37NY	**B737**	**23976**	N55FB	DC-8	45678	N71PW	B737	21960	N88WZ	737NG	29441
N37PV	SE210	255	N55JT	1-11	075	N71SW	B737	22358	**N88ZL**	**B707**	**18928**
N37RT	F.28	11009	N55NW	CV880	22-00-7	N71UA	DC-8	45381	(N89AF)	B737	22803
N37WF	MD11	48453	N55SW	B737	21593	N71WF	MD11	48485	N89CD	B737	29001
N38VP	**DO328**	**3174**	N56AF	B737	22369	N72AF	DC-9	47015	**N89LD**	**E145**	**145648**
N38WF	MD11	48634	N56B	1-11	055	N73AF	B737	21186	**N89S**	**DC-9**	**47042**
N39BL	B737	21957	N56CD	B737	29000	N73AF	B737	21720	N89SM	DC-9	45775
N39KA	B727	18324	N56FA	DC-8	45663	N73AF	DC-9	47013	N89SW	B737	22904
N40	**B727**	**19854**	N56SW	B737	21721	N73AF	DC-9	47152	(N90AF)	B737	22804
N40AF	B727	18741	N56UA	DC-9	47754	N73FS	B737	21765	N90AM	1-11	BAC.111
N40AF	B737	19769	N57AF	B737	22370	N73GQ	B737	19770	N90AX	B727	20040

Reg	Type	c/n	Reg	Type	c/n	Reg	Type	c/n	Reg	Type	c/n
N90CD	737NG	30272	N101TV	DC-10	46800	N105NK	B737	26105	N110CK	L1011	193N-1132
(N90MJ)	B707	17697	N101UN	737NG	28089	N105QS	737NG	33102	N110DL	B767	22222
N90R	**737NG**	**32775**	N101UW	A320	0936	N105RK	B727	19122	N110DS	B707	18063
N90S	DC-9	47244	N102AA	DC-10	46502	N105SW	B737	23249	N110ER	B737	23065
N90SW	B737	22905	N102AB	B767	24729	N105TR	B747	22768	N110FE	B727	19806
N90TF	1-11	080	N102AN	B737	27285	**N105UA**	**B747**	**26473**	**N110HM**	**MD80**	**49787**
N91CD	737NG	30274	N102CK	L1011	193N-1198	**N105UW**	**A320**	**0868**	**N110HQ**	**E170**	**17000172**
N91S	DC-9	47063	N102DA	B767	22214	N105WA	DC-10	46891	N110KC	DC-10	48200
N91SW	B737	22963	N102EV	A300	193	N105WA	DC-10	46987	N110ML	F.100	11486
N92GS	B707	18452	N102EW	F.28	11187	N105WP	DC-8	46095	N110NE	B727	18952
N92GS	B727	18892	N102EX	1-11	009	N106AA	DC-10	46506	N110QS	737NG	33036
(N92JF)	B737	19606	N102FE	B727	19193	N106BN	B707	18069	(N110TA)	1-11	BAC.236
N92S	DC-9	47064	N102GP	1-11	060	N106BV	B707	19415	N110UR	F.28	11182
N92SW	B737	22964	N102GU	B737	23535	N106CK	L1011	193N-1211	**N110UW**	**A320**	**1112**
N92TA	L1011	193U-1201	**N102HQ**	**E170**	**17000157**	N106DA	B767	22218	N111AA	DC-10	46511
N92TB	L1011	193U-1203	**N102KH**	**B737**	**23538**	N106EX	1-11	013	N111AC	1-11	BAC.111
N92TT	L1011	193U-1223	N102ME	1-11	067	N106FE	B727	19201	N111AK	B727	21010
N93EV	**MD80**	**49393**	N102NC	A300	102	**N106HQ**	**E170**	**17000164**	N111DN	B767	22223
N93GS	B727	18893	N102QS	737NG	32628	**N106KH**	**B737**	**24916**	N111EK	B727	19253
(N93PJ)	SE210	102	N102RK	B727	21343	N106ML	F.100	11477	N111FE	B727	19805
N93S	DC-9	47078	(N102RW)	146	E1010	N106TR	B747	22769	N111FL	1-11	073
N93SW	B737	22965	N102SW	B737	23108	**N106UA**	**B747**	**26474**	N111GS	1-11	BAC.126
N94AA	CNCRD	206	N102TR	B737	21335	N106UR	F.28	11149	**N111HQ**	**E170**	**17000173**
N94AB	CNCRD	208	N102TV	DC-10	46801	**N106US**	**A320**	**1044**	N111JL	B727	18998
N94AD	CNCRD	210	N102UA	DC-10	46905	N106WA	DC-10	46905	**N111JX**	**1-11**	**BAC.163**
N94AE	CNCRD	212	N102UN	737NG	29076	N107AA	DC-10	46507	**N111KH**	**B737**	**23708**
N94AF	CNCRD	216	**N102UW**	**A320**	**0844**	N107BN	B707	18739	N111LP	1-11	068
N94EV	**DC-9**	**49394**	N103AA	DC-10	46503	N107BV	B707	19321	N111MD	MD11	48401
N94FA	CNCRD	205	N103AZ	B727	21260	N107CK	L1011	193N-1182	N111MF	B707	18338
N94FB	CNCRD	207	N103CK	L1011	193N-1212	N107DL	B767	22219	(N111MF)	B727	22687
N94FC	CNCRD	209	N103DA	B767	22215	(N107EV)	MD11	48546	N111NA	1-11	055
N94FD	CNCRD	211	**N103EV**	**MD11**	**48415**	N107EX	1-11	085	N111NA	1-11	060
N94GS	B727	18892	N103EW	F.28	11062	N107FE	B727	19202	N111NA	1-11	065
N94S	DC-9	47204	N103EX	1-11	010	**N107HQ**	**E170**	**17000165**	**N111NB**	**737NG**	**36027**
N94SD	CNCRD	213	N103FE	B727	19199	**N107KH**	**B737**	**24022**	N111NS	1-11	078
N94SW	B737	23053	N103GU	B737	23388	N107ML	F.100	11450	N111QA	1-11	015
N95GS	B727	18895	**N103HA**	**B737**	**21186**	N107PY	MD80	49671	N111RZ	1-11	056
N95S	DC-9	47205	**N103HQ**	**E170**	**17000159**	N107TR	B737	20807	(N111UR)	F.28	11185
N95SW	B737	23054	**N103KH**	**B737**	**24020**	**N107UA**	**B747**	**26900**	**N111US**	**A320**	**1114**
N96	KC135	18006	N103ML	F.100	11444	N107UR	F.28	11159	**N111VM**	**737NG**	**36090**
N96AC	B767	25536	N103MU	B727	18324	**N107US**	**A320**	**1052**	N112	CV880	22-7-3-55
N96B	B727	18365	N103QS	737NG	32970	N107WA	DC-10	46836	N112AA	DC-10	46512
N96S	DC-9	47206	(N103RW)	146	E1011	N108AA	DC-10	46508	N112AK	DC-9	47151
N96SW	B737	23055	N103SW	B737	23109	N108BN	B707	18740	(N112BV)	B707	19350
N97	B727	18360	N103TR	B737	21336	N108BV	B707	18940	N112CG	A319	2431
(N97GA)	1-11	058	N103TV	DC-10	46802	N108CK	L1011	193N-1204	N112CK	L1011	193N-1146
N97JF	1-11	089	N103UN	737NG	29077	N108DE	A321	1008	N112DL	B767	22224
N97KR	1-11	005	**N103US**	**A320**	**0861**	N108DL	B767	22220	N112FE	B727	19890
N97NK	B737	26097	N103WA	DC-10	46975	N108FE	B727	19204	N112HM	B707	19869
N97S	DC-9	47245	N104AA	DC-10	46504	**N108HQ**	**E170**	**17000166**	**N112HQ**	**E170**	**17000174**
N97XS	DC-9	47597	N104AQ	A321	1042	**N108KH**	**B737**	**24902**	N112NA	1-11	059
N98	KC135	17969	N104CK	L1011	193C-1193	N108ML	F.100	11484	N112NA	1-11	088
N98KT	SE210	102	N104DA	B767	22216	**N108MS**	**737NG**	**33102**	**N112PS**	**DC-9**	**47013**
N98NG	B737	24098	N104EW	F.28	11099	N108RA	B707	20315	(N112TA)	B707	17696
N98WS	B707	18338	N104EX	1-11	011	N108RD	DC-8	45663	N112TR	B737	24070
N99WT	B707	17606	N104FE	B727	19198	N108UA	B747	26903	(N112UR)	F.28	11185
N99XS	DC-9	47599	N104GA	A300	178	N108UR	F.28	11173	**N112US**	**A320**	**1134**
N99YA	DC-9	45702	**N104HQ**	**E170**	**17000160**	**N108UW**	**A320**	**1061**	N112WA	DC-10	47820
N99ZL	737NG	32915	**N104HR**	**B727**	**21525**	N108WA	DC-10	46837	N113	B707	18066
N100CC	1-11	059	N104ML	F.100	11445	N109AA	DC-10	46509	**N113**	**B727**	**18935**
N100FS	B757	25054	N104NK	B737	26104	N109AP	B737	21445	N113AA	DC-10	46513
N100JJ	DC-8	45763	N104NL	L1011	193U-1203	N109BV	B707	19433	N113AH	B737	22113
N100ME	DC-9	47309	(N104QS)	737NG	33010	N109CK	L1011	193N-1205	N113AW	B737	24302
N100MU	B727	19534	N104SW	B737	23110	N109DL	B767	22221	N113CA	B727	19243
N100UN	737NG	28088	N104TR	B747	21446	N109FE	B727	19205	N113DA	B767	22225
N101AA	DC-10	46500	**N104UA**	**B747**	**26902**	**N109HQ**	**E170**	**17000168**	N113FE	B727	19894
N101AA	DC-10	46501	**N104UW**	**A320**	**0863**	N109HT	B727	18998	**N113HQ**	**E170**	**17000177**
N101DA	B767	22213	**N104VR**	**B737**	**27925**	N109KM	B727	21155	**N113UW**	**A320**	**1141**
N101EX	1-11	007	N104WA	DC-10	46727	N109ML	F.100	11485	N113WA	DC-10	47821
N101FE	B727	19197	N104WA	DC-10	46986	N109QS	737NG	33434	N113YT	B737	23113
N101GA	A300	253	N105AA	DC-10	46505	N109RD	DC-8	45674	N114AA	DC-10	46514
N101GU	B737	23766	N105BN	B707	18068	N109TH	1-11	067	N114AW	B737	24304
N101HQ	**E170**	**17000156**	N105BV	B707	20297	N109TR	B737	21694	N114DL	B767	22226
N101LF	A319	2396	N105CK	L1011	193Y-1178	N109UA	B747	26906	N114FE	B727	19527
N101LF	B737	28055	N105DA	B767	22217	N109UR	F.28	11181	N114HM	B707	19871
N101LF	B757	26332	N105EV	MD11	48544	**N109UW**	**A320**	**1065**	**N114HQ**	**E170**	**17000179**
N101MP	A310	549	N105EX	1-11	012	N109WA	DC-10	46933	N114M	1-11	BAC.119
(N101MU)	B727	18255	N105FE	B727	19194	N109WA	DC-10	47819	**N114M**	**146**	**E1068**
(N101MU)	B727	18802	**N105HQ**	**E170**	**17000163**	N110AA	DC-10	46510	N114MX	1-11	BAC.119
N101MU	B727	18858	**N105KH**	**B737**	**24462**	N110AC	B727	19253	**N114UW**	**A320**	**1148**
N101PC	1-11	073	N105ML	F.100	11475	N110AV	F.28	11097	N114WA	DC-10	46999
N101RW	146	E1002				N110BV	B707	19177			

Reg	Type	Serial
N115AA	DC-10	46515
N115AD	B737	22115
N115AW	B737	24305
N115DA	B727	22227
N115FE	B727	19814
N115FS	B757	25155
N115GB	B737	24450
N115HQ	E170	17000182
N115TA	B727	20327
N115US	A320	1171
N115WA	DC-10	47818
(N116AW)	B737	24462
N116DL	B767	23275
N116FE	B727	19298
N116HQ	E170	17000183
N116KB	B747	23027
N116TA	B727	20328
N116UA	B747	26908
N116US	A320	1210
N116WA	DC-10	47906
N117AA	DC-10	46517
(N117AW)	B737	23923
N117DF	B737	23800
N117DL	B767	23276
N117FE	B727	19299
N117GB	DC-10	48318
N117HQ	E170	17000184
N117JB	B727	20993
N117KC	B747	23028
N117MR	1-11	065
N117TA	B727	20513
N117TR	146	E1017
N117UA	B747	28810
N117UR	F.28	11222
N117UW	A320	1224
N117WA	DC-10	48318
N118AA	DC-10	46518
N118CH	A321	2060
N118DF	B727	21344
N118DL	B767	23277
N118FE	B727	19300
N118KD	B747	23029
N118RW	B737	23040
N118UA	B747	28811
N118UR	F.28	11224
N118US	A320	1264
N119	DC-9	45732
N119AA	DC-10	46519
N119CH	737NG	30296
N119DA	1-11	072
N119DL	B767	23278
N119FE	B727	19301
N119GA	1-11	072
N119GA	B727	21068
N119KE	B747	23030
N119SW	B737	21226
N119UA	B747	28812
N119UR	F.28	11226
N119US	A320	1268
N119WF	B757	23119
N120AA	DC-10	46520
N120AF	B737	28491
N120DL	B767	23279
N120ED	A321	1204
N120FE	B727	19356
N120KF	B747	23031
N120NE	DC-9	45731
N120NJ	B737	22979
N120SR	B737	22120
N120TA	1-11	056
(N120UA)	B747	28813
N120UA	B747	29166
N120UP	A300	805
N120UR	F.28	11231
N120US	A320	1286
N121AA	DC-10	46521
N121DE	B767	23435
N121FE	B737	19357
N121GA	DC-8	45632
N121GU	B737	20583
N121KG	B747	23032

Reg	Type	Serial
N121NJ	B737	21735
N121SR	B737	22121
N121UA	B747	29167
N121UP	A300	806
N121UR	F.28	11237
N121UW	A320	1294
N122AA	DC-10	46522
N122DL	B767	23436
N122FE	B727	19358
N122GU	B737	20586
N122KH	B747	23033
(N122NA)	B737	23121
N122NJ	B737	22120
N122UA	B747	29168
N122UP	A300	807
N122UR	F.28	11238
N122US	A320	1298
N123AA	DC-10	46523
N123AF	DC-8	46108
N123AQ	B737	22123
N123DN	B767	23437
N123FE	B727	19359
N123GU	B737	20587
N123H	1-11	BAC.163
N123KJ	B747	23243
N123NJ	B737	22121
N123UW	A320	1310
N123YR	B727	18366
N124	B727	18821
N124AA	DC-10	46524
N124AD	B737	22124
N124AF	DC-8	46140
N124AJ	DC-8	45626
N124AN	A300	024
N124AS	B727	18821
N124DE	B767	23438
N124FE	B727	19360
N124GU	B737	20588
N124KK	B747	23244
N124LS	E145	14500948
N124NJ	B737	22122
N124UP	A300	808
N124US	A320	1314
N125AA	DC-10	46525
N125DL	B767	24075
N125DT	L1011	193L-1079
N125FE	B727	19717
N125GU	B737	23849
N125KL	B747	23245
N125NJ	B737	22882
(N125TW)	B747	20271
N125UP	A300	809
N126AA	DC-10	46947
N126AD	B737	22126
N126AT	737NG	32679
N126AW	B737	20959
N126DL	B767	24076
N126FE	B727	19718
N126GU	B737	20582
N126NJ	B737	22884
N126NK	DC-9	47303
(N126TW)	B747	20273
N126UP	A300	810
N127	B727	19176
N127AA	DC-10	46948
N127AD	B737	22127
N127AG	A321	1227
N127AW	B737	20922
N127DL	B767	24077
N127FE	B727	19719
N127GE	DC-9	48127
N127GU	B737	22074
N127LC	B747	25127
N127MA	B757	25133
N127NJ	B737	22886
N127NK	DC-9	47361
N127QS	737NG	30327
N127UA	B747	28813
N127UP	A300	811
N128AA	DC-10	46984
N128AD	B737	22128

Reg	Type	Serial
N128AN	A300	028
N128AW	B737	20958
N128BP	B747	19729
N128CF	1-11	061
N128DL	B767	24078
N128FE	B727	19720
N128GA	1-11	BAC.117
N128GE	DC-9	48128
N128NA	B727	20879
N128NJ	B737	22892
N128NK	DC-9	47307
N128QS	737NG	30328
N128TA	1-11	BAC.117
N128TW	B747	19729
N128UA	B747	30023
N128UP	A300	812
N129AA	DC-10	46996
N129AW	B737	21115
N129CA	B727	19501
N129DL	B767	24079
N129GE	DC-9	48129
N129JK	B727	18933
N129NA	B727	20880
N129NK	DC-9	47305
N129QS	737NG	30329
N129SW	B737	22340
N129TW	B747	21141
N129UM	DO328	3129
N129UP	A300	813
N130AA	DC-10	46989
N130AN	A300	030
N130AW	B727	20521
N130DL	B767	24080
N130FA	DC-10	46554
N130FE	B727	19721
N130KR	B707	18071
N130ML	F.100	11329
N130NJ	MD80	49222
N130NK	DC-9	47604
N130QS	737NG	30330
N130SW	B737	22699
N130UP	A300	814
N131AA	DC-10	46994
N131AW	B737	20956
N131DN	B767	24852
N131EA	B707	18713
N131FE	B727	19722
N131LF	A320	0491
N131ML	F.100	11323
N131NJ	MD80	49846
N131NK	DC-9	47605
N131UP	A300	815
N132AA	DC-10	47827
N132AW	B737	21186
N132DN	B767	24981
N132EA	B707	19566
N132FE	B727	19850
N132KR	B767	25132
N132ML	F.100	11321
N132NJ	MD80	49780
N132NK	DC-9	47202
N132SW	B737	21227
N133AA	DC-10	47828
N133AD	B737	22133
N133AW	B737	21735
N133CA	B727	18844
N133DN	B767	24982
N133FE	B727	19851
N133JC	DC-10	46752
N133ML	F.100	11330
(N133NA)	B737	23122
N133NK	DC-9	48111
N133TW	B747	19957
N133UP	A300	816
N134AA	B737	25134
N134AA	DC-10	47829
N134AR	737NG	29749
N134AS	B727	18371
N134AT	A320	0024
N134AW	B737	22576
N134CA	B727	18744
N134DL	B767	25123

Reg	Type	Serial
N134FE	B727	19852
N134TW	B747	19958
N134UP	A300	817
N135AA	DC-10	47830
N135AW	B737	19940
N135BC	CRJ	7075
N135CA	B727	19393
N135DL	B767	25145
N135FE	B727	19853
N135JM	E145	145412
N135NJ	MD80	49440
N135SF	737NG	30135
N135SG	E145	145706
N135SH	E145	14500973
N135SL	E145	145711
N135SW	B737	21932
N135TA	B737	19940
N135TR	146	E1035
N135UP	A300	818
N136AA	DC-10	47846
N136AA	DC-9	47553
N136AW	B737	19708
N136CV	B757	24136
N136DL	B767	25146
N136FE	B727	19855
N136JV	146	E2136
N136NJ	MD80	49413
N136SE	CRJ	7136
N136SW	B737	21933
N136TR	146	E2136
N136UP	A300	819
N137AA	DC-10	47847
N137AW	B737	23148
N137DL	B767	25306
(N137FE)	B727	19856
N137GP	B747	27137
N137NJ	MD80	49229
N137UP	A300	820
N138AA	DC-10	46911
N138AT	A320	0026
N138AW	B727	22792
N138DE	E145	145129
N138DL	B767	25409
(N138FE)	B727	19857
N138JV	146	E2138
N138MJ	B707	17696
(N138MJ)	B707	17697
N138SR	B707	17697
N138TA	B707	17696
N138TR	146	E2138
N138UP	A300	821
N139AA	DC-10	46711
N139AW	B737	22370
N139DL	B767	25984
N139SW	B747	21934
N139UP	A300	822
N140AA	DC-10	46712
N140AV	DC-9	47140
N140AW	B737	22371
N140LL	B767	25988
N140NJ	MD80	49931
N140SC	L1011	193E-1067
N140UA	B747	21022
(N140UP)	A300	805
N140UP	A300	823
N140WC	CRJ	7140
N140WE	DC-10	46920
N141AA	DC-10	46713
N141AC	146	E2051
N141AW	B737	21955
N141CY	B737	29141
N141LF	A320	0405
N141LF	B737	24961
N141LF	B737	26315
N141LF	B737	24150
N141NJ	MD80	49932
N141RD	DC-8	45669
N141RF	A300	160
N141UA	B747	21023
(N141UP)	A300	806
N141UP	A300	824
N141US	DC-10	46750

Reg.	Type	C/n	Reg.	Type	C/n	Reg.	Type	C/n	Reg.	Type	C/n
N141WE	DC-10	46661	N150AW	B737	23218	(N156KH)	B727	20664	N162GJ	CRJ7	10254
N142AA	DC-10	46714	N150FE	B727	19141	N156PL	MD80	49759	N162GL	B707	20089
N142AC	146	E2053	N150FN	B737	19166	N156QS	737NG	30756	N162JT	B747	24162
N142AW	B737	20449	N150FV	B737	23168	N156TR	146	E2156	N162PL	MD80	49765
N142RF	A300	244	N150SE	CRJ	7152	N156UA	B747	20105	N162QS	DC-8	45956
N142SW	B747	22302	N150UA	B737	21992	N156UP	A300	845	N162UP	A300	851
N142UA	B747	21024	N150UP	A300	833	N156US	DC-10	46765	N162US	DC-10	46771
N142UP	A300	825	N150US	DC-10	46759	N157AW	B737	23779	N162UW	A321	1412
N142US	DC-10	46751	N151AA	DC-10	46706	N157DM	DC-10	46920	N162W	1-11	087
N142WE	DC-10	46966	N151AW	B737	23219	N157FE	B727	18314	N163AA	DC-10	46914
N143AA	DC-10	46555	N151FE	B727	19147	(N157FN)	B727	18804	N163AT	L1011	293A-1229
N143AW	B737	22453	N151FN	B727	18805	N157GJ	CRJ7	10230	N163AW	B737	23785
N143AZ	B727	22043	N151FV	B737	23169	(N157KH)	B727	21512	N163BS	MD80	53466
N143CA	B727	18743	N151GJ	CRJ7	10216	N157PL	MD80	49760	N163CA	DC-8	45955
N143DA	B767	25991	N151GX	B757	24451	N157UA	DC-10	47106	(N163FE)	B727	18319
N143EV	A300	143	N151LF	737NG	30635	N157UP	A300	846	N163GJ	CRJ7	10255
N143FE	B727	19136	N151LF	B737	26317	N157US	DC-10	46766	(N163GL)	B707	20179
N143G	MD80	49670	N151LF	B757	26275	N158AW	B737	23780	N163GP	B737	21193
N143MC	L1011	193A-1043	N151SY	DC-10	48295	(N158FE)	B727	18315	N163PL	MD80	49766
N143RF	A300	239	N151UA	B747	23736	N158FN	B727	18812	N163PM	F.28	11163
N143UA	B747	21025	N151UP	A300	834	N158GE	A300	158	N163UA	B747	21353
N143UP	A300	826	N151US	DC-10	46760	N158GJ	CRJ7	10237	N163UP	A300	852
N143US	DC-10	46752	N152AA	DC-10	46707	(N158KH)	B727	21513	N163US	146	E2022
N144AA	DC-10	47848	N152AS	B727	19535	N158PL	MD80	49761	N163US	A321	1417
N144AC	146	E2054	N152AW	B737	23387	N158UA	B747	21054	N164AA	DC-10	46950
N144AW	B737	19074	N152DL	B767	24984	N158UP	A300	847	N164AT	L1011	293A-1238
N144DA	B767	27584	N152FE	B727	18285	N158US	DC-10	46767	N164AW	B737	23625
N144FE	B727	19137	N152FN	B727	19167	N158VA	B737	22959	N164BS	MD80	53488
N144JC	DC-10	46753	N152FV	B737	23171	N159AD	F.28	11227	(N164FE)	B727	18861
(N144NA)	B737	23123	N152GJ	CRJ7	10218	N159AW	B737	23781	N164GJ	CRJ7	10256
N144SP	B707	19209	N152LM	B707	19210	(N159FE)	B727	18316	(N164GL)	B707	20069
N144UA	B747	21026	N152SY	DC-10	48289	(N159FN)	B727	18811	N164LF	737NG	30694
N144UP	A300	827	N152UA	B747	23737	N159GJ	CRJ7	10238	N164LF	B767	26257
N144US	DC-10	46753	N152UP	A300	835	(N159KH)	B727	20997	N164PL	B737	22735
N145AA	DC-10	46700	N152US	DC-10	46761	N159PL	B737	21186	N164RJ	737NG	30328
N145AC	146	E2055	N153AA	DC-10	46708	(N159PL)	MD80	49762	N164UA	B747	21657
(N145AC)	146	E2067	N153AF	DC-8	45682	N159UA	B747	21140	N164UP	A300	853
N145AW	B737	20194	N153AW	B737	23406	N159UP	A300	848	N164UW	A321	1425
N145FE	B727	19109	N153DL	B767	24985	N159US	DC-10	46768	N164W	1-11	090
N145SP	B707	20174	N153FA	DC-8	45755	N160AA	DC-10	46710	N165AT	L1011	193J-1183
N145UA	B747	21441	N153FE	B727	18286	N160AT	L1011	293A-1217	N165AW	B737	23626
N145UP	A300	828	N153FN	B727	18846	N160AW	B737	23782	N165BS	MD80	53520
N145US	DC-10	46754	N153FV	B737	23172	N160BS	MD80	53463	(N165FE)	B727	18862
N146AA	DC-10	46701	N153GJ	CRJ7	10219	(N160FE)	B727	18317	N165GJ	CRJ7	10257
N146AC	146	E2057	N153SY	DC-10	48276	N160FN	B727	18942	N165MD	CRJ7	10165
N146AP	146	E1013	N153UA	B747	20102	N160GE	B757	26160	N165PL	A300	584
N146AW	B737	20195	N153UP	A300	839	N160GJ	CRJ7	10239	N165UA	B747	21658
N146FE	B727	19110	N153US	DC-10	46762	N160GL	B707	20026	N165UP	A300	854
N146FT	146	E2056	N154AA	DC-10	46709	N160PL	MD80	49763	N165US	146	E2023
N146JS	B737	20688	N154AW	B737	23776	N160UA	B747	21237	N165US	A321	1431
N146PZ	146	E3149	N154DL	B767	25241	N160UP	A300	849	N165W	B737	19605
N146QT	146	E2056	N154FE	B727	18287	N160US	DC-10	46769	N166AA	DC-10	46908
N146RF	B747	22711	N154FN	B727	18815	N161AA	DC-10	46942	N166AT	737NG	33917
N146SB	146	E2074	N154FV	B737	23225	N161AN	B737	25161	N166AW	B737	23627
N146SP	B707	20016	N154GJ	CRJ7	10224	N161AT	L1011	293A-1219	N166DE	DC-9	47152
N146UA	B747	21547	(N154KH)	B727	21269	N161AW	B737	23783	N166FE	B727	18863
N146UK	146	E3120	N154LR	CRJ	7154	N161BS	MD80	53464	N166PL	A300	603
N146UP	A300	829	N154SF	CRJ	7154	N161DB	DC-8	45980	N166PL	MD80	49928
N146US	DC-10	46755	N154SY	DC-10	48259	N161DF	B737	22161	N166UP	A300	861
N147AA	DC-10	46702	N154UA	B747	20103	N161FN	B737	20521	N166US	146	E2024
N147AW	B737	22630	N154UP	A300	840	N161GE	A300	161	N166US	A321	1436
N147FE	B727	19080	N154US	DC-10	46763	N161GE	B757	26161	N166WP	B737	22024
N147SP	B707	20085	N155AW	B737	23777	N161GJ	CRJ7	10253	N167AA	DC-10	46930
N147UA	B747	21548	N155DL	B767	25269	N161GL	B707	20172	N167AS	MD80	49414
N147UP	A300	830	N155FE	B727	18288	N161JT	B737	24161	N167AT	737NG	33918
N147US	DC-10	46756	(N155FN)	B727	18816	N161KB	B757	28161	N167AW	B737	23628
N148AA	DC-10	46703	N155FW	B727	22381	N161LF	737NG	28224	N167FE	B727	18864
N148AC	146	E2058	N155GJ	CRJ7	10225	N161LF	B737	25162	N167MD	CRJ7	10167
N148AW	B737	22340	(N155KH)	B727	20041	N161LF	B737	26283	N167PL	B737	22531
N148CA	DC-9	47656	(N155MA)	B727	23124	N161LF	B757	26274	N167UP	A300	862
N148FE	B727	19086	N155MC	L1011	193A-1055	N161NG	1-11	067	N167US	146	E2025
N148UA	B747	21648	N155MW	CRJ	7021	N161PL	MD80	49764	N167US	A321	1442
N148UP	A300	831	(N155PA)	B737	20440	N161UA	B747	21352	N167WP	B737	21717
N148US	DC-10	46757	N155UA	B747	20104	N161UP	A300	850	N168AA	DC-10	46938
N149AT	737NG	32681	N155UP	A300	841	N161US	DC-10	46770	N168AT	737NG	32653
N149AW	B737	22575	N155US	DC-10	46764	N161UW	A321	1403	N168AW	B737	23629
N149DM	B707	19773	N156AW	B737	23778	N162AA	DC-10	46943	N168BN	A320	0168
N149FE	B727	19087	N156DL	B767	25354	N162AT	L1011	293A-1220	N168CK	CRJ	7099
N149FN	B727	18814	N156FE	B727	18289	N162AW	B737	23784	N168CL	B747	29906
N149UA	B747	21649	N156FN	B727	18943	N162BS	MD80	53465	N168FE	B727	18865
N149UP	A300	832	N156GJ	CRJ7	10227	N162CA	DC-8	45956	N168GB	A320	0476
N149US	DC-10	46758				(N162FE)	B727	18318	N168MD	CRJ7	10168

Reg	Type	Serial	Reg	Type	Serial	Reg	Type	Serial	Reg	Type	Serial
N168PL	MD80	53174	N176AA	B757	32395	N183UA	B747	25379	N191AJ	MD80	53191
N168UP	A300	863	N176AS	MD80	49411	N183US	146	E2043	N191AN	B757	32385
N168US	A321	1447	N176AT	737NG	32654	N183UW	A321	1539	N191AP	B737	25191
N168WP	B737	22728	N176DN	B767	25061	N184AN	B757	29594	N191AT	L1011	193C-1084
N169AT	737NG	32744	(N176DZ)	B767	29695	N184AS	MD80	49412	N191CB	B727	20822
N169AW	B737	23630	N176DZ	B767	29697	N184AT	737NG	32656	N191DN	B767	28448
N169DZ	B767	29689	N176SE	CRJ	7176	N184AT	DC-10	46751	N191FE	B727	19084
N169FE	B727	18866	N176UA	B747	24383	N184AW	B737	22651	N191FH	B737	23832
N169KT	B727	22359	N176UW	A321	1499	N184DN	B767	27111	(N191FS)	B727	19262
N169PL	MD80	53175	N177AN	B757	32396	N184FE	B727	18870	N191G	B737	25191
N169UP	A300	864	N177DN	B767	25122	N184JB	E190	19000008	N191LF	B737	24332
N169UW	A321	1455	(N177DZ)	B767	29696	N184QS	737NG	30884	N191LF	MD80	49822
(N170AW)	B737	23122	N177DZ	B767	29698	N184SK	DC-8	45981	N191LS	B737	25191
N170FE	1-11	057	N177MD	CRJ7	10177	N184UA	B747	25380	N191PL	A300	713
N170PL	B737	22733	N177UA	B747	24384	N184US	146	E2044	N191QS	737NG	30791
N170RJ	146	E1199	N177US	146	E2039	N184US	A321	1651	N191RD	B727	22290
N170UP	A300	865	N177US	A321	1517	N185AN	B757	32379	N191UA	B747	26880
N170US	A321	1462	(N178AA)	B757	32397	N185AT	L1011	193C-1052	N191US	146	E2073
N171AA	DC-10	46906	N178AA	B757	32398	N185AW	B737	22652	N191US	DC-9	45718
N171AW	B737	21599	N178AT	L1011	193A-1008	N185DN	B767	27961	N191UW	A321	1447
N171DN	B767	24759	N178AW	B737	22645	N185FE	B727	18871	N192AJ	MD80	53192
N171DZ	B767	29690	N178DN	B767	25143	N185FR	B737	25185	N192AN	B757	32386
N171FE	1-11	061	(N178DZ)	B767	29697	N185UA	B747	25395	N192AT	B737	23449
N171G	B727	21071	N178DZ	B767	30596	N185US	146	E2045	N192AT	L1011	193C-1057
N171LF	737NG	30666	N178EE	B737	22728	N185UW	A321	1666	N192DN	B767	28449
N171LF	B737	26286	N178JB	E190	19000004	N186AN	B757	32380	N192FE	B727	19085
N171LF	B767	26262	N178UA	B747	24385	N186AT	L1011	193C-1074	N192GP	B737	21192
N171MD	CRJ7	10171	N178US	146	E2040	N186AW	B737	22653	N192JB	E190	19000014
N171PL	B737	22734	N178US	A321	1519	N186DN	B767	27962	N192PL	A300	715
N171QS	737NG	30572	N179AA	B757	32397	N186FE	B727	18872	N192SA	DC-9	47418
N171TR	146	E1071	(N179AA)	B757	32398	N186LS	B737	25186	N192UA	B747	26881
N171UA	B747	24322	N179AT	L1011	193L-1120	N186UA	B747	26875	N192US	146	E2074
N171UK	C-17	UK.1	N179AW	B737	22646	N186US	A321	1701	N192US	DC-9	47156
N171UP	A300	866	N179DE	DC-9	47011	N187AN	B757	32381	N192UW	A321	1496
N171US	146	E2028	N179DN	B767	25144	N187AS	MD80	49888	N193AN	B757	32387
N171US	A321	1465	(N179DZ)	B767	29698	N187AT	L1011	193C-1077	N193AT	B737	23450
N172AJ	B757	32400	N179DZ	B767	30597	N187AW	B737	22654	N193AT	L1011	193C-1071
N172AW	B737	23631	N179FE	1-11	075	N187DN	B757	27582	N193DN	B767	28450
N172DN	B767	24775	N179JB	E190	19000006	N187FE	B727	19079	N193FE	B727	19142
N172DZ	B767	29691	N179PC	B727	22052	N187JB	E190	19000009	N193JB	E190	19000017
N172FE	1-11	056	N179UA	B747	25158	N187SK	DC-8	46202	N193UA	B747	26890
N172PL	B737	19711	N179US	146	E2041	N187UA	B747	26876	N193US	146	E2075
N172UA	B747	24363	N179UW	A321	1521	N187US	146	E2046	N193US	DC-9	45828
N172UK	C-17	UK.2	N180AD	737NG	30496	N187US	A321	1704	N194AA	B757	32388
N172UP	A300	867	N180AW	B737	22647	N188AN	B757	32382	N194AS	MD80	53377
N172US	146	E2030	N180AX	B727	20041	N188AT	L1011	193C-1078	N194AT	L1011	193B-1230
N172US	A321	1472	N180DN	B767	25985	N188AW	B737	22655	(N194AW)	B737	19552
N173AN	B757	32399	N180FE	B727	18867	N188CL	B727	18893	N194CA	B707	17663
N173AT	737NG	32661	N180RN	B737	22628	N188DN	B767	27583	N194DN	B767	28451
N173AW	B737	23632	N180SM	737NG	30496	N188FE	B727	19081	N194FE	B727	19143
N173DN	B767	24000	N180UA	B747	25224	N188LF	B737	23766	N194UA	B747	26892
N173DZ	B767	29692	N180US	A321	1525	N188SC	A300	188	N194US	DC-9	47016
N173FE	1-11	087	N181AN	B757	29591	N188UA	B747	26877	N195AN	B757	32389
N173PL	B737	20236	N181AT	L1011	193L-1125	N188US	146	E2047	N195AT	L1011	193C-1041
N173UA	B747	24380	N181AW	B737	22648	N188US	A321	1724	N195AW	B737	21500
N173UK	C-17	UK.3	N181DN	B767	25986	N189AN	B757	32383	N195CA	B707	17668
N173UP	A300	868	N181FE	B727	18868	N189AS	MD80	49933	N195DN	B767	28452
N173US	146	E2031	N181LF	B737	24208	N189AT	L1011	193C-1081	N195FE	B727	19144
N173US	A321	1481	N181LF	B767	26261	N189AW	B737	22656	N195UA	B747	26899
N174AA	B757	31308	N181LF	B777	28692	N189AX	DC-10	48277	N195US	DC-9	47017
N174AT	737NG	32667	N181SK	DC-8	45910	N189CB	B727	20739	N196AA	B757	32390
N174AW	B737	23633	N181UA	B747	25278	N189DN	B767	25990	N196AJ	B727	20838
N174DN	B767	29689	N181US	146	E2042	N189FE	B727	19082	N196AT	B747	23244
N174DZ	B767	29693	N181UW	A321	1531	N189GE	MD80	49189	N196AT	L1011	193B-1076
N174FE	1-11	BAC.127	N182AN	B757	29592	N189NK	B737	25189	N196AU	B737	21196
N174GM	B747	21141	N182AW	B737	22649	N189UA	B747	26878	N196AW	B737	21501
N174UA	B747	24381	N182DN	B767	25987	N189US	146	E2048	N196CA	B707	17610
N174UK	C-17	UK.4	N182GE	B737	25182	N189UW	A321	1425	N196DN	B767	28453
N174UP	A300	869	(N182QS)	737NG	30496	N190AA	B757	32384	N196FE	B727	19145
N174US	146	E2034	N182QS	737NG	32575	N190AJ	B727	18878	N196UA	B747	28715
N174US	A321	1492	N182SK	DC-8	45817	N190AN	MD80	53190	N196US	DC-9	47155
N175AN	B757	32394	N182UA	B747	25279	N190AT	L1011	193C-1086	N197AL	B737	20300
N175AT	737NG	32652	N182UW	A321	1536	(N190AW)	B737	20364	N197AN	B757	32391
N175AW	B737	23634	N183AN	B757	29593	(N190CB)	B727	20545	N197AT	L1011	193P-1082
N175DN	B767	24803	N183AT	DC-10	46501	N190DN	B767	28447	N197AW	B737	19709
(N175DZ)	B767	29694	N183AT	L1011	193A-1153	N190FE	B727	19083	N197CA	B707	17672
N175DZ	B767	29696	N183AW	B737	22650	N190FH	B737	23831	N197DN	B767	28454
N175MD	CRJ7	10178	N183DN	B767	27110	N190JB	E190	19000011	(N197FE)	B727	19146
(N175SG)	E145	145775	(N183FE)	B727	18869	N190PL	A300	709	N197JB	E190	19000020
N175UA	B747	24382	N183JB	E190	19000007	N190UA	B747	26879	N197JQ	B737	20196
N175US	146	E2036	N183NA	MD80	49808	N190US	146	E2072	N197QQ	B737	21184
N175US	A321	1496	N183SK	DC-8	45904	N190UW	A321	1436	N197SS	B737	20711

Registration	Type	S/N
N197UA	B747	26901
N197US	DC-9	47154
N198AA	B757	32392
N198AT	L1011	193B-1111
N198AW	B737	19710
N198CA	B707	17661
N198DN	B767	28455
N198FE	B727	19154
N198JB	E190	19000021
N198PC	B727	22053
N198UA	B747	28716
N198US	DC-9	47045
N199AJ	B727	21426
N199AM	B727	19262
N199AN	B757	32393
N199AW	B737	19712
N199DN	B767	28456
N199FE	B727	19509
N199NA	B737	19949
N199UA	B747	28717
N199US	DC-9	47153
N200AU	B737	19418
N200AV	B727	21930
N200CC	1-11	068
N200EE	1-11	083
N200GE	B767	26200
N200JX	1-11	015
N200KG	B737	24060
N200LR	B727	21945
N200NE	B737	20440
N200UU	B757	27809
N200WN	737NG	32482
N201CP	E145	145726
N201EA	A300	041
N201FE	B727	22924
N201FE	B737	21926
(N201LF)	737NG	30595
N201LF	B767	24448
N201LV	737NG	29854
N201US	B727	22154
N201UU	B757	27810
N201YT	B737	21192
N202AC	B767	25280
N202AE	B747	21097
N202AP	A300	056
N202AU	B737	19419
N202AV	B727	21931
(N202BN)	F.100	11257
N202CP	E145	145728
N202DJ	B707	20017
N202EA	A300	042
N202GA	A300	209
N202KG	B737	24059
N202ME	DC-9	47672
N202PA	A300	195
N202PH	B747	20888
N202PS	CRJ	7858
N202RC	L1011	193B-1013
N202UA	B737	24717
N202US	B727	22155
"N202UU"	B757	27811
N202UW	B757	27811
N202WN	737NG	33999
N203AA	MD80	49145
N203AE	B747	21098
N203AU	B737	19420
N203AV	B727	22474
N203EA	A300	043
N203FE	B727	22925
N203FE	B737	21927
N203JB	E190	19000023
N203ME	DC-9	47673
N203PA	A300	227
N203UA	B737	24718
N203US	B727	22543
N203UW	B757	30548
N203WN	737NG	32483
N203YT	B737	22802
N204AE	B747	21099
N204AM	MD80	49404
N204AU	B737	19603
N204AV	B727	22475
N204EA	A300	044
N204FE	B727	22926
N204GE	B767	26204
N204ME	DC-9	47680
N204P	F.28	11227
N204PA	A300	198
N204RC	L1011	193B-1215
N204UA	B727	28713
N204US	B727	22544
N204UW	B757	30886
N204WN	737NG	29855
N205AA	MD80	49155
N205AM	MD80	49405
N205AU	B737	19421
N205AV	B727	22476
N205EA	A300	065
N205FE	B727	22927
N205FE	B737	21929
N205ME	DC-9	47601
N205P	F.28	11228
N205PA	A300	247
N205UA	B777	28714
N205US	B727	20392
N205US	DC-9	47690
N205UW	B757	30887
N205WN	737NG	34010
N206AU	B737	19422
(N206BN)	F.100	11292
N206EA	A300	066
N206FE	B727	22928
N206FE	B737	21959
N206JB	E190	19000025
N206ME	DC-9	47791
N206P	F.28	11229
N206PA	A300	234
N206PS	CRJ	7860
N206UA	B777	30212
N206US	B727	20393
N206UW	B757	27808
N206WN	737NG	34011
N207AA	MD80	49158
N207AE	B747	21516
N207AU	B737	19423
N207BA	B747	22482
(N207BN)	F.100	11299
N207EA	A300	067
N207FE	B727	22929
(N207FX)	D0328	3207
N207ME	DC-9	47794
N207P	F.28	11230
N207PA	A300	236
N207PS	CRJ	7873
N207UA	B777	30213
N207US	B727	20302
N207US	B727	21699
N207US	DC-9	47355
N207WN	737NG	34012
N208AA	MD80	49159
N208AE	B747	21517
N208AU	B737	19547
N208BC	CRJ	7283
N208EA	A300	068
N208FE	B727	22930
N208LS	B767	25208
N208P	F.28	11233
N208PA	A300	304
N208UA	B777	30214
N208UP	B727	21701
N208US	B727	20303
N208US	DC-9	47220
N208WN	737NG	29856
N209EA	A300	086
N209FE	B727	22931
N209ME	DC-9	47730
N209P	F.28	11234
N209PA	A300	305
N209PK	B737	24209
N209PS	CRJ	7874
N209UA	B777	30215
N209UP	B727	21698
N209US	B737	19548
N209WN	737NG	32484
N210AA	MD80	49161
(N210BN)	F.100	11294
N210DS	B707	18167
N210EA	A300	087
N210FE	B727	22932
N210G	SE210	138
N210NE	B727	18903
(N210NE)	B727	18905
N210PA	A300	238
N210TN	A300	210
N210UA	B777	30216
N210UP	B727	21697
N210US	B737	19555
N210WN	737NG	34162
(N211BN)	F.100	11298
N211DB	B727	20766
N211FL	B727	19807
N211JL	B747	22989
N211MD	MD11	48402
N211NW	DC-10	46868
N211PA	A300	235
N211PL	B737	20681
N211UA	B777	30217
N211UP	B727	21700
N211US	B737	20211
N211WN	737NG	34163
(N212BN)	F.100	11301
N212EA	A300	091
N212FE	B727	22934
N212JL	B747	23067
N212ME	DC-9	47701
N212PA	A300	208
N212PL	B737	20776
N212UA	B777	30218
N212UP	B727	21392
N212US	B737	20212
N212WN	737NG	32485
(N213BN)	F.100	11302
N213EA	A300	092
N213FE	B727	22935
N213JL	B747	23068
N213MT	B737	21356
N213MX	A320	3123
N213PA	A300	210
N213PP	B737	21130
N213PS	CRJ	7879
N213UA	B777	30219
N213UP	B727	21341
N213US	B737	20213
N213WN	737NG	34217
N214AA	MD80	49162
N214AM	MD80	49585
N214AU	B737	20214
(N214BN)	F.100	11317
N214F	B727	21455
N214P	F.28	11235
N214UA	B777	30220
N214UP	B727	21342
N214WN	737NG	32486
N215AA	MD80	49163
N215BA	B747	22291
N215EA	A300	108
N215FE	B727	22936
N215ME	DC-9	47744
N215P	F.28	11240
N215PS	CRJ	7880
N215UA	B777	30221
N215US	B737	20095
N215US	DC-9	47480
N215WN	737NG	32487
N215YC	C-15	?
N216AA	MD80	49167
N216AM	MD80	49586
N216AP	B727	21600
(N216BN)	F.100	11322
N216EA	A300	118
N216FE	B727	22937
N216JB	E190	19000026
N216ME	DC-9	47740
N216PA	A300	204
N216PS	CRJ	7882
N216UA	B777	30549
N216US	B737	19954
(N216WN)	737NG	32488
N216WR	737NG	32488
(N217BN)	F.100	11341
N217CA	1-11	063
N217EA	A300	119
N217FE	B727	22938
N217JC	737NG	34232
N217UA	B777	30550
N217US	B737	20215
(N217WN)	737NG	34232
N218AA	MD80	49168
N218BA	B747	20827
N218CA	1-11	089
N218CT	B737	25218
N218FE	B727	21101
N218PS	CRJ	7885
N218TA	B737	20218
N218TT	B727	19684
N218UA	B777	30222
N218US	B737	20216
N218WN	737NG	32489
N219AA	MD80	49171
N219AS	B737	22119
N219BA	B747	22293
N219EA	A300	120
N219FE	B727	21102
N219PA	B737	19956
N219TY	B737	24219
N219UA	B777	30551
N219US	B737	20414
N219WN	737NG	32490
N220AM	B707	17696
N220AN	A320	0022
N220AU	DC-10	46501
N220EA	A300	124
N220FE	B727	20934
N220LS	B737	22090
N220NE	B727	18905
N220NW	DC-10	46577
N220PR	DC-10	46577
N220PS	CRJ	7887
N220RB	DC-8	45280
N220UA	B777	30223
N220US	B737	20453
(N220WL)	B737	22597
N220WN	737NG	32491
N221AA	MD80	49172
N221AL	B727	22044
N221AW	B737	20125
N221CN	1-11	BAC.111
N221DL	B737	23970
N221EA	A300	152
N221FE	B727	20764
N221FE	B727	20932
N221FL	B727	19805
N221GE	B747	22995
N221GF	B747	22996
N221LF	A300	743
N221LF	B737	25373
N221LF	B737	26283
N221LF	B767	27136
N221MP	B737	20120
N221NW	DC-10	46579
N221PS	CRJ	7889
N221UA	B777	30552
N221US	B737	20454
N221WN	737NG	34259
N222AW	B737	23789
N222AW	B737	24791
N222DZ	B737	23971
N222EA	A300	153
N222FE	B727	20765
N222FE	B727	20933
N222KW	A300	236
N222TM	B737	24791
N222UA	B777	30553
N222WN	737NG	34290
N223AA	MD80	49173
N223AW	B737	24790

Reg	Type	C/n	Reg	Type	C/n	Reg	Type	C/n	Reg	Type	C/n
N223BA	B747	24975	N229KW	A300	261	N236WA	B737	23184	N243BA	B747	22294
N223DZ	B737	23972	N229NW	DC-10	46551	N236WN	737NG	34631	N243FE	B727	21480
N223EA	A300	154	N229PS	CRJ	7898	N237AA	MD80	49253	N243NW	DC-10	48315
N223FB	DC-8	45985	N229UA	B777	30557	N237BA	737NG	33500	N243TR	B737	23503
(N223FE)	B727	20766	N229US	B737	21818	N237CT	B737	23750	N243US	B737	22445
N223FE	B727	20935	N229WN	737NG	32498	(N237DH)	B727	19192	N243WA	B737	23517
N223JS	CRJ	7892	N230AL	B747	23048	N237FE	B727	21331	N243WN	737NG	34863
N223KW	A300	227	N230AM	A320	0023	N237G	B707	19133	N244AA	MD80	49256
N223NW	DC-10	46580	N230AN	A320	0023	N237NW	DC-10	47844	N244FE	B727	21647
N223UA	B777	30224	N230AU	B737	21975	N237PS	CRJ	7906	N244NW	DC-10	48316
N223US	B737	21665	N230BA	A310	669	N237TA	B737	21645	N244PS	CRJ	7912
N223WN	737NG	32492	N230EA	A300	216	N237TR	B737	23007	N244SR	B737	29244
N224AA	MD80	49174	N230GE	B737	23065	N237US	B737	22353	N244TR	B737	23003
N224BA	MD80	53469	N230MR	B747	23056	N237WA	B737	23185	N244US	B737	22752
N224DA	B737	24269	N230NE	B727	18907	N237WN	737NG	34632	N244WA	B737	23518
N224EA	A300	155	N230NW	DC-10	46552	N238AT	B727	19150	N244WN	737NG	34864
N224JT	B737	21666	N230PS	CRJ	7904	N238BA	B747	22594	N245AA	MD80	49257
N224KW	A300	073	N230RX	A320	0230	N238CT	B737	23812	N245AC	B707	18068
N224NW	DC-10	46581	(N230UW)	A320	2193	N238JB	E190	19000039	N245AY	B767	23897
N224TA	737NG	30496	(N230WL)	B737	23001	N238NW	DC-10	48267	N245BA	B747	22595
N224UA	B777	30225	N230WN	737NG	34592	N238RX	A320	0238	N245FE	B727	22016
N224US	B737	21666	N231DN	B737	23717	N238TA	B737	22075	N245HG	DC-8	45662
N224WN	737NG	32493	N231EA	A300	220	"N238TR"	A310	552	N245PS	CRJ	7919
N225AA	MD80	49175	N231FL	B727	19205	N238TR	B737	23349	N245TR	B737	23793
N225AG	B737	22516	N231JB	E190	19000033	(N238TZ)	B727	19150	N245US	B737	22751
N225DL	B737	25069	N231TA	B737	22596	N238US	B737	22398	N245WA	B737	23519
N225EA	A300	158	N231US	B737	21976	N238WA	B737	23186	N245WN	737NG	32506
N225GE	A300	158	N231US	DC-9	48114	N238WN	737NG	34713	N246AA	MD80	49258
N225KW	A300	093	(N231UW)	A320	2312	N239CT	B737	23980	N246AY	B767	23898
N225LF	A321	0604	N231WN	737NG	32499	N239DW	B737	23977	N246BA	B757	24738
N225LF	A330	087	N232AA	MD80	49179	N239JB	E190	19000040	N246FE	B727	22068
N225NW	DC-10	46582	N232BA	A310	654	N239NW	DC-10	48290	N246LV	737NG	32507
N225RX	A320	0225	N232DZ	B737	24220	N239TA	B737	23789	N246PS	CRJ	7920
N225UA	B777	30554	N232EA	A300	259	N239TR	B737	23002	N246SS	146	E1003
N225US	B737	21667	N232NW	DC-10	46961	N239US	B737	22354	N246ST	B737	24696
N225VV	DC-8	45765	N232TA	B737	22277	N239WA	B737	23187	N246TR	B737	23010
N225WN	737NG	34333	N232US	B737	22018	N239WN	737NG	34714	N246US	B737	22753
N226AA	MD80	49176	(N232UW)	A320	2359	N240AT	737NG	32657	N246WA	B737	23520
N226AW	B737	25010	N232WN	737NG	32500	N240AU	B737	22355	N247JB	E190	19000042
N226EA	A300	161	N233AA	MD80	49180	N240BA	B777	28281	N247JM	A300	247
N226G	B757	25491	(N233BA)	B747	22709	N240FE	B727	20978	N247JS	CRJ	7922
N226GE	A300	161	N233BC	B737	24788	N240LA	B757	24367	N247RX	A320	0247
N226JS	CRJ	7895	N233EA	A300	261	N240LF	B737	24070	N247SP	B747	21023
N226KW	A300	095	N233FE	B727	21327	N240MC	B737	24069	N247TN	A300	247
N226MT	B767	26206	N233LV	737NG	32501	N240NE	B727	18906	N247TR	B737	23011
N226NW	DC-10	46583	N233NW	DC-10	46640	N240NW	DC-10	48319	N247US	B737	22754
N226UA	B777	30226	N233TA	B737	22601	(N240PR)	B737	19424	N247WA	B737	23521
N226US	B737	21815	N233TM	B737	23043	N240RC	B727	21474	N247WN	737NG	32508
N226VV	DC-8	45766	N233US	B737	22273	(N240RC)	SE210	87	N248AA	MD80	49259
N226WN	737NG	32494	N233UW	A320	2405	N240SE	A320	0024	N248AY	B767	23900
N227AA	MD80	49177	N234AA	MD80	49181	N240SZ	B767	24086	N248BA	B747	22712
N227AN	B757	23227	N234AN	B737	24234	N240TA	B737	21729	N248FS	CRJ	7926
N227AU	B737	21816	N234DC	DC-10	46940	N240TF	B737	24030	N248US	B737	22755
N227AW	B737	25011	N234EA	A300	271	N240TR	B737	23504	N248WA	B737	23602
N227BA	MD80	53487	N234FA	B707	20069	N240WA	B737	23188	N248WN	737NG	32509
N227EA	A300	204	N234FE	B727	21328	N240WN	737NG	32503	N249AA	MD80	49269
N227JL	B727	20875	N234GD	B737	24234	N241AA	MD80	49254	N249AU	B767	23901
N227KW	A300	274	N234GE	B737	23444	N241AG	B737	24103	N249BA	B747	24309
N227MT	B767	26207	N234NW	DC-10	46912	N241CV	B757	24122	N249JB	E190	19000045
N227NW	DC-10	46969	N234TR	B737	23004	N241DL	B737	23833	N249JW	B737	25249
N227UA	B777	30555	N234US	B737	22274	N241FE	B727	20979	N249PS	CRJ	7926
N227VV	B707	19212	(N234UW)	A320	2422	N241LF	B737	24132	N249TR	B737	22598
N227WN	737NG	34450	N234WN	737NG	32502	N241LF	B757	26247	N249US	B737	22756
N228AA	MD80	49178	N235EA	A300	274	N241MT	B737	24131	N249WA	B737	23603
N228AW	B737	25032	N235FE	B727	21329	N241NW	DC-10	48282	N249WN	737NG	34951
N228EA	A300	207	N235NW	DC-10	46915	(N241PR)	B737	20221	N249WP	B767	24952
N228G	B727	20533	N235SC	B757	24235	N241PS	CRJ	7909	N250AP	B767	25000
N228JB	E190	19000030	N235TA	B737	21765	N241TC	DC-9	45775	N250AT	B737	25071
N228KW	A300	207	N235US	B737	22443	N241US	B737	22443	N250AY	B767	23902
N228NW	DC-10	46578	(N235UW)	A320	2430	N241WA	B737	23189	N250GE	B737	25017
N228PR	DC-10	46578	N235WA	B737	22859	N241WN	737NG	32504	N250LA	B757	24291
N228PS	CRJ	7897	N235WN	737NG	34630	N242AA	MD80	49255	N250MY	B767	23306
N228UA	B777	30556	N236AA	MD80	49251	N242BA	B747	24226	N250NE	B727	20112
N228US	B737	21817	N236BA	737NG	33434	N242DL	B737	23834	N250PS	CRJ	7929
N228VV	B707	18714	(N236DH)	B727	19191	N242FE	B727	21178	N250TR	B737	22597
N228WN	737NG	32496	N236FE	B727	21330	N242GD	B737	24234	N250UP	MD11	48745
N228Z	DC-9	47151	N236GX	737NG	32363	N242JS	CRJ	7911	N250WN	737NG	34972
N229AN	A320	0229	N236JB	E190	19000035	N242NW	DC-10	47845	N251AA	MD80	49270
N229BA	A310	570	N236NW	DC-10	46934	N242TR	B737	23009	N251AU	B737	22757
N229DE	DC-9	45826	N236TA	B737	19708	N242US	B737	22444	N251AY	B767	24764
N229EA	A300	211	N236US	B737	22352	N242WA	B737	23516	N251DH	B727	19968
N229JB	E190	19000032	N236UW	A320	2482	N242WN	737NG	32505	N251FL	B727	19204

Reg	Type	Serial	Reg	Type	Serial	Reg	Type	Serial	Reg	Type	Serial
N251LF	B737	22408	(N259WA)	B737	23609	N267WN	737NG	32525	N274AU	B737	22886
N251MY	B767	23280	N259WN	737NG	35554	N268AT	737NG	33920	N274AW	DC-9	47236
N251PA	CRJ	7931	N260AU	B737	22866	N268AU	B737	22880	N274AY	A330	342
N251RY	B737	25180	N260AV	A320	1564	N268AV	A320	2175	(N274BN)	B727	20548
N251TR	B737	23792	N260BD	CRJ	7039	N268FE	B727	21674	(N274CL)	B727	20641
N251UP	MD11	48744	N260FA	L1011	193A-1158	N268SK	E145	145270	N274FE	B727	22039
N251US	B727	19970	N260GS	B727	19261	N268US	B727	20290	N274JB	E190	19000082
N251WN	737NG	32510	N260JS	CRJ	7957	N268WN	737NG	32524	N274N	F.28	11107
N252AU	B737	22758	N260MY	B767	23057	N269AA	MD80	49292	N274SK	E145	145344
N252AU	B767	24765	N260NE	B727	20113	N269AU	B737	22881	N274UP	MD11	48575
N252MY	B767	23973	N260SE	A320	0026	N269AV	A320	2187	N274US	B727	20296
N252RL	B727	21456	N260SE	CRJ	7140	N269FE	B727	21675	N274US	B737	22280
N252TR	B737	23001	N260SK	E145	145128	N269SK	E145	145293	N274WA	MD11	48633
N252UP	MD11	48768	N260UP	MD11	48418	N269US	B727	20291	N274WC	B727	20548
N252US	B727	19971	N260US	B727	19979	N269WN	737NG	32526	N274WN	737NG	32529
N252WN	737NG	34973	N260WN	737NG	32518	N270AE	B757	22185	N275AA	MD80	49272
N253AA	MD80	49286	N261AT	737NG	32660	N270AU	B737	22882	N275AF	B727	22092
N253AU	B737	22795	N261AU	B737	22867	N270AV	A320	2325	N275AU	B737	22887
N253AY	B767	24894	N261AV	A320	1615	N270AW	B737	24027	N275AW	B757	25495
N253CT	B757	25053	N261BD	CRJ	7137	N270AX	B727	19170	N275AY	A330	370
N253DV	B737	23800	N261LF	B737	26294	N270AX	DC-10	48318	N275B	B707	20060
N253FA	DC-8	45660	N261LF	B767	26261	N270AY	A330	315	(N275BN)	B727	20549
N253MY	B767	23974	N261LR	B737	22402	N270AZ	B737	27086	N275FE	B727	22040
N253PS	CRJ	7934	N261PS	CRJ	7959	N270BC	B747	22704	N275SK	E145	145345
N253SE	CRJ	7099	N261PW	B757	22176	N270E	1-11	BAC.120	N275UP	MD11	48774
N253TR	B737	23005	N261SK	E145	145144	N270FE	B727	22035	N275US	B727	21154
N253UP	MD11	48439	N261US	B727	19980	N270FL	B737	22733	N275WA	MD11	48631
N253US	B727	19972	N261WN	737NG	32517	N270PC	B727	22167	N275WC	B727	20549
N253WN	737NG	32511	N262AA	MD80	49290	N270SE	A320	0027	N275WN	737NG	36153
N254AU	B737	22796	N262AU	B737	22868	N270SK	E145	145304	N276AA	MD80	49273
N254DG	B757	25488	N262AV	A320	1725	N270UP	MD11	48576	N276AG	B727	22276
N254FE	B727	20936	N262CT	B757	26246	N270US	B727	20292	N276AT	737NG	32664
N254PS	CRJ	7935	N262FE	B727	21624	N270WN	737NG	29089	N276AU	B737	22888
N254RY	B737	24690	N262GE	A300	262	N271AA	MD80	49293	N276AW	B767	27376
N254SJ	737NG	30572	N262KS	B737	26282	N271AE	B757	23227	N276AY	A330	375
N254UP	MD11	48406	N262PS	CRJ	7962	N271AF	B727	22003	(N276BN)	B727	20550
N254US	B727	19973	N262SK	E145	145168	N271AU	B737	22883	N276C	DC-8	45641
(N254WA)	B737	23604	N262SR	B757	26244	N271AV	A320	2327	N276FE	B727	22041
N254WN	737NG	32512	N262US	B727	19981	N271AY	A330	323	(N276FL)	B737	23040
N255AA	MD80	49287	N262WN	737NG	32519	N271AZ	B727	27168	N276HE	B737	24276
N255AU	B737	22797	N263AU	B737	22869	N271CH	737NG	30271	N276SK	E145	145348
N255AY	B767	25257	N263AV	A320	1860	N271FE	B727	22036	N276UP	MD11	48579
N255CF	B737	24255	N263FE	B727	21625	N271FL	B727	22734	N276US	B727	21155
N255KD	B767	27255	N263LF	B737	26333	N271LF	B737	23788	N276WA	MD11	48632
N255RY	737NG	28619	N263LF	B757	26248	N271LF	B737	26286	N276WC	B727	20550
N255UP	MD11	48404	N263PC	1-11	068	N271LF	B757	26249	N276WN	737NG	32530
N255US	B727	19974	(N263PS)	CRJ	7963	N271LR	B737	22636	N277AU	B737	22889
(N255WA)	B737	23605	N263SK	E145	145199	N271LV	737NG	29090	N277AW	DC-9	47230
N255WN	737NG	32513	N263US	B727	19982	N271N	F.28	11105	N277AY	A330	380
N256AU	B737	22798	N263WN	737NG	32520	N271RX	A320	0271	N277CH	737NG	30277
N256AY	B767	26847	N264AU	B737	22961	N271SK	E145	145305	N277FE	B727	22042
N256PS	CRJ	7937	N264AV	A320	1867	N271SW	B767	23106	N277HE	B737	24277
N256UP	MD11	48405	N264FE	B727	21626	N271UP	MD11	48572	N277NS	1-11	057
N256US	B727	19975	N264LV	737NG	32521	N271US	B727	20293	N277SK	E145	145355
(N256WA)	B737	23606	N264MT	B767	24448	N271WA	MD11	48518	N277UP	MD11	48578
N256WN	737NG	32514	N264SK	E145	145221	N272AF	B727	22004	N277US	B727	21156
N257AU	B737	22799	N264US	B727	19983	N272AT	737NG	33921	"N277US"	B737	22009
N257DR	B737	25740	N265AU	B737	22962	N272AU	B737	22884	N277WA	MD11	48743
N257FE	B727	20939	N265AV	A330	0427	N272AY	A330	333	N277WN	737NG	32531
N257JQ	E145	14500812	N265CT	B737	26538	N272FE	B727	22037	N278AA	MD80	49294
N257PS	CRJ	7939	N265FE	B727	21671	N272LF	B757	26250	N278AT	737NG	32665
N257RX	A320	0257	N265JB	E190	19000049	N272N	F.28	11095	N278AU	B737	22890
N257UP	MD11	48451	N265LF	B767	26265	N272SK	E145	145306	N278AY	A330	388
N257US	B727	19976	N265SK	E145	145226	N272UP	MD11	48571	N278C	DC-8	45643
(N257WA)	B737	23607	N265US	B727	19984	N272US	B727	20294	N278FE	B727	22345
N257WN	737NG	32515	N265WN	737NG	32522	N272WA	MD11	48437	N278HE	B737	24278
N258AA	MD80	49288	N266AA	MD80	49291	N272WN	737NG	32527	N278SK	E145	146370
N258FE	B727	20940	N266AU	B737	228/8	N273AF	B727	22005	N278UP	MD11	48577
N258JB	E190	19000047	N266AV	A320	1152	N273AT	737NG	32662	N278US	B727	21157
N258JQ	E145	145768	N266BA	A310	634	N273AU	B737	22885	N278WA	MD11	48746
(N258KP)	B727	19977	N266FE	B727	21672	N273AY	A330	337	N278WN	737NG	36441
N258PS	CRJ	7941	N266JB	E190	19000054	N273FE	B727	22038	N279AA	MD80	49295
N258UP	MD11	48416	N266SK	E145	145241	N273JB	E190	19000073	N279AD	B737	22279
N258US	B727	19977	N266US	B727	19977	N273N	F.28	11106	N279AN	B767	27909
(N258WA)	B737	23608	N266WN	737NG	32523	N273SK	E145	145331	N279AP	B737	22279
N258WN	737NG	32516	N267AT	737NG	33919	N273UP	MD11	48574	N279AT	737NG	32666
N259AA	MD80	49289	N267AU	B737	22807	N273US	B727	20295	N279AU	B737	22891
N259AU	B737	22806	N267AV	A320	1198	N273WA	MD11	48519	N279AX	DC-10	47816
N259JQ	E145	145763	N267FE	B727	21673	(N273WC)	B727	20978	N279FE	B727	22346
N259PS	CRJ	7945	N267JB	E190	19000065	N273WN	737NG	32528	N279HE	B737	24279
N259UP	MD11	48417	N267SK	E145	145268	N274AA	MD80	49271	N279JB	E190	19000090
N259US	B727	19978	N267US	B727	20289	N274AF	B727	22091	N279SK	E145	145379

Registration	Type	Serial
N279UP	MD11	48573
N279US	B727	21158
N279WA	MD11	48756
N279WN	737NG	32532
N280AU	B737	22892
N280CD	B737	25595
N280FE	B727	22347
N280FH	F.28	11048
(N280FH)	F.28	11049
N280N	F.28	11061
N280NE	B727	18971
N280RX	A320	0280
N280SK	E145	145381
N280UP	MD11	48634
N280US	B727	21159
N280WA	MD11	48458
N280WN	737NG	32533
N281AT	737NG	33922
N281AU	B737	23114
N281FE	B727	22348
N281FH	F.28	11016
N281JB	E190	19000103
N281KH	B727	21105
N281LF	B737	22071
N281MP	F.28	11221
N281N	F.28	11075
N281SC	B727	21949
N281SK	E145	145391
N281UP	MD11	48538
N281US	B727	21160
N281WN	737NG	36528
N281ZV	B727	19281
N282AD	B737	20282
N282AU	B737	23115
N282FE	B727	22349
N282FH	F.28	11018
N282LF	B737	28200
N282MP	F.28	11223
N282N	F.28	11032
N282SC	B727	22558
N282SK	E145	145409
N282UP	MD11	48452
N282US	B727	21161
N282WA	B727	21484
N282WN	737NG	32534
N283A	B737	24283
N283AA	MD80	49296
N283AT	737NG	34479
N283AT	B727	19150
N283AU	B737	23116
N283CD	B737	29000
N283DH	B727	18275
N283FE	B727	22350
N283FH	F.28	11020
(N283MP)	F.28	11226
N283N	F.28	11035
N283SC	B727	22559
N283SK	E145	145424
N283TR	A310	552
N283UP	MD11	48484
N283US	B727	21322
N283WA	B727	21485
N283WN	737NG	36610
N284AN	B737	27284
N284AN	B767	28495
N284AT	737NG	32668
N284AT	B727	19151
N284AU	B737	23131
N284CD	B737	29001
N284CH	B737	28492
N284FE	B727	22621
N284FH	F.28	11024
N284KH	B727	21108
(N284MP)	F.28	11231
N284N	F.28	11036
N284SC	B727	21438
N284SK	E145	145427
N284TR	B737	22259
(N284TZ)	B727	19151
N284UP	MD11	48541
N284US	B727	21323
N284WA	B727	21697
N284WN	737NG	32535
N285AA	MD80	49297
N285AT	737NG	32670
N285AT	B727	19152
N285AU	B737	23132
N285AW	DC-9	47231
N285BA	A310	589
N285CD	E145	145098
N285CR	DC-10	48285
N285FE	B727	22622
(N285FH)	F.28	11032
N285FH	F.28	11033
N285MM	B737	28555
N285MT	B737	28563
N285SC	B727	21676
N285SK	E145	145435
N285SW	B747	22485
N285TR	B737	22260
(N285TZ)	B727	19152
N285UP	MD11	48457
N285US	B727	21324
N285WN	737NG	32536
N286AA	MD80	49298
N286AT	737NG	34480
N286AT	B727	19153
N286AU	B737	23133
N286AW	DC-9	47311
N286CD	B757	26240
N286CH	B737	28664
N286FE	B727	22623
N286FH	F.28	11038
N286N	F.28	11044
N286SC	B727	21601
N286SK	E145	145443
N286TR	B737	22266
N286UP	MD11	48453
N286US	B727	21325
N286WA	B727	21699
N286WN	737NG	32471
N287AA	MD80	49299
N287AT	737NG	32671
N287AT	B727	18805
N287AU	B737	23134
N287CH	B737	28761
N287FE	B727	21849
N287FH	F.28	11043
N287KB	MD80	49768
N287MD	MD80	49389
N287N	F.28	11087
N287SC	B727	21345
N287SK	E145	145460
N287TR	B737	22341
N287UP	MD11	48539
N287US	B727	21375
N287WA	B727	21699
N287WN	737NG	32537
N288AA	MD80	49300
N288AS	B727	22003
N288AT	737NG	33924
N288AT	B727	18943
N288AU	B737	23135
N288BA	B747	22710
N288BA	MD80	53468
N288CD	B737	20211
N288FE	B727	21850
N288FH	F.28	11044
N288N	F.28	11054
N288SC	B727	20765
N288SK	E145	145461
N288TR	B737	22342
N288UP	MD11	48540
N288US	B727	21376
N288WA	B727	21700
N288WN	737NG	36611
N289AA	MD80	49301
N289AN	B757	24289
N289AS	B727	22004
N289AT	737NG	32673
N289AT	B727	18942
N289CD	737NG	30278
N289CT	737NG	36633
N289FH	F.28	11047
N289MT	B727	22467
N289N	F.28	11064
(N289SC)	B727	21979
N289SC	B727	22475
N289SK	E145	145463
N289TR	B737	22159
N289UP	MD11	48455
N289US	B727	21377
N289WA	B727	21701
N290AA	MD80	49302
N290AN	B757	24290
N290AS	B727	21510
N290AT	737NG	33925
N290AT	B727	18812
N290N	F.28	11063
N290NE	B727	18972
N290RB	CRJ7	10029
N290SC	B727	20764
N290SE	A320	0029
N290SK	E145	145474
N290TR	B737	21713
N290UE	146	E2080
N290UP	MD11	48456
N290US	B727	21378
N290WA	B727	22108
N290WN	737NG	36632
N291AA	MD80	49303
N291AN	B757	24291
N291AS	B727	21511
N291AT	737NG	32675
N291EA	A300	049
N291LF	A321	0597
N291MX	A320	0291
N291N	F.28	11043
N291SC	B727	22770
N291SK	E145	145486
N291SR	B737	29122
N291SZ	B737	29122
N291TR	B737	22807
N291UE	146	E2084
N291UP	MD11	48477
N291US	B727	21379
N291WA	B727	22109
N291WN	737NG	32539
N292AA	MD80	49304
N292AS	B727	21458
N292AT	737NG	33926
N292BA	B747	22292
N292EA	A300	051
N292MX	A320	0292
N292SK	E145	145488
N292SZ	B737	29245
N292UE	146	E2087
N292UP	MD11	48566
N292US	B727	21503
N292WA	B727	22110
N292WN	737NG	32538
N293AA	MD80	49305
N293AS	B727	19534
N293AS	B727	21348
N293AW	B757	24293
N293N	F.28	11037
N293SK	E145	145500
N293UE	146	E2097
N293UP	MD11	48473
N293US	B727	21504
N293WA	B727	22111
N293WN	737NG	36612
N294AA	MD80	49306
N294AS	B727	22146
N294N	F.28	11101
N294SC	B727	21202
N294SK	E145	145497
N294UE	146	E2107
N294US	B727	21505
N294WA	B727	22112
N294WN	737NG	32540
N295AA	MD80	49307
N295AS	B727	22147
N295AT	737NG	32677
(N295MD)	B717	55001
N295SK	E145	145513
N295UE	146	E2108
N295US	B727	21506
N295WA	B727	22532
N295WN	737NG	32541
N296AA	MD80	49308
N296AJ	B727	21156
N296AS	B727	21459
N296AT	737NG	34861
N296CR	DC-10	48296
N296N	F.28	11096
N296SC	B727	22449
N296SK	E145	145514
N296US	B727	21788
N296WA	B727	22533
N296WN	737NG	36613
N297AA	MD80	49309
N297AS	B727	21608
N297BN	B727	19391
N297N	F.28	11098
N297SK	E145	145522
N297US	B727	21789
N297WA	B727	22534
N297WN	737NG	32542
N298AA	MD80	49310
N298AS	B727	21426
N298BA	B757	24748
N298BN	B727	19392
N298JD	B747	24195
N298N	F.28	11103
N298SK	E145	145508
N298US	B727	22152
N298WN	737NG	32543
N299AJ	B727	21427
N299AS	B727	21427
N299AT	737NG	32678
N299BN	B727	19393
N299BS	CRJ	7299
N299JD	B747	24196
N299LA	B737	19121
N299NY	B737	24299
N299SK	E145	145532
N299US	B727	22153
N299WN	737NG	36614
N300AA	B727	18856
N300AR	B737	24700
N300AT	737NG	33923
N300AU	B737	23228
N300AW	L1011	193P-1134
N300BN	B727	19394
N300DK	B727	18998
N300FV	A300	147
N300ME	DC-9	46718
N300ML	A320	0317
N300NE	B727	18974
N300SW	B737	22940
N301AA	B767	22307
N301AC	B737	23228
N301AL	B737	23841
N301AM	B757	30045
N301AR	B767	24728
N301AS	B707	18376
N301AT	A320	0030
N301AU	B737	23229
N301AW	B737	24008
N301BN	B727	19395
N301DE	B737	25994
N301DL	B737	23073
N301EA	L1011	193A-1002
N301EA	L1011	193A-1003
N301FE	DC-10	46800
(N301FE)	DC-10	47807
(N301FL)	B737	23257
N301FV	DC-10	46955
N301FV	DC-10	48258
N301JD	B747	24194
N301LF	737NG	28212
N301LF	B777	28689
N301ME	DC-9	47190
N301ML	A320	0315
N301NB	A319	1058
N301P	B737	23228
N301RC	MD80	48054

Reg	Type	Serial
N301SA	A320	0354
N301SW	**B737**	**22941**
N301TW	B747	20501
N301TZ	**737NG**	**28239**
N301UA	**B737**	**23642**
N301UP	**B767**	**27239**
N301US	**A320**	**0031**
(N301US)	B747	23719
N301XV	B737	20253
N302AA	B767	22308
N302AL	B737	23943
N302AR	B737	21014
N302AS	**737NG**	**30017**
N302AS	B707	18377
N302AU	B737	23230
N302AW	**B737**	**24009**
N302BN	B727	19242
N302DE	B737	25995
N302DL	B737	23074
N302EA	L1011	193A-1003
N302FE	**DC-10**	**46801**
(N302FE)	DC-10	47808
(N302FL)	B737	23177
N302FV	B727	21442
N302GC	E145	145600
N302LS	737NG	30231
N302MB	L1011	193P-1129
N302ME	DC-9	47102
N302ML	A320	0338
N302NB	**A319**	**1062**
N302RC	MD80	48055
(N302RP)	MD80	48054
N302SA	A320	0357
N302SW	**B737**	**22942**
N302TW	B747	20502
N302TZ	737NG	32576
N302UA	**B737**	**23643**
N302UP	**B767**	**27240**
N302US	A320	0032
(N302US)	B747	23720
N302VA	B737	20126
N302WA	B737	23182
N302XV	B737	20254
N303AA	B767	22309
N303AC	B737	23289
N303AL	B737	23499
N303AR	B737	22505
N303AS	**737NG**	**30016**
N303AS	B707	18042
N303AW	**B737**	**24010**
N303BN	B727	18897
N303DE	B737	25996
N303DL	B737	23075
N303EA	L1011	193A-1004
N303FE	**DC-10**	**46802**
(N303FE)	DC-10	47809
N303FL	**B737**	**25039**
N303FV	B727	21619
N303GA	A300	377
N303GC	E145	145608
N303ML	A320	0304
N303NB	A319	1071
N303P	B737	23229
(N303RP)	MD80	48055
N303SA	A320	0411
N303SW	**B737**	**22943**
N303TW	B747	20116
N303TZ	737NG	28648
N303UA	**B737**	**23644**
N303UP	**B767**	**27241**
N303US	**A320**	**0034**
(N303US)	B747	23818
N303VA	B737	20125
N303WA	B737	23183
N303WL	**DC-10**	**46917**
N303XV	B737	20255
N304AA	B767	22310
N304AC	B737	23290
N304AL	B737	23500
N304AS	B737	18049
N304AS	B727	22005
N304AW	B737	24011
N304BN	B727	20217
N304DE	B737	25997
N304DL	B737	23076
N304EA	L1011	193A-1005
N304FE	**DC-10**	**46992**
(N304FE)	DC-10	47810
N304FL	B737	27633
N304FV	A300	105
N304H	B757	22195
N304ML	**A320**	**0373**
N304NB	A319	1078
N304P	B737	23230
N304RC	MD80	48056
(N304RP)	MD80	48056
N304RX	A320	0304
N304SP	**DC-10**	**46540**
N304SW	**B737**	**22944**
N304TW	B747	20117
N304TZ	**737NG**	**30675**
N304UA	**B737**	**23665**
N304UP	**B737**	**27242**
N304US	**A320**	**0040**
(N304US)	B747	23819
N304VA	B737	19617
N304WA	B737	23345
N304WL	**DC-10**	**47928**
N304XV	B737	20256
N305AA	B767	22311
N305AS	**737NG**	**30013**
N305AS	B727	22091
N305AW	**B737**	**24012**
N305BN	B727	18794
N305CC	CRJ	7099
N305DE	B737	25998
N305DL	B737	23077
N305EA	L1011	193A-1006
N305FA	B737	28662
N305FE	DC-10	47870
N305FV	DC-10	47868
N305GB	L1011	193P-1127
N305NB	A319	1090
N305P	B737	23257
N305PA	**DC-9**	**45740**
(N305RP)	MD80	48057
N305SW	**B737**	**22945**
N305TW	B737	20742
N305TZ	**737NG**	**30706**
N305UA	**B737**	**23666**
N305UP	**B767**	**27243**
N305US	**A320**	**0041**
(N305US)	B747	23820
N305VA	B737	19606
N305WA	B737	23346
N306AA	B737	23291
N306AA	B737	22312
N306AS	**737NG**	**30014**
N306AS	B727	21997
N306AW	**B737**	**24633**
N306BN	B727	18795
N306DL	B737	23078
N306EA	L1011	193A-1007
N306FE	**DC-10**	**48287**
N306FL	B737	28563
N306FV	DC-10	47889
N306GB	L1011	193U-1138
N306GE	B737	23066
N306NB	A319	1091
N306P	B737	23258
N306RC	MD80	48057
(N306RP)	MD80	48086
N306SW	**B737**	**22946**
(N306TW)	B747	19655
N306TW	B737	20398
N306TZ	737NG	32348
N306UA	**B737**	**23667**
N306UP	**B767**	**27759**
N306US	A320	0060
(N306US)	B747	23821
N306VA	B737	19609
N306WA	B737	23347
N307AA	B767	22313
N307AC	B737	23251
N307AS	**737NG**	**30015**
N307AS	B727	22000
N307AT	**737NG**	**34862**
N307AW	**B737**	**24634**
N307BN	B727	18796
N307DL	B737	23079
N307EA	L1011	193A-1008
N307FE	**DC-10**	**48291**
N307FL	B737	28760
N307FV	A300	235
N307GB	L1011	193U-1131
N307JT	MD80	48086
(N307ML)	E145	145174
N307MT	B767	23072
N307NB	A319	1126
N307P	B737	23259
N307RC	MD80	48086
(N307RP)	MD80	48087
N307SW	**B737**	**22947**
N307TA	737NG	30783
N307TW	B747	20009
N307TZ	737NG	28653
N307UA	**B737**	**23668**
N307UP	**B767**	**27760**
N307US	A320	0106
(N307US)	B747	24222
N307VA	B737	19600
N307WA	B737	23440
N308AA	**B767**	**22314**
N308AC	B737	23252
N308AS	**B727**	**22002**
N308AT	**737NG**	**35109**
N308AW	**B737**	**24710**
N308BN	B727	19827
N308DL	B737	23080
N308EA	L1011	193A-1009
N308FE	**DC-10**	**48297**
N308FL	B737	28738
N308FV	A300	304
N308GB	L1011	193U-1133
N308NB	A319	1129
(N308RC)	MD80	48089
N308RX	A320	0308
N308SA	**B737**	**23498**
N308TA	737NG	30785
N308TZ	**737NG**	**28244**
N308UA	**B737**	**23669**
N308UP	**B767**	**27761**
N308US	A320	0107
(N308US)	B747	24223
N308VA	B737	19613
N308WA	B737	23441
N309AC	B737	23253
N309AS	**737NG**	**30857**
N309AS	B727	21947
N309AT	**737NG**	**33929**
N309AW	**B737**	**24711**
N309BN	B727	19808
N309DL	B737	23081
N309EA	L1011	193A-1010
N309EL	B707	18692
N309FE	**DC-10**	**48298**
N309FL	B737	28734
N309FV	B727	20661
N309GB	L1011	193P-1156
N309JT	MD80	48088
N309NB	A319	1131
N309P	B737	23260
N309RC	MD80	48088
N309SW	**B737**	**22948**
N309TZ	737NG	32577
N309UA	**B737**	**23670**
N309UP	**B767**	**27740**
N309US	**A320**	**0118**
(N309US)	B747	24224
N309VA	B737	19614
N309WA	B737	23442
N310AC	B737	23505
N310AN	B767	27310
N310AS	B727	21948
N310AU	B737	22878
N310BN	B727	19008
N310DA	B737	23082
N310EA	L1011	193A-1011
N310EL	1-11	072
N310FE	**DC-10**	**48299**
N310FL	**B737**	**26440**
N310FV	B757	25488
N310GA	A300	371
N310GB	L1011	193P-1155
N310MJ	DC-9	45740
N310NB	A319	1149
N310NE	B727	20241
N310NW	A320	0121
N310SS	L1011	193C-1096
N310SW	**B737**	**22949**
N310TZ	**737NG**	**28243**
N310UA	**B737**	**23671**
N310UP	**B767**	**27762**
(N310US)	B737	23257
N310VA	B737	21501
(N311AC)	B737	23752
N311AG	**B727**	**20512**
(N311AS)	B707	17650
N311AT	**737NG**	**33930**
N311AU	B737	22879
N311AW	**B737**	**24712**
N311BN	B727	19012
N311DL	B737	23083
N311EA	L1011	193A-1012
N311FE	**DC-10**	**46871**
N311FL	B737	24856
N311FV	**MD80**	**49855**
N311JT	MD80	48089
N311MD	MD11	48458
N311ML	737NG	30051
N311NB	A319	1164
N311RC	MD80	48089
N311SW	**B737**	**23333**
N311TZ	737NG	32578
N311UA	**B737**	**23672**
N311UP	**B767**	**27741**
N311US	**A320**	**0125**
(N311US)	B747	24225
N311VA	B737	21500
N311WA	B737	23597
N311XV	B737	19709
N312AA	B767	22315
N312AT	**737NG**	**35110**
N312AU	B737	22880
N312AW	**B737**	**24060**
N312DL	B737	23084
N312EA	L1011	193M-1019
N312FE	**DC-10**	**48300**
N312FL	B737	24569
N312GB	L1011	193P-1100
N312LA	**B767**	**32572**
N312ML	737NG	28613
N312NB	A319	1167
N312NE	B727	20193
N312P	B737	23261
N312RC	MD80	48090
N312SF	B757	25493
N312SW	**B737**	**23334**
N312TT	MD80	48003
N312TZ	737NG	32579
N312UA	**B737**	**23673**
N312UP	**B767**	**27763**
N312US	**A320**	**0152**
N312VA	B737	20236
N312WA	B737	23598
N312XV	B737	19710
N313AA	B767	22316
N313AT	**737NG**	**33927**
N313AU	B737	22881
N313AW	**B737**	**23712**
N313DL	B737	23085
N313EA	L1011	193A-1020
N313FE	**DC-10**	**48311**
N313FL	B737	26442
N313ML	737NG	29893
N313NB	**A319**	**1186**

N313NE	B727	19702	**N317AS**	**737NG**	**30856**	**N320NP**	**A319**	**1494**	N324UA	B737	23956
N313P	737NG	33010	**N317AT**	**737NG**	**35789**	N320P	B737	23237	**N324UP**	**B767**	**27750**
N313P	B737	23231	N317AU	B737	22885	N320PA	B727	18998	**N324US**	**A320**	**0273**
N313RC	MD80	48091	N317AW	B737	23388	**N320SW**	**B737**	**23341**	**N325AA**	**B767**	**22326**
N313SW	**B737**	**23335**	**N317CA**	**CRJ7**	**10055**	(N320TZ)	737NG	30643	N325AS	B727	20267
N313TZ	737NG	32580	N317DL	B737	23089	N320TZ	737NG	32610	N325AU	B737	23114
N313UA	**B737**	**23674**	N317EA	L1011	193A-1038	N320UA	B737	23952	N325AW	B737	23260
N313UP	**B767**	**27764**	N317F	B707	19004	**N320UP**	**B767**	**27747**	N325CT	737NG	33025
N313US	**A320**	**0153**	**N317FE**	**DC-10**	**46835**	**N320US**	**A320**	**0213**	N325DL	B737	23097
N313VA	B737	19711	(N317FE)	DC-10	48317	**N321AA**	**B767**	**22322**	N325EA	L1011	193A-1051
N313WA	B737	23599	N317FL	B737	25263	N321AU	B737	22889	N325F	B707	19355
N313XV	B737	19712	N317FV	A300	105	**N321DL**	**B737**	**23093**	(N325FE)	DC-10	47812
N314AS	B727	18992	**N317NB**	**A319**	**1324**	N321E	B707	18423	N325FV	DC-9	47725
N314AU	B737	22882	(N317NE)	B727	19489	N321EA	L1011	193A-1043	**N325JF**	**E145**	**145499**
N314AW	**B737**	**23733**	N317NE	B727	21945	**N321FE**	**DC-10**	**47836**	**N325NB**	**A319**	**1483**
N314DA	B737	23086	N317P	B737	23235	N321LF	B757	26269	N325P	B737	23514
N314EA	L1011	193A-1022	N317PA	B727	18995	**N321NB**	**A319**	**1414**	N325PA	B727	19007
N314FE	**DC-10**	**48312**	N317RX	A320	0317	N321P	B737	23510	**N325SW**	**B737**	**23689**
N314FL	B737	25256	**N317TZ**	**737NG**	**28246**	N321PA	B727	18999	(N325TZ)	737NG	32882
N314FV	MD80	49402	N317UA	B737	23949	**N321SW**	**B737**	**23342**	N325TZ	737NG	32884
N314LA	**B767**	**32573**	**N317UP**	**B767**	**27745**	**N321TZ**	**737NG**	**28249**	**N325UA**	**B737**	**23957**
N314ML	737NG	30271	**N317US**	**A320**	**0197**	N321UA	B737	23953	**N325UP**	**B767**	**27751**
N314NB	**A319**	**1191**	**N317WN**	**B737**	**24068**	N321US	A320	0262	**N325US**	**A320**	**0281**
N314NE	B727	19495	**N318AS**	**737NG**	**30018**	N321XV	B737	19929	N325V	1-11	086
N314P	B737	23232	N318AS	B727	18996	**N322AA**	**B767**	**22323**	N326AS	B727	20268
N314PA	B727	18992	**N318AT**	**737NG**	**33931**	N322AS	B727	21364	**N326AT**	**737NG**	**33933**
N314RC	MD80	49110	N318AU	B737	22886	N322AU	B737	22890	N326AU	B737	23115
N314RX	A320	0314	N318AW	B737	23506	**N322AW**	**B737**	**25400**	N326AW	B737	23258
N314ST	B757	22211	N318CM	B737	22088	**N322DL**	**B737**	**23094**	N326CT	737NG	33026
N314SW	**B737**	**23336**	N318DL	B737	23090	N322EA	L1011	193A-1044	**N326DL**	**B737**	**23098**
N314TZ	**737NG**	**30640**	N318EA	L1011	193A-1039	N322F	B707	18975	N326EA	L1011	193A-1054
N314UA	**B737**	**23675**	N318F	B707	18880	N322FE	DC-10	47908	N326FE	DC-10	47813
N314UP	**B767**	**27742**	**N318FE**	**DC-10**	**46837**	N322FV	MD80	49571	N326FV	DC-9	47614
N314US	**A320**	**0160**	(N318FE)	DC-10	48318	**N322K**	**F.70**	**11521**	N326MR	B767	23326
N315AA	B767	22317	N318FL	B737	26293	**N322NB**	**A319**	**1434**	**N326NB**	**A319**	**1498**
N315AS	**737NG**	**30019**	N318FV	A300	147	N322P	B737	23511	N326P	B737	23515
N315AT	**737NG**	**35788**	N318ML	737NG	32582	**N322SW**	**B737**	**23343**	N326PA	B727	19035
N315AU	B737	22883	**N318NB**	**A319**	**1325**	(N322TZ)	737NG	28249	**N326SW**	**B737**	**23690**
N315AW	**B737**	**23734**	N318PA	B727	18996	N322TZ	737NG	32611	N326TZ	737NG	32612
N315DL	B737	23087	N318SR	B767	24318	N322UA	B737	23954	**N326UA**	**B737**	**23958**
N315EA	L1011	193M-1023	**N318SW**	**B737**	**23339**	**N322UP**	**B767**	**27748**	**N326UP**	**B767**	**27752**
N315FE	**DC-10**	**48313**	**N318TZ**	**737NG**	**28247**	**N322US**	**A320**	**0263**	**N326US**	**A320**	**0282**
N315FL	B737	25159	**N318UA**	**B737**	**23950**	N322XV	B737	19930	**N327AA**	**B767**	**22327**
N315FV	**MD80**	**49707**	**N318UP**	**B767**	**27746**	**N323AA**	**B767**	**22324**	N327AS	B727	21345
N315ML	737NG	32244	**N318US**	**A320**	**0206**	**N323AS**	**737NG**	**30021**	N327AU	B737	23116
N315NB	**A319**	**1230**	**N319AA**	**B767**	**22320**	N323AS	B727	21365	N327AW	B737	23507
N315NE	B727	20190	**N319AS**	**737NG**	**33679**	N323AT	737NG	36073	N327DL	B737	23099
N315P	B737	23233	N319AU	B737	22887	N323AU	B737	22891	N327EA	L1011	193A-1055
N315PA	B727	18993	N319AW	B737	23838	N323AW	B737	23684	(N327FE)	DC-10	47819
N315RX	A320	0315	N319DL	B737	23091	N323CT	737NG	33023	N327FV	DC-9	47627
N315SC	B737	23766	N319EA	L1011	193A-1040	N323DL	B737	23095	(N327JL)	B727	20513
N315ST	B757	22611	N319F	B707	19415	N323EA	L1011	193A-1045	N327MR	B767	23327
N315SW	**B737**	**23337**	**N319FE**	**DC-10**	**47820**	N323F	B707	18976	**N327NB**	**A319**	**1501**
N315TS	**737NG**	**30772**	N319FL	B737	26301	N323FE	DC-10	47811	**N327NW**	**A320**	**0297**
N315TZ	**737NG**	**28245**	N319FV	B747	21939	N323MC	B747	21782	N327P	B737	23550
N315UA	**B737**	**23947**	**N319NB**	**A319**	**1346**	**N323NB**	**A319**	**1453**	N327PA	B727	19036
N315UP	**B767**	**27743**	**N319NE**	**B727**	**21349**	N323P	B737	23512	**N327SW**	**B737**	**23691**
N315US	**A320**	**0171**	N319P	B737	23236	N323PA	B727	19005	N327TZ	737NG	32613
N316AA	B767	22318	N319PA	B727	18997	**N323SW**	**B737**	**23344**	**N327UA**	**B737**	**24147**
N316AS	B727	18994	**N319SW**	**B737**	**23340**	**N323TZ**	**737NG**	**30033**	**N327UP**	**B767**	**27753**
N316AT	**737NG**	**33928**	**N319TZ**	**737NG**	**30643**	N323UA	B737	23955	N327US	B737	23255
N316AU	B737	22884	(N319TZ)	737NG	28654	**N323UP**	**B767**	**27749**	**N327US**	**DC-9**	**47414**
N316AW	**B737**	**23713**	N319UA	B737	23951	**N323US**	**A320**	**0272**	**N328AA**	**B767**	**22328**
N316CA	DC-9	47301	**N319UP**	**B767**	**27758**	N323XV	B737	20156	N328AB	D0328	3198
N316DL	B737	23088	**N319US**	**A320**	**0208**	**N324AA**	**B767**	**22325**	**N328AC**	**D0328**	**3132**
N316EA	L1011	193A-1037	**N320AA**	**B767**	**22321**	N324AS	B727	19006	N328AS	B727	21601
N316FE	DC-10	48314	N320AS	737NG	33680	N324AS	B727	20264	**N328AT**	**737NG**	**33934**
N316FL	B737	25264	N320AS	B727	18998	N324AU	B737	22892	N328AU	B737	23131
N316FV	MD80	49399	N320AT	737NG	33932	N324AW	B737	23261	N328AW	B737	23377
(N316GA)	B737	20365	N320AU	B737	22888	N324CA	B737	21970	(N328BC)	D0328	3200
N316LA	**B767**	**30842**	N320AW	A320	0397	N324DL	B737	23096	**N328BH**	**D0328**	**3137**
N316ML	737NG	28654	N320AW	B737	23942	N324EA	L1011	193A-1050	(N328CD)	D0328	3201
N316NB	**A319**	**1249**	N320CH	A320	1935	N324F	B707	19354	N328CR	D0328	3160
N316NE	B727	19475	**N320DL**	**B737**	**23092**	N324FV	DC-9	47624	**N328DA**	**D0328**	**3171**
N316P	B737	23234	N320EA	L1011	193A-1042	N324JM	B727	22703	(N328DE)	D0328	3203
N316PA	B727	18994	**N320FE**	**DC-10**	**47835**	**N324K**	**F.70**	**11545**	N328DL	B737	23100
N316SW	**B737**	**23338**	N320FV	MD80	49630	**N324NB**	**A319**	**1456**	N328DP	D0328	3169
N316TZ	737NG	32609	N320HG	B727	20533	N324P	B737	23513	N328DR	D0328	3176
N316UA	B737	23948	(N320K)	F.100	11368	N324PA	B727	19006	N328EA	L1011	193A-1056
N316UP	**B767**	**27744**	N320MJ	B707	20028	**N324SW**	**B737**	**23414**	N328EF	D0328	3206
N316US	**A320**	**0192**	N320MW	A320	1686	(N324TZ)	737NG	32612	(N328FD)	D0328	3116
N317AA	B767	22319	**N320NB**	**A319**	**1392**	N324TZ	737NG	32882	N328FD	D0328	3183

Reg	Type	S/N	Reg	Type	S/N	Reg	Type	S/N	Reg	Type	S/N
N328FD	D0328	3196	N331SW	B737	23695	N339BA	737NG	30572	N346UA	B737	24250
(N328FG)	D0328	3207	N331TZ	737NG	30660	N339CA	DC-9	47306	N346US	B737	23515
N328FV	B727	21455	N331UA	B737	24192	N339EA	L1011	193A-1158	N347AN	B767	33086
N328GH	D0328	3208	N331UP	B767	27757	N339LF	B737	26288	(N347KA)	A320	0347
N328GT	D0328	3183	(N331US)	B737	23260	N339LF	B767	24150	N347NB	A319	1800
N328HJ	D0328	3210	N331XV	B737	19743	N339NB	A319	1709	N347NW	A320	0408
N328JT	D0328	3105	N332AA	B767	22331	N339NW	A320	0367	N347PA	B727	21895
N328JT	D0328	3129	N332AU	B737	23135	N339PA	B727	19134	N347PS	146	E2023
(N328KL)	D0328	3211	N332AW	B737	23384	N339SW	B737	24090	N347SW	B737	24374
(N328LM)	D0328	3212	N332DL	B737	23104	N339UA	B737	24243	N347TM	A320	0347
(N328MN)	D0328	3215	N332EA	L1011	193A-1123	N339US	B737	23236	N347UA	B737	24251
N328MT	B767	23328	N332FV	DC-9	47632	(N340AN)	B737	23550	N347US	B737	23550
N328NB	A319	1520	N332MX	A320	0332	N340CA	CRJ7	10062	N348AN	B767	33087
N328NP	D0328	3216	N332NB	A319	1570	N340DR	B727	19253	N348AU	B737	23507
N328NW	A320	0298	N332NW	A320	0319	N340LA	A320	0425	N348BA	737NG	29791
N328P	B737	23551	N332SW	B737	23696	N340LV	B737	23738	N348NB	A319	1810
N328PA	B727	19037	N332TZ	737NG	30679	N340NB	A319	1714	N348NW	A320	0410
N328PA	D0328	3197	N332UA	B737	24193	N340NW	A320	0372	N348P	B737	23559
N328PD	D0328	3105	N332UP	B767	32843	N340P	B737	23556	N348PA	B727	21921
N328PM	D0328	3184	(N332US)	B737	23261	N340PA	B727	19135	N348PS	146	E2024
N328PQ	D0328	3217	(N332XV)	B737	20336	N340UA	B737	24244	N348SW	B737	24375
N328PT	D0328	3199	N333EA	L1011	193A-1126	N340US	B737	23237	N348UA	B737	24252
N328QR	D0328	3218	N333GB	1-11	076	N341A	B707	18014	N348US	B737	23551
N328RS	D0328	3219	N333NB	A319	1582	(N341AN)	B767	29430	N349AN	B767	33088
N328SW	B737	23692	N333NW	A320	0329	N341CA	B737	23847	N349BA	737NG	30789
N328TZ	737NG	32614	(N333RN)	B737	19682	N341LF	737NG	28210	N349NB	A319	1815
(N328TZ)	737NG	32884	(N333RN)	B737	19770	N341LF	B757	25044	N349NW	A320	0417
N328UA	B737	24148	N333SW	B737	23697	N341NB	A319	1738	N349P	B737	23560
N328UP	B767	27754	N333TZ	737NG	30673	N341NW	A320	0380	N349PA	B727	21898
(N328US)	B737	23258	N333UA	B737	24228	N341P	B737	23557	N349PS	146	E2025
N328VA	D0328	3170	N334AA	B767	22332	N341PA	B727	19136	N349SW	B737	24408
N328WW	D0328	3116	N334AW	B737	23748	N341SW	B737	24091	N349UA	B737	24253
N329AA	B767	22329	N334CT	737NG	33014	N341TC	1-11	BAC.126	N349US	B737	23552
N329AS	B727	22295	N334DL	B737	23105	N341TC	B727	19148	N350AN	B767	33089
N329AT	737NG	33034	N334EA	L1011	193A-1141	N341UA	B737	24245	N350AU	B737	22950
N329AT	737NG	36091	N334FV	B727	20662	N341US	B737	23510	N350LP	737NG	30050
N329AU	B737	23132	N334NB	A319	1659	N342A	B707	18953	N350NA	A320	0418
N329AW	B737	23500	N334NW	A320	0339	(N342AN)	B767	29431	N350NB	A319	1819
N329BS	CRJ	7329	N334P	B737	23552	N342AN	B767	33081	N350P	B737	23739
N329DL	B737	23101	N334SW	B737	23938	N342CA	B767	23848	N350PS	146	E2027
N329EA	L1011	193A-1085	N334UA	B737	24229	N342NB	A319	1746	N350SW	B737	24409
N329FV	DC-9	47629	N334UP	B767	32844	N342NW	A320	0381	N350UA	B737	24301
N329K	737NG	30753	N334US	B737	23231	N342P	B737	23558	N350US	B737	23553
N329K	B727	19557	N335AA	B767	22333	N342PA	B727	19137	N351AA	B767	24032
N329NB	A319	1543	N335AW	B737	28740	N342PA	B727	21893	N351AS	B747	21705
N329NW	A320	0306	N335EA	L1011	193A-1142	N342SP	B727	21024	N351AU	A320	0347
N329PA	B727	19038	N335FV	B757	24135	N342SW	B737	24133	N351BA	CRJ	7351
N329QS	B727	19038	N335NB	A319	1662	N342UA	B737	24246	N351EJ	CRJ	7351
N329SN	L1011	193A-1085	N335NW	A320	0340	N342US	B737	23511	N351LF	A310	562
N329SW	B737	23693	N335P	B737	23553	N343A	B707	20456	N351LF	B737	26293
N329TZ	737NG	32615	N335SJ	DC-10	47843	(N343AN)	B767	29432	N351NB	A319	1820
N329UA	B737	24149	N335SW	B737	23939	N343AN	B767	33082	N351NW	A320	0766
N329UP	B767	27755	N335UA	B737	24230	N343NB	A319	1752	N351PA	B727	20614
N329US	B737	23256	N335US	B737	23232	N343NW	A320	0387	N351PS	146	E2028
N330AA	B767	22330	N336AA	B767	22334	N343PA	B727	21894	N351SK	D0328	3108
N330AT	737NG	36399	N336AW	B737	23707	N343SW	B737	24151	N351SR	B707	18586
N330AU	B737	23133	N336EA	L1011	193A-1143	N343UA	B737	24747	N351SW	B727	24672
N330AW	B737	23499	N336NB	A319	1683	N343US	B737	23512	N351UA	B737	24319
N330DL	B737	23102	N336NW	A320	0355	N344AN	B767	33083	N351US	B707	18584
N330DS	B707	18455	N336P	B737	23554	N344NB	A319	1766	N351US	B737	23554
N330EA	L1011	193A-1087	N336SW	B737	23940	N344NW	A320	0388	(N351US)	DC-10	46922
N330FV	DC-9	47630	N336UA	B737	24240	N344SW	B737	24152	N351WA	DC-10	48283
N330K	737NG	30755	N336US	B737	23233	N344TM	B737	23044	N352AA	B767	24033
N330LF	B767	24448	N337EA	L1011	193A-1152	N344UA	B737	24248	N352AU	B737	22952
N330NB	A319	1549	N337NB	A319	1685	N344US	B737	23513	N352BA	146	E2060
N330NW	A320	0307	N337NW	A320	0358	N345AN	B767	33084	N352NB	A319	1824
N330SF	737NG	33005	N337P	B737	23555	N345AW	MD80	53093	N352NW	A320	0778
N330SW	B737	23694	N337SW	B737	23959	N345FA	B707	20069	N352P	B737	23740
N330TZ	737NG	32616	N337UA	B737	24241	N345HC	DC-10	48265	N352PA	B727	20616
N330UA	B737	24191	N337US	B737	23234	N345JW	DC-8	46042	N352PS	146	E2030
N330UP	B767	27756	N338AA	B767	22335	N345NB	A319	1774	N352SK	D0328	3111
(N330US)	B737	23259	N338AW	B737	23627	N345NW	A320	0399	N352SW	B737	24888
N331AT	737NG	33935	N338CA	DC-9	47360	N345SA	B737	23786	N352UA	B737	24320
N331AU	B737	23134	N338EA	L1011	193A-1153	N345UA	B737	24249	N352US	B707	18585
N331AW	B737	23747	N338NB	A319	1693	N345US	B737	23514	N352US	B737	23555
N331CA	CRJ7	10061	N338NW	A320	0360	N346AN	B767	33085	N352WL	DC-10	47838
N331DL	B737	23103	N338RX	A320	0338	N346NB	A319	1796	N353AA	B767	24034
N331EA	L1011	193A-1121	N338SW	B737	23960	N346NW	A320	0400	N353AS	DC-8	45924
N331FV	DC-10	47843	N338UA	B737	24242	N346PA	B727	21904	N353AU	B737	22953
N331LF	737NG	28219	N338US	B737	23234	N346PS	146	E2022	N353CT	B737	24353
N331NB	A319	1567	N339AA	B767	22336	(N346SS)	146	E1004	N353FA	DC-8	45624
N331NW	A320	0318	N339AW	B737	23629	N346SW	B737	24153	N353NB	A319	1828

Reg	Type	Serial	Reg	Type	Serial	Reg	Type	Serial	Reg	Type	Serial
N353NW	A320	0786	N357UA	B737	24378	N362AU	B737	23312	N367G	737NG	28579
N353P	B737	23741	N357US	B707	18747	N362BJ	737NG	33964	N367ML	737NG	30742
N353PA	B727	20622	N357US	B737	23560	N362DH	A300	084	N367NB	A319	2028
N353PS	146	E2031	N358AA	B767	24039	N362FC	B747	22304	N367NW	A320	0988
N353SK	DO328	3122	N358AS	B737	21278	N362FE	DC-10	48261	N367PA	B727	22539
N353SW	B737	24889	N358AS	B747	19732	N362ML	737NG	30737	N367PS	146	E2073
N353UA	B737	24321	N358AU	B737	22958	N362NB	A319	1982	N367SK	DO328	3167
N353US	B707	18586	N358BJ	737NG	33542	N362NW	A320	0911	N367SW	B737	26578
N353US	B737	23556	N358FE	DC-10	46633	(N362P)	B737	23935	N367UA	B737	24536
N353WL	DC-10	48318	N358NB	A319	1897	N362PA	B727	21106	N367US	B707	19168
N354AA	B767	24035	N358NW	A320	0832	N362PA	B727	21850	N368AA	B767	25195
N354AS	B747	21189	N358PA	B737	19260	N362PR	B737	26301	N368AP	B737	22368
N354AU	B737	22954	N358PA	B727	20674	N362PS	146	E2045	N368AU	B737	23318
N354CA	CRJ7	10064	"N358PA"	B727	20676	N362SW	B737	26573	N368BJ	737NG	34809
N354FC	B747	23394	N358PS	146	E2041	N362UA	B737	24455	N368CA	CRJ7	10075
N354MC	B747	23394	N358QS	B727	19005	N362US	B707	18922	N368CE	B737	27456
N354NB	A319	1833	N358SK	DO328	3188	(N362US)	B737	23743	N368CG	B757	24368
N354NW	A320	0801	N358SW	B737	26595	N363AA	B767	24044	N368DE	B727	22279
N354P	B737	23742	N358UA	B737	24379	N363AU	B737	23313	N368DH	A300	207
N354PA	B727	20624	N358US	B707	18748	N363BJ	737NG	33986	N368DL	B737	21776
N354PS	146	E2034	N358US	B737	23739	N363DH	A300	085	N368EC	B737	22736
N354SK	DO328	3126	N359AA	B767	24040	N363FE	DC-10	48263	N368FE	DC-10	46606
N354SW	B737	25219	N359AS	B737	21528	N363ML	737NG	30738	N368ML	737NG	30743
N354UA	B737	24360	N359AS	B747	20520	N363NB	A319	1990	N368MM	B737	22368
N354US	B707	18693	N359AU	B737	22959	N363NW	A320	0923	N368MX	A320	0368
N354US	B737	23557	N359BJ	737NG	33476	N363PA	B727	22535	N368NB	A319	2039
N355AA	B767	24036	N359FE	DC-10	46635	N363PS	146	E2046	N368NW	A320	0996
N355AS	B747	19729	N359MT	B737	21359	N363SW	B737	26574	N368PA	B727	22540
N355AU	B737	22955	N359NB	A319	1923	N363UA	B737	24532	N368PS	146	E2074
N355BJ	737NG	33499	N359NW	A320	0846	N363US	B707	18964	N368SW	B737	26579
N355CA	CRJ7	10067	N359P	B737	23932	N364AU	B737	23314	N368UA	B737	24537
N355MC	B747	23395	N359PA	B727	19261	N364BJ	737NG	33987	N368US	B707	19209
N355NB	A319	1839	N359PA	B727	20789	N364DH	A300	141	N368WA	B707	19716
N355NW	A320	0807	N359PS	146	E2042	N364FE	DC-10	46600	N369AA	B767	25196
N355P	B737	23743	N359QS	B727	19007	N364LF	B757	25622	N369AP	B737	22369
N355PA	B727	19257	N359SK	DO328	3202	N364ML	737NG	30739	N369AU	B737	23319
N355PA	B727	20625	N359SW	B737	26596	N364NB	A319	2002	N369AX	B757	28161
N355PS	146	E2036	N359UA	B737	24452	N364NW	A320	0962	N369BJ	737NG	35478
N355Q	DC-8	45668	N359US	B707	18888	(N364P)	B737	23936	N369CA	CRJ7	10079
N355QS	B727	19257	N359US	B737	23740	N364PA	B727	21107	N369DL	B737	21776
N355SK	DO328	3124	N360AA	B767	24041	N364PA	B727	22536	N369FA	B727	21851
N355SW	B737	25250	N360AU	B737	23310	N364PS	146	E2047	N369FE	DC-10	46607
(N355TA)	B747	23033	N360AX	DC-10	46706	N364SW	B737	26575	N369LS	B737	22369
N355UA	B737	24361	N360BJ	737NG	33963	N364UA	B737	24533	N369ML	737NG	30744
N355US	B707	18710	N360FE	DC-10	46636	N364US	B707	19034	N369MX	A320	0369
N355US	B737	23558	N360NB	A319	1959	N365AU	B737	23315	N369NB	A319	2047
N356AS	B747	19730	N360NW	A320	0903	N365BJ	737NG	34807	N369NW	A320	1011
N356AU	B737	22956	(N360P)	B737	23933	N365DH	A300	149	N369PA	B727	21950
N356BA	146	E2066	N360PA	B727	19262	N365FE	DC-10	46601	N369PA	B727	22541
N356BJ	737NG	33962	N360PA	B727	20676	N365ML	737NG	30740	N369PS	146	E2075
N356NB	A319	1870	N360PR	B737	28742	N365NB	A319	2013	N369SW	B737	26580
N356NW	A320	0818	N360PS	146	E2043	N365NW	A320	0964	N369UA	B737	24538
N356PA	B727	19258	N360SK	DO328	3136	(N365P)	B737	23937	N369US	B707	19210
N356PA	B727	20626	N360SW	B737	26571	N365PA	B727	20628	N369WA	B707	19715
N356PS	146	E2039	N360UA	B737	24453	N365PA	B727	22537	N370AA	B767	25197
N356QS	B727	19258	N360US	B707	18889	N365PS	146	E2048	N370AU	B737	23376
N356SK	DO328	3163	N360US	B737	23741	N365SK	DO328	3165	N370BC	B737	23468
N356SW	B737	25251	N360WA	B737	23553	N365SR	B767	25365	N370BJ	737NG	36106
N356UA	B737	24362	N361AA	B767	24042	N365SW	B737	26576	N370FE	DC-10	46608
N356US	B707	18746	N361AU	B737	23311	N365UA	B737	24534	N370ML	737NG	30745
N356US	B737	23559	N361AW	B767	27377	N365US	B707	19163	N370NB	A319	2087
N356WS	DC-8	45668	N361BJ	737NG	33477	N366AA	B767	25193	N370NW	A320	1037
N357AA	B767	24038	N361DA	A320	0361	N366AU	B737	23316	N370PA	B727	22542
N357AS	B747	19731	N361DH	A300	071	N366BJ	737NG	34808	N370PC	A300	134
N357AT	L1011	193B-1221	N361FC	B747	22442	N366DH	A300	249	N370SK	E145	145515
N357AU	B737	22957	N361FE	DC-10	48260	N366FE	DC-10	46602	N370SW	B737	26597
N357BJ	737NG	33500	N361KP	B727	20627	N366G	737NG	28581	N370UA	B737	24539
N357BJ	737NG	34622	N361LF	737NG	30737	N366ML	737NG	30741	N370US	B707	19263
N357FE	DC-10	46939	N361LF	B767	27136	N366NB	A319	2026	N370WA	B707	19442
N357KP	B727	20675	N361ML	737NG	30736	N366NW	A320	0981	N370WL	B737	24011
N357NB	A319	1875	N361NB	A319	1976	N366PA	B727	22538	N371AA	B767	25198
N357NE	B727	19405	N361NW	A320	0907	N366PS	146	E2072	N371AU	B737	23377
N357NW	A320	0830	(N361P)	B737	23934	N366SW	B737	26577	N371BC	737NG	32971
N357P	B737	23930	N361PA	B727	20623	N366UA	B737	24535	N371BJ	737NG	29051
N357PA	B727	19259	N361PA	B727	21849	N366US	B707	19164	N371CA	CRJ7	10082
N357PA	B727	20627	N361PR	B737	26293	N367AU	B737	23317	N371DA	737NG	29619
N357PA	B727	21896	N361PS	146	E2044	N367BJ	737NG	33965	N371EA	B737	20012
N357PS	146	E2040	N361SW	B737	26572	N367CA	CRJ7	10069	N371EA	L1011	193A-1008
N357QS	B727	19259	N361UA	B737	24454	N367DH	A300	265	N371FA	B737	23631
N357SK	DO328	3164	N361US	B707	18921	N367DL	B737	21774	N371FE	DC-10	46609
N357SW	B737	26594	N361US	B737	23742	N367EC	B737	22367	N371LF	737NG	28056
N357TC	B747	23751	N362AA	B767	24043	N367FE	DC-10	46605	N371LF	B767	23057

Reg	Type	S/N	Reg	Type	S/N	Reg	Type	S/N	Reg	Type	S/N
N371ML	737NG	30746	N375DL	B737	23602	N380PA	B737	20670	N387AU	B737	23704
N371NB	A319	2095	N375FE	DC-10	46613	N380PS	B737	19920	N387DA	737NG	30374
N371NW	A320	1535	N375NB	A319	2474	N380RM	B757	29380	N387FE	DC-10	46621
N371PA	B727	20248	N375NC	A320	1789	N380SK	E145	145613	N387PA	B737	22276
N371PA	B737	23543	N375PA	B727	20875	N380SW	B737	26587	N387SW	B737	26602
N371PC	A300	157	N375PA	B737	23812	N380UA	B737	24655	N387UA	B737	24662
N371SK	E145	145535	N375SK	E145	145569	N380US	B707	19636	N387US	B737	22959
N371SW	B737	26598	N375SW	B737	26583	N380WA	MD11	48407	N388AA	B767	27448
N371TA	B737	24834	N375TA	B737	23787	N380WL	B737	23218	N388AU	B737	23705
N371UA	B737	24540	N375UA	B737	24640	N381AC	B737	23481	N388DA	737NG	30375
N371US	B707	19411	N375US	B707	19631	N381AN	B767	25450	N388FE	DC-10	46622
N371US	B737	22950	N375US	B737	22954	N381AU	B737	23595	N388LS	L1011	293A-1249
N371WA	B707	19441	N375WA	B707	18707	N381DA	737NG	30350	N388PA	B727	19818
N372AA	B767	25199	N376AN	B767	25445	N381DL	B737	23608	N388PA	B727	22277
N372AU	B737	23378	N376AU	B737	23382	N381DN	737NG	30350	N388SW	B737	26591
N372BC	737NG	32805	N376BJ	737NG	32775	N381FE	DC-10	46615	N388UA	B737	24663
N372BC	DC-10	46976	N376CA	CRJ7	10092	(N381KP)	B727	21578	N388US	B737	23310
N372BJ	737NG	30829	N376DA	737NG	29624	N381LF	A320	0640	N389AA	B767	27449
N372BJ	737NG	36118	N376DL	B737	23603	(N381LF)	B737	23506	N389AU	B737	23706
N372DA	737NG	29620	(N376FE)	DC-10	46614	N381LF	B757	24367	N389DA	737NG	30376
(N372EA)	B747	20011	N376NB	A319	2618	N381PA	B737	20588	N389FE	DC-10	46623
N372EA	L1011	193R-1033	N376NW	A320	1812	N381PS	B737	19921	N389LS	L1011	193G-1250
N372FE	DC-10	46610	N376PA	B727	20169	N381SK	E145	145619	N389PA	B727	19819
N372NB	A319	2369	N376SK	E145	145578	N381UA	B737	24656	N389PA	B727	20293
N372NW	A320	1633	N376SW	B737	26584	N381US	B707	19872	N389PA	B737	22516
N372PA	B727	20249	N376UA	B737	24641	N381WA	MD11	48523	N389SW	B737	26592
N372PA	B737	23546	N376US	B707	19632	N382AN	B767	25451	N389UA	B737	24664
N372PC	A300	196	N376US	B737	22955	N382AU	B737	23699	N389US	B737	23311
N372SK	E145	145538	N376WA	B707	18991	N382DA	737NG	30345	N390AA	B767	27450
N372SW	B737	26599	N377AK	B737	20588	N382DL	B737	23609	N390AU	B737	23856
N372TA	B737	24856	N377AN	B767	25446	(N382FE)	DC-10	47969	N390BA	1-11	BAC.129
N372UA	B737	24637	N377AU	B737	23383	N382JT	MD80	49110	N390CA	CRJ7	10106
N372US	B707	19412	N377DA	737NG	29625	(N382KP)	B727	21579	N390DA	737NG	30536
N372US	B737	22951	N377DL	B737	23604	N382PA	B737	19921	N390EA	DC-10	47862
N372WA	B707	19179	N377FE	DC-10	47965	N382PS	B737	20155	N390FE	DC-10	46624
N373AA	B767	25200	N377JC	737NG	33367	N382SK	E145	145624	N390LS	MD80	49390
N373AU	B737	23379	N377NB	A319	2641	N382SW	B737	26588	N390PA	B727	20899
N373BJ	737NG	32627	N377NW	A320	2082	N382UA	B737	24657	N390SW	B737	26593
N373DA	737NG	29621	N377PA	B727	19992	N382US	B707	19773	N390UA	B737	24665
N373DL	B737	23520	N377PA	B737	23718	N383AN	B767	26995	N390US	B737	23312
N373FE	DC-10	46611	N377SK	E145	145579	N383AU	B737	23700	N390WL	B737	23219
N373JM	737NG	33405	N377UA	B737	24642	N383DA	737NG	30346	N391AA	B767	27451
N373NB	A319	2373	N377US	B707	19633	N383FE	DC-10	46616	N391AU	B737	23857
N373NW	A320	1641	N378AN	B767	25447	(N383KP)	B727	21580	N391CA	CRJ7	10108
N373PA	B727	20678	N378AU	B737	23384	N383PA	B737	20205	N391DA	737NG	30560
N373PA	B737	23749	N378BC	737NG	33474	N383SW	B737	26589	N391EA	DC-10	47866
N373PC	A300	218	N378BJ	737NG	32916	N383UA	B737	24658	N391FE	DC-10	46625
N373RB	E145	14500957	N378CA	CRJ7	10097	N383US	B707	19774	N391LF	A320	0428
N373S	COMET	06018	N378DA	737NG	30265	N383US	B737	22956	N391LF	A320	0676
N373SK	E145	145543	N378DL	B737	23605	N384AA	B767	26996	N391LS	B737	29201
N373SW	B737	26581	(N378FE)	DC-10	47966	N384AU	B737	23701	N391PA	B727	20900
N373TA	B737	26283	N378NW	A320	2092	N384DA	737NG	30347	N391SW	B737	27378
N373UA	B737	24638	N378PA	B727	20392	N384FE	DC-10	46617	N391UA	B737	24666
N373US	B707	19434	N378PS	B737	19681	N384PA	B727	20303	N391US	B737	23313
N373US	B737	22952	N378SK	E145	145593	(N384PA)	B737	21231	N392AN	B767	29429
N373WA	B707	18582	N378SW	B737	26585	N384PS	B727	20437	N392AS	B737	22116
N374AA	B767	25201	N378UA	B737	24653	N384SW	B737	26590	N392AU	B737	23858
N374AU	B737	23380	N378US	B707	19634	N384UA	B737	24659	N392BA	1-11	BAC.131
N374BC	737NG	33080	N379AA	B767	25448	N384US	B707	19775	N392DA	737NG	30561
N374BJ	737NG	32451	N379AU	B737	23385	N384US	B737	22957	N392EA	DC-10	47867
N374CA	CRJ7	10090	N379BC	737NG	33473	N385AM	B767	27059	N392FE	DC-10	46626
N374DA	737NG	29622	N379BC	B737	26284	N385AU	B737	23702	N392LS	B737	29202
N374DL	B737	23521	N379BJ	737NG	32777	N385DN	737NG	30348	N392PA	B727	20901
N374FD	A300	374	N379CA	CRJ7	10102	N385FE	DC-10	46619	N392SW	B737	27379
N374FE	DC-10	46612	(N379DA)	737NG	30266	N385PA	B727	20393	N392UA	B737	24667
N374GE	MD80	49374	N379DA	737NG	30349	N385PA	B737	21719	N392US	B737	23314
N374MC	737NG	30076	N379DL	B737	23606	N385SW	B737	26600	N393AN	B767	29430
N374NB	A319	2464	(N379FE)	DC-10	47967	N385UA	B737	24660	N393AU	B737	23859
N374NW	A320	1646	N379PA	B727	20302	N385US	B707	19776	N393DA	737NG	30377
N374PA	B727	20679	N379PS	B737	19682	N385US	B737	22958	N393FE	DC-10	46627
N374PA	B737	28333	N379SK	E145	145606	N386AA	B767	27060	N393NY	A320	0393
N374SK	E145	145544	N379SW	B737	26586	N386AU	B737	23703	N393PA	B727	20902
N374SW	B737	26582	N379UA	B737	24654	N386CH	E145	145467	N393PA	DC-9	47392
N374TA	B737	26286	N379US	B707	19635	N386DA	737NG	30373	N393UA	B737	24668
N374UA	B737	24639	N380AC	B737	23117	N386FE	DC-10	46620	N393US	B737	23315
N374US	B707	19443	N380AN	B767	25449	N386PA	B727	19973	N394AN	B767	29431
N374US	B737	22953	N380AU	B737	23594	(N386PA)	B727	20785	N394AU	B737	23860
N374WA	B707	18583	N380BG	B737	28038	N386SW	B737	26601	N394DA	737NG	30562
N375AU	B737	23381	N380DA	737NG	30266	N386UA	B737	24661	N394DL	B737	27394
N375BC	737NG	33079	N380DL	B737	23607	N386US	B707	19777	N394FE	DC-10	46628
N375BJ	737NG	32807	(N380FE)	DC-10	47968	N386US	B707	19872			
N375DA	737NG	29623	(N380KP)	B727	21453	N387AM	B767	27184	(N394PA)	B727	20903

Reg	Type	S/N	Reg	Type	S/N	Reg	Type	S/N	Reg	Type	S/N
N394PA	DC-9	47376	N401UA	A320	0435	N405DA	B727	21149	(N408PA)	F.100	11299
N394SW	B737	27380	N401UP	B757	23723	N405EA	DC-9	47688	N408PE	B737	19025
N394UA	B737	24669	(N401US)	B727	18797	N405EV	B747	27142	N408SW	CRJ	7055
N394US	B737	23316	N401WN	737NG	29813	N405FE	A310	237	N408TW	B717	55075
N395AJ	B727	21100	N401XV	146	E2059	N405FE	DC-8	46090	N408UA	A320	0457
N395AN	B767	29432	N402A	MD80	49313	N405FJ	D0328	3155	N408UP	B757	23730
N395AU	B737	23861	N402AL	B737	25664	N405GT	B737	29405	(N408US)	B727	18804
N395DN	737NG	30773	N402AW	B737	25505	N405JS	B757	29380	N408US	B737	23878
N395FE	DC-10	46629	N402AW	CRJ	7281	N405KW	B737	24704	N408WN	737NG	27895
(N395MD)	B717	55002	N402BN	B727	20393	N405MX	A320	0405	N408XV	146	E2077
(N395PA)	B727	20906	N402DA	B727	21146	(N405P)	B737	23877	N409AA	MD80	49320
N395SW	B737	27689	N402EA	DC-9	47683	N405PA	B707	18836	N409AN	A310	309
N395UA	B737	24670	N402FE	A310	201	(N405PA)	B727	20618	N409AT	A310	309
N395US	B737	23317	(N402FE)	DC-8	46059	N405PE	B737	19022	N409AW	CRJ	7447
N396AD	B737	22396	N402FE	DC-8	46073	N405SW	CRJ	7029	N409BN	B727	20162
N396AN	B767	29603	N402FJ	D0328	3147	N405TW	B717	55072	N409CA	CRJ	7441
N396AU	B737	23862	N402JR	DC-10	47831	N405UA	A300	066	N409DA	B727	21153
N396DA	737NG	30378	N402KW	B737	26285	N405UA	A320	0452	N409EA	DC-9	47728
N396FE	DC-10	46630	(N402P)	B737	23886	N405UP	B757	23727	N409EV	B747	28093
N396GE	MD80	49396	N402PA	B707	18833	(N405US)	B727	18801	N409FE	A310	273
N396SW	B737	27690	(N402PD)	B707	18833	N405US	B737	23885	N409FJ	D0328	3161
N396UA	B737	24671	N402PE	B737	19019	N405WN	737NG	27893	N409MC	B747	30558
N396US	B737	23318	N402SY	B747	24405	N405XV	146	E2066	N409MX	A320	0409
N397AJ	B727	22608	N402TW	B717	55069	N406A	MD80	49317	(N409P)	B737	23881
N397AN	B767	29604	N402TZ	B737	24667	N406AW	CRJ	7402	N409PA	B707	18840
N397DA	737NG	30537	N402UA	A300	120	N406BN	B727	19991	N409PE	B737	19026
N397FE	DC-10	46631	N402UA	A320	0439	N406DA	B727	21150	N409SW	CRJ	7056
N397MC	B737	23977	N402UP	B757	23724	N406EA	DC-9	47686	N409TW	B717	55076
N397P	B737	23256	(N402US)	B727	18798	N406EV	B747	27898	N409UA	A320	0462
N397PA	B727	20918	N402WN	737NG	29814	N406FJ	D0328	3156	N409UP	B757	23731
N397SW	B737	27691	N402XV	146	E2060	N406KW	B737	24709	(N409US)	B727	18805
N397UA	B737	24672	N403A	MD80	49314	(N406P)	B737	23878	N409US	B737	23879
N397US	B737	23319	N403AW	B737	25506	N406PA	B707	18837	N409WN	737NG	27896
N398AN	B767	29605	N403AW	CRJ	7288	(N406PA)	B727	20619	(N409XV)	146	E2092
N398CA	CRJ7	10112	N403BN	B727	20394	(N406PA)	F.100	11292	N410AA	MD80	49321
N398DA	737NG	30774	N403CA	CRJ	7428	N406PE	B737	19023	N410AM	DC-9	47010
N398FE	DC-10	46634	N403DA	B727	21147	N406SW	CRJ	7030	N410AN	A310	410
N398SW	B737	27692	N403EA	DC-9	47685	N406TW	B717	55073	N410AW	CRJ	7490
N398UA	B737	24673	N403EV	B747	27141	N406UA	A320	0454	N410BN	B727	20608
N398US	B737	23507	N403FE	A310	230	N406UP	B757	23728	N410BN	B727	21387
N399AN	B767	29606	N403FJ	D0328	3149	(N406US)	B727	18802	N410DA	B727	21222
N399DA	737NG	30379	N403JS	B757	27351	N406WN	737NG	27894	N410EA	DC-9	47731
N399FE	DC-10	48262	N403KW	B737	24234	N406XV	146	E2062	N410FE	A310	356
N399P	B737	23255	(N403P)	B737	23885	N407AA	MD80	49318	N410FJ	D0328	3165
N399UA	B737	24674	N403PE	B737	19020	N407AW	CRJ	7424	(N410P)	B737	23882
N399WN	B737	27693	N403SW	CRJ	7028	N407BN	B727	19992	N410PA	B707	18841
N400AA	MD80	49311	N403TW	B717	55070	N407DA	B727	21151	N410PE	B737	19027
N400DA	B727	21144	N403TZ	B737	24664	N407EA	DC-9	47692	N410SW	CRJ	7066
N400JR	DC-10	46976	N403UA	A300	068	N407EV	B747	27899	N410UA	A320	0463
N400KL	B757	25268	N403UA	A320	0442	N407FE	A310	254	N410UP	B767	23732
N400ME	DC-9	45727	N403UP	B757	23725	N407FE	DC-8	46089	(N410US)	B727	18806
N400MJ	CRJ	7309	(N403US)	B727	18799	N407FJ	D0328	3157	N410WN	737NG	27897
N400MS	CRJ7	10004	N403WN	737NG	29815	N407KW	B737	24703	(N410XV)	146	E2094
N400RG	B727	19149	N403XV	146	E2061	(N407P)	B737	23879	N410Z	D0328	3125
N400WN	737NG	27891	N404AW	B737	25507	N407PA	B707	18838	N411AA	MD80	49322
N401	B707	18832	N404AW	CRJ	7294	(N407PA)	B727	20620	N411BN	B727	20609
N401AL	B737	25663	N404BN	B727	20302	N407PE	B737	23879	N411DA	B727	21223
N401AW	B737	25603	N404DA	B727	21148	N407SW	CRJ	7034	N411EA	DC-9	47732
N401AW	CRJ	7280	N404EA	DC-9	47665	N407TW	B717	55074	N411FE	A310	359
N401BN	B727	20392	N404FE	A310	233	N407U	A300	124	N411FJ	D0328	3166
N401DA	B727	21145	N404FE	DC-8	46001	N407UA	A300	124	N411LF	737NG	28224
N401EA	DC-9	47682	N404FJ	D0328	3150	N407UA	A320	0456	N411LF	B737	26306
N401FE	A310	191	N404KW	B737	25371	N407UP	B757	23729	N411MD	MD11	48419
N401FE	DC-8	46117	(N404P)	B737	23876	(N407US)	B727	18803	(N411PA)	F.100	11294
N401FJ	D0328	3145	N404PA	B707	18835	N407US	B737	23877	N411PE	B737	19028
N401JR	DC-10	46590	(N404PB)	B707	18835	N407WN	737NG	29817	N411SW	CRJ	7067
N401JS	B757	26332	N404PE	B737	19021	N407XV	146	E2069	N411TW	B717	55078
N401KW	B767	26281	N404UA	A300	065	N408AA	MD80	49319	N411UA	A320	0464
N401LF	B737	28202	N404UA	A320	0450	N408AW	CRJ	7568	N411UP	B757	23851
N401LF	B767	28206	N404UP	B757	23726	N408BN	B727	19993	(N411US)	B727	18807
N401ME	DC-9	47133	(N404US)	B727	18800	N408CA	CRJ	7440	N411US	B737	23880
N401MG	B737	21763	N404US	B737	23886	N408CE	B737	19408	N411WN	737NG	29821
N401MJ	CRJ	7316	N404WN	737NG	27892	N408DA	B727	21152	(N411XV)	146	E2098
N401PA	B707	18832	N404XV	146	E2064	N408EA	DC-9	47693	N411ZW	CRJ	7569
(N401PA)	B727	20615	N405A	MD80	49316	N408EV	B747	28092	N412AA	MD80	49323
N401PW	B727	23719	N405AW	B737	25508	N408FE	A310	257	N412AW	CRJ	7592
N401SH	B737	20584	N405AW	CRJ	7362	N408FJ	D0328	3160	N412BN	B727	20610
N401SK	1-11	073	N405BC	B737	23405	N408MC	B747	29261	N412CE	B737	20412
N401SY	A340	24315	N405BN	B727	20303	(N408P)	B737	23880	N412CT	B737	24124
N401TW	B717	55058	N405CC	CRJ	7099	N408PA	B707	18839	N412DA	B727	21232
N401TZ	B737	24663				(N408PA)	B727	20621	N412EA	DC-9	47733
N401UA	A300	118							N412FE	A310	360

Reg.	Type	No.	Reg.	Type	No.	Reg.	Type	No.	Reg.	Type	No.
N412FJ	D0328	3167	N416PE	B737	19033	N420UP	B757	23907	N426FE	A310	245
N412MC	B747	30559	N416SW	CRJ	7089	N420US	B737	23987	N426FJ	D0328	3190
(N412P)	B737	23883	N416TW	B717	55083	N420WN	737NG	29825	N426PA	B707	19361
N412PA	B707	18842	N416UA	A320	0479	N421AJ	DC-8	45421	N426SW	CRJ	7468
(N412PA)	F.100	11298	N416UP	B757	23903	N421AV	B767	25421	N426TW	B717	55093
N412PE	B737	19029	N416US	B737	23884	N421BN	B727	20734	N426UA	A320	0510
(N412SW)	CRJ	7090	N416WN	737NG	32453	N421DA	B727	21274	N426UP	B757	25457
N412SW	CRJ	7101	N417AA	MD80	49328	N421EA	DC-9	47679	N426US	B737	24548
N412TW	B717	55079	N417AW	CRJ	7610	N421EX	B727	19099	N426WN	737NG	29830
N412UA	A320	0465	N417BN	B727	20730	N421FE	A310	342	N427AA	MD80	49339
N412UP	B757	23852	N417DA	B727	21259	N421FJ	D0328	3179	N427BN	B727	20773
N412US	B737	23881	N417DG	DC-10	46936	N421LV	737NG	32452	N427CA	CRJ	7460
N412WN	737NG	29818	N417EA	DC-9	47753	N421MA	B707	18049	(N427DA)	B727	21308
(N412XV)	146	E2103	N417EX	B727	19290	N421PA	B707	19266	N427EX	B727	19090
N413AA	MD80	49324	N417FE	A310	333	N421UA	A320	0500	N427FB	DC-8	45684
N413AW	CRJ	7585	N417FJ	D0328	3174	N421UP	B757	25281	N427FE	A310	362
N413BN	B727	20611	N417GE	MD80	49417	N421US	B737	23988	N427FJ	D0328	3192
N413DA	B727	21233	N417MA	B707	18082	N421ZW	CRJ	7346	N427LF	B737	26319
N413EA	DC-9	47745	N417PA	B707	18959	N422AA	MD80	49334	N427MA	B707	17607
N413EX	B727	19206	(N417PA)	F.100	11309	N422AW	CRJ	7341	N427PA	B707	19362
N413FE	A310	397	N417PE	B737	19794	N422BN	B727	20735	N427SB	B767	27427
N413FJ	D0328	3168	N417SW	CRJ	7400	(N422DA)	B727	21303	N427SW	CRJ	7497
N413JG	B737	23148	N417UA	A320	0483	N422EX	B727	19094	N427UA	A320	0512
N413LT	MD11	48413	N417UP	B757	23904	N422FE	A310	346	N427UP	B757	25458
(N413PA)	F.100	11301	N417US	B737	23984	N422FJ	D0328	3180	N427US	B737	24549
N413PE	B737	19030	N417WN	737NG	29822	N422PA	B707	19275	N427WN	737NG	29831
(N413SW)	CRJ	7093	N418AA	MD80	49329	(N422PA)	F.100	11322	N427ZW	CRJ	7685
N413SW	CRJ	7102	N418AW	CRJ	7618	N422TW	B717	55089	N428AA	MD80	49340
N413TW	B717	55080	N418BN	B727	20731	N422UA	A320	0503	N428AW	CRJ	7695
N413UA	A320	0470	N418DA	B727	21271	N422UP	B757	25324	N428BN	B727	20774
N413UP	B757	23853	N418EA	DC-9	47676	N422US	B737	23989	(N428DA)	B727	21309
N413US	B737	23882	N418EX	B727	18946	N422WN	737NG	29826	N428EX	B727	19097
N413WN	737NG	29819	N418FE	A310	343	N423AA	MD80	49335	N428FE	A310	248
(N413XV)	146	E2107	N418FJ	D0328	3176	N423AW	CRJ	7636	N428FJ	D0328	3193
N414BN	B727	20612	N418GE	MD80	49418	N423BN	B727	20736	N428MX	A320	0428
N414DA	B727	21256	N418JW	B737	25418	N423BN	B727	20738	N428PA	B707	19363
N414EA	DC-9	47746	N418LA	B767	34246	(N423DA)	B727	21304	N428TW	B717	55095
N414EX	B727	18899	N418MC	B747	32840	N423EX	B727	19314	N428UA	A320	0523
N414FE	A310	400	N418PA	B707	18960	N423FE	A310	281	N428UP	B757	25459
N414FJ	D0328	3169	(N418PA)	F.100	11317	N423FJ	D0328	3181	N428US	B737	24550
N414LT	MD11	48414	N418SW	CRJ	7446	N423MA	B707	18083	N428WN	737NG	29844
(N414P)	B737	23884	N418TW	B717	55085	N423PA	B707	19276	N429AA	MD80	49341
N414PA	B707	18956	N418UA	A320	0485	(N423PA)	F.100	11341	N429AW	CRJ	7711
(N414PA)	F.100	11302	N418UP	B757	23905	N423SW	CRJ	7456	N429BN	B727	20775
N414PE	B737	19031	N418US	B737	23985	N423TW	B717	55090	(N429DA)	B727	21310
N414UA	A320	0472	N418WN	737NG	29823	N423UA	A320	0504	N429EX	B727	19100
N414UP	B757	23854	N419AA	MD80	49331	N423UP	B757	25325	N429FE	A310	264
N414WN	737NG	29820	N419AW	CRJ	7633	N423US	B737	23990	N429FJ	D0328	3194
(N414XV)	146	E2111	N419B	B707	19351	N423WN	737NG	29827	N429MX	A319	1429
N414ZW	CRJ	7586	N419BN	B727	20732	N424AA	MD80	49336	N429RX	A320	0429
N415AA	MD80	49326	N419CT	B737	25419	N424AW	CRJ	7656	N429SW	CRJ	7518
N415AM	DC-9	47015	N419DA	B727	21272	N424BN	B727	20737	N429TW	B717	55096
N415AW	CRJ	7593	N419EA	DC-9	47677	(N424DA)	B727	21305	N429UA	A320	0539
N415BN	B727	20613	N419EX	B727	18947	N424EX	B727	20042	N429UP	B757	25460
N415DA	B727	21257	N419FE	A310	345	N424FE	A310	241	N429US	B737	24551
N415EA	DC-9	47749	N419FJ	D0328	3173	N424FJ	D0328	3185	N429WN	737NG	33658
N415EX	B727	18945	N419GE	737NG	33419	N424GB	B737	19424	N430AA	MD80	49342
N415FE	A310	349	N419GE	MD80	49419	N424PA	B707	19277	N430AW	CRJ	7719
N415FJ	D0328	3170	N419MA	B707	18082	N424TW	B717	55091	N430BN	B727	20837
N415MC	B747	32837	N419MT	MD80	49419	N424UA	A320	0506	N430CA	CRJ	7461
N415MX	A320	0415	N419PA	B707	19264	N424UP	B757	25369	(N430DA)	B727	21311
N415PA	B707	18957	(N419PA)	F.100	11319	N424US	B737	23991	N430EX	B727	19101
(N415PA)	F.100	11304	N419UA	A320	0487	N424WN	737NG	29828	N430FE	A310	394
N415PE	B737	19032	N419UP	B757	23906	N425AN	B737	25425	N430FJ	D0328	3209
N415TW	B717	55082	N419US	B737	23986	N425AW	CRJ	7663	N430SW	CRJ	7523
N415UA	A320	0475	N419WN	737NG	29824	N425BN	B727	20738	N430TW	B717	55097
N415UP	B757	23855	N420AA	MD80	49332	(N425DA)	B727	21306	N430UA	A320	0568
N415US	B737	23883	N420AJ	DC-8	45419	N425EX	B727	19095	N430UP	B757	25461
N415WN	737NG	29836	N420AW	CRJ	7640	N425FE	A310	264	N430US	B737	24552
(N415XV)	146	E2119	N420BN	B727	20733	N425FJ	D0328	3189	N430WN	737NG	33659
N416AA	MD80	49327	N420CA	CRJ	7451	N425LV	737NG	29829	N430Z	D0328	3127
N416AW	CRJ	7603	N420DA	B727	21273	N425MA	B707	17689	N431AA	MD80	49343
N416BN	B727	20729	N420DS	B747	24108	N425PA	B707	19278	N431AV	DC-10	46557
N416CA	CRJ	7450	N420EA	DC-9	47689	N425UA	A320	0508	N431AW	CRJ	7256
N416DA	B727	21258	N420EX	B727	19102	N425UP	B757	25370	N431BN	B727	20838
N416EA	DC-9	47751	N420FE	A310	339	N425US	B737	23992	N431CA	CRJ	7472
N416EX	B727	19287	N420FJ	D0328	3178	N426AA	MD80	49338	(N431DA)	B727	21312
N416FE	A310	288	N420GE	SE210	42	N426AW	CRJ	7669	N431EX	B727	19103
N416FJ	D0328	3171	N420LA	B767	34627	N426BN	B727	20772	N431FE	A310	316
N416MC	B747	32838	N420PA	B707	19265	(N426DA)	B727	21307	N431LF	A310	309
N416PA	B707	18958	N420TW	B717	55087	N426EX	B727	19089	N431LF	A320	0361
(N416PA)	F.100	11305	N420UA	A320	0489	N426FB	DC-8	45667	N431LT	MD11	48431

Reg	Type	No.	Reg	Type	No.	Reg	Type	No.	Reg	Type	No.
N431MA	B707	17597	N437UP	B757	25468	N445SW	CRJ	7651	N451GX	B757	24451
N431PE	B737	19884	N437US	B737	24559	N445UA	A320	0826	N451LF	A320	0525
N431SW	CRJ	7536	N437WN	737NG	29832	N445UP	B757	27390	N451LF	A321	0591
N431UA	A320	0571	N438AA	MD80	49456	N445US	B737	24863	N451PA	B707	19273
N431UP	B757	25462	N438AW	CRJ	7748	N445WN	737NG	29841	N451PA	B747	30809
N431US	B737	24553	N438SW	CRJ	7574	N446AA	MD80	49472	N451RN	B707	19273
N431WN	737NG	29845	N438UA	A320	0678	N446AN	A320	0446	N451TA	A320	0733
N432AA	MD80	49350	N438UP	B757	25469	N446AW	CRJ	7806	N451UA	A320	0865
N432AW	CRJ	7257	N438US	B737	24560	N446BN	B727	21247	N451UP	B757	27739
N432BN	B727	20839	N438WN	737NG	29833	(N446CA)	CRJ	7503	N451US	F.28	11103
(N432DA)	B727	21313	N439AA	MD80	49457	N446CA	CRJ	7546	N451UW	B737	24934
N432EX	B727	19867	N439AW	CRJ	7753	N446CT	B737	24461	N451WN	737NG	32495
N432FE	A310	326	N439BN	B727	21118	N446FE	A310	224	N452AA	MD80	49553
(N432PA)	F.100	11371	N439SW	CRJ	7578	N446GE	B757	32446	N452AT	A310	352
N432PE	B737	19885	N439UA	A320	0683	N446PA	B707	19268	N452AW	CRJ	7835
N432SW	CRJ	7548	N439UP	B757	25470	N446SW	CRJ	7666	N452BN	B727	21366
N432UA	A320	0587	N439US	B737	24781	N446UA	A320	0834	N452DA	B727	20634
N432UP	B757	25463	N439WN	737NG	29834	N446UP	B757	27735	N452FE	A310	313
N432US	B737	24554	N440AA	MD80	49459	N446US	B737	24873	N452FJ	DO328	3214
N432WN	737NG	33715	N440AN	B757	25044	N446WN	737NG	29842	N452PA	B707	19274
N433AA	MD80	49451	N440AW	CRJ	7766	N447AA	MD80	49473	N452PA	B747	30810
N433AW	CRJ	7289	N440BN	B727	21119	N447AW	CRJ	7812	N452SW	CRJ	7716
N433BN	B727	20840	N440DR	B727	19253	N447BN	B727	21248	N452TA	A320	0741
(N433DA)	B727	21314	N440DS	B707	18977	(N447CA)	CRJ	7504	N452UA	A320	0955
N433EX	B727	19868	N440GB	B737	21440	N447CA	CRJ	7552	N452UP	B757	25473
N433FE	A310	335	N440LV	737NG	29835	N447DN	A310	447	N452US	F.28	11105
N433LV	737NG	33716	N440SW	CRJ	7589	N447FE	A310	251	N452UW	B737	24979
N433MA	B707	18084	N440UA	A320	0702	N447GE	B757	32447	N452WN	737NG	29846
N433PA	B707	19364	N440UP	B757	25471	N447MX	A320	0447	N453AA	MD80	49558
N433PE	B737	19886	N440US	B737	24811	N447PA	B707	19269	N453AC	B737	19931
N433SW	CRJ	7550	N440XS	A310	440	N447SW	CRJ	7677	N453AW	CRJ	7838
N433UA	A320	0589	N441AA	MD80	49460	N447TM	A320	0447	N453BN	B727	21394
N433UP	B757	25464	N441BN	B727	21242	N447UA	A320	0836	N453DA	B727	20635
N433US	B737	24555	N441J	DC-8	45988	N447UP	B757	27736	N453FA	DC-8	45601
N433ZV	B727	20433	N441KA	A320	0441	N447US	B737	24874	N453FE	A310	267
N434AA	MD80	49452	N441LF	A310	352	N447WN	737NG	33720	(N453FJ)	DO328	3215
N434AW	CRJ	7322	N441LF	A320	0405	N448AA	MD80	49474	N453LS	B737	22453
N434BN	B727	21041	N441LF	B737	24988	N448AW	CRJ	7814	N453PA	B707	19374
(N434DA)	B727	21315	N441SW	CRJ	7602	N448BN	B727	21249	N453PA	B747	30811
N434EX	B727	18898	N441UA	A320	0751	N448DR	B727	19253	N453SW	CRJ	7743
N434FE	A310	355	N441UP	B757	27386	N448FE	A310	260	N453TA	A320	0747
N434KC	DC-10	48201	N441US	B737	24812	N448M	B707	19270	N453UA	A320	1001
N434PA	B707	19365	N441WN	737NG	29837	N448PA	B707	19270	N453UP	B757	25474
N434PE	B737	19887	N441ZW	CRJ	7777	N448SW	CRJ	7678	N453US	F.28	11106
N434UA	A320	0592	N442AA	MD80	49468	N448UA	A320	0842	N453UW	B737	24980
N434UP	B757	25465	N442AW	CRJ	7778	N448UP	B757	27737	N453WN	737NG	29847
N434US	B737	24556	N442BN	B727	21243	N448US	B737	24892	N454AA	MD80	49559
N434WN	737NG	32454	N442CA	CRJ	7483	(N448WA)	B707	19271	N454AW	CRJ	7842
(N434ZV)	B727	20434	N442FE	A310	353	N448WN	737NG	33721	N454BN	B727	21395
N435AA	MD80	49453	N442LV	737NG	32459	N449AA	MD80	49475	N454DA	B727	20636
N435AW	CRJ	7724	N442SW	CRJ	7609	N449AW	CRJ	7818	N454FE	A310	278
N435BN	B727	21042	N442UA	A320	0780	N449BN	B727	21363	(N454FJ)	DO328	3212
N435CA	CRJ	7473	N442UP	B757	27387	N449FE	A310	217	N454PA	B707	19376
N435EX	B727	19288	N442US	B737	24841	N449GE	B757	32449	N454PA	B747	30812
N435FE	A310	369	N442WN	737NG	32459	N449J	B707	18954	N454PC	B707	18839
N435MA	B707	18085	N443AA	MD80	49469	N449PA	B707	19271	N454SW	CRJ	7749
N435PA	B707	19366	N443AW	CRJ	7781	N449RX	A320	0449	N454TA	A320	0789
N435PE	B737	19888	N443BN	B727	21244	N449SW	CRJ	7699	N454UA	A320	1104
N435SW	CRJ	7555	(N443CA)	CRJ	7496	N449UA	A320	0851	N454UP	B757	25475
N435UA	A320	0613	N443CA	CRJ	7539	N449UP	B757	27738	N454US	F.28	11107
N435UP	B757	25466	N443FE	A310	283	N449US	B737	24893	N454UW	B737	24996
N435US	B737	24557	N443RR	A320	443	N449WN	737NG	32469	N454WN	737NG	29851
N435WN	737NG	32455	N443SW	CRJ	7638	N450AA	MD80	49476	N455AA	MD80	49560
N435XS	A310	435	N443UA	A320	0820	N450AW	CRJ	7823	N455AW	CRJ	7848
N436AA	MD80	49454	N443UP	B757	27388	N450AX	DC-10	46942	N455BN	B727	21461
N436AW	CRJ	7734	N443US	B737	24842	N450BN	B727	21364	N455CA	CRJ	7592
N436BN	B727	21043	N443WN	737NG	29838	N450FE	A310	162	(N455CC)	B727	21455
N436CA	CRJ	7482	N444BN	B727	21245	N450ML	DC-10	47831	N455DA	B727	20637
"N436DH"	B727	22641	(N444CM)	B727	19665	N450PA	B707	19272	N455FE	A310	331
N436EX	B727	19289	N444RX	A320	0444	N450PA	B747	30808	(N455FJ)	DO328	3217
N436FE	A310	454	N444SA	B727	19987	N450UA	A320	0857	N455PA	B707	19378
N436NA	DC-8	46082	N444UA	A320	0824	N450UP	B757	25472	N455SW	CRJ	7760
N436UA	A320	0638	N444UP	B757	27389	N450US	F.28	11101	N455TA	A320	0874
N436UP	B757	25467	N444US	B737	24862	N450UW	B737	24933	N455UA	A320	1105
N436US	B737	24558	N444WN	737NG	29839	N450WN	737NG	32470	N455UP	B757	25476
N436WN	737NG	32456	N444ZW	CRJ	7788	N451AA	MD80	49477	N455UW	B737	24997
N437AA	MD80	49455	N445AA	MD80	49471	N451AW	CRJ	7832	N455WN	737NG	32462
N437AW	CRJ	7744	N445AW	CRJ	7804	N451BN	B727	21365	N456AA	MD80	49561
N437BN	B727	21044	N445BN	B727	21246	N451CA	CRJ	7562	N456AW	MD80	53182
N437RX	A320	0437	N445FE	A310	297	N451DJ	E145	145789	N456BN	B727	21462
N437SW	CRJ	7564	N445PA	B707	19267	N451FE	A310	303	N456DA	B727	20638
N437UA	A320	0655				N451FJ	DO328	3205	N456FE	A310	318

Reg	Type	S/N	Reg	Type	S/N	Reg	Type	S/N	Reg	Type	S/N
(N456FJ)	D0328	3218	N461AW	CRJ	7870	N465FE	B727	21289	N470TA	A320	1400
N456MT	E145	145789	N461BN	B727	21488	N465GB	B737	19713	N470TA	B737	19611
N456TM	B737	20336	(N461DA)	B727	20634	N465SM	CRJ	7612	N470UA	A320	1427
N456UA	A320	1128	N461DA	B727	20643	N465SW	CRJ	7845	N470UP	B757	25486
N456UP	B757	25477	N461EA	146	E2097	N465TA	A320	1374	N470US	B727	18806
N456US	F.28	11035	N461FE	B727	22548	N465UA	A320	1341	N470US	F.28	11098
N456UW	B737	25020	N461GB	B737	19306	N465UP	B757	28269	N470WN	737NG	33860
N456WN	737NG	32463	N461LF	737NG	30635	N465US	B727	18801	N470ZW	CRJ	7927
N456ZW	CRJ	7849	N461LF	A300	677	N465WN	737NG	33829	N471AA	MD80	49601
N457AA	MD80	49562	N461PA	B707	19371	N466AA	MD80	49596	N471AS	A300	069
(N457AC)	B737	19598	N461PR	B737	28882	N466AC	B737	19601	N471BN	B727	21669
N457AN	B737	27457	N461RD	B727	19461	(N466AT)	B727	21279	N471CA	CRJ	7655
N457AW	CRJ	7854	N461S	B727	21149	N466AW	CRJ	7899	(N471DA)	B727	20644
N457BN	B727	21463	N461SW	CRJ	7811	N466BN	B727	21493	N471DA	B727	20748
N457CA	CRJ	7612	N461TA	A320	1300	N466CA	CRJ	7627	N471EV	B747	20651
N457DA	B727	20639	N461UA	A320	1266	(N466DA)	B727	20639	N471GB	B737	19680
(N457FJ)	D0328	3219	N461UP	B757	28265	N466DA	B727	20743	N471LF	A320	0814
N457GE	B767	24457	N461US	B727	18797	N466FE	B727	21292	N471LF	B737	26288
N457PA	B707	19367	N461WN	737NG	32465	N466SW	CRJ	7856	N471SM	CRJ	7613
N457PC	B707	20178	N462AA	MD80	49592	N466UA	A320	1343	N471TA	A319	1066
N457SW	CRJ	7773	N462AC	B737	19307	N466UP	B757	25482	N471UA	A320	1432
N457TA	A320	0902	N462AP	146	E1017	N466US	B727	18802	N471UP	B757	28842
N457TM	B737	20156	N462AT	B737	22631	N466US	F.28	11075	N471US	B727	18807
N457UA	A320	1146	N462AU	F.28	11054	N466WN	737NG	30677	N471WN	737NG	32471
N457UP	B757	25478	N462AW	CRJ	7875	N467AA	MD80	49597	N472AA	MD80	49647
N457US	F.28	11036	N462BN	B727	21489	N467AT	B737	22055	N472AS	A300	125
N457UW	B737	25021	N462DA	B727	20644	N467AW	CRJ	7900	N472BN	B727	21670
N457WN	737NG	33856	N462EA	146	E2107	N467BN	B727	21529	N472CA	CRJ	7667
N458AA	MD80	49563	N462FE	B727	22550	N467CA	CRJ	7637	(N472DA)	B727	20645
"N458AC"	B707	18068	N462GB	B737	19307	(N467DA)	B727	20640	N472DA	B727	20749
N458AC	B737	21720	N462GE	MD80	49642	N467DA	B727	20744	N472EV	B747	20320
N458AN	B737	27458	N462PA	B707	19372	N467FE	B727	21449	N472GB	B737	19679
N458AW	CRJ	7861	N462PR	B737	28494	N467GB	B737	19714	N472GE	A310	472
N458BN	B727	21464	N462TA	A320	1334	N467HE	B737	24467	N472TA	A319	1113
N458CA	CRJ	7613	N462UA	A320	1272	N467RX	A320	0467	N472UA	A320	1435
N458DA	B727	20640	N462UP	B757	28266	N467UA	A320	1359	N472UP	B757	28843
N458PA	B707	19368	N462US	B727	18798	N467UP	B757	25483	N472US	B727	18943
N458TA	A320	0912	N462WN	737NG	32466	N467US	B727	18803	N472WN	737NG	33831
N458UA	A320	1163	N463AA	MD80	49593	N467US	F.28	11087	N473AA	MD80	49648
N458UP	B757	25479	(N463AC)	B737	19308	N467WN	737NG	33830	N473AC	B737	19614
N458US	F.28	11037	N463AP	146	E1063	N468AA	MD80	49598	N473AS	A300	203
N458UW	B737	25022	(N463AT)	B737	21355	N468AC	B737	20334	N473BN	B727	21996
N458WN	737NG	33857	N463AU	F.28	11061	N468AT	B737	19074	N473CA	CRJ	7668
N459AA	MD80	49564	N463AW	CRJ	7878	N468AW	CRJ	7916	(N473DA)	B727	20646
N459AC	B737	19072	N463BN	B727	21490	N468BN	B727	21530	N473DA	B727	20750
N459AW	CRJ	7863	(N463DA)	B727	20636	N468CA	CRJ	7649	N473EV	B747	19657
N459AX	B757	25621	N463DA	B727	20645	(N468DA)	B727	20641	N473MM	E145	14500983
N459BN	B727	21465	N463FE	B727	22551	N468DA	B727	20745	N473PA	B707	19375
N459DA	B727	20641	N463GB	B737	19308	N468FE	B727	21452	N473RN	B707	19375
N459JS	B747	20459	N463PA	B707	19373	N468UA	A320	1363	N473SC	A300	203
N459PA	B707	19369	N463SW	CRJ	7820	N468UP	B757	25484	N473TA	A319	1140
N459SW	CRJ	7782	N463TA	A320	1339	N468US	B727	18804	N473UA	A320	1469
N459TA	A320	0916	N463UA	A320	1282	N468US	F.28	11054	N473UP	B757	28846
N459UA	A320	1192	N463UP	B757	28267	N468WN	737NG	33858	N473US	B727	18943
N459UP	B757	25480	N463US	B727	18799	N469AA	MD80	49599	N473WN	737NG	33832
N459US	F.28	11043	N463WN	737NG	32467	N469AC	B727	20335	N474	MD80	49649
N459UW	B737	25023	N464AA	MD80	49594	(N469AT)	B737	21513	N474AS	A300	210
N459WN	737NG	32497	N464AC	B737	19309	N469AW	CRJ	7917	N474BN	B727	21997
N460AA	MD80	49565	N464AT	B737	21278	N469BN	B727	21531	(N474DA)	B727	20647
N460AC	B737	20158	N464AW	CRJ	7890	(N469DA)	B727	20642	N474DA	B727	20751
N460AT	B737	20158	N464BA	B737	23464	N469DA	B727	20746	N474EV	B747	19637
N460AU	F.28	11044	N464BN	B727	21491	N469FE	B727	21581	N474PA	B707	19377
N460AW	CRJ	7867	(N464DA)	B727	20637	N469NA	B737	23469	N474TA	A319	1159
N460BN	B727	21466	N464DA	B727	20646	N469SM	CRJ	7650	N474UA	A320	1475
N460DA	B727	20642	N464FE	B727	21288	N469UA	A320	1409	N474UP	B757	28844
N460DN	DC-8	46066	N464GB	B737	19309	N469UP	B757	25485	N474US	B727	18944
N460PA	B707	19370	N464SW	CRJ	7827	N469US	B727	18805	N474WN	737NG	33861
N460PR	B737	28881	N464TA	A320	1353	N469V	DC-10	46923	N475AA	MD80	49650
N460SW	CRJ	7803	N464UA	A320	1290	N469WN	737NG	33859	N475AC	MD80	48027
N460TA	A320	1007	N464UP	B757	28268	N470AA	MD80	49600	N475AU	F.28	11222
N460TF	B737	24460	N464US	B727	18800	N470AC	B737	20126	N475BN	B727	21998
N460UA	A320	1248	N464US	F.28	11063	(N470AC)	B737	20336	N475DA	B727	20752
N460UP	B757	25481	N464WN	737NG	32468	N470AS	A300	063	N475DC	CRJ	7137
N460US	B737	18910	N465A	MD80	49595	N470AT	B737	21501	N475EV	B747	19638
N460UW	B737	25024	N465AC	B737	19713	N470BN	B727	21532	N475GE	A310	475
N460WN	737NG	32464	N465AT	B737	21528	N470CA	CRJ	7650	N475HA	B717	55121
N461AA	MD80	49566	N465AU	F.28	11064	(N470DA)	B727	20643	N475PA	B707	19379
(N461AC)	B737	19306	N465AW	CRJ	7893	N470DA	B727	20747	N475TA	A319	1575
N461AC	B737	20976	N465BN	B727	21492	N470EV	B747	20653	N475UA	A320	1495
N461AP	146	E1015	(N465DA)	B727	20638	N470KB	B737	24470	N475UP	B757	28845
N461AT	B737	20976	N465DA	B727	20647	N470PC	B707	18839	N475US	B727	19121
N461AU	F.28	11032							N475WN	737NG	32474

Registration	Type	Serial
N476AA	MD80	49651
N476AC	MD80	48028
N476BN	B727	21999
N476DA	B727	20753
N476DC	CRJ	7139
N476EV	B747	19655
N476HA	B717	55118
(N476TA)	A319	1608
N476TA	A319	1934
N476UA	A320	1508
N476US	B727	19122
N476US	F.28	11224
N476WN	737NG	32475
N477AA	MD80	49652
N477AC	MD80	48062
N477AN	B767	27477
N477AU	F.28	11226
N477BN	B727	22000
N477CA	CRJ	7670
N477DA	B727	20754
N477EV	B747	20784
N477FE	B727	21394
N477GX	737NG	30477
N477HA	B717	55122
(N477TA)	A319	1703
N477TA	A319	1952
N477UA	A320	1514
N477US	B727	19123
N477WN	737NG	33988
N478AA	MD80	49653
N478AC	MD80	48063
N478BN	B727	22001
N478CA	CRJ	7671
N478CT	DC-10	47819
N478DA	B727	20755
N478EV	B747	21033
N478FE	B727	21395
N478HA	B717	55123
N478RX	A320	0478
N478TA	A319	2339
N478UA	A320	1533
N478US	B727	19124
N478US	F.28	11227
N478WN	737NG	33989
N479AA	MD80	49654
N479AC	MD80	48066
N479AU	F.28	11228
N479BN	B727	22002
N479CA	CRJ	7675
N479DA	B727	20756
N479EV	B747	19808
N479FE	B727	21461
N479HA	B717	55124
N479TA	A319	2444
N479UA	A320	1538
N479US	B727	19125
N479WN	737NG	33990
N480AA	MD80	49655
N480AC	MD80	48008
N480AC	MD80	49112
N480AU	F.28	11229
N480BN	B727	22003
N480CT	MD80	48069
N480DA	B727	20860
N480EV	B747	20348
N480FE	B727	21462
N480GX	B747	19746
N480HA	B717	55125
N480LP	MD80	48003
N480RX	A320	0480
N480TA	A319	3057
N480UA	A320	1555
N480US	B727	19126
"N480US"	F.28	11229
N480WN	737NG	33998
N481AA	MD80	49656
N481AC	MD80	49113
N481BN	B727	22004
N481CM	DC-9	48105
N481DA	B727	20861
N481EV	B747	19896
N481FE	B727	21463
N481GX	A320	0131
N481HA	B717	55126
N481SF	DC-9	48125
N481SG	DC-9	48126
N481TA	A320	1500
N481UA	A320	1559
N481US	F.28	11230
N481WN	737NG	29853
N482AA	MD80	49675
N482AC	MD80	49126
N482BN	B727	22005
N482CR	DC-10	48288
N482DA	B727	20862
N482EV	B747	20713
N482FE	B727	21464
N482GX	A320	0132
N482HA	B717	55127
N482TA	A320	1482
N482UA	A320	1584
N482US	F.28	11231
N482WN	737NG	29852
N483A	MD80	49676
N483AC	MD80	49127
(N483AS)	B727	18331
N483BN	B727	22091
N483CA	CRJ	7689
N483DA	B727	20863
(N483EV)	B747	20351
N483FE	B727	21465
N483GX	A320	0189
N483GX	B767	24973
N483HA	B717	55128
N483TA	A320	1509
N483UA	A320	1586
N483US	F.28	11233
N483WN	737NG	32472
N484AA	MD80	49677
N484BN	B727	22092
N484CA	CRJ	7702
N484DA	B727	20864
(N484EV)	B747	20352
N484FE	B727	21466
N484GX	A320	0190
N484HA	B717	55129
N484TA	A320	1523
N484TC	B767	24844
N484UA	A320	1609
N484US	F.28	11234
N484WN	737NG	33841
N485AA	MD80	49678
N485EV	B747	20712
N485FE	B727	21488
N485GX	A320	0343
N485HA	B717	55130
N485LS	MD11	48500
N485TA	A320	1624
N485UA	A320	1617
N485US	F.28	11235
N485WN	737NG	33842
N486AA	MD80	49679
N486CA	CRJ	7707
N486DA	B727	20866
N486EV	B747	20888
N486FE	B727	21489
N486GX	A320	0346
N486HA	B717	55131
(N486TA)	A320	1676
N486UA	A320	1620
N486US	F.28	11237
N486WN	737NG	33852
N487AA	MD80	49680
N487CA	CRJ	7729
N487CT	B767	24087
N487DA	B727	20867
N487EV	B747	23286
N487FE	B727	21490
N487GS	B737	19600
N487GX	B747	20493
N487HA	B717	55132
N487TA	A320	2084
N487UA	A320	1669
N487US	F.28	11238
N487WN	737NG	33854
N488AA	MD80	49681
(N488AS)	B727	18852
N488CA	CRJ	7730
N488DA	B727	21018
N488EV	B747	23287
N488FE	B727	21491
N488GX	B747	20372
N488TA	A320	2118
N488UA	A320	1680
N488US	B727	19867
N488US	F.28	11240
N488WN	737NG	33853
N489AA	MD80	49682
N489CA	CRJ	7755
N489DA	B727	21019
N489EV	B747	23393
N489FE	B727	21492
N489GX	MD11	48458
N489NC	MD80	48009
N489TA	A320	2102
N489UA	A320	1702
N489US	B727	19868
N489US	F.28	11149
N489WN	737NG	33855
N490AA	MD80	49683
N490AM	B757	25490
N490AN	B757	25490
N490DA	B727	21020
N490FE	B727	21493
N490GE	B737	28490
N490GX	A320	0331
N490GX	B747	19650
N490SA	DC-9	45798
N490ST	1-11	083
N490TA	A320	2282
N490UA	A320	1728
N490US	B727	18898
N490US	F.28	11152
N490W	B727	19091
N490WN	737NG	32476
N491AA	MD80	49684
N491CA	CRJ	7756
N491DA	B727	21060
N491FE	B727	21529
N491GX	A320	0288
N491GX	B747	19641
N491GX	MD80	49602
N491MC	B747	29252
N491PA	B707	19693
N491SA	DC-9	45799
N491SH	MD80	49150
N491ST	1-11	056
N491TA	A320	2301
N491UA	A320	1741
N491US	B727	18899
N491US	F.28	11156
N491WC	B737	21820
N491WN	737NG	33867
N492AA	MD80	49730
N492CA	CRJ	7763
N492DA	B727	21061
N492FE	B727	21530
N492GD	B737	24492
(N492GX)	B747	20350
N492KR	B737	24492
N492MC	B747	29253
N492PA	B707	19694
N492SW	CRJ	7168
N492TA	A320	2434
N492UA	A320	1755
N492US	B727	18945
N492US	F.28	11159
N492WC	B737	21821
N492WN	737NG	33866
N493AA	MD80	49731
N493AG	737NG	36493
N493AN	B737	24093
N493AP	MD80	49373
N493DA	B727	21062
N493FE	B727	21531
N493GX	A320	0234
N493GX	B747	19647
N493MC	B747	29254
N493PA	B707	19695
N493SW	CRJ	7450
N493TA	A319	2657
N493TA	A320	2917
N493UA	A320	1821
N493US	B727	18946
N493US	F.28	11161
N493WC	B737	21822
N493WN	737NG	32477
N494AA	MD80	49732
N494AC	B737	24494
N494AP	MD80	49442
N494CA	CRJ	7765
N494DA	B727	21074
N494FE	B727	21532
N494GX	A320	0235
N494GX	B747	19648
N494MC	B747	29255
N494PA	B707	19696
(N494TA)	A319	2666
N494TA	A320	3042
N494TG	E145	145678
N494UA	A320	1840
N494US	B727	18947
N494US	F.28	11167
N494WN	737NG	33868
N495	B707	19697
N495AA	MD80	49733
N495AJ	B727	20937
N495CA	CRJ	7774
N495DA	B727	21075
N495FE	B727	21669
N495MC	B747	29256
(N495MC)	B747	29261
(N495MD)	B717	55003
N495PA	B707	19697
(N495TA)	A320	2791
N495TA	A320	3103
N495UA	A320	1842
N495US	B727	19206
N495US	F.28	11168
N495WC	B727	19092
N495WN	737NG	33869
N496AA	MD80	49734
N496AN	B737	24096
N496CA	CRJ	7791
N496DA	B727	21076
N496FE	B727	21670
(N496MC)	B747	29256
N496MC	B747	29257
N496PA	B707	19698
N496SW	CRJ	7473
N496TA	A320	3113
N496UA	A320	1845
N496US	B727	19287
N496US	F.28	11169
N496WC	B727	19098
N496WN	737NG	32478
N497AA	MD80	49735
N497AN	B737	24097
N497DA	B727	21077
N497FE	B727	20866
N497GX	B757	24497
(N497MC)	B747	29257
N497MC	B747	29258
N497PA	B707	19699
N497PJ	MD80	49777
N497SR	B737	24097
N497SW	CRJ	7482
N497TF	737NG	28497
N497UA	A320	1847
N497US	B727	19288
N497US	F.28	11173
N497WC	B727	19096
N497WN	737NG	32479
N498AA	MD80	49736
N498AW	737NG	28498

Reg	Type	c/n	Reg	Type	c/n	Reg	Type	c/n	Reg	Type	c/n
N498CA	CRJ	7792	(N502FJ)	D0328	3206	N505NK	A319	2485	N509MD	MD80	49784
N498DA	B727	21142	N502GX	B767	24973	N505PA	L1011	193Y-1184	N509MJ	CRJ7	10094
N498FE	B727	20867	N502MD	DC-9	47363	(N505PE)	B727	20638	N509MM	146	E3248
N498GA	B707	19695	N502ME	DC-9	48132	N505SW	B737	24182	N509NK	A319	2603
(N498MC)	B747	29258	N502MG	B727	19391	N505T	B727	20115	N509PA	L1011	193Y-1188
N498MC	B747	29259	N502MJ	CRJ7	10050	N505TA	A300	271	(N509PE)	B727	20642
N498SW	CRJ	7483	N502NK	A319	2433	N505UA	B757	24626	N509SW	B737	24186
N498UA	A320	1865	(N502PE)	B727	20635	N505US	B757	23194	N509UA	B757	24763
N498US	B727	19289	N502RA	DC-9	19391	N505XJ	146	E2313	N509US	B757	23198
N498US	F.28	11181	N502SR	B747	20208	N506AE	CRJ7	10056	N509XJ	146	E2321
N498WC	B727	19093	N502SW	B737	24179	(N506AE)	E145	145194	N510	F.28	11167
N498WN	737NG	32480	N502T	1-11	083	N506AU	B737	23381	N510AE	CRJ7	10105
N499AA	MD80	49737	N502TA	A300	075	N506CA	CRJ	7793	N510AM	MD80	49804
N499AY	B737	23499	N502UA	B757	24623	N506DA	B727	21308	N510AU	B737	23385
N499BN	B727	20162	N502US	B757	23251	N506DC	B747	21251	N510CA	CRJ	7802
N499DA	B727	21143	N502UW	B737	23232	N506EA	B757	22196	N510DA	B727	21312
N499FE	B727	21018	(N502VL)	A319	2780	N506FE	B727	18277	N510EA	B757	22200
N499HE	MD11	48499	N502XJ	146	E2307	"N506GX"	B737	23772	N510FE	B727	18282
N499MC	B747	29260	N503AE	CRJ7	10021	N506JB	A320	1235	N510FP	B757	24290
N499SW	CRJ	7398	(N503AE)	E145	145173	N506MC	B747	21252	N510JB	A320	1280
N499US	B727	19290	N503AU	B737	23378	N506MD	DC-9	47431	N510MD	MD11	48421
N499US	F.28	11182	N503AV	B737	20227	N506MJ	CRJ7	10073	N510MJ	CRJ7	10101
N499WN	737NG	32481	N503DA	B727	21305	N506MM	146	E3244	N510MM	146	E3250
N500AE	CRJ7	10025	N503EA	B757	22193	N506NA	B757	24771	N510NK	A319	2622
N500AL	B737	21206	N503FE	B727	18273	N506NK	A319	2490	N510PA	L1011	193Y-1194
N500AV	B727	21021	(N503FJ)	D0328	3207	(N506PE)	B727	20639	(N510PE)	B727	20643
N500AY	B737	23500	N503JB	A320	1123	N506SW	B737	24183	(N510RG)	E145	145224
N500CS	1-11	086	N503MD	DC-9	47430	N506TA	A300	207	N510SK	B727	24289
N500FJ	D0328	3197	N503MG	B727	19392	N506UA	B757	24627	N510SW	B737	24187
N500GX	737NG	28824	N503MJ	CRJ7	10058	N506US	B757	23195	N510TA	A300	100
N500GX	B757	24176	N503NK	A319	2470	N506XJ	146	E2314	N510UA	B757	24780
N500JJ	B707	17699	N503PA	L1011	193Y-1177	N507AE	CRJ7	10059	N510XJ	146	E2323
N500JJ	B727	18951	(N503PE)	B727	20636	(N507AE)	E145	145195	N511AE	CRJ7	10107
(N500LE)	E145	145156	N503RA	B727	19395	N507AU	B737	23382	(N511AE)	E145	145235
N500LS	737NG	29054	N503SW	B737	24180	N507CA	CRJ	7796	N511AU	B737	23594
N500LS	B727	20115	N503T	1-11	BAC.183	N507DA	B727	21309	N511DA	B727	21313
N500ME	DC-9	45711	N503UA	B757	24624	N507DC	DC-8	45855	N511DB	B727	19139
N500MH	B737	23174	N503US	B757	23192	N507EA	B757	22197	N511EA	B757	22201
N500MH	DC-8	45812	N503UW	B737	23237	N507FE	B727	18278	N511FE	B727	18283
N500PR	CRJ	7846	N503XJ	146	E2310	N507JB	A320	1240	N511HE	B737	24511
N500TR	MD80	49144	N504	F.28	11152	N507MC	B747	21380	N511JZ	MD80	49511
N500WN	F.28	11016	N504AE	CRJ7	10044	N507MD	DC-9	47474	N511LF	A321	0614
N501AA	MD80	49738	(N504AE)	E145	145174	N507MJ	CRJ7	10077	N511MD	MD11	48420
N501AM	MD80	49188	N504AU	B737	23379	N507MM	146	E3245	N511MJ	CRJ7	10104
N501AU	B737	23376	N504AV	B727	20726	N507NK	A319	2560	N511MM	146	E3255
N501AV	B737	20128	N504DA	B727	21306	N507PA	L1011	193Y-1185	N511NK	A319	2659
N501BG	CRJ7	10017	N504DC	B747	21316	(N507PE)	B727	20640	N511P	B747	21162
(N501BN)	B747	20207	N504EA	B757	22194	N507SW	B737	24184	N511PA	L1011	193Y-1195
N501DA	B727	21303	N504FE	B727	18274	N507UA	B757	24743	N511PE	B727	20634
N501DC	B727	20739	N504JB	A320	1156	N507US	B757	23196	(N511PE)	B727	20644
N501EA	B757	22191	N504MD	DC-9	47468	N507XJ	146	E2316	N511RP	MD80	49793
N501FR	MD11	48501	N504MG	B727	19395	N508AE	CRJ7	10072	N511SW	B737	24188
N501GB	L1011	193J-1183	N504MJ	CRJ7	10066	(N508AE)	E145	145205	N511TA	A300	173
N501GX	737NG	28825	N504MM	146	E3221	N508AU	B737	23383	N511UA	B757	24799
N501LS	CRJ	7008	N504NK	A319	2473	N508DA	B727	21310	N511US	B757	23199
N501LS	CRJ	7584	N504PA	L1011	193Y-1181	N508DC	DC-8	45935	N511XJ	146	E2325
N501ME	DC-9	47132	(N504PE)	B727	20637	N508FA	B757	22198	N512	F.28	11168
N501MH	B757	22176	N504RA	B727	19395	N508FE	B727	18279	N512AE	CRJ7	10110
N501MJ	CRJ7	10047	N504SW	B737	24181	N508JB	A320	1257	(N512AE)	E145	145247
(N501MR)	E145	145162	N504T	1-11	084	N508MC	B747	21644	N512AT	B757	25493
N501NG	B737	22395	N504TA	A300	216	N508MD	DC-9	47477	N512AU	B737	23595
N501NK	A319	2424	N504UA	B757	24625	N508MJ	CRJ7	10087	N512DA	B727	21314
N501PA	L1011	193Y-1176	N504US	B757	23193	N508MM	146	E3247	N512DC	B747	21252
(N501PE)	B727	20634	N504XJ	146	E2311	N508NA	B757	26244	N512EA	B757	22202
N501RR	A310	050	N505	F.28	11156	N508NK	A319	2567	(N512FE)	B727	18435
N501SR	DC-8	45994	N505AA	MD80	49799	N508PA	L1011	193Y-1186	N512FE	B727	19131
N501SW	B737	24178	N505AE	CRJ7	10053	(N508PE)	B727	20641	(N512FE)	B727	19389
N501TR	A300	053	(N505AE)	E145	145184	N508RL	A319	3253	N512FP	DC-8	46075
N501UA	B757	24622	N505AU	B737	23380	N508SW	B737	24185	N512GE	B737	24512
N501US	B757	23190	N505AV	B737	20277	N508UA	B757	24744	N512MC	B747	21220
N501UW	B737	23231	N505C	B727	20115	N508US	B757	24115	N512MJ	CRJ7	10109
(N501VL)	A319	2771	N505DA	B727	21307	N508XJ	146	E2318	N512MM	146	E3263
N501VL	A319	2979	N505EA	B757	22195	N509	F.28	11161	N512NA	B757	26962
N501XJ	146	E2208	N505FB	DC-8	45410	N509AE	CRJ7	10078	N512NK	A319	2673
N502AE	CRJ7	10018	N505FE	B727	18276	(N509AE)	E145	145211	N512PA	L1011	193Y-1197
(N502AE)	E145	145164	N505JB	A320	1173	N509AU	B737	23384	N512PE	B727	20635
N502AU	B737	23377	N505LS	B727	20115	N509DA	B727	21311	(N512PE)	B727	20645
N502AV	B727	20580	(N505MC)	B747	21048	N509DC	B737	23636	N512SW	B737	24189
N502CG	CRJ	7283	N505MC	B747	21251	N509EA	B757	22199	N512TA	A300	183
N502DA	B727	21304	N505MD	MD80	49149	N509FE	B727	18280	N512TZ	B757	26635
N502EA	B757	22192	N505MJ	CRJ7	10070	N509JB	A320	1270	N512UA	B757	24809
N502FE	B727	18271	N505MM	146	E3242	N509MC	B747	21221	N512US	B757	23200

Reg	Type	Serial
N512XJ	146	E2326
N513	F.28	11169
N513AA	MD80	49890
N513AE	CRJ7	10114
(N513AE)	E145	145249
N513AT	B757	32449
N513AU	B737	23699
N513DA	B727	21315
N513EA	B757	22203
(N513FE)	B727	18847
N513FE	B727	19388
N513HC	MD80	49513
N513HE	B737	24513
N513JB	A320	1802
N513MJ	CRJ7	10111
N513NA	B757	23895
N513PA	L1011	193Y-1208
N513PE	B727	20636
(N513PE)	B727	20646
N513SW	B737	24190
N513UA	B757	24810
N513US	B757	23201
N513XJ	146	E2329
N514AE	CRJ7	10119
(N514AE)	E145	145260
N514AT	B757	27971
N514AU	B737	23700
N514CA	CRJ	7809
N514DA	B727	21430
N514DC	B747	21162
N514EA	B757	22204
(N514FE)	B727	19131
N514FE	B727	19389
N514MD	MD11	48411
N514MJ	CRJ7	10116
N514NK	A319	2679
N514PA	L1011	193Y-1210
N514PE	B727	20637
(N514PE)	B727	20647
N514SW	B737	25153
N514UA	B757	24839
N514US	B757	23202
N514XJ	146	E2330
N515AE	CRJ7	10121
(N515AE)	E145	145262
N515AT	B757	27598
N515AU	B737	23701
N515DA	B727	21431
(N515DL)	B767	22567
N515EA	B757	22205
(N515FF)	R727	19180
N515FE	B727	19428
N515GM	737NG	30782
N515HC	MD80	49515
N515JT	E145	14500950
N515MD	DC-9	47225
N515MJ	CRJ7	10117
N515NA	B737	19437
N515NK	A319	2698
N515PE	B727	20638
N515SW	B737	25154
N515UA	B757	24840
N515US	B757	23203
N515XJ	146	E2333
N516AE	CRJ7	10123
N516AM	MD80	49893
N516AT	B757	27972
N516AU	B737	23702
N516DA	B727	21432
N516EA	B757	22206
(N516FE)	B727	19182
N516FE	B727	19431
N516JB	A320	1302
N516LR	CRJ7	10258
N516MC	B747	22507
N516MD	DC-9	47128
N516NK	A319	2704
N516PE	B727	20639
N516UA	B757	24860
N516US	B757	23204
N516XJ	146	E2334
N517AE	CRJ7	10124
N517AT	B757	27973
N517AU	B737	23703
N517DA	B727	21433
N517EA	B757	22207
N517FE	B727	18429
(N517FE)	B727	19166
N517JB	A320	1327
N517MA	B707	20017
N517MC	B747	23300
N517NA	B757	24260
N517NK	A319	2711
N517PE	B727	20640
N517UA	B757	24861
N517US	B757	23205
N517XJ	146	E2335
N518AE	CRJ7	10126
N518AT	B757	27974
N518AU	B737	23704
N518CA	CRJ	7816
N518DA	B727	21469
N518EA	B757	22208
N518FE	B727	18435
(N518FE)	B727	19167
N518LR	CRJ7	10259
N518MC	B747	23476
N518MD	DC-10	46999
N518NK	A319	2718
N518PE	B727	20641
N518PM	B727	18435
N518UA	B757	24871
N518US	B757	23206
N518XJ	146	E2337
N519AE	CRJ7	10131
N519AP	B737	24519
N519AT	B757	27975
N519AU	B737	23705
N519DA	B727	21470
N519EA	B757	22209
(N519FE)	B727	19387
N519GA	B707	17646
N519JB	A320	1398
N519LR	CRJ7	10260
N519MD	DC-10	47818
N519NK	A319	2723
N519PE	B727	20642
N519SW	B737	25318
N519UA	B757	24872
N519US	B757	23207
N519XJ	146	E2344
N520AT	B757	27976
N520AU	B737	23706
N520DA	B727	214/1
N520DC	CRJ7	10140
N520EA	B757	22210
(N520FE)	B727	19388
N520JB	A320	1446
N520L	B737	20194
N520NK	A319	2784
N520PE	B727	20643
N520SW	B737	25319
N520TA	A319	3248
N520UA	B757	24890
N520UP	B747	21943
N520US	B757	23208
N520XJ	146	E2345
(N521)	F.28	11175
N521AE	CRJ7	10142
N521AT	B757	24368
N521AU	B737	23856
N521DA	B727	21472
N521DB	B727	21266
N521EA	B757	22211
N521FE	MD11	48478
N521JB	A320	1452
N521LF	B737	24234
N521LR	CRJ7	10261
N521MD	DC-9	47428
N521NA	B757	25592
N521NK	A319	2797
N521PE	B727	20644
N521SW	B737	25320
"N521SX"	A319	2773
N521TX	DC-9	47521
N521UA	B757	24891
N521UP	B747	21944
N521US	B757	23209
N521VA	A319	2773
N521XJ	146	E2346
(N522)	F.28	11176
N522AE	CRJ7	10147
N522AT	B757	29330
N522AU	B737	24260
N522AX	DC-10	48315
N522DA	B727	21582
N522EA	B757	22611
(N522FE)	B727	19390
N522FE	MD11	48476
N522JB	A320	1464
N522LR	CRJ7	10262
N522MC	B747	21783
N522MD	DC-9	47323
N522NA	B757	25133
N522NK	A319	2893
N522PE	B727	20645
N522SW	B737	26564
"N522SX"	A319	2811
N522TX	DC-9	47524
N522UA	B757	24931
N522UP	B747	21936
N522US	B757	23616
N522VA	A319	2811
N522XJ	146	E2347
(N523)	F.28	11177
N523AC	1-11	015
N523AE	CRJ7	10152
N523AT	B757	30232
N523AU	B737	23858
N523CA	CRJ	7821
N523DA	B727	21583
N523EA	B757	22612
(N523FE)	B727	19428
N523FE	MD11	48479
N523JB	A320	1506
N523MC	B747	21782
N523MD	DC-9	47320
N523NA	B757	30043
N523NK	A319	2898
N523NY	DC-9	47520
N523PE	B727	20646
N523SJ	B707	20546
N523SW	B737	26565
N523TX	DC-9	47520
N523UA	B757	24932
N523UP	B747	22301
N523US	B757	23617
N523VA	A319	3181
N523XJ	146	E2348
(N524)	F.28	11184
N524AC	1-11	BAC.120
N524AE	CRJ7	10154
N524AT	B757	30233
N524AU	B737	23859
N524DA	B727	21584
N524EA	B757	22688
(N524FE)	B727	19430
N524FE	MD11	48480
N524JB	A320	1528
N524MC	B747	21784
N524MD	DC-10	46999
N524NK	A319	2929
N524PE	B727	20647
N524SJ	B707	19789
N524SW	B737	26566
N524TX	DC-9	47539
N524UA	B757	24977
N524UP	B747	21446
N524US	B737	23618
N524VA	A319	3204
N524XJ	146	E2349
N525AT	B757	30548
N525AU	B737	23860
N525DA	B727	21585
N525EA	B757	22689
N525EJ	B707	19417
(N525FE)	B727	19431
N525FE	MD11	48565
N525MD	DC-10	46550
N525NK	A319	2942
N525NY	DC-9	47531
N525SJ	B707	20084
N525SW	B737	26567
N525TX	DC-9	47531
N525UA	B757	24978
N525UP	B747	21939
N525US	B757	23619
N525XJ	146	E2350
N526AT	B757	30735
N526AU	B737	23861
N526CA	CRJ	7824
N526DA	B727	21586
(N526EA)	B757	22690
N526EJ	B707	19664
(N526FE)	B727	19834
N526FE	MD11	48600
N526JB	A320	1546
N526MC	B747	22337
N526MD	B727	20725
N526MD	DC-10	46998
N526NA	B757	24794
N526NK	A319	2963
N526PC	B727	20370
N526PH	B767	22526
N526SJ	B707	19621
N526SW	B737	26568
N526UA	B757	24994
N526UP	B747	21937
N526US	B757	23620
N526XJ	146	E2351
N527AD	B737	23527
N527AT	B757	30886
N527AU	B737	23862
(N527AU)	B737	24410
N527DA	B727	21587
(N527EA)	B757	22691
N527EJ	B707	19986
(N527FE)	B727	19836
N527FE	MD11	48601
N527GN	B737	23527
N527JB	A320	1557
N527MC	B747	22471
N527MD	B727	20466
N527MD	DC-9	47274
N527NK	A319	2978
N527PC	B727	19665
N527SJ	B707	20016
N527SW	B737	26669
N527UA	B757	24995
N527UP	B747	21730
N527US	B757	23842
N527XJ	146	E2352
N528AT	B757	30887
N528AU	B737	24410
(N528AU)	B737	24411
N528CA	CRJ	7841
N528D	B727	21426
N528DA	B727	21702
N528E	B727	21427
N528FD	A310	528
(N528FE)	B727	18429
N528FE	MD11	48623
N528JB	A320	1591
N528JS	B727	21455
N528MC	B747	22472
N528MD	B727	20468
N528MD	DC-9	47284
N528NK	A319	2983
N528PC	B727	19597
N528PS	B727	19683
N528SJ	B707	20085
N528SW	B737	26570
N528UA	B757	25018
N528UP	B747	24071
N528UP	B747	24195
N528UP	B747	24196
N528US	B757	23843
N528XJ	146	E2353

Registration	Type	Serial
N528YV	F.70	11528
N529AC	B727	20327
N529AU	**B737**	**24411**
(N529AU)	B737	24412
N529DA	B727	21703
N529DB	**CRJ**	**7152**
N529FE	**MD11**	**48624**
N529JB	**A320**	**1610**
N529MD	DC-9	47262
N529NK	**A319**	**3007**
N529PA	B747	21992
N529PP	**737NG**	**36756**
N529PS	B727	19684
N529UA	**B757**	**25019**
N529US	**B757**	**23844**
N529XJ	146	E2363
N530AU	**B737**	**24412**
(N530AU)	B737	24478
N530DA	B727	21813
N530EA	B727	19685
N530EJ	B727	19618
N530KF	B727	19176
N530MD	B727	20571
N530MD	DC-9	47260
N530NK	**A319**	**3017**
N530PA	B747	21022
N530PS	B727	19685
N530UA	**B757**	**25043**
N530US	**B757**	**23845**
N530XJ	146	E2364
N531AU	**B737**	**24478**
(N531AU)	B737	24479
N531AW	B747	19922
N531AX	**DC-10**	**48316**
N531DA	B727	21814
N531EA	B727	19686
N531EJ	B727	19619
N531JB	A320	1650
N531LF	A320	0371
N531LS	MD80	53199
N531MD	B727	20728
N531MD	MD80	49101
N531NK	**A319**	**3026**
N531PA	B747	21023
N531PS	B727	19686
N531TA	**B727**	**22669**
N531TX	DC-9	45847
N531UA	**B757**	**25042**
N531US	**B757**	**23846**
N531XJ	146	E2365
N532AU	**B737**	**24479**
(N532AU)	B737	24515
N532AW	B747	19923
N532CA	CRJ	7712
N532DA	B727	22045
N532FA	B727	19687
N532MD	MD80	48011
N532MD	MD80	53121
N532NK	**A319**	**3165**
N532PA	B747	21024
N532PS	B727	19687
N532TX	DC-9	45791
N532UA	**B757**	**25072**
N532US	**B757**	**24263**
N532XJ	146	E2366
N533AU	**B737**	**24515**
(N533AU)	B737	24516
N533AW	B747	19924
N533CA	CRJ	7251
N533DA	B727	22046
"N533DL"	B727	22046
N533JB	**A320**	**1652**
N533MD	DC-10	46553
N533PA	B747	21025
N533PS	B727	19688
N533TX	DC-9	47281
N533UA	**B757**	**25073**
N533US	**B757**	**24264**
N533XJ	146	E2367
N534AU	**B737**	**24516**
N534AW	B747	20398
N534DA	B727	22047
N534EA	B727	19689
N534JB	**A320**	**1705**
N534MC	B747	21832
N534MD	DC-9	47065
N534MD	MD90	53552
N534PA	B747	21026
N534PS	B727	19689
N534RR	A310	534
N534TX	DC-9	47110
N534UA	**B757**	**25129**
N534US	**B757**	**24265**
N534XJ	146	E2370
N535AW	B767	25535
N535DA	B727	22048
N535FC	**B747**	**21833**
N535GE	B737	23535
N535JB	**A320**	**1739**
N535KR	A310	535
N535MC	B747	21833
N535MD	DC-9	47003
N535MD	MD90	53553
N535PA	B747	20651
N535PS	B727	20161
N535TX	DC-9	47111
N535UA	**B757**	**25130**
N535US	**B757**	**26482**
N535XJ	146	E2371
N536CA	CRJ	7635
N536DA	B727	22049
N536EA	B727	20438
N536JB	**A320**	**1784**
N536MC	B747	21576
N536MD	DC-9	47496
N536PA	B747	21441
N536PS	B727	20162
N536PS	B727	20438
N536TX	DC-9	47113
N536UA	**B757**	**25156**
N536US	**B757**	**26483**
N536XJ	146	E2372
N537DA	B727	22073
N537JB	**A320**	**1785**
N537MC	**B747**	**22403**
N537MD	DC-10	47818
N537MD	DC-9	47004
N537PA	B747	21547
N537PS	B727	20163
N537TX	DC-9	47112
N537UA	**B757**	**25157**
N537US	**B757**	**26484**
N537YV	F.70	11537
N538DA	B727	22076
N538MC	B747	21964
N538MD	DC-9	47545
N538MD	MD11	48503
N538PA	B747	21548
N538PS	B727	20164
N538TX	DC-9	47218
N538UA	**B757**	**25222**
N538US	**B757**	**26485**
N539DA	B727	22385
N539MC	B747	21965
N539MD	DC-9	47565
N539MD	MD11	48504
N539NY	DC-9	45792
N539PA	B747	21648
N539PS	B727	20165
N539TX	DC-9	45792
N539UA	**B757**	**25223**
N539US	**B757**	**26486**
N540AX	DC-10	46595
N540DA	B727	22386
N540MC	**B747**	**22508**
N540MD	DC-9	47325
N540MD	MD11	48502
N540PA	B747	21649
N540PS	B727	20166
N540RD	A300	089
N540UA	**B757**	**25252**
N540US	**B757**	**26487**
N541BN	1-11	015
N541DA	B727	22387
N541LF	A320	0397
N541NA	B757	24291
N541NY	DC-9	45793
N541PS	B727	20167
N541SA	DC-10	46541
N541TX	DC-9	45793
N541UA	**B757**	**25253**
N541US	**B757**	**26488**
N542DA	B727	22391
N542JB	**A320**	**1802**
N542LF	A320	0542
N542NA	B757	26245
N542PS	B727	20168
N542TX	DC-9	47535
N542UA	**B757**	**25276**
N542US	**B757**	**26489**
N543BA	737NG	33826
N543DA	B727	22392
N543JB	**A320**	**1823**
N543NA	B757	28161
N543NY	DC-9	45789
N543TX	DC-9	45789
N543UA	**B757**	**25698**
N543US	**B757**	**26490**
N544DA	B727	22493
N544JB	**A320**	**1835**
N544LF	B757	24544
N544NA	B757	29942
N544PS	B727	20367
N544TX	DC-9	47219
N544UA	**B757**	**25322**
N544US	**B757**	**26491**
N545DA	B727	22494
N545NA	B757	29944
N545NK	B737	24545
N545NY	DC-9	47094
N545PS	B727	20169
N545TX	DC-9	47094
N545UA	**B757**	**25323**
N545US	**B757**	**26492**
N546AS	737NG	30022
N546DA	B727	22677
(N546FE)	DC-10	46906
N546JB	**A320**	**1827**
N546NA	B757	29945
N546PS	B727	20366
N546UA	**B757**	**25367**
N546US	**B757**	**26493**
N547EA	B727	20250
N547JB	**A320**	**1849**
N547NA	B757	29946
N547PS	B727	20250
N547UA	**B757**	**25368**
N547US	**B757**	**26494**
N548AS	737NG	30020
N548EA	B727	20251
N548EA	B727	20437
N548JB	**A320**	**1868**
N548PS	B727	20251
N548UA	**B757**	**25396**
N548US	**B757**	**26495**
N549AS	737NG	30824
N549AX	B757	24528
N549EA	B727	20252
N549NA	B757	24544
N549PS	B727	20252
N549UA	**B757**	**25397**
N549US	**B757**	**26496**
N550BR	A321	0550
N550DS	B707	18417
N550FA	B757	23411
N550FE	**DC-10**	**46521**
N550JB	**A320**	**1891**
N550NW	**B757**	**26497**
N550PS	B727	20678
N550SW	B747	20924
N550TZ	**B757**	**32584**
N550UA	**B757**	**25398**
N550WN	**737NG**	**30279**
N551AS	**737NG**	**34593**
N551FA	B737	23412
N551LF	B737	24986
N551NA	B757	25621
N551NW	**B757**	**26498**
N551PE	DC-9	20772
N551PS	B727	20679
N551SX	**A319**	**1901**
N551TZ	B757	32585
N551UA	**B757**	**25399**
N551VB	E145	14500913
N551WN	**737NG**	**30280**
N552AA	MD80	53034
N552AS	**737NG**	**34595**
N552JB	**A320**	**1861**
N552NA	B727	20706
N552NW	**B757**	**26499**
N552PE	B727	20773
N552PS	B727	20706
N552SW	B747	22066
N552SX	**A319**	**1884**
N552TZ	B757	32586
N552UA	**B757**	**26641**
N553AA	**MD80**	**53083**
N553AS	**737NG**	**34594**
N553JB	**A320**	**1896**
N553NA	B727	20707
N553NW	**B757**	**26500**
N553PE	B727	20774
N553PS	B727	20707
N553SW	B747	22067
N553SX	A319	3171
N553TZ	B757	32587
N553UA	**B757**	**25277**
N554AA	**MD80**	**53084**
N554FE	**DC-10**	**46708**
N554JB	**A320**	**1898**
N554NW	**B757**	**26501**
N554PE	B727	20775
N554PS	B727	20875
N554SW	B747	20529
N554TZ	B757	32588
N554UA	**B757**	**26644**
N555AN	**MD80**	**53085**
N555BN	B727	20370
N555NW	**B757**	**33391**
N555PE	B727	20837
N555PS	B727	21512
N555SL	SE210	102
N555TZ	B757	32589
N555UA	**B757**	**26647**
N556AA	**MD80**	**53086**
N556AS	**737NG**	**35175**
N556FE	DC-10	46710
N556JB	**A320**	**1904**
N556JT	**E145**	**14500989**
N556NW	**B757**	**33392**
N556NY	DC-9	47423
N556PE	B727	20838
N556GS	B727	21613
N556SW	B747	19825
N556TZ	B757	32590
N556UA	**B757**	**26650**
N556WP	L1011	193T-1118
N557AN	**MD80**	**53087**
N557AS	737NG	35176
N557AS	DC-9	47013
N557FE	DC-10	46525
N557NA	**B757**	**22191**
N557NW	**B757**	**33393**
N557NY	DC-9	47424
N557PE	B727	20839
N557PS	B727	21691
N557SW	B747	20531
N557TZ	B757	32591
N557UA	**B757**	**26653**
N558AA	**MD80**	**53088**
N558AS	**737NG**	**35177**
N558AU	B737	23512
(N558FE)	DC-10	46908
N558HA	DC-9	47045
N558JB	**A320**	**1915**
(N558NA)	B757	32446
N558PE	B727	20840
N558PS	B727	21692

Reg	Type	Serial	Reg	Type	Serial	Reg	Type	Serial	Reg	Type	Serial
N558SW	B747	19824	N567FE	DC-10	46994	N574GE	737NG	28574	N581PE	B727	22052
N558TZ	B757	32592	N567HE	B737	28567	N574ML	CRJ	7242	N581UA	B757	26701
N558UA	B757	26654	N567KM	B767	23179	N574PE	B727	21267	N581US	B737	23259
N559AA	MD80	53089	N567PC	DC-9	47153	N574PJ	MD80	49574	N582AA	MD80	53159
N559AS	737NG	35178	N567PE	B727	21243	N574RP	E145	14500845	N582FE	MD11	48420
N559AU	B737	23513	N567RP	E145	145698	N574SW	B767	23178	N582HA	B767	28139
N559EV	B747	21035	N567TA	A321	2610	N574UA	B757	26686	N582HE	737NG	28582
N559FE	DC-10	46930	N567UA	B757	26673	N574UP	B747	35663	N582JB	A320	2147
N559JB	A320	1917	N568AA	MD80	49349	N574US	B737	23739	N582ML	CRJ	7322
(N559NA)	B757	32447	N568AS	737NG	35183	N575AM	MD80	53152	N582NW	B757	32981
N559PE	B727	21041	N568BA	146	E1015	N575FE	MD11	48500	N582PE	B727	22053
N559PS	B727	21958	N568FE	DC-10	47827	N575GE	737NG	28575	N582UA	B757	26702
N559SW	B747	20333	N568JB	A320	2063	N575GP	B747	25075	N582US	B737	23260
N559TZ	B757	32593	N568PC	DC-9	47086	N575ML	CRJ	7256	N583AA	MD80	53160
N559UA	B757	26657	N568PE	B727	21244	N575PE	B727	21268	N583AN	MD80	53183
N560AA	MD80	53090	N568TA	A321	2687	N575RP	E145	14500847	N583AS	737NG	35681
N560AS	737NG	35179	N568UA	B757	26674	N575SW	B767	23180	N583CC	1-11	015
N560AU	B737	23514	N569AA	MD80	49351	N575UA	B757	26689	N583CC	B737	21069
N560FE	DC-10	46938	N569AS	737NG	35184	N575UP	B747	35664	N583CQ	1-11	015
N560MD	MD80	48000	N569FE	DC-10	47828	N575US	B737	23740	N583FE	MD11	48421
N560PE	B727	21042	N569JB	A320	2075	N576AA	MD80	53153	N583HA	B767	25531
N560TZ	B757	33525	N569NB	B767	27569	N576DF	B727	22576	N583HE	737NG	28583
N560UA	B757	26660	N569PE	B727	21245	N576FE	MD11	48501	N583JB	A320	2150
N561AA	MD80	53091	N569RP	E145	14500816	N576GE	737NG	28576	N583MD	MD80	49659
(N561FE)	DC-10	46943	N569UA	B757	26677	N576ML	CRJ	7257	N583ML	CRJ	7327
N561JB	A320	1927	N570AA	MD80	49352	N576PE	B727	21269	N583NK	A321	1195
N561LF	B737	24987	N570AS	737NG	35185	N576RP	E145	14500856	N583NW	B757	32983
N561PC	DC-9	47014	N570C	B727	22165	N576UA	B757	26690	N583PE	B727	22165
N561PE	B727	21043	N570FE	DC-10	47829	N576UP	B747	35665	N583SF	737NG	32583
N561RP	E145	145447	N570GB	B737	20070	N576US	B737	23741	N583UA	B757	26705
N561TZ	B757	33526	N570JB	A320	2099	N577AA	MD80	53154	N583US	B737	23261
N561UA	B757	26661	N570LL	B737	24570	N577AS	737NG	35186	N584AA	MD80	53247
N562AA	MD80	49344	N570ML	CRJ	7206	N577FE	MD11	48469	N584AS	737NG	35682
N562AS	737NG	35091	N570PE	B727	21246	N577GE	737NG	28577	N584FE	MD11	48436
N562AU	B737	23550	N570RP	E145	14500821	N577JB	B727	19401	N584HA	B767	24258
N562FE	DC-10	46947	N570SW	B747	19823	N577ML	CRJ	7269	N584JB	A320	2149
N562JB	A320	1948	N570UA	B757	26678	N577PE	B727	21270	N584ML	CRJ	7330
N562PC	DC-9	47012	N570UP	B747	35667	N577RP	E145	14500862	N584NK	A321	1408
N562PE	B727	21044	N571AA	MD80	49353	N577UA	B757	26693	N584NW	B757	32984
N562RP	E145	145451	N571CA	B757	24456	N577UP	B747	35666	N584PE	B727	22166
N562UA	B757	26664	N571FE	DC-10	47830	N577US	B737	23742	N584SR	737NG	28584
N563AA	MD80	49345	N571GB	B737	20071	N578AA	MD80	53155	N584UA	B757	26706
N563AS	737NG	35180	N571GX	737NG	30571	N578FE	MD11	48458	N584US	B737	23743
N563AU	B737	23551	N571JB	A320	2125	N578GE	737NG	28578	N585AA	MD80	53248
N563FE	DC-10	46948	N571LF	B737	26284	N578JC	DC-8	45275	N585AS	737NG	35683
N563JB	A320	2006	N571ML	CRJ	7209	N578ML	CRJ	7270	N585FE	MD11	48481
N563PC	DC-9	47055	N571PE	B727	21264	N578PE	B727	21661	N585HA	B767	24257
N563PE	B727	21045	N571RP	E145	14500827	N578RP	E145	14500865	N585HE	737NG	28585
N563RP	E145	145509	N571RY	DC-10	46645	N578UA	B757	26694	N585JB	A320	2159
N563UA	B757	26665	N571SC	DC-10	46645	N578US	B737	23257	N585ML	CRJ	7334
N564AA	MD80	49346	N571SW	A310	461	N579AA	MD80	53156	N585NK	A321	1438
N564AS	737NG	35103	N571UA	B757	26681	N579AS	737NG	35187	N585NW	B757	32985
N564FE	DC-10	46984	N572AA	MD80	49458	N579FE	MD11	48470	N585PE	B727	22167
N564JB	A320	2020	N572CA	B757	24868	N579JB	A320	2132	N585UA	B757	26709
N564PC	DC-9	47062	N572GB	B737	20072	N579JC	DC-8	45289	N585US	B737	23930
N564PE	B727	21118	N572ML	CRJ	7224	N579ML	CRJ	7277	N586AA	MD80	53249
N564RP	E145	145524	N572PE	B727	21265	N579PE	B727	21662	N586AS	737NG	35189
N564SR	B737	28564	N572RP	E145	14500828	N579RP	E145	14500871	N586FE	MD11	48487
N564TA	A321	2862	N572RY	DC-10	46977	N579UA	B757	26697	N586HA	B767	24259
N564UA	B757	26666	N572SC	DC-10	46977	N579US	B737	23258	N586JB	A320	2160
N565AA	MD80	49347	N572SW	A310	455	N580AA	MD80	53157	N586ML	CRJ	7341
N565AS	737NG	35181	N572UA	B757	26682	N580CR	B727	20580	N586NK	A321	1794
N565FE	DC-10	46996	N572UP	B747	35669	N580FE	MD11	48471	N586NW	B757	32987
N565JB	A320	2031	N573AA	MD80	53092	N580HA	B767	28140	N586PE	B727	22168
N565LS	B737	28565	N573CA	B757	24971	N580HE	737NG	28580	N586RP	E145	145800
N565PC	DC-9	47240	N573DC	A320	0573	N580JB	A320	2136	N586UA	B757	26710
N565PE	B727	21119	N573FB	DC-8	45765	N580JC	DC-8	45594	N586US	B737	23931
N565RP	E145	145679	N573GB	B737	20073	N580ML	CRJ	7289	N587A	B707	18023
N565UA	B757	26669	N573JW	B767	23180	N580ML	E145	14500990	N587AA	MD80	53250
N566AA	MD80	49348	N573LS	B737	28573	N580PE	B727	21663	N587AS	737NG	35684
N566AN	B757	24566	N573ML	CRJ	7227	N580UA	B757	26698	N587FE	MD11	48489
N566AS	737NG	35182	N573PE	B727	21266	N581AA	MD80	53158	N587HA	B767	33421
N566FE	DC-10	46989	N573RP	E145	14500837	N581AS	737NG	35188	N587JB	A320	2177
N566HE	B737	28566	N573SC	DC-10	46905	N581FE	MD11	48419	N587ML	CRJ	7346
N566JB	A320	2042	N573SW	B727	23179	N581HA	B767	28141	N587NK	A321	2476
N566PC	DC-9	45828	N573UA	B757	26685	N581JB	A320	2141	N587NW	B757	32986
N566PE	B727	21242	N573UP	B747	35662	N581LF	B767	28111	N587SW	CRJ	7062
N566RP	E145	145691	N573US	B737	23560	N581LF	DC-10	46970	N587UA	B757	26713
N566TA	A321	2553	N574AA	MD80	53151	N581LT	MD11	48581	N587US	B737	23932
N566UA	B757	26670	(N574CA)	B757	24635	N581ML	CRJ	7303	N588AA	MD80	53251
N567AM	MD80	53293	N574FE	MD11	48499	N581NW	B757	32982	N588AS	737NG	35685
N567AW	MD80	53183	N574GB	B737	20074	(N581PE)	B727	21664	N588FE	MD11	48490

Reg	Type	c/n	Reg	Type	c/n	Reg	Type	c/n	Reg	Type	c/n
N588HA	B767	33466	N596HA	B767	23276	N602ME	DC-9	48133	N605DA	DC-10	47969
N588JB	A320	2201	N596NW	B757	32996	N602NW	DC-9	47046	N605DL	B757	22812
N588ML	CRJ	7368	N596PE	B757	28749	N602PE	B727	21682	N605FE	MD11	48514
N588MX	A319	0588	N597AA	MD80	53287	N602PR	B747	19779	N605FF	B747	20271
N588NK	A321	2590	N597FE	MD11	48596	N602QX	CRJ7	10010	N605GC	DC-10	47925
N588NW	B757	32988	N597HA	B767	23277	N602RC	B757	23322	N605JB	A320	2368
N588SW	CRJ	7069	N597JB	A320	2307	N602RP	F.100	11246	N605NW	DC-9	47223
N588UA	B757	26717	N597SW	CRJ	7293	N602SW	B737	27953	N605PE	B747	20520
N588US	B737	23933	N597UA	B757	28750	N602TR	F.100	11247	N605QX	CRJ7	10022
N589AA	MD80	53252	N598AA	MD80	53288	N602TW	B767	22565	N605RC	B757	23567
N589AS	737NG	35686	N598AJ	B727	21947	N602UA	B767	21863	N605RR	E145	145059
N589HA	B767	33422	N598FE	MD11	48597	N602US	B747	19779	N605SW	B737	27956
N589JB	A320	2215	N598HA	B767	23278	N602XJ	CRJ	8045	N605TW	B767	22568
N589ML	CRJ	7376	N598JB	A320	2314	N603AA	B757	27054	N605UA	B767	21866
N589NW	B757	32989	N598UA	B757	28751	N603AE	E145	145055	N605US	B747	19782
N589SW	CRJ	7072	N599AA	MD80	53289	N603AL	DC-8	46003	N605WG	E145	14500980
N589UA	B757	28707	N599FE	MD11	48598	N603AR	B727	19862	(N605XJ)	CRJ	8049
N589US	B737	23934	N599JB	A320	2336	N603AT	B717	55127	N606AA	B757	27057
N590AA	MD80	53253	N599MP	146	E3194	N603AU	B757	22198	N606AE	E145	145062
N590AS	737NG	35687	N600AU	B757	22192	N603AW	146	E2018	N606AL	DC-8	46044
N590CA	B727	20098	N600BK	E145	145044	N603AW	A320	0661	N606AR	B727	19544
N590FE	MD11	48505	N600CS	B707	19739	N603AX	DC-10	48267	N606AU	B757	22202
N590HA	B767	33467	N600DF	MD80	49619	N603BN	B747	21785	N606AW	146	E2033
N590JB	A320	2231	N600GC	DC-10	46965	N603CA	MD80	49508	N606BN	B747	21992
N590ML	CRJ	7385	N600JJ	B707	17702	N603CZ	E170	17000176	N606CZ	E170	17000188
N590NW	B757	32990	N600LR	CRJ9	15142	N603DA	DC-10	47967	N606DL	B757	22813
(N590RB)	E145	14500913	N600ME	DC-9	45725	N603DC	DC-9	47784	N606FE	MD11	48602
N590SW	CRJ	7077	N600ML	B737	23404	N603DJ	B737	19955	N606FF	B747	20273
N590UA	B757	28708	N600QX	CRJ7	10005	N603DL	B757	22810	N606GC	DC-10	47929
N590US	B737	23935	N600SK	B737	25261	N603FE	MD11	48459	N606JB	A320	2384
N591AA	MD80	53254	N600TR	DC-9	47783	N603FF	B747	19746	N606NW	DC-9	47225
N591DB	B727	21349	N600WN	B737	27694	N603GC	DC-10	47922	N606PB	B747	19783
N591FE	MD11	48527	N600XL	E145	14500965	N603JB	A320	2352	N606PE	B747	19730
N591HA	B767	33423	N601AA	B747	21962	N603NW	DC-9	47101	N606QX	CRJ7	10023
N591JB	A320	2246	N601AN	B757	27052	N603P	B767	23897	N606RC	B757	23568
N591KB	A321	0591	N601AP	DC-9	47658	N603PE	B747	19729	N606SK	CRJ7	10250
N591LF	DC-10	46973	N601AR	B727	19865	N603QX	CRJ7	10011	N606SW	B737	27926
N591ML	CRJ	7388	N601AU	B757	22193	N603RC	B757	23323	N606TA	B737	26067
N591NW	B757	32991	N601AW	146	E2012	N603SK	CRJ7	10248	N606TW	B767	22569
N591SW	CRJ	7079	N601AW	A320	1935	N603SW	B737	27954	N606UA	B767	21867
N591UA	B757	28142	N601BN	B747	20207	N603TW	B767	22566	N606US	B747	19783
N591US	B737	23936	N601DA	DC-10	47965	N603UA	B767	21864	N607AE	E145	145064
N592AA	MD80	53255	N601DL	B757	22808	N603US	B747	19780	N607AM	B757	27058
N592AS	737NG	35190	N601EV	B767	25076	(N603XJ)	CRJ	8047	N607AS	737NG	29751
N592FE	MD11	48550	N601FE	MD11	48401	N604AA	B757	27055	N607AU	B757	22203
N592HA	B767	33468	N601FF	B747	20207	N604AJ	B727	21453	N607AW	146	E2052
N592JB	A320	2259	N601GC	DC-10	47921	N604AL	DC-8	46047	(N607BN)	B747	22234
N592KA	B757	25592	N601GH	E145	145046	N604AR	B727	20409	N607DL	B757	22814
N592ML	CRJ	7410	N601LF	A320	0525	N604AT	B717	55128	N607FE	MD11	48547
N592NW	B757	32992	N601LF	B767	28206	N604AU	B757	22199	N607FF	B747	20011
N592SW	CRJ	7279	N601LS	CRJ	7008	N604AW	146	E2020	N607GC	DC-10	46978
N592UA	B757	28143	N601ME	MD80	49762	N604AW	A320	1196	N607JB	A320	2386
N592US	B737	23937	N601NW	DC-9	47038	N604BN	B747	21786	N607NW	DC-9	47232
N593AA	MD80	53256	N601QX	CRJ7	10009	N604BX	DC-8	46046	N607P	B767	23899
N593AN	MD80	53093	N601RC	B757	23321	N604CZ	E170	17000181	N607PE	B747	20011
N593FE	MD11	48551	N601TR	B757	25178	N604DA	DC-10	47968	N607QX	CRJ7	10024
N593HA	B767	33424	N601TW	B767	22564	N604DG	E145	145058	N607SK	CRJ7	10251
N593JB	A320	2280	N601UA	B767	21862	N604DL	B757	22811	N607SW	B737	27927
N593KA	B757	25593	N601US	B747	19778	N604FE	MD11	48460	N607TW	B767	22570
N593ML	CRJ	7465	N601WN	B737	27695	N604FF	B747	19659	N607UA	B767	21868
N593NW	B757	32993	N601XJ	CRJ	8044	N604GC	DC-10	47924	N607US	B747	19784
N593RA	B757	25593	N602AA	B747	21963	(N604NA)	B727	18807	N608AA	B757	27446
N593UA	B757	28144	N602AE	E145	145048	N604NA	B727	19124	N608AE	E145	145068
N594AA	MD80	53284	N602AL	DC-8	45991	N604NW	DC-9	47222	N608AU	B757	22204
N594FE	MD11	48552	N602AN	B757	27053	N604P	B767	23898	N608AW	146	E2049
N594HA	B767	23275	N602AR	B727	20075	N604PE	B747	19731	(N608BN)	B747	22302
(N594HA)	B767	33469	N602AU	B757	22196	N604QX	CRJ7	10019	N608DA	B757	22815
N594JB	A320	2284	N602AW	146	E2014	N604RC	B757	23566	N608FE	MD11	48548
N594NW	B757	32994	N602AW	A320	0565	N604SK	CRJ7	10249	N608FF	B747	19672
N594RC	A310	594	N602BN	B747	20208	N604SW	B737	27955	N608GC	DC-10	46921
N594SW	CRJ	7285	N602BN	B747	21682	N604TW	B767	22567	N608JB	A320	2415
N594UA	B757	28145	N602CA	MD80	49415	N604UA	B767	21865	N608NW	DC-9	47233
N595AA	MD80	53285	N602CZ	E170	17000171	N604US	B747	19781	N608P	B767	23900
N595FE	MD11	48553	N602DA	DC-10	47966	(N604XJ)	CRJ	8048	N608PE	B767	20012
N595HA	B767	33425	N602DC	DC-10	46976	N605AA	B757	27056	N608QX	CRJ7	10026
N595JB	A320	2286	N602DF	B757	24398	N605AL	DC-8	46106	N608SK	CRJ7	10252
N595NW	B757	32995	N602DG	F.100	11263	N605AR	B727	19545	N608SW	B737	27928
N595SW	CRJ	7292	N602DL	B757	22809	N605AU	B757	22201	N608TW	B767	22571
N595UA	B757	28748	N602EV	B767	25117	N605AW	146	E2016	N608UA	B767	21869
N596AA	MD80	53286	N602FE	MD11	48402	N605AW	A320	0543	N608US	B747	19785
N596AH	L1011	193J-1196	N602FF	B747	19734	N605BN	B747	21991	N609AA	B757	27447
N596FE	MD11	48554	N602GC	DC-10	47923	N605CZ	E170	17000186	N609AE	E145	145069

Reg	Type	Serial	Reg	Type	Serial	Reg	Type	Serial	Reg	Type	Serial
N609AG	B727	20705	N613AU	B757	27144	N618DL	B757	22908	N623AC	B737	23157
N609AS	737NG	29752	N613DL	B757	22820	N618FE	MD11	48754	N623AE	E145	145109
N609AU	B757	22205	N613FE	MD11	48749	N618FF	B747	21937	N623AS	737NG	30166
N609AW	146	E2070	N613FF	B747	19647	N618JB	A320	2489	N623AU	B757	27244
N609DC	DC-10	46932	N613JB	A320	2449	N618MX	A319	1618	N623AV	B737	22384
N609DL	B757	22816	N613NW	DC-9	47438	N618NW	DC-9	47433	N623BR	CRJ	7192
N609FE	MD11	48549	N613QX	CRJ7	10045	N618QX	CRJ7	10205	N623DH	B727	20895
N609FF	B747	20354	N613SK	CRJ7	10038	N618SH	B767	29618	N623DL	B757	22913
N609GC	DC-10	46932	N613SW	B737	27931	(N618SW)	B737	28034	N623EV	B767	27194
N609HA	DC-9	47676	N613UA	B767	21874	N618UA	B767	21878	N623FE	B747	19897
N609KW	B727	21950	N613US	B747	20358	N618US	B747	21122	N623FE	MD11	48794
N609LP	737NG	28609	N614AA	B757	24490	N618WN	B737	28034	N623FF	B747	22382
N609NW	DC-9	47234	N614AE	E145	145086	N619AA	B757	24577	N623JB	A320	2504
N609PE	B747	20534	N614AG	B727	22377	N619AE	E145	145101	N623NW	DC-9	47591
N609QX	CRJ7	10031	N614AR	B747	20009	N619AS	737NG	30164	N623SW	B737	27933
N609SK	CRJ7	10020	N614AS	737NG	30343	(N619AS)	737NG	30166	N623US	B747	21705
N609SW	B737	27929	N614AU	B757	27145	N619AU	B757	27198	N623VA	A320	2740
N609TW	B767	22572	N614AW	146	E3132	N619AW	A320	0527	N624AA	B757	24582
N609UA	B767	21870	N614DL	B757	22821	N619DB	MD80	49151	N624AC	B737	23161
N609US	B747	19786	N614FE	MD11	48528	N619DL	B757	22909	N624AE	E145	145111
N610AA	B757	24486	N614FF	B747	20534	N619FE	MD11	48770	N624AJ	A320	0624
N610AE	E145	145073	N614GB	VFW	G-014	N619FF	B747	21316	N624AS	737NG	30778
N610AG	B727	21068	N614GC	DC-10	46931	N619HA	DC-9	47677	N624AU	B757	27245
N610AR	B747	20800	N614LS	737NG	28614	N619NW	DC-9	47518	N624AW	A320	0055
N610AU	B757	27122	N614NW	DC-9	47128	N619QX	CRJ7	10246	N624BR	CRJ	7211
N610AW	146	E2082	N614P	B767	23901	N619SW	B737	28035	N624DH	B727	20709
N610BN	B747	19746	N614PA	B727	20738	N619UA	B767	21879	N624DL	B757	22914
N610DL	B757	22817	N614QX	CRJ7	10049	N619US	B747	21321	N624FE	B747	20246
N610FE	MD11	48603	N614SK	CRJ7	10051	N620AA	B757	24578	(N624FE)	B747	20349
N610FF	B747	20501	N614SW	B737	28033	N620AE	E145	145102	N624FE	MD11	48443
N610G	B757	29304	N614UA	B767	21875	N620AU	B757	27199	N624FF	B747	21439
N610NW	DC-9	47432	N614US	B747	20359	N620AW	A320	0052	N624FT	DC-8	45929
N610PE	B747	20535	N615AE	E145	145087	N620BN	B747	20927	N624JB	A320	2520
N610PH	DC-10	46584	N615AM	B757	24491	N620BR	CRJ	7179	N624PL	B747	20246
N610QX	CRJ7	10033	(N615AR)	B747	20543	N620DL	B757	22910	N624SW	B737	27934
N610TF	DC-10	46661	N615AS	737NG	30344	(N620FE)	B747	19733	N624US	B747	21706
N610TW	B767	22573	N615AU	B757	27146	(N620FE)	B747	20013	N624VA	A320	2778
N610UA	B767	21871	N615AW	146	E3141	N620FE	MD11	48791	N624VA	B727	20327
N610US	B747	19787	N615DL	B757	22822	N620FF	B747	21162	N625AA	B757	24583
N610WN	B737	27696	N615FE	MD11	48767	N620NW	DC-9	47533	N625AC	B737	23165
N610XS	DC-9	47610	N615FF	B747	19638	N620PC	B737	19708	N625AE	E145	145115
N611AE	E145	145074	N615JB	A320	2461	N620SW	B737	28036	N625AS	737NG	30792
N611AM	B757	24487	N615NW	DC-9	47129	N620UA	B767	21880	(N625AU)	B757	27246
N611AN	A300	611	N615PA	B727	21266	N620US	B747	19918	N625AW	A320	0064
N611AR	B747	19749	N615PG	E145	14501004	N621AC	B737	23156	N625BR	CRJ	7214
N611AS	737NG	29753	N615QX	CRJ7	10065	N621AE	E145	145105	N625CA	CRJ7	10113
N611AU	B757	27123	N615SW	B737	27698	N621AM	B757	24579	N625DH	B727	20780
N611AW	146	E3120	N615UA	B767	21876	N621AU	B757	27200	N625DL	B757	22915
N611BN	B747	20527	N615US	B747	20360	N621AW	A320	0053	N625EV	B767	27195
N611DL	B757	22818	N616AA	B757	24524	N621AX	DC-10	48319	N625FE	B747	20247
N611FE	MD11	48604	N616AE	E145	145092	N621BR	CRJ	7186	(N625FE)	B747	20353
N611FF	B747	20502	N616AU	B757	27147	N621DL	B757	22911	N625FE	MD11	48444
N611LF	B737	24299	N616AW	146	E3145	N621EV	B767	27192	N625FT	DC-8	45928
N611NA	DC-9	47435	N616DL	B757	22823	(N621FE)	B747	19661	N625JB	A320	2535
(N611PE)	B747	19732	N616FE	MD11	48747	N621FE	B747	20014	N625PL	B747	20247
N611QX	CRJ7	10041	N616FF	B747	21939	N621FE	MD11	48792	N625SA	L1011	193L-1125
N611SK	CRJ7	10035	N616NW	DC-9	47229	(N621FF)	B747	19729	N625SW	B737	27701
N611SW	B737	27697	N616PA	B727	20055	N621FF	B747	21730	N625US	B747	21707
N611UA	B767	21872	N616QX	CRJ7	10128	N621JB	A320	2491	N625VA	A320	2800
N611US	B747	20356	N616SW	B737	27699	N621LF	B737	24705	N625VJ	B757	27246
N612AA	B757	24488	N616US	B747	21120	N621NW	DC-9	47544	N626AA	B757	24584
N612AE	E145	145079	N617AE	E145	145093	N621SW	B737	28037	N626AC	B737	23620
N612AG	B727	21297	N617AM	B757	24525	N621US	B747	19919	N626AE	E145	145117
N612AR	B747	19752	(N617AS)	737NG	30164	N621VA	A320	2616	N626AJ	A320	0626
N612AS	737NG	30162	N617AS	737NG	30542	N622AA	B757	24580	N626AS	737NG	30793
N612AU	B757	27124	N617AU	B757	27148	N622AE	E145	145108	N626AU	B757	27303
N612AW	146	E3122	N617DL	B757	22907	N622AS	737NG	30165	N626AW	A320	0065
N612AX	DC-10	48290	N617FE	MD11	48748	N622AU	B757	27201	N626BR	CRJ	7225
N612DL	B757	22819	N617FF	B747	19650	N622AW	A320	0054	N626DH	B727	20905
N612FE	MD11	48605	N617NW	DC-9	47235	N622BR	CRJ	7187	N626DH	B727	22644
N612GC	DC-10	47840	N617P	B767	23902	N622DG	B737	23662	N626DL	B757	22916
N612JB	A320	2447	N617QX	CRJ7	10130	N622DH	B727	20896	N626FE	B747	20349
N612MX	A319	1612	N617SW	B737	27700	N622DL	B757	22912	(N626FE)	B747	20391
N612NW	DC-9	47436	N617UA	B767	21877	N622DS	A300	659	N626FE	MD11	48445
N612QX	CRJ7	10042	N617US	B747	21121	N622EV	B767	27193	N626NW	B747	21708
N612SW	B737	27930	N617WA	E145	14500884	N622FF	B747	22496	N626SW	B737	27702
N612UA	B767	21873	N618AA	B757	24526	N622NW	DC-9	47575	N626TX	DC-9	45726
N612US	B747	20357	N618AE	E145	145097	N622RG	A320	657	N626US	B747	21708
N613AA	B757	24489	(N618AS)	737NG	30165	N622SW	B737	27932	N626VA	A320	2830
N613AE	E145	145081	N618AS	737NG	30543	N622US	B747	21704	N627AA	B757	24585
N613AN	A300	613	N618AU	B757	22210	N622VA	A320	2674	N627AE	E145	145121
N613AS	737NG	30163	N618AW	A320	0304	N623AA	B757	24581	N627AS	737NG	30794

Reg	Type	No.	Reg	Type	No.	Reg	Type	No.	Reg	Type	No.
N627AU	B757	27805	N632CT	MD80	49632	N637TW	B767	25403	N643JB	A320	2871
N627AW	A320	0066	N632DL	B757	23613	N637US	B747	23548	N643NW	B747	22245
N627BR	CRJ	7233	(N632FE)	B747	20827	N638AA	B757	24596	N643RW	E170	17000060
N627DH	B727	22424	N632FE	B747	22245	N638AE	E145	145172	N643SH	737NG	28643
N627DH	B727	22641	(N632FE)	MD11	48455	N638AW	A320	0280	N643SW	B737	27716
N627DL	B757	22917	N632JB	A320	2647	N638AW	A320	0455	N643UA	B767	25093
(N627FE)	B747	20246	N632NW	B747	23112	N638BR	CRJ	7311	N643UW	B757	30886
N627FE	B747	20353	N632RW	E170	17000050	N638DL	B757	23761	(N644AA)	B737	19601
N627FE	MD11	48446	N632SW	B737	27707	N638FE	B747	21841	N644AA	B757	24602
N627JB	A320	2577	N632TW	B767	24953	(N638FE)	B747	22245	N644AE	E145	145204
N627SW	B737	27935	N632US	B747	23112	N638JB	A320	2802	N644AS	737NG	30795
N627US	B747	21709	N632VA	A320	3155	N638RW	E170	17000053	N644AW	A320	0317
N627VA	A320	2851	N633AA	B757	24591	N638SW	B737	27711	N644BR	CRJ	7379
N628AA	B757	24586	N633AE	E145	145148	N638TW	B767	26205	N644DL	B757	23998
N628AE	E145	145124	N633AN	A300	633	N638US	B747	23549	(N644FE)	MD11	48538
N628AJ	A320	0628	N633AU	B757	27811	N639AA	B757	24597	N644JB	A320	2880
N628AU	B757	27806	N633AW	A320	0082	N639AE	E145	145182	N644NW	B747	24177
N628AW	A320	0067	N633BR	CRJ	7274	N639AW	A320	0471	N644RW	E170	17000061
N628BR	CRJ	7240	N633DL	B757	23614	N639AX	B757	24368	N644SW	B737	28329
N628DL	B757	22918	(N633FE)	B747	21650	N639AX	B757	25597	N644UA	B767	25094
N628FE	B747	19661	N633FE	B747	22237	N639BR	CRJ	7313	N644UW	B757	30887
(N628FE)	B747	20247	(N633FE)	MD11	48484	N639DL	B757	23993	(N645AA)	B737	19614
N628FE	MD11	48447	N633GP	B737	22633	N639FE	B747	21650	N645AA	B757	24603
(N628GA)	B737	19945	N633JB	A320	2671	(N639FE)	B747	22237	N645AE	E145	145212
N628SW	B737	27703	N633RW	E170	17000054	N639HA	DC-9	47689	(N645AM)	B757	24603
N628TX	DC-9	45727	N633SW	B737	27936	N639JB	A320	2814	N645AS	737NG	33011
N628US	B747	22389	N633US	B747	21991	N639RW	E170	17000057	N645AW	A320	0238
N628VA	A320	2993	N633VA	A320	3230	N639SH	737NG	28639	N645BR	CRJ	7383
N629AA	B757	24587	N634AA	B757	24592	N639SW	B737	27712	N645DL	B757	24216
N629AE	E145	145130	N634AE	E145	145150	N639TW	B767	26208	(N645FE)	MD11	48539
N629AS	737NG	30626	N634AW	A320	0091	N639US	B747	23887	N645JB	A320	2900
N629AU	B757	27807	N634BR	CRJ	7287	N640A	B757	24598	N645NW	B747	23736
N629AW	A320	0076	N634DL	B757	23615	N640AD	B737	22640	N645RW	E170	17000064
N629BR	CRJ	7251	(N634FE)	B747	21764	N640AE	E145	145183	N645SW	B737	28330
N629DL	B757	22919	N634FE	B747	22150	N640AW	A320	0448	N645UA	B767	25280
(N629F)	B747	20013	(N634FE)	MD11	48456	N640BR	CRJ	7340	N645US	B767	23897
N629FE	B747	20391	N634JB	A320	2710	N640DL	B757	23994	(N646AA)	B737	20126
(N629FE)	MD11	48452	N634MX	A319	1634	N640FE	B747	20826	N646AA	B757	24604
N629HA	DC-9	47679	N634RW	E170	17000055	(N640FE)	B747	22150	N646AE	E145	145213
N629JB	A320	2580	N634SW	B737	27937	N640JB	A320	2832	N646AW	A320	0271
N629SW	B737	27704	(N634TW)	B767	25209	N640KS	A310	640	N646BR	CRJ	7392
N629US	B747	22388	N634TW	B767	28132	N640RD	A300	169	N646DL	B757	24217
N629VA	A320	3037	N634US	B747	22234	N640RW	E170	17000058	(N646FE)	MD11	48540
N630AA	B757	24588	N635AA	B757	24593	N640SW	B737	27713	N646JB	A320	2945
N630AE	E145	145132	N635AE	E145	145158	N640TW	B767	25411	N646LS	B737	24646
N630AJ	A320	0630	N635AW	A320	0092	N640US	B747	23888	N646NW	B747	23737
N630AU	B757	27808	N635BR	CRJ	7295	(N641AA)	B737	19680	N646RW	E170	17000066
N630AX	DC-10	46596	"N635DA"	B757	23762	N641AA	B757	24599	N646SW	B737	28331
N630BR	CRJ	7255	N635DL	B757	23762	N641AE	E145	145191	N646UA	B767	25283
N630DL	B757	22920	(N635FE)	B747	21841	N641AW	A320	0453	N646US	B767	23898
N630FE	B747	19733	N635FE	B747	22151	N641BR	CRJ	7349	(N647AA)	B757	24605
(N630FE)	B747	20653	(N635FE)	MD11	48457	N641CA	CRJ7	10122	N647AE	E145	145222
(N630FE)	MD11	48453	N635GE	737NG	28635	N641DL	B757	23995	N647AM	B757	24605
N630GE	737NG	28630	N635GS	B757	26635	N641FE	B747	20827	N647AS	737NG	33012
N630JB	A320	2640	N635JB	A320	2725	(N641FE)	B747	22150	N647AW	A320	0762
N630LT	MD11	48630	N635RW	E170	17000056	N641JB	A320	2848	N647BR	CRJ	7399
N630SJ	B747	19733	N635SW	B737	27708	N641LF	B737	26321	N647DL	B757	24218
N630US	B747	21668	N635TW	B767	28207	N641NW	B747	21941	(N647FE)	MD11	48634
N630VA	A320	3101	N635US	B747	21682	N641RW	E170	17000062	N647RW	E170	17000067
N630WN	B737	27705	N635VX	A320	1635	N641SW	B737	27714	N647SW	B737	27717
N631AA	B757	24589	N636AE	E145	145160	N641UA	B767	25091	N647UA	B767	25284
N631AE	E145	145139	N636AM	B757	24594	N642AA	B757	24600	N647US	B767	23899
N631AU	B757	27809	N636AN	B737	23636	N642AE	E145	145193	(N648AA)	B737	19307
(N631AW)	146	E1003	N636AW	A320	0098	N642AG	E145	145642	N648AA	B757	24606
N631AW	A320	0077	N636BR	CRJ	7307	N642AW	A320	0584	N648AE	E145	145225
N631BR	CRJ	7261	N636DL	B757	23763	N642BR	CRJ	7356	N648AS	737NG	30662
N631DL	B757	23612	N636FE	B747	21764	N642CA	CRJ7	10125	N648AW	A320	0770
(N631FE)	B747	20826	(N636FE)	B747	21827	N642DL	B757	23996	N648BR	CRJ	7406
N631FE	B747	21827	N636JB	A320	2755	(N642FE)	MD11	48485	N648DL	B757	24372
N631FE	MD11	48454	N636RW	E170	17000052	N642KS	A310	642	(N648FE)	MD11	48541
N631LF	B737	24708	N636TW	B767	30301	N642NW	B747	21942	N648JB	A320	2970
N631NW	B747	23111	N636US	B747	23547	N642RW	E170	17000063	N648RW	E170	17000068
N631RW	E170	17000007	N636WN	B737	27709	N642UA	B767	25092	N648SW	B737	27718
N631SW	B737	27706	N637AD	B727	22637	N642UN	B757	30548	N648UA	B767	25285
N631US	B747	23111	N637AE	E145	145170	N642WN	B737	27715	N648US	B767	23900
N631VA	A320	3135	N637AM	B757	24595	(N643AA)	B737	19598	(N649AA)	B737	19308
N632AA	B757	24590	N637AW	A320	0099	N643AA	B757	24601	N649AA	B757	24607
N632AE	E145	145143	N637BR	CRJ	7308	N643AE	E145	145200	N649AS	737NG	30663
N632AU	B757	27810	N637DL	B757	23760	N643AW	A320	0315	N649AW	A320	0803
(N632AW)	146	E1063	N637JB	A320	2781	N643BR	CRJ	7363	N649BR	CRJ	7414
N632AW	A320	0081	N637RW	E170	17000051	N643DL	B757	23997	N649DL	B757	24389
N632BR	CRJ	7268	N637SW	B737	27710	(N643FE)	MD11	48486	N649HA	DC-9	47712

Registration	Type	C/N
N649HA	DC-9	47715
N649JB	A320	2977
N649PP	E145	145234
N649RW	E170	17000070
N649SW	B737	27719
N649UA	B767	25286
N649US	B767	23901
(N650AA)	B737	19309
N650AA	B757	24608
N650AE	E145	145417
N650AW	A320	0856
N650BR	CRJ	7418
N650DH	1-11	059
N650DL	B757	24390
N650FE	A300	726
N650HA	DC-9	47714
N650ML	CRJ	7137
N650RW	E170	17000071
N650SW	B737	27720
N650TW	B767	23057
N650UA	B767	25287
N650UG	DC-9	47418
N650US	B767	23902
(N651AA)	B737	19713
N651AA	B757	24609
N651AE	E145	145422
N651AW	A320	0866
N651BR	CRJ	7426
N651DL	B757	24391
N651FE	A300	728
N651JB	A320	2992
N651LF	B737	25790
N651LF	B757	26275
N651MG	B757	23651
N651ML	CRJ	7139
N651RW	E170	17000072
N651SW	B737	27721
N651TF	B707	18586
N651TW	B767	23058
N651TX	DC-9	45714
N651UA	B767	25288
N651US	B767	24764
(N652AA)	B737	19714
N652AA	B757	24610
N652AW	A320	0953
N652BR	CRJ	7429
N652DL	B757	24392
N652FE	A300	735
N652JB	A320	3029
N652ML	CRJ	7036
N652PA	B747	20347
N652RS	E145	145432
N652RW	E170	17000075
N652SJ	B747	20347
N652SW	B737	27722
N652TX	DC-9	45715
N652UA	B767	25390
N652US	B767	24765
(N653A)	B737	20035
N653A	B757	24611
N653AE	E145	145433
N653AW	A320	1003
N653BR	CRJ	7438
N653CA	CRJ7	10129
N653DL	B757	24393
N653FE	A300	736
N653JB	A320	3039
N653ML	CRJ	7039
N653PA	B747	20348
N653RW	E170	17000076
N653SW	B737	28398
N653TX	DC-9	45716
N653UA	B767	25391
N653US	B767	24894
(N654A)	B737	19707
N654A	B757	24612
N654AE	E145	145437
N654AW	A320	1050
N654BR	CRJ	7454
N654DL	B757	24394
N654FE	A300	738
N654PA	B747	20349
N654RW	E170	17000104
N654SW	B737	28399
N654TX	DC-9	45735
N654UA	B767	25392
N654US	B767	25225
(N655AA)	B737	19931
N655AA	B757	24613
N655AE	E145	145452
N655BR	CRJ	7457
N655CA	CRJ7	10134
N655CC	CRJ	7152
N655DL	B757	24395
N655FE	A300	742
N655JB	A320	3072
N655PA	B747	20350
N655RW	E170	17000105
N655TX	DC-9	45736
N655UA	B767	25393
N655US	B767	25257
N655WN	B737	28400
(N656AA)	B737	20158
N656AA	B757	24614
N656AE	E145	145740
N656AW	A320	1079
N656BR	CRJ	7485
N656CA	CRJ7	10143
N656DL	B757	24396
N656FE	A300	745
N656JB	A320	3091
N656PA	B747	20351
N656RW	E170	17000113
N656SW	B737	28401
N656UA	B767	25394
N656US	B767	26847
N657AE	E145	145744
N657AM	B757	24615
N657AW	A320	1083
N657BR	CRJ	7491
N657DL	B757	24419
N657FE	A300	748
N657JB	A320	3119
N657PA	B747	20352
N657RW	E170	17000115
N657SW	B737	23331
N657UA	B767	27112
N658AA	B757	24616
N658AE	E145	145760
N658AW	A320	1110
N658BR	CRJ	7500
N658CA	CRJ7	10148
N658DL	B757	24420
N658FE	A300	752
N658JB	A320	3150
N658PA	B747	20353
N658SW	B737	23332
N658UA	B767	27113
(N659AA)	B737	22051
N659AA	B757	24617
N659AE	E145	145762
N659AW	A320	1166
N659BR	CRJ	7509
N659CA	CRJ7	10153
N659DG	B737	23659
N659DL	B757	24421
N659FE	A300	757
N659HA	DC-9	47713
N659JB	A320	3190
N659PA	B747	20354
N659SW	B737	23229
N659UA	B767	27114
N660AM	B757	25294
(N660AT)	L1011	193B-1036
N660AW	A320	1234
N660CL	E145	145764
N660DL	B757	24422
N660FE	A300	759
N660HA	DC-9	48122
N660SW	B737	23230
N660UA	B767	27115
N660VV	DC-10	46660
N660YT	B737	22660
(N661AA)	B737	21066
N661AA	B757	25295
N661AV	DC-8	45969
N661AW	A320	1284
N661BR	CRJ	7520
N661DN	B757	24972
N661FE	A300	760
N661HA	DC-9	47796
N661JA	E145	145766
N661JB	A320	3228
N661LF	B737	26333
N661SW	B737	23173
N661UA	B767	27158
N661US	B747	23719
(N662AA)	B737	19072
(N662AA)	B737	21067
N662AA	B747	20101
N662AA	B757	25296
N662AR	A320	0662
N662AW	A320	1274
N662BR	CRJ	7526
N662DN	B757	24991
N662EH	E145	145777
N662FE	A300	761
N662HA	DC-9	47742
N662JB	A320	3263
N662SW	B737	23255
N662UA	B767	27159
N662US	B747	23720
N662VV	DC-10	46662
N663AL	B737	25663
N663AM	B757	25297
N663AR	E145	145778
N663AW	A320	1419
N663BR	CRJ	7527
N663DN	B757	24992
N663FE	A300	766
N663JB	A320	3287
N663SW	B737	23256
N663UA	B767	27160
N663US	B747	23818
N664AA	B757	25298
N664AL	B737	25664
N664AW	A320	1621
N664BR	CRJ	7528
N664DN	B757	25012
N664FE	A300	768
N664MS	E145	145779
N664NA	B767	29236
N664US	B747	23819
N664WN	B737	23495
N665AA	B757	25299
N665AW	A320	1644
N665BC	E145	145783
N665BR	CRJ	7534
N665DN	B757	25013
N665FE	A300	769
N665UA	B767	29237
N665US	B747	23820
N665WN	B737	23497
N666A	B757	25034
N666DN	B757	25034
N666UA	B767	29238
N666US	B747	23821
N667AW	A320	1710
N667BR	CRJ	7535
N667DN	B757	25035
N667FE	A300	771
N667GB	E145	145784
N667SW	B737	23063
N667UA	B767	29239
N667US	B747	24222
N667YT	B737	22667
N668AA	B757	25333
N668AW	A320	1764
N668BR	CRJ	7544
N668CA	CRJ7	10162
N668DN	B757	25141
N668FE	A300	772
N668HH	E145	145785
N668SW	B737	23060
N668UA	B767	30024
N668US	B747	24223
N669AA	B757	25334
N669AW	A320	1792
N669BR	CRJ	7545
N669CA	CRJ7	10176
N669DN	B757	25142
N669FE	A300	774
N669HA	DC-9	47654
N669HA	DC-9	47714
N669MB	E145	145788
N669SW	B737	23752
N669UA	B767	30025
N669US	B747	24224
N670AA	B757	25335
N670AE	E145	145790
N670AW	A320	2029
N670BR	CRJ	7561
N670DN	B757	25331
N670FE	A300	777
N670MA	B737	23121
N670MC	DC-9	47659
N670SW	B737	23784
N670UA	B767	29240
N670US	B747	24225
N670UW	A330	315
N671	B737	23122
N671AA	B757	25336
N671AE	E145	145793
(N671AS)	737NG	30017
N671AW	A320	2077
N671AW	B737	23122
N671BR	CRJ	7572
N671DN	B757	25332
N671FE	A300	778
N671MA	B737	23122
N671MC	DC-9	47660
N671SR	B737	28671
N671SW	B737	23785
N671UA	B767	30026
N671UP	B747	20323
(N671US)	B747	26473
N671US	B747	26477
N671UW	A330	323
N672AA	B757	25337
N672AE	E145	145794
N672AS	737NG	30016
N672AW	A320	2193
N672BR	CRJ	7594
N672DL	B757	25977
N672FE	A300	779
N672FH	B737	24672
N672MA	B737	23123
N672MC	DC-9	47661
N672RY	B737	24672
N672SW	B737	23406
N672UA	B767	30027
N672UP	B747	20324
(N672US)	B747	26474
N672US	B747	30267
N672UW	A330	333
N673AA	B737	23251
N673AE	E145	145797
N673AN	B757	29423
(N673AS)	737NG	30013
N673AW	A320	2312
N673BF	B767	23402
N673BR	CRJ	7599
N673DL	B757	25978
N673FE	A300	780
N673HC	MD80	49673
N673MA	B737	23124
N673MC	DC-9	47726
N673UA	B767	29241
N673UP	B747	20325
N673US	B747	30268
N673UW	A330	337
N674AA	B737	23252
N674AN	B757	29424
(N674AS)	737NG	30014
N674AW	A320	2359
N674BR	CRJ	7601

N674DL	B757	25979	N680BR	CRJ	7679	N688DL	B757	27587	(N696DA)	B757	29728
N674FE	A300	781	N680DA	B757	26956	N688FE	A300	874	N696DL	B757	29728
N674MA	B737	23292	N680EM	B757	24923	N688GX	B757	22688	N696SW	B737	23064
N674MC	DC-9	47735	N680FE	A300	794	N688MV	B737	26688	N696WA	B727	19987
N674MG	B727	21450	N680FM	B727	18970	N688SW	B737	23254	N697A	146	E2055
(N674PA)	B747	20326	N680FP	B757	24923	N688UP	B747	20784	N697AB	E145	14500875
N674RJ	E145	14500801	N680MV	B737	26680	N689AA	B757	25731	N697AN	B757	26977
N674UA	B767	29242	N680SW	B747	23244	N689BR	CRJ	7737	N697BJ	DC-9	47799
N674UP	B747	20100	N680UP	B747	20923	N689CA	CRJ9	15133	N697BR	CRJ	7787
N674US	B747	30269	(N681AA)	B737	23752	N689DL	B757	27172	N697CA	B727	23052
N674UW	A330	342	N681AA	B757	25338	N689EC	E145	14500853	N697DL	B757	30318
N675AA	B737	23253	N681AE	E145	14500824	N689FE	A300	875	N697SW	B737	23838
N675AE	E145	14500806	N681BR	CRJ	7680	N689GX	B757	22689	N698AA	146	E2057
N675AN	B757	29425	N681CA	B727	22020	N689HA	DC-9	47663	N698AN	B757	26980
(N675AS)	737NG	30015	N681DA	B757	26957	N689MA	B737	24124	N698BR	CRJ	7799
N675AW	A320	2405	N681FE	A300	799	N689SW	B737	23387	N698CB	E145	14500877
N675BR	CRJ	7635	N681LF	A320	0760	N689UP	B747	21033	N698DL	B757	29911
N675DL	B757	25980	N681MA	B737	24376	N690AA	E145	14500858	N698QS	DC-8	45886
(N675FE)	A300	782	N681SW	B747	23245	N690BR	CRJ	7739	N698SN	DC-8	45886
N675FE	A300	789	N681UP	B747	19661	N690CA	CRJ7	10182	N698SS	B727	21369
N675MA	B737	23065	N682AA	B757	25339	N690DL	B757	27585	N698SW	B737	23176
N675MC	DC-9	47651	N682AE	E145	14500826	N690FE	A300	876	N699AA	146	E2058
N675MG	B727	22553	N682BR	CRJ	7691	N690MA	B737	24165	N699AE	E145	14500883
N675NW	B747	33001	N682CA	B727	22019	N690SW	B737	23783	N699AN	B757	27051
N675UA	B767	29243	N682DA	B757	26958	N690UP	B747	20348	N699BR	CRJ	7801
N675UP	B747	20390	N682FE	A300	800	N690WA	B727	19504	N699DL	B757	29970
N675US	A330	370	N682FM	B727	18970	N691AA	B757	25697	N699HA	DC-9	47763
N676AA	B737	23288	N682G	B727	19254	N691AE	E145	14500860	N699PU	B727	24699
N676AE	E145	14500807	N682GE	B737	24682	N691AN	E145	145699	N699SW	B737	23826
N676AN	B757	29426	N682MA	B737	25071	N691BR	CRJ	7740	N700AZ	737NG	28497
N676AW	A320	2422	N682RW	1-11	061	N691FE	A300	877	N700CK	B747	22990
N676BR	CRJ	7644	N682RW	DC-9	47733	N691GE	B737	24691	N700EW	737NG	28436
N676CA	CRJ9	15127	N682SH	B767	22682	N691LF	B767	25137	N700FW	B707	18711
N676DL	B757	25981	N682SW	B757	23496	N691MA	B737	24166	N700GS	737NG	27835
N676FE	A300	790	N682UP	B747	20349	N691MV	B737	26691	N700JA	1-11	059
N676MA	B737	23066	N683A	B757	25340	N691UP	B747	19641	N700JZ	B737	26070
N676MC	DC-9	47652	N683AE	E145	14500833	N691WA	B727	19505	N700LE	E145	145156
N676MG	B727	22554	N683BR	CRJ	7692	N691WN	B737	23781	N700ME	DC-9	45696
N676NW	B747	33002	N683CA	B727	22490	N692AA	B757	26972	N700ML	B737	23404
N676SW	B737	23288	N683DA	B757	27103	N692AE	E145	14500866	N/OUNW	CV880	22-00-63
N676TC	E145	145699	N683FE	A300	801	N692AF	B727	18816	N700TE	B727	18365
N676UA	B767	30028	N683GE	B737	24683	N692BR	CRJ	7759	N700TS	L1011	193B-1066
N676UP	B747	20101	N683MV	B737	26683	(N692DA)	B757	29724	N700UP	DC-8	45900
N676UW	A330	375	N683SW	B737	24008	N692DL	B757	29724	N700UW	A319	0885
N677AA	B737	23289	N683UP	B747	20353	N692FE	A300	878	N700WH	737NG	29142
N677AE	E145	14500810	N684AA	B757	25341	N692SW	B737	23062	N701AA	B727	22459
N677AN	B757	29427	N684BR	CRJ	7708	N692WA	B727	19506	N701AW	B737	19013
N677AW	A320	2430	N684CA	B727	22491	(N693)	B727	19507	N701BR	CRJ	7448
N677BR	CRJ	7652	N684DA	B757	27104	N693AA	B757	26973	N701CK	B747	19725
N677DL	B757	25982	N684FE	A300	802	N693AE	E145	14500868	N701CK	B727	21730
N677FE	A300	791	N684JW	E145	14500835	N693BR	CRJ	7761	N701DA	L1011	193C-1041
N677MC	DC-9	47756	N684WN	B737	23941	(N693DA)	B757	29725	N701DH	B727	19011
N677R	B707	19774	N685AA	B757	25342	N693DL	B757	29725	N701DN	B777	29740
N677UA	B767	30029	N685AE	E145	14500836	N693SW	B737	23174	N701EV	B727	19310
N677UP	B747	20391	N685BR	CRJ	7712	N693WA	B727	19507	N701EV	CRJ7	10020
N677UW	A330	380	N685CA	B727	22492	N693YT	B737	21693	N701EW	737NG	28437
N678AA	B737	23290	N685DA	B757	27588	N694AA	146	E2051	N701FT	DC-8	46117
N678AE	E145	14500813	N685FE	A300	803	N694AE	E145	14500869	N701GC	MD11	48434
N678AN	B757	29428	N685MA	B737	23791	N694AN	B757	26974	N701GS	737NG	27836
N678AW	A320	2482	N685SW	B737	23401	N694BR	CRJ	7768	N701JZ	B737	26072
N678BR	CRJ	7653	N686AA	B757	25343	(N694DA)	B757	29726	N701LF	B757	24367
N678CA	CRJ9	15125	N686AE	E145	14500843	N694DL	B757	29726	N701ME	MD80	49760
N678DL	B757	25983	N686BR	CRJ	7715	N694SW	B737	23061	N701MG	B757	22197
N678FE	A300	792	N686CA	B727	22021	N694WA	B727	19508	N701MH	E145	145162
N678MG	B727	22555	N686DA	B757	27589	N695AA	146	E2053	N701ML	B737	23405
N678US	A330	388	N686FE	A300	804	N695AE	E145	14500870	N701NE	B727	22459
N679AA	B737	23291	N686MA	B737	24795	N695AN	B757	26975	N701PA	B707	17674
N679AE	E145	14500814	N686RL	1-11	1686	N695BR	CRJ	7772	N701PC	B707	17639
N679AN	B757	29589	N686SG	E145	145686	N695CA	B727	20661	N701PJ	B737	19013
N679AW	A320	2613	N686SW	B737	23175	(N695DA)	B757	29727	N701SK	CRJ7	10133
N679BR	CRJ	7662	N687AA	B757	25695	N695DL	B757	29727	N701SW	B747	20826
N679CA	CRJ9	15132	N687BR	CRJ	7720	N695LC	A321	0956	N701TA	B747	22791
N679DA	B757	26955	(N687DL)	B757	27172	N695SW	B737	23506	N701TT	L1011	193C-1041
N679FE	A300	793	N687DL	B757	27586	N695WA	B727	19509	N701UW	B757	28160
N679HA	DC-9	47662	N687FE	A300	873	N696AA	146	E2054	N701UP	DC-8	45938
N679HA	DC-9	47715	N687JS	E145	14500846	N696AE	E145	14500874	N701US	B727	19444
N679MG	B727	22557	N687SW	B737	23388	N696AN	B757	26976	N701UW	A319	0890
N680AA	B737	23505	N688AA	B757	25730	N696BJ	B737	24470	N702	B707	17677
N680AE	E145	14500820	N688AE	E145	14500849	N696BR	CRJ	7779	N702AA	B727	22460
N680AM	B727	18970	N688BR	CRJ	7723	N696CA	B727	22574	N702AE	E145	145164
N680AN	B757	29590	N688CA	B727	22344				N702AW	B737	19015
N680AW	A320	2630	N688CZ	B777	27606						

Reg	Type	C/n	Reg	Type	C/n	Reg	Type	C/n	Reg	Type	C/n
N702AX	B767	22566	N705CA	B727	19479	N707HP	B707	18985	N709DH	B727	19968
N702BA	B777	27108	N705CK	B747	21032	N707HT	B707	19271	N709EV	CRJ7	10068
N702BC	MD11	48504	N705CK	B747	21034	N707HT	B707	19821	N709GB	E145	145211
N702BR	CRJ	7462	N705DA	L1011	193C-1071	N707HW	B707	19294	N709HA	DC-9	47764
N702CK	B747	20332	N705DH	B727	19191	N707JJ	B707	19352	(N709HK)	E145	145157
N702CM	E145	14500925	N705EB	CRJ	7057	N707JT	B707	18740	N709ML	B737	20336
N702CT	DC-9	47702	N705EV	B727	19009	N707JU	B707	21956	N709PA	B707	17588
N702DA	L1011	193C-1046	N705EV	CRJ7	10051	(N707KH)	B747	21541	N709PC	B707	20175
N702DH	B727	19793	N705FT	DC-8	46090	N707KN	B707	20919	N709PS	CRJ7	10165
N702DN	B777	29741	N705FW	B707	19270	N707KS	B707	17702	N709SK	CRJ7	10159
N702DR	E145	14500925	N705GC	MD11	48412	N707KS	B707	20025	N709SP	B737	19770
N702EV	CRJ7	10035	N705ML	B737	22055	N707KV	B707	19632	N709SW	737NG	27843
N702FT	DC-8	46073	N705PA	B707	17686	N707LE	B707	19361	N709TW	B757	28168
N702GC	MD11	48435	N705PC	B707	19587	N707LG	B707	21092	N709UP	DC-8	45914
N702ML	B737	22054	N705PS	CRJ7	10144	N707MB	B707	19294	N709US	B727	20139
N702NE	B727	22460	N705PS	DC-9	45846	N707MB	B707	19986	N709UW	A319	0997
N702PA	B707	17677	N705S	B737	21800	N707ME	B707	19530	N710AA	B727	22467
N702PC	B707	17645	N705SK	CRJ7	10145	N707MJ	B707	21104	N710BA	B747	20771
N702PJ	B737	19015	N705SW	737NG	27839	N707MQ	B707	21368	N710BR	CRJ	7852
N702PS	CRJ7	10135	(N705SW)	B747	22150	N707N	B707	20008	N710CA	CRJ	7241
N702PT	B707	17677	N705TA	B747	22725	(N707NR)	B707	19574	N710CK	B747	21097
N702SK	CRJ7	10136	(N705TW)	B757	28165	N707PA	B707	17587	N710DA	L1011	193C-1084
N702SW	B747	20827	N705TW	B757	28479	N707PD	B707	19964	(N710EV)	B727	22078
N702TA	B707	17677	N705TZ	DC-10	46915	N707PM	B707	19352	N710EV	CRJ7	10071
N702TA	B747	22722	N705UP	DC-8	45949	N707PS	DC-9	47023	N710FW	B707	20017
N702TT	L1011	193C-1046	N705US	B727	19447	N707QJ	B707	21261	(N710HV)	L1011	193A-1141
N702TW	B757	28162	N705UW	A319	0929	N707QT	B707	21956	N710NA	CV990	30-10-29
N702TZ	DC-10	46912	N706AA	B727	22463	(N707R)	B707	17691	N710PA	B707	17589
N702UP	DC-8	45902	N706AS	B737	28894	N707RZ	B707	18375	N710PS	CRJ7	10167
N702US	B727	19445	N706BA	737NG	30282	N707SA	737NG	27841	N710SK	CRJ7	10170
N702UW	A319	0896	N706BR	CRJ	7553	N707SH	B707	19353	N710SW	737NG	27844
N703	B707	17680	N706CA	B727	19496	N707SK	B707	17702	N710SY	737NG	30629
N703AA	B727	22461	N706CK	B747	20010	N707SK	CRJ7	10003	N710TB	E145	145224
N703AM	B757	27203	N706CK	B747	21827	N707TW	B757	27625	N710TS	CRJ7	10247
N703AS	B737	28893	N706CT	DC-9	47706	(N707TW)	B757	28479	N710TW	B757	28169
N703BA	B777	27109	N706DA	L1011	193C-1074	N707UM	B707	24503	N710UW	A319	1019
N703BC	737NG	33434	N706DH	B727	19192	N707UP	DC-8	45907	N711	B707	17590
N703BR	CRJ	7467	N706EV	CRJ7	10054	N707US	B727	19448	N711BE	B727	20724
N703CK	B747	19727	N706FT	DC-8	46001	N707UW	A319	0949	N711DA	L1011	193C-1086
N703CK	B747	21939	N706JP	B727	19835	(N707V)	B707	17692	N711GN	B727	19401
N703CL	B747	30761	N706MX	A319	1706	(N707W)	B707	17693	N711HK	737NG	27845
N703DA	L1011	193C-1052	N706PA	B707	17689	N707WJ	B707	20301	N711LF	A320	0645
N703DH	B727	19010	N706PC	B707	20177	N707XS	DC-9	47777	N711LF	B757	28833
N703EV	B727	19311	N706PS	CRJ7	10150	N707XX	B707	18740	N711LF	DC-8	45260
N703EV	CRJ7	10038	N706PS	DC-9	47020	(N707Y)	B707	17694	N711NA	CV990	30-10-1
N703FT	DC-8	46059	N706RB	B747	27066	(N707Z)	D707	17695	N711PA	B707	17590
N703GC	MD11	48411	N706RG	E145	145194	N707ZS	B707	20261	N711PC	B707	20172
(N703ME)	E145	145173	N706SK	CRJ7	10149	N708A	B707	20060	N711PH	E145	145235
(N703ML)	B737	22055	N706SW	737NG	27840	N708AA	B727	22465	(N711RC)	B727	22019
N703ML	B737	22529	(N706SW)	B747	22151	N708AE	E145	145205	N711ST	1-11	058
N703MR	E145	145173	N706TA	B707	17689	N708AS	B737	28895	N711SW	DC-9	45740
N703PA	B707	17680	(N706TW)	B757	27625	N708AW	B737	19771	N711SY	737NG	30642
N703PC	B707	19335	N706TW	B757	28165	N708AX	B767	22571	N711UT	B707	17601
N703PS	CRJ7	10137	N706TZ	DC-10	46582	N708BA	B747	22484	N711UW	A319	1033
N703S	B737	22529	N706UP	DC-8	46056	N708BC	737NG	33500	N711WM	CRJ	7140
N703SK	CRJ7	10139	N706US	A319	0946	N708BBR	CRJ	7575	N711ZX	B757	28481
N703SW	737NG	27837	N707AA	B727	22464	N708CA	CRJ	7235	N712AA	B727	22468
N703SW	B747	21764	N707AD	B707	19529	N708CK	B747	21543	N712AE	E145	145247
N703TA	B747	22724	N707AR	B707	17634	N708DA	L1011	193C-1078	N712BA	737NG	30285
N703TT	L1011	193P-1103	N707AR	B707	20029	N708DH	B727	18275	N712CA	CRJ	7244
N703TW	B757	27620	N707AX	B767	22570	N708EV	CRJ7	10060	N712CK	B747	19754
N703UP	DC-8	45939	N707BZ	737NG	32970	N708KS	B737	24708	N712CK	B747	21098
N703US	B727	19446	N707CA	B707	18586	N708PA	B707	17586	N712DA	L1011	193C-1088
N703UW	A319	0904	N707CA	B727	20662	N708PC	B707	20170	N712DH	B727	19401
N704A	B727	19504	"N707CK"	B747	19658	N708PS	CRJ7	10160	N712EV	CRJ7	10074
N704CK	B727	20528	N707CK	B747	21541	N708PS	DC-9	47068	N712NA	CV990	30-10-37
N704CK	B747	22299	N707CK	B747	21681	N708SK	CRJ7	10156	N712PA	B707	17591
N704CT	DC-9	47704	N707DA	L1011	193C-1077	N708SP	B737	19771	N712PC	B707	20176
N704DA	L1011	193C-1057	N707DH	B727	18321	N708SW	737NG	27842	N712PS	CRJ7	10168
N704PA	B707	17683	N707DY	B707	19412	N708TW	B757	28480	N712RC	B727	22020
N704PG	E145	145174	N707EB	E145	145195	N708UP	DC-8	46048	N712S	B737	23038
N704SW	737NG	27838	N707EL	B707	19869	N708US	B727	19449	N712SK	CRJ7	10172
N704SW	B747	21841	N707EV	CRJ7	10057	N708UW	A319	0972	N712SW	737NG	27846
N704US	A319	0922	N707FR	B707	19740	N709AA	B727	22466	N712SY	737NG	30642
N704X	B757	28163	N707FT	DC-8	46089	N709AS	B737	28896	N712TW	B757	27624
N705A	B727	19134	N707GB	B707	18808	N709AW	B737	19770	N712UA	DC-8	45416
N705AA	B727	22462	N707GE	B707	17608	N709AX	B767	22572	N712US	A319	1038
N705AE	E145	145184	N707GE	B707	18840	N709BA	B747	22483	N713A	B737	23467
N705AS	B737	29318	N707HD	B707	18084	N709BR	CRJ	7850	N713AA	B727	22469
N705BA	MD80	53486	N707HE	B707	20124	N709CA	CRJ	7238	N713AE	E145	145249
N705BC	B747	22705	N707HG	B707	19353	N709CK	B747	20247	N713AS	B737	30161
N705BR	CRJ	7470	N707HL	B707	19417	N709DA	L1011	193C-1081	N713AX	B767	23058

N713BA	B747	22169	N717PA	B707	17595	N720US	A319	1089	N723US	B727	20167
N713CA	**CRJ**	**7245**	N717QS	B707	20717	N720US	B727	20164	**N723UW**	**A319**	**1109**
N713CK	**B747**	**21099**	**N717SA**	**737NG**	**27851**	N720V	B707	18376	**N724AE**	**E145**	**145301**
N713DA	L1011	193C-1089	**N717TW**	**B757**	**28485**	N720W	B707	18377	(N724CK)	B727	19491
N713EV	**CRJ7**	**10081**	N717UA	DC-8	45390	**N720WN**	**737NG**	**27854**	(N724CK)	B727	20184
N713NA	CV990	30-10-29	N717US	B727	19995	N720ZK	B727	21849	**N724CK**	**B727**	**20383**
(N713RC)	B727	22021	**N717UW**	**A319**	**1069**	N721AA	B727	20729	**N724CL**	**B727**	**19121**
N713SK	**CRJ7**	**10174**	N717XA	B717	55000	**N721CA**	**CRJ**	**7259**	N724DA	L1011	193C-1151
N713SW	**737NG**	**27847**	N717XB	B717	55001	**N721CX**	**DC-8**	**46013**	N724DH	B727	19862
N713TW	**B757**	**28173**	N717XC	B717	55002	N721DA	L1011	193C-1139	N724EV	B727	19109
N713UA	DC-8	45389	N717XD	B717	55003	N721DH	B727	19545	**N724EV**	**CRJ7**	**10138**
N713UP	DC-8	46014	N717XE	B717	55004	N721EV	B727	18897	**N724FD**	**A300**	**530**
N713US	B727	20140	N718AA	B727	20611	N721EW	MD80	49767	N724HB	DC-9	47690
N713UW	**A319**	**1040**	**N718AE**	**E145**	**145275**	**N721FD**	**A300**	**477**	N724JE	B727	19010
N714	B707	17592	**N718BA**	**B747**	**27042**	N721GS	B707	19377	N724ML	B737	23790
N714A	B737	23405	N718CT	B737	23718	**N721HS**	**E145**	**145283**	N724PA	B707	17602
N714AW	A320	0714	N718DA	L1011	193C-1097	N721JE	B727	18843	N724PA	B747	21316
N714AX	B767	22314	**N718EV**	**CRJ7**	**10095**	N721LF	A320	0542	N724PL	B727	19135
N714BZ	E145	145260	**N718FD**	**A300**	**365**	N721LF	B737	26307	N724RW	B727	21457
N714CB	**737NG**	**27848**	N718PA	B707	17596	**N721MF**	**B727**	**22687**	N724SK	B727	21234
N714CK	**B747**	**22446**	**N718PS**	**CRJ7**	**10175**	N721ML	B727	22697	**N724SK**	**CRJ7**	**10189**
N714DA	L1011	193C-1090	N718RC	B727	22344	N721MM	MD80	49767	**N724SW**	**737NG**	**27856**
N714FC	B707	17592	**N718SK**	**CRJ7**	**10184**	N721PA	B707	17599	(N724SW)	737NG	29276
N714NA	C-141	6110	**N718SW**	**737NG**	**27852**	N721PC	B727	18997	N724TW	B757	28488
N714P	B757	28482	**N718TW**	**B757**	**28486**	N721RC	B727	22492	N724US	B707	18354
N714PA	B707	17592	N718UA	DC-8	45384	**N721RR**	**B747**	**23721**	**N724UW**	**A319**	**1122**
N714PT	B707	17592	**N718UP**	**DC-8**	**46018**	N721RW	B727	21200	**N724YS**	**B727**	**21474**
(N714RC)	B727	22344	N718US	B727	20161	N721SK	B727	21298	N725AA	B727	20732
N714US	**A319**	**1046**	N718UW	A319	1077	**N721TW**	**B757**	**29954**	**N725AE**	**E145**	**145312**
N715A	B737	21928	N719A	B737	22679	N721UA	DC-8	45753	N725AL	B727	19665
N715AA	**B727**	**22470**	N719AA	B727	20612	N721US	B707	18351	N725AL	B737	22051
N715AE	**E145**	**145262**	N719AE	E145	145276	N721US	B727	20165	N725CA	B707	17603
N715BA	737NG	32371	**N719BA**	**737NG**	**36107**	N721UW	A319	1095	(N725CK)	B727	19183
N715CK	**B747**	**22447**	N719BC	B757	25131	N721WN	B737	22697	N725DA	L1011	193C-1162
N715CL	DC-9	47068	**N719CA**	**CRJ**	**7253**	N721ZK	B727	21850	N725DT	B727	20046
N715DA	L1011	193C-1092	N719CK	B727	19481	N722AA	B727	20730	N725EV	B727	19112
N715DH	B727	19618	**N719CK**	**B747**	**20923**	**N722AE**	**E145**	**145287**	N725FD	A300	572
N715FW	B707	19789	N719DA	L1011	193C-1135	N722CK	B727	19485	N725FW	B707	20085
(N715NA)	B737	19437	**N719EV**	**CRJ7**	**10099**	**N722CK**	**B727**	**20948**	N725JE	B727	19793
N715PA	A300	023	**N719FD**	**A300**	**388**	N722CX	DC-8	46130	N725ML	B737	23791
N715PA	B707	17593	N719PA	B707	17597	N722DA	L1011	193C-1147	N725PA	B707	17603
N715RC	B727	22019	**N719PS**	**CRJ7**	**10177**	N722DH	B727	19861	N725PA	B747	19898
N715SF	**CRJ**	**7115**	N719QS	B707	20719	N722EV	B727	19136	N725PL	B727	19191
N715SK	**CRJ7**	**10179**	N719RC	B727	22490	**N722EV**	**CRJ7**	**10127**	**N725PS**	**CRJ7**	**10186**
N715SW	737NG	27849	**N719SK**	**CRJ7**	**10188**	**N722FD**	**A300**	**479**	N725RW	B727	21502
N715TW	B757	28483	**N719SW**	**737NG**	**27853**	N722GS	B707	19373	N725S	B737	22051
N715UA	DC-8	45386	(N719TA)	146	E2136	N722JE	B727	19807	N725SA	B747	21550
N715UP	**DC-8**	**45915**	N719TW	B757	28487	**N722LA**	**B727**	**22992**	N725SK	B737	25168
N715US	B727	19994	N719US	A319	1084	N722ML	B737	22698	**N725SW**	**737NG**	**27857**
N715UW	**A319**	**1051**	N719US	B727	20163	N722PA	B707	17600	(N725SW)	737NG	29277
N716A	B737	21929	N720A	B737	21926	N722RW	B727	21201	N725TW	B757	30338
N716AA	B727	20608	N720AA	B727	20613	N722S	B727	20449	N725US	B707	18355
N716AE	**E145**	**145264**	N720AC	B707	18016	N722SK	B727	20940	**N725UW**	**A319**	**1135**
N716AN	B767	24716	**N720AE**	**E145**	**145279**	N722TW	B757	29385	N726AA	B727	20733
N716AW	A320	0716	**N720AX**	**DC-10**	**48252**	N722UA	DC-8	45767	**N726AE**	**E145**	**145314**
N716BA	737NG	33879	N720BA	146	E1002	**N722US**	**A319**	**1097**	N726AL	B727	19666
N716CA	**CRJ**	**7250**	N720BC	B707	18251	N722US	B707	18352	N726AL	B737	22426
N716CK	**B747**	**19753**	N720BG	B707	18033	N722US	B727	20166	N726BA	B737	29035
N716DA	L1011	193C-1095	N720CC	B707	17915	N722WN	B737	22698	N726DA	L1011	193C-1163
N716EV	**CRJ7**	**10084**	**N720CH**	**737NG**	**29866**	N723AA	B727	20731	N726DH	B727	20409
N716FD	**A300**	**358**	N720CK	B727	19487	**N723AE**	**E145**	**145288**	N726EV	B727	19311
N716HH	B707	17594	**N720CK**	**B727**	**21298**	N723BA	B757	24747	**N726FD**	**A300**	**575**
N716PA	B707	17594	N720DA	L1011	193C-1136	N723BC	B767	24797	N726JE	B727	19815
N716PS	**CRJ7**	**10171**	N720DC	B727	19253	N723CK	B727	20191	N726NS	A320	0726
N716RC	B727	22021	N720DH	B727	19544	**N723CK**	**B727**	**20545**	N726PA	B707	17604
N716SA	B747	24067	**N720EV**	**CRJ7**	**10115**	N723DA	L1011	193C-1150	N726PA	B747	21048
N716SK	**CRJ7**	**10180**	N720FD	A300	417	N723EV	B727	19137	N726PL	B727	19192
N716SW	**737NG**	**27850**	N720FW	B707	19263	**N723EV**	**CRJ7**	**10132**	N726RW	B727	21655
N716TW	**B757**	**28484**	N720FW	B707	20085	**N723FD**	**A300**	**543**	**N726SK**	**CRJ7**	**10190**
N716UA	DC-8	45385	N720GS	B707	19370	N723GS	B707	19986	**N726SW**	**737NG**	**27858**
N716US	B727	20141	N720GT	B707	18384	N723JE	B727	18896	(N726SW)	737NG	29278
N716UW	**A319**	**1055**	N720H	B707	18384	N723ML	B737	23789	N726TW	B757	30339
N717AA	B727	20610	N720JE	B727	19618	N723PA	B707	17601	N726US	A319	1136
N717AE	**E145**	**145272**	N720JR	B707	18451	N723PA	B727	21439	N726US	B707	18356
N717BA	737NG	33880	**N720MM**	**737NG**	**33010**	**N723PS**	**CRJ7**	**10181**	N726VA	B727	20739
N717CK	**B747**	**20325**	N720PA	B707	17598	N723RW	B727	21202	N727AA	B727	20734
N717DA	L1011	193C-1096	**N720PS**	**CRJ7**	**10178**	N723SK	B727	20545	**N727AE**	**E145**	**145326**
N717DH	B727	19389	N720PW	B707	18021	**N723SW**	**737NG**	**27855**	**N727AH**	**B727**	**19261**
N717EV	**CRJ7**	**10088**	N720RC	B727	22491	(N723SW)	737NG	29275	N727AK	B727	19123
N717FD	**A300**	**361**	(N720SA)	B747	21590	N723TA	B727	22723	N727AL	B727	19807
N717JL	**B717**	**55042**	**N720SW**	**CRJ**	**7297**	N723TW	B757	29378	N727AN	B727	22543
N717NA	DC-8	46082	N720TW	B757	30319	N723US	B707	18353	(N727AW)	B727	19401

N727BB	B727	19136	N728AL	B737	21719	N730US	B707	18381	N735TW	B707	17662
N727BE	B727	18933	N728AL	B737	22629	N730US	B727	20367	N735US	B707	18688
N727BE	B727	20764	N728BA	B747	24066	N731	B707	17607	**N736BP**	**B737**	**23465**
N727CD	B727	18849	N728BE	B727	20765	N731AA	B727	20738	**N736DT**	**E145**	**145388**
N727CF	B727	18323	**N728CG**	**B767**	**24728**	(N731AE)	E145	145356	N736DY	L1011	193C-1227
N727CH	B727	18371	N728CK	B727	18847	N731BA	B707	17607	N736N	B737	19420
N727CH	B727	18933	N728DA	L1011	193C-1173	**N731BE**	**E145**	**145356**	N736PA	B747	19643
N727CK	B727	19195	N728EV	B727	18794	N731EV	B727	19113	N736S	B737	23752
N727CK	B747	22478	**N728FD**	**A300**	**581**	**N731FD**	**A300**	**709**	(N736SA)	737NG	27863
N727CR	B727	18894	N728FV	B727	22537	N731JP	B707	17607	**N736SA**	**737NG**	**27868**
N727DA	L1011	193C-1167	N728JE	B727	18368	N731L	DC-9	47326	N736T	B707	18064
N727DG	B727	19261	N728JE	B737	19594	N731PA	B747	19637	N736TW	B707	17663
N727DH	B727	20204	N728PA	B707	17606	N731PL	DC-8	46023	N736US	A319	1209
N727EC	**B727**	**18365**	N728PA	B747	20712	N731Q	B707	20031	N736US	B707	18792
N727EC	B727	19318	**N728PH**	**E145**	**14500985**	(N731RW)	B727	21824	**N737A**	**737NG**	**30181**
N727EV	B727	19500	N728PL	DC-8	45918	(N731SA)	737NG	27858	**N737AG**	**737NG**	**30496**
N727FD	**A300**	**579**	N728Q	B707	20025	**N731SA**	**737NG**	**27863**	N737AL	B707	19416
N727FH	B727	20489	N728RW	B727	21741	N731T	B707	18423	N737AP	B737	19956
N727FV	B727	22536	N728SA	B747	21982	N731TW	B707	17658	N737AR	B737	24212
N727GB	B727	19136	**N728SK**	**CRJ7**	**10192**	N731US	B707	18382	N737BF	737NG	30076
N727GC	B727	20938	(N728SW)	737NG	27855	**N731VA**	**B737**	**27456**	N737BG	B737	19612
N727GG	**B727**	**19252**	**N728SW**	**737NG**	**27860**	N731XL	B737	24095	N737BJ	B737	21957
N727GP	B727	19260	"N728SW"	737NG	29491	N732AL	B727	19808	N737BX	737NG	27981
N727GS	B727	18893	"N728U"	B707	18689	**N732BJ**	**737NG**	**36108**	N737BZ	737NG	29102
N727HC	B727	19835	N728US	B707	18421	**N732DH**	**E145**	**145358**	**N737CC**	**737NG**	**29135**
N727JE	B727	19011	N728US	B727	20168	N732FD	A300	713	N737D	L1011	193C-1228
N727JH	B727	20942	N728UW	A319	1155	**N732MA**	**737NG**	**30618**	**N737DB**	**737NG**	**35990**
N727JR	B727	18366	N728VA	B727	22537	N732PA	B747	19638	**N737DX**	**B737**	**24804**
(N727KA)	B727	20371	N728ZV	B727	20710	N732Q	B707	20034	**N737ER**	**737NG**	**30754**
N727KS	B727	20489	N729AA	B727	20736	N732S	B737	23406	N737FA	B737	24300
N727LA	B727	19260	**N729AE**	**E145**	**145343**	**N732SK**	**CRJ7**	**10194**	**N737GG**	**737NG**	**29136**
N727LJ	B727	19137	N729AL	B737	22630	(N732SW)	737NG	27859	**N737GQ**	**737NG**	**35792**
N727LS	B727	20941	N729BC	B737	25049	**N732SW**	**737NG**	**27864**	(N737JW)	737NG	27864
N727M	B727	19313	N729BE	B737	20766	N732TW	B707	17659	**N737JW**	**737NG**	**27869**
N727M	B727	22541	**N729CA**	**CRJ**	**7265**	N732TW	B737	22731	N737KD	B737	19945
N727MB	B727	19318	N729CK	B727	19482	**N732US**	**A319**	**1203**	**N737M**	**737NG**	**33361**
(N727MJ)	B727	18365	N729DA	L1011	193C-1180	N732US	B707	18383	N737MC	737NG	30076
N727MJ	B727	19313	N729DH	B727	22080	N733AR	B737	23466	**N737MW**	**E145**	**145396**
N727MJ	B727	21595	N729EV	B727	19116	N733BA	B747	24061	N737N	B737	19421
N727NK	**B727**	**21945**	**N729FD**	**A300**	**657**	N733DS	L1011	193C-1224	N737PA	B747	19644
N727NY	B727	20646	N729JP	B707	17607	N733FD	A300	715	N737Q	B737	19758
N727PA	B707	17605	N729PA	B707	17607	**N733KR**	**E145**	**145368**	N737Q	B737	21279
N727PA	B747	21162	N729PA	B747	20713	N733MA	737NG	30619	N737RD	B737	20365
N727PJ	B727	18752	N729PL	DC-8	45921	N733MA	B737	23062	N737SP	737NG	29272
N727PL	B727	19195	N729Q	B707	20029	**N733PA**	**B737**	**23466**	N737SP	737NG	33361
N727PL	B727	20643	N729RW	B727	21742	N733PA	B747	19640	N737TW	B707	17664
N727PN	**B727**	**20327**	N729SA	B747	22379	N733Q	B707	19621	N737TW	B707	20257
(N727PR)	B727	21950	(N729SW)	737NG	27856	(N733SA)	737NG	27860	**N737US**	**A319**	**1245**
N727PX	B727	19261	**N729SW**	**737NG**	**27861**	**N733SA**	**737NG**	**27865**	N737US	B707	18793
N727RE	B727	20228	(N729TA)	146	E2138	N733T	B707	18581	"N737VU"	B737	19041
N727RE	B727	22430	**N729UP**	**DC-8**	**46029**	N733TW	B707	17660	**N737WH**	**737NG**	**29142**
N727RF	B727	19261	N729US	A319	1170	**N733TW**	**B737**	**22732**	N737WH	B737	22431
N727RL	B727	18253	N729US	B707	18422	N733US	B707	18384	N737X	737NG	27841
N727RW	B727	21656	N729US	B727	20366	**N733UW**	**A319**	**1205**	N737X	737NG	30017
N727S	B727	18998	N730AA	B727	20737	N734AB	B737	27143	**N738A**	**737NG**	**30182**
N727SA	B727	20906	N730AL	B727	22631	N734EB	1-11	005	**N738AL**	**737NG**	**28499**
N727SG	B727	19260	N730AS	B737	22577	**N734EK**	**E145**	**145371**	N738AL	B707	20076
N727SH	B727	20005	N730BC	B737	24326	**N734MA**	**737NG**	**30039**	N738AP	B737	21766
N727SK	**CRJ7**	**10191**	**N730BH**	**E145**	**145367**	(N734MA)	737NG	30786	(N738CB)	737NG	27865
N727SN	B727	21100	N730DA	L1011	193C-1199	N734MA	B737	23387	**N738CB**	**737NG**	**27870**
N727SR	B727	20006	N730EV	B727	19110	N734N	B737	19418	**N738EV**	**CRJ7**	**10146**
N727SW	**737NG**	**27859**	**N730EV**	**CRJ7**	**10141**	N734PA	B747	19641	(N738MA)	737NG	30787
(N727SW)	737NG	29279	**N730FD**	**A300**	**659**	(N734Q)	B707	18886	**N738MA**	**737NG**	**32799**
N727TA	B727	19122	N730FW	B707	19212	**N734SA**	**737NG**	**27866**	N738N	B737	19422
N727TG	B727	19503	N730JP	B707	17671	N734SH	737NG	32734	**N738NR**	**E145**	**145401**
N727TW	**B757**	**30340**	**N730KW**	**E145**	**145346**	(N734SW)	737NG	27861	N738PA	B747	19645
N727UD	B727	18367	N730MA	B737	23506	N734T	B707	18041	**N738SK**	**CRJ7**	**10195**
N727US	B707	18420	N730PA	B737	27608	N734T	B707	18065	N738TW	B707	17665
N727UW	A319	1147	N730PA	B737	27924	N734TW	B707	17661	**N738US**	**A319**	**1254**
N727VA	B727	20675	N730PA	B747	20888	N734US	B707	18687	**N739A**	**737NG**	**30183**
N727VA	B727	20765	N730PL	DC-8	46161	**N735CA**	**CRJ**	**7267**	N739AA	B737	22055
N727VA	B727	22536	N730Q	B707	20022	N735D	L1011	193C-1226	**N739AE**	**E145**	**145402**
N727VJ	**B727**	**19318**	N730RW	B727	21823	N735LA	B737	20574	**N739AL**	**737NG**	**28500**
N727WE	B727	19262	N730S	B737	23506	N735MA	B737	23289	N739AL	B707	20077
N727WF	B727	20045	N730SA	B747	22380	N735N	B737	19419	**N739AX**	**B767**	**22216**
N727X	B727	19394	**N730SK**	**CRJ7**	**10193**	N735PA	B747	19642	N739BN	B727	20739
N727XL	B727	20533	(N730SW)	737NG	27857	N735PL	DC-8	46153	**N739CA**	**CRJ**	**7273**
N727YK	**B727**	**19806**	**N730SW**	**737NG**	**27862**	(N735SA)	737NG	27862	**N739GB**	**737NG**	**29275**
N727ZV	B727	19249	N730T	B707	18154	N735SA	737NG	27867	**N739MA**	**737NG**	**30670**
N728A	DC-8	46081	N730TJ	B737	20364	N735SJ	B747	19642	N739PA	B747	19646
N728AA	B727	20735	**N730UP**	**DC-8**	**46030**	N735T	B707	17662	N739TW	B707	17666
N728AE	**E145**	**145328**	**N730US**	**A319**	**1182**	**N735TS**	**E145**	**145386**	N739US	A319	1263

Reg	Type	Serial	Reg	Type	Serial	Reg	Type	Serial	Reg	Type	Serial
N740AL	737NG	28640	N743DH	B727	22438	N747BH	B747	21162	N750AG	MD80	53577
N740AP	B737	21500	N743EV	B727	19088	N747BJ	B747	21316	N750AL	737NG	32743
N740AS	B737	22578	N743N	B737	20212	(N747BJ)	B747	27141	N750AN	B777	30259
N740AX	B767	22213	N743NV	737NG	30137	N747BJ	B747	27646	(N750AN)	B777	30261
N740CK	B747	22064	N743PA	B747	19650	N747BJ	B757	22209	(N750AS)	B737	28895
N740DA	L1011	193C-1244	N743PR	B747	21834	N747BK	B747	21439	(N750AS)	B737	29318
N740DH	B727	21930	N743SA	B747	22671	N747BK	B747	21604	N750AT	B757	23126
N740EH	737NG	34596	N743SC	A300	045	N747BL	B747	19732	N750AX	B767	22227
N740EV	B727	19252	N743SK	CRJ7	10199	N747BL	B747	20781	N750DH	B727	21951
N740EV	CRJ7	10151	N743SW	737NG	29279	N747BL	B747	21605	N750EV	B727	19010
N740FD	A300	559	N743TV	B747	22403	(N747BL)	B747	27142	N750EV	CRJ7	10161
N740FW	B707	19411	N743TW	B707	17670	N747BM	B747	20011	N750FW	B707	19353
N740N	B737	19423	N743UN	B747	23640	N747BN	B747	20012	N750MX	A319	1750
N740PA	B747	19647	N743US	B727	20285	N747BN	B747	20782	N750NA	B757	26277
N740PA	B757	24497	N743UW	A319	1277	N747BX	737NG	30276	N750NW	DC-9	47114
N740RD	A300	174	N744AL	737NG	32582	N747BZ	B747	25880	N750PA	B747	19654
N740RW	B727	21824	N744AS	B737	21822	N747CK	B747	21743	N750RA	MD80	49777
N740SA	B747	21380	N744AX	B767	22221	N747DH	B727	22253	N750SA	737NG	29802
N740SC	A300	047	N744BC	MD90	53553	N747ER	B747	32909	N750SJ	B747	24177
N740SJ	B747	22477	(N744CK)	B727	19483	N747FT	B747	20712	N750SK	CRJ7	10207
N740SK	CRJ7	10196	N744CK	B747	22065	N747FU	B747	21992	N750TW	B707	18389
N740SW	737NG	29276	N744EV	B727	19827	N747GE	B747	19651	N750UA	B727	19319
N740TW	B707	17667	N744EV	CRJ7	10157	N747GT	B747	22995	N750UP	DC-8	45950
N740UN	B747	23482	N744MA	B737	23200	N747KS	B747	21133	N750US	B727	21512
N740US	B727	20467	N744N	B737	20213	N747KV	B747	21133	N750UW	A319	1315
N740UW	A319	1265	N744P	A319	1287	N747MC	B747	23348	N750VJ	B727	20302
N741AL	737NG	28641	N744PA	B747	19651	N747N	B737	20216	N750WA	B747	19733
N741AS	B737	21959	N744PR	B747	22382	N747NA	B747	21441	N750WL	B757	23928
N741AX	B767	22215	N744SA	B747	22363	N747PA	B747	19639	N751AA	B737	21771
(N741CK)	B727	20187	(N744SJ)	B727	22245	N747QC	B747	19639	N751AF	A320	1211
N741CK	B747	21679	N744SK	CRJ7	10200	N747SA	737NG	29799	N751AL	737NG	30674
N741DA	L1011	193C-1245	N744SW	737NG	29490	N747SP	B747	21022	(N751AN)	B777	30262
N741DH	B727	21931	N744TW	B707	17671	N747TA	B747	20712	N751AN	B777	30798
N741EV	CRJ7	10155	N744UP	DC-8	45944	N747TW	B707	18386	(N751AS)	B737	28896
N741L	DC-9	47418	N744US	A319	1287	N747US	B727	20569	N751AT	B757	23125
N741LA	B747	19824	N744US	B727	20286	N747UT	B747	21934	N751DA	L1011	193W-1166
N741N	B737	20211	N745A	737NG	30185	N747UW	A319	1301	N751DH	B727	22982
N741PA	B747	19648	N745AL	737NG	29904	N747VC	B747	22872	N751EV	CRJ7	10163
N741PA	B757	24737	N745AM	B777	32718	N747WA	B747	20651	N751L	B737	23507
N741PR	B747	21832	N745AP	B737	21767	N747WR	B747	20651	N751LF	A321	0604
N741RW	B727	21951	N745AS	B737	20794	N747ZZ	B747	23222	N751LF	B757	26274
N741SA	737NG	29277	N745AX	B767	22222	N748AL	737NG	30050	N751MA	B707	19582
N741SC	A300	023	N745BC	B757	25131	(N748AS)	B737	29318	N751N	B737	19548
N741SJ	B747	19648	N745CK	B747	21680	N748AX	B767	22225	N751NA	B757	28164
N741SJ	B747	22063	N745DH	B727	20665	N748CK	B747	21744	N751NW	DC-9	47115
N741TV	B747	21964	N745EV	B727	19283	N748DH	B727	22440	N751PA	B747	19655
N741TW	B707	17668	N745LA	B747	20527	N748EV	B727	19793	N751PA	B757	23928
N741UN	B747	24156	N745N	B737	20214	N748EV	CRJ7	10158	N751PR	B747	27261
N741US	B727	20509	N745SA	B747	22382	N748FD	A300	633	N751RA	MD80	49779
N741UW	A319	1269	N745SJ	B747	20888	N748FT	B747	20713	N751SA	B747	22678
N742AL	737NG	30830	N745SK	CRJ7	10201	N748LA	B747	23150	N751SK	CRJ7	10208
N742AP	B737	21955	N745SW	737NG	29491	N748MA	B737	23064	N751SW	737NG	29803
N742AS	B737	23136	N745TW	B707	17672	N748PA	B747	19652	N751TA	B707	17649
N742AX	B767	22217	N745US	B727	20510	N748SA	B747	21110	N751TW	B707	18390
N742CK	B747	22745	N745UW	A319	1289	N748SK	CRJ7	10203	N751UA	DC-8	46139
N742DH	B727	21290	N745VJ	A319	1289	N748SW	737NG	29800	N751US	B727	21513
N742EV	B727	19140	N746AL	737NG	29905	N748TA	B747	20713	N751UW	A319	1317
N742MA	B737	23200	N746AM	B777	32719	N748TW	B707	18387	N751VJ	B727	20303
N742PA	B747	19649	N746AP	B737	21770	N748UP	DC-8	45948	N752AN	B777	30260
N742PA	B757	24402	N746AS	B737	23123	N748US	B727	20570	(N752AN)	B777	30263
N742PB	737NG	29200	N746BA	737NG	34477	N748UW	A319	1311	N752AP	B737	21769
N742PR	B747	21833	N746DH	B727	22252	N748WA	B747	20652	N752AT	B757	23128
N742PS	A319	1275	N746EV	B727	20078	N749AL	737NG	32738	N752AX	B767	23434
N742RW	B727	21952	N746N	B737	20215	N749AP	B737	21768	N752BC	737NG	30755
N742SA	B747	22669	N746SA	B747	21111	N749AP	B737	23749	N752DA	L1011	193C-1172
N742SC	A300	019	N746SK	CRJ7	10202	(N749AS)	B737	28894	N752DH	B727	22466
N742SJ	B747	21827	N746SW	737NG	29798	N749AX	B767	22226	N752EV	CRJ7	10166
N742SK	CRJ7	10197	N746TW	B707	18385	N749DH	B727	22013	N752MA	B737	23063
N742SW	737NG	29278	N746US	B727	20568	N749FD	A300	536	N752MA	B737	28198
N742TV	B747	21965	N746UW	A319	1297	N749FT	B747	20888	N752N	B737	19073
N742TW	B707	17669	N747AS	B737	23124	N749N	B737	19547	N752NA	B757	28174
N742TW	B737	21186	N747AS	B737	28893	N749PA	B747	19653	N752NW	DC-9	47116
N742UN	B747	24019	N747AV	B747	19734	N749R	B747	20310	N752PA	B747	19656
N742US	A319	1275	N747AX	B767	22224	N749SW	737NG	29801	N752PR	B727	27262
N742VA	B737	24773	N747BA	B747	19734	(N749TA)	146	E2156	N752RA	MD80	49780
N743A	737NG	30184	N747BA	B747	20770	N749TA	B747	20888	N752SA	B747	21255
N743AL	737NG	28654	N747BA	B747	27645	N749TW	B707	18388	N752SK	CRJ7	10209
N743AS	B737	21821	N747BC	B747	20771	N749UN	B747	22991	N752SW	737NG	29804
N743AX	B767	22218	N747BC	B747	21048	N749US	A319	1313	N752TA	B707	17648
N743BC	MD90	53552	N747BC	B747	25879	N749US	B727	21393	N752TW	B707	18391
(N743CK)	B727	19486	N747BH	B737	23752	N749WA	B747	20653	N752UA	DC-8	45956
N743CK	B747	22746	N747BH			(N750AC)	B747	21543	N752UP	DC-8	45952

Registration	Type	S/N
N752US	A319	1319
N752US	B727	21691
N753AL	B727	19203
N753AN	B777	30261
(N753AN)	B777	30264
N753AS	B727	19203
N753DA	L1011	193W-1189
N753DH	B727	22468
N753EB	CRJ	7053
N753EV	CRJ7	10169
N753JM	B757	32982
N753MA	B737	23060
N753MA	B737	28053
N753N	B737	20453
N753NA	B757	24544
N753NW	DC-9	47117
N753PA	B747	19657
N753PR	B747	27828
N753RA	MD80	49587
N753SA	B747	21787
N753SK	CRJ7	10214
N753SW	737NG	29848
N753UA	DC-8	46024
N753US	A319	1326
N753US	B727	21692
N754AN	B777	30262
N754AS	B737	25095
N754AT	B757	24964
N754BC	737NG	30753
N754DH	B727	22008
N754DL	L1011	193Y-1181
N754EV	CRJ7	10173
N754N	B737	20454
N754NA	B757	29381
N754NW	DC-9	47178
N754PA	B747	19658
N754PR	B747	27663
N754RA	MD80	49641
N754SA	B747	21576
N754SK	CRJ7	10215
N754SW	737NG	29849
N754TW	B707	18392
N754UA	B737	19707
N754US	A320	0283
N754US	B727	21958
N754UW	A319	1328
N755AN	B777	30263
N755AS	B737	25096
N755AT	B757	24965
N755DH	B727	21857
N755DL	L1011	193Y-1184
N755EV	CRJ7	10185
(N755FT)	DC-8	46088
N755MA	B737	23406
N755MX	B757	24964
N755NA	B757	30043
N755NW	DC-9	47179
N755PA	B747	19659
(N755PR)	B747	28959
N755RA	MD80	49727
N755SA	737NG	27871
N755SK	CRJ7	10220
N755TW	B707	18393
N755UA	DC-8	45888
N755UP	DC-8	46055
N755US	A319	1331
N756AF	B757	24923
N756AM	B777	30264
N756AS	B737	25097
N756AT	B757	27351
N756DR	L1011	193Y-1185
N756NA	B757	32448
N756NW	DC-9	47180
N756PR	B747	27602
N756SA	737NG	27872
N756SK	CRJ7	10221
N756TW	B707	18394
N756UA	DC-8	45921
N756US	A319	1340
N757A	B757	22212
N757AF	B757	25155
N757AG	B757	29306
N757AN	B777	32636
N757AT	B757	23127
N757AV	B757	25493
(N757B)	B757	22172
(N757BC)	B757	22212
N757BJ	B757	22176
N757GA	B757	24260
N757HW	B757	22194
N757LV	737NG	29850
N757MA	B757	28463
N757NA	B757	24567
N757PA	B707	18083
(N757PR)	B747	28960
N757SS	B757	22176
N757TW	B707	18395
N757UW	A319	1342
N757X	B757	29016
N758AN	B777	32637
N758BC	B737	24165
N758EV	CRJ7	10210
N758MA	B737	23752
N758MX	B757	24965
N758N	B737	19603
N758NW	DC-9	47286
N758PA	B707	18084
N758SA	B747	23138
N758SK	CRJ7	10222
N758SL	A320	0758
N758SW	737NG	27873
N758TW	B707	18396
N758US	A319	1348
N759AN	B777	32638
N759BA	146	E2059
N759CA	CRJ	7279
N759DA	L1011	193Y-1176
N759EV	CRJ7	10211
N759GS	737NG	30544
N759N	B737	19954
N759NW	DC-9	47287
N759PA	B707	18085
N759TW	B707	18397
N760AL	B727	21953
N760AN	B777	31477
N760AS	B737	25098
N760AT	B727	21954
N760BE	B737	25017
N760DH	L1011	193P-1194
N760EV	CRJ7	10212
N760FW	B707	19442
N760NA	B767	26257
N760NC	DC-9	47708
N760NW	DC-9	47288
N760PA	B707	18335
N760SA	B747	21221
(N760SJ)	B747	21964
N760SK	CRJ7	10223
N760SW	737NG	27874
N760TW	B707	18913
N760US	A319	1354
N760US	B727	21954
N761AJ	B777	31478
N761DA	L1011	193Y-1208
N761LF	A321	0614
N761LF	B737	23811
N761N	B737	21665
N761NC	DC-9	47709
N761ND	CRJ7	10213
N761PA	B707	18336
N761RR	737NG	27875
N761SA	B747	21832
(N761SJ)	B747	22403
N761TW	B707	17673
N761U	B707	19820
N762AL	B727	21954
N762AN	B777	31479
N762AS	B737	25099
N762AT	B727	22162
N762BE	L1011	193P-1070
(N762BT)	B767	24728
N762DA	L1011	193Y-1210
(N762HA)	L1011	193P-1070
N762MX	B757	29442
N762N	B737	21666
N762NC	DC-9	47710
N762NW	DC-9	47395
N762PA	B707	18337
(N762SJ)	B747	21965
N762SK	CRJ7	10226
N762SW	737NG	27876
N762TA	B767	23623
N762TB	B707	18337
N762TT	B767	33687
(N762TW)	B707	17674
N762TW	B707	17675
N762U	B707	19821
N762UA	DC-8	45906
N762US	A319	1358
N762US	B727	22162
N763AA	B737	22367
N763AB	B707	17676
N763AN	B777	31480
N763AS	B737	25100
N763AT	B727	22983
N763BA	B737	22736
N763BE	L1011	193P-1082
(N763BT)	B767	24475
N763DL	L1011	193Y-1197
N763MX	B757	29443
N763N	B737	21667
N763NC	DC-9	47716
N763NW	DC-9	47396
N763PA	B707	18338
N763SK	CRJ7	10228
N763SW	737NG	27877
N763TT	B767	33844
(N763TW)	B707	17675
N763TW	B707	17676
N763U	B707	19822
N763US	A319	1360
N763US	B727	22983
N763W	B707	18338
N764AN	B777	32439
N764AS	B737	25101
N764AT	B727	22984
N764BA	146	E2064
N764BC	MD80	48046
N764BE	L1011	193P-1103
N764BE	L1011	193P-1113
N764DA	L1011	193H-1202
(N764HA)	L1011	193P-1113
N764MA	B737	23838
N764MX	B767	26517
N764NC	DC-9	47717
N764PA	B707	18339
N764SE	B707	18339
N764SK	CRJ7	10229
N764SW	737NG	27878
N764TA	B737	25764
N764TT	B767	33688
(N764TW)	B707	17676
N764TW	B707	17678
N764US	A319	1369
N764US	B727	22984
(N765AB)	B707	17679
N765AN	B777	32879
N765AS	B727	19534
N765AS	B737	25102
N765AT	B727	23014
N765B	1-11	067
N765BC	MD90	53576
N765BE	L1011	193P-1105
N765CF	1-11	067
N765DA	L1011	193H-1206
(N765HA)	L1011	193P-1105
N765MX	B757	30044
N765NA	B767	28098
N765NC	DC-9	47718
N765PA	B707	18579
N765SA	B747	21660
N765SK	CRJ7	10231
N765SW	737NG	29805
N765TA	B737	25765
N765TT	B767	33689
(N765TW)	B707	17677
N765TW	B707	17679
N765US	A319	1371
N765US	B727	23014
N766AN	B777	32880
N766AS	B737	19728
N766AT	B727	21999
N766BC	MD80	49662
N766BE	L1011	193P-1112
N766DA	L1011	193H-1207
(N766HA)	L1011	193P-1112
N766JS	B727	19535
N766NC	DC-9	47739
N766PA	B707	18580
N766RD	DC-8	46015
N766SK	CRJ7	10232
N766ST	B737	23766
N766SW	737NG	29806
N766TT	B767	34433
(N766TW)	B707	17678
N766TW	B707	17681
N766UA	B777	26917
N766US	A319	1378
N766US	B727	21999
N767A	B767	33685
N767AB	B707	17682
N767AJ	B777	33539
N767AN	B757	23767
N767AN	B767	27476
N767AS	B737	27081
N767AT	B727	22001
N767AT	B767	22694
N767AX	B767	22785
N767BA	B767	22233
N767BE	B767	23057
N767CA	CRJ	7285
N767DA	L1011	193H-1209
N767ER	B767	23178
N767GE	B767	23764
N767JA/501	B767	27385
N767JB/502	B767	27391
N767JC	B767	28016
N767JD	B767	28017
N767KS	B767	28270
N767LJ		
N767MW	B767	22694
N767N	B737	20095
N767NA	B767	27569
N767NC	DC-9	47724
N767PA	B707	18591
N767PW	B767	27351
N767QT	B767	23804
N767RV	1-11	DAC.111
N767RV	B727	20512
N767S	B767	23215
N767SK	CRJ7	10233
N767SW	737NG	29807
N767TA	B767	23494
N767TT	B767	33686
(N767TW)	B707	17679
N767TW	B707	17682
N767TW	B737	20258
N767UA	B777	26918
N767US	B727	22001
N767UW	A319	1382
N767VA	B767	21870
N768AA	B777	33540
N768AS	B737	27082
N768AT	B727	21996
N768AX	B767	22786
N768BC	B737	24166
N768BE	B767	23058
N768DL	L1011	193H-1216
N768N	B737	21815
N768NA	B767	29898
N768NC	DC-9	47729
N768QT	B767	23803
N768SK	CRJ7	10234
N768SW	737NG	30587
N768TA	B767	25535
N768TT	B767	33958
(N768TW)	B707	17680
N768TW	B707	17684

N768UA	**B777**	**26919**	**N773AS**	B737	25106	**N777UA**	**B777**	**26916**	N781WN	737NG	30601
N768US	**A319**	**1389**	N773AT	B727	22004	N777VV	SE210	87	N782AL	B727	21996
N768US	B727	21996	**N773AX**	B767	22788	N777WA	COMET	6443	N782AL	DC-8	45929
N769AS	**B737**	**25103**	N773BE	B727	20877	"N778"	B707	17903	**N782AN**	**B777**	**30003**
N769AT	B727	21998	N773CT	B737	23773	**N778AN**	**B777**	**29587**	**N782AS**	**B737**	**25113**
N769AX	**B767**	**22787**	N773FT	DC-8	45966	**N778AS**	**B737**	**25110**	N782AT	B727	21972
N769BC	B767	23624	N773N	B737	21818	N778AT	B727	22005	N782AU	B737	25021
N769BE	B707	18418	**N773NC**	**DC-9**	**47775**	N778AU	B737	24980	**N782DH**	**B727**	**21998**
N769BE	B757	24118	N773RA	B737	23976	N778BA	B747	22481	N782DL	L1011	193A-1006
N769CA	CRJ	7292	**N773SA**	737NG	27881	N778CA	CRJ	7297	N782FT	DC-8	46002
N769DL	L1011	193H-1218	**N773SK**	CRJ7	10236	N778FT	DC-8	46049	N782JA	MD80	49103
(N769HA)	L1011	193B-1091	N773SR	B737	25773	N778JA	MD80	48080	N782N	B737	22352
N769N	B737	21816	(N773TW)	B707	17685	N778MA	B737	23785	**N782NC**	**DC-9**	**48107**
N769NA	**B767**	**28039**	N773TW	B707	18405	N778N	B737	22018	N782PA	B707	18037
N769NC	**DC-9**	**47757**	**N773UA**	**B777**	**26929**	**N778NC**	**DC-9**	**48100**	**N782SA**	737NG	29808
N769QT	**B767**	**23801**	N773WD	B767	23402	N778PA	B707	17903	N782TW	B707	18401
N769SW	**737NG**	**30588**	N774AL	B727	22984	**N778SK**	CRJ7	10242	**N782UA**	**B777**	**26948**
N769TA	B767	26608	**N774AM**	B737	28689	**N778SW**	737NG	27883	(N782UA)	B777	26951
(N769TW)	B707	17681	**N774AN**	**B777**	**29581**	(N778TW)	B707	17689	N783AL	B727	21998
N769TW	B707	17685	**N774AS**	**B737**	**25107**	N778TW	B707	18409	N783AL	DC-8	45927
N769UA	**B777**	**26921**	N774AT	B737	21510	**N778UA**	**B777**	**26940**	**N783AN**	**B777**	**30004**
N769US	**A319**	**1391**	**N774AX**	B767	22789	N778YY	B737	24970	**N783AS**	**B737**	**25114**
N769US	B727	21998	**N774BC**	MD11	48502	N779AL	B727	23052	N783AT	B727	22000
N770AL	B727	22162	N774BE	B727	20878	**N779AN**	**B777**	**29955**	N783AU	B737	25022
N770AN	**B777**	**29578**	(N774BE)	B747	27828	**N779AS**	**B737**	**25111**	**N783AX**	B767	23016
N770AT	**B727**	**21953**	N774C	DC-8	45634	N779AT	B727	22091	**N783CA**	CRJ	7315
N770BB	**B757**	**25220**	N774CT	B737	23774	N779AU	B737	24996	N783DC	B737	24023
N770BE	B707	18419	N774EC	737NG	32774	N779C	DC-8	45644	**N783DH**	**B727**	**21999**
N770BE	B757	24119	N774FT	DC-8	46087	**N779CA**	CRJ	7306	N783DL	L1011	193A-1009
N770FW	B707	20016	N774N	B737	21975	N779FT	DC-8	45989	N783FT	DC-8	46003
N770JS	B707	19626	**N774NC**	**DC-9**	**47776**	N779JA	MD80	48079	N783JA	MD80	49104
N770NC	**DC-9**	**47758**	**N774SK**	CRJ7	10240	N779MA	B737	23784	N783N	B737	22353
N770PA	B747	19660	**N774SW**	737NG	27882	N779N	B737	22273	**N783NC**	**DC-9**	**48108**
N770PC	B747	25074	(N774TW)	B707	17686	**N779NC**	**DC-9**	**48101**	N783PA	B707	18057
N770PL	**B727**	**22434**	N774TW	B707	18406	N779PA	B707	17904	**N783SW**	737NG	29809
N770QT	**B767**	**23802**	**N774UA**	**B777**	**26936**	**N779SW**	737NG	27884	N783TW	B707	18402
N770SA	**737NG**	**30589**	N774WD	B767	23403	(N779TW)	B707	17690	**N783TW**	**DC-9**	**47010**
(N770SG)	E145	145770	N775AA	B737	23775	N779TW	B707	18764	(N783UA)	**B777**	26937
N770SK	**CRJ7**	**10243**	N775AL	B727	23014	**N779UA**	**B777**	**26941**	**N783UA**	**B777**	**26950**
N770TA	B767	25221	**N775AN**	**B777**	**29584**	N779UP	DC-8	45979	N783UP	DC-8	45973
N770TT	**B767**	**35498**	**N775AS**	**B737**	**25108**	N780AL	B727	21999	**N784AL**	**DC-8**	**46135**
(N770TW)	B707	17682	N775AT	B727	21511	N780AL	DC-8	45928	**N784AN**	**B777**	**29588**
N770TW	B707	17687	N775AU	B737	24933	**N780AN**	**B777**	**29956**	**N784AS**	**B737**	**28199**
N770UA	B777	26925	**N775AX**	B767	22790	**N780AS**	**B737**	**25112**	N784AT	B727	21393
N770UW	**A319**	**1393**	N775BE	B727	20727	N780AT	B727	22295	(N784AU)	B737	25023
N770WD	B767	23306	N775MA	B737	23174	N780AU	B737	24997	**N784AX**	B767	23017
N771AL	B727	22163	N775N	B737	21976	**N780BA**	**B747**	**24310**	**N784CA**	CRJ	7319
N771AN	**B777**	**29579**	**N775NC**	**DC-9**	**47785**	**N780DH**	**B727**	**22006**	N784DA	L1011	193A-1038
N771AS	**B737**	**25104**	**N775SM**	E145	14500971	N780EC	B707	18033	N784DC	B737	24024
N771BE	B707	18793	N775SR	B737	25775	N780EG	MD80	49780	**N784DH**	**B727**	**22001**
N771CA	DC-8	46022	**N775SW**	737NG	30590	N780FT	DC-8	45990	N784FT	DC-8	46004
N771NC	**DC-9**	**47769**	(N775TW)	B707	17687	N780JA	MD80	49126	(N784JA)	MD80	49370
N771PA	B747	19661	N775TW	B707	18407	(N780JS)	B707	19574	N784JA	MD80	49386
N771SA	**737NG**	**27879**	**N775UA**	**B777**	**26947**	"N780KS"	B737	24708	N784MA	B737	23781
N771SK	**CRJ7**	**10244**	N775US	B727	21953	N780MA	B737	23254	N784N	B737	22354
(N771TW)	B707	17683	N776AL	B727	22770	N780N	B737	22274	**N784NC**	**DC-9**	**48109**
N771TW	B707	17688	**N776AN**	**B777**	**29582**	**N780NC**	**DC-9**	**48102**	N784PA	B707	18059
N771UA	**D777**	**26932**	**N776AS**	B737	25109	N780PA	B707	18033	**N784SW**	737NG	29810
N771WD	B767	23309	N776AT	B727	21608	N780SG	E145	145760	N784TW	B707	18403
(N772AB)	B707	17690	N776AU	B737	24934	**N780SW**	737NG	27885	**N784TW**	**DC-9**	**47014**
N772AB	B757	24772	N776BA	B747	22486	N780T	B747	19746	(N784UA)	B777	26948
N772AL	B727	22164	N776CA	CRJ	7293	N780TJ	B737	20197	**N784UA**	**B777**	**26951**
N772AN	**B777**	**29580**	N776FT	DC-8	46112	N780TW	B707	18914	N785AL	DC-8	46149
N772AS	**B737**	**25105**	N776MA	B737	23252	**N780UA**	**B777**	**26944**	**N785AN**	**B777**	**30005**
N772AT	B727	22003	N776N	B737	20414	N781AL	B727	22001	**N785AS**	**B737**	**27628**
N772BC	**737NG**	**29102**	**N776NC**	**DC-9**	**47786**	N781AL	DC-8	45926	**N785AT**	**B727**	**21691**
N772BC	MD80	53231	**N776SK**	CRJ7	10241	**N781AN**	**B777**	**29586**	N785AU	B737	25024
N772BE	B727	20876	(N776TW)	B707	17688	N781AU	B737	25020	N785AW	B737	24933
N772CA	DC-8	46131	N776TW	B707	18408	N781BC	CRJ	7299	**N785AX**	B767	23018
N772FT	DC-8	46109	**N776UA**	**B777**	**26937**	**N781CA**	CRJ	7312	N785BC	CRJ	7283
N772N	B737	21817	**N776WN**	737NG	30591	**N781DH**	**B727**	**21996**	**N785CA**	CRJ	7326
N772NC	**DC-9**	**47774**	**N777AN**	**B777**	**29585**	N781DL	L1011	193A-1003	N785DL	L1011	193A-1121
N772SK	**CRJ7**	**10235**	**N777AS**	**B777**	**29271**	N781FT	DC-8	45991	N785FT	DC-8	46005
N772SW	**737NG**	**27880**	N777AU	B737	24979	N781JA	MD80	49111	(N785JA)	MD80	49371
(N772TW)	B707	17684	(N777EC)	B737	19309	(N781L)	B737	23387	N785JA	MD80	49387
N772TW	B707	17690	N777FB	B707	18711	N781L	B737	23506	N785MA	B737	23783
N772UA	**B777**	**26930**	N777FB	B737	19210	N781N	B737	22275	N785N	B737	22355
N772UP	**DC-8**	**46072**	**N777KY**	B727	21068	**N781NC**	**DC-9**	**48121**	**N785NC**	**DC-9**	**48110**
N772WD	B767	23896	**N777NC**	**DC-9**	**47787**	N781PA	B707	18036	N785PA	B707	18060
N772WH	B737	19772	N777NW	B707	17647	**N781TS**	737NG	28581	**N785SW**	737NG	30602
N773AL	B727	22983	**N777QC**	737NG	30592	N781TW	B707	18400	N785TW	B707	18404
N773AN	**B777**	**29583**	N777SJ	DC-10	46978	**N781UA**	**B777**	**26945**	**N785TW**	**DC-9**	**47015**

N785UA	B777	26954	N790TW	B707	18738	N795N	B737	22756	N800GK	737NG	30751
N786AL	DC-8	46121	N790UA	B777	26943	N795PA	B707	18765	**N800KS**	**737NG**	**30782**
N786AN	**B777**	**30250**	(N790UA)	B777	28713	N795RN	B707	18765	N800MC	1-11	062
N786AS	**B737**	**24795**	(N791AL)	DC-8	45924	**N795SW**	**737NG**	**30606**	N800MC	1-11	078
N786AT	**B727**	**21692**	N791AL	DC-8	46150	N795TW	B707	18384	N800ME	DC-9	45842
N786AW	B737	24786	**N791AN**	**B777**	**30254**	N795TW	B707	18758	N800NA	737NG	28215
N786AX	**B767**	**23019**	**N791AS**	**B737**	**28886**	**N795UA**	**B777**	**26927**	N800NK	MD80	49144
N786BA	737NG	34865	N791AW	B737	24791	(N795UA)	B777	26946	N800NW	CV880	22-00-17
N786BC	CRJ	7329	**N791AX**	**B767**	**23141**	N796AL	DC-8	46054	N800PA	DC-8	45253
N786CA	**CRJ**	**7333**	N791BA	B727	20505	**N796AN**	**B777**	**30796**	N800PW	1-11	078
N786DL	L1011	193A-1123	N791FT	DC-8	46045	**N796AS**	**B737**	**28891**	**N800SK**	**CRJ9**	**15060**
N786FT	DC-8	46006	N791L	B727	21608	**N796AX**	**B767**	**23146**	N800SY	737NG	30627
N786JA	MD80	49426	N791LF	B747	24956	**N796CA**	**CRJ**	**7338**	N800US	MD80	48034
N786N	B737	22443	(N791N)	B737	22751	N796FT	DC-8	46104	N800WA	B737	20255
N786NC	**DC-9**	**48148**	N791N	B737	22752	(N796N)	B737	22756	N800WR	DC-10	46955
N786PA	B707	18248	N791PA	B707	18715	N796N	B737	22757	**N801AE**	**E145**	**145469**
N786PT	DC-10	47865	N791SA	B707	17698	N796PA	B707	18766	N801AJ	CV880	22-00-3
N786SW	**737NG**	**29811**	**N791SW**	**737NG**	**27886**	**N796SW**	**737NG**	**27889**	N801AL	B737	19426
N786TA	737NG	30786	N791TW	B707	18381	N796TW	B707	18759	N801AL	DC-10	46933
N786TW	B707	18711	N791TW	B707	18756	**N796UA**	**B777**	**26931**	N801AM	B757	25624
N786UA	**B777**	**26938**	**N791UA**	**B777**	**26933**	(N796UA)	B777	26953	N801AT	DC-9	47275
(N786UA)	B777	26951	(N791UA)	B777	28714	N797AJ	B727	22609	**N801AW**	**A319**	**0889**
N787AL	**B777**	**30010**	N792A	B727	19195	N797AL	DC-8	46163	N801AX	DC-8	46077
N787AL	DC-8	45999	N792AL	DC-8	46041	**N797AN**	**B777**	**30012**	**N801AY**	**CRJ**	**8001**
N787AW	B737	24787	**N792AN**	**B777**	**30253**	N797AS	B727	19169	N801BN	DC-8	46082
N787AX	**B767**	**23020**	**N792AS**	**B737**	**28887**	**N797AS**	**B737**	**28892**	N801CK	DC-8	45816
N787BA	**B787**	**?**	**N792AX**	**B767**	**23142**	**N797AX**	**B767**	**23147**	**N801DE**	**MD11**	**48472**
N787BC	CRJ	7139	N792BA	B747	23026	N797BA	MD11	48744	**N801DH**	**DC-8**	**46033**
N787CT	DC-9	47707	N792FA	DC-9	47701	N797BB	B737	24020	**N801DM**	**B757**	**26240**
N787DL	L1011	193A-1126	N792FT	DC-8	46046	**N797CA**	**CRJ**	**7344**	N801E	DC-8	45408
N787FT	DC-8	46007	(N792N)	B737	22752	(N797FT)	DC-8	46138	**N801EA**	**B727**	**22432**
N787JA	MD80	49427	N792N	B737	22753	N797FT	DC-8	46140	N801EV	DC-8	45750
N787M	L1011	193L-1064	N792PA	B707	18716	**N797MX**	**737NG**	**27890**	N801FB	DC-8	45965
N787N	B737	22444	N792SA	B707	17701	(N797N)	B737	22757	**N801FD**	**A310**	**539**
N787NC	**DC-9**	**48149**	**N792SW**	**737NG**	**27887**	N797N	B737	22758	**N801FR**	**A318**	**1939**
N787PA	B707	18250	N792TW	B707	18382	**N797PA**	**B707**	**18767**	N801FT	B747	20101
N787RR	**B747**	**21966**	N792TW	B707	18757	N797TW	B707	18760	N801GP	DC-8	46039
N787SA	737NG	29812	**N792UA**	**B777**	**26934**	**N797UA**	**B777**	**26924**	**N801HK**	**E145**	**145053**
N787TM	737NG	30787	(N792UA)	B777	26943	(N797UA)	B777	26927	N801KH	B747	21541
N787TW	B707	18712	**N793A**	**B727**	**20774**	N797UP	DC-8	45897	N801LF	737NG	28210
N787UA	**B777**	**26939**	N793AL	DC-8	46097	N798AL	DC-8	46129	**N801MA**	**E170**	**17000012**
N787WH	**B737**	**22431**	**N793AN**	**B777**	**30255**	(N798AN)	B777	30259	N801MG	DC-8	45986
N788AL	DC-8	45999	**N793AS**	**B737**	**28888**	**N798AN**	**B777**	**30797**	N801MJ	B727	18449
N788AN	**B777**	**30011**	**N793AX**	**B767**	**23143**	N798AS	B727	19170	N801ML	MD80	49724
N788AS	**B727**	**28885**	N793BA	B747	23029	N798AW	B767	23431	N801NK	MD80	48048
N788AT	**B727**	**21958**	N793DG	MD80	49793	**N798AX**	**B767**	**23431**	**N801NW**	**A330**	**524**
N788AX	**B767**	**23021**	**N793DH**	**B727**	**21393**	N798BA	MD11	48745	N801NY	MD80	49127
N788BA	737NG	30476	N793FT	DC-8	46047	N798BB	B737	24022	N801PA	A310	248
N788BR	B727	20710	(N793N)	B737	22753	**N798CA**	**CRJ**	**7348**	N801PA	DC-8	45254
N788DL	L1011	193A-1141	N793N	B737	22754	N798FT	DC-8	46108	**N801PG**	**B767**	**27427**
N700FT	DC 8	46008	N793NA	B707	17700	N798N	B737	22751	N801PH	F.28	11097
N788LS	**B737**	**24220**	N793PA	B707	18717	(N798N)	B737	22758	N801RW	146	E1002
N788N	B737	22445	N793SA	B707	17700	N798PA	B707	18790	N801SW	DC-8	45692
N788PA	B707	18251	N793SA	B707	17700	(N798PA)	B707	18825	**N801SY**	**737NG**	**30332**
N788SA	**737NG**	**30603**	N793TW	B707	18383	**N798SW**	**737NG**	**28436**	**N801TJ**	**B737**	**24892**
N788TW	B707	18713	N793TW	B707	18915	N798TW	B707	18761	N801TW	CV880	22-00-1
N788UA	**B777**	**26942**	(N793UA)	B777	26933	**N798UA**	**B777**	**26928**	N801TW	CV880	22-00-42
N789AL	DC-8	46063	**N793UA**	**B777**	**26946**	(N798UA)	B777	26931	N801U	DC-8	45939
N789AN	**B777**	**30252**	(N793UA)	B777	26947	**N798UP**	**DC-8**	**45898**	**N801UA**	**A319**	**0686**
N789AX	**B767**	**23022**	N794	B707	18718	**N799AL**	**DC-8**	**45922**	**N801UP**	**DC-8**	**46101**
N789BA	B757	23917	N794AJ	B727	21243	**N799AN**	**B777**	**30258**	N801US	DC-8	45602
N789BV	MD80	49789	N794AL	DC-8	45923	(N799AN)	B777	30260	N801US	MD80	48037
N789CF	**1-11**	**BAC.119**	**N794AN**	**B777**	**30256**	**N799AS**	**B737**	**29270**	N801VV	MD80	48046
N789DL	L1011	193A-1142	**N794AS**	**B737**	**28889**	**N799AX**	**B767**	**23432**	N801WA	B737	21763
N789FT	DC-8	45858	**N794AX**	**B767**	**23144**	N799BA	MD11	48769	N801WA	DC-8	46133
N789LS	**B737**	**24269**	N794EP	B707	18718	N799BB	B737	25015	**N802AE**	**E145**	**145471**
N789N	B737	22398	N794FT	DC-8	46086	N799FT	DC-8	46001	N802AJ	CV880	22-00-6
N789SW	**737NG**	**29816**	(N794N)	B737	22754	N799N	B737	22795	(N802AL)	B737	20364
N789TM	B737	23046	N794N	B737	22755	N799PA	B707	18824	N802AL	B737	22148
N789TW	B707	18709	N794PA	B707	18718	(N799PA)	B707	18826	N802AM	B757	26270
N789UA	B777	26935	N794RN	B707	18718	**N799SW**	**737NG**	**28209**	N802AT	DC-9	47177
N790AL	DC-8	46093	**N794SW**	**737NG**	**30605**	N799TW	B707	18762	**N802AW**	**A319**	**0924**
N790AN	**B777**	**30251**	N794TW	B707	20429	**N799UA**	**B777**	**26926**	N802AX	DC-8	46134
N790AX	**B767**	**23140**	(N794UA)	B777	26934	**N800AE**	**E145**	**145425**	N802BN	DC-8	45909
N790CC	B737	23790	**N794UA**	**B777**	**26953**	**N800AK**	**B727**	**20045**	**N802BV**	**A321**	**0802**
N790DL	L1011	193A-1143	N795AL	DC-8	46136	**N800AY**	**CRJ**	**8000**	N802CK	DC-8	45679
N790FA	B707	17697	**N795AN**	**B777**	**30257**	N800CZ	B767	26389	N802DE	MD11	48473
N790FT	DC-8	46044	**N795AS**	**B737**	**28890**	N800DH	F.28	11176	**N802DH**	**DC-8**	**46076**
N790PA	B707	17697	**N795AX**	**B767**	**23145**	N800DM	1-11	079	N802E	DC-8	45409
N790SA	B707	17697	N795BA	737NG	30275	N800DM	DC-9	47466	N802EA	B727	22433
N790SW	**737NG**	**30604**	N795FT	DC-8	46103	N800EV	DC-8	45301	**N802FD**	**A310**	**542**
N790TS	**CRJ**	**7990**	(N795N)	B737	22755	N800FT	B747	20100	**N802FR**	**A318**	**1991**

Reg	Type	S/N	Reg	Type	S/N	Reg	Type	S/N	Reg	Type	S/N
N802FT	B747	20323	N804BR	A319	2296	N806BN	DC-8	45911	N808EA	B727	22439
N802HK	E145	145066	N804CA	CRJ	7352	N806BR	A319	2362	N808FD	A310	439
N802MA	B727	22433	N804CE	D0328	3184	N806CA	CRJ	7359	N808FR	A318	3038
N802MD	E170	17000013	N804CK	DC-8	45689	N806CK	DC-8	45808	N808FT	B747	22245
N802MG	DC-8	46098	N804DE	MD11	48475	N806CK	DC-8	45932	N808GE	B737	21808
N802ML	MD80	49725	N804DH	DC-8	46124	N806DE	MD11	48477	N808HK	E145	145157
N802N	B737	22796	N804DL	A310	345	N806DH	DC-8	46002	N808MA	B727	21988
N802NA	737NG	28587	N804E	DC-8	45411	N806E	DC-8	45413	N808MC	B747	21048
N802NK	MD80	53168	N804EA	B727	22435	N806EA	B727	22437	N808MD	E170	17000021
N802NW	A330	533	N804EV	DC-8	45303	N806FD	A310	458	N808ME	MD80	48070
N802NY	MD80	49222	N804FD	A310	549	N806FR	A318	2218	N808ML	MD80	49780
N802PA	A310	333	N804FR	A318	2051	N806FT	B727	21827	N808NK	MD80	49504
N802PA	DC-8	45255	N804FT	B747	20246	N806HE	B767	23806	N808NW	A330	591
N802PH	F.28	11017	N804HK	E145	145082	N806HK	E145	145112	N808NY	MD80	49262
N802RW	146	E1010	N804MA	B727	22435	N806MA	B727	22437	N808PA	DC-8	45261
N802SC	B727	18802	N804MD	E170	17000016	N806MD	E170	17000019	N808SY	737NG	33021
N802SK	CRJ9	15061	N804ME	MD80	48030	N806ME	MD80	48032	N808TW	CV880	22-00-10
N802SW	DC-8	45818	N804ML	MD80	49727	N806ML	MD80	49778	N808UA	A319	0804
N802SY	737NG	30628	N804MS	B767	27255	N806N	B737	22806	N808UP	DC-8	46008
N802TJ	B737	24874	N804N	B737	22798	N806NK	MD80	48051	(N808US)	DC-8	45630
N802TW	CV880	22-00-2	N804NK	MD80	49104	N806NW	A330	578	N808US	MD80	48040
N802U	DC-8	45950	N804NW	A330	549	N806NY	MD80	49260	N808WC	B737	23808
N802UA	A319	0690	N804NY	MD80	49246	N806PA	A310	342	(N808ZS)	B707	19695
N802UP	DC-8	46100	N804PA	A310	345	N806PA	DC-8	45259	N809AE	E145	145521
N802US	DC-8	45603	N804PA	DC-8	45257	N806SK	CRJ9	15070	N809AJ	CV880	22-00-19
N802US	MD80	48036	N804RA	MD80	48048	N806SW	DC-8	45883	N809AL	B737	21720
N802VV	MD80	48048	N804SK	CRJ9	15067	N806SY	737NG	28215	N809AM	B757	27351
N802WA	DC-8	46146	N804SW	DC-8	45816	(N806SY)	737NG	30629	N809AT	DC-9	47322
N803AE	E145	145483	N804SY	737NG	30689	N806TW	CV880	22-00-8	N809AW	A319	1111
N803AJ	CV880	22-00-8	N804TW	CV880	22-00-5	N806UA	A319	0788	N809BR	A319	2404
N803AL	B737	20206	N804U	DC-8	45938	N806UP	DC-8	46006	N809CA	CRJ	7366
N803AM	B757	26268	N804UA	A319	0759	(N806US)	DC-8	45628	N809CK	DC-8	45803
N803AT	DC-9	47261	N804UP	DC-8	46004	N806US	MD80	48038	N809CK	DC-8	46095
N803AW	A319	0931	N804US	DC-8	45605	N806WA	DC-8	46145	N809DE	MD11	48480
N803AX	DC-8	45917	N804US	MD80	48052	N806YT	B737	20806	N809DH	DC-8	46047
N803BR	A319	2277	N804WA	DC-8	46137	N807AE	E145	145506	N809E	DC-8	45649
N803CK	B707	20315	N805AE	E145	145489	N807AJ	CV880	22-00-13	N809EA	B727	22440
N803CK	DC-8	45610	N805AL	B737	21809	N807AL	B737	23443	N809FD	A310	449
N803CK	DC-8	46085	N805AM	B757	26272	(N807AM)	B767	26261	N809FR	A318	3092
N803DE	MD11	48474	N805AT	DC-9	47378	N807AN	B767	23807	N809FT	B747	19733
N803DH	DC-8	46123	N805AW	A319	1049	N807AT	DC-9	47444	N809FT	B747	21650
N803E	DC-8	45410	N805AX	DC-8	45906	N807AW	A319	1064	N809FT	B747	21827
N803EA	B727	22434	N805AY	CRJ	8005	N807AX	DC-8	45953	(N809FT)	B747	22237
N803FD	A310	378	N805AZ	DC-10	47855	N807BR	A319	2383	N809HA	MD80	48044
N803FR	A318	2017	N805BR	A319	2335	N807CA	CRJ	7364	N809HK	E145	145187
N803FT	B747	19897	N805CA	CRJ	7354	N807CK	DC-8	45767	N809M	1-11	BAC.126
N803HE	B767	23803	N805CK	DC-8	45649	N807DE	MD11	48478	N809MC	B747	20887
N803HK	E145	145077	N805DE	MD11	48476	N807DH	DC-8	45990	N809MD	E170	17000022
N803MA	B727	22434	N805DH	DC-8	46125	N807E	DC-8	45645	N809ME	MD80	48071
N803MD	E170	17000015	N805E	DC-8	45412	N807EA	B727	22438	N809ML	MD80	49931
N803ME	MD80	48029	N805EA	B727	22436	N807FD	A310	492	N809N	B737	22867
N803MG	DC-8	45910	N805FD	A310	456	N807FR	A318	2276	N809NK	MD80	49503
N803ML	MD80	49726	N805FR	A318	1660	N807FT	B747	21828	N809NW	A330	663
N803N	B737	22797	N805FT	B747	20247	"N807FV"	MD80	49777	N809NY	MD80	49263
N803NK	MD80	48087	N805HE	B767	23805	N807HK	E145	145119	N809PA	DC-8	45262
N803NW	A330	542	N805HK	E145	145096	N807MD	E170	17000020	N809SC	E145	14500809
N803NY	MD80	49229	N805MD	E170	17000018	N807ME	MD80	48033	N809SK	CRJ9	15086
N803PA	A310	343	N805ME	MD80	48031	N807ML	MD80	49779	N809SY	737NG	30683
N803PA	DC-8	45256	N805ML	MD80	49777	N807N	B737	22799	N809TD	E145	14500809
N803PH	F.28	11031	N805N	B737	22799	N807NK	MD80	49777	N809TW	CV880	22-00-12
N803SC	B727	19534	N805NK	MD80	48058	N807NW	A330	588	N809UA	A319	0825
N803SK	CRJ9	15062	N805NW	A330	552	N807NY	MD80	49261	N809UP	DC-8	46109
N803SR	B737	22803	N805NY	MD80	49249	N807PA	A310	346	(N809US)	DC-8	45631
N803SW	DC-8	45821	N805PA	A310	339	N807PA	DC-8	45260	N809US	MD80	48041
N803SY	737NG	28241	N805PA	DC-8	45258	N807SK	CRJ9	15082	N810AE	E145	145525
N803TW	CV880	22-00-3	N805RA	MD80	48087	(N807SY)	737NG	30642	N810AJ	CV880	22-00-20
N803U	DC-8	45900	N805SK	CRJ9	15069	N807SY	737NG	33016	N810AL	B737	24031
N803UA	A319	0748	N805SW	DC-8	45817	N807TW	CV880	22-00-9	N810AT	146	E2062
N803UP	DC-8	46073	N805SY	737NG	30032	N807UA	A319	0798	N810AT	DC-9	47277
N803US	DC-8	45604	N805TW	CV880	22-00-6	N807UP	DC-8	46007	N810AW	A319	1116
N803US	MD80	48035	N805U	DC-8	45817	(N807US)	DC-8	45629	N810AX	DC-10	48265
N803VV	MD80	48087	N805UA	A319	0783	N807US	MD80	48039	N810BN	DC-8	45905
N803WA	DC-8	46149	N805UP	DC-8	46117	N808AE	E145	145519	N810BR	A319	2414
N804AE	E145	145487	N805US	CV880	22-00-15	N808AJ	CV880	22-00-15	N810CA	CRJ	7370
N804AJ	B727	21021	N805US	MD80	48053	N808AL	B737	23445	N810CK	DC-8	45814
N804AJ	CV880	22-00-10	N805WA	DC-8	46143	N808AM	B767	26262	N810DE	MD11	48565
N804AL	B737	21719	N806AE	E145	145503	N808AW	A319	1088	N810E	DC-8	45650
N804AM	B757	26271	N806AJ	CV880	22-00-12	N808AX	DC-8	45954	N810EA	B727	22441
N804AW	A319	1043	N806AL	B737	21927	N808BR	A319	2396	N810EV	DC-8	45902
N804AX	DC-8	45987	N806AM	B757	26273	N808CK	DC-8	45817	N810FD	A310	452
N804AZ	DC-10	47823	N806AT	DC-9	47379	N808DE	MD11	48479	N810FR	A318	3110
			N806AW	A319	1056	N808E	DC-8	45646	N810FT	B747	22237

Reg	Type	c/n	Reg	Type	c/n	Reg	Type	c/n	Reg	Type	c/n
N810GB	DC-8	45878	N812PA	A310	442	N815E	DC-8	45689	N818EA	B727	22555
N810HK	E145	145231	N812PA	DC-8	45265	N815EA	B727	22552	N818EV	DC-8	46113
N810MD	E170	17000026	N812SK	CRJ9	15098	N815EV	DC-8	46002	N818FD	A310	654
N810ME	MD80	48072	N812TC	DC-8	45764	N815FD	A310	638	N818FT	B747	20353
N810ML	MD80	49932	N812TW	CV880	22-00-15	N815FT	B747	22150	N818HK	E145	145059
N810N	B737	22868	N812UA	A319	0850	N815HK	E145	145048	N818MD	E170	17000039
N810NA	CV990	30-10-29	N812UP	DC-8	46112	N815MD	E170	17000034	N818NK	MD80	48018
N810NK	MD80	48015	N812US	MD80	48092	(N815ML)	MD80	53066	N818NW	A330	857
N810NW	A330	674	N812ZA	DC-8	46028	N815NK	MD80	49415	N818NY	MD80	49478
N810NY	MD80	49264	N813AE	E145	145539	N815NW	A330	817	N818PA	A310	455
N810PA	DC-8	45263	N813AJ	CV880	22-00-24	N815NY	MD80	49113	N818PA	DC-8	45271
N810SK	CRJ9	15093	N813AT	DC-9	47318	N815PA	A310	451	N818SJ	MD80	48058
N810SY	737NG	29635	N813AW	A319	1223	N815PA	DC-8	45268	N818TW	CV880	22-00-24
N810TW	CV880	22-00-13	N813AX	DC-8	46136	N815PG	737NG	32406	N818UA	A319	0882
N810U	B747	20208	N813AY	CRJ	8013	N815SK	CRJ9	15101	N818UP	DC-8	46108
N810UA	A319	0843	N813BN	DC-8	45642	N815TW	CV880	22-00-20	N818US	MD80	48098
N810UP	DC-8	46001	N813CK	DC-8	45893	N815UA	A319	0867	N819AE	E145	145566
(N810US)	DC-8	45632	N813DE	MD11	48600	N815UP	DC-8	46002	N819AJ	CV880	22-00-36
N810US	MD80	48042	N813E	DC-8	45688	N815US	MD80	48095	N819AL	B737	23791
N810ZA	DC-8	46162	N813EA	B727	22550	N815ZA	DC-8	46024	N819AT	DC-9	47260
N811AD	B757	22197	N813FD	A310	500	N816AE	E145	145552	N819AW	A319	1395
N811AE	E145	145529	N813FT	B747	21764	N816AJ	CV880	22-00-40	N819AX	DC-8	45927
N811AJ	CV880	22-00-22	N813HK	E145	145044	N816AL	B737	23122	N819AY	CRJ	8019
N811AL	DC-8	46099	N813MA	E170	17000031	N816AS	146	E2087	N819CA	CRJ	7415
N811AN	B737	23811	N813ME	MD80	48007	N816AT	DC-9	47445	(N819CK)	DC-8	46098
N811AT	DC-9	47285	N813N	B737	22961	N816AW	A319	1350	N819E	DC-8	45806
N811AX	DC-8	46113	N813NW	A330	799	N816AX	DC-8	46093	N819EA	B727	22556
N811BN	DC-8	45634	N813NY	MD80	48066	N816CA	CRJ	7398	N819EV	DC-8	46126
N811BR	A319	2431	N813PA	A310	449	N816CK	DC-8	45892	N819F	DC-8	45437
N811CA	CRJ	7380	N813PA	DC-8	45266	N816E	DC-8	45690	N819FD	A310	669
N811CK	DC-8	46147	N813SK	CRJ9	15099	N816EA	B727	22553	N819FT	B747	19661
N811DE	MD11	48566	N813TL	MD80	45732	N816EV	DC-8	45990	N819HK	E145	145062
N811E	DC-8	45672	N813TW	CV880	22-00-18	N816FD	A310	593	N819MD	E170	17000040
N811EA	B727	22548	N813UA	A319	0858	N816FT	B747	22151	N819NK	MD80	48016
N811EV	DC-8	46051	N813UP	DC-8	46059	N816HK	E145	145055	N819NW	A330	858
N811FD	A310	457	N813US	MD80	48093	N816MA	E170	17000037	N819NY	MD80	49479
N811FT	B747	20826	N813ZA	DC-8	46139	N816NK	MD80	49140	N819PA	A310	456
N811GB	DC-8	46154	N814AE	E145	145552	N816NW	A330	827	N819PA	DC-8	45272
N811HK	E145	145256	N814AJ	CV880	22-00-32	N816NY	MD80	49370	N819SL	DC-8	45854
N811LF	A320	0579	N814AS	146	E2080	N816PA	A310	452	N819TW	CV880	22-00-25
N811MD	E170	17000028	N814AW	A319	1281	N816PA	DC-8	45269	N819UA	A319	0893
N811ML	MD80	49889	N814AX	DC-8	46041	N816PG	B757	24714	N819UP	DC-8	46019
N811N	B737	22869	N814BN	DC-8	45644	N816SK	CRJ9	15105	N819US	MD80	48099
N811NK	MD80	48017	N814BR	A319	2467	N816TW	CV880	22-00-22	N820AE	E145	145576
N811NW	A330	690	N814CA	CRJ	7387	N816UA	A319	0871	N820AJ	CV880	22-00-39
N811NY	MD80	49265	(N814CK)	DC-8	45986	N816UP	DC-8	45990	N820AL	B737	22138
N811PA	A310	439	N814CK	DC-8	46127	N816US	MD80	48096	N820AS	CRJ	7188
N811PA	DC-8	45264	N814DE	MD11	48623	N816ZA	DC-8	46068	N820AT	A320	0028
N811SL	DC-10	46921	N814E	DC-8	45687	N817AE	E145	145554	N820AW	A319	1397
N811SY	737NG	29660	N814EA	B727	22551	N817AJ	CV880	22-00-4	N820AX	DC-8	46155
N811TC	DC-8	45883	N814FD	A310	534	N817AL	B737	23292	N820AY	CRJ	8020
N811TW	CV880	22-00-14	N814FT	B747	21841	N817AT	DC-9	47323	N820BX	DC-8	46065
N811UA	A319	0847	N814GB	DC-8	45913	N817AW	A319	1373	N820E	DC-8	45815
N811UP	DC-8	46089	N814HK	E145	145046	N817AX	DC-8	45928	N820EA	B727	22557
N811US	MD80	48043	N814MD	E170	17000033	N817CK	DC-8	45887	N820F	DC-8	45435
N811UT	B707	17692	N814ME	MD80	48010	N817E	DC-8	45807	N820FT	B747	20391
N811ZA	DC-8	46154	(N814ML)	MD80	53065	N817EA	B727	22554	N820HK	E145	145064
N812AE	E145	145531	N814N	B737	22962	N817EV	DC-8	46022	N820MD	E170	17000041
N812AJ	CV880	22-00-23	N814NK	MD80	49619	N817FD	A310	552	N820NK	MD80	49126
N812AR	B737	23655	N814NW	A330	806	N817FT	B747	20349	N820NW	A330	859
N812AS	146	E2074	N814NY	MD80	49112	N817HK	E145	145058	N820NY	MD80	49480
N812AW	A319	1178	N814PA	A310	450	N817MD	E170	17000038	N820PA	A310	457
N812AX	DC-8	46126	N814PA	DC-8	45267	N817NA	DC-8	46082	N820PA	DC-8	45273
N812AY	CRJ	8012	N814PG	MD80	49848	N817NK	MD80	49141	N820SC	A300	154
N812BN	DC-8	45635	N814RW	DC-9	47011	N817NW	A330	843	N820SK	CRJ9	15108
N812BR	A319	2452	(N814SD)	L1011	193A-1006	N817NY	MD80	49371	N820TC	DC-8	45999
N812CA	CRJ	7381	N814SK	CRJ9	15100	N817PA	A310	453	N820TW	CV880	22-00-26
N812CK	DC-8	45890	N814TW	CV880	22-00-19	N817PA	DC-8	45270	N820UA	A319	0898
N812DE	MD11	48624	N814UA	A319	0862	N817SJ	MD80	48051	N820US	MD80	49119
N812E	DC-8	45673	N814US	MD80	48094	N817SK	CRJ9	15107	N821AE	E145	145577
N812EA	B727	22549	N814ZA	DC-8	45956	N817TW	CV880	22-00-23	N821AJ	B737	23155
N812FD	A310	467	N815AE	E145	145545	N817UA	A319	0873	N821AS	CRJ	7194
N812FR	A318	3163	N815AJ	CV880	22-00-35	N817US	MD80	48097	N821AT	DC-9	47284
N812FT	B747	20827	N815AS	146	E2084	N818AE	E145	145561	N821AW	A319	1406
N812HK	E145	145373	N815AT	DC-9	47443	N818AJ	CV880	22-00-9	N821AX	DC-8	46116
N812MD	E170	17000030	N815AW	A319	1323	N818AL	B737	22117	N821AY	CRJ	8021
N812ME	MD80	48006	N815AX	DC-8	46097	N818AT	DC-9	47320	N821BX	DC-8	45811
N812ML	MD80	53017	N815BR	A319	2468	N818AW	A319	1375	N821CA	CRJ	7420
(N812ML)	MD80	53064	N815CA	CRJ	7397	N818AX	DC-8	46075	N821CC	DC-10	46554
N812NK	MD80	48021	N815CK	DC-8	46151	N818CA	CRJ	7408	N821E	DC-8	45877
N812NW	A330	784	N815DE	MD11	48624	N818CK	DC-8	45961	N821EA	B727	22558
N812NY	MD80	49250				N818E	DC-8	45808			

Reg	Type	Ser	Reg	Type	Ser	Reg	Type	Ser	Reg	Type	Ser
N821F	DC-8	45433	**N825AW**	**A319**	**1527**	N829NK	MD80	49931	N833NK	MD80	49449
N821HK	**E145**	**145068**	N825AX	DC-8	46115	**N829RN**	**E145**	**145361**	N833PC	B737	19308
N821JT	MD80	48091	**N825AY**	**CRJ**	**8025**	N829SC	A300	074	N833RA	MD80	53045
N821L	B737	21687	**N825BX**	**DC-8**	**45978**	(N829TW)	CV880	22-00-39	**N833RP**	**E145**	**145687**
N821L	DC-10	47848	N825E	DC-8	45944	**N829UA**	**A319**	**1211**	N833TW	B727	18903
N821LF	B747	24957	**N825HK**	**E145**	**145510**	N829US	MD80	49429	**N833UA**	**A319**	**1401**
N821MD	**E170**	**17000042**	**N825MH**	**B767**	**29703**	**N830AE**	**E145**	**145615**	N834AC	B737	19309
N821NK	MD80	49508	**N825MJ**	**E145**	**145179**	**N830AS**	**CRJ**	**7236**	**N834AE**	**E145**	**145631**
N821NW	**A330**	**865**	N825NK	MD80	53012	N830AT	DC-9	47723	**N834AL**	**B737**	**20917**
N821PA	A310	458	(N825PA)	A310	574	**N830AW**	**A319**	**1565**	**N834AS**	**CRJ**	**7254**
N821RA	MD80	49931	**N825SC**	**A300**	**129**	**N830AY**	**CRJ**	**8030**	N834AT	DC-9	47488
N821SC	**A300**	**211**	N825SG	E145	14500825	**N830BX**	**DC-8**	**45973**	N834AU	MD80	53165
N821SK	**CRJ9**	**15109**	N825TW	CV880	22-00-32	N830DS	B747	24106	**N834AW**	**A319**	**2302**
N821TC	DC-8	46127	**N825UA**	**A319**	**0980**	N830FT	B747	19642	**N834AY**	**CRJ**	**8034**
N821TW	CV880	22-00-27	N825US	MD80	49237	**N830HK**	**E145**	**145313**	N834BE	146	E1225
N821UA	**A319**	**0944**	N825VV	DC-10	47825	**N830MH**	**B767**	**29701**	N834F	MD80	48004
N821US	MD80	49138	**N826AE**	**E145**	**145592**	**N830MJ**	**E145**	**145259**	**N834HK**	**E145**	**145269**
N822AE	**E145**	**145581**	**N826AL**	**B737**	**23051**	N830NK	MD80	49943	N834LA	DC-10	46946
N822AL	B747	20402	**N826AS**	**CRJ**	**7210**	N830TW	CV880	22-00-40	**N834MH**	**B767**	**29707**
N822AN	MD80	49822	N826AT	DC-9	47359	**N830UA**	**A319**	**1243**	**N834MJ**	**E145**	**145340**
N822AW	**A319**	**1410**	**N826AW**	**A319**	**1534**	N830US	MD80	49443	N834N	B727	18858
N822AX	DC-8	46079	**N826AX**	**DC-8**	**46061**	N830VV	MD80	49397	N834NK	MD80	49847
N822BX	**DC-8**	**45813**	**N826AY**	**CRJ**	**8026**	N830WA	B727	21482	N834RA	MD80	53124
N822DE	L1011	193A-1152	N826BG	B737	27826	**N831AE**	**E145**	**145616**	**N834RP**	**E145**	**145696**
N822E	DC-8	45907	N826BX	DC-8	45998	N831AL	DC-8	46149	**N834UA**	**A319**	**1420**
N822EA	B727	22559	N826CR	L1011	193A-1141	N831AT	DC-9	47674	N834VX	A320	1834
N822FT	B747	19733	N826E	DC-8	45979	**N831AW**	**A319**	**1576**	N835A	B737	23835
N822HK	**E145**	**145069**	N826GR	L1011	193A-1141	**N831AY**	**CRJ**	**8031**	N835AB	A310	650
N822MD	**E170**	**17000043**	**N826HK**	**E145**	**145016**	N831F	DC-8	45606	**N835AE**	**E145**	**145634**
N822ME	**MD80**	**49759**	**N826MD**	**E170**	**17000046**	N831FT	B747	19648	**N835AL**	**B737**	**21613**
N822NK	MD80	49392	**N826MH**	**B767**	**29713**	**N831HK**	**E145**	**145232**	**N835AS**	**CRJ**	**7258**
N822PA	A310	467	**N826MJ**	**E145**	**145214**	N831L	B727	21826	N835AT	DC-9	47534
N822RA	MD80	49932	N826NK	MD80	49391	**N831LA**	**DC-10**	**46936**	N835AU	MD80	53166
N822TW	CV880	22-00-28	(N826PA)	A310	576	N831LF	MD80	53050	**N835AW**	**A319**	**2458**
N822UA	**A319**	**0948**	N826SC	A300	100	**N831MH**	**B767**	**29702**	**N835AY**	**CRJ**	**8035**
N822US	MD80	49139	N826TW	CV880	22-00-33	N831MJ	E145	145273	**N835BA**	**737NG**	**30572**
N822V	DC-10	47822	**N826UA**	**A319**	**0989**	N831NK	MD80	49617	(N835BE)	146	E1230
N823AE	**E145**	**145582**	N826US	MD80	48026	N831PC	B737	19306	N835F	MD80	48005
N823AL	**B737**	**23154**	N826VV	DC-10	47826	**N831RP**	**E145**	**145663**	**N835HK**	**E145**	**145670**
N823AS	**CRJ**	**7196**	**N827AE**	**E145**	**145602**	N831RV	B727	19093	**N835MH**	**B767**	**29708**
N823AT	DC-9	47529	N827AL	B737	23913	N831TW	B727	18902	**N835MJ**	**E145**	**145353**
N823AW	**A319**	**1463**	**N827AS**	**CRJ**	**7212**	**N831UA**	**A319**	**1291**	(N835N)	B727	19252
N823AX	DC-8	46122	N827AT	DC-9	47486	N831US	MD80	53162	N835NK	MD80	53044
N823AY	**CRJ**	**8023**	**N827AW**	**A319**	**1547**	N831WA	B727	21483	(N835PC)	B737	19713
N823BX	**DC-8**	**46064**	N827AX	DC-8	45901	**N832AE**	**E145**	**145627**	**N835RP**	**E145**	**145702**
N823E	DC-8	45914	**N827AY**	**CRJ**	**8027**	N832AL	DC-8	46063	**N835UA**	**A319**	**1426**
N823HK	**E145**	**145475**	N827BX	DC-8	45971	**N832AS**	**CRJ**	**7243**	N836AB	A310	660
N823MD	**E170**	**17000044**	**N827HK**	**E145**	**145021**	N832AT	DC-9	47451	(N836AB)	A310	676
N823ME	MD80	49766	**N827MD**	**E170**	**17000047**	N832AU	MD80	53163	**N836AE**	**E145**	**145635**
N823NK	MD80	48020	**N827MH**	**B767**	**29705**	**N832AW**	**A319**	**1643**	**N836AL**	**B737**	**23225**
N823NS	MD80	49823	**N827MJ**	**E145**	**145217**	**N832AY**	**CRJ**	**8032**	**N836AS**	**CRJ**	**7263**
N823PA	A310	539	N827NK	MD80	49793	N832BE	146	E1223	N836AT	DC-9	47397
N823RA	MD80	49889	N827SC	A300	183	N832F	MD80	48002	N836AU	MD80	53167
N823SC	A300	207	N827TW	CV880	22-00-34	N832FT	B747	20347	**N836AW**	**A319**	**2570**
N823TW	CV880	22-00-30	**N827UA**	**A319**	**1022**	**N832HK**	**E145**	**145771**	**N836AY**	**CRJ**	**8036**
N823UA	**A319**	**0952**	N827US	MD80	48049	N832LA	DC-10	46931	**N836BA**	**737NG**	**30756**
N823US	MD80	49142	**N828AE**	**E145**	**145604**	N832MH	B767	29704	(N836BE)	146	E1249
N824AE	**E145**	**145584**	**N828AL**	**B737**	**23168**	N832MJ	E145	145310	N836EV	DC-8	46051
N824AL	**B737**	**23045**	**N828AS**	**CRJ**	**7213**	N832NK	MD80	49618	**N836HK**	**E145**	**145695**
N824AS	**CRJ**	**7203**	N828AT	DC-9	47274	N832PC	B737	19307	**N836MH**	**B767**	**29709**
N824AT	DC-9	47278	**N828AW**	**A319**	**1552**	N832RA	MD80	53044	**N836MJ**	**E145**	**145359**
N824AW	**A319**	**1490**	**N828AX**	**DC-8**	**45999**	**N832RP**	**E145**	**145676**	N836N	B727	18850
N824AX	DC-8	46141	**N828BX**	**DC-8**	**45993**	N832RV	B727	19098	N836NK	MD80	53045
N824AY	**CRJ**	**8024**	**N828MD**	**E170**	**17000048**	(N832SG)	E145	14500832	(N836PC)	B737	19714
N824BX	DC-8	45946	**N828MH**	**B767**	**29699**	**N832UA**	**A319**	**1321**	**N836RA**	**MD80**	**53046**
N824DS	B747	24107	**N828MJ**	**E145**	**145218**	N833AA	DC-10	47833	**N836RP**	**E145**	**145713**
N824E	DC-8	45915	N828NK	MD80	49823	**N833AE**	**E145**	**145629**	**N836UA**	**A319**	**1460**
N824HK	**E145**	**145498**	N828SC	A300	078	**N833AS**	**CRJ**	**7246**	N836UP	DC-8	45936
N824MD	**E170**	**17000045**	"N828SC"	A300	100	N833AT	DC-9	47489	(N836Y)	B737	21980
N824NK	MD80	53015	N828TW	CV880	22-00-35	N833AU	MD80	53164	N836Y	B737	23836
N824PA	A310	542	**N828UA**	**A319**	**1031**	**N833AW**	**A319**	**1844**	N837AB	A310	674
N824RA	MD80	53017	N828US	MD80	48028	**N833AY**	**CRJ**	**8033**	(N837AB)	A310	676
N824SC	A300	271	**N829AE**	**E145**	**145609**	N833BE	146	E1224	**N837AE**	**E145**	**145647**
N824TW	CV880	22-00-31	**N829AS**	**CRJ**	**7232**	N833DA	DC-8	45380	**N837AL**	**B737**	**23169**
N824UA	**A319**	**0965**	**N829AW**	**A319**	**1563**	N833FA	DC-8	45378	**N837AS**	**CRJ**	**7271**
N824US	MD80	49143	**N829AY**	**CRJ**	**8029**	**N833HK**	**E145**	**145240**	N837AT	DC-9	45774
N824VV	DC-10	47824	**N829BX**	**DC-8**	**45994**	**N833LA**	**DC-10**	**46937**	N837AT	DC-9	47442
N825AC	1-11	065	N829HA	MD80	48051	**N833MH**	**B767**	**29706**	N837AU	MD80	53168
N825AE	**E145**	**145589**	**N829HK**	**E145**	**145281**	**N833MJ**	**E145**	**145327**	**N837AW**	**A319**	**2595**
N825AQ	1-11	065	**N829MD**	**E170**	**17000049**	N833N	B727	18935	(N837BE)	146	E1252
N825AS	**CRJ**	**7207**	**N829MH**	**B767**	**29700**	N833NA	B707	18066	**N837HK**	**E145**	**145255**
N825AT	DC-9	47319	**N829MJ**	**E145**	**145228**				**N837MH**	**B767**	**29710**

Reg	Type	Serial	Reg	Type	Serial	Reg	Type	Serial	Reg	Type	Serial
N837MJ	E145	145367	N843AA	B727	20984	N849TW	B727	18750	N854SY	B727	20791
N837N	B727	18802	N843AB	A310	689	N849UA	A319	1649	N854TW	B727	18573
N837RP	E145	145715	N843AE	E145	145680	N850AA	B727	20991	N854UA	A319	1731
N837UA	A319	1474	N843AS	CRJ	7310	N850AE	E145	145722	N854US	F.100	11282
N837Y	B737	23837	N843AX	DC-8	46017	N850AM	737NG	33786	N854WT	B737	26850
N838AB	A310	676	N843BB	B737	25843	N850AS	CRJ	7355	N855AA	B727	20996
N838AE	E145	145651	N843HK	E145	14500822	N850AX	DC-8	45894	N855AE	E145	145747
N838AM	MD80	49397	N843MH	B767	29716	N850BB	B737	25850	N855AM	737NG	33792
N838AS	CRJ	7276	N843MJ	E145	145478	N850FJ	CRJ	7448	N855AS	CRJ	7395
N838AU	MD80	53169	N843RA	MD80	49615	N850FT	B747	19755	N855BC	DC-8	45804
N838AW	A319	2615	N843RP	E145	145599	N850HK	E145	145003	N855FT	B747	19733
N838HK	E145	145321	N843TC	B767	24843	N850MJ	E145	145568	N855MJ	E145	145614
N838MH	B767	29711	N843UA	A319	1573	N850RJ	CRJ	8055	N855N	B727	20163
N838MJ	E145	145384	N844AA	B727	20985	N850SY	B727	21114	N855NW	A330	621
N838N	B727	18803	N844AE	E145	145682	N850TS	CRJ	8056	N855RW	E170	17000077
N838RP	E145	145720	N844AS	CRJ	7317	N850TW	B727	18569	N855TW	B727	18574
N838UA	A319	1477	N844AX	DC-8	45848	N850UA	A319	1653	N855UA	A319	1737
N839AD	A310	678	N844HK	E145	14500838	N850US	F.100	11276	N855US	F.100	11283
N839AE	E145	145653	N844MH	B767	29717	N851AA	B727	20992	N856AA	B727	20997
N839AS	CRJ	7284	N844MJ	E145	145481	N851AE	E145	145734	N856AE	E145	145748
N839AT	DC-9	47089	N844RA	MD80	49423	N851AL	B727	21851	N856AS	CRJ	7404
N839AU	MD80	53170	N844RP	E145	145620	N851AM	737NG	29363	N856FT	B747	19897
N839AV	DC-9	45839	N844TW	B727	18755	N851AS	CRJ	7360	N856MJ	E145	145626
N839AW	A319	2669	N844UA	A319	1581	N851AX	DC-8	45940	N856N	B727	20164
N839AY	CRJ	8039	N845AA	B727	20986	N851F	DC-8	45824	N856NW	A330	631
N839HA	MD80	48058	N845AE	E145	145685	N851FJ	CRJ	7462	N856RW	E170	17000078
N839HK	E145	14500829	N845AS	CRJ	7324	N851FT	B747	19756	N856TW	B727	18575
N839MH	B767	29712	N845AT	DC-9	47238	N851JB	B707	20084	N856US	F.100	11286
N839MJ	E145	145416	N845AX	DC-8	46157	N851L	B737	22657	N856V	DC-10	47856
N839RP	E145	145724	N845CP	MD80	49845	N851LF	B737	23788	N857AA	B727	21084
N839TW	B727	18904	N845HK	E145	14500842	N851MA	B707	19212	N857AE	E145	145752
N839UA	A319	1507	N845MH	B767	29719	N851MA	B707	19411	N857AM	737NG	33793
N840AB	A310	682	N845MJ	E145	145502	N851MA	L1011	193A-1158	N857AS	CRJ	7411
N840AE	E145	145656	N845RA	MD80	49380	N851MJ	E145	145572	N857FT	B747	20246
N840AL	B737	23124	N845RP	E145	145551	N851NW	A330	609	N857MJ	E145	145765
N840AS	CRJ	7290	N845TW	B727	18754	N851SY	B727	20792	N857N	B727	20165
N840AT	DC-9	47523	N845UA	A319	1585	N851TW	B727	18570	N857NW	A330	633
N840AU	MD80	53171	N846AA	B727	20987	N851UA	A319	1664	N857RW	E170	17000079
N840AW	A319	2690	N846AE	E145	145692	N851UP	DC-8	46051	N857TW	B727	18576
N840AY	CRJ	8040	N846AG	737NG	36846	N851US	F.100	11278	N857US	F.100	11289
N840HK	E145	145341	N846AS	CRJ	7328	N852AA	B727	20993	N857V	DC-10	47857
N840MH	B767	29718	N846AT	DC-9	47226	N852AE	E145	145736	N858AA	B727	21085
N840MJ	E145	145429	N846AX	DC-8	46158	N852AK	737NG	34620	N858AE	E145	145754
N840OMT	B767	30840	N846HK	E145	14500855	N852AM	737NG	33787	N858AS	CRJ	7417
N840RA	MD80	49424	N846MJ	E145	145507	N852AS	CRJ	7369	N858FT	B747	20109
N840RP	E145	145725	N846PR	CRJ	7846	N852AX	DC-8	46016	N858MJ	E145	145767
N840TW	B727	18905	N846RP	E145	145600	N852CT	B737	26852	N858N	B727	20161
N840UA	A319	1522	N846TW	B727	18753	N852F	DC-8	45856	N858NW	A330	718
N840UP	DC-8	46140	N846UA	A319	1600	N852FJ	CRJ	7467	N858RW	E170	17000080
N841AB	A310	686	N847AA	B727	20988	N852FT	B747	19757	N858TW	B727	18577
N841AF	E145	145667	N847AE	E145	145707	N852MJ	E145	145567	N858US	F.100	11291
N841AL	B737	23123	N847AG	737NG	36847	N852NW	A330	614	N858V	DC-10	40301
N841AS	CRJ	7300	N847AS	CRJ	7335	N852SY	B727	20790	N859AA	B727	21086
N841AX	DC-8	45908	N847AT	DC-9	47555	N852TW	B727	18571	N859AS	CRJ	7421
N841AY	CRJ	8041	N847AX	DC-8	46031	N852UA	A319	1671	N859CT	B737	24859
N841HK	E145	145382	N847HK	E145	14500857	N852UP	DC-8	46052	N859FT	B747	20326
N841L	B737	19955	N847MJ	E145	145517	N852US	F.100	11280	N859HA	MD80	48074
N841L	B737	23255	N847RP	E145	145608	N852V	DC-10	47852	N859MJ	E145	145769
N841LF	B737	23811	N847SF	B767	30847	N853AA	B727	20994	N859N	B727	20366
N841LF	B737	24988	N847TA	B737	19847	N853AE	E145	145742	N859NW	A330	722
(N841LF)	B737	26301	N847TW	B727	18752	N853AM	737NG	33791	N859RW	E170	17000082
N841MH	B767	29714	N847UA	A319	1627	N853AS	CRJ	7374	N859TW	B727	18578
N841MJ	E145	145448	N848AA	B727	20989	N853AX	DC-8	46037	N859US	F.100	11293
N841MM	B727	18368	N848AE	E145	145710	N853CH	A310	378	N860AA	B727	21087
N841N	B727	18324	N848AS	CRJ	7339	N853FJ	CRJ	7470	N860AS	CRJ	7433
N841RA	MD80	49421	N848AT	DC-9	47559	N853FT	B747	19753	N860AT	B727	22981
N841RP	E145	145737	N848AX	DC-8	46032	N853MJ	E145	145464	(N860AT)	DC-9	47067
N841TW	B727	18906	N848CP	MD80	49848	N853NW	A330	618	N860DA	B777	29951
N841UA	A319	1545	N848MJ	E145	145530	N853SY	B727	21113	N860FT	DC-8	45938
N842AB	A310	687	N848TW	B727	18751	N853TW	B727	18572	N860GA	MD80	49786
N842AE	E145	145673	N848UA	A319	1647	N853UA	A319	1688	N860MJ	E145	145773
N842AM	737NG	32842	N849AA	B727	20990	N853US	F.100	11281	N860N	B727	20166
N842AS	CRJ	7304	N849AE	E145	145716	N853VV	DC-10	47853	N860NW	A330	778
N842AX	DC-8	46015	N849AL	DC-8	45849	N854AA	B727	20995	N860PA	A300	220
N842HK	E145	14500830	N849AS	CRJ	7347	N854AE	E145	145743	N860RW	E170	17000084
(N842L)	B737	19940	N849AT	DC-9	47484	(N854AM)	737NG	28262	N860SY	B727	20905
N842MH	B767	29715	N849AX	DC-8	45891	N854AS	CRJ	7382	N860US	F.100	11295
N842MJ	E145	145457	N849AX	DC-8	45981	N854FT	B747	19754	N861AA	B727	21088
N842RA	MD80	49604	N849HA	MD80	48073	N854MJ	E145	145490	N861AS	CRJ	7445
N842RP	E145	145661	N849HK	E145	145002	N854NW	A330	620	N861AT	B767	22692
N842TW	B727	18907	N849MJ	E145	145534	N854SA	CRJ	8053	N861BX	B707	19293
N842UA	A319	1569				N854SG	E145	14500854	N861DA	B777	29952

Reg	Type	Serial	Reg	Type	Serial	Reg	Type	Serial	Reg	Type	Serial
N861FT	DC-8	45900	**N867UP**	DC-8	45967	N875AA	B727	21387	N884US	F.100	11338
N861GA	MD80	49557	N867US	F.100	11312	**N875AS**	CRJ	7559	N885AA	B727	21524
N861L	B737	22760	N868AA	B727	21373	(N875BX)	B727	19504	**N885AS**	CRJ	7521
N861LF	MD80	49826	N868AC	B737	23868	N875C	DC-8	45635	N885DV	146	E3163
N861MC	146	E1068	N868AN	B757	24868	N875GA	MD80	53468	N885JM	DC-9	47265
N861N	B727	20167	**N868AS**	CRJ	7474	N875RA	MD80	53182	N885PA	B707	20024
N861NW	A330	796	N868BX	DC-8	46034	(N875RW)	E170	17000156	N885US	F.100	11345
N861PA	A300	216	**N868CA**	CRJ	7427	N875SJ	DC-8	46063	N886AA	B727	21525
N861PL	DC-8	45964	N868F	DC-8	45950	N875UM	B747	20305	**N886AS**	CRJ	7531
N861RW	E170	17000094	N868FT	DC-8	45950	N876AA	B727	21388	N886DV	146	E3165
N861SY	B737	20588	**N868GA**	MD80	49554	N876AS	CRJ	7576	**N886GA**	MD80	49931
N861US	F.100	11297	**N868RW**	E170	17000131	N876GA	MD80	53469	N886JM	DC-9	47289
N862AA	B727	21089	**N868UP**	DC-8	45968	N876RA	MD80	53183	N886MA	B727	21855
N862AS	CRJ	7476	N868US	F.100	11313	(N876RW)	E170	17000157	N886PA	B707	20025
N862AT	B767	22695	N869AA	B727	21374	N876UM	B727	20430	N886US	F.100	11346
N862BX	B707	19625	N869AP	B737	23869	N877AA	B727	21389	N887AA	B727	21526
N862DA	B777	29734	**N869AS**	CRJ	7479	**N877AS**	CRJ	7579	(N887DV)	146	E3169
N862FT	DC-8	45948	N869BX	DC-8	46035	N877C	DC-8	45642	**N887GA**	MD80	49932
N862GA	MD80	49556	N869DC	B737	26069	**N877GA**	MD80	53467	N887JM	DC-9	47290
N862N	B727	20568	N869F	DC-8	45913	N877SE	CRJ	7075	N887MA	B727	21857
N862PA	A300	211	**N869GA**	MD80	53294	N877UM	B727	20525	N887PA	B707	20026
N862RW	E170	17000098	(N869HA)	MD80	49119	N878AA	B727	21390	N887US	F.100	11349
N862SY	B737	20670	N869N	B727	20467	**N878AS**	CRJ	7590	**N888AQ**	737NG	35977
N862US	F.100	11300	**N869RW**	E170	17000133	**N878GA**	MD80	53487	N888AU	F.100	11357
N863AA	B727	21090	N869US	F.100	11314	N878RA	MD80	53184	N888CQ	A320	0978
N863AS	CRJ	7487	N870AA	B727	21382	N878UM	B727	20431	(N888DV)	146	E3193
N863AT	B767	22696	**N870AS**	CRJ	7530	N879AA	B727	21391	**N888GW**	737NG	30751
N863BX	B707	19270	N870BX	DC-8	46036	**N879AS**	CRJ	7600	N888KH	B747	21827
N863DA	B777	29735	N870GA	MD80	53191	**N879GA**	MD80	53486	**N888ML**	E145	14500818
N863E	DC-8	45999	N870GX	B737	28870	N879RA	MD80	53185	N888NW	B707	17705
N863F	DC-8	46001	N870N	B727	20285	N879UM	B727	20526	**N888NY**	737NG	30751
N863FT	DC-8	45949	N870PA	B707	20016	N880AA	B727	21519	**N888TY**	737NG	29749
N863GA	MD80	49911	**N870RW**	E170	17000138	N880AJ	CV880	22-00-1	N888VT	B727	20371
N863N	B727	20510	N870SJ	DC-8	46039	**N880AS**	CRJ	7606	N888WA	COMET	6424
N863PA	A300	053	N870TV	DC-8	46086	N880DP	1-11	079	**N888YF**	737NG	33036
N863RW	E170	17000100	N871AA	B727	21383	**N880DP**	DC-9	47635	N889AA	B727	21527
N863SY	B727	18323	**N871AS**	CRJ	7537	N880DV	146	E2062	**N889AS**	CRJ	7538
N863US	F.100	11303	N871DP	MD80	49412	**N880EP**	CV880	22-00-38	(N889CC)	B737	22889
N864AA	B727	21369	N871GA	MD80	53192	**N880GA**	MD80	49625	(N889DV)	146	E3213
N864AS	CRJ	7502	**N871GA**	MD80	53296	N880JT	CV880	22-7-8-60	N889FT	B747	21725
N864AT	B767	22980	N871L	B737	23256	N880NW	CV880	22-00-11	N889MA	B727	21854
N864BX	B707	19375	N871LF	B757	24543	N880P	1-11	079	N889ME	DC-9	47293
N864DA	B777	29736	N871MY	DC-8	45970	N880PA	B707	20019	**N889NC**	737NG	30070
N864F	DC-8	46087	N871PA	B707	20017	N880RA	MD80	53186	N889TW	B737	19228
N864FT	DC-8	45952	N871RA	MD80	49788	N880RB	DC-9	47635	N889US	F.100	11350
N864GA	MD80	49912	**N871RW**	E170	17000140	N880SR	CV880	22-00-7	N890AA	B727	22006
N864N	B727	20286	N871SJ	DC-8	45977	**N880UP**	DC-8	46080	N890FS	B737	23467
N864PA	A300	075	N871TV	DC-8	45968	N880US	F.100	11331	N890FT	B747	20013
N864RW	E170	17000117	N871TW	CV880	22-00-1	N880WA	CV880	22-00-51	**N890GA**	MD80	49371
N864US	F.100	11306	N871UM	DC-9	47434	N880WF	B747	21827	N890JA	DC-9	47294
N865AA	B727	21370	N872AA	B727	21384	N881AA	B727	21520	N890PA	B707	20027
N865AS	CRJ	7507	**N872AS**	CRJ	7542	N881AN	B737	24881	N890TW	B727	19229
N865BX	B707	18766	(N872BX)	B707	19584	**N881AS**	CRJ	7496	N890US	F.100	11365
N865DA	B777	29737	N872CV	A320	0872	N881DV	146	E2074	N891AA	B727	22007
N865F	DC-8	46088	N872DP	MD80	49414	**N881GA**	MD80	49708	**N891AT**	B717	55043
N865GA	MD80	49998	**N872GA**	MD80	53295	N881JM	DC-9	47199	N891DB	B727	22770
N865N	B727	20570	**N872MX**	A319	1872	N881LF	B737	23506	N891DL	MD11	48411
N865PA	A300	259	N872PA	B707	20018	**N881LF**	MD80	53051	N891FS	B737	23468
N865RW	E170	17000122	N872RA	MD80	49793	N881PA	B707	20020	**N891GA**	MD80	49423
N865US	F.100	11308	**N872RW**	E170	17000143	N881RA	MD80	49941	**N891JM**	DC-9	47354
N866AA	B727	21371	**N872SJ**	DC-8	46040	N881US	F.100	11333	N891L	B737	23388
N866AS	CRJ	7517	N872TV	DC-8	46001	N882AA	B727	21521	N891LF	B747	24896
N866AT	DC-9	47168	N872UM	DC-9	47437	**N882AS**	CRJ	7503	N891PA	B707	20028
N866DA	B777	29738	N873AA	B727	21385	N882DV	146	E2136	N891TW	B727	19230
N866F	DC-8	46112	**N873AS**	CRJ	7549	N882JM	DC-9	47292	N891US	F.100	11366
N866GA	MD80	49910	(N873BX)	B707	19585	N882MX	A319	1882	N892AA	B727	22008
N866MX	A319	1866	N873DP	MD80	49411	N882PA	B707	20021	(N892AF)	DC-8	45618
N866N	B727	20569	**N873GA**	MD80	49658	N882RA	MD80	49949	**N892AT**	B717	55044
N866RW	E170	17000129	N873JC	D0328	3118	N882US	F.100	11334	(N892DB)	B727	22770
N866SY	B727	20905	N873RA	MD80	53093	N883AA	B727	21522	N892DL	MD11	48412
N866UP	DC-8	45966	**N873RW**	E170	17000144	**N883AS**	CRJ	7504	N892FS	B737	23469
N866US	F.100	11310	N873SJ	DC-8	46091	N883DV	146	E2138	**N892GA**	MD80	49826
N867AA	B727	21372	N873UM	DC-9	47436	**N883GA**	MD80	49710	N892JM	DC-9	47422
N867AS	CRJ	7463	N874AA	B727	21386	N883JM	DC-9	47611	N892PA	B707	20029
N867AT	DC-9	47170	**N874AS**	CRJ	7551	N883LA	DC-10	46958	N892TW	B727	19231
N867BG	B737	28867	(N874BX)	B727	19134	N883PA	B707	20022	N892US	F.100	11372
N867BX	DC-8	46049	**N874GA**	MD80	49643	N883US	F.100	11337	N892VX	A320	1892
N867DA	B777	29743	**N874RW**	E170	17000148	N884AA	B727	21523	N893AA	B727	22009
N867F	DC-8	45939	N874SJ	DC-8	46149	**N884AS**	CRJ	7513	N893AF	DC-8	45619
N867FT	DC-8	45939	(N874UM)	B727	19863	N884DV	146	E2156	**N893AT**	B717	55045
N867N	B727	20509	N874UM	B747	20014	N884JM	DC-9	47024	N893GA	MD80	53051
N867RW	E170	17000130	**N874UP**	DC-8	46074	N884PA	B707	20023	N893JM	DC-9	47546

Registration	Type	Serial
N893PA	B707	20030
N893TW	B727	19232
N893US	F.100	11373
N894AA	B727	22010
N894AT	**B717**	**55046**
N894GA	**MD80**	**49660**
N894JM	DC-9	47554
N894PA	B707	20031
N894TW	B727	19233
N894UP	**DC-8**	**46094**
N894US	F.100	11379
N895AA	B727	22011
N895AJ	B727	20660
N895AT	**B717**	**55047**
N895GA	**MD80**	**49667**
N895JM	DC-9	47557
N895N	B727	20168
N895NC	B747	24895
N895PA	B707	20032
N895SY	B707	20032
N895TW	B727	19234
N895US	F.100	11380
N896AA	B727	22012
N896AS	CRJ	7428
N896AT	**B717**	**55048**
N896JM	DC-9	47560
N896N	B727	20367
N896PA	B707	20033
N896US	F.100	11391
N897AA	B727	22013
N897AS	CRJ	7460
N897JM	DC-9	47592
N897PA	B707	20034
N897US	F.100	11392
N897WA	B707	18339
N898AA	**B727**	**22014**
N898AS	CRJ	7461
N898ED	B737	24898
N898GE	B767	29898
N898JM	**B737**	**22873**
N898PC	B727	19620
N898US	F.100	11398
N898WA	B707	19502
N899AA	**B727**	**22015**
N899AT	**B717**	**55049**
N899JM	**B737**	**22874**
N899TH	B747	20929
N899US	F.100	11399
N900AE	**E145**	**14500885**
N900AX	**DC-9**	**47380**
N900CH	B727	19835
N900CL	DC-8	45265
N900D	L1011	193A-1056
N900DE	**MD80**	**53372**
N900DP	**E145**	**14500903**
N900EM	**E145**	**14500976**
N900ER	737NG	35680
N900EV	**CRJ**	**7608**
N900ME	DC-9	45841
N900ML	DC-9	45710
N900NW	CV880	22-00-62
N900PC	**B757**	**28446**
N900PG	B737	21794
N900SA	DC-9	45775
(N900UW)	B757	22192
N900WN	**737NG**	**32544**
N901AK	DC-9	45846
N901AN	**737NG**	**29503**
N901AW	**B757**	**23321**
N901AX	DC-9	47381
N901B	DC-9	45731
N901BN	A320	0052
N901CK	DC-9	47154
(N901CL)	DC-8	45274
N901DA	**MD90**	**53381**
N901DC	DC-9	47038
N901DC	MD90	53367
N901DE	**MD80**	**53378**
N901DL	**MD80**	**49532**
N901EV	**CRJ**	**7616**
N901FD	**B757**	**27122**
N901FR	**A319**	**1488**
N901H	DC-9	45717
N901ML	DC-9	47104
N901MW	SE210	62
N901PA	B747	20391
N901PG	B727	21978
N901RA	MD90	53489
N901RF	B727	22476
N901TS	B727	18257
N901TW	MD80	49166
N901UA	**B737**	**25001**
(N901UW)	B757	22193
N901VJ	DC-9	47275
N901WA	DC-10	46908
N901WN	**737NG**	**32545**
N901XJ	**CRJ9**	**15130**
N902AN	**737NG**	**29504**
N902AW	**B757**	**23322**
N902AX	DC-9	47426
N902BC	**E145**	**14500887**
N902BN	A320	0053
N902CK	DC-9	47045
N902CL	DC-10	46905
(N902CL)	DC-8	45276
N902DA	**MD90**	**53382**
N902DC	DC-9	47039
N902DC	MD90	53381
N902DE	**MD80**	**53379**
N902DL	MD80	49533
N902EV	**CRJ**	**7620**
N902FD	B757	27123
N902FJ	**CRJ9**	**15002**
N902FR	**A319**	**1515**
N902H	DC-9	45724
N902JW	DC-10	46905
N902LX	**E145**	**145495**
N902ME	**B717**	**55166**
N902ML	DC-9	47105
N902MW	SE210	88
N902PA	B747	19896
N902PG	**B727**	**20725**
N902PG	B737	21795
N902PJ	MD80	49401
N902R	DC-8	45767
N902RA	MD90	53490
N902RF	B727	22549
N902RQ	B707	18689
N902TS	B727	18267
N902TW	MD80	49153
N902UA	**B737**	**25002**
N902UP	B727	18898
(N902UW)	B757	22196
N902VJ	DC-9	47177
N902VX	A320	1902
N902WA	DC-10	46928
N902WC	B737	19613
N902WG	**B737**	**22620**
N902WN	**737NG**	**36615**
N902XJ	**CRJ9**	**15131**
N903AK	DC-9	47023
N903AN	**737NG**	**29505**
N903AW	**B757**	**23323**
N903AX	**DC-9**	**47427**
N903BN	A320	0054
N903CL	DC-8	45382
N903DA	**MD80**	**53383**
N903DC	DC-9	47046
N903DE	**MD80**	**53380**
N903DL	**MD80**	**49534**
N903EV	**CRJ**	**7621**
N903FD	**B757**	**27124**
N903FJ	**CRJ9**	**15003**
N903FR	**A319**	**1560**
N903H	DC-9	47149
N903LC	B737	19612
N903ME	**B717**	**55167**
N903ML	MD80	49759
N903MW	SE210	89
N903PA	B747	20100
N903PG	B727	20466
N903PG	B757	24370
N903R	DC-8	45647
N903RA	MD90	53551
N903RC	B737	19598
N903RF	B727	21609
N903SW	**CRJ**	**7425**
N903TS	**B727**	**18272**
N903TW	MD80	49154
N903UA	**B737**	**25003**
N903UP	B727	18945
N903VJ	DC-9	47261
N903WA	DC-10	46929
N903WN	**737NG**	**32457**
N903XJ	**CRJ9**	**15134**
N904AK	DC-9	47068
N904AM	**737NG**	**28262**
N904AN	**737NG**	**29506**
N904AW	**B757**	**23566**
N904AX	**DC-9**	**47040**
N904BN	A320	0055
N904CL	DC-8	45376
N904DA	**MD90**	**53384**
N904DC	DC-9	47047
N904DE	**MD80**	**53409**
N904DL	**MD80**	**49535**
N904EV	**CRJ**	**7628**
N904FD	B757	27144
N904FJ	**CRJ9**	**15004**
N904FR	**A319**	**1579**
N904LP	737NG	29904
N904LX	**E145**	**145780**
N904MA	737NG	29051
N904ME	**B717**	**55168**
N904ML	MD80	49766
N904MW	SE210	93
N904PA	B747	21743
N904PG	B727	20468
N904R	DC-8	46000
N904RA	MD90	53570
N904RF	B727	21781
N904TS	B727	18291
N904TW	MD80	49156
N904UA	**B737**	**25004**
N904UP	B727	18946
N904VJ	DC-9	47377
N904WA	DC-10	46930
N904WN	**737NG**	**36616**
N904XJ	**CRJ9**	**15135**
N905AF	B737	24905
N905AJ	**B727**	**21989**
N905AN	**737NG**	**29507**
N905AW	**B757**	**23567**
N905AX	**DC-9**	**47147**
N905DN	A320	0064
N905CL	DC-8	45274
N905DA	**MD90**	**53385**
N905DC	DC-9	47101
N905DE	**MD80**	**53376**
N905DL	**MD80**	**49536**
N905EV	**CRJ**	**7632**
N905FD	B757	27145
N905FR	**A319**	**1583**
N905H	DC-9	47150
N905HB	**D0328**	**3178**
N905J	**CRJ9**	**15005**
N905JH	**E145**	**14500892**
N905LP	737NG	29905
N905LX	**E145**	**145775**
N905ME	**B717**	**55169**
N905ML	MD80	53044
N905MW	SE210	95
N905NA	**B747**	**20107**
N905PA	B747	21744
N905PG	B727	20571
N905PG	B757	24371
N905RA	MD90	53573
N905RF	B727	20595
N905SW	CRJ	7437
N905TA	**MD80**	**49905**
N905TS	B727	18966
N905TW	MD80	49157
N905UA	**B737**	**25005**
N905UP	B727	18947
N905VJ	DC-9	47378
N905WA	DC-10	46938
N905WN	**737NG**	**36617**
N905XJ	**CRJ9**	**15137**
N906AE	**E145**	**14500894**
(N906AK)	DC-9	47070
N906AM	**737NG**	**29356**
N906AN	**737NG**	**29508**
N906AT	**B717**	**55087**
N906AW	**B757**	**23568**
N906AX	**DC-9**	**47072**
N906BN	A320	0065
N906CG	MD80	49906
N906CL	DC-8	45276
N906DA	**MD90**	**53386**
N906DC	DC-9	47129
N906DE	**MD80**	**53415**
N906DL	MD80	49537
N906EV	**CRJ**	**7642**
N906FD	**B757**	**27148**
N906FJ	**CRJ9**	**15006**
N906FR	**A319**	**1684**
N906H	DC-9	47171
N906HB	**D0328**	**3179**
N906LX	**E145**	**14500825**
N906MA	737NG	29052
N906ME	**B717**	**55170**
N906ML	MD80	53045
N906PG	B727	20728
N906R	**DC-8**	**46087**
N906RF	B727	20606
N906SW	**CRJ**	**7510**
N906TS	B727	18967
N906TW	MD80	49160
N906UA	**B737**	**25006**
N906UP	B727	19314
N906VJ	DC-9	47379
N906WA	DC-10	46939
N906WN	**737NG**	**36887**
N906XJ	**CRJ9**	**15138**
N907AE	**E145**	**14500895**
N907AN	**737NG**	**29509**
N907AW	**B757**	**22691**
N907AX	**DC-9**	**47203**
(N907BN)	A320	0066
N907CL	DC-8	45967
N907DA	**MD90**	**53387**
N907DC	DC-9	47476
N907DE	**MD80**	**53416**
N907DL	**MD80**	**49538**
N907EV	**CRJ**	**7648**
N907FD	B757	27198
N907FJ	**CRJ9**	**15007**
N907FR	**A319**	**1743**
N907GP	A320	0066
N907H	DC-9	47362
N907LX	**E145**	**14500966**
N907MD	MD80	49934
N907ME	**B717**	**55171**
N907ML	MD80	53046
N907MW	SE210	129
N907PG	B727	22164
N907R	DC-8	45764
N907RF	B727	20811
N907SW	CRJ	7511
N907TS	B727	18973
N907TW	MD80	49165
N907UA	**B737**	**25007**
N907UP	B727	19118
N907VJ	DC-9	47444
N907WA	DC-10	46946
N907XJ	**CRJ9**	**15139**
N908AE	**E145**	**14500897**
N908AM	**737NG**	**30038**
N908AN	**737NG**	**29510**
N908AW	**B757**	**24233**
N908AX	**DC-9**	**47008**
(N908BN)	A320	0067
N908CL	DC-8	45903
(N908CL)	DC-8	45968
N908DA	**MD90**	**53388**
N908DC	DC-9	45721
N908DE	**MD80**	**53417**

N908DL	MD80	49539	N911GP	A320	0077	N914LF	DC-9	45695	**N917FR**	A319	1890			
N908EV	CRJ	7654	N911KM	DC-9	45740	**N914ME**	B717	55177	N917GP	A320	0099			
N908FD	B757	27199	(N911LX)	E145	14500966	(N914PG)	B727	20725	N917JW	DC-10	46727			
N908FJ	CRJ9	15008	**N911NA**	B747	20781	N914PG	B727	22603	**N917ME**	B717	55179			
N908FR	A319	1759	N911R	DC-8	45817	N914RW	DC-9	47362	N917PG	B727	22605			
N908GP	A320	0067	N911RW	DC-9	47149	N914TS	B727	20251	N917R	DC-8	46099			
N908H	DC-9	47517	(N911SY)	DC-9	45731	N914TW	MD80	49185	N917R	DC-9	47015			
N908JE	B727	20115	N911TS	B727	19689	**N914UA**	B737	25381	N917RW	DC-9	47145			
N908LX	E145	145528	N911TW	MD80	49182	N914UP	B727	19246	**N917SW**	CRJ	7641			
N908ME	B717	55172	N911UA	B737	25255	N914VJ	DC-9	47068	N917TS	B727	20149			
N908PG	B727	20951	N911UP	B727	19119	N914VV	DC-9	47486	N917TW	MD80	49366			
N908RF	B727	21611	N911VV	DC-9	47285	N914WA	DC-10	47832	(N917U)	DC-9	47409			
N908SW	CRJ	7540	**N912AN**	737NG	29513	**N915AN**	737NG	29516	N917UA	B737	25384			
N908TS	B727	19685	(N912BN)	A320	0081	**N915AT**	B717	55085	N917UP	B727	19310			
N908TW	MD80	49169	**N912CA**	CRJ	7011	**N915AW**	B757	22209	**N917UW**	B757	22193			
N908UA	B737	25008	N912CL	DC-8	45908	(N915BN)	A320	0092	N917VV	DC-9	47323			
N908UP	B727	19114	N912CW	E145	145412	N915BV	DC-8	45981	**N918AE**	E145	14500902			
N908VJ	DC-9	47321	**N912DE**	MD80	49997	**N915CA**	CRJ	7013	**N918AN**	737NG	29519			
N908WA	DC-10	46977	**N912DL**	MD80	49543	**N915CK**	DC-9	47086	**N918CA**	CRJ	7018			
N909AE	E145	14500899	**N912DN**	MD90	53392	N915CL	DC-8	45894	N918CH	B737	29189			
N909AM	737NG	29511	(N912DN)	MD90	53393	**N915DE**	MD80	53420	N918CL	DC-8	45648			
N909AW	B757	24522	**N912EV**	CRJ	7728	**N915DL**	MD80	49546	**N918DE**	MD80	49959			
N909AX	DC-9	47148	**N912FJ**	CRJ9	15012	**N915DN**	MD90	53395	**N918DL**	MD80	49583			
(N909BN)	A320	0076	**N912FR**	A319	1803	(N915DN)	MD90	53396	**N918FJ**	CRJ9	15018			
N909CH	1-11	067	N912GP	A320	0081	**N915EV**	CRJ	7754	**N918FR**	A319	1943			
(N909CL)	DC-8	46092	**N912JC**	E145	14501015	N915F	DC-9	47061	**N918ME**	B717	55180			
N909DA	MD90	53389	**N912LX**	E145	14500993	**N915FD**	B757	24120	N918PG	B727	21823			
N909DC	DC-9	47410	"N912M"	B737	19607	**N915FJ**	CRJ9	15015	**N918RW**	DC-9	47158			
N909DE	MD80	53418	**N912ME**	B717	55175	**N915FR**	A319	1851	**N918SW**	CRJ	7645			
N909DL	MD80	49540	N912MP	B737	19607	N915GP	A320	0092	N918TS	B727	20445			
N909EV	CRJ	7658	N912PG	B737	21496	N915MJ	DC-9	47151	N918TW	MD80	49367			
N909FD	B757	27200	N912R	DC-8	45908	N915PG	B727	21689	(N918U)	DC-9	47410			
N909FJ	CRJ9	15009	N912RW	DC-9	47150	N915PJ	MD80	49619	**N918UA**	B737	25385			
N909FR	A319	1761	**N912SW**	CRJ	7595	N915R	DC-8	45916	N918UP	B727	19008			
(N909FR)	A319	1770	N912TS	B727	20438	N915R	DC-9	47086	**N918UW**	B757	22196			
(N909GP)	A320	0076	N912TW	MD80	49183	**N915RW**	DC-9	47139	N918VJ	DC-9	48138			
N909LH	B737	20195	**N912UA**	B737	25290	**N915SW**	CRJ	7615	N918VV	DC-9	47619			
N909LX	E145	14500942	N912UP	B727	19244	N915TS	B727	20252	**N919AN**	737NG	29520			
N909ME	B717	55173	N912VJ	DC-9	47020	N915TW	MD80	49186	**N919AT**	B717	55084			
N909PG	B727	21852	N912VV	DC-9	47359	(N915U)	DC-9	47407	N919CL	DC-8	46106			
(N909RF)	B727	21610	N912WA	DC-10	46645	N915UA	B737	25382	**N919DE**	MD80	53422			
N909SH	B767	27909	**N913AN**	737NG	29514	N915UP	B727	19533	**N919DL**	MD80	49584			
N909SW	CRJ	7558	**N913AW**	B757	22207	N915VV	DC-9	47443	**N919EV**	CRJ	7780			
N909TS	B727	19686	(N913BN)	A320	0082	N915WA	DC-10	47833	**N919FJ**	CRJ9	15019			
N909TW	MD80	49170	**N913DE**	MD80	49956	**N916AN**	737NG	29517	**N919FR**	A319	1980			
N909UA	B737	25009	**N913DL**	MD80	49544	N916AW	B757	24291	N919JW	DC-8	46106			
N909UP	B727	19115	**N913DN**	MD90	53393	(N916BN)	A320	0098	**N919ME**	B717	55181			
N909VJ	DC-9	47322	(N913DN)	MD90	53394	**N916CA**	CRJ	7014	N919PG	B727	22604			
N909WA	DC-10	46983	**N913EV**	CRJ	7731	N916CL	DC-10	46906	N919PJ	DC-9	47663			
N909XJ	CRJ9	15141	**N913FJ**	CRJ9	15013	**N916DE**	MD80	53421	N919RW	DC-9	47162			
N910AN	737NG	29512	**N913FR**	A319	1863	**N916DL**	MD80	49591	**N919SW**	CRJ	7657			
N910AT	B717	55086	N913GP	A320	0082	**N916DN**	MD90	53396	N919TS	B727	20447			
N910AW	B757	24523	**N913LX**	E145	14501007	**N916EV**	CRJ	7757	N919TW	MD80	49368			
(N910BN)	A320	0077	**N913ME**	B717	55176	N916F	DC-9	47044	**N919UA**	B737	25386			
N910BW	B747	20529	N913PG	B737	21498	N916FD	B757	24137	N919UP	B727	19012			
N910CL	DC-8	46094	N913PM	L1011	193U–1223	**N916FJ**	CRJ9	15016	**N919UW**	B757	22198			
(N910DA)	MD90	53390	N913R	DC-8	46128	**N916FR**	A319	1876	N919VJ	DC-9	48139			
N910DE	MD80	53419	N913RW	DC-9	47171	N916GP	A320	0098	N919VV	DC-9	47260			
N910DL	MD80	49541	**N913SW**	CRJ	7597	N916JW	DC-10	46906	N919VV	DC-9	47723			
N910DN	MD90	53390	N913TS	B727	20250	**N916ME**	B717	55178	**N920AN**	737NG	29521			
N910EV	CRJ	7727	N913TW	MD80	49184	N916PG	B727	21690	**N920AT**	B717	55083			
N910FJ	CRJ9	15010	**N913UA**	B737	25291	N916R	DC-8	45753	**N920CA**	CRJ	7022			
N910FR	A319	1781	N913UP	B727	19245	N916R	DC-9	47010	N920CL	DC-8	46058			
N910GP	A320	0076	N913VJ	DC-9	45846	**N916RW**	DC-9	47144	**N920DE**	MD80	53423			
N910LX	E145	14500952	N913VV	DC-10	46913	**N916SW**	CRJ	7634	**N920DL**	MD80	49644			
N910ME	B717	55174	N913VV	DC-9	47318	N916TS	B727	20437	**N920EV**	CRJ	7810			
N910PC	B707	20171	N913WA	DC-10	46646	N916TW	MD80	49187	**N920FJ**	CRJ9	15020			
N910PG	B727	22606	**N914AN**	737NG	29515	(N916U)	DC-9	47408	**N920FR**	A319	1997			
N910R	DC-8	45854	**N914AW**	B757	22208	N916UA	B737	25383	N920FT	B747	22237			
N910SF	DC-10	46524	(N914BN)	A320	0091	N916UP	B727	19808	N920L	DC-9	47734			
N910SW	CRJ	7566	N914BV	DC-8	45912	**N916UW**	B757	22192	N920LG	DC-9	47797			
N910TS	B727	19687	**N914CA**	CRJ	7012	N916VJ	DC-9	47023	**N920ME**	B717	55182			
N910UA	B737	25254	N914CH	B737	29140	N916VV	DC-9	47445	N920PG	B727	21688			
N910UP	B727	19117	N914CL	DC-8	45912	N917AC	MD80	48028	N920PJ	DC-9	47677			
(N910UW)	B757	27123	**N914DE**	MD80	49957	**N917AN**	737NG	29518	N920PS	MD80	48051			
N910VJ	DC-9	47277	**N914DL**	MD80	49545	(N917BN)	A320	0099	N920RW	DC-9	47163			
N911AW	B757	24543	**N914DN**	MD90	53394	**N917CA**	CRJ	7017	**N920SW**	CRJ	7660			
N911CL	DC-8	45981	(N914DN)	MD90	53395	N917CL	DC-10	46727	N920TS	B727	20448			
N911DA	MD90	53391	**N914EV**	CRJ	7752	**N917DE**	MD80	49958	N920TW	MD80	49369			
N911DE	MD80	49967	**N914FJ**	CRJ9	15014	**N917DL**	MD80	49573	N920UA	B737	25387			
N911DL	MD80	49542	**N914FR**	A319	1841	**N917EV**	CRJ	7769	N920UP	B727	19873			
N911FJ	CRJ9	15011	N914GP	A320	0091	**N917FJ**	CRJ9	15017	**N920UW**	B757	22199			

Registration	Type	No.
(N920UW)	B757	27303
N920VJ	DC-9	47682
N920VJ	DC-9	48140
N920VV	DC-9	47262
N920VV	DC-9	47674
N920WA	B737	21791
N921AN	**737NG**	**29522**
N921AT	**B717**	**55082**
N921AW	B737	24921
N921CL	DC-8	45643
N921DL	**MD80**	**49645**
N921EV	**CRJ**	**7819**
N921FJ	**CRJ9**	**15021**
N921FR	**A319**	**2010**
N921FT	**B747**	**21575**
N921L	DC-9	47107
N921LF	A320	0453
N921LG	DC-9	47798
N921ME	**B717**	**55183**
N921NB	B737	23921
N921PG	B737	21796
N921R	**DC-8**	**46145**
N921RW	**DC-9**	**47164**
N921TS	B727	22043
N921TW	MD80	49101
N921UA	**B737**	**25388**
N921UP	B727	19874
N921UW	**B757**	**22202**
(N921UW)	B757	27806
N921VJ	DC-9	47683
N921VJ	DC-9	48141
N921VV	DC-9	47284
N921VV	DC-9	47451
N921WA	B737	23039
N922AB	B737	23922
N922AE	**E145**	**14500906**
N922AN	**737NG**	**29523**
N922AT	**B717**	**55050**
N922AV	B737	24922
N922BV	DC-8	45925
N922CL	DC-8	45925
N922DL	**MD80**	**49646**
N922EV	**CRJ**	**7822**
N922FJ	**CRJ9**	**15022**
N922FR	**A319**	**2012**
N922FT	B747	22768
N922L	DC-9	47108
N922LG	DC-9	47281
N922ME	**B717**	**55184**
N922PG	B737	21798
N922RW	**DC-9**	**47182**
N922TS	B727	20415
N922TW	MD80	48013
N922UA	**B737**	**26642**
N922UP	B727	19231
N922UW	**B757**	**22202**
(N922UW)	B757	27807
N922VJ	DC-9	47685
N922VJ	DC-9	48142
N922VV	DC-9	47274
N922VV	DC-9	47489
N923AE	**E145**	**14500907**
N923AN	**737NG**	**29524**
N923AP	B737	23923
N923AT	**B717**	**55051**
N923AX	DC-9	47165
N923BV	DC-8	45943
N923CL	DC-8	45920
N923DL	**MD80**	**49705**
N923EV	**CRJ**	**7826**
N923FJ	**CRJ9**	**15023**
N923FR	**A319**	**2019**
N923FT	**B747**	**22769**
N923L	DC-9	47109
N923LG	DC-9	47110
N923ME	**B717**	**55185**
N923PG	B727	22163
N923R	DC-8	46077
N923R	DC-9	47014
N923RW	**DC-9**	**47183**
N923SW	**CRJ**	**7664**
N923TS	B727	20441
N923TW	MD80	49379
N923UA	**B737**	**26643**
N923UP	B727	19229
N923UW	**B757**	**22203**
N923VJ	DC-9	47665
N923VJ	DC-9	48143
N923VV	DC-9	47488
N923VV	DC-9	47529
N923WA	B737	21800
N924AN	**737NG**	**29525**
N924AT	**B717**	**55080**
N924AW	B757	24924
N924AX	**DC-9**	**47403**
N924BV	DC-8	45920
N924CA	**CRJ**	**7026**
N924CL	DC-8	46134
N924DL	**MD80**	**49711**
N924EV	**CRJ**	**7830**
N924FJ	**CRJ9**	**15024**
N924FR	**A319**	**2030**
N924FT	B747	21730
N924L	DC-9	47324
N924LG	DC-9	47765
N924ME	**B717**	**55190**
N924PG	B727	21968
N924PG	B747	21938
N924PS	MD80	48034
N924RW	**DC-9**	**47185**
N924SW	**CRJ**	**7681**
N924TS	B727	21041
N924TW	MD80	49100
N924UA	**B737**	**26645**
N924UP	B727	19234
N924UW	**B757**	**22204**
(N924UW)	B757	27810
N924VJ	DC-9	47688
N924VJ	DC-9	48144
N924VV	DC-9	47228
N924VV	DC-9	47534
N925AE	**E145**	**14500908**
N925AN	**737NG**	**29526**
N925AT	**B717**	**55079**
(N925AX)	DC-9	45718
N925AX	DC-9	45728
N925BV	DC-8	45885
N925DL	**MD80**	**49712**
(N925DS)	B727	20046
N925EV	**CRJ**	**7831**
N925FJ	**CRJ9**	**15025**
N925FR	**A319**	**2103**
(N925FT)	B747	21841
N925L	DC-9	47357
N925LG	DC-9	47788
N925ME	**B717**	**55191**
N925MX	**A319**	**1925**
N925PG	B737	23164
N925PS	MD80	48035
N925SW	**CRJ**	**7682**
N925TS	B727	21244
N925TW	MD80	49357
N925UA	**B737**	**26646**
N925UP	B727	19230
N925US	**DC-9**	**47472**
N925UW	**B757**	**22205**
(N925UW)	B757	27811
N925VJ	DC-9	47686
N925VJ	DC-9	48145
N925VV	DC-9	47319
N925VV	DC-9	47397
N926AN	**737NG**	**29527**
N926AT	**B717**	**55078**
N926AX	DC-9	47002
N926CA	**CRJ**	**7027**
N926CL	DC-8	46092
N926DL	**MD80**	**49713**
N926EV	**CRJ**	**7843**
N926FM	**E145**	**145466**
N926FR	**A319**	**2198**
(N926FT)	B747	21650
N926JS	**B757**	**24964**
N926L	DC-9	47172
N926LG	DC-9	47799
N926LR	**CRJ9**	**15026**
N926ME	**B717**	**55192**
N926NW	**DC-9**	**47425**
N926PG	B737	23165
N926PS	MD80	48036
N926RC	DC-9	47473
N926SW	**CRJ**	**7687**
N926TS	B727	20774
N926TW	MD80	49356
N926UA	B737	26648
N926UP	B727	19233
(N926UW)	B757	27122
N926VA	L1011	193U-1140
N926VJ	DC-9	47692
N926VJ	DC-9	48146
N926VV	DC-9	45774
N927AN	**737NG**	**30077**
N927AT	**B717**	**55077**
N927AX	DC-9	45717
N927CA	**CRJ**	**7031**
N927DA	**MD80**	**49714**
N927DS	B727	20046
N927EV	**CRJ**	**7844**
N927FR	**A319**	**2209**
N927L	DC-9	48123
N927LR	**CRJ9**	**15027**
N927ME	**B717**	**55193**
N927PG	B737	23168
N927PS	MD80	48037
N927RC	DC-9	47469
N927SW	**CRJ**	**7693**
N927TS	B727	20837
N927TW	MD80	49358
N927UA	**B737**	**26649**
N927UP	B727	19232
N927UW	**B757**	**27123**
N927VJ	DC-9	47693
N927VJ	DC-9	48154
N927VV	DC-9	47442
N928AE	**E145**	**14500911**
N928AN	**737NG**	**29528**
N928AT	**B717**	**55076**
N928AX	DC-9	45718
N928AX	**DC-9**	**47392**
N928CT	B737	24928
N928CW	E145	145528
N928DL	**MD80**	**49715**
N928EV	**CRJ**	**8006**
N928FR	**A319**	**2236**
N928L	DC-9	48124
N928LR	**CRJ9**	**15028**
N928ME	**D717**	**55194**
N928ML	DC-9	47326
N928PG	B727	22438
N928PS	MD80	48038
N928PS	MD80	48052
N928SW	**CRJ**	**7701**
N928TW	MD80	48012
N928UA	**B737**	**26651**
N928UP	B727	19091
N928UW	B757	27124
N928VJ	DC-9	48131
N929AN	**737NG**	**30078**
N929AT	**B717**	**55075**
N929AX	**DC-9**	**45874**
N929CA	**CRJ**	**7035**
N929DL	**MD80**	**49716**
N929EV	**CRJ**	**8007**
N929FR	**A319**	**2240**
N929L	DC-9	47174
N929LR	**CRJ9**	**15029**
N929ML	DC-9	47418
N929PS	MD80	48053
N929R	DC-8	45901
N929RD	**B757**	**23929**
N929SW	**CRJ**	**7703**
N929TW	MD80	48014
N929UA	**B737**	**26652**
N929UP	B727	19092
N929UW	**B757**	**27144**
N929VJ	DC-9	48118
N930AN	**737NG**	**29529**
N930AS	MD80	49231
N930AT	**B717**	**55072**
N930AX	**DC-9**	**47363**
N930BB	DC-9	47521
N930CA	B737	21358
N930DL	**MD80**	**49717**
N930EA	DC-9	45730
N930EV	**CRJ**	**8014**
N930FR	**A319**	**2241**
N930FT	B727	19387
N930LR	**CRJ9**	**15030**
N930MC	MD80	48056
N930ML	DC-9	47527
N930NA	**KC135**	**17969**
N930PG	B737	23171
N930RC	DC-9	45729
N930RD	B757	22210
N930SW	**CRJ**	**7713**
N930TL	F.28	11016
N930UA	**B737**	**26655**
N930UP	B727	19096
N930UW	**B757**	**27145**
N930VJ	DC-9	45868
N930VV	DC-9	47723
N930WA	B737	28732
N931AE	**E145**	**14500912**
N931AN	**737NG**	**30079**
N931AS	MD80	49232
N931AX	DC-9	47384
N931CA	**CRJ**	**7037**
(N931CA)	CRJ	7038
N931DL	**MD80**	**49718**
N931EA	DC-9	45698
N931EV	**CRJ**	**8015**
N931F	DC-9	47040
N931F	DC-9	47192
N931FR	**A319**	**2253**
N931FT	B727	19390
N931JT	MD80	48057
N931L	DC-9	47173
N931LF	A320	0448
N931LR	**CRJ9**	**15031**
N931MC	MD80	48057
N931ML	DC-9	47202
N931NA	**KC135**	**18615**
N931NU	B737	25247
N931PG	B727	19151
N931PS	MD80	48039
N931TW	**MD80**	**49527**
N931UA	B737	26656
N931UP	B727	19858
N931UW	B757	27148
N931VJ	DC-9	47188
N931VV	DC-9	47674
N931WA	B737	28733
N932AE	**E145**	**14500915**
N932AN	**737NG**	**29530**
N932AS	MD80	49233
N932AT	**B717**	**55073**
N932AX	**DC-9**	**47465**
N932CA	**CRJ**	**7038**
(N932CA)	CRJ	7040
N932DL	**MD80**	**49719**
N932EA	DC-9	45699
N932EV	**CRJ**	**8016**
N932F	DC-9	47041
N932F	DC-9	47355
N932FR	**A319**	**2258**
N932FT	B727	19834
N932HA	B737	29326
N932L	DC-9	47669
N932LR	**CRJ9**	**15032**
N932MC	MD80	49120
N932MJ	DC-9	48156
N932ML	**DC-9**	**47547**
N932NA	**DC-9**	**47476**
N932NU	B737	25248
(N932PG)	B727	19152
N932PS	MD80	48040
N932RD	**MD80**	**49233**
N932SW	**CRJ**	**7714**
N932UA	**B737**	**26658**

Reg	Type	Serial	Reg	Type	Serial	Reg	Type	Serial	Reg	Type	Serial
N932UP	B727	19856	N936AN	737NG	29532	N939PS	MD80	48099	N943AS	MD80	53018
N932UW	B757	27198	N936AS	MD80	49363	N939SW	CRJ	7742	N943AT	B717	55006
N932VJ	DC-9	47189	N936AT	B717	55058	N939UA	B737	26672	N943AX	DC-9	47528
N932VV	DC-9	47451	N936AX	DC-9	47269	N939UP	B727	19532	N943CA	CRJ	7062
N933AN	737NG	30080	N936CA	CRJ	7043	N939UW	B757	27303	N943DL	MD80	49816
N933AS	MD80	49234	(N936CA)	CRJ	7046	N939VJ	DC-9	48120	N943FR	A319	2518
N933AT	B717	55071	N936DL	MD80	49723	N939VV	DC-9	47089	N943ML	DC-9	47133
N933AX	DC-9	47291	N936EV	CRJ	8038	N940AA	DC-9	48147	N943MT	MD80	49943
N933CA	CRJ	7040	N936F	DC-9	47408	(N940AN)	737NG	29534	N943N	DC-9	47647
(N933CA)	CRJ	7042	N936FR	A319	2392	N940AN	737NG	30598	N943PG	B737	23411
N933DL	MD80	49720	N936FT	B727	19836	N940AS	MD80	49825	N943PS	MD80	48098
N933EV	CRJ	8022	N936L	DC-9	47711	N940AT	B717	55004	N943SW	CRJ	7762
N933F	DC-9	47147	N936MC	MD80	49444	N940CA	CRJ	7048	N943U	DC-9	48132
N933F	DC-9	47191	N936ML	DC-9	47501	(N940CA)	CRJ	7052	N943UA	B737	26680
N933FR	A319	2260	N936PG	B727	22441	N940DL	MD80	49813	N943UP	B727	19102
N933FT	B727	19182	N936PS	MD80	48092	N940F	DC-9	47414	N943VJ	DC-9	47058
N933JK	DC-9	48159	N936SW	CRJ	7726	N940FR	A319	2465	N944AA	DC-9	48120
N933JN	E145	14500918	N936UA	B737	26667	(N940FT)	B727	19389	N944AM	MD80	49440
N933L	DC-9	47617	N936UP	B727	19503	N940JW	DC-8	46155	N944AN	737NG	29535
N933LR	CRJ9	15033	N936UW	B757	27244	(N940MC)	MD80	49662	(N944AN)	737NG	29536
N933MC	MD80	49121	N936VJ	DC-9	48116	N940ML	DC-9	47102	N944AS	MD80	53019
N933ML	DC-9	47548	N936VV	DC-9	47397	N940N	DC-9	47572	N944AT	B717	55007
N933NU	B737	25226	N937AN	737NG	30082	N940PG	DC-10	46944	N944AX	DC-9	47550
N933PS	MD80	48041	N937AS	MD80	49364	N940PS	MD80	48095	N944DL	MD80	49817
N933UA	B737	26659	N937AT	B717	55091	N940UA	B737	26675	N944F	DC-9	47194
N933UP	B727	19857	N937AX	DC-9	47074	N940UP	B727	19826	N944FR	A319	2700
N933UW	B757	27199	N937CA	CRJ	7044	N940UW	B757	27805	(N944FT)	B727	18435
N933VJ	DC-9	47216	(N937CA)	CRJ	7048	N940VJ	DC-9	47053	N944JW	B707	18336
N933VV	DC-9	47489	N937DL	MD80	49810	N940VV	DC-9	47523	N944ML	DC-9	47132
N934AN	737NG	29531	N937EV	CRJ	8042	N941AA	DC-9		N944PS	MD80	49119
N934AS	MD80	49235	N937F	DC-9	47409	N941AN	737NG	29534	N944SW	CRJ	7764
N934AT	B717	55070	N937FR	A319	2400	N941AS	MD80	49925	N944U	DC-9	48133
N934AX	DC-9	47462	N937FT	B727	18847	N941AX	DC-9	47419	N944UA	B737	26683
N934CA	CRJ	7042	N937MC	MD80	49450	N941CA	CRJ	7050	N944UP	B727	19103
(N934CA)	CRJ	7045	N937ML	DC-9	47005	(N941CA)	CRJ	7055	N944UW	E190	19000058
N934DL	MD80	49721	N937PG	B737	23170	N941DL	MD80	49814	N945AA	DC-9	48119
N934EV	CRJ	8028	N937PS	MD80	48093	N941F	DC-9	47193	N945AN	737NG	30085
N934F	DC-9	47148	N937SW	CRJ	7735	N941FR	A319	2483	(N945AN)	737NG	30086
N934FJ	CRJ9	15034	N937UA	B737	26668	N941FT	B727	19428	N945AS	MD80	49643
N934FR	A319	2287	N937UP	B727	19302	N941JW	DC-8	45988	N945AT	B717	55008
(N934FT)	B727	18429	N937UW	B757	27245	N941LF	A320	0461	N945AX	DC-9	47551
N934FT	B727	19430	N937VJ	DC-9	48117	N941LT	E145	14500926	N945CA	CRJ	7069
N934L	DC-9	47618	N937VV	DC-9	45774	(N941MC)	MD80	49663	N945DL	MD80	49818
N934LK	DC-9	48157	N938AN	737NG	29533	N941ML	DC-9	47131	N945F	DC-9	47279
N934MC	MD80	49122	N938AS	MD80	49365	N941MT	MD80	49941	N945FR	A319	2751
N934MD	MD90	53552	N938AT	B717	55098	N941N	DC-9	47540	N945GE	DC-8	45945
N934ML	DC-9	47526	N938AX	DC-9	47009	N941NE	DC-9	47633	N945L	DC-9	45728
N934NA	DC-9	47428	N938CA	CRJ	7046	N941PG	B737	21799	N945MA	MD80	49725
N934NU	B737	27830	(N938CA)	CRJ	7050	N941PS	MD80	48096	N945ML	DC-9	47168
N934PG	B737	24366	N938DL	MD80	49811	N941SW	CRJ	7750	N945N	DC-9	47664
N934PS	MD80	48042	(N938EV)	CRJ	8043	N941TD	F.28	11073	N945PG	B737	23412
N934SW	CRJ	7722	N938F	DC-9	47221	N941UA	B737	26676	N945PS	B737	49138
N934UA	B737	26662	N938FR	A319	2406	N941UP	B727	19196	N945SW	CRJ	7770
N934UP	B727	19135	(N938FT)	B727	19131	N941UW	B757	27806	N945UA	B737	26684
N934UW	B757	27200	N938GA	B747	21938	N941VJ	DC-9	47054	N945UP	B727	19069
N934VJ	DC-9	48114	N938LR	CRJ9	15038	N941VV	DC-9	47666	N945UW	E190	19000062
N934VV	DC-9	47488	N938MC	MD80	49525	N942AA	DC-9	48118	N945VJ	DC-9	47066
N935AF	F145	14500920	N938ML	DC-9	47007	(N942AN)	737NG	29535	N945VV	DC-9	47238
N935AN	737NG	30081	N938PG	B737	23169	N942AN	737NG	30084	N945WP	B737	24212
N935AS	MD80	49236	N938PR	DC-9	47098	N942AS	MD80	53052	N946AN	737NG	30600
N935AT	B717	55069	N938PS	MD80	48094	N942AT	B717	55005	N946AS	MD80	49658
N935AX	DC-9	47413	N938SW	CRJ	7741	N942AX	DC-9	47552	N946AT	B717	55009
N935DL	MD80	49722	N938UA	B737	26671	N942DL	MD80	49815	N946AX	DC-9	47003
N935DS	DC-9	48158	N938UP	B727	19506	N942F	DC-9	47408	N946CA	CRJ	7072
N935EV	CRJ	8037	N938UW	B757	27246	N942FR	A319	2497	N946DL	MD80	49819
N935F	DC-9	47220	N938VJ	DC-9	48119	N942FT	B727	19431	N946FR	A319	2763
N935F	DC-9	47407	N938VV	DC-9	47442	N942LL	E145	14500930	N946L	DC-9	45729
N935FR	A319	2318	N939AE	E145	14500923	N942LR	CRJ9	15042	N946LL	DC-10	46946
N935FT	B727	19180	N939AJ	E145	14500939	N942ML	DC-9	47190	N946ML	DC-9	47170
N935L	DC-9	47603	N939AN	737NG	30083	N942ML	DC-9	47478	N946PG	DC-10	46542
N935LR	CRJ9	15035	N939AS	MD80	49657	N942N	DC-9	47459	N946PS	MD80	49139
N935MC	MD80	49125	N939AT	B717	55099	(N942PG)	B727	22603	N946SW	CRJ	7776
N935MD	MD90	53553	N939AX	DC-9	47201	N942PG	B737	21716	N946UA	B737	26687
N935ML	DC-9	47549	N939DL	MD80	49812	N942PS	MD80	48097	N946UP	B727	19721
N935PG	B727	21628	N939F	DC-9	47413	N942UA	B737	26679	N946UW	E190	19000072
N935PS	MD80	48043	N939FR	A319	2448	N942UP	B727	19101	N946VJ	DC-9	47026
N935SW	CRJ	7725	N939FT	B727	19388	N942UW	B757	27807	N946VV	DC-9	47226
N935UA	B737	26663	N939LR	CRJ9	15039	N942VJ	DC-9	47057	N946WP	B737	23173
N935UP	B727	20143	N939MC	MD80	49526	N942VV	DC-9	47648	N947AC	B767	24947
N935UW	B757	27201	N939ML	DC-9	45710	N943AA	DC-9	48141	N947AN	737NG	29536
N935VJ	DC-9	48115	N939PG	B737	23225	(N943AN)	737NG	30085	N947AS	MD80	53020
N935VV	DC-9	47534	N939PR	DC-9	47120	N943AN	737NG	30599	N947AT	B717	55010

Reg	Type	S/N	Reg	Type	S/N	Reg	Type	S/N	Reg	Type	S/N
N947AX	DC-9	47004	N951PG	B757	22185	N957AS	MD80	49126	N963DE	A321	0963
N947CA	CRJ	7077	N951PS	MD80	49429	N957AT	B717	55019	N963DL	MD80	49982
N947DL	MD80	49878	N951R	DC-8	46092	N957AX	DC-9	47759	(N963HA)	DC-9	47735
N947FR	A319	2806	N951SW	CRJ	7795	N957CA	CRJ	7109	N963ML	DC-9	45872
N947L	DC-9	45730	N951TW	MD80	53470	N957DL	MD80	49976	N963N	DC-9	47415
N947ML	DC-9	47514	N951U	MD80	49245	(N957HA)	DC-9	47784	N963PG	MD80	49568
N947PG	B737	21806	N951UA	B737	26696	N957N	DC-9	47253	N963R	DC-8	45901
(N947PS)	MD80	49140	N951UP	B727	19850	N957PG	B767	24349	N963SW	CRJ	7865
N947PS	MD80	49142	N951UW	E190	19000112	N957R	DC-8	46137	N963TW	MD80	53613
N947SW	CRJ	7786	N951VJ	DC-9	47576	N957SW	CRJ	7829	N963VJ	DC-9	47508
N947UA	B737	26688	N951VV	DC-9	47305	N957U	MD80	49702	N963WP	B737	28868
N947UP	B727	19722	N951WP	B737	22951	N957UA	B737	26707	N964AN	737NG	30093
N947UW	E190	19000078	N952AA	737NG	30088	N958AN	737NG	30091	N964AS	MD80	53078
N947VV	DC-9	47555	N952AT	B717	55014	N958AS	MD80	53024	N964AT	B717	55025
N947WP	B737	23376	N952AX	DC-9	47615	N958AT	B717	55020	N964AX	DC-9	47781
N948AL	E145	145450	N952CA	CRJ	7092	N958AX	DC-9	47760	N964CA	CRJ	7129
N948AN	737NG	30086	N952DL	MD80	49883	N958CA	CRJ	7111	N964DL	MD80	49983
N948AS	MD80	53021	N952N	DC-9	47073	N958DL	MD80	49977	(N964HA)	DC-9	47726
N948AT	B717	55011	N952PG	B737	23226	N958N	DC-9	47254	N964ML	DC-9	45873
N948AV	B767	24948	N952PS	MD80	49443	N958PG	B757	24118	N964N	DC-9	47416
N948AX	DC-9	47065	N952R	DC-8	46061	N958SW	CRJ	7833	N964PG	B767	23764
N948CA	CRJ	7079	N952SW	CRJ	7805	N958U	MD80	49703	N964R	DC-8	46000
N948DL	MD80	49879	N952U	MD80	49266	N958VJ	DC-9	47351	N964SW	CRJ	7868
N948FR	A319	2836	N952UA	B737	26699	N959AN	737NG	30828	N964TW	MD80	53614
N948GE	B767	24948	N952VJ	DC-9	47574	N959AT	B717	55021	N964VJ	DC-9	47373
N948L	DC-9	47049	N952VV	DC-9	47303	N959AX	DC-9	47761	N964VV	DC-9	47555
N948MA	MD80	49778	N952WP	B737	23378	N959CA	CRJ	7116	N964WP	B737	28869
N948ML	DC-9	47169	N953AN	737NG	29539	N959DL	MD80	49978	N965AN	737NG	29544
N948PG	B737	23172	N953AS	MD80	49386	(N959HA)	DC-9	47658	N965AS	MD80	53079
(N948PS)	MD80	49141	N953AT	B717	55015	N959N	DC-9	47255	N965AT	B717	55026
N948PS	MD80	49143	N953AX	DC-9	47608	N959PG	MD80	49741	N965AX	DC-9	47498
N948SW	CRJ	7789	N953DL	MD80	49884	N959R	DC-8	46143	N965CA	CRJ	7131
N948TW	MD80	49575	N953N	DC-9	47083	N959SW	CRJ	7840	N965DL	MD80	49984
N948UA	B737	26691	N953PG	MD80	49846	N959U	MD80	49704	(N965HA)	DC-9	47661
N948UP	B727	19357	N953SW	CRJ	7813	N959VJ	DC-9	47352	N965ML	DC-9	45874
N948UW	E190	19000081	N953U	MD80	49267	N960AN	737NG	29542	N965N	DC-9	47417
N948VV	DC-9	47559	N953UA	B737	26700	N960AS	MD80	53074	N965PG	B727	20639
N948WP	B737	23259	N953VJ	DC-9	47583	N960AT	B717	55022	N965SW	CRJ	7871
N949AN	737NG	29537	N953WP	B737	23384	N960AX	DC-9	47762	N965TW	MD80	53615
N949AS	MD80	53022	N954AN	737NG	30089	N960CA	CRJ	7117	N965VJ	DC-9	47374
N949AT	B717	55003	N954AS	MD80	49387	N960CC	B707	17634	N965VV	DC-9	47202
N949AX	DC-9	47325	N954AT	B717	55016	N960DL	MD80	49979	N965WP	B737	28870
N949CA	CRJ	7080	N954AX	DC-9	47612	N960JS	B747	19960	N966AN	737NG	30094
N949DL	MD80	49880	N954CA	CRJ	7100	N960N	DC-9	47256	N966AS	MD80	49104
N949FR	A319	2857	N954DL	MD80	49885	N960PG	MD80	49904	N966AT	B717	55027
N949L	DC-9	45844	N954N	DC-9	47159	N960SW	CRJ	7853	N966AX	DC-9	47510
N949MA	MD80	49779	N954PG	B737	21795	N960TW	MD80	49231	N966C	A300	117
N949N	DC-9	47566	N954R	DC-8	45908	N960VJ	DC-9	47505	N966CA	CRJ	7132
N949PG	B737	23159	N954SW	CRJ	7815	N960VV	DC-9	47067	N966DL	MD80	53115
N949PS	MD80	49237	N954U	MD80	49426	N960WP	B737	23331	(N966HA)	DC-9	47654
N949UA	B737	26692	N954UA	B737	26739	N961AN	737NG	30092	N966ML	DC-9	47217
N949UP	B727	19717	N954UP	B727	19827	N961AS	MD80	53075	N966PG	737NG	28577
N949UW	E190	19000102	N954VJ	DC-9	47590	N961AT	B717	55023	N966TW	MD80	53616
N949VV	DC-9	47484	(N954WP)	B737	23787	N961DL	MD80	49980	N966VJ	DC-9	47420
N949WP	B737	23230	N955AN	737NG	29540	N961GF	DC-10	46961	N966VV	DC-9	47168
N950AN	737NG	30087	N955AS	MD80	48080	N961LF	A320	0453	N966WP	B737	28871
N950AS	MD80	53023	N955AT	B717	55017	N961N	DC-9	47405	N967AN	737NG	29545
N950AT	B717	55012	N955AX	DC-9	47619	N961PG	B737	23161	N967AS	MD80	49103
N950CC	1-11	086	N955DL	MD80	49886	N961R	DC-8	46133	N967AT	B717	55028
N950DL	MD80	49881	N955N	DC-9	47160	N961SW	CRJ	7857	N967AX	DC-9	47509
N950FR	A319	3028	N955PG	B757	24371	N961TW	MD80	53611	N967C	A300	121
N950JW	DC-8	46058	N955SW	CRJ	7817	N961VJ	DC-9	47506	N967CA	CRJ	7134
(N950L)	DC-9	47246	N955U	MD80	49427	N961WP	B737	23332	N967DL	MD80	53116
N950PB	DC-9	47394	N955UA	B737	26703	N962AN	737NG	30858	N967ML	DC-9	45875
N950PG	B737	23160	N955VJ	DC-9	47593	N962AS	MD80	53076	N967N	DC-9	47573
N950PS	MD80	48028	N955WP	B737	24463	N962AX	DC-9	47768	N967PG	DC-10	46945
N950R	DC-8	45903	N956AN	737NG	30090	N962CA	CRJ	7123	N967PR	DC-9	47121
N950U	MD80	49230	N956AS	MD80	48079	N962CW	E145	145462	N967SW	CRJ	7872
N950UA	B737	26695	N956AT	B717	55018	N962DL	MD80	49981	N967TW	MD80	53617
N950UP	B727	19718	N956AX	DC-9	47620	N962GF	DC-10	46640	N967VJ	DC-9	47375
N950UW	E190	19000106	N956CA	CRJ	7105	N962ML	DC-9	45871	N967VV	DC-10	46967
N950VJ	DC-9	47564	N956DL	MD80	49887	N962N	DC-9	47406	N967VV	DC-9	47170
(N950VV)	DC-9	47307	N956LR	CRJ9	15056	N962PG	B757	24119	(N967WP)	B737	28873
N950WP	B737	23229	N956N	DC-9	47252	N962SW	CRJ	7859	N968AN	737NG	30095
N951AA	737NG	29538	N956PG	B737	23166	N962TW	MD80	53612	N968AS	MD80	53016
N951AS	MD80	49111	N956PT	DC-10	47956	N962VJ	DC-9	47507	N968AT	B717	55029
N951AT	B717	55013	N956SW	CRJ	7825	N962WP	B737	23748	N968AX	DC-9	47499
N951AX	DC-9	47616	N956U	MD80	49701	N963AN	737NG	29543	N968C	A300	126
N951CA	CRJ	7091	N956UA	B737	26704	N963AS	MD80	53077	N968DL	MD80	53161
N951DL	MD80	49882	N956VJ	DC-9	47588	N963AT	B717	55024	N968E	DC-9	45786
N951LF	A320	0460	N956WP	B737	24299	N963AX	DC-9	47780	N968ML	DC-9	45876
N951N	DC-9	47067	N957AN	737NG	29541	N963CA	CRJ	7127			

(N968PG)	B737	20909	**N974AX**	**DC-9**	**47623**	N978TW	MD80	53628	N983PG	B737	22761
N968TW	MD80	53618	N974C	A300	126	N978UA	B737	21509	N983PS	B737	20156
N968VJ	DC-9	47429	**N974DL**	MD80	53242	N978VJ	DC-9	47371	**N983SW**	**CRJ**	**7961**
(N968WP)	B737	28872	**N974EV**	**CRJ**	**7594**	N978Z	DC-9	47250	**N983TW**	MD80	53633
N969AN	737NG	29546	N974ML	DC-9	47119	**N979AL**	B727	21979	N983UA	B737	21641
N969AS	MD80	53063	N974NE	DC-9	47066	(N979AN)	737NG	29551	N983US	DC-9	47282
N969AT	**B717**	**55030**	N974PG	B737	21496	**N979AS**	MD80	53471	N983VJ	DC-9	48159
N969AX	**DC-9**	**47464**	N974PS	B727	18798	**N979AT**	**B717**	**55038**	N983Z	DC-9	47411
N969CA	**CRJ**	**7141**	N974PS	B727	18912	**N979AX**	**DC-9**	**47492**	(N984AN)	737NG	29553
N969DL	MD80	53172	N974RP	E145	145203	N979CA	CRJ	7159	**N984AN**	**B767**	**24357**
(N969HA)	DC-9	47763	N974RY	737NG	28617	**N979DL**	MD80	53266	(N984AT)	B717	55043
N969ML	DC-9	47268	**N974TW**	MD80	53624	**N979EV**	**CRJ**	**7737**	N984AX	A300	47258
N969PG	B727	22269	N974UA	B737	21597	N979NE	DC-9	47097	(N984C)	A300	108
N969SW	**CRJ**	**7876**	N974VJ	DC-9	47130	N979PG	B767	26608	**N984CA**	**CRJ**	**7171**
N969TW	MD80	53619	N974VV	DC-10	46974	**N979RP**	E170	17000088	**N984DL**	MD80	53311
N969VJ	DC-9	47421	N974Z	DC-9	47034	**N979SW**	**CRJ**	**7954**	N984PS	B737	20157
N969Z	DC-9	47001	**N975AN**	737NG	29549	**N979TW**	MD80	53629	N984PS	B737	22762
N970AN	737NG	30096	**N975AS**	MD80	53451	N979U	B737	21544	N984RT	B727	21984
N970AT	**B717**	**55031**	**N975AT**	**B717**	**55035**	N979VJ	DC-9	47372	**N984TW**	MD80	53634
N970AX	**DC-9**	**47494**	**N975AX**	**DC-9**	**47512**	N979Z	DC-9	47343	N984UA	B737	21642
N970C	A300	250	N975CA	CRJ	7150	**N980AL**	DC-9	47383	**N984US**	**DC-9**	**47383**
N970DL	MD80	53173	**N975DL**	MD80	53243	(N980AN)	737NG	30101	N984VJ	DC-9	47207
N970EV	**CRJ**	**7527**	**N975EV**	**CRJ**	**7599**	**N980AT**	**B717**	**55039**	N984Z	DC-9	47412
(N970HA)	DC-9	47764	N975ML	DC-9	47271	**N980AX**	**DC-9**	**47176**	(N985AM)	737NG	30901
N970ML	DC-9	47269	N975NE	DC-9	47075	(N980C)	A300	086	**N985AN**	**B767**	**24618**
N970NE	DC-9	47053	N975PG	B737	21498	N980DC	MD80	48000	(N985AT)	B717	55044
N970PS	B727	18908	N975PS	B727	18990	**N980DL**	MD80	53267	**N985AT**	**B717**	**55090**
N970SW	**CRJ**	**7881**	N975RP	E145	145337	**N980EV**	**CRJ**	**7759**	**N985AX**	**DC-9**	**47522**
N970TW	MD80	53620	N975RY	737NG	28592	N980GC	MD80	49888	(N985C)	A300	119
N970VJ	DC-9	47050	**N975SW**	**CRJ**	**7951**	N980NE	DC-9	47134	**N985DL**	MD80	53312
N970Z	DC-9	45772	**N975TW**	MD80	53625	N980PG	B727	21629	N985PG	B737	21718
N971AN	737NG	29547	N975VJ	DC-9	47146	N980SB	MD80	48051	N985PS	B737	20158
N971AT	**B717**	**55032**	N975Z	DC-9	47035	**N980SW**	**CRJ**	**7955**	N985UA	B737	21747
N971AX	**DC-9**	**47497**	**N976AL**	DC-8	45976	**N980TW**	MD80	53630	N985US	DC-9	47479
N971C	A300	262	**N976AN**	737NG	30099	N980UA	B737	21545	N985VJ	DC-9	47208
N971CA	**CRJ**	**7145**	**N976AS**	MD80	53452	N980VJ	DC-9	48156	N985Z	DC-9	47491
N971DL	MD80	53214	**N976AX**	**DC-9**	**47596**	N980Z	DC-9	47344	**N986AM**	737NG	29554
N971EV	**CRJ**	**7528**	N976CA	CRJ	7151	(N981AN)	737NG	30897	**N986AN**	**B767**	**24835**
N971GT	A320	0179	**N976DL**	MD80	53257	**N981AS**	MD80	53472	(N986AT)	B717	55045
N971ML	DC-9	47270	**N976EV**	**CRJ**	**7601**	**N981AT**	**B717**	**55040**	**N986AT**	**B717**	**55089**
N971NE	DC-9	47054	N976ML	DC-9	47272	N981AX	DC-9	47273	**N986AX**	**DC-9**	**47543**
N971PG	B747	25422	N976NE	DC-9	47082	(N981C)	A300	087	(N986C)	A300	154
N971PS	B727	18909	N976PG	B737	20521	**N981CA**	**CRJ**	**7163**	**N986CA**	**CRJ**	**7174**
N971RP	E145	145426	N976PS	B727	18799	**N981DL**	MD80	53268	**N986DL**	MD80	53313
N971SW	**CRJ**	**7947**	N976PS	B727	19398	**N981EV**	**CRJ**	**7768**	N986PG	B737	22659
N971TW	MD80	53621	N976RP	E145	145322	**N981JM**	B747	21162	N986PS	B737	20159
N971VJ	DC-9	47051	**N976SW**	**CRJ**	**7952**	N981LR	A320	0558	**N986SW**	**CRJ**	**7967**
N971Z	DC-9	45773	**N976TW**	MD80	53626	N981NE	DC-9	47135	N986UA	B737	21748
N972AN	737NG	30097	N976UA	B737	21598	N981PG	B727	21634	N986US	DC-9	47480
N972AS	MD80	53448	N976VJ	DC-9	48147	N981PS	DC-9	47006	N986VJ	DC-9	47209
N972AT	**B717**	**55033**	N976Z	DC-9	47248	N981SB	MD80	48058	N986Z	DC-9	47589
N972AX	**DC-9**	**47631**	**N977AN**	737NG	29550	(N981TW)	MD80	53631	**N987AA**	B707	18825
N972C	A300	289	**N977AS**	MD80	53453	N981UA	B737	21546	**N987AN**	B757	25494
N972DL	MD80	53215	**N977AT**	**B717**	**55036**	N981VJ	DC-9	48157	N987AS	CV990	30-10-13
N972EV	**CRJ**	**7534**	**N977AX**	**DC-9**	**47513**	N981Z	DC-9	47207	(N987AT)	B717	55046
N972ML	DC-9	47036	N977CA	CRJ	7157	(N982AN)	737NG	29552	**N987AT**	**B717**	**55088**
N972NE	DC-9	47057	**N977DL**	MD80	53258	**N982AS**	MD80	53473	N987AX	DC-9	47364
N972PG	A320	0916	**N977EV**	**CRJ**	**7720**	**N982AT**	**B717**	**55041**	(N987C)	A300	155
N972PS	B727	18910	N977ML	DC-9	47329	**N982AX**	**DC-9**	**47317**	**N987CA**	**CRJ**	**7199**
N972RP	E145	145440	N977MP	B737	21518	(N982C)	A300	091	**N987DL**	MD80	53338
N972TW	MD80	53622	N977NE	DC-9	47095	**N982CA**	**CRJ**	**7168**	N987PG	B747	24883
N972VJ	DC-9	47052	N977PG	MD80	49877	**N982DL**	MD80	53273	N987PS	B737	20160
N972Z	DC-9	45841	N977PS	B727	18800	**N982JM**	B727	21695	N987UA	B737	21749
N973AN	737NG	29548	N977PS	B727	19815	N982NE	DC-9	47136	**N987US**	**DC-9**	**47458**
N973AS	MD80	53449	**N977RP**	E145	145185	N982PG	B737	22256	N987VJ	DC-9	47210
N973AX	**DC-9**	**47511**	**N977RY**	737NG	32740	N982PS	DC-9	47251	N987Z	DC-9	47137
N973CA	**CRJ**	**7146**	**N977UA**	B737	21508	**N982SW**	**CRJ**	**7956**	**N988AM**	737NG	29561
N973DL	MD80	53241	N977VJ	DC-9	48155	**N982TW**	MD80	53632	**N988AN**	**B767**	**24742**
N973EV	**CRJ**	**7575**	N977Z	DC-9	47249	N982UA	B737	21640	**N988AT**	**B717**	**55068**
N973ML	DC-9	47074	N978AL	B727	21978	N982US	DC-9	45790	N988AX	DC-9	47084
N973NE	DC-9	47058	**N978AN**	737NG	30100	N982VJ	DC-9	48158	(N988C)	A300	216
N973PG	B727	20640	N978AS	MD80	53470	(N982Z)	DC-9	47561	**N988CA**	**CRJ**	**7204**
N973PS	B727	18797	**N978AT**	**B717**	**55037**	(N983AN)	737NG	30899	**N988DL**	MD80	53339
N973PS	B727	18911	**N978AX**	**DC-9**	**47628**	N983AT	B717	55042	N988PG	MD11	48408
N973RP	E145	145444	N978CA	CRJ	7158	**N983AT**	**B717**	**55052**	N988PS	B737	20368
N973SW	**CRJ**	**7949**	**N978DL**	MD80	53259	N983AX	DC-9	47257	N988UA	B737	21750
N973TW	MD80	53623	**N978EV**	**CRJ**	**7723**	(N983C)	A300	092	N988US	DC-9	47480
N973VJ	DC-9	47099	N978NE	DC-9	47096	**N983CA**	**CRJ**	**7169**	N988VJ	DC-9	47211
N973Z	DC-9	47033	N978PG	MD80	49668	**N983DL**	MD80	53274	N988Z	DC-9	47134
N974AN	737NG	30098	N978PS	B727	18801	**N983JC**	E145	14500977	**N989AN**	B757	24293
N974AS	MD80	53450	**N978RP**	E145	145169	N983MQ	B757	23983	**N989AT**	**B717**	**55152**
N974AT	**B717**	**55034**	**N978SW**	**CRJ**	**7953**	N983NE	DC-9	47137	**N989AX**	**DC-9**	**47314**

Reg	Type	Ser	Reg	Type	Ser	Reg	Type	Ser	Reg	Type	Ser
(N989C)	A300	220	N997AM	737NG	30283	N1005T	MD80	49425	N1070T	DC-9	45784
N989CA	CRJ	7215	N997AT	B717	55141	N1005U	MD80	49428	N1074T	MD80	49727
N989DL	MD80	53341	N997CF	DC-8	46154	(N1005U)	SE210	89	N1075T	MD80	49724
(N989PG)	MD11	48410	N997DL	MD80	53364	N1005U	SE210	90	N1100P	L1011	193B-1016
N989PG	MD80	49845	N997EA	DC-9	47749	N1005V	MD80	49149	"N1101N"	737NG	29441
N989PS	B737	20369	N997GA	DC-10	46997	N1005W	MD80	49662	N1105X	C-17	P.105
N989UA	B737	21751	N997GE	DC-8	45997	N1006F	737NG	30782	N1112J	1-11	030
N989VJ	DC-9	47212	N997PG	B727	21343	N1006K	B757	30423	N1113J	1-11	031
N989Z	DC-9	47135	N997UA	B737	22457	(N1006U)	SE210	90	N1114J	1-11	032
N990AB	CV990	30-10-2	N997VJ	DC-9	47336	N1006U	SE210	91	N1115J	1-11	082
N990AC	CV990	30-10-5	N997Z	DC-9	47029	(N1007U)	SE210	91	N1116J	1-11	BAC.098
N990AM	737NG	29556	N998AA	B727	21344	N1007U	SE210	92	N1117J	1-11	BAC.099
N990AT	B717	55134	N998AM	737NG	29555	(N1008U)	SE210	92	N1118J	1-11	BAC.100
N990AX	DC-9	47493	N998AT	B717	55142	N1008U	SE210	93	N1119J	1-11	BAC.101
(N990C)	A300	259	N998CF	DC-8	46139	(N1009U)	SE210	93	N1120J	1-11	BAC.102
N990CF	DC-8	46068	N998DL	MD80	53370	N1009U	SE210	94	N1122J	1-11	BAC.103
N990DL	MD80	53342	N998EA	DC-9	47751	(N1010U)	SE210	94	N1123J	1-11	BAC.104
N990E	CV990	30-10-16	N998GP	B747	24998	N1010U	SE210	95	N1124J	1-11	BAC.134
N990PG	MD80	49448	N998PG	B727	21502	N1011	L1011	193A-1001	N1125J	1-11	BAC.135
N990SE	A320	0990	N998R	DC-9	47030	N1011N	737NG	29273	N1126J	1-11	BAC.179
N990UA	B737	21980	N998UA	B737	22741	N1011N	737NG	29441	N1127J	1-11	BAC.180
N990Z	DC-9	47136	N999AM	737NG	29560	(N1011U)	SE210	95	N1128J	1-11	BAC.181
N991AT	B717	55135	N999BW	1-11	BAC.120	N1011U	SE210	96	N1129J	1-11	BAC.182
N991CA	CRJ	7216	N999CA	CRJ	7230	N1012N	B757	29012	N1130J	1-11	BAC.096
N991CF	DC-8	45801	N999CZ	B737	25604	N1012U	SE210	96	N1131J	1-11	BAC.097
(N991DB)	B727	22163	N999DN	MD80	53371	N1012U	SE210	97	N1132J	1-11	BAC.105
N991DL	MD80	53343	N999EA	DC-9	47753	(N1013U)	SE210	97	N1134J	1-11	045
N991EA	DC-9	47728	N999UA	B737	22742	N1013U	SE210	98	N1135J	1-11	046
(N991JM)	B737	23249	N999WA	COMET	6425	N1014S	737NG	29078	N1136J	1-11	071
N991LR	A320	0561	"N1001N"	737NG	29273	(N1014U)	SE210	98	N1181L	L1011	193R-1033
N991PG	MD80	48079	N1001U	SE210	86	N1014U	SE210	99	N1181Z	B707	19693
N991UA	B737	21981	N1002D	DC-10	46970	N1014X	737NG	30476	N1186Z	B727	19134
N991VJ	DC-9	47310	N1002G	MD80	48001	N1015B	737NG	30413	N1187Z	B727	18323
N991Z	DC-9	47096	N1002N	DC-9	47782	N1015B	B737	29210	N1200K	B767	28457
N992AJ	B727	19428	N1002R	737NG	28107	N1015U	SE210	100	N1201P	B767	28458
N992AM	737NG	29557	N1002R	737NG	30587	(N1015U)	SE210	99	N1235E	B727	21270
N992AT	B717	55136	N1002R	B757	29018	N1015X	B737	28596	N1238E	B737	21296
N992CF	DC-8	45884	(N1002U)	SE210	62	(N1016U)	SE210	100	N1239E	B727	22078
N992DL	MD80	53344	N1002U	SE210	87	N1016U	SE210	101	N1239E	B747	21251
N992EA	DC-9	47731	N1002W	MD80	48015	(N1017U)	SE210	101	N1243E	B737	21283
N992MS	B747	21961	N1002X	DC-10	46583	N1017U	SE210	102	N1246E	B727	21297
N992PG	MD80	49229	N1002Y	DC-10	46584	N1018N	B757	29304	N1248E	B747	21468
N992UA	B737	22089	N1003G	MD80	48050	(N1018U)	SE210	102	N1252E	B747	21537
N992Z	DC-9	47095	N1003L	DC-10	48258	N1018U	SE210	103	N1253E	B727	21539
N993AM	737NG	29558	N1003M	737NG	28288	(N1019U)	SE210	103	N1261E	B727	21540
N993AT	B717	55137	N1003M	737NG	29980	N1019U	SE210	104	N1261L	DC-9	47317
N993CF	DC-8	46028	N1003M	B757	29023	N1020A	B757	30824	N1262E	B737	21716
N993DL	MD80	53345	N1003M	B757	30178	N1020L	B737	28737	N1262L	DC-9	47257
N993EA	DC-9	47732	N1003N	737NG	28580	N1020L	B757	30061	N1263L	DC-9	47258
N993PG	MD80	49120	N1003N	737NG	29979	(N1020U)	SE210	104	N1264L	DC-9	47259
N993UA	B737	22383	N1003N	DC-10	48276	N1020U	SE210	114	N1265L	DC-9	47260
N993VJ	DC-9	47332	N1003P	DC-9	48160	N1023C	F145	145550	N1266L	DC-9	47261
N993Z	DC-9	47082	N1003U	DC-9	48151	N1024A	B737	28739	N1267L	DC-9	47262
N994AJ	B727	20942	(N1003U)	SE210	87	N1024A	B757	29305	N1268L	DC-9	47284
N994AT	B717	55138	N1003U	SE210	88	N1026G	737NG	30752	N1269E	B737	21723
N994CF	DC-8	45956	N1003W	737NG	30756	N1026G	B737	28741	N1269E	B737	21763
N994DL	MD80	53346	N1003W	B737	29208	N1031F	DC-10	46825	N1269L	DC-9	47285
N994EA	DC-9	47733	N1003W	DC-10	48289	N1032F	DC-10	46826	N1269Y	B727	21269
N994UA	B737	22384	N1003X	MD80	48067	(N1033F)	DC-10	46827	N1270L	DC-9	47318
N994VJ	DC-9	47333	N1003Y	MD80	48068	N1033F	DC-10	46960	N1271L	DC-9	47319
N994Z	DC-9	47097	N1003Z	MD80	48069	N1034F	DC-10	46962	N1272L	DC-9	47320
N995AM	737NG	29559	N1004A	DC-10	48294	N1035F	DC-10	46992	N1273E	B727	21930
N995AT	B717	55139	N1004B	DC-10	48295	N1041W	DC-8	45669	N1273L	DC-9	47321
N995CA	CRJ	7229	N1004D	MD80	48089	N1051T	DC-9	45714	N1274E	B737	21599
N995CF	DC-8	46024	N1004F	MD80	48090	N1052T	DC-9	45715	N1274L	DC-9	47322
N995CW	E145	145495	N1004G	MD80	48091	N1053T	DC-9	45716	N1275E	B737	21790
N995DL	MD80	53362	N1004L	MD80	49110	N1054T	DC-9	45735	N1275L	DC-9	47323
N995EA	DC-9	47745	N1004N	MD80	49111	N1055T	DC-9	45736	N1276L	DC-9	47324
N995UA	B737	22399	N1004S	MD80	48088	N1056T	DC-9	45737	N1277L	DC-9	47356
N995VJ	DC-9	47334	N1004S	MD80	49140	N1057T	DC-9	45738	N1278L	DC-9	47357
N995WL	DC-8	45603	N1004U	MD80	49102	N1058T	DC-9	45739	N1279E	B727	21971
N995Z	DC-9	47027	(N1004U)	SE210	88	N1059T	DC-9	45740	N1279L	DC-9	47358
N996AT	B717	55140	N1004U	SE210	89	N1060T	DC-9	45741	N1280E	B727	21972
N996CF	DC-8	46162	N1004W	MD80	48022	N1061T	DC-9	45775	N1280L	DC-9	47359
N996DL	MD80	53363	N1004Y	MD80	49373	N1062T	DC-9	45776	N1281L	DC-9	47377
N996EA	DC-9	47746	N1005A	MD80	49103	N1063T	DC-9	45777	N1282L	DC-9	47378
N996GE	DC-8	45996	N1005B	MD80	49104	N1064T	DC-9	45778	N1283L	DC-9	47379
N996SE	A320	1996	N1005G	MD80	49142	N1065T	DC-9	45779	N1284L	DC-9	47380
N996UA	B737	22456	N1005J	MD80	49143	N1066T	DC-9	45780	N1285E	B737	21790
N996VJ	DC-9	47335	N1005N	MD80	49374	N1067T	DC-9	45781	N1285L	DC-9	47381
N996Z	DC-9	47028	N1005S	737NG	30572	N1068T	DC-9	45782	N1286L	DC-9	47426
N997AA	B727	21343	N1005S	MD80	49355	N1069T	DC-9	45783	N1287L	DC-9	47427

Reg	Type	MSN
N1288	B737	20195
N1288E	B747	21668
(N1288E)	B747	21832
N1288L	DC-9	47443
(N1289E)	B727	21971
(N1289E)	B747	21833
N1289E	B747	22272
N1289L	DC-9	47444
(N1290E)	B727	21972
(N1290E)	B747	21834
N1290E	B747	22107
N1290L	DC-9	47445
N1291L	DC-9	47466
N1292L	DC-9	47529
N1293L	DC-9	47486
N1294L	DC-9	47516
N1295E	B747	22376
N1295L	DC-9	47525
N1298E	B747	22379
N1300L	DC-8	46014
N1301E	B747	22302
N1301L	DC-8	46018
N1301L	L1011	193A-1002
N1301T	DC-9	45695
N1302L	DC-8	46029
N1302T	DC-9	47043
N1303L	DC-8	46030
N1303T	DC-9	47044
N1304E	B747	21934
N1304L	DC-8	46048
N1304T	DC-9	47045
N1305E	B747	22428
N1305L	DC-8	46072
N1305T	DC-9	47055
N1306L	DC-8	46055
N1306T	DC-9	47061
N1307L	DC-8	46056
N1307T	DC-9	47062
N1308T	DC-9	47315
N1309E	B747	22380
N1309T	**DC-9**	**47316**
N1310T	DC-9	47487
N1311T	DC-9	47490
N1330U	DC-9	47411
N1331U	DC-9	47412
N1332U	**DC-9**	**47404**
N1334U	**DC-9**	**47280**
N1335U	DC-9	47393
N1336U	DC-9	47522
N1337U	DC-10	46704
N1338U	DC-10	46705
N1339U	DC-10	46550
N1340U	DC-10	46575
N1341U	DC-10	46850
N1342U	DC-10	46551
N1343U	DC-9	47570
N1345U	DC-9	47562
N1346U	DC 9	47563
N1346U	F.28	11173
N1347U	DC-9	47567
N1348U	DC-10	46727
N1349U	DC-10	46554
N1350U	DC-10	46851
N1352B	B747	20235
N1355B	B727	19527
N1355B	B727	20465
N1359B	B737	19758
N1400H	F.100	11340
N1401G	F.100	11352
N1402A	**B767**	**25989**
N1402K	F.100	11353
N1403M	F.100	11354
N1404D	F.100	11355
N1405J	F.100	11356
N1406A	F.100	11359
N1407D	F.100	11360
N1408B	F.100	11361
N1409B	F.100	11367
N1410E	F.100	11368
N1411G	F.100	11369
N1412A	F.100	11370
N1413A	F.100	11376
N1414D	F.100	11377
N1415K	F.100	11385
N1416A	F.100	11395
N1417D	F.100	11396
N1418A	F.100	11397
N1419D	F.100	11402
N1420D	F.100	11403
N1421K	F.100	11404
N1422J	F.100	11405
N1423A	F.100	11406
N1424M	F.100	11407
N1425A	F.100	11408
N1426A	F.100	11411
N1427A	F.100	11412
N1428D	F.100	11413
N1429G	F.100	11414
N1430D	F.100	11415
N1431B	F.100	11416
N1432A	F.100	11417
N1433B	F.100	11418
N1434A	F.100	11419
N1435D	F.100	11425
N1436A	F.100	11426
N1437B	F.100	11427
N1438H	F.100	11428
N1439A	F.100	11434
N1440A	F.100	11435
N1441A	F.100	11436
N1442E	F.100	11437
N1443A	F.100	11446
N1444N	F.100	11447
N1444Z	B737	20227
N1445B	F.100	11448
N1446A	F.100	11449
N1447L	F.100	11456
N1448A	F.100	11457
N1449D	F.100	11458
N1450A	F.100	11459
N1450Z	B737	20277
N1451N	F.100	11460
N1451Z	B737	20226
N1452B	F.100	11464
N1453D	F.100	11465
N1454D	F.100	11466
N1455K	F.100	11467
N1456D	F.100	11468
N1457B	F.100	11469
N1458H	F.100	11478
N1459A	F.100	11479
N1460A	F.100	11480
N1461C	F.100	11481
N1462C	F.100	11482
N1463A	F.100	11483
N1464A	F.100	11490
N1465K	F.100	11491
N1466A	F.100	11498
N1467A	F.100	11499
N1468A	F.100	11501
N1469D	F.100	11502
N1470K	F.100	11506
N1471G	F.100	11507
N1472B	F.100	11514
N1473K	F.100	11515
N1474D	F.100	11520
N1486B	B707	19809
N1501P	**B767**	**24983**
N1501U	DC-8	45822
N1501W	B707	19963
N1502U	DC-8	45823
N1502W	B707	19964
N1503U	DC-8	45903
N1503W	B707	19965
N1504U	DC-8	45901
N1504W	B707	19966
N1505U	DC-8	45909
N1505W	B707	19967
N1506W	B707	20315
N1507W	B707	20316
N1508W	B707	20317
N1509U	DC-8	45858
N1509W	B707	20318
N1510W	B707	20319
N1541	1-11	015
N1542	1-11	016
N1543	1-11	017
N1544	1-11	018
N1545	1-11	019
N1546	1-11	020
N1547	1-11	041
N1548	1-11	042
N1549	1-11	043
N1550	1-11	044
N1551	1-11	045
N1552	1-11	046
N1553	1-11	070
N1554	1-11	071
N1602	**B767**	**29694**
N1603	**B767**	**29695**
N1604R	**B767**	**30180**
N1605	**B767**	**30198**
N1607B	B747	22234
N1607B	**B767**	**30388**
N1608	**B767**	**30573**
N1608B	B747	22302
N1609	**B767**	**30574**
N1610D	**B767**	**30594**
N1611B	**B767**	**30595**
N1612T	**B767**	**30575**
N1613B	**B767**	**32776**
N1631	B727	18850
N1632	B727	18858
N1633	B727	19249
N1634	B727	19250
N1635	B727	19251
N1636	B727	19252
N1637	B727	19595
N1638	B727	19596
N1639	B727	19444
N1640	B727	19445
(N1640A)	B737	19679
N1641	B727	19446
N1642	B727	19447
N1643	B727	19448
N1644	B727	19449
N1645	B727	20139
N1646	B727	20140
N1647	B727	20141
N1648	B727	19994
N1649	B727	19995
N1650	B727	20248
N1673B	B707	19810
N1709B	B707	20830
N1714T	B737	21714
N1715Z	B737	21715
N1716B	B737	23766
N1727T	B727	19859
N1728T	B727	19860
N1731D	L1011	193C-1200
N1732D	L1011	193C-1213
N1733B	B737	20300
N1734D	L1011	193C-1225
N1738D	L1011	193C-1234
N1739D	L1011	193C-1237
N1748B	B727	19994
N1750B	MD11	48419
N1751A	MD11	48420
N1752K	MD11	48421
N1753	MD11	48487
N1754	MD11	48489
N1755	MD11	48490
N1756	**MD11**	**48491**
N1757	B757	24923
N1757A	MD11	48505
N1758B	MD11	48527
N1759	MD11	48481
(N1759)	MD11	48528
N1760A	MD11	48550
N1761R	MD11	48551
N1762B	MD11	48552
N1763	MD11	48553
N1764B	MD11	48554
N1765B	MD11	48596
N1766A	MD11	48597
N1767A	MD11	48598
N1768D	MD11	48436
N1776Q	B707	18041
N1776R	DC-8	45602
N1779B	737NG	28592
N1779B	737NG	29136
N1779B	737NG	29188
N1779B	737NG	29441
N1779B	737NG	29635
N1779B	737NG	29866
N1779B	737NG	33666
N1779B	737NG	34807
N1779B	737NG	35114
N1779B	737NG	36714
N1779B	B727	20525
N1779B	B727	20552
N1779B	B727	20764
N1779B	B727	22664
N1779B	B737	22777
N1779B	B737	22793
N1779B	B737	24463
N1779B	B737	29130
N1780B	737NG	28009
N1780B	737NG	28292
N1780B	737NG	28585
N1780B	737NG	28822
N1780B	737NG	29054
N1780B	737NG	30373
N1780B	737NG	30695
N1780B	737NG	34303
N1780B	737NG	35050
N1780B	737NG	35133
N1780B	737NG	35215
N1780B	737NG	35711
N1780B	B727	20217
N1780B	B727	20286
N1780B	B727	20432
N1780B	B727	20608
N1780B	B727	22263
N1780B	B727	22665
N1780B	B737	19679
N1780B	B737	22638
N1780B	B747	21515
N1780B	B747	21652
N1781B	737NG	28497
N1781R	737NG	28641
N1781B	737NG	29490
N1781B	737NG	30203
N1781B	737NG	30240
N1781B	737NG	30403
N1781B	737NG	30474
N1781B	737NG	30745
N1781B	737NG	30799
N1781B	737NG	30813
N1781B	737NG	30835
N1781B	737NG	32358
N1781B	737NG	33063
N1781B	737NG	33665
N1781B	737NG	33874
N1781B	737NG	34260
N1781B	B727	19524
N1781B	B727	19525
N1781B	B727	19526
N1781B	B727	19527
N1781B	B727	20243
N1781B	B727	20421
N1781B	B727	20426
N1781B	B727	20463
N1781B	B727	20464
N1781B	B727	20465
N1781B	B727	20468
N1781B	B727	20469
N1781B	B727	20540
N1781B	B737	19680
N1781B	B737	28993
N1781B	B747	23071
N1781B	B747	23150
N1781B	B767	22682
N1781B	B767	23018
N1782B	737NG	28219
N1782B	737NG	28322
N1782B	737NG	28787
N1782B	737NG	28824

Reg	Type	Serial	Reg	Type	Serial	Reg	Type	Serial	Reg	Type	Serial
N1782B	737NG	29043	N1785B	B747	25866	N1787B	737NG	28381	N1787B	737NG	30121
N1782B	737NG	29080	N1785B	B747	27163	N1787B	737NG	28382	N1787B	737NG	30125
N1782B	737NG	29142	N1785B	B747	28959	N1787B	737NG	28402	N1787B	737NG	30126
N1782B	737NG	29620	N1785B	B767	22981	N1787B	737NG	28500	N1787B	737NG	30134
N1782B	737NG	30265	N1785B	B767	23021	N1787B	737NG	28536	N1787B	737NG	30139
N1782B	737NG	30377	N1785B	B767	23178	N1787B	737NG	28581	N1787B	737NG	30162
N1782B	737NG	30477	N1785B	B767	27392	N1787B	737NG	28615	N1787B	737NG	30181
N1782B	737NG	30674	N1786B	737NG	30688	N1787B	737NG	28617	N1787B	737NG	30194
N1782B	737NG	30700	N1786B	737NG	30713	N1787B	737NG	28641	N1787B	737NG	30196
N1782B	737NG	33797	N1786B	737NG	32507	N1787B	737NG	28642	N1787B	737NG	30207
N1782B	737NG	34182	N1786B	737NG	32532	N1787B	737NG	28643	N1787B	737NG	30208
N1782B	737NG	35096	N1786B	737NG	32692	N1787B	737NG	28648	N1787B	737NG	30231
N1782B	737NG	35121	N1786B	737NG	32772	N1787B	737NG	28652	N1787B	737NG	30235
N1782B	B727	20244	N1786B	737NG	32834	N1787B	737NG	28653	N1787B	737NG	30236
N1782B	B727	22605	N1786B	737NG	33935	N1787B	737NG	28768	N1787B	737NG	30238
N1782B	B737	20779	N1786B	737NG	34277	N1787B	737NG	28788	N1787B	737NG	30271
N1782B	B737	22114	N1786B	737NG	34413	N1787B	737NG	28790	N1787B	737NG	30272
N1782B	B737	22776	N1786B	737NG	34414	N1787B	737NG	28792	N1787B	737NG	30275
N1782B	B737	24790	N1786B	737NG	34415	N1787B	737NG	28794	N1787B	737NG	30277
N1782B	B747	21681	N1786B	737NG	35050	N1787B	737NG	28795	N1787B	737NG	30279
N1782B	B747	22502	N1786B	737NG	35175	N1787B	737NG	28796	N1787B	737NG	30280
N1782B	B747	22614	N1786B	737NG	35212	N1787B	737NG	28822	N1787B	737NG	30286
N1783B	B727	20245	N1786B	737NG	35215	N1787B	737NG	28824	N1787B	737NG	30328
N1783B	B747	21255	N1786B	B707	20043	N1787B	737NG	28825	N1787B	737NG	30329
N1783B	B747	22479	N1786B	B727	20596	N1787B	737NG	28826	N1787B	737NG	30332
N1783B	B767	22527	N1786B	B727	22076	N1787B	737NG	28827	N1787B	737NG	30344
N1784B	737NG	28178	N1786B	B727	22158	N1787B	737NG	28935	N1787B	737NG	30356
N1784B	737NG	28224	N1786B	B737	20397	N1787B	737NG	28943	N1787B	737NG	30357
N1784B	737NG	28239	N1786B	B737	20917	N1787B	737NG	28945	N1787B	737NG	30358
N1784B	737NG	28307	N1786B	B737	22416	N1787B	737NG	28946	N1787B	737NG	30376
N1784B	737NG	28404	N1786B	B737	22505	N1787B	737NG	28951	N1787B	737NG	30404
N1784B	737NG	28595	N1786B	B737	22779	N1787B	737NG	28953	N1787B	737NG	30406
N1784B	737NG	28823	N1786B	B737	23522	N1787B	737NG	28954	N1787B	737NG	30411
N1784B	737NG	28825	N1786B	B737	23809	N1787B	737NG	28986	N1787B	737NG	30414
N1784B	737NG	28945	N1786B	B737	24912	N1787B	737NG	29036	N1787B	737NG	30417
N1784B	737NG	29103	N1786B	B737	24946	N1787B	737NG	29037	N1787B	737NG	30418
N1784B	737NG	29134	N1786B	B737	25150	N1787B	737NG	29054	N1787B	737NG	30458
N1784B	737NG	29904	N1786B	B737	25607	N1787B	737NG	29078	N1787B	737NG	30459
N1784B	737NG	30076	N1786B	B737	25608	N1787B	737NG	29082	N1787B	737NG	30460
N1784B	737NG	30159	N1786B	B737	28898	N1787B	737NG	29094	N1787B	737NG	30468
N1784B	737NG	30279	N1786B	B747	21220	N1787B	737NG	29106	N1787B	737NG	30474
N1784B	737NG	30495	N1786B	B747	23151	N1787B	737NG	29136	N1787B	737NG	30478
N1784B	737NG	30686	N1786B	B757	25133	N1787B	737NG	29142	N1787B	737NG	30497
N1784B	737NG	30751	N1786B	B757	25495	N1787B	737NG	29188	N1787B	737NG	30498
N1784B	737NG	30772	N1786B	B757	26160	N1787B	737NG	29246	N1787B	737NG	30543
N1784B	737NG	32488	N1786B	B757	26249	N1787B	737NG	29250	N1787B	737NG	30560
N1784B	737NG	32583	N1786B	B757	26254	N1787B	737NG	29273	N1787B	737NG	30567
N1784B	737NG	32774	N1786B	B757	28836	N1787B	737NG	29274	N1787B	737NG	30583
N1784B	737NG	33645	N1786B	B757	29609	N1787B	737NG	29317	N1787B	737NG	30593
N1784B	737NG	33921	N1786B	B757	30178	N1787B	737NG	29365	N1787B	737NG	30610
N17R4B	737NG	33994	N1786B	B757	30187	N1787B	737NG	29441	N1787B	737NG	30611
N1784B	737NG	34010	N1786B	B757	30397	N1787B	737NG	29444	N1787B	737NG	30617
N1784B	737NG	34297	N1786E	B737	25069	N1787B	737NG	29501	N1787B	737NG	30618
N1784B	737NG	34620	N1787B	737NG	27841	N1787B	737NG	29595	N1787B	737NG	30637
N1784B	B727	18464	N1787B	737NG	27844	N1787B	737NG	29596	N1787B	737NG	30638
N1784B	B737	25603	N1787B	737NG	27854	N1787B	737NG	29598	N1787B	737NG	30664
N1784B	B737	25604	N1787B	737NG	27855	N1787B	737NG	29619	N1787B	737NG	30684
N1784B	B737	26071	N1787B	737NG	27856	N1787B	737NG	29622	N1787B	737NG	30687
N1784B	B747	22705	N1787B	737NG	27860	N1787B	737NG	29660	N1787B	737NG	30706
N1784B	B747	23070	N1787B	737NG	27864	N1787B	737NG	29749	N1787B	737NG	30727
N1784B	B747	23222	N1787B	737NG	27865	N1787B	737NG	29769	N1787B	737NG	30742
N1784B	B767	22523	N1787B	737NG	27871	N1787B	737NG	29770	N1787B	737NG	30743
N1784B	B767	22785	N1787B	737NG	27878	N1787B	737NG	29778	N1787B	737NG	30753
N1784B	B767	22788	N1787B	737NG	27892	N1787B	737NG	29780	N1787B	737NG	30756
N1784B	B767	23020	N1787B	737NG	27896	N1787B	737NG	29788	N1787B	737NG	30781
N1785B	737NG	29274	N1787B	737NG	27984	N1787B	737NG	29807	N1787B	737NG	30790
N1785B	737NG	29809	N1787B	737NG	28009	N1787B	737NG	29808	N1787B	737NG	30794
N1785B	737NG	30173	N1787B	737NG	28056	N1787B	737NG	29811	N1787B	737NG	30816
N1785B	737NG	30182	N1787B	737NG	28221	N1787B	737NG	29836	N1787B	737NG	30829
N1785B	737NG	30243	N1787B	737NG	28225	N1787B	737NG	29848	N1787B	737NG	30878
N1785B	737NG	30736	N1787B	737NG	28239	N1787B	737NG	29849	N1787B	737NG	31591
N1785B	B707	20741	N1787B	737NG	28240	N1787B	737NG	29893	N1787B	737NG	31632
N1785B	B707	20761	N1787B	737NG	28244	N1787B	737NG	29912	N1787B	737NG	32277
N1785B	B727	19995	N1787B	737NG	28291	N1787B	737NG	29920	N1787B	737NG	32348
N1785B	B727	20430	N1787B	737NG	28293	N1787B	737NG	29923	N1787B	737NG	32354
N1785B	B727	20753	N1787B	737NG	28294	N1787B	737NG	29947	N1787B	737NG	32357
N1785B	B737	20396	N1787B	737NG	28299	N1787B	737NG	29980	N1787B	737NG	32374
N1785B	B737	23443	N1787B	737NG	28304	N1787B	737NG	30007	N1787B	737NG	32375
N1785B	B747	21516	N1787B	737NG	28305	N1787B	737NG	30031	N1787B	737NG	32406
N1785B	B747	22547	N1787B	737NG	28308	N1787B	737NG	30032	N1787B	737NG	32419
N1785B	B747	22616	N1787B	737NG	28309	N1787B	737NG	30070	N1787B	737NG	32425
N1785B	B747	22668	N1787B	737NG	28310	N1787B	737NG	30072	N1787B	737NG	32450

Reg	Type	No	Reg	Type	No	Reg	Type	No	Reg	Type	No
N1787B	737NG	32483	N1788B	B747	23814	N1795B	737NG	27866	N1796B	737NG	28930
N1787B	737NG	32499	N1788B	B747	23824	N1795B	737NG	28073	N1796B	737NG	29084
N1787B	737NG	32576	N1788B	B747	27602	N1795B	737NG	28216	N1796B	737NG	29601
N1787B	737NG	32579	N1788B	B767	23016	N1795B	737NG	28241	N1796B	737NG	30389
N1787B	737NG	32581	N1788B	B767	23179	N1795B	737NG	28301	N1796B	737NG	30783
N1787B	737NG	32599	N1788B	B767	24338	N1795B	737NG	28306	N1796B	B737	28894
N1787B	737NG	32628	N1788B	B767	26984	N1795B	737NG	28320	N1796B	B737	28895
N1787B	737NG	32635	N1789B	737NG	28100	N1795B	737NG	28322	N1796B	B747	19730
N1787B	737NG	32673	N1789B	737NG	29924	N1795B	737NG	28585	N1796B	B747	20771
N1787B	737NG	32738	N1789B	B727	20600	N1795B	737NG	28587	N1796U	DC-9	47450
N1787B	737NG	32754	N1789B	B737	23449	N1795B	737NG	28595	N1797B	B737	20299
N1787B	737NG	32807	N1789B	B737	23636	N1795B	737NG	28645	N1797U	DC-9	47442
N1787B	737NG	33014	N1789B	B737	24970	N1795B	737NG	28786	N1798B	737NG	30772
N1787B	737NG	33057	N1789B	B737	25115	N1795B	737NG	28787	N1798B	B747	19762
N1787B	737NG	33576	N1789B	B747	21725	N1795B	737NG	28823	N1798B	B747	20770
N1787B	737NG	33663	N1789B	B757	25495	N1795B	737NG	29366	N1798U	DC-9	47369
N1787B	737NG	33797	N1789B	B757	27621	N1795B	737NG	29771	N1799B	737NG	27851
N1787B	737NG	33873	N1789B	B757	28172	N1795B	737NG	29781	N1799B	737NG	30493
N1787B	737NG	33975	N1789B	B767	23017	N1795B	737NG	29818	N1799B	B737	20967
N1787B	737NG	34247	N1789B	B767	23180	N1795B	737NG	29820	N1799B	B737	25134
N1787B	737NG	34410	N1789B	B767	24350	N1795B	737NG	29857	N1799B	B737	28737
N1787B	737NG	34540	N1790	B737	20453	N1795B	737NG	29904	N1799B	B737	28739
N1787B	737NG	34559	N1790B	B727	20539	N1795B	737NG	29959	N1799B	B737	28741
N1787B	737NG	34630	N1790B	B727	20572	N1795B	737NG	29988	N1799B	B747	19761
N1787B	737NG	34701	N1790B	B727	20601	N1795B	737NG	30138	N1799B	B747	20704
N1787B	737NG	35219	N1790B	B737	20453	N1795B	737NG	30374	N1799B	B757	28484
N1787B	737NG	36714	N1790B	B737	23444	N1795B	737NG	30377	N1799B	B757	29380
N1787B	B727	20553	N1790B	B737	23450	N1795B	737NG	30378	N1799B	B757	29724
N1787B	B727	20595	N1790B	B737	24123	N1795B	737NG	30496	**N1799U**	**DC-9**	**47370**
N1787B	B727	20790	N1790B	B737	25508	N1795B	737NG	30499	N1800	DC-8	45274
N1787B	B727	21264	N1790B	B737	26539	N1795B	737NG	30571	N1800B	737NG	28535
N1787B	B737	20299	N1790B	B737	27333	N1795B	737NG	30576	N1800B	737NG	29621
N1787B	B737	20412	N1790B	B737	28740	N1795B	737NG	30652	N1800B	737NG	29913
N1787B	B737	21278	N1790B	B737	28881	N1795B	737NG	30792	N1800B	B737	22138
N1787B	B737	21279	N1790B	B747	21238	N1795B	737NG	30819	N1800B	B737	22505
N1787B	B737	21774	N1790B	B757	26436	N1795B	737NG	30836	N1800B	B737	22601
N1787B	B737	23000	N1790B	B757	28989	N1795B	737NG	31590	N1800B	B737	29408
N1787B	B737	25609	N1790U	DC-9	45785	N1795B	737NG	32482	N1800B	B747	19746
N1787B	B737	26069	N1791	B737	20454	N1795B	737NG	32492	N1800B	B747	20530
N1787B	B737	27460	N1791B	737NG	28110	N1795B	737NG	32582	N1800B	B747	21758
N1787B	B737	28590	N1791B	737NG	28238	N1795B	737NG	32583	N1800B	B757	29589
N1787B	B737	28602	N1791B	B707	21956	N1795B	737NG	32684	N1801	DC-8	45276
N1787B	B737	28740	N1791B	B727	20592	N1795B	737NG	32777	N1801U	DC-10	46600
N1787B	B737	28873	N1791B	B737	20454	N1795B	737NG	33542	N1802	DC-8	45277
N1787B	B737	28896	N1791B	B737	23397	N1795B	737NG	33932	N1802U	DC-10	46601
N1787B	B737	28918	N1791B	B737	23445	N1795B	737NG	34703	N1803	DC-8	45895
N1787B	B737	28990	N1791B	B737	23870	N1795B	B737	25606	N1803U	DC-10	46602
N1787B	B737	29130	N1791B	B747	21189	N1795B	B737	28872	N1804	DC-8	45896
N1787B	B737	29203	N1791B	B747	22672	N1795B	B737	29264	N1804U	DC-10	46603
N1787B	B737	29265	N1791B	B757	24567	N1795B	B737	29750	N1805	DC-8	45899
N1787B	B737	29267	N1791B	B767	22521	N1795B	B747	20237	N1805U	DC-10	46604
N1787B	B737	29332	N1791B	B767	22684	N1795B	B747	20781	N1806	DC-8	45911
N1787B	B737	29333	N1791B	B767	22696	N1795B	B757	26247	N1806U	DC-10	46605
N1787B	B737	29336	N1791B	B767	23019	N1795B	B757	28174	N1807	DC-8	45904
N1787B	B737	29341	N1791U	DC-9	45786	N1795B	B757	29020	N1807U	DC-10	46606
N1787B	B737	29342	N1792B	737NG	27837	N1795B	B757	29283	N1808E	DC-8	46105
N1787B	B737	30102	N1792B	B737	23302	N1795B	B757	29308	N1808U	DC-10	46607
N1787B	B737	30161	N1792B	B737	23446	N1795B	B757	29380	N1809E	DC-8	46107
N1787B	B757	28488	N1792B	B737	25124	N1795B	B757	29385	N1809U	DC-10	46608
N1787B	B757	28751	N1792B	B737	27917	N1795B	B757	29589	N1810U	DC-10	46609
N1787B	B757	28835	N1792B	B737	28732	N1795B	B757	29727	N1811U	DC-10	46610
N1787B	B757	28967	N1792B	B747	21659	N1795B	B757	29728	N1812U	DC-10	46611
N1787B	B757	29428	N1792B	B747	21831	N1795B	B757	29941	N1813U	DC-10	46612
N1787B	B757	29590	N1792B	B757	24014	N1795B	B757	29942	N1814U	DC-10	46613
N1787B	B757	29594	N1792B	B757	24471	N1795B	B757	29943	N1815U	DC-10	46614
N1787B	B757	30030	N1792B	B757	25488	N1795B	B757	29946	N1816U	DC-10	46615
N1787B	B757	30043	N1792B	B757	27203	N1795B	B757	29970	N1817U	DC-10	46616
N1787B	B757	30061	N1792B	B767	23022	N1795B	B757	30318	N1818U	DC-10	46617
N1788B	B727	20540	N1792B	B767	23106	N1795B	B757	30319	N1819U	DC-10	46618
N1788B	B727	20568	N1792N	B767	22789	N1795B	B757	30351	N1820U	DC-10	46619
N1788B	B727	20595	N1792U	DC-9	45712	N1795B	B757	30396	N1821U	DC-10	46620
N1788B	B727	20596	N1793T	B707	20428	N1795B	B757	30548	N1822U	DC-10	46621
N1788B	B727	20597	N1793U	DC-9	45787	N1795B	B757	30757	N1823U	DC-10	46622
N1788B	B727	20598	N1794B	737NG	34157	N1795B	B757	32242	N1824U	DC-10	46623
N1788B	B727	20599	N1794B	B747	20373	N1795B	B757	32989	N1825U	DC-10	46624
N1788B	B727	20603	N1794B	B747	20801	N1795B	B757	32990	N1826U	DC-10	46625
N1788B	B727	20606	N1794B	B747	28961	N1795B	B757	33098	N1827U	DC-10	46626
N1788B	B727	20607	N1794B	B767	27189	N1795B	B757	33099	N1828U	DC-10	46627
N1788B	B737	20300	N1794B	B767	27376	N1795B	B757	33966	N1829U	DC-10	46628
N1788B	B737	20496	N1794B	B767	27393	N1795U	DC-9	47451	N1830U	DC-10	46629
N1788B	B737	20561	N1794U	DC-9	47304	N1796B	737NG	28315	N1831U	DC-10	46630
N1788B	B737	20786	N1795B	737NG	27862	N1796B	737NG	28378	N1832U	DC-10	46631

N1833U	DC-10	47965	N1992	B727	18448	N2806W	B727	20268	N3254D	B727	19618
N1834U	DC-10	47966	N1993	B727	18449	N2807W	B727	20579	N3281G	DC-9	47003
N1835U	DC-10	47967	N1994	B727	18450	N2808W	B727	20580	N3281K	DC-9	47004
N1836U	DC-10	47968	N1995	B727	18900	N2809W	B727	20581	N3281N	DC-9	47325
N1837U	DC-10	47969	N1996	B727	18901	N2810W	B727	20648	N3281R	DC-9	47065
N1838U	DC-10	46632	N1997	B727	19128	N2811W	B727	20649	N3281U	B737	23477
N1839U	DC-10	46633	N1998	B727	19129	N2812W	B727	20868	(N3281V)	B737	23625
N1841U	DC-10	46634	N1999L	B737	21184	N2813W	B727	20869	(N3281W)	B737	23626
N1842U	DC-10	46635	N2034	B727	21155	N2814W	B727	20870	(N3281Y)	B737	23627
N1843U	DC-10	46636	**N2061L**	**B747**	**20826**	N2815W	B727	20871	(N3282G)	B737	23628
N1844U	DC-10	48260	N2089	B737	22089	N2816W	B727	20872	(N3282N)	B737	23629
N1845U	DC-10	48261	N2090B	B707	19291	N2817W	B727	20873	(N3282P)	B737	23630
N1846U	DC-10	48262	N2111J	1-11	029	N2818W	B727	20874	(N3282R)	B737	23631
N1847U	DC-10	48263	N2117X	B737	19424	N2819W	B727	21057	(N3282V)	B737	23632
N1848U	DC-10	48264	**N2121**	**737NG**	**34683**	N2820W	B727	21058	(N3282W)	B737	23633
(N1849U)	DC-10	46543	(N2132M)	B727	21322	N2821W	B727	21059	(N3282X)	B737	23634
N1849U	DC-10	46939	"N2138T"	B707	18835	N2822W	B727	21327	N3282Y	B737	23635
(N1850U)	DC-10	48285	N2143H	B707	17644	N2823W	B727	21328	N3283G	B737	23636
(N1851U)	DC-10	48288	N2143J	B707	18451	N2824W	B727	21329	N3301	B737	23181
N1852U	DC-10	47811	(N2178F)	B707	19293	N2825W	B727	21330	N3301L	DC-9	45696
N1853U	DC-10	47812	N2213E	B707	20027	N2826W	B727	21331	N3302L	DC-9	45697
N1854U	DC-10	47813	N2215Y	B707	19129	N2827W	B727	21392	N3303L	DC-9	45698
N1855U	DC-10	47837	N2235W	B707	17631	N2828W	B727	21393	N3304L	DC-9	45699
N1856U	DC-10	46975	N2248F	DC-9	47657	N2829W	B727	21481	N3305L	DC-9	45700
N1857U	DC-10	46986	N2257	B737	22257	N2892Q	DC-9	45841	N3306L	DC-9	45701
N1858U	DC-10	46987	N2264	B737	22264	N2896W	DC-9	45722	N3307L	DC-9	45702
N1859U	DC-10	47819	N2276X	B707	17602	N2913	B727	20045	N3308L	DC-9	45703
N1901	B727	19130	N2282C	B737	19013	N2914	B727	20046	N3309L	DC-9	45704
N1902	B727	19131	N2286C	B737	19014	N2915	B727	20143	N3310L	DC-9	45705
N1903	B727	19132	N2289C	B737	19015	N2919N	DC-8	46052	N3311L	DC-9	45706
N1905	B727	19180	(N2292Z)	737NG	29536	N2920	CV990	30-10-35	N3312L	DC-9	45707
N1906	B727	19181	(N2294B)	737NG	30086	N2941W	B737	22596	N3313L	DC-9	45708
N1907	B727	19182	(N2296N)	SE210	102	N2969G	B727	19304	N3314L	DC-9	45709
N1908	B727	19183	N2310	B737	23596	N2969V	B727	19137	N3315L	DC-9	45710
N1909	B727	19184	N2310B	DC-8	45765	N2977G	B727	18897	N3316L	DC-9	47025
N1910	B727	19385	N2332Q	B737	24570	N2978G	B707	18924	N3317L	DC-9	47026
N1924N	B747	21924	N2371	B737	23718	N2979G	B727	19305	N3318L	DC-9	47027
N1928	B727	19386	N2393W	B737	24571	N3001D	MD80	49936	N3319L	DC-9	47028
N1929	B727	19387	N2404A	B717	55071	N3002A	MD80	49941	N3320L	DC-9	47029
N1930	B727	19388	N2405T	DC-9	47309	N3004C	MD80	49935	N3321L	DC-9	47030
N1931	B727	19389	N2409N	B737	20496	N3005	E145	145770	N3322L	DC-9	47031
N1932	B727	19390	N2410W	B717	55077	N3010C	MD80	49903	N3323L	DC-9	47032
N1933	B727	19428	N2414E	B717	55081	N3010G	MD80	49808	**N3324L**	**DC-9**	**47103**
N1934	B727	19429	N2417F	B717	55084	N3016Z	DC-10	48266	N3325L	DC-9	47104
N1935	B727	19430	N2419C	B717	55086	N3024W	DC-10	48318	N3325T	DC-8	45754
(N1938R)	DC-9	47098	N2421A	B717	55088	**N3075A**	**A300**	**606**	N3326L	DC-9	47105
(N1939R)	DC-9	47120	N2423N	B717	25594	N3124Z	B707	18157	N3327L	DC-9	47106
N1955	B727	19431	N2425A	B717	55092	(N3126H)	1-11	BAC.122	N3328L	DC-9	47107
N1956	B727	19432	N2427A	B717	55094	(N3126Q)	1-11	BAC.123	N3329L	DC-9	47108
N1957	B727	19833	N2464C	B707	18381	N3127K	B707	20028	N3330L	DC-9	47109
N1958	B727	19834	N2464K	B707	18382	N3128H	DC-8	45672	N3331L	DC-9	47172
N1959	B727	19835	N2471	B727	19524	N3134C	737NG	27852	N3332L	DC-9	47173
N1962	B727	19836	N2472	B727	19525	N3134C	B737	28736	N3333L	DC-9	47174
N1963	B727	19837	N2473	B727	19526	N3140D	L1011	193G-1233	N3333M	B737	20194
N1964	B727	19838	N2474	B727	19527	N3154	B707	18827	N3334L	DC-9	47175
N1965	B727	19839	N2475	B727	19528	N3155	B707	18828	N3335L	DC-9	47176
N1969	B727	20044	N2484B	B767	24846	N3156	B707	18829	N3336L	DC-9	47177
N1970	B727	18426	N2547R	DC-8	46084	N3157	B707	18830	N3337L	DC-9	47273
N1971	B727	18427	(N2550)	B727	20045	N3158	B707	18963	N3338L	DC-9	47274
"N1971B"	737NG	28110	N2606Z	MD80	49626	N3159	B707	19160	N3339L	DC-9	47275
N1972	B727	18428	N2613M	B727	21853	N3160	B707	19161	N3340L	DC-9	47276
N1973	B727	18429	N2628Y	B707	18165	N3160M	B737	20197	(N3401A)	A340	013
N1974	B727	18430	(N2655Y)	B737	21538	N3161	B707	19207	(N3402N)	A340	015
N1975	B727	18431	N2674U	DC-8	46062	N3162	B707	19208	(N3403G)	A340	016
N1976	B727	18432	N2679T	DC-9	47476	N3163	B707	19413	(N3404G)	A340	035
N1976P	DC-8	45435	N2688Z	B727	19318	N3164	B707	19414	(N3405N)	A340	039
N1977	B727	18433	N2689E	B727	19318	N3165	B707	19438	(N3406A)	A340	040
N1978	B727	18434	N2697V	B707	18066	N3166	B707	19439	(N3407G)	A340	041
N1979	B727	18435	N2703J	B727	18367	N3167	B707	19523	(N3408A)	A340	044
N1980	B727	18436	N2703Y	F.28	11223	N3182B	B727	19536	N3439F	B747	23439
N1981	B727	18437	N2711R	B737	19426	N3183B	B707	18158	N3459D	B727	20554
N1982	B727	18438	(N2727)	B727	19244	N3183B	B707	21956	N3502P	737NG	27979
N1983	B727	18439	N2741A	B727	18990	(N3201)	B747	19676	N3502P	737NG	28099
N1984	B727	18440	**N2767**	**B767**	**23896**	(N3202)	B747	19677	N3502P	B757	24635
N1985	B727	18441	N2777	B727	19176	(N3203)	B747	19678	N3502P	B757	25054
N1986	B727	18442	N2786S	DC-9	47283	N3203Y	B747	19751	N3502P	B757	26436
N1987	B727	18443	N2786T	DC-9	47223	N3206T	146	E1144	N3504T	DC-9	47638
N1987B	B707	21103	N2801W	B727	20263	N3209Y	B727	20540	N3505T	DC-9	45788
N1988	B727	18444	N2802W	B727	20264	N3211M	B727	18951	N3506T	DC-9	47765
N1989	B727	18445	N2803W	B727	20265	N3213T	B737	25744	**N3507A**	**MD80**	**49801**
N1990	B727	18446	N2804W	B727	20266	N3238N	B707	19996	N3507T	DC-9	47788
N1991	B727	18447	N2805W	B727	20267	N3238S	B707	20199	N3508T	DC-9	47797

Reg	Type	No.	Reg	Type	No.	Reg	Type	No.	Reg	Type	No.
N3509J	737NG	27980	N3951A	B707	17647	N4530W	B737	20134	N4742	B727	19462
N3509J	B737	26069	N3951B	DC-8	45417	(N4530W)	B737	22505	N4743	B727	19463
N3509J	B737	28729	N3991C	DC-9	47175	N4532N	B727	22687	N4744	B727	19464
N3509J	B757	28707	N4002M	B727	20327	N4544F	B747	22939	N4745	B727	19465
N3509N	DC-9	47798	N4003G	L1011	193Y-1177	N4546U	B727	19597	N4746	B727	19466
N3510T	DC-9	47799	N4003G	L1011	193Y-1194	N4548M	B747	23056	N4747	B727	19467
N3512T	DC-9	48111	N4005X	L1011	193Y-1176	N4549V	DC-9	47639	N4748	B727	19468
N3513T	DC-9	48112	N4039W	B737	21112	N4550T	1-11	BAC.135	N4749	B727	19469
N3514T	DC-9	48113	N4051L	B747	20010	N4551N	B747	23137	N4750	B727	19470
N3515	MD80	49892	N4094	B707	20342	N4554N	B727	22982	N4751	B727	19471
N3519L	B737	25743	(N4111X)	1-11	054	N4555E	B727	22983	N4752	B727	19472
N3519L	B757	24845	N4113D	B737	25788	N4555W	B727	19793	N4753	B727	19473
N3519L	B757	29025	N4115J	B707	19295	N4556L	B737	22800	N4753B	B727	18287
N3519M	B757	26160	N4131G	B707	19622	N4556W	B727	18282	N4754	B727	19474
N3519M	B757	29026	N4141A	C-141	6110	N4558L	B727	18282	N4761G	DC-8	45917
N3521N	737NG	28209	N4157A	DC-9	47039	N4561B	DC-8	45610	N4768G	DC-8	45679
N3521N	737NG	28213	N4225J	B707	18809	N4561K	B737	22802	N4769F	DC-8	45686
N3521N	B737	24815	N4228G	B737	18425	N4562N	B737	22859	N4769G	DC-8	45860
N3521N	B737	25179	N4245S	B727	19282	N4563H	B737	22700	N4805J	DC-8	46063
N3521N	B757	26161	N4249R	B737	25116	N4569N	B737	22701	N4809E	DC-8	45762
N3605	B727	18942	N4264Y	B737	20158	N4570B	B737	22875	N4863T	DC-8	45951
N3606	B727	18943	(N4278L)	B737	21763	N4571A	B737	22876	N4864T	DC-8	46059
N3618F	A319	2748	N4292P	DC-8	45985	N4571M	B737	22793	N4865T	DC-8	46073
(N3727)	B727	19245	N4320B	B737	25124	N4574P	DC-8	46116	N4866T	DC-8	46089
N3730B	737NG	30538	N4339D	CV880	22-7-9-61	N4575L	B767	22923	N4867T	DC-8	46090
N3731T	737NG	30775	N4360W	B737	23866	N4578C	DC-8	45943	N4868T	DC-8	46091
N3732J	737NG	30380	N4361R	B737	21800	N4582N	DC-8	45982	N4869T	DC-8	46117
N3733Z	737NG	30539	N4361V	B737	26851	N4585L	B727	19010	N4901C	DC-8	45274
N3734B	737NG	30776	(N4367J)	B727	18796	(N4591Y)	B707	17591	N4902C	DC-8	45276
N3735D	737NG	30381	N4408F	B707	18839	N4593U	B707	17590	N4902W	B737	20440
N3736C	737NG	30540	N4450Z	B707	18831	(N4594A)	B707	17589	(N4903C)	DC-8	45277
N3737C	737NG	30799	N4451B	B707	18086	N4602D	B727	18843	N4904C	DC-8	45668
N3738B	737NG	30382	N4465C	B707	18413	N4605D	B707	18335	N4905C	DC-8	45805
N3739P	737NG	30541	N4465D	B707	18411	N4610	B727	18811	N4905W	B737	20917
N3740C	737NG	30800	(N4466C)	B707	18963	N4611	B727	18812	N4906	B737	20138
N3741S	737NG	30487	N4476F	B767	24476	N4612	B727	18813	N4906C	DC-8	45862
N3742C	737NG	30835	N4476S	737NG	33010	N4613	B727	18814	N4907	B737	19594
N3743H	737NG	30836	N4489M	DC-8	45618	N4614	B727	18815	N4907C	DC-8	45967
N3744F	737NG	30837	N4501Q	B747	22381	N4615	B727	18816	N4908C	DC-8	45968
N3745B	737NG	32373	N4501W	B737	19598	N4616	B727	18817	N4909C	DC-8	46060
N3746E	B707	18060	N4502R	B747	22496	N4617	B727	18845	N4910C	DC-8	46094
N3746H	737NG	30488	N4502W	B737	19599	N4618	B727	18846	N4929U	DC-8	45296
N3747D	737NG	32374	N4503W	B737	19600	N4619	B727	18847	N4934Z	DC-8	46079
N3748Y	737NG	30489	N4504	B737	19601	N4620	B727	19165	N4935C	DC-8	45931
N3749D	737NG	30490	N4504W	B737	19601	N4621	B727	19166	N4936S	B727	19311
N3750D	737NG	32375	N4505W	B737	19602	N4622	B727	19167	N4951W	B737	21066
N3751B	737NG	30491	N4506H	B747	22794	(N4646S)	B727	18933	N4952W	B737	21067
N3751X	DC-8	45619	N4506W	B737	19603	N4655Y	DC-10	46651	(N4980Y)	DC-8	45614
(N3751Y)	B707	18707	N4507W	B737	19604	N4655Z	DC-10	46552	N5002K	737NG	28289
N3752	737NG	30492	N4508E	B747	22678	N4703U	B747	19753	N5002K	737NG	28290
N3753	737NG	32626	N4508H	B747	22547	N4704U	B747	19754	N5002K	737NG	34477
N3754A	737NG	29626	N4508W	B737	19605	N4710U	B747	19755	N5002K	B737	28735
N3755D	737NG	29627	N4509	B727	19242	N4711U	B747	19756	N5002K	B757	24971
N3756	737NG	30493	N4509W	B737	19606	N4712U	B747	19757	N5002K	B757	25054
N3756F	1-11	005	N4510W	B737	19607	N4713U	B747	19875	N5005C	B767	25834
N3757D	737NG	30813	N4511W	B737	19608	N4714U	B747	19876	N5014K	B777	27107
N3758Y	737NG	30814	N4512W	B737	19609	N4717U	B747	19877	N5014K	B777	27507
N3759	737NG	30815	N4513W	B737	19610	N4718U	B747	19878	N5014K	B777	29735
N3760C	737NG	30816	N4514W	B737	19611	N4719U	B747	19879	N5014K	B777	32648
N3761R	737NG	29628	N4515W	B737	19612	N4720U	B747	19880	N5014K	B777	32857
N3762Y	737NG	30817	N4516W	B737	19613	N4723U	B747	19881	N5014K	B777	32963
N3763D	737NG	29629	N4517W	B737	19614	N4724U	B747	19882	N5014K	B777	33711
N3764D	737NG	30818	N4518W	B737	19615	(N4727)	B727	19246	N5015	1-11	055
N3765	737NG	30819	N4519W	B737	19616	N4727U	B747	19883	N5015G	A320	0087
N3766	737NG	30820	N4520W	B737	19617	N4728U	B747	19925	N5016	1-11	056
N3767	737NG	30821	N4521W	B737	20125	N4729U	B747	19926	N5016R	B777	27027
N3768	737NG	29630	N4522	B727	20126	N4730	B727	19450	N5016R	B777	27485
N3769L	737NG	30822	N4522V	B747	22805	N4731	B727	19451	N5016R	B777	27506
N3771K	737NG	29632	N4522W	B737	20126	N4732	B727	19452	N5016R	B777	28360
(N3774C)	737NG	30824	N4523W	B737	20127	N4732U	B747	19927	N5016R	B777	32431
(N3775)	737NG	30826	N4524W	B737	20128	N4733	B727	19453	N5016R	B777	32705
N3791G	B707	17598	N4525W	B737	20129	N4734	B727	19454	N5016R	B777	32714
N3831X	B707	18059	N4526W	B737	20130	N4735	B727	19455	N5016R	B777	35160
N3833L	B707	19523	N4527W	B737	20131	N4735U	B747	19928	N5017	1-11	057
N3842X	B707	17692	N4528W	B737	20132	N4736	B727	19456	N5017Q	B747	32866
N3878F	DC-10	47864	(N4528N)	B767	23623	N4737	B727	19457	N5017Q	B777	28275
N3878M	DC-10	47863	N4528Y	B767	23624	N4738	B727	19458	N5017Q	B777	30302
N3878P	DC-10	47861	N4529T	B767	23623	N4739	B727	19459	N5017Q	B777	32723
N3931A	DC-8	45961	(N4529T)	B767	23624	N4740	B727	19460	N5017Q	B777	32845
N3931G	DC-8	45986	N4529W	B737	20133	N4741	B727	19461	N5017Q	B777	36083
N3939V	1-11	054	**N4529W**	**B737**	**20785**				N5017V	B777	27358
N3946A	B727	19394	N4529W	B737	22504				N5017V	B777	27505

N5017V	B777	27641	N5093	B727	19175	N5573P	B737	23448	N6005C	B747	23823
N5017V	B777	28361	N5093K	B707	17619	N5573P	B747	21759	N6005C	B747	23824
N5017V	B777	28408	N5094K	B707	17708	N5573P	B747	23223	N6005C	B747	23864
N5017V	B777	32430	N5094Q	DC-8	46009	N5573P	B757	25598	N6005C	B747	23967
N5017V	B777	32709	N5095K	B707	17918	N5573S	B747	23817	N6005C	B747	23969
N5017V	B777	32710	N5100X	CRJ	7008	N5573S	B747	27163	N6005C	B747	24062
N5017V	B777	32714	N5111Y	B727	18270	N5573S	B767	27394	N6005C	B747	24071
N5017V	B777	33863	N5129K	L1011	193G-1250	N5601	CV990	30-10-1	N6005C	B747	24108
N5017V	B777	36300	**N5175U**	**B737**	**20689**	N5601	CV990	30-10-33	N6005C	B747	24138
N5018	1-11	058	**N5176Y**	**B737**	**20692**	N5601G	CV990	30-10-1	N6005C	B747	24226
N5019	1-11	059	**N5177C**	**B737**	**20693**	N5602	CV990	30-10-2	N6005C	B747	24447
(N5019K)	SE210	146	**N5294E**	**B737**	**20691**	N5602	CV990	30-10-34	N6005C	B747	24885
N5020	1-11	060	**N5294M**	**B737**	**20694**	N5602G	CV990	30-10-2	N6005C	B747	25068
N5020K	B747	32912	N5341L	DC-9	47277	N5603	CV990	30-10-13	N6005C	B747	25278
N5020K	B777	27252	N5342L	DC-9	47278	N5603	CV990	30-10-3	N6005C	B747	25544
N5020K	B777	27950	N5366Y	DC-9	19377	N5603	CV990	30-10-35	N6005C	B747	25546
N5020K	B777	28371	N5373G	DC-9	47015	N5603G	CV990	30-10-3	N6005C	B747	25632
N5020K	B777	32317	N5375S	B737	23273	(N5604)	B727	19124	N6005C	B747	28339
N5020K	B777	34481	N5381X	B707	18928	N5604	CV990	30-10-36	N6005C	B747	30455
N5020K	B777	34598	N5458E	B727	18896	N5604	CV990	30-10-4	N6005C	B767	23145
N5020K	B777	36302	N5463Y	DC-10	47814	N5604G	CV990	30-10-4	N6005C	B767	23147
N5021	1-11	061	N5464M	DC-10	47815	N5605	CV990	30-10-9	N6005C	B767	23216
N5022	1-11	062	N5472	B727	19525	N5606	CV990	30-10-10	N6005C	B767	23432
N5022E	B747	32897	N5473	B727	19526	N5606	CV990	30-10-34	N6005C	B767	23756
N5022E	B747	33748	N5474	B727	19527	N5607	B727	18804	N6005C	B767	23805
N5022E	B747	35804	N5475	B727	19524	N5607	CV990	30-10-16	N6005C	B767	23807
N5022E	B777	27483	N5487N	B707	18380	N5608	B727	18805	N6005C	B767	23961
N5022E	B777	27604	(N5517U)	B707	18842	N5608	CV990	30-10-18	N6005C	B767	24143
N5022E	B777	27607	N5517Z	B707	18842	N5609	B727	18806	N6005C	B767	24145
N5022E	B777	28529	N5519U	B707	18836	N5609	CV990	30-10-21	N6005C	B767	24316
N5022E	B777	28698	N5519V	B707	18834	N5610	CV990	30-10-22	N6005C	B767	24317
N5022E	B777	29734	N5537L	737NG	32777	N5611	CV990	30-10-23	N6005C	B767	24340
N5022E	B777	33781	N5573B	737NG	28069	N5612	CV990	30-10-24	N6005C	B767	24948
N5022E	B777	36084	N5573B	737NG	28102	N5612	CV990	30-10-36	N6005C	B767	25761
N5023	1-11	063	N5573B	B737	22598	N5613	CV990	30-10-25	N6005C	B767	27477
N5023Q	B767	35814	N5573B	B737	23303	N5614	CV990	30-10-26	N6005C	B767	27600
N5023Q	B777	27484	N5573B	B737	23447	N5615	CV990	30-10-27	N6005C	B767	28370
N5023Q	B777	28345	N5573B	B737	23654	N5616	CV990	30-10-25	N6005C	B767	29129
N5023Q	B777	28530	N5573B	B737	24237	N5616	CV990	30-10-28	N6005F	B747	23348
N5023Q	B777	32891	N5573B	B747	22709	N5617	CV990	30-10-29	N6006C	B747	23026
N5023Q	B777	34206	N5573B	B747	23120	N5618	CV990	30-10-30	N6009F	B737	22802
N5024	1-11	064	N5573B	B747	23149	N5619	CV990	30-10-31	N6009F	B747	22489
N5025	1-11	065	N5573B	B747	24061	N5620	CV990	30-10-32	N6009F	B747	23263
N5026	1-11	066	N5573B	B757	24015	N5623	CV990	30-10-20	N6009F	B747	23300
N5027	1-11	067	N5573B	B757	24472	N5624	CV990	30-10-16	N6009F	B747	23390
N5028	1-11	068	N5573B	B757	24923	N5625	CV990	30-10-19	N6009F	B747	23395
N5028V	B777	27250	N5573B	B767	22790	N5700N	B737	21800	N6009F	B747	23413
N5028Y	B767	35816	N5573E	B727	22621	N5700T	B747	22616	N6009F	B747	23482
N5028Y	B777	27250	N5573F	B747	22481	N5701E	B737	22397	N6009F	B747	23638
N5028Y	B777	27605	N5573K	737NG	28006	(N5710)	B707	19566	N6009F	B747	23639
N5028Y	B777	29150	N5573K	737NG	28101	N5711E	B727	22084	N6009F	B747	23640
N5028Y	B777	30874	N5573K	B737	22113	N5720	DC-9	45726	N6009F	B747	23676
N5028Y	B777	32327	N5573K	B737	22127	N5728	DC-9	45727	N6009F	B747	23919
N5028Y	B777	32850	N5573K	B737	22667	N5768X	DC-8	45768	N6009F	B747	24053
N5028Y	B777	36301	N5573K	B737	23396	N5771T	B707	19212	N6009F	B747	24055
N5029	1-11	069	N5573K	B737	23451	N5772T	B707	19213	N6009F	B747	24088
N5030	1-11	072	N5573K	B737	23830	N5772T	B727	21655	N6009F	B747	24134
N5031	1-11	073	N5573K	B737	24462	N5773T	B707	19214	N6009F	B747	24227
N5032	1-11	074	N5573K	B737	24650	N5774T	B707	19435	N6009F	B747	24619
N5033	1-11	075	N5573K	B737	27179	N5791	B707	18756	N6009F	B747	24779
N5033	B737	25033	N5573K	B737	28735	N5824A	DC-8	45824	N6009F	B747	24836
N5034	1-11	076	N5573K	B747	22991	N5828B	146	E1002	N6009F	B747	24850
N5035	1-11	077	N5573K	B757	23863	N5858	CV880	22-00-46M	N6009F	B747	24887
N5036	1-11	078	N5573K	B757	24016	N5863	CV880	22-00-48M	N6009F	B747	24896
N5037	1-11	079	N5573K	B757	27623	N5865	CV880	22-7-5-57	N6009F	B747	24976
N5038	1-11	080	N5573K	B767	22980	N5866	CV880	22-7-9-61	N6009F	B747	24990
N5038	B707	17652	N5573K	B767	23141	N5879X	DC-8	45879	N6009F	B747	25046
N5039	1-11	081	N5573L	737NG	28584	N5973L	B747	22293	N6009F	B747	25075
N5040	1-11	086	N5573L	737NG	28628	N6004U	F.28	11193	N6009F	B747	25315
N5041	1-11	087	N5573L	737NG	29091	N6005C	B747	22616	N6009F	B747	25641
N5042	1-11	088	N5573L	737NG	29139	N6005C	B747	22704	N6009F	B747	25813
N5043	1-11	089	N5573L	737NG	29149	N6005C	B747	22725	N6009F	B747	25819
N5044	1-11	090	N5573L	737NG	29346	N6005C	B747	23224	N6009F	B747	26409
N5055	B727	19173	N5573L	737NG	29916	N6005C	B747	23262	N6009F	B747	26426
N5065T	B707	19519	N5573L	737NG	30695	N6005C	B747	23266	N6009F	B747	26552
N5073L	B727	18936	N5573L	737NG	32670	N6005C	B747	23268	N6009F	B747	27663
N5088K	B707	17704	N5573L	737NG	33014	N6005C	B747	23392	N6009F	B747	27915
N5089K	B707	17722	N5573L	B737	22660	N6005C	B747	23394	N6009F	B747	28342
N5090K	B707	17905	N5573L	B737	29750	N6005C	B747	23407	N6009F	B747	29899
N5091K	B707	17705	N5573L	B757	28846	N6005C	B747	23439	N6009F	B767	23305
N5092	B727	19174	N5573P	737NG	27977	N6005C	B747	23688	N6009F	B767	23306
N5092K	B707	17706	N5573P	737NG	28210	N6005C	B747	23769	N6009F	B767	23328

Reg	Type	Ser	Reg	Type	Ser	Reg	Type	Ser	Reg	Type	Ser
N6009F	B767	23431	N6018N	B767	25826	N6046P	B767	24083	N6067B	B767	23140
N6009F	B767	23745	N6018N	B767	26915	N6046P	B767	24257	N6067E	737NG	29054
N6009F	B767	23764	N6018N	B777	34568	N6046P	B767	24318	N6067E	737NG	29364
N6009F	B767	23765	N6018N	B777	34569	N6046P	B767	24334	N6067E	737NG	35178
N6009F	B767	23801	N6018N	B777	34597	N6046P	B767	24716	N6067E	B737	28734
N6009F	B767	23804	N6018N	B777	36300	N6046P	B767	24742	N6067E	B767	23072
N6009F	B767	23896	N6018P	B767	30850	N6046P	B767	24983	N6067H	737NG	34474
N6009F	B767	23916	N6038E	B737	22804	N6046P	B767	25273	N6067U	737NG	32631
N6009F	B767	24013	N6038E	B747	23269	N6046P	B767	26205	N6067U	737NG	34474
N6009F	B767	24085	N6038E	B747	23287	N6046P	B767	26986	N6067U	737NG	34559
N6009F	B767	24142	N6038E	B747	23391	N6046P	B767	30851	N6067U	B737	23274
N6009F	B767	24239	N6038E	B747	23509	N6055C	B767	23698	N6067U	B757	23454
N6009F	B767	24323	N6038E	B747	23534	N6055C	B767	29129	N6067U	B767	29703
N6009F	B767	24324	N6038E	B747	23652	N6055X	737NG	29274	N6069D	B737	24692
N6009F	B767	24333	N6038E	B747	23920	N6055X	737NG	32796	N6069D	B737	25289
N6009F	B767	24407	N6038E	B747	23982	N6055X	737NG	35679	N6069D	B737	28739
N6009F	B767	24768	N6038E	B747	24019	N6055X	B747	23267	N6069D	B747	22487
N6009F	B767	25533	N6038E	B747	24161	N6055X	B747	23286	N6069D	B757	24402
N6009F	B767	26208	N6038E	B747	24194	N6055X	B747	23408	N6069D	B757	29015
N6009F	B767	26913	N6038E	B747	24195	N6055X	B747	23410	N6069E	B737	28735
N6009F	B767	27048	N6038E	B747	24196	N6055X	B747	23501	N6069P	B737	23635
N6009F	B767	27377	N6038E	B747	24198	N6055X	B747	23508	N6069R	B737	28738
N6009F	B767	27960	N6038E	B747	24215	N6055X	B747	23711	N6069R	MD11	48805
N6009F	B767	28392	N6038E	B747	24731	N6055X	B747	23751	N6108N	B747	22791
N6009F	B767	28495	N6038E	B747	25705	N6055X	B747	23799	N6108N	B747	23480
N6009F	B767	29390	N6038E	B747	26407	N6055X	B747	23816	N6108N	B767	24349
N6009F	B767	30846	N6038E	B747	26547	N6055X	B747	23968	N6140A	DC-9	47049
N6009F	B777	32645	N6038E	B747	27828	N6055X	B747	24158	(N6141A)	DC-9	47050
N6009F	B777	34576	N6038E	B767	22524	N6055X	B747	24730	(N6142A)	DC-9	47051
N6018N	B737	22803	N6038E	B767	22921	N6055X	B747	25544	(N6143A)	DC-9	47052
N6018N	B747	23221	N6038E	B767	23142	N6055X	B747	25647	(N6144A)	DC-9	47099
N6018N	B747	23301	N6038E	B767	23144	N6055X	B747	27827	(N6145A)	DC-9	47130
N6018N	B747	23350	N6038E	B767	23213	N6055X	B747	28551	(N6146A)	DC-9	47146
N6018N	B747	23389	N6038E	B767	23214	N6055X	B767	22525	N6150Z	DC-10	47889
N6018N	B747	23709	N6038E	B767	23280	N6055X	B767	23146	N6161A	DC-8	45969
N6018N	B747	23746	N6038E	B767	23433	N6055X	B767	23304	**N6161C**	**DC-8**	**45856**
N6018N	B747	23911	N6038E	B767	23645	N6055X	B767	23327	N6161M	DC-8	45762
N6018N	B747	23999	N6038E	B767	23757	N6055X	B767	23758	N6162A	DC-8	46061
N6018N	B747	24018	N6038E	B767	23759	N6055X	B767	23963	N6163A	DC-8	46062
N6018N	B747	24067	N6038E	B767	23962	N6055X	B767	24004	N6164A	DC-8	46144
N6018N	B747	24107	N6038E	B767	24003	N6055X	B767	24082	(N6165A)	DC-8	46133
N6018N	B747	24159	N6038E	B767	24084	N6055X	B767	24086	(N6166A)	DC-8	46146
N6018N	B747	24162	N6038E	B767	24087	N6055X	B767	24146	(N6167A)	DC-8	46149
N6018N	B747	24359	N6038E	B767	24150	N6055X	B767	24498	N6167D	B727	22430
N6018N	B747	24761	N6038E	B767	24325	N6055X	B767	25532	N6186	B747	21439
N6018N	B747	24855	N6038E	B767	27205	N6055X	B767	25534	(N6189)	B747	20273
N6018N	B747	24883	N6038E	B767	28270	N6055X	B767	25762	N6200N	B717	55135
N6018N	B747	24955	N6038N	B767	23271	N6055X	B767	26544	N6200N	DC-10	48292
N6018N	B747	24998	N6046B	B747	22990	N6055X	B767	27569	N6200N	MD11	48439
N6018N	B747	25045	N6046P	737NG	32416	N6055X	B767	27908	N6200N	MD80	49399
N6018N	B747	25547	N6046P	737NG	32883	N6055X	B777	29956	N6200N	MD80	49401
N6018N	B747	25780	N6046P	B747	22750	N6056X	B767	27175	N6200N	MD80	49417
N6018N	B747	26344	N6046P	B747	23139	N6063S	B737	29122	N6200N	MD80	49439
N6018N	B747	27178	N6046P	B747	23264	N6063S	B767	25865	N6200N	MD80	49483
N6018N	B747	27442	N6046P	B747	23265	N6065A	B777	33781	N6200N	MD80	49604
N6018N	B747	27899	N6046P	B747	23270	N6065Y	737NG	32905	N6200N	MD80	49807
N6018N	B747	28552	N6046P	B747	23393	N6065Y	737NG	32921	N6200N	MD80	53603
N6018N	B747	32909	N6046P	B747	23611	N6065Y	B747	23409	N6200N	MD90	53514
N6018N	B767	22786	N6046P	B747	23621	N6065Y	B767	23107	N6202D	B717	55136
N6018N	B767	22923	N6046P	B747	23622	N6065Y	B767	23307	N6202D	MD11	48555
N6018N	B767	22973	N6046P	B747	23721	N6066B	B757	24052	N6202D	MD80	49393
N6018N	B767	22974	N6046P	B747	23735	N6066U	737NG	30000	N6202D	MD80	49441
N6018N	B767	23058	N6046P	B747	24106	N6066U	737NG	33916	N6202D	MD80	49900
N6018N	B767	23143	N6046P	B747	24156	N6066U	B747	22472	N6202D	MD80	53010
N6018N	B767	23309	N6046P	B747	24160	N6066U	B747	23048	N6202D	MD90	53498
N6018N	B767	23326	N6046P	B747	24177	N6066U	B767	22528	N6202D	MD90	53517
N6018N	B767	23402	N6046P	B747	24201	N6066U	B767	23250	N6202F	B717	55138
N6018N	B767	23802	N6046P	B747	24202	N6066Z	737NG	33103	N6202S	B717	55057
N6018N	B767	23806	N6046P	B747	24354	N6066Z	B737	22657	N6202S	B717	55135
N6018N	B767	23965	N6046P	B747	24777	N6066Z	B737	28733	N6202S	B717	55151
N6018N	B767	23966	N6046P	B747	24966	N6066Z	B747	23138	N6202S	B717	55152
N6018N	B767	23974	N6046P	B747	25546	N6066Z	B757	30061	N6202S	B717	55153
N6018N	B767	24006	N6046P	B747	28849	N6066Z	B767	22972	N6202S	MD11	48601
N6018N	B767	24144	N6046P	B747	30401	N6066Z	B777	33782	N6202S	MD80	49398
N6018N	B767	24157	N6046P	B757	29305	N6067B	B737	25714	N6202S	MD80	49901
N6018N	B767	24336	N6046P	B767	22975	N6067B	B737	28737	N6202S	MD80	53118
N6018N	B767	24727	N6046P	B767	23212	N6067B	B747	22870	N6202S	MD90	53552
N6018N	B767	24854	N6046P	B767	23403	N6067B	B757	24401	N6203D	MD11	48743
N6018N	B767	25316	N6046P	B767	23434	N6067B	B757	29017	N6203D	MD80	49218
N6018N	B767	25363	N6046P	B767	23964	N6067B	B767	22922	N6203D	MD80	49442
N6018N	B767	25535	N6046P	B767	23973						
N6018N	B767	25536	N6046P	B767	24005						

Reg	Type	c/n	Reg	Type	c/n	Reg	Type	c/n	Reg	Type	c/n
N6203D	MD80	53064	N6804	B727	19479	N7034E	DC-8	45658	N7088U	B727	19152
N6203D	MD80	53119	N6805	B727	19480	N7034U	B727	18326	N7089U	B727	19153
N6203D	MD80	53581	N6806	B727	19481	N7035T	L1011	193B-1231	N7090U	B727	19154
N6203D	MD90	53495	N6807	B727	19482	N7035U	B727	18327	N7095	B707	19104
N6203D	MD90	53509	N6808	B727	19483	N7036T	L1011	193B-1232	N7096	B707	19105
N6203D	MD90	53518	N6809	B727	19484	N7036U	B727	18328	N7097	B707	19106
N6203U	B717	55059	N6810	B727	19485	N7037U	B727	18329	N7098	B707	19107
N6203U	DC-10	48267	N6811	B727	19486	N7038U	B727	18330	N7099	B707	19108
N6203U	MD11	48766	N6812	B727	19487	N7039U	B727	18331	N7100	B707	19440
N6203U	MD80	49612	N6813	B727	19488	N7040U	B727	18332	N7102	B707	19529
N6203U	MD80	49708	N6814	B727	19489	N7041U	B727	18848	N7103	B707	19530
N6203U	MD80	53126	N6815	B727	19490	N7042U	B727	18849	N7104	B707	19531
N6203U	MD90	53510	N6816	B727	19491	N7043U	B727	18850	N7128T	B727	20286
N6203U	MD90	53553	N6817	B727	19492	N7043U	DC-8	46042	N7152J	B727	20937
N6204C	B717	55068	N6818	B727	19493	N7044U	B727	18851	N7158T	B707	20036
N6204C	MD80	49965	N6819	B727	19494	N7045U	B727	18852	N7158Z	B707	20179
N6204C	MD90	53554	N6820	B727	19495	N7046A	B727	18877	N7181C	DC-8	45602
N6204N	DC-10	48310	N6821	B727	19496	N7046G	DC-8	45885	N7182C	DC-8	45603
N6204N	MD80	49966	N6822	B727	19700	N7046H	DC-8	46011	N7183C	DC-8	45605
N6206F	MD80	49823	N6823	B727	19701	N7046U	B727	18853	N7184C	DC-8	45606
N6206F	MD80	49945	N6824	B727	19702	N7047U	B727	18854	N7201U	B707	17907
N6206F	MD80	53120	N6825	B727	19703	N7048U	B727	18855	N7202U	B707	17908
N6206F	MD90	53569	N6826	B727	19704	N7049U	B727	18856	N7203U	B707	17909
N6241	B737	19847	**N6827**	**B727**	**20180**	N7050U	B727	18857	N7204U	B707	17910
N6254X	A300	053	N6828	B727	20181	(N7051U)	B727	18858	N7205U	B707	17911
N6254Y	A300	075	N6829	B727	20182	N7052U	B727	18859	N7206U	B707	17912
N6293N	B727	19432	N6830	B727	20183	N7053U	B727	18860	N7207U	B707	17913
N6373P	B767	23280	N6831	B727	20184	N7054U	B727	18861	N7208Q	A300	052
N6373Q	A300	018	N6832	B727	20185	**N7055A**	**A300**	**462**	N7208U	B707	17914
N6388Z	DC-9	47713	N6833	B727	20186	N7055U	B727	18862	N7209U	B707	17915
N6393X	B727	22641	N6834	B727	20187	N7056U	B727	18863	N7210U	B707	17916
(N6403X)	DC-9	47018	N6835	B727	20188	N7057U	B727	18864	N7211U	B707	17917
N6410B	L1011	193A-1040	N6836	B727	20189	N7058U	B727	18865	N7212U	B707	18044
N6504K	B707	20035	N6837	B727	20190	N7059U	B727	18866	N7213U	B707	18045
N6546L	B707	19296	N6838	B727	20191	N7060U	B727	18867	N7214U	B707	18046
N6571C	DC-8	45391	N6839	B727	20192	N7061U	B727	18868	N7215U	B707	18047
N6572C	DC-8	45392	N6841	B727	20193	**N7062A**	**A300**	**474**	N7216U	B707	18048
N6573C	DC-8	45393	N6842	B727	20241	N7062U	B727	18869	N7217U	B707	18049
(N6574C)	DC-8	45394	N6842	DC-8	45803	N7063U	B727	18870	N7218U	B707	18050
(N6575C)	DC-8	45395	N6843	CV990	30-10-30	N7064U	B727	18871	(N7219)	B707	18072
(N6576C)	DC-8	45396	N6844	CV990	30-10-18	N7065U	B727	18872	N7219U	B707	18072
N6577C	DC-8	45442	N6845	CV990	30-10-25	N7066U	B727	19079	N7220U	B707	18073
N6578C	DC-8	45443	N6846	CV990	30-10-24	N7067U	B727	19080	N7221U	B707	18074
N6598W	B707	19133	N6857X	DC-10	46991	N7068U	B727	19081	N7222U	B707	18075
N6658Y	B737	20221	(N7000Y)	B707	18891	N7069U	B727	19082	N7223U	B707	18076
N6666U	B757	23452	N7001U	B727	18293	N7070U	B727	19083	N7224U	B707	18077
N6700	**B757**	**30337**	N7002U	B727	18294	N7071	B707	17691	N7225U	B707	18078
N6701	**B757**	**30187**	N7003U	B727	18295	N7071U	B717	55044	N7226U	B707	18079
N6702	**B757**	**30188**	N7003U	B727	18791	N7071U	B727	19084	N7227U	B707	18080
N6703D	**B757**	**30234**	N7004U	B727	18296	N7072	B707	17692	N7228U	B707	18081
N67047	**B757**	**30396**	N7005U	B727	18297	N7072U	B727	19085	N7229L	B707	18159
N6705Y	**B757**	**30397**	N7006U	B727	18298	N7073	B707	17693	N7229U	B707	18082
N6706Q	**B757**	**30422**	N7007U	B727	18299	N7073U	B727	19086	"N7230T"	B707	19572
N6707A	**B757**	**30395**	N7008U	B727	18300	N7074	B707	17694	N7231T	B707	19572
N6708D	**B757**	**30480**	N7009U	B727	18301	N7074U	B727	19087	N7232X	B707	19570
N6709	**B757**	**30481**	N7010U	B727	18302	N7075	B707	17695	N7251U	B727	21398
N6710E	**B757**	**30482**	N7011U	B727	18303	N7075U	B727	19088	N7252U	B727	21399
N6711M	**B757**	**30483**	N7012U	B727	18304	N7076	B707	18064	N7253U	B727	21400
N6712B	**B757**	**30484**	N7013U	B727	18305	**N7076A**	**A300**	**610**	N7254U	B727	21401
N6713Y	**B757**	**30777**	N7014U	B727	18306	N7076U	B727	19140	N7255U	B727	21402
N6714Q	**B757**	**30485**	N7015Q	DC-8	45882	N7077	B707	18065	N7256U	B727	21403
N6715C	**B757**	**30486**	N7015U	B727	18307	N7077U	B727	19141	N7257U	B727	21404
N6716C	**B757**	**30838**	N7016U	B727	18308	N7078	B707	18066	N7258U	B727	21405
N6720	B707	18986	N7017U	B727	18309	N7078	B707	18154	N7259U	B727	21406
N6721	B707	18987	N7018U	B727	18310	N7078U	B727	19142	N7260U	B727	21407
N6722	B707	18988	N7019U	B727	18311	N7079	B727	18423	N7261U	B727	21408
N6723	B707	18989	N7020U	B727	18312	N7079S	B757	22206	N7262U	B727	21409
N6724	B707	19215	N7021U	B727	18313	N7079U	B727	19143	N7263U	B727	21410
N6726	B707	19216	N7022U	B727	18314	N7080	B727	18581	N7264U	B727	21411
N6727	B707	19217	N7023U	B727	18315	N7080U	B727	19144	**N7264V**	**CRJ**	**7264**
N6728	B707	19218	N7024U	B727	18316	N7081	B707	18042	N7265U	B727	21412
N6729	B707	19219	N7025U	B727	18317	N7081U	B727	19145	N7266U	B727	21413
(N6757A)	B737	21720	N7026U	B727	18318	N7082	B707	18043	N7267U	B727	21414
N6763T	B707	19220	N7027U	B727	18319	**N7082A**	**A300**	**643**	N7268U	B727	21415
N6764T	B707	19221	N7028U	B727	18320	N7082U	B727	19146	N7269U	B727	21416
N6771T	B707	19222	N7029U	B727	18321	N7083	B707	18041	N7270	B727	19109
N6789T	B707	19223	N7030U	B727	18322	**N7083A**	**A300**	**645**	**N7270B**	**B727**	**20641**
N6790T	B707	19436	N7031A	B727	21219	N7083U	B727	19147	N7270C	B727	18897
N6800	B727	19475	N7031F	B737	21445	N7084U	B727	19148	N7270F	B727	19391
N6801	B727	19476	N7031U	B727	18323	N7085U	B727	19149	N7270L	B727	19536
N6802	B727	19477	N7032U	B727	18324	N7086U	B727	19150	(N7270Q)	B727	20250
N6803	B727	19478	N7033U	B727	18325	N7087U	B727	19151	N7270U	B727	21417

Reg	Type	MSN	Reg	Type	MSN	Reg	Type	MSN	Reg	Type	MSN	Reg	Type	MSN
N7271	B727	19110	N7348F	B737	21981	N7422U	B727	19197	N7525A	B707	17652			
N7271F	B727	19392	N7349F	B737	22089	N7423U	B727	19198	**N7525A**	**MD80**	**49917**			
N7271P	B727	18933	N7350F	B737	22383	N7424U	B727	19199	N7526A	B707	18054			
N7271F	B727	18998	N7351F	B737	22384	N7425U	B727	19200	**N7526A**	**MD80**	**49918**			
(N7271P)	B727	19243	N7352F	B737	22399	N7426U	B727	19201	N7527A	B707	18013			
(N7271Q)	B727	20251	N7353F	B737	22456	N7427U	B727	19202	**N7527A**	**MD80**	**49919**			
N7271U	B727	21418	N7354F	B737	22457	N7428U	B727	19203	N7528A	B707	18014			
N7272	B727	19111	N7355F	B737	22741	N7429U	B727	19204	**N7528A**	**MD80**	**49920**			
N7272F	B727	19393	N7356F	B737	22742	N7430U	B727	19205	N7529A	B707	18015			
(N7272Q)	B727	20252	N7357F	B737	22743	N7431U	B727	19805	**N7530**	**MD80**	**49922**			
N7272U	B727	21419	N7358F	B737	22744	N7432U	B727	19806	N7530A	B707	18016			
N7273	B727	19112	N7359F	B737	23023	N7433U	B727	19890	N7531A	B707	18017			
N7273F	B727	19394	N7360F	B737	20222	N7434U	B727	19891	**N7531A**	**MD80**	**49923**			
N7273U	B727	21420	N7361F	B737	20223	N7435U	B727	19892	N7532A	B707	18018			
N7274	B727	19113	N7362F	B737	21131	N7436U	B727	19893	**N7532A**	**MD80**	**49924**			
N7274F	B727	19395	N7363F	B737	20133	N7437U	B727	19894	N7533A	B707	18019			
N7274U	B727	21421	N7370F	B737	20073	N7438U	B727	19895	**N7533A**	**MD80**	**49987**			
N7275	B727	19114	(N7371F)	B737	20070	N7441U	B727	21895	N7534A	B707	18020			
N7275F	B727	19995	N7371F	B737	20074	N7442U	B727	21896	**N7534A**	**MD80**	**49988**			
N7275U	B727	21422	(N7372F)	B737	20071	N7443U	B727	21897	N7535A	B707	18021			
N7276	B727	19115	N7372F	B737	20072	N7444U	B727	21898	**N7535A**	**MD80**	**49989**			
N7276F	B727	19991	(N7373F)	B737	20072	N7445U	B727	21899	N7536A	B707	18022			
N7276U	B727	21423	N7373F	B737	20361	N7446U	B727	21900	**N7536A**	**MD80**	**49990**			
N7277	B727	19116	(N7374F)	B737	20073	N7447U	B727	21901	N7537A	B707	18023			
N7277F	B727	19992	N7374F	B737	20362	N7448U	B727	21902	**N7537A**	**MD80**	**49991**			
N7277U	B727	21424	N7374F	B737	21980	N7449U	B727	21903	N7538A	B707	18024			
N7278	B727	19117	**N7375A**	**B767**	**25202**	N7450U	B727	21904	**N7538A**	**MD80**	**49992**			
N7278F	B727	19993	(N7375F)	B737	20074	N7451U	B727	21905	N7539A	B707	18025			
N7278U	B727	21425	N7375F	B737	20363	N7452U	B727	21906	**N7539A**	**MD80**	**49993**			
N7279	B727	19118	N7376	737NG	28296	N7453U	B727	21907	N7540A	B707	18026			
N7279F	B727	19994	N7376F	B737	20364	N7454U	B727	21908	**N7540A**	**MD80**	**49994**			
N7279F	B727	20162	N7377F	B737	20365	N7455U	B727	21909	N7541A	B707	18027			
N7279U	B727	21557	N7378F	B737	20070	N7456U	B727	21910	**N7541A**	**MD80**	**49995**			
N7280	B727	19119	N7378P	737NG	29272	N7457U	B727	21911	N7542A	B707	18028			
N7280U	B727	21558	N7379F	B737	20071	N7458U	B727	21912	**N7542A**	**MD80**	**49996**			
N7281	B727	19120	N7380F	B737	19681	N7459U	B727	21913	N7543A	B707	18029			
N7281U	B727	21559	N7381	B707	18977	N7460U	B727	21914	**N7543A**	**MD80**	**53025**			
N7282	B727	19243	N7381F	B737	20369	N7461U	B727	21915	N7544A	B707	18030			
N7282U	B727	21560	N7382F	B737	20492	N7462U	B727	21916	**N7544A**	**MD80**	**53026**			
N7283U	B727	21561	N7383F	B737	19075	N7463U	B727	21917	N7545A	B707	18031			
N7284	B727	19244	N7384F	B737	20129	N7464U	B727	21918	N7546A	B707	18032			
N7284U	B727	21562	N7385F	B737	21069	N7465B	DC-9	47465	**N7546A**	**MD80**	**53028**			
N7285U	B727	21563	N7386F	B737	20368	N7465U	B727	21919	N7547A	B707	18033			
N7286	B727	19245	N7387F	B737	19682	N7466U	B727	21920	**N7547A**	**MD80**	**53029**			
N7286U	B727	21564	(N7388F)	B737	19758	N7467U	B727	21921	N7548A	B707	18034			
N7287	B727	19246	N7388F	B737	19920	N7470	B747	20235	**N7548A**	**MD80**	**53030**			
N7287U	B727	21565	N7389F	B737	19937	N7486B	B707	21261	N7549A	B707	18035			
N7287V	B727	22080	N7390F	B737	19945	N7501A	B707	17628	**N7549A**	**MD80**	**53031**			
N7288	B727	19497	N7391F	B737	21508	N7502A	B707	17629	**N7550**	**MD80**	**53032**			
N7288U	B727	21566	N7392F	B737	21509	N7503A	B707	17630	N7550A	B707	18036			
N7289	B727	19499	N7393F	B737	21544	N7504A	B707	17631	N7551A	B707	18882			
N7289U	B727	21567	N7394F	B737	21545	N7505A	B707	17632	N7551A	B707	18037			
N7290	B727	19500	N7395F	B737	21546	**N7506**	**MD80**	**49800**	N7551A	B707	18883			
N7290U	B727	21568	N7396F	B737	21640	N7506A	B707	17633	N7552A	B707	18884			
N7291U	B727	21569	N7397F	B737	21641	N7507A	B707	17634	N7553A	B707	18885			
N7291Z	**CRJ**	**7291**	N7398F	B737	21642	**N7508**	**MD80**	**49802**	N7554A	B707	19185			
N7292	B727	19501	N7399F	B737	23024	N7508A	B707	17635	N7555A	B707	18689			
N7292U	B727	21570	(N7401Q)	B747	20080	**N7509**	**MD80**	**49003**	N7556A	D707	18690			
N7293	B727	19534	N7401U	B727	19089	N7509A	B707	17636	N7557A	B707	18691			
N7293U	B727	21571	(N7402Q)	B747	20081	N7510A	B707	17637	N7558A	B707	18692			
N7294	B727	19535	N7402U	B727	19090	N7511A	B707	17638	N7559A	B707	18938			
N7294U	B727	21572	(N7403Q)	B747	20082	N7512A	B707	17639	N7560A	B707	18939			
N7295	B727	19532	N7403U	B727	19091	**N7512A**	**MD80**	**49806**	N7561A	B707	18940			
N7295U	B727	21573	(N7404Q)	B747	20083	N7513A	B707	17640	N7562A	B707	19235			
N7296	B727	19533	N7404U	B727	19092	N7514A	B707	17641	N7563A	B707	19236			
N7296U	B727	21574	N7405U	B727	19093	**N7514A**	**MD80**	**49891**	N7563Q	B727	22424			
N7297U	B727	21892	N7406U	B727	19094	N7515A	B707	17642	N7564A	B707	19237			
N7298U	B727	21893	N7407U	B727	19095	N7516A	B707	17643	N7565A	B707	19380			
N7299U	B727	21894	N7408U	B727	19096	N7517A	B707	17644	N7567A	B707	19381			
N7302F	B737	19758	N7409U	B727	19097	**N7517A**	**MD80**	**49894**	N7567A	B707	19382			
N7305V	**CRJ**	**7305**	N7410U	B727	19098	N7518A	B707	17645	N7568A	B707	19383			
N7310F	B737	20344	N7411U	B727	19099	**N7518A**	**MD80**	**49895**	N7569A	B707	19384			
N7321S	B707	19840	N7412U	B727	19100	N7519A	B707	17646	N7570A	B707	19186			
N7322S	B707	19841	N7413U	B727	19101	**N7519A**	**MD80**	**49896**	N7571A	B707	19187			
N7323S	B707	19842	N7414U	B727	19102	N7520A	B707	17647	N7572A	B707	19188			
N7340F	B737	21597	N7415U	B727	19103	**N7520A**	**MD80**	**49897**	N7573A	B707	19323			
N7341F	B737	21598	N7416U	B727	19191	N7521A	B707	17648	N7574A	B707	19324			
N7342F	B737	21747	N7417U	B727	19192	**N7521A**	**MD80**	**49898**	N7575A	B707	19325			
N7343F	B737	21748	N7418U	B727	19193	N7522A	B707	17649	N7576A	B707	19326			
N7344F	B737	21749	N7419U	B727	19194	**N7522A**	**MD80**	**49899**	N7577A	B707	19327			
N7345F	B737	21750	N7420U	B727	19195	N7523A	B707	17650	N7578A	B707	19328			
N7346F	B737	21751	N7421U	B727	19196	N7524A	B707	17651	N7579A	B707	19329			

Registration	Type	Serial
N7580A	B707	19330
N7581A	B707	19331
N7582A	B707	19332
N7583A	B707	19333
N7584A	B707	19334
N7585A	B707	19335
N7586A	B707	19336
N7587A	B707	19337
N7588A	B707	19338
N7589A	B707	19339
N7590A	B707	19340
N7591A	B707	19341
N7592A	B707	19342
N7593A	B707	19343
N7594A	B707	19344
N7595A	B707	19515
N7596A	B707	19516
N7597A	B707	19517
N7598A	B707	19518
N7599A	B707	19519
N7600K	**737NG**	**32628**
N7620U	B727	19537
N7621U	B727	19538
N7622U	B727	19539
N7623U	B727	19540
N7624U	B727	19541
N7625U	B727	19542
N7626U	B727	19899
N7627U	B727	19900
N7628U	B727	19901
N7629U	B727	19902
N7630U	B727	19903
N7631U	B727	19904
N7632U	B727	19905
N7633U	B727	19906
N7634U	B727	19907
N7635U	B727	19908
N7636U	B727	19909
N7637U	B727	19910
N7638U	B727	19911
N7639U	B727	19912
N7640U	B727	19913
N7641U	B727	19914
N7642U	B727	19915
N7643U	B727	20037
N7644U	B727	20038
N7645U	B727	20039
N7646U	B727	20040
N7647U	B727	20041
(N7660A)	B737	22426
N7667A	**B757**	**25301**
"N7667AB"	B707	17682
N7667D	D707	21307
N7771	B777	27116
N7772	B777	26936
N7773	B777	26932
N7774	B777	26929
N7821B	MD11	48543
N7829A	DC-8	20217
N7852Q	L1011	193K-1024
N7876	CV990	30-10-4
N7878	CV990	30-10-37
(N7888)	B707	18713
N7890	B727	20112
N7892	B727	20114
N7893	B727	20115
N8001U	DC-8	45278
N8002U	DC-8	45279
N8003U	DC-8	45280
N8004U	DC-8	45281
N8005U	DC-8	45282
N8006U	DC-8	45283
N8007U	1-11	054
N8007U	DC-8	45284
N8008D	DC-8	45252
N8008F	DC-8	45669
N8008U	DC-8	45285
N8009U	DC-8	45286
N8010U	DC-8	45287
N8011U	DC-8	45288
N8012U	DC-8	45289
N8013U	DC-8	45290
N8014U	DC-8	45588
N8015U	DC-8	45589
N8016	DC-8	45254
N8016U	DC-8	45590
N8017U	DC-8	45591
N8018D	DC-8	45278
N8018U	DC-8	45291
N8019U	DC-8	45592
N8020U	DC-8	45593
N8021U	DC-8	45594
N8021V	DC-8	45612
N8022U	DC-8	45595
N8023U	DC-8	45292
N8024U	DC-8	45293
N8025U	DC-8	45294
N8026U	DC-8	45295
N8027	DC-8	45255
"N8027U"	B747	19883
N8027U	DC-8	45296
N8028D	DC-8	45279
N8028U	DC-8	45297
N8029U	DC-8	45298
N8030H	B727	18816
N8030U	DC-8	45596
N8031U	DC-8	45299
N8032M	B737	22022
N8032U	DC-8	45597
N8033U	DC-8	45300
N8034T	L1011	193B-1230
N8034U	DC-8	45301
N8035U	DC-8	45302
N8036U	DC-8	45303
N8037U	DC-8	45304
N8038A	DC-8	45256
N8038D	DC-8	45280
N8038U	DC-8	45305
N8039U	DC-8	45306
N8040U	DC-8	45307
N8041U	DC-8	45675
N8042U	DC-8	45676
N8043B	B727	19254
N8043E	B727	20228
N8043U	DC-8	45677
N8044U	DC-8	45800
N8045U	DC-8	45801
N8046U	DC-8	45802
N8047U	DC-8	45880
N8048U	DC-8	45881
N8049U	DC-8	45886
N8050U	DC-8	45884
N8051U	DC-8	45885
N8052U	DC-8	46009
N8053U	DC-8	46010
N8054U	DC-8	46011
N8055U	DC-8	46012
N8060U	DC-8	45693
N8061U	DC-8	45694
N8062U	DC-8	45757
N8063U	DC-8	45758
N8064U	DC-8	45759
N8065U	DC-8	45756
N8066U	DC-8	45850
N8067A	**A300**	**510**
N8067U	DC-8	45851
N8068D	DC-8	45255
N8068U	DC-8	45852
N8069U	DC-8	45853
N8070U	DC-8	45810
N8071B	MD80	49661
N8071U	DC-8	45811
N8072U	DC-8	45812
N8073U	DC-8	45813
N8074U	DC-8	45849
N8075U	DC-8	45940
N8076U	DC-8	45941
N8077U	DC-8	45945
N8078H	B747	21922
N8078M	B747	21606
N8078Q	B747	21923
N8078U	DC-8	45946
N8079U	DC-8	45947
N8080U	DC-8	45970
N8081U	DC-8	45971
N8082U	DC-8	45972
N8083N	B737	28083
N8083U	DC-8	45973
N8084U	DC-8	45974
N8085U	DC-8	45975
N8086U	DC-8	45976
N8087U	DC-8	45977
N8088U	DC-8	45978
N8089U	DC-8	45993
N8090P	B707	18921
N8090Q	B707	19434
N8090U	DC-8	45994
N8091J	B707	19776
N8091U	DC-8	45995
N8092U	DC-8	45996
N8093U	DC-8	45997
N8094L	DC-10	46556
N8094P	DC-10	46953
N8094U	DC-8	45998
N8094Z	DC-10	46982
N8095U	DC-8	45298
N8095V	DC-10	47980
N8096U	DC-8	46040
N8097U	DC-8	46064
N8098U	DC-8	46065
N8099U	DC-8	46066
N8101N	B727	18252
N8102N	B727	18253
N8103N	B727	18254
N8104E	B727	18255
N8104N	B727	18255
N8105N	B727	18256
N8106N	B727	18257
N8107N	B727	18258
N8108N	B727	18259
N8109N	B727	18260
N8110N	B727	18261
N8111N	B727	18262
N8112N	B727	18263
N8113N	B727	18264
N8114N	B727	18265
N8115N	B727	18266
N8116N	B727	18267
N8117N	B727	18268
N8118N	B727	18269
N8119N	B727	18270
N8120N	B727	18271
N8121N	B727	18272
N8122N	B727	18273
N8123N	B727	18274
N8124N	B727	18275
N8125N	B727	18276
N8126N	B727	18277
N8127N	B727	18278
N8128N	B727	18279
N8128R	B737	28128
N8129L	B737	28129
N8129N	B727	18280
N8130J	B737	28130
N8130N	B727	18281
N8131N	B727	18282
N8132N	B727	18283
N8133N	B727	18284
N8134N	B727	18285
N8135N	B727	18286
N8136N	B727	18287
N8137N	B727	18288
N8138N	B727	18289
N8139N	B727	18290
N8140G	B727	19393
N8140N	B727	18291
N8140P	B727	18744
N8140V	B727	18743
N8141N	B727	18965
N8142N	B727	18966
N8143N	B727	18967
N8144N	B727	18968
N8145N	B727	18969
N8146N	B727	18970
N8147N	B727	18971
N8148A	DC-8	45267
N8148N	B727	18972
N8149N	B727	18973
N8150N	B727	18974
N8151G	B727	19298
N8152G	B727	19299
N8153G	B727	19300
N8154G	B727	19301
N8155G	B727	19302
N8156G	B727	19356
N8157G	B727	19357
N8158G	B727	19358
N8159G	B727	19359
N8160C	CV990	30-10-9
N8160G	B727	19360
N8161G	B727	19717
N8162G	B727	19718
N8163G	B707	18746
N8163G	B727	19719
N8164G	B727	19720
N8165G	B727	19721
N8166A	DC-8	45269
N8166G	B727	19722
N8167G	B727	19850
N8168G	B727	19851
N8169G	B727	19852
N8170A	DC-8	45270
N8170G	B727	19853
N8171G	B727	19854
N8172G	B727	19855
N8173G	B727	19856
N8174G	B727	19857
N8175G	B727	19858
N8177U	DC-8	45983
(N8183E)	B727	19404
N8184A	DC-8	45271
(N8190U)	B707	19321
N8207U	DC-8	45275
N8209U	DC-8	45260
N8215Q	B707	18688
N8215U	DC-8	45261
N8217U	DC-8	45263
N8228P	DC-10	46937
N8240U	DC-8	45257
N8243U	DC-8	45258
N8245U	DC-8	45259
N8246U	DC-8	45262
N8251R	737NG	29047
N8252U	DC-8	45264
N8253J	737NG	29049
N8253V	737NG	29050
N8254G	737NG	29051
(N8254Q)	737NG	29052
N8256C	CV990	30-10-19
N8258U	DC-8	45387
N8259C	CV990	30-10-20
N8266U	DC-8	45388
N8270A	DC-9	47037
N8270H	DC-9	47089
N8274H	DC-8	45274
N8275H	DC-8	45275
N8276H	DC-8	45276
N8277H	DC-8	45277
N8277V	B737	21176
N8277V	B737	21443
N8277V	B737	21507
N8277V	B747	22704
N8277V	B767	22921
(N8277Z)	B727	19132
N8278V	B727	22349
N8278V	B727	22641
N8278V	B737	22057
N8278V	B747	22870
N8278V	B767	22692
N8279V	B737	22596
N8279V	B737	22635
N8279V	B747	22970
N8279V	B747	23026
N8280V	B727	22167
N8280V	B737	21804
N8280V	B737	22276
N8280V	B747	21239
N8280V	B747	22305

Reg	Type	Ser
N8281V	B727	22394
N8281V	B747	22486
N8281V	B747	22498
N8282V	B737	22087
N8283V	B737	22607
N8284V	B727	22261
N8284V	B727	22268
N8284V	B747	21991
N8284V	B747	22477
N8284V	B747	22502
N8285V	B727	21346
N8285V	B727	22430
N8285V	B737	22589
N8285V	B747	21241
N8285V	B747	22234
N8286V	B727	22262
N8286V	B727	22271
N8286V	B737	22602
N8286V	B747	21604
N8286V	B767	22923
N8287V	B767	22694
N8288V	B727	22081
N8288V	B727	22288
N8288V	B737	22160
N8288V	B737	22778
N8289V	B737	21791
N8289V	B747	19735
N8289V	B747	22969
N8289V	B767	22695
N8289V	B767	22980
N8290V	B727	21853
N8290V	B737	22283
N8291V	B727	22359
N8291V	B737	22281
N8291V	B737	22408
N8291V	B747	21590
N8292V	B727	22374
N8292V	B737	22282
N8292V	B737	22338
N8292V	B767	22693
N8293V	B727	20903
N8293V	B737	22031
N8293V	B737	22653
N8293V	B747	21514
N8293V	B757	22184
N8294V	B757	22185
N8295V	B727	22375
N8295V	B737	22406
N8295V	B737	22739
N8295V	B747	21352
N8296V	B737	22120
N8296V	B747	22614
N8296V	B747	22764
N8296V	B747	22971
N8297V	B737	22137
N8297V	B747	20977
N8297V	B747	21111
N8297V	B747	21134
N8298V	B737	22119
N8298V	B737	22132
N8320	B727	19526
N8356C	CV990	30-10-27
N8357C	CV990	30-10-24
N8390A	CRJ	7390
N8396A	CRJ	7396
N8400	B707	19433
N8401	B707	19581
N8402	B707	19582
N8403	B707	19583
N8404	B707	19584
N8405	B707	19585
N8406	B707	19586
N8408	B707	19587
N8409	B707	19588
N8409N	CRJ	7409
N8410	B707	19589
N8411	B707	19574
N8412	B707	19575
N8412F	CRJ	7412
N8413	B707	19576
N8414	B707	19577
N8415	B707	20087
N8416	B707	20088
N8416A	B707	20088
N8416B	CRJ	7416
N8417	B707	20089
"N8417A"	B707	20089
N8418	DC-8	45600
N8418A	B707	17637
N8420A	B707	17638
N8423C	CRJ	7423
N8431	B707	20170
N8432	B707	20171
N8432A	CRJ	7432
N8433	B707	20172
N8434	B707	20173
N8434B	DC-8	45609
N8435	B707	20174
N8436	B707	20175
N8437	B707	20176
N8438	B707	20177
N8439	B707	20178
N8440	B707	20179
N8444F	CRJ	7444
N8458A	CRJ	7458
N8459	B707	20630
N8475B	CRJ	7475
N8477H	CV880	22-7-2-54
N8477R	CRJ	7477
N8478H	CV880	22-00-5
N8479H	CV880	22-00-8
N8480H	CV880	22-00-12
N8481H	CV880	22-00-20
N8482H	CV880	22-00-22
N8483H	CV880	22-00-23
(N8484H)	CV990	30-10-14
N8484H	CV990	30-10-5
N8485H	CV990	30-10-6
N8486H	CV880	22-00-44M
N8487H	CV880	22-00-37M
N8488D	CRJ	7488
N8488H	CV880	22-7-4-56
N8489H	CV880	22-00-1
N8489H	CV880	22-00-47M
N8490H	CV880	22-7-1-53
N8491H	CV880	22-00-46M
N8491H	CV880	22-00-49M
N8492C	CRJ	7492
N8492H	CV880	22-00-9
N8493H	CV880	22-00-18
N8494H	CV880	22-00-34
N8495B	CRJ	7495
N8495H	CV880	22-00-39
N8497H	CV990	30-10-7
N8498H	CV990	30-10-8
N8498S	B707	18424
N8498T	B707	18425
N8499H	CV990	30-10-11
N8500	DC-9	45731
N8501F	CRJ	7501
N8505Q	CRJ	7505
N8506C	CRJ	7506
N8515F	CRJ	7515
N8516C	CRJ	7516
N8524A	CRJ	7524
N8525B	CRJ	7525
N8527S	B737	20194
N8532G	CRJ	7532
N8533D	CRJ	7533
N8536Z	B737	22075
N8541D	CRJ	7541
N8543F	CRJ	7543
N8550F	B737	28550
N8554A	CRJ	7554
N8560F	CRJ	7560
N8577D	CRJ	7577
N8580A	CRJ	7580
N8587E	CRJ	7587
N8588D	CRJ	7588
N8596C	B727	21946
N8598B	CRJ	7598
N8601	DC-8	45422
N8602	DC-8	45423
N8603	DC-8	45424
N8604	DC-8	45425
N8604C	CRJ	7604
N8605	DC-8	45426
N8606	DC-8	45427
N8607	DC-8	45428
N8608	DC-8	45429
N8609	DC-8	45430
N8610	DC-8	45431
N8611	DC-8	45432
N8611A	CRJ	7611
N8612	DC-8	45433
N8613	DC-8	45434
N8614	DC-8	45435
N8615	DC-8	45436
N8617	DC-8	45437
(N8618)	DC-8	45438
(N8619)	DC-8	45439
N8623A	CRJ	7623
N8630	DC-8	46101
N8631	DC-8	45936
N8631E	CRJ	7631
N8632	DC-8	45966
N8633	DC-8	46020
N8634	DC-8	46021
N8635	DC-8	46050
N8636	DC-8	46051
N8637	DC-8	46052
N8638	DC-8	46053
N8639	DC-8	46049
N8641	DC-8	46106
N8642	DC-8	46109
N8646A	CRJ	7646
(N8647A)	B737	19306
N8659B	CRJ	7659
N8665A	CRJ	7665
N8672A	CRJ	7672
N8673D	CRJ	7673
N8674A	CRJ	7674
N8683B	CRJ	7683
N8688C	CRJ	7688
N8694A	CRJ	7694
N8696C	CRJ	7696
N8698A	CRJ	7698
N8700H	B727	18321
N8701E	B707	18155
N8702E	B707	18156
N8702Q	DC-10	46920
N8703E	B707	18157
N8703Q	DC-10	46923
N8704Q	DC-10	46921
N8705E	B707	18159
N8705Q	DC-10	46660
N8705T	B707	18916
N8706E	B707	18160
N8706Q	DC-9	47661
N8707E	B707	18161
N8707Q	DC-10	46959
N8708E	B707	18162
N8708Q	DC-10	46961
N8709A	CRJ	7709
N8709E	B707	18163
N8709Q	DC-9	47697
N8710A	CRJ	7710
N8710E	B707	18164
N8710Q	DC-9	47761
N8711E	B707	18240
N8712E	B707	18241
N8712Q	DC-10	46976
N8713E	B707	18242
N8713Q	DC-9	47772
N8714E	B707	18243
N8714Q	DC-9	47773
N8715E	B707	18244
N8715T	B707	18917
(N8717U)	DC-8	46118
N8718E	CRJ	7718
N8721B	CRJ	7721
(N8724U)	DC-8	46119
N8725T	B707	18918
N8729	B707	20058
N8730	B707	20059
N8730B	C-14	?
N8731	B707	20060
(N8731U)	DC-8	46120
N8731U	DC-8	46130
N8732	B707	20060
N8733	B707	20062
N8733G	CRJ	7733
N8734	B707	20063
N8735	B707	20064
N8736	B707	20065
N8736A	CRJ	7736
N8737	B707	20066
N8738	B707	20067
(N8739)	B707	18408
N8740	C-14	?
N8740	DC-8	45668
N8745B	CRJ	7745
N8747B	CRJ	7747
N8751D	CRJ	7751
N8755	DC-8	46097
N8756	DC-8	46096
N8757	DC-8	46095
N8758	DC-8	46093
N8758D	CRJ	7758
N8759	DC-8	46058
N8760	DC-8	46074
N8762	DC-8	46038
N8763	DC-8	46037
N8764	DC-8	46017
N8765	DC-8	46016
N8766	DC-8	46015
N8767	DC-8	45992
N8768	DC-8	45983
N8769	DC-8	45982
N8770	DC-8	45913
N8771	DC-8	45912
N8771A	CRJ	7771
N8772	DC-8	45943
N8773	DC-8	45942
N8774	DC-8	45894
N8775	DC-8	45889
N8775A	CRJ	7775
N8776	DC-8	45888
N8777	DC-8	45887
N8778	DC-8	45848
N8779R	DC-8	45760
N8780R	DC-8	45628
N8781R	DC-8	45648
N8782R	DC-8	45667
N8783E	CRJ	7783
N8783R	DC-8	45684
N8784R	DC-8	45769
N8785R	DC-8	45803
N8786R	DC-8	45897
N8787R	DC-8	45898
N8788R	DC-8	45952
N8789R	B707	19410
N8789R	B727	20143
N8790A	CRJ	7790
N8790R	B707	18043
N8790R	B727	20240
N8791R	B727	20241
N8794B	CRJ	7794
N8797A	CRJ	7797
N8800G	CRJ	7800
N8801E	CV880	22-00-4
N8802E	CV880	22-00-7
N8803E	CV880	22-00-11
N8804E	CV880	22-00-16
N8805E	CV880	22-00-17
N8806E	CV880	22-00-21
N8807E	CV880	22-00-29
N8808E	CV880	22-00-36
N8808H	CRJ	7808
N8809E	CV880	22-00-38
N8810E	CV880	22-00-41
N8811E	CV880	22-00-50
N8812E	CV880	22-00-51
N8813E	CV880	22-00-52
N8814E	CV880	22-00-62
N8815E	CV880	22-00-63
N8816E	CV880	22-00-64

Reg	Type	Serial	Reg	Type	Serial	Reg	Type	Serial	Reg	Type	Serial
N8817E	CV880	22-00-65	N8888Z	B727	21857	N8940E	CRJ	7940	N8979E	DC-9	47328
N8825E	B727	20144	N8889Z	B727	21858	N8940E	DC-9	47163	N8980A	CRJ	7980
N8826E	B727	20145	N8890Z	B727	21859	N8941E	DC-9	47164	N8980E	DC-9	47329
N8827E	B727	20146	N8891A	CRJ	7891	N8942A	CRJ	7942	N8981E	DC-9	47330
N8828D	CRJ	7828	N8891Z	B727	21860	N8942E	DC-9	47165	N8982A	CRJ	7982
N8828E	B727	20147	N8892Z	B727	21861	N8943A	CRJ	7943	N8982E	DC-9	47331
N8829E	B727	20148	N8894A	CRJ	7894	N8943E	DC-9	47166	N8983E	DC-9	47399
N8830E	B727	20149	N8896A	CRJ	7896	N8944B	CRJ	7944	N8984E	DC-9	47400
N8831E	B727	20150	N8901	DC-9	45826	N8944E	DC-9	47167	N8985E	DC-9	47401
N8832E	B727	20151	N8901E	DC-9	45742	N8945E	DC-9	47181	N8985V	B737	22059
N8833E	B727	20152	N8902	DC-9	47010	N8946A	CRJ	7946	N8986B	CRJ	7986
N8834E	B727	20153	N8902E	DC-9	45743	N8946E	DC-9	47182	N8986E	DC-9	47402
N8835E	B727	20154	N8903	DC-9	47011	N8947E	DC-9	47183	N8987E	DC-9	47403
N8836A	CRJ	7836	N8903A	CRJ	7903	N8948B	CRJ	7948	N8988E	DC-9	47098
N8836E	B727	20379	N8903E	DC-9	45744	N8948E	DC-9	47184	N8989E	DC-9	47121
N8837B	CRJ	7837	N8904	DC-9	47012	N8949E	DC-9	47185	N8990E	DC-9	47120
N8837E	B727	20380	N8904E	DC-9	45745	N8950E	DC-9	47186	N9001D	MD80	53138
N8838E	B727	20381	N8905	DC-9	47013	N8951E	DC-9	47187	N9001L	MD80	53137
N8839E	B727	20382	N8905E	DC-9	45746	N8952E	DC-9	45867	N9001U	B737	19039
N8839E	CRJ	7839	N8905F	CRJ	7905	N8953E	DC-9	45868	N9002U	B737	19040
N8840A	B707	19247	N8906	DC-9	47014	N8953U	DC-9	45797	N9003U	B737	19041
N8840E	B727	20383	N8906E	DC-9	45747	N8954E	DC-9	47188	N9004U	B737	19042
N8841E	B727	20415	N8907	DC-9	47015	N8954U	DC-8	45878	N9005U	B737	19043
N8842E	B727	20416	N8907A	CRJ	7907	N8955E	DC-9	47189	N9006U	B737	19044
N8843E	B727	20441	N8907E	DC-9	45748	N8955U	DC-8	45948	N9007U	B737	19045
N8844E	B727	20442	N8908	DC-9	47152	N8956E	DC-9	47214	N9008U	B737	19046
N8845E	B727	20443	N8908D	CRJ	7908	N8956U	DC-8	45949	N9009U	B737	19047
N8846E	B727	20444	N8908E	DC-9	45749	N8957E	DC-9	47215	N9010L	B717	55060
N8847A	CRJ	7847	N8909	DC-9	47016	N8958E	DC-9	47216	N9010L	MD90	53494
N8847E	B727	20445	N8909E	DC-9	45770	N8959E	DC-9	47157	N9010L	MD90	53513
N8848E	B727	20446	N8910	DC-9	47153	N8960A	CRJ	7960	N9010U	B737	19048
N8849E	B727	20447	N8910E	DC-9	45771	N8960E	DC-9	45869	N9011U	B737	19049
N8850E	B727	20448	N8911	DC-9	47017	N8960T	DC-8	45938	N9012J	B717	55054
N8851E	B727	20614	N8911E	DC-9	45825	N8960U	DC-9	47114	N9012J	MD80	49952
N8852E	B727	20615	N8912	DC-9	47154	N8961	DC-9	45842	N9012J	MD80	53121
N8853E	B727	20616	N8912E	DC-9	45829	N8961E	DC-9	45870	N9012J	MD80	53235
N8855A	CRJ	7855	N8913	DC-9	47018	N8961T	DC-8	45902	N9012S	B717	55055
N8855E	B727	20617	N8913A	CRJ	7913	N8961U	DC-9	47115	N9012S	MD80	53065
N8856E	B727	20618	N8913E	DC-9	45830	N8962	DC-9	45843	N9012S	MD80	53479
N8857E	B727	20619	N8914	DC-9	47155	N8962E	DC-9	45871	N9012S	MD90	53491
N8858E	B727	20620	N8914A	CRJ	7914	N8962T	DC-8	45900	N9012S	MD90	53496
N8859E	B727	20621	N8914E	DC-9	45831	N8963	DC-9	45844	N9012S	MD90	53505
N8860	DC-9	45797	N8915	DC-9	47086	N8963E	DC-9	45872	N9012S	MD90	53569
N8860E	B727	20622	N8915E	DC-9	45832	N8963U	DC-9	47192	N9012U	B737	19050
N8861E	B727	20623	N8916	DC-9	47156	N8964	DC-9	47048	N9013U	B737	19051
N8862E	B727	20624	N8916E	DC-9	45733	N8964E	CRJ	7964	N9014S	B717	55064
N8863E	B727	20625	N8917	DC-9	47087	N8964E	DC-9	45873	N9014S	MD90	53493
N8864E	B727	20626	N8917E	DC-9	45734	N8964U	DC-8	45961	N9014S	MD90	53515
N8865E	B727	20627	N8918	DC-9	45828	N8965E	CRJ	7965	N9014U	B737	19052
N8866E	B727	20628	N8918B	CRJ	7918	N8965E	DC-9	45874	N9015U	B737	19053
N8867E	B727	20823	N8918E	DC-9	45833	N8965U	DC-9	47301	N9016U	B737	19054
N8869B	CRJ	7869	N8919	DC-9	47240	N8966E	DC-9	47217	N9017P	MD80	53124
N8869E	B727	20824	N8919E	DC-9	45834	N8966U	DC-8	46067	N9017U	B737	19055
N8870A	B707	18873	N8920E	DC-9	45835	N8967E	DC-9	47267	N9018U	B737	19056
N8870Z	B727	21288	N8921B	CRJ	7921	N8967U	DC-8	46068	N9019U	B737	19057
N8871Z	B727	21289	N8921E	DC-9	45836	N8968E	CRJ	7968	N9020Q	MD11	48504
N8872Z	B727	21290	N8922E	DC-9	45837	N8968E	DC-9	45875	N9020Q	MD11	48746
N8873Z	B727	21291	N8923A	CRJ	7923	N8968U	DC-8	46069	N9020Q	MD11	48758
N8874Z	B727	21292	N8923E	DC-9	45838	N8969A	CRJ	7969	N9020Q	MD11	48781
N8875Z	B727	21293	N8924B	CRJ	7924	N8969E	DC-9	45876	N9020U	B737	19058
N8876Z	B727	21449	N8924E	DC-9	45839	N8969U	DC-8	46070	N9020U	MD11	48428
N8877A	CRJ	7877	N8925E	DC-9	45840	N8970D	CRJ	7970	N9020U	MD11	48503
N8877Z	B727	21450	N8926E	DC-9	45863	N8970E	DC-9	47268	N9020Z	MD11	48426
N8878Z	B727	21451	N8927E	DC-9	45864	N8970U	DC-8	46071	N9020Z	MD11	48427
N8879Z	B727	21452	N8928A	CRJ	7928	N8971A	CRJ	7971	N9020Z	MD11	48533
N8880A	B707	18708	N8928E	DC-9	45865	N8971E	DC-9	47269	N9021U	B737	19059
N8880Z	B727	21453	N8929E	DC-9	45866	N8971U	DC-8	46081	N9022U	B737	19060
N8881Z	B727	21578	N8930E	CRJ	7930	N8972E	CRJ	7972	N9023U	B737	19061
N8882Z	B727	21579	N8930E	DC-9	47139	N8972E	DC-9	47270	N9024U	B737	19062
N8883E	CRJ	7883	N8931E	DC-9	47140	N8972U	DC-8	46084	N9025U	B737	19063
N8883Z	B727	21021	N8932C	CRJ	7932	N8973E	DC-9	47036	N9026U	B737	19064
N8883Z	B727	21580	N8932E	DC-9	47141	N8973U	DC-8	46085	N9027U	B737	19065
N8884E	CRJ	7884	N8933B	CRJ	7933	N8974C	CRJ	7974	N9028U	B737	19066
N8884Z	B727	21581	N8933E	DC-9	47142	N8974E	DC-9	47074	N9029U	B737	19067
N8885Z	B727	21854	N8934E	DC-9	47143	N8974U	DC-8	46110	N9030Q	MD11	48790
N8886A	CRJ	7886	N8935E	DC-9	47144	N8975E	DC-9	47119	N9030U	B737	19068
N8886Z	B727	21855	N8936A	CRJ	7936	N8975U	DC-8	46111	N9031U	B737	19069
N8887Z	B727	21856	N8936E	DC-9	47145	N8976E	CRJ	7976	N9032U	B737	19070
N8888B	A300	677	N8937E	DC-9	47158	N8976E	DC-9	47271	N9033U	B737	19071
N8888B	DC-8	45860	N8938A	CRJ	7938	N8977A	CRJ	7977	N9034U	B737	19072
N8888D	CRJ	7888	N8938E	DC-9	47161	N8977E	DC-9	47272	N9035C	MD80	53139
N8888P	A300	555	N8939E	DC-9	47162	N8978E	DC-9	47327	N9035U	B737	19073

Reg	Type	c/n	Reg	Type	c/n	Reg	Type	c/n	Reg	Type	c/n
N9036U	B737	19074	N9333	DC-9	47246	N9669	B747	20108	N11109	E145	145657
N9037U	B737	19075	N9334	DC-9	47247	N9670	B747	20109	N11113	E145	145662
N9038U	B737	19076	N9335	DC-9	47337	N9671	B747	20323	N11119	E145	145677
N9039U	B737	19077	N9336	DC-9	47338	N9672	B747	20324	N11121	E145	145683
N9040U	B737	19078	N9337	DC-9	47346	N9673	B747	20325	N11127	E145	145697
N9041U	B737	19547	N9338	DC-9	47347	N9674	B747	20326	N11137	E145	145721
N9042U	B737	19548	N9339	DC-9	47382	N9675	B747	20390	N11140	E145	145732
N9043U	B737	19549	N9340	DC-9	47389	N9676	B747	20101	N11150	E145	145756
N9044U	B737	19550	N9341	DC-9	47390	N9676	B747	20391	N11155	E145	145782
N9045U	B737	19551	N9342	DC-9	47391	N9677W	MD80	53627	N11164	E145	14500817
N9046U	B737	19552	N9343	DC-9	47439	N9681B	MD80	53631	N11165	E145	14500819
N9047F	DC-8	45445	N9344	DC-9	47440	N9683Z	DC-8	45750	N11176	E145	14500881
N9047U	B737	19553	N9345	DC-9	47441	N9684Z	DC-9	45711	N11181	1-11	BAC.096
N9048U	B737	19554	N9346	DC-9	47376	N9727N	B747	21575	N11181	E145	14500904
N9049U	B737	19555	N9347	DC-9	45827	N9743Z	DC-9	47201	N11182	1-11	BAC.097
N9050U	B737	19556	N9348	DC-9	45787	"N9748C"	B727	20113	N11183	1-11	BAC.105
N9051U	B737	19932	N9349	DC-9	47016	N9801F	MD80	49116	N11184	E145	14500917
N9052U	B737	19933	N9350	DC-9	47153	N9802F	MD80	49117	N11187	E145	14500927
N9053N	DC-10	48294	N9351	DC-9	47240	N9803F	MD80	49118	N11189	E145	14500931
N9053U	B737	19934	N9352	DC-9	47017	N9804F	MD80	49114	N11191	E145	14500935
N9054U	B737	19935	N9353	DC-9	47154	N9805F	MD80	49102	N11192	E145	14500938
N9055U	B737	19936	N9354	DC-9	47018	(N9806F)	MD80	49391	N11193	E145	14500940
N9056U	B737	19937	N9355	DC-9	47155	N9806F	MD80	49444	N11194	E145	14500953
N9057U	B737	19938	N9356	DC-9	47086	N9807F	MD80	49450	N11199	E145	145411
N9058U	B737	19939	N9357	DC-9	47156	N9896	B747	19896	N11206	737NG	30578
N9059U	B737	19940	N9358	DC-9	47087	N9897	B747	19897	N11244	B737	20073
N9060U	B737	19941	N9359	DC-9	45828	N9898	B747	19898	N11412	B727	18874
N9061U	B737	19942	N9401	B747	22245	N9899	B747	20246	N11415	B727	19122
N9062U	B737	19943	N9401W	MD80	53137	N9900	B747	20247	N11526	E145	145410
N9063U	B737	19944	N9402W	MD80	53138	N9985F	B707	18056	N11535	E145	145518
N9064U	B737	19945	N9403W	MD80	53139	(N9986F)	B707	17718	N11536	E145	145520
N9065U	B737	19946	N9404V	MD80	53140	N10022	MD80	48024	N11539	E145	145536
N9066U	B737	19947	N9405T	MD80	53141	(N10023)	B747	20012	N11544	E145	145557
N9067U	B737	19948	N9405W	MD80	53141	N10024	B747	20534	N11547	E145	145563
N9068U	B737	19949	N9406W	MD80	53126	N10027	MD80	48025	N11548	E145	145565
N9069U	B737	19950	N9407R	MD80	49400	N10028	DC-9	48137	N11551	E145	145411
N9070L	146	E3147	(N9408R)	MD80	49575	N10028	MD80	48026	N11556	E145	145621
N9070N	A320	0088	N9409F	MD80	53121	N10028	MD80	48046	N11612	B737	27325
N9070U	B737	19951	N9412W	MD80	53187	N10029	MD80	48049	(N11612)	B737	27326
N9071U	B737	19952	N9413T	MD80	53188	N10033	MD80	48083	N11641	B737	28902
N9072U	B737	19953	N9414W	MD80	53189	N10034	MD80	48056	N11651	B727	20249
N9073U	B737	19954	(N9415G)	MD80	53562	N10035	MD80	48057	N11651	B737	28912
N9074U	B737	19955	(N9416G)	MD80	53563	N10037	MD80	49114	N11656	B737	28917
N9075H	MD80	53140	(N9417C)	MD80	53564	N10038	DC-10	48275	(N11843)	MD80	49661
N9075H	MD90	53516	(N9418B)	MD80	53565	N10038	MD11	48533	N11984	A300	108
N9075H	MD90	53519	(N9419N)	MD80	53566	N10040	737NG	30790	N11995	A300	119
N9075U	B737	19956	N9420D	MD80	49824	N10045	DC-10	48259	N12061	DC-10	47851
N9076Y	MD11	48502	N9500H	C-17	F.169/CA.2	(N10046)	MD80	48026	N12064	DC-10	47862
N9086L	146	E3135	N9515T	B727	19874	N10046	MD80	49141	N12081	DC-10	47981
N9093P	MD11	48532	N9516T	B727	19873	N10060	DC-10	46970	N12089	DC-10	46550
N9101	DC-9	45794	(N9530)	B717	55000	N10112	L1011	193L-1064	N12109	B757	27299
N9102	DC-9	45795	N9601Z	DC-8	45567	N10114	L1011	193L-1079	(N12109)	B757	27300
N9103	DC-9	45796	N9603Z	DC-8	45383	N10115	L1011	193L-1114	N12114	B757	27556
N9104	DC-9	47081	N9604Z	DC-8	45623	N10116	L1011	193L-1120	N12116	B757	27558
(N9105)	DC-9	47138	N9605Z	DC-8	45614	N10117	L1011	193L-1125	N12122	E145	145684
(N9106)	DC-9	47263	N9607Z	DC-8	45607	N10156	E145	145786	(N12125)	B757	27567
(N9107)	DC-9	47264	N9608Z	DC-8	45608	N10199	YAK40	9940360	N12125	B757	28967
N9110V	DC-8	45817	N96097	DC-8	45640	N10236	B737	19937	N12126	E145	145693
N9115G	L1011	193A-1042	N9612Z	DC-8	45653	(N10240)	B737	20368	N12135	E145	145718
N9134D	MD11	48520	N9615W	MD80	53562	N10242	B737	20071	N12136	E145	145719
N9134D	MD11	48768	N9616G	MD80	53563	N10248	B737	20344	N12142	E145	145735
N9166N	MD11	48769	N9617R	MD80	53564	(N10249)	B737	20369	N12145	E145	145745
N9166N	MD11	48777	N9618A	MD80	53565	N10251	B737	20361	N12157	E145	145787
N9166N	MD11	48782	N9619V	MD80	53566	N10323	B737	23374	N12160	E145	145799
N9166N	MD11	48803	N9620D	MD80	53591	N10328	B737	19682	N12163	E145	14500811
N9166X	MD11	48406	N9621A	MD80	53592	(N10408)	B727	21661	N12166	E145	14500831
N9184X	B727	20894	N9622A	MD80	53593	(N10409)	B727	21662	N12167	E145	14500834
N9187D	B737	23320	N9624T	MD80	53594	N10556	DC-9	47423	N12172	E145	14500864
N9194M	B707	17713	N9625W	MD80	53595	N10575	E145	145640	N12175	E145	14500878
(N9221R)	DC-8	45901	N9626F	MD80	53596	N10698	B767	23072	N12195	E145	14500943
N9230Z	B707	17683	N9627R	MD80	53597	N10756	B727	21042	N12216	737NG	28776
N9233Z	B727	18366	N9628W	MD80	53598	N10791	B727	20645	N12218	737NG	28778
N9234Z	B727	18368	N9629H	MD80	53599	N10801	MD80	49127	N12221	737NG	28930
N9302B	MD80	49528	N9630A	MD80	53561	N10834	MD80	49494	N12225	737NG	28934
N9303K	MD80	49529	N9661	B747	20100	N10970	A300	250	N12230	B737	19884
N9304C	MD80	49530	N9662	B747	20101	N11002	L1011	193B-1014	N12231	B737	19885
N9305N	MD80	49395	N9663	B747	20102	N11003	L1011	193B-1015	N12238	737NG	28804
N9306T	MD80	49567	N9664	B747	20103	N11004	L1011	193B-1016	N12301	B727	19558
N9307R	MD80	49663	N9665	B747	20104	N11005	L1011	193B-1017	N12302	B727	19559
N9330	DC-9	47138	N9666	B747	20105	N11006	L1011	193B-1018	N12303	B727	19560
N9331	DC-9	47263	N9667	B747	20106	N11060	A300	470	N12304	B727	19561
N9332	DC-9	47264	N9668	B747	20107	N11106	E145	145650			
						N11107	E145	145654			

Reg	Type	No.	Reg	Type	No.	Reg	Type	No.	Reg	Type	No.	Reg	Type	No.
N12305	B727	19562	N13627	MD80	53015	N14174	E145	14500876	N14652	B737	28913
N12306	B727	19563	N13627	MD80	53199	N14177	E145	14500888	N14653	B737	28914
N12307	B727	19564	N13665	B737	28926	N14179	E145	14500896	N14654	B737	28915
N12308	B727	19565	(N13666)	B737	28927	N14180	E145	14500900	N14655	B737	28916
N12313	B737	23364	N13699	DC-9	45711	N14186	E145	14500924	N14660	B737	28921
N12318	B737	23369	N13716	737NG	28787	N14188	E145	14500929	N14662	B737	28923
N12319	B737	23370	N13718	737NG	28937	N14198	E145	14500951	N14664	B737	28925
N12322	B737	23373	N13720	737NG	28939	N14203	E145	14500964	N14667	B737	28927
N12327	B737	23457	(N13738)	737NG	28791	N14204	E145	14500968	(N14667)	B737	28928
N12335	B737	19758	(N13744)	737NG	28798	N14206	B737	19023	N14668	B737	28928
N12349	B737	23587	N13750	737NG	28941	N14208	B737	19025	N14704	737NG	28765
N12411	B727	22052	N13759	B727	21044	N14209	B737	19026	N14708	MD80	49670
N12450	737NG	28957	N13780	B727	20635	N14211	B737	19028	N14731	737NG	28799
N12505	DC-9	45788	(N13809)	MD80	49263	N14212	B737	19029	(N14731)	737NG	28936
N12507	DC-9	47788	N13881	MD80	48045	N14214	737NG	28774	(N14735)	737NG	28940
N12508	DC-9	47797	N13891	MD80	49102	(N14216)	B737	19033	N14735	737NG	28950
N12510	DC-9	47799	N13903	E145	145479	N14219	737NG	28781	(N14741)	737NG	28797
N12514	DC-9	48113	N13908	E145	145465	N14228	737NG	28792	N14760	B727	21118
N12519	E145	145366	N13913	E145	145438	N14230	737NG	28794	N14788	B727	20642
N12528	E145	145504	N13914	E145	145430	N14231	737NG	28795	N14791	B707	18810
N12530	E145	145533	N13929	E145	145009	(N14233)	B737	19887	N14810	MD80	49264
N12532	DC-9	45791	N13935	E145	145022	N14235	737NG	28947	N14814	MD80	49112
N12536	DC-9	47113	N13936	E145	145025	N14237	737NG	28802	N14816	MD80	49370
N12538	DC-9	47218	N13949	E145	145057	N14237	B737	19945	N14818	MD80	49478
N12539	DC-9	45792	N13955	E145	145075	N14239	B737	19920	N14831	MD80	49491
N12540	E145	145537	N13956	E145	145078	N14240	737NG	28952	N14839	MD80	49635
N12552	E145	145583	N13958	E145	145085	N14241	B737	20070	N14840	MD80	49580
N12563	E145	145612	N13964	E145	145123	N14242	737NG	28805	(N14845)	MD80	49668
N12564	E145	145618	N13965	E145	145125	N14245	B737	20074	(N14846)	MD80	49701
N12567	E145	145623	N13968	E145	145138	N14246	B737	20129	(N14848)	MD80	49703
N12569	E145	145630	N13969	E145	145141	N14247	B737	20133	N14871	MD80	48022
N12657	B737	28918	N13970	E145	145146	N14249	737NG	28809	N14879	MD80	49526
(N12746)	737NG	28948	N13971	A300	262	(N14250)	B737	20492	N14880	MD80	48044
N12811	MD80	49265	N13972	A300	289	N14307	B737	23358	(N14886)	MD80	48063
N12826	B727	19826	"N-13972"	A300	289	N14308	B737	23359	N14889	MD80	49118
N12827	B727	19827	N13974	A300	126	N14320	B737	23371	N14890	MD80	49114
(N12844)	MD80	49667	N13975	E145	145163	N14324	B737	23375	N14902	E145	145496
N12900	E145	145511	N13978	E145	145180	N14325	B737	23455	N14904	E145	145477
N12921	E145	145354	N13979	E145	145181	N14334	B737	23572	N14905	E145	145476
N12922	E145	145338	N13983	A300	092	N14335	B737	23573	N14907	E145	145468
N12924	E145	145311	N13988	E145	145265	N14336	B737	23574	N14916	E145	145415
N12934	E145	145019	N13989	E145	145271	N14337	B737	23575	N14920	E145	145380
N12946	E145	145052	N13990	E145	145277	N14341	B737	23579	N14923	E145	145318
N12957	E145	145080	N13992	E145	145284	N14342	B737	23580	N14925	E145	145004
N12967	E145	145133	N13994	E145	145291	N14346	B737	23584	N14930	B747	20103
N12996	E145	145296	N13995	E145	145295	N14347	B737	23585	N14930	E145	145011
N13066	DC-10	46591	N13997	E145	145298	N14358	B737	23943	N14931	E145	145013
N13067	DC-10	47866	N14024	B747	20534	N14381	B737	26310	N14933	E145	145018
N13086	DC-10	46917	N14053	A300	420	N14383	B737	26312	N14936	B747	20105
N13088	DC-10	46850	N14056	A300	463	N14384	B737	26313	N14937	B747	20106
N13110	B757	27300	N14061	A300	471	(N14405)	B727	21268	N14937	E145	145026
(N13110)	B757	27301	N14062	DC-10	47863	N14416	B727	22168	N14938	E145	145029
N13113	B757	27555	N14063	DC-10	47864	N14505	E145	145192	N14939	B747	20108
N13118	E145	145675	N14065	A300	508	N14508	E145	145220	N14939	E145	145030
N13123	E145	145688	N14068	A300	511	N14514	E145	145303	N14940	E145	145033
N13124	E145	145689	N14074	DC-10	46911	N14516	E145	145323	N14942	E145	145037
N13132	E145	145708	N14075	DC-10	46922	N14522	E145	145383	N14943	B747	20102
N13133	E145	145712	N14077	A300	612	N14524	DC-9	47539	N14943	E145	145040
N13138	B757	30351	N14079	DC-10	46927	N14534	DC-9	47110	N14945	E145	145049
N13161	E145	14500805	N14090	DC-10	46553	N14542	E145	145547	N14947	E145	145054
N13202	E145	14500962	N14102	B757	27292	N14543	E145	145553	N14950	E145	145061
N13227	737NG	28788	(N14102)	B757	27293	N14551	MD80	53033	N14952	E145	145067
N13234	B737	19888	N14105	E145	145649	N14558	E145	145598	N14953	E145	145071
N13248	737NG	28808	N14106	B757	27296	N14562	E145	145611	N14959	E145	145091
N13331	B737	23569	(N14106)	B757	27297	N14564	DC-9	47490	N14960	E145	145100
N13512	DC-9	48111	N14107	B757	27297	N14568	E145	145628	N14966	A300	117
N13538	E145	145527	(N14107)	B757	27298	N14570	E145	145632	N14968	A300	153
N13550	E145	145575	N14115	B757	27557	N14573	E145	145638	N14969	A300	207
N13553	E145	145585	N14116	E145	145672	N14601	B737	27314	N14972	E145	145151
N13566	E145	145622	N14117	E145	145674	(N14601)	B737	27315	N14973	A300	211
N13614	DC-9	45713	N14118	B757	27560	N14604	B737	27317	N14974	E145	145161
N13624	B737	27528	N14120	B757	27562	(N14604)	B737	27318	N14975	A300	261
N13627	DC-10	47855	N14121	B757	27563	N14605	B737	27318	N14976	A300	271
N13627	DC-10	48259	N14125	E145	145690	(N14605)	B737	27319	N14977	A300	274
N13627	DC-8	45618	N14143	E145	145739	N14609	B737	27322	N14977	E145	145175
N13627	DC-9	47651	N14148	E145	145751	(N14609)	B737	27323	N14980	A300	086
N13627	DC-9	47784	N14153	E145	145761	N14613	B737	27326	N14991	E145	145278
N13627	MD80	48015	N14158	E145	145791	(N14613)	B737	27327	N14993	E145	145289
N13627	MD80	48024	N14162	E145	14500808	N14628	B737	27532	N14998	E145	145302
N13627	MD80	49193	N14168	E145	14500840	N14629	B737	27533	N15017	L1011	193B-1063
N13627	MD80	49826	N14171	E145	14500859	N14639	B737	28900	N15069	DC-10	46584
N13627	MD80	49951	N14173	E145	14500872	N14645	B737	28906	N15255	B737	21069

Reg	Type	S/N	Reg	Type	S/N	Reg	Type	S/N	Reg	Type	S/N
N15335	DC-9	45725	N16703	737NG	28764	N17244	737NG	28954	(N18401)	B727	21264
N15509	E145	145238	N16709	737NG	28779	N17245	737NG	28955	N18476	B727	19173
N15512	B727	18897	N16713	737NG	28784	N17252	B737	20362	N18477	B727	18361
N15525	DC-9	47531	(N16732)	737NG	28937	N17275	CRJ	7275	N18478	B727	18364
N15527	E145	145413	N16732	737NG	28948	N17306	B737	23357	N18479	B727	19174
N15555	E145	145594	(N16737)	737NG	28790	N17309	B737	23360	N18480	B727	18741
N15572	E145	145636	N16738	B707	19568	N17316	B737	23367	N18513	DC-9	48112
N15574	E145	145639	N16739	B707	19569	N17317	B737	23368	N18544	DC-9	47219
N15659	B737	28920	N16758	B727	21043	N17321	B707	18825	N18556	E145	145595
N15710	737NG	28780	N16761	B727	21119	N17321	B737	23372	N18557	E145	145596
N15710	B707	19566	N16762	B727	21245	N17322	B707	18826	N18563	DC-9	47487
N15711	B707	19567	N16764	B727	18936	N17323	B707	18886	N18611	B737	27324
N15712	737NG	28783	N16765	B727	18361	N17324	B707	18887	(N18611)	B737	27325
N15712	B707	20068	N16766	B727	18364	N17325	B707	19177	N18622	B737	27526
N15713	B707	20069	N16767	B727	18365	N17326	B707	19178	N18658	B737	28919
(N15740)	737NG	28796	N16768	B727	18363	N17326	B737	23456	N18701	B707	18978
(N15742)	737NG	28944	(N16778)	B727	21246	N17327	B707	19350	N18702	B707	18979
(N15747)	737NG	28800	N16784	B727	20639	N17328	B707	19351	N18703	B707	18980
(N15749)	737NG	28950	N16802	MD80	49222	N17328	B737	23458	N18704	B707	18981
(N15772)	B727	21041	N16804	MD80	49246	N17329	B707	19352	N18706	B707	18982
N15774	B727	21242	N16806	MD80	49260	N17329	B737	23459	N18707	B707	18983
N15781	B727	20636	N16807	MD80	49261	N17337	CRJ	7337	N18708	B707	18984
N15790	B727	20644	N16808	MD80	49262	N17344	B737	23582	N18709	B707	18985
N15820	MD80	49480	N16813	MD80	48066	N17345	B737	23583	N18710	B707	19224
N15841	MD80	49581	N16815	MD80	49113	N17356	B737	23942	N18711	B707	19225
N15910	E145	145455	N16883	MD80	48073	N17358	CRJ	7358	N18712	B707	19226
N15912	E145	145439	N16884	MD80	48074	N17386	B737	26321	N18713	B707	19227
N15926	E145	145005	(N16885)	MD80	48062	N17402	B727	21265	N18786	B727	20641
N15932	E145	145015	N16887	MD80	49116	(N17403)	B727	21266	N18813	1-11	BAC.126
N15941	E145	145035	N16892	MD80	49391	N17406	B727	21269	N18814	1-11	BAC.119
N15948	E145	145056	N16893	MD80	49392	N17407	B727	21270	N18815	B747	20887
N15967	A300	121	N16894	MD80	49393	N17410	B727	21663	N18833	MD80	49493
N15973	E145	145159	N16895	MD80	49394	N17413	B727	22165	N18835	MD80	49439
N15980	E145	145202	N16911	E145	145446	(N17418)	B727	21855	N18982	E145	145223
N15983	E145	145239	N16918	E145	145397	(N17480)	B727	21661	N19059	A300	469
N15985	E145	145248	N16919	E145	145393	N17507	E145	145215	N19072	DC-10	46576
N15986	E145	145254	N16927	E145	145006	N17513	E145	145292	N19117	B757	27559
N16065	B767	30199	N16944	E145	145045	N17521	E145	145378	(N19118)	B757	27560
N16112	E145	145660	N16949	DC-10	46949	N17524	E145	145399	N19130	B757	28970
N16147	E145	145749	N16951	E145	145063	N17531	DC-9	45847	N19136	B757	29285
N16149	E145	145753	N16954	E145	145072	N17533	DC-9	47281	N19141	B757	30354
N16151	E145	145758	N16961	E145	145103	N17535	DC-9	47111	N19357	B737	23839
N16170	E145	14500850	N16963	E145	145116	(N17541)	DC-9	45793	N19357	B737	23841
N16178	E145	14500889	N16976	E145	145171	N17543	DC-9	45789	N19382	B737	26311
N16183	E145	14500914	N16981	E145	145208	N17557	DC-9	47424	N19503	E145	145176
(N16203)	B737	19020	N16982	A300	091	N17560	DC-9	47067	N19504	DC-9	47638
N16217	737NG	28777	N16987	E145	145261	N17560	E145	145605	N19554	E145	145587
N16232	B737	19886	N16999	E145	145307	N17614	B737	27327	N19621	B737	27334
N16234	737NG	28946	N17010	B747	19729	(N17614)	B737	27328	N19622	B737	27527
N16254	B737	20365	N17011	B747	19730	N17619	B737	27332	N19634	B737	26319
N16301	B737	23352	N17025	B747	20535	(N17619)	B737	27333	N19636	B737	26340
N16310	B737	23361	N17085	DC-10	47957	N17620	B737	27333	N19638	B737	28899
N16339	B737	23577	N17087	DC-10	47928	(N17620)	B737	27334	(N19743)	737NG	28945
N16501	E145	145145	N17104	B757	27294	N17627	B737	27531	(N19745)	737NG	28799
N16502	E145	145166	(N17104)	B757	27295	N17640	B737	28901	N19066	E145	145131
N16510	E145	145251	N17105	B757	27295	N17644	B737	28905	(N20171)	B757	32398
N16511	E145	145267	(N17105)	B757	27296	N17663	B737	28924	N20205	B737	19022
N16520	E145	145372	N17108	E145	145655	N17719	737NG	28938	(N20410)	B757	32397
N16521	DC-9	47521	N17115	E145	145666	N17730	737NG	28798	N20643	B737	28904
N16525	E145	145403	N17117	B737	19768	(N17739)	737NG	28941	N20727	B737	20276
N16541	E145	145542	N17122	B757	27564	N17773	B727	21045	(N21037)	B707	20097
N16545	MD80	53027	N17125	B747	20271	(N17775)	B727	21243	(N21100)	B757	27291
N16546	E145	145562	N17126	B747	20273	(N17776)	B727	21244	N21108	B757	27298
N16559	E145	145603	N17126	B757	27566	(N17777)	B727	20634	N21108	B757	27299
N16561	E145	145610	N17128	B757	27567	N17789	B727	20643	N21129	E145	145703
N16571	E145	145633	N17133	B757	29282	N17804	DC-10	47861	N21130	E145	145704
N16607	B737	27320	N17138	E145	145727	N17812	MD80	49250	N21144	E145	145741
(N16607)	B737	27321	N17139	B757	30352	(N17843)	MD80	49365	N21154	E145	145772
N16617	B737	27330	N17146	E145	145746	N17928	E145	145007	N21197	E145	14500947
(N16617)	B737	27331	N17156	CRJ	7156	N17984	E145	145246	N21537	E145	145523
N16618	B737	27331	N17159	E145	145792	N18066	A300	509	N21555	MD80	49780
(N16618)	B737	27332	N17169	E145	14500844	N18101	E145	145590	N21723	737NG	28790
N16632	B737	27900	N17175	CRJ	7175	N18102	E145	145643	(N22055)	B707	20340
N16642	B737	28903	N17185	E145	14500922	N18112	B757	27302	N22134	B727	20903
N16646	B737	28907	N17196	E145	14500945	N18114	E145	145664	N22620	B737	22620
N16647	B737	28908	N17207	B707	19002	N18119	B757	27561	N22679	L1011	193A-1008
N16648	B707	17661	N17208	B707	19003	N18120	E145	145681	N22909	E145	145459
N16648	B737	28909	(N17217)	B737	19794	N18220	737NG	28929	N22971	E145	145149
N16649	B707	17668	N17217	CRJ	7217	N18223	737NG	28932	N23139	E145	145731
N16649	B737	28910	N17229	737NG	28793	N18243	737NG	28806	N23657	B737	28918
N16650	B737	28911	N17231	CRJ	7231	N18350	B737	23588	N23661	B737	28922
N16701	737NG	28762	N17233	737NG	28943	N18359	B737	23841	N23707	737NG	28768

Reg.	Type c/n	Reg.	Type c/n	Reg.	Type c/n	Reg.	Type c/n
N23708	737NG 28769	(N27734)	737NG 28939	N32724	B727 20654	N37078	DC-10 46926
N23721	737NG 28940	N27734	737NG 28949	N32725	B727 20655	(N37165)	B767 30430
(N23748)	737NG 28949	N27783	B727 20638	N32824	B707 18071	(N37166)	B767 30431
(N23842)	MD80 49363	N27962	E145 145110	N32831	B757 23686	(N37167)	B767 30432
N24089	B737 20455	N28366	B747 20800	N32836	B737 23752	(N37168)	B767 30433
N24103	E145 145645	N28518	E145 145334	N33021	B747 20520	(N37169)	B767 30434
N24128	E145 145700	N28529	E145 145512	N33069	A300 512	(N37170)	B767 30435
N24202	737NG 30429	N28714	B707 18408	N33103	B757 27293	N37178	CRJ 7178
N24211	737NG 28771	N28724	B707 19570	(N33103)	B757 27294	N37208	CRJ 7208
N24212	737NG 28772	N28726	B707 19571	N33132	B757 29281	N37218	CRJ 7218
N24213	B737 19030	N28727	B707 19572	N33182	E145 14500909	N37228	CRJ 7228
N24224	737NG 28933	N28728	B707 19573	N33202	B737 19019	N37252	737NG 30583
N24343	B727 21630	N28888	B747 20542	N33203	737NG 30613	N37253	737NG 30584
N24517	E145 145332	N28899	B747 20543	N33209	737NG 30581	N37255	737NG 30610
N24633	B737 27901	N28903	B747 20541	(N33210)	B737 19027	N37263	737NG 31583
N24666	B707 18383	N29124	B757 27565	N33262	737NG 32402	N37267	737NG 31586
N24702	737NG 28763	(N29124)	B757 27566	N33264	737NG 31584	N37270	B727 19846
N24706	737NG 28767	N29129	B757 28969	N33266	737NG 32403	N37273	737NG 31591
N24715	737NG 28786	N29180	DC-8 46095	N33284	737NG 31635	N37274	737NG 31592
N24728	B727 20657	N29259	DC-9 45739	N33286	737NG 31600	N37277	737NG 31595
N24729	737NG 28945	N29515	E145 145309	N33289	737NG 31607	N37281	737NG 31599
(N24729)	B727 20658	N29549	DC-8 45803	N33292	737NG 33455	N37287	737NG 31636
(N24730)	B727 20659	N29717	737NG 28936	N33294	737NG 34000	N37290	737NG 31601
(N24736)	737NG 28789	N29730	B727 19209	N33341	B737 24681	N37293	737NG 33453
N24736	737NG 28803	N29796	B707 19209	N33414	MD80 49325	N37298	737NG 34004
N24837	B747 24837	N29879	737NG 29043	N33502	MD80 49739	N37342	CRJ 7342
N25034	B767 24999	N29887	737NG 29044	N33506	DC-9 47765	N37408	737NG 30125
N25071	A300 514	N29895	B727 19251	N33608	B737 27321	N37409	737NG 30126
N25134	E145 145714	N29906	E145 145472	(N33608)	B737 27322	N37413	737NG 31664
N25201	737NG 28958	N29917	E145 145414	N33635	B737 26339	N37615	B737 27328
N25504	E145 145186	N29922	DC-8 45754	N33637	B737 27540	(N37615)	B737 27329
N25621	B757 25621	N29953	DC-8 45691	N33714	737NG 28785	N37681	B707 17608
N25705	737NG 28766	N29954	DC-8 45859	N33785	B727 20640	N37700	737NG 29631
N25729	B727 20658	N29959	B707 17646	N33805	MD80 49249	N37777	B707 18044
(N26123)	B757 27565	(N29959)	1-11 009	N33817	MD80 49371	N37882	MD80 48027
N26123	B757 28966	(N29967)	737NG 29045	N34078	A300 615	N38257	737NG 30612
N26141	E145 145733	N29975	737NG 29046	N34110	E145 145658	N38268	737NG 31587
N26175	DC-9 47172	N29976	A300 087	N34111	E145 145659	N38383	B757 25491
N26208	737NG 30580	N29981	MD80 49563	N34131	B757 28971	N38403	737NG 30120
N26210	737NG 28770	N30008	MD80 49937	N34137	B757 30229	N38641	DC-9 47060
N26215	737NG 28775	N30010	MD80 49940	N34222	737NG 28931	N38727	737NG 28797
N26226	737NG 28935	N30016	MD11 48474	(N34256)	B737 22743	(N38819)	MD80 49479
N26232	737NG 28942	N30075	737NG 30118	(N34257)	B737 22744	N39081	DC-10 47861
N26545	E145 145558	N30401	L1011 193A-1002	N34282	737NG 31634	N39297	737NG 34003
N26549	E145 145571	N31001	L1011 193B-1013	N34315	B737 23366	N39305	DC-8 46098
N26565	B737 18370	N31001	L1011 193B-1026	N34415	B727 22167	N39307	DC-8 45910
(N26600)	B737 27314	N31007	L1011 193B-1028	N34838	MD80 49634	N39340	B737 23578
N26729	B727 21348	N31008	L1011 193B-1029	N35030	737NG 27982	N39343	B737 23581
N26861	B747 19733	N31009	L1011 193B-1030	N35030	B737 25017	N39356	B767 24037
N26862	B747 19734	N31010	L1011 193B 1031	N35030	B757 26242	N39364	B767 24045
N26863	B747 19735	N31011	L1011 193B-1035	N35050	B737 28882	N39365	B767 24046
N26864	B747 20305	N31013	L1011 193B-1036	N35084	DC-10 46991	N39367	B767 25194
N26877	B727 19319	N31014	L1011 193B-1059	N35108	737NG 27836	N39415	737NG 32826
N26879	B727 20475	N31015	L1011 193B-1060	N35108	B737 26071	N39416	737NG 37093
N26902	DC-9 47514	N31016	L1011 193B-1065	N35108	B737 26100	N39726	737NG 28796
N27015	B777 28678	N31018	L1011 193B-1066	N35108	B757 25220	N39728	737NG 28944
N27152	E145 145759	N31019	L1011 193B-1075	N35135	737NG 28297	N40061	DC-10 46973
N27172	CRJ 7172	N31021	L1011 193B-1076	N35135	B737 24785	N40064	A300 507
N27173	CRJ 7173	N31022	L1011 193B-1080	N35153	737NG 28004	N40102	B707 18158
N27185	CRJ 7185	N31023	L1011 193B-1091	N35153	737NG 28068	N40104	B727 21091
N27190	E145 14500934	N31024	L1011 193B-1109	N35153	B737 28898	N40108	B747 19896
N27191	CRJ 7191	N31029	L1011 193B-1111	N35153	B757 24749	N40112	B737 21302
N27200	E145 14500956	N31030	L1011 193B-1115	N35153	B757 25345	N40115	B727 21266
N27205	737NG 30577	N31031	L1011 193B-1124	N35161	737NG 27978	N40116	B747 21141
N27213	737NG 28773	(N31032)	L1011 193B-1215	N35161	737NG 28005	N40120	B737 21282
N27239	737NG 28951	N31032	L1011 193B-1130	N35198	B737 27381	N40467	B747 19725
N27246	737NG 28956	(N31033)	L1011 193B-1221	N35204	737NG 30576	N40481	B727 18329
N27314	CRJ 7314	N31033	E145 145705	N35236	737NG 28801	N40482	B727 18330
N27318	CRJ 7318	N31131	DC-10 47889	N35260	737NG 30855	N40483	B727 18331
N27358	B737 23840	N31208	B707 17696	N35271	737NG 31589	N40483	B747 19727
(N27417)	B727 21854	N31239	B707 17718	N35407	737NG 30124	N40484	B727 18791
N27506	E145 145206	N31240	B707 17703	N35674	B707 17918	N40485	B727 18332
N27509	DC-9 47798	N31241	737NG 30129	N35832	MD80 49492	N40486	B727 18848
N27512	E145 145274	N31412	737NG 30121	N35836	MD80 49441	N40487	B727 18849
N27522	DC-9 47524	N32404	B737 27530	N35888	MD80 49117	N40488	B727 18852
N27523	E145 145389	N32626	B727 20385	N36207	737NG 30579	N40489	B727 18854
N27610	B737 27323	N32716	B727 20386	N36247	737NG 28807	N40490	B747 20528
(N27610)	B737 27324	N32717	B727 20387	N36272	737NG 31590	N40495	B727 18860
N27722	737NG 28789	N32718	B727 20388	N36280	737NG 31598	N41012	B737 24021
N27724	737NG 28791	N32719	B727 20463	N36915	E145 145421	N41016	L1011 193B-1034
N27733	737NG 28800	N32721	B727 20464	N37018	B777 31680	N41020	L1011 193B-1060
(N27733)	737NG 28938	N32722	B727 20465	N37077	DC-10 46981		L1011 193B-1072

Reg.	Type	c/n
N41033	B727	21269
N41035	B747	21025
N41063	**A300**	**506**
N41068	DC-10	47867
N41069	B737	25787
N41104	**E145**	**145646**
N41135	**B757**	**29284**
N41140	**B757**	**30353**
N42086	DC-8	46132
N42783	DC-10	47868
N42920	DC-8	45752
N43265	DC-9	47222
N43537	DC-9	47112
N44214	B737	19031
(N44253)	B737	20363
N44316	B727	20049
N44503	**MD80**	**49797**
N45090	DC-8	45908
N45191	DC-8	45981
N45224	B747	20520
N45498	B727	19665
N45733	B737	23059
N45742	B767	22922
N45793	B727	20647
N45814	DC-8	45814
N45908	DC-8	45416
N45914	DC-8	45389
N46625	**B737**	**27529**
N46793	B727	20489
N46916	DC-10	46916
N47142	B727	19135
N47202	**CRJ**	**7202**
N47239	CRJ	7239
N47330	B707	19353
N47331	B707	19869
N47332	B707	19870
N47332	**B737**	**23570**
(N47333)	B707	19871
N47401	DC-9	47401
(N47403)	B767	29448
N47414	**737NG**	**32826**
N47691	DC-8	45861
N47816	DC-10	47816
N47831	DC-10	47831
N47888	**DC-10**	**47888**
N47904	B767	27568
N47978	DC-8	46162
N48054	B727	21082
N48054	B727	21946
N48058	CV880	22-00-43M
N48059	CV880	22-00-44M
N48060	CV880	22-00-47M
N48062	CV880	22-7-2-54
N48063	CV880	22-7-4-56
N48075	DC-9	45723
N48127	**B757**	**28968**
N48200	DC-9	45721
N48258	DC-10	48258
N48277	DC-10	48277
N48354	L1011	193H-1246
N48354	L1011	193U-1144
N48354	L1011	193V-1157
(N48901)	B767	27392
N48901	**E145**	**145501**
N49082	**DC-10**	**47927**
(N49725)	737NG	28941
(N49803)	DC-8	45613
(N50022)	B747	20011
N50051	**A300**	**459**
N50074	A319	1429
N50089	737NG	30807
N50217	B747	35234
N50217	B767	33850
N50217	B777	27947
N50217	B777	28344
N50217	B777	28409
N50217	B777	29736
N50217	B777	32849
N50217	B777	33169
N50217	B777	33374
N50281	B777	29067
N50281	B777	29395
N50281	B777	30457
N50881	B737	24680
N51387	1-11	BAC.126
"N52022E"	B777	27607
N52309	B727	19828
N52310	B727	19829
N52311	B727	19830
N52312	B727	19831
N52313	B727	19832
N52616	**B737**	**27329**
(N52616)	B737	27330
N52845	DC-8	45981
N52958	DC-8	45883
(N53030)	737NG	27982
N53110	B747	19676
N53111	B747	19677
N53112	B747	19678
N53116	B747	20321
N53302	B707	19004
N54241	**737NG**	**28953**
N54325	B727	20232
N54326	B727	20233
N54327	B727	20234
N54329	B727	20306
N54330	B727	20307
N54331	B727	20308
N54332	B727	20309
N54333	B727	20310
N54334	B727	20460
N54335	B727	20461
N54336	B727	20462
N54337	B727	20490
N54338	B727	20491
N54339	B727	20843
N54340	B727	20845
N54341	B727	21628
N54342	B727	21629
N54344	B727	21631
N54345	B727	21632
N54348	B727	21967
N54349	B727	21968
N54350	B727	21969
N54351	B727	21983
N54352	B727	21984
N54353	B727	21985
N54354	**B727**	**21986**
N54627	DC-10	46925
N54629	DC-10	46852
N54631	DC-9	47588
N54631	DC-9	47597
N54633	DC-10	47886
N54634	DC-10	47887
N54635	DC-9	47600
N54638	DC-9	47649
N54639	DC-10	46853
N54640	DC-10	46921
N54641	DC-9	47654
N54642	DC-9	47655
N54643	DC-10	46949
N54644	DC-10	47928
N54645	DC-9	47619
N54646	DC-10	46952
N54648	DC-9	45722
N54649	DC-10	46854
N54652	DC-10	46661
N54652	DC-10	46913
N54711	**737NG**	**28782**
N56807	B737	22265
N56807	B737	22648
N56807	B767	23017
N56859	**B757**	**32818**
N57000	B727	22038
N57001	B727	22270
N57001	B737	21710
N57001	B727	22277
N57001	B727	22365
N57002	B727	22036
N57002	B727	22039
N57002	B727	22642
N57004	B747	22376
N57004	B747	22442
N57008	B727	21950
N57008	B727	22040
N57008	B737	21957
N57008	B737	22267
N57008	B737	22431
N57008	B757	22216
N57008	B767	23057
N57016	**B777**	**28679**
N57111	**B757**	**27301**
(N57111)	B757	27302
N57201	B707	18416
N57202	B707	18417
N57202	B747	21962
N57203	B707	18418
N57203	B747	21963
N57204	B707	18419
N57205	B707	18587
N57206	B707	18763
N57837	MD80	49582
N57852	**B757**	**32811**
N57855	**B757**	**32814**
N57857	**B757**	**32816**
N57863	**B757**	**32587**
N57864	**B757**	**32588**
N57868	**B757**	**32590**
N57869	**B757**	**32593**
N58101	**B757**	**27291**
(N58101)	B757	27292
N58201	B747	21961
N58414	B727	22166
N58541	DC-9	45793
N58545	DC-9	47094
N58606	**B737**	**27319**
(N58606)	B737	27320
(N58849)	MD80	49704
(N58902)	B767	27393
N58937	B707	18334
N59053	**B767**	**29448**
N59081	**A300**	**639**
N59083	DC-10	47926
N59101	A300	101
N59106	A300	106
N59107	A300	107
N59123	A300	123
N59139	A300	139
N59140	A300	140
(N59207)	B737	19024
(N59274)	A300	274
N59302	**B737**	**23353**
N59338	**B737**	**23576**
(N59404)	B727	21267
N59412	B727	22053
N59523	**MD80**	**49915**
N59630	**B737**	**27534**
(N59792)	B727	20646
(N59842)	MD80	49660
(N60274)	B727	20161
(N60282)	B727	20163
N60312	B737	23363
(N60362)	B727	20164
N60436	737NG	28447
N60436	737NG	28929
N60436	737NG	28948
N60436	737NG	29078
N60436	737NG	29135
N60436	B737	19932
N60436	B737	28729
N60436	B737	28742
N60436	B737	29267
N60436	B737	29795
(N60446)	B727	20165
N60468	B747	27044
(N60471)	B727	20166
(N60507)	B727	20167
N60655	B747	23908
N60656	737NG	30624
N60659	737NG	30210
N60659	B747	23502
N60659	B747	23610
N60659	B747	23813
N60659	B747	23825
N60659	B747	26408
N60659	B747	26425
N60659	B747	26473
N60659	B747	26563
N60659	B747	32910
N60659	B757	29434
N60659	B767	22522
N60659	B767	23217
N60659	B767	23281
N60659	B767	23308
N60659	B767	23744
N60659	B767	24947
N60659	B767	25058
N60659	B767	26389
N60659	B767	27391
N60659	B767	27427
N60659	B767	30341
N60665	B747	25873
N60668	737NG	32470
N60668	737NG	33471
N60668	B747	23461
N60668	B747	23637
N60668	B747	23722
N60668	B747	24066
N60668	B747	24518
N60668	B747	24740
N60668	B747	25152
N60668	B747	25213
N60668	B747	28960
N60668	B757	30046
N60668	B757	32343
N60668	B767	22787
N60668	B767	23282
N60668	B767	23803
N60668	B767	24002
N60668	B767	24007
N60668	B767	27049
N60668	B767	27428
N60668	B767	29230
N60668	B767	30342
N60669	B737	24231
N60688	B747	26474
(N60690)	B727	20168
N60697	B747	23610
N60697	B747	24870
N60697	B747	26056
N60697	B747	27117
N60697	B747	27137
N60697	B747	28468
N60697	B747	28705
N60697	B767	24846
N60697	B767	27385
N60697	B767	22053
N60697	B777	32725
(N60747)	B727	20366
(N60819)	B727	20367
N61304	**B737**	**23355**
N61699	B707	17661
(N61699)	B707	17662
N61944	B727	18894
N62020	DC-10	48205
N62020	MD80	49847
N62025	MD80	49282
N62119	B727	18934
N62215	B707	18080
N62355	L1011	193P-1103
N62357	L1011	193P-1105
N62393	B707	21049
(N62510)	MD80	49804
(N62576)	A300	011
N62631	**B737**	**27535**
N62683	A300	081
(N62846)	A300	010
N63050	MD80	49668
N63063	B727	22425
N63305	**B737**	**23356**
N63305	B747	20799
N63584	B727	18920
N63661	A300	031
N64315	B727	20048
N64319	B727	20052
N64320	B727	20053
N64321	B727	20054

Reg	Type	MSN	Reg	Type	MSN	Reg	Type	MSN	Reg	Type	MSN	Reg	Type	MSN
N64322	B727	20055	N68646	B707	18745	**N73270**	737NG	31632	**N76064**	B767	29459			
N64323	B727	20098	N68649	B727	18360	**N73275**	737NG	31593	**N76065**	B767	29460			
N64324	B727	20099	N68650	B727	18295	**N73276**	737NG	31594	N76073	DC-10	46940			
N64339	B727	20844	N68655	B707	18873	**N73283**	737NG	31606	N76151	B767	30430			
N64346	B727	21633	N68657	B707	19000	**N73291**	737NG	33454	N76153	B767	30432			
N64347	B727	21634	N68782	B727	20637	**N73299**	737NG	34005	N76156	B767	30435			
N64696	B707	18073	N68903	B767	27394	N73380	B737	26309	**N76200**	MD80	53290			
N64739	B707	17719	**N69020**	B777	31687	N73385	B737	26314	**N76201**	MD80	53291			
N64740	B707	17694	**N69059**	B767	29454	**N73406**	737NG	30123	**N76202**	MD80	53292			
(N64757)	B707	17692	**N69063**	B767	29458	**N73444**	MD80	49470	N76254	737NG	30779			
N64799	DC-8	45598	**N69154**	B767	30433	**N73529**	737NG	30803	N76265	737NG	31585			
N64804	DC-8	45600	**N69311**	B737	23362	N73700	B737	19437	N76269	737NG	31588			
N64854	L1011	193E-1058	**N69333**	B737	23571	N73700	B737	22950	N76288	737NG	33451			
N64854	L1011	193E-1067	**N69348**	B737	23586	N73700	B737	23886	**N76354**	B737	23592			
N64854	L1011	193E-1069	**N69351**	B737	23589	N73700	B737	24178	**N76355**	B737	23593			
N64854	L1011	193E-1073	N69523	DC-9	47520	N73711	737NG	29749	N76360	B737	23941			
N64854	L1011	193H-1247	**N69602**	B737	27315	N73711	B737	20209	N76361	B737	23942			
N64854	L1011	193N-1083	(N69602)	B737	27316	N73712	737NG	28090	N76362	B737	23943			
N64854	L1011	193T-1118	**N69603**	B737	27316	N73712	A340	117	N76400	B767	29703			
N64854	L1011	193U-1110	(N69603)	B737	27317	N73712	B737	20210	N76400	B767	29705			
N64911	L1011	193G-1250	**N69735**	B727	20664	N73713	737NG	28091	(N76401)	B737	29446			
N64911	L1011	193Y-1176	N69736	B727	20665	N73713	B737	20242	**N76502**	737NG	31603			
N64959	L1011	293A-1248	"N69736PG"	B727	20665	**N73713**	**B747**	**24315**	**N76503**	737NG	33461			
N64996	L1011	293A-1249	**N69739**	B727	20667	N73714	B737	19072	**N76504**	737NG	31604			
N65010	B707	19163	N69740	B727	20668	N73714	B737	19552	**N76505**	737NG	32834			
N65358	DC-9	47048	N69741	B727	22250	(N73714)	B737	20344	N76508	737NG	31639			
N65516	DC-8	46143	N69742	B727	22251	**N73714**	**B747**	**24405**	N76752	B727	21248			
N65517	DC-8	46145	N69803	MD80	49229	N73715	737NG	30031	N76753	B727	21249			
N65518	DC-8	46137	N69826	MD80	49486	N73715	B737	19679	N76823	MD80	49483			
N65858	**MD80**	**49578**	N70051	DC-8	45609	(N73715)	B737	20345	**N77006**	B777	29476			
N65894	B727	19501	**N70054**	A300	461	N73717	B737	19680	**N77012**	B777	29860			
N65910	B727	19243	**N70072**	A300	515	N73717	B737	20345	**N77014**	B777	29862			
N66051	**B767**	**29446**	**N70073**	A300	516	(N73717)	B737	20346	**N77019**	B777	35547			
N66056	**B767**	**29451**	**N70074**	A300	517	N73717	B747	22969	**N77066**	B767	29461			
N66057	**B767**	**29452**	**N70079**	A300	619	N73718	B737	20128	**N77080**	A300	626			
N66480	MD80	49900	**N70330**	B737	23460	N73718	B747	23301	**N77181**	CRJ	7181			
N66510	B727	18742	**N70352**	B737	23590	N73721	737NG	29139	**N77195**	CRJ	7195			
N66651	B707	18716	**N70353**	B737	23591	N73721	737NG	32806	N77204	B737	19021			
N66656	DC-8	45953	**N70401**	MD80	49312	N73724	B757	24254	N77215	B737	19032			
N66726	B727	20656	**N70404**	MD80	49315	**N73728**	737NG	31596	**N77258**	737NG	30802			
N66731	B727	20660	N70415	B727	22643	N73729	MD80	53467	**N77260**	CRJ	7260			
N66732	B727	20661	**N70425**	MD80	49337	N73730	B767	24541	**N77261**	737NG	31582			
N66733	B727	20662	**N70504**	MD80	49798	N73741	B747	23600	**N77278**	CRJ	7278			
N66734	B727	20663	**N70524**	MD80	49916	N73749	737NG	30279	**N77286**	CRJ	7286			
N67052	**B767**	**29447**	**N70529**	MD80	49921	N73750	737NG	30280	**N77295**	737NG	34001			
N67058	**B767**	**29453**	N70542	DC-9	47535	N73751	B727	21247	**N77296**	737NG	34002			
N67134	**B757**	**29283**	N70611	1-11	083	N73791	737NG	32773	**N77302**	CRJ	7302			
N67157	D7G7	30436	**N70700**	B707	17168	N73793	737NG	30281	**N77303**	R737	23354			
N67158	**B767**	**30437**	N70708	B727	19813	N73795	B747	21925	**N77331**	CRJ	7331			
N67161	**B757**	**30839**	N70720	B737	21112	N73797	A340	149	**N77421**	MD80	49333			
(N6725B)	B737	23023	N70721	B737	21500	**N74007**	**B777**	**29477**	N77771	B777	27106			
N67333	B707	19871	N70722	B737	21501	N74317	B727	20050	N77772	B747	19918			
N68041	**DC-10**	**46900**	N70723	B737	21739	N74318	B727	20051	(N77772)	B777	26936			
N68042	DC-10	46901	N70724	B737	21740	N74612	B707	18012	N77772	B777	27265			
N68043	DC-10	46902	N70755	B727	21366	N74613	B707	17903	N77773	B747	19919			
N68044	DC-10	46903	N70773	B707	17904	N74614	B707	17904	(N77773)	B777	26932			
N68045	DC-10	46904	N70774	B707	17610	N74615	B707	17615	N77773	B777	27266			
N68046	DC-10	47800	N70775	B707	17611	**N74856**	**B757**	**32815**	(N77774)	B777	26929			
N68047	DC-10	47801	N70785	B707	17612	N74989	A300	220	(N77775)	B777	26930			
N68048	DC-10	47802	N70798	B707	17605	N75356	B737	23838	(N77776)	B777	26917			
N68049	**DC-10**	**47803**	N71314	B737	23365	**N75410**	737NG	30127	N77779	B777	27105			
N68050	**DC-10**	**47804**	**N71411**	737NG	30128	N75429	B727	21427	N77780	B727	20635			
N68051	DC-10	47805	N71828	MD80	49488	**N75851**	**B757**	**32810**	N77827	MD80	49487			
N68052	DC-10	47806	N72381	B727	22644	**N75853**	**B757**	**32812**	(N77847)	MD80	49702			
N68053	**DC-10**	**47807**	**N72405**	737NG	30122	**N75854**	**B757**	**32813**	**N77865**	B757	32589			
N68054	**DC-10**	**47808**	N72488	DC-8	45444	**N75858**	**B757**	**32817**	**N77867**	B757	32592			
N68055	DC-10	47809	N72700	B727	18368	**N75861**	**B757**	**32585**	**N78001**	B777	27577			
N68056	**DC-10**	**47810**	N72700	B727	18464	**N75983**	CRJ	7481	**N78002**	B777	27578			
N68057	**DC-10**	**48264**	N72821	MD80	49481	**N75984**	CRJ	7489	**N78003**	B777	27579			
N68058	**DC-10**	**46705**	N72822	MD80	49482	**N75987**	CRJ	7405	**N78004**	B777	27580			
N68059	**DC-10**	**46907**	N72824	MD80	49484	**N75991**	CRJ	7422	**N78005**	B777	27581			
N68060	DC-10	47850	N72825	MD80	49485	**N75992**	CRJ	7401	**N78008**	B777	29478			
N68061	**B767**	**29456**	N72829	MD80	49489	**N75993**	CRJ	7372	**N78009**	B777	29479			
N68065	DC-10	46590	N72830	MD80	49490	**N75994**	CRJ	7367	**N78013**	B777	29861			
N68096	A310	589	N72986	A300	154	**N75995**	CRJ	7361	**N78017**	B777	31679			
N68097	A310	634	N72987	A300	155	**N75996**	CRJ	7357	(N78018)	B777	31680			
N68142	A300	142	N72988	A300	216	**N75998**	CRJ	7336	N78019	B747	20527			
N68155	**B767**	**30434**	N72990	A300	259	**N75999**	CRJ	7471	N78020	B747	19731			
N68159	**B767**	**30438**	**N73152**	B767	30431	**N76010**	B777	29480	**N78060**	B767	29455			
N68160	**B767**	**30439**	N73243	B737	20072	**N76054**	B767	29449	**N78285**	737NG	33452			
N68173	A300	173	**N73251**	737NG	30582	**N76055**	B767	29450	**N78501**	737NG	31602			
N68644	B727	18297	**N73256**	737NG	30611	**N76062**	B767	29457	**N78506**	737NG	32832			

Reg	Type	c/n	Reg	Type	c/n	Reg	Type	c/n	Reg	Type	c/n
N78509	**737NG**	**31638**	**N89427**	**B727**	**21365**	N99548	B727	20512	OB-1568	YAK40	9140220
N78866	**B757**	**32591**	**N90070**	**A300**	**513**	N99763	B727	20772	OB-1569	YAK40	9141020
N79011	**B777**	**29859**	N90125	MD80	53347	N99862	DC-8	45303	OB-1570	B727	19153
N79279	**737NG**	**31597**	N90126	MD80	53042	N99890	B737	20693	OB-1570-P	B727	19153
N79402	**737NG**	**30119**	N90126	MD80	53561				OB-1572	B727	20525
N79711	**737NG**	**30547**	N90178	MD11	48600				OB-1572	B737	19714
N79712	B747	20652	N90178	MD11	48789	Peru			OB-1573	B727	20728
N79713	B747	20373	N90178	MD11	48805				OB-1588	B727	18942
N79715	737NG	30754	N90178	MD11	48572	(OB-)	B727	18744	OB-1590	B727	22164
N79743	B727	22252	N90187	MD11	48573	(OB-)	B727	18844	OB-1592	B707	20301
N79744	B727	22253	N90187	MD11	48616	(OB-)	B727	19243	OB-1596	A300	204
N79745	B727	22448	N90187	MD11	48745	(OB-)	B727	19501	OB-1601	B727	18943
N79746	B727	22449	N90187	MD11	48773	OB-	DC-10	46975	OB-1601-P	B727	18943
N79748	B727	22450	N90287	B707	17921	OB-	DC-10	47834	OB-1606	YAK40	9041860
N79749	B727	22451	N90450	CV880	22-00-36	(OB-)	B737	23168	OB-1611	A300	216
N79750	B727	22452	N90452	CV880	22-00-9	OB-1018	F.28	11065	OB-1615	B737	19408
N79751	B727	21457	N90455	CV880	22-00-39	OB-1019	F.28	11066	OB-1618	DC-8	46132
N79754	B727	21363	(N90498)	B707	17719	OB-1141	B727	19312	OB-1619	B737	19616
N79771	B727	20840	N90498	B707	17721	OB-1210	DC-8	46142	OB-1620	B737	19615
N80052	**A300**	**460**	**N90511**	**MD80**	**49805**	OB-1222	DC-8	45992	OB-1631	A300	154
N80057	**A300**	**465**	N90549	B767	23057	OB-1223	DC-8	45420	OB-1634	A300	259
N80058	**A300**	**466**	N90557	B727	18935	OB-1244	DC-8	45763	OB-1635	B737	19554
N80084	**A300**	**675**	N90558	B727	18362	OB-1248	DC-8	46027	OB-1636	F.28	11009
N80703	B707	17599	N90651	B707	17928	OB-1249	DC-8	46132	OB-1637	B737	19059
N80946	DC-10	47834	**N91050**	**A300**	**423**	OB-1256	B727	19305	OB-1642	B727	18432
N81025	L1011	193B-1098	N91078	MD11	48776	OB-1260	DC-8	46102	OB-1647	B727	22606
N81026	L1011	193B-1104	N91392	B727	18997	OB-1267	DC-8	45851	OB-1653	YAK40	9041860
N81027	L1011	193B-1107	(N91516)	MD80	49893	OB-1268	DC-8	45853	OB-1658	B737	19014
N81028	L1011	193B-1108	N91566	MD11	48559	OB-1277	B727	19400	OB-1659	L1011	193A-1004
(N81826)	B727	19405	N91566	MD11	48571	OB-1287	DC-8	45759	OB-1661	B727	20422
(N81827)	B727	19406	N91566	MD11	48775	OB-1288	B727	19769	OB-1670	B737	20128
(N81871)	B727	18445	N91891	B727	18741	OB-1296	DC-8	45285	OB-1672	B737	19059
N81906	DC-8	45854	(N92038)	B707	18792	OB-1300	DC-8	45861	OB-1688	L1011	193A-1005
N82521	737NG	29048	N92874	MD80	49122	OB-1301	B727	20263	OB-1696	B707	18711
N82702	DC-9	47090	N93101	B747	19667	OB-1303	B727	20266	OB-1697	B727	19561
N83071	DC-10	48293	N93102	B747	19668	OB-1314	B737	19425	OB-1697	B727	21690
N83428	B727	21426	N93103	B747	19669	OB-1316	DC-8	45384	OB-1699	B707	20084
N83658	B707	18686	N93104	B747	19670	OB-1317	B737	19610	OB-1711	B737	23161
N83870	MD80	48056	N93105	B747	19671	OB-1323	DC-8	45953	OB-1712	B737	23164
N83872	MD80	49120	N93106	B747	19672	OB-1344	L1011	193A-1002	OB-1713	B737	19707
N83873	MD80	49121	N93107	B747	19673	OB-1371	B707	19575	OR-1715	B737	23165
N84355	B727	21987	N93108	B747	19674	OB-1372	DC-8	46078	OB-1716	B707	20017
N84356	B727	21988	N93109	B747	19675	OB-1373	DC-8	45984	OB-1718	B737	19424
N84357	B727	21989	(N93110)	B747	19676	OB-1396	F.28	11100	OB-1719	B737	20221
N84790	CV880	22-7-3-55	(N93111)	B747	19677	OB-1400	B707	19434	OB-1723	B737	19712
(N84905)	B767	27569	(N93112)	B747	19678	OB-1401	B707	18921	OB-1724	B737	23042
(N85877)	MD80	49450	N93113	B747	20080	OB-1407	DC-8	46038	OB-1728	B737	18433
N86330	B727	22642	N93114	B747	20081	OB-1421	DC-8	45752	OB-1728-P	B737	21002
N86425	**B727**	**21459**	N93115	B747	20320	OB-1438	DC-8	45985	OB-1729	B737	20128
(N86425)	B727	21947	N93117	B747	20322	OB-1451	B737	19072	OB-1729-P	B737	20128
N86426	B727	21364	N93118	B747	20082	OB-1452	DC-8	46038	OB-1730	B737	19422
N86430	B727	21947	N93119	B747	20083	OB-1455	L1011	193A-1002	OB-1730-P	B737	19422
N86740	B707	20056	N93134	B707	18067	OB-1456	DC-8	45272	OB-1731	B727	18432
N86741	B707	20057	N93135	B707	18069	OB-1465	B727	18845	OB-1733	B737	19059
N87070	DC-10	48292	N93136	B707	18165	OB-1476	B737	20492	OB-1738	B727	19432
N87353	**CRJ**	**7353**	N93137	B707	18250	OB-1485	AN7x	72095907	OB-1738-P	B737	19432
(N87402)	B767	29447	N93138	B707	18245	OB-1486	AN7x	72096911	OB-1742	B737	19616
(N87404)	B767	29449	N93141	B707	18061	OB-1487	AN7x	72096912	OB-1742-P	B737	19616
N87507	**737NG**	**31637**	N93142	B707	18062	OB-1489	TU134	1351203	(OB-1743)	B737	21226
N87569	B737	21006	N93143	B707	18063	OB-1490	TU134	60525	OB-1745	B737	19014
N87790	B727	20903	N93144	B707	18167	OB-1493	B737	19712	OB-1746	B737	20277
N88131	B737	28131	N93145	B707	18451	OB-1504	L1011	193A-1087	OB-1746-P	B737	20277
N88701	B727	19510	N93146	B707	18452	OB-1511	B737	20277	OB-1747	B737	20414
N88702	B727	19511	N93147	B707	18453	OB-1512	B727	19499	OB-1748	B737	19547
N88703	B727	19512	N93148	B707	18588	OB-1533	B727	19836	OB-1748-P	B737	19547
N88704	B727	19513	N93149	B707	18589	OB-1536	B737	20128	**OB-1749**	**DC-10**	**46891**
N88705	B727	19514	N93150	B707	18590	OB-1537	B727	21071	OB-1750	F.28	11097
N88706	B727	19797	N93151	B707	18749	OB-1538	B737	21206	OB-1750-P	F.28	11097
N88707	B727	19798	N93152	B707	18818	OB-1541	B727	21072	OB-1751	B737	19409
N88708	B727	19799	N93153	B707	18820	OB-1543	B727	18846	OB-1751-P	B737	19409
N88709	B727	19800	N93738	B727	20666	OB-1544	B737	20956	**OB-1752-P**	**B737**	**20711**
N88710	B727	19801	N93875	MD80	49125	OB-1544-P	B737	20956	OB-1753	B737	20214
N88711	B727	19802	N94104	B747	22376	OB-1545	L1011	193B-1075	OB-1754	B737	20215
N88712	B727	19803	N94280	CV990	30-10-12(2)	OB-1546	B737	19150	OB-1755	B737	19955
N88713	B727	19804	N94284	CV880	22-00-43M	OB-1546-P	B727	19150	OB-1758	B767	23057
N88714	B727	20243	N94285	CV880	22-00-45M	OB-1547	B727	19151	OB-1758-P	B767	23057
N88715	B727	20384	N94314	B727	20047	OB-1548	B727	19152	OB-1759	B727	19152
N88770	B727	20839	N94417	B737	23512	OB-1552	TU134	60215	OB-1759-P	B727	19152
N88777	B727	19798	N94454	DC-9	47291	OB-1553	TU134	60206	OB-1763	B737	19059
N88881	A300	743	**N97325**	**CRJ**	**7325**	OB-1559	YAK40	9640251	OB-1764	B737	20212
N88887	A300	625	N97891	B727	20113	OB-1560	B727	20903	OB-1764-P	B737	20212
N88931	B747	20798	N98876	MD80	49444	OB-1561	B737	19059			

Reg	Type	Serial
OB-1765	B767	24448
OB-1765-P	B767	24448
OB-1766	B767	24150
OB-1766-P	B767	24150
OB-1779P	F.28	11006
OB-1780P	F.28	11087
OB-1781-P	B737	21002
OB-1783-P	B737	19955
OB-1788-P	B757	24451
OB-1793-P	B737	20583
OB-1794-P	B737	23039
OB-1794-T	B737	23039
OB-1799-T	B737	23789
OB-1800-P	B737	21641
OB-1802-P	B737	20536
OB-1804-P	B737	21747
OB-1804-T	B737	21747
OB-1808-P	B737	22582
OB-1809-P	B737	22580
OB-1816-P	F.100	11377
OB-1821-P	F.100	11376
OB-1823	B737	22793
OB-1831P	F.100	11414
OB-1832-P	B737	21716
OB-1837-P	B737	22113
OB-1839-P	B737	22640
OB-1841-P	B737	22058
OB-1843-P	B737	21718
OB-1851-P	B737	22133
OB-OAG-728	CV990	30-10-5
(OB-R-231)	F.28	11035
(OB-R-232)	F.28	11036
(OB-R-233)	F.28	11039
OB-R-390	F.28	11032
OB-R-397	F.28	11059
OB-R-398	F.28	11065
OB-R-399	F.28	11066
OB-R-728	CV990	30-10-5
OB-R-765	CV990	30-10-2
OB-R-902	B727	19846
OB-R-925	CV990	30-10-24
OB-R-931	DC-8	45619
OB-R-953	1-11	BAC.239
OB-R-962	DC-8	45629
(OB-R-)	B737	19611
OB-R-1018	F.28	11065
OD R 1019	F.28	11066
OB-R-1020	F.28	11059
OB-R-1030	F.28	11032
OB-R-1080	1-11	BAC.241
OB-R-1081	B727	18269
OB-R-1083	DC-8	45768
OB-R-1084	DC-8	45879
OB-R-1115	B727	18879
OB-R-1115	B727	19115
OB-R-1116	DC-8	45629
OB-R-1123	DC-8	45760
OB-R-1124	DC-8	45648
OB-R-1125	DC-8	45643
OB-R-1135	B727	19506
OB-R-1141	B727	19312
OB-R-1142	DC-8	45612
OB-R-1143	DC-8	45598
OB-R-1173	1-11	BAC.193
OB-R-1181	DC-8	45760
OB-R-1200	DC-8	45882
OB-R-1205	DC-8	45442
OB-R-1210	DC-8	46142
OB-R-1214	DC-8	45600
OB-R-1222	DC-8	45992
OB-R-1223	DC-8	45420
OB-R-1243	B707	19375
OB-R-1248	DC-8	46027
OB-R-1249	DC-8	46132
OB-R-1256	B727	19305
OB-R-1259	DC-8	45659
OB-R-1260	DC-8	46102
OB-R-1263	B737	20449
OB-R-1267	DC-8	45851
OB-R-1268	DC-8	45853
OB-R-1269	DC-8	45852
OB-R-1270	DC-8	45757
OB-R-1277	B727	19400
OB-R-1287	DC-8	45759
OB-R-1288	B737	19769
OB-R-1296	DC-8	45285
OB-R-1300	DC-8	45861
OB-R-1301	B727	20263
OB-R-1303	B727	20266
OB-R-1314	B737	19425
OB-R-1317	B737	19610
OB-R-1323	DC-8	45953
OB-R1137	1-11	BAC.193
OB-T-1244	DC-8	45763
OB-T-1264	B707	19294
OB-T-1316	DC-8	45384

Lebanon

Reg	Type	Serial
(OD-ADK)	COMET	6445
OD-ADQ	COMET	6446
OD-ADR	COMET	6445
OD-ADS	COMET	6448
OD-ADT	COMET	6450
OD-ADY	SE210	83
OD-ADZ	SE210	51
OD-AEE	SE210	153
OD-AEF	SE210	157
OD-AEM	SE210	23
OD-AEO	SE210	174
OD-AEV	COMET	6414
OD-AEW	CV990	30-10-31
OD-AEX	CV990	30-10-10
OD-AFA	VC10	803
OD-AFB	B707	20224
OD-AFC	B707	20225
OD-AFD	B707	20259
OD-AFE	B707	20260
OD-AFF	CV990	30-10-18
OD-AFG	CV990	30-10-30
OD-AFH	CV990	30-10-25
OD-AFI	CV990	30-10-35
OD-AFJ	CV990	30-10-33
OD-AFK	CV990	30-10-26
OD-AFL	B707	18034
OD-AFM	B707	18027
OD-AFN	B707	18030
OD-AFO	B707	18035
OD-AFP	B707	18017
OD-AFQ	B707	18024
OD-AFR	B707	18018
OD-AFS	B707	18019
OD-AFT	B707	18020
OD-AFU	B707	18029
OD-AFW	B707	18026
OD-AFX	B707	19107
OD-AFY	B707	19108
OD-AFZ	B707	18025
OD-AGB	B707	18021
OD-AGC	B747	20391
OD-AGD	B707	18939
OD-AGE	B707	18963
OD-AGF	B707	18830
OD-AGG	B707	18828
OD-AGH	B747	21097
OD-AGI	B747	21098
OD-AGJ	B747	21099
OD-AGM	B747	20390
OD-AGN	B707	18938
OD-AGO	B707	19269
OD-AGP	B707	19274
OD-AGQ	B707	19160
OD-AGR	B707	19161
OD-AGS	B707	19214
OD-AGT	B707	19213
OD-AGU	B707	19966
OD-AGV	B707	19967
OD-AGW	B707	19440
OD-AGX	B707	19104
OD-AGY	B707	19105
OD-AGZ	B707	19531
OD-AHB	B707	19588
OD-AHC	B707	19589
OD-AHD	B707	19515
OD-AHE	B707	19516
OD-AHF	B707	20170
(OD-APA)	B707	19590
(OD-HEO)	L1011	193P-1103
OD-JOE	L1011	293B-1243
OD-LMB	B737	23082
OD-MAC	B737	23109
OD-MIR	L1011	193H-1246
OD-NOR	B737	22754
OD-WOL	B737	23083
OD-ZEE	L1011	293B-1239

Austria

Reg	Type	Serial
OE-BRL	146	E1002
(OE-FGW)	B737	23601
OE-HAA	D0328	3200
(OE-HAB)	D0328	3210
OE-HCM	D0328	3199
OE-HMS	D0328	3121
OE-HTG	D0328	3162
OE-HTJ	D0328	3114
OE-IAS	E145	14500832
OE-IBO	DC-8	46088
OE-IDA	B707	20043
OE-IDB	E145	14500999
OE-IEB	B707	18339
OE-IFA	MD80	49809
OE-IGR	E145	14500967
OE-IIB	F.100	11403
OE-IIC	F.100	11406
OE-IID	F.100	11368
OE-IKB	MD80	49448
OE-ILC	1-11	BAC.255
OE-ILD	1-11	BAC.256
(OE-ILD)	DC-10	47870
OE-ILE	B737	22023
OE-ILF	B737	23601
OE-ILG	B737	24081
OE-ILI	CRJ	8048
OE-ILX	737NG	32777
OE-INA	B707	18069
OE-IRA	B707	18068
OE-IRK	E145	14500916
OE-ISA	CRJ	8043
OE-ISN	E145	14500851
OE-ITA	B737	27924
OE-IWP	E145	14500841
(OE-L..)	A319	0910
(OE-L..)	A330	275
OE-LAA	A310	489
(OE-LAA)	B767	23765
OE-LAB	A310	492
OE-LAC	A310	568
OE-LAD	A310	624
OE-LAE	B767	30383
OE-LAG	A340	075
OE-LAH	A340	081
OE-LAK	A340	169
OE-LAL	A340	263
OE-LAM	A330	223
"OE-LAM"	B777	28698
OE-LAN	A330	195
OE-LAO	A330	181
OE-LAP	A330	317
OE-LAS	B767	27909
OE-LAT	B767	25273
OE-LAU	B767	23765
OE-LAW	B767	26417
OE-LAX	B767	27095
OE-LAY	B767	29867
OE-LAZ	B767	30331
OE-LBA	A321	0552
OE-LBA	B707	18374
OE-LBB	A321	0570
OE-LBC	A321	0581
OE-LBD	A321	0920
OE-LBE	A321	0935
OE-LBF	A321	1458
OE-LBN	A320	0768
OE-LBO	A320	0776
OE-LBP	A320	0797
OE-LBQ	A320	1137
OE-LBR	A320	1150
OE-LBS	A320	1189
OE-LBT	A320	1387
OE-LBU	A320	1478
OE-LCA	SE210	161
OE-LCE	SE210	156
OE-LCF	CRJ	7094
OE-LCG	CRJ	7103
OE-LCH	CRJ	7110
OE-LCI	CRJ	7133
OE-LCI	SE210	166
OE-LCJ	CRJ	7142
(OE-LCK)	CRJ	7133
OE-LCK	CRJ	7148
(OE-LCL)	CRJ	7142
OE-LCL	CRJ	7167
OE-LCM	CRJ	7205
OE-LCN	CRJ	7365
OE-LCO	CRJ	7371
OE-LCO	SE210	167
OE-LCP	CRJ	7480
OE-LCQ	CRJ	7605
OE-LCR	CRJ	7910
OE-LCU	SE210	136
OE-LDA	A319	2131
OE-LDA	DC-9	47521
OE-LDB	A319	2174
OE-LDB	DC-9	47524
OE-LDC	A319	2262
OE-LDC	DC-9	47520
OE-LDD	A319	2416
OE-LDD	DC-9	47539
OE-LDE	A319	2494
OE-LDE	DC-9	47531
OE-LDF	A319	2547
OE-LDF	DC-9	47458
OE-LDG	A319	2652
OE-LDG	DC-9	47484
OE-LDH	DC-9	47555
OE-LDI	DC-9	47559
OE-LDK	DC-9	47651
OE-LDL	DC-9	47652
OE-LDM	DC-9	47726
OE-LDN	DC-9	47735
OE-LDO	DC-9	47756
OE-LDP	MD80	48015
(OE-LDQ)	MD80	49279
OE-LDR	MD80	48016
OE-LDS	MD80	48017
OE-LDT	MD80	48018
OE-LDU	MD80	48019
OE-LDV	MD80	48020
OE-LDW	MD80	48059
OE-LDX	MD80	48021
(OE-LDY)	MD80	48022
OE-LDY	MD80	49115
OE-LDZ	MD80	49164
OE-LEA	A320	2529
OE-LEE	A320	2749
OE-LEK	A319	3019
OE-LEO	A320	2668
OE-LEU	A320	2902
OE-LEX	A320	2867
OE-LFG	F.70	11549
OE-LFH	F.70	11554
OE-LFI	F.70	11529
OE-LFJ	F.70	11532
OE-LFK	F.70	11555
OE-LFL	F.70	11573
OE-LFO	F.70	11559
OE-LFP	F.70	11560
OE-LFQ	F.70	11568
OE-LFR	F.70	11572
OE-LFS	F.70	11528

Reg	Type	c/n
OE-LFT	F.70	11537
OE-LGS	A319	3046
OE-LHG	MD80	49790
OE-LJE	MD80	49966
OE-LJR	D0328	3213
OE-LMA	MD80	49278
OE-LMB	MD80	49279
OE-LMC	MD80	49372
OE-LMD	MD80	49933
OE-LME	MD80	53377
OE-LMH	MD80	49933
OE-LMI	MD80	49823
OE-LMK	MD80	49411
OE-LML	MD80	49412
OE-LMM	MD80	49413
OE-LMM	MD80	53377
OE-LMN	MD80	49414
OE-LMO	MD80	49888
OE-LMP	A310	410
OE-LNH	B737	25147
OE-LNI	B737	27094
OE-LNJ	737NG	28177
(OE-LNJ)	B767	29867
OE-LNK	737NG	28178
OE-LNL	737NG	30137
OE-LNM	737NG	30138
OE-LNN	737NG	30418
OE-LNO	737NG	30419
OE-LNP	737NG	30420
OE-LNQ	737NG	30421
OE-LNR	737NG	33833
OE-LNS	737NG	34262
OE-LNT	737NG	33834
OE-LOE	A320	0659
OE-LOF	A320	0667
OE-LOG	MD80	49359
OE-LOR	A320	1459
OE-LOS	A321	1487
OE-LPA	B777	28698
OE-LPB	B777	28699
OE-LPC	B777	29313
OE-LPD	B777	35960
OE-LRA	CRJ	7032
OE-LRB	CRJ	7033
OE-LRC	CRJ	7036
OE-LRD	CRJ	7052
OE-LRE	CRJ	7059
OE-LRF	CRJ	7061
OE-LRG	CRJ	7063
OE-LRH	CRJ	7125
(OE-LRM)	MD80	49568
OE-LRQ	CRJ	7039
OE-LRW	MD80	49629
OE-LSC	CRJ	7299
OE-LSD	CRJ	7329
OE-LSE	CRJ	7990
OE-LSF	CRJ7	10217
OE-LSM	E145	145322
OE-LSP	E145	145337
OE-LSR	E145	145203
OE-LSS	CRJ	7283
OE-LTU	A320	1504
OE-LTV	A320	1553
OE-LVA	F.100	11490
OE-LVB	F.100	11502
OE-LVC	F.100	11446
OE-LVD	F.100	11515
OE-LVE	F.100	11499
OE-LVF	F.100	11483
OE-LVG	F.100	11520
OE-LVH	F.100	11456
OE-LVI	F.100	11468
OE-LVJ	F.100	11359
(OE-LVK)	F.100	11361
OE-LVK	F.100	11397
OE-LVL	F.100	11404
OE-LVM	F.100	11361
OE-LVN	F.100	11367
OE-LYM	MD80	48022
OE-UNA	B707	18069
OE-URA	B707	18068

Finland

Reg	Type	c/n
OH-AFI	B757	26330
OH-AFJ	B757	26269
OH-AFK	B757	25622
OH-BLC	MD90	53459
OH-BLD	MD90	53544
OH-BLU	MD90	53458
OH-EBE	E145	145351
OH-EBF	E145	145387
OH-KDM	DC-8	45628
OH-KSA	B747	20117
OH-LAA	A300	299
OH-LAB	A300	302
OH-LBO	B757	28172
OH-LBR	B757	28167
OH-LBS	B757	27623
OH-LBT	B757	28170
OH-LBU	B757	29377
OH-LBV	B757	30046
OH-LBX	B757	29382
OH-LEA	SE210	21
OH-LEB	SE210	22
OH-LEC	SE210	27
OH-LED	SE210	116
OH-LEE	E170	17000093
OH-LEF	E170	17000106
OH-LEG	E170	17000107
OH-LEH	E170	17000112
OH-LEI	E170	17000120
OH-LEK	E170	17000127
OH-LEL	E170	17000139
OH-LEM	E170	17000141
OH-LEN	E170	17000146
OH-LEO	E170	17000150
OH-LER	SE210	162
OH-LFR	DC-8	46013
OH-LFS	DC-8	46043
OH-LFT	DC-8	46013
OH-LFV	DC-8	46043
OH-LFY	DC-8	46130
OH-LFZ	DC-8	45987
OH-LGA	MD11	48449
OH-LGB	MD11	48450
OH-LGC	MD11	48512
OH-LGD	MD11	48513
OH-LGE	MD11	48780
OH-LGF	MD11	48766
OH-LGG	MD11	48763
OH-LHA	DC-10	47956
OH-LHB	DC-10	47957
(OH-LHC)	DC-10	48265
OH-LHD	DC-10	47865
OH-LHE	DC-10	46978
OH-LKE	E190	19000059
OH-LKF	E190	19000066
OH-LKG	E190	19000079
OH-LKH	E190	19000086
OH-LMA	MD80	49403
OH-LMB	MD80	49404
OH-LMC	MD80	49405
OH-LMG	MD80	49625
OH-LMH	MD80	53245
OH-LMN	MD80	49150
OH-LMO	MD80	49151
OH-LMP	MD80	49152
OH-LMR	MD80	49284
OH-LMS	MD80	49252
OH-LMT	MD80	49877
OH-LMU	MD80	49741
OH-LMV	MD80	49904
OH-LMW	MD80	49905
OH-LMX	MD80	49906
OH-LMY	MD80	53244
OH-LMZ	MD80	53246
OH-LNA	DC-9	47603
OH-LNB	DC-9	47604
OH-LNC	DC-9	47613
OH-LND	DC-9	47606
OH-LNE	DC-9	47605
OH-LNF	DC-9	47614
OH-LPA	MD80	49900

Reg	Type	c/n
OH-LPB	MD80	49966
OH-LPC	MD80	49965
OH-LPD	MD80	49710
OH-LPE	MD80	49401
OH-LPF	MD80	49574
OH-LPG	MD80	49708
OH-LPH	MD80	49623
OH-LQB	A340	835
OH-LQC	A340	844
OH-LQD	A340	921
OH-LSA	SE210	181
OH-LSB	SE210	182
OH-LSC	SE210	185
OH-LSD	SE210	187
OH-LSE	SE210	189
OH-LSF	SE210	188
OH-LSG	SE210	169
OH-LSH	SE210	211
OH-LSI	SE210	259
OH-LSK	SE210	212
OH-LVA	A319	1073
OH-LVB	A319	1107
OH-LVC	A319	1309
OH-LVD	A319	1352
OH-LVE	A319	1791
OH-LVF	A319	1808
OH-LVG	A319	1916
OH-LVH	A319	1184
OH-LVI	A319	1364
OH-LVK	A319	2124
OH-LVL	A319	2266
OH-LXA	A320	1405
OH-LXB	A320	1470
OH-LXC	A320	1544
OH-LXD	A320	1588
OH-LXE	A320	1678
OH-LXF	A320	1712
OH-LXG	A320	1735
OH-LXH	A320	1913
OH-LXI	A320	1989
OH-LXK	A320	2065
OH-LXL	A320	2146
OH-LXM	A320	2154
OH-LYA	DC-9	45713
OH-LYB	DC-9	45712
OH-LYC	DC-9	45711
OH-LYD	DC-9	45725
OH-LYE	DC-9	45729
OH-LYG	DC-9	45730
OH-LYH	DC-9	47044
OH-LYI	DC-9	47045
OH-LYK	DC-9	45841
OH-LYN	DC-9	47694
OH-LYO	DC-9	47695
OH-LYP	DC-9	47696
OH-LYR	DC-9	47736
OH-LYS	DC-9	47737
OH-LYT	DC-9	47738
OH-LYU	DC-9	47771
OH-LYV	DC-9	47772
OH-LYW	DC-9	47773
OH-LYX	DC-9	48134
OH-LYY	DC-9	48135
OH-LYZ	DC-9	48136
OH-LZA	A321	0941
OH-LZB	A321	0961
OH-LZC	A321	1185
OH-LZD	A321	1241
OH-LZE	A321	1978
OH-LZF	A321	2208
OH-SAH	146	E2383
OH-SAI	146	E2385
OH-SAJ	146	E2388
OH-SAK	146	E2389
OH-SAL	146	E2392
OH-SAM	146	E2386
OH-SAN	146	E2387
OH-SAO	146	E2393
OH-SAP	146	E2394
OH-SOA	DC-8	45606
OH-SOB	DC-8	45602

Czech Republic

Reg	Type	c/n
(OK-)	B767	30564
OK-020	YAK40	9431436
OK-9522	TU134	2351602
OK-ABD	IL62	10902
OK-AFA	TU134	1351406
OK-AFB	TU134	1351410
OK-AFD	TU134	1351407
OK-BGQ	B737	28494
OK-BYA	TU154	80A-420
OK-BYC	TU154	81A-517
OK-BYD	TU154	84A-601
OK-BYE	YAK40	9440338
OK-BYF	YAK40	9230823
OK-BYG	YAK40	9230723
OK-BYH	YAK40	9321128
OK-BYI	YAK40	9321028
OK-BYJ	YAK40	9821257
OK-BYK	YAK40	9940260
OK-BYL	YAK40	9940560
OK-BYO	TU154	89A-803
OK-BYP	TU154	90A-858
OK-BYQ	TU134	1351409
OK-BYR	TU134	1351408
OK-BYS	TU134	1351503
OK-BYT	TU134	73.49858
OK-BYV	IL62	3850145
OK-BYV	IL62	41805
OK-BYW	IL62	4037425
OK-BYZ	IL62	2647737
OK-BYZ	TU154	96A-1016
OK-CEC	A321	0674
OK-CED	A321	0684
OK-CFC	TU134	2351504
OK-CFD	TU134	2351505
OK-CFE	TU134	2351602
OK-CFF	TU134	2351603
OK-CFG	TU134	2351710
OK-CFH	TU134	2351801
OK-CGH	B737	28469
OK-CGI	B737	28882
OK-CGJ	B737	28470
OK-CGK	B737	28471
OK-CGT	B737	28549
OK-DBE	IL62	31501
OK-DBF	IL62	31502
OK-DFI	TU134	3351908
OK-DGB	B737	28997
OK-DGC	B737	29235
OK-DGL	B737	28472
OK-DGM	B737	28473
OK-DGN	B737	28474
OK-DHA	YAK40	9341230
OK-DYA	YAK40	9341230
OK-EBG	IL62	41602
OK-EEA	YAK40	9431436
OK-EEB	YAK40	9431536
OK-EEC	YAK40	9440737
OK-EED	YAK40	9440837
OK-EEF	YAK40	9440937
OK-EEG	YAK40	9441037
OK-EFJ	TU134	23128
OK-EFK	TU134	23130
OK-EGK	B727	21021
OK-EGO	B737	28475
OK-EGP	B737	28476
OK-EXB	YAK40	9431436
OK-FAN	B737	27469
OK-FBF	IL62	41805
OK-FEH	YAK40	9510340
OK-FEI	YAK40	9510440
OK-FEJ	YAK40	9510540
OK-FGR	B737	28477
OK-FGS	B737	28478
OK-FIT	B737	28590
OK-FUN	B737	27910
OK-GBH	IL62	..62404
OK-GEA	A320	1439
OK-GEB	A320	1450
OK-GEK	YAK40	9641050
OK-GEL	YAK40	9640651

Reg	Type	Serial
OK-GEM	YAK40	9640851
OK-GEN	YAK40	9641251
OK-GEO	YAK40	9641451
OK-GGG	E145	14500986
OK-HEP	YAK40	9730555
OK-HEQ	YAK40	9741056
OK-HER	YAK40	9741156
OK-HFL	TU134	49913
OK-HFM	TU134	73.60142
OK-IEL	F.28	11138
OK-IFN	TU134	83.60282
OK-JBI	IL62	2932748
OK-JBJ	IL62	4933456
(OK-JEM)	F.28	11139
(OK-JEN)	F.28	11140
(OK-JGT)	B727	21690
OK-JGY	B727	21623
OK-KBK	IL62	1035435
OK-KBN	IL62	4037425
(OK-KGZ)	B737	22115
OK-KKG	E145	14500873
OK-LCS	TU154	81A-517
OK-LDA	TU104	76600503
OK-LDB	TU104	76600601
OK-LDC	TU104	76600602
OK-LEE	A320	2719
OK-LEF	A320	2758
OK-LEG	A320	2789
(OK-LFN)	MD80	48087
(OK-LFO)	MD80	48048
(OK-LGZ)	B737	22667
OK-MDE	TU104	86601202
OK-MEH	A320	3031
OK-MEI	A320	3060
OK-MEJ	A320	3097
OK-MEK	A319	3043
OK-MEL	A319	3094
OK-MEO	F.28	11176
(OK-MGS)	B727	22605
OK-NDD	TU104	96601803
OK-NDF	TU104	9350801
OK-OBL	IL62	4445032
OK-PBM	IL62	1545951
OK-SCA	TU154	87A-765
OK-SLN	E145	145796
OK-SUN	E145	14500963
OK-SWU	B737	26703
OK-SWV	B737	26696
OK-SWY	B737	24815
OK-SWZ	B737	24816
OK-TCB	TU154	88A-770
OK-TCC	TU154	88A-789
OK-TCD	TU154	88A-792
OK-TEA	TU124	4351503
OK-TEB	TU124	4351504
OK-TGX	B727	18798
OK-TVA	737NG	32243
OK-TVB	737NG	32362
OK-TVC	737NG	30278
OK-TVD	737NG	28595
OK-TVE	737NG	30294
OK-TVF	737NG	29669
OK-TVG	737NG	30719
OK-TVP	B737	24234
OK-TVQ	737NG	28618
OK-TVR	B737	23870
OK-TVS	B737	24911
OK-UCE	TU154	89A-804
OK-UCF	TU154	89A-807
OK-UEC	TU124	5351607
(OK-UGA)	B727	18443
OK-UGZ	B727	18444
OK-VCG	TU154	90A-838
OK-VCP	TU154	90A-858
OK-VGZ	B737	24769
OK-WAA	A310	564
OK-WAB	A310	567
OK-WGD	B737	25065
OK-WGF	B737	24903
OK-WGG	B737	24693
OK-WGX	B737	25349
OK-WGY	B737	25839
OK-XFJ	B707	19570
OK-XGA	B737	26539
OK-XGB	B737	26540
OK-XGC	B737	26541
OK-XGD	B737	26542
OK-XGE	B737	26543
OK-XGV	B737	26445
OK-XGW	B737	26446
OK-YAC	A310	672
OK-YAD	A310	674
OK-YBA	IL62	90602
OK-YBB	IL62	90603
OK-YGA	B737	26290
OK-YGU	B737	26289
OK-ZBC	IL62	00701

Slovakia

Reg	Type	Serial
OM-AAA	B737	24256
OM-AAA	TU154	98A-1014
OM-AAB	TU154	98A-1015
(OM-AAC)	F.100	11373
OM-AAC	F.100	11460
OM-AAC	TU154	98A-1018
OM-AAD	B737	23636
OM-AAE	B737	23601
OM-AHK	B727	20525
OM-ALK	B737	23157
OM-ASA	B757	24370
OM-ASB	B757	24371
OM-ASC	B737	23601
OM-BWJ	B737	22116
OM-BYE	YAK40	9440338
OM-BYL	YAK40	9940560
OM-BYO	TU154	89A-803
OM-BYR	TU154	98A-1012
OM-CHD	B727	20526
OM-DGK	B757	24772
OM-DYA	YAK40	9341230
OM-ERA	B737	21722
OM-GAT	TU134	63.48565
OM-NGA	737NG	32684
OM-NGB	737NG	32695
OM-NGC	737NG	32696
OM-NGD	737NG	32674
OM-NGE	737NG	32676
OM-NGF	737NG	32680
OM-NGG	737NG	34753
OM-NGH	737NG	34754
OM-NGJ	737NG	34755
OM-NGK	737NG	34756
OM-NGL	737NG	34757
(OM-NGM)	737NG	34758
OM-NGN	737NG	34759
OM-NGP	737NG	34760
OM-NGQ	737NG	34761
OM-NGR	737NG	34762
OM-NSH	B767	22569
OM-RAN	B737	23156
OM-SEA	B737	25186
OM-SEB	B737	25191
OM-SEC	B737	25288
OM-SED	B737	24826
OM-SEE	B737	24827
OM-SEF	B737	25185
OM-SEG	B737	25289
OM-SNA	B757	24135
OM-UFB	B707	18839
OM-VEA	TU154	90A-859
OM-VEA	TU154	91A-866
OM-WFA	B707	19335

Belgium

Reg	Type	Serial
OO-	A320	0345
(OO-)	B737	20808
OO-ABA	B707	18746
OO-ABB	B737	21359
(OO-AEY)	A320	0301
OO-AEY	A320	0348
OO-AEZ	A320	0349
OO-AMI	DC-8	45376
OO-ATJ	B727	19011
(OO-BAI)	B707	18746
(OO-BTA)	B737	24020
(OO-BTB)	B737	24021
(OO-BTC)	B737	24022
(OO-BTD)	B737	24023
(OO-BTE)	B737	24024
OO-CAH	B727	22609
OO-CBA	B747	24158
OO-CDE	B707	19590
OO-CMB	DC-8	45382
OO-COF	A320	0542
(OO-COG)	A320	0543
OO-COH	A320	0543
OO-COL	A320	0344
OO-CPS	A321	0591
OO-CTA	B767	27477
OO-CTB	MD11	48766
OO-CTC	MD11	48780
OO-CTG	B737	28491
(OO-CTJ)	A300	630
OO-CTQ	B767	28159
OO-CTR	B767	28495
OO-CTS	MD11	48756
OO-CTT	A300	755
OO-CTU	A300	758
OO-CTV	B737	29000
OO-CTW	B737	29001
OO-CTX	B737	23718
OO-CVA	SE210	97
OO-CYE	B737	23787
OO-CYH	737NG	30278
OO-CYI	737NG	30274
OO-CYN	737NG	30272
OO-CYS	737NG	28644
OO-DHK	B727	22643
OO-DHM	B727	20114
OO-DHN	B727	20113
OO-DHO	B727	20112
OO-DHP	B727	19166
OO-DHQ	B727	19167
OO-DHR	B727	19834
OO-DHS	B727	20189
OO-DHT	B727	19489
OO-DHU	B727	20992
OO-DHV	B727	21084
OO-DHW	B727	20993
OO-DHX	B727	20994
OO-DHY	B727	20905
OO-DHZ	B727	22424
OO-DIB	A300	274
OO-DIC	A300	220
OO-DID	A300	235
OO-DIF	A300	148
OO-DJA	F.28	11163
OO-DJB	F.28	11184
OO-DJC	146	E2069
OO-DJD	146	E2077
OO-DJE	146	E2164
OO-DJF	146	E2167
OO-DJG	146	E2180
OO-DJH	146	E2172
OO-DJJ	146	E2196
OO-DJK	146	E2271
OO-DJL	146	E2273
OO-DJN	146	E2275
OO-DJO	146	E2279
OO-DJP	146	E2287
OO-DJQ	146	E2289
OO-DJR	146	E2290
OO-DJS	146	E2292
OO-DJT	146	E2294
OO-DJV	146	E2295
OO-DJW	146	E2296
OO-DJX	146	E2297
(OO-DJY)	146	E2069
OO-DJY	146	E2302
(OO-DJZ)	146	E2077
OO-DJZ	146	E2305
OO-DLB	B727	22642
OO-DLC	A300	152
OO-DLD	A300	259
OO-DLE	A300	236
OO-DLG	A300	208
OO-DLI	A300	234
(OO-DLJ)	B727	22644
OO-DLJ	B757	24971
OO-DLK	B757	24635
OO-DLL	A300	093
OO-DLN	B757	22172
OO-DLO	B757	22180
OO-DLP	B757	22179
OO-DLQ	B757	22175
OO-DLR	A300	095
OO-DLT	A300	250
OO-DLU	A300	289
OO-DLV	A300	150
OO-DLW	A300	199
OO-DLY	A300	116
OO-DLZ	A300	219
OO-DPB	B757	22183
OO-DPF	B757	22173
OO-DPI	B757	24102
OO-DPJ	B757	23493
OO-DPK	B757	23492
OO-DPL	B757	24267
OO-DPM	B757	22189
OO-DPN	B757	23533
OO-DPO	B757	23398
OO-DWA	146	E3308
OO-DWB	146	E3315
OO-DWC	146	E3322
OO-DWD	146	E3324
OO-DWE	146	E3327
OO-DWF	146	E3332
OO-DWG	146	E3336
OO-DWH	146	E3340
OO-DWI	146	E3342
OO-DWJ	146	E3355
OO-DWK	146	E3360
OO-DWL	146	E3361
(OO-EAG)	B767	24848
OO-HPN	DC-10	48294
(OO-HVA)	DC-10	46891
OO-IHV	B767	30584
OO-IID	B737	24255
(OO-IIE)	B737	23748
OO-ILF	B737	23401
OO-ILG	B737	23388
OO-ILH	B737	24234
OO-ILI	B757	24528
OO-ILJ	B737	25262
OO-ILK	B737	23766
OO-ING	A300	066
OO-JAA	B727	18951
OO-JAF	737NG	35133
OO-JAM	B737	28867
OO-JAT	B737	24927
OO-JOT	DC-10	46850
(OO-LEA)	DC-10	46554
OO-LLS	B727	22608
OO-LRM	DC-10	46998
OO-LTA	B737	24020
OO-LTB	B737	24021
OO-LTC	B737	24022
(OO-LTD)	B737	24023
OO-LTD	B737	24376
(OO-LTE)	B737	24024
OO-LTE	B737	24377
(OO-LTF)	B737	24376
OO-LTF	B737	25015
(OO-LTG)	B737	24377
OO-LTG	B737	25016
(OO-LTH)	B737	24413
(OO-LTH)	B737	25017
(OO-LTI)	B737	24414
OO-LTJ	B737	25039
OO-LTK	B737	25040

Reg	Type	Serial
OO-LTL	B737	25041
OO-LTM	B737	25070
OO-LTN	B737	25071
OO-LTO	B737	25011
OO-LTP	B737	25032
OO-LTQ	B737	25844
OO-LTR	B737	25116
OO-LTS	B737	25860
OO-LTT	B737	24708
OO-LTU	B737	27455
OO-LTV	B737	23924
OO-LTW	B737	25010
OO-LTX	B737	24131
OO-LTY	B737	23925
OO-MJE	146	E2192
OO-MKO	A300	065
(OO-MYD)	DO328	3121
OO-PHA	DC-8	45854
OO-PHC	B737	20221
OO-PHE	B737	19424
OO-PHF	B737	19549
OO-PHG	B737	19554
OO-PHN	DC-10	46554
OO-PLH	B737	20128
"OO-PS1"	B707	19378
OO-PSA	B707	19378
OO-PSI	B707	19378
OO-RMV	B737	24352
OO-RVM	B737	22453
OO-SBJ	B737	24573
OO-SBM	B737	25729
OO-SBN	B737	23979
OO-SBQ	B737	21596
OO-SBQ	SE210	123
OO-SBR	B707	17921
OO-SBS	B737	21839
OO-SBT	B737	21840
OO-SBU	B707	19442
OO-SBW	B707	17930
OO-SBX	B737	25040
OO-SBY	B767	27310
OO-SBZ	B737	23775
OO-SCA	A310	303
OO-SCB	A310	313
OO-SCC	A310	437
OO-SCI	A310	331
OO-SCW	A340	014
OO-SCX	A340	022
OO-SCY	A340	047
OO-SCZ	A340	051
OO-SDA	B737	20907
OO-SDB	B737	20908
OO-SDC	B737	20909
OO-SDD	B737	20910
OO-SDE	B737	20911
OO-SDF	B737	20912
(OO-SDG)	B737	20913
OO-SDG	B737	21135
OO-SDH	B737	20914
OO-SDJ	B737	20915
OO-SDK	B737	20916
OO-SDL	B737	21136
OO-SDM	B737	21137
OO-SDN	B737	21176
OO-SDO	B737	21177
OO-SDP	B737	21139
(OO-SDQ)	B737	21138
OO-SDR	B737	21738
OO-SDV	B737	23771
OO-SDW	B737	23772
OO-SDX	B737	23773
OO-SDY	B737	23774
OO-SEJ	B737	24221
OO-SFM	A330	030
OO-SFN	A330	037
OO-SFO	A330	045
OO-SFP	A330	230
OO-SFQ	A330	290
OO-SFR	A330	296
OO-SFS	A330	300
OO-SFT	A330	322
OO-SFU	A330	324
OO-SFW	A330	082
OO-SFX	A330	096
OO-SGA	B747	20401
OO-SGB	B747	20402
OO-SGC	B747	23439
OO-SGD	B747	24837
OO-SJA	B707	17623
OO-SJB	B707	17624
OO-SJC	B707	17625
OO-SJD	B707	17626
OO-SJE	B707	17627
OO-SJF	B707	18374
(OO-SJG)	B707	18375
OO-SJG	B707	18460
OO-SJH	B707	18890
OO-SJJ	B707	19162
OO-SJK	B707	19211
OO-SJL	B707	19996
OO-SJM	B707	20198
OO-SJN	B707	20199
OO-SJO	B707	20200
OO-SJP	B707	17686
OO-SJR	B707	19706
OO-SLA	DC-10	47906
OO-SLB	DC-10	47907
OO-SLC	DC-10	47908
OO-SLD	DC-10	47835
OO-SLE	DC-10	47836
OO-SLF	A340	010
(OO-SLG)	A340	014
OO-SLG	DC-10	47926
(OO-SLH)	A340	022
OO-SLH	DC-10	47927
(OO-SLI)	A340	047
(OO-SLJ)	A340	051
OO-SLK	B737	29072
(OO-SLR)	B737	24221
OO-SLR	B767	30563
OO-SLS	B767	30566
OO-SLT	B767	25208
OO-SLW	B737	24474
OO-SNE	A320	1054
OO-SNF	A320	1081
OO-SNG	A320	1370
OO-SNH	A320	1413
OO-SNI	A320	1439
OO-SNJ	A320	1450
(OO-SQA)	A340	1364
(OO-SQA)	B737	24355
(OO-SQB)	A340	395
(OO-SQB)	B737	24356
OO-SRA	SE210	64
OO-SRB	SE210	65
OO-SRC	SE210	66
OO-SRD	SE210	69
OO-SRE	SE210	67
OO-SRF	SE210	76
OO-SRG	SE210	70
OO-SRH	SE210	78
OO-SRI	SE210	175
OO-SRK	SE210	196
OO-SSA	A319	1048
OO-SSB	A319	1068
OO-SSC	A319	1086
OO-SSD	A319	1102
OO-SSE	A319	1124
OO-SSF	A319	1145
OO-SSG	A319	1160
OO-SSH	A319	1184
OO-SSI	A319	1283
OO-SSJ	A319	1305
OO-SSK	A319	1336
OO-SSL	A319	1364
OO-SSM	A319	1388
OO-SSN	A319	1429
OO-SSO	A319	1494
(OO-SSP)	A319	1618
(OO-SSQ)	A319	1634
OO-STA	B727	19400
OO-STB	B727	19402
OO-STC	B727	19401
OO-STD	B727	19403
OO-STE	B727	19987
OO-STF	B767	27212
OO-SUA	A321	0970
OO-SUB	A321	0995
OO-SUC	A321	1012
OO-SYA	B737	24355
OO-SYB	B737	24356
OO-SYC	B737	25226
OO-SYD	B737	25247
OO-SYE	B737	25218
OO-SYF	B737	25248
OO-SYG	B737	25249
OO-SYH	B737	25418
OO-SYI	B737	25419
OO-SYJ	B737	26537
OO-SYK	B737	26538
(OO-SYL)	B737	26539
(OO-SYM)	B737	26540
(OO-SYN)	B737	26541
(OO-SYO)	B737	26542
(OO-SYP)	B737	26543
OO-TAA	146	E3151
OO-TAD	146	E3166
OO-TAE	146	E3182
OO-TAF	146	E3186
OO-TAH	146	E3168
OO-TAJ	146	E3153
OO-TAK	146	E3150
(OO-TAQ)	146	E2102
OO-TAR	146	E2067
(OO-TAS)	146	E2109
OO-TAS	146	E3154
OO-TAU	146	E2100
OO-TAW	146	E2089
OO-TAY	146	E2211
OO-TAZ	146	E2188
OO-TBI	B757	25133
(OO-TC)	A320	0313
OO-TCB	A320	0357
OO-TCC	A320	0411
OO-TCE	A320	0394
OO-TCF	A320	0354
OO-TCG	A320	0443
OO-TCH	A320	1929
OO-TCI	A320	1975
OO-TCJ	A320	1787
OO-TCK	A320	0343
OO-TCL	A320	0436
OO-TCM	A320	0420
OO-TCN	A320	0426
OO-TCP	DC-8	45265
OO-TEA	B707	18155
OO-TEB	B707	18043
OO-TEC	B707	17659
OO-TED	B707	17665
OO-TEE	B707	17666
OO-TEF	A300	002
OO-TEG	A300	017
OO-TEH	B737	21231
OO-TEJ	B737	21131
OO-TEK	B737	21719
OO-TEL	B737	21736
OO-TEM	B737	21735
OO-TEN	B737	21955
OO-TEO	B737	22090
(OO-TEZ)	B737	20908
OO-THA	B747	35232
OO-THB	B747	35234
OO-THC	B747	35235
OO-TJA	B747	29255
OO-TJN	B727	19011
OO-TJO	A300	204
OO-TNA	B737	23569
OO-TNB	B737	23578
OO-TNC	B737	23513
OO-TND	B737	23515
OO-TNE	B737	23535
OO-TNF	B737	24131
OO-TNG	B737	24255
OO-TNH	B737	23930
OO-TNI	B737	23512
OO-TNJ	B737	23260
OO-TNK	B737	23258
OO-TUA	B737	24127
OO-TUB	B737	27831
OO-TUC	B767	24844
OO-TUF	F.100	11373
OO-TUI	B737	24125
OO-TUM	B737	24750
OO-TYA	B707	18384
(OO-TYB)	B707	18832
OO-TYB	B737	21359
OO-TYC	B707	19291
OO-TYD	B737	21774
OO-TZA	A300	155
OO-TZB	A300	261
OO-TZC	A300	210
OO-TZD	A300	247
OO-VAC	737NG	33014
OO-VAS	737NG	30285
OO-VAS	B767	25535
OO-VBR	B737	24314
OO-VDO	B737	24915
OO-VEA	B737	28332
OO-VEB	B737	28333
OO-VEC	B737	28549
OO-VED	B737	28550
OO-VEE	B737	23922
OO-VEF	B737	27000
OO-VEG	B737	28568
OO-VEH	B737	28571
OO-VEJ	B737	24271
OO-VEK	B737	24270
OO-VEN	B737	28586
OO-VEO	B737	24688
OO-VEP	B737	28489
OO-VES	B737	28493
OO-VEX	B737	28670
OO-VGM	B707	18073
OO-VJO	B737	23980
OO-XTG	B737	25016
OO-YCK	B707	19621
OO-YCL	B707	19622

Denmark

Reg	Type	Serial
OY-ANI	CV990	30-10-25
OY-ANL	CV990	30-10-36
OY-APA	B737	28083
OY-APB	B737	28084
(OY-APC)	B737	28128
OY-APC	B737	28129
OY-APD	B737	28130
OY-APG	B737	21278
OY-APG	B737	28131
OY-APH	B737	21279
OY-APH	B737	28721
OY-API	B737	21528
OY-API	B737	28722
OY-APJ	B737	21685
OY-APK	B737	21686
OY-APK	B737	28995
OY-APL	B737	22070
OY-APL	B737	28996
(OY-APN)	B707	18421
OY-APN	B737	22071
OY-APN	B737	28997
(OY-APO)	B707	18422
OY-APO	B737	22072
(OY-APP)	B707	18384
OY-APP	B737	22406
OY-APP	B737	29234
OY-APR	B737	22407
OY-APR	B737	29235
OY-APS	B737	22408
OY-APU	B707	18792
OY-APV	B707	18793
OY-APW	B707	18422
OY-APY	B707	18421

Registration	Type	Serial
OY-APZ	B707	18384
OY-ASA	VFW	G-8
OY-BRM	F.28	11143
OY-BRN	F.28	11151
OY-CNA	A300	079
OY-CNB	A320	0221
OY-CNC	A320	0222
OY-CND	A320	0163
OY-CNE	A320	0164
OY-CNF	A320	0168
OY-CNG	A320	0169
OY-CNH	A320	0179
OY-CNI	A320	0193
OY-CNK	A300	094
OY-CNL	A300	128
OY-CNM	A320	0301
OY-CNN	A320	0348
OY-CNO	DC-10	46990
OY-CNP	A320	0294
OY-CNR	A320	0349
OY-CNS	DC-10	46646
OY-CNT	DC-10	47833
OY-CNU	DC-10	47832
OY-CNW	A320	0299
OY-CNY	DC-10	46983
OY-CRG	146	E2075
OY-CRW	146	E2115
OY-CTA	DC-9	47655
OY-CTB	DC-9	47657
OY-CTD	DC-9	47658
OY-DSK	B707	18157
OY-DSL	B707	18159
OY-DSM	B707	18161
OY-DSP	B707	18241
OY-DSR	B707	18243
OY-FJE	146	E3234
OY-GRL	B757	25620
OY-GRN	A330	230
OY-JTA	B737	23631
OY-JTB	B737	24464
OY-KAA	A300	122
OY-KBA	A340	435
OY-KBB	A340	1642
(OY-KBC)	A321	1675
OY-KBC	A340	467
OY-KBD	A340	470
OY-KBE	A321	1798
OY-KBF	A321	1807
OY-KBH	A321	1675
OY-KBI	A340	430
OY-KBK	A321	1587
OY-KBL	A321	1619
OY-KBM	A340	450
OY-KBN	A330	496
OY-KBO	A319	2850
OY-KBP	A319	2888
OY-KBR	A319	3231
OY-KBT	A319	3292
OY-KDA	DC-10	46870
OY-KDB	DC-10	46933
OY-KDC	DC-10	46959
OY-KDH	B767	24358
OY-KDI	B767	24475
OY-KDK	B767	24476
OY-KDL	B767	24477
OY-KDM	B767	25088
OY-KDN	B767	24848
OY-KDO	B767	24849
(OY-KFA)	B747	20121
OY-KGA	DC-9	47115
OY-KGB	DC-9	47178
OY-KGC	DC-9	47286
OY-KGD	DC-9	47302
OY-KGE	DC-9	47305
OY-KGF	DC-9	47308
OY-KGG	DC-9	47395
OY-KGH	DC-9	47493
OY-KGI	DC-9	47494
OY-KGK	DC-9	47510
OY-KGL	DC-9	47597
OY-KGM	DC-9	47624
OY-KGN	DC-9	47628
OY-KGO	DC-9	47632
OY-KGP	DC-9	47646
OY-KGR	DC-9	47725
OY-KGS	DC-9	47766
OY-KGT	MD80	49380
OY-KGU	DC-9	47110
OY-KGW	DC-9	47113
OY-KGY	MD80	49420
OY-KGZ	MD80	49381
OY-KHA	B747	20121
(OY-KHB)	B747	22381
OY-KHC	MD80	49436
(OY-KHD)	MD80	49555
OY-KHE	MD80	49604
OY-KHF	MD80	49609
OY-KHG	MD80	49613
OY-KHI	MD80	49614
(OY-KHK)	MD80	49610
OY-KHK	MD80	49910
OY-KHL	MD80	49911
OY-KHM	MD80	49914
OY-KHN	MD80	53000
OY-KHO	MD80	53003
OY-KHP	MD80	53007
OY-KHR	MD80	53275
OY-KHS	MD80	53001
(OY-KHS)	MD80	53010
OY-KHT	MD80	53296
OY-KHU	MD80	53336
OY-KHW	MD80	53348
OY-KIA	DC-9	47301
OY-KIB	DC-9	47307
OY-KIC	DC-9	47361
OY-KID	DC-9	47360
OY-KIE	DC-9	47306
OY-KIF	DC-9	47303
OY-KIG	MD80	48006
OY-KIH	MD80	48007
OY-KII	MD80	48008
OY-KIK	MD80	48004
OY-KIL	MD90	53458
OY-KIM	MD90	53460
OY-KIN	MD90	53544
(OY-KK.)	737NG	28320
(OY-KK.)	737NG	30468
OY-KKA	737NG	28289
OY-KKB	737NG	28293
OY-KKC	737NG	28298
OY-KKD	737NG	28299
OY-KKE	737NG	28305
OY-KKF	737NG	30189
OY-KKG	737NG	28300
(OY-KKG)	737NG	28311
OY-KKH	737NG	28301
(OY-KKH)	737NG	28312
(OY-KKI)	737NG	28313
OY-KKI	737NG	28315
(OY-KKK)	737NG	28314
(OY-KKK)	737NG	28316
(OY-KKL)	737NG	28319
(OY-KKL)	737NG	28321
OY-KKM	737NG	30193
(OY-KKN)	737NG	30194
OY-KKN	737NG	30469
(OY-KKO)	737NG	30195
OY-KKP	737NG	28312
OY-KKR	737NG	28316
OY-KKS	737NG	28322
OY-KKT	737NG	30468
OY-KKU	737NG	28320
OY-KKY	737NG	28306
(OY-KKZ)	737NG	30467
(OY-KLB)	737NG	28318
OY-KLC	737NG	28319
(OY-KLD)	737NG	28323
(OY-KLF)	737NG	30194
OY-KRA	SE210	6
OY-KRB	SE210	14
OY-KRC	SE210	29
OY-KRD	SE210	47
OY-KRE	SE210	49
OY-KRF	SE210	170
OY-KRG	SE210	191
OY-KTA	DC-8	45384
OY-KTB	DC-8	45387
OY-KTC	DC-8	45804
OY-KTD	DC-8	45906
OY-KTE	DC-8	45922
OY-KTF	DC-8	46041
OY-KTG	DC-8	46093
OY-KTH	DC-8	46097
(OY-KVA)	CV990	30-10-14
(OY-KVA)	CV990	30-10-17
(OY-KVA)	CV990	30-10-5
OY-LQA	A340	058
OY-MAA	B737	24778
OY-MAB	B737	24805
OY-MAC	B737	24859
OY-MAD	B737	24928
OY-MAE	B737	25066
OY-MAF	B737	28128
OY-MAK	B737	26440
OY-MAL	B737	26441
OY-MAM	B737	26442
OY-MAN	B737	27061
OY-MAO	B737	27336
OY-MAP	B737	27337
OY-MAR	B737	27833
OY-MAS	B737	27834
OY-MAT	B737	27924
OY-MAU	B737	27925
OY-MAV	CRJ	7386
OY-MBI	CRJ	7436
OY-MBJ	CRJ	7442
OY-MBK	B737	24911
OY-MBL	B737	25190
OY-MBN	B737	25033
OY-MBO	CRJ	7226
OY-MBP	CRJ	7247
OY-MBR	CRJ	7248
OY-MBS	CRJ	7283
OY-MBT	CRJ	7617
OY-MBU	CRJ	7373
OY-MBV	B737	22735
OY-MBW	B737	22734
OY-MBZ	B737	22733
(OY-MEY)	737NG	29076
(OY-MEZ)	737NG	29077
OY-MLW	737NG	29078
OY-MLY	737NG	29076
OY-MLZ	737NG	29077
OY-MMD	B737	24569
OY-MME	B737	24570
OY-MMF	B737	24571
OY-MMK	B737	23331
OY-MML	B737	23332
OY-MMM	B737	23717
OY-MMN	B737	23718
OY-MMO	B737	24219
(OY-MMO)	B737	24928
OY-MMP	B737	24220
OY-MMR	B737	24221
(OY-MMW)	B737	24778
OY-MMW	B737	25125
(OY-MMY)	B737	24805
OY-MMY	B737	25150
(OY-MMZ)	B737	24859
(OY-MMZ)	B737	25360
OY-MRA	737NG	28004
OY-MRB	737NG	28005
OY-MRC	737NG	28006
OY-MRD	737NG	28007
OY-MRE	737NG	28008
OY-MRF	737NG	28009
OY-MRG	737NG	28010
OY-MRH	737NG	28013
OY-MRI	737NG	28014
OY-MRJ	737NG	28015
OY-MRK	737NG	28012
OY-MRL	737NG	28011
OY-MRO	737NG	28497
OY-MRP	737NG	34401
OY-MRR	737NG	34402
OY-NCL	DO328	3192
OY-NCM	DO328	3190
OY-NCN	DO328	3193
OY-NCO	DO328	3210
OY-NCP	DO328	3219
OY-RCA	146	E2045
OY-RCB	146	E2094
OY-RCC	146	E3357
OY-RCD	146	E2235
OY-RCZ	146	E2041
(OY-RGB)	VFW	G-014
(OY-RGB)	VFW	G-018
(OY-RGT)	VFW	G-014
OY-RJA	CRJ	7413
OY-RJB	CRJ	7419
OY-RJC	CRJ	7015
OY-RJD	CRJ	7007
OY-RJE	CRJ	7009
OY-RJF	CRJ	7019
OY-RJG	CRJ	7104
OY-RRW	VFW	G-019
OY-SA	B727	20764
OY-SAA	SE210	270
OY-SAB	SE210	271
OY-SAC	SE210	269
OY-SAD	SE210	272
OY-SAE	SE210	273
OY-SAF	SE210	275
OY-SAG	SE210	276
OY-SAH	SE210	88
OY-SAJ	SE210	104
OY-SAK	SE210	99
OY-SAL	SE210	89
OY-SAM	SE210	95
OY-SAN	SE210	98
OY-SAO	SE210	101
OY-SAP	SE210	90
OY-SAR	SE210	103
OY-SAS	B727	20765
OY-SAT	B727	20766
OY-SAU	B727	20764
OY-SAY	SE210	255
OY-SAZ	SE210	263
OY-SBA	B727	20706
OY-SBB	B727	20707
OY-SBC	B727	21438
OY-SBD	B727	21676
OY-SBE	B727	22079
OY-SBF	B727	22080
OY-SBG	B727	22574
OY-SBH	B727	22164
OY-SBI	B727	23052
OY-SBJ	B727	21040
OY-SBK	DC-8	45923
OY-SBL	DC-8	46054
OY-SBM	DC-8	45924
OY-SBN	B727	22163
OY-SBO	B727	22770
OY-SBP	B727	21080
OY-SBV	SE210	91
OY-SBW	SE210	93
OY-SBY	SE210	94
OY-SBZ	SE210	114
OY-SCA	B727	20739
OY-SCB	B727	22536
OY-SCC	B727	21945
OY-SEA	737NG	28213
OY-SEB	737NG	28214
OY-SEC	737NG	28221
OY-SED	737NG	28237
OY-SEE	B737	24463
OY-SEF	B737	25162
OY-SEG	B737	26419
OY-SEH	737NG	29444
OY-SEI	737NG	29445
OY-SEJ	737NG	30289
OY-SEK	737NG	30292
OY-SEL	737NG	33018
OY-SEM	737NG	33019

Reg	Type	c/n
OY-SER	B727	20639
OY-SES	B727	19977
OY-SET	B727	21245
OY-SEU	B727	21269
OY-SEV	B727	20571
OY-SEW	B727	21688
OY-SEY	B727	20659
OY-SEZ	B727	21202
OY-SHA	B757	25155
OY-SHB	B757	25220
OY-SHE	B757	24135
OY-SHF	B757	24136
OY-SHI	B757	24137
OY-SRF	B767	23327
OY-SRG	B767	23328
OY-SRH	B767	24457
OY-SRI	B767	27193
OY-SRJ	B767	27195
OY-SRK	B767	23072
OY-SRL	B767	22219
OY-SRM	B767	27192
OY-SRN	B767	23326
OY-SRO	B767	27194
OY-SRP	B767	22220
OY-STA	SE210	183
OY-STB	SE210	186
OY-STC	SE210	212
OY-STD	SE210	238
OY-STE	SE210	249
OY-STF	SE210	257
OY-STG	SE210	259
OY-STH	SE210	262
OY-STI	SE210	265
(OY-STI)	SE210	266
OY-STK	SE210	266
(OY-STK)	SE210	267
OY-STL	SE210	267
OY-STM	SE210	268
OY-TNT	B727	20725
OY-TOR	VFW	G-4
OY-UPA	B727	19233
OY-UPB	B727	19874
OY-UPC	B727	19230
OY-UPD	B727	19103
OY-UPJ	B727	19102
OY-UPM	B727	19229
OY-UPS	B727	19232
OY-UPT	B727	19094
OY-USA	B757	25462
OY-USB	B757	25463
OY-USC	B757	25464
OY-USD	B757	25465
OY-VKA	A321	1881
OY-VKB	A321	1921
OY-VKC	A321	1932
OY-VKD	A321	1960
OY-VKE	A321	1887
OY-VKF	A330	309
OY-VKG	A330	349
OY-VKH	A330	356
OY-VKI	A330	357
OY-VKL	A320	1780
OY-VKM	A320	1889
OY-VKN	A320	2114
OY-VKO	A320	2162
OY-VKP	A320	2183
OY-VKR	A320	1942
OY-VKS	A320	1954
OY-YVI	CRJ	8046

North Korea

Reg	Type	c/n
P-551	TU154	75A-129
P-552	TU154	76A-143
P-553	TU154	77A-191
P-561	TU154	83A-573
P-618	IL62	2546624
P-813	TU134	66215
P-814	TU134	66368
P-880	IL62	2241758
P-881	IL62	3647853
P-882	IL62	2850236
P-885	IL62	3933913
P-912	IL76	1003403104
P-913	IL76	1003404126
P-914	IL76	1003404146
P-2040	B737	23157

Netherlands

Reg	Type	c/n
(PH-)	B737	23922
PH-AAI	DC-10	46971
PH-AAJ	DC-10	46972
PH-AAK	DC-10	46982
PH-AAL	B767	24150
PH-AAM	B767	25221
PH-AAP	737NG	29079
PH-AAQ	737NG	29081
PH-AAR	B757	24792
PH-AAU	B737	25262
PH-AAV	737NG	30465
PH-AAW	737NG	32903
PH-ABE	737NG	30466
PH-ABF	A300	105
PH-ABI	A320	0978
PH-ADA	DC-8	45750
PH-AFO	F.100	11497
PH-AFQ	F.100	11503
PH-AGA	A310	241
PH-AGB	A310	245
PH-AGC	A310	248
PH-AGD	A310	264
PH-AGE	A310	283
PH-AGF	A310	297
(PH-AGG)	A310	352
PH-AGG	A310	353
(PH-AGG)	A310	370
(PH-AGH)	A310	360
PH-AGH	A310	362
PH-AGI	A310	364
(PH-AGI)	A310	375
PH-AGK	A310	394
(PH-AGL)	A310	436
(PH-AGM)	A310	439
(PH-AGN)	A310	442
PH-AHB	B727	20739
(PH-AHC)	B737	24911
PH-AHD	B727	20822
PH-AHE	B757	24135
PH-AHF	B757	24136
PH-AHI	B757	24137
PH-AHK	B757	24291
PH-AHL	B757	24838
(PH-AHM)	B767	24736
PH-AHM	B767	25058
PH-AHN	B757	24771
(PH-AHN)	B767	25139
PH-AHO	B757	22781
PH-AHP	B757	24528
PH-AHQ	B767	24477
PH-AHR	B767	27136
PH-AHS	B757	25622
(PH-AHS)	B757	27237
PH-AHT	B757	27237
PH-AHX	B767	24847
PH-AHY	B767	24848
PH-AHZ	B727	21021
(PH-AIR)	F.28	11164
PH-AOA	A330	682
PH-AOB	A330	686
PH-AOC	A330	703
PH-AOD	A330	738
PH-AOE	A330	770
PH-AOF	A330	801
PH-AOH	A330	811
PH-AOI	A330	819
PH-AOK	A330	834
PH-AOL	A330	900
(PH-ARN)	SE210	30
PH-BBV	F.28	11127
PH-BDA	B737	23537
PH-BDB	B737	23538
PH-BDC	B737	23539
PH-BDD	B737	23540
PH-BDE	B737	23541
PH-BDG	B737	23542
PH-BDH	B737	23543
PH-BDI	B737	23544
PH-BDK	B737	23545
PH-BDL	B737	23546
PH-BDN	B737	24261
PH-BDO	B737	24262
PH-BDP	B737	24404
PH-BDR	B737	24514
PH-BDS	B737	24529
PH-BDT	B737	24530
PH-BDU	B737	24857
PH-BDW	B737	24858
PH-BDY	B737	24959
PH-BDZ	B737	25355
"PH-BEN"	DC-8	46122
PH-BFA	B747	23999
PH-BFB	B747	24000
PH-BFC	B747	23982
PH-BFD	B747	24001
PH-BFE	B747	24201
PH-BFF	B747	24202
PH-BFG	B747	24517
PH-BFH	B747	24518
PH-BFI	B747	25086
PH-BFK	B747	25087
PH-BFL	B747	25356
PH-BFM	B747	26373
PH-BFN	B747	26372
PH-BFO	B747	25413
PH-BFP	B747	24792
PH-BFR	B747	27202
PH-BFS	B747	28195
PH-BFT	B747	28459
PH-BFU	B747	28196
PH-BFV	B747	28460
PH-BFW	B747	30454
PH-BFY	B747	30455
PH-BGA	737NG	37593
PH-BGB	737NG	37594
PH-BMC	A320	1081
PH-BMD	A320	1370
PH-BPA	B737	23865
PH-BPB	B737	24344
PH-BPC	B737	24468
PH-BPD	B737	24231
PH-BPE	B737	24232
PH-BPF	B737	24813
PH-BPG	B737	24814
PH-BQA	B777	33711
PH-BQB	B777	33712
PH-BQC	B777	29397
PH-BQD	B777	33713
PH-BQE	B777	28691
PH-BQF	B777	29398
PH-BQG	B777	32704
PH-BQH	B777	32705
PH-BQI	B777	33714
PH-BQK	B777	29399
PH-BQL	B777	34711
PH-BQM	B777	34712
PH-BQN	B777	32720
PH-BQO	B777	35295
PH-BQP	B777	32721
(PH-BQR)	B777	35671
PH-BTA	B737	25412
PH-BTB	B737	25423
PH-BTC	B737	25424
PH-BTD	B737	27420
PH-BTE	B737	27421
PH-BTF	B737	27232
PH-BTG	B737	27233
PH-BTH	B737	28719
PH-BTI	B737	28720
PH-BUA	B747	19922
PH-BUB	B747	19923
PH-BUC	B747	19924
PH-BUD	B747	20398
PH-BUE	B747	20399
PH-BUF	B747	20400
PH-BUG	B747	20427
PH-BUH	B747	21110
PH-BUI	B747	21111
PH-BUK	B747	21549
PH-BUL	B747	21550
PH-BUM	B747	21659
PH-BUN	B747	21660
PH-BUO	B747	21848
PH-BUP	B747	22376
PH-BUR	B747	22379
PH-BUT	B747	22380
PH-BUU	B747	23056
PH-BUV	B747	23137
PH-BUW	B747	23508
PH-BVA	B777	35671
PH-BVB	B777	36145
PH-BXA	737NG	29131
PH-BXB	737NG	29132
PH-BXC	737NG	29133
PH-BXD	737NG	29134
PH-BXE	737NG	29595
PH-BXF	737NG	29596
PH-BXG	737NG	30357
PH-BXH	737NG	29597
PH-BXI	737NG	30358
PH-BXK	737NG	29598
PH-BXL	737NG	30359
PH-BXM	737NG	30355
PH-BXN	737NG	30356
PH-BXO	737NG	29599
PH-BXP	737NG	29600
PH-BXR	737NG	29601
PH-BXS	737NG	29602
PH-BXT	737NG	32944
PH-BXU	737NG	33028
PH-BXV	737NG	30370
PH-BXW	737NG	30360
PH-BXZ	737NG	30368
PH-BZA	B767	27957
PH-BZB	B767	27958
PH-BZC	B767	26263
PH-BZD	B767	27610
PH-BZE	B767	28098
PH-BZF	B767	27959
PH-BZG	B767	27960
PH-BZH	B767	27611
PH-BZI	B767	27612
PH-BZK	B767	27614
PH-BZM	B767	28884
PH-BZO	B767	30393
PH-CDI	F.100	11245
PH-CFA	F.100	11323
PH-CFB	F.100	11324
PH-CFC	F.100	11325
PH-CFD	F.100	11326
PH-CFE	F.100	11327
PH-CFF	F.100	11328
PH-CFG	F.100	11329
PH-CFH	F.100	11330
PH-CHB	F.28	11138
PH-CHD	F.28	11139
PH-CHF	F.28	11140
PH-CHI	F.28	11141
PH-CHN	F.28	11176
PH-CKA	B747	33694
PH-CKB	B747	33695
PH-CKC	B747	33696
PH-CKD	B747	35233
PH-CLA	A300	044
PH-CXA	F.100	11276
PH-CXB	F.100	11278
PH-CXC	F.100	11280
PH-CXD	F.100	11281
PH-CXE	F.100	11300
PH-CXF	F.100	11303
PH-CXG	F.100	11306
PH-CXH	F.100	11308

Reg.	Type	c/n	Reg.	Type	c/n	Reg.	Type	c/n	Reg.	Type	c/n
PH-CXI	F.100	11310	PH-DTG	DC-10	46556	PH-EXO	F.28	11184	PH-EXW	F.28	11192
PH-CXJ	F.100	11312	PH-DTH	DC-10	46557	PH-EXO	F.28	11195	PH-EXX	F.28	11020
PH-CXK	F.100	11313	PH-DTI	DC-10	46933	PH-EXO	F.28	11201	PH-EXX	F.28	11119
PH-CXL	F.100	11314	PH-DTK	DC-10	46914	PH-EXO	F.28	11205	PH-EXX	F.28	11132
PH-CXM	F.100	11331	(PH-DTK)	DC-10	46934	PH-EXO	F.28	11210	PH-EXX	F.28	11150
PH-CXN	F.100	11333	PH-DTL	DC-10	46952	PH-EXP	F.28	11070	PH-EXX	F.28	11155
PH-CXO	F.100	11334	(PH-DTM)	DC-10	46958	PH-EXP	F.28	11084	PH-EXX	F.28	11172
PH-CXP	F.100	11337	PH-DVR	A320	0190	PH-EXP	F.28	11122	PH-EXX	F.28	11179
PH-CXQ	F.100	11338	PH-EAN	A300	041	PH-EXP	F.28	11125	PH-EXX	F.28	11189
(PH-CXR)	F.100	11296	PH-EUS	F.100	11477	PH-EXP	F.28	11141	PH-EXX	F.28	11207
PH-CXR	F.100	11391	PH-EXA	F.28	11013	PH-EXP	F.28	11149	PH-EXY	F.28	11036
PH-CXS	F.100	11399	PH-EXA	F.28	11023	PH-EXP	F.28	11168	PH-EXY	F.28	11076
PH-DBA	B757	24747	PH-EXA	F.28	11026	PH-EXP	F.28	11185	PH-EXY	F.28	11094
PH-DBB	B757	24738	PH-EXA	F.28	11028	PH-EXP	F.28	11198	PH-EXY	F.28	11100
(PH-DBC)	B757	24748	PH-EXA	F.28	11043	PH-EXP	F.28	11203	PH-EXY	F.28	11120
PH-DBH	B757	24748	PH-EXA	F.28	11992	PH-EXR	F.28	11044	PH-EXY	F.28	11124
PH-DCA	DC-8	45376	PH-EXB	F.28	11032	PH-EXR	F.28	11071	PH-EXY	F.28	11142
PH-DCB	DC-8	45377	PH-EXB	F.28	11056	PH-EXR	F.28	11113	PH-EXY	F.28	11156
PH-DCC	DC-8	45378	PH-EXB	F.28	11079	PH-EXR	F.28	11128	PH-EXY	F.28	11162
PH-DCD	DC-8	45379	PH-EXB	F.28	11994	PH-EXR	F.28	11135	PH-EXY	F.28	11166
PH-DCE	DC-8	45380	PH-EXC	F.28	11024	PH-EXR	F.28	11152	PH-EXZ	F.28	11024
PH-DCF	DC-8	45381	PH-EXC	F.28	11080	PH-EXR	F.28	11164	PH-EXZ	F.28	11078
PH-DCG	DC-8	45382	PH-EXD	F.28	11049	PH-EXR	F.28	11171	PH-EXZ	F.28	11102
PH-DCH	DC-8	45383	PH-EXD	F.28	11061	PH-EXR	F.28	11177	PH-EXZ	F.28	11111
PH-DCI	DC-8	45613	PH-EXD	F.28	11064	PH-EXR	F.28	11193	PH-EXZ	F.28	11123
PH-DCK	DC-8	45614	PH-EXD	F.28	11081	PH-EXR	F.28	11204	PH-EXZ	F.28	11134
PH-DCL	DC-8	45615	PH-EXD	F.28	11106	PH-EXS	F.28	11072	PH-EXZ	F.28	11143
PH-DCM	DC-8	45616	PH-EXE	F.28	11037	PH-EXS	F.28	11097	PH-EXZ	F.28	11157
PH-DCN	DC-8	45629	PH-EXE	F.28	11063	PH-EXS	F.28	11129	PH-EXZ	F.28	11180
PH-DCO	DC-8	45632	PH-EXE	F.28	11107	PH-EXS	F.28	11137	PH-EXZ	F.28	11183
(PH-DCP)	DC-8	45607	PH-EXE	F.28	11993	PH-EXS	F.28	11144	PH-EXZ	F.28	11191
PH-DCP	DC-8	45608	PH-EXF	F.28	11025	PH-EXS	F.28	11161	PH-EXZ	F.28	11194
PH-DCR	DC-8	45607	PH-EXF	F.28	11035	PH-EXS	F.28	11165	PH-EXZ	F.28	11212
PH-DCS	DC-8	45683	PH-EXF	F.28	11041	PH-EXS	F.28	11181	PH-EZA	F.100	11245
PH-DCT	DC-8	45691	PH-EXF	F.28	11048	PH-EXS	F.28	11186	PH-EZA	F.100	11257
PH-DCU	DC-8	45859	PH-EXF	F.28	11053	PH-EXS	F.28	11197	PH-EZA	F.100	11321
PH-DCV	DC-8	45766	PH-EXF	F.28	11108	PH-EXT	F.28	11073	PH-EZA	F.100	11353
PH-DCW	DC-8	45762	PH-EXF	F.28	11209	PH-EXT	F.28	11085	PH-EZA	F.100	11364
PH-DCY	DC-8	45765	PH-EXF	F.28	11992	PH-EXT	F.28	11091	PH-EZA	F.100	11434
PH-DCZ	DC-8	45804	PH-EXG	F.28	11074	PH-EXT	F.28	11127	PH-EZA	F.100	11456
PH-DEA	DC-8	45903	PH-EXG	F.28	11101	PH-EXT	F.28	11138	PH-EZA	F.100	11478
PH-DEB	DC-8	45901	PH-EXG	F.28	11109	PH-EXT	F.28	11148	PH-EZA	F.100	11484
PH-DEC	DC-8	45999	PH-EXH	F.28	11037	PH-EXT	F.28	11159	PH-EZA	F.28	11037
PH-DED	DC-8	46000	PH-EXH	F.28	11056	PH-EXT	F.28	11162	PH-EZA	F.28	11111
PH-DEE	DC-8	46019	PH-EXH	F.28	11090	PH-EXT	F.28	11169	PH-EZA	F.28	11213
PH-DEF	DC-8	46080	PH-EXH	F.28	11096	PH-EXT	F.28	11175	PH-EZA	F.28	11236
PH-DEG	DC-8	46092	PH-EXH	F.28	11103	PH-EXT	F.28	11202	PH-EZA	F.70	11539
PH-DEH	DC-8	46075	PH-EXI	F.28	11047	PH-EXT	F.28	11208	PH-EZA	F.70	11569
PH-DEK	DC-8	46121	PH-EXI	F.28	11068	PH-EXU	F.28	11077	PH-EZB	F.100	11244
PH-DEL	DC-8	46122	PH-EXI	F.28	11088	PH-EXU	F.28	11086	PH-EZB	F.100	11246
PH-DEM	DC-8	46141	PH-EXI	F.28	11098	PH-EXU	F.28	11104	PH-EZB	F.100	11274
PH-DNA	DC-9	45718	PH-EXK	F.28	11069	PH-EXU	F.28	11114	PH-EZB	F.100	11297
PH-DNB	DC-9	45719	PH-EXK	F.28	11112	PH-EXU	F.28	11130	PH-EZB	F.100	11318
PH-DNC	DC-9	45720	PH-EXL	F.28	11067	PH-EXU	F.28	11139	PH-EZB	F.100	11330
PH-DND	DC-9	45721	PH-EXL	F.28	11089	PH-EXU	F.28	11151	PH-EZB	F.100	11349
PH-DNE	DC-9	45722	PH-EXL	F.28	11099	PH-EXU	F.28	11162	PH-EZB	F.100	11369
PH-DNF	DC-9	45723	PH-EXL	F.28	11110	PH-EXU	F.28	11170	PH-EZB	F.100	11391
PH-DNG	DC-9	47102	PH-EXM	F.28	11038	PH-EXU	F.28	11176	PH-EZB	F.100	11404
PH-DNH	DC-9	47131	PH-EXM	F.28	11043	PH-EXU	F.28	11190	PH-EZB	F.100	11411
PH-DNI	DC-9	47132	PH-EXM	F.28	11075	PH-EXU	F.28	11196	PH-EZB	F.100	11435
PH-DNK	DC-9	47133	PH-EXM	F.28	11115	PH-EXU	F.28	11206	PH-EZB	F.100	11457
PH-DNL	DC-9	47190	PH-EXN	F.28	11035	PH-EXU	F.28	11211	PH-EZB	F.100	11479
PH-DNM	DC-9	47191	PH-EXN	F.28	11065	PH-EXV	F.28	11044	PH-EZB	F.100	11485
PH-DNN	DC-9	47192	PH-EXN	F.28	11082	PH-EXV	F.28	11075	PH-EZB	F.28	11214
PH-DNO	DC-9	47193	PH-EXN	F.28	11118	PH-EXV	F.28	11087	PH-EZB	F.28	11226
PH-DNP	DC-9	47194	PH-EXN	F.28	11136	PH-EXV	F.28	11105	(PH-EZB)	F.70	11540
PH-DNR	DC-9	47279	PH-EXN	F.28	11140	PH-EXV	F.28	11116	PH-EZB	F.70	11575
PH-DNS	DC-9	47168	PH-EXN	F.28	11146	PH-EXV	F.28	11126	PH-EZC	F.100	11247
PH-DNT	DC-9	47169	PH-EXN	F.28	11158	PH-EXV	F.28	11145	PH-EZC	F.100	11250
PH-DNV	DC-9	47170	PH-EXN	F.28	11173	PH-EXV	F.28	11153	PH-EZC	F.100	11300
PH-DNW	DC-9	47201	PH-EXN	F.28	11182	PH-EXV	F.28	11165	PH-EZC	F.100	11323
PH-DNY	DC-9	47462	PH-EXN	F.28	11188	PH-EXV	F.28	11200	PH-EZC	F.100	11354
PH-DNZ	DC-9	47476	PH-EXN	F.28	11199	PH-EXW	F.28	11018	PH-EZC	F.100	11365
PH-DOA	DC-9	48132	PH-EXO	F.28	11066	PH-EXW	F.28	11032	PH-EZC	F.100	11395
PH-DOB	DC-9	48133	PH-EXO	F.28	11083	PH-EXW	F.28	11117	PH-EZC	F.100	11412
PH-DTA	DC-10	46550	PH-EXO	F.28	11095	PH-EXW	F.28	11131	PH-EZC	F.100	11436
PH-DTB	DC-10	46551	PH-EXO	F.28	11121	PH-EXW	F.28	11147	PH-EZC	F.100	11458
PH-DTC	DC-10	46552	PH-EXO	F.28	11133	PH-EXW	F.28	11154	PH-EZC	F.100	11480
PH-DTD	DC-10	46553	PH-EXO	F.28	11160	PH-EXW	F.28	11163	PH-EZC	F.100	11486
PH-DTE	DC-10	46554	PH-EXO	F.28	11167	PH-EXW	F.28	11178	PH-EZC	F.28	11215
PH-DTF	DC-10	46555	PH-EXO	F.28	11174	PH-EXW	F.28	11187	PH-EZC	F.28	11227

Reg	Type	c/n	Reg	Type	c/n	Reg	Type	c/n	Reg	Type	c/n
PH-EZC	F.70	11568	PH-EZI	F.100	11513	PH-EZP	F.100	11366	PH-EZY	F.70	11574
PH-EZD	F.100	11248	PH-EZI	F.28	11103	PH-EZP	F.100	11406	PH-EZZ	F.100	11295
PH-EZD	F.100	11251	PH-EZI	F.28	11233	PH-EZP	F.100	11428	PH-EZZ	F.100	11352
PH-EZD	F.100	11258	PH-EZI	F.70	11578	PH-EZP	F.100	11448	PH-EZZ	F.100	11417
PH-EZD	F.100	11303	PH-EZJ	F.100	11259	PH-EZP	F.100	11495	PH-EZZ	F.100	11477
PH-EZD	F.100	11334	PH-EZJ	F.100	11310	PH-EZP	F.100	11504	PH-EZZ	F.100	11514
PH-EZD	F.100	11344	PH-EZJ	F.100	11326	PH-EZP	F.28	11218	PH-EZZ	F.28	11217
PH-EZD	F.100	11370	PH-EZJ	F.100	11356	PH-EZP	F.28	11229	PH-EZZ	F.28	11230
PH-EZD	F.100	11392	PH-EZJ	F.100	11368	PH-EZP	F.70	11555	PH-EZZ	F.70	11539
PH-EZD	F.100	11425	PH-EZJ	F.100	11398	PH-EZR	F.100	11283	PH-EZZ	F.70	11553
PH-EZD	F.100	11459	PH-EZJ	F.100	11414	PH-EZR	F.100	11313	PH-EZZ	F.70	11570
PH-EZD	F.100	11481	PH-EZJ	F.100	11432	PH-EZR	F.100	11335	PH-FDI	F.100	11351
PH-EZD	F.100	11488	PH-EZJ	F.100	11465	PH-EZR	F.100	11470	(PH-FNQ)	A300	069
PH-EZD	F.28	11216	PH-EZJ	F.100	11497	PH-EZR	F.28	11219	PH-FPT	F.28	11994
PH-EZD	F.28	11231	(PH-EZJ)	F.100	11510	PH-EZR	F.28	11238	PH-FYA	F.100	11253
PH-EZD	F.70	11572	PH-EZJ	F.28	11105	PH-EZR	F.70	11532	PH-FYB	F.100	11255
PH-EZE	F.100	11249	PH-EZJ	F.28	11234	PH-EZR	F.70	11561	PH-FZK	F.100	11332
PH-EZE	F.100	11252	PH-EZK	F.100	11260	PH-EZR	F.70	11564	(PH-GCL)	A320	0436
PH-EZE	F.100	11262	PH-EZK	F.100	11261	(PH-EZS)	F.100	11284	(PH-GCX)	A320	0420
PH-EZE	F.100	11311	PH-EZK	F.100	11466	(PH-EZS)	F.100	11309	PH-GIR	A300	042
PH-EZE	F.100	11345	PH-EZK	F.100	11492	PH-EZS	F.100	11338	PH-HSP	F.100	11485
PH-EZE	F.100	11372	PH-EZK	F.100	11498	PH-EZS	F.100	11361	PH-HSX	737NG	28225
PH-EZE	F.100	11396	PH-EZK	F.100	11519	PH-EZS	F.100	11377	**PH-HSY**	**737NG**	**32672**
PH-EZE	F.100	11408	PH-EZK	F.28	11095	PH-EZS	F.100	11407	PH-HVF	B737	23411
PH-EZE	F.100	11426	PH-EZK	F.28	11240	PH-EZS	F.100	11449	PH-HVG	B737	23412
PH-EZE	F.100	11460	PH-EZK	F.70	11551	PH-EZS	F.28	11220	PH-HVI	B737	24098
PH-EZE	F.100	11482	PH-EZK	F.70	11579	PH-EZS	F.70	11528	PH-HVJ	B737	23738
PH-EZE	F.100	11489	PH-EZL	F.100	11264	PH-EZS	F.70	11540	PH-HVK	B737	23786
PH-EZE	F.28	11063	PH-EZL	F.100	11327	PH-EZT	F.100	11285	PH-HVM	B737	24326
PH-EZE	F.28	11096	PH-EZL	F.100	11357	PH-EZT	F.100	11331	PH-HVN	B737	24327
PH-EZE	F.28	11217	PH-EZL	F.100	11373	PH-EZT	F.100	11362	PH-HVT	B737	24328
PH-EZE	F.28	11237	PH-EZL	F.100	11399	PH-EZT	F.100	11451	PH-HVV	B737	24329
PH-EZE	F.70	11571	PH-EZL	F.100	11415	PH-EZT	F.100	11461	**PH-HZA**	**737NG**	**28373**
PH-EZF	F.100	11253	PH-EZL	F.100	11438	PH-EZT	F.28	11221	**PH-HZB**	**737NG**	**28374**
PH-EZF	F.100	11263	PH-EZL	F.100	11467	PH-EZT	F.28	11241	**PH-HZC**	**737NG**	**28375**
(PH-EZF)	F.100	11276	PH-EZL	F.100	11499	PH-EZT	F.70	11563	**PH-HZD**	**737NG**	**28376**
PH-EZF	F.100	11306	PH-EZL	F.28	11098	PH-EZU	F.100	11286	**PH-HZE**	**737NG**	**28377**
PH-EZF	F.100	11315	PH-EZL	F.28	11162	PH-EZU	F.100	11312	**PH-HZF**	**737NG**	**28378**
PH-EZF	F.100	11454	PH-EZL	F.28	11239	(PH-EZU)	F.100	11339	**PH-HZG**	**737NG**	**28379**
PH-EZF	F.100	11483	PH-EZL	F.70	11529	PH-EZU	F.100	11452	**PH-HZI**	**737NG**	**28380**
PH-EZF	F.100	11506	PH-EZL	F.70	11580	PH-EZU	F.100	11472	**PH-HZJ**	**737NG**	**30389**
PH-EZF	F.100	11509	PH-EZM	F.100	11265	PH-EZU	F.100	11490	**PH-HZK**	**737NG**	**30390**
PH-EZF	F.28	11017	PH-EZM	F.100	11328	PH-EZU	F.28	11222	**PH-HZL**	**737NG**	**30391**
PH-EZF	F.28	11087	PH-EZM	F.100	11358	PH-EZU	F.28	11235	**PH-HZM**	**737NG**	**30392**
PH-EZF	F.70	11576	PH-EZM	F.100	11379	PH-EZV	F.100	11275	**PH-HZN**	**737NG**	**32943**
PH-EZG	F.100	11254	PH-EZM	F.100	11402	PH-EZV	F.100	11296	(PH-HZO)	737NG	32944
PH-EZG	F.100	11278	PH-EZM	F.100	11419	PH-EZV	F.100	11329	**PH-HZO**	**737NG**	**34169**
PH-EZG	F.100	11289	PH-EZM	F.100	11439	PH-EZV	F.100	11363	PH-HZQ	737NG	32354
PH-EZG	F.100	11292	PH-EZM	F.100	11468	PH-EZV	F.100	11463	**PH-HZR**	**737NG**	**32693**
PH-EZG	F.100	11324	PH-EZM	F.100	11501	PH-EZV	F.100	11473	PH-HZS	737NG	32357
PH-EZG	F.100	11359	PH-EZM	F.100	11523	PH-EZV	F.100	11491	PH-HZT	737NG	32355
PH-EZG	F.100	11380	PH-EZM	F.28	11106	PH-EZV	F.100	11520	PH-HZU	737NG	32358
PH-EZG	F.100	11405	PH-EZM	F.70	11543	PH-EZV	F.28	11223	**PH-HZV**	**737NG**	**30650**
PH-EZG	F.100	11427	PH-EZM	F.70	11581	PH-EZV	F.70	11537	**PH-HZW**	**737NG**	**29345**
PH-EZG	F.100	11455	PH-EZM	F.70	11585	PH-EZV	F.70	11559	**PH-HZX**	**737NG**	**28248**
PH-EZG	F.100	11507	PH-EZN	F.100	11266	PH-EZW	F.100	11277	**PH-HZY**	**737NG**	**30646**
PH-EZG	F.100	11522	PH-EZN	F.100	11288	PH-EZW	F.100	11316	PH-HZZ	737NG	32356
PH-EZG	F.28	11054	PH-EZN	F.100	11446	PH-EZW	F.100	11333	PH-INA	F.100	11249
PH-EZG	F.28	11232	PH-EZN	F.100	11469	PH-EZW	F.100	11474	PH-INC	F.100	11244
PH-EZG	F.70	11577	PH-EZN	F.100	11487	PH-EZW	F.28	11224	PH-ITA	B757	26243
PH-EZH	F.100	11255	PH-EZN	F.100	11500	PH-EZW	F.70	11549	PH-JCA	F.100	11480
PH-EZH	F.100	11280	PH-EZN	F.100	11502	PH-EZW	F.70	11560	PH-JCB	F.100	11481
PH-EZH	F.100	11291	PH-EZN	F.100	11527	PH-EZW	F.70	11573	PH-JCC	F.100	11482
PH-EZH	F.100	11314	PH-EZN	F.28	11107	PH-EZX	F.100	11279	PH-JCD	F.100	11483
PH-EZH	F.100	11332	PH-EZN	F.70	11541	(PH-EZX)	F.100	11304	**PH-JCH**	**F.70**	**11528**
(PH-EZH)	F.100	11508	PH-EZN	F.70	11554	PH-EZX	F.100	11307	PH-JCJ	F.100	11505
PH-EZH	F.100	11512	PH-EZO	F.100	11267	PH-EZX	F.100	11462	PH-JCK	F.100	11511
PH-EZH	F.28	11064	(PH-EZO)	F.100	11305	PH-EZX	F.100	11475	PH-JCL	F.100	11516
PH-EZH	F.28	11101	PH-EZO	F.100	11337	PH-EZX	F.100	11517	PH-JCM	F.100	11518
PH-EZH	F.70	11536	PH-EZO	F.100	11346	PH-EZX	F.28	11225	PH-JCO	F.100	11500
PH-EZH	F.70	11545	PH-EZO	F.100	11360	PH-EZX	F.70	11538	PH-JCP	F.100	11496
PH-EZI	F.100	11256	PH-EZO	F.100	11376	PH-EZX	F.70	11565	**PH-JCT**	**F.70**	**11537**
PH-EZI	F.100	11281	PH-EZO	F.100	11403	PH-EZY	F.100	11293	PH-JHG	F.28	11001
PH-EZI	F.100	11308	PH-EZO	F.100	11418	(PH-EZY)	F.100	11301	**PH-JLC**	**A300**	**107**
PH-EZI	F.100	11325	PH-EZO	F.100	11447	PH-EZY	F.100	11340	PH-JLH	A300	123
PH-EZI	F.100	11355	PH-EZO	F.100	11471	PH-EZY	F.100	11385	(PH-JLI)	A300	129
PH-EZI	F.100	11367	PH-EZO	F.100	11494	PH-EZY	F.100	11416	PH-JPV	F.28	11130
PH-EZI	F.100	11397	PH-EZO	F.100	11503	PH-EZY	F.100	11476	PH-JXP	F.100	11371
PH-EZI	F.100	11413	PH-EZO	F.28	11228	PH-EZY	F.100	11493	PH-JXR	F.100	11375
PH-EZI	F.100	11437	PH-EZP	F.100	11282	PH-EZY	F.100	11515	PH-JXS	F.100	11382
PH-EZI	F.100	11464	PH-EZP	F.100	11290	PH-EZY	F.28	11043			

Registration	Type	c/n
PH-JXT	F.100	11383
(PH-JXU)	F.100	11383
PH-JXU	F.100	11384
PH-JXV	F.100	11389
PH-JXW	F.100	11390
PH-JXX	F.100	11374
PH-JXY	F.100	11381
PH-JXZ	F.100	11386
PH-KBX	F.70	11547
PH-KCA	MD11	48555
PH-KCB	MD11	48556
PH-KCC	MD11	48557
PH-KCD	MD11	48558
PH-KCE	MD11	48559
PH-KCF	MD11	48560
PH-KCG	MD11	48561
PH-KCH	MD11	48562
PH-KCI	MD11	48563
PH-KCK	MD11	48564
PH-KLC	F.100	11268
PH-KLD	F.100	11269
PH-KLE	F.100	11270
PH-KLG	F.100	11271
PH-KLH	F.100	11272
PH-KLI	F.100	11273
(PH-KLK)	F.100	11274
(PH-KLL)	F.100	11275
(PH-KLM)	F.100	11242
(PH-KLN)	F.100	11277
(PH-KLO)	F.100	11279
(PH-KRK)	F.100	11242
PH-KXA	F.100	11378
PH-KXB	F.100	11387
PH-KXC	F.100	11388
PH-KXI	F.100	11394
PH-KXJ	F.100	11400
PH-KXK	F.100	11401
PH-KXL	F.100	11393
PH-KXP	F.100	11409
PH-KXR	F.100	11410
PH-KXZ	F.100	11423
PH-KZA	F.70	11567
PH-KZB	F.70	11562
PH-KZC	F.70	11566
PH-KZD	F.70	11582
PH-KZE	F.70	11576
PH-KZF	F.70	11577
PH-KZG	F.70	11578
PH-KZH	F.70	11583
PH-KZI	F.70	11579
PH-KZK	F.70	11581
PH-KZL	F.70	11536
PH-KZM	F.70	11561
PH-KZN	F.70	11553
PH-KZO	F.70	11538
PH-KZP	F.70	11539
PH-KZR	F.70	11551
PH-LEX	F.28	11179
PH-LMF	F.100	11257
PH-LMG	F.100	11292
PH-LMH	F.100	11267
PH-LMI	F.100	11284
PH-LMK	F.100	11285
PH-LML	F.100	11287
PH-LMM	F.100	11294
PH-LMN	F.100	11298
PH-LMO	F.100	11299
PH-LMU	F.100	11288
PH-LMV	F.100	11301
PH-LMW	F.100	11302
PH-LMX	F.100	11304
PH-LMY	F.100	11305
PH-LMZ	F.100	11309
PH-LNA	F.100	11317
PH-LNB	F.100	11319
PH-LND	F.100	11320
PH-LNE	F.100	11322
PH-LNF	F.100	11336
PH-LNG	F.100	11339
PH-LNH	F.100	11341
PH-LNI	F.100	11340
PH-LNJ	F.100	11342
PH-LNK	F.100	11343
PH-LNL	F.100	11347
PH-LNM	F.100	11348
PH-LNN	F.100	11350
PH-LNO	F.100	11351
(PH-LNP)	F.100	11323
(PH-LNR)	F.100	11324
(PH-LNT)	F.100	11325
PH-LXA	F.100	11429
PH-LXB	F.100	11430
PH-LXC	F.100	11431
PH-LXD	F.100	11440
PH-LXG	F.100	11420
PH-LXH	F.100	11421
PH-LXI	F.100	11422
PH-LXS	F.100	11441
PH-LXV	F.100	11424
PH-MAN	DC-9	47291
PH-MAO	DC-9	47363
PH-MAR	DC-9	47410
PH-MAS	DC-8	45824
PH-MAT	F.28	11008
PH-MAU	DC-8	45856
PH-MAX	DC-9	47514
PH-MBG	DC-10	46891
PH-MBH	DC-8	45818
PH-MBN	DC-10	46924
PH-MBP	DC-10	46956
PH-MBT	DC-10	46985
PH-MBY	MD80	48048
PH-MBZ	MD80	49144
PH-MCA	A310	281
PH-MCB	A310	349
(PH-MCC)	A310	433
PH-MCD	MD80	48022
PH-MCE	B747	23652
PH-MCF	B747	24134
(PH-MCG)	A310	362
PH-MCG	B767	24428
PH-MCH	B767	24429
PH-MCI	B767	25312
PH-MCJ	B767	25535
PH-MCK	B767	25273
PH-MCL	B767	26469
PH-MCM	B767	26470
PH-MCN	B747	25266
PH-MCO	DC-10	46998
PH-MCP	MD11	48616
PH-MCR	MD11	48617
PH-MCS	MD11	48618
PH-MCT	MD11	48629
PH-MCU	MD11	48757
PH-MCV	B767	27619
PH-MCW	MD11	48788
PH-MCY	MD11	48445
PH-MKC	F.100	11243
PH-MKC	F.70	11243
PH-MKH	F.100	11242
PH-MKS	F.70	11521
PH-MOL	F.28	11003
PH-MPD	A320	1944
PH-MPE	A320	1945
PH-MPF	A320	2167
PH-MPP	B747	24061
PH-MPQ	B747	24975
PH-MPR	B747	24226
PH-MPS	B747	24066
PH-MXA	F.100	11433
PH-MXB	F.100	11443
PH-MXC	F.100	11444
PH-MXD	F.100	11445
PH-MXK	F.100	11442
PH-MXL	F.100	11450
PH-MXM	F.70	11557
PH-MXN	F.70	11553
PH-MXO	F.100	11453
PH-MXW	F.100	11471
(PH-NMB)	B737	24377
PH-NXA	F.100	11433
PH-OFA	F.100	11246
PH-OFB	F.100	11247
PH-OFC	F.100	11263
PH-OFD	F.100	11259
PH-OFE	F.100	11260
PH-OFF	F.100	11274
PH-OFG	F.100	11259
PH-OFH	F.100	11277
PH-OFI	F.100	11279
PH-OFJ	F.100	11248
PH-OFK	F.100	11249
PH-OFL	F.100	11444
PH-OFM	F.100	11475
PH-OFN	F.100	11477
PH-OFO	F.100	11462
PH-OFP	F.100	11472
PH-ONS	F.100	11517
PH-OZA	B737	23718
PH-OZB	B737	23921
(PH-OZB)	B737	24911
PH-OZC	B737	28559
PH-PBX	F.28	11045
PH-RAL	B737	21736
PH-RRA	F.28	11219
PH-RRB	F.28	11223
(PH-RRC)	F.100	11321
PH-RRC	F.28	11203
PH-RRG	F.100	11316
PH-RRH	F.100	11318
PH-RRI	F.100	11321
PH-RRJ	F.28	11118
(PH-RRM)	F.28	11099
PH-RRN	F.100	11452
PH-RRS	F.70	11540
PH-RRT	F.70	11541
PH-RRU	F.70	11543
PH-RRV	F.70	11556
PH-RRW	F.70	11558
(PH-RST)	A300	212
PH-RST	L1011	193W-1189
PH-RVE	F.70	11571
PH-RXA	E145	145216
PH-RXB	E145	145320
PH-RXC	E145	145106
(PH-RXD)	E145	145411
PH-SEM	F.100	11265
PH-SEZ	MD80	49903
(PH-SFK)	A300	211
PH-SFL	A300	220
PH-SFM	A300	274
PH-SIX	F.28	11092
(PH-SWA)	F.100	11243
PH-SXI	F.100	11335
(PH-TAB)	A300	003
PH-TAB	F.100	11290
PH-TAC	F.100	11296
(PH-TEV)	A300	017
(PH-TFA)	737NG	35100
PH-THY	F.100	11264
PH-TIR	F.28	11124
PH-TKA	B757	26633
PH-TKB	B757	26634
PH-TKC	B757	26635
PH-TKD	B757	26330
PH-TKY	B757	24118
PH-TKZ	B757	24119
PH-TRF	B707	19664
PH-TRH	SE210	96
PH-TRM	SE210	21
PH-TRN	SE210	191
PH-TRO	SE210	33
PH-TRP	SE210	43
PH-TRR	SE210	48
PH-TRS	SE210	100
PH-TRU	SE210	102
PH-TRV	B707	19107
PH-TRW	B707	19416
PH-TRX	SE210	92
PH-TRY	SE210	87
PH-TSA	B737	22738
PH-TSB	B737	22739
PH-TSD	B737	21797
PH-TSE	B737	21793
PH-TSI	B737	22737
PH-TSR	B737	24023
PH-TSU	B737	24905
PH-TSW	B737	24219
PH-TSX	B737	26318
PH-TSY	B737	28085
PH-TSZ	B737	27635
PH-TVA	B707	17646
PH-TVC	B737	20836
PH-TVD	B737	20943
PH-TVE	B737	20944
PH-TVF	B737	20282
PH-TVG	B737	19711
(PH-TVG)	F.28	11124
PH-TVH	B737	19955
PH-TVI	B737	19940
PH-TVK	B707	20198
PH-TVL	A300	008
(PH-TVM)	A300	003
(PH-TVM)	B737	21131
PH-TVN	B737	21193
PH-TVO	B737	21196
PH-TVP	B737	21397
PH-TVR	B737	22025
PH-TVS	B737	22296
PH-TVT	SE210	93
PH-TVU	B737	22906
PH-TVV	SE210	44
PH-TVW	SE210	36
(PH-TVW)	SE210	44
(PH-TVW)	SE210	93
PH-TVX	B737	22023
PH-TVZ	SE210	91
PH-VAB	F.28	11099
PH-VAC	A320	0645
PH-VAD	A320	0525
PH-VAE	A320	0579
PH-VGR	F.28	11124
PH-WEV	F.28	11002
PH-WOL	F.100	11475
PH-WXA	F.70	11570
PH-WXB	F.70	11575
PH-WXC	F.70	11475
PH-WXD	F.70	11563
PH-WXE	F.70	11573
PH-WXF	F.70	11529
PH-WXG	F.70	11532
PH-XRA	737NG	30784
PH-XRB	737NG	28256
PH-XRC	737NG	29347
PH-XRD	737NG	30659
PH-XRE	737NG	30668
PH-XRV	737NG	34170
PH-XRW	737NG	33465
PH-XRX	737NG	33464
PH-XRY	737NG	33463
PH-XRZ	737NG	33462
PH-YAA	B737	25040
PH-ZAA	F.28	11004
PH-ZAB	F.28	11006
(PH-ZAC)	F.28	11008
PH-ZAD	F.28	11009
PH-ZAE	F.28	11010
PH-ZAF	F.28	11011
PH-ZAG	F.28	11012
PH-ZAH	F.28	11013
PH-ZAI	F.28	11014
PH-ZAK	F.28	11015
PH-ZAL	F.28	11016
PH-ZAM	F.28	11017
PH-ZAN	F.28	11018
PH-ZAO	F.28	11019
PH-ZAP	F.28	11020
PH-ZAR	F.28	11991
PH-ZAS	F.28	11021
PH-ZAT	F.28	11022
(PH-ZAU)	F.28	11992
PH-ZAU	F.28	11993
(PH-ZAV)	F.28	11023
PH-ZAV	F.28	11032

Reg	Type	c/n
(PH-ZAW)	F.28	11024
PH-ZAW	F.28	11052
PH-ZAX	F.28	11053
(PH-ZAX)	F.28	11993
PH-ZBA	F.28	11057
(PH-ZBA)	F.28	11994
PH-ZBB	F.28	11058
PH-ZBC	F.28	11060
(PH-ZBD)	F.28	11029
PH-ZBD	F.28	11059
PH-ZBE	F.28	11062
PH-ZBF	F.28	11037
PH-ZBG	F.28	11027
PH-ZBH	F.28	11031
PH-ZBI	F.28	11034
PH-ZBJ	F.28	11163
PH-ZBK	F.28	11079
PH-ZBL	F.28	11093
PH-ZBM	F.28	11048
PH-ZBN	F.28	11097
PH-ZBO	F.28	11110
PH-ZBP	F.28	11125
PH-ZBR	F.28	11136
PH-ZBS	F.28	11137
PH-ZBT	F.28	11135
PH-ZBU	F.28	11133
PH-ZBV	F.28	11153
PH-ZBW	F.28	11157
PH-ZBX	F.28	11159
PH-ZBY	F.28	11169
PH-ZBZ	F.28	11167
PH-ZCA	F.28	11164
PH-ZCB	F.28	11166
PH-ZCC	F.28	11168
PH-ZCD	F.28	11177
PH-ZCE	F.28	11184
PH-ZCF	F.28	11185
PH-ZCG	F.28	11165
PH-ZCH	F.28	11220
PH-ZCI	F.100	11276
PH-ZCK	F.100	11274
PH-ZCL	F.100	11275
PH-ZCM	F.100	11277
PH-ZCN	F.100	11279
PH-ZDJ	F.100	11451
PH-ZFA	F.100	11486
PH-ZFB	F.100	11490
PH-ZFE	F.100	11502
PH-ZFF	F.100	11446
PH-ZFG	F.100	11515
PH-ZFH	F.100	11499
PH-ZFI	F.100	11483
PH-ZFJ	F.100	11520
PH-ZFL	F.100	11468
PH-ZFM	F.100	11359
PH-ZFN	F.100	11361
PH-ZFO	F.100	11367
PH-ZFP	F.100	11396
PH-ZFQ	F.100	11397
PH-ZFR	F.100	11404
PH-ZFS	F.100	11460
PH-ZKF	F.100	11456

Philippines
(see also RP-)

Reg	Type	c/n
PI-C1121	1-11	091
PI-C1131	1-11	092
PI-C1141	1-11	094
PI-C1151	1-11	BAC.157
PI-C1151	1-11	BAC.161
PI-C1161	1-11	BAC.213
PI-C1171	1-11	BAC.215
PI-C1181	1-11	BAC.226
PI-C1191	1-11	BAC.231
(PI-C295)	DC-10	46892
PI-C7071	B707	17661
PI-C7072	B707	17668
PI-C7073	B707	17680
PI-C801	DC-8	45607
PI-C801	DC-8	45608
PI-C802	DC-8	45762
PI-C803	DC-8	45937
PI-C804	DC-8	45607
PI-C827	DC-8	45378
(PI-C827)	DC-8	46121
PI-C829	DC-8	45380
(PI-C829)	DC-8	46122
PI-C969	SE210	103
PI-C970	SE210	90

Netherlands Antilles

Reg	Type	c/n
PJ-BOA	B727	19506
PJ-DAA	F.100	11310
PJ-DAB	F.100	11331
PJ-DNA	DC-9	45722
PJ-DNB	DC-9	45723
PJ-DNC	DC-9	45721
PJ-MDA	MD80	49449
PJ-SEF	MD80	49123
PJ-SEG	MD80	49124
PJ-SEH	MD80	49661
PJ-SNA	DC-9	47648
PJ-SNB	DC-9	47666
PJ-SNC	DC-9	47669
PJ-SND	DC-9	47639
PJ-SNE	DC-9	47175
PJ-SNK	DC-9	48144
PJ-SNL	DC-9	48154
PJ-SNM	DC-9	48139
PJ-SNN	DC-9	48138

Indonesia

Reg	Type	c/n
(PK-)	B727	18970
PK-	B727	19480
(PK-)	B727	22045
PK-	B727	22559
(PK-)	B737	19070
(PK-)	B737	19076
(PK-)	B737	19948
(PK-)	B737	19950
(PK-)	B737	19952
PK-AIG	B737	22364
PK-ALC	B737	23320
PK-ALF	MD80	49985
PK-ALG	MD80	49986
PK-ALH	B737	21732
PK-ALH	MD80	48066
PK-ALI	MD80	49112
PK-ALJ	MD80	49113
PK-ALK	B737	22032
PK-ALN	B737	23132
PK-ALV	B737	23135
PK-AWA	A310	410
PK-AWD	A310	437
PK-AWE	A320	0542
PK-AWN	B737	26442
PK-AWO	B737	24659
PK-AWP	B737	24905
PK-AWQ	B737	23376
PK-AWR	A310	409
PK-AWS	B737	24856
PK-AWT	B737	23345
PK-AWU	B737	23257
PK-AWV	B737	23552
PK-AWW	B737	23554
PK-BAR	B727	18970
PK-BPT	B727	20736
PK-BPW	B737	23157
PK-BYA	B737	23796
PK-BYD	B737	21518
PK-BYX	B737	24197
PK-CDA	B737	20255
PK-CJA	B737	22301
PK-CJC	B737	24025
PK-CJD	B737	22057
PK-CJE	B737	23446
PK-CJF	B737	22343
PK-CJG	B737	23320
PK-CJH	B737	22883
PK-CJI	B737	23135
PK-CJJ	B737	22880
PK-CJK	B737	22032
PK-CJL	B737	21301
PK-CJM	B737	22884
PK-CJN	B737	23134
PK-CJO	B737	22300
PK-CJP	B737	23132
PK-CJR	B737	21225
PK-DTA	146	E1144
(PK-DTC)	146	E1152
PK-DTD	146	E2170
PK-EPV	B727	22702
PK-FEA	MD80	49766
PK-FEC	MD80	49759
PK-FED	MD80	53199
(PK-FTT)	MD80	49759
PK-GAA	A300	159
PK-GAC	A300	164
PK-GAD	A300	165
PK-GAE	A300	166
PK-GAF	A300	167
PK-GAG	A300	168
PK-GAH	A300	213
PK-GAI	A300	214
PK-GAJ	A300	215
PK-GAK	A300	611
PK-GAL	A300	613
PK-GAM	A300	625
PK-GAN	A300	630
PK-GAO	A300	633
PK-GAP	A300	657
PK-GAQ	A300	659
PK-GAR	A300	664
PK-GAS	A300	668
PK-GAT	A300	677
PK-GAU	B707	21092
(PK-GBA)	B747	22246
(PK-GBB)	B747	22247
(PK-GBC)	B747	22248
(PK-GBD)	B747	22249
PK-GEA	DC-8	45765
PK-GEB	DC-8	45766
PK-GEC	DC-8	45632
PK-GEE	737NG	32361
PK-GEF	737NG	32363
PK-GFQ	F.28	11117
PK-GFR	F.28	11113
PK-GFS	F.28	11119
PK-GFT	F.28	11120
PK-GFU	F.28	11131
PK-GFV	F.28	11132
PK-GFW	F.28	11134
PK-GGA	B737	28726
PK-GGC	B737	28727
PK-GGD	B737	28728
PK-GGE	B737	28729
PK-GGF	B737	28730
PK-GGG	B737	28731
(PK-GGH)	B737	28732
(PK-GGI)	B737	28733
(PK-GGJ)	B737	28734
(PK-GGK)	B737	28738
(PK-GGK)	B737	28740
(PK-GGL)	B737	28735
(PK-GGL)	B737	28742
(PK-GGM)	B737	28736
(PK-GGM)	B737	28740
PK-GGN	B737	28735
(PK-GGN)	B737	28738
PK-GGO	B737	28736
(PK-GGO)	B737	28737
PK-GGP	B737	28737
(PK-GGP)	B737	28739
PK-GGQ	B737	28739
(PK-GGQ)	B737	28741
PK-GGR	B737	28741
(PK-GGR)	B737	28742
PK-GGS	B737	25138
PK-GGT	B737	28566
PK-GGU	B737	28567
PK-GGV	B737	26293
PK-GGW	B737	28332
PK-GGX	B737	28573
PK-GGY	B737	28555
(PK-GHA)	F.28	11154
(PK-GHB)	F.28	11155
(PK-GHC)	F.28	11157
(PK-GHD)	F.28	11158
(PK-GHE)	F.28	11160
PK-GHQ	B737	29108
PK-GHR	B737	29109
PK-GHS	B737	24698
PK-GHT	B737	24680
PK-GHU	B737	24681
PK-GHV	B737	24914
PK-GIA	DC-10	46918
PK-GIB	DC-10	46919
PK-GIC	DC-10	46964
PK-GID	DC-10	46951
PK-GIE	DC-10	46685
PK-GIF	DC-10	46686
PK-GIG	MD11	48502
PK-GIH	MD11	48500
PK-GII	MD11	48503
PK-GIJ	MD11	48504
PK-GIK	MD11	48753
PK-GIL	MD11	48755
PK-GIM	MD11	48758
PK-GJA	CV990	30-10-3
PK-GJB	CV990	30-10-4
PK-GJC	CV990	30-10-37
(PK-GJC)	DC-8	45766
PK-GJD	DC-8	45765
PK-GJE	DC-9	47385
PK-GJF	DC-9	47386
PK-GJG	DC-9	47481
PK-GJH	DC-9	47463
PK-GJI	DC-9	47561
PK-GJJ	DC-9	47569
"PK-GJK"	B737	29206
PK-GJK	DC-9	47601
PK-GJN	DC-8	45766
PK-GJP	F.28	11078
PK-GJQ	F.28	11075
PK-GJR	F.28	11037
PK-GJS	F.28	11064
PK-GJT	F.28	11063
PK-GJU	F.28	11061
PK-GJV	F.28	11055
PK-GJW	F.28	11054
PK-GJX	F.28	11039
PK-GJY	F.28	11036
PK-GJZ	F.28	11035
PK-GKA	F.28	11154
PK-GKB	F.28	11155
PK-GKC	F.28	11157
PK-GKD	F.28	11158
PK-GKE	F.28	11160
PK-GKF	F.28	11170
PK-GKG	F.28	11171
PK-GKH	F.28	11174
PK-GKI	F.28	11188
PK-GKJ	F.28	11189
PK-GKK	F.28	11193
PK-GKL	F.28	11175
PK-GKM	F.28	11177
PK-GKN	F.28	11196
PK-GKO	F.28	11198
PK-GKP	F.28	11199
PK-GKQ	F.28	11201
PK-GKR	F.28	11202
PK-GKS	F.28	11206
PK-GKT	F.28	11209
PK-GKU	F.28	11210
PK-GKV	F.28	11211
PK-GKW	F.28	11213
PK-GKX	F.28	11214
PK-GKY	F.28	11215

Reg	Type	S/N	Reg	Type	S/N	Reg	Type	S/N	Reg	Type	S/N
PK-GKZ	F.28	11216	PK-GWN	B737	25716	PK-JGQ	B727	20989	PK-LFM	737NG	35715
PK-GNA	DC-9	47385	PK-GWO	B737	25717	PK-JGR	B737	23157	PK-LFP	737NG	35717
PK-GNB	DC-9	47386	PK-GWP	B737	25718	PK-JGS	B737	19949	PK-LIA	B737	21440
PK-GNC	DC-9	47481	PK-GWQ	B737	25719	PK-JGT	B727	20580	PK-LID	B737	20363
PK-GND	DC-9	47463	PK-GWR	B737	20458	PK-JGU	B727	20612	PK-LIF	B737	24467
PK-GNE	DC-9	47561	PK-GWT	B737	26316	PK-JGV	B737	21227	PK-LIG	B737	24513
PK-GNF	DC-9	47569	PK-GWU	B737	24708	PK-JGW	B737	21226	PK-LIH	B737	20206
PK-GNG	DC-9	47601	PK-GWV	B737	24512	PK-JGX	B727	21586	PK-LIH	B737	24520
PK-GNH	DC-9	47635	PK-GWW	B737	24683	PK-JGY	B737	21791	PK-LII	B737	24123
PK-GNI	DC-9	47636	PK-GWX	B737	24691	PK-JHA	B737	20450	PK-LIJ	B737	24682
PK-GNJ	DC-9	47672	PK-GWY	B737	28490	PK-JHC	B737	20506	PK-LIK	MD90	53570
PK-GNK	DC-9	47673	PK-GWZ	B737	28881	PK-JHD	B737	20451	PK-LIL	MD90	53573
PK-GNL	DC-9	47680	PK-GZA	B737	25663	PK-JHE	B737	20452	PK-LIM	MD90	53489
PK-GNM	DC-9	47701	PK-GZC	B737	25664	PK-JHF	B737	20508	PK-LIO	MD90	53490
PK-GNN	DC-9	47722	PK-GZF	B737	29201	PK-JHG	B737	20507	PK-LIP	MD90	53551
PK-GNO	DC-9	47730	PK-GZG	B737	29202	PK-JHH	B737	22131	PK-LIQ	B737	24911
PK-GNP	DC-9	47740	PK-GZH	B737	29203	PK-JHI	B737	22132	PK-LIR	B737	24692
PK-GNQ	DC-9	47741	PK-GZI	B737	29204	PK-JIA	A300	198	PK-LIS	B737	24513
PK-GNR	DC-9	47744	PK-GZJ	B737	29205	PK-JIC	A300	195	PK-LIT	B737	24512
PK-GNS	DC-9	47789	PK-GZK	B737	29206	PK-JID	A300	238	PK-LIU	B737	23218
PK-GNT	DC-9	47790	PK-GZL	B737	29207	PK-JIE	A300	247	PK-LIV	B737	23219
PK-GNU	DC-9	47791	PK-GZM	B737	29208	PK-JKM	F.28	11116	PK-LIW	B737	24684
PK-GNV	DC-9	47792	PK-GZN	B737	29209	PK-KAD	B737	22338	PK-LME	MD80	53481
PK-GNW	DC-9	47793	PK-GZO	B737	29210	PK-KAO	B737	22339	PK-LMF	MD80	53147
PK-GNX	DC-9	47794	PK-GZP	B737	28661	PK-KAR	B737	23796	PK-LMG	MD80	49417
PK-GNY	DC-9	47795	PK-HAS	B737	24197	PK-KAT	B737	23134	PK-LMH	MD80	49419
PK-GPA	A330	138	PK-HHS	B737	21957	PK-KDK	A300	633	PK-LMI	MD80	49263
PK-GPC	A330	140	PK-HNH	F.28	11218	PK-KDN	A310	500	PK-LMJ	MD80	49262
PK-GPD	A330	144	PK-HNJ	F.28	11134	PK-KDP	A300	677	PK-LMK	MD80	49788
PK-GPE	A330	148	PK-HNK	F.28	11129	PK-KDW	A310	534	PK-LML	MD80	48083
PK-GPF	A330	153	PK-HNN	F.28	11119	PK-KFD	F.28	11168	PK-LMM	MD80	48069
PK-GPG	A330	165	PK-HNP	F.28	11216	PK-KJK	B737	21195	PK-LMN	MD80	49189
PK-GQA	F.28	11217	PK-IAA	B737	23528	PK-KJL	B737	21227	PK-LMO	MD80	49373
PK-GQB	F.28	11218	PK-IAB	B737	23527	PK-KJM	B737	21732	PK-LMP	MD80	49102
PK-GSA	B747	22246	PK-IAF	B727	21702	PK-KJN	B737	22599	PK-LMQ	MD80	49117
PK-GSB	B747	22247	PK-IAT	B747	23245	PK-KJO	B737	22406	PK-LMR	MD80	49116
PK-GSC	B747	22248	PK-IAU	B747	22067	PK-KKA	B737	28565	PK-LMS	MD80	49114
PK-GSD	B747	22249	PK-IJA	B737	19408	PK-KKC	B737	26071	PK-LMT	MD80	49118
PK-GSE	B747	22768	PK-IJC	B737	20412	PK-KKD	B737	23978	PK-LMU	MD80	49429
PK-GSF	B747	22769	PK-IJD	B737	20631	PK-KKE	B737	23773	PK-LMV	MD80	49190
PK-GSG	B747	25704	PK-IJE	B737	20926	PK-KKF	B737	22299	PK-LMW	MD80	49443
PK-GSH	B747	25705	PK-IJF	B737	21732	PK-KKG	B737	25134	PK-LMY	MD80	49250
PK-GSI	B747	24956	PK-IJG	B737	23320	PK-KKH	B737	24069	PK-LYA	B737	23054
PK-GVA	F.28	11035	PK-IJH	B737	21397	PK-KKI	B737	24234	PK-MAW	A310	539
PK-GVC	F.28	11039	PK-IJI	B737	22125	PK-KKJ	B737	22637	PK-MAX	A310	542
PK-GVD	F.28	11036	PK-IJJ	B737	22130	PK-KKL	B737	23188	PK-MAY	A300	344
PK-GVD	F.20	11054	PK-IJK	B737	22143	(PK-KKM)	B737	22113	PK-MBA	B707	18739
PK-GVE	F.28	11055	PK-IJL	B737	23039	PK-KKM	B737	24791	PK-MBC	B737	22129
PK-GVF	F.28	11061	PK-IJM	B737	22131	PK-KKN	B737	22161	PK-MBD	B737	22141
PK-GVG	F.28	11063	PK-IJN	B737	22132	PK-KKP	B737	24103	PK-MBE	B737	22142
PK-GVH	F.28	11064	PK-IJO	B737	21732	PK-KKQ	B737	22396	PK-MBF	B737	22368
PK-GVI	F.28	11037	PK-IJP	B737	22339	PK-KKR	B737	24569	PK-MBG	B737	22369
PK-GVJ	F.28	11075	PK-IJQ	B737	22338	PK-KKS	B737	23980	PK-MBH	B737	22279
PK-GVK	F.28	11078	PK-IJR	B737	22300	PK-KKT	B737	24353	PK-MBJ	B737	22576
PK-GVL	F.28	11087	PK-IJS	B737	22301	PK-KKU	B737	23923	PK-MBK	B737	24689
PK-GVM	F.28	11032	PK-IMC	MD80	49113	PK-KKV	B737	27284	PK-MBL	B737	24467
PK-GVN	F.28	11043	PK-IMD	MD80	49112	PK-KKW	B737	24070	PK-MBM	B737	24513
PK-GVO	F.28	11044	PK-IME	MD80	48066	PK-KKY	B737	24059	PK-MBN	B737	24304
PK-GVP	F.28	11094	PK-JAC	B727	21587	PK-KKZ	B737	24300	(PK-MBN)	B737	24692
PK-GVQ	F.28	11096	PK-JAE	B727	21310	PK-KMA	B737	23981	PK-MBO	B737	24305
PK-GVR	F.28	11098	PK-JGA	B737	22399	PK-KMC	B737	24493	PK-MBP	B737	23632
PK-GVS	F.28	11101	PK-JGA	F.100	11264	PK-KMD	B737	24469	PK-MBQ	B737	22260
PK-GVT	F.28	11095	PK-JGC	F.100	11265	PK-KME	B737	23977	PK-MBR	B737	22341
PK-GVU	F.28	11103	PK-JGC	B727	20736	(PK-LAF)	737NG	35679	PK-MBS	B737	22342
PK-GVV	F.28	11105	PK-JGD	F.100	11266	(PK-LAG)	737NG	35680	PK-MBU	B737	22259
PK-GVW	F.28	11106	PK-JGE	F.100	11301	(PK-LAH)	737NG	35710	PK-MBV	B727	21310
PK-GVX	F.28	11107	PK-JGF	F.100	11347	(PK-LAI)	737NG	35711	PK-MBW	B727	21306
PK-GWA	B737	24403	PK-JGG	F.100	11336	(PK-LAJ)	737NG	35712	PK-MBX	B737	23005
(PK-GWA)	DC-10	46918	(PK-JGG)	F.100	11339	(PK-LAK)	737NG	35713	PK-MBY	B737	23004
(PK-GWA)	DC-10	46952	(PK-JGG)	F.100	11348	(PK-LAL)	737NG	35714	PK-MBZ	B737	23007
(PK-GWB)	DC-10	46919	(PK-JGH)	F.100	11336	(PK-LAM)	737NG	35715	PK-MDC	B737	21685
PK-GWD	B737	24470	PK-JGH	F.100	11339	(PK-LAP)	737NG	35717	PK-MDH	B737	23932
PK-GWE	B737	24492	(PK-JGH)	F.100	11350	PK-LEO	A310	410	PK-MDJ	B737	23931
PK-GWF	B737	24698	PK-JGI	F.70	11529	PK-LEP	A310	437	(PK-MGA)	F.28	11154
PK-GWG	B737	24699	PK-JGJ	F.70	11532	PK-LFF	737NG	35679	PK-MGC	F.28	11155
PK-GWH	B737	24700	(PK-JGL)	F.70	11566	PK-LFG	737NG	35680	PK-MGD	F.28	11157
PK-GWI	B737	24701	PK-JGM	B727	21519	PK-LFH	737NG	35710	PK-MGE	F.28	11158
PK-GWJ	B737	24702	PK-JGN	B727	21384	PK-LFI	737NG	35711	(PK-MGF)	F.28	11160
PK-GWK	B737	25713	(PK-JGN)	F.70	11582	PK-LFJ	737NG	35712	PK-MGG	F.28	11170
PK-GWL	B737	25714	PK-JGO	B727	21584	PK-LFK	737NG	35713	PK-MGH	F.28	11171
PK-GWM	B737	25715	PK-JGP	B737	22364	PK-LFL	737NG	35714	PK-MGI	F.28	11174

Reg	Type	c/n
PK-MGJ	F.28	11175
PK-MGK	F.28	11188
PK-MGL	F.28	11189
PK-MGM	F.28	11199
PK-MGN	F.28	11202
(PK-MGO)	F.28	11209
PK-MGP	F.28	11213
(PK-MGQ)	F.28	11214
PK-MGR	F.28	11215
(PK-MGS)	F.28	11177
(PK-MGT)	F.28	11193
(PK-MGU)	F.28	11196
(PK-MGV)	F.28	11198
(PK-MGW)	F.28	11201
(PK-MGX)	F.28	11206
(PK-MGY)	F.28	11211
PK-MGZ	F.28	11217
PK-MJA	F.100	11453
PK-MJC	F.100	11463
PK-MJD	F.100	11474
PK-MJE	F.100	11512
PK-MJF	F.100	11517
PK-MJG	F.100	11527
PK-MSU	F.28	11139
PK-MSV	F.28	11140
PK-MSW	F.28	11138
PK-MSX	F.28	11176
PK-MTA	146	E1004
PK-NAD	B737	24197
PK-NAI	F.28	11142
PK-NAJ	F.28	11133
PK-NAM	F.28	11234
PK-OCF	B737	19601
PK-OCG	B737	20335
PK-OCI	B737	20255
PK-OCP	B737	23794
PK-OCQ	B737	21687
PK-OCT	MD80	49889
PK-OCU	MD80	53017
PK-OME	E145	145516
PK-OSP	146	E1124
PK-PFE	F.70	11553
PK-PFF	F.100	11475
PK-PFG	F.100	11477
PK-PFZ	F.100	11486
PK-PJC	1-11	BAC.166
PK-PJF	1-11	065
PK-PJJ	146	E2239
PK-PJK	F.28	11192
PK-PJL	F.28	11111
PK-PJM	F.28	11178
PK-PJN	F.100	11288
PK-PJO	F.100	11444
PK-PJP	146	E2050
PK-PJP	B727	21091
PK-PJQ	B707	21092
PK-PJS	F.28	11030
PK-PJT	F.28	11042
PK-PJU	F.28	11029
PK-PJV	F.28	11073
(PK-PJW)	F.28	11095
PK-PJW	F.28	11148
PK-PJX	F.100	11445
(PK-PJX)	F.28	11042
PK-PJY	F.28	11146
PK-RGE	F.100	11445
(PK-RI.)	B737	22875
PK-RIA	B737	21357
PK-RIC	B737	22278
PK-RID	B737	22803
PK-RIE	B737	22804
PK-RIF	B737	21685
PK-RIH	B737	23868
PK-RII	B737	22876
PK-RIJ	B737	21820
PK-RIK	B737	22531
PK-RIL	B737	22137
PK-RIM	B737	22136
PK-RIN	B737	21732
PK-RIO	B737	23913
(PK-RIP)	B737	22903
PK-RIQ	B737	23023

Reg	Type	c/n
PK-RIR	B737	22735
PK-RIT	B737	23979
PK-RIV	B737	23796
PK-RIW	B737	22396
PK-RIY	B727	21585
PK-RIZ	B727	21587
PK-RJG	E145	14500969
PK-RJI	F.100	11328
PK-RJW	F.28	11045
PK-RMA	A320	0279
PK-RMC	A320	0391
PK-RME	A320	3264
PK-RPH	B737	20943
PK-RPI	B737	20944
PK-RPX	B737	20256
PK-TAL	1-11	BAC.259
PK-TMA	B727	21697
PK-TRU	1-11	BAC.262
PK-TSR	1-11	BAC.126
PK-TST	1-11	BAC.118
PK-TWA	F.28	11234
PK-TWI	F.100	11293
PK-TWM	F.28	11183
PK-TWN	F.100	11335
PK-TXA	B737	23134
PK-TXC	B737	22884
PK-TXD	B737	22400
PK-TXE	B737	21301
PK-TXF	B737	21302
PK-VBA	B727	18970
PK-VFA	F.28	11142
PK-VFY	F.28	11179
PK-WIF	MD80	49481
PK-WIG	MD80	49489
PK-WIH	MD80	49582
PK-YCM	F.28	11168
PK-YGF	B737	21822
PK-YGI	B727	20185
PK-YGM	B737	20206
PK-YGR	B727	20993
PK-YGZ	B727	20112
PK-YHK	F.28	11116
PK-YPJ	F.28	11148
PK-YPT	F.28	11163
PK-YPV	F.28	11124
PK-YRT	B737	22599
PK-YTA	B737	21192
PK-YTC	B737	22090
PK-YTD	B737	22802
PK-YTE	B737	25303
PK-YTF	B737	22397
PK-YTG	B737	22453
PK-YTH	B737	20806
PK-YTI	B737	22407
PK-YTJ	B737	21693
PK-YTK	B737	24687
PK-YTL	B737	23113
PK-YTM	B737	22957
PK-YTN	B737	22659
PK-YTO	B737	22660
PK-YTP	B737	24345
PK-YTQ	B737	21767
PK-YTR	B737	21766
PK-YTS	B737	22055
PK-YTT	B737	22667
PK-YTU	B737	25604
PK-YTV	B737	21955
PK-YTW	B737	23318
PK-YTX	B737	22953
PK-YTY	B737	22955
PK-YTZ	B737	23869
PK-YVA	A319	2648
PK-YVC	A319	2660
PK-YVD	A320	0449
PK-YVE	A320	0441
PK-YVU	B737	24097
PK-YVV	B737	23316
PK-YVW	B737	23319
PK-YVX	B737	24093
PK-YVY	B737	22952
PK-YVZ	B737	23317

Brazil

Reg	Type	c/n
(PP-)	B737	25787
(PP-)	B737	25788
PP-ABS	DC-8	45810
PP-AIU	B727	20580
PP-AIV	B727	20874
PP-AIW	B727	22079
PP-AIY	DC-8	46070
PP-AJM	DC-10	47929
(PP-AJN)	DC-10	48258
PP-AJP	B707	20069
(PP-AMS)	B737	20132
(PP-ARR)	B727	20710
PP-BEL	DC-8	46047
PP-BET	DC-8	46103
PP-BEX	DC-8	46104
PP-BLR	B727	21661
PP-BLS	B727	20655
PP-BMS	B737	20134
PP-BRB	B707	18925
PP-BRG	B707	19586
PP-BRH	B707	19774
PP-BRI	B707	19776
(PP-BRR)	B707	19375
PP-BRR	B707	20088
PP-BSE	B707	19317
PP-CJA	SE210	129
PP-CJB	SE210	133
PP-CJC	SE210	62
PP-CJD	SE210	168
PP-CJE	B727	20418
PP-CJF	B727	20419
PP-CJG	B727	20420
PP-CJH	B727	19305
PP-CJH	B727	20421
PP-CJI	B727	19242
PP-CJJ	B727	19400
PP-CJK	B727	18969
PP-CJL	MD80	49149
PP-CJN	B737	21012
PP-CJO	B737	21013
PP-CJP	B737	21014
PP-CJR	B737	21015
PP-CJS	B737	21016
PP-CJT	B737	21017
PP-CLA	A300	109
PP-CLB	A300	110
PP-DGP	DC-8	45953
PP-DGX	DC-8	45953
PP-ITA	B727	18968
PP-ITL	B727	20078
PP-ITM	B727	19507
PP-ITP	B727	19313
PP-ITR	B727	22549
PP-ITV	B727	22476
PP-JUB	B727	21242
PP-LBF	B727	20705
PP-LBN	B707	19239
PP-LBO	B727	22377
PP-LBY	B727	21297
(PP-MCA)	B707	19586
PP-MLM	B727	21299
PP-MTA	DC-10	47908
PP-NAC	B737	24690
PP-OOO	DC-10	48258
PP-OPR	B727	22146
PP-PDS	DC-8	45272
PP-PDT	DC-8	45273
PP-PDU	SE210	118
PP-PDV	SE210	120
PP-PDX	SE210	126
PP-PDZ	SE210	131
PP-PEA	DC-8	45253
PP-PEF	DC-8	45271
PP-PHB	B707	18711
PP-PSD	A310	437
PP-PSE	A310	535
PP-SDH	E170	17000002
PP-SDP	1-11	BAC.192
PP-SDQ	1-11	BAC.228

Reg	Type	c/n
PP-SDR	1-11	BAC.230
PP-SDS	1-11	BAC.236
PP-SDT	1-11	BAC.193
PP-SDU	1-11	BAC.211
PP-SDV	1-11	BAC.199
PP-SFA	MD11	48768
PP-SFB	DC-10	46575
PP-SFC	B727	21071
PP-SFD	MD11	48769
PP-SFE	B727	22166
PP-SFF	B727	20880
PP-SFG	B727	22425
PP-SFH	A310	552
PP-SFI	B737	21478
PP-SFJ	B737	24212
PP-SFK	B737	28868
PP-SFL	B737	23787
PP-SFM	B737	24299
PP-SFN	B737	27925
(PP-SFO)	MD11	48755
(PP-SFP)	MD11	48758
PP-SFQ	B727	22079
(PP-SFS)	B737	22736
PP-SLS	B737	26104
PP-SLT	B737	26105
PP-SMA	B737	20092
PP-SMB	B737	20093
PP-SMC	B727	20094
PP-SMC	E170	17000004
PP-SMD	B737	20095
PP-SME	B737	20096
PP-SMF	B737	20589
PP-SMG	B737	20777
PP-SMH	B737	20778
PP-SMK	B727	21348
PP-SMP	B737	20779
PP-SMQ	B737	20155
PP-SMR	B737	20157
PP-SMS	B737	20159
PP-SMT	B737	20160
PP-SMU	B737	20967
PP-SMV	B737	20968
PP-SMW	B737	20346
PP-SMX	B737	20969
PP-SMY	B737	20970
PP-SMZ	B737	20971
PP-SNA	B737	21094
PP-SNB	B737	21095
PP-SNC	B737	21187
PP-SND	B737	21188
PP-SNE	B727	21341
PP-SNF	B727	21342
(PP-SNG)	B727	21343
PP-SNG	B727	21345
(PP-SNH)	B727	21344
PP-SNH	B727	21346
PP-SNI	B727	21600
(PP-SNI)	B737	21597
PP-SNJ	B727	21601
(PP-SNJ)	B737	21598
PP-SNK	B727	21345
(PP-SNK)	B737	21599
PP-SNK	B737	21686
PP-SNL	A300	202
(PP-SNL)	B727	21348
PP-SNM	A300	205
(PP-SNM)	B727	21600
PP-SNN	A300	225
(PP-SNN)	B727	21601
PP-SNO	B737	21685
PP-SNP	B737	21206
PP-SNQ	B737	23173
PP-SNR	B737	23174
PP-SNS	B737	23175
PP-SNT	B737	23176
PP-SNU	B737	23177
PP-SNV	B737	23826
PP-SNW	B737	22580
PP-SNW	B737	24096
(PP-SNX)	B737	24097
PP-SNY	B737	20218
PP-SNY	B737	23415

Reg	Type	Serial
PP-SNZ	B737	24097
PP-SOA	B737	23747
PP-SOB	B737	23748
PP-SOC	B737	24790
PP-SOD	B737	24791
PP-SOE	B737	25010
PP-SOF	B737	25011
PP-SOG	B737	25032
PP-SOH	B737	24683
PP-SOI	B737	24691
PP-SOJ	B737	24911
PP-SOK	B737	25057
PP-SOL	B737	25119
PP-SOM	DC-10	46940
PP-SON	DC-10	47868
PP-SOO	DC-8	45974
PP-SOP	DC-8	45976
PP-SOQ	DC-8	45941
PP-SOR	B737	25125
PP-SOT	B737	25150
PP-SOU	B737	25360
PP-SOV	DC-10	47889
PP-SOW	MD11	48413
PP-SOZ	MD11	48414
PP-SPA	B737	23464
PP-SPB	B737	23465
PP-SPC	B737	23466
PP-SPD	MD11	48411
PP-SPE	MD11	48412
PP-SPF	B737	21073
PP-SPG	**B737**	**21616**
PP-SPH	B737	22070
PP-SPI	B737	21476
PP-SPJ	B737	21236
PP-SPK	MD11	48744
PP-SPL	MD11	48745
PP-SPM	MD11	48563
(PP-SPN)	MD11	48768
PP-SQB	E145	14500828
PP-SQC	E145	14500829
PP-SQD	E145	14500830
PP-SQE	E145	14500831
PP-SQF	E145	14500833
PP-SQG	E145	14500834
PP-SQH	E145	14500835
PP-SQI	E145	14500836
PP-SRK	B727	21347
PP-SRT	1-11	BAC.119
PP-SRU	1-11	BAC.126
PP-SRV	B737	22296
PP-SRW	B737	22058
PP-SRX	B737	19425
PP-SRY	B727	19310
PP-SRZ	B727	19311
PP-SSH	B737	29122
(PP-STB)	E190	19000002
(PP-S)	B737	22367
(PP-S)	B737	22736
PP-TAR	DC-8	45668
(PP-TLM)	B727	20580
PP-TNZ	DC-8	45768
PP-TPC	DC-8	45752
PP-VJA	B707	17905
PP-VJB	B707	17906
PP-VJC	SE210	10
PP-VJD	SE210	15
PP-VJE	CV990	30-10-13
PP-VJF	CV990	30-10-19
PP-VJG	CV990	30-10-20
PP-VJH	B707	20008
PP-VJI	SE210	20
PP-VJJ	B707	18694
PP-VJK	B707	19822
PP-VJR	B707	19320
PP-VJS	B707	19321
PP-VJT	B707	19322
PP-VJX	B707	19842
PP-VJY	B707	19840
PP-VJZ	B707	19841
PP-VLA	B727	20422
PP-VLB	B727	20423
PP-VLC	B727	20424
PP-VLD	B727	20425
PP-VLE	B727	19666
PP-VLE	B727	20426
PP-VLF	B727	20422
PP-VLG	B727	20423
PP-VLH	B727	20424
PP-VLI	B707	19433
PP-VLJ	B707	19106
PP-VLK	B707	19870
PP-VLL	B707	19871
PP-VLM	B707	19869
PP-VLN	B707	19177
PP-VLO	B707	19350
PP-VLP	B707	18940
PP-VLQ	B727	19595
PP-VLR	B727	19596
PP-VLS	**B727**	**19508**
PP-VLT	B727	19250
PP-VLU	B707	19235
PP-VLV	B727	19009
PP-VLW	B727	19507
PP-VMA	DC-10	46944
PP-VMB	DC-10	46945
(PP-VMC)	DC-10	46941
PP-VMD	DC-10	46916
PP-VME	B737	21000
PP-VMF	B737	21001
PP-VMG	B737	21002
PP-VMH	B737	21003
PP-VMI	B737	21004
PP-VMJ	B737	21005
PP-VMK	B737	21006
PP-VML	B737	21007
PP-VMM	**B737**	**21008**
PP-VMN	B737	21009
PP-VMO	DC-10	46540
PP-VMP	DC-10	46541
PP-VMQ	DC-10	46941
PP-VMR	DC-10	47817
PP-VMS	DC-10	47818
PP-VMT	**DC-10**	**47841**
PP-VMU	**DC-10**	**47842**
PP-VMV	DC-10	47843
PP-VMW	DC-10	47844
PP-VMX	DC-10	47845
PP-VMY	DC-10	48282
PP-VMZ	DC-10	46999
PP-VNA	B747	22105
PP-VNB	B747	22106
PP-VNC	B747	22107
PP-VND	A300	143
PP-VNE	A300	194
PP-VNF	B737	22504
PP-VNG	B737	22505
PP-VNH	B747	23394
PP-VNI	B747	23395
PP-VNL	B767	23057
PP-VNM	B767	23058
PP-VNN	B767	23803
PP-VNO	B767	23801
PP-VNP	B767	23802
PP-VNQ	B767	23804
PP-VNR	B767	23805
PP-VNS	B767	23806
PP-VNT	**B737**	**23828**
PP-VNU	B737	23797
PP-VNV	B737	23798
PP-VNW	B747	20238
PP-VNX	**B737**	**23829**
PP-VNY	**B737**	**24864**
PP-VNZ	**B737**	**24869**
PP-VOA	B747	24106
PP-VOB	B747	24107
PP-VOC	B747	24108
PP-VOD	B737	24275
PP-VOE	B737	24276
PP-VOF	B737	24277
PP-VOG	B737	24278
PP-VOH	B737	24279
PP-VOI	**B767**	**24752**
PP-VOJ	**B767**	**24753**
PP-VOK	B767	24843
PP-VOL	B767	24844
PP-VOM	B737	23922
PP-VON	**B737**	**24935**
PP-VOO	**B737**	**24936**
PP-VOP	MD11	48434
PP-VOQ	MD11	48435
PP-VOR	B737	24093
PP-VOS	**B737**	**25048**
PP-VOT	B737	25049
PP-VOU	B737	25050
PP-VOV	B737	25051
PP-VOW	B737	24961
PP-VOX	B737	24962
PP-VOY	**B737**	**25210**
PP-VOZ	**B737**	**25239**
PP-VPA	B737	26852
(PP-VPB)	B737	26853
PP-VPB	**B737**	**26856**
(PP-VPC)	B737	26854
PP-VPC	**B737**	**26857**
PP-VPD	B737	21518
PP-VPD	B737	26855
PP-VPE	B737	21130
(PP-VPE)	B737	26856
PP-VPF	B737	24834
(PP-VPF)	B737	26857
PP-VPG	B747	24956
PP-VPH	B747	24957
PP-VPI	B747	24896
PP-VPJ	MD11	48404
PP-VPK	MD11	48405
PP-VPL	MD11	48406
PP-VPM	MD11	48439
PP-VPN	MD11	48499
PP-VPO	MD11	48500
PP-VPP	MD11	48501
PP-VPQ	B737	28664
PP-VPR	B737	28761
PP-VPS	B737	28671
PP-VPT	B737	28566
PP-VPU	B737	28567
(PP-VPU)	B737	28672
PP-VPV	**B767**	**24086**
PP-VPW	B767	24087
PP-VPX	B737	28870
PP-VPY	**B737**	**28871**
PP-VPZ	B737	29245
PP-VQA	737NG	28580
PP-VQD	737NG	28582
PP-VQC	737NG	28583
PP-VQD	737NG	28584
PP-VQE	737NG	28585
PP-VQF	MD11	48502
PP-VQG	**MD11**	**48503**
PP-VQH	MD11	48504
PP-VQI	MD11	48753
PP-VQJ	MD11	48755
PP-VQK	MD11	48758
PP-VQL	MD11	48413
PP-VQM	MD11	48414
PP-VQN	**B737**	**24098**
PP-VQO	**B737**	**24377**
PP-VQP	B737	28564
PP-VQQ	B737	24467
PP-VQR	B737	24511
PP-VQS	B737	24513
PP-VQT	B737	24692
PP-VQU	**B727**	**20880**
PP-VQV	**B727**	**22166**
PP-VQW	B737	23787
PP-VQX	MD11	48769
PP-VQY	**DC-10**	**46949**
PP-VQZ	B737	27284
PP-VRA	B777	28689
PP-VRB	B777	28692
PP-VRC	B777	27108
PP-VRD	B777	27109
PP-VRE	B777	30213
PP-VRF	B777	30214
PP-VRI	B777	26918
PP-VRJ	B777	26925
PP-VSA	737NG	30571
PP-VSB	737NG	30477
PP-VTA	**B737**	**23797**
PP-VTB	**B737**	**23798**
PP-VTC	**B767**	**25411**
PP-VTE	**B767**	**26208**
PP-VTF	MD11	48444
PP-VTG	MD11	48446
PP-VTH	MD11	48457
PP-VTI	MD11	48456
PP-VTJ	MD11	48455
PP-VTK	MD11	48540
PP-VTL	B737	25116
PP-VTM	B737	23977
PP-VTN	B737	25764
PP-VTO	B737	25765
PP-VTP	MD11	48539
PP-VTQ	B757	26247
PP-VTR	B757	26248
PP-VTS	B757	26249
PP-VTT	B757	26250
PP-VTU	MD11	48541
(PP-VTV)	MD11	48453
PP-VTW	**B737**	**24366**
(PP-V)	B767	30341
(PP-V)	B767	30342
PP-XGM	E145	145462
PP-XHL	E145	145374
PP-XIT	E145	145729
PP-XJA	E170	17000005
PP-XJB	**E170**	**17000003**
PP-XJC	E170	17000002
PP-XJD	**E170**	**17000014**
PP-XJE	**E170**	**17000001**
PP-XJF	**E170**	**17000004**
PP-XJG	E170	17000017
PP-XJI	E170	17000007
PP-XJM	E145	145723
PP-XJN	E145	145190
PP-XJO	**E145**	**145363**
PP-XJR	E145	145757
PP-XJS	E170	17000006
PP-XJU	E145	145671
PP-XJV	E145	145694
PP-XKN	E145	145003
PP-XMA	**E190**	**19000001**
PP-XMB	E145	145770
PP-XMB	**E190**	**19000002**
PP-XMC	E190	19000004
PP-XMD	E190	19000006
PP-XMI	**E190**	**19000003**
PP-XMJ	**E190**	**19000005**
PP-XOL	**E190**	**19000109**
PP-XRJ	E170	17000001
PP-XRS	E145	145140
PP-XRT	E145	145154
PP-XRU	E145	145257
PP-XSA	E145	145104
PP-XSB	E145	145122
PP-XSC	E145	145263
PP-XSE	E145	145392
PP-XSW	E145	145412
PR-ABA	DC-8	45980
PR-ABB	**B767**	**29881**
PR-ABD	**B767**	**34245**
PR-AIB	**B727**	**21363**
PR-BBS	**737NG**	**32575**
PR-BME	DC-10	47819
PR-BRA	B737	23830
PR-BRB	**B737**	**24210**
PR-BRC	**B737**	**25262**
PR-BRD	**B737**	**24376**
PR-BRE	B737	24213
PR-BRF	**B737**	**25051**
PR-BRG	**B737**	**25050**
PR-BRH	**B737**	**24511**
PR-BRI	B737	24494
(PR-BRJ)	B737	24212
PR-BRK	**B737**	**23787**
PR-BRV	**B767**	**22569**
PR-BRW	**B737**	**25403**
PR-BRY	**B737**	**23830**
(PR-CMA)	B737	20138

Reg	Type	S/N	Reg	Type	S/N	Reg	Type	S/N	Reg	Type	S/N
(PR-DMA)	B737	20218	PR-GTN	737NG	34267	PR-MHK	A320	3058	PT-LEQ	146	E1011
PR-DPF	E145	145127	PR-GTO	737NG	34964	PR-MHL	A320	3037	PT-MCN	F.100	11452
PR-GGA	737NG	35063	PR-GTP	737NG	34965	PR-MHM	A320	3211	PT-MCO	F.100	11471
PR-GGB	737NG	35064	PR-GTQ	737NG	36146	PR-MHN	A320	3240	PT-MDF	DC-8	46132
PR-GGC	737NG	35065	PR-GTR	737NG	34966	PR-MHP	A320	3266	PT-MDG	B727	19319
PR-GGD	737NG	34275	PR-GTT	737NG	34268	PR-MHQ	A320	3284	PT-MNC	B737	25165
PR-GIA	737NG	28653	PR-GTU	737NG	34269	PR-MHR	A320	3313	PT-MND	B737	24786
PR-GIB	737NG	32348	PR-GTV	737NG	34270	PR-MHS	A320	3325	PT-MNE	B737	24787
PR-GIC	737NG	32576	PR-GTW	737NG	34272	PR-MTC	DC-10	46540	PT-MNH	B737	26067
PR-GID	737NG	29904	PR-GTX	737NG	34271	PR-MTD	B727	21248	PT-MNI	B737	25425
PR-GIE	737NG	33027	PR-GTY	737NG	34273	PR-MTG	B737	22255	PT-MNJ	B737	25057
PR-GIF	737NG	29076	PR-GTZ	737NG	34274	PR-MTH	B737	23102	PT-MNK	B737	27457
PR-GIG	737NG	29077	PR-LEG	E145	145495	PR-NAC	B737	23405	PT-MNL	B737	27458
PR-GIH	737NG	32743	PR-LGB	B727	21341	PR-NAD	B737	21000	PT-MQA	F.100	11296
PR-GII	737NG	28011	PR-LGC	B727	21342	PR-NAE	B737	21009	PT-MQB	F.100	11350
PR-GIJ	737NG	28012	PR-LGD	MD11	48408	PR-NCT	B737	23404	PT-MQC	F.100	11371
PR-GIK	737NG	28224	PR-LGE	MD11	48410	PR-OAD	F.100	11370	PT-MQD	F.100	11383
PR-GIL	737NG	30635	PR-LGF	B757	24235	(PR-OAE)	F.100	11376	PT-MQE	F.100	11389
PR-GIM	737NG	30238	PR-LGG	B757	23767	PR-OAE	F.100	11426	PT-MQF	F.100	11401
PR-GIN	737NG	30242	PR-LGH	B757	22211	(PR-OAF)	F.100	11377	PT-MQG	F.100	11527
PR-GIO	737NG	30477	PR-LGI	B757	22611	PR-OAF	F.100	11415	PT-MQH	F.100	11512
PR-GIP	737NG	30571	PR-LGJ	B757	22210	PR-OAG	F.100	11412	PT-MQI	F.100	11517
PR-GIQ	737NG	28616	PR-LGK	B757	22689	PR-OAH	F.100	11413	PT-MQJ	F.100	11347
PR-GIR	737NG	28213	PR-LGO	DC-10	46921	PR-OAI	F.100	11417	PT-MQK	F.100	11336
PR-GLA	B737	23527	(PR-LGP)	B727	20879	PR-OAJ	F.100	11418	PT-MQL	F.100	11394
(PR-GLB)	B737	23525	(PR-LGQ)	B727	21971	PR-OAK	F.100	11425	PT-MQM	F.100	11301
PR-GLB	B737	24452	PR-LSW	B737	20219	PR-OAL	F.100	11435	PT-MQN	F.100	11409
(PR-GLC)	B737	23526	PR-MAA	A320	1595	PR-OAM	F.100	11436	PT-MQO	F.100	11423
PR-GLC	B737	24453	PR-MAB	A320	1663	PR-OAQ	F.100	11467	PT-MQP	F.100	11430
PR-GLD	B737	24248	PR-MAC	A320	1672	PR-OAT	F.100	11411	PT-MQQ	F.100	11265
PR-GLE	B737	24249	PR-MAD	A320	1771	PR-OAU	F.100	11427	PT-MQR	F.100	11421
PR-GLF	B737	24666	PR-MAE	A320	1804	PR-OAV	F.100	11419	PT-MQS	F.100	11431
PR-GLG	B737	24455	PR-MAF	A320	0249	PR-ONA	B767	25280	PT-MQT	F.100	11429
PR-GLH	B737	24532	PR-MAG	A320	1832	PR-ORE	E145	145625	PT-MQU	F.100	11264
PR-GLI	B737	23955	PR-MAH	A319	1608	PR-PLH	B727	22434	PT-MQV	F.100	11326
PR-GLJ	B737	23956	PR-MAI	A319	1703	"PR-PRC"	B737	25262	PT-MQW	F.100	11332
PR-GLK	B737	24668	PR-MAJ	A320	1818	PR-RIO	E145	145717	PT-MRA	F.100	11284
PR-GLM	B737	24670	PR-MAK	A320	1825	PR-RLA	B737	21009	PT-MRB	F.100	11285
PR-GLN	B737	24379	PR-MAL	A319	1801	(PR-RLB)	B737	21008	PT-MRC	F.100	11320
PR-GLO	B737	23952	PR-MAM	A319	1826	PR-RLB	B737	23766	PT-MRD	F.100	11322
PR-GLQ	B737	24247	PR-MAN	A319	1831	PR-RLC	B737	21000	PT-MRE	F.100	11348
PR-GMA	B727	20659	PR-MAO	A319	1837	PR-SAA	737NG	30277	PT-MRF	F.100	11351
(PR-GO.)	737NG	32734	PR-MAP	A320	1857	(PR-SAB)	737NG	30135	PT-MRG	F.100	11304
PR-GOA	737NG	28005	PR-MAQ	A319	1855	(PR-SAC)	737NG	32734	PT-MRH	F.100	11305
PR-GOB	737NG	28099	PR-MAR	A320	1888	(PR-SAD)	737NG	33005	PT-MRI	F.100	11442
PR-GOC	737NG	28101	PR-MAS	A320	2372	PR-SAE	737NG	29078	PT-MRJ	F.100	11451
PR-GOD	737NG	28105	(PR-MAT)	A320	2393	PR-SAF	737NG	30635	PT-MRK	F.100	11440
PR-GOE	737NG	28106	(PR-MAV)	A319	1952	PR-SAG	737NG	28224	PT-MRL	F.100	11441
PR-GOF	737NG	30273	PR-MAV	A320	2393	PR-SAH	737NG	30211	PT-MRM	F.100	11422
PR-GOG	737NG	30275	PR-MAW	A320	2417	PR-SKC	DC-8	46143	PT-MRN	F.100	11443
PR-GOH	737NG	32440	PR-MAX	A320	2602	PR-SKI	DC-8	46154	PT-MRO	F.100	11470
PR-GOI	737NG	32574	PR-MAY	A320	2661	PR-SKM	DC-8	46137	PT-MRP	F.100	11472
PR-GOJ	737NG	32359	PR-MAZ	A320	2513	(PR-SKY)	DC-8	45635	PT-MRQ	F.100	11473
PR-GOK	737NG	32360	PR-MBA	A320	2734	PR-TTR	B727	22007	PT-MRR	F.100	11461
PR-GOL	737NG	28004	PR-MBB	A320	2737	PR-TTO	B727	21200	PT-MRS	F.100	11462
PR GOM	737NG	28613	PR-MBC	A320	2783	PR-VAA	B767	27909	PT-MRT	F.100	11505
PR-GON	737NG	30051	PR-MBD	A320	2838	PR-VAB	B767	24477	PT-MRU	F.100	11511
PR-GOO	737NG	30135	PR-MBE	A320	2859	PR-VAB	B767	27477	PT-MRV	F.100	11516
PR-GOP	737NG	30621	PR-MBF	A320	2896	PR-VAC	B767	27048	PT-MRW	F.100	11518
PR-GOQ	737NG	33417	PR-MBG	A320	1459	PR-VAD	B767	26204	PT-MRX	F.100	11341
PR-GOR	737NG	33380	PR-MBH	A320	2904	PR-VAE	B767	27619	(PT-MRX)	F.100	11508
PR-GOT	737NG	30625	PR-MBI	A319	1575	PR-VAF	B767	25132	PT-MRY	F.100	11343
PR-GOU	737NG	28219	PR-MBJ	A320	2445	PR-VAH	B767	25208	(PT-MRY)	F.100	11510
PR-GOV	737NG	28580	PR-MBK	A320	0789	PR-VAI	B767	25221	PT-MRZ	F.100	11290
PR-GOW	737NG	28584	PR-MBL	A320	0916	PR-VAJ	B767	24999	PT-MSD	A330	334
PR-GOX	737NG	28088	PR-MBM	A320	1339	PR-VAK	B767	24947	(PT-MSG)	A330	501
PR-GOY	737NG	28089	PR-MBN	A319	3032	PR-VBA	737NG	29916	PT-MSH	MD11	48755
PR-GOZ	737NG	28648	PR-MBO	A320	3156	PR-VBB	737NG	29917	PT-MSI	MD11	48758
PR-GPT	DC-8	45970	PR-MBP	A320	1215	PR-VBC	737NG	29918	PT-MSJ	MD11	48769
PR-GTA	737NG	34474	PR-MGA	B737	20282	PR-VBD	737NG	29919	PT-MST	B707	18711
PR-GTB	737NG	34475	PR-MH.	A320	3278	PR-VBE	737NG	29920	PT-MTA	B737	20220
PR-GTC	737NG	34277	PR-MHA	A320	2924	PT-	E145	14500921	PT-MTB	B737	20254
PR-GTD	737NG	34653	PR-MHB	A320	1692	PT-	E145	14500928	PT-MTC	B727	20409
PR-GTE	737NG	34278	PR-MHC	A320	1717	PT-	E145	14500932	PT-MTC	B737	20282
PR-GTF	737NG	34279	PR-MHD	A320	1775	PT-	E145	14500949	PT-MTE	B707	20017
PR-GTG	737NG	34654	PR-MHE	A320	3111	PT-	E145	14500958	PT-MTF	B737	21007
PR-GTH	737NG	34655	(PR-MHF)	A320	2740	PT-	E170	17000191	(PT-MTG)	B737	21017
PR-GTI	737NG	34280	PR-MHF	A320	3180	PT-AIY	DC-8	46070	PT-MTQ	B727	22053
PR-GTJ	737NG	34656	PR-MHG	A320	3002	PT-BLR	B727	21661	PT-MTR	B707	20084
PR-GTK	737NG	34281	PR-MHH	A320	2740	"PT-DGX"	DC-8	45953	PT-MTT	B727	22167
PR-GTL	737NG	34962	PR-MHI	A320	3035	PT-DUW	SE210	86	PT-MVA	A330	232
PR-GTM	737NG	34963	PR-MHJ	A320	3047	PT-LEP	146	E1010	PT-MVB	A330	238

Reg	Type	Serial
PT-MVC	**A330**	**247**
PT-MVD	**A330**	**259**
PT-MVE	**A330**	**361**
PT-MVF	**A330**	**466**
PT-MVG	**A330**	**472**
PT-MVH	**A330**	**477**
PT-MVK	**A330**	**486**
PT-MVL	**A330**	**700**
PT-MVM	**A330**	**869**
PT-MVN	**A330**	**876**
PT-MXA	**A321**	**3222**
PT-MXB	**A321**	**3229**
(PT-MYA)	DC-8	46137
(PT-MYB)	DC-8	46143
PT-MZA	**A319**	**0976**
PT-MZB	**A319**	**1010**
PT-MZC	**A319**	**1092**
PT-MZD	**A319**	**1096**
PT-MZE	**A319**	**1103**
PT-MZF	**A319**	**1139**
PT-MZG	**A320**	**1143**
PT-MZH	**A320**	**1158**
PT-MZI	**A320**	**1246**
PT-MZJ	**A320**	**1251**
PT-MZK	**A320**	**1368**
PT-MZL	**A320**	**1376**
PT-MZM	**A320**	**0453**
PT-MZN	**A320**	**0440**
PT-MZO	**A320**	**0250**
PT-MZP	**A320**	**0243**
PT-MZQ	**A320**	**0335**
PT-MZR	**A320**	**0334**
PT-MZS	**A320**	**0251**
PT-MZT	**A320**	**1486**
PT-MZU	**A320**	**1518**
PT-MZV	**A320**	**0758**
PT-MZW	**A320**	**1580**
PT-MZX	**A320**	**1613**
PT-MZY	**A320**	**1628**
PT-MZZ	**A320**	**1593**
PT-S	**E145**	**14500992**
PT-S	**E145**	**14501005**
PT-S	**E145**	**14501019**
PT-S	E145	145079
PT-S	E145	145080
PT-S	E145	145081
PT-S	E145	145082
PT-S	E145	145004
PT-S	E145	145085
PT-S	E145	145086
PT-S	E145	145087
PT-S	E145	145088
PT-S	E145	145091
PT-S	E145	145092
PT-S	E145	145101
PT-S	E145	145102
PT-S	E145	145103
PT-S	E145	145105
PT-S	E145	145106
PT-S	E145	145107
PT-S	E145	145108
PT-S	E145	145109
PT-S	E145	145110
PT-S	E145	145111
PT-S	E145	145158
PT-S	E145	145159
PT-S	E145	145160
PT-S	E145	145161
PT-S	E145	145163
PT-S	E145	145167
PT-S	E145	145168
PT-S	E145	145169
PT-S	E145	145170
PT-S	E145	145172
PT-S	E145	145200
PT-SA	E145	145077
PT-SA	E145	145078
PT-SAB	E145	145412
PT-SAB	E170	17000100
PT-SAC	E145	145462
PT-SAC	E170	17000101
PT-SAD	E145	145484
PT-SAE	E145	145061
PT-SAF	E145	145062
PT-SAF	E145	145505
PT-SAG	E145	145063
PT-SAG	E145	145516
PT-SAH	E145	145064
PT-SAH	E145	145528
PT-SAH	E170	17000102
PT-SAI	E145	145065
PT-SAI	E145	145540
PT-SAI	E170	17000103
PT-SAJ	E145	145066
PT-SAJ	E145	145549
PT-SAK	E145	145067
PT-SAK	E145	145555
PT-SAK	E170	17000104
PT-SAM	E145	145068
PT-SAM	E170	17000105
PT-SAN	E145	145069
PT-SAO	E145	145070
PT-SAO	E170	17000106
PT-SAP	E145	145071
PT-SAP	E145	145637
PT-SAP	E170	17000107
PT-SAQ	E145	145072
PT-SAQ	E145	145642
PT-SAQ	E170	17000108
PT-SAR	E145	145073
PT-SAR	E145	145644
PT-SAR	E170	17000109
PT-SAS	E145	145074
PT-SAS	E145	145678
PT-SAS	E170	17000110
PT-SAT	E145	145075
PT-SAT	E145	145686
PT-SAT	E170	17000111
PT-SAU	E145	145076
PT-SAV	B727	19497
PT-SAW	B727	19393
PT-SAX	E145	145706
PT-SAX	E170	17000112
PT-SAY	E145	145711
PT-SAY	E170	17000113
PT-SAZ	E145	145717
PT-SAZ	E170	17000114
PT-SBB	E145	145565
PT-SBC	E145	145566
PT-SBD	E145	145567
PT-SBE	E145	145568
PT-SBF	E145	145569
PT-SBG	E145	145570
PT-SBH	E145	145571
PT-SBI	E145	145572
PT-SBJ	E145	145573
PT-SBK	E145	145574
PT-SBL	E145	145575
PT-SBM	E145	145576
PT-SBN	E145	145577
PT-SBO	E145	145578
PT-SBP	E145	145093
PT-SBP	E145	145579
PT-SBQ	E145	145094
PT-SBR	E145	145095
PT-SBR	E145	145580
PT-SBS	E145	145096
PT-SBS	E145	145581
PT-SBT	E145	145097
PT-SBT	E145	145582
PT-SBU	E145	145098
PT-SBU	E145	145583
PT-SBV	E145	145099
PT-SBV	E145	145584
PT-SBW	E145	145100
PT-SBW	E145	145585
PT-SBX	E145	145587
PT-SBY	E145	145588
PT-SBZ	E145	145589
PT-SCA	E145	14500931
PT-SCA	E145	145592
PT-SCB	E145	14500933
PT-SCC	E145	14500934
PT-SCC	E145	145593
PT-SCD	E145	145594
PT-SCE	E145	145595
PT-SCF	E145	145596
PT-SCG	E145	14500935
PT-SCG	E145	145598
PT-SCH	E145	14500936
PT-SCH	E145	145597
PT-SCI	E145	14500937
PT-SCI	E145	145599
PT-SCJ	E145	14500938
PT-SCJ	E145	145600
PT-SCK	E145	14500939
PT-SCK	E145	145601
PT-SCL	E145	14500940
PT-SCL	E145	145602
PT-SCM	E145	14500941
PT-SCM	E145	145603
PT-SCN	E145	14500942
PT-SCN	E145	145604
PT-SCO	E145	14500943
PT-SCO	E145	145112
PT-SCO	E145	145605
PT-SCP	E145	14500944
PT-SCP	E145	145113
PT-SCP	E145	145606
PT-SCQ	E145	14500945
PT-SCQ	E145	145607
PT-SCR	**E145**	**14500946**
PT-SCR	E145	145115
PT-SCR	E145	145608
PT-SCS	E145	14500947
PT-SCS	E145	145116
PT-SCS	E145	145609
PT-SCT	E145	14500948
PT-SCT	E145	145117
PT-SCT	E145	145610
PT-SCU	E145	145118
PT-SCV	E145	145119
PT-SCV	E145	145611
PT-SCW	E145	145120
PT-SCW	E145	145612
PT-SCX	E145	14500950
PT-SCX	E145	145121
PT-SCX	E145	145613
PT-SCZ	E145	14500951
PT-SCZ	E145	145123
PT-SCZ	E145	145614
PT-SDA	E145	145124
PT-SDB	E145	145125
PT-SDC	E170	17000115
PT-SDD	E145	145126
PT-SDD	E145	145615
PT-SDD	E170	17000116
PT-SDE	E145	145127
PT-SDE	E145	145616
PT-SDE	E170	17000117
PT-SDF	E145	145128
PT-SDF	E145	145617
PT-SDF	E170	17000118
PT-SDG	E145	145129
PT-SDG	E145	145618
PT-SDG	E170	17000119
PT-SDH	E145	145130
PT-SDH	E145	145619
PT-SDI	E145	145131
PT-SDI	E145	145620
PT-SDI	E170	17000120
PT-SDJ	E145	145132
PT-SDJ	E145	145621
PT-SDJ	E170	17000121
PT-SDK	E145	145133
PT-SDK	E145	145622
PT-SDK	E170	17000122
PT-SDL	E145	145134
PT-SDL	E145	145623
PT-SDM	E145	145135
PT-SDM	E145	145624
PT-SDM	E170	17000123
PT-SDN	E145	145136
PT-SDN	E145	145625
PT-SDN	E170	17000124
PT-SDO	E145	145137
PT-SDO	E145	145626
PT-SDO	E170	17000125
PT-SDP	E145	145138
PT-SDP	E145	145627
PT-SDP	E170	17000126
PT-SDQ	E145	145139
PT-SDQ	E145	145628
PT-SDQ	E170	17000127
PT-SDR	E145	145141
PT-SDR	E145	145629
PT-SDR	E170	17000128
PT-SDS	E145	145142
PT-SDS	E145	145630
PT-SDS	E170	17000129
PT-SDT	E145	145143
PT-SDT	E145	145631
PT-SDT	E170	17000130
PT-SDU	E145	145144
PT-SDU	E145	145632
PT-SDU	E170	17000131
PT-SDV	E145	145145
PT-SDV	E145	145633
PT-SDV	E170	17000132
PT-SDW	E145	145146
PT-SDW	E145	145634
PT-SDW	E170	17000133
PT-SDX	E145	145147
PT-SDX	E145	145635
PT-SDX	E170	17000134
PT-SDY	E145	145148
PT-SDY	E145	145636
PT-SDY	E170	17000135
PT-SDZ	E145	145149
PT-SDZ	E145	145638
PT-SDZ	E170	17000136
PT-SEB	E145	145150
PT-SEB	E145	145639
PT-SEB	E170	17000137
PT-SEC	E145	145151
PT-SEC	E145	145640
PT-SEC	E170	17000138
PT-SED	E145	145152
PT-SED	E145	145641
PT-SED	E170	17000139
PT-SEE	E145	145153
PT-SEE	E145	145643
PT-SEE	E170	17000140
PT-SEF	E145	145645
PT-SEF	E170	17000141
PT-SEG	E145	145646
PT-SEG	E170	17000142
PT-SEH	E145	145647
PT-SEH	E170	17000143
PT-SEI	E145	145648
PT-SEI	E170	17000144
PT-SEJ	E145	145155
PT-SEJ	E145	145649
PT-SEJ	E170	17000145
PT-SEK	E145	145157
PT-SEK	E145	145650
PT-SEK	E170	17000146
PT-SEL	E145	145651
PT-SEL	E170	17000147
PT-SEM	E145	145652
PT-SEM	E170	17000148
PT-SEN	E145	145653
PT-SEN	E170	17000149
PT-SEO	E145	145654
PT-SEO	E170	17000150
PT-SEP	E145	145655
PT-SEP	E170	17000151
PT-SEQ	E145	145656
PT-SEQ	E170	17000152
PT-SER	E145	145657
PT-SER	E170	17000153
PT-SES	E145	145658
PT-SES	E170	17000155
PT-SET	E145	145659
PT-SET	E170	17000154
PT-SEU	E145	145210
PT-SEU	E145	145660

Reg.	Type	Serial	Reg.	Type	Serial	Reg.	Type	Serial	Reg.	Type	Serial
PT-SEU	E170	17000156	PT-SGA	E145	145695	PT-SHG	E145	145730	PT-SIV	E145	14500891
PT-SEV	E145	145171	PT-SGA	E190	19000026	PT-SHH	E145	14500975	PT-SIV	E145	145262
PT-SEV	E145	145661	PT-SGB	E145	145179	PT-SHH	E145	145222	PT-SIW	E145	14500903
PT-SEV	E170	17000157	PT-SGB	E145	145696	PT-SHI	E145	145731	PT-SIW	E145	145264
PT-SEW	E145	145662	PT-SGB	E190	19000027	PT-SHI	E145	14500976	PT-SIX	E145	14500901
PT-SEW	E170	17000158	PT-SGC	E145	145180	PT-SHI	E145	145223	PT-SIX	E145	145265
PT-SEX	E145	145175	PT-SGC	E145	145697	PT-SHI	E145	145732	PT-SIY	E145	14500910
PT-SEX	E145	145663	PT-SGC	E190	19000028	PT-SHJ	E145	145225	PT-SIY	E145	145266
PT-SEX	E170	17000159	PT-SGD	E145	145181	PT-SHJ	E145	145733	PT-SIZ	E145	14500913
PT-SEY	E145	145177	PT-SGD	E145	145698	PT-SHK	E145	14500977	PT-SIZ	E145	145267
PT-SEY	E145	145664	PT-SGD	E190	19000029	PT-SHK	E145	145734	PT-SJA	E145	145741
(PT-SEY)	E170	17000017	PT-SGE	E145	145182	PT-SHL	E145	145226	PT-SJA	E190	19000062
PT-SEZ	E145	145178	PT-SGE	E145	145700	PT-SHL	E145	145735	PT-SJB	E145	145742
PT-SEZ	E145	145665	PT-SGE	E190	19000030	PT-SHM	E145	14500978	PT-SJB	E190	19000063
PT-SFA	E145	14500953	PT-SGF	E145	145183	PT-SHM	E145	145227	PT-SJC	E145	145743
PT-SFA	E145	145666	PT-SGF	E145	145701	PT-SHM	E145	145736	PT-SJC	E190	19000064
PT-SFB	E145	14500952	PT-SGF	E190	19000031	PT-SHQ	E145	14500979	PT-SJD	E145	145744
PT-SFB	E145	145667	PT-SGG	E145	145185	PT-SHQ	E145	145228	PT-SJD	E190	19000065
PT-SFC	E145	14500954	PT-SGG	E145	145702	PT-SHQ	E145	145737	PT-SJE	E145	145745
PT-SFC	E145	145156	PT-SGG	E190	19000032	PT-SHS	E145	14500980	PT-SJE	E190	19000066
PT-SFC	E145	145668	PT-SGH	E145	145187	PT-SHS	E145	145229	PT-SJF	E145	145243
PT-SFD	E145	14500955	PT-SGH	E145	145703	PT-SHS	E145	145738	PT-SJF	E145	145746
PT-SFD	E145	145162	PT-SGH	E190	19000033	PT-SHT	E145	14500981	PT-SJG	E145	145247
PT-SFD	E145	145669	PT-SGI	E145	145704	**PT-SHT**	**E145**	**145230**	PT-SJG	E145	145747
PT-SFE	E145	14500956	PT-SGI	E190	19000034	PT-SHT	E145	145739	PT-SJG	E190	19000067
PT-SFE	E145	145164	PT-SGJ	E145	145191	**PT-SHV**	**E145**	**14500982**	PT-SJH	E145	145249
PT-SFE	E145	145670	PT-SGJ	E145	145705	PT-SHV	E145	145231	PT-SJH	E145	145748
PT-SFF	E145	14500957	PT-SGJ	E190	19000035	PT-SHV	E145	145740	PT-SJH	E190	19000068
PT-SFF	E145	145166	PT-SGK	E145	145193	PT-SHW	E145	145232	PT-SJI	E145	145251
PT-SFF	E145	145672	PT-SGK	E145	145707	PT-SHX	E145	145233	PT-SJI	E145	145749
PT-SFG	E145	14500959	PT-SGK	E190	19000036	PT-SHZ	E145	145234	PT-SJI	E190	19000069
PT-SFG	E145	145173	PT-SGL	E145	145196	PT-SIA	E145	145235	PT-SJJ	E145	145252
PT-SFG	E145	145673	PT-SGL	E145	145708	PT-SIA	E145	145699	PT-SJJ	E145	145750
PT-SFH	E145	14500960	PT-SGL	E190	19000037	PT-SIA	E190	19000051	PT-SJJ	E190	19000070
PT-SFH	E145	145174	PT-SGN	E145	145197	PT-SIB	E145	145236	PT-SJK	E145	145268
PT-SFH	E145	145674	PT-SGN	E145	145709	PT-SIB	E145	145770	PT-SJK	E145	145751
PT-SFI	E145	14500961	PT-SGN	E190	19000038	PT-SIB	E190	19000052	PT-SJK	E190	19000071
PT-SFI	E145	145675	PT-SGO	E145	145710	PT-SIC	E145	145237	PT-SJL	E145	145269
PT-SFJ	E145	14500962	PT-SGO	E190	19000039	PT-SIC	E145	145775	PT-SJL	E145	145752
PT-SFJ	E145	145184	PT-SGP	E145	145199	PT-SIC	E190	19000053	PT-SJL	E190	19000072
PT-SFJ	E145	145676	PT-SGP	E145	145712	PT-SID	E145	145238	PT-SJM	E145	145270
PT-SFK	E145	14500963	PT-SGP	E190	19000040	PT-SID	E145	145780	PT-SJM	E145	145753
PT-SFK	E145	145186	PT-SGQ	E145	145201	PT-SID	E190	19000054	PT-SJM	E190	19000073
PT-SFK	E145	145677	PT-SGQ	E145	145713	PT-SIE	E145	145239	PT-SJN	E145	145271
PT-SFL	E145	14500964	PT-SGQ	E190	19000041	PT-SIE	E145	145789	PT-SJN	E145	145754
PT-SFL	E145	145188	PT-SGR	E145	145714	PT-SIE	E190	19000055	PT-SJN	E190	19000074
PT-SFL	E145	145679	PT-SGR	E190	19000042	PT-SIF	E145	145240	PT-SJO	E145	145272
PT-SFM	E145	145189	PT-SGS	E145	145715	PT-SIF	E145	145796	PT-SJO	E145	145760
PT-SFM	E145	145680	PT-SGS	E190	19000043	PT-SIF	E190	19000056	PT-SJP	E145	145273
PT-SFN	E145	14500965	PT-SGT	E145	145716	PT-SIG	E145	14500802	PT-SJP	E145	145756
PT-SFN	E145	145192	PT-SGT	E190	19000044	PT-SIG	E145	145241	PT-SJP	E190	19000075
PT-SFN	E145	145681	PT-SGU	E145	145203	PT-SIH	E145	145242	PT-SJQ	E145	145274
PT-SFO	E145	145194	PT-SGU	E145	145718	PT-SII	E145	14500809	PT-SJQ	E145	145758
PT-SFO	E145	145682	PT-SGU	E190	19000045	PT-SII	E145	145244	PT-SJR	E145	145275
PT-SFP	E145	14500966	PT-SGV	E145	145719	PT-SII	E190	19000057	PT-SJR	E145	145759
PT-SFP	E145	145195	PT-SGV	E190	19000046	PT-SIJ	E145	145245	PT-SJR	E190	19000076
PT-SFP	E145	145683	PT-SGW	E145	145204	PT-SIK	E145	14500825	PT-SJS	E145	145276
PT-SFQ	E145	14500967	PT-SGW	E145	145720	PT-SIK	E145	145246	PT-SJS	E145	145761
PT-SFQ	E145	145198	PT-SGW	E190	19000047	PT-SIL	E145	14500832	PT-SJS	E190	19000077
PT-SFQ	E145	145684	PT-SGX	E145	145207	PT-SIL	E145	145248	PT-SJT	E145	145277
PT-SFR	E145	145205	PT-SGX	E145	145721	PT-SIL	E190	19000058	PT-SJT	E145	145762
PT-SFR	E145	145685	PT-SGX	E190	19000048	PT-SIM	E145	14500818	PT-SJU	E145	145278
PT-SFT	E145	14500968	PT-SGY	E145	145208	PT-SIM	E145	145250	PT-SJU	E145	145763
PT-SFT	E145	145202	PT-SGY	E145	145722	PT-SIM	E190	19000059	PT-SJU	E190	19000078
PT-SFT	E145	145687	PT-SGY	E190	19000049	PT-SIN	E145	14500841	PT-SJV	E145	145279
PT-SFU	E145	145688	PT-SGZ	E145	145723	PT-SIN	E145	145253	PT-SJV	E145	145764
PT-SFV	E145	145211	PT-SGZ	E190	19000050	PT-SIN	E190	19000060	PT-SJV	E190	19000079
PT-SFV	E145	145689	PT-SHA	E145	14500973	PT-SIO	E145	14500851	PT-SJW	E145	145280
PT-SFW	E145	14500969	PT-SHA	E145	145213	PT-SIO	E145	145254	PT-SJW	E145	145765
PT-SFW	E145	145215	PT-SHA	E145	145724	PT-SIO	E190	19000061	PT-SJW	E190	19000080
PT-SFW	E145	145690	PT-SHB	E145	145214	PT-SIP	E145	14500854	PT-SJX	E145	145281
PT-SFX	E145	14500970	PT-SHB	E145	145725	PT-SIP	E145	145255	PT-SJX	E145	145766
PT-SFX	E145	145209	PT-SHC	E145	145216	PT-SIQ	E145	14500863	PT-SJX	E190	19000081
PT-SFX	E145	145691	PT-SHC	E145	145726	PT-SIQ	E145	145256	PT-SJY	E145	145282
PT-SFY	E145	14500971	PT-SHD	E145	14500974	PT-SIR	E145	14500867	PT-SJY	E145	145767
PT-SFY	E145	145176	PT-SHD	E145	145217	PT-SIR	E145	145258	PT-SJY	E190	19000082
PT-SFY	E145	145220	PT-SHD	E145	145727	PT-SIS	E145	14500873	PT-SJZ	E145	145283
PT-SFY	E145	145692	PT-SHE	E145	145218	PT-SIS	E145	145259	PT-SKA	E145	14500983
PT-SFZ	E145	14500972	PT-SHE	E145	145728	PT-SIT	E145	14500880	PT-SKA	E170	17000008
PT-SFZ	E145	145224	PT-SHF	E145	145219	PT-SIT	E145	145260	PT-SKB	E145	14500985
PT-SFZ	E145	145693	PT-SHF	E145	145729	PT-SIU	E145	14500884	PT-SKB	E145	145284
			PT-SHG	E145	145221	PT-SIU	E145	145261			

PT-SKB	E170	17000009	PT-SMD	E145	145773	PT-SNH	E145	145341	PT-SPA	E145	145020
PT-SKC	E145	14500986	PT-SME	E145	145313	PT-SNI	E145	14500806	PT-SPB	E145	145023
PT-SKC	E145	145285	PT-SME	E145	145774	PT-SNI	E145	145342	PT-SPC	E145	145027
PT-SKD	E170	17000010	PT-SME	E170	17000162	PT-SNI	E190	19000089	PT-SPD	E145	145028
PT-SKD	E145	14500988	PT-SMF	E145	145314	PT-SNJ	E145	14500807	PT-SPE	E145	145032
PT-SKD	E170	17000011	PT-SMF	E145	145776	PT-SNJ	E145	145343	PT-SPF	E145	145034
PT-SKE	E145	14500984	PT-SMF	E170	17000163	PT-SNJ	E190	19000090	PT-SPG	E145	145038
PT-SKE	E145	145287	PT-SMG	E145	145315	PT-SNK	E145	14500808	PT-SPH	E145	145060
PT-SKE	E170	17000012	PT-SMG	E145	145777	PT-SNK	E145	145344	PT-SPI	E145	145065
PT-SKF	E145	14500987	PT-SMG	E170	17000164	PT-SNK	E190	19000091	PT-SPJ	E145	145083
PT-SKF	E145	145288	PT-SMH	E145	145316	PT-SNL	E145	14500810	PT-SPK	E145	145089
PT-SKF	E170	17000013	PT-SMH	E145	145778	PT-SNL	E145	145345	PT-SPL	E145	145090
PT-SKG	E145	145289	PT-SMH	E170	17000165	PT-SNL	E190	19000092	PT-SPM	E145	145114
PT-SKH	E145	145290	PT-SMI	E145	145317	PT-SNM	E145	145346	PT-SPN	E145	145127
PT-SKI	E145	145291	PT-SMI	E145	145779	PT-SNN	E145	14500811	PT-SPO	E145	145137
PT-SKI	E170	17000015	PT-SMI	E170	17000166	PT-SNN	E145	145347	PT-SPP	E145	145350
PT-SKJ	E145	14500989	PT-SMJ	E145	145318	PT-SNN	E190	19000093	PT-SQA	E145	145376
PT-SKJ	E145	145292	PT-SMJ	E145	145782	PT-SNO	E145	14500812	PT-SQA	E190	19000106
PT-SKJ	E170	17000016	PT-SMJ	E170	17000167	PT-SNO	E145	145348	PT-SQB	E145	145377
PT-SKK	E145	14500990	PT-SMK	E145	145319	PT-SNO	E190	19000094	PT-SQB	E190	19000107
PT-SKK	E145	145293	PT-SMK	E145	145783	PT-SNP	E145	14500813	PT-SQC	E145	145378
PT-SKL	E145	14500991	PT-SMK	E170	17000168	PT-SNP	E145	145349	PT-SQC	E190	19000108
PT-SKL	E145	145294	PT-SML	E145	145320	PT-SNP	E190	19000095	PT-SQD	E145	145379
PT-SKL	E170	17000018	PT-SML	E145	145784	PT-SNQ	E145	14500814	PT-SQD	E190	19000109
PT-SKM	E145	14500993	PT-SML	E170	17000169	PT-SNQ	E190	19000096	PT-SQE	E145	145380
PT-SKM	E145	145295	PT-SMM	E145	145321	PT-SNR	E145	14500816	PT-SQE	E190	19000110
PT-SKM	E170	17000019	PT-SMM	E145	145785	PT-SNR	E145	145352	PT-SQF	E145	145381
PT-SKN	E145	14500994	PT-SMM	E170	17000170	PT-SNR	E190	19000097	PT-SQF	E190	19000111
PT-SKN	E145	145296	PT-SMN	E145	145322	PT-SNS	E145	14500817	PT-SQG	E145	145382
PT-SKN	E170	17000020	PT-SMN	E145	145786	PT-SNS	E145	145353	PT-SQG	E145	145393
PT-SKO	E145	14500995	PT-SMN	E170	17000171	PT-SNS	E190	19000098	PT-SQG	E190	19000112
PT-SKO	E145	145297	PT-SMP	E145	145323	PT-SNT	E145	14500819	PT-SQH	E145	145383
PT-SKO	E170	17000021	PT-SMP	E145	145787	PT-SNT	E145	145354	PT-SQH	E190	19000113
PT-SKP	E145	14500997	PT-SMP	E170	17000172	PT-SNT	E190	19000099	PT-SQI	E145	145384
PT-SKP	E145	145298	PT-SMQ	E145	145324	PT-SNU	E145	14500820	**PT-SQI**	**E190**	**19000114**
PT-SKP	E170	17000022	PT-SMQ	E145	145788	PT-SNU	E145	145355	PT-SQJ	E145	14500837
PT-SKQ	E145	14500998	PT-SMQ	E170	17000173	PT-SNU	E190	19000100	PT-SQJ	E145	145385
PT-SKQ	E145	145299	PT-SMR	E145	145325	PT-SNV	E145	14500821	**PT-SQJ**	**E190**	**19000115**
PT-SKQ	E170	17000023	PT-SMR	E145	145790	PT-SNV	E145	145356	PT-SQK	E145	14500838
PT-SKR	E145	14500999	PT-SMR	E170	17000174	PT-SNV	E190	19000101	PT-SQK	E145	145386
PT-SKR	E145	145300	PT-SMS	E145	145326	PT-SNW	E145	14500822	**PT-SQK**	**E190**	**19000116**
PT-SKR	E170	17000024	PT-SMS	E145	145791	PT-SNW	E145	145357	PT-SQL	E145	14500840
PT-SKS	E145	14501001	PT-SMS	E170	17000175	PT-SNW	E190	19000102	PT-SQL	E145	145387
PT-SKS	E145	145301	PT-SMT	E145	145327	PT-SNX	E145	14500824	**PT-SQL**	**E190**	**19000117**
PT-SKS	E170	17000025	PT-SMT	E170	17000176	PT-SNX	E145	145358	PT-SQM	E145	14500842
PT-SKT	E145	14501002	PT-SMU	E145	145328	PT-SNX	E190	19000103	PT-SQM	E145	145388
PT-SKT	E145	145302	PT-SMU	E170	17000177	PT-SNY	E145	14500826	**PT-SQM**	**E190**	**19000118**
PT-SKT	E170	17000026	PT-SMV	E145	145329	PT-SNY	E145	145359	PT-SQN	E145	14500843
PT-SKU	E145	14501003	PT-SMV	E145	145793	PT-SNY	E190	19000104	PT-SQN	E145	145389
PT-SKU	E145	145303	PT-SMV	E170	17000178	PT-SNZ	E145	14500827	**PT-SQN**	**E190**	**19000119**
PT-SKU	E170	17000027	PT-SMW	E145	145330	PT-SNZ	E145	145360	PT-SQO	E145	14500844
PT-SKV	E145	145304	PT-SMW	E145	145795	PT-SNZ	E190	19000105	PT-SQO	E145	145390
PT-SKV	E145	14501004	PT-SMW	E170	17000179	PT-SOA	E145	14500839	**PT-SQO**	**E190**	**19000120**
PT-SKV	E170	17000028	PT-SMX	E145	145331	PT-SOB	E145	14500848	PT-SQP	E145	14500845
PT-SKW	**E145**	**14501006**	PT-SMX	E145	145797	PT-SOC	E145	14500882	PT-SQP	E145	145391
PT-SKW	E145	145305	PT-SMX	E170	17000180	PT-SOD	E145	14500898	**PT-SQP**	**E190**	**19000121**
PT-SKW	E170	17000029	PT-SMY	E145	145332	PT-SOE	E145	14500905	PT-SQQ	E145	14500846
PT-SKX	E145	14501007	PT-SMY	E145	145798	PT-SOM	E145	14500916	**PT-SQQ**	**E190**	**19000122**
PT-SKX	E145	145306	PT-SMY	E170	17000181	PT-SOM	E145	145361	PT-SQR	E145	14500847
PT-SKX	E170	17000007	PT-SMZ	E145	145333	PT-SON	E145	14500919	PT-SQR	E145	145394
PT-SKY	**E145**	**14501008**	PT-SMZ	E145	145799	PT-SON	E145	145362	PT-SQS	E145	14500849
PT-SKY	E145	145307	PT-SMZ	E170	17000182	PT-SOO	E145	14500925	PT-SQS	E145	145395
PT-SKY	E170	17000030	PT-SNA	E145	145334	PT-SOP	E145	14500925	**PT-SQS**	**E190**	**19000123**
PT-SKZ	**E145**	**14501010**	PT-SNA	E145	145755	PT-SOQ	E145	145366	PT-SQT	E145	14500850
PT-SKZ	E145	145308	PT-SNA	E190	19000083	PT-SOR	E145	145367	PT-SQT	E145	145396
PT-SKZ	E170	17000031	PT-SNB	E145	145335	PT-SOT	E145	14500992	**PT-SQT**	**E190**	**19000124**
PT-SLM	B737	25115	PT-SNB	E145	145781	PT-SOT	E145	14500922	PT-SQU	E145	14500852
PT-SLN	B737	26075	PT-SNB	E190	19000084	PT-SOT	E145	145368	PT-SQU	E145	145397
PT-SLP	B737	26097	PT-SNC	E145	145336	PT-SOU	E145	14500996	**PT-SQU**	**E190**	**19000125**
PT-SLU	B737	25186	PT-SND	E145	145337	PT-SOU	E145	14500923	PT-SQV	E145	145398
PT-SLV	B737	25189	PT-SND	E190	19000085	PT-SOU	E145	145369	**PT-SQV**	**E190**	**19000126**
PT-SLW	B737	24922	PT-SNE	E145	145338	PT-SOV	E145	14500924	PT-SQW	E145	145399
PT-SMA	E145	145309	PT-SNE	E145	145800	PT-SOV	E145	145370	PT-SQW	E145	145399
PT-SMA	E145	145769	PT-SNE	E190	19000086	PT-SOW	E145	14500926	**PT-SQW**	**E190**	**19000127**
PT-SMA	E170	17000160	PT-SNF	E145	14500801	PT-SOW	E145	145371	PT-SQX	E145	145856
PT-SMB	E145	145310	PT-SNF	E145	145339	PT-SOX	E145	14500927	PT-SQX	E145	145400
PT-SMB	E145	145771	PT-SNF	E190	19000087	PT-SOX	E145	145372	**PT-SQX**	**E190**	**19000128**
PT-SMB	E170	17000161	PT-SNG	E145	14500803	PT-SOY	E145	14500929	PT-SQY	E145	14500857
PT-SMC	E145	145311	PT-SNG	E145	145340	PT-SOY	E145	145373	PT-SQY	E145	145401
PT-SMC	E145	145772	PT-SNG	E190	19000088	PT-SOZ	E145	14500930	**PT-SQY**	**E190**	**19000129**
PT-SMD	E145	145312	PT-SNH	E145	14500805	PT-SOZ	E145	145375	PT-SQZ	E145	14500859

Reg	Type	No.	Reg	Type	No.	Reg	Type	No.	Reg	Type	No.
PT-SQZ	E145	145402	PT-SUD	E145	145432	PT-SVO	E170	17000063	PT-SYB	E145	145509
PT-SQZ	**E190**	**19000130**	PT-SUD	E170	17000034	PT-SVP	E145	145470	PT-SYC	E145	145006
PT-SSA	B737	25192	PT-SUD	E170	17000186	PT-SVP	E170	17000064	PT-SYC	E145	14500889
PT-SSB	B737	27629	PT-SUE	E145	145433	PT-SVQ	E145	145471	PT-SYC	E145	145510
PT-SSC	B737	27634	PT-SUE	E170	17000035	PT-SVQ	E170	17000065	PT-SYD	E145	145007
PT-SSD	B737	28565	PT-SUF	E145	145434	PT-SVR	E145	145472	PT-SYD	E145	14500890
PT-SSE	B737	28052	PT-SUF	E170	17000036	PT-SVR	E170	17000066	PT-SYD	E145	145511
PT-SSF	B737	28201	PT-SUG	E145	145435	PT-SVS	E145	145473	PT-SYE	E145	145008
PT-SSG	B737	28055	PT-SUG	E170	17000037	PT-SVS	E170	17000067	PT-SYE	E145	14500892
PT-SSI	B737	24785	PT-SUG	E170	17000187	PT-SVT	E145	145474	PT-SYE	E145	145512
PT-SSJ	B737	24791	PT-SUH	E145	145436	PT-SVT	E170	17000068	PT-SYF	E145	14500893
PT-SSK	**B737**	**23922**	PT-SUH	E170	17000038	PT-SVU	E145	145475	PT-SYF	E145	145009
PT-SSL	B737	25185	PT-SUH	E170	17000188	PT-SVU	E170	17000069	PT-SYF	E145	145513
PT-SSM	B737	25191	PT-SUI	E145	145437	**PT-SVV**	**E145**	**14501018**	PT-SYG	E145	14500894
PT-SSN	B737	24881	PT-SUI	E170	17000039	PT-SVV	E145	145476	PT-SYG	E145	145010
PT-SSO	B737	24921	**PT-SUI**	**E170**	**17000189**	PT-SVV	E170	17000070	PT-SYG	E145	145514
PT-SSP	B737	24097	PT-SUJ	E145	145438	**PT-SVW**	**E145**	**14501020**	PT-SYH	E145	14500895
PT-SSQ	B737	27454	PT-SUJ	E170	17000040	PT-SVW	E145	145477	PT-SYH	E145	145011
PT-STA	E145	145403	PT-SUK	E145	145439	PT-SVW	E170	17000071	PT-SYH	E145	145515
(PT-STA)	E145	145495	PT-SUK	E170	17000041	**PT-SVX**	**E145**	**14501021**	PT-SYI	E145	14500896
PT-STB	E145	145404	PT-SUL	E145	145440	PT-SVX	E145	145478	PT-SYI	E145	145012
PT-STC	E145	145405	PT-SUL	E170	17000042	PT-SVX	E170	17000072	PT-SYI	E145	145517
PT-STD	E145	145406	PT-SUM	E145	145441	PT-SVY	E145	145479	PT-SYJ	E145	14500897
PT-STD	E190	19000004	PT-SUM	E170	17000043	PT-SVY	E170	17000073	PT-SYJ	E145	145013
PT-STE	E145	145407	PT-SUN	E145	145442	PT-SVZ	E145	145480	PT-SYJ	E145	145518
PT-STF	E145	145408	PT-SUN	E170	17000044	PT-SVZ	E170	17000074	**PT-SYJ**	**E190**	**19000131**
PT-STF	E190	19000006	PT-SUO	E145	145443	PT-SWX	E145	145027	PT-SYK	E145	14500899
PT-STG	E145	145409	PT-SUO	E170	17000045	PT-SWY	E145	145028	PT-SYK	E145	145014
PT-STG	E190	19000007	PT-SUP	E145	145444	PT-SXA	E145	14500860	PT-SYK	E145	145519
PT-STH	E145	145410	PT-SUP	E170	17000046	**PT-SXA**	**E170**	**17000195**	**PT-SYK**	**E190**	**19000132**
PT-STH	E190	19000008	PT-SUQ	E145	145445	PT-SXB	E145	14500861	PT-SYL	E145	14500900
PT-STI	E145	145411	PT-SUQ	E170	17000047	PT-SXB	E145	145482	PT-SYL	E145	145015
PT-STI	E190	19000009	**PT-SUQ**	**E170**	**17000190**	PT-SXC	E145	14500862	PT-SYL	E145	145520
PT-STJ	E145	145413	PT-SUR	E145	145446	PT-SXC	E145	145483	PT-SYM	E145	14500902
PT-STJ	E190	19000010	PT-SUR	E170	17000048	PT-SXD	E145	14500864	PT-SYM	E145	145016
PT-STK	E145	145414	PT-SUS	E145	145447	PT-SXE	E145	14500865	PT-SYM	E145	145521
PT-STK	E190	19000011	PT-SUT	E145	145448	PT-SXE	E145	145485	PT-SYN	E145	14500904
PT-STL	E145	145415	PT-SUT	E170	17000049	PT-SXF	E145	14500866	PT-SYN	E145	145017
PT-STL	E190	19000012	**PT-SUT**	**E170**	**17000192**	PT-SXF	E145	145486	PT-SYN	E145	145522
PT-STM	E145	145416	PT-SUU	E145	145449	**PT-SXF**	**E170**	**17000196**	PT-SYO	E145	145018
PT-STM	E190	19000013	PT-SUU	E170	17000050	PT-SXG	E145	14500868	PT-SYO	E145	145523
PT-STO	E145	145417	PT-SUV	E145	145450	PT-SXG	E145	145487	PT-SYP	E145	14500906
PT-STO	E190	19000014	PT-SUV	E170	17000051	PT-SXH	E145	14500870	PT-SYP	E145	145019
PT-STP	E145	145418	**PT-SUV**	**E170**	**17000193**	PT-SXH	E145	145488	PT-SYP	E145	145524
PT-STP	E190	19000015	PT-SUW	E145	145451	PT-SXI	E145	14500871	PT-SYQ	E145	14500907
PT-STQ	E145	145419	PT-SUX	E145	145452	PT-SXI	E145	145489	PT-SYQ	E145	145020
PT-STQ	E190	19000016	PT-SUY	E145	145453	PT-SXJ	E145	145490	PT-SYQ	E145	145525
PT-STR	E145	145420	PT-SUY	E170	17000053	PT-SXK	E145	14500872	PT-SYR	E145	14500908
PT-STR	E145	145526	**PT-SUY**	**E170**	**17000194**	PT-SXK	E145	145491	PT-SYR	E145	145021
PT-STR	E190	19000017	PT-SUZ	E145	145454	PT-SXL	E145	14500823	PT-SYS	E145	14500909
PT-STS	E145	145421	PT-SUZ	E170	17000054	PT-SXL	E145	145492	PT-SYS	E145	145022
PT-STS	E145	145527	PT-SVA	E145	145455	PT-SXM	E145	14500858	PT-SYT	E145	14500911
PT-STS	E190	19000018	PT-SVB	E145	145456	PT-SXM	E145	145493	PT-SYT	E145	145023
PT-STT	E145	145422	PT-SVC	E145	145457	PT-SXN	E145	14500869	PT-SYU	E145	14500912
PT-STT	E145	145529	**PT-SVD**	**E145**	**14501016**	PT-SXN	E145	145494	PT-SYU	E145	145024
PT-STT	E190	19000019	PT-SVD	E145	145458	PT-SXO	E145	14500874	PT-SYV	E145	14500914
PT-STU	E145	145423	PT-SVD	E170	17000006	PT-SXO	E145	145496	PT-SYV	E145	145025
PT-STU	E145	145530	**PT-SVE**	**E145**	**14501011**	PT-SXQ	E145	14500875	PT-SYW	E145	14500915
PT-STU	E190	19000020	PT-SVE	E145	145459	PT-SXQ	E145	145497	PT-SYW	E145	145026
PT-STV	E145	145424	PT-SVE	E170	17000055	PT-SXR	E145	14500876	PT-SYX	E145	14500917
PT-STV	E145	145531	PT-SVF	E145	145460	PT-SXR	E145	145498	PT-SYX	E145	145029
PT-STV	E190	19000021	PT-SVF	E170	17000056	PT-SXS	E145	14500877	PT-SYY	E145	14500918
PT-STW	E145	145425	**PT-SVG**	**E145**	**14501012**	PT-SXS	E145	145499	PT-SYY	E145	145030
PT-STW	E145	145532	PT-SVG	E145	145461	PT-SXT	E145	14500878	PT-SYZ	E145	14500920
PT-STW	E190	19000022	PT-SVG	E170	17000057	PT-SXT	E145	145500	PT-SYZ	E145	145031
PT-STX	E145	145426	**PT-SVH**	**E145**	**14501014**	PT-SXU	E145	14500879	PT-SZA	E145	145033
PT-STX	E145	145533	PT-SVH	E145	145462	PT-SXU	E145	145501	PT-SZA	E145	145536
PT-STX	E190	19000023	PT-SVH	E170	17000058	PT-SXV	E145	14500881	PT-SZA	E170	17000075
PT-STY	E145	145427	PT-SVI	E145	14501015	PT-SXV	E145	145502	PT-SZB	E145	145035
PT-STY	E145	145534	PT-SVI	E145	145463	PT-SXW	E145	14500883	PT-SZB	E145	145537
PT-STY	E190	19000024	PT-SVI	E170	17000059	PT-SXW	E145	145503	PT-SZB	E170	17000076
PT-STZ	E145	145428	PT-SVJ	E145	145464	PT-SXX	E145	14500885	PT-SZC	E145	145036
PT-STZ	E145	145535	**PT-SVK**	**E145**	**14501017**	PT-SXX	E145	145504	PT-SZC	E170	17000077
PT-STZ	E190	19000025	PT-SVK	E145	145465	PT-SXY	E145	14500886	PT-SZD	E145	145539
PT-SUA	E145	145429	PT-SVK	E170	17000052	PT-SXY	E145	145506	PT-SZD	E170	17000078
PT-SUA	E170	17000032	PT-SVL	E145	145466	PT-SXZ	E145	14500887	PT-SZE	E145	145039
PT-SUA	E170	17000183	PT-SVL	E170	17000060	PT-SXZ	E145	145507	PT-SZE	E170	17000079
PT-SUB	E145	145430	PT-SVM	E145	145467	PT-SYA	E145	145004	PT-SZF	E145	145040
PT-SUB	E170	17000033	PT-SVM	E170	17000061	PT-SYA	E145	14500888	PT-SZF	E145	145542
PT-SUB	E170	17000184	PT-SVN	E145	145468	PT-SYB	E145	145005			
PT-SUC	E145	145431	PT-SVN	E170	17000062						
PT-SUC	E170	17000185	PT-SVO	E145	145469						

Reg	Type	Serial
PT-SZF	E170	17000080
PT-SZG	E145	145041
PT-SZG	E145	145543
PT-SZH	E145	145042
PT-SZH	E145	145544
PT-SZH	E170	17000082
PT-SZI	E145	145043
PT-SZI	E145	145545
PT-SZI	E170	17000083
PT-SZJ	E145	145044
PT-SZJ	E145	145546
PT-SZJ	E170	17000084
PT-SZK	E145	145045
PT-SZK	E145	145547
PT-SZK	E170	17000085
PT-SZL	E145	145046
PT-SZL	E145	145548
PT-SZL	E170	17000086
PT-SZM	E145	145047
PT-SZM	E145	145550
PT-SZM	E170	17000087
PT-SZN	E145	145048
PT-SZN	E145	145551
PT-SZN	E170	17000005
PT-SZO	E145	145049
PT-SZO	E145	145552
PT-SZO	E170	17000081
PT-SZO	E170	17000088
PT-SZP	E145	145050
PT-SZP	E145	145553
PT-SZP	E170	17000089
PT-SZQ	E145	145051
PT-SZQ	E145	145554
PT-SZQ	E170	17000090
PT-SZR	E145	145052
PT-SZR	E145	145556
PT-SZR	E170	17000091
PT-SZS	E145	145053
PT-SZS	E145	145557
PT-SZS	E170	17000092
PT-SZT	E145	145054
PT-SZT	E145	145558
PT-SZT	E170	17000093
PT-SZU	E145	145055
PT-SZU	E145	145559
PT-SZU	E170	17000094
PT-SZV	E145	145056
PT-SZV	E145	145560
PT-SZV	E170	17000095
PT-SZW	E145	145057
PT-SZW	E145	145561
PT-SZW	E170	17000096
PT-SZX	E145	145058
PT-SZX	E145	145562
PT-SZX	E170	17000097
PT-SZY	E145	145059
PT-SZY	E145	145563
PT-SZY	E170	17000098
PT-SZZ	E145	145564
PT-SZZ	E170	17000099
(PT-T)	B737	23787
(PT-T)	B737	26068
PT-TAA	B767	22921
PT-TAB	B767	22922
PT-TAC	B767	22923
PT-TAD	B767	24947
PT-TAE	B767	24948
PT-TAF	B767	25411
PT-TAG	B767	24150
PT-TAH	B767	23624
PT-TAI	B767	24727
PT-TAJ	B767	24728
PT-TAK	B767	25421
PT-TAL	B767	23764
PT-TAM	B767	24349
PT-TCA	B727	19136
PT-TCB	B727	19137
PT-TCC	B727	18844
PT-TCD	B727	18744
PT-TCE	B727	18743
(PT-TCE)	B727	22424
PT-TCF	B727	18742

Reg	Type	Serial
(PT-TCF)	B727	22425
PT-TCG	B727	19136
PT-TCH	B727	19088
PT-TCI	B727	19140
PT-TCJ	B707	19529
PT-TCK	B707	19519
PT-TCL	B707	19517
PT-TCM	B707	19317
PT-TCN	B707	20088
PT-TCO	B707	18932
PT-TCP	B707	19416
PT-TCQ	B707	20456
PT-TCR	B707	20018
PT-TCS	B707	19354
"PT-TCT"	B707	19296
(PT-TCU)	B707	20316
PT-TDA	B737	24690
(PT-TDA)	B757	24635
PT-TDB	B737	24685
(PT-TDB)	B757	24868
PT-TDC	B737	24690
PT-TDD	B737	24689
PT-TDE	B737	24545
PT-TDE	B747	21033
PT-TDF	B737	24682
PT-TDG	B727	19319
PT-TDG	B737	25180
PT-TDH	B737	24124
(PT-TE.)	B737	25190
PT-TEA	B737	23499
PT-TEB	B737	23500
PT-TEC	B737	23708
PT-TED	B737	23750
PT-TEE	B737	23808
PT-TEF	B737	24208
PT-TEG	B737	24209
PT-TEH	B737	24210
PT-TEI	B737	23812
PT-TEJ	B737	23926
PT-TEK	B737	23927
PT-TEL	B737	24467
PT-TEM	B737	24511
(PT-TEN)	B737	24512
PT-TEN	B737	24513
(PT-TEO)	B737	24676
PT-TEO	B737	24692
(PT-TEP)	B737	24790
PT-TEP	B737	28364
PT-TEQ	B737	25057
PT-TER	B737	25119
PT-TET	B737	25015
PT-TEU	B737	23797
PT-TEV	B737	23798
PT-TEW	B737	24221
PT-TEX	B737	23827
PT-TYH	B727	19497
PT-TYI	B727	19827
PT-TYJ	B727	19393
PT-TYK	B727	19499
PT-TYL	B727	19501
PT-TYM	B727	19500
PT-TYN	B727	19243
PT-TYO	B727	19116
PT-TYP	B727	19113
PT-TYQ	B727	19110
PT-TYR	B727	18794
PT-TYS	B727	19111
PT-TYT	B727	19112
PT-TYU	B727	19109
PT-TYV	1-11	BAC.200
PT-TYW	1-11	BAC.206
PT-TYY	1-11	BAC.240
PT-WBA	B737	21685
PT-WBB	B737	21206
PT-WBC	B737	21686
PT-WBD	B737	23173
PT-WBE	B737	23175
PT-WBF	B737	23176
PT-WBG	B737	23177
PT-WBH	B737	23747
PT-WBI	B737	23826
PT-WBJ	B737	24911

Reg	Type	Serial
PT-WBK	DC-8	45941
PT-WBL	DC-8	45974
PT-WBM	DC-8	45976
PT-WHK	F.100	11452
PT-WHL	F.100	11471
PT-WJE	B707	19585
(PT-WRM)	F.100	11422
PT-WSM	B707	19773
(PT-WSM)	B707	20124
(PT-WSY)	B707	19774
PT-WSZ	**B707**	**18808**
PT-WUS	**B707**	**19352**
PT-XGF	E145	145425
PT-XHF	E145	145590
PT-ZJA	E145	145801
PT-ZJB	E145	145001
PT-ZJC	E145	145002
PT-ZJD	E145	145003

Suriname

Reg	Type	Serial
PZ-TCG	MD80	49671
PZ-TCK	DC-9	47655
PZ-TCL	**MD80**	**49444**
PZ-TCM	**B747**	**23508**

Papua New Guinea

Reg	Type	Serial
P2-ANA	A310	378
P2-ANA	B707	19622
P2-ANA	F.100	11358
P2-ANB	**F.100**	**11349**
P2-ANB	F.28	11049
P2-ANC	**F.100**	**11471**
P2-ANC	F.28	11089
P2-AND	**F.100**	**11473**
P2-AND	F.28	11118
P2-ANE	**F.100**	**11264**
P2-ANE	F.28	11033
P2-ANF	**F.100**	**11351**
P2-ANF	F.28	11038
P2-ANG	A300	134
P2-ANG	A310	549
P2-ANG	B707	18014
P2-ANG	**B767**	**24875**
P2-ANH	B707	19294
P2-ANH	F.28	11022
P2-ANI	F.28	11223
P2-ANJ	F.28	11219
P2-ANL	F.28	11003
P2-ANR	F.28	11207
P2-ANS	F.28	11195
P2-ANU	F.28	11041
P2-ANW	F.28	11056
P2-ANY	F.28	11070
P2-ANZ	F.28	11034

Aruba

Reg	Type	Serial
(P4-)	B707	19585
P4-AAA	B757	24771
(P4-AAU)	L1011	193B-1013
(P4-ABA)	B767	22694
P4-ABF	B727	22425
P4-ABU	A310	431
P4-AFE	B747	21962
P4-AIR	**MD80**	**49412**
P4-AKW	B707	20123
P4-AMO	1-11	086
P4-ARA	B737	20277
P4-ARB	B737	19616
P4-ARC	B737	19712
P4-ARL	**A319**	**2192**
P4-ASA	B737	19014
P4-BAA	B737	18433
"P4-BAB"	B727	18433
P4-BAB	B727	19432
P4-BAC	B727	18432

Reg	Type	Serial
P4-BAS	737NG	30627
P4-BBJ	737NG	32777
P4-BDL	MD11	48766
P4-CAD	B737	19422
P4-CAS	737NG	30629
P4-CBH	1-11	088
P4-CBI	1-11	061
P4-CCC	B707	19585
P4-CCG	B707	18766
P4-CCG?	B707	20315
P4-CCL	1-11	078
P4-CRJ	**CRJ**	**7176**
P4-CZT	737NG	30076
P4-DAS	737NG	30642
P4-DCA	DC-9	47638
P4-DCB	DC-9	48112
P4-DCE	DC-8	46071
P4-DPD	A310	431
P4-DRS	B707	21104
P4-EAS	**B757**	**29488**
P4-ESP	B707	19292
P4-FAS	**B757**	**29489**
P4-FDH	B707	18586
P4-FLY	**B727**	**19148**
P4-FSH	**B747**	**21963**
P4-FZT	B737	24970
P4-GAS	**B757**	**28112**
P4-GFA	B747	19763
P4-GFB	B747	20953
P4-GFC	B747	21300
P4-GFD	B747	22298
P4-GFE	B747	20504
P4-GJC	737NG	30751
P4-IAH	L1011	193A-1040
P4-IVM	**E145**	**145686**
P4-JAA	L1011	193B-1013
P4-JAB	L1011	193B-1215
P4-JCC	B707	18948
P4-JLB	1-11	BAC.260
P4-JLD	B727	19620
P4-JLI	B727	21853
P4-KAZ	**737NG**	**32774**
P4-KCA	**B767**	**27612**
P4-KCB	**B767**	**27614**
P4-MAS	**B757**	**28833**
(P4-MAS)	B757	29306
P4-MDA	MD80	49759
P4-MDB	MD80	53045
P4-MDC	MD80	49766
P4-MDD	DC-9	47271
P4-MDE	MD80	49950
P4-MDF	MD90	53578
P4-MDG	MD90	53579
P4-MDH	MD90	53580
P4-MED	L1011	193L-1064
(P4-MER)	B727	21460
P4-MES	**B767**	**33425**
P4-MIS	**A319**	**3133**
P4-MMG	**B727**	**18368**
P4-MSG	**E145**	**14500913**
P4-NAS	**A321**	**1042**
(P4-NAS)	B757	29307
P4-NEN	B737	20925
P4-NJR	B707	18453
P4-NRA	**E145**	**14500960**
P4-NSN	B757	23454
P4-NVB	**E145**	**14501002**
P4-OAS	**A321**	**1204**
P4-OMC	**B737**	**22050**
P4-ONE	B727	19148
P4-OOO	B707	19435
P4-OYX	B737	19059
P4-PAS	**A320**	**2128**
P4-PHS	B737	24970
P4-PTA	B737	20365
P4-RMB	B737	20364
P4-RUS	**737NG**	**34622**
P4-SAO	**E145**	**14500994**
P4-SAS	**A320**	**2016**
P4-SIS	**E145**	**145586**
P4-SKI	B727	21460
P4-SWM	MD11	48780

P4-TAS	A320	2828	RA-42379	YAK42 1014543	RA-64010	TU204	64010	RA-65056	TU134 49860
P4-TBN	737NG	29791	RA-42380	YAK42 2014549	RA-64011	TU204 1364011		RA-65057	TU134 49865
P4-TBN	B707	21049	RA-42382	YAK42 2016196	RA-64012	TU204 2364012		RA-65059	TU134 49870
P4-TKA	MD11	48756	RA-42384	YAK42 3016230	RA-64013	TU204 3364013		RA-65060	TU134 49872
P4-TSO	B747	22723	RA-42385	YAK42 3016309	RA-64014	TU204 4364014		RA-65062	TU134 49875
P4-UAS	A320	2987	RA-42386	YAK42 4016310	RA-64015	TU204 1464015		RA-65063	TU134 49880
P4-VAS	A320	3141	RA-42387	YAK42 4016436	RA-64016	TU204 3464016		RA-65064	TU134 49886
P4-VML	A319	2921	RA-42388	YAK42 4016510	RA-64017	TU204 2564017		RA-65065	TU134 49890
P4-VNF	A320	0726	RA-42389	YAK42 4016542	RA-64018	TU204 1964018		RA-65066	TU134 49898
P4-VVP	E145	145549	RA-42390	YAK42 4016557	RA-64019	TU204 1064019		RA-65067	TU134 49905
P4-YJR	B727	18366	RA-42391	YAK42 1316562	RA-64020	TU204 3164020		RA-65068	TU134 49907
P4-YYY	B707	20069	RA-42401	YAK42 1116567	RA-64021	TU204 2964021		RA-65069	TU134 49908
			RA-42402	YAK42 2116583	RA-64022	TU204 2064022		RA-65070	TU134 49912
			RA-42406	YAK42 4116683	RA-64024	TU204 1364024		RA-65074	TU134 49987
Russia			RA-42408	YAK42 4116698	RA-64025	TU204 3164025		RA-65079	TU134 60054
(see also CCCP-, RF-)			RA-42409	YAK42 1216709	RA-64026	TU204 3164026		RA-65080	TU134 60065
			RA-42411	YAK42 1219043	RA-64027	TU204 3764027		RA-65082	TU134 60081
RA-19	TU134	?	RA-42412	YAK42 2219055	RA-64028	TU204 3764028		RA-65083	TU134 60090
RA-10200	DC-10	46891	RA-42413	YAK42 2219066	RA-64029	TU204 3164029		RA-65084	TU134 60115
RA-21500	YAK40 9741356		RA-42414	YAK42 2219073	RA-64030	TU204 3664030		RA-65086	TU134 60130
RA-21501	YAK40 9741756		RA-42415	YAK42 2219089	RA-64032	TU204 2264032		RA-65087	TU134 60155
RA-21502	YAK40 9831858		RA-42417	YAK42 3219110	RA-64036	TU204	64036	RA-65088	TU134 60172
RA-21503	YAK40 9820358		RA-42418	YAK42 3219118	RA-64038	TU204 4464038		RA-65090	TU134 83 60185
RA-21504	YAK40 9831758		RA-42421	YAK42 2303017	RA-64039	TU204 1564039		RA-65091	TU134 60195
RA-21505	YAK40 9830159		RA-42422	YAK42 4304017	RA-64040	TU204 4564040		RA-65093	TU134 60215
RA-21506	YAK40 9840259		RA-42423	YAK42 4216606	RA-64451	TU134 66550		RA-65096	TU134 60257
RA-21511	BE200 002'		RA-42424	YAK42 1302016	RA-64454	TU134 66140		RA-65097	TU134 60540
RA-21512	BE200 003'		RA-42425	YAK42 1303016	RA-64501	TU214 44524001		RA-65099	TU134 63700
RA-21515	BE200 10101		RA-42426	YAK42 4305016	RA-64502	TU214 42625002		RA-65100	TU134 60258
RA-21516	BE200 10102?		RA-42427	YAK42 2305016	RA-64503	TU214 43103003		RA-65101	TU134 60260
RA-21517	BE200 2501?	"RA-42427"	YAK42 2306016	RA-64504	TU214 41203004		RA-65102	TU134 60267
RA-28929	YAK40 9310927		RA-42428	YAK42 4116683	RA-64505	TU214 42204005		RA-65103	TU134 60297
RA-42316	YAK42 2202030		RA-42429	YAK42 3407016	RA-64506	TU214 44204006		RA-65104	TU134 60301
RA-42318	YAK42 3402051		RA-42430	YAK42 3408016	RA-64507	TU214 42305007		RA-65105	TU134 60308
RA-42320	YAK42 1302075		RA-42431	YAK42 409016	RA-64508	TU214	008	RA-65108	TU134 60332
RA-42321	YAK42 3402088		RA-42432	YAK42 4410016	RA-64509	TU214 42305009		RA-65109	TU134 60339
RA-42322	YAK42 3402108		RA-42433	YAK42 1301017	RA-64510	TU214 42305010		RA-65110	TU134 60343
RA-42323	YAK42 3402116		RA-42434	YAK42 4305017	RA-64511	TU214	011	RA-65112	TU134 60350
RA-42324	YAK42 1402125		RA-42435	YAK42 4306017	RA-64512	TU214 42305012		RA-65113	TU134 60380
RA-42325	YAK42 4402148		RA-42436	YAK42 1605018	RA-64513	TU214	013	RA-65116	TU134 60420
RA-42326	YAK42 4402154		RA-42437	YAK42 3606018	RA-64514	TU214	014	RA-65117	TU134 60450
RA-42327	YAK42 4402161		RA-42438	YAK42 3609018	RA-64515	TU214	015	RA-65118	TU134 60462
RA-42328	YAK42 1505058		RA-42439	YAK42 3904019	RA-64516	TU214	016	RA-65122	TU134 60518
RA-42329	YAK42 2505093		RA-42440	YAK42 10018	RA-64517	TU214	017	RA-65124	TU134 60560
RA-42330	YAK42 2505122		RA-42441	YAK42 1402018	RA-64518	TU214	018	RA-65126	TU134 60588
RA-42331	YAK42 4505128		RA-42442	YAK42 2002016	RA-64615	TU134 64615		RA-65127	TU134 60627
RA-42332	YAK42 4505135		RA-42443	YAK42 4116664	RA-65002	TU134 44020		RA-65128	TU134 60628
RA-42333	YAK42 2606156		RA-42443	YAK42 ?	RA-65004	TU134 44060		RA-65131	TU134 60637
RA-42335	YAK42 2606204		RA-42444	YAK42 4116677	RA-65005	TU134 44065		RA-65132	TU134 60639
RA-42336	YAK42 2606220		RA-42445	YAK42 4116669	RA-65007	TU134 46100		RA-65136	TU134 60885
RA-42337	YAK42 3606235		RA-42446	YAK42 3308017	RA-65008	TU134 46105		RA-65137	TU134 60890
RA-42339	YAK42 4606267		RA-42450	YAK42 4601019	RA-65009	TU134 46120		RA-65139	TU134 60915
RA-42340	YAK42 4606270		RA 42451	YAK42 2708018	RA-65010	TU134 46130		RA-65141	TU134 60945
RA-42341	YAK42 1706292		RA-42452	YAK42 409016	RA-65011	TU134 46140		RA-65143	TU134 60967
RA-42342	YAK42 1706302		RA-42524	YAK42 11030603	RA-65012	TU134 46175		RA-65144	TU134 60977
RA-42343	YAK42 1708285		RA-42526	YAK42 11040803	RA-65015	TU134 48325		RA-65146	TU134 61000
RA-42344	YAK42 2708295		RA-42528	YAK42 11041003	RA-65016	TU134 48340		RA-65148	TU134 61025
RA-42345	YAK42 2708304		RA-42538	YAK42 11130404	RA-65017	TU134 48360		RA-65550	TU134 66200
RA-42346	YAK42 3708311		RA-42539	YAK42 11140504	RA-65018	TU134 48365		RA-65552	TU134 66270
RA-42347	YAK42 3711322		RA-42541	YAK42 11140704	RA-65019	TU134 48375		RA-65553	TU134 66300
RA-42350	YAK42 4711372		RA-42542	YAK42 11140804	RA-65020	TU134 48380		RA-65554	TU134 66320
RA-42352	YAK42 1811395		RA-42543	YAK42 11250904	RA-65021	TU134 48390		RA-65555	TU134 66350
RA-42353	YAK42 4711396		RA-42549	YAK42 11040105	RA-65024	TU134 48420		RA-65557	TU134 66380
RA-42354	YAK42 4711397		RA-42550	YAK42 11140205	RA-65025	TU134 48450		RA-65559	TU134 73 49909
RA-42355	YAK42 4711399		RA-42551	YAK42 11140305	RA-65026	TU134 48470		RA-65560	TU134 60321
RA-42356	YAK42 2811400		RA-42557	YAK42 3302017	RA-65027	TU134 48485		RA-65562	TU134 2350204
RA-42357	YAK42 2811408		RA-42640	YAK42 3914323	RA-65028	TU134 48490		RA-65563	TU134 60035
RA-42359	YAK42 3811417		RA-48110	YAK40 9230623	RA-65029	TU134 48500		RA-65564	TU134 63165
RA-42360	YAK42 3811421		RA-48111	YAK40 9211420	RA-65033	TU134 48540		RA-65565	TU134 63998
RA-42361	YAK42 3811427		RA-48112	YAK40 9211520	RA-65034	TU134 63 48565		RA-65566	TU134 63952
RA-42362	YAK42 4811431		RA-63757	TU134 63757	RA-65035	TU134 48590		RA-65567	TU134 63967
RA-42363	YAK42 4811438		RA-63775	TU134 63775	RA-65038	TU134 48950		RA-65568	TU134 66135
RA-42364	YAK42 4811442		RA-63832	TU134 63832	RA-65040	TU134 63 49100		RA-65569	TU134 63340
RA-42365	YAK42 4811447		RA-63950	TU134 63950?	RA-65042	TU134 49350		RA-65570	TU134 66550
RA-42367	YAK42 1914133		RA-63975	TU134 63975	RA-65043	TU134 49400		RA-65571	TU134 63955
RA-42368	YAK42 2914166		RA-64001	TU204 64001	RA-65045	TU134 49500		RA-65572	TU134 63295
RA-42370	YAK42 2914203		RA-64003	TU204 64003	RA-65046	TU134 49550		RA-65573	TU134 13 63761
RA-42371	YAK42 2914225		RA-64004	TU204 1164004	RA-65047	TU134 49600		RA-65575	TU134 62350
RA-42373	YAK42 3914323		RA-64006	TU204 3164006	RA-65052	TU134 49755		RA-65579	TU134 63295
RA-42374	YAK42 3914340		RA-64007	TU204 1264007	RA-65054	TU134 49825		RA-65604	TU134 62561
RA-42375	YAK42 4914410		RA-64008	TU204 3264008	RA-65054	TU134 49840		RA-65605	TU134 09070
RA-42378	YAK42 1014494		RA-64009	TU204 4264009	RA-65055	TU134 49856		RA-65606	TU134 46300

Reg	Type	Serial
RA-65607	TU134	48560
RA-65608	TU134	38040
RA-65609	TU134	46155
RA-65610	TU134	40150
RA-65611	TU134	3351903
RA-65612	TU134	3352102
RA-65613	TU134	3352106
RA-65614	TU134	4352207
RA-65615	TU134	4352205
RA-65616	TU134	4352206
RA-65617	TU134	08068
RA-65618	TU134	12095
RA-65619	TU134	31218
RA-65620	TU134	35180
RA-65621	TU134	48320
RA-65622	TU134	60495
RA-65623	TU134	73 49985
RA-65626	TU134	9350704
RA-65651	TU134	0351007
RA-65653	TU134	0351009
RA-65661	TU134	0351107
RA-65666	TU134	1351202
RA-65667	TU134	1351207
RA-65669	TU134	9350916
RA-65671	TU134	1351208
RA-65679	TU134	23249
RA-65680	TU134	49020
RA-65681	TU134	49760
RA-65682	TU134	62120
RA-65684	TU134	62205
RA-65685	TU134	62375
RA-65688	TU134	62575
RA-65689	TU134	62655
RA-65690	TU134	62805
RA-65691	TU134	63195
RA-65692	TU134	63215
RA-65693	TU134	63221
RA-65694	TU134	63235
RA-65697	TU134	63307
RA-65701	TU134	63365
RA-65712	TU134	63515
RA-65715	TU134	63536
RA-65716	TU134	63595
RA-65717	TU134	63657
RA-65719	TU134	63637
RA-65720	TU134	62820
RA-05721	TU134	66130
RA-65722	TU134	66420
RA-65723	TU134	66440
RA-65724	TU134	66445
RA-65725	TU134	66472
RA-65726	TU134	63720
RA-65727	TU134	64820
RA-65728	TU134	73 49858
RA-65729	TU134	63961
RA-65737	TU134	64195
RA-65737	TU134	?
RA-65738	TU134	2351507
RA-65740	TU134	2351510
RA-65751	TU134	61066
RA-65753	TU134	61099
RA-65755	TU134	62165
RA-65756	TU134	62179
RA-65758	TU134	62230
RA-65759	TU134	62239
RA-65760	TU134	62187
RA-65762	TU134	62279
RA-65769	TU134	62415
RA-65770	TU134	62430
RA-65771	TU134	62445
RA-65775	TU134	62530
RA-65777	TU134	62552
RA-65780	TU134	62622
RA-65781	TU134	62645
RA-65783	TU134	62708
RA-65784	TU134	62715
RA-65785	TU134	62750
RA-65786	TU134	62775
RA-65790	TU134	63100
RA-65792	TU134	63121
RA-65793	TU134	63128
RA-65794	TU134	63135
RA-65796	TU134	63150
RA-65797	TU134	63173
RA-65798	TU134	63179
RA-65800	TU134	3352009
RA-65801	TU134	3352010
RA-65802	TU134	3352101
RA-65805	TU134	3352105
RA-65811	TU134	3352202
RA-65813	TU134	3352204
RA-65815	TU134	4352209
RA-65819	TU134	4352304
RA-65823	TU134	09073
RA-65824	TU134	09074
RA-65825	TU134	09078
RA-65827	TU134	12084
RA-65828	TU134	12086
RA-65829	TU134	12087
RA-65830	TU134	12093
RA-65834	TU134	17109
RA-65837	TU134	17114
RA-65838	TU134	18116
RA-65840	TU134	18118
RA-65842	TU134	18121
RA-65843	TU134	18123
RA-65845	TU134	23131
RA-65846	TU134	23132
RA-65847	TU134	23135
RA-65851	TU134	23241
RA-65852	TU134	23244
RA-65854	TU134	23248
RA-65855	TU134	23252
RA-65859	TU134	23264
RA-65860	TU134	28265
RA-65861	TU134	1351407
RA-65862	TU134	28270
RA-65863	TU134	28283
RA-65866	TU134	28292
RA-65867	TU134	28296
RA-65868	TU134	28305
RA-65869	TU134	28306
RA-65870	TU134	28310
RA-65872	TU134	29312
RA-65880	TU134	35200
RA-65881	TU134	35220
RA-65885	TU134	36160
RA-65887	TU134	36170
RA-65889	TU134	38010
RA-65891	TU134	38030
RA-65894	TU134	40130
RA-65897	TU134	42210
RA-65898	TU134	42220
RA-65899	TU134	42225
RA-65901	TU134	63731
RA-65902	TU134	63742
RA-65903	TU134	63750
RA-65904	TU134	63953
RA-65905	TU134	63965
RA-65906	TU134	66175
RA-65907	TU134	63996
RA-65908	TU134	63870
RA-65911	TU134	63972
RA-65912	TU134	63985
RA-65914	TU134	66109
RA-65915	TU134	66120
RA-65916	TU134	66152
RA-65917	TU134	63991
RA-65918	TU134	63995
RA-65919	TU134	66168
RA-65921	TU134	63997
RA-65926	TU134	66101
RA-65927	TU134	66198
RA-65928	TU134	66491
RA-65929	TU134	66495
RA-65930	TU134	66500
RA-65931	TU134	66185
RA-65932	TU134	66405
RA-65934	TU134	66143
RA-65935	TU134	66180
RA-65939	TU134	1351409
RA-65940	TU134	3351906
RA-65941	TU134	60642
RA-65942	TU134	17103
RA-65943	TU134	63580
RA-65944	TU134	12096
RA-65945	TU134	64010
RA-65950	TU134	2351702
RA-65954	TU134	2351707
RA-65955	TU134	2351708
RA-65956	TU134	2351709
RA-65958	TU134	3351804
RA-65960	TU134	3351806
RA-65961	TU134	3351807
RA-65962	TU134	3351901
RA-65966	TU134	3351902
RA-65967	TU134	3351905
RA-65969	TU134	3351909
RA-65970	TU134	3351910
RA-65971	TU134	3352001
RA-65972	TU134	3352002
RA-65973	TU134	3352003
RA-65976	TU134	3352007
RA-65976	TU134	63976
RA-65977	TU134	63245
RA-65978	TU134	63357
RA-65979	TU134	63158
RA-65980	TU134	63207
RA-65981	TU134	63250
RA-65982	TU134	63315
RA-65983	TU134	63350
RA-65984	TU134	63400
RA-65986	TU134	63475
RA-65987	TU134	63505
RA-65988	TU134	63550
RA-65989	TU134	63605
RA-65990	TU134	63690
RA-65991	TU134	63845
RA-65992	TU134	63850
RA-65994	TU134	66207
RA-65995	TU134	66400
RA-65996	TU134	63825
(RA-71430)	B737	22028
RA-72390	AN7x	72070678
RA-72901	AN7x	72020358
RA-72905	AN7x	72030430
RA-72908	AN7x	76094880
RA-72909	AN7x	72040550
RA-72913	AN7x	72030477
RA-72914	AN7x	72030479
RA-72915	AN7x	72040520
RA-72916	AN7x	72010526
RA-72917	AN7x	72040530
RA-72918	AN7x	72040548
RA-72919	AN7x	72040565
RA-72920	AN7x	72040570
RA-72922	AN7x	72040560
RA-72924	AN7x	72060600
RA-72925	AN7x	72040563
RA-72926	AN7x	72060620
RA-72928	AN7x	72060640
RA-72929	AN7x	72060653
RA-72934	AN7x	72080777
RA-72935	AN7x	72080778
RA-72936	AN7x	72060642?
RA-72938	AN7x	72070693
RA-72939	AN7x	72080780
RA-72940	AN7x	72080781
RA-72943	AN7x	72080787
RA-72944	AN7x	72090796
RA-72945	AN7x	72090799
RA-72946	AN7x	72090801
RA-72947	AN7x	72090803
RA-72950	AN7x	72091819
RA-72952	AN7x	72091823
RA-72954	AN7x	72090795
RA-72955	AN7x	72090807
RA-72958	AN7x	72092841
RA-72960	AN7x	72093865
RA-72961	AN7x	72093866
RA-72962	AN7x	72091831
RA-72963	AN7x	72092845
RA-72964	AN7x	72093860
RA-72965	AN7x	72093863
RA-72967	AN7x	72091837
RA-72968	AN7x	72092838
RA-72969	AN7x	72092848
RA-72970	AN7x	76093870
RA-72971	AN7x	72093873
RA-72972	AN7x	72094883
RA-72973	AN7x	72094877
RA-72974	AN7x	72094878
RA-72976	AN7x	72094884
RA-72979	AN7x	72095908
RA-72982	AN7x	72096914
RA-72983	AN7x	72096912
RA-72991	AN7x	72010949
RA-72992	AN7x	?
RA-73000	B737	21443
RA-73000	B737	21444
RA-73000	B737	22032
RA-73001	B737	21444
RA-73001	B737	22028
RA-73002	B737	22034
RA-73003	B737	19611
RA-73003	B737	22859
RA-73005	B737	19408
RA-73005	B737	23100
RA-73007	B757	24749
RA-73008	B757	25436
RA-73009	B757	25437
RA-73010	B757	25438
RA-73011	B757	25439
RA-73012	B757	25440
RA-73013	B757	25441
RA-73015	B757	25901
RA-73016	B757	26433
RA-73017	B757	26434
RA-73018	B757	26435
RA-73019	B757	26436
RA-74000	AN7x	47060649
RA-74001	AN7x	47070655
RA-74003	AN7x	47070690
RA-74004	AN7x	47094890
RA-74005	AN7x	47094892
RA-74006	AN7x	47095896
RA-74008	AN7x	47095900
RA-74009	AN7x	47095898
RA-74011	AN7x	47136013
RA-74012	AN7x	47098959
RA-74013	AN7x	47195015
RA-74014	AN7x	47098968
RA-74015	AN7x	47195015
RA-74016	AN7x	470991034
RA-74017	AN7x	47195015
RA-74020	AN7x	47195014
RA-74024	AN7x	47096918
RA-74025	AN7x	47095905
RA-74027	AN7x	47096920
RA-74029	AN7x	47097940
RA-74030	AN7x	47098957
RA-74031	AN7x	47098961
RA-74032	AN7x	47098962
RA-74033	AN7x	?
RA-74034	AN7x	47136012
RA-74035	AN7x	47098963
RA-74036	AN7x	47098965
RA-74037	AN7x	47098950
RA-74039	AN7x	47097931
RA-74040	AN7x	47097930
RA-74041	AN7x	47096924
RA-74043	AN7x	47096923
RA-74044	AN7x	47097936
RA-74045	AN7x	47097938
RA-74046	AN7x	47097935
RA-74047	AN7x	47097941
RA-74048	AN7x	47098943
RA-74050	AN7x	47181011
RA-74052	AN7x	47098944
RA-74056	AN7x	47098951
RA-74058	AN7x	47098956
RA-74060	AN7x	47098966
RA-76350	IL76	1023410344
RA-76352	IL76	1023411378
RA-76354	IL76	1023409280
RA-76355	IL76	1023408265
RA-76356	IL76	?
RA-76357	IL76	1023414467

Reg.	Type	c/n	Reg.	Type	c/n	Reg.	Type	c/n	Reg.	Type	c/n
RA-76360	IL76	1033414492	RA-76478	IL76	0053459788	RA-76639	IL76	0053460805	RA-76799	IL76	1003403075
RA-76361	IL76	1033415497	RA-76479	IL76	0053460790	RA-76640	IL76	0053460811	RA-76800	IL76	0093493810
RA-76362	IL76	1033416533	RA-76481	IL76	0053460795	RA-76641	IL76	0053460813	RA-76801	IL76	0093495866
RA-76363	IL76	1033417540	RA-76482	IL76	0053460832	RA-76643	IL76	0053460822	RA-76802	IL76	0093495874
RA-76366	IL76	1043418628	RA-76483	IL76	0063468042	RA-76648	IL76	0053461848	RA-76803	IL76	0093497927
RA-76367	IL76	1033414474	RA-76484	IL76	0063469081	RA-76649	IL76	0053462864	RA-76804	IL76	0093497931
RA-76368	IL76	0033447364	RA-76485	IL76	0063470088	RA-76650	IL76	0053462865	RA-76806	IL76	1003403121
RA-76369	IL76	1033414480	RA-76486	IL76	0073476281	RA-76659	IL76	0053463908	RA-76807	IL76	1013405176
RA-76370	IL76	1023414458	RA-76487	IL76	0073479367	RA-76666	IL76	0053464934	RA-76808	IL76	1013405177
RA-76372	IL76	073410279	RA-76488	IL76	0073479371	RA-76668	IL76	0053465946	RA-76809	IL76	1013408252
RA-76373	IL76	1033415507	RA-76489	IL76	0083485554	RA-76669	IL76	0063465949	RA-76812	IL76	1013407230
RA-76378?	IL76	1033417553	RA-76490	IL76	093416506	RA-76672	IL76	0063466981	RA-76814	IL76	1013408269
RA-76379	IL76	1033417569	RA-76491	IL76	093421630	RA-76686	IL76	0063468045	RA-76817	IL76	1023412387
RA-76380	IL76	0043450493	RA-76492	IL76	093418548	RA-76693	IL76	0063470100	RA-76818	IL76	1013408264
RA-76380	IL76	1033418578	RA-76493	IL76	0043456700	RA-76701	IL76	0063471139	RA-76819	IL76	1013409274
RA-76381	IL76	1033418596	RA-76494	IL76	0063465956	RA-76702	IL76	0063471142	RA-76820	IL76	1013409295
RA-76382	IL76	0023436048	RA-76495	IL76	073410292	RA-76708	IL76	0063473171	RA-76822	IL76	0093499982
RA-76383	IL76	0023437076	RA-76496	IL76	073410301	RA-76710	IL76	0063473182	RA-76823	IL76	0023441189
RA-76386	IL76	1033418600	RA-76497	IL76	073410320	RA-76712	IL76	0063473190	RA-76825	IL76	1003404136
RA-76388	IL76	1013406204	RA-76498	IL76	0023442218	RA-76713	IL76	0063474193	RA-76826	IL76	1003404143
RA-76389	IL76	1013407212	RA-76499	IL76	0023441186	RA-76714	IL76	0063474198	RA-76828	IL76	1003405164
RA-76391	IL76	0043453568	RA-76504	IL76	073411328	RA-76718	IL76	0073474219	RA-76829	IL76	1003405172
RA-76400	IL76	1023413438	RA-76505	IL76	073411331	RA-76719	IL76	0073474226	RA-76832	IL76	1023410360
RA-76401	IL76	1023412399	RA-76506	IL76	073411334	RA-76720	IL76	0073475229	RA-76833	IL76	1023411363
RA-76402	IL76	1023413430	RA-76507	IL76	073411338	RA-76722	IL76	0073475242	RA-76834	IL76	1023409319
RA-76403	IL76	1023412414	RA-76508	IL76	083413412	RA-76723	IL76	0073475245	RA-76835	IL76	1013408244
RA-76404	IL76	0063471150	RA-76509	IL76	083413415	RA-76724	IL76	0073475250	RA-76837	IL76	1023409316
RA-76405	IL76	1023412402	RA-76510	IL76	083414432	RA-76725	IL76	0073475253	RA-76838	IL76	1023411370
RA-76406	IL76	1023414463	RA-76512	IL76	083414447	RA-76726	IL76	0073475261	RA-76839	IL76	1023411375
RA-76407	IL76	1023413435	RA-76513	IL76	084514451	RA-76731	IL76	0073476290	RA-76840	IL76	1033417553
RA-76409	IL76	1023410355	RA-76514	IL76	083415453	RA-76733	IL76	0073476304	RA-76841	IL76	1033418601
RA-76411	IL76	1023411384	RA-76515	IL76	093417526	RA-76735	IL76	0073476314	RA-76842	IL76	1033418616
RA-76412	IL76	0083488638	RA-76516	IL76	093418556	RA-76737	IL76	0073477323	RA-76843	IL76	1013408269
RA-76413	IL76	1013407215	RA-76517	IL76	093418560	RA-76738	IL76	0073477326	RA-76843	IL76	1033418584
RA-76414	IL76	0083482478	RA-76518	IL76	093420594	RA-76739	IL76	0073477332	RA-76845	IL76	1043420696
RA-76415	IL76	0083481440	RA-76519	IL76	093420599	RA-76740	IL76	0073477335	RA-76848	IL76	0033448390
RA-76416	IL76	043402041	RA-76520	IL76	093420605	RA-76741	IL76	0073478337	RA-76849	IL76	0023440161
RA-76417	IL76	043402046	RA-76521	IL76	0003423699	RA-76743	IL76	0073478349	RA-76900	IL76	1053417563
RA-76418	IL76	073409237	RA-76522	IL76	0003424707	RA-76745	IL76	0073479362	RA-76950	IL76	1063420697
RA-76419	IL76	1023414470	RA-76523	IL76	0003425732	RA-76746	IL76	0073479374	RA-76951	IL76	?
RA-76420	IL76	1023413446	RA-76524	IL76	0003425746	RA-76747	IL76	0073479381	RA-77114	TU144	100802
RA-76421	IL76	1033415504	RA-76525	IL76	0003427787	RA-76750	IL76	0083485561	RA-78731	IL76	0013428831
RA-76423	IL76	0053457720	RA-76526	IL76	0003427792	RA-76751	IL76	0083487610	RA-78734	IL76	1013409303
RA-76424	IL76	0063470096	RA-76527	IL76	0003427796	RA-76752	IL76	0093498967	RA-78738	IL76	0033442247
RA-76425	IL76	1003405167	RA-76528	IL76	073410293	RA-76753	IL76	0083481461	RA-78750	IL76	0083483510
RA-76426	IL76	1013405184	RA-76529	IL76	073410308	RA-76754	IL76	093421637	RA-78757	IL76	0083484547
RA-76428	IL76	083415464	RA-76530	IL76	0023441180	RA-76755	IL76	0013433984	RA-78762	IL76	0083486574
RA-76429	IL76	1043419639	RA-76533	IL76	0023442205	RA-76756	IL76	0013428839	RA-78764	IL76	0083486586
RA-76430	IL76	073410300	RA-76538	IL76	0023442231	RA-76757	IL76	0013433990	RA-78766	IL76	0083486595
RA-76430	IL76	093415475	RA-76542	IL76	0033443249	RA-76758	IL76	0073474203	RA-78770	IL76	0083487603
RA-76431	IL76	0063467020	RA-76544	IL76	0033443262	RA-76759	IL76	093418543	RA-78770	IL76	008348/617
(RA-76432)	IL76	0053465946	RA-76545	IL76	0033443266	RA-76761	IL76	0073479401	RA-78776	IL76	0083489652
RA-76433	IL76	0053460827	RA-76546	IL76	0033443272	RA-76762	IL76	0073480406	RA-78777	IL76	0083489654
RA-76436	IL76	1023411360	RA-76547	IL76	0033443273	RA-76763	IL76	0073480413	RA-78782	IL76	0083489659
RA-76440	IL76	1023413423	RA-76548	IL76	0033443278	RA-76764	IL76	0073480424	RA-78784	IL76	0083489678
RA-76443	IL76	0043452534	RA-76549	IL76	0033444283	RA-76765	IL76	0073481426	RA-78788	IL76	0083489687
RA-76444	IL76	0063470113	RA-76550	IL76	0033445306	RA-76766	IL76	0083481431	RA-78789	IL76	0083490703
RA-76445	IL76	1023410330	RA-76551	IL76	0033445309	RA-76767	IL76	0073481436	RA-78790	IL76	0083490706
RA-76446	IL76	1023412418	RA-76552	IL76	0033445313	RA-76768	IL76	0073481448	RA-78791	IL76	0083490712
RA-76450	IL76	0053463900	RA-76553	IL76	0033445318	RA-76769	IL76	0073481452	RA-78792	IL76	0083490718
RA-76451	IL76	0053464938	RA-76554	IL76	0033445324	RA-76770	IL76	0073481456	RA-78794	IL76	0093490726
RA-76453	IL76	0063466995	RA-76556	IL76	0033445294	RA-76771	IL76	0083482466	RA-78795	IL76	0093491729
RA-76457	IL76	093421621	RA-76558	IL76	0033446333	RA-76772	IL76	0083482472	RA-78796	IL76	0093491735
RA-76458	IL76	0013430888	RA-76572	IL76	0033449434	RA-76773	IL76	0083482473	RA-78797	IL76	0093491742
RA-76459	IL76	0013430890	RA-76577	IL76	0043449462	RA-76776	IL76	0083482486	RA-78798	IL76	0093491747
RA-76460	IL76	0013431928	RA-76578	IL76	0043449468	RA-76779	IL76	0083483505	RA-78803	IL76	0093492774
RA-76461	IL76	0013431935	RA-76584	IL76	0043450493	RA-76780	IL76	0013430901	RA-78805	IL76	0093492783
RA-76462	IL76	0013432955	RA-76588	IL76	0043451530	RA-76781	IL76	0023439133	RA-78807	IL76	0093493791
RA-76463	IL76	0013432960	RA-76591	IL76	0043452546	RA-76783	IL76	0093498974	RA-78809	IL76	0093493807
RA-76464	IL76	0023437090	RA-76592	IL76	0043452555	RA-76785	IL76	0093495863	RA-78810	IL76	0093493814
RA-76465	IL76	0023438101	RA-76599	IL76	0043453593	RA-76786	IL76	0093496923	RA-78811	IL76	0093494823
RA-76467	IL76	0023440157	RA-76604	IL76	0043454625	RA-76787	IL76	0093495854	RA-78812	IL76	0093494826
RA-76468	IL76	0023441195	RA-76605	IL76	0043454631	RA-76788	IL76	0013433996	RA-78813	IL76	0093494830
RA-76469	IL76	0033444286	RA-76612	IL76	0043455660	RA-76788	IL76	0033446325	RA-78814	IL76	0093494838
RA-76470	IL76	0033444291	RA-76613	IL76	0043455664	RA-76789	IL76	0013433999	RA-78815	IL76	0093494842
RA-76471	IL76	0033446345	RA-76615	IL76	0043455672	RA-76790	IL76	0093496903	RA-78816	IL76	0093495846
RA-76472	IL76	0033446350	RA-76616	IL76	0043455676	RA-76791	IL76	0093497936	RA-78817	IL76	0093495855
RA-76473	IL76	0033448404	RA-76623	IL76	0053457705	RA-76792	IL76	0093497942	RA-78818	IL76	0093495858
RA-76474	IL76	0033448407	RA-76632	IL76	0053459757	RA-76795	IL76	0093498962	RA-78819	IL76	0093495883
RA-76475	IL76	0043451523	RA-76634	IL76	0053459770	RA-76796	IL76	1003499994	RA-78820	IL76	0093496907
RA-76476	IL76	0043451528	RA-76635	IL76	0053459775	RA-76797	IL76	1003403052			
RA-76477	IL76	0043453575	RA-76638	IL76	0053460802	RA-76798	IL76	1003403063			

Registration	Type	Serial
RA-78825	IL76	1013495871
RA-78828	IL76	1003401004
RA-78829	IL76	1013401006
RA-78830	IL76	1003401010
RA-78831	IL76	1003401017
RA-78833	IL76	1003401025
RA-78834	IL76	1003401032
RA-78835	IL76	1003402033
RA-78838	IL76	1003402044
RA-78840	IL76	1003403056
RA-78842	IL76	1003403069
RA-78844	IL76	1003403092
RA-78845	IL76	1003403095
RA-78847	IL76	1003404132
RA-78850	IL76	1013405196
RA-78851	IL76	1013406204
RA-78852	IL76	1013407212
RA-78854	IL76	1013407220
RA-82003	AN124	19530502792
RA-82006	AN124	19530501004
RA-82010	AN124	977305361601
RA-82011	AN124	977305461602
RA-82012	AN124	977305273202
RA-82013	AN124	977305373203
RA-82014	AN124	977305473203
RA-82020	AN124	19530502001
RA-82021	AN124	19530502002
RA-82022	AN124	19530502003
RA-82023	AN124	19530502012
RA-82024	AN124	19530502033
RA-82025	AN124	19530502106
RA-82026	AN124	19530502127
RA-82028	AN124	19530502599
RA-82030	AN124	977305473204
RA-82031	AN124	977305183204
RA-82032	AN124	977305283205
RA-82033	AN124	977305283205
RA-82034	AN124	977305383205
RA-82035	AN124	977305483206
RA-82036	AN124	977305483206
RA-82037	AN124	977305295507
RA-82038	AN124	977305495507
RA-82039	AN124	977305205508
RA-82040	AN124	977305305508
RA-82041	AN124	977305405508
RA-82042	AN124	977305405509
RA-82043	AN124	977305415510
RA-82044	AN124	977305415510
RA-82045	AN124	977305225511
RA-82046	AN124	977305225511
RA-82047	AN124	977305325912
RA-82067	AN124	977305225511
RA-82068	AN124	977305135912
RA-82069	AN124	977305 5912
RA-82070	AN124	977305135912
RA-82071	AN124	977305435913
RA-82072	AN124	977305335913
RA-82073	AN124	977305435913
RA-82074	AN124	977305145914
RA-82075	AN124	977305345914
RA-82077	AN124	977305445915
RA-82078	AN124	977305455915
RA-82079	AN124	977305206215
RA-82080	AN124	977305146216
RA-82081	AN124	977305146216
RA-85007		70M007
RA-85007	TU154	88A-777
RA-85013	TU154	71A-013
RA-85013	TU154	90A-840
RA-85016	TU154	71A-016
RA-85016	TU154	90A-844
RA-85018	TU154	71A-018
RA-85018	TU154	90A-852
RA-85019	TU154	A-1019
RA-85019	TU154	71A-019
RA-85028	TU154	72A-028
RA-85031	TU154	72A-031
RA-85033	TU154	72A-033
RA-85034	TU154	72A-034
RA-85037	TU154	73A-037
RA-85038	TU154	73A-038
RA-85041	TU154	73A-041
RA-85042	TU154	73A-042
RA-85043	TU154	73A-043
RA-85051	TU154	73A-051
RA-85052	TU154	73A-052
RA-85056	TU154	74A-056
RA-85056	TU154	90A-845
RA-85057	TU154	74A-057
RA-85060	TU154	74A-060
RA-85061	TU154	74A-061
RA-85062	TU154	74A-062
RA-85064	TU154	74A-064
RA-85069	TU154	74A-069
RA-85069	TU154	90A-863
RA-85070	TU154	74A-070
RA-85075	TU154	74A-075
RA-85078	TU154	74A-078
RA-85080	TU154	74A-080
RA-85081	TU154	74A-081
RA-85081	TU154	85A-717
RA-85084	TU154	74A-084
RA-85085	TU154	90A-855
RA-85089	TU154	74A-089
RA-85089	TU154	90A-838
RA-85091	TU154	75A-091
RA-85092	TU154	75A-092
RA-85092	TU154	89A-799
RA-85094	TU154	75A-094
RA-85096	TU154	75A-096
RA-85096	TU154	89A-800
RA-85098	TU154	75A-098
RA-85099	TU154	75A-099
RA-85101	TU154	75A-101
RA-85101	TU154	88A-783
RA-85104	TU154	75A-104
RA-85106	TU154	75A-106
RA-85107	TU154	75A-107
RA-85109	TU154	75A-109
RA-85109	TU154	88A-790
RA-85110	TU154	75A-110
RA-85112	TU154	75A-112
RA-85114	TU154	75A-114
RA-85114	TU154	89A-814
RA-85115	TU154	75A-115
RA-85117	TU154	75A-117
RA-85123	TU154	75A-123
RA-85124	TU154	75A-124
RA-85130	TU154	75A-130
RA-85133	TU154	78A-133
RA-85135	TU154	76A-135
RA-85135	TU154	92A-922
RA-85136	TU154	88A-791
RA-85139	TU154	76A-139
RA-85140	TU154	76A-140
RA-85140	TU154	85A-716
RA-85141	TU154	76A-141
RA-85142	TU154	76A-142
RA-85145	TU154	76A-145
RA-85146	TU154	76A-146
RA-85146	TU154	86A-724
RA-85149	TU154	89A-797
RA-85150	TU154	76A-150
RA-85153	TU154	76A-153
RA-85155	TU154	76A-155
RA-85156	TU154	76A-156
RA-85157	TU154	76A-157
RA-85159	TU154	?
RA-85160	TU154	76A-160
RA-85164	TU154	76A-164
RA-85165	TU154	76A-165
RA-85167	TU154	76A-167
RA-85171	TU154	76A-171
RA-85171	TU154	91A-893
RA-85172	TU154	76A-172
RA-85174	TU154	76A-174
RA-85176	TU154	76A-176
RA-85178	TU154	76A-178
RA-85180	TU154	76A-180
RA-85181	TU154	76A-181
RA-85182	TU154	76A-182
RA-85183	TU154	76A-183
RA-85184	TU154	76A-184
RA-85185	TU154	76A-185
RA-85185	TU154	91A-894
RA-85187	TU154	76A-187
RA-85187	TU154	92A-919
RA-85190	TU154	76A-190
RA-85193	TU154	77A-193
RA-85195	TU154	77A-195
RA-85201	TU154	77A-201
RA-85202	TU154	77A-202
RA-85204	TU154	77A-204
RA-85204	TU154	91A-886
RA-85205	TU154	77A-205
RA-85206	TU154	77A-206
RA-85207	TU154	77A-207
RA-85212	TU154	77A-212
RA-85213	TU154	77A-213
RA-85215	TU154	77A-215
RA-85216	TU154	77A-216
RA-85217	TU154	77A-217
RA-85219	TU154	77A-219
RA-85220	TU154	77A-220
RA-85223	TU154	77A-223
RA-85226	TU154	77A-226
RA-85228	TU154	77A-228
RA-85229	TU154	77A-229
RA-85235	TU154	77A-235
RA-85236	TU154	77A-236
RA-85237	TU154	77A-237
RA-85238	TU154	77A-238
RA-85242	TU154	77A-242
RA-85253	TU154	78A-253
RA-85255	TU154	78A-255
RA-85256	TU154	78A-256
RA-85261	TU154	78A-261
RA-85263	TU154	78A-263
RA-85264	TU154	78A-264
RA-85265	TU154	78A-265
RA-85266	TU154	78A-266
RA-85267	TU154	78A-267
RA-85273	TU154	78A-273
RA-85275	TU154	78A-275
RA-85280	TU154	78A-280
RA-85283	TU154	78A-283
RA-85284	TU154	78A-284
RA-85285	TU154	78A-285
RA-85287	TU154	78A-287
RA-85289	TU154	78A-289
RA-85291	TU154	78A-291
RA-85292	TU154	78A-292
RA-85293	TU154	78A-293
RA-85295	TU154	78A-295
RA-85296	TU154	78A-296
RA-85298	TU154	78A-298
RA-85299	TU154	78A-299
RA-85300	TU154	78A-300
RA-85301	TU154	78A-301
RA-85302	TU154	78A-302
RA-85303	TU154	78A-303
RA-85304	TU154	78A-304
RA-85305	TU154	78A-305
RA-85306	TU154	78A-306
RA-85307	TU154	78A-307
RA-85308	TU154	78A-308
RA-85309	TU154	78A-309
RA-85310	TU154	78A-310
RA-85312	TU154	78A-312
RA-85314	TU154	78A-314
RA-85315	TU154	78A-315
RA-85317	TU154	78A-317
RA-85318	TU154	79A-318
RA-85319	TU154	79A-319
RA-85324	TU154	79A-324
RA-85328	TU154	79A-328
RA-85330	TU154	79A-330
RA-85332	TU154	79A-332
RA-85333	TU154	79A-333
RA-85334	TU154	79A-334
RA-85335	TU154	79A-335
RA-85336	TU154	79A-336
RA-85337	TU154	79A-337
RA-85340	TU154	79A-340
RA-85341	TU154	79A-341
RA-85343	TU154	79A-343
RA-85346	TU154	79A-346
RA-85347	TU154	79A-347
RA-85348	TU154	79A-348
RA-85349	TU154	79A-349
RA-85351	TU154	79A-351
RA-85354	TU154	79A-354
RA-85357	TU154	79A-357
RA-85358	TU154	79A-358
RA-85360	TU154	79A-360
RA-85361	TU154	79A-361
RA-85363	TU154	79A-363
RA-85365	TU154	79A-365
RA-85366	TU154	79A-366
RA-85367	TU154	79A-367
RA-85371	TU154	79A-371
RA-85373	TU154	79A-373
RA-85374	TU154	79A-374
RA-85375	TU154	79A-375
RA-85376	TU154	79A-376
RA-85377	TU154	79A-377
RA-85378	TU154	79A-378
RA-85380	TU154	79A-380
RA-85381	TU154	79A-381
RA-85382	TU154	79A-382
RA-85384	TU154	79A-384
RA-85386	TU154	79A-386
RA-85388	TU154	79A-388
RA-85389	TU154	80A-389
RA-85390	TU154	80A-390
RA-85392	TU154	80A-392
RA-85393	TU154	80A-393
RA-85395	TU154	80A-395
RA-85400	TU154	80A-400
RA-85402	TU154	80A-402
RA-85404	TU154	80A-404
RA-85409	TU154	80A-409
RA-85412	TU154	80A-412
RA-85414	TU154	80A-414
RA-85417	TU154	80A-417
RA-85418	TU154	80A-418
RA-85421	TU154	80A-421
RA-85425	TU154	80A-425
RA-85426	TU154	81A-426
RA-85427	TU154	80A-427
RA-85429	TU154	80A-429
RA-85432	TU154	80A-432
RA-85434	TU154	80A-434
RA-85435	TU154	80A-435
RA-85436	TU154	80A-436
RA-85437	TU154	80A-437
RA-85439	TU154	80A-439
RA-85441	TU154	80A-441
RA-85443	TU154	80A-443
RA-85446	TU154	80A-446
RA-85448	TU154	80A-448
RA-85450	TU154	80A-450
RA-85451	TU154	80A-451
RA-85452	TU154	80A-452
RA-85453	TU154	80A-453
RA-85454	TU154	80A-454
RA-85456	TU154	80A-456
RA-85457	TU154	80A-457
RA-85458	TU154	80A-458
RA-85459	TU154	80A-459
RA-85461	TU154	80A-461
RA-85462	TU154	80A-462
RA-85467	TU154	81A-467
RA-85468	TU154	81A-468
RA-85470	TU154	81A-470
RA-85471	TU154	81A-471
RA-85472	TU154	81A-472
RA-85477	TU154	81A-477
RA-85479	TU154	?
RA-85479?	TU154	91A-895
RA-85481	TU154	81A-481
RA-85485	TU154	81A-485
RA-85486	TU154	81A-486
RA-85488	TU154	81A-488
RA-85489	TU154	81A-489
RA-85494	TU154	81A-494
RA-85495	TU154	81A-495
RA-85498	TU154	81A-498

Registration	Type	Serial
RA-85500	TU154	81A-500
RA-85502	TU154	81A-502
RA-85503	TU154	81A-503
RA-85504	TU154	81A-504
RA-85505	TU154	81A-505
RA-85506	TU154	81A-506
RA-85508	TU154	81A-508
RA-85510	TU154	82A-510
RA-85512	TU154	81A-512
RA-85514	TU154	81A-514
RA-85520	TU154	81A-520
RA-85522	TU154	81A-522
RA-85523	TU154	81A-523
RA-85525	TU154	82A-525
RA-85527	TU154	82A-527
RA-85529	TU154	82A-529
RA-85530	TU154	82A-530
RA-85534	TU154	82A-534
RA-85540	TU154	82A-540
RA-85541	TU154	?
RA-85542	TU154	82A-542
RA-85550	TU154	82A-550
RA-85551	TU154	82A-551
RA-85552	TU154	82A-552
RA-85553	TU154	82A-553
RA-85554	TU154	82A-554
RA-85555	TU154	82A-555
RA-85556	TU154	82A-556
RA-85557	TU154	82A-557
RA-85559	TU154	82A-559
RA-85562	TU154	82A-562
RA-85563	TU154	82A-563
RA-85564	TU154	82A-564
RA-85565	TU154	82A-565
RA-85567	TU154	83A-567
RA-85568	TU154	83A-568
RA-85570	TU154	83A-570
RA-85571	TU154	83A-571
RA-85572	TU154	83A-572
RA-85574	TU154	83A-574
RA-85577	TU154	83A-577
RA-85579	TU154	83A-579
RA-85583	TU154	83A-583
RA-85584	TU154	83A-584
RA-85585	TU154	83A-585
RA-85586	TU154	83A-586
RA-85587	TU154	83A-587
RA-85588	TU154	83A-588
RA-85592	TU154	83A-592
RA-85594	TU154	83A-594
RA-85595	TU154	83A-595
RA-85596	TU154	84A-596
RA-85597	TU154	84A-597
RA-85602	TU154	84A-602
RA-85603	TU154	84A-603
RA-85604	TU154	84A-604
RA-85605	TU154	84A-605
RA-85606	TU154	84A-701
RA-85607	TU154	84A-702
RA-85610	TU154	84A-705
RA-85611	TU154	85A-715
RA-85612	TU154	85A-721
RA-85613	TU154	85A-722
RA-85614	TU154	86A-723
RA-85615	TU154	86A-731
RA-85616	TU154	86A-732
RA-85618	TU154	86A-737
RA-85619	TU154	86A-738
RA-85620	TU154	86A-739
RA-85621	TU154	86A-742
RA-85622	TU154	87A-746
RA-85623	TU154	87A-749
RA-85624	TU154	87A-750
RA-85625	TU154	87A-752
RA-85626	TU154	87A-753
RA-85627	TU154	87A-756
RA-85628	TU154	87A-757
RA-85629	TU154	87A-758
RA-85630	TU154	87A-759
RA-85631	TU154	87A-760
RA-85632	TU154	87A-761
RA-85633	TU154	87A-762
RA-85634	TU154	87A-763
RA-85635	TU154	87A-764
RA-85636	TU154	87A-766
RA-85637	TU154	87A-767
RA-85638	TU154	87A-768
RA-85639	TU154	88A-771
RA-85640	TU154	88A-772
RA-85641	TU154	88A-773
RA-85642	TU154	88A-778
RA-85643	TU154	88A-779
RA-85644	TU154	88A-780
RA-85645	TU154	88A-782
RA-85646	TU154	88A-784
RA-85647	TU154	88A-785
RA-85648	TU154	88A-786
RA-85649	TU154	88A-787
RA-85650	TU154	88A-788
RA-85651	TU154	88A-793
RA-85652	TU154	88A-794
RA-85653	TU154	88A-795
RA-85654	TU154	88A-796
RA-85655	TU154	89A-798
RA-85656	TU154	89A-801
RA-85657	TU154	89A-802
RA-85658	TU154	89A-808
RA-85659	TU154	89A-809
RA-85660	TU154	89A-810
RA-85661	TU154	89A-811
RA-85662	TU154	89A-816
RA-85663	TU154	89A-817
RA-85665	TU154	89A-819
RA-85666	TU154	89A-820
RA-85667	TU154	89A-825
RA-85668	TU154	89A-826
RA-85669	TU154	89A-827
RA-85670	TU154	89A-828
RA-85671	TU154	89A-829
RA-85672	TU154	89A-830
RA-85673	TU154	90A-833
RA-85674	TU154	90A-834
RA-85675	TU154	90A-835
RA-85676	TU154	90A-836
RA-85677	TU154	90A-839
RA-85678	TU154	90A-841
RA-85679	TU154	90A-842
RA-85680	TU154	90A-843
RA-85681	TU154	90A-848
RA-85682	TU154	90A-849
RA-85683	TU154	90A-850
RA-85684	TU154	90A-851
RA-85685	TU154	90A-853
RA-85686	TU154	90A-854
RA-85687	TU154	90A-857
RA-05688	TU154	90A-859
RA-85689	TU154	90A-860
RA-85690	TU154	90A-861
RA-85693	TU154	91A-866
RA-85694	TU154	91A-867
RA-85695	TU154	91A-868
RA-85696	TU154	91A-869
RA-85697	TU154	91A-870
RA-85699	TU154	91A-874
RA-85700	TU154	91A-875
RA-85702	TU154	91A-877
RA-85704	TU154	91A-879
RA-85705	TU154	91A-880
RA-85708	TU154	91A-883
RA-85709	TU154	91A-884
RA-85710	TU154	91A-885
RA-85712	TU154	91A-888
RA-85713	TU154	91A-889
RA-85714	TU154	91A-890
RA-85715	TU154	91A-891
RA-85716	TU154	91A-892
RA-85719	TU154	91A-901
RA-85720	TU154	91A-902
RA-85721	TU154	87A-751
RA-85722	TU154	91A-904
RA-85723	TU154	91A-905
RA-85724	TU154	91A-906
RA-85725	TU154	91A-907
RA-85726	TU154	86A-725
RA-85726	TU154	92A-908
RA-85727	TU154	92A-909
RA-85728	TU154	92A-910
RA-85730	TU154	92A-912
RA-85731	TU154	92A-913
RA-85733	TU154	92A-915
RA-85734	TU154	86A-734
RA-85735	TU154	92A-917
RA-85736	TU154	92A-918
RA-85739	TU154	92A-925
RA-85740	TU154	91A-895
RA-85742	TU154	79A-320
RA-85743	TU154	92A-926
RA-85744	TU154	92A-927
RA-85745	TU154	92A-928
RA-85746	TU154	92A-929
RA-85747	TU154	92A-930
RA-85749	TU154	92A-931
RA-85750	TU154	92A-932
RA-85751	TU154	92A-933
RA-85752	TU154	92A-934
RA-85753	TU154	92A-935
RA-85754	TU154	92A-936
RA-85755	TU154	92A-937
RA-85756	TU154	92A-938
RA-85757	TU154	92A-939
RA-85758	TU154	92A-940
RA-85759	TU154	92A-941
RA-85760	TU154	92A-942
RA-85761	TU154	92A-944
RA-85762	TU154	92A-945
RA-85763	TU154	93A-946
RA-85764	TU154	93A-947
RA-85765	TU154	90A-832
RA-85766	TU154	92A-923
RA-85767	TU154	93A-948
RA-85768	TU154	93A-949
RA-85769	TU154	93A-951
RA-85770	TU154	93A-952
RA-85771	TU154	93A-953
RA-85772	TU154	93A-954
RA-85773	TU154	93A-955
RA-85774	TU154	93A-956
RA-85775	TU154	93A-957
RA-85777	TU154	93A-959
RA-85778	TU154	93A-962
RA-85779	TU154	93A-963
RA-85780	TU154	93A-964
RA-85782	TU154	93A-966
RA-85783	TU154	93A-967
RA-85784	TU154	93A-968
RA-85785	TU154	93A-969
RA-85786	TU154	93A-970
RA-85787	TU154	93A-971
RA-85788	TU154	93A-972
RA-85789	TU154	93A-973
RA-85790	TU154	93A-974
RA-85791	TU154	93A-975
RA-85792	TU154	93A-976
RA-85793	TU154	93A-977
RA-85794	TU154	93A-978
RA-85795	TU154	93A-979
RA-85796	TU154	94A-980
RA-85797	TU154	93A-981
RA-85798	TU154	93A-982
RA-85799	TU154	94A-983
RA-85800	TU154	94A-984
RA-85801	TU154	93A-960
RA-85802	TU154	93A-961
RA-85803	TU154	89A-822
RA-85804	TU154	81A-517
RA-85805	TU154	94A-986
RA-85806	TU154	94A-987
RA-85807	TU154	94A-988
RA-85808	TU154	94A-989
RA-85809	TU154	94A-985
RA-85810	TU154	89A-824
RA-85811	TU154	90A-831
RA-85812	TU154	94A-1005
RA-85813	TU154	95A-990
RA-85814	TU154	95A-994
RA-85816	TU154	95A-1006
RA-85817	TU154	95A-1007
RA-85818	TU154	85A-719
RA-85819	TU154	97A-1008
RA-85820	TU154	98A-995
RA-85821	TU154	89A-805
RA-85822	TU154	89A-806
RA-85823	TU154	88A-775
RA-85824	TU154	87A-769
RA-85825	TU154	88A-776
RA-85826	TU154	89A-812
RA-85827	TU154	87A-745
RA-85828	TU154	97A-1009
RA-85829	TU154	87A-755
RA-85830	TU154	89A-821
RA-85831	TU154	88A-774
RA-85832	TU154	92A-908
RA-85833	TU154	01A-1020
RA-85834	TU154	98A-1014
RA-85835	TU154	98A-1015
RA-85836	TU154	98A-1018
RA-85837	TU154	91A-876
RA-85840	TU154	98A-1011
RA-85841	TU154	90A-858
RA-85842	TU154	80A-420
RA-85843	TU154	01A-991
RA-85844	TU154	03A-992
RA-85845	TU154	86A-735
RA-85846	TU154	89A-807
RA-85847	TU154	88A-792
RA-85848	TU154	89A-804
RA-85849	TU154	89A-815
RA-85851	TU154	82A-531
RA-86002	IL86	0103
RA-86004	IL86	51483200002
RA-86006	IL86	51483200004
RA-86007	IL86	51483200005
RA-86010	IL86	51483201008
RA-86011	IL86	51483201009
RA-86012	IL86	51483201010
RA-86013	IL86	51483201011
RA-86015	IL86	51483202013
RA-86017	IL86	51483202015
RA-86018	IL86	51483202016
RA-86020	IL76	083413403
RA-86022	IL76	083413417
RA-86023	IL76	083413422
RA-86025	IL76	083414433
RA-86026	IL76	083414439
RA-86027	IL76	083415459
RA-86032	IL76	093415482
RA-86033	IL76	093416488
RA-86034	IL76	093416489
RA-86035	IL76	093416494
RA-86037	IL76	093417514
RA-86038	IL76	093417514
RA-86040	IL76	093417521
RA-86041	IL76	093417532
RA-86042	IL76	093417535
RA-86043	IL76	093418539
RA-86044	IL76	093418552
RA-86045	IL76	093418564
RA-86048	IL76	093419573
RA-86049	IL76	093419580
RA-86050	IL86	51483202017
RA-86051	IL86	51483202018
RA-86053	IL86	51483202020
RA-86054	IL86	51483203021
RA-86055	IL86	51483203022
RA-86058	IL86	51483203025
RA-86059	IL86	51483203026
RA-86060	IL86	51483203027
RA-86061	IL86	51483203028
RA-86062	IL86	51483203029
RA-86063	IL86	51483203030
RA-86065	IL86	51483204032
RA-86066	IL86	51483204033
RA-86067	IL86	51483204034
RA-86070	IL86	51483204037
RA-86073	IL86	51483204040
RA-86074	IL86	51483205041
RA-86075	IL86	51483205044
RA-86078	IL86	51483205049

Reg.	Type	Serial	Reg.	Type	Serial	Reg.	Type	Serial	Reg.	Type	Serial
RA-86079	IL86	51483205050	RA-86480	IL62	2828354	RA-86590	IL62	2647737	RA-86847	IL76	0003426769
RA-86080	IL86	51483206051	RA-86481	IL62	2829415	RA-86597	IL62	2932748	RA-86848	IL76	0003426776
RA-86081	IL86	51483206052	RA-86482	IL62	2829526	RA-86600	IL76	033401022	RA-86849	IL76	0003426779
RA-86082	IL86	51483206053	RA-86483	IL62	2829637	RA-86604	IL76	043402039	RA-86850	IL76	0003427782
RA-86084	IL86	51483206055	RA-86484	IL62	4727324	RA-86611	IL62	41803	RA-86851	IL76	0003424715
RA-86085	IL86	51483206056	RA-86485	IL62	3830912	RA-86618	IL62	3520422	RA-86853	IL76	0003424723
RA-86087	IL86	51483206058	RA-86486	IL62	3830123	RA-86620	IL62	3520345	RA-86855	IL76	0003425734
RA-86088	IL86	51483206059	RA-86487	IL62	3830234	RA-86621	IL62	3520556	RA-86856	IL76	0003425740
RA-86089	IL86	51483206060	RA-86488	IL62	4830345	RA-86622	IL62	4521617	RA-86857	IL76	0003425744
RA-86091	IL86	51483207062	RA-86489	IL62	4830456	RA-86623	IL62	4521728	RA-86858	IL76	0003426759
RA-86092	IL86	51483207063	RA-86490	IL62	4831739	RA-86625	IL76	063405130	RA-86860	IL76	0003426759
RA-86093	IL86	51483207064	RA-86491	IL62	1931142	RA-86627	IL76	063405137	RA-86861	IL76	0003427804
RA-86094	IL86	51483207065	RA-86492	IL62	4140324	RA-86628	IL76	063405144	RA-86862	IL76	0003427806
RA-86095	IL86	51483207066	RA-86493	IL62	4140748	RA-86642	IL76	073409248	RA-86863	IL76	0003428809
RA-86096	IL86	51483207067	RA-86494	IL62	4140859	RA-86646	IL76	1003403115	RA-86865	IL76	0003428817
RA-86097	IL86	51483207068	RA-86495	IL62	2726628	RA-86647	IL76	043402060	RA-86866	IL76	0003428821
RA-86102	IL86	51483207070	RA-86496	IL62	3829859	RA-86649	IL62	00703	RA-86867	IL76	0013428828
RA-86103	IL86	51483208071	RA-86497	IL62	1931253	RA-86656	IL62	00901	RA-86868	IL76	0013428833
RA-86104	IL86	51483208072	RA-86498	IL62	1932314	RA-86657	IL62	10904	RA-86869	IL76	0013428844
RA-86105	IL86	51483208073	RA-86499	IL62	2932637	RA-86673	IL62	3154416	RA-86870	IL76	0013429847
RA-86106	IL86	51483208074	RA-86501	IL62	3933121	RA-86674	IL62	80304	RA-86871	IL76	0013434002
RA-86107	IL86	51483208075	RA-86502	IL62	3933345	RA-86675	IL62	80305	RA-86872	IL76	0013434008
RA-86108	IL86	51483208076	RA-86503	IL62	4934512	RA-86692	IL62	11102	RA-86873	IL76	0013429850
RA-86109	IL86	51483208077	RA-86504	IL62	4934623	RA-86693	IL62	11103	RA-86874	IL76	0013429853
RA-86110	IL86	51483208078	RA-86506	IL62	1035234	RA-86699	IL62	21304	RA-86875	IL76	0013429859
RA-86111	IL86	51483208079	RA-86507	IL62	2035546	RA-86700	IL62	31503	RA-86876	IL76	0013429861
RA-86112	IL86	51483208080	RA-86509	IL62	2036829	RA-86701	IL62	31504	RA-86877	IL76	0013429867
RA-86113	IL86	51483209081	RA-86510	IL62	1035213	RA-86702	IL62	31505	RA-86880	IL76	0013430871
RA-86114	IL86	51483209082	RA-86511	IL62	3036142	RA-86703	IL62	31601	RA-86881	IL76	0013431906
RA-86115	IL86	51483209083	RA-86512	IL62	3037314	RA-86705	IL62	41605	RA-86882	IL76	0013431917
RA-86119	IL86	51483209087	RA-86514	IL62	4037647	RA-86706	IL62	21105	RA-86883	IL76	0013431921
RA-86120	IL86	51483209088	RA-86515	IL62	2138657	RA-86706	IL62	41802	RA-86884	IL76	0013431932
RA-86121	IL86	51483209089	RA-86516	IL62	2139524	RA-86707	IL62	41604	RA-86885	IL76	0013431939
RA-86122	IL86	51483209090	RA-86517	IL62	3139732	RA-86709	IL62	62204	RA-86886	IL76	0013431943
RA-86123	IL86	51483210091	RA-86518	IL62	3139956	RA-86710	IL62	2647646	RA-86887	IL76	0013431945
RA-86124	IL86	51483210092	RA-86519	IL62	4140212	RA-86711	IL62	4648414	RA-86888	IL76	0013432966
RA-86125	IL86	51483210093	RA-86520	IL62	1241314	RA-86712	IL62	4648339	RA-86891	IL76	093421628
RA-86126	IL62	4154535	RA-86521	IL62	1241425	RA-86715	IL76	053403072	RA-86893	IL76	0013432975
RA-86127	IL62	1254851	RA-86522	IL62	2241536	RA-86720	IL76	073409267	RA-86894	IL76	0013432977
RA-86128	IL62	2255719	RA-86523	IL62	2241647	RA-86726	IL76	083412380	RA-86895	IL76	0013433985
RA-86129	IL62	2255525	RA-86524	IL62	3242321	RA-86727	IL76	083413383	RA-86896	IL76	0013434018
RA-86130	IL62	3255333	RA-86525	IL62	4851612	RA-86731	IL76	083413391	RA-86897	IL76	0013434023
RA-86131	IL62	4255244	RA-86526	IL62	2951447	RA-86733	IL76	083413396	RA-86898	IL76	0023435028
RA-86136	IL86	51483210094	RA-86530	IL62	3242543	RA-86734	IL76	083413397	RA-86900	IL76	0023435034
RA-86137	IL86	51483210095	RA-86531	IL62	4242654	RA-86736	IL76	083411342	RA-86901	IL76	0023436038
RA-86138	IL86	51483210096	RA-86532	IL62	4243111	RA-86737	IL76	083411347	RA-86902	IL76	0023436043
RA-86139	IL86	51483210098	RA-86533	IL62	1343123	RA-86738	IL76	083411352	RA-86906	IL76	0023436064
RA-86140	IL86	51483211102	RA-86534	IL62	1343332	RA-86740	IL76	083412358	RA-86907	IL76	0023436065
RA-86141	IL86	51483211103	RA-86535	IL62	2444555	RA-86741	IL76	083412361	RA-86908	IL76	0023437077
RA-86142	IL86	51483210097	RA-86536	IL62	4445948	RA-86742	IL76	083412365	RA-86910	IL76	0023437077
RA-86143	IL86	51483210099	RA-86537	IL62	3546733	RA-86743	IL76	083412369	RA-86925	IL76	0093492766
RA-86144	IL86	51483210035	RA-86538	IL62	2241758	RA-86744	IL76	083412376	RA-86926	IL86	51483210100
RA-86145	IL86	51483210097	RA-86539	IL62	2344615	RA-86746	IL76	063407165	RA-86931	IL62	3344724
RA-86145	IL86	51483211101	RA-86540	IL62	3546548	RA-86747	IL76	063407170	RA-86935	IL62	1545951
RA-86146	IL86	514832050422?	RA-86541	IL62	3951359	RA-86748	IL76	063407175	RA-86945	IL62	3850145
RA-86147	IL86	514832050432?	RA-86542	IL62	3952714	RA-86749	IL76	063407179	RA-87200	YAK40	9811956
RA-86148	IL86	514832050462?	RA-86552	IL62	2052345	RA-86805	IL76	053403073	RA-87203	YAK40	9741456
RA-86149	IL86	514832050482?	RA-86553	IL62	3052657	RA-86806	IL76	053403078	RA-87204	YAK40	9810157
RA-86450	IL62	3623856	RA-86554	IL62	4053514	RA-86809	IL76	053404091	RA-87209	YAK40	9810657
RA-86452	IL62	1622212	RA-86555	IL62	4547315	RA-86810	IL76	053404094	RA-87210	YAK40	9810757
RA-86453	IL62	1622323	RA-86557	IL62	2725456	RA-86812	IL76	053404103	RA-87211	YAK40	9440737
RA-86454	IL62	1622434	RA-86558	IL62	1052128	RA-86813	IL76	053404105	RA-87216	YAK40	9510440
RA-86455	IL62	2622656	RA-86559	IL62	2153258	RA-86814	IL76	053405110	RA-87219	YAK40	9932059
RA-86457	IL62	2623822	RA-86560	IL62	2153347	RA-86825	IL76	093419581	RA-87221	YAK40	9831958
RA-86459	IL62	3623945	RA-86561	IL62	4154842	RA-86826	IL76	093419588	RA-87222	YAK40	9832058
RA-86461	IL62	3624711	RA-86562	IL62	4831517	RA-86827	IL76	093419589	RA-87223	YAK40	9840359
RA-86462	IL62	3624623	RA-86563	IL62	3036931	RA-86828	IL76	093420604	RA-87224	YAK40	9841459
RA-86463	IL62	4624434	RA-86564	IL62	4934734	RA-86829	IL76	0003427798	RA-87225	YAK40	9841359
RA-86464	IL62	4624151	RA-86565	IL62	2546812	RA-86830	IL76	093421626	RA-87226	YAK40	9841259
RA-86465	IL62	4625315	RA-86566	IL62	4255152	RA-86832	IL76	0003421646	RA-87227	YAK40	9841559
RA-86466	IL62	2749316	RA-86567	IL62	4256314	RA-86833	IL76	0003422650	RA-87228	YAK40	9841659
RA-86467	IL62	3749733	RA-86568	IL62	4256223	RA-86835	IL76	0003422658	RA-87229	YAK40	9841759
RA-86468	IL62	4749857	RA-86570	IL62	1356344	RA-86836	IL76	0003422661	RA-87232	YAK40	9531742
RA-86469	IL62	1725121	RA-86571	IL62	?	RA-86837	IL76	0003423668	RA-87234	YAK40	9531942
RA-86471	IL62	2725345	RA-86572	IL62	3154624	RA-86838	IL76	0003423669	RA-87235	YAK40	9530143
RA-86472	IL62	2726517	RA-86575	IL62	1647928	RA-86839	IL76	0003423684	RA-87238	YAK40	9530543
RA-86473	IL62	3726641	RA-86576	IL62	4546257	RA-86840	IL76	0003423688	RA-87239	YAK40	9530743
RA-86474	IL62	3726952	RA-86577	IL62	2748552	RA-86841	IL76	0003423690	RA-87240	YAK40	9530743
RA-86475	IL62	3727213	RA-86579	IL62	2951636	RA-86842	IL76	0003423694	RA-87241	YAK40	9530943
RA-86476	IL62	4728229	RA-86583	IL62	1356851	RA-86843	IL76	0003423701	RA-87244	YAK40	9531243
RA-86478	IL62	4727657	RA-86584	IL62	?	RA-86844	IL76	0003424711	RA-87245	YAK40	9531343
RA-86479	IL62	4728118	RA-86586	IL62	3357947	RA-86845	IL76	0003426762			
						RA-86846	IL76	0003426765			

Reg.	Type	c/n	Reg.	Type	c/n	Reg.	Type	c/n	Reg.	Type	c/n
RA-87247	YAK40	9531543	RA-87407	YAK40	9421933	RA-87575	YAK40	9220722	RA-87944	YAK40	9540845
RA-87248	YAK40	9540144	RA-87410	YAK40	9420234	RA-87576	YAK40	9220822	RA-87947	YAK40	9621145
RA-87251	YAK40	9310826	RA-87414	YAK40	9420634	RA-87577	YAK40	9220922	RA-87949	YAK40	9621345
RA-87252	YAK40	9310926	RA-87416	YAK40	9420834	RA-87578	YAK40	9221022	RA-87950	YAK40	9810857
RA-87253	YAK40	9321026	RA-87417	YAK40	9420934	RA-87580	YAK40	9221222	RA-87952	YAK40	9811057
RA-87254	YAK40	9311126	RA-87418	YAK40	9421034	RA-87581	YAK40	9221322	RA-87953	YAK40	9811157
RA-87255	YAK40	9311226	RA-87422	YAK40	9421834	RA-87582	YAK40	9221422	RA-87954	YAK40	9811357
RA-87256	YAK40	9311326	RA-87423	YAK40	9421934	RA-87583	YAK40	9221522	RA-87956	YAK40	9821757
RA-87260	YAK40	9311126A	RA-87424	YAK40	9422034	RA-87586	YAK40	9221822	RA-87957	YAK40	9821857
RA-87261	YAK40	9311726	RA-87425	YAK40	9420135	RA-87587	YAK40	9221922	RA-87958	YAK40	9821957
RA-87262	YAK40	9321826	RA-87428	YAK40	9420435	RA-87588	YAK40	9222022	RA-87959	YAK40	9822057
RA-87266	YAK40	9310227	RA-87429	YAK40	9420535	RA-87606	YAK40	9120518	RA-87962	YAK40	9820558
RA-87268	YAK40	9310427	RA-87431	YAK40	9420735	RA-87611	YAK40	9121018	RA-87965	YAK40	9820858
RA-87270	YAK40	9310627	RA-87433	YAK40	9420935	RA-87615	YAK40	9131618	RA-87966	YAK40	9820958
RA-87272	YAK40	9330827	RA-87436	YAK40	9431235	RA-87621	YAK40	9130219	RA-87968	YAK40	9841258
RA-87277	YAK40	9311327	RA-87438	YAK40	9431435	RA-87625	YAK40	9130619	RA-87969	YAK40	9831358
RA-87279	YAK40	9321527	RA-87439	YAK40	9431535	RA-87640	YAK40	9140120	RA-87970	YAK40	9831458
RA-87280	YAK40	9322025	RA-87440	YAK40	9431635	RA-87645	YAK40	9140620	RA-87971	YAK40	9831558
RA-87281	YAK40	9311627	RA-87443	YAK40	9432035	RA-87646	YAK40	9140720	RA-87972	YAK40	9921658
RA-87284	YAK40	9311927	RA-87444	YAK40	9430136	RA-87647	YAK40	9140820	RA-87973	YAK40	9041860
RA-87286	YAK40	9310128	RA-87447	YAK40	9430436	RA-87648	YAK40	9140920	RA-87974	YAK40	9041960
RA-87287	YAK40	9320228	RA-87449	YAK40	9430636	RA-87651	YAK40	9141220	RA-87977	YAK40	9321128
RA-87288	YAK40	9320328	RA-87450	YAK40	9430736	RA-87652	YAK40	9141320	RA-87981	YAK40	9540444
RA-87290	YAK40	9320528	RA-87452	YAK40	9430936	RA-87653	YAK40	9211620	RA-87983	YAK40	9540644
RA-87292	YAK40	9320728	RA-87456	YAK40	9431336	RA-87655	YAK40	9211820	RA-87984	YAK40	9540744
RA-87294	YAK40	9320928	RA-87460	YAK40	9431936	RA-87656	YAK40	9211920	RA-87986	YAK40	9540944
RA-87295	YAK40	9321228	RA-87462	YAK40	9430137	RA-87659	YAK40	9240325	RA-87988	YAK40	9541244
RA-87297	YAK40	9321428	RA-87464	YAK40	9430337	RA-87662	YAK40	9240625	RA-87991	YAK40	9541544
RA-87299	YAK40	9341528	RA-87465	YAK40	9430437	RA-87663	YAK40	9240725	RA-87992	YAK40	9541644
RA-87300	YAK40	9321628	RA-87467	YAK40	9440637	RA-87665	YAK40	9240925	RA-87993	YAK40	9541744
RA-87303	YAK40	9321928	RA-87468	YAK40	9441337	RA-87667	YAK40	9241525	RA-87994	YAK40	9541844
RA-87304	YAK40	9322028	RA-87471	YAK40	9441637	RA-87669	YAK40	9021760	RA-87997	YAK40	9540145
RA-87307	YAK40	9320329	RA-87473	YAK40	9441837	RA-87755	YAK40	9021011	RA-87999	YAK40	9540345
RA-87311	YAK40	9320629	RA-87474	YAK40	9441937	RA-87801	YAK40	9220423	RA-88144	YAK40	?
RA-87315	YAK40	9331429	RA-87476	YAK40	9440438	RA-87802	YAK40	9230523	RA-88150	YAK40	9610346
RA-87317	YAK40	9331629	RA-87481	YAK40	9440938	RA-87802	YAK40	9411333	RA-88153	YAK40	9610746
RA-87319	YAK40	9331829	RA-87482	YAK40	9441038	RA-87805	YAK40	9231123	RA-88155	YAK40	9610946
RA-87321	YAK40	9332029	RA-87483	YAK40	9441138	RA-87807	YAK40	9231723	RA-88156	YAK40	9611046
RA-87324	YAK40	9330330	RA-87484	YAK40	9441238	RA-87809	YAK40	9231923	RA-88159	YAK40	9611346
RA-87325	YAK40	9330430	RA-87486	YAK40	9441438	RA-87810	YAK40	9232023	RA-88160	YAK40	9611446
RA-87326	YAK40	9330530	RA-87487	YAK40	9441538	RA-87814	YAK40	9230524	RA-88163	YAK40	9611746
RA-87332	YAK40	9510339	RA-87489	YAK40	9512038	RA-87815	YAK40	9230624	RA-88164	YAK40	9611846
RA-87334	YAK40	9510738	RA-87493	YAK40	9611645	RA-87820	YAK40	9231224	RA-88165	YAK40	9611946
RA-87336	YAK40	9510539	RA-87494	YAK40	9541745	RA-87821	YAK40	9241324	RA-88166	YAK40	9612046
RA-87339	YAK40	9510839	RA-87495	YAK40	9541845	RA-87822	YAK40	9241424	RA-88168	YAK40	9610647
RA-87340	YAK40	9510939	RA-87496	YAK40	9541945	RA-87823	YAK40	9241524	RA-88170	YAK40	9620847
RA-87341	YAK40	9521039	RA-87497	YAK40	9542045	RA-87828	YAK40	9242024	RA-88171	YAK40	9620947
RA-87342	YAK40	9511139	RA-87499	YAK40	9610246	RA-87829	YAK40	9240125	RA-88172	YAK40	9631047
RA-87343	YAK40	9511239	RA-87500	YAK40	9511939	RA-87834	YAK40	9241125	RA-88175	YAK40	9621347
RA-87344	YAK40	9511339	RA-87502	YAK40	9510140	RA-87837	YAK40	9240326	RA-88176	YAK40	9621447
RA-87348	YAK40	9511739	RA-87503	YAK40	9520240	RA-87838	YAK40	9240426	RA-88177	YAK40	9621747
RA-87350	YAK40	9331930	RA-87505	YAK40	9510740	RA-87839	YAK40	9240526	RA-88179	YAK40	9621947
RA-87351	YAK40	9412030	RA-87506	YAK40	9520840	RA-87840	YAK40	9240626	RA-88180	YAK40	9622047
RA-87352	YAK40	9330131	RA-87507	YAK40	9520940	RA-87842	YAK40	9331030	RA-88182	YAK40	9620248
RA-87353	YAK40	9330231	RA-87510	YAK40	9621240	RA-87843	YAK40	9331130	RA-88184	YAK40	9620448
RA-87357	YAK40	9340631	RA-87511	YAK40	9521340	RA-87844	YAK40	9331230	RA-88186	YAK40	9620648
RA 87358	YAK40	9340731	RA-87513	YAK40	9521540	RA-87845	YAK40	9331430	RA-88188	YAK40	9620848
RA-87359	YAK40	9340831	RA-87514	YAK40	9521640	RA-87847	YAK40	9331630	RA-88190	YAK40	9621048
RA-87362	YAK40	9341131	RA-87516	YAK40	9521840	RA-87849	YAK40	9331830	RA-88193	YAK40	9621348
RA-87364	YAK40	9341331	RA-87517	YAK40	9521940	RA-87900	YAK40	9720254	RA-88200	YAK40	9630149
RA-87365	YAK40	9341531	RA-87518	YAK40	9520040	(RA-87901)	YAK40	9720354	RA-88201	YAK40	9630349
RA-87368	YAK40	9341831	RA-87519	YAK40	9520141	RA-87903	YAK40	9720654	RA-88204	YAK40	9630649
RA-87371	YAK40	9340232	RA-87520	YAK40	9520241	RA-87904	YAK40	9720854	RA-88205	YAK40	9630749
RA-87372	YAK40	9340332	RA-87524	YAK40	9520641	RA-87905	YAK40	9730954	RA-88206	YAK40	9630949
RA-87373	YAK40	9410732	RA-87527	YAK40	9520941	RA-87906	YAK40	9731054	RA-88207	YAK40	9631149
RA-87374	YAK40	9410832	RA-87530	YAK40	9521241	RA-87907	YAK40	9731254	RA-88209	YAK40	9710353
RA-87375	YAK40	9410932	RA-87533	YAK40	9541741	RA-87908	YAK40	9721354	RA-88210	YAK40	9631649
RA-87376	YAK40	9411032	RA-87534	YAK40	9521841	RA-87910	YAK40	9731654	RA-88212	YAK40	9631849
RA-87380	YAK40	9421225	RA-87535	YAK40	9521941	RA-87912	YAK40	9732054	RA-88213	YAK40	9631949
RA-87381	YAK40	9411232	RA-87541	YAK40	9530642	RA-87915	YAK40	9730455	RA-88215	YAK40	9630150
RA-87382	YAK40	9411332	RA-87546	YAK40	9531142	RA-87916	YAK40	9730555	RA-88216	YAK40	9630250
RA-87383	YAK40	9411432	RA-87550	YAK40	9210121	RA-87917	YAK40	9730755	RA-88218	YAK40	9630450
RA-87385	YAK40	9411632	RA-87551	YAK40	9210221	RA-87919	YAK40	9730955	RA-88220	YAK40	9630650
RA-87388	YAK40	9412032	RA-87552	YAK40	9210321	RA-87921	YAK40	9731155	RA-88222	YAK40	9630850
RA-87392	YAK40	9410433	RA-87556	YAK40	9210721	RA-87924	YAK40	9731555	RA-88223	YAK40	9640950
RA-87393	YAK40	9410533	RA-87558	YAK40	9210921	RA-87925	YAK40	9731655	RA-88224	YAK40	9641150
RA-87395	YAK40	9410733	RA-87560	YAK40	9211521	RA-87936	YAK40	9740756	RA-88225	YAK40	9641250
RA-87397	YAK40	9410933	RA-87565	YAK40	9211721	RA-87938	YAK40	9710153	RA-88226	YAK40	9641350
RA-87400	YAK40	9421233	RA-87568	YAK40	9222021	RA-87939	YAK40	9640352	RA-88227	YAK40	9641550
RA-87404	YAK40	9411633	RA-87569	YAK40	9220222	RA-87940	YAK40	9540445	RA-88228	YAK40	9641750
RA-87405	YAK40	9421733	RA-87572	YAK40	9220422	RA-87941	YAK40	9540545	RA-88229	YAK40	9641850
RA-87406	YAK40	9421833	RA-87573	YAK40	9220522	RA-87942	YAK40	9610645	RA-88231	YAK40	9642050

RA-88232	YAK40	9640151
RA-88234	YAK40	9640351
RA-88236	YAK40	9640551
RA-88238	YAK40	9640951
RA-88239	YAK40	9641051
RA-88240	YAK40	9641151
RA-88241	YAK40	9641351
RA-88243	YAK40	9641651
RA-88244	YAK40	9641751
RA-88246	YAK40	9641951
RA-88247	YAK40	9642051
RA-88251	YAK40	9710552
RA-88254	YAK40	9710952
RA-88255	YAK40	9711052
RA-88257	YAK40	9711252
RA-88258	YAK40	9711352
RA-88261	YAK40	9711652
RA-88263	YAK40	9711852
RA-88264	YAK40	9711952
RA-88265	YAK40	9722052
RA-88269	YAK40	9720753
RA-88270	YAK40	9720853
RA-88273	YAK40	9721153
RA-88274	YAK40	9721253
RA-88275	YAK40	9721353
RA-88276	YAK40	9721453
RA-88278	YAK40	9722053
RA-88280	YAK40	9820658
RA-88285	YAK40	?
RA-88287	YAK40	9940360
RA-88291	YAK40	9530541
RA-88292	YAK40	9610446
RA-88293	YAK40	9510138
RA-88294	YAK40	9331029
RA-88295	YAK40	9331329
RA-88296	YAK40	9421634
RA-88297	YAK40	9530142
RA-88298	YAK40	9930160
RA-88300	YAK40	9641451
RA-88301	YAK40	9641251
RA-88304	YAK40	9510439
RA-88306	YAK40	9640651
RA-88307	YAK40	9421334
RA-88308	YAK40	9230224
RA-93876	AN7x	72093876
RA-93926	TU134	1351204
RA-93927	TU134	2351508
RA-94001	TU334	01001
RA-94005	TU334	01005
RA-96000	IL96	0101
RA-96001	IL96	0103
RA-96002	IL96	74393201001
RA-96005	IL96	74393201002
RA-96006	IL96	74393201003
RA-96007	IL96	74393201004
RA-96008	IL96	74393201005
RA-96009	IL96	74393201006
RA-96010	IL96	74393201007
RA-96011	IL96	74393201008
RA-96012	IL96	74393201009
(RA-96013)	IL96	74393202010
RA-96013	IL96	74393202013
(RA-96014)	IL96	74393202011
RA-96014	IL96	74393202014
RA-96015	IL96	74393202012
RA-96016	IL96	74393202017
RA-96017	IL96	74393202011
RA-96018	IL96	74393202018
RA-96101	IL96	?
RA-96102	IL96	0102?
RA-98106	YAK40	9740656
RA-98109	YAK40	9740956
RA-98110	YAK40	9741556
RA-98111	YAK40	9741656
RA-98113	YAK40	9710253

Croatia
(see also 9A-)

RC-CTA	B737	22119
RC-CTB	B737	22116
RC-CTC	B737	22118

Laos
(see also XW-)

RDPL-34001	YAK40	9431835
RDPL-34002	YAK40	9840559
RDPL-34018	AN7x	470991005
RDPL-34125	B737	20363
RDPL-34126	B737	19553
RDPL-34133	B737	21440
RDPL-34138	IL76	0033447365
RDPL-34141	IL76	0053465941
RDPL-34146	IL76	0043449468
RDPL-34148	IL76	1013409310

Russia
(see also CCCP-, RA-)

RF-21512	BE200	003'
RF-31112	AN7x	47136012
RF-32765	BE200	10101
RF-32768	BE200	?
RF-32769	BE200	?
RF-72011	AN7x	?
RF-72016	AN7x	?
RF-72025	AN7x	?
RF-76325	IL76	0093493810
RF-76326	IL76	?
RF-87659	YAK40	9240325
RF-88301	YAK40	9641251
RK3448	IL76	?
RK3449	IL76	?
RK3450	IL76	?
RK3453	IL76	?
RK3454	IL76	?

Philippines
(see also PI-)

RP-1177	F.28	11153
RP-1250	F.28	11153
RP-C	B737	19951
(RP-C)	A320	0868
(RP-C)	A320	0870
(RP-C)	A320	0886
(RP-C)	A320	0909
(RP-C)	A320	0919
(RP-C)	A320	0925
RP-C1	1-11	BAC.120
(RP-C)	B737	19948
RP-C345	DC-8	45807
RP-C348	DC-8	45755
RP-C349	DC-8	45660
RP-C479	146	E3168
RP-C480	146	E3166
RP-C481	146	E2109
RP-C482	146	E2112
RP-C801	DC-8	45608
RP-C803	DC-8	45937
RP-C804	DC-8	45607
RP-C827	DC-8	45378
RP-C829	DC-8	45380
RP-C830	DC-8	45688
RP-C831	DC-8	45690
RP-C832	DC-8	45806
RP-C837	DC-8	45646
RP-C840	DC-8	45645
RP-C843	DC-8	45683
RP-C911	B707	17606
RP-C970	SE210	90
RP-C1161	1-11	BAC.213
RP-C1171	1-11	BAC.215
RP-C1177	F.28	11153
RP-C1181	1-11	BAC.226
RP-C1182	1-11	BAC.246
RP-C1183	1-11	BAC.248
RP-C1184	1-11	BAC.190
RP-C1185	1-11	BAC.195
RP-C1186	1-11	BAC.188
RP-C1187	1-11	BAC.189
RP-C1188	1-11	BAC.209
RP-C1189	1-11	BAC.204

RP-C1193	1-11	BAC.231
RP-C1194	1-11	BAC.199
RP-C123	SE210	257
RP-C1240	B727	19691
RP-C1241	B727	19692
(RP-C1383)	B737	22278
RP-C1503	DC-9	47789
RP-C1504	DC-9	47792
RP-C1505	DC-9	47793
RP-C1506	DC-9	47795
RP-C1507	DC-9	47069
RP-C1508	DC-9	47070
RP-C1509	DC-9	47071
RP-C1535	DC-9	47266
RP-C1536	DC-9	47353
RP-C1537	DC-9	47570
RP-C1538	DC-9	47239
RP-C1539	DC-9	47485
RP-C1540	DC-9	47734
RP-C1541	DC-9	48143
RP-C1542	DC-9	48115
RP-C1543	DC-9	48116
RP-C1544	DC-9	48117
RP-C1545	DC-9	48132
RP-C1546	DC-9	48133
RP-C1886	B707	19034
RP-C1938	B737	19553
RP-C2000	B737	25996
(RP-C2000)	DC-10	46958
RP-C2003	DC-10	46958
(RP-C2004)	DC-10	47838
RP-C2020	B737	19943
RP-C2021	B737	19039
RP-C2022	B737	19942
RP-C2023	B737	19947
RP-C2024	B737	19056
RP-C2025	B737	19077
RP-C2026	B737	19949
RP-C2114	DC-10	47838
RP-C2695	YAK40	9522041
RP-C2714	B757	24370
RP-C2715	B757	24371
RP-C2716	B757	25597
RP-C2803	YAK40	9430537
RP-C2805	YAK40	9342031
RP-C2906	B737	20458
RP-C2986	MD80	49483
RP-C2994	146	E1005
RP-C2997	146	E2178
RP-C2999	146	E1009
RP-C3001	A300	003
RP-C3002	A300	069
RP-C3003	A300	125
RP-C3004	A300	203
RP-C3005	A300	219
RP-C3006	A300	222
RP-C3007	A300	083
RP-C3008	A300	262
RP-C3010	B737	21447
RP-C3011	B737	21533
RP-C3012	B737	21448
RP-C3015	B737	21534
RP-C3189	A319	2556
RP-C3190	A319	2586
RP-C3191	A319	2625
RP-C3192	A319	2638
RP-C3193	A319	2786
RP-C3194	A319	2790
RP-C3195	A319	2831
RP-C3196	A319	2821
RP-C3197	A319	2852
RP-C3198	A319	2876
RP-C3221	A320	0706
RP-C3222	A320	0708
RP-C3223	A320	0745
RP-C3224	A320	0753
(RP-C3225)	A320	0844
RP-C3225	A320	1063
(RP-C3226)	A320	0861
RP-C3226	A320	2162
(RP-C3227)	A320	0863
RP-C3227	A320	2183
RP-C3228	A320	2162

RP-C3229	A320	0936
RP-C3230	A320	1171
RP-C3231	A320	1210
RP-C3240	A320	2419
RP-C3241	A320	2439
RP-C3242	A320	2994
RP-C3243	A320	3048
RP-C3244	A320	3272
RP-C4005	B737	24060
RP-C4006	B737	24059
RP-C4007	B737	25996
RP-C4008	B737	25033
RP-C4010	B737	24464
RP-C4011	B737	24770
RP-C5353	B727	19131
RP-C5475	B747	21941
RP-C5476	B747	21943
(RP-C5751)	B747	27261
(RP-C5752)	B747	27262
RP-C7073	B707	17680
RP-C7074	B707	17604
RP-C7075	B707	18336
RP-C7076	B707	18335
RP-C8001	B737	23116
RP-C8002	B737	22886
RP-C8003	B737	22888
RP-C8004	B737	22882
RP-C8006	B737	22882
RP-C8007	B737	22878
RP-C8009	B737	22879
RP-C8011	B737	23606
RP-C8015	B737	20536
RP-C8017	B727	19289
RP-C8018	B727	19288
RP-C8019	B727	21249
RP-C8022	B737	23607
RP-C8168	B747	27827
RP-C8600	A319	2878
RP-C8601	A319	2925
RP-C8602	A319	2954
RP-C8603	A319	3108
RP-C8604	A320	3087
RP-C8605	A320	3107
RP-C8606	A320	3187
RP-C8607	A320	3205
RP-C8608	A320	3273
RP-C8777	B737	23088
RP-C8820	B747	21834
RP-C8830	B747	21517
RP-C8850	B747	21516
RP-C8881	A300	009
RP-C8882	A300	046
RP-C8883	A300	271
RP-C8884	A300	154
RP-C8886	B737	20130
RP-C8887	B737	20132
RP-C8890	B737	19711
RP-C8891	B737	20236

Sweden

(SE-)	B737	23811
(SE-D)	L1011	193K-1032
SE-DAA	SE210	4
SE-DAB	SE210	11
SE-DAC	SE210	25
SE-DAD	SE210	34
SE-DAE	SE210	56
SE-DAF	SE210	112
SE-DAG	SE210	172
SE-DAH	SE210	193
SE-DAI	SE210	210
SE-DAK	DC-9	47492
SE-DAL	DC-9	47498
SE-DAM	DC-9	47499
SE-DAN	DC-9	47464
SE-DAO	DC-9	47509
SE-DAP	DC-9	47512
SE-DAR	DC-9	47596
SE-DAS	DC-9	47610
SE-DAT	DC-9	47625
SE-DAU	DC-9	47627

Registration	Type	c/n
SE-DAW	DC-9	47629
SE-DAX	DC-9	47631
SE-DAY	CV990	30-10-8
SE-DAZ	CV990	30-10-17
SE-DBA	DC-8	45386
SE-DBB	DC-8	45389
SE-DBC	DC-8	45390
SE-DBD	DC-8	45753
SE-DBE	DC-8	45823
SE-DBF	DC-8	45905
SE-DBG	DC-8	45921
SE-DBH	DC-8	45924
SE-DBI	DC-8	46129
SE-DBK	DC-8	46136
SE-DBL	DC-8	46163
SE-DBM	DC-9	47633
SE-DBN	DC-9	47413
SE-DBO	DC-9	47361
SE-DBP	DC-9	47360
SE-DBR	DC-9	47306
SE-DBS	DC-9	47303
SE-DBT	DC-9	47288
SE-DBU	DC-9	47180
SE-DBW	DC-9	47117
SE-DBX	DC-9	47114
SE-DBY	DC-9	47112
SE-DBZ	DC-9	47094
SE-DCR	DC-8	45628
SE-DCT	DC-8	45648
SE-DDA	B727	19691
SE-DDB	B727	19692
SE-DDC	B727	20042
SE-DDD	B727	19313
SE-DDK	CV990	30-10-34
SE-DDL	B747	20120
SE-DDP	DC-9	47747
SE-DDR	DC-9	47750
SE-DDS	DC-9	47777
SE-DDT	DC-9	47779
SE-DDU	DC-8	45906
(SE-DEA)	DC-10	46869
(SE-DEB)	DC-10	46872
SE-DEB	SE210	247
SE-DEC	SE210	263
(SE-DEF)	B747	21575
SE-DEH	SE210	188
SE-DEI	146	E2086
SE-DFD	DC-10	46869
SE-DFE	DC-10	46872
SE-DFF	DC-10	47815
SE-DFG	DC-10	46554
SE-DFH	DC-10	46954
SE-DFK	A300	094
SE-DFL	A300	128
SE-DFN	DC-9	47657
SE-DFO	DC-9	47658
(SE-DFP)	MD80	49556
SE-DFR	MD80	49422
SE-DFS	MD80	49384
SE-DFT	MD80	49385
SE-DFU	MD80	49421
SE-DFV	MD80	49422
(SE-DFW)	MD80	49422
SE-DFX	MD80	49424
SE-DFY	MD80	49438
SE-DFZ	B747	21575
SE-DGA	F.28	11067
SE-DGB	F.28	11068
SE-DGC	F.28	11069
(SE-DGD)	F.28	11080
SE-DGD	F.28	11111
(SE-DGE)	F.28	11081
SE-DGE	F.28	11112
SE-DGF	F.28	11115
SE-DGG	F.28	11116
SE-DGH	F.28	11120
SE-DGI	F.28	11122
SE-DGK	F.28	11123
SE-DGL	F.28	11126
SE-DGM	F.28	11128
SE-DGN	F.28	11130
SE-DGO	F.28	11190
SE-DGP	F.28	11191
SE-DGR	F.28	11204
SE-DGS	F.28	11236
SE-DGT	F.28	11239
SE-DGU	F.28	11241
SE-DGX	F.28	11225
SE-DHA	SE210	259
SE-DHB	MD80	49396
SE-DHC	MD80	49397
SE-DHD	MD80	49578
SE-DHF	MD80	49642
SE-DHG	MD80	49389
SE-DHI	MD80	49706
SE-DHM	146	E2109
SE-DHN	MD80	49623
SE-DHS	DC-10	46646
SE-DHT	DC-10	47833
SE-DHU	DC-10	47832
SE-DHX	DC-10	46645
SE-DHY	DC-10	46983
SE-DHZ	DC-10	46977
SE-DIA	MD80	49603
SE-DIB	MD80	49605
SE-DIC	MD80	49607
SE-DID	MD80	49615
(SE-DIE)	MD80	49728
SE-DIF	MD80	49606
SE-DIH	MD80	49608
SE-DII	MD80	49909
SE-DIK	MD80	49728
SE-DIL	MD80	49913
SE-DIM	146	E3150
(SE-DIM)	MD80	49998
SE-DIN	MD80	49999
(SE-DIP)	MD80	53001
SE-DIP	MD80	53010
SE-DIR	MD80	53004
SE-DIS	MD80	53006
SE-DIT	146	E3151
SE-DIU	MD80	53011
SE-DIX	MD80	49998
SE-DIY	MD80	53008
SE-DIZ	MD80	53294
SE-DJE	MD80	49846
SE-DJF	MD80	49568
SE-DJN	146	E2231
SE-DJO	146	E2226
SE-DJP	146	E1254
SE-DJX	146	E1223
SE-DJY	146	E1224
SE-DJZ	146	E1225
SE-DKG	B737	19408
SE-DKH	B737	20412
SE-DKO	B767	24318
SE-DKP	B767	24471
(SE-DKR)	B767	24477
SE-DKR	B767	24846
SE-DKS	B767	24848
SE-DKT	B767	24849
SE-DKU	B767	24729
SE-DKX	B767	25365
SE-DKY	B767	25411
SE-DKZ	B767	24952
SE-DLA	B737	24300
(SE-DLA)	B737	24694
(SE-DLB)	B737	24695
SE-DLC	DC-9	47493
SE-DLD	B737	20711
SE-DLG	B737	23388
SE-DLH	DC-8	45994
SE-DLM	DC-8	45971
SE-DLN	B737	23747
SE-DLO	B737	23748
SE-DLP	B737	19409
(SE-DLR)	B737	20197
SE-DLS	B737	53198
SE-DLU	MD80	53199
SE-DLV	MD80	49965
SE-DLX	MD80	49966
SE-DMA	MD80	53009
SE-DMB	MD80	53314
SE-DMC	MD80	53340
SE-DMD	MD80	53347
SE-DME	MD80	53366
SE-DMF	MD90	53457
SE-DMG	MD90	53461
SE-DMH	MD90	53543
SE-DMT	MD80	48003
SE-DMU	MD80	48005
SE-DMX	MD80	48002
SE-DMY	MD80	48010
SE-DMZ	MD80	48009
SE-DNA	B737	24694
SE-DNB	B737	24695
SE-DNC	B737	24754
(SE-DNC)	B737	25038
SE-DND	B737	25038
(SE-DND)	B737	25065
SE-DNE	B737	25065
SE-DNF	B737	25160
SE-DNG	B737	25166
SE-DNH	B737	25167
SE-DNI	B737	26419
SE-DNK	B737	26421
SE-DNL	B737	26422
SE-DNM	737NG	28288
SE-DNM	B737	27268
SE-DNN	737NG	28291
SE-DNO	737NG	28292
SE-DNP	737NG	28295
SE-DNR	737NG	28296
SE-DNS	737NG	28297
SE-DNT	737NG	28302
SE-DNU	737NG	28303
SE-DNX	737NG	28304
SE-DNY	737NG	28308
SE-DNZ	737NG	30190
SE-DOA	B767	24475
SE-DOB	B767	24476
SE-DOC	B767	26544
(SE-DOF)	B767	24358
SE-DOI	DC-9	47599
SE-DOK	DC-9	47626
SE-DOL	DC-9	47630
SE-DOM	DC-9	47634
SE-DON	DC-9	47748
SE-DOO	DC-9	47778
SE-DOR	737NG	28305
SE-DOT	737NG	28306
SE-DPA	B737	25401
SE-DPB	B737	25402
SE-DPC	B737	25426
SE-DPH	MD80	49663
SE-DPI	MD80	49557
SE-DPM	L1011	193N-1145
SE-DPN	B737	23783
(SE-DPN)	L1011	193B-1072
SE-DPO	B737	23783
SE-DPP	L1011	193B-1072
(SE-DPP)	L1011	193B-1221
SE-DPR	L1011	193B-1231
SE-DPS	MD80	49398
SE-DPU	MD80	49938
SE-DPV	L1011	193B-1030
SE-DPX	L1011	193B-1091
SE-DRA	146	E2115
SE-DRB	146	E2057
SE-DRC	146	E2053
SE-DRD	146	E2094
SE-DRE	146	E2051
SE-DRF	146	E2055
SE-DRG	146	E2054
SE-DRH	146	E1006
SE-DRI	146	E2058
SE-DRK	146	E2108
SE-DRL	146	E2138
SE-DRM	146	E2196
SE-DRN	146	E2113
SE-DRR	B737	24690
SE-DRU	MD80	49442
SE-DSB	L1011	193B-1059
SE-DSC	L1011	193B-1065
SE-DSD	L1011	193B-1215
SE-DSE	L1011	193B-1013
SE-DSF	A300	220
SE-DSG	A300	259
SE-DSH	A300	207
SE-DSK	B757	25592
SE-DSL	B757	25593
SE-DSM	B757	24528
SE-DSN	B757	25133
SE-DSO	146	E3221
SE-DSP	146	E3242
SE-DSR	146	E3244
SE-DSS	146	E3245
SE-DST	146	E3247
SE-DSU	146	E3248
SE-DSV	146	E3250
SE-DSX	146	E3255
SE-DSY	146	E3263
SE-DTA	B737	24068
SE-DTB	B737	24911
SE-DTC	L1011	193A-1050
SE-DTD	L1011	193R-1033
SE-DTF	737NG	28309
(SE-DTG)	737NG	28311
SE-DTG	737NG	30191
(SE-DTH)	737NG	28313
SE-DTH	737NG	28313
SE-DTI	737NG	28314
(SE-DTI)	737NG	30191
SE-DTK	737NG	28318
(SE-DTK)	737NG	30192
(SE-DTL)	737NG	28317
SE-DTL	737NG	28319
(SE-DTM)	737NG	28318
SE-DTM	737NG	28320
(SE-DTN)	737NG	28322
SE-DTN	737NG	30467
(SE-DTO)	737NG	28323
SE-DTO	737NG	30194
(SE-DTP)	737NG	30467
SE-DTP	737NG	30468
(SE-DTR)	737NG	30470
(SE-DTR)	737NG	30471
SE-DTR	737NG	32277
(SE-DTS)	737NG	30196
SE-DTS	737NG	30197
SE-DTT	737NG	28324
(SE-DTT)	737NG	28326
(SE-DTT)	737NG	30471
SE-DTU	737NG	28311
SE-DTV	B737	20363
SE-DTX	737NG	28321
SE-DTY	737NG	30193
SE-DTZ	737NG	28322
SE-DUA	F.100	11321
SE-DUB	F.100	11323
SE-DUC	F.100	11324
SE-DUD	F.100	11325
SE-DUE	F.100	11326
SE-DUF	F.100	11329
SE-DUG	F.100	11330
SE-DUH	F.100	11350
SE-DUI	F.100	11371
SE-DUK	B757	25054
SE-DUL	B757	26151
SE-DUN	B757	22612
SE-DUO	B757	24792
SE-DUP	B757	24793
SE-DUR	F.100	11332
SE-DUS	B737	24255
SE-DUT	B737	25165
SE-DUU	F.100	11286
SE-DUX	CRJ	7010
SE-DUY	CRJ	7023
SE-DVF	L1011	293B-1241
(SE-DVH)	A320	0190
SE-DVI	L1011	293A-1248
SE-DVM	L1011	193J-1183
(SE-DVN)	L1011	193J-1196
SE-DVO	737NG	28822
SE-DVR	737NG	28826
SE-DVU	737NG	28825
SE-DVX	L1011	193J-1183
SE-DYA	737NG	28323
(SE-DYC)	737NG	30469
(SE-DYC)	737NG	32276
(SE-DYD)	737NG	28328
(SE-DYD)	737NG	30195

Reg	Type	Serial
(SE-DYD)	737NG	30471
(SE-DYG)	737NG	30470
SE-DYG	737NG	32278
SE-DYH	737NG	30196
(SE-DYI)	A330	353
(SE-DYK)	A330	362
SE-DYM	737NG	28325
(SE-DYN)	737NG	28326
(SE-DYP)	737NG	28327
(SE-DYR)	737NG	32277
SE-DYT	737NG	28328
SE-DZA	E145	145070
SE-DZB	**E145**	**145113**
SE-DZC	E145	145169
SE-DZD	E145	145185
SE-DZF	B767	25221
SE-DZG	B767	28042
SE-DZH	**737NG**	**28227**
SE-DZI	**737NG**	**28229**
SE-DZK	**737NG**	**28231**
(SE-DZK)	737NG	30465
SE-DZL	737NG	30465
SE-DZM	737NG	30466
SE-DZN	**737NG**	**32903**
SE-DZO	B767	28883
SE-DZV	**737NG**	**32904**
SE-RAA	**E145**	**145210**
SE-RAB	**E145**	**145453**
SE-RAC	**E145**	**145098**
(SE-RAN)	B737	25790
SE-RBA	**MD80**	**49403**
SE-RBE	**MD80**	**49152**
SE-RBF	**A330**	**353**
SE-RBG	**A330**	**362**
SE-RBH	B747	21316
(SE-RBH)	B747	21439
SE-RBI	MD80	49402
SE-RBL	MD80	49707
SE-RBN	B747	21162
SE-RBP	B747	20009
SE-RBR	MD80	49399
SE-RBS	MD80	49617
SE-RBT	MD80	49618
SE-RBU	MD80	49855
SE-RBV	B767	24150
SE-RCB	A320	1787
SE-RCC	A320	0288
SE-RCD	A320	1130
SE-RCE	B757	24176
SE-RCF	A320	0978
SE-RCG	A320	0132
(SE-RCH)	A320	0764
SE-RCO	B737	23635
SE-RCP	B737	24025
SE-RCR	B737	24026
SE-RCS	B737	24299
SE-RDE	**MD80**	**49857**
SE-RDF	**MD80**	**49769**
SE-RDG	**MD80**	**49856**
SE-RDH	MD80	49949
SE-RDI	**MD80**	**49631**
SE-RDL	MD80	53014
SE-RDM	**MD80**	**49662**
SE-RDN	**A321**	**2211**
SE-RDO	**A321**	**2216**
SE-RDP	**A321**	**2410**
SE-RDR	**MD80**	**49151**
SE-RDS	**MD80**	**49401**
SE-RDT	MD80	49278
SE-RDU	MD80	49372
SE-RDV	**MD80**	**49574**
SE-REA	A340	413
SE-REB	A340	424
(SE-REC)	A340	430
SE-REE	**A330**	**515**
SE-REG	A321	1848
(SE-REI)	A321	1587
(SE-REK)	A321	1619
(SE-REL)	A319	2850
(SE-REM)	A321	1798
SE-RFB	**MD80**	**53246**
SE-RFC	**MD80**	**49900**
SE-RFD	**MD80**	**53244**

Reg	Type	Serial
(SE-RGA)	CRJ	7958
SE-RGO	MD80	49708
SE-RGP	MD80	49710
(SE-XBK)	SE210	33
(SE-XBL)	SE210	38
(SE-XBM)	SE210	43
(SE-XBN)	SE210	48

Slovenia
(see also S5-)

Reg	Type	Serial
SL-AAA	A320	0043
SL-AAB	A320	0113
SL-AAC	A320	0114
SL-ABA	MD80	48048
SL-ABB	MD80	48087
SL-ABC	MD80	49379
SL-ABD	MD80	49440
SL-ABE	MD80	48046
SL-ABF	DC-9	47239
SL-ABG	DC-9	47530
SL-ABH	DC-9	47570

Poland

Reg	Type	Serial
(SP-FVK)	B757	24747
SP-FVO	B737	28590
SP-FVP	B757	24965
SP-FVR	**B757**	**25490**
SP-FYS	YAK40	9412032
SP-FYT	YAK40	9641851
SP-FYU	YAK40	9211821
SP-GEA	YAK40	9230224
SP-KEI	B737	24125
SP-KEI	B737	24126
SP-KEK	B737	24127
SP-KEN	B737	24128
(SP-KEW)	L1011	193H-1207
SP-KPI	B737	28202
SP-KPK	B737	26306
SP-KPL	B737	24659
SP-LAA	IL62	11004
SP-LAB	IL62	21105
SP-LAC	IL62	31401
SP-LAD	IL62	41604
SP-LAE	IL62	41802
SP-LAF	IL62	62204
SP-LAG	IL62	2725456
SP-LBA	IL62	2932526
SP-LBB	IL62	1034152
SP-LBC	IL62	3036253
SP-LBD	IL62	1138234
SP-LBE	IL62	1138546
SP-LBF	IL62	2343554
SP-LBG	IL62	3344942
SP-LBH	IL62	1748445
SP-LBI	IL62	4934623
SP-LBR	IL62	4727546
SP-LCA	TU154	86A-727
SP-LCB	TU154	86A-733
SP-LCC	TU154	87A-745
SP-LCD	TU154	87A-755
SP-LCE	TU154	87A-769
SP-LCF	TU154	88A-774
SP-LCG	TU154	88A-775
SP-LCH	TU154	88A-776
SP-LCI	TU154	89A-805
SP-LCK	TU154	89A-806
SP-LCL	TU154	89A-812
SP-LCM	TU154	89A-824
SP-LCN	TU154	90A-831
SP-LCO	TU154	90A-862
SP-LDA	**E170**	**17000023**
SP-LDB	**E170**	**17000024**
SP-LDC	**E170**	**17000025**
SP-LDD	**E170**	**17000027**
SP-LDE	**E170**	**17000029**
SP-LDF	**E170**	**17000035**
SP-LDG	**E170**	**17000065**
SP-LDH	**E170**	**17000069**
SP-LDI	**E170**	**17000073**

Reg	Type	Serial
SP-LDK	**E170**	**17000074**
SP-LEA	YAK40	9021660
SP-LEB	YAK40	9541843
SP-LEC	YAK40	9541943
SP-LED	YAK40	9542043
SP-LEE	YAK40	9021560
SP-LGA	E145	145155
SP-LGA	TU134	8350602
SP-LGB	E145	145165
SP-LGB	TU134	8350603
SP-LGC	E145	145227
SP-LGC	TU134	9350804
SP-LGD	**E145**	**145244**
SP-LGD	TU134	9350805
SP-LGE	**E145**	**145285**
SP-LGE	TU134	9350806
SP-LGF	**E145**	**145308**
SP-LGG	**E145**	**145319**
SP-LGH	**E145**	**145329**
SP-LGI	E145	145336
SP-LGK	E145	145339
SP-LGL	**E145**	**145406**
SP-LGM	**E145**	**145408**
SP-LGN	**E145**	**145441**
SP-LGO	**E145**	**145560**
SP-LHA	TU134	3351808
SP-LHB	TU134	3351809
SP-LHC	TU134	3351810
SP-LHD	TU134	48400
SP-LHE	TU134	48405
SP-LHF	TU134	3352005
SP-LHG	TU134	3352008
SP-LHI	TU134	73.49985
SP-LIA	**E170**	**17000125**
SP-LIB	**E170**	**17000132**
SP-LIC	**E170**	**17000134**
SP-LID	**E170**	**17000136**
SP-LIE	**E170**	**17000153**
SP-LIF	**E170**	**17000154**
SP-LKA	**B737**	**27416**
SP-LKB	**B737**	**27417**
SP-LKC	**B737**	**27418**
SP-LKD	**B737**	**27419**
SP-LKE	**B737**	**27130**
SP-LKF	**B737**	**27368**
SP-LKG	B737	24825
SP-LKH	B737	24826
SP-LKI	B737	24827
SP-LKK	B737	28996
SP-LLA	**B737**	**27131**
SP-LLB	**B737**	**27156**
SP-LLC	**B737**	**27157**
SP-LLD	**B737**	**27256**
SP-LLE	**B737**	**27914**
SP-LLF	**B737**	**28752**
SP-LLG	**B737**	**28753**
SP-LLH	B737	25594
SP-LLI	**B737**	**24706**
SP-LMB	B737	23535
SP-LMC	**B737**	**28668**
SP-LMD	**B737**	**28669**
SP-LME	**B737**	**28590**
SP-LOA	**B767**	**24733**
SP-LOB	**B767**	**24734**
SP-LPA	**B767**	**24865**
SP-LPB	**B767**	**27902**
SP-LPC	**B767**	**28656**
SP-LPD	B767	24484
SP-LPE	**B767**	**24843**
SP-LPF	**B767**	**24876**
SP-PGA	YAK40	9510138

Sudan

Reg	Type	Serial
ST-AAW	COMET	6457
ST-AAX	COMET	6463
ST-AFA	**B707**	**20897**
ST-AFB	B707	20898
ST-AFK	B737	21169
ST-AFL	B737	21170
ST-AHG	B707	17651
ST-AIB	B737	22859

Reg	Type	Serial
ST-AIM	B707	19410
ST-AIR	IL76	1033414474
ST-AIX	B707	20086
ST-AIY	IL76	1023410344
ST-AJD	DC-8	45764
ST-AJR	DC-8	46009
ST-AKR	B707	19521
ST-AKW	**B707**	**20123**
ST-ALK	B707	18976
ST-ALL	B707	19622
ST-ALM	B707	19367
ST-ALP	B707	19295
ST-ALX	B707	18715
ST-AMF	**B707**	**19367**
ST-ANP	B707	19632
ST-APS	**IL76**	**1023409316**
ST-APY	B707	19412
ST-AQA	**IL76**	**0023442218**
ST-AQB	**IL76**	**0053460795**
ST-AQI	B707	19999
ST-AQL	B747	20504
ST-AQN	B747	20333
ST-AQR	**IL76**	**0043453575**
ST-AQW	**B707**	**20517**
ST-AQY	IL76	0033448404
ST-AQZ	**YAK42**	**2306016**
ST-ARI	**B707**	**20720**
ST-ARK	**YAK40**	**9841659**
ST-ASE	A300	559
ST-ASS	A300	252
ST-AST	**A310**	**437**
ST-ASX	**IL76**	**0073479392**
ST-ATA	**A300**	**775**
ST-ATB	**A300**	**666**
ST-ATH	**IL76**	**0063472158**
ST-ATI	IL76	1033418596
ST-ATX	IL76	0063473182
ST-AWR	**IL76**	**0033447365**
ST-BDA	AN7x	47098968
ST-BDE	B737	1013408252
ST-BDK	**AN7x**	**720606042?**
ST-BDK	**AN7x**	**?**
ST-BUE	IL76	?
ST-CAC	IL76	0023437076
ST-DRS	B707	21104
ST-EWA	IL76	?
ST-EWB	IL76	0023438122
ST-EWC	**IL76**	**0023438129**
ST-EWD	**IL76**	**0063466989**
ST-EWX	**IL76**	**1013409282**
ST-GFF	**AN7x**	**?**
ST-GLD	B707	19821
ST-JCC	B707	18948
ST-MRS	**TU134**	**63333**
ST-NSR	B707	18931
ST-PRA	**IL62**	**2357711**
ST-PRB	**AN7x**	**47096918**
ST-SAC	B707	19377
ST-SDA	**B737**	**23274**
ST-SDB	**B737**	**23273**
ST-SFT	IL76	073410292
ST-SMS	**YAK40**	**9311526**
ST-UAA	DC-8	46162
ST-WTA	**IL76**	**1023410355**
ST-WTB	**IL76**	**1003499994**
ST-WTS	**AN7x**	**47098960**
ST-YAK	YAK40	9510439

Egypt

Reg	Type	Serial
(SU-)	MD80	53012
SU-ALC	COMET	6439
SU-ALD	COMET	6441
SU-ALE	COMET	6444
SU-ALL	COMET	6454
SU-ALM	COMET	6458
SU-AMV	COMET	6462
SU-AMW	COMET	6464
SU-ANC	COMET	6466
SU-ANI	COMET	6475
SU-AOU	B707	19844
SU-AOW	B707	19845

Reg	Type	c/n
SU-APD	B707	20341
SU-APE	B707	20342
SU-ARN	IL62	00801
SU-ARO	IL62	00705
SU-ARW	IL62	90501
SU-ARX	IL62	80305
SU-AVL	IL62	00804
SU-AVU	IL62	00802
SU-AVW	IL62	00805
SU-AVX	B707	20760
SU-AVY	B707	20761
SU-AVZ	B707	20762
SU-AWJ	IL62	00803
SU-AXA	B707	20763
SU-AXB	TU154	73A-048
SU-AXC	TU154	73A-049
SU-AXD	TU154	73A-050
SU-AXE	TU154	73A-051
SU-AXF	TU154	73A-052
SU-AXG	TU154	74A-053
SU-AXH	TU154	74A-054
SU-AXI	TU154	74A-055
SU-AXJ	B707	20919
SU-AXK	B707	20920
SU-AYH	B737	21191
SU-AYI	B737	21192
SU-AYJ	B737	21193
SU-AYK	**B737**	**21194**
SU-AYL	B737	21195
SU-AYM	B737	21196
SU-AYN	B737	21226
SU-AYO	B737	21227
SU-AYT	B737	20222
SU-AYX	B737	19425
SU-AZY	A300	025
SU-BAG	B707	18765
SU-BAO	B707	19775
SU-BBA	B707	18810
SU-BBS	A300	017
SU-BBU	SE210	154
SU-BBV	SE210	254
SU-BBW	B737	21196
SU-BBX	B737	21193
SU-BCA	A300	115
SU-BCB	A300	116
SU-BCC	A300	150
(SU-BCD)	A300	199
(SU-BCE)	A300	200
SU-BCJ	B737	22071
SU-BDF	A300	199
SU-BDG	**A300**	**200**
SU-BKK	DC-9	47656
SU-BLC	B737	23786
(SU-BLI)	B707	19001
(SU-BLJ)	B707	18880
(SU-BLK)	B707	19378
SU-BLL	B737	23001
SU-BLM	B737	24345
SU-BLN	B737	23252
SU-BLR	B737	23786
SU-BME	**MD80**	**49628**
SU-BMF	MD80	53199
SU-BMM	A300	175
SU-BMQ	MD90	53576
SU-BMR	MD90	53552
(SU-BMR)	MD90	53601
SU-BMS	MD90	53553
SU-BMT	MD90	53601
SU-BMV	B707	20260
(SU-BMZ)	A300	123
SU-BNN	MD90	53554
SU-BOW	A310	437
SU-BOY	**MD80**	**53191**
SU-BOZ	MD80	53192
SU-BPG	**737NG**	**32669**
SU-BPH	**737NG**	**34257**
SU-BPM	**AN7x**	**47098977**
SU-BPU	**A320**	**2937**
SU-BPV	**A320**	**2966**
SU-BPY	**B757**	**24965**
SU-BPZ	**737NG**	**35213**
SU-BQA	**737NG**	**35220**
SU-DAA	B707	19916
SU-DAB	B707	19521
SU-DAC	B707	19843
SU-DAD	B707	20517
SU-DAE	B707	19622
(SU-DAF)	B707	19621
SU-DAI	B707	19590
SU-DAJ	B707	18686
SU-DAK	MD80	49661
SU-DAL	MD80	49845
SU-DAM	MD80	49848
SU-DAN	A300	192
SU-DAO	MD80	49779
SU-DAP	MD80	49724
SU-DAQ	MD80	49780
SU-DAR	A300	175
SU-DAS	A300	145
SU-DAT	B707	19775
SU-EAF	**TU204**	**3764027**
SU-EAG	**TU204**	**3764028**
SU-EAH	**TU204**	**3164023**
SU-EAI	**TU204**	**3164025**
SU-EAJ	**TU204**	**3164029**
SU-FAA	B707	18069
SU-FAB	B707	18068
SU-FAC	B707	20087
SU-GAA	A300	239
SU-GAB	A300	240
SU-GAC	**A300**	**255**
SU-GAH	B767	23178
SU-GAI	B767	23179
SU-GAJ	B767	23180
SU-GAK	B747	20117
SU-GAL	B747	24161
SU-GAM	B747	24162
SU-GAN	B737	21226
SU-GAO	B767	24541
SU-GAP	B767	24542
SU-GAR	A300	557
SU-GAS	**A300**	**561**
SU-GAT	A300	572
SU-GAU	A300	575
SU-GAV	A300	579
SU-GAW	A300	581
SU-GAX	A300	601
SU-GAY	**A300**	**607**
SU-GAZ	A300	616
SU-GBA	**A320**	**0165**
SU-GBB	**A320**	**0166**
SU-GBC	**A320**	**0178**
SU-GBD	**A320**	**0194**
SU-GBE	**A320**	**0198**
SU-GBF	**A320**	**0351**
SU-GBG	**A320**	**0366**
SU-GBH	**B737**	**25084**
SU-GBI	B737	25307
SU-GBJ	**B737**	**25352**
SU-GBK	**B737**	**26052**
SU-GBL	**B737**	**26051**
SU-GBM	**A340**	**156**
SU-GBN	**A340**	**159**
SU-GBO	**A340**	**178**
SU-GBP	**B777**	**28423**
SU-GBR	**B777**	**28424**
SU-GBS	**B777**	**28425**
SU-GBT	**A321**	**0680**
SU-GBU	**A321**	**0687**
SU-GBV	**A321**	**0715**
SU-GBW	**A321**	**0725**
SU-GBX	**B777**	**32629**
SU-GBY	**B777**	**32630**
SU-GBZ	**A320**	**2070**
SU-GCA	**A320**	**2073**
SU-GCB	**A320**	**2079**
SU-GCC	**A320**	**2088**
SU-GCD	**A320**	**2094**
SU-GCE	**A330**	**600**
SU-GCF	**A330**	**610**
SU-GCG	**A330**	**666**
SU-GCH	**A330**	**683**
SU-GCI	**A330**	**696**
SU-GCJ	**A330**	**709**
SU-GCK	**A330**	**726**
SU-GCL	**A320**	**0322**
SU-GCM	**737NG**	**35558**
SU-GCN	**737NG**	**35559**
SU-GCO	**737NG**	**35561**
SU-GCP	**737NG**	**35560**
SU-GCT	**E170**	**17000167**
SU-GCU	**E170**	**17000169**
SU-GCV	**E170**	**17000170**
SU-GCW	**E170**	**17000175**
SU-GCX	**E170**	**17000178**
SU-GGG	**A340**	**061**
SU-HMD	B737	24474
SU-KBA	**A320**	**0937**
SU-KHM	**B737**	**26438**
SU-LBA	A320	0371
SU-LBB	A320	0814
SU-LBC	A320	0937
SU-LBD	A320	1372
SU-LBE	A320	1413
SU-LBF	A319	0629
SU-LBG	**A320**	**0743**
SU-LBH	**A320**	**0739**
SU-LBI	**A320**	**0667**
SU-MBA	B737	26283
SU-MWA	A310	652
SU-MWB	A310	671
SU-OAA	IL76	1013409297
SU-OAB	IL76	1023409321
SU-OAC	TU154	91A-898
SU-OAD	TU154	91A-899
SU-PBA	B707	19843
SU-PBB	B707	19916
SU-PBC	B707	19967
SU-PBD	A320	0026
SU-PBE	A320	0024
SU-PBO	**DC-9**	**48131**
SU-PMA	B737	19064
SU-PTA	B737	25740
SU-RAA	A320	0322
SU-RAB	A320	0326
SU-RAC	A320	0478
(SU-RAC)	B757	27203
SU-RAD	A320	0344
(SU-RAD)	B757	27204
SU-RAG	A320	0344
SU-SAA	B737	24124
SU-SAB	B737	24124
SU-SMA	B737	23868
SU-YAK	B727	21621
SU-ZCA	MD80	53190
SU-ZCC	A310	267
SU-ZCD	B737	26286
SU-ZCE	B737	26283
SU-ZCF	A320	0366
SU-ZDA	IL62	4445827
SU-ZDB	**IL62**	**3242432**
SU-ZDC	**IL62**	**3749224**

Greece

Reg	Type	c/n
(SX-)	B737	24570
SX-BAQ	MD80	49710
SX-BAR	1-11	BAC.096
SX-BAS	A320	0043
SX-BAT	A320	0113
SX-BAU	A320	0114
SX-BAV	MD80	49706
SX-BAW	MD80	49389
SX-BAX	A320	0361
SX-BAY	A300	208
SX-BAZ	A300	210
SX-BBT	B737	25011
SX-BBU	**B737**	**25743**
SX-BBV	MD80	48048
SX-BBW	MD80	48087
SX-BBY	B757	26151
SX-BBZ	B757	24792
SX-BCA	B737	21224
SX-BCB	B737	21225
SX-BCC	B737	21301
SX-BCD	B737	21302
SX-BCE	B737	22300
SX-BCF	B737	22301
SX-BCG	B737	22338
SX-BCH	B737	22339
SX-BCI	B737	22343
SX-BCK	B737	22400
SX-BCL	B737	22401
SX-BEB	A300	046
SX-BEC	A300	056
SX-BED	A300	058
SX-BEE	A300	103
SX-BEF	A300	105
SX-BEG	A300	148
SX-BEH	A300	184
SX-BEI	A300	189
SX-BEK	A300	632
SX-BEL	A300	696
SX-BEM	**A300**	**603**
SX-BEU	**MD80**	**49848**
SX-BEV	**MD80**	**49668**
SX-BFA	B737	26300
SX-BFI	A300	204
(SX-BFM)	B727	21978
(SX-BFN)	B727	21851
SX-BFO	MD80	49396
SX-BFP	B737	25062
SX-BFS	DC-9	47305
SX-BFT	B737	24470
SX-BFV	B737	27004
SX-BFX	B737	21440
SX-BGH	**B737**	**23866**
SX-BGI	B737	27061
SX-BGJ	**B737**	**25595**
SX-BGK	**B737**	**24679**
SX-BGL	F.100	11387
SX-BGM	F.100	11476
SX-BGN	B737	28753
SX-BGQ	**B737**	**25177**
SX-BGR	**B737**	**25063**
SX-BGS	**B737**	**26279**
SX-BGV	**B737**	**26308**
SX-BGW	**B737**	**29264**
SX-BGX	**B737**	**24124**
SX-BGY	**B737**	**29100**
SX-BGZ	**B737**	**29265**
SX-BKA	**B737**	**25313**
SX-BKB	**B737**	**25314**
SX-BKC	**B737**	**25361**
SX-BKD	**B737**	**25362**
SX-BKE	**B737**	**25417**
SX-BKF	**B737**	**25430**
SX-BKG	**B737**	**27149**
SX-BKH	**B737**	**24703**
SX-BKI	**B737**	**24704**
SX BKK	B737	25371
SX-BKL	B737	24915
SX-BKM	**B737**	**24709**
SX-BKN	**B737**	**26281**
SX-BKP	E145	145671
SX-BKQ	E145	145729
SX-BKR	E145	145757
SX-BKT	**B737**	**25377**
SX-BKX	**B737**	**27000**
SX-BLA	B737	28869
SX-BLB	B737	25015
SX-BLC	**B737**	**26303**
SX-BLM	**B737**	**24813**
SX-BLN	B737	24688
SX-BLO	E145	145426
SX-BLP	E145	145440
SX-BLR	E145	145444
SX-BLT	737NG	28090
SX-BLU	737NG	28091
SX-BLV	B757	26278
SX-BLW	B757	24397
SX-BLX	A320	0029
SX-BMA	B737	27171
SX-BMB	B737	27213
SX-BMC	**B737**	**27143**
SX-BMP	MD80	49279
SX-BOA	B717	55056
SX-BOB	B717	55053
SX-BOC	B717	55065
SX-BSH	A320	0225

SX-BSJ	A320	0230	S2-ABQ	B707	19441	S7-AHM	B767	26328	**Turkey**
SX-BSQ	**MD80**	**49372**	S2-ACA	B707	19434	**S7-ASA**	**A320**	**0590**	
SX-BSV	A320	0449	S2-ACA	B707	19776	S7-ASB	A320	0594	TC-
SX-BSW	**MD80**	**49949**	S2-ACF	B707	18921	S7-ASC	A320	0601	TC-
SX-BTN	**B737**	**28494**	S2-ACG	B707	19354	S7-ASD	A320	0605	(TC-)
SX-BTO	**B737**	**25033**	S2-ACH	F.28	11172	S7-ASE	A320	0607	(TC-)
SX-BVA	**A320**	**0425**	(S2-ACI)	F.28	11180	S7-ASF	A320	0611	**TC-AAB**
SX-BVB	A320	1992	S2-ACJ	F.28	11180	S7-ASG	A320	0617	**TC-AAD**
SX-BVC	A320	2016	S2-ACK	B707	20018	S7-ASH	A320	0619	**TC-AAE**
SX-BVD	**A320**	**0142**	**S2-ACO**	**DC-10**	**46993**	S7-ASI	A320	0648	TC-AAE
SX-BVM	B757	24451	**S2-ACP**	**DC-10**	**46995**	**S7-ASJ**	**A320**	**0650**	**TC-AAF**
SX-BVN	B757	24497	**S2-ACQ**	**DC-10**	**47817**	S7-ASK	MD80	53481	**TC-AAG**
SX-CAO	B727	21978	**S2-ACR**	**DC-10**	**48317**	**S7-ASY**	**B767**	**29386**	**TC-AAH**
SX-CAR	B727	21851	**S2-ACS**	**DC-10**	**46543**	S7-LAS	B707	20179	**TC-AAK**
SX-CBA	B727	20003	**S2-ACV**	**F.28**	**11124**	S7-RGA	A310	573	**TC-AAP**
SX-CBB	B727	20004	**S2-ACW**	**F.28**	**11148**	S7-RGJ	A321	0604	TC-ABA
SX-CBC	B727	20005	S2-ADA	DC-10	46999	S7-RGK	A321	0614	TC-ABB
SX-CBD	B727	20006	S2-ADB	DC-10	47818	S7-RGL	A320	0542	TC-ABC
SX-CBE	B727	20201	S2-ADE	A310	698	S7-RGL	B737	24208	TC-ABD
SX-CBF	B727	19536	**S2-ADF**	**A310**	**700**	S7-RGM	B737	24299	TC-ABE
SX-CBG	B727	20918	S2-ADG	A310	433	S7-RGN	A310	437	TC-ABF
SX-CBH	B727	20790	**S2-ADH**	**A310**	**650**	S7-RGO	A300	584	TC-ABG
SX-CBI	B727	20791	**S2-ADK**	**A310**	**594**	S7-RGP	A310	549	TC-ABH
SX-CDK	**E145**	**14500998**	**S2-ADM**	**MD80**	**53147**	S7-RGQ	A310	410	**TC-ABK**
(SX-CPH)	DC-10	48294	**S2-ADN**	**DC-10**	**46542**	S7-RGR	A310	409	TC-ACA
SX-CVA	L1011	193H-1246	**S2-ADO**	**MD80**	**53481**	S7-RGR	A310	410	**TC-ACB**
SX-CVB	L1011	293B-1239	S2-ADR	L1011	193P-1129	S7-RGS	B767	27427	**TC-ACC**
SX-CVC	DC-10	47843	S2-ADT	B747	21541	S7-RGT	B767	27428	**TC-ACD**
SX-CVD	L1011	293F-1236	**S2-ADU**	**B707**	**20803**	S7-RGU	B767	27568	TC-ACI
SX-CVE	L1011	193N-1198	**S2-ADY**	**F.28**	**11120**	S7-RGV	B767	27392	**TC-ACT**
SX-CVH	DC-10	48258	**S2-ADZ**	**F.28**	**11123**	S7-RGW	B767	27393	TC-ACT
SX-CVP	DC-10	48294	S2-AEA	B737	24304	S7-RGX	A320	0238	**TC-ACU**
SX-DAK	COMET	6437	S2-AEB	B737	24305	S7-SEZ	737NG	30727	TC-ACV
SX-DAL	COMET	6438	S2-AEK	DC-8	45888	S7-SIA	DC-8	45629	TC-ACY
SX-DAN	COMET	6440				S7-SIS	DC-8	46141	**TC-ACZ**
SX-DAO	COMET	6447							TC-ADA
SX-DBA	B707	18948	**Slovenia**						(TC-ADA)
SX-DBB	B707	18949	(see also SL-)			**Sao Tome**			(TC-AEA)
SX-DBC	B707	18950							(TC-AEB)
SX-DBD	B707	19760	**S5-AAA**	**A320**	**0043**	(S9-)	B727	18805	(TC-AEC)
SX-DBE	B707	20035	**S5-AAB**	**A320**	**0113**	S9-BAC	IL76	0013428839	TC-AFA
SX-DBF	B707	20036	**S5-AAC**	**A320**	**0114**	**S9-BAE**	**B727**	**18903**	TC-AFB
SX-DBG	B707	18352	**S5-AAD**	**CRJ**	**7166**	S9-BAG	B727	19313	TC-AFC
SX-DBH	B707	18353	**S5-AAE**	**CRJ**	**7170**	S9-BAH	B727	19507	TC-AFD
SX-DBI	B707	18355	**S5-AAF**	**CRJ**	**7272**	S9-BAI	B727	20078	TC-AFE
SX-DBK	B707	18356	**S5-AAG**	**CRJ**	**7384**	**S9-BAP**	**YAK40**	**9441937**	TC-AFG
SX-DBL	B707	18420	**S5-AAH**	**CRJ**	**7032**	S9-BAQ	B727	19093	TC-AFJ
SX-DBM	B707	10607	**S5-AAI**	**CRJ**	**7248**	**S9-BAR**	**B727**	**19098**	TC-AFK
SX-DBN	B707	18688	**S5-AAJ**	**CRJ**	**8010**	**S9-BAU**	**B727**	**19358**	TC-AFL
SX-DBO	B707	19164	**S5-AAK**	**CRJ9**	**15128**	**S9-BAV**	**B727**	**21383**	TC-AFM
SX-DBP	B707	19163	**S5-AAL**	**CRJ9**	**15129**	S9-BOC	B727	18447	TC-AFN
SX-DFA	**A340**	**235**	S5-ABA	MD80	48048	S9-BOD	B727	18968	TC-AFO
SX-DFB	**A340**	**239**	S5-ABB	MD80	48087	**S9-BOE**	**B727**	**19192**	TC-AFP
SX-DFC	**A340**	**280**	S5-ABC	MD80	49379	S9-BOG	B727	19170	TC-AFR
SX-DFD	**A340**	**292**	S5-ABD	MD80	49440	S9-BOM	IL76	073410279	TC-AFS
SX-DIE	**B747**	**23509**	S5-ABE	MD80	48046	S9-BOU	AN7x	72095907	TC-AFT
SX-DVA	146	E3341	S5-ABF	DC-9	47239	**S9-CAA**	**B727**	**19836**	TC-AFU
SX-DVB	**146**	**E3343**	S5-ABG	DC-9	47530	S9-CAB	B727	19182	TC-AFV
SX-DVC	**146**	**E3358**	S5-ABH	DC-9	47570	S9-CAH	B727	18849	TC-AFY
SX-DVD	**146**	**E3362**	S5-ACC	MD80	48095	S9-DAA	DC-9	47368	TC-AGA
SX-DVE	**146**	**E3374**	S5-ACD	MD80	49143	**S9-DAB**	**DC-9**	**47313**	**TC-AGK**
SX-DVF	**146**	**E3375**				S9-DAE	IL76	0083483513	TC-AHA
SX-DVG	**A320**	**3033**				S9-DBH	DC-9	47731	TC-AJA
SX-DVH	**A320**	**3066**	**Seychelles**			**S9-DBM**	**B727**	**18323**	TC-AJK
SX-DVI	**A320**	**3074**				**S9-DBR**	**IL76**	**0063471147**	TC-AJR
(SX-ERA)	B767	24716	S7-	B787	35307	**S9-GRE**	**AN7x**	**?**	TC-AJS
(SX-ERB)	B767	24742	S7-	B787	35309	S9-IAO	B727	19358	TC-AJT
(SX-ERC)	B767	24762	(S7-1HM)	B767	24448	S9-NAB	DC-8	45421	TC-AJU
SX-FIN	**B747**	**21575**	(S7-2HM)	B707	19869	S9-NAG	DC-8	45259	TC-AJV
SX-IFA	**MD80**	**49809**	S7-4HM	B707	19871	S9-NAN	DC-8	45433	TC-AJY
SX-OAA	B747	20742	S7-AAB	B767	27427	S9-NAS	DC-8	45435	TC-AJZ
SX-OAB	B747	20825	S7-AAQ	B767	26387	S9-NAZ	B727	19404	TC-AKA
SX-OAC	B747	21683	S7-AAS	B767	24448	**S9-PAC**	**B727**	**20475**	TC-AKA
SX-OAD	B747	21684	S7-AAV	B767	26388	**S9-PSC**	**B727**	**21526**	TC-AKB
SX-OAE	B747	21935	S7-AAW	A300	033	**S9-PSD**	**DC-8**	**45820**	TC-AKD
SX-TID	**B747**	**23502**	S7-AAX	B757	25622	**S9-PSR**	**DC-9**	**47706**	**TC-AKL**
			S7-AAY	A300	035	**S9-PST**	**B727**	**19859**	**TC-AKM**
			S7-AAZ	A300	055	**S9-ROI**	**B727**	**18933**	**TC-AKN**
Bangladesh			(S7-AAZ)	B767	26328	**S9-SVE**	**B727**	**18366**	TC-AKP
			S7-ABA	B737	24305	S9-TAE	1-11	084	TC-AKV
			S7-ABB	B737	24302	**S9-TAN**	**B727**	**18893**	TC-ALA
S2-AAL	B707	17903	S7-ABC	B737	24304	**S9-TAO**	**B727**	**19390**	**TC-ALB**
S2-ABM	B707	17680	S7-ABD	B737	24303	(S9-TBA)	B727	18801	**TC-ALC**
S2-ABN	B707	19168							

Additional Turkey (TC-) entries continued in right column:

TC-	737NG	35700
TC-	A300	106
(TC-)	B737	23870
(TC-)	B737	25124
TC-AAB	**737NG**	**28620**
TC-AAD	**B737**	**28201**
TC-AAE	**737NG**	**35700**
TC-AAE	B737	28055
TC-AAF	**B737**	**29122**
TC-AAG	**B737**	**29234**
TC-AAH	**737NG**	**35701**
TC-AAK	**737NG**	**35094**
TC-AAP	**737NG**	**32736**
TC-ABA	SE210	253
TC-ABB	A321	0597
TC-ABC	A321	0591
TC-ABD	A300	611
TC-ABE	A300	613
TC-ABF	A300	633
TC-ABG	A320	0313
TC-ABH	A320	0345
TC-ABK	**A300**	**101**
TC-ACA	B737	24519
TC-ACB	**A300**	**121**
TC-ACC	**A300**	**147**
TC-ACD	**A300**	**075**
TC-ACI	TU154	90A-834
TC-ACT	**A300**	**083**
TC-ACT	TU154	86A-739
TC-ACU	**A300**	**183**
TC-ACV	TU154	90A-833
TC-ACY	A300	107
TC-ACZ	**A300**	**105**
TC-ADA	B737	23866
(TC-ADA)	B737	24911
(TC-AEA)	B737	21275
(TC-AEB)	B737	21276
(TC-AEC)	B737	20575
TC-AFA	B737	26306
TC-AFB	B727	19864
TC-AFC	B727	19863
TC-AFD	B727	21113
TC-AFE	B727	21114
TC-AFG	B727	21988
TC-AFJ	B737	23979
TC-AFK	B737	24684
TC-AFL	B737	24690
TC-AFM	B727	26279
TC-AFN	B727	21619
TC-AFO	B727	21620
TC-AFP	B727	21442
TC-AFR	B727	21621
TC-AFS	B737	23981
TC-AFT	B727	21618
TC-AFU	B737	26081
TC-AFV	B727	20905
TC-AFY	B737	24705
TC-AGA	B737	24512
TC-AGK	**A300**	**117**
TC-AHA	B757	24121
TC-AJA	B757	24771
TC-AJK	B737	22090
TC-AJR	B727	19393
TC-AJS	B727	18744
TC-AJT	B727	18743
TC-AJU	B727	18951
TC-AJV	B727	20265
TC-AJY	B727	19993
TC-AJZ	B727	18802
TC-AKA	1-11	BAC.255
TC-AKA	SE210	239
TC-AKB	1-11	BAC.253
TC-AKD	B727	20930
TC-AKL	**MD80**	**53184**
TC-AKM	**MD80**	**53185**
TC-AKN	**MD80**	**53186**
TC-AKP	A310	352
TC-AKV	A310	309
TC-ALA	SE210	250
TC-ALB	**B727**	**20431**
TC-ALC	**B737**	**19424**

Reg	Type	Serial	Reg	Type	Serial	Reg	Type	Serial	Reg	Type	Serial	Reg	Type	Serial
(TC-ALD)	B727	20526	TC-FLG	A300	110	TC-JAU	DC-10	46705	TC-JER	B737	26073			
TC-ALF	B727	20430	TC-FLH	B737	24300	TC-JAV	DC-10	46704	TC-JES	B737	26074			
TC-ALG	A300	259	TC-FLI	B737	24069	TC-JAY	DC-10	46907	TC-JET	B737	26077			
TC-ALK	B727	20430	TC-FLJ	A300	082	TC-JAZ	F.28	11032	TC-JEU	B737	26078			
TC-ALL	A321	0604	TC-FLK	A300	151	TC-JBA	B707	17587	TC-JEV	B737	26085			
TC-ALM	B727	20431	TC-FLL	A300	256	TC-JBA	B727	20463	TC-JEY	B737	26086			
TC-ALN	A300	065	TC-FLM	A300	176	TC-JBB	B707	17589	TC-JEZ	B737	26088			
TC-ALO	A321	0614	TC-FLN	MD80	53149	TC-JBB	B727	20464	TC-JFA	B727	20434			
TC-ALP	A300	153	TC-FLO	MD80	53150	TC-JBC	B707	17590	TC-JFB	B727	20433			
TC-ALR	A300	155	TC-FLR	E145	145155	TC-JBC	B727	20465	TC-JFC	737NG	29765			
TC-ALS	A300	066	TC-GAA	A320	0238	TC-JBD	B707	17591	TC-JFD	737NG	29766			
TC-ALS	B737	25844	TC-GAB	A320	0280	TC-JBE	B707	17903	TC-JFE	737NG	29767			
TC-ALT	B737	20221	TC-GAC	A310	278	TC-JBF	B727	20980	TC-JFF	737NG	29768			
TC-ALU	A300	211	TC-GEN	B757	22206	TC-JBG	B727	20981	TC-JFG	737NG	29769			
TC-ALU	TU134	1351206	TC-GHA	B707	19869	TC-JBH	B727	20982	TC-JFH	737NG	29770			
TC-ALV	A300	261	TC-GHA	B707	20069	TC-JBJ	B727	20983	TC-JFI	737NG	29771			
TC-ALV	TU134	1351204	TC-GHB	B707	19871	TC-JBK	DC-9	47674	TC-JFJ	737NG	29772			
TC-ALY	YAK42	4410016	TC-GHB	B737	24791	TC-JBL	DC-9	47723	TC-JFK	737NG	29773			
TC-ANA	A319	1002	TC-GHC	737NG	28004	TC-JBM	B727	21260	TC-JFL	737NG	29774			
TC-ANH	B737	25375	TC-GLA	B757	30044	TC-JBN	B707	17697	TC-JFM	737NG	29775			
TC-ANI	A300	046	TC-GRA	TU154	86A-739	TC-JBP	B707	17697	TC-JFN	737NG	29776			
(TC-ANI)	B737	23868	TC-GRB	TU154	90A-833	TC-JBP	B727	17701	TC-JFO	737NG	29777			
TC-ANL	B737	25374	TC-GRC	TU154	90A-834	TC-JBR	B727	21603	TC-JFO	A310	257			
TC-ANM	B757	24122	TC-GRD	TU134	66109	TC-JBS	B707	18834	TC-JFP	737NG	29778			
TC-ANN	B757	24136	TC-GRE	TU134	66120	TC-JBT	B707	18836	TC-JFR	737NG	29779			
TC-APA	B737	25595	TC-GTA	A300	054	TC-JBU	B707	18842	TC-JFT	737NG	29780			
TC-APB	B737	26290	TC-GTB	A300	127	TC-JBV	DC-8	45429	TC-JFU	737NG	29781			
TC-APC	B737	24345	TC-GTC	A300	048	TC-JBY	DC-8	45694	TC-JFV	737NG	29782			
TC-APD	B737	29107	(TC-GTD)	A300	057	TC-JBZ	DC-8	45693	TC-JFY	737NG	29783			
TC-APF	737NG	28642	TC-GUL	B757	22209	TC-JCA	B727	22992	TC-JFZ	737NG	29784			
TC-APG	737NG	29329	TC-GUL	DC-8	46159	TC-JCB	B727	22993	TC-JGA	737NG	29785			
TC-APH	737NG	29250	TC-IAA	B737	29000	TC-JCC	B707	18715	TC-JGB	737NG	29786			
TC-API	737NG	32732	TC-IAB	B737	29001	TC-JCD	B727	22998	TC-JGC	737NG	29787			
TC-APJ	737NG	32735	TC-IAC	B737	24450	TC-JCE	B727	22999	TC-JGD	737NG	29788			
TC-APK	737NG	28643	TC-IAD	B737	25033	TC-JCF	B707	17601	TC-JGE	737NG	29789			
TC-APL	737NG	30231	TC-IAE	B737	24571	TC-JCF	B707	19271	TC-JGF	737NG	29790			
TC-APM	737NG	28403	TC-IAF	B737	28490	TC-JCK	B727	21664	TC-JGG	737NG	34405			
TC-APN	737NG	28628	TC-IAG	B737	28491	TC-JCL	A310	338	TC-JGH	737NG	34406			
TC-APP	B737	28202	TC-IAH	737NG	28591	TC-JCM	A310	375	TC-JGI	737NG	34407			
TC-APR	B737	24685	(TC-IAJ)	737NG	28592	TC-JCN	A310	379	TC-JGJ	737NG	34408			
TC-APT	B737	24687	(TC-IAK)	737NG	28595	TC-JCO	A310	386	TC-JGK	737NG	34409			
TC-APU	737NG	29344	TC-IEA	737NG	32361	TC-JCP	1-11	BAC.254	TC-JGL	737NG	34410			
TC-APV	737NG	28639	TC-IEB	737NG	32363	TC-JCR	A310	370	TC-JGM	737NG	34411			
TC-APY	737NG	28591	TC-IEC	F.100	11410	TC-JCS	A310	389	TC-JGN	737NG	34412			
TC-APZ	737NG	29103	TC-IEC	F.100	11420	TC-JCT	A310	502	TC-JGO	737NG	34413			
TC-ARA	B757	26962	TC-IED	F.100	11420	TC-JCU	A310	390	TC-JGP	737NG	34414			
TC-ARI	1-11	BAC.253	TC-IEE	F.100	11326	TC-JCV	A310	476	TC-JGR	737NG	34415			
TC-ARI	SE210	235	TC-IEF	A321	0968	TC-JCY	A310	478	TC-JGS	737NG	34416			
TC-ASA	SE210	222	TC-IEG	A321	0974	TC-JCZ	A310	480	TC-JGT	737NG	34417			
TC-ASK	B767	23280	TC-IEH	A321	0963	TC-JDA	A310	496	TC-JGU	737NG	34418			
TC-ATA	B737	24687	(TC-IEI)	A321	1008	TC-JDB	A310	497	TC-JGV	737NG	34419			
TC-ATE	B737	20521	TC-IHO	B727	20430	TC-JDC	A310	537	TC-JHA	MD90	53552			
TC-ATU	B727	18742	TC-IKO	B727	20431	TC-JDD	A310	586	TC-JHB	MD90	53553			
TC-ATU	B737	21736	TC-INA	MD80	49943	TC-JDE	B737	24904	TC-JIH	A340	270			
TC-AVA	B737	25594	TC-INB	MD80	49936	TC-JDF	B737	24917	TC-JII	A340	331			
TC-AYA	B737	24683	TC-INC	MD80	49792	TC-JDG	B737	25181	TC-JKA	B737	26300			
TC-AZA	B737	24691	TC-IND	MD80	49940	TC-JDH	B737	25184	TC-JKB	B737	23981			
TC-BIR	B737	25040	TC-IQA	A321	0970	TC-JDI	B737	25372	TC-JKC	B737	24469			
TC-COA	A300	128	TC-IYA	B727	22999	TC-JDJ	A340	023	TC-JKD	B737	24493			
TC-CYO	B737	23415	TC-IYB	B727	21664	TC-JDK	A340	025	TC-JKF	A310	356			
TC-DEL	B727	22439	TC-IYC	B727	21260	TC-JDL	A340	057	TC-JLA	A320	0545			
TC-ESA	B737	23411	TC-IYI	YAK42	1304016	TC-JDM	A340	115	TC-JLB	A320	0562			
TC-ESB	B737	23412	TC-IZH	A319	2452	TC-JDN	A340	180	TC-JLC	A320	0566			
TC-ESC	B737	23165	TC-IZM	A319	2404	TC-JDT	B737	25261	TC-JLD	A320	0574			
TC-ETB	CRJ9	15063	TC-IZR	A319	2414	TC-JDU	B737	25288	TC-JLE	A320	0992			
TC-ETC	CRJ9	15064	TC-JAA	DC-9	47048	TC-JDV	B737	25289	TC-JLF	A320	1413			
TC-ETD	CRJ9	15065	TC-JAB	DC-9	45774	TC-JDY	B737	26065	TC-JLG	A320	1054			
TC-FAR	YAK42	1014494	TC-JAC	DC-9	47213	TC-JDZ	B737	26066	TC-JLH	A320	0553			
TC-FBB	MD80	53185	TC-JAD	DC-9	47488	TC-JEA	B737	27143	TC-JLI	A320	0559			
TC-FBD	MD80	53186	TC-JAE	DC-9	47489	TC-JEC	B727	22287	TC-JLJ	A320	1856			
TC-FBE	A320	0132	TC-JAF	DC-9	47451	TC-JED	B737	25740	TC-JLK	A320	1909			
TC-FBF	A320	0288	TC-JAG	DC-9	47442	TC-JEE	B737	26290	TC-JLL	A320	1996			
TC-FBG	A321	0771	TC-JAH	B707	17593	TC-JEF	B737	26291	TC-JLM	A319	2738			
TC-FBG	MD80	53184	TC-JAJ	B707	17603	TC-JEG	B737	25374	TC-JLN	A319	2739			
TC-FBT	A321	0855	TC-JAK	DC-9	47397	TC-JEH	B737	26320	TC-JMA	A321	0522			
TC-FBT	MD80	49949	TC-JAL	DC-9	47534	TC-JEI	B737	26298	TC-JMB	A321	0541			
TC-FBY	A320	0283	TC-JAM	B707	17607	TC-JEJ	B737	26375	TC-JMC	A321	0806			
TC-FLA	A300	127	TC-JAN	B707	17594	TC-JEK	B737	26299	TC-JMD	A321	0810			
TC-FLB	B757	24122	TC-JAO	F.28	11057	TC-JEL	B737	26300	TC-JME	A321	1219			
TC-FLC	B757	24136	TC-JAP	F.28	11058	TC-JEM	B737	26302	TC-JMF	A321	1233			
TC-FLD	B757	26244	TC-JAR	F.28	11060	TC-JEN	B737	25376	TC-JMG	A321	2060			
TC-FLE	A300	163	TC-JAS	F.28	11070	TC-JEO	B737	25377	TC-JNA	A330	697			
TC-FLF	A300	194	TC-JAT	F.28	11071	TC-JEP	B737	25378	TC-JNB	A330	704			

Reg	Type	Serial
TC-JNC	A330	742
TC-JND	A330	754
TC-JNE	A330	774
TC-JPA	A320	2609
TC-JPB	A320	2626
TC-JPC	A320	2928
TC-JPD	A320	2934
TC-JPE	A320	2941
TC-JPF	A320	2984
TC-JPG	A320	3010
TC-JPH	A320	3185
TC-JPI	A320	3208
TC-JPJ	A320	3239
TC-JPK	A320	3257
TC-JRA	A321	2823
TC-JRB	A321	2868
TC-JRC	A321	2999
TC-JRD	A321	3015
TC-JRE	A321	3126
TC-JRF	A321	3207
TC-JTB	B737	23781
TC-JTC	B737	23783
TC-JUC	B727	20430
TC-JUH	B727	20431
TC-JUN	SE210	259
TC-JUP	B737	19408
TC-JUR	B737	20412
TC-JUS	B737	22453
TC-JUT	B737	20197
TC-JUU	B737	23404
TC-JUV	A300	161
TC-JUY	A300	158
TC-JYK	A310	172
TC-KTA	MD90	53552
TC-KTB	MD90	53553
TC-KTC	A321	1451
(TC-KTC)	MD90	53554
TC-KTD	A321	2117
TC-KTY	A321	1012
TC-KZT	A300	139
TC-KZU	A300	173
TC-KZV	A300	041
TC-KZY	A300	044
TC-MAB	DC-8	46016
TC-MAO	737NG	28645
TC-MCA	A300	269
TC-MCB	A300	304
TC-MIO	B737	23714
TC-MNA	A300	019
TC-MNB	A300	292
TC-MNC	A300	277
TC-MND	A300	212
TC-MNE	A300	222
TC-MNF	B737	24126
TC-MNG	A300	083
TC-MNH	B737	24773
TC-MNI	B737	24128
TC-MNJ	A300	123
TC-MNL	B737	25374
TC-MNM	B737	25375
TC-MNN	A300	126
TC-MNO	MD80	49138
TC-MNP	MD80	49142
TC-MNR	MD80	48097
TC-MNS	MD80	48098
TC-MNT	MD80	48096
TC-MNU	A300	047
TC-MNY	A300	299
TC-MNZ	A300	302
TC-MSO	737NG	29246
TC-MZZ	737NG	29247
TC-OAA	A300	744
TC-OAB	A300	749
TC-OAC	A320	0313
TC-OAD	A320	0345
TC-OAE	A321	0663
TC-OAF	A321	0668
TC-OAG	A300	747
TC-OAH	A300	584
TC-OAI	A321	0787
TC-OAK	A321	0954
TC-OAL	A321	1004
TC-OAN	A321	1421
TC-OAO	A300	764
TC-OAP	A321	0604
TC-OAR	A321	0614
TC-OAS	MD80	53465
TC-OAT	MD80	53466
TC-OAU	MD80	53488
TC-OAV	MD80	53520
TC-OAY	A300	677
TC-OBB	A300	302
TC-OBC	A300	299
TC-OGA	B757	22688
TC-OGB	B757	22689
TC-OGC	B757	23983
TC-OGD	B757	24176
TC-OGE	A320	0764
TC-OGF	A320	0978
TC-OGG	B757	23983
TC-OGH	B757	22688
TC-OGI	A320	0640
TC-OGJ	A320	0676
TC-OGK	A320	0460
TC-OGL	A320	0272
TC-OGM	CRJ7	10028
TC-OGN	CRJ7	10039
TC-OGO	A320	2423
TC-OGP	A320	2453
TC-OGR	A320	2457
TC-OGS	B757	29307
TC-OGT	B757	29308
TC-OGU	A319	2631
TC-OGV	A319	2655
TC-OIM	A300	094
TC-ONA	A320	0288
TC-ONB	A320	0331
TC-ONC	A320	0289
TC-OND	A320	0371
TC-ONE	A320	0453
TC-ONE	A320	0528
TC-ONF	A320	0444
TC-ONG	A320	0361
TC-ONH	A321	0591
TC-ONI	A321	0597
TC-ONJ	A321	0385
TC-ONK	A300	086
TC-ONL	A300	087
TC-ONM	MD80	53546
TC-ONN	MD80	53547
TC-ONO	MD80	53548
TC-ONP	MD80	53549
TC-ONR	MD80	53550
TC-ONS	A321	0364
TC-ONT	A300	138
TC-ONU	A300	192
TC-ONY	A300	037
TC-ORH	A300	083
TC-ORI	A300	183
TC-ORK	A300	173
TC-OYC	A300	079
TC-RAA	A300	017
TC-RAB	A300	102
TC-RAC	B727	20792
TC-RAD	TU154	91A-890
TC-RAE	A300	029
TC-RAF	B737	20196
TC-RAG	L1011	193A-1004
(TC-RJA)	146	E3341
(TC-RJB)	146	E3343
TC-RTU	MD80	49708
TC-RUT	B727	20904
TC-SAL	A320	0347
TC-SAN	A320	0373
TC-SGA	A300	090
TC-SGB	A310	562
TC-SGC	A310	519
TC-SGD	B737	25773
TC-SGE	B737	25775
TC-SKA	B737	23865
TC-SKB	B737	27004
TC-SKC	737NG	30478
TC-SKD	B737	25372
TC-SKE	B737	25163
TC-SKF	B737	26291
TC-SKG	B737	25371
TC-SKH	737NG	29644
TC-SNA	B757	25624
TC-SNB	B757	26271
TC-SNC	B757	26273
TC-SND	B757	26268
TC-SNS	B737	24494
TC-SUA	737NG	28612
TC-SUB	737NG	28614
TC-SUC	737NG	28616
TC-SUD	737NG	28620
TC-SUE	737NG	29079
TC-SUF	737NG	29083
TC-SUG	737NG	32365
TC-SUH	737NG	32366
TC-SUI	737NG	32367
TC-SUJ	737NG	32368
TC-SUK	B737	26431
TC-SUL	737NG	28822
TC-SUM	737NG	28826
TC-SUN	B737	24676
TC-SUO	737NG	30272
TC-SUP	B737	24908
TC-SUR	B737	24910
TC-SUS	B737	27007
TC-SUT	B737	25190
TC-SUU	737NG	30274
TC-SUV	737NG	30807
TC-SUY	737NG	30806
TC-TCA	B727	21113
TC-TCB	A319	1002
TC-TCB	B727	21114
TC-THA	146	E3232
TC-THB	146	E3234
TC-THC	146	E3236
TC-THD	146	E3237
TC-THE	146	E3238
TC-THF	146	E3240
TC-THG	146	E3241
TC-THH	146	E3243
TC-THI	146	E1229
TC-THJ	146	E1230
TC-THL	146	E1249
TC-THM	146	E3264
TC-THN	146	E1252
TC-THO	146	E3265
TC-TJA	B737	24699
TC-TJB	B737	27633
TC-TJC	B737	25374
TC-TJD	B737	25375
TC-TKA	A300	086
TC-TKB	A300	087
TC-TKC	A300	091
TC-TMT	A310	418
TC-TRU	MD80	49442
TC-TTA	MD80	48096
TC-TTB	MD80	49144
TC-TUA	MD80	49138
TC-TUB	A321	0604
TC-TUC	A321	0614
TC-TUR	B727	20792
TC-VAA	B737	19424
TC-VAB	B737	20221

Iceland

Reg	Type	Serial
(TF-)	B747	19744
TF-ABA	B747	22530
TF-ABD	B737	20417
TF-ABD	L1011	193B-1221
TF-ABE	B737	23122
TF-ABE	L1011	193A-1022
TF-ABF	B737	20258
TF-ABF	B737	21184
TF-ABG	B737	21192
TF-ABG	B737	20377
TF-ABG	L1011	193A-1005
TF-ABH	B737	19553
TF-ABH	L1011	193A-1054
TF-ABI	B737	23023
TF-ABI	B747	20924
TF-ABJ	B737	19594
TF-ABK	B737	23922
TF-ABK	B747	20116
TF-ABL	B737	23525
TF-ABL	B747	20117
TF-ABM	L1011	193A-1044
TF-ABM	L1011	193B-1072
TF-ABM	L1011	193B-1221
TF-ABN	B737	22278
(TF-ABN)	B747	19730
(TF-ABN)	B747	19745
TF-ABN	B747	21962
TF-ABO	B747	20208
TF-ABP	B747	22429
TF-ABP	L1011	193A-1045
TF-ABQ	B747	20529
TF-ABQ	B747	20543
TF-ABR	B747	20014
TF-ABS	B747	20305
TF-ABT	B737	20458
TF-ABT	L1011	193B-1231
TF-ABU	B737	21686
TF-ABU	L1011	193A-1051
TF-ABV	B737	22137
TF-ABV	L1011	193R-1033
TF-ABW	B747	20376
TF-ABX	B737	20257
TF-ABY	B737	22136
TF-ABY	B747	21030
TF-ABZ	B747	21316
TF-ACV	DC-8	45989
(TF-ADF)	B747	21351
(TF-ADI)	B747	21830
(TF-ADJ)	B747	21831
(TF-ADK)	B747	22303
(TF-ADL)	B747	22305
(TF-ADO)	B747	23799
TF-AEA	B707	18714
TF-AEB	B707	19621
TF-AEC	B707	19622
TF-AED	DC-8	45817
TF-AIA	B727	20951
TF-AIC	B737	21184
TF-AIC	B737	23253
TF-AMA	B747	24063
TF-AMB	B747	24065
TF-AMC	B747	21835
TF-AMD	B747	23476
TF-AME	B747	23032
TF-AMF	B747	23286
TF-AMH	B747	23393
TF-AMI	B747	27066
TF-AMJ	B747	23030
TF-AMK	B747	23028
TF-AMO	B747	28367
TF-AMP	B747	24801
TF-ANC	B707	18746
TF-ARA	B767	28206
TF-ARB	B767	26265
TF-ARD	B757	22211
TF-ARE	B757	22611
TF-ARF	B747	22305
TF-ARG	B747	22303
TF-ARH	B747	22669
TF-ARI	B757	25240
TF-ARJ	B747	23735
TF-ARK	B757	22612
TF-ARL	B747	22671
TF-ARM	B747	22363
TF-ARN	B747	22382
TF-ARO	B747	23301
TF-ARP	B747	23348
TF-ARQ	B747	22380
TF-ARR	B747	23621
TF-ARS	B747	22996
TF-ARU	B747	22970
TF-ARV	B747	24138
TF-ARW	B747	24071
TF-ARY	B747	24837
TF-ATA	B747	20527
TF-ATB	B747	19824
TF-ATC	B747	22149
TF-ATD	B747	21966
(TF-ATE)	B747	19825

Reg	Type	c/n
TF-ATE	B747	20531
TF-ATF	B747	19825
TF-ATG	B747	23244
TF-ATH	B747	24106
TF-ATI	**B747**	**24107**
TF-ATJ	**B747**	**24108**
TF-ATK	B747	22872
TF-ATL	B747	22454
TF-ATM	B747	22455
TF-ATN	B747	22723
TF-ATO	B767	24013
TF-ATP	B767	24239
TF-ATR	B767	24457
TF-ATS	B747	23245
TF-ATT	B767	24358
(TF-ATU)	B747	23250
TF-ATU	B767	26204
TF-ATV	B747	23048
TF-ATW	B747	22724
TF-ATX	**B747**	**23711**
TF-ATY	B767	23072
TF-ATZ	B747	24088
TF-AVB	CV880	22-00-48M
TF-AYA	B707	18792
TF-AYB	B707	18422
TF-AYC	B707	18421
TF-AYD	B707	18793
TF-AYE	B707	18716
TF-AYF	B707	20097
TF-AYG	B707	19004
TF-BBA	**B737**	**28271**
TF-BBA	DC-8	45954
TF-BBB	**B737**	**28334**
TF-BBB	DC-8	46162
TF-BBC	B737	24209
TF-BBC	DC-8	46154
TF-BBD	**B737**	**24463**
TF-BBD	DC-8	46028
TF-BBE	**B737**	**25256**
TF-BBF	**B737**	**25264**
TF-BBG	**B737**	**25263**
TF-BBX	B737	23499
TF-BBY	B737	23500
TF-BCV	DC-8	45900
TF-BCV	DC-8	46002
TF-CCV	DC-8	45990
TF-CIB	**B757**	**26962**
TF-ECV	DC-8	45445
TF-ELA	A300	788
TF-ELA	B737	25401
TF-ELB	A300	659
TF-ELB	A300	666
TF-ELC	A300	775
TF-ELC	B737	25041
TF-ELD	A300	536
TF-ELD	B737	24124
TF-ELE	**A300**	**767**
TF-ELE	A310	502
TF-ELF	**A300**	**529**
TF-ELG	**A300**	**758**
TF-ELJ	B737	24573
TF-ELK	**A300**	**557**
TF-ELL	B737	20138
TF-ELM	B737	21736
TF-ELM	B737	24021
TF-ELN	B737	23766
TF-ELO	B737	24028
TF-ELP	B737	23522
TF-ELP	B737	25729
TF-ELQ	B737	23535
TF-ELR	A310	624
TF-ELR	B737	23523
TF-ELR	B737	23775
TF-ELS	A310	552
TF-ELU	A300	657
TF-ELV	B737	24796
TF-ELW	**A300**	**755**
TF-ELY	B737	25168
TF-ELZ	B737	23980
TF-FDA	B737	24700
TF-FIA	B727	19826
TF-FIA	B737	24352
TF-FIA	**B757**	**29310**
TF-FIA	B767	24953
TF-FIB	B737	24353
TF-FIB	**B767**	**25365**
TF-FIC	B737	24804
TF-FIC	**B767**	**24846**
TF-FID	B737	25063
TF-FID	**B757**	**24567**
TF-FIE	B727	19503
TF-FIE	B737	23811
TF-FIE	B737	24795
TF-FIE	**B757**	**24566**
TF-FIG	**B757**	**24456**
TF-FIH	**B757**	**24739**
TF-FII	**B757**	**24760**
TF-FIJ	**B757**	**25085**
TF-FIK	B757	24771
TF-FIK	B757	26276
TF-FIN	**B757**	**28989**
TF-FIO	**B757**	**29436**
TF-FIP	**B757**	**30423**
TF-FIR	**B757**	**26242**
TF-FIS	**B757**	**26245**
TF-FIT	B757	24868
TF-FIT	**B757**	**26244**
TF-FIU	**B757**	**26243**
TF-FIV	**B757**	**30424**
TF-FIW	B757	24838
TF-FIX	**B757**	**29434**
TF-FIY	**B757**	**29312**
TF-FIZ	**B757**	**30052**
TF-FLA	DC-8	46020
TF-FLB	DC-8	45753
TF-FLB	DC-8	45936
TF-FLC	DC-8	46049
TF-FLC	DC-8	46088
TF-FLE	DC-8	46042
TF-FLE	DC-8	46101
TF-FLF	DC-8	46062
TF-FLF	DC-8	46112
TF-FLG	B727	19826
TF-FLH	B727	19503
TF-FLI	B727	22295
TF-FLJ	B727	19619
TF-FLK	B727	20951
TF-FLT	DC-8	46075
TF-FLU	DC-8	45999
TF-FLV	DC-8	46121
TF-GCV	DC-8	45640
TF-GRL	B757	25620
TF-ISA	B737	20156
TF-ISA	DC-8	45980
TF-ISB	B737	20521
TF-ISB	DC-8	45964
TF-IUC	B707	19133
TF-IUD	B707	19628
TF-IUE	B707	18708
TF-IUE	B707	19372
TF-IUF	DC-8	46016
TF-IUG	B707	19133
TF-JXA	**MD80**	**49555**
TF-JXB	**MD80**	**49909**
TF-JXC	**MD80**	**49627**
TF-JXD	**737NG**	**30688**
TF-JXE	**737NG**	**30722**
TF-JXF	**737NG**	**33419**
TF-LLA	**B767**	**24541**
TF-LLK	DC-8	45818
TF-LLZ	**B757**	**22691**
TF-MDA	MD80	48003
TF-MDB	MD80	49449
TF-MDC	MD80	53014
TF-MDE	MD80	49823
TF-MIK	**DO328**	**3147**
TF-MIL	DO328	3149
TF-MIM	DO328	3161
TF-MIO	**DO328**	**3181**
TF-MKG	DC-8	46027
TF-MKH	DC-8	46153
TF-NPA	**DO328**	**3220**
TF-NPB	**DO328**	**3161**
(TF-RMR)	B727	21581
TF-SUN	B737	23535
TF-VLA	B707	18163
(TF-VLB)	B707	18082
TF-VLB	B707	18827
TF-VLC	B707	18820
TF-VLG	B707	19964
TF-VLJ	B707	19351
TF-VLK	B737	22453
TF-VLL	B707	19270
TF-VLM	B737	21715
TF-VLP	B707	18964
TF-VLR	B707	18881
TF-VLS	B727	18893
TF-VLT	B737	20458
TF-VLV	B707	18962
TF-VLW	DC-8	45912
TF-VLX	B707	19664
TF-VLY	DC-8	46019
TF-VLZ	DC-8	46080
TF-VVA	B707	18082
TF-VVB	B707	18075
(TF-VVC)	B707	18073
TF-VVE	B707	18163

Guatemala

Reg	Type	c/n
TG-ALA	B727	19302
TG-ALA	B737	20583
TG-ALA	B737	20586
TG-ALE	**DC-9**	**48135**
TG-AMA	B737	23388
TG-AOA	B727	18742
TG-AOA	B737	20582
TG-ARA	1-11	BAC.205
TG-AVA	1-11	BAC.206
TG-AYA	1-11	BAC.211
TG-AYA	B727	19506
TG-AYA	B737	20587
TG-AZA	1-11	BAC.231
TG-CAO	F.28	11048
TG-DHP	B727	19166
TG-JII	DC-9	48136
TG-LKA	B727	19393
TG-TJF	1-11	089
TG-TJK	1-11	063
TG-URY	DC-9	47529
TG-URY	**DC-9**	**48150**
TG-YAK	YAK40	9011160

Costa Rica

Reg	Type	c/n
TI-1055C	1-11	BAC.162
TI-1056C	1-11	BAC.108
TI-1084C	1-11	BAC.237
TI-1095C	1-11	BAC.242
TI-1096C	1-11	BAC.244
(TI-)	B737	23527
(TI-)	B737	24453
(TI-)	B737	24455
(TI-)	B737	24532
(TI-)	B737	24666
(TI-)	B737	24668
TI-AZS	DC-9	47301
TI-BBH	**MD80**	**49486**
TI-LRC	B727	18856
TI-LRF	1-11	BAC.237
TI-LRI	1-11	BAC.242
TI-LRJ	1-11	BAC.244
TI-LRK	1-11	BAC.208
TI-LRL	1-11	BAC.237
TI-LRP	DC-8	45672
TI-LRQ	B727	21945
TI-LRR	B727	21349
TI-VEL	DC-8	45435

Cameroon

Reg	Type	c/n
(TJ-)	F.28	11183
TJ-AAC	B737	23624
TJ-AAM	B727	21636
TJ-AIO	B737	21139
TJ-ALC	F.28	11204
TJ-ALD	**F.28**	**11226**
TJ-ALE	F.28	11225
TJ-ALG	**F.28**	**11227**
TJ-CAA	B707	20629
TJ-CAB	B747	22378
TJ-CAC	**B767**	**28138**
TJ-CAD	B767	22564
TJ-CAE	B747	23033
TJ-CAF	B757	24868
TJ-CAG	**B757**	**24293**
TJ-CAH	B757	24924
TJ-CBA	B737	20590
TJ-CBB	B737	20591
TJ-CBD	B737	21295
TJ-CBE	B737	23386
TJ-CBF	B737	23535
TJ-CBG	B737	27458
TJ-CBH	B737	27457
(TJ-CBI)	CRJ	7584
TJ-CGB	B737	27458

Central African Republic

Reg	Type	c/n
TL-	B737	23518
TL-AAI	SE210	10
TL-AAK	DC-8	45803
TL-ABB	SE210	249
TL-ABC	AN7x	72095909
TL-ABW	TU154	91A-895
TL-ACF	IL62	3052657
TL-ACL	IL62	3036142
TL-ACM	B737	22264
TL-ACN	IL76	053403072
TL-ACO	YAK40	9632049
TL-ACP	YAK40	9511639
TL-ACQ	YAK40	9411639
TL-ACU	IL76	043402039
TL-ACV	**AN7x**	**72080777**
TL-ACW	**AN7x**	**72090706**
TL-ACY	IL76	0003426765
TL-ADF	**AN7x**	**?**
TL-ADH	IL76	073411334
TL-ADJ	B707	20200
TL-ADO	B737	22264
TL-ADR	**B737**	**21281**
TL-AHI	DC-8	45300
TL-ALM	B707	20200
TL-FCA	SE210	42
TL-KAB	SE210	42

Congo Brazzaville

Reg	Type	c/n
TN-ACP	F.28	11072
TN-AEB	B727	21655
TN-AEE	B737	21538
TN-AFS	**IL76**	**1033415504**
TN-AFY	B727	19833
TN-AFZ	**B727**	**19839**
TN-AGO	B707	19519
TN-AGR	B737	20197
TN-AHI	**B737**	**23609**
TN-TAC	**B737**	**22264**
TN-WHK	**B737**	**21687**

Gabon

Reg	Type	c/n
TR-LCR	F.100	11258
TR-LEJ	B767	23280
TR-LEV	B727	22083
TR-LFH	B767	23178
TR-LFU	B737	24353
TR-LFZ	B737	23750
TR-LGP	**F.28**	**11126**
TR-LGQ	**F.100**	**11424**
TR-LHG	**DC-9**	**47198**
TR-LHP	**B767**	**21877**
TR-LQR	DC-8	45821
TR-LST	**F.28**	**11080**
TR-LSU	F.28	11081
TR-LTR	F.28	11104

```
TR-LTS    F.28    11102
TR-LTZ    DC-8    46053
TR-LVK    DC-8    45805
TR-LWD    SE210   114
TR-LXK    B747    21468
TR-LXL    B737    21467


Tunisia

TS-IAX    A300    601
TS-IAY    A300    354
TS-IAZ    A300    616
TS-IEA    B737    23320
TS-IEB    B737    22407
TS-IEB    B737    24905
TS-IEC    B737    23716
TS-IEC    B737    25010
TS-IED    B737    24141
TS-IED    B737    25032
TS-IEE    B737    24790
TS-IEF    B737    26309
TS-IEG    B737    29116
TS-IEJ    B737    24655
TS-IGU    A310    295
TS-IGV    A310    306
TS-IKM    SE210   84
TS-IMA    A300    188
TS-IMB    A320    0119
TS-IMC    A320    0124
TS-IMD    A320    0205
TS-IME    A320    0123
TS-IMF    A320    0370
TS-IMG    A320    0390
TS-IMH    A320    0402
TS-IMI    A320    0511
TS-IMJ    A319    0869
TS-IMK    A319    0880
TS-IML    A320    0958
TS-IMM    A320    0975
TS-IMN    A320    1187
TS-IMO    A319    1479
TS-IMP    A320    1700
TS-IMQ    A319    3096
TS-INA    A320    1121
TS-INB    A320    1175
TS-TNC    A320    1744
TS-IND    A320    0348
TS-INE    A320    0222
TS-INF    A320    0299
TS-ING    A320    0140
TS-INH    A320    0157
TS-INI    A320    0301
TS-INJ    A320    0025
TS-INK    A320    0112
TS-INL    A320    0400
TS-INM    A320    0246
TS-INN    A320    0793
TS-IOC    B737    21973
TS-IOD    B737    21974
TS-IOE    B737    22624
TS-IOF    B737    22625
TS-IOG    B737    26639
TS-IOH    B737    26640
TS-IOI    B737    27257
TS-IOJ    B737    27912
TS-IOK    737NG   29496
TS-IOL    737NG   29497
TS-IOM    737NG   29498
TS-ION    737NG   29499
TS-IOO    737NG   29149
TS-IOP    737NG   29500
TS-IOQ    737NG   29501
TS-IOR    737NG   29502
TS-IPA    A300    558
TS-IPB    A300    563
TS-IPC    A300    505
TS-IQB    A321    0995
TS-ISA    CRJ9    15091
TS-ITU    SE210   246
TS-JEA    B727    22665
TS-JEB    B727    22666
TS-JHN    B727    20545


TS-JHO    B727    20739
TS-JHP    B727    20822
TS-JHQ    B727    20948
TS-JHR    B727    21179
TS-JHS    B727    21234
TS-JHT    B727    21235
TS-JHU    B727    21318
TS-JHV    B727    21319
TS-JHW    B727    21320
TS-MAC    SE210   207
TS-TAR    SE210   178


Tchad

(TT-AAD)  SE210   100
TT-AAM    SE210   100
TT-DAE    L1011   193N-1101
(TT-DSZ)  B727    20470
TT-DWE    L1011   193N-1093
TT-EAP    B707    19964
TT-EAS    F.28    11173
TT-EAS    F.28    11204
TT-WAB    B707    19964


Ivory Coast

(TU-...)  DC-10   46891
TU-TAC    A310    571
TU-TAD    A310    651
TU-TAE    A310    652
TU-TAF    A310    671
TU-TAG    A300    657
TU-TAH    A300    744
TU-TAI    A300    749
TU-TAJ    B737    26333
TU-TAK    B737    28200
TU-TAL    DC-10   46890
TU-TAM    DC-10   46892
TU-TAN    DC-10   46997
TU-TAO    A300    137
TU-TAP    B747    22169
TU-TAQ    A300    659
TU-TAR    A310    440
TU-TAS    A300    243
TU-TAT    A300    282
TU-TAU    A310    435
TU-TAV    B737    19048
TU-TAX    A330    358
TU-TAY    A330    364
TU-TAZ    A310    595
(TU-TBD)  DC-10   46892
TU-TBX    DC-8    45604
TU-TBY    B707    17922
TU-TCA    DC-8    45670
TU-TCB    DC-8    45671
TU-TCC    DC-8    45857
TU-TCD    DC-8    45627
TU-TCE    DC-8    45569
TU-TCF    DC-8    46135
(TU-TCG)  DC-10   46890
TU-TCG    DC-8    45669
TU-TCH    DC-8    45883
TU-TCN    SE210   199
TU-TCO    SE210   215
TU-TCP    DC-8    45568
TU-TCY    SE210   219
TU-TDB    B707    18245
TU-TDC    B707    17924
TU-TIJ    F.28    11118
TU-TIK    F.28    11121
TU-TIM    F.28    11097
TU-TIN    F.28    11099
TU-TIR    F.28    11124
TU-TIS    F.100   11318
TU-TIV    F.100   11316
TU-TIW    F.28    11233
TU-TIX    F.28    11237
TU-TIY    F.28    11238
TU-TIZ    F.28    11099
TU-TXA    B707    18457
TU-TXB    B707    18457


TU-TXF    B707    18458
TU-TXG    DC-8    45819
TU-TXI    B707    18686
TU-TXJ    B707    18458
TU-TXK    DC-8    45819
TU-TXL    B707    19291
TU-TXM    B707    18686
TU-TXN    B707    19291
TU-TXQ    SE210   201
TU-TXR    SE210   78
TU-TXT    DC-8    46096
TU-VAA    F.100   11245
TU-VAA    F.28    11097
TU-VAB    F.28    11099
TU-VAH    F.28    11118
TU-VAJ    F.28    11124
TU-VAN    F.28    11121
(TU-VAZ)  F.28    11124


Benin

TY-AAM    B707    18084
TY-BBM    B707    20457
TY-BBN    F.28    11184
TY-BBR    B707    20457
TY-BBW    B707    18084


Mali

TZ-ADL    B737    20544
TZ-ADR    B727    19509
TZ-ADS    SE210   184
TZ-ADT    146     E1009
TZ-ASH    F.28    11003
TZ-BSB    1-11    086
TZ-NBA    B727    21853
TZ-TAC    B707    21049


Kiribati

T3-ATB    B727    19311
T3-VAL    B737    20158


Bosnia-Herzegovina

T9-AAC    MD80    48093
T9-ABC    YAK42   11140604
T9-ABC    YAK42   11151004
T9-ABD    YAK42   2016201
T9-ABE    AN7x    47097932
T9-ABF    YAK42   4402161
T9-ABH    YAK42   4814047
T9-CAB    IL76    1023408265
T9-CAC    IL76    0023437076
T9-QAA    IL76    0023437076
T9-QAB    IL76    1023408265


Uzbekistan

UK 31001  A310    574
UK 31002  A310    576
UK 31003  A310    706
UK 63979  TU134   63979
UK 67000  B767    35796
UK 75700  B757    28338
(UK 75701) B757   30060
UK 75702  B757    30061
UK 76351  IL76    1013408240
UK 76352  IL76    1023411378
UK 76353  IL76    1023414454
UK 76358  IL76    1023410339
UK 76359  IL76    1033414483
UK 76364  IL76    1043419657
UK 76365  IL76    1043420667
UK 76375  IL76    1033414496
UK 76376  IL76    1033417541
UK 76377  IL76    1033417545
UK 76386  IL76    1033418600


UK 76426  IL76    1043419644
UK 76427  IL76    1013406207
UK 76428  IL76    1043419648
UK 76447  IL76    1023412389
UK 76448  IL76    1023413443
UK 76449  IL76    1023403058
(UK 76701) B767   28370
(UK 76702) B767   28392
UK 76782  IL76    0093498971
UK 76793  IL76    0093498951
UK 76794  IL76    0093498954
UK 76805  IL76    1003403109
UK 76811  IL76    1013407223
UK 76813  IL76    1013408246
UK 76821  IL76    0023441200
UK 76824  IL76    1023410327
UK 76831  IL76    1013409287
UK 76844  IL76    1033416525
UK 76900  IL76    1053417563
UK 80001  146     E2312
UK 80002  146     E2309
UK 80003  146     E2319
UK 85050  TU154   73A-050
UK 85189  TU154   76A-189
UK 85245  TU154   77A-245
UK 85248  TU154   77A-248
UK 85249  TU154   78A-249
UK 85272  TU154   78A-272
UK 85286  TU154   78A-286
UK 85322  TU154   79A-322
UK 85344  TU154   79A-344
UK 85356  TU154   79A-356
UK 85370  TU154   79A-370
UK 85397  TU154   80A-397
UK 85398  TU154   80A-398
UK 85401  TU154   80A-401
UK 85416  TU154   80A-416
UK 85423  TU154   80A-423
UK 85438  TU154   80A-438
UK 85449  TU154   80A-449
UK 85575  TU154   83A-575
UK 85578  TU154   83A-578
UK 85600  TU154   84A-600
UK 85711  TU154   91A-887
UK 85764  TU154   93A-947
UK 85776  TU154   93A-958
UK 86012  IL86    51483201010
UK 86016  IL86    51483202014
UK 86052  IL86    51483202019
UK 86053  IL86    51483202020
UK 86056  IL86    51483203023
UK 86057  IL86    51483203024
UK 86064  IL86    51483204031
UK 86072  IL86    51483204039
UK 86083  IL86    51483206054
UK 86090  IL86    51483207061
UK 86569  IL62    1356234
UK 86573  IL62    4140536
UK 86574  IL62    3344833
UK 86575  IL62    1647928
UK 86576  IL62    4546257
UK 86577  IL62    2748552
UK 86578  IL62    1951525
UK 86579  IL62    2951636
UK 86610  IL62    41801
UK 86659  IL62    31404
UK 86664  IL62    11104
UK 86704  IL62    41603
UK 86932  IL62    3242432
UK 86933  IL62    3749224
UK 86934  IL62    4445827
UK 87263  YAK40   9311926
UK 87264  YAK40   9312026
UK 87289  YAK40   9320428
UK 87296  YAK40   9321328
UK 87309  YAK40   9320529
UK 87349  YAK40   9511839
UK 87367  YAK40   9341731
UK 87373  YAK40   9411425
UK 87396  YAK40   9410833
UK 87457  YAK40   9431636
UK 87515  YAK40   9521740
UK 87539  YAK40   9530442
```

Reg	Type	Serial
UK 87540	YAK40	9530542
UK 87542	YAK40	9530742
UK 87564	YAK40	9211621
UK 87799	YAK40	9040316
UK 87830	YAK40	9241625
UK 87846	YAK40	9331530
UK 87848	YAK40	9331730
UK 87923	YAK40	9741455
UK 87985	YAK40	9540844
UK 87989	YAK40	9541344
UK 87996	YAK40	9542044
UK 88185	YAK40	9620548
UK 88194	YAK40	9621448
UK 88217	YAK40	9630350
UK 88242	YAK40	9641551

Kazakhstan

Reg	Type	Serial
UN-001	B747	21962
UN-002	B757	23454
UN-10200	DC-10	46891
UN-42323	YAK42	3402116
UN-42337	YAK42	3606235
UN-42338	YAK42	3606256
UN-42342	YAK42	1706302
UN-42373	YAK42	3914323
UN-42401	YAK42	1116567
UN-42407	YAK42	4116690
UN-42410	YAK42	1219029
UN-42423	YAK42	4216606
UN-42424	YAK42	1302016
UN-42428	YAK42	2306016
UN-42430	YAK42	3408016
UN-42446	YAK42	3308017
UN-42447	YAK42	4309017
UN-42448	YAK42	3310017
UN-42460	YAK42	3914323
UN-42557	YAK42	3302017
UN-42558	YAK42	3307017
UN-42641	YAK42	3302017
UN-42712	YAK42	4309017
UN-42721	YAK42	3310017
UN-42730	YAK42	3307017
UN-65025	TU134	48450
UN-65069	TU134	49908
UN-65070	TU134	49912
UN-65083	TU134	60090
UN-65115	TU134	60405
UN-65121	TU134	60505
UN-65130	TU134	60635
UN-65138	TU134	60907
UN-65147	TU134	61012
UN-65551	TU134	66212
UN-65610	TU134	40150
UN-65619	TU134	31218
UN-65683	TU134	62199
UN-65694?	TU134	63235
UN-65695	TU134	63285
UN-65699	TU134	63333
UN-65720	TU134	62820
UN-65767	TU134	62335
UN-65776	TU134	62545
UN-65787	TU134	62798
UN-65799	TU134	63187
UN-65900	TU134	63684
UN-72850	AN7x	?
UN-72859	AN7x	?
UN-72904	AN7x	72030425
UN-72950	AN7x	?
UN-74031	AN7x	47098961
UN-76001	IL76	0033448407
UN-76002	IL76	0023442218
UN-76003?	IL76	?
UN-76004	IL76	0013434018
UN-76005	IL76	0073479392
UN-76006	IL76	0013434018
UN-76007	IL76	0003426765
UN-76007	IL76	?
UN-76008	IL76	0033448404
UN-76008	IL76	093420599
UN-76009	IL76	1003499994
UN-76010	IL76	?
UN-76011	IL76	?
UN-76020	IL76	?
UN-76021	IL76	0013430890
UN-76023	IL76	?
UN-76024	IL76	1033414480
UN-76077	IL76	?
UN-76371	IL76	1033414485
UN-76374	IL76	1033416520
UN-76384	IL76	1033401015
UN-76385	IL76	1033416515
UN-76410	IL76	1023412411
UN-76434	IL76	1023412395
UN-76435	IL76	1023413428
UN-76442	IL76	1023414450
UN-76472	IL76	0033446350
UN-76485	IL76	0063470088
UN-76487	IL76	0073479367
UN-76496	IL76	073410301
UN-76497	IL76	043402039
UN-76499	IL76	0023441186
UN-76810	IL76	1013409282
UN-78734	IL76	1013409303
UN-85066	TU154	74A-066
UN-85076	TU154	74A-076
UN-85111	TU154	75A-111
UN-85113	TU154	75A-113
UN-85151	TU154	76A-151
UN-85173	TU154	76A-173
UN-85194	TU154	77A-194
UN-85221	TU154	77A-221
UN-85230	TU154	77A-230
UN-85231	TU154	77A-231
UN-85240	TU154	77A-240
UN-85271	TU154	78A-271
UN-85276	TU154	78A-276
UN-85324	TU154	79A-324
UN-85385	TU154	79A-385
UN-85387	TU154	79A-387
UN-85396	TU154	80A-396
UN-85422	TU154	80A-422
UN-85431	TU154	80A-431
UN-85455	TU154	80A-455
UN-85463	TU154	80A-463
UN-85464	TU154	80A-464
UN-85478	TU154	81A-478
UN-85509	TU154	81A-509
UN-85516	TU154	81A-516
UN-85521	TU154	81A-521
UN-85537	TU154	82A-537
UN-85539	TU154	82A-539
UN-85558	TU154	82A-558
UN-85569	TU154	82A-569
UN-85570	TU154	87A-754
UN-85589	TU154	83A-589
UN-85713	TU154	91A-889
UN-85719	TU154	91A-901
UN-85742	TU154	79A-320
UN-85744	TU154	92A-927
UN-85775	TU154	93A-957
UN-85777	TU154	78A-262
UN-85780	TU154	93A-964
UN-85781	TU154	93A-965
UN-85782	TU154	93A-966
UN-85835	TU154	85A-716
UN-85836	TU154	85A-717
UN-85837	TU154	86A-724
UN-85852	TU154	86A-726
UN-85853	TU154	86A-728
UN-85854	TU154	86A-729
UN-85855	TU154	89A-823
UN-86068	IL86	51483204035
UN-86071	IL86	51483204038
UN-86077	IL86	51483205047
UN-86086	IL86	51483206057
UN-86101	IL86	51483207069
UN-86116	IL86	51483209084
UN-86125?	IL86	51483210093
UN-86130	IL62	3255333
UN-86501	IL62	4831628
UN-86502	IL62	21305
UN-86503	IL62	51902
UN-86505	IL62	4934847
UN-86506	IL62	1138234
UN-86507	IL62	4242654
UN-86524	IL62	3242321
UN-86558	IL62	1052128
UN-86586	IL62	3357947
UN-86935	IL62	1545951
UN-87202	YAK40	9812056
UN-87204	YAK40	9810157
UN-87208	YAK40	9810557
UN-87213	YAK40	9641050
UN-87233	YAK40	9531842
UN-87249	YAK40	9530244
UN-87251	YAK40	9421334
UN-87274	YAK40	9310727
UN-87274	YAK40	9311027
UN-87282	YAK40	9321727
UN-87305	YAK40	9320229
UN-87312	YAK40	9320729
UN-87314	YAK40	9330929
UN-87337	YAK40	9510639
UN-87359	YAK40	9340831
UN-87377	YAK40	9411132
UN-87403	YAK40	9411533
UN-87408	YAK40	9422033
UN-87420	YAK40	9421234
UN-87438	YAK40	9431435
UN-87471	YAK40	9441637
UN-87480	YAK40	9441938
UN-87488	YAK40	9441638
UN-87491	YAK40	9621647
UN-87492	YAK40	9541545
UN-87498	YAK40	9540146
UN-87501	YAK40	9512039
UN-87533	YAK40	9541741
UN-87537	YAK40	9520242
UN-87543	YAK40	9530842
"UN-87590"	YAK40	9110416
UN-87652	YAK40	9141320
UN-87654	YAK40	9211720
UN-87661	YAK40	9240525
UN-87662	YAK40	9240625
UN-87816	YAK40	9230724
UN-87850	YAK40	9441738
UN-87909	YAK40	9721454
UN-87912	YAK40	9732054
UN-87913	YAK40	9730255
UN-87920	YAK40	9731055
UN-87926	YAK40	9741755
UN-87927	YAK40	9741855
UN-87929	YAK40	9742055
UN-87931	YAK40	9740256
UN-87932	YAK40	9740356
UN-87933	YAK40	9740456
UN-87934	YAK40	9740556
UN-87935	YAK40	9811856
UN-87990	YAK40	9541444
UN-88154	YAK40	9610846
UN-88162	YAK40	9611646
UN-88173	YAK40	9621147
UN-88181	YAK40	9620148
UN-88189	YAK40	9620948
UN-88191	YAK40	9621148
UN-88195	YAK40	9631648
UN-88197	YAK40	9631948
UN-88198	YAK40	9632048
UN-88221	YAK40	9630750
UN-88248	YAK40	9640152
UN-88249	YAK40	9640252
UN-88259	YAK40	9711452
UN-88260	YAK40	9711552
UN-88266	YAK40	9710453
UN-88268	YAK40	9720653
UN-88271	YAK40	9720953
UN-88277	YAK40	9721953
UN-88294	YAK40	9331029
UN-A1901	A319	2592
UN-A3101	A310	399
UN-A3102	A310	412
UN-B1110	1-11	078
UN-B1111	1-11	078
UN-B2701	B727	22045
UN-B2702	B727	21861
UN-B2703	B727	21584
UN-B3703	B737	23444
UN-B3704	B737	24103
UN-B3705	B737	22453
UN-B3706	B737	22090
UN-B3707	B737	22123
UN-B3708	B737	22650
UN-B6701	B767	32954
UN-B7501	B757	23454

Ukraine

Reg	Type	Serial
(UR-)	B737	21616
UR-ABA	A319	3260
UR-AIS	YAK40	9211821
UR-BFA	B737	21685
UR-BVY	B737	22760
UR-BVZ	B737	22453
UR-BWE	YAK40	9530943
UR-BWF	YAK40	9711352
UR-BWH	YAK40	9640951
UR-BXQ	IL76	1023410360
UR-BXR	IL76	1023411384
UR-BXS	IL76	1023411368
UR-BYH	AN7x	47098946
UR-BYL	DC-9	47657
UR-BYY	TU134	62820
UR-BZY	TU134	63.48565
UR-CAC	AN7x	47136013
UR-CAE	AN7x	?
UR-CAN	MD80	49822
UR-CAP	IL76	0063466989
UR-CAR	YAK40	9530541
UR-CAR	YAK40	9741756
UR-CAT	IL76	0053464922
UR-CAW	YAK40	9341230
UR-CBN	MD80	49490
UR-CBO	MD80	49483
UR-CBR	IL76	?
UR-CBV	DC-9	47772
UR-CBY	DC-9	47773
UR-CCG	TU134	63960
UR-CCK	DC-9	48134
UR-CCR	DC-9	47736
UR-CCS	DC-9	47737
UR-CCT	DC-9	47696
UR-CCX	AN124	19530502..3
UR-CDA	MD80	49278
UR-CDI	MD80	49279
UR-CDU	YAK42	4811431
UR-CDW	YAK40	9610546
UR-CEL	MD80	49390
UR-CER	YAK42	3914323
UR-CCS	AN7x	47098977
UR-CEW	MD80	49634
UR-CFA	YAK42	3016269
UR-CFE	MD80	49222
UR-CFF	MD80	49845
UR-CFG	MD80	49370
UR-CLA	YAK40	9731155
UR-CLB	YAK40	9731555
UR-DAA	A320	0085
UR-DAB	A320	0230
UR-DAP	YAK40	9521241
UR-DNA	E145	145088
UR-DNB	E145	145094
UR-DWC	YAK40	9541144
UR-DWE	YAK40	9240326
UR-ECL	YAK40	9932059
UR-EEE	YAK40	9340632
UR-ETG	YAK40	9531143
UR-FRU	YAK40	9440737
UR-FVV	TU154	86A-725
UR-GAA	B737	26069
UR-GAB	B737	26071
UR-GAC	B737	23188
UR-GAD	B737	22802
UR-GAE	B737	24907
UR-GAF	B737	24237
UR-GAG	B737	24238
UR-GAH	B737	29130
UR-GAI	B737	25218
UR-GAJ	B737	25192
UR-GAK	B737	26075

Reg	Type	Serial
UR-GAL	B737	24275
UR-GAM	B737	25190
UR-GAN	B737	28569
UR-GAO	B737	25147
UR-GAP	B737	27094
UR-GAQ	B737	28869
UR-GAR	B737	26081
UR-GAS	B737	25236
UR-GAT	B737	25237
UR-GAU	B737	25182
UR-GAV	B737	26437
UR-GAW	B737	24898
UR-IBE	YAK40	?
UR-ISD	YAK40	9530541
UR-IVK	B737	24571
UR-KBR	YAK42	3403018
UR-KIV	B737	24686
UR-LAZ	YAK40	?
UR-LDK	AN7x	47098984
UR-LEV	YAK40	9720154
UR-LRZ	YAK40	9641851
UR-LUX	YAK40	9541542
UR-MAY	YAK40	?
UR-MHG	YAK40	?
UR-MIG	YAK40	9641250
UR-MMH	YAK40	?
UR-MMK	YAK40	9521540
UR-NTA	AN148	01-01
UR-NTB	AN148	01-02
UR-ORG	YAK40	9740656
UR-ORG	YAK40	9812056
UR-PIT	YAK40	9610647
UR-PST?	YAK40	9610647
UR-PVS	YAK40	?
UR-RPC	YAK40	9721353
UR-RTS	YAK40	?
UR-SAL	TU134	62315
UR-SAN	YAK40	9542043
UR-UAP	AN124	19530502792
UR-UAS	YAK40	?
UR-UAS?	YAK40	9420835
UR-UCA	IL76	0073479394
UR-UCB	IL76	0063467003
UR-UCC	IL76	0083489647
UR-UCD	IL76	0083488643
UR-UCE	IL76	0083484522
UR-UCF	IL76	0083488638
UR-UCG	IL76	0083482478
UR-UCH	IL76	0083484536
UR-UCI	IL76	0083481440
"UR-UCI"	IL76	083414444
UR-UCJ	IL76	0083484531
UR-UCL	IL76	0043456692
UR-UCO	IL76	0053458749
UR-UCQ	IL76	0063465963
UR-UCR	IL76	0073475270
UR-UCS	IL76	0063470113
UR-UCT	IL76	0063470089
UR-UCU	IL76	0073476275
UR-UCV	IL76	0043451517
UR-UCW	IL76	0053458733
UR-UCX	IL76	0063470112
UR-UCY	IL76	0083485566
UR-UCZ	TU154	82A-561
UR-UDB	IL76	0043455686
UR-UDC	IL76	0063467011
UR-UES	TU134	66472
UR-UFB	A320	0027
UR-VVA	B737	24492
UR-VVB	B737	26537
UR-VVC	B737	26538
UR-VVD	B737	25419
UR-VVE	B737	24521
UR-VVF	B767	24476
UR-VVG	B767	24729
UR-VVH	B737	27156
UR-VVI	B737	24461
UR-VVJ	B737	24474
UR-VVK	B737	26280
UR-VVL	B737	25052
UR-VVM	B737	25736
UR-VVN	B737	24903
UR-VVO	B767	24475
UR-VVP	B737	26290
UR-VVQ	B737	29235
UR-WOG	DO328	3118
UR-XYZ	YAK40	9610946
UR-YVA	AN7x	47098984
UR-ZPR	YAK40	9240426
UR-ZVA	IL76	0063468036
UR-ZVB	IL76	0053463902
UR-ZVC	IL76	0053463891
UR-ZYD	AN124	19530502..3
UR-	YAK40	9131618
UR-42308	YAK42	11040303
UR-42310	YAK42	11040403
UR-42317	YAK42	2202039
UR-42318	YAK42	3402051
UR-42319	YAK42	3402062
UR-42327	YAK42	4402161
UR-42330	YAK42	2505122
UR-42334	YAK42	2606164
UR-42337	YAK42	3606235
UR-42343	YAK42	1708285
UR-42348	YAK42	3711342
UR-42352	YAK42	1811395
UR-42358	YAK42	2811413
UR-42366	YAK42	4814047
UR-42369	YAK42	2914190
UR-42372	YAK42	3914266
UR-42376	YAK42	4914477
UR-42377	YAK42	1014479
UR-42381	YAK42	2014576
UR-42383	YAK42	2016201
UR-42403	YAK42	2116588
UR-42405	YAK42	3116624
UR-42409	YAK42	1216709
UR-42410	YAK42	1219029
UR-42416	YAK42	3219102
UR-42419	YAK42	3201016
UR-42426	YAK42	1304016
UR-42449	YAK42	1401018
UR-42527	YAK42	11040903
	YAK42	11120204
UR-42540	YAK42	11140604
UR-42544	YAK42	11151004
UR-42703	YAK42	4116690
UR-480182	AN225	19530503763
UR-63957	TU134	63957
UR-65023	TU134	48415
UR-65037	TU134	48850
UR-65048	TU134	49750
UR-65049	TU134	49980
UR-65076	TU134	60001
UR-65077	TU134	60028
UR-65081	TU134	60076
UR-65089	TU134	60180
UR-65092	TU134	60206
UR-65093	TU134	60215
UR-65107	TU134	60328
UR-65109	TU134	60339
UR-65114	TU134	60395
UR-65123	TU134	60525
UR-65134	TU134	60647
UR-65135	TU134	60648
UR-65556	TU134	66372
UR-65718	TU134	63668
UR-65752	TU134	61079
UR-65757	TU134	62215
UR-65761	TU134	62244
UR-65764	TU134	62305
UR-65765	TU134	62315
UR-65773	TU134	62495
UR-65782	TU134	62672
UR-65790	TU134	63100
UR-65841	TU134	18120
UR-65864	TU134	28284
UR-65877	TU134	31250
UR-65888	TU134	36175
UR-65917	TU134	63991
UR-72959	AN7x	72092858
UR-72984	AN7x	76096926
UR-74004	AN7x	47094890
UR-74007	AN7x	47095903
UR-74008	AN7x	47095900
UR-74010	AN7x	47030450
UR-74011	AN7x	47136013
UR-74025	AN7x	47095905
UR-74026	AN7x	47096919
UR-74027	AN7x	47096920
UR-74028	AN7x	47010947
UR-74031	AN7x	47098961
UR-74032	AN7x	47098962
UR-74033	AN7x	?
UR-74038	AN7x	47097933
UR-74042	AN7x	47097932
UR-74044	AN7x	47097936
UR-74053	AN7x	47098946
UR-74055	AN7x	47098959
UR-74057	AN7x	47098960
UR-74300	AN7x	47098984
UR-76316	IL76	0043454633
UR-76317	IL76	0053458733
UR-76318	IL76	0023438127
UR-76319	IL76	0023438129
UR-76320	IL76	0043455686
UR-76321	IL76	0053457713
UR-76322	IL76	0053462873
UR-76323	IL76	0063466988
UR-76390	IL76	0043453562
UR-76391	IL76	0043453568
UR-76392	IL76	0043454602
UR-76393	IL76	0043455653
UR-76394	IL76	0063466989
UR-76395	IL76	0033443255
UR-76396	IL76	0043451508
UR-76397	IL76	0043451517
UR-76398	IL76	0083484522
UR-76399	IL76	0083485566
UR-76408	IL76	0053460820
UR-76412	IL76	0083488638
UR-76413	IL76	1013407215
UR-76414	IL76	0083482478
UR-76415	IL76	0083481440
UR-76423	IL76	0053457720
UR-76424	IL76	0043470096
UR-76429	IL76	083415465
UR-76433	IL76	0053460827
UR-76437	IL76	0083484527
UR-76438	IL76	0083483513
UR-76441	IL76	0043455677
UR-76443	IL76	0043452534
UR-76444	IL76	0063470113
UR-76532	IL76	0023441201
UR-76534	IL76	0023442210
UR-76535	IL76	0023442213
UR-76536	IL76	0023442221
UR-76537	IL76	0033442225
UR-76539	IL76	0033442234
UR-76541	IL76	0033442241
UR-76555	IL76	0033446325
UR-76560	IL76	0033446341
UR-76561	IL76	0033447364
UR-76562	IL76	0033447365
UR-76563	IL76	0033447372
UR-76568	IL76	0033448420
UR-76570	IL76	0033448427
UR-76571	IL76	0033448429
UR-76573	IL76	0033449437
UR-76574	IL76	0033449441
UR-76576	IL76	0043449449
UR-76578	IL76	0043449468
UR-76579	IL76	0043449471
UR-76580	IL76	0043450476
UR-76581	IL76	0043450484
UR-76582	IL76	0043450487
UR-76583	IL76	0043450491
UR-76585	IL76	0043451503
UR-76590	IL76	0043452544
UR-76595	IL76	0043453571
UR-76601	IL76	0043454606
UR-76603	IL76	0043454623
UR-76609	IL76	0043453597
UR-76610	IL76	0043454640
UR-76614	IL76	0043455665
UR-76618	IL76	0043455682
UR-76620	IL76	0043456692
UR-76622	IL76	0053457702
UR-76624	IL76	0053457710
UR-76628	IL76	0053458741
UR-76629	IL76	0053458745
UR-76630	IL76	0053458749
UR-76633	IL76	0053459764
UR-76636	IL76	0053459781
UR-76637	IL76	0053460797
UR-76646	IL76	0053461837
UR-76647	IL76	0053461843
UR-76651	IL76	0053462872
UR-76653	IL76	0053462879
UR-76654	IL76	0053462884
UR-76655	IL76	0053463885
UR-76656	IL76	0053463891
UR-76658	IL76	0053463902
UR-76662	IL76	0053464919
UR-76663	IL76	0053464922
UR-76664	IL76	0053464926
UR-76667	IL76	0053465941
UR-76670	IL76	0063465958
UR-76671	IL76	0063465963
UR-76676	IL76	0063467003
UR-76677	IL76	0063467005
UR-76680	IL76	0063467020
UR-76681	IL76	0063467021
UR-76682	IL76	0063467027
UR-76683	IL76	0063468029
UR-76684	IL76	0063468036
UR-76687	IL76	0063469051
UR-76688	IL76	0063469062
UR-76689	IL76	0063469066
UR-76690	IL76	0063469080
UR-76691	IL76	0063470089
UR-76694	IL76	0063470107
UR-76695	IL76	0063470112
UR-76697	IL76	0063470118
UR-76698	IL76	0063471123
UR-76699	IL76	0063471131
UR-76700	IL76	0063471134
UR-76704	IL76	0063471150
UR-76705	IL76	0063472158
UR-76706	IL76	0083472163
UR-76707	IL76	0063472166
UR-76715	IL76	0073479394
UR-76716	IL76	0073474211
UR-76717	IL76	0073474216
UR-76721	IL76	0073475239
UR-76727	IL76	0073475268
UR-76728	IL76	0073475270
UR-76729	IL76	0073476275
UR-76730	IL76	0073476277
UR-76732	IL76	0073476296
UR-76742	IL76	0073478346
UR-76744	IL76	0073478359
UR-76748	IL76	0073479386
UR-76759	IL76	0083485558
UR-76759	IL76	0083485558
UR-76760	IL76	0073479400
UR-76767	IL76	0083487598
UR-76777	IL76	0083482490
UR-76778	IL76	0083483502
UR-78130	IL76	0043454611
UR-78734	IL76	1013409303
UR-78752	IL76	0083483519
UR-78755	IL76	0083484541
UR-78756	IL76	0083484536
UR-78758	IL76	0083484551
UR-78772	IL76	0083487627
UR-78774	IL76	0083484643
UR-78775	IL76	0083489647
UR-78785	IL76	0083489691
UR-78786	IL76	0083490693
UR-78820	IL76	0093496907
UR-78821	IL76	0093496914
UR-82003	AN124	19530502792
UR-82007	AN124	19530501005
UR-82008	AN124	19530501006
UR-82009	AN124	19530501007
UR-82027	AN124	19530502288
UR-82029	AN124	19530502984
UR-82060	AN225	19530503763
UR-82066	AN124	19530502761
UR-82070	AN124	977305135912

Reg	Type	Serial
UR-82072	AN124	977305335913
UR-82073	AN124	977305435913
UR-85009	TU154	70M009
UR-85068	TU154	74A-068
UR-85074	TU154	74A-074
UR-85075	TU154	74A-075
UR-85093	TU154	75A-093
UR-85116	TU154	75A-116
UR-85118	TU154	75A-118
UR-85132	TU154	76A-132
UR-85137	TU154	76A-137
UR-85148	TU154	76A-148
UR-85152	TU154	76A-152
UR-85154	TU154	76A-154
UR-85179	TU154	76A-179
UR-85218	TU154	77A-218
UR-85232	TU154	77A-232
UR-85288	TU154	78A-288
UR-85316	TU154	78A-316
UR-85350	TU154	79A-350
UR-85362	TU154	79A-362
UR-85368	TU154	79A-368
UR-85379	TU154	79A-379
UR-85395	TU154	80A-395
UR-85399	TU154	80A-399
UR-85407	TU154	80A-407
UR-85424	TU154	80A-424
UR-85445	TU154	80A-445
UR-85460	TU154	80A-460
UR-85476	TU154	81A-476
UR-85482	TU154	81A-482
UR-85490	TU154	81A-490
UR-85499	TU154	81A-499
UR-85513	TU154	81A-513
UR-85526	TU154	82A-526
UR-85535	TU154	82A-535
UR-85546	TU154	82A-546
UR-85561	TU154	82A-561
UR-85700	TU154	91A-875
UR-85701	TU154	91A-876
UR-85707	TU154	91A-882
UR-85710	TU154	91A-885
UR-86132	IL62	1034152
UR-86133	IL62	1138234
UR-86134	IL62	1138546
UR-86135	IL62	1748445
UR-86451	IL62	4521152
UR-86527	IL62	4037758
UR-86528	IL62	4038111
UR-86529	IL62	4038625
UR-86580	IL62	2343554
UR-86581	IL62	2932526
UR-86582	IL62	3036253
UR-86903	IL76	0023436048
UR-86916	IL76	0023430120
UR-86920	IL76	0023440152
UR-86921	IL76	0023440161
UR-86924	IL76	0023441174
UR-87215	YAK40	9510540
UR-87230	YAK40	9541542
UR-87237	YAK40	9530343
UR-87245	YAK40	9531343
UR-87266	YAK40	9310227
UR-87276	YAK40	9311227
UR-87298	YAK40	9321325
UR-87308	YAK40	9320429
UR-87327	YAK40	9330630
UR-87345	YAK40	9511439
UR-87389	YAK40	9410133
UR-87405	YAK40	9421733
UR-87421	YAK40	9421734
UR-87432	YAK40	9420835
UR-87435	YAK40	9431135
UR-87440	YAK40	9431635
UR-87463	YAK40	9430237
UR-87469	YAK40	9441437
UR-87479	YAK40	9441838
UR-87508	YAK40	9521040
UR-87512	YAK40	9521440
UR-87528	YAK40	9521041
UR-87547	YAK40	9531242
UR-87562	YAK40	9211321
UR-87566	YAK40	9211821
UR-87574	YAK40	9220622
UR-87590	YAK40	9741156
UR-87591	YAK40	9741056
UR-87592	YAK40	9730555
UR-87615	YAK40	9131618
UR-87624	YAK40	9130519
UR-87641	YAK40	9140220
UR-87642	YAK40	9140320
UR-87649	YAK40	9141020
UR-87660	YAK40	9240425
"UR-87685"	YAK40	9840502
UR-87806	YAK40	9231223
UR-87814	YAK40	9230524
UR-87818	YAK40	9230924
UR-87832	YAK40	9241825
UR-87841	YAK40	9330930
UR-87918	YAK40	9730855
UR-87951	YAK40	9810957
UR-87961	YAK40	9820458
UR-87964	YAK40	9820758
UR-87965	YAK40	9820858
UR-87987	YAK40	9541144
UR-87998	YAK40	9540245
UR-88151	YAK40	9610546
UR-88203	YAK40	9630549
UR-88219	YAK40	9630550
UR-88237	YAK40	9640751
UR-88290	YAK40	9840459
UR-88299	YAK40	9321028
UR-88309	YAK40	9840859
UR-88310	YAK40	9940760

Australia

Reg	Type	Serial
(VH-)	B747	21162
(VH-)	B747	21316
VH-AFR	B717	55062
VH-AHT	F.28	11183
"VH-AKK"	B707	20517
VH-ANA	B727	22641
VH-ANA	B747	24062
VH-ANB	B727	22642
VH-ANB	B747	24064
VH-ANE	B727	22643
VH-ANF	B727	22644
VH-ANO	E170	17000099
VH-ATD	F.28	11047
VH-ATE	F.28	11082
VH-ATG	F.28	11084
VH-AUP	B727	21695
VH-AWE	B757	24635
VH-BRN	B757	24868
VH-BWF	A300	633
VH-BZF	B767	27569
VH-BZI	B767	28495
VH-BZL	B767	26387
VH-BZM	B767	26388
(VH-BZN)	B767	26389
VH-CLL	A300	690
VH-CLM	A300	688
VH-CZA	B737	23653
VH-CZA	DC-9	47003
VH-CZB	B737	23654
VH-CZB	DC-9	47004
VH-CZC	B737	23655
VH-CZC	DC-9	47005
VH-CZD	B737	23656
VH-CZD	DC-9	47065
VH-CZE	B737	23657
VH-CZE	DC-9	47202
VH-CZF	B737	23658
VH-CZF	DC-9	47325
VH-CZG	B737	23659
VH-CZG	DC-9	47501
VH-CZH	B737	23660
VH-CZH	DC-9	47526
VH-CZI	B737	23661
VH-CZI	DC-9	47527
VH-CZJ	B737	23662
VH-CZJ	DC-9	47547
VH-CZK	B737	23663
VH-CZK	DC-9	47548
VH-CZL	B737	23664
VH-CZL	DC-9	47549
VH-CZM	B737	22645
VH-CZN	B737	24302
VH-CZN	B737	22646
VH-CZN	B737	24303
VH-CZO	B737	22647
VH-CZO	B737	24304
VH-CZP	B737	22648
VH-CZP	B737	24305
VH-CZQ	B737	22649
VH-CZQ	B737	24461
VH-CZR	B737	22650
VH-CZR	B737	24460
VH-CZS	B737	22651
VH-CZS	B737	24030
VH-CZT	B737	22652
VH-CZT	B737	27454
VH-CZU	B737	22653
VH-CZU	B737	27267
VH-CZV	B737	22654
VH-CZV	B737	23831
VH-CZW	B737	22655
VH-CZW	B737	23832
VH-CZX	B737	22656
VH-CZX	B737	24029
VH-DHE	B727	22080
VH-DHF	B727	22998
VH-EAA	B707	19621
VH-EAA	B747	22495
VH-EAB	B707	19622
VH-EAB	B747	22672
VH-EAC	B707	19623
VH-EAD	B707	19624
VH-EAE	B707	19625
VH-EAF	B707	19626
VH-EAG	B707	19627
VH-EAH	B707	19628
VH-EAI	B707	19629
VH-EAJ	B707	19630
VH-EAJ	B767	23304
VH-EAK	B767	23305
VH-EAL	B767	23306
(VH-EAM)	B767	23307
VH-EAM	B767	23309
(VH-EAN)	B767	23308
VH-EAN	B767	23402
(VH-EAO)	B767	23309
VH-EAO	B767	23403
VH-EAQ	B767	23306
VH-EBA	A330	508
VH-EBA	B707	17696
VH-EBA	B747	20009
VH-EBB	A330	522
VH-EBB	B707	17697
VH-EBB	B747	20010
VH-EBC	A330	506
VH-EBC	B707	17698
VH-EBC	B747	20011
VH-EBD	A330	513
VH-EBD	B707	17699
VH-EBD	B747	20012
VH-EBE	A330	842
VH-EBE	B707	17700
VH-EBE	B747	20534
VH-EBF	A330	853
VH-EBF	B707	17701
VH-EBF	B747	20535
VH-EBG	B707	17702
VH-EBG	B747	20841
VH-EBH	B707	18067
VH-EBH	B747	20842
VH-EBI	B707	18068
VH-EBI	B747	20921
VH-EBJ	B707	18069
VH-EBJ	B747	21054
VH-EBK	B707	18334
VH-EBK	B747	21140
VH-EBL	B707	18739
VH-EBL	B747	21237
VH-EBM	B707	18740
VH-EBM	B747	21352
VH-EBN	B707	18808
VH-EBN	B747	21353
VH-EBO	B707	18809
VH-EBO	B747	21657
VH-EBP	B707	18810
VH-EBP	B747	21658
VH-EBQ	B707	18953
VH-EBQ	B747	22145
VH-EBR	B707	18954
VH-EBR	B747	22614
VH-EBS	B707	18955
VH-EBS	B747	22616
VH-EBT	B707	19293
VH-EBT	B747	23222
VH-EBU	B707	19294
VH-EBU	B747	23223
VH-EBV	B707	19295
VH-EBV	B747	23224
VH-EBW	B707	19296
VH-EBW	B747	23408
VH-EBX	B707	19297
VH-EBX	B747	23688
VH-EBY	B747	23823
VH-EBZ	B707	19354
VH-ECA	B747	21354
VH-ECB	B747	21977
VH-ECC	B747	22615
VH-EEI	B747	20108
VH-EFG	A330	887
VH-EFW	A300	630
(VH-EWA)	F.28	11173
VH-EWA	F.28	11195
(VH-EWB)	F.28	11181
VH-EWB	F.28	11205
VH-EWC	F.28	11207
VH-EWD	F.28	11208
VH-EWF	F.28	11143
VH-EWG	F.28	11151
VH-EWH	F.28	11186
VH-EWI	146	E3171
VH-EWJ	146	E3173
VH-EWK	146	E3175
VH-EWL	146	E3177
VH-EWM	146	E3179
VH-EWN	146	E3190
VH-EWR	146	E3195
VH-EWS	146	E3197
VH-FKA	F.100	11345
VH-FKA	F.28	11021
VH-FKB	F.28	11022
VH-FKC	F.100	11349
VH-FKC	F.28	11025
VH-FKD	F.100	11357
VH-FKE	F.28	11026
VH-FKE	F.100	11358
VH-FKE	F.28	11040
VH-FKF	F.100	11365
VH-FKF	F.28	11008
(VH-FKF)	F.28	11041
(VH-FKF)	F.28	11056
VH-FKG	F.100	11366
VH-FKG	F.28	11031
VH-FKI	F.28	11183
VH-FKJ	F.100	11372
VH-FKJ	F.28	11186
VH-FKK	F.100	11379
(VH-FKK)	F.28	11082
VH-FKL	F.100	11380
VH-FKN	F.28	11207
VH-FKO	F.28	11212
(VH-FKP)	F.28	11151
VH-FNJ	F.100	11489
VH-FNR	F.100	11488
VH-FNT	F.100	11461
VH-FNY	F.100	11484
(VH-FRB)	146	E2034
VH-FWH	F.100	11316
VH-FWI	F.100	11318
VH-HTC	B707	18937
VH-HYA	A320	0022
VH-HYB	A320	0023
VH-HYC	A320	0024
VH-HYD	A320	0025
VH-HYE	A320	0026

Reg	Type	Serial
VH-HYF	A320	0027
VH-HYG	A320	0029
VH-HYH	A320	0030
(VH-HYI)	A320	0059
VH-HYI	A320	0140
(VH-HYJ)	A320	0068
VH-HYJ	A320	0142
(VH-HYK)	A320	0073
VH-HYK	A320	0157
VH-HYL	A320	0229
VH-HYN	A320	0726
VH-HYO	A320	0547
VH-HYQ	A320	0615
VH-HYR	A320	0622
VH-HYS	A320	0632
VH-HYT	A320	0662
VH-HYX	A320	0288
VH-HYY	A320	0331
(VH-ICA)	E145	145095
(VH-ICD)	E145	145099
VH-IGF	A300	613
VH-IMD	B717	55055
VH-IMP	B717	55054
VH-INH	B747	23026
VH-INJ	B747	23029
VH-INK	B747	23028
VH-INU	B737	23684
VH-IPC	DC-9	47193
VH-IPF	DC-9	47408
VH-ITA	B767	27376
VH-ITB	B767	27377
(VH-ITH)	B767	27468
VH-IWD	A300	611
VH-JBN	A300	630
VH-JJP	146	E2037
VH-JJQ	146	E2038
VH-JJS	146	E2093
VH-JJT	146	E2098
VH-JJU	146	E2116
VH-JJW	146	E2110
VH-JJX	146	E2127
VH-JJY	146	E2113
VH-JJZ	146	E2114
VH-JNE	B737	25119
VH-JQG	A320	2169
VH-JQL	A320	2185
VH-JQX	A320	2197
VH-JSF	146	E1160
VH-KDF	CRJ	7489
VH-KJF	CRJ	7336
VH-KJG	CRJ	7357
VH-KJJ	CRJ	7361
VH-KJN	CRJ	7367
VH-KJQ	CRJ	7372
VH-KJS	CRJ	7401
VH-KJU	CRJ	7405
VH-KJV	CRJ	7422
VH-KJX	CRJ	7471
VH-KJY	CRJ	7481
VH-KXJ	CRJ	7508
VH-LAP	B727	18270
VH-LAR	F.28	11212
VH-LAX	B717	55057
VH-LEF	CRJ	8060
VH-LNH	MD80	49938
VH-LNI	MD80	53121
VH-LNJ	MD80	49383
VH-LNK	MD80	49423
VH-LNL	MD80	49437
(VH-LNN)	MD80	53118
VH-MMJ	F.28	11013
(VH-NJA)	146	E1003
VH-NJA	146	E1004
VH-NJC	146	E1013
VH-NJD	146	E1160
VH-NJE	146	E1104
VH-NJE	B737	23766
VH-NJF	146	E3198
VH-NJG	146	E2170
VH-NJH	146	E2178
VH-NJJ	146	E2184
VH-NJL	146	E3213
VH-NJM	146	E3194
VH-NJN	146	E3217
VH-NJQ	146	E2072
VH-NJQ	146	E2176
VH-NJR	146	E1152
VH-NJT	146	E1228
VH-NJU	146	E2073
VH-NJV	146	E1002
VH-NJW	146	E1223
VH-NJW	146	E2034
VH-NJX	146	E1003
VH-NJY	146	E1005
VH-NJZ	146	E1009
VH-NLH	B747	24050
VH-NOA	B767	27909
VH-NOA	B767	28495
VH-NOE	B767	25535
VH-NOF	B757	24566
VH-NOL	B727	27477
VH-NXB	B717	55002
VH-NXC	B717	55151
VH-NXD	B717	55062
VH-NXE	B717	55063
VH-NXF	B717	55001
VH-NXG	B717	55057
VH-NXH	B717	55055
VH-NXI	B717	55054
VH-NXK	B717	55092
VH-NXL	B717	55093
VH-NXM	B717	55094
VH-NXO	B717	55096
VH-NXQ	B717	55097
VH-OAM	B737	25010
VH-OAN	B737	25011
VH-OBN	B737	21137
VH-OEB	B747	25778
VH-OEC	B747	24836
VH-OED	B747	25126
VH-OEE	B747	32909
VH-OEF	B747	32910
VH-OEG	B747	32911
VH-OEH	B747	32912
VH-OEI	B747	32913
VH-OEJ	B747	32914
VH-OGA	B767	24146
VH-OGB	B767	24316
VH-OGC	B767	24317
VH-OGD	B767	24407
VH-OGE	B767	24531
VH-OGF	B767	24853
VH-OGG	B767	24929
VH-OGH	B767	24930
VH-OGI	B767	25246
VH-OGJ	B767	25274
VH-OGK	B767	25316
VH-OGL	B767	25363
VH-OGM	B767	25575
VH-OGN	B767	25576
VH-OGO	B767	25577
VH-OGP	B767	28153
VH-OGQ	B767	28154
VH-OGR	B767	28724
VH-OGS	B767	28725
VH-OGT	B767	29117
VH-OGU	B767	29118
VH-OGV	B767	30186
VH-OJA	B747	24354
VH-OJB	B747	24373
VH-OJC	B747	24406
VH-OJD	B747	24481
VH-OJE	B747	24482
VH-OJF	B747	24483
VH-OJG	B747	24779
VH-OJH	B747	24806
VH-OJI	B747	24887
VH-OJJ	B747	24974
VH-OJK	B747	25067
VH-OJL	B747	25151
VH-OJM	B747	25245
VH-OJN	B747	25315
VH-OJO	B747	25544
VH-OJP	B747	25545
VH-OJQ	B747	25546
VH-OJR	B747	25547
VH-OJS	B747	25564
VH-OJT	B747	25565
VH-OJU	B747	25566
VH-OPW	A300	668
VH-OQA	A380	014
VH-OQB	A380	015
VH-OQC	A380	022
VH-OQD	A380	026
VH-OQE	A380	027
VH-OZD	B737	20911
VH-OZQ	B737	20907
VH-OZU	B737	21176
VH-OZX	B737	21177
VH-OZX	B747	22302
VH-PAE	B727	21455
VH-PWD	A300	664
VH-QPA	A330	553
VH-QPB	A330	558
VH-QPC	A330	564
VH-QPD	A330	574
VH-QPE	A330	593
VH-QPF	A330	595
VH-QPG	A330	603
VH-QPH	A330	695
VH-QPI	A330	705
VH-QPJ	A330	712
VH-RMA	B767	24742
VH-RMC	B767	23326
VH-RMD	B727	18844
VH-RMD	B767	22692
VH-RME	B727	18743
VH-RME	B767	22693
VH-RMF	B727	18744
VH-RMF	B767	22694
VH-RMG	B767	22695
VH-RMH	B767	22696
VH-RMK	B727	21178
VH-RMK	B767	22981
VH-RML	B727	21480
VH-RML	B767	22980
VH-RMM	B727	21647
VH-RMM	B767	24973
VH-RMN	B727	21695
VH-RMO	B727	22016
VH-RMO	B767	23807
VH-RMP	B727	22068
VH-RMR	B727	19253
VH-RMS	B727	20278
VH-RMT	B727	20370
VH-RMU	B727	20518
VH-RMV	B727	20549
VH-RMW	B727	20550
VH-RMX	B727	20551
VH-RMY	B727	20978
VH-RMZ	B727	20979
VH-RON	B737	26960
VH-SMH	B717	55063
VH-SWO	E170	17000081
VH-TAA	A300	134
VH-TAB	A300	151
VH-TAB	B737	26282
VH-TAC	A300	157
VH-TAD	A300	196
VH-TAE	A300	218
VH-TAF	B737	23477
VH-TAG	B737	23478
VH-TAH	B737	23479
VH-TAI	B737	23483
VH-TAJ	B737	23484
VH-TAK	B737	23485
VH-TAU	B737	23486
VH-TAV	B737	23487
VH-TAW	B737	23488
VH-TAX	B737	23489
VH-TAY	B737	23490
VH-TAZ	B737	23491
VH-TBG	B727	20552
VH-TBH	B727	20553
VH-TBI	B727	20554
VH-TBJ	B727	20555
VH-TBK	B727	20950
VH-TBL	B727	20951
VH-TBM	B727	21171
VH-TBN	B727	21479
VH-TBO	B727	21646
VH-TBP	B727	21696
VH-TBQ	B727	22017
VH-TBR	B727	22069
VH-TBS	B727	20278
VH-TJA	B727	18741
VH-TJA	B737	24295
VH-TJB	B727	18742
VH-TJB	B737	24296
VH-TJC	B727	18843
VH-TJC	B737	24297
VH-TJD	B727	19254
VH-TJD	B737	24298
VH-TJE	B727	20228
VH-TJE	B737	24430
VH-TJF	B727	20371
VH-TJF	B737	24431
VH-TJG	B737	24432
VH-TJH	B737	24433
VH-TJI	B737	24434
VH-TJJ	B737	24435
VH-TJJ	DC-9	47007
VH-TJK	B737	24436
VH-TJK	DC-9	47008
VH-TJL	B737	24437
VH-TJL	DC-9	47009
VH-TJM	B737	24438
VH-TJM	DC-9	47072
VH-TJN	B737	24439
VH-TJN	DC-9	47203
VH-TJO	B737	24440
VH-TJO	DC-9	47326
VH-TJP	B737	24441
VH-TJP	DC-9	47418
VH-TJQ	B737	24442
VH-TJQ	DC-9	47419
VH-TJR	B737	24443
VH-TJR	DC-9	47528
VH-TJS	B737	24444
VH-TJS	DC-9	47550
VH-TJT	B737	24445
VH-TJT	DC-9	47551
VH-TJU	B737	24446
VH-TJU	DC-9	47552
VH-TJV	B737	25163
VH-TJW	B737	26961
VH-TJX	B737	28150
VH-TJY	B737	28151
VH-TJZ	B737	28152
VH-TXE	B727	21456
VH-TXH	B727	20549
VH-VBA	737NG	28238
VH-VBB	737NG	28240
VH-VBC	737NG	30638
VH-VBD	737NG	30707
VH-VBF	737NG	30630
VH-VBH	737NG	30641
VH-VBI	737NG	30644
VH-VBJ	737NG	30647
VH-VBK	737NG	30648
VH-VBL	737NG	30633
VH-VBM	737NG	32734
VH-VBN	737NG	33005
VH-VBO	737NG	33418
VH-VBP	737NG	30743
VH-VBQ	737NG	30744
VH-VBR	737NG	30745
VH-VBS	737NG	30746
VH-VBT	737NG	30740
VH-VBU	737NG	30288
VH-VBV	737NG	33015
VH-VBW	737NG	29091
VH-VBX	737NG	29092
VH-VBY	737NG	34323
VH-VBZ	737NG	34322
VH-VGA	B737	28489
VH-VGA	B777	35302
VH-VGB	B737	25740
VH-VGC	B737	28549
VH-VGD	B737	23980
VH-VGE	B737	28493
VH-VHD	A319	1999

Registration	Type	c/n
(VH-VLD)	B727	21455
(VH-VLE)	B727	20549
VH-VLF	B727	21695
VH-VLG	B727	20551
VH-VLH	**B727**	**22642**
VH-VLI	**B727**	**22641**
VH-VNC	**A320**	**3275**
VH-VND	**A320**	**3296**
VH-VOA	**737NG**	**30620**
VH-VOB	**737NG**	**30622**
VH-VOC	**737NG**	**30623**
VH-VOD	**737NG**	**30624**
VH-VOE	737NG	30272
VH-VOF	737NG	30274
VH-VOG	**737NG**	**28644**
VH-VOH	**737NG**	**29884**
VH-VOI	737NG	30786
VH-VOJ	737NG	30787
VH-VOK	**737NG**	**33758**
VH-VOL	**737NG**	**33759**
VH-VOM	**737NG**	**33794**
VH-VON	**737NG**	**33795**
VH-VOO	737NG	33796
VH-VOP	737NG	33797
VH-VOQ	**737NG**	**33798**
VH-VOR	737NG	33799
VH-VOS	**737NG**	**33800**
VH-VOT	**737NG**	**33801**
VH-VOU	**737NG**	**30665**
VH-VOV	**737NG**	**30658**
VH-VOW	**737NG**	**32798**
VH-VOX	**737NG**	**33017**
VH-VOY	737NG	33996
VH-VOZ	B737	26302
VH-VQA	**A320**	**2604**
VH-VQA	B717	55001
VH-VQB	B717	55002
VH-VQC	B717	55151
VH-VQD	B717	55062
VH-VQE	B717	55063
VH-VQF	B717	55092
VH-VQG	**A320**	**2787**
VH-VQG	B717	55093
VH-VQH	**A320**	**2766**
VH-VQH	B717	55094
VH-VQI	**A320**	**2717**
VH-VQI	B717	55095
VH-VQJ	**A320**	**2703**
VH-VQJ	B717	55096
VH-VQK	**A320**	**2651**
VH-VQK	B717	55097
VH-VQL	**A320**	**2642**
VH-VQM	**A320**	**2608**
VH-VQN	**A320**	**2600**
VH-VQO	**A320**	**2587**
VH-VQP	**A320**	**2573**
VH-VQQ	**A320**	**2537**
VH-VQR	**A320**	**2526**
VH-VQS	**A320**	**2515**
VH-VQT	**A320**	**2475**
VH-VQU	**A320**	**2455**
VH-VQV	**A320**	**2338**
VH-VQW	**A320**	**2329**
VH-VQX	**A320**	**2322**
VH-VQY	**A320**	**2299**
VH-VQZ	**A320**	**2292**
VH-VUA	**737NG**	**33997**
VH-VUB	**737NG**	**34013**
VH-VUC	**737NG**	**34014**
VH-VUD	**737NG**	**34015**
VH-VUE	**737NG**	**34167**
VH-VUF	**737NG**	**34168**
VH-VUG	**737NG**	**34438**
VH-VUH	**737NG**	**34440**
VH-VUI	**737NG**	**34441**
VH-VUJ	**737NG**	**34443**
VH-VUK	**737NG**	**36602**
VH-VUL	**737NG**	**36603**
VH-VUM	**737NG**	**29675**
VH-VUN	**737NG**	**29676**
VH-VXA	**737NG**	**29551**
VH-VXB	**737NG**	**30101**
VH-VXC	**737NG**	**30897**
VH-VXD	**737NG**	**29552**
VH-VXE	**737NG**	**30899**
VH-VXF	**737NG**	**29553**
VH-VXG	**737NG**	**30901**
VH-VXH	**737NG**	**33478**
VH-VXI	**737NG**	**33479**
VH-VXJ	**737NG**	**33480**
VH-VXK	**737NG**	**33481**
VH-VXL	**737NG**	**33482**
VH-VXM	**737NG**	**33483**
VH-VXN	**737NG**	**33484**
VH-VXO	**737NG**	**33485**
VH-VXP	**737NG**	**33722**
VH-VXQ	**737NG**	**33723**
VH-VXR	**737NG**	**33724**
VH-VXS	**737NG**	**33725**
VH-VXT	**737NG**	**33760**
VH-VXU	**737NG**	**33761**
VH-VYA	**737NG**	**33762**
VH-VYB	**737NG**	**33763**
VH-VYC	**737NG**	**33991**
VH-VYD	**737NG**	**33992**
VH-VYE	**737NG**	**33993**
VH-VYF	**737NG**	**33994**
VH-VYG	**737NG**	**33995**
VH-VYH	**737NG**	**34180**
VH-VYI	**737NG**	**34181**
VH-VYJ	**737NG**	**34182**
VH-VYK	**737NG**	**34183**
VH-VYL	**737NG**	**34184**
VH-VZA	**737NG**	**34195**
VH-XBA	B707	17696
VH-XMB	**B737**	**23478**
VH-XML	**B737**	**23486**
VH-XMO	**B737**	**23488**
VH-XMR	**B737**	**23490**
VH-XNG	F.28	11038
VH-YAD	**146**	**E2097**
VH-YAE	**146**	**E2107**
VH-YAF	146	E2040
VH-YMA	A300	584
VH-YMB	A300	603
VH-YMI	A310	425
VH-YMJ	A300	540
VH-YMK	A300	556
VH-YQF	B717	55092
VH-YQG	B717	55093
VH-YQH	B717	55094
VH-YQI	**B717**	**55095**
VH-YQJ	B717	55096
VH-YQK	B717	55097
VH-ZHA	**E170**	**17000180**
VH-ZHB	**E170**	**17000187**
VH-ZHC	**E170**	**17000191**
VH-ZXA	**B767**	**24337**
VH-ZXB	**B767**	**24338**
VH-ZXC	**B767**	**24339**
VH-ZXD	**B767**	**24342**
VH-ZXE	**B767**	**24343**
VH-ZXF	**B767**	**25203**
VH-ZXG	**B767**	**25443**

Vietnam
(see also XV-)

Registration	Type	c/n
VN-	A330	087
VN-81416	B707	18832
VN-83415	B707	19821
VN-A102	TU134	60925
VN-A104	TU134	61055
VN-A106	TU134	49752
VN-A108	TU134	63.48430
VN-A110	TU134	62144
VN-A112	TU134	62458
VN-A114	TU134	66220
VN-A116	TU134	66230
VN-A118	TU134	66360
VN-A120	TU134	66360
VN-A122	TU134	49900
VN-A123	A320	0024
VN-A124	TU134	60108
VN-A126	TU134	60435
VN-A128	TU134	60612
VN-A130	TU134	62259
VN-A132	TU134	63260
VN-A141	**B777**	**28688**
VN-A142	**B777**	**32701**
VN-A143	**B777**	**33502**
VN-A144	**B777**	**33503**
VN-A145	**B777**	**33504**
VN-A146	**B777**	**33505**
VN-A147	**B777**	**27607**
(VN-A147)	B777	32716
VN-A149	**B777**	**32716**
VN-A150	**B777**	**32717**
VN-A151	**B777**	**27608**
VN-A168	A320	0789
VN-A189	**B737**	**28490**
VN-A190	**B737**	**27383**
VN-A302	**A320**	**0594**
VN-A303	**A320**	**0601**
VN-A304	**A320**	**0605**
VN-A304	B707	17929
VN-A305	**A320**	**0607**
VN-A306	**A320**	**0611**
VN-A307	**A320**	**0617**
VN-A308	**A320**	**0619**
VN-A309	**A320**	**0648**
VN-A341	A321	0557
VN-A342	A321	0591
VN-A343	A321	0956
VN-A344	**A321**	**2255**
VN-A345	**A321**	**2261**
VN-A346	A321	0597
VN-A347	**A321**	**2267**
VN-A348	**A321**	**2303**
VN-A349	**A321**	**2480**
VN-A350	**A321**	**2974**
VN-A351	**A321**	**3005**
VN-A352	**A321**	**3013**
VN-A353	**A321**	**3022**
VN-A354	**A321**	**3198**
VN-A369	**A330**	**255**
VN-A370	**A330**	**262**
VN-A441	YAK40	9421334
VN-A442	YAK40	9421434
VN-A443	YAK40	9421534
VN-A445	YAK40	9421634
VN-A446	YAK40	9631748
VN-A449	YAK40	9631848
VN-A450	YAK40	9920960
VN-A452	YAK40	9920860
VN-A502	**F.70**	**11580**
VN-A504	**F.70**	**11585**
VN-A761	B767	27477
VN A762	B767	27392
VN-A763	B767	26261
VN-A764	B767	27393
VN-A765	B767	27568
VN-A766	B767	27909
VN-A768	B767	27310
VN-A769	B767	26262
VN-B1416	B707	18832
VN-B3415	B707	19821

Bermuda
(see also VR-B)

Registration	Type	c/n
VP-B	**CRJ9**	**15126**
VP-BAA	**B727**	**19123**
VP-BAB	B727	19254
VP-BAF	A310	472
VP-BAG	**A310**	**475**
VP-BAH	B737	29201
VP-BAI	B737	29202
VP-BAJ	B737	29203
VP-BAL	B737	29204
VP-BAM	B737	29205
VP-BAN	B737	29206
VP-BAO	B737	29207
VP-BAP	**B727**	**19260**
VP-BAP	B737	29208
VP-BAQ	B737	29209
VP-BAR	B737	29210
VP-BAS	B777	27607
VP-BAT	B747	21648
VP-BAU	B747	27608
VP-BAV	**B767**	**30107**
VP-BAX	**B767**	**30109**
VP-BAY	**B767**	**30110**
VP-BAZ	**B767**	**30111**
VP-BBA	1-11	BAC.126
VP-BBG	**B737**	**23543**
VP-BBH	**B737**	**23546**
VP-BBJ	**737NG**	**29273**
VP-BBL	B737	22743
VP-BBL	B737	23183
VP-BBM	B737	23024
VP-BBN	**B737**	**23442**
VP-BBN	B737	23527
VP-BBO	B737	22367
VP-BBP	B737	22736
(VP-BBQ)	A320	2165
VP-BBR	B757	29305
VP-BBS	B737	30824
VP-BBT	737NG	29089
VP-BBU	737NG	29090
VP-BBW	**737NG**	**30076**
VP-BBY	E145	14500970
VP-BCC	**CRJ**	**7717**
VP-BCI	**CRJ**	**7351**
VP-BCJ	A320	1491
VP-BCK	A320	1568
VP-BCL	**CRJ7**	**10247**
VP-BCN	1-11	BAC.188
VP-BCO	1-11	BAC.189
VP-BCP	1-11	034
VP-BCQ	1-11	BAC.198
VP-BCS	A319	1256
VP-BCS	A320	1854
VP-BCU	A310	594
VP-BCY	1-11	BAC.121
VP-BCZ	1-11	BAC.157
VP-BDB	B737	23261
VP-BDE	B707	17700
VP-BDE	**DC-10**	**47823**
VP-BDF	B707	18085
VP-BDF	**DC-10**	**47855**
VP-BDG	B707	18084
VP-BDG	**DC-10**	**46661**
VP-BDH	**DC-10**	**46966**
VP-BDI	1-11	074
VP-BDI	**B767**	**29618**
VP-BDJ	1-11	089
VP-BDJ	B737	20046
VP-BDK	**A320**	**2106**
VP-BDM	**A319**	**2069**
VP-BDN	1-11	062
VP-BDN	**A319**	**2072**
VP-BDO	**A319**	**2091**
VP-BDP	1-11	063
(VP-BDP)	A319	2093
(VP-BEA)	1-11	BAC.195
VP-BEB	1-11	BAC.226
(VP-BEC)	1-11	BAC.196
(VP-BED)	1-11	BAC.200
(VP-BEF)	B737	19934
VP-BEL	737NG	29139
VP-BEP	B737	19953
VP-BEY	**A319**	**2675**
VP-BFA	**737NG**	**30884**
VP-BFB	**B737**	**26067**
VP-BFE	737NG	30753
VP-BFI	**B757**	**24838**
VP-BFJ	**B737**	**24859**
VP-BFK	**B737**	**24928**
VP-BFM	**B737**	**24921**
VP-BFN	**B737**	**24922**
VP-BFO	737NG	30755
VP-BFT	**737NG**	**36714**
VP-BGH	**MD80**	**49937**
VP-BGI	**MD80**	**49940**
VP-BGP	**B737**	**24691**
VP-BGQ	**B737**	**24683**
VP-BGR	**B737**	**25790**
VP-BGU	**B747**	**23482**
VP-BGW	**B727**	**18366**

VP-BHF	A319	1819
VP-BHG	A319	1870
VP-BHI	A319	2028
VP-BHJ	A319	2369
VP-BHK	A319	2373
VP-BHM	DC-8	46111
VP-BHN	737NG	32438
VP-BHP	A319	2618
VP-BHQ	A319	2641
VP-BHV	A319	2474
VP-BIA	B747	22545
VP-BIB	B747	22506
VP-BIC	B747	24837
VP-BID	B747	23139
VP-BIF	B727	20533
VP-BIG	B747	35420
VP-BII	B747	24576
VP-BIJ	B747	25171
VP-BIK	B747	35421
VP-BIL	B727	20533
VP-BIM	B747	23237
VP-BIZ	737NG	34477
VP-BJB	737NG	30330
VP-BJR	DC-8	46067
VP-BJV	B737	23507
VP-BJW	B737	23551
VP-BJX	B737	23557
VP-BJY	B737	23559
VP-BKC	B727	20533
VP-BKS	B767	27254
VP-BLF	B737	25232
VP-BLG	B737	25233
VP-BLG	DC-8	46071
VP-BLK	B747	21961
VP-BMC	737NG	30751
(VP-BMC)	B727	18323
VP-BNA	B727	19262
"VP-BNH"	737NG	32438
VP-BNZ	737NG	35959
(VP-BOC)	737NG	28976
VP-BOC	B737	24970
VP-BOO	MD80	49778
VP-BOP	MD80	49725
VP-BOU	B737	25049
VP-BPA	B737	25037
VP-BPD	B737	25062
VP-BPE	B737	26445
VP BPF	737NG	29441
VP-BPF	B737	26446
VP-BPX	B747	22872
VP-BQA	B747	22723
VP-BQB	B747	22724
VP-BQC	B747	22725
VP-BQE	B747	22722
VP-BQH	B747	22791
VP-BQI	B737	25186
VP-BQL	B737	25185
(VP-BQM)	B767	27611
VP-BQP	A320	2875
VP-BQR	A321	2903
VP-BQS	A321	2912
VP-BQT	A321	2965
VP-BQU	A310	535
VP-BQV	A320	2920
VP-BQW	A320	2947
VP-BQX	A321	2957
VP-BQY	A320	0140
VP-BQZ	A320	0157
VP-BRB	A320	0528
VP-BRE	B737	24827
VP-BRG	B737	24826
VP-BRH	B777	29953
VP-BRI	B737	25289
VP-BRK	B737	25288
VP-BRM	737NG	28976
VP-BRN	B737	25191
VP-BRP	B737	25651
VP-BRQ	B737	25230
VP-BRS	B737	25231
VP-BRS	B747	22485
VP-BRT	737NG	32970
VP-BRU	B737	25206
VP-BRV	B737	25227

VP-BRW	A321	3191
VP-BRX	A320	3063
VP-BRY	A320	3052
VP-BRZ	A320	3157
VP-BSQ	B737	26672
VP-BSU	B737	26675
VP-BSV	B737	26692
VP-BSW	B737	26695
VP-BSX	B737	26699
VP-BSY	A310	430
VP-BSZ	A310	468
VP-BTA	B737	21443
VP-BTA	B737	25168
VP-BTB	B737	21444
VP-BTD	B737	25001
VP-BTE	B737	25008
VP-BTF	B737	25009
VP-BTG	B737	25383
VP-BTH	B737	24231
VP-BTI	B737	25387
VP-BTJ	A310	520
VP-BTK	A310	427
VP-BTL	A310	487
VP-BTM	A310	486
VP-BTN	A319	1126
VP-BTO	A319	1129
VP-BTP	A319	1131
VP-BTQ	A319	1149
VP-BTS	A319	1164
VP-BTT	A319	1167
VP-BTU	A319	1071
VP-BTV	A319	1078
VP-BTW	A319	1090
VP-BTX	A319	1091
VP-BUB	B757	30060
VP-BUD	B757	30061
VP-BUE	B767	33469
VP-BUF	B767	33078
VP-BUH	B757	30339
VP-BUI	B757	28487
VP-BUJ	B757	28488
VP-BUZ	E145	28392
VP-BVA	A320	0739
VP-BVB	A320	0743
VP-BVC	A320	0839
VP-BVD	A320	0892
VP-BVS	E145	14500979
VP-BWA	A319	2052
VP-BWD	A320	2116
VP-BWE	A320	2133
VP-BWF	A320	2144
VP-BWG	A319	2093
VP-BWH	A320	2151
VP-BWI	A320	2163
VP-BWJ	A319	2179
VP-BWK	A319	2222
VP-BWL	A319	2243
VP-BWM	A320	2233
VP-BWN	A321	2330
VP-BWO	A321	2337
VP-BWP	A321	2342
VP-BWQ	B767	30342
VP-BWR	737NG	29317
VP-BWT	B767	29617
VP-BWU	B767	25076
VP-BWV	B767	25117
VP-BWW	B767	27959
VP-BWX	B767	27960
VP-BWY	B737	27305
VP-BWZ	B737	27304
VP-BXC	B747	22254
VP-BXD	B747	23348
VP-BXP	B747	20827
VP-BXT	A320	3164
VP-BYA	737NG	29972
VP-BZL	737NG	32915

Cayman Islands

(VP-C)	B737	21957
VP-C	MD80	53577
VP-CAJ	A319	0913

VP-CAL	B737	22022
VP-CAN	A319	1886
VP-CAU	B757	25220
VP-CAY	B737	26286
VP-CBA	B737	22628
(VP-CBB)	737NG	30031
VP-CBB	737NG	32806
VP-CBQ	B727	21460
VP-CCC	A340	779
VP-CCG	1-11	081
VP-CCJ	A319	2421
VP-CDA	1-11	BAC.259
VP-CDL	B727	21655
VP-CEC	737NG	30031
VP-CFA	E145	145637
VP-CGF	L1011	193Y-1195
VP-CHK	B737	21957
VP-CHM	1-11	BAC.260
VP-CHP	E145	14500802
VP-CIE	A319	1589
VP-CJL	1-11	086
VP-CJN	B727	20371
VP-CKA	B727	20489
VP-CKS	A318	3238
VP-CKX	B737	23162
VP-CKY	B737	26282
VP-CLI	E145	14501003
VP-CLL	737NG	35977
VP-CLM	1-11	072
VP-CLR	737NG	34865
VP-CME	B767	22567
VP-CMI	1-11	BAC.183
VP-CMM	B727	18368
VP-CMN	B727	19282
VP-CMS	A320	2403
VP-CNG	E145	14500854
VP-CNI	MD80	49767
VP-CRJ	CRJ	7136
VP-CSA	B737	22628
VP-CSK	737NG	34620
VP-CSL	E145	145495
VP-CUP	E145	145555
VP-CVD	E145	145528
VP-CVX	A319	1212
VP-CWC	B727	19620
VP-CYB	B737	21929
VP-CZA	E145	145021
VP-CZB	E145	145016
VP-CZT	737NG	30076
VP-CZY	B727	21595

British Honduras
(see also HR-)

VP-HCM	B707	18046
VP-HCN	B707	18074
VP-HCO	B707	18045
VP-HCP	B707	17917
VP-HCQ	B707	18076

Kenya
(see also 5Y-)

VP-KPJ	COMET	6431
VP-KPK	COMET	6433
VP-KRL	COMET	6472

British Virgin Islands

VP-LAK	1-11	BAC.205
VP-LAN	1-11	BAC.198
VP-LAP	1-11	BAC.188
VP-LAR	1-11	BAC.189

St Vincent & Grenadines
(see also J8-)

"VP-VNG"	B737	22505

Rhodesia
(see also Z-)

VP-WGA	B707	20110
VP-WKR	B707	18819
VP-WKS	B707	18923
VP-WKT	B707	18929
VP-WKU	B707	18930
VP-WKV	B707	18927
VP-WKW	B707	18891
VP-WMJ	DC-8	45821
VP-YNL	B707	18162
VP-YNM	B707	18242
VP-YNN	B707	18244
VP-YXA	1-11	039
VP-YXB	1-11	040

Fiji/Tonga
(see also DQ-)

(VQ-FBQ)	1-11	BAC.245

Bermuda
(see also VP-B)

(VR-B)	B727	19088
(VR-B)	B747	20305
VR-BAC	1-11	017
VR-BAT	B727	20371
VR-BAT	B747	21648
VR-BBW	B707	18372
VR-BBZ	B707	18373
VR-BCP	B707	19590
VR-BCU	A310	594
VR-BDJ	B727	20046
VR-BEA	1-11	BAC.195
VR-BEB	1-11	BAC.226
VR-BEC	1-11	BAC.196
VR-BED	1-11	BAC.200
VR-BEG	B737	21957
VR-BEH	B737	20194
VR-BGW	B727	18366
VR-BHK	B727	18933
VR-BHM	DC-8	46111
VR-BHN	B727	18370
VR-BHO	B727	19251
VR-BHP	B727	18371
VR-BHS	1-11	076
VR-BIA	DC-8	45658
VR-BJR	DC-8	46067
VR-BKC	B727	20533
VR-BKO	B737	21957
(VR-BLC)	B757	24527
VR-BLG	DC-8	46071
VR-BMC	B727	18323
VR-BMG	DC-9	47006
VR-BMH	MD80	49628
VR-BMI	MD80	49629
VR-BMJ	MD80	49791
VR-BMP	DC-10	46578
VR-BMR	DC-8	46071
VR-BMU	A310	594
VR-BMV	B707	18586
VR-BMX	B737	23404
VR-BNA	B727	19262
VR-BNC	F.28	11016
VR-BNK	A300	247
VR-BOC	B737	24970
VR-BOO	MD80	49778
VR-BOP	MD80	49725
VR-BOR	B707	18586
VR-BOU	A310	638
VR-BOX	B737	21206
VR-BQU	A310	535
VR-BRR	B727	20371
VR-BSA	B727	20046
VR-BUA	B767	28370
VR-BZA	B707	20375

Cayman Islands
(see also VP-C)

Reg	Type	c/n
VR-CAA	B737	25371
VR-CAB	1-11	BAC.237
VR-CAB	B737	24519
VR-CAL	1-11	BAC.211
VR-CAL	B737	22022
VR-CAL	B737	24512
VR-CAM	1-11	069
(VR-CAM)	B727	20371
VR-CAN	B707	18067
VR-CAO	B707	18586
VR-CAQ	1-11	005
VR-CAR	B707	18748
VR-CAU	B757	25220
VR-CBA	B727	18935
VR-CBE	B727	19282
VR-CBG	B727	19620
VR-CBI	1-11	057
VR-CBN	B707	20028
VR-CBQ	B727	21460
VR-CBV	B727	19620
VR-CBX	1-11	084
VR-CBY	1-11	BAC.183
VR-CBZ	1-11	083
VR-CBZ	B737	23800
VR-CCA	B727	21010
VR-CCB	B727	20228
VR-CCD	B737	23800
VR-CCG	1-11	081
VR-CCJ	1-11	BAC.126
VR-CCS	1-11	069
VR-CCW	B737	23387
VR-CDB	B727	19139
VR-CDL	B727	21655
VR-CEF	B737	23162
VR-CGF	L1011	193Y-1195
VR-CHS	B727	18934
VR-CHS	B727	20228
VR-CKA	B727	20489
VR-CKA	DC-8	46095
VR-CKE	DC-9	47151
VR-CKL	B727	19253
VR-CKL	DC-8	46095
VR-CKO	DC-9	47151
VR-CKX	B737	23162
VR-CLM	B727	19282
VR-CMA	B727	21105
VR-CMB	B727	21106
VR-CMC	B727	21107
VR-CMD	B727	21108
VR-CMI	1-11	BAC.183
VR-CMM	B727	18368
VR-CMN	B727	19282
VR-CNN	B737	21518
VR-COJ	B727	21948
VR-CRB	B727	19139
VR-CRC	B737	25040
VR-CRJ	CRJ	7136
VR-CRK	B757	23454
VR-CTM	1-11	081
VR-CWC	B727	19620
VR-CYB	B737	22074
VR-CZZ	L1011	293A-1249

Hong Kong
(see also B-H)

Reg	Type	c/n
VR-HFS	CV880	22-00-47M
VR-HFT	CV880	22-00-43M
VR-HFX	CV880	22-00-37M
VR-HFY	CV880	22-7-2-54
VR-HFZ	CV880	22-7-1-53
VR-HGA	CV880	22-00-44M
VR-HGC	CV880	22-7-4-56
VR-HGF	CV880	22-7-6-58
VR-HGG	CV880	22-7-8-60
VR-HGH	B707	18584
VR-HGI	B707	18585
VR-HGN	B707	18693
VR-HGO	B707	18586
(VR-HGP)	B707	18921
VR-HGP	B707	18922
(VR-HGQ)	B707	18922
VR-HGQ	B707	18964
VR-HGR	B707	18921
(VR-HGR)	B707	18964
(VR-HGS)	B707	19034
VR-HGU	B707	19034
VR-HHB	B707	18747
VR-HHD	B707	18748
VR-HHE	B707	18888
VR-HHG	L1011	193A-1056
VR-HHJ	B707	18889
(VR-HHK)	B707	19263
VR-HHK	L1011	193T-1118
(VR-HHL)	B707	19412
VR-HHL	L1011	193T-1122
VR-HHV	L1011	193K-1024
VR-HHW	L1011	193K-1032
VR-HHX	L1011	193A-1054
VR-HHY	L1011	193A-1051
VR-HIA	B747	21966
VR-HIB	B747	22149
VR-HIC	B747	22429
VR-HID	B747	22530
VR-HIE	B747	22872
VR-HIF	B747	23048
VR-HIH	B747	23120
VR-HII	B747	23221
(VR-HIJ)	B747	23221
VR-HIJ	B747	23392
VR-HIK	B747	23534
VR-HKB	B747	19642
(VR-HKC)	B707	20456
VR-HKC	B747	20247
VR-HKG	B747	21746
VR-HKK	B707	20517
VR-HKL	B707	19367
VR-HKM	B747	20246
VR-HKN	B747	19897
VR-HKO	B747	22237
VR-HKP	B737	22071
VR-HLA	A330	071
VR-HLB	A330	083
VR-HLC	A330	099
VR-HLD	A330	102
VR-HLE	A330	109
VR-HLF	A330	113
VR-HLG	A330	118
VR-HLH	A330	121
VR-HLI	A330	155
VR-HLJ	A330	012
VR-HLK	A330	017
VR-HMD	B747	22105
VR-HME	B747	22106
VR-HMF	B747	22107
VR-HMR	A340	063
VR-HMS	A340	074
VR-HMT	A340	080
VR-HMU	A340	085
VR-HMV	L1011	193R-1033
VR-HMW	L1011	193N-1094
VR-HNA	B777	27265
VR-HNB	B777	27266
VR-HNC	B777	27263
VR-HND	B777	27264
VR-HOA	L1011	193A-1022
VR-HOB	L1011	193A-1037
VR-HOC	L1011	193A-1042
VR-HOD	L1011	193A-1043
VR-HOE	L1011	193E-1021
VR-HOF	L1011	193E-1027
VR-HOG	L1011	193A-1045
VR-HOH	L1011	193A-1050
VR-HOI	L1011	193A-1039
VR-HOJ	L1011	193A-1044
VR-HOK	L1011	193A-1055
VR-HOL	B747	23709
VR-HOM	B747	23920
VR-HON	B747	24215
VR-HOO	B747	23814
VR-HOP	B747	23815
VR-HOR	B747	24631
VR-HOS	B747	24850
VR-HOT	B747	24851
VR-HOU	B747	24925
VR-HOV	B747	25082
VR-HOW	B747	25211
VR-HOX	B747	24955
VR-HOY	B747	25351
VR-HOZ	B747	25871
VR-HTC	B707	18937
VR-HUA	B747	25872
VR-HUB	B747	25873
VR-HUD	B747	25874
VR-HUE	B747	27117
VR-HUF	B747	25869
VR-HUG	B747	25870
VR-HUH	B747	27175
VR-HUI	B747	27230
VR-HUJ	B747	27595
VR-HUK	B747	27503
VR-HVX	B747	24568
VR-HVY	B747	22306
VR-HVZ	B747	23864
VR-HXA	A340	136
VR-HXB	A340	137
VR-HXC	A340	142
VR-HXD	A340	147
VR-HXE	A340	157
VR-HXF	A340	160
VR-HYA	A330	098
VR-HYB	A330	106
VR-HYC	A330	111
VR-HYD	A330	132
VR-HYE	A330	177
VR-HYK	B737	22660
VR-HYL	B737	22408
VR-HYM	B737	22734
VR-HYN	B737	22733
VR-HYO	A320	0393
VR-HYP	A320	0394
VR-HYR	A320	0414
VR-HYS	A320	0430
VR-HYT	A320	0443
VR-HYU	A320	0447
VR-HYV	A320	0415
VR-HYZ	B737	22453

Tanganyika
(see also 5H-)

Reg	Type	c/n
"VR-TBV"	B727	19620

Brunei
(see also VS-/V8-)

Reg	Type	c/n
VR-UEB	B737	20913
VR-UEC	B737	21138
VR-UED	B737	21809
VR-UHM	B727	18371

Brunei
(see also VR-U/V8-)

Reg	Type	c/n
VS-1HB	B727	21010
VS-HB1	B727	21010
VS-UEB	B737	20913
VS-UEB	B737	21809
VS-UEC	B737	21138
VS-UHM	B727	18371

India

Reg	Type	c/n
VT-	737NG	35289
VT-	A340	886
VT-	A320	3256
VT-	A340	894
(VT-)	B737	24519
VT-ADR	A320	2922
VT-ADS	A320	2914
VT-ADT	A320	2908
VT-ADU	A320	2874
VT-ADV	A320	2366
VT-ADW	A320	2376
VT-ADX	A320	0932
VT-ADY	A320	0943
VT-ADZ	A320	0977
VT-AIA	A310	665
VT-AIB	A310	680
VT-AIC	B747	24198
VT-AID	B747	24621
VT-AIE	B747	24226
VT-AIF	B747	24066
VT-AIG	A310	669
VT-AIH	A310	654
VT-AIJ	B777	26943
VT-AIK	B777	28714
VT-AIL	B777	26935
VT-AIM	B747	25074
VT-AIN	A310	684
VT-AIO	A310	693
VT-AIP	A310	697
VT-AIQ	B747	24975
VT-AIR	B777	26917
VT-AIS	B747	25703
VT-ALA	B777	36300
VT-ALB	B777	36301
VT-ALC	B777	36302
VT-ALD	B777	36303
VT-ALE	B777	36304
VT-ALJ	B777	36308
VT-ALK	B777	36309
VT-ALL	B777	36310
VT-ALM	B777	36311
VT-ALN	B777	36312
VT-AXA	737NG	30296
VT-AXB	737NG	33023
VT-AXC	737NG	33024
VT-AXD	737NG	30696
VT-AXE	737NG	29368
VT-AXF	737NG	29369
VT-AXG	737NG	30701
VT-AXH	737NG	36323
VT-AXI	737NG	36324
VT-AXJ	737NG	36325
VT-AXM	737NG	36326
VT-AXN	737NG	36327
VT-AXP	737NG	36328
VT-AXQ	737NG	36329
VT-AXR	737NG	36330
VT-AXT	737NG	36331
VT-AXU	737NG	36332
VT-AXV	737NG	36333
VT-BDE	B737	21163
VT-BDF	B737	21164
VT-BDG	B737	22415
VT-BDH	B737	24236
VT-BDI	B737	23272
VT-BDJ	B757	24102
VT-BDK	B757	24267
VT-BSF	E145	14500901
VT-DJI	B707	17722
VT-DJJ	B707	17723
VT-DJK	B707	17724
VT-DKR	A320	2731
VT-DKS	A320	2747
VT-DKT	A320	2753
VT-DKU	A320	2676
VT-DKV	A320	2645
VT-DKW	A320	2029
VT-DKX	A320	2077
VT-DKY	A320	2564
VT-DKZ	A320	2524
VT-DMN	B707	18055
VT-DNW	A320	3219
VT-DNX	A320	3183
VT-DNY	A320	3162
VT-DNY	B707	18414
VT-DNZ	A320	3012
VT-DNZ	B707	18415
VT-DPM	B707	18708
VT-DPN	SE210	155
VT-DPO	SE210	128
VT-DPP	SE210	130

Reg	Type	C/n	Reg	Type	C/n	Reg	Type	C/n	Reg	Type	C/n
VT-DSB	SE210	134	VT-EPF	A320	0049	VT-INA	A320	2844	VT-JNA	737NG	28578
VT-DSI	B707	18873	VT-EPG	A320	0050	VT-INB	A320	2863	VT-JNB	737NG	28575
VT-DUH	SE210	203	VT-EPH	A320	0051	VT-INC	A320	2883	VT-JNC	737NG	29036
VT-DUI	SE210	204	VT-EPI	A320	0056	VT-IND	A320	2911	VT-JND	737NG	29037
VT-DVA	B707	19247	VT-EPJ	A320	0057	VT-INE	A320	2958	VT-JNE	737NG	29043
VT-DVB	B707	19248	VT-EPK	A320	0058	VT-INF	A320	2990	VT-JNF	737NG	29044
VT-DVI	SE210	213	VT-EPL	A320	0074	VT-ING	A320	3004	VT-JNG	737NG	29045
VT-DVJ	SE210	216	VT-EPM	A320	0075	VT-INH	A320	3050	VT-JNH	737NG	29046
VT-DWN	SE210	231	VT-EPN	A320	0079	VT-INI	A320	3086	VT-JNJ	737NG	29038
VT-DXT	B707	19988	VT-EPO	A320	0080	VT-INJ	A320	3159	VT-JNL	737NG	29039
VT-EAG	B737	20480	VT-EPP	A320	0089	VT-INK	A320	3192	VT-JNM	737NG	29040
VT-EAH	B737	20481	VT-EPQ	A320	0090	VT-INL	A320	3227	VT-JNN	737NG	29041
VT-EAI	B737	20482	VT-EPR	A320	0095	VT-IOA	CRJ	7379	VT-JNP	737NG	28630
VT-EAJ	B737	20483	VT-EPS	A320	0096	VT-IOB	CRJ	7363	VT-JNQ	737NG	28635
VT-EAK	B737	20484	VT-EPT	A320	0097	VT-J	A330	885	VT-JNR	737NG	30403
VT-EAL	B737	20485	VT-EPW	B747	24159	VT-JAA	B737	24790	VT-JNS	737NG	28498
VT-EAM	B737	20486	VT-EPX	B747	24160	VT-JAB	B737	24791	VT-JNT	737NG	28609
VT-EBD	B747	19959	VT-EQG	B737	20492	VT-JAC	B737	24096	VT-JNU	737NG	30404
VT-EBE	B747	19960	VT-EQH	B737	22744	VT-JAD	B737	24097	VT-JNV	737NG	30405
VT-EBN	B747	20459	VT-EQI	B737	23023	VT-JAE	B737	27086	VT-JNW	737NG	30406
VT-EBO	B747	20558	VT-EQJ	B737	23024	VT-JAF	B737	27168	VT-JNX	737NG	30407
VT-ECG	SE210	70	VT-EQS	A310	538	VT-JAG	B737	24345	(VT-JNY)	737NG	30279
VT-ECH	SE210	78	VT-EQT	A310	544	VT-JAH	B737	24682	VT-JNY	737NG	30408
VT-ECI	SE210	237	VT-ERN	B737	19553	VT-JAI	B737	24165	(VT-JNZ)	737NG	30280
VT-ECP	B737	20960	VT-ERS	B707	18159	VT-JAJ	B737	24166	VT-JNZ	737NG	30409
VT-ECQ	B737	20961	VT-ESA	A320	0396	VT-JAK	B737	24687	VT-JWA	A340	643
VT-ECR	B737	20962	VT-ESB	A320	0398	VT-JAL	B737	25191	VT-JWB	A340	646
VT-ECS	B737	20963	VT-ESC	A320	0416	VT-JAM	B737	25773	VT-JWC	A340	651
VT-EDR	B737	21163	VT-ESD	A320	0423	VT-JAN	B737	25775	VT-JWD	A330	751
VT-EDS	B737	21164	VT-ESE	A320	0431	(VT-JAO)	B737	29032	VT-JWE	A330	807
VT-EDU	B747	21182	VT-ESF	A320	0432	VT-JAP	B737	25664	VT-JWF	A330	825
VT-EDV	A300	034	VT-ESG	A320	0451	(VT-JAP)	B737	29033	VT-JWG	A330	831
VT-EDW	A300	036	VT-ESH	A320	0469	VT-JAQ	B737	25663	VT-JWH	A330	882
VT-EDX	A300	038	VT-ESI	A320	0486	VT-JAR	B737	29032	VT-KFA	A320	2413
VT-EDY	A300	059	VT-ESJ	A320	0490	VT-JAS	B737	29033	VT-KFB	A320	2443
VT-EDZ	A300	060	VT-ESK	A320	0492	VT-JAT	B737	29034	VT-KFC	A320	2496
VT-EFJ	B747	21446	VT-ESL	A320	0499	VT-JAU	B737	29035	VT-KFD	A320	2502
VT-EFK	B737	21496	VT-ESM	B747	27078	VT-JAV	B737	26447	VT-KFE	A320	2522
VT-EFL	B737	21497	VT-ESN	B747	27164	VT-JAW	B737	27354	VT-KFF	A320	2531
VT-EFM	B737	21498	VT-ESO	B747	27165	(VT-JAX)	B737	26454	VT-KFG	A320	2576
VT-EFO	B747	21473	VT-ESP	B747	27214	(VT-JAY)	B737	26456	VT-KFH	A319	2621
VT-EFU	B747	21829	VT-EVA	B747	28094	VT-JAZ	B737	27355	VT-KFI	A319	2634
VT-EFV	A300	088	VT-EVB	B747	28095	VT-JBA	B737	29035	VT-KFJ	A319	2664
VT-EFW	A300	111	VT-EVC	A300	262	VT-JBB	737NG	36846	VT-KFK	A320	2670
VT-EFX	A300	113	VT-EVD	A300	240	VT-JBC	737NG	36847	VT-KFL	A320	2817
VT-EGA	B747	21993	VT-EVE	A310	501	VT-JBD	737NG	35099	VT-KFM	A320	2856
VT-EGB	B747	21994	VT-EVF	A310	548	VT-JEA	B777	35157	VT-KFN	A321	2916
VT-EGC	B747	21995	VT-EVG	A310	447	VT-JEB	B777	35158	VT-KFP	A321	2919
VT-EGD	B737	22280	VT-EVH	A310	481	VT-JEC	D777	35159	VT-KFQ	A321	2927
VT-EGE	B737	22281	VT-EVI	A310	519	VT-JED	B777	35160	VT-KFR	A321	2933
VT-EGF	B737	22282	VT-EVJ	B747	24199	VT-JEE	B777	35164	VT-KFS	A321	3034
VT-EGG	B737	22283	VT-EVO	A320	0247	VT-JEF	B777	35162	VT-KFT	A320	3089
VT-EGH	B737	22284	VT-EVP	A320	0257	VT-JEG	B777	35163	VT-KFV	A320	3105
VT-EGI	B737	22285	VT-EVQ	A320	0327	VT-JEH	B777	35166	VT-KFW	A321	3120
VT-EGJ	B737	22286	VT-EVR	A320	0336	VT-JEJ	B777	35161	VT-KFX	A321	3270
VT-EGM	B737	22473	VT-EVS	A320	0308	VT-JEK	B777	35165	VT-LCA	B727	22052
VT-EHC	A300	181	VT-EVT	A320	0314	(VT-JGA)	737NG	30408	VT-LCB	B727	22053
VT-EHD	A300	182	VT-EVU	A310	634	VT-JGA	737NG	30410	VT-LCC	B727	22167
VT-EHE	B737	22860	VT-EVW	A310	598	(VT-JGB)	737NG	30409	VT-LCI	B727	22168
VT-EHF	B737	22861	VT-EVX	A310	695	VT-JGB	737NG	30411	VT-MDL	146	E1229
VT-EHG	B737	22862	VT-EVY	A310	589	(VT-JGC)	737NG	30410	VT-MDM	146	E1230
VT-EHH	B737	22863	VT-EWA	B737	20956	VT-JGC	737NG	30412	VT-MGA	B737	22120
VT-EHN	A300	177	VT-EWB	B737	22703	VT-JGD	737NG	33740	VT-MGB	B737	22121
VT-EHO	A300	180	VT-EWC	B737	22576	VT-JGE	737NG	32663	VT-MGC	B737	22122
VT-EHQ	A300	190	VT-EWD	B737	22633	VT-JGF	737NG	29639	VT-MGD	B737	22117
VT-EHW	B737	23036	VT-EWF	B737	22396	VT-JGG	737NG	29668	VT-MGE	B737	23865
VT-EHX	B737	23037	VT-EWH	B737	21714	VT-JGH	737NG	32577	VT-MGF	B737	24344
VT-EJG	A310	406	VT-EWI	B737	21715	VT-JGJ	737NG	32578	VT-MGG	B737	24468
VT-EJH	A310	407	VT-EWJ	B737	22279	VT-JGK	737NG	32579	VT-PAB	E170	17000005
VT-EJI	A310	413	VT-EWL	B737	23866	VT-JGL	737NG	32738	VT-PAC	E170	17000002
(VT-EJJ)	A310	392	VT-EYA	A320	0376	VT-JGM	737NG	32614	VT-PAD	E170	17000126
VT-EJJ	A310	428	VT-EYB	A320	0386	VT-JGN	737NG	32616	VT-PAE	E170	17000137
VT-EJK	A310	429	VT-EYC	A320	0362	VT-JGP	737NG	34798	VT-PAF	E170	17000147
VT-EJL	A310	392	VT-EYD	A320	0168	VT-JGQ	737NG	34797	VT-PDA	B737	22415
VT-EKC	B737	20943	VT-EYE	A320	0179	VT-JGR	737NG	34799	VT-PDB	B737	22416
VT-EKD	B737	20944	VT-EYF	A320	0225	VT-JGS	737NG	34800	VT-PDC	B737	23042
VT-ELV	A300	022	VT-EYG	A320	0326	VT-JGT	737NG	34801	VT-PDD	B737	23041
VT-ELW	A300	026	VT-EYH	A320	0344	VT-JGU	737NG	34802	VT-PPA	A321	3130
VT-ENQ	B747	21936	VT-EYI	A320	0478	VT-JGV	737NG	34803	VT-PPB	A321	3146
VT-EPB	A320	0045	VT-EYJ	A320	0354	VT-JGW	737NG	34804	VT-PPD	A321	3212
VT-EPC	A320	0046	VT-EYK	A320	0411	VT-JGX	737NG	34805	(VT-S)	B737	24492
VT-EPD	A320	0047	VT-EYL	A320	0480	VT-JGY	737NG	34806	(VT-S)	B737	27000
VT-EPE	A320	0048	VT-HSS	737NG	29102	VT-JGZ	737NG	35218	(VT-S)	B737	27001

Reg	Type	C/N
VT-SAL	CRJ	7224
VT-SAO	CRJ	7227
VT-SAP	CRJ	7242
VT-SAQ	CRJ	7345
VT-SAR	CRJ	7393
VT-SAS	CRJ	7434
VT-SAU	CRJ	7469
VT-SAW	B737	29055
VT-SAX	B737	29056
VT-SAY	B737	25161
VT-SCA	A319	2593
VT-SCB	A319	2624
VT-SCC	A319	2629
VT-SCD	A319	1668
VT-SCE	A319	1718
VT-SCF	A319	2907
VT-SCG	A319	3271
VT-SCH	A319	3278
VT-SDL	B767	25280
VT-SIA	B737	21763
VT-SIB	B737	22161
VT-SIC	B737	24708
VT-SID	B737	24705
VT-SIE	B737	22415
VT-SIE	B737	24707
VT-SIF	B737	22416
VT-SIG	737NG	28497
VT-SIH	B737	24165
VT-SII	B737	24166
VT-SIJ	737NG	29049
VT-SIK	737NG	29050
VT-SIQ	B737	24234
VT-SIR	737NG	30279
VT-SIS	737NG	30280
VT-SIU	737NG	28090
VT-SIV	737NG	28091
VT-SIW	B737	29056
VT-SIX	B737	29055
VT-SIY	B737	24166
VT-SIZ	737NG	33025
VT-SJA	737NG	33026
VT-SJB	B737	28202
VT-SJC	B737	28491
VT-SJD	B737	29141
VT-SJE	737NG	30727
VT-SJF	737NG	28610
VT-SJG	737NG	30694
VT-SJH	737NG	30695
VT-SJI	737NG	34399
VT-SJJ	737NG	34400
VT-SPC	737NG	28824
VT-SPD	737NG	28827
VT-SPE	737NG	28621
VT-SPF	737NG	34896
VT-SPG	737NG	32672
VT-SPH	737NG	30660
VT-SPI	737NG	32693
VT-SPJ	737NG	34897
VT-SPK	737NG	34898
VT-SPL	737NG	34899
VT-SPM	737NG	34900
(VT-SPN)	737NG	34901
(VT-SPO)	737NG	34902
VT-SPO	737NG	35216
VT-SPP	737NG	35217
VT-SPQ	737NG	34903
VT-SPR	737NG	34904
VT-SPS	737NG	34905
VT-SPT	737NG	34952
VT-SPU	737NG	34953
VT-SPY	737NG	28375
VT-SPZ	737NG	29345
VT-VJM	A319	2650
VT-WAA	A320	0455
VT-WAB	A320	0471
VT-WAC	A320	1482
VT-WAD	A320	1509
VT-WAV	A320	1597
VT-WAW	A320	1657
VT-WAX	A320	1767
VT-WAY	A320	1767
VT-WAZ	A320	1597

Antigua & Barbuda

Reg	Type	C/N
V2-LDT	B737	20582
V2-LDX	A300	204
V2-LDY	A300	065
V2-LEA	DC-10	46554
V2-LEC	A310	539
V2-LED	A310	542
V2-LEH	DC-10	47861
V2-LEJ	L1011	193H-1246
V2-LEK	L1011	293A-1248
V2-LEM	L1011	193K-1032
V2-LEN	L1011	193T-1122
V2-LEO	L1011	293B-1240
V2-LER	DC-10	48294
V2-LEX	DC-10	48258
(V2-LFB)	DC-10	48275
V2-LFQ	L1011	193N-1212
V2-SKY	DC-10	48275

St Kitts & Nevis

Reg	Type	C/N
(V4-CGC)	B727	20679
(V4-THB)	B737	21184

Namibia

Reg	Type	C/N
V5-ANA	B737	23790
V5-ANB	B737	21686
V5-AND	B737	21790
V5-ANE	B737	21805
V5-KEA	F.28	11151
V5-KEX	F.28	11143
V5-NMA	B747	28551
V5-NMB	B767	25535
(V5-NMC)	DO328	3200
V5-NMC	MD11	48484
(V5-NMD)	DO328	3201
V5-NMD	MD11	48453
V5-NME	A340	051
V5-NMF	A340	047
V5-SPE	B747	21254
V5-SPF	B747	21263
(V5-TST)	B747	22971

Brunei-Darrusalum
(see also VR-U/VS-)

Reg	Type	C/N
V8-	B777	26918
V8-AC1	B747	21649
(V8-AC2)	B747	29101
V8-AC3	A340	204
V8-AL1	B747	26426
V8-AM1	A340	009
V8-BG1	B727	18371
V8-BG1	B727	22362
V8-BG2	B727	18371
V8-BKH	A340	009
V8-BKH	A340	046
V8-DPD	A310	431
V8-HB1	B727	21010
V8-HB1	B757	23454
V8-HB3	A340	204
V8-HM1	A310	431
V8-HM1	B727	22362
V8-HM2	B727	22362
(V8-HM8)	A340	204
V8-JBB	A340	151
V8-JBB	B747	21649
V8-JP1	A340	009
V8-JP1	B747	21649
V8-MHB	B767	25537
V8-MJB	B767	25537
V8-PJB	A340	046
V8-RB3	F.100	11253
V8-RB4	F.100	11255
V8-RBA	B757	23452
V8-RBB	B757	23453
V8-RBC	B757	23454
V8-RBD	B767	24742
V8-RBE	B767	25346
V8-RBF	B767	25530
V8-RBG	B767	25532
V8-RBH	B767	25534
V8-RBJ	B767	25533
V8-RBK	B767	25536
V8-RBL	B767	27189
V8-RBM	B767	27428
V8-RBN	B767	27427
V8-RBP	A319	2023
V8-RBR	A319	2032
V8-RBS	A320	2135
V8-RBT	A320	2139
V8-RBU	B777	30213
V8-UB1	B727	22362
V8-UEB	B737	20913
V8-UEB	B737	21809
V8-UEC	B737	21138
V8-UHM	B727	18371

Mexico

Reg	Type	C/N
X.-	B727	19913
(X.-)	B737	22959
X.-	B737	23312
X.-	B737	23707
X.-	B737	23747
X.-	B787	35304
X.-	B787	35306
X.-	B787	35308
X.-	DO328	3125
(XA-)	737NG	28577
XA-	A320	3286
(XA-)	B707	19773
(XA-)	B727	20383
(XA-)	B727	21851
(XA-)	B727	22982
(XA-)	B727	22983
(XA-)	B727	22984
(XA-)	B727	23014
XA-	B737	22866
(XA-)	B747	20402
XA-	CRJ	7363
XA-AAD	737NG	33783
XA-AAQ	B727	21628
XA-AAS	DO328	3127
XA-AAU	B737	24211
XA-AAV	B737	24214
XA-ABC	B727	23467
XA-ABG	B707	20315
XA-ABL	B727	20640
XA-ADM	B727	21978
XA-ABQ	DC-9	48119
XA-ABR	DC-9	48120
XA-ABS	DC-9	48118
XA-ABT	DC-9	48141
XA-ABU	B707	19585
XA-ABX	B727	20917
XA-ACO	A320	1322
XA-ACP	B737	23065
XA-ACZ	DC-9	47514
XA-ADA	DC-9	48112
XA-ADC	1-11	084
XA-ADC	1-11	BAC.183
XA-ADK	DC-9	47131
XA-ADV	B737	23066
XA-AEB	DC-9	48147
XA-AEC	DC-9	48155
XA-AEP	737NG	32406
XA-AEQ	737NG	32407
XA-AEX	737NG	32774
XA-AFB	B727	21149
XA-AFC	B727	20383
XA-AGM	737NG	35786
XA-AGS	DC-9	45786
XA-AIJ	A320	1179
XA-ALI	E145	145795
XA-ALM	A320	1308
XA-AMA	DC-9	48125
XA-AMB	DC-9	48126
XA-AMC	DC-9	48127
XA-AMD	DC-9	48128
XA-AME	DC-9	48129
XA-AMF	DC-9	48130
(XA-AMG)	DC-9	48150
XA-AMH	B737	24300
(XA-AMH)	DC-9	48151
(XA-AMI)	MD80	48067
(XA-AMJ)	MD80	48068
(XA-AMK)	MD80	48069
(XA-AML)	MD80	48083
(XA-AMM)	DC-10	48275
(XA-AMN)	DC-10	48276
XA-AMO	B737	49149
XA-AMO	MD80	49188
XA-AMP	DC-8	45687
(XA-AMP)	MD80	49150
XA-AMP	MD80	49189
(XA-AMQ)	MD80	49151
XA-AMQ	MD80	49190
XA-AMR	DC-10	46931
XA-AMR	DC-8	45955
XA-AMS	DC-8	45911
(XA-AMS)	MD80	49152
XA-AMS	MD80	49926
XA-AMT	DC-8	45909
XA-AMT	MD80	49927
XA-AMU	MD80	49928
XA-AMV	MD80	49929
XA-APB	B737	20631
XA-APB	B767	27618
XA-ASS	B727	18800
XA-AVL	B737	24787
XA-AVO	B737	24881
XA-BAM	737NG	33784
XA-BBI	B727	19528
XA-BCS	DC-9	47043
XA-BCS	DC-9	47061
XA-BDM	DC-9	47087
XA-BLI	E145	145798
XA-BTO	B727	18853
XA-CAM	737NG	33785
XA-CAS	E737	23948
XA-CLI	E145	14500803
XA-CMA	A319	2066
XA-CMG	1-11	079
XA-CSL	DC-9	45743
XA-CTG	737NG	35123
XA-CUE	B727	20709
XA-CUE	B727	20710
XA-CUN	B727	20780
XA-CYM	737NG	35124
XA-DAM	737NG	33786
XA-DAT	B727	20787
XA-DEI	DC-9	47650
XA-DEJ	DC-9	47594
XA-DEK	DC-9	47602
XA-DEL	DC-9	47607
XA-DEM	DC-9	47609
XA-DEN	DC-9	47621
XA-DEO	DC-9	47622
XA-DEV	DC-9	47048
XA-DIA	B757	23928
XA-DLI	E145	14500852
XA-DLP	CRJ	7653
XA-DOD	DC-8	45641
XA-DOE	DC-8	45252
XA-DUG	DC-10	46936
XA-DUH	DC-10	46937
XA-DUI	B727	20894
XA-DUJ	B727	20895
XA-DUK	B727	20896
XA-EAM	737NG	29360
XA-ECA	B737	24024
XA-ECD	CRJ	7662
XA-ELI	E145	14500861
XA-FAA	B727	18911
XA-FAC	B727	19427
XA-FAM	737NG	33787
XA-FID	B727	21071
XA-FIE	B727	21072
XA-FLI	E145	145203
XA-FNP	B737	23603
XA-FPV	MD80	49846

Reg	Type	C/n	Reg	Type	C/n	Reg	Type	C/n	Reg	Type	C/n
XA-GAM	737NG	33788	XA-MEL	B727	22413	XA-RJZ	A320	0320	XA-SGF	F.100	11384
XA-GBM	B737	19017	XA-MEM	B727	22414	XA-RKA	A320	0321	XA-SGJ	B737	24030
XA-GBP	B737	18252	XA-MEN	B727	18797	XA-RKB	A320	0353	XA-SGS	F.100	11390
XA-GDL	DC-9	47085	XA-MEP	B727	18800	XA-RKI	B767	26200	XA-SGT	F.100	11400
XA-GGB	B737	24023	XA-MEQ	B727	22424	XA-RKJ	B767	26204	XA-SGY	B727	19497
XA-GHC	CRJ	7739	XA-MER	B727	22425	XA-RKM	F.100	11341	XA-SHG	F.100	11410
XA-GLI	E145	145444	(XA-MET)	DC-10	48259	XA-RKN	F.100	11343	XA-SHH	F.100	11420
XA-GMV	737NG	35118	(XA-MEU)	DC-10	48289	XA-RKP	B737	25186	XA-SHI	F.100	11309
XA-GOJ	DC-9	45721	XA-MEW	DC-10	48294	XA-RKQ	B737	25189	XA-SHJ	F.100	11319
XA-GOK	DC-9	45722	(XA-MEX)	DC-10	48258	XA-RKT	DC-9	47122	XA-SHK	F.100	11333
XA-GOL	737NG	35785	XA-MEX	DC-10	48295	XA-RLI	E145	145559	XA-SHL	F.100	11337
XA-GRO	B727	21634	XA-MEZ	B727	22676	XA-RLM	B727	18326	XA-SHR	DC-9	47284
XA-GUU	B727	20328	XA-MIA	737NG	35119	XA-RLM	B757	24566	XA-SHT	B727	18742
XA-GUV	B727	20513	XA-MLI	E145	145065	XA-RLV	A300	140	XA-SHV	DC-9	47214
XA-HAM	737NG	33789	XA-MMX	B757	25054	XA-RLV	B727	20383	XA-SHW	DC-9	47166
XA-HLI	E145	145337	XA-MRM	MD80	53066	XA-RMO	146	E2060	XA-SHX	DC-9	47187
XA-HOH	B727	21577	XA-MRV	F.100	11320	XA-RNQ	DC-9	47059	XA-SIA	DC-8	45878
XA-HON	B727	21617	XA-MTY	B757	25240	XA-RPH	MD80	49792	XA-SIB	DC-8	45855
XA-HOV	B727	21637	XA-MXA	A319	2078	XA-RRA	B727	18911	XA-SID	DC-8	45935
XA-HOX	B727	21638	XA-MXA	B727	22661	XA-RRB	B727	19427	XA-SIE	B727	22069
(XA-IAM)	737NG	33790	XA-MXB	B727	22662	XA-RRY	DC-9	45785	XA-SIH	B737	23786
XA-IEU	B727	21836	XA-MXB	B767	24475	XA-RSQ	DC-9	45730	XA-SIJ	B727	22017
(XA-IEV)	B727	21837	XA-MXC	B727	22663	XA-RST	146	E1015	XA-SIK	B757	25624
(XA-IEW)	B727	21838	XA-MXC	B767	24349	XA-RSW	B737	19794	XA-SIR	B727	18743
XA-IJA	A320	1244	XA-MXD	A320	1229	XA-RSY	B737	19027	XA-SIV	B727	22424
XA-IJT	A320	1132	XA-MXD	B727	22664	XA-RSZ	B737	19033	XA-SIW	B737	22370
XA-ILI	E145	145564	XA-MXE	A321	21457	XA-RTI	146	E2066	XA-SIX	B737	22371
XA-INJ	A320	1162	XA-MXE	B767	23764	XA-RTK	MD80	49938	XA-SIY	B737	23747
XA-IOV	DC-9	47006	XA-MXF	A320	0566	XA-RTN	1-11	085	XA-SIZ	B737	23748
XA-ITJ	A320	1259	XA-MXF	B727	21346	XA-RUO	MD80	49673	XA-SJD	B757	26270
XA-IUP	B727	18910	XA-MXG	A319	1630	XA-RVY	B767	24762	XA-SJE	B727	21479
XA-JAM	737NG	33791	XA-MXG	B727	21600	XA-RVZ	B767	24716	XA-SJI	B737	20588
XA-JBC	B767	24762	XA-MXH	A319	1673	XA-RWG	B727	18572	XA-SJK	B727	20525
XA-JBP	B757	30758	XA-MXH	B727	20876	XA-RWW	B767	24952	XA-SJM	B727	20162
XA-JEB	DC-9	47394	XA-MXI	A319	1742	XA-RWX	B767	24953	XA-SJU	B727	20552
XA-JEC	DC-9	47106	XA-MXI	B727	21346	XA-RXG	DC-9	45714	XA-SKA	DC-9	47060
XA-JED	DC-9	47356	XA-MXJ	A319	1805	XA-RXI	B727	20150	XA-SKC	B727	19181
XA-JJA	B727	18326	XA-MXJ	B727	21600	XA-RXJ	B727	20154	XA-SKQ	B757	25490
XA-JLI	E145	145440	XA-NAB	COMET	6420	XA-RYI	B727	19228	XA-SKR	B757	25489
XA-JOY	737NG	35121	XA-NAD	B727	19815	XA-RYQ	A320	0259	XA-SKY	B767	25411
XA-JPM	CRJ	7113	(XA-NAD)	COMET	6457	XA-RYS	A320	0260	XA-SLC	B737	22055
XA-JXT	F.100	11303	(XA-NAE)	COMET	6443	XA-RYT	A320	0261	XA-SLG	B727	21171
XA-JXW	F.100	11390	XA-NAF	B737	23470	XA-RZI	B727	20151	XA-SLI	E145	145580
XA-KAC	E145	145322	XA-NAK	B737	23474	XA-RZU	A320	0252	XA-SLK	B737	23412
XA-KAM	737NG	33792	XA-NAM	737NG	33790	XA-SAB	B737	25187	XA-SLM	B727	21696
XA-KLI	E145	145426	XA-NAP	COMET	6418	XA-SAC	B737	25192	XA-SLY	B737	24098
XA-KWK	B757	26151	XA-NAR	COMET	6424	XA-SAD	B757	25598	XA-SMB	B727	21646
XA-KXJ	F.100	11400	XA-NAS	COMET	6425	XA-SAM	B727	21130	XA-SMD	B757	25490
XA-KXR	F.100	11410	XA-NAT	COMET	6443	XA-SAS	B737	26191	XA-SME	B757	25489
XA-LAC	DC-9	47126	XA-NAV	B737	23472	XA-SBH	F.100	11350	XA-SMI	DC-9	47018
XA-LAM	737NG	33793	XA-NAZ	COMET	6418	XA-SCA	B737	23979	XA-SMJ	B757	26268
XA-LBM	B737	19014	XA-NCA	A319	2126	XA-SCB	B757	26151	XA-SMK	B757	26271
XA-LEX	B727	18325	XA-NLI	E145	145083	XA-SCD	F.100	11371	XA-SML	B757	26272
XA-LLI	E145	145060	XA-NMB	B737	21016	XA-SDF	DC-9	47006	XA-SMM	B757	26273
XA-LMM	DC-9	45736	XA-NOV	B737	23521	XA-SDH	B727	18743	XA-SNC	B737	24377
XA-LSA	DC-8	45296	XA-NPF	B727	22663	XA-SDL	B707	18072	XA-SNR	DC-9	45699
XA-LXG	F.100	11420	XA-NUS	DC-8	45633	XA-SDR	B727	20555	XA-SNW	B727	18450
XA-MAA	B737	23655	XA-OAM	B767	26471	XA-SEA	B727	18911	XA-SOA	DC-9	47059
XA-MAA	DC-8	45980	XA-OCI	B737	21640	XA-SEB	B727	18821	XA-SOB	DC-9	47085
XA-MAB	B737	21016	XA-OHC	B737	22257	(XA-SEC)	B757	22691	XA-SOC	DC-9	47100
XA-MAC	B737	21014	XA-OLI	E145	145089	XA-SEJ	B727	19255	XA-SOD	DC-9	47122
XA-MAD	B737	19409	XA-PAL	B727	18800	XA-SEK	B727	18912	XA-SOE	DC-9	47123
XA-MAD	B737	22652	XA-PAM	737NG	34293	XA-SEL	B727	19256	XA-SOF	DC-9	47124
XA-MAE	B737	22648	XA-PBA	B737	20631	XA-SEM	B727	19427	XA-SOG	DC-9	47125
XA-MAF	B737	22505	XA-PEI	DC-8	45652	XA-SEM	B737	23924	XA-SOH	DC-9	47126
XA-MAG	B737	21184	XA-PIK	DC-8	45685	XA-SEN	B727	19398	XA-SOI	DC-9	47127
(XA-MAH)	737NG	35121	XA-PLI	E145	145090	XA-SEO	B737	23925	XA-SOJ	DC-9	45785
XA-MAH	737NG	35122	XA-POW	COMET	6420	XA-SEP	B727	18912	XA-SOM	B737	20197
XA-MAI	B737	24537	XA-PPG	CRJ	7652	XA-SER	B727	18908	XA-SOY	DC-9	47085
XA-MAK	B737	21816	XA-QAM	737NG	34294	XA-SEU	B727	18909	XA-SPA	DC-9	45698
XA-MAS	B707	19585	XA-QLI	E145	145588	XA-SEW	B727	20217	XA-SPG	B757	25155
XA-MAS	DC-8	45976	XA-RAN	B727	19165	XA-SFF	B727	19462	XA-SPH	B727	22146
XA-MAX	DC-8	45810	XA-RBC	B737	22647	XA-SFG	B727	19474	XA-SPK	B727	19497
XA-MEB	B727	21837	XA-RBD	B737	22649	XA-SFK	MD80	48068	XA-SPU	B727	20181
XA-MEC	B727	21838	XA-RIY	DC-10	47861	XA-SFL	MD80	48069	XA-SQO	B727	18752
XA-MED	B727	22156	XA-RJP	B737	24255	XA-SFM	MD80	49149	XA-SRC	B727	19911
XA-MEE	B727	22157	XA-RJR	B737	25179	XA-SFO	MD80	49673	XA-SSW	DC-9	45735
XA-MEF	B727	22158	XA-RJS	B737	25185	XA-SFR	B737	19707	XA-SSZ	DC-9	45715
XA-MEG	B727	18743	XA-RJT	MD80	49777	(XA-SGA)	A320	0368	XA-STB	B737	20128
XA-MEH	B727	22409	XA-RJV	B727	20525	(XA-SGB)	A320	0376	XA-STE	B737	20808
XA-MEI	B727	22410	XA-RJW	A320	0275	(XA-SGC)	A320	0386	XA-STM	B737	23411
XA-MEJ	B727	22411	XA-RJX	A320	0276	(XA-SGD)	A320	0433	XA-STN	B737	23412
XA-MEK	B727	22412	XA-RJY	A320	0296	XA-SGE	F.100	11382	XA-SVQ	B737	23786

Reg	Type	Serial
XA-SVZ	DC-9	47125
XA-SWG	**DC-9**	**47230**
XA-SWH	DC-9	47236
XA-SWL	B737	20711
XA-SWO	B737	27284
XA-SWW	MD80	49848
XA-SXC	B727	20619
XA-SXE	B727	20615
XA-SXJ	MD80	49845
XA-SXO	B727	20268
XA-SXS	DC-9	45713
XA-SXT	DC-9	45719
XA-SXV	DC-9	45715
XA-SXZ	B727	18436
XA-SYA	B727	19432
XA-SYD	**DC-9**	**47283**
XA-SYE	DC-10	46990
XA-SYF	DC-9	45780
XA-SYG	A300	211
XA-SYI	B727	20264
XA-SYQ	DC-9	45702
XA-SYT	B737	19409
XA-SYX	B737	19059
XA-SZC	DC-9	45739
XA-TAA	B727	20432
XA-TAB	B727	20433
XA-TAC	B727	20434
XA-TAE	B727	18800
XA-TAE	B757	25268
XA-TAF	**DC-9**	**47039**
XA-TBO	A300	207
XA-TBQ	**DC-9**	**47553**
XA-TBX	DC-9	45716
XA-TCD	B757	22691
XA-TCG	**F.100**	**11374**
XA-TCH	**F.100**	**11375**
XA-TCP	B727	21278
XA-TCP	**F.100**	**11341**
XA-TCQ	B737	21528
XA-TCT	DC-9	47274
XA-TCW	B727	20580
XA-TCX	B727	22440
XA-TDC	DC-10	46891
XA-TDI	DC-10	48259
XA-TDV	DC-9	47156
XA-TDZ	B707	19774
XA-TFM	DC-10	47861
XA-TFO	DC-9	48151
XA-TGJ	DC-9	45783
XA-TGP	B727	22604
XA-TGU	B727	20876
XA-THB	**DC-9**	**47648**
XA-THC	**DC-9**	**47666**
XA-THP	MD80	53191
XA-THQ	MD80	53192
XA-THU	B727	20625
XA-TIM	**DC-9**	**45778**
XA-TIZ	DC-9	45782
XA-TJC	B757	25133
XA-TJD	B767	25411
XA-TJS	DC-9	45784
XA-TKM	B727	24234
XA-TKN	DC-9	47418
XA-TKO	B727	22536
XA-TKP	**F.100**	**11266**
XA-TKR	**F.100**	**11339**
XA-TKV	B727	22537
XA-TLH	**MD80**	**53119**
XA-TLI	**E145**	**145601**
XA-TLJ	B737	20926
XA-TLZ	B727	22163
XA-TMA	B727	22164
XA-TMB	B737	24492
(XA-TMG)	B767	27618
XA-TMU	B757	26330
XA-TMY	B727	21987
XA-TNS	B767	24728
XA-TNT	**DC-9**	**48113**
XA-TOJ	**B767**	**24727**
XA-TOR	MD80	49710
(XA-TPK)	B727	21343
XA-TPM	**MD80**	**49671**

Reg	Type	Serial
XA-TPV	B727	19493
XA-TQI	B737	24096
XA-TQJ	B737	24097
XA-TQT	B727	20188
XA-TQU	B757	27203
XA-TQV	DC-9	47765
XA-TRA	B757	24737
XA-TRB	B727	20706
XA-TRD	MD80	48079
XA-TRR	B727	21629
XA-TRW	B737	19743
XA-TSW	MD80	49741
XA-TTC	MD80	49904
XA-TTM	**B737**	**22753**
XA-TTP	**B727**	**22868**
XA-TUE	A300	078
XA-TUK	**B737**	**22867**
XA-TUP	MD80	49877
XA-TUR	MD80	49642
XA-TUR	MD80	49708
XA-TUY	B727	19815
XA-TVB	DC-9	48145
XA-TVC	DC-9	48146
XA-TVD	**B737**	**22758**
XA-TVE	B727	19562
XA-TVL	**B737**	**22869**
XA-TVN	**B737**	**22752**
XA-TVU	**A300**	**074**
XA-TWA	**MD80**	**49780**
XA-TWF	737NG	28577
XA-TWG	**B737**	**23412**
XA-TWJ	**B737**	**23471**
XA-TWL	MD80	49120
XA-TWM	**MD80**	**49568**
XA-TWO	**B737**	**23475**
XA-TWP	**B737**	**21738**
XA-TWQ	A300	045
XA-TWR	**B737**	**21812**
XA-TWT	**MD80**	**49706**
XA-TWV	**B737**	**23473**
XA-TXC	**MD00**	**49389**
XA-TXD	**B737**	**22018**
XA-TXF	**B727**	**22961**
XA-TXG	DC-9	48114
XA-TXH	**MD80**	**49413**
XA-TXS	**DC-8**	**46054**
XA-TXT	**A320**	**0430**
XA-TXU	B727	21343
XA-TYB	MD80	49229
XA-TYC	**B737**	**22962**
XA-TYI	**B737**	**22757**
XA-TYO	**B737**	**22756**
XA-TYT	B727	19534
XA-UAA	**B737**	**22755**
XA-UAH	**A320**	**0447**
XA-UAK	B737	21130
XA-UAQ	**A319**	**1598**
XA-UBB	**B737**	**21750**
XA-UBQ	**A318**	**2328**
XA-UBR	**A318**	**2333**
XA-UBS	**A318**	**2358**
XA-UBT	**A318**	**2367**
XA-UBU	**A318**	**2377**
XA-UBV	**A318**	**2394**
XA-UBW	**A318**	**2523**
XA-UBX	**A318**	**2544**
XA-UBY	**A318**	**2552**
XA-UBZ	**A318**	**2575**
XA-UCG	**B737**	**22445**
XA-UCL	B737	24460
XA-UCP	B737	24030
XA-UCY	B737	23500
XA-UCZ	**A320**	**0357**
XA-UDA	**DC-9**	**47170**
XA-UDB	DC-9	47238
XA-UDC	**DC-9**	**47523**
XA-UDD	DC-9	47534
XA-UDE	**DC-9**	**47673**
XA-UDF	**DC-9**	**47674**
XA-UDG	**DC-9**	**47740**
XA-UDH	**DC-9**	**47791**
XA-UDQ	B737	23499

Reg	Type	Serial
XA-UDS	**DC-9**	**47680**
XA-UDT	A320	2347
XA-UDU	A320	2248
XA-UEG	**DC-9**	**47794**
XA-UEI	DC-9	47723
XA-UEL	**B737**	**22963**
XA-UER	**A319**	**2662**
XA-UFD	**CRJ**	**7164**
XA-UFH	**B737**	**23377**
XA-UFW	**B737**	**23558**
XA-UFX	**CRJ**	**7144**
XA-UGE	**B737**	**23555**
XA-UGF	**B737**	**23556**
XA-UGL	**B737**	**22958**
XA-UGS	**CRJ**	**7467**
XA-UGU	**CRJ**	**7470**
XA-UGW	**CRJ**	**7016**
XA-UHB	**CRJ**	**7025**
XA-UHE	**A320**	**3149**
XA-UHF	**CRJ**	**7006**
XA-UHM	**CRJ**	**7004**
XA-UHN	**CRJ**	**7329**
XA-UHU	**CRJ**	**7299**
XA-ULI	**E145**	**145570**
XA-VAI	**A320**	**3160**
XA-VAM	**737NG**	**34295**
XA-VIA	**B737**	**23856**
XA-VIV	**B737**	**23560**
XA-VIY	**B737**	**22959**
XA-VLI	**E145**	**145574**
XA-VOA	**A319**	**2771**
XA-VOB	**A319**	**2780**
XA-VOC	**A319**	**2997**
XA-VOD	**A319**	**3045**
XA-VOE	**A319**	**3069**
XA-VOF	**A319**	**3077**
XA-VOG	**A319**	**3175**
XA-VOI	**A319**	**2657**
XA-VOL	**A319**	**2666**
XA-WAM	**737NG**	**34296**
XA-WLI	**E145**	**145434**
(XA-XAM)	737NG	34297
XA-XAX	DC-8	45432
XA-XLI	**E145**	**145456**
(XA-YAM)	737NG	34298
XA-YLI	**E145**	**145400**
XA-ZAM	**737NG**	**35120**
XA-ZLI	**E145**	**145420**
XB-GBP	B727	18252
XB-GRP	B737	20197
XB-IBV	B737	19772
XB-JSC	1-11	BAC.183
XB-KCE	**1-11**	**BAC.183**
XB-LCR	B737	19772
XB-MUO	1-11	005
XB-UJD	B727	20383
XC-BCO	DC-9	47087
XC-BDM	DC-9	47154
XC-CBD	B757	22690
XC-FAD	B727	18912
XC-FAY	B727	18908
XC-FAZ	B727	18909
XC-FPA	**B727**	**22413**
XC-IJI	B737	20127
XC-LJG	**B737**	**24361**
XC-LJZ	DC-9	45775
XC-MPF	**B727**	**22664**
XC-OPF	**B727**	**22676**
XC-PFA	B727	22413
XC-UJA	B727	19123
XC-UJA	B727	19123
XC-UJB	B727	19121
XC-UJB	**B737**	**24095**
XC-UJI	B737	20127
XC-UJL	B737	19772
XC-UJM	**B757**	**22690**

Burkina Faso

Reg	Type	Serial
XT-ABX	B707	18925
XT-ABZ	B707	18837

Reg	Type	Serial
XT-BBE	B727	18990
XT-BBF	B707	19521
XT-BBH	B707	18837
XT-BFA	**B727**	**22430**
XT-DMK	**B747**	**21316**
XT-DMS	B747	20009
XT-FCB	**IL76**	**1023408265**
XT-FDC	F.28	11173
XT-FZP	F.28	11163
XT-FZP	**F.28**	**11185**
XT-TIB	**F.28**	**11108**

Cambodia

Reg	Type	Serial
XU-	MD80	49395
XU-AKA	MD80	49952
XU-AKB	B757	27204
XU-JTA	SE210	145
XU-JTB	SE210	53
XU-RJK	B727	20989
XU-RKA	B737	22061
XU-RKB	B737	22674
XU-RKC	B727	22903
XU-RKF	B727	19494
"XU-RKG"	B727	19475
XU-RKH	B737	23105
XU-RKK	B737	23054
XU-U4B	B737	20450
XU-U4D	MD80	49390
XU-U4F	B737	22074
XU-001	F.28	11012
XU-100	L1011	193P-1156
XU-101	TU134	49890
XU-102	TU134	66550
XU-122	L1011	193B-1221
XU-123	B757	24528
XU-200	L1011	193C-1200
XU-211	YAK40	?
XU-222	L1011	193C-1225
XU-229	IL62	4445032
XU-234	B757	23651
XU-299	**IL62**	**4933456**
XU-300	L1011	193P-1129
XU-600	L1011	193A-1043
XU-700	L1011	193A-1055
XU-711	B737	20218
XU-756	B737	26319
XU-800	L1011	193A-1040
XU-888	F.28	11012
XU-900	L1011	193P 1070

Vietnam
(see also VN-)

Reg	Type	Serial
XV-NJA	SE210	10
XV-NJB	B727	19818
XV-NJC	B727	19819
XV-NJD	B707	17683

Laos
(see also RDPL-)

Reg	Type	Serial
XW-PNH	SE210	83

Myanmar

Reg	Type	Serial
XY-ADR	B727	19620
XY-ADU	F.28	11019
XY-ADV	F.28	11017
XY-ADW	**F.28**	**11114**
XY-AGA	F.28	11232
XY-AGB	F.28	11184
XY-AGC	F.100	11327
XY-AGD	A310	419
XY-AGE	A310	320
XY-AGF	F.100	11282

Afghanistan

Reg	Type	Serial
YA-AQS	B767	23745
YA-BAB	A300	180
YA-BAC	A300	190
YA-BAD	A300	177
YA-EAG	B747	21352
(YA-EAH)	B747	21054
(YA-F)	B727	21090
YA-FAK	B727	21370
YA-FAL	B727	21089
YA-FAM	B727	21088
YA-FAR	B727	19690
YA-FAS	B727	21388
YA-FAU	B727	20343
YA-FAW	B727	19619
YA-FAX	B727	22290
YA-FAY	B727	22289
YA-FAZ	B727	22288
YA-GAA	B727	18798
YA-GAB	B737	22650
YA-GAC	B737	22074
YA-GAD	B727	22702
YA-GAE	B737	23519
YA-GAF	B707	19177
YA-GAG	1-11	011
YA-HBA	B707	18060
YA-KAB	YAK40	9120417
YA-KAD	YAK40	9120517
YA-KAE	YAK40	9441037
YA-KAF	YAK40	9120617
YA-KAM	B767	21879
YA-KAM	YAK40	9441438
YA-LAS	DC-10	47888
YA-PAM	B707	19350
YA-TAP	TU154	87A-747
YA-TAR	TU154	87A-748
YA-TAT	TU154	84A-600
YA-YAA?	IL76	0013434018

Iraq

Reg	Type	Serial
YI-AEA	TRDNT	2125
YI-AEB	TRDNT	2127
YI-AEC	TRDNT	2129
YI-ACD?	TU134	9350916
YI-AEL	TU124	5351610?
YI-AEY	TU124	5351609?
YI-AGE	B707	20889
YI-AGF	B707	20890
YI-AGG	B707	20891
YI-AGH	B737	20892
YI-AGI	B737	20893
YI-AGJ	B737	21183
YI-AGK	B727	21197
YI-AGL	B727	21198
YI-AGM	B727	21199
YI-AGN	B747	21180
YI-AGO	B747	21181
YI-AGP	B747	22366
YI-AGQ	B727	22261
YI-AGR	B727	22262
YI-AGS	B727	22263
YI-AIK	IL76	073410292
YI-AIL	IL76	073410293
YI-AIM	IL76	073410320
YI-AIN	IL76	073410301
YI-AIO	IL76	073410315
YI-AIP	IL76	073410308
YI-AKO	IL76	093416506
YI-AKP	IL76	093421630
YI-AKQ	IL76	093421635
YI-AKS	IL76	093418543
YI-AKT	IL76	093418548
YI-AKU	IL76	093421637
YI-AKV	IL76	0013428831
YI-AKW	IL76	0013428839
YI-AKX	IL76	0013433990
YI-ALL	IL76	0013433984
YI-ALM	B747	22858
YI-ALO	IL76	0013433996
YI-ALP	IL76	0013433999
YI-ALQ	IL76	0023441189
YI-ALR	IL76	0023441200
YI-ALS	IL76	0033442247
YI-ALT	IL76	0033448393
YI-ALU	IL76	0033448398
YI-ALV	IL76	0033448409
YI-ALW	IL76	0033448416
YI-ALX	IL76	0043449455
YI-ANA	IL76	0063469055
YI-ANB	IL76	0063469071
YI-ANC	IL76	0063470102
YI-AND	IL76	0063471155
YI-ANE	IL76	0073474224
YI-ANF	IL76	0073475236
YI-ANG	IL76	0073476288
YI-ANH	IL76	0073476307
YI-ANI	IL76	0073481442
YI-ANJ	IL76	0083482481
YI-ANK	IL76	0083482495
YI-ANL	IL76	0083484542
YI-ANM	IL76	0093495886
YI-ANN	IL76	0093496894
YI-ANO	IL76	1003403087
YI-AOA	A310	318
YI-AOB	A310	276
YI-AOC	A310	267
YI-AOD	A310	331
YI-AOE	A310	278
YI-AOE	B727	21235
YI-AOF	B737	20451
YI-AOW	B727	20666
YI-AOX	B747	22298
YI-AOY	B727	21318
YI-AOZ	B727	20598

Vanuatu

Reg	Type	Serial
YJ-AV18	B737	28054
YJ-AV19	737NG	30734

Syria

Reg	Type	Serial
(YK-)	A320	0866
YK-AFA	SE210	184
YK-AFB	SE210	190
YK-AFC	SE210	183
YK-AFD	SE210	186
YK-AGA	B727	21203
YK-AGB	B727	21204
YK-AGC	B727	21205
YK-AGD	B727	22360
YK-AGE	B727	22361
YK-AGF	B727	22763
YK-AHA	B747	21174
YK-AHB	B747	21175
YK-AIA	TU154	85A-708
YK-AIB	TU154	85A-709
YK-AIC	TU154	85A-710
YK-AKA	A320	0886
YK-AKB	A320	0918
YK-AKC	A320	1032
YK-AKD	A320	1076
YK-AKE	A320	1085
YK-AKF	A320	1117
YK-AQA	YAK40	9341932
YK-AQB	YAK40	9530443
YK-AQC	YAK40	9531743?
YK-AQD	YAK40	9830158
YK-AQE	YAK40	9830258
YK-AQF	YAK40	9931859
YK-AQG	YAK40	9941959
YK-AQH	YAK40	9930160
YK-ATA	IL76	093421613
YK-ATB	IL76	093421619
YK-ATC	IL76	0013431911
YK-ATD	IL76	0013431915
YK-AYA	TU134	63992
YK-AYB	TU134	63994
YK-AYC	TU134	63989
YK-AYD	TU134	63990
YK-AYE	TU134	66187
YK-AYF	TU134	66190
YK-BBK	B737	29332
YK-DEL	B727	21179
YK-DGL	B727	21385
YK-DLC	L1011	293B-1242
YK-KEC	L1011	193C-1225
YK-KEQ	L1011	193C-1199
YK-KEU	L1011	193C-1226

Latvia

Reg	Type	Serial
YL-BAA	B737	22028
YL-BAA	DC-9	47016
YL-BAB	B737	22032
YL-BAC	B737	22034
YL-BAE	B727	18900
YL-BAF	B727	18440
YL-BAK	146	E1223
YL-BAL	146	E1224
YL-BAN	146	E1225
YL-BBA	B737	24646
YL-BBB	B737	24273
YL-BBC	A320	0142
YL-BBD	B737	29075
YL-BBE	B737	29073
YL-BBF	B737	24878
YL-BBG	B737	24919
YL-BBH	B737	24968
YL-BBI	B737	27454
YL-BBL	B737	29334
YL-BBM	B737	26680
YL-BBN	B737	26683
YL-BBP	B737	26688
YL-BBQ	B737	26691
YL-BCB	A320	0726
YL-KSA	AN7x	47098957
YL-KSB	AN7x	47136013
YL-LAA	TU154	78A-133
YL-LAB	TU154	81A-515
YL-LAC	B737	22034
YL-LAC	TU154	81A-516
YL-LAD	TU154	82A-556
YL-LAE	TU154	82A-546
YL-LAF	TU154	82A-539
YL-LAG	TU154	82A-524
YL-LAH	TU154	82A-558
YL-LAI	TU154	91A-895
YL-LAJ	IL76	083414432
YL-LAJ	IL76	1013409295
YL-LAK	IL76	0003424707
YL-LAL	IL76	0013433984
YL-LAR	IL76	1033416525
YL-LBA	TU134	61000
YL-LBB	TU134	63215
YL-LBC	TU134	63221
YL-LBD	TU134	63235
YL-LBE	TU134	63285
YL-LBF	TU134	63295
YL-LBG	TU134	63333
YL-LBH	TU134	63340
YL-LBI	TU134	63365
YL-LBJ	TU134	63410
YL-LBK	TU134	63425
YL-LBL	TU134	63515
YL-LBM	TU134	63536
YL-LBN	TU134	63187
YL-LBT	YAK42	4404018
YL-LBU	YAK42	3403018
YL-LBV	YAK42	4116664
YL-LBY	YAK42	4116677
YL-LBZ	YAK42	4116669
YL-LCA	A320	0333
YL-LCB	A320	0384
YL-LCC	A320	0310
YL-LCD	A320	0359
YL-LCE	A320	0311
YL-LCY	B767	24952
YL-LCZ	B767	25000
YL-RAF	AN7x	47095905
YL-TRA	YAK40	9510939
YL-TRB	YAK40	9721353
YL-TRN	YAK40	?

Nicaragua

(see also AN-)

Reg	Type	Serial
YN-BSQ	B727	18843
(YN-BWL)	B707	17675
YN-BWX	B727	18742
YN-BXW	B727	18284
YN-BYI	B707	18688
YN-CBT	TU154	89A-821
YN-CCN	B707	18054
YN-CDE	B707	19335
YN-CEV	IL76	1023411384
YN-CEW	IL76	1023410360
YN-CEX	IL76	1023411368

Romania

Reg	Type	Serial
(YR-)	B737	22354
YR-ABA	B707	20803
YR-ABB	B707	20804
YR-ABC	B707	20805
YR-ABD	B707	21651
YR-ABM	B707	19272
YR-ABN	B707	19379
YR-ASA	A318	2931
YR-ASB	A318	2955
YR-ASC	A318	3220
YR-ASD	A318	3225
YR-BAA	B737	27267
YR-BAB	B737	24785
YR-BAC	B737	23653
YR-BAD	B737	25429
YR-BCA	1-11	BAC.130
YR-BCB	1-11	BAC.156
YR-BCC	1-11	BAC.167
YR-BCD	1-11	BAC.159
YR-BCE	1-11	BAC.165
YR-BCF	1-11	BAC.168
YR-BCG	1-11	077
YR-BCH	1-11	BAC.161
YR-BCI	1-11	BAC.252
YR-BCJ	1-11	BAC.253
YR-BCK	1-11	BAC.254
YR-BCL	1-11	BAC.255
YR-BCM	1-11	BAC.256
YR-BCN	1-11	BAC.266
YR-BCO	1-11	BAC.272
YR-BCP	1-11	BAC.162
YR-BCR	1-11	BAC.267
YR-BEA	146	E2227
YR-BEB	146	E2220
YR-BGA	B737	27179
YR-BGB	B737	27180
YR-BGC	B737	27181
YR-BGD	B737	27182
YR-BGE	B737	27395
YR-BGF	737NG	28440
YR-BGG	737NG	28442
YR-BGH	737NG	28438
YR-BGI	737NG	28439
YR-BGT	B737	28083
YR-BGU	B737	27284
YR-BGX	B737	29326
YR-BGY	B737	28332
YR-BGZ	B737	24878
YR-BRA	1-11	BAC.401
YR-BRB	1-11	BAC.402
YR-BRC	1-11	BAC.403
YR-BRD	1-11	BAC.404
YR-BRE	1-11	BAC.405
YR-BRF	1-11	BAC.406
YR-BRG	1-11	BAC.407
YR-BRH	1-11	BAC.408
YR-BRI	1-11	BAC.409
YR-CJL	1-11	086
YR-FKA	F.100	11369
YR-FKB	F.100	11340
YR-GPA	CRJ	7137
(YR-GPB)	CRJ	7138
YR-GPC	CRJ	7139
(YR-GPD)	CRJ	7149
(YR-GPD)	CRJ	7170

YR-HRS	**1-11**	**BAC.259**
YR-IRA	IL62	21302
YR-IRB	IL62	21305
YR-IRC	IL62	51902
YR-IRD	IL62	4727546
YR-IRE	IL62	4831628
YR-JBA	1-11	BAC.234
YR-JBB	1-11	BAC.238
YR-JCA	B707	19530
YR-JCB	B707	20022
YR-JCC	B707	18948
YR-JTX	**B707**	**21049**
YR-LCA	**A310**	**636**
YR-LCB	A310	644
YR-LCC	A310	450
YR-MDJ	**MD80**	**48053**
YR-MDK	**MD80**	**49139**
YR-MDL	**MD80**	**48079**
YR-MDM	**MD80**	**49119**
YR-MDR	**MD80**	**48097**
YR-MDS	MD80	48098
YR-MIA	**1-11**	**BAC.260**
YR-TPA	TU154	76A-159
YR-TPB	TU154	76A-161
YR-TPC	TU154	76A-175
YR-TPD	TU154	77A-224
YR-TPE	TU154	77A-225
YR-TPF	TU154	77A-239
YR-TPG	TU154	78A-262
YR-TPH	TU154	78A-277
YR-TPI	TU154	79A-342
YR-TPJ	TU154	80A-408
YR-TPK	TU154	80A-415
YR-TPL	TU154	80A-428
YR-VGA	YAK40	9810757

El Salvador

YS-	**DC-9**	**45732**
(YS-)	B767	25221
YS-01C	1-11	BAC.108
YS-08C	B737	21599
YS-17C	1-11	093
YS-18C	1-11	BAC.106

Yugoslavia/Montenegro

YU-AGA	B707	17601
(YU-AGB)	DC-8	45883
YU-AGD	B707	19866
YU-AGE	B707	19284
YU-AGF	B707	19286
YU-AGG	B707	19285
YU-AGH	B707	17594
YU-AGI	B707	19210
YU-AGJ	B707	19411
YU-AGL	146	E2210
YU-AGM	146	E2220
YU-AHA	SE210	139
YU-AHB	SE210	135
YU-AHD	SE210	151
YU-AHE	SE210	194
YU-AHF	SE210	218
YU-AHG	SE210	233
YU-AHH	TU134	9350701
YU-AHI	TU134	9350705
YU-AHJ	DC-9	47239
YU-AHK	SE210	237
YU-AHL	DC-9	47425
YU-AHM	DC-9	47469
YU-AHN	DC-9	47470
YU-AHO	DC-9	47472
YU-AHP	DC-9	47473
YU-AHR	DC-9	47503
YU-AHS	TU134	0350921
YU-AHT	DC-9	47482
YU-AHU	DC-9	47532
YU-AHV	DC-9	47460
YU-AHW	DC-9	47530
YU-AHX	TU134	1351203
YU-AHY	TU134	1351204
YU-AHZ	TU134	1351205
YU-AJA	TU134	1351206
YU-AJB	DC-9	47392
YU-AJD	TU134	2351508
YU-AJE	SE210	209
YU-AJF	DC-9	47570
YU-AJG	SE210	191
YU-AJH	DC-9	47562
YU-AJI	DC-9	47563
YU-AJJ	**DC-9**	**47567**
YU-AJK	**DC-9**	**47568**
YU-AJL	DC-9	47571
YU-AJM	DC-9	47582
YU-AJN	DC-9	47579
YU-AJO	DC-9	47457
YU-AJP	DC-9	47408
YU-AJR	DC-9	47649
YU-AJS	TU134	63.48370
YU-AJT	DC-9	47697
YU-AJU	DC-9	47754
YU-AJV	TU134	60035
YU-AJW	TU134	60321
YU-AJX	DC-9	47172
YU-AJY	DC-9	47172
YU-AJZ	MD80	48046
YU-AKA	B727	20930
YU-AKB	B727	20931
YU-AKD	B727	21040
YU-AKE	B727	21037
YU-AKF	B727	21038
YU-AKG	B727	21039
YU-AKH	B727	21080
YU-AKI	B727	22393
YU-AKJ	B727	22394
YU-AKK	B727	22665
YU-AKL	B727	22666
YU-AKM	B727	22702
YU-AKN	1-11	BAC.266
YU-AKO	B727	20951
YU-AKP	**YAK40**	**9120717**
YU-AKR	B727	20549
YU-AKT	**YAK40**	**9222020**
YU-AKV	**YAK40**	**9630849**
YU-AKW	**YAK40**	**9731255**
YU-AMA	DC-10	46981
YU-AMB	DC-10	46988
YU-AMC	DC-10	46578
YU-AMD	DC-10	46554
YU-AMI	**IL76**	**0093499982**
YU-AMJ	**IL76**	**1013409303**
YU-ANA	MD80	48047
YU-ANB	MD80	48048
YU-ANC	MD80	48087
YU-AND	**B737**	**23329**
YU-ANE	TU134	63165
YU-ANF	**B737**	**23330**
YU-ANG	MD80	49379
YU-ANH	**B737**	**23415**
YU-ANI	**B737**	**23416**
YU-ANJ	**B737**	**23714**
YU-ANK	**B737**	**23715**
YU-ANL	**B737**	**23716**
YU-ANM	1-11	BAC.266
YU-ANN	1-11	BAC.272
YU-ANO	MD80	49440
YU-ANP	**B737**	**23912**
YU-ANR	1-11	BAC.401
YU-ANS	1-11	BAC.403
YU-ANT	1-11	BAC.404
YU-ANU	B737	24139
YU-ANV	**B737**	**24140**
YU-ANW	**B737**	**24141**
YU-ANX	B737	20227
YU-ANY	B737	20277
YU-ANZ	B737	20956
YU-AOA	A320	0043
YU-AOB	A320	0028
YU-AOD	A320	0113
YU-AOE	A320	0114
YU-AOF	B737	22596
YU-AOG	B737	22601
YU-AOH	F.28	11184
YU-AOI	F.28	11176
YU-AOJ	**F.28**	**11187**
YU-AOK	**F.100**	**11272**
YU-AOL	F.100	11268
YU-AOM	**F.100**	**11321**
YU-AON	**B737**	**24208**
YU-AOO	B737	24070
YU-AOP	**F.100**	**11332**
(YU-AOQ)	B737	24165
YU-AOR	**B737**	**24550**
YU-AOS	**B737**	**24551**
YU-AOT	**F.100**	**11350**

Venezuela

YV-	**DC-9**	**48141**
YV-	DC-9	47249
YV-	**DC-9**	**47282**
YV-	DC-9	47343
YV-	**DC-9**	**47479**
YV-	**DC-9**	**48119**
YV-	**DC-9**	**48147**
YV-01C	DC-9	47309
YV-01C	MD80	49822
YV-02C	DC-9	47002
YV-02C	MD80	48067
YV-03C	DC-9	47000
YV-04C	MD80	49103
YV-05C	MD80	49393
YV-06C	MD80	49394
YV-10C	**DC-9**	**47713**
YV-11C	**DC-9**	**47306**
YV-12C	**DC-9**	**47360**
YV-13C	DC-9	47301
YV-14C	DC-9	47738
YV-15C	**DC-9**	**47771**
(YV-17C)	B727	20548
YV-18C	B727	21984
YV-18C	DC-9	47001
YV-19C	DC-9	47394
YV-20C	DC-9	47705
YV-21C	DC-9	47719
YV-22C	DC-9	47703
YV-23C	DC-9	47720
YV-24C	DC-9	47727
YV-25C	DC-9	47721
YV-32C	DC-9	47770
YV-33C	DC-9	47782
YV-35C	DC-9	47712
YV-36C	MD80	49395
YV-37C	DC-9	47752
YV-38C	MD80	49567
YV-39C	MD80	49659
YV-40C	B727	21632
YV-40C	DC-9	47783
YV-41C	B727	21968
YV-41C	DC-9	47784
YV-42C	**DC-9**	**47656**
YV-42C	MD80	49793
YV-43C	**DC-9**	**47695**
YV-43C	MD80	49788
YV-44C	**DC-9**	**47694**
YV-44C	MD80	53046
YV-46C	DC-9	47535
YV-47C	**DC-9**	**47490**
YV-48C	**DC-9**	**45847**
YV-49C	DC-9	47539
YV-50C	DC-10	46945
YV-51C	DC-10	46944
YV-51C	DC-9	47006
YV-52C	B737	23161
YV-52C	DC-9	47048
YV-57C	DC-9	47060
YV-60C	DC-10	47867
YV-65C	DC-9	45723
YV-66C	DC-9	45710
YV-67C	DC-9	47025
YV-68C	DC-9	47031
YV-69C	DC-10	46944
YV-69C	DC-9	47309
YV-70C	DC-9	47103
YV-71C	DC-9	47104
YV-72C	DC-9	47105
YV-73C	DC-9	47106
YV-74C	B727	22043
YV-74C	B737	20909
YV-75C	B727	22044
YV-76C	B727	20394
YV-77C	B727	21457
YV-77C	B757	23227
YV-78C	B757	22185
YV-79C	B727	18800
YV-79C	**B737**	**20908**
YV-80C	B727	18326
YV-80C	DC-9	47692
YV-81C	B727	18327
YV-82C	B727	18325
YV-82C	DC-9	47121
YV-85C	DC-9	47683
YV-87C	B727	18853
YV-87C	DC-9	47685
YV-88C	B727	18855
YV-89C	B727	18851
YV-90C	B727	18856
YV-90C	B727	19815
YV-90C	DC-9	47665
YV-91C	B727	19165
YV-92C	B727	20724
YV-93C	B727	20876
YV-94C	B727	20877
YV-95C	B727	20878
YV-96C	B727	20727
YV-97C	B727	20885
YV-99C	B737	24463
YV-125C	B727	20596
YV-125C	DC-8	46042
YV-126C	B727	20594
YV-126C	DC-8	46063
YV-127C	B727	20597
YV-127C	DC-8	45377
YV-128C	B727	20605
YV-128C	DC-8	45381
YV-128C	DC-8	45861
YV-129C	B727	20599
YV-129C	DC-8	45616
YV-130C	DC-8	46052
YV-131C	B727	21823
YV-131C	DC-8	45613
YV-132C	B727	22604
YV-132C	DC-8	45614
YV-133C	DC-10	46555
YV-134C	DC-10	46556
YV-135C	DC-10	46971
YV-136C	DC-10	46972
YV-136T	**DC-9**	**47738**
YV-137C	DC-10	46982
YV-138C	DC-10	46557
YV-139C	DC-10	46953
YV-139C	DC-9	47476
(YV-139C)	DC-10	46952
YV-145C	CV880	22-00-64
YV-156T	B727	20114
(YV-158C)	MD80	49103
(YV-159C)	MD80	49104
YV-160C	A300	053
YV-161C	A300	075
YV-1663	**DC-9**	**48144**
YV-215C	B737	21231
YV-216C	B737	21774
YV-231T	DC-9	47133
YV-243T	**DC-9**	**48120**
YV-392C	DC-8	45603
YV-405C	B737	19771
YV-445C	DC-8	45663
YV-447C	DC-8	45684
YV-448C	B727	18270
YV-458C	DC-9	47527
YV-459C	DC-9	47548
YV-460C	DC-8	45640
YV-461C	DC-8	45878
YV-462C	B727	20303
YV-463C	B727	20248
YV-464C	B727	20392
YV-465C	B727	19992
YV-466C	B727	19973
YV-480C	B727	18270

Reg	Type	Serial
YV-495C	DC-9	47047
YV-496C	DC-9	47653
YV-497C	DC-9	47237
YV-499C	DC-8	45686
YV-504C	DC-8	45663
YV-505C	DC-8	45410
YV-594C	YAK40	9841159
YV-598C	YAK40	9641450
YV-599C	YAK40	9731754
YV-608C	B727	20394
YV-612C	DC-9	45710
YV-613C	DC-9	47104
YV-614C	DC-9	47105
YV-643C	B737	21970
YV-671C	B707	19435
YV-703C	DC-9	45798
(YV-704C)	DC-9	45799
YV-705C	DC-9	45867
YV-706C	DC-9	45875
YV-707C	DC-9	47272
YV-708C	DC-9	45864
YV-709C	DC-9	47005
YV-710C	DC-9	47271
YV-714C	DC-9	47007
YV-715C	DC-9	47323
YV-716C	DC-9	47358
YV-717C	DC-9	47320
YV-718C	DC-9	47187
YV-719C	DC-9	47157
YV-720C	DC-9	45837
YV-728C	B727	18270
YV-760C	DC-9	47098
YV-762C	B727	22268
YV-763C	B727	18327
YV-764C	DC-9	47331
YV-765C	B727	18855
YV-766C	DC-9	47679
YV-767C	DC-9	47745
YV-768C	B727	21457
YV-770C	DC-9	47330
YV-810C	DC-8	45410
YV-813C	B727	19393
YV-815C	DC-9	45875
YV-816C	DC-9	47272
YV-817C	DC-9	47036
YV-818C	DC-9	47399
YV-819C	DC-9	47401
YV-820C	DC-9	47743
YV-821C	B727	19534
YV-822C	B727	22270
YV-823C	B727	22269
YV-830C	DC-9	45699
(YV-837C)	B727	18853
YV-838C	B727	19165
YV-839C	B727	18325
YV-840C	B727	19815
YV-843C	B727	20876
YV-844C	B727	22270
YV-845C	B727	19534
YV-846C	B727	19167
YV-848C	B727	20114
YV-852C	DC-9	45745
YV-855C	B727	20905
YV-856C	B727	20614
YV-857C	DC-9	45776
YV-880C	B727	20665
YV-881C	DC-9	45789
YV-905C	B727	20992
YV-907C	B727	20895
YV-909C	B727	19561
YV-910C	B727	19979
YV-917C	B737	21665
YV-937C	MD80	49567
YV-977C	DC-9	45745
(YV-1006C)	B767	25287
YV-1040C	DC-10	47867
YV-1052C	DC-10	46944
YV-1052C	YAK40	?
YV-1052CP	YAK40	9631548
YV-1056C	B727	22269
YV-1070CP	YAK40	9412032
YV-1072C	YAK40	9841059
YV-1072C	YAK40	?

Reg	Type	Serial
YV-1100CP	YAK40	9441137
YV-1100CP	YAK40	?
YV-1121C	DC-9	47281
YV-1122C	DC-9	47219
YV-1155C	B737	21776
YV-1174C	B727	21968
YV-1178C	B737	25118
YV-1382	DC-9	45745
YV-C-AAA	DC-9	47309
YV-C-ANP	DC-9	47000
YV-C-ANV	DC-9	47002
YV-C-AVB	DC-9	45703
YV-C-AVC	DC-9	47048
YV-C-AVD	DC-9	47243
YV-C-AVI	SE210	20
YV-C-AVM	DC-9	47056
YV-C-AVR	DC-9	47060
YV-C-LEV	DC-9	47006
YV-C-VIA	CV880	22-7-1-53
YV-C-VIA	DC-8	46042
YV-C-VIB	CV880	22-7-4-56
YV-C-VIB	DC-8	46063
YV-C-VIC	CV880	22-00-37M
YV-C-VIC	DC-8	45879
YV-C-VID	DC-8	45768
YV-C-VIE	DC-8	45377
YV-C-VIF	DC-8	45381
YV-C-VIG	DC-8	45616
YV-C-VIM	DC-8	45816
YV-C-VIN	DC-8	46052
YV	DC-9	48155
YV111T	DC-9	48154
YV114T	DC-9	48139
YV115T	DC-9	48138
YV116T	DC-9	45867
YV117T	DC-9	47272
YV118T	DC-9	47005
YV119T	DC-9	47271
YV122T	DC-9	45875
YV130T	MD80	49822
YV131T	MD80	48067
YV132T	MD80	49103
YV133T	MD80	49393
YV134T	MD80	49394
YV135T	DC-9	47712
YV141T	DC-9	47705
YV143T	DC-9	47539
YV154T	B727	20895
YV155T	B727	20992
YV169T	B737	21776
YV170T	B737	21231
YV174T	B727	21968
YV187T	B737	22964
YV241T	DC-9	48118
YV253T	MD80	49392
YV268T	B737	23099
YV286T	DC-9	47473
YV287T	B727	22728
YV295T	B737	21717
YV296T	B737	22024
YV302T	B737	23087
YV1004	A340	031
YV1007	B737	23949
YV1120	DC-9	47705
YV1121	DC-9	47719
YV1122	DC-9	47703
YV1123	DC-9	47727
YV1124	DC-9	47721
YV1125	DC-9	47770
YV1126	DC-9	47782
YV1127	DC-9	47752
YV1327	MD80	49103
YV1360	B737	23055
YV1361	B737	22826
YV1381	B737	21774
YV1404	YAK40	9441137
YV1879	DC-9	48139
YV1921	DC-9	48154
YV1922	DC-9	48138
YV2242	B757	24119
YV2243	B757	24118
YV2309	B727	20114

Zimbabwe
(see also VP-Y)

Reg	Type	Serial
Z-ALT	DC-10	47818
Z-ARL	DC-10	47907
Z-AVT	DC-10	46590
Z-NAL	B737	22408
Z-WKR	B707	18819
Z-WKS	B707	18923
Z-WKT	B707	18929
Z-WKU	B707	18930
Z-WKV	B707	18927
Z-WMJ	DC-8	45821
Z-WPA	B737	23677
Z-WPB	B737	23678
Z-WPC	B737	23679
Z-WPD	146	E2065
Z-WPE	B767	24713
Z-WPF	B767	24867
Z-WSB	DC-8	45805
Z-WST	B707	18747
Z-WTV	IL76	073410279
Z-WYY	B727	18370
Z-WZL	DC-8	45975
Z-YNL	B707	18162
Z-YNN	B707	18244

Albania

Reg	Type	Serial
ZA-ARB	MD80	48095
ZA-ARC	F.100	11268
ZA-ARD	MD80	49104
ZA-AVA	F.100	11272
ZA-MAK	146	E1085
ZA-MAL	146	E2054
ZA-MEV	146	E3197

New Zealand

Reg	Type	Serial
ZK-CZR	B737	24460
ZK-CZS	B737	24030
ZK-CZU	B737	27267
ZK-FDM	B737	25016
ZK-FRE	B737	28742
(ZK-ILF)	B747	24896
ZK-JJD	B737	21732
ZK-JNA	B737	23490
ZK-JNB	B737	23491
ZK-JNC	B737	24296
ZK-JND	B737	24297
ZK-JNE	B737	25119
ZK-JNF	B737	23486
ZK-JNG	B737	23478
ZK-JNH	B737	23488
ZK-JNN	B737	24295
ZK-JNO	B737	24298
(ZK-JTP)	B737	24435
ZK-JTP	B737	24441
ZK-JTQ	B737	24442
ZK-JTR	B737	24439
ZK-NAA	B737	22638
ZK-NAB	B737	22364
ZK-NAC	B737	19929
ZK-NAD	B737	19930
ZK-NAD	B737	23040
ZK-NAE	B737	19931
ZK-NAF	B737	22038
ZK-NAH	B737	23039
ZK-NAI	B737	22365
ZK-NAJ	B737	20344
ZK-NAK	B737	20156
ZK-NAL	B737	20158
ZK-NAL	B737	21138
ZK-NAM	B737	19758
ZK-NAP	B737	21130
ZK-NAQ	B737	21131
ZK-NAQ	B737	22022
ZK-NAR	B737	21645
ZK-NAS	B737	22088
(ZK-NAT)	B737	22657
ZK-NAT	B737	23470

Reg	Type	Serial
ZK-NAU	B737	23471
ZK-NAV	B737	23472
ZK-NAW	B737	23473
ZK-NAX	B737	23474
ZK-NAY	B737	23475
ZK-NAZ	B737	20913
ZK-NBA	B767	23326
ZK-NBB	B767	23327
ZK-NBC	B767	23328
ZK-NBD	B767	23058
ZK-NBE	B767	24150
ZK-NBF	B767	22681
ZK-NBH	B767	22682
ZK-NBI	B767	23072
ZK-NBJ	B767	23250
ZK-NBS	B747	24386
ZK-NBT	B747	24855
ZK-NBU	B747	25605
ZK-NBV	B747	26910
ZK-NBW	B747	29375
ZK-NCE	B767	24875
ZK-NCF	B767	24876
ZK-NCG	B767	26912
ZK-NCH	B767	26264
ZK-NCI	B767	26913
ZK-NCJ	B767	26915
ZK-NCK	B767	26971
ZK-NCL	B767	28745
ZK-NCM	B767	26389
ZK-NCN	B767	29388
ZK-NCO	B767	30586
(ZK-NCP)	B767	28206
ZK-NEA	B737	19013
ZK-NEB	B737	19015
ZK-NED	B737	19770
ZK-NEE	B737	20195
ZK-NEF	B737	22575
ZK-NGA	B737	28873
ZK-NGB	B737	29140
ZK-NGC	B737	29189
ZK-NGD	B737	28732
ZK-NGE	B737	28733
ZK-NGF	B737	28734
ZK-NGG	B737	25606
ZK-NGH	B737	25607
ZK-NGI	B737	25608
ZK-NGJ	B737	25609
ZK-NGK	B737	26318
ZK NGM	B737	28085
(ZK-NGN)	B737	28738
ZK-NGN	B737	29072
(ZK-NGO)	B737	27635
ZK-NGO	B737	28548
ZK-NQC	B737	22994
ZK-NZA	146	E2116
ZK-NZA	DC-8	45750
ZK-NZB	146	E2127
ZK-NZB	DC-8	45751
ZK-NZC	146	E2119
ZK-NZC	DC-8	45752
ZK-NZD	DC-8	45932
(ZK-NZE)	B747	24386
ZK-NZE	DC-8	45985
ZK-NZF	146	E3134
ZK-NZF	DC-8	45303
ZK-NZG	146	E3135
ZK-NZG	DC-8	45301
ZK-NZH	146	E3137
ZK-NZI	146	E3143
ZK-NZJ	146	E3147
ZK-NZK	146	E3190
ZK-NZL	146	E3175
ZK-NZL	DC-10	47846
ZK-NZM	146	E3173
ZK-NZM	DC-10	47847
ZK-NZN	146	E3177
ZK-NZN	DC-10	47848
ZK-NZP	DC-10	46910
ZK-NZQ	DC-10	46911
ZK-NZR	DC-10	47849
ZK-NZS	DC-10	46950
ZK-NZT	DC-10	46950
ZK-NZV	B747	22722

Reg	Type	c/n	Reg	Type	c/n	Reg	Type	c/n	Reg	Type	c/n
ZK-NZW	B747	22723	ZS-DYN	B727	18893	ZS-NUG	1-11	BAC.237	ZS-PBI	B767	26200
ZK-NZX	B747	22724	ZS-DYO	B727	18894	ZS-NUH	1-11	BAC.257	ZS-PDL	B727	20466
ZK-NZY	B747	22725	ZS-DYP	B727	18895	ZS-NUI	1-11	BAC.258	ZS-PGL	DC-9	47643
ZK-NZZ	B747	22791	ZS-DYR	B727	18896	ZS-NUJ	1-11	BAC.261	(ZS-PIL)	B727	21291
ZK-OJA	A320	2085	ZS-EKV	B707	19133	(ZS-NVH)	B727	18443	(ZS-PIU)	B737	21729
ZK-OJB	A320	2090	ZS-EKW	B727	19318	ZS-NVR	B727	20673	ZS-PIU	B737	21765
ZK-OJC	A320	2112	ZS-EKX	B727	19319	ZS-NWA	B727	20757	(ZS-PIV)	B737	21765
ZK-OJD	A320	2130	ZS-EUW	B707	19705	ZS-NYX	B727	19811	ZS-PIV	B737	22071
ZK-OJE	A320	2148	ZS-EUX	B707	19706	ZS-NYY	B727	19251	ZS-PIW	B737	22408
ZK-OJF	A320	2153	(ZS-EUY)	B737	19707	ZS-NYZ	1-11	BAC.132	(ZS-PIW)	B737	25418
ZK-OJG	A320	2173	(ZS-EUZ)	B737	19708	ZS-NZP	A320	0203	(ZS-PIY)	B737	25418
ZK-OJH	A320	2257	(ZS-FKG)	B707	20230	ZS-NZR	A320	0220	(ZS-PJH)	B747	22872
ZK-OJI	A320	2297	(ZS-FKH)	B737	20229	ZS-NZS	A320	0221	(ZS-PJI)	B747	21351
ZK-OJJ	A320	2403	(ZS-FKT)	B707	20110	ZS-NZT	A320	0222	(ZS-PJI)	B747	23048
ZK-OJK	A320	2445	ZS-GAG	DC-9	47190	ZS-NZV	B727	20792	ZS-PKU	B737	25249
ZK-OJL	A320	2500	ZS-GAL	DC-9	47601	ZS-OAA	B737	26960	ZS-PKV	B737	25418
ZK-OJM	A320	2533	ZS-GAR	DC-9	47132	ZS-OAF	1-11	BAC.114	ZS-PNJ	F.28	11173
ZK-OJN	A320	2594	ZS-GAS	DC-10	47832	ZS-OAF	B737	25116	ZS-PNL	F.28	11136
ZK-OJO	A320	2663	ZS-GAT	DC-9	47797	ZS-OAG	1-11	066	ZS-PNU	B737	21729
ZK-OKA	B777	29404	ZS-GAU	DC-9	47798	ZS-OAH	1-11	BAC.115	ZS-POL	DC-8	46110
ZK-OKB	B777	34376	ZS-GAV	F.28	11156	ZS-OAO	B727	21978	ZS-PRD	DC-8	46000
ZK-OKC	B777	34377	ZS-GAV	F.28	11191	ZS-OAZ	B727	21851	ZS-PUI	B737	22890
ZK-OKD	B777	29401	ZS-GAW	DC-10	46983	ZS-OBF	MD80	48019	ZS-PUL	146	E2064
ZK-OKE	B777	32712	ZS-IAC	B727	21247	ZS-OBG	MD80	48020	ZS-PUM	146	E2059
ZK-OKF	B777	34378	ZS-IJE	B727	18443	ZS-OBH	MD80	48059	ZS-PUZ	146	E2074
ZK-OKG	B777	29403	ZS-IJF	B727	18444	ZS-OBI	MD80	48016	ZS-PVU	B737	21959
ZK-OKH	B777	34379	ZS-IJG	B727	18433	ZS-OBJ	MD80	48018	ZS-PVX	B727	22825
ZK-PBA	737NG	33796	ZS-IJH	B727	19813	ZS-OBK	MD80	49115	ZS-RSA	737NG	32627
ZK-PBB	737NG	33797	ZS-IJI	B707	19517	ZS-OBL	MD80	49164	ZS-SAA	B707	17928
ZK-PBC	737NG	33017	ZS-IJJ	B737	20591	ZS-OBM	B727	22044	ZS-SAA	B747	22170
ZK-PBD	737NG	33996	ZS-IJK	B737	19176	ZS-OBO	B727	21623	ZS-SAB	B707	17929
ZK-PBF	737NG	33799	ZS-IJN	F.28	11118	ZS-ODO	B727	20843	(ZS-SAB)	B747	22171
ZK-PLU	B737	24094	ZS-IJS	B727	21260	(ZS-ODZ)	B727	19813	ZS-SAC	B707	17930
ZK-POL	B737	22575	ZS-IOC	D0328	3219	ZS-OEZ	B737	22118	ZS-SAC	B747	23031
ZK-SHH	146	E1005	(ZS-IRS)	B727	21519	(ZS-OGB)	CRJ	7351	ZS-SAD	B707	18891
ZK-SJB	B737	28868	ZS-JAL	F.28	11151	ZS-OGH	CRJ	7351	ZS-SAE	B707	19133
ZK-SJC	B737	28738	ZS-JAP	F.28	11143	ZS-OGN	B727	20637	ZS-SAF	B707	19706
ZK-SJE	B737	27635	ZS-JAS	F.28	11225	ZS-OIV	B737	22634	ZS-SAG	B707	20110
ZK-SLA	B737	23653	ZS-JAV	F.28	11161	ZS-OKB	B737	23477	ZS-SAH	B707	20230
ZK-SUH	B747	24896	ZS-JAV	F.28	11183	ZS-OKC	B737	23484	ZS-SAI	B707	20283
ZK-SUI	B747	24957	ZS-JEN	F.28	11204	ZS-OKD	B737	21803	ZS-SAJ	B747	23027
ZK-SUJ	B747	27602	ZS-JES	F.28	11236	ZS-OKE	B737	21807	ZS-SAK	B747	28468
ZK-TGA	B747	21782	ZS-LSF	B707	20283	ZS-OKF	B737	21686	ZS-SAL	B747	20237
ZK-TLA	B737	23383	ZS-LSH	B707	19577	ZS-OKG	B737	23483	ZS-SAM	B747	20238
ZK-TLB	B737	24209	(ZS-LSI)	B707	19575	ZS-OKH	B737	23479	ZS-SAN	B747	20239
ZK-TLC	B737	23705	ZS-LSI/1415	B707	19522	ZS-OKI	B737	23489	ZS-SAO	B747	20556
ZK-TLD	B737	23706	(ZS-LSJ)	B707	19723	ZS-OKJ	B737	23487	ZS-SAP	B747	20557
			(ZS-LSK)	B707	19917	ZS-OKK	B737	23485	ZS-SAR	B747	22170
			ZS-LSL	B707	19706	ZS-OKK	B747	23244	ZS-SAS	B747	22171
Paraguay			ZS-MRJ	DC-9	47466	ZS-OLA	B737	23163	ZS-SAT	B747	22970
			ZS-NCA	146	E1002	ZS-OLB	B737	23167	ZS-SAU	B747	22971
ZP-CAB	B737	21130	ZS-NCB	146	E2148	ZS-OLC	B737	22119	ZS-SAV	B747	24976
ZP-CAC	B737	21518	ZS-NGB	F.28	11219	ZS-OLN	DC-9	47218	ZS-SAW	B747	25152
ZP-CCE	B707	18841	ZS-NLJ	B707	19964	ZS-OMG	B737	22140	ZS-SAX	B747	26637
ZP-CCF	B707	18957	ZS-NLN	D737	21686	ZS-OOC	B727	22856	ZS-SAY	B747	26638
ZP-CCG	B707	19264	ZS-NMC	CRJ	7225	ZS-OOD	B737	22857	ZS-SAZ	B747	29119
ZP-CCH	DC-8	46115	ZS-NMD	CRJ	7233	ZS-OOS	B727	21190	ZS-SBA	B727	18892
ZP-CCR	DC-8	46037	ZS-NME	CRJ	7240	ZS-OPC	B727	20382	ZS-SBA	B737	26070
ZP-CCY	146	E3149	ZS-NMI	CRJ	7153	ZS-OPS	F.28	11241	ZS-SBB	B727	18893
			ZS-NMJ	CRJ	7161	ZS-OPT	B727	20183	ZS-SBC	B727	18894
			ZS-NMK	CRJ	7198	ZS-OPU	MD80	48021	ZS-SBD	B727	18895
South Africa			ZS-NML	CRJ	7201	ZS-OPX	MD80	53012	ZS-SBE	B727	18896
			ZS-NMM	CRJ	7234	ZS-OPZ	MD80	49617	ZS-SBF	B727	19318
ZS-	B727	22165	ZS-NMN	CRJ	7237	ZS-OSI	DC-8	46098	ZS-SBG	B727	19319
(ZS-)	B737	20590	ZS-NMS	1-11	BAC.186	ZS-OTF	B737	25305	ZS-SBH	B727	20475
ZS-	B767	21878	ZS-NMT	1-11	BAC.201	ZS-OTG	B737	25840	ZS-SBI	B727	20476
ZS-	DC-9	47730	ZS-NMW	B727	18849	ZS-OTH	B737	25841	ZS-SBJ	B747	24177
ZS-	DC-9	48111	ZS-NMX	B727	18426	(ZS-OTJ)	B737	25849	ZS-SBK	B747	28959
ZS-	MD80	49165	ZS-NMY	B727	18447	ZS-OTM	E145	145485	ZS-SBL	B737	19707
ZS-	MD80	49831	ZS-NMZ	B727	19129	ZS-OTN	E145	145491	ZS-SBM	B737	19708
(ZS-AGR)	B737	20197	ZS-NNG	B737	21793	(ZS-OTW)	B747	23028	ZS-SBN	B737	20229
ZS-ANA	B737	23790	ZS-NNH	B737	21797	ZS-OUV	E145	145493	ZS-SBO	B737	20329
ZS-ANX	DC-9	45799	ZS-NNM	1-11	BAC.108	ZS-OVE	B737	23006	ZS-SBP	B737	20330
ZS-BAL	F.28	11190	ZS-NNN	DC-9	47516	ZS-OVF	B737	23008	ZS-SBR	B737	20331
ZS-CKC	B707	17928	ZS-NOU	B727	21113	ZS-OVG	B737	21800	ZS-SBS	B747	28960
ZS-CKD	B707	17929	ZS-NOV	B727	21114	ZS-OVO	B737	20205	ZS-SDA	A300	032
ZS-CKE	B707	17930	ZS-NPX	B727	19131	ZS-OWM	B737	21711	ZS-SDB	A300	037
ZS-DBH	DC-9	47384	(ZS-NPZ)	DC-10	46578	(ZS-OZH)	DC-10	45802	ZS-SDC	A300	039
ZS-DPE	B727	22643	ZS-NRA	DC-9	47430	ZS-OZP	B727	20572	ZS-SDD	A300	040
ZS-DPF	B727	22644	ZS-NRB	DC-9	47468	ZS-OZR	B727	20573	ZS-SDE	A300	138
ZS-DRF	F.28	11239	ZS-NRC	DC-9	47090	ZS-OZV	DC-8	45986	ZS-SDF	A300	192
ZS-DYL	B707	18891	ZS-NRD	DC-9	47037	ZS-PAE	DC-8	46012	ZS-SDG	A300	212
ZS-DYM	B727	18892	ZS-NSA	B727	19130	ZS-PAK	DC-9	47368	ZS-SDH	A300	222

ZS-SDI	A300	269	
ZS-SFD	**A319**	**2268**	
ZS-SFE	**A319**	**2281**	
ZS-SFF	**A319**	**2308**	
ZS-SFG	**A319**	**2326**	
ZS-SFH	**A319**	**2355**	
ZS-SFI	**A319**	**2375**	
ZS-SFJ	**A319**	**2379**	
ZS-SFK	**A319**	**2418**	
ZS-SFL	**A319**	**2438**	
ZS-SFM	**A319**	**2469**	
ZS-SFN	**A319**	**2501**	
ZS-SHA	A320	0243	
ZS-SHB	A320	0249	
ZS-SHC	A320	0250	
ZS-SHD	A320	0251	
ZS-SHE	A320	0334	
ZS-SHF	A320	0335	
ZS-SHG	A320	0440	
ZS-SIA	B737	22580	
ZS-SIB	B737	22581	
ZS-SIC	**B737**	**22582**	
ZS-SID	**B737**	**22583**	
ZS-SIE	B737	22584	
ZS-SIF	**B737**	**22585**	
ZS-SIG	**B737**	**22586**	
ZS-SIH	**B737**	**22587**	
ZS-SII	B737	22588	
ZS-SIJ	B737	22589	
ZS-SIK	**B737**	**22590**	
ZS-SIL	**B737**	**22591**	
ZS-SIM	**B737**	**22828**	
(ZS-SIN)	B707	20283	
ZS-SIN	**B737**	**21802**	
(ZS-SIO)	B707	19706	
ZS-SIO	**B737**	**21792**	
ZS-SIP	**B737**	**22116**	
ZS-SIR	B737	21805	
ZS-SIS	B737	21801	
ZS-SIT	B737	21790	
ZS-SIU	B737	22026	
ZS-SIV	B737	22029	
ZS-SIW	B737	22031	
ZS-SJA	**737NG**	**29248**	
ZS-SJB	**737NG**	**29249**	
ZS-SJC	**737NG**	**28828**	
ZS-SJD	**737NG**	**28829**	
ZS-SJE	**737NG**	**28830**	
ZS-SJF	**737NG**	**30006**	
ZS-SJG	**737NG**	**32353**	
ZS-SJH	**737NG**	**32354**	
ZS-SJI	**737NG**	**30007**	
ZS-SJJ	**737NG**	**30567**	
ZS-SJK	**737NG**	**32355**	
ZS-SJL	**737NG**	**32356**	
ZS-SJM	**737NG**	**30476**	
ZS-SJN	**737NG**	**30569**	
ZS-SJO	**737NG**	**32357**	
ZS-SJP	**737NG**	**32358**	
ZS-SJR	**737NG**	**32631**	
ZS-SJS	**737NG**	**32632**	
ZS-SJT	**737NG**	**32633**	
ZS-SJU	**737NG**	**32634**	
ZS-SJV	**737NG**	**32635**	
ZS-SJW	**E145**	**145423**	
ZS-SJX	**E145**	**145428**	
ZS-SKA	B747	22996	
ZS-SKB	B747	22995	
ZS-SLA	**A340**	**008**	
ZS-SLB	**A340**	**011**	
ZS-SLC	**A340**	**018**	
ZS-SLD	**A340**	**019**	
ZS-SLE	**A340**	**021**	
ZS-SLF	**A340**	**006**	
ZS-SNA	**A340**	**410**	
ZS-SNB	**A340**	**417**	
ZS-SNC	**A340**	**426**	
ZS-SND	**A340**	**531**	
ZS-SNE	**A340**	**534**	
ZS-SNF	**A340**	**547**	
ZS-SNG	**A340**	**557**	
ZS-SNH	**A340**	**626**	
ZS-SNI	**A340**	**630**	

ZS-SPA	B747	21132	
ZS-SPB	B747	21133	
ZS-SPC	B747	21134	
ZS-SPD	B747	21253	
ZS-SPE	B747	21254	
ZS-SPF	B747	21263	
ZS-SRA	B767	26471	
ZS-SRB	B767	23179	
ZS-SRC	B767	23180	
ZS-STO	B737	20197	
ZS-SXA	**A340**	**544**	
ZS-SXB	**A340**	**582**	
ZS-SXC	**A340**	**590**	
ZS-SXD	**A340**	**643**	
ZS-SXE	**A340**	**646**	
ZS-SXF	**A340**	**651**	
ZS-TGL	**DC-9**	**47102**	
ZS-TGR	**DC-9**	**47672**	
(ZS-TIC)	MD80	49233	
(ZS-TOC)	MD80	49234	
ZS-TRA	**B727**	**20660**	
(ZS-TRA)	B737	20197	
ZS-TRC	B737	21186	
ZS-TRD	**MD80**	**48022**	
ZS-TRE	**MD80**	**49387**	
ZS-TRF	**MD80**	**49440**	
ZS-XGU	F.28	11231	
ZS-XGV	**F.28**	**11128**	
ZS-XGW	**F.28**	**11130**	
ZS-XGX	F.28	11115	

Macedonia

Z3-AAA	B737	23416	
Z3-AAB	DC-9	47571	
Z3-AAC	MD80	49442	
Z3-AAD	MD80	49373	
Z3-AAE	F.100	11272	
Z3-AAF	**B737**	**23858**	
Z3-AAG	**CRJ9**	**15001**	
Z3-ARA	DC-9	47530	
Z3-ARB	MD80	48046	
Z3-ARC	DC-9	47613	
Z3-ARD	DC-9	47568	
Z3-ARD	DC-9	47606	
Z3-ARE	DC-9	47567	
Z3-ARF	B737	23716	

Mauritius

3B-	**A330**	**883**	
(3B-)	B727	18903	
3B-AGC	MD80	49809	
3B-LXM	B737	21732	
3B-NAE	B707	18891	
3B-NAF	B707	19133	
3B-NAG	B747	21134	
3B-NAI	B747	20238	
3B-NAJ	B747	21132	
3B-NAK	B767	23973	
3B-NAL	B767	23974	
3B-NAO	B747	21263	
3B-NAQ	B747	21786	
3B-NAR	B747	21254	
3B-NAS	B747	22170	
3B-NAT	A340	048	
3B-NAU	**A340**	**076**	
3B-NAV	**A340**	**094**	
3B-NAY	**A340**	**152**	
3B-NAZ	B767	27427	
3B-NBD	**A340**	**194**	
3B-NBE	**A340**	**268**	
3B-NBF	**A319**	**1592**	
3B-NBH	**A319**	**1936**	
3B-NBI	**A340**	**793**	
3B-NBJ	**A340**	**800**	
3B-NBK	**A340**	**883**	
3B-RGY	A320	0376	
3B-RGZ	A320	0386	
3B-SMC	B747	24063	
3B-STI	A310	347	
3B-STJ	A310	350	

3B-STK	A310	357	
3B-THK	A300	035	
3B-THM	A300	055	

Equatorial Guinea

3C-4GE	YAK40	9940660	
3C-AAJ	B737	19075	
3C-ABH	B707	18056	
3C-ABT	B707	17721	
3C-CDA	DC-9	47643	
3C-CGA	**YAK40**	**9411132**	
3C-CGE	**YAK40**	**9821557**	
3C-CSB	B707	19179	
3C-EGE	**737NG**	**33367**	
3C-FNK	DC-8	45683	
3C-GFB	B747	20953	
3C-GFC	B747	21300	
3C-GFD	B747	22298	
3C-GFE	B747	20504	
3C-GIG	B707	19179	
3C-HAC	**B737**	**20211**	
3C-HAV	IL76	0073479386	
3C-JJJ	IL76	073411334	
3C-JZU	YAK40	9512038	
3C-JZW	B707	18747	
3C-KKE	IL76	1023411368	
3C-KKF	IL76	1023411384	
3C-KKG	IL76	1023410360	
3C-LGF	IL76	0073479386	
3C-LGP	**F.28**	**11156**	
3C-LKI	**1-11**	**BAC.158**	
3C-LLF	**F.28**	**11073**	
3C-LLL	YAK42	2306016	
3C-LQC	**B727**	**19152**	
3C-MNB	YAK40	9821557	
3C-NGK	B707	19415	
3C-QQC	L1011	193A-1152	
3C-QQD	IL76	073410279	
3C-QQH	**E145**	**145076**	
3C-QQO	AN7x	72096914	
3C-QQR	IL62	4648414	
3C-QQS	AN7x	72080789	
3C-QQZ	IL62	3052657	
3C-QRA	IL76	043402039	
3C-QRB	**IL76**	**073411334**	
3C-QRF	DC-8	45858	
3C-QRF	1-11	061	
3C-QRL	L1011	193N-1093	
3C-QRO	B707	19411	
3C-QRQ	L1011	193N-1101	
3C-QTA	AN7x	72060653	
3C-RIM	**YAK40**	**9530244**	
3C-SIR	**YAK40**	**9720653**	
3C-VQT	**YAK40**	**9611646**	
3C-ZZM	B737	20590	

Swaziland

(3D-)	B727	21089	
(3D-)	DC-8	45888	
3D-AAB	L1011	193U-1201	
3D-AAJ	B737	19075	
3D-AAK	B727	21089	
3D-ABQ	B727	21742	
3D-ABV	MD80	49119	
3D-ADA	B737	19708	
3D-ADK	B707	19335	
3D-ADV	DC-8	45858	
3D-ADV	DC-8	46012	
3D-AFR	**DC-8**	**45802**	
3D-AFX	DC-8	45886	
3D-AIA	DC-8	45803	
3D-AIA	DC-8	45854	
3D-AIA	DC-8	46098	
3D-AJG	DC-8	46110	
3D-AKU	B707	18930	
3D-ALB	B727	20600	
3D-ALJ	B737	18689	
3D-ALM	F.100	11335	
3D-ALN	F.28	11136	

3D-ASB	B707	19519	
3D-ASC	B707	19706	
3D-AUG	SE210	264	
3D-AVC	**B727**	**21155**	
3D-BBQ	B727	21741	
3D-BGA	**B737**	**21722**	
3D-BOA	DC-9	47731	
3D-BOB	B727	21235	
3D-BOC	B727	18323	
3D-BOE	B727	18933	
3D-BOX	B747	21054	
3D-CDG	**DC-8**	**45821**	
3D-CDL	DC-8	45986	
3D-CNA	SE210	240	
3D-CSB	B707	19179	
3D-DAW	F.28	11118	
3D-DPT	B727	18370	
3D-ETM	DC-8	45663	
3D-FAK	B727	21370	
3D-FNK	DC-8	45683	
3D-GFA	B747	19763	
3D-GFB	B747	20333	
3D-GFC	B747	21300	
3D-GFD	B747	22298	
3D-GFE	B747	20504	
3D-GFG	B707	20517	
3D-ITC	**B727**	**21260**	
3D-JAA	B707	20022	
3D-JAB	B727	21318	
3D-JES	DC-9	47198	
3D-JET	MD80	48053	
3D-JJM	B727	20053	
3D-JNM	B727	19139	
3D-JOE	L1011	293B-1243	
3D-JOY	B727	21090	
3D-KIK	SE210	251	
3D-KMJ	B727	19892	
(3D-KRU)	DC-8	45821	
3D-MDJ	MD80	48039	
3D-MES	**DC-9**	**47598**	
3D-MRJ	DC-9	47466	
3D-MRK	DC-9	47601	
3D-MRL	DC-9	47102	
3D-MRM	DC-9	47190	
3D-MRN	DC-9	47672	
3D-MRO	DC-9	47132	
3D-MRQ	DC-10	46983	
3D-MRR	DC-10	46646	
3D-MRS	DC-10	47832	
3D-MRT	DC-10	47707	
3D-MRU	DC-9	47798	
3D-NEC	L1011	193C-1096	
3D-NED	B747	20009	
3D-NEE	B747	21162	
3D-NEF	B747	21316	
3D-NEG	L1011	193B-1066	
3D-NGK	B707	19415	
3D-PAH	B747	20333	
3D-PAI	B727	21320	
3D-PAJ	B747	20504	
3D-PAJ	B747	21300	
3D-PHS	**B737**	**20575**	
3D-ROK	B707	19587	
3D-RTA	IL76	0003426765	
3D-RTI	IL62	3036142	
3D-RTP	TU154	91A-895	
3D-RTT	IL76	053403072	
3D-RTV	AN7x	72080777	
3D-RTW	AN7x	72090796	
3D-RTX	IL76	043402039	
3D-SEP	SE210	251	
3D-SGF	B707	19999	
3D-SGG	B707	20517	
3D-SGH	B727	20666	
3D-WKU	B707	18930	
3D-YAC	YAK40	9510439	
3D-YAH	YAK40	9632049	
3D-YAK	YAK40	9511639	
3D-YAQ	YAK40	9411333	
3D-ZZM	**B737**	**20590**	
3D-ZZN	B727	19176	

Guinea

Reg	Type	c/n
(3X-)	B737	20156
3X-CGA	YAK40	?
3X-GAW	YAK40	9440637
3X-GAZ	B707	18748
3X-GCA	B727	19120
3X-GCB	B737	22627
(3X-GCC)	B707	18685
3X-GCC	B707	19291
3X-GCH	B727	19120
3X-GCM	B737	23469
3X-GDM	B727	21089
3X-GDO	B727	21370

Azerbaijan
(see also AHY-/AL-)

Reg	Type	c/n
4K-325	TU154	79A-325
4K-401	B707	19584
4K-473	TU154	81A-473
4K-474	**TU154**	**81A-474**
4K-555	DC-8	45885
4K-727	TU154	86A-727
4K-733	TU154	86A-733
4K-4201	B727	19460
4K-8888	**B727**	**22543**
4K-65496	TU134	63468
4K-65702	TU134	63375
4K-65703	TU134	63383
4K-65704	**TU134**	**63410**
4K-65705	TU134	63415
4K-65708	TU134	63447
4K-65709	TU134	63484
4K-65710	TU134	63490
4K-65711	TU134	63498
4K-65712	**TU134**	**63515**
4K-65713	**TU134**	**63520**
4K-65714	**TU134**	**63527**
4K-65985	TU134	63468
4K-76671	IL76	0063465963
4K-76677	IL76	0063467005
4K-76717	IL76	0073474216
4K-78129	**IL76**	**0083489683**
4K-78130	IL76	0043454611
4K-85147	TU154	76A-147
4K-85158	TU154	76A-158
4K-85177	TU154	76A-177
4K-85192	TU154	77A-192
4K-85199	TU154	77A-199
4K-85211	TU154	77A-211
4K-85214	TU154	77A-214
4K-85250	TU154	77A-250
4K-85274	TU154	78A-274
4K-85329	TU154	79A-329
4K-85362	TU154	79A-362
4K-85364	TU154	79A-364
4K-85391	TU154	80A-391
4K-85395	TU154	80A-395
4K-85474	TU154	81A-474
4K-85524	**TU154**	**82A-524**
4K-85538	TU154	82A-538
4K-85548	TU154	82A-548
4K-85698	TU154	91A-871
4K-85729	**TU154**	**92A-911**
4K-85732	**TU154**	**92A-914**
4K-85734	**TU154**	**92A-916**
4K-85738	**TU154**	**92A-921**
4K-86810	**IL76**	**053404094**
4K-87218	**YAK40**	**9440937**
4K-87257	**YAK40**	**9311426**
4K-87278	YAK40	9311427
4K-87413	YAK40	9420534
4K-87415	YAK40	9420734
4K-87478	YAK40	9440638
4K-87504	YAK40	9510640
4K-87644	**YAK40**	**9140520**
4K-87812	**YAK40**	**9230424**
4K-87817	YAK40	9230824
4K-87946	YAK40	9611045
4K-88174	YAK40	9621247

Reg	Type	c/n
4K-AZ1	B727	19460
4K-AZ2	B727	19461
4K-AZ3	B707	19321
4K-AZ4	B707	19415
4K-AZ8	B727	20525
4K-AZ22	B727	22543
4K-AZ01	**A319**	**2487**
4K-AZ03	**A319**	**2516**
4K-AZ04	**A319**	**2588**
4K-AZ05	**A319**	**2788**
4K-AZ10	**TU154**	**98A-1013**
(4K-AZ11)	B757	29304
4K-AZ11	IL76	1023409280
4K-AZ12	B757	29305
(4K-AZ13)	B757	30824
4K-AZ14	**IL76**	**1023412389**
4K-AZ15	**IL76**	**1033417569**
4K-AZ16	**IL76**	**1023412411**
4K-AZ17	**TU154**	**85A-718**
4K-AZ19	**IL76**	**0053460820**
4K-AZ22	IL76	0053464926
4K-AZ25	DC-8	45920
4K-AZ26	**IL76**	**1033416525**
4K-AZ27	IL76	0053460827
4K-AZ28	IL76	0063471147
4K-AZ29	DC-8	46085
4K-AZ31	**IL76**	**1013405184**
4K-AZ38	**B757**	**26246**
4K-AZ40	**IL76**	**1043419632**
4K-AZ41	**IL76**	**1063420673**
4K-AZ42	B727	20525
4K-AZ43	**B757**	**23453**
4K-AZ54	**A320**	**0331**
4K-AZ55	**IL76**	**1063420680**
4K-AZ62	**IL76**	**0023441200**
4K-AZ100	**IL76**	**2073421708**
4K-AZ101	**IL76**	**20.3421716**
(4K-BEK)	B707	19521

Georgia
(see also GR-)

Reg	Type	c/n
4L-AAA	B737	23708
4L-AAB	TU134	63340
4L-AAC	TU134	63536
4L-AAD	TU134	63295
4L-AAE	TU134	83.60282
4L-AAF	TU154	91A-890
4L-AAH	TU154	82A-558
4L-AAI	TU134	63179
4L-AAJ	**TU134**	**63860**
4L-AAK	YAK40	9531043
4L-AAL	**AN7x**	**?**
4L-AAM	YAK42	3116579
4L-AAR	YAK42	3116650
4L-AIL	IL76	0063471147
4L-AVC	YAK40	9342031
4L-AVD	YAK40	9430537
4L-AVK	YAK40	9311526
4L-AVP	YAK40	?
4L-AVR	YAK40	?
4L-GAF	**CRJ**	**8046**
4L-GAL	**CRJ**	**7076**
4L-GNA	TU134	62820
4L-GND	**CRJ**	**7644**
4L-MGC	YAK40	9320129
4L-MGC	YAK40	?
4L-MMB	**IL76**	**093418543**
4L-SAS	AN7x	720606427
4L-TGA	**B737**	**25218**
4L-TGG	**YAK42**	**3116579**
4L-TGL	**B737**	**23859**
4L-TGM	**YAK42**	**3116650**
4L-TGN	**YAK40**	**9611246**
4L-TGT	**B737**	**26306**
4L-VAS	**AN7x**	**?**
4L-VIP	**YAK40**	**9320129**
4L-ZIL	IL76	0053464926
4L-65061	TU134	49874
4L-65730	**TU134**	**1351310**
4L-65750	TU134	61042
4L-65774	TU134	62519
4L-65798	TU134	63179
4L-65857	TU134	23255
4L-65865	TU134	28286
4L-65879	TU134	31265
4L-65993	TU134	63860
4L-76445	IL76	1023410330
4L-85168	TU154	76A-168
4L-85188	TU154	76A-188
4L-85197	TU154	77A-197
4L-85359	TU154	79A-359
4L-85430	TU154	80A-430
4L-85496	TU154	81A-496
4L-85518	TU154	81A-518
4L-85547	TU154	82A-547
4L-85558	TU154	82A-558
4L-85713	TU154	91A-889
4L-86558	IL62	1052128
4L-87212	YAK40	9431536
4L-87242	YAK40	9531043
4L-87258	YAK40	9311526
4L-87305	YAK40	9320129
4L-87322	YAK40	9330130
4L-87358	YAK40	9340731
4L-87370	YAK40	9342031
4L-87374	YAK40	9410832
4L-87466	YAK40	9430537
4L-88152	YAK40	9610646
4L-88158	YAK40	9611246
4L-88183	YAK40	9620348

Sri Lanka

Reg	Type	c/n
(4R-...)	A330	365
(4R-...)	A330	372
4R-ABA	A320	0374
4R-ABB	**A320**	**0406**
4R-ABC	**A320**	**0304**
4R-ABD	**A320**	**0315**
4R-ABE	**A320**	**0169**
4R-ABF	**A320**	**0164**
4R-ACN	TRDNT	2135
4R-ACQ	DC-8	45604
4R-ACS	B707	18013
4R-ACT	DC-8	45445
4R-ADA	**A340**	**032**
4R-ADB	**A340**	**033**
4R-ADC	**A340**	**034**
4R-ADD	**A340**	**036**
4R-ADE	**A340**	**367**
4R-ADF	**A340**	**374**
4R-ALA	**A320**	**303**
4R-ALA	B707	19738
4R-ALB	**A330**	**306**
4R-ALB	B707	19737
4R-ALC	**A330**	**311**
4R-ALC	B737	21278
4R-ALD	**A330**	**313**
4R-ALD	B737	20913
4R-ALE	A330	336
4R-ALE	L1011	193E-1047
4R-ALF	A330	341
4R-ALF	L1011	193P-1053
(4R-ALG)	A330	348
4R-ALG	L1011	193E-1025
4R-ALH	L1011	193P-1061
4R-EXJ	**DC-8**	**46049**
4R-PAA	YAK40	9331630
4R-PLA?	YAK40	9331630
4R-SEM	B727	19494
4R-TNJ	L1011	193E-1067
4R-TNK	L1011	193E-1069
4R-TNL	L1011	193E-1073
4R-ULA	L1011	293F-1235
4R-ULB	L1011	293F-1236
4R-ULC	L1011	193P-1053
4R-ULD	L1011	193P-1061
4R-ULE	L1011	193P-1062
4R-ULF	B747	20009
4R-ULG	B747	20010
4R-ULH	B737	19742
4R-ULJ	L1011	193E-1021
4R-ULK	L1011	193E-1027
4R-ULL	B737	20195
4R-ULM	L1011	193N-1211
4R-ULN	L1011	193Y-1178
4R-ULO	B737	21192

Yemen Arab Republic
(see also 70-)

Reg	Type	c/n
4W-ABZ	B737	21296
4W-ACF	B727	21844
4W-ACG	B727	21845
4W-ACH	B727	21846
4W-ACI	B727	21847
4W-ACJ	B727	21842

Israel

Reg	Type	c/n
4X-ABA	B707	18424
4X-ABB	B707	18425
4X-ABJ	737NG	29079
(4X-ABK)	B737	21955
4X-ABL	B737	21736
4X-ABM	B737	22090
4X-ABN	B737	22856
4X-ABO	B737	22857
4X-ABR	737NG	29081
4X-ACN	B707	17665
(4X-ACN)	B707	18012
4X-ACU	B707	17666
4X-AGI	IL76	0093486579
4X-AGJ	B727	19011
4X-AGT	B707	17661
4X-AGU	B707	17668
4X-AOT	**B737**	**21740**
4X-AOX	B737	20794
4X-AOY	B707	19517
4X-ATA	B707	18070
4X-ATB	B707	18071
4X-ATC	B707	18357
4X-ATD	B707	18985
4X-ATE	B707	18456
4X-ATF	B707	19277
4X-ATG	B707	20174
4X-ATR	B707	19004
4X-ATS	B707	19502
4X-ATT	B707	20097
4X-ATU	B707	20122
4X-ATX	B707	20122
4X-ATY	B707	20301
4X-AXA	B747	20135
4X-AXB	B747	20274
4X-AXC	B747	20704
4X-AXD	B747	21190
4X-AXF	**B747**	**21594**
4X-AXG	B747	21737
4X-AXH	B747	22254
4X-AXK	**B747**	**22151**
4X-AXL	**B747**	**22150**
4X-AXM	**B747**	**22485**
4X-AXQ	**B747**	**20841**
4X-AXZ	B747	19735
4X-BAA	B737	21820
4X-BAB	B737	22875
4X-BAC	B737	22876
4X-BAE	B727	19249
4X-BAF	B737	20413
4X-BAG	B737	20276
4X-BAR	1-11	BAC.230
4X-BAS	1-11	BAC.199
(4X-BAS)	1-11	BAC.236
4X-BAU	**B757**	**30178**
4X-BAW	**B757**	**30179**
4X-BAY	B757	26151
4X-BAZ	B757	24121
4X-BMA	B707	18014
4X-BMB	B707	18013
4X-BMC	B707	20456
4X-BYA	B707	18012
4X-BYC	B707	19291
4X-BYD	B707	17667
4X-BYG	B707	18013

Reg	Type	Serial
4X-BYH	B707	17668
4X-BYH	B707	20721
4X-BYI	B707	17661
4X-BYK	B707	18246
4X-BYL	B707	17612
4X-BYL	B707	18374
4X-BYM	B707	18460
4X-BYN	B707	17619
4X-BYN	B707	20716
4X-BYQ	B707	20110
4X-BYR	B707	20629
4X-BYS	B707	20230
4X-BYT	B707	17625
4X-BYV	B707	17615
4X-BYW	B707	17617
4X-BYX	B707	17922
4X-BYY	B707	20428
4X-BYZ	B707	17596
4X-EAA	B767	22972
4X-EAB	B767	22973
4X-EAC	B767	22974
4X-EAD	B767	22975
4X-EAE	B767	24832
4X-EAF	B767	24854
4X-EAJ	B767	25208
(4X-EAP)	B767	23106
4X-EAP	B767	24953
4X-EAR	B767	26262
4X-EBF	B757	24136
4X-EBI	B757	27622
4X-EBL	B757	23917
4X-EBM	B757	23918
4X-EBO	B757	24120
4X-EBR	B757	24254
4X-EBS	B757	24884
4X-EBT	B757	25036
4X-EBU	B757	26053
4X-EBV	B757	26054
4X-EBY	B757	24137
4X-ECA	B777	30831
4X-ECB	B777	30832
4X-ECC	B777	30833
4X-ECD	B777	33169
4X-ECE	B777	36083
4X-ECF	B777	36084
4X-EKA	737NG	29957
4X-EKB	737NG	29958
4X-EKC	737NG	29959
4X-EKD	737NG	29960
4X-EKE	737NG	29961
4X-EKI	737NG	28587
4X-EKO	737NG	30287
4X-EKP	737NG	30639
4X-ELA	B747	26055
4X-ELB	B747	26056
4X-ELC	B747	27915
4X-ELD	B747	29328
4X-ELS	B747	27132
4X-ICL	B747	21964
4X-ICM	B747	21965
4X-ICN	B747	22485
(4X-JAA)	B707	18012
(4X-JAD)	B707	17667
4X-JYB	B707	20629
4X-JYL	B707	17612
4X-JYQ	B707	20110
4X-JYR	B707	20629
4X-JYS	B707	20230

Jordan
(see also JY-)

Reg	Type	Serial
4YB-CAB	B707	18716
4YB-CAC	B707	20890

Libya

Reg	Type	Serial
5A-	YAK40	9540345
(5A-...)	A300	195
(5A-...)	A300	198
(5A-...)	A300	227

Reg	Type	Serial
5A-...	CRJ9	15055
5A-CVA	B707	17719
5A-DAA	SE210	158
5A-DAB	SE210	162
5A-DAE	SE210	221
5A-DAH	B727	20244
5A-DAI	B727	20245
5A-DAK	B707	21228
5A-DBU	737NG	32796
5A-DDQ	1-11	BAC.158
5A-DGK	DC-8	45300
5A-DGL	DC-8	45417
5A-DGN	DC-8	45382
5A-DHL	B707	18765
5A-DHM	B707	17647
5A-DHO	B707	17647
5A-DIA	B727	21050
5A-DIB	B727	21051
5A-DIC	B727	21052
5A-DID	B727	21229
5A-DIE	B727	21230
5A-DIF	B727	21332
5A-DIG	B727	21333
5A-DIH	B727	21539
5A-DII	B727	21540
5A-DIJ	B747	22105
5A-DIK	B707	18881
5A-DIK	B747	22106
(5A-DIL)	B747	22107
5A-DIX	B707	18880
5A-DIY	B707	19001
5A-DIZ	B707	18746
5A-DJD	DC-8	45417
5A-DJM	B707	19378
5A-DJO	B707	18955
5A-DJP	DC-8	45659
5A-DJS	B707	18964
5A-DJT	B707	18888
5A-DJU	B707	18889
5A-DJV	B707	19590
5A-DKA	B707	19212
5A-DKG	YAK40	?
5A-DKH	YAK40	?
5A-DKI	YAK40	?
5A-DKJ	YAK40	9631149
5A-DKK	IL76	0003423675
5A-DKK	YAK40	9420235
5A-DKL	AN124	19530502761
5A-DKN	AN124	19530502792
5A-DKO	1-11	BAC.126
5A-DKO	IL76	?
5A-DKP	YAK40	?
5A-DKR	IL62	4053514
5A-DKS	IL76	1033418584
5A-DKT	IL62	4648414
5A-DKY	B737	22766
5A-DLA	A310	295
5A-DLB	A310	306
5A-DLL	IL76	0093493799
5A-DLL	IL76	093421612
5A-DLT	B707	18686
5A-DLU	F.28	11197
5A-DLV	F.28	11200
5A-DLW	F.28	11194
5A-DLY	A300	601
5A-DLZ	A300	616
5A-DMG	737NG	34948
5A-DMH	737NG	34949
5A-DMM	IL76	0003423679
5A-DMN	B727	22287
5A-DMO	B727	20983
5A-DMP	B727	20981
5A-DMQ	IL76	0073479392
5A-DMU	B737	21212
5A-DMV	B737	21286
5A-DNA	IL76	0023439140
5A-DNB	IL76	0023437086
5A-DNC	IL76	0023437084
5A-DND	IL76	0033445299
5A-DNE	IL76	0013432952
5A-DNF	IL76	0033445302
5A-DNG	IL76	0013432961
5A-DNH	IL76	0033446356

Reg	Type	Serial
5A-DNI	IL76	0013430878
5A-DNJ	IL76	0013430869
5A-DNK	IL76	0013430800
5A-DNL	IL76	0033447357
5A-DNO	IL76	0043451509
5A-DNP	IL76	0043451516
5A-DNQ	IL76	0043454641
5A-DNS	IL76	0023439145
5A-DNT	IL76	0023439141
5A-DNU	IL76	0043454651
5A-DNV	IL76	0043454645
5A-DNW	IL76	0043450479?
5A-DNY	IL62	3052657
5A-DQA	IL76	1003405167
5A-DRR	IL76	083415469
5A-DRS	IL76	1003403063
5A-DRT	IL76	?
5A-DSO	F.28	11110
5A-DTF	B707	19628
5A-DTG	F.28	11139
5A-DTH	F.28	11140
5A-DTI	F.28	11187
5A-DZZ	IL76	093416501
5A-IAY	A300	354
5A-LAA	CRJ9	15120
5A-LAB	CRJ9	15121
5A-LAC	CRJ9	15122
5A-ONA	A320	3224
5A-ONB	A320	3236
5A-ONE	A340	151
5A-SOC	E170	17000162

Cyprus

Reg	Type	Serial
(5B-)	B737	24127
5B-	L1011	193N-1198
(5B-AUC)	B747	23501
5B-AUD	B747	23502
(5B-CAC)	DC-8	45303
5B-CIO	B737	23921
5B-DAA	TRDNT	2154
5B-DAB	TRDNT	2155
5B-DAC	TRDNT	2141
5B-DAD	TRDNT	2114
5B-DAE	TRDNT	2134
5B-DAF	1-11	BAC.201
5B-DAG	1-11	BAC.257
5B-DAH	1-11	BAC.258
5B-DAJ	1-11	BAC.261
5B-DAK	B707	17632
5B-DAL	B707	17631
5B-DAM	B707	17628
5B-DAO	B707	18054
5B-DAP	B707	17635
5B-DAQ	A310	300
5B-DAR	A310	309
5B-DAS	A310	352
5B-DAT	A320	0028
5B-DAU	A320	0035
5B-DAV	A320	0037
5B-DAW	A320	0038
5B-DAX	A310	486
5B-DAY	B707	19622
5B-DAZ	B707	19521
5B-DBA	A320	0180
5B-DBB	A320	0256
5B-DBC	A320	0295
5B-DBD	A320	0316
5B-DBE	B727	18371
5B-DBF	B737	23040
5B-DBG	B737	24682
5B-DBH	737NG	30806
5B-DBI	737NG	30807
5B-DBJ	A320	0414
5B-DBK	A320	0430
5B-DBO	A319	1729
5B-DBP	A319	1768
(5B-DBQ)	1-11	BAC.408
(5B-DBR)	1-11	BAC.409
5B-DBR	737NG	30720
5B-DBS	A330	505
5B-DBT	A330	526

Reg	Type	Serial
5B-DBV	737NG	30654
5B-DBW	737NG	30671
5B-DBX	737NG	33699
5B-DBY	B737	29099
5B-DBZ	737NG	33030
5B-DCE	737NG	33029

Tanzania
(see also VR-T)

Reg	Type	Serial
5H-AAF	COMET	6433
5H-ARS	B727	19687
5H-ATC	B737	21710
5H-CCM	F.28	11137
5H-JAS	F.28	11225
5H-KRA	B737	21186
5H-MMT	VC10	882
5H-MOG	VC10	885
5H-MOI	DC-9	47430
(5H-MRF)	B737	21711
5H-MRK	B737	21711
5H-MUZ	B737	22029
5H-MVA	B737	22031
5H-MVK	F.28	11236
5H-MVV	B737	23520
5H-MVZ	B737	23602
5H-TCA	B737	24790
5H-ZAS	F.28	11225

Nigeria

Reg	Type	Serial
(5N-)	1-11	BAC.184
(5N-)	1-11	BAC.210
(5N-)	1-11	BAC.253
(5N-)	B727	20600
5N-	B727	22052
5N-	F.28	11191
5N-AAA	B747	19745
5N-ABD	VC10	804
5N-ABJ	B707	20474
5N-ABK	B707	20669
5N-AGN	F.28	11049
5N-AGY	B727	22825
5N-AKR	B727	20984
5N-AMM	B727	20604
5N-ANA	F.28	11093
5N-ANB	F.28	11053
5N-ANC	B737	20671
5N-AND	B737	20672
5N-ANF	F.28	11090
5N-ANH	F.28	11091
5N-ANI	F.28	11108
5N-ANJ	F.28	11109
5N-ANK	F.28	11110
5N-ANN	DC-10	46957
5N-ANO	B707	21428
(5N-ANO)	DC-10	46968
5N-ANP	B727	21426
5N-ANQ	B727	21427
5N-ANR	DC-10	46968
5N-ANU	F.28	11142
5N-ANV	F.28	11144
5N-ANW	B737	22771
5N-ANX	B737	22772
5N-ANY	B737	22773
5N-ANZ	B737	22774
5N-AOK	1-11	BAC.113
5N-AOL	YAK40	?
5N-AOM	1-11	BAC.122
5N-AON	DC-8	45954
5N-AOO	B707	19263
5N-AOO	B707	19590
5N-AOP	1-11	BAC.109
5N-AOQ	B707	19664
5N-AOS	1-11	BAC.123
5N-AOT	1-11	BAC.133
5N-AOW	1-11	094
5N-AOY	SE210	180
5N-AOZ	1-11	BAC.107
5N-ARH	DC-8	45859
5N-ARO	B707	18924

Reg	Type	c/n
5N-ARQ	B707	18809
5N-ASY	B707	18922
5N-ATS	DC-8	45817
5N-ATY	DC-8	45858
5N-ATZ	DC-8	45965
5N-AUA	B737	22985
5N-AUB	B737	22986
5N-AUE	A310	270
5N-AUF	A310	285
5N-AUG	A310	329
5N-AUH	A310	340
(5N-AUI)	DC-10	48318
5N-AUS	DC-8	45854
5N-AVO	SE210	256
5N-AVP	SE210	260
5N-AVQ	SE210	220
5N-AVR	DC-8	45758
5N-AVS	DC-8	45756
5N-AVX	1-11	BAC.167
5N-AVY	DC-8	45688
5N-AWE	DC-8	45753
5N-AWF	SE210	206
5N-AWG	SE210	111
5N-AWH	B727	19120
5N-AWK	SE210	50
5N-AWO	B707	19372
5N-AWO	SE210	217
5N-AWQ	SE210	219
5N-AWT	SE210	215
5N-AWV	B727	18254
5N-AWX	B727	18256
5N-AWY	B727	18258
5N-AWZ	DC-8	46012
5N-AXQ	1-11	BAC.157
5N-AXT	1-11	BAC.121
5N-AXV	1-11	BAC.159
5N-AYJ	B707	19168
5N-AYR	1-11	BAC.162
5N-AYS	1-11	BAC.129
5N-AYT	1-11	BAC.131
5N-AYU	1-11	062
5N-AYV	1-11	BAC.128
5N-AYW	1-11	BAC.166
5N-AYY	1-11	043
5N-AYZ	DC-8	45421
5N-BAA	1-11	041
5N-BAB	1-11	BAC.127
5N-BBA	DC-9	47217
5N-BBB	B747	19726
5N-BBB	L1011	193P-1068
5N-BBC	DC-9	45871
5N-BBD	B707	19625
5N-BBE	DC-9	45872
5N-BBF	B727	20049
5N-BBG	B727	20054
5N-BBH	B727	20050
5N-BBJ	B737	20197
5N-BBP	1-11	BAC.202
5N-BBQ	1-11	BAC.230
5N-BBU	1-11	BAC.252
5N-BCF	B727	21655
5N-BCG	1-11	BAC.141
5N-BCH	1-11	BAC.140
5N-BCY	B727	19461
5N-BDC	1-11	BAC.111
5N-BDE	B727	21346
5N-BDF	B727	21457
5N-BDG	B727	22558
5N-BDU	1-11	BAC.193
5N-BDV	1-11	BAC.233
5N-BEC	B727	20975
5N-BED	B737	22638
5N-BEE	B737	22365
5N-BEG	B727	20602
5N-BEI	B737	19708
5N-BEJ	B727	21044
5N-BEU	B727	22559
5N-BEV	B737	22658
5N-BEW	B737	22865
5N-BEY	B737	22504
5N-BFA	DC-8	48142
5N-BFD	DC-9	47562
5N-BFJ	B737	22890
5N-BFK	B737	22891
5N-BFM	B737	22733
5N-BFN	B737	22734
5N-BFQ	B737	22892
5N-BFS	DC-9	48140
5N-BFX	B737	23024
5N-BFY	B727	22542
5N-BGA	B737	22456
5N-BGB	B737	22457
5N-BGG	B767	23805
5N-BGH	B767	23806
5N-BGL	MD80	48099
5N-BGM	B737	22889
5N-BGQ	B727	21455
5N-BGU	B737	22881
5N-BHA	B737	23283
5N-BHC	DC-9	47704
5N-BHI	B737	22864
5N-BHV	B727	21364
5N-BHY	B737	24669
5N-BHZ	B737	24671
5N-BID	B737	23791
5N-BIF	B737	23043
5N-BIG	B737	23044
5N-BIH	B737	23046
5N-BII	MD80	49482
5N-BIN	1-11	BAC.265
5N-BIZ	B737	24558
5N-BJA	B737	24873
5N-BJI	CRJ	7772
5N-BJJ	CRJ	7779
5N-BJK	CRJ	7787
5N-BJM	E145	14500984
5N-BJN	B727	22540
5N-BJT	E145	14500987
5N-BLV	DC-9	47276
5N-BOS	YAK40	9341431
5N-BVU	A300	633
5N-CCC	1-11	069
5N-CEO	F.100	11295
5N-CMB	B727	20757
5N-COE	DC-9	47276
5N-COO	F.100	11297
5N-DAN?	YAK40	9340632
5N-DAO	YAK40	?
5N-DBP	B737	23114
5N-DIO	B737	19549
5N-ECI	1-11	BAC.241
5N-EDE	B727	19972
5N-EDO	B747	19726
5N-EEE	B747	19732
5N-EEO	B707	19270
5N-EHI	1-11	074
5N-ENO	1-11	BAC.208
5N-ESA	1-11	DAC.174
"5N-ESB"	1-11	BAC.174
5N-ESB	1-11	BAC.175
5N-ESD	1-11	BAC.402
5N-ESE	1-11	BAC.254
5N-ESF	1-11	BAC.266
5N-EYI	1-11	BAC.211
5N-FGN	B727	22825
5N-FGT	737NG	34260
5N-FSY	1-11	017
5N-GAB	B747	21141
5N-GBA	B727	20677
5N-GGG	1-11	BAC.154
5N-GIN	DC-9	47161
5N-HAS	DC-8	45912
5N-HHH	1-11	064
5N-HHS	B747	19644
5N-HTA	1-11	051
5N-HTB	1-11	052
5N-HTC	1-11	049
5N-HTD	1-11	050
5N-IFY	B737	22797
5N-IMM	B727	20603
5N-IMO	1-11	BAC.229
5N-INZ	DC-9	47402
5N-JEA	CRJ9	15058
5N-JEB	CRJ9	15059
5N-JEC	CRJ9	15054
5N-JED	CRJ9	15114
5N-JIL	B707	18922
5N-JJJ	B747	19766
5N-JNR	B727	21056
5N-KAY	DC-9	47259
5N-KBA	1-11	BAC.179
5N-KBC	1-11	BAC.104
5N-KBD	1-11	BAC.102
(5N-KBE)	1-11	030
5N-KBG	1-11	082
5N-KBM	1-11	BAC.105
5N-KBO	1-11	BAC.180
5N-KBR	1-11	093
5N-KBS	1-11	031
5N-KBT	1-11	BAC.100
5N-KBV	1-11	032
5N-KBW	1-11	BAC.106
5N-KBX	B727	20444
5N-KBY	B727	20442
5N-KGB	1-11	082
5N-KHA	B707	19967
5N-KKK	1-11	BAC.160
5N-KMA	B707	20805
5N-LLL	B727	20654
5N-MAM	B727	18801
5N-MAR	YAK40	9421225
5N-MAS	B707	18718
5N-MBM	1-11	068
5N-MCI	B737	19554
5N-MJA	B737	24454
5N-MJB	B737	24360
5N-MJC	737NG	33932
5N-MJD	737NG	36073
5N-MKE	DC-8	45753
5N-MML	B727	20906
5N-MMM	B727	20656
5N-MXX	B707	18940
5N-MZE	1-11	BAC.110
5N-NCZ	F.28	11241
5N-NEC	B727	20673
5N-NNN	B747	21189
5N-NRC	1-11	BAC.124
5N-NYA	B73/	22799
5N-NZA	B737	22798
5N-NZA	B737	22806
5N-OAL	1-11	BAC.214
5N-OCL	B707	19631
5N-OCM	DC-8	45753
(5N-OGI)	DC-10	46928
5N-OKA	1-11	BAC.168
5N-OMO	1-11	034
5N-ONE	B707	19353
5N-OOO	B747	20952
5N-ORI	B727	18330
5N-ORO	1-11	DAC.264
5N-OSA	1-11	BAC.153
5N-OTI	B727	22534
5N-OVE	1-11	BAC.112
5N-PAL	B727	20679
5N-PAX	B727	20678
5N-PDP	B747	20842
5N-PPP	B747	20921
5N-QQQ	B727	20658
5N-RIR	B727	21087
5N-RKY	B727	21055
5N-RRR	B747	19765
5N-RSG	E145	14500891
5N-SDP	1-11	BAC.125
5N-SEO	1-11	BAC.267
5N-SKS	1-11	BAC.100
5N-SKS	1-11	BAC.243
5N-SMA	B727	19388
5N-SPE	D0328	3151
5N-SPM	D0328	3141
5N-SPN	D0328	3120
5N-SSS	B727	20147
5N-SSZ	F.28	11190
5N-TAS	B707	19375
5N-THG	B747	19640
5N-TKE	B727	19406
5N-TKT	B727	18330
5N-TNO	B707	20085
5N-TOM	1-11	BAC.124
5N-TSA	B737	23110
5N-TTK	B727	20432
5N-TTT	B727	20463
5N-UDE	1-11	BAC.259
5N-UJC	1-11	BAC.255
5N-USE	1-11	BAC.151
5N-USE	1-11	BAC.235
5N-VNA	B737	28563
5N-VNB	B737	29339
5N-VNC	B737	29338
5N-VND	B737	29337
5N-VNE	B737	29340
5N-VNF	B737	29341
5N-VNG	B737	29342
5N-VRG	B707	19664
5N-VVV	1-11	080
5N-VWE	DC-9	47259
5N-YMM	B737	22590
"5N-ZAX"	F.28	11053
5N-ZZZ	B747	19744

Madagascar

Reg	Type	c/n
5R-MFA	B737	20231
5R-MFB	B737	20680
5R-MFC	B767	25403
5R-MFD	B767	29898
5R-MFE	B767	23624
5R-MFF	B767	25221
5R-MFG	B767	25088
5R-MFH	B737	26305
5R-MFI	B737	26301
5R-MFK	B707	18686
5R-MFT	B747	21614
5R-MRM	B737	24081
5R-MUA	YAK40	9840859
5R-MUB	YAK40	9940760
5R-MVZ	B767	25403

Mauritania

Reg	Type	c/n
5T-AUE	B747	23509
5T-CJW	SE210	91
5T-CLF	F.28	11092
5T-CLG	F.28	11093
5T-CLH	F.28	11138
5T-CLI	A300	069
5T-CLK	737NG	28210
5T-CLM	737NG	30037
5T-CLP	B727	22044
5T-MAL	SE210	91
5T-RIM	SE210	91

Niger

Reg	Type	c/n
5U-ACE	B747	20527
5U-ACF	B747	23150
5U-BAG	B737	21499
(5U-MAF)	B737	21499

Togo

Reg	Type	c/n
5V-MAB	F.28	11079
5V-SBB	B727	22165
5V-TAB	F.28	11079
5V-TAD	B707	19523
5V-TAF	DC-8	45692
5V-TAG	B707	19739
5V-TAI	F.28	11079
5V-TGE	B707	21049
5V-TGF	DC-8	46071
5V-TPA	B727	22165
5V-TPB	B727	19565
5V-TPC	B727	19970
5V-TPO	F.28	11027
5V-TPX	B727	18366
5V-TTK	DC-9	47198
5V-TTT	A300	069

Samoa

5W-FAX	B737	23788
5W-ILF	B737	26282
5W-PAL	B737	22575
5W-SAM	737NG	30039
5W-SAO	737NG	30639
5W-TEA	B767	23280

Uganda

5X-	DC-10	46541
5X-AAL	L1011	193U-1201
5X-AAO	COMET	6431
5X-AMM	B727	20371
5X-AMW	B707	20723
5X-ARJ	B707	19632
5X-BON	DC-10	46921
5X-CAU	B707	17713
5X-DAR	B707	18825
5X-DAS	DC-10	46541
5X-EAA	**B737**	**22741**
5X-EOT	B707	19821
5X-GLA	B707	19821
5X-JCR	B707	18832
5X-JCR	DC-10	47831
5X-JEF	B707	19821
5X-JET	B707	19411
5X-JOE	**DC-10**	**47906**
5X-JON	B707	20546
5X-JOS	DC-10	46976
5X-ONE	DC-10	46952
5X-ROY	DC-10	47818
5X-TON	B727	22540
5X-TRA	B707	20722
5X-TRE	**DC-9**	**47746**
5X-TWO	**DC-9**	**47732**
5X-UAC	B707	18747
5X-UAL	B707	18580
(5X-UAL)	B707	18765
5X-UBC	B707	19630
5X-UCM	B707	19177
5X-USM	B737	24785
5X-UVA	VC10	881
5X-UVJ	VC10	884
5X-UVY	DC-9	47478
5X-UWM	B707	10001

Kenya

5Y-	**737NG**	**35286**
5Y-AAA	COMET	6472
5Y-ADA	VC10	883
5Y-ADD	COMET	6413
5Y-AKX	DC-9	45787
5Y-ALD	COMET	6412
5Y-ALF	COMET	6406
5Y-ALR	DC-9	47468
5Y-AMT	COMET	6405
(5Y-ANA)	B707	19521
5Y-ASA	DC-8	45379
5Y-AXA	B707	19621
5Y-AXB	B727	19565
5Y-AXC	B707	18746
5Y-AXD	B727	22165
5Y-AXD	**DC-9**	**47088**
5Y-AXE	**B727**	**21611**
5Y-AXF	**DC-9**	**47093**
5Y-AXG	B707	19369
5Y-AXH	F.28	11027
5Y-AXI	B707	18927
5Y-AXM	B707	18819
5Y-AXR	B707	19634
5Y-AXS	B707	19133
5Y-AXW	B707	19366
5Y-BAS	DC-8	45629
(5Y-BAT)	DC-8	46122
5Y-BBH	DC-9	47430
5Y-BBI	B707	19634
5Y-BBJ	B707	19633
5Y-BBK	B707	19872

5Y-BBR	DC-9	47478
5Y-BBX	B707	18588
5Y-BEL	A310	416
5Y-BEN	A310	426
5Y-BFB	B707	18964
5Y-BFC	B707	18881
5Y-BFF	B707	20179
5Y-BFT	A310	519
5Y-BGI	B757	24566
(5Y-BHF)	B757	24923
(5Y-BHG)	B757	24924
5Y-BHV	B737	21193
5Y-BHW	B737	21196
5Y-BMW	B727	18255
5Y-BNJ	B707	19498
5Y-BOR	B707	19415
5Y-BPI	B737	21356
5Y-BPP	B737	22161
5Y-BPZ	B737	21733
5Y-BRC	B737	24103
5Y-BRV	B707	19999
5Y-CCC	B767	24948
5Y-CGO	B727	18896
5Y-EEE	**F.28**	**11229**
5Y-GFC	B747	21300
5Y-GFD	B747	22298
5Y-GFE	B747	20504
5Y-GFF	B707	19999
5Y-GFG	B707	20517
5Y-GFH	B707	19999
5Y-JAP	**B737**	**20915**
5Y-JLA	F.28	11093
5Y-JLC	**CRJ**	**7183**
5Y-KQA	**B737**	**28746**
5Y-KQB	**B737**	**28747**
5Y-KQC	**B737**	**29088**
5Y-KQD	**B737**	**29750**
5Y-KQE	**737NG**	**30133**
5Y-KQF	**737NG**	**30136**
5Y-KQG	**737NG**	**32371**
5Y-KQH	**737NG**	**32372**
5Y-KQJ	B737	21714
5Y-KQK	**B737**	**21715**
5Y-KQL	A310	485
5Y-KQM	A310	600
5Y-KQN	B737	20915
5Y-KQP	**B767**	**24797**
5Y-KQQ	**B767**	**27310**
5Y-KQR	B767	24484
5Y-KQS	**B777**	**33683**
5Y-KQT	**B777**	**33682**
5Y-KQU	**B777**	**33681**
5Y-KQV	B767	26206
5Y-KQW	B767	26207
5Y-KQX	**B767**	**30854**
5Y-KQY	**B767**	**30841**
5Y-KQZ	**B767**	**30853**
5Y-KYA	**737NG**	**35069**
5Y-KYB	**737NG**	**35070**
5Y-KYC	**737NG**	**35071**
5Y-KYJ	**E170**	**17000128**
5Y-KYK	E170	17000111
5Y-KYZ	**B777**	**36124**
5Y-LKL	B707	19133
5Y-LLL	F.28	11239
5Y-MBA	DC-10	46952
5Y-MNT	F.28	11229
5Y-NNN	F.28	11231
5Y-NNT	F.28	11231
5Y-QQQ	B767	27619
(5Y-QSR)	DC-8	45629
5Y-RAA	B737	24097
5Y-RAB	B737	24096
5Y-RUM	L1011	193C-1200
5Y-SIM	B707	20517
5Y-VIP	**A310**	**620**
5Y-XXA	**DC-9**	**45725**
5Y-XXB	**DC-9**	**45711**
(5Y-XXC)	DC-9	45696
(5Y-XXD)	DC-9	45799
5Y-ZEB	DC-8	46122

Somalia

60-SAU	B707	18013
60-SAW	B707	18015
60-SAX	B707	18031
60-SBM	B707	18953
60-SBN	B707	18954
60-SBS	B707	19315
60-SBT	B707	19316
60-SCG	B727	22430

Senegal

6V-AAR	SE210	5
(6V-ACP)	SE210	5
6V-AEF	**B727**	**21091**
6V-AHK	**B737**	**22767**
6V-AHM	B737	25062
6V-AHN	**737NG**	**30738**
6V-AHO	**737NG**	**30739**
6V-AHT	B737	24652
6V-AHU	**737NG**	**34263**
(6V-BFC?)	SE210	5

Jamaica

(6Y-J)	A300	208
(6Y-J)	A300	210
6Y-JAB	A310	676
6Y-JAC	A310	678
6Y-JAD	A310	682
6Y-JAE	A310	686
6Y-JAF	**A320**	**0624**
6Y-JAG	**A320**	**0626**
6Y-JAI	**A320**	**0628**
6Y-JAJ	A320	0630
6Y-JGA	DC-9	47351
6Y-JGB	DC-9	47352
6Y-JGC	DC-8	45963
6Y-JGD	DC-8	45760
6Y-JGE	DC-8	45648
6Y-JGF	DC-8	45643
6Y-JGG	DC-8	45894
6Y-JGH	DC-8	45912
6Y-JII	DC-8	46084
6Y-JIJ	DC-9	47639
6Y-JIP	B727	21105
6Y-JIQ	B727	21106
6Y-JIR	B727	21107
6Y-JIS	B727	21108
6Y-JMA	A320	0528
6Y-JMA	B727	21105
6Y-JMB	**A320**	**0422**
6Y-JMB	B727	21106
6Y-JMC	A340	048
6Y-JMC	B727	21107
6Y-JMD	**A321**	**0666**
6Y-JMD	B727	21108
6Y-JME	**A321**	**0775**
6Y-JME	DC-8	45442
6Y-JMF	**A320**	**1213**
6Y-JMF	DC-8	45612
6Y-JMG	**A320**	**1390**
6Y-JMG	B727	22036
6Y-JMH	**A321**	**1503**
6Y-JMH	B727	20936
6Y-JMI	**A320**	**1747**
6Y-JMJ	A300	127
6Y-JMJ	A320	1751
6Y-JMK	A300	131
6Y-JMK	**A320**	**2048**
6Y-JML	B727	20978
6Y-JMM	**A340**	**216**
6Y-JMM	B727	21105
6Y-JMN	B727	21106
6Y-JMO	B727	21107
6Y-JMP	**A340**	**257**
6Y-JMP	B727	20935
6Y-JMP	B727	21108
6Y-JMQ	B727	22347
6Y-JMR	A300	109

6Y-JMR	**A321**	**1905**
6Y-JMS	A300	143
6Y-JMS	**A321**	**1966**
6Y-JMW	**A321**	**1988**

Yemen
(see also 4W-)

70-	**A310**	**568**
70-ABQ	B707	18032
70-ABY	B707	19777
70-ACI	B737	21763
70-ACJ	B707	18737
70-ACN	TU154	81A-501
70-ACO	B707	20374
70-ACP	B707	18016
70-ACQ	**B737**	**23129**
70-ACR	B737	23130
70-ACS	B707	20547
70-ACT	TU154	89A-822
70-ACU	B737	21296
70-ACV	B727	21844
70-ACW	B727	21845
70-ACX	B727	21846
70-ACY	B727	21847
70-ADA	**B727**	**21842**
70-ADF	**IL76**	**1033418578**
70-ADG	**IL76**	**1023412402**
70-ADH	IL76	1033415497
70-ADJ	**A310**	**535**
70-ADL	**737NG**	**30645**
70-ADM	**737NG**	**28252**
70-ADN	**737NG**	**30661**
70-ADO	IL76	?
70-ADP	**A330**	**625**
70-ADQ	**737NG**	**30730**
70-ADT	**A330**	**632**
70-YMN	**B747**	**21786**

Lesotho

7P-DPT	B727	18370
7P-LAA	B727	21155
7P-LAN	B707	19517

Malawi

7Q-YKE	1-11	039
7Q-YKF	1-11	BAC.243
7Q-YKG	1-11	BAC.245
7Q-YKH	VC10	819
7Q-YKI	1-11	BAC.214
7Q-YKJ	1-11	BAC.240
7Q-YKK	1-11	BAC.235
7Q-YKL	B747	21133
7Q-YKP	**B737**	**25056**
(7Q-YKR)	B737	25604
7Q-YKW	**B737**	**25384**

Algeria

7T-	**IL76**	**1013408244**
(7T-)	B737	22383
(7T-)	B767	27255
(7T-V..)	B747	21991
(7T-V..)	B747	22234
7T-VAE	SE210	51
7T-VAG	SE210	18
7T-VAI	SE210	28
7T-VAK	SE210	73
7T-VAL	SE210	75
(7T-VCO)	B737	22089
(7T-VCQ)	B737	22384
7T-VEA	B727	20472
7T-VEB	B727	20473
7T-VEC	B737	20544
7T-VED	B737	20650
7T-VEE	B737	20758
7T-VEF	B737	20759

Reg	Type	c/n
7T-VEG	B737	20884
7T-VEH	B727	20955
7T-VEI	B727	21053
7T-VEJ	B737	21063
7T-VEK	B737	21064
7T-VEL	B737	21065
7T-VEM	**B727**	**21210**
7T-VEN	**B737**	**21211**
7T-VEO	B737	21212
7T-VEP	**B727**	**21284**
7T-VEQ	**B737**	**21285**
7T-VER	B737	21286
7T-VES	**B727**	**21287**
7T-VET	**B727**	**22372**
7T-VEU	B727	22373
7T-VEV	**B727**	**22374**
7T-VEW	B727	22375
7T-VEX	**B727**	**22765**
7T-VEY	B727	22766
7T-VEZ	B737	22700
7T-VJA	**B737**	**22800**
7T-VJB	**B737**	**22801**
7T-VJC	**A310**	**291**
7T-VJD	**A310**	**293**
7T-VJE	A310	295
7T-VJF	**A310**	**306**
7T-VJG	**B767**	**24766**
7T-VJH	**B767**	**24767**
7T-VJI	**B767**	**24768**
7T-VJJ	**737NG**	**30202**
7T-VJK	**737NG**	**30203**
7T-VJL	**737NG**	**30204**
7T-VJM	**737NG**	**30205**
7T-VJN	**737NG**	**30206**
7T-VJO	**737NG**	**30207**
7T-VJP	**737NG**	**30208**
7T-VJQ	**737NG**	**30209**
7T-VJR	**737NG**	**30545**
7T-VJS	**737NG**	**30210**
7T-VJT	**737NG**	**30546**
7T-VJU	**737NG**	**30211**
7T-VJV	**A330**	**644**
7T-VJW	**A330**	**647**
7T-VJX	**A330**	**650**
7T-VJY	**A330**	**653**
7T-VJZ	**A330**	**667**
7T-VKA	**737NG**	**34164**
7T-VKB	**737NG**	**34165**
7T-VKC	**737NG**	**34166**
7T-VKL	A340	117
7T-VKM	A340	139
7T-VKN	A340	149
7T-VKO	A320	0094
7T-VKP	B777	27108
7T-VKQ	B777	27109
7T-VRA	L1011	193G-1250
7T-VVA	B737	20440
7T-WIA	**IL76**	**0083489674**
7T-WIB	**IL76**	**0093493803**
7T-WIC	**IL76**	**1003405154**
7T-WID	**IL76**	**1023414470**
7T-WIE	**IL76**	**1023414463**
7T-WIF	IL76	?
7T-WIG	**IL76**	**1023413435**
7T-WIH	IL76	?
7T-WIL	**IL76**	**0043454640**
7T-WIN	**IL76**	**0063469080**
7T-WIP	**IL76**	**1043419636**
7T-WIQ	**IL76**	**0053462879**
7T-WIR	IL76	?
7T-WIT	IL76	?
7T-WIU	**IL76**	**1023413423**
7T-WIV	**IL76**	**1043419649**

Barbados

Reg	Type	c/n
8P-CAC	B707	19412
8P-CAD	B707	19632
8P-GUL	B757	22206
8P-PLC	DC-8	46042

Maldives

Reg	Type	c/n
8Q-CA003	DC-8	45649
8Q-CA004	DC-8	45808
8Q-CA005	DC-8	45689
8Q-PNB	DC-8	45649
8Q-PNC	DC-8	45808

Guyana

Reg	Type	c/n
8R-GGA	TU154	85A-719
8R-UCJ	AN7x	?

Croatia

Reg	Type	c/n
(9A-ADL)	TU134	63952
(9A-ADP)	TU134	63967
(9A-ADR)	TU134	66135
9A-BTD	**F.100**	**11407**
9A-BTE	**F.100**	**11416**
9A-CBC	MD80	49143
9A-CBD	MD80	48095
9A-CBE	MD80	53149
9A-CBF	**MD80**	**49221**
9A-CBG	MD80	49430
9A-CBH	**MD80**	**49220**
9A-CBI	MD80	49631
9A-CBJ	MD80	49449
9A-CDA	**MD80**	**49602**
9A-CDB	**MD80**	**49986**
9A-CDC	**MD80**	**49112**
9A-CDD	**MD80**	**49113**
9A-CDE	**MD80**	**48066**
9A-CTA	B737	22119
9A-CTB	B737	22116
9A-CTC	B737	22118
9A-CTD	B737	22140
9A-CTE	B737	22634
9A-CTF	**A320**	**0258**
9A-CTG	**A319**	**0767**
9A-CTH	**A319**	**0833**
9A-CTI	**A319**	**1029**
9A-CTJ	**A320**	**1009**
9A-CTK	**A320**	**1237**
9A-CTL	**A319**	**1252**
9A-CTM	**A320**	**0671**

Ghana

Reg	Type	c/n
9G-...	**DC-8**	**46097**
9G-ABO	VC10	823
9G-ABP	VC10	824
(9G-ABQ)	VC10	825
(9G-ABZ)	F.28	11062
9G-ACA	F.28	11077
9G-ACB	B707	17593
(9G-ACB)	F.28	11062
9G-ACD	B707	17603
9G-ACG	DC-8	45256
9G-ACJ	B707	17903
9G-ACK	B707	17721
9G-ACM	DC-9	47755
9G-ACN	B707	17640
9G-ACO	B707	17651
9G-ACR	B707	19001
9G-ACX	B707	19498
9G-ACY	B707	19212
9G-ACZ	B707	19369
(9G-ACZ)	B707	19843
9G-ADA	F.28	11187
9G-ADB	B707	20457
9G-ADL	B707	19369
9G-ADM	A320	0112
9G-ADN	DC-9	47276
9G-ADS	B707	19587
9G-ADT	DC-9	47665
9G-ADU	DC-9	47692
9G-ADY	DC-9	47679
9G-ALG	B707	19415
9G-ANA	DC-10	48286

Reg	Type	c/n
9G-ANB	DC-10	46959
9G-ANC	DC-10	46933
9G-AND	DC-10	46712
9G-ANE	DC-10	46713
9G-AXA	**DC-8**	**46113**
9G-AYO	B707	19519
9G-BAN	DC-8	45904
9G-CDG	DC-8	45821
9G-CJM	B707	20760
(9G-DUC)	B707	19350
9G-EBK	B707	19372
9G-ESI	B707	19372
9G-FAB	**DC-8**	**46121**
9G-FIA	B707	20069
9G-IRL	B707	20805
9G-JET	B707	19372
9G-JNR	B707	19353
9G-LAD	**B707**	**18940**
9G-LIL	**DC-8**	**46147**
9G-MAN	B707	19212
9G-MKA	DC-8	45804
9G-MKB	DC-8	45860
9G-MKC	DC-8	45692
9G-MKD	DC-8	45965
9G-MKE	DC-8	45753
9G-MKF	DC-8	45820
9G-MKG	DC-8	46027
9G-MKH	DC-8	46153
9G-MKI	B747	22063
9G-MKJ	B747	22170
9G-MKK	DC-8	46022
(9G-MKL)	B747	20888
9G-MKL	**B747**	**21650**
9G-MKM	**B747**	**22482**
9G-MKN	DC-8	46151
9G-MKO	DC-8	46147
9G-MKP	**B747**	**21841**
9G-MKQ	B747	22169
9G-MKR	**B747**	**22481**
9G-MKS	B747	22486
9G-MKT	**DC-8**	**45764**
9G-NHA	DC-8	45924
9G-OAL	**B707**	**19350**
9G-OLD	B707	19350
9G-OLF	B707	19821
9G-OLU	B707	19519
9G-ONE	B707	19821
9G-OOD	DC-8	46085
9G-PEL	DC-8	46085
9G-PHN	DC-10	46554
9G-RBO	B707	18746
9G-RCA	B707	18746
(9G-REM)	DC-0	45910
9G-RMF	DC-8	45920
9G-ROX	B707	19521
9G-SGF	B707	19372
(9G-TOO)	B707	20517
9G-TOP	**DC-8**	**46151**
9G-TWO	B707	20517
9G-WON	B707	19821

Malta

Reg	Type	c/n
9H-AAK	B707	18063
9H-AAL	B707	18167
9H-AAM	B707	18378
9H-AAN	B707	18380
9H-AAO	B707	18829
9H-ABA	B737	23038
9H-ABB	B737	23039
9H-ABC	B737	23040
9H-ABE	B737	23847
9H-ABF	B737	23848
9H-ABG	B737	24031
9H-ABQ	A320	0293
9H-ABR	B737	25613
9H-ABS	B737	25614
9H-ABT	B737	25615
(9H-ABW)	146	E1254
(9H-ABX)	146	E1258
9H-ABX	A320	0289

Reg	Type	c/n
(9H-ABY)	146	E1260
(9H-ABZ)	146	E1267
9H-ACM	146	E1254
9H-ACN	146	E1258
9H-ACO	146	E1260
9H-ACP	146	E1267
9H-ACS	B737	23827
9H-ACT	B737	23830
9H-ADH	**B737**	**27459**
9H-ADI	**B737**	**27460**
9H-ADJ	B737	27353
9H-ADK	B737	27673
9H-ADL	B737	27674
9H-ADM	B737	24365
9H-ADN	B737	25161
9H-ADO	B737	27003
9H-ADP	B737	23718
(9H-ADR)	B737	23921
9H-ADY	A320	1769
9H-ADZ	A320	0331
9H-AED	A320	0288
9H-AEF	**A320**	**2142**
9H-AEG	**A319**	**2113**
9H-AEH	**A319**	**2122**
9H-AEI	**A320**	**2189**
9H-AEJ	**A319**	**2186**
9H-AEK	**A320**	**2291**
9H-AEL	**A319**	**2332**
9H-AEM	**A319**	**2382**
9H-AEN	**A320**	**2665**
9H-AEO	**A320**	**2768**
9H-AEP	**A320**	**3056**
9H-AEQ	**A320**	**3068**
9H-AER	A320	2178
9H-AFE	**A320**	**0350**
9H-AHN	F.100	11351

Zambia

Reg	Type	c/n
9J-ABR	DC-8	45599
9J-ADY	B707	18976
9J-ADZ	B737	19424
(9J-AEA)	B737	21236
9J-AEB	B707	19263
9J-AEC	B707	19354
9J-AEG	B737	21236
9J-AEL	B707	19295
9J-AEQ	B707	19367
9J-AFL	DC-8	46099
9J-AFM	B737	22744
(9J-AFN)	DC-10	47922
9J-AFO	B757	24635
9J-AFT	B707	19964
9J-AFU	B737	19075
9J-AFW	B737	19426
9J-JCN	**B737**	**22588**
9J-JOY	**B737**	**22584**
9J-MKK	**DC-8**	**46022**
9J-RCH	1-11	039
9J-RCI	1-11	040

Kuwait

Reg	Type	c/n
(9K-...)	A300	755
(9K-...)	A300	758
9K-ACA	COMET	6465
9K-ACE	COMET	6474
9K-ACF	TRDNT	2114
9K-ACG	TRDNT	2118
9K-ACH	TRDNT	2134
(9K-ACI)	1-11	033
9K-ACI	COMET	6427
(9K-ACJ)	1-11	034
9K-ACJ	B707	20084
(9K-ACK)	1-11	035
9K-ACK	B707	20085
9K-ACL	B707	20086
9K-ACM	B707	20546
9K-ACN	B707	20547
9K-ACO	1-11	035
9K-ACS	B707	20016

9K-ACU	B707	20018	9L-LDR	L1011	193G-1179
9K-ACV	B737	21206	(9L-LDS)	L1011	193G-1233
9K-ACX	B707	19789	9L-LDS	YAK42	2003019
9K-ADA	B747	21541	9L-LDT	YAK42	..10018
9K-ADB	B747	21542	9L-LDU	B707	19179
9K-ADC	B747	21543	"9L-LDV"	B727	21611
9K-ADD	B747	22740	9L-LDV	L1011	193C-1200
9K-ADE	B747	27338	(9L-LDY)	B727	20600
(9K-ADF)	B747	27663	9L-LDY	YAK40	9441137
9K-AFA	B727	22359	9L-LDZ	L1011	193N-1212
9K-AFB	B727	22360	9L-LED	L1011	193G-1222
9K-AFC	B727	22361	9L-LEE	YAK40	9810757
9K-AFD	B727	22763	9L-LEF	B727	21482
9K-AGC	MD80	49809	"9L-LEG"	B727	21245
9K-AHA	A310	267	9L-LEG	B737	22885
9K-AHB	A310	276	9L-LEK	B727	19288
9K-AHC	A310	278	9L-LEL	B727	21483
9K-AHD	A310	318	9L-LEN	B727	20600
9K-AHE	A310	331	9L-LEO	B727	21484
9K-AHF	A300	327	9L-LEQ	L1011	193C-1199
9K-AHG	A300	332	9L-LEU	L1011	193C-1226
9K-AHH	A300	339	9L-LFA	B737	22354
9K-AHI	A300	344	9L-LFB	L1011	193P-1156
9K-AHJ	A310	342	9L-LFC	L1011	193C-1225
9K-AHK	A310	346	9L-LFD	B727	21245
9K-AIA	B767	23280	9L-LFE	B737	22274
9K-AIB	B767	23281	9L-LFF	B767	22526
9K-AIC	B767	23282	9L-LFI	B727	22057
9K-AKA	A320	0181	9L-LFJ	B727	19289
9K-AKB	A320	0182	(9L-LFK)	DC-9	47707
9K-AKC	A320	0195	9L-LFV	B737	23114
9K-AKD	A320	2046	9L-LOR	B747	20929
9K-ALA	A310	647			
9K-ALB	A310	649			
9K-ALC	A310	663	**Malaysia**		
9K-ALD	A310	648			
9K-AMA	A300	673	9M-	MD11	48446
9K-AMB	A300	694	9M-...	A320	3299
9K-AMC	A300	699	(9M-...)	B707	17594
9K-AMD	A300	719	9M-A..	A320	3261
9K-AME	A300	721	9M-AAA	B737	24907
9K-ANA	A340	089	9M-AAB	B737	23718
9K-ANB	A340	090	9M-AAB	B737	28555
9K-ANC	A340	101	9M-AAC	B737	28200
9K-AND	A340	104	9M-AAD	B737	24905
9K-AOA	B777	28743	9M-AAE	B737	24570
9K-AOB	B777	28744	9M-AAF	B737	24096
9K-CAA	A320	2569	9M-AAG	B737	27061
9K-CAB	A320	2584	9M-AAI	B737	23510
9K-CAC	A320	2792	9M-AAJ	B737	23511
9K-CAD	A320	2822	9M-AAK	B737	23236
9K-CAE	A320	3016	9M-AAL	B737	23235
9K-MKU	B747	22237	9M-AAM	B737	23233
			9M-AAN	B737	23234
			9M-AAO	B737	23365
Sierra Leone			9M-AAP	B737	23367
			9M-AAQ	B737	23368
9L-	YAK40	9320528	9M-AAR	B737	23358
9L-LAZ	B707	18251	9M-AAS	B737	23357
9L-LBK	IL76	0023437076	9M-AAT	B737	25071
9L-LBO	IL76	1023408265	9M-AAU	B737	23257
9L-LBW	B727	21044	9M-AAV	B737	23552
9L-LCK	B727	20814	9M-AAW	B737	23554
9L-LCS	B727	20598	9M-AAX	B737	24547
9L-LCU	B727	20818	9M-AAY	B737	24678
9L-LCW	IL76	0033448404	9M-AEA	B737	24659
9L-LCX	IL76	0043453575	9M-AEB	B737	24465
(9L-LCY)	B727	20600	9M-AEC	B737	24677
9L-LCY	IL76	1003499994	9M-AED	B737	26442
9L-LDC	L1011	193B-1231	(9M-AEE)	B737	23259
9L-LDE	L1011	193C-1244	9M-AFA	A320	2612
9L-LDF	DC-9	47088	9M-AFB	A320	2633
9L-LDG	DC-9	47093	9M-AFC	A320	2656
9L-LDH	DC-9	47643	9M-AFD	A320	2683
9L-LDI	YAK40	9542043	9M-AFE	A320	2699
9L-LDJ	1-11	BAC.242	9M-AFF	A320	2760
(9L-LDK)	1-11	BAC.203	9M-AFG	A320	2816
9L-LDK	YAK40	9331229	9M-AFH	A320	2826
9L-LDL	1-11	BAC.232	9M-AFI	A320	2842
9L-LDM	B727	21179	9M-AFJ	A320	2881
9L-LDM	B727	21235	9M-AFK	A320	2885
9L-LDN	L1011	193B-1221	9M-AFL	A320	2926
9L-LDP	YAK42	2007018	9M-AFM	A320	2944

9M-AFN	A320	2956	9M-MFI	B737	27356
9M-AFO	A320	2989	(9M-MFZ)	B737	27125
9M-AFP	A320	3000	9M-MHA	A300	073
9M-AFQ	A320	3018	9M-MHB	A300	093
9M-AFR	A320	3064	9M-MHC	A300	095
9M-AFS	A320	3117	9M-MHD	A300	147
9M-AFT	A320	3140	9M-MHG	B747	22724
9M-AFU	A320	3154	9M-MHH	B747	22791
9M-AFV	A320	3173	9M-MHI	B747	22304
9M-AFX	A320	3182	9M-MHJ	B747	22442
9M-AFY	A320	3194	9M-MHK	B747	23600
9M-AFZ	A320	3201	9M-MHL	B747	24315
9M-AHA	A320	3223	9M-MHM	B747	24405
9M-AHB	A320	3232	9M-MHN	B747	24836
9M-AHD	A320	3291	9M-MHO	B747	25126
9M-AMZ	F.28	11168	(9M-MHP)	B747	27042
9M-AOA	COMET	6401	9M-MHZ	B747	22671
9M-AOB	COMET	6403	9M-MJA	B737	24703
9M-AOC	COMET	6404	9M-MJB	B737	24704
9M-AOD	COMET	6405	9M-MJC	B737	24705
9M-AOE	COMET	6406	9M-MJD	B737	24706
9M-AOT	B707	19738	9M-MJE	B737	24707
9M-AOU	B737	19768	9M-MJF	B737	24708
9M-AOV	B737	19770	9M-MJG	B737	24709
9M-AOW	B737	19772	9M-MJH	B737	24686
9M-AQB	B707	19529	9M-MJI	B737	24688
9M-AQC	B737	20521	9M-MJJ	B737	24163
9M-AQD	B707	17592	9M-MJK	B737	24682
9M-AQL	B737	20582	9M-MJL	B737	24344
9M-AQM	B737	20583	9M-MJM	B737	24693
9M-AQN	B737	20584	9M-MJN	B737	24903
9M-AQO	B737	20585	9M-MJO	B737	24906
9M-AQP	B737	20586	9M-MJP	B737	24915
9M-AQQ	B737	20587	9M-MJQ	B737	24912
9M-ARG	B737	20631	9M-MJR	B737	24683
9M-ASO	B707	18955	9M-MJS	B737	24691
9M-ASQ	B707	18953	9M-MJT	B737	24915
9M-ASR	B737	20926	9M-MKA	A330	067
9M-ATR	B707	18954	9M-MKB	A330	068
9M-BBJ	737NG	29274	9M-MKC	A330	069
9M-CHG	B737	27456	9M-MKD	A330	073
9M-EKC	CRJ	7089	9M-MKE	A330	077
9M-LKY	B737	27456	9M-MKF	A330	100
9M-MAS	DC-10	46955	9M-MKG	A330	107
9M-MAT	DC-10	46640	9M-MKH	A330	110
(9M-MAT)	DC-10	46957	9M-MKI	A330	116
9M-MAV	DC-10	48283	9M-MKJ	A330	119
9M-MAW	DC-10	46959	9M-MKR	A330	095
9M-MAX	DC-10	46961	9M-MKS	A330	143
9M-MAZ	DC-10	46933	9M-MKT	A330	262
9M-MBA	B737	20582	9M-MKU	A330	255
9M-MBB	B737	20583	9M-MKV	A330	296
9M-MBC	B737	20584	9M-MKW	A330	300
9M-MBD	B737	20585	9M-MKX	A330	290
9M-MBE	B737	20586	9M-MKY	A330	143
9M-MBF	B737	20587	9M-MKZ	A330	096
9M-MBG	B737	20631	(9M-ML.)	B737	25348
9M-MBH	B737	20926	9M-MLA	B737	24164
9M-MBI	B737	21109	9M-MLB	B737	24167
9M-MBJ	B737	21732	9M-MLC	B737	23865
9M-MBK	B737	22620	9M-MLD	B737	24434
9M-MBL	B737	23320	9M-MLE	B737	24432
9M-MBM	B737	23849	9M-MLF	B737	25116
9M-MBN	B737	21231	9M-MLG	B737	25595
9M-MBO	B737	22395	9M-MLH	B737	25134
9M-MBP	B737	21176	9M-MLI	B737	24344
9M-MBQ	B737	21138	9M-MLJ	B737	25594
9M-MBY	B737	21686	9M-MLK	B737	25303
9M-MBZ	B737	21685	9M-MLL	B737	24644
9M-MCQ	B707	18953	9M-MMA	B737	26443
9M-MCR	B707	18954	9M-MMB	B737	26444
9M-MCS	B707	18955	9M-MMC	B737	26453
9M-MFA	B737	26445	9M-MMD	B737	26464
9M-MFB	B737	26446	9M-MME	B737	26465
9M-MFC	B737	26448	9M-MMF	B737	26466
(9M-MFD)	B737	26449	9M-MMG	B737	26467
9M-MFD	B737	26450	9M-MMH	B737	27084
(9M-MFE)	B737	26450	9M-MMI	B737	27096
9M-MFE	B737	26454	9M-MMJ	B737	27097
(9M-MFF)	B737	26451	9M-MMK	B737	27083
9M-MFF	B737	26456	9M-MML	B737	27085
9M-MFG	B737	27354	(9M-MMM)	B737	27086
9M-MFH	B737	27355	9M-MMM	B737	27166

Reg	Type	Serial
(9M-MMN)	B737	27087
9M-MMN	**B737**	**27167**
(9M-MMO)	B737	26468
9M-MMO	B737	27086
9M-MMP	B737	27168
(9M-MMQ)	B737	26447
9M-MMQ	**B737**	**27087**
9M-MMR	**B737**	**26468**
9M-MMS	**B737**	**27169**
9M-MMT	**B737**	**27170**
9M-MMU	**B737**	**26447**
9M-MMV	**B737**	**26449**
9M-MMW	**B737**	**26451**
9M-MMX	**B737**	**26452**
9M-MMY	**B737**	**26455**
9M-MMZ	**B737**	**26457**
(9M-MNA)	B737	26458
(9M-MNB)	B737	26459
(9M-MNC)	B737	26460
(9M-MND)	B737	26461
9M-MPA	B747	27042
9M-MPB	**B747**	**25699**
9M-MPC	B747	25700
9M-MPD	**B747**	**25701**
9M-MPE	B747	25702
9M-MPF	**B747**	**27043**
9M-MPG	B747	25703
9M-MPH	**B747**	**27044**
9M-MPI	**B747**	**27672**
9M-MPJ	**B747**	**28426**
9M-MPK	**B747**	**28427**
9M-MPL	**B747**	**28428**
9M-MPM	**B747**	**28435**
9M-MPN	**B747**	**28432**
9M-MPO	**B747**	**28433**
9M-MPP	**B747**	**29900**
9M-MPQ	B737	20254
9M-MPQ	**B747**	**29901**
9M-MPR	**B747**	**28434**
9M-MPS	**B747**	**29902**
9M-MQA	**B737**	**26458**
9M-MQB	**B737**	**26459**
9M-MQC	**B737**	**26460**
9M-MQD	**B737**	**26461**
9M-MQE	**B737**	**26462**
9M-MQF	**B737**	**26463**
9M-MQG	**B737**	**27190**
9M-MQH	B737	27352
9M-MQI	**B737**	**27353**
9M-MQJ	B737	27383
9M-MQK	**B737**	**27384**
9M-MQL	B737	27191
9M-MQM	**B737**	**27306**
9M-MQN	**B737**	**27673**
9M-MQO	**B737**	**27674**
9M-MQP	**B737**	**28038**
9M-MQQ	**B737**	**24915**
9M-MRA	**B777**	**28408**
9M-MRB	**B777**	**28409**
9M-MRC	**B777**	**28410**
9M-MRD	**B777**	**28411**
9M-MRE	**B777**	**28412**
9M-MRF	**B777**	**28413**
9M-MRG	**B777**	**28414**
9M-MRH	**B777**	**28415**
9M-MRI	**B777**	**28416**
9M-MRJ	**B777**	**28416**
9M-MRK	**B777**	**28418**
9M-MRL	**B777**	**29065**
9M-MRM	**B777**	**29066**
9M-MRN	**B777**	**28419**
9M-MRO	**B777**	**28420**
9M-MRP	**B777**	**28421**
9M-MRQ	**B777**	**28422**
9M-MZA	B737	27125
9M-MZB	B737	27347
9M-NAA	**A319**	**2949**
9M-PML	**B737**	**21116**
9M-PMM	**B737**	**20458**
9M-PMP	B737	20220
9M-PMR	B737	19553
9M-PMU	B737	23124
9M-PMW	**B737**	**24197**

Reg	Type	Serial
9M-PMY	B737	23913
9M-PMZ	B737	23796
9M-SAS	B727	18371
9M-TDM	B707	21049
9M-TGA	B727	22993
9M-TGB	**B727**	**22998**
9M-TGE	B727	21697
9M-TGF	**B727**	**21698**
9M-TGG	**B727**	**21699**
9M-TGH	**B727**	**21701**
9M-TGJ	B727	21700
9M-TGK	B727	21392
9M-TGM	**B727**	**22549**
9M-TGP	**MD11**	**48444**
9M-TGR	**MD11**	**48485**
9M-TGS	**MD11**	**48486**
9M-TOM	B727	20710
9M-VMB	B737	22703
9M-VWJ	B737	22279
9M-XAA	**A330**	**054**

Nepal

Reg	Type	Serial
(9N-)	146	E3362
(9N-ABA)	B727	19813
9N-ABD	B727	20421
9N-ABN	B727	19813
9N-ABV	B727	18879
9N-ABW	B727	18878
9N-ABY	B727	19113
9N-ACA	**B757**	**23850**
9N-ACB	**B757**	**23863**
9N-AHG	F.100	11485
9N-AHI	F.100	11450
9N-AHO	F.100	11264

Democratic Republic of Congo

Reg	Type	Serial
(9Q-)	B707	17905
9Q-	**DC-9**	**48126**
(9Q-)	MD80	49856
(9Q-)	MD80	49857
(9Q-ARW)	B747	19637
9Q-CAD	DC-8	46000
9Q-CAN	**DC-8**	**45858**
(9Q-CAR)	B727	18877
9Q-CAU	B727	20424
9Q-CAV	**B727**	**18967**
9Q-CAY	F.28	11136
9Q-CBD	B707	17658
9Q-CBD	**MD80**	**48018**
9Q CBF	**B727**	**19139**
9Q-CBF	DC-8	45629
9Q-CBG	B727	18367
9Q-CBL	B707	19266
9Q-CBP	B727	21320
9Q-CBS	B707	20200
9Q-CBS	B727	19319
9Q-CBT	B727	19138
9Q-CBW	B707	20200
9Q-CCP	SE210	229
9Q-CDA	B707	19294
9Q-CDC	**B727**	**18934**
9Q-CDG	DC-8	45821
9Q-CDJ	**B727**	**20424**
9Q-CDM	**B727**	**18919**
9Q-CDM	DC-8	45686
9Q-CDO	**DC-9**	**48125**
9Q-CDT	**DC-9**	**48128**
9Q-CDY	**1-11**	**BAC.261**
9Q-CEH	1-11	057
9Q-CFN	SE210	254
9Q-CFT	B707	18043
9Q-CGC	B707	19531
9Q-CGC	SE210	119
9Q-CGI	B747	21543
9Q-CGO	B707	17602
9Q-CGU	IL76	?
9Q-CGV	**IL76**	**0033449441**
9Q-CGV	IL76	?
9Q-CHA	L1011	193C-1227

Reg	Type	Serial
9Q-CHC	**L1011**	**193H-1209**
9Q-CHD	**B727**	**22494**
9Q-CHE	**B727**	**21310**
9Q-CHF	**B727**	**22677**
9Q-CHG	**B727**	**21586**
9Q-CHK	**B727**	**19401**
9Q-CHN	**DC-9**	**47731**
9Q-CJB	**MD80**	**48016**
9Q-CJD	**B767**	**23178**
9Q-CJL	**DC-8**	**45909**
9Q-CJT	B707	19335
9Q-CJW	B707	17602
9Q-CJW	B707	19844
9Q-CKB	B707	19519
9Q-CKB	B707	19844
9Q-CKB	B707	20761
9Q-CKG	B707	19844
9Q-CKI	1-11	BAC.177
9Q-CKI	B707	19801
9Q-CKI	DC-8	45683
9Q-CKK	B707	19577
(9Q-CKK)	B707	19844
9Q-CKK	B707	20761
9Q-CKP	1-11	BAC.191
9Q-CKP	B707	17658
9Q-CKR	**B707**	**19411**
9Q-CKS	B707	19415
9Q-CKY	1-11	BAC.176
9Q-CKZ	B737	19309
9Q-CLB	YAK40	9231623
9Q-CLC	SE210	240
9Q-CLD	SE210	251
9Q-CLE	DC-8	45266
9Q-CLF	DC-8	45268
9Q-CLG	DC-8	46151
9Q-CLH	DC-8	46147
9Q-CLI	DC-10	47886
9Q-CLK	**B707**	**17702**
9Q-CLP	SE210	115
9Q-CLT	DC-10	46932
9Q-CLV	DC-8	45610
9Q-CLY	B707	20517
9Q-CMA	B707	17606
9Q-CMC	B727	18371
9Q-CMD	B707	18694
9Q-CMD	SE210	74
9Q-CMG	DC-8	45683
9Q-CMK	SE210	254
9Q-CMP	**B727**	**19892**
9Q-CNA	SE210	240
9Q-CNI	**B707**	**19369**
9Q-CNI	B737	20793
9Q-CNJ	B737	20794
9Q-CNK	B737	20795
9Q-CNL	B737	20276
9Q-COB	**AN7x**	**72020362**
9Q-COW	B737	20808
9Q-CPI	SE210	169
9Q-CPI	SE210	183
9Q-CPJ	**B727**	**19088**
9Q-CPM	B707	18357
9Q-CPS	SE210	21
9Q-CPY	SE210	169
9Q-CQM	DC-8	45607
9Q-CRA	B707	19844
9Q-CRA	B727	18877
9Q-CRG	B727	18361
9Q-CRS	**B727**	**19687**
9Q-CRT	B707	17718
9Q-CRU	SE210	71
9Q-CRW	B707	17713
9Q-CRY	B707	17601
9Q-CSB	B707	19179
9Q-CSE	B727	18361
9Q-CSF	B727	18332
9Q-CSG	B727	18369
9Q-CSH	B727	19558
9Q-CSH	B707	19844
9Q-CSJ	**1-11**	**013**
9Q-CSJ	DC-8	45686
9Q-CSS	DC-10	46928
9Q-CSV	**B737**	**20276**
9Q-CSW	B707	19375

Reg	Type	Serial
9Q-CSY	B727	19180
9Q-CSZ	B707	19577
9Q-CTD	B707	18162
(9Q-CTD)	TRDNT	2308
9Q-CTE	TRDNT	2307
9Q-CTI	TRDNT	2305
9Q-CTK	B707	18413
9Q-CTM	B707	18078
(9Q-CTM)	TRDNT	2304
9Q-CTS	L1011	193B-1066
(9Q-CTY)	TRDNT	2308
(9Q-CTZ)	TRDNT	2322
9Q-CUG	1-11	057
9Q-CVG	B707	19162
9Q-CVG	B707	20122
9Q-CVH	DC-8	45862
9Q-CVN	L1011	193U-1201
9Q-CVO	SE210	209
9Q-CVT	**DC-9**	**48127**
9Q-CWA	B727	20775
9Q-CWB	**B707**	**20259**
9Q-CWD	**B727**	**19562**
9Q-CWE	**DC-9**	**47701**
9Q-CWF	DC-9	47531
9Q-CWG	**B707**	**19587**
9Q-CWH	**DC-9**	**47744**
9Q-CWK	**B707**	**20022**
9Q-CWR	B707	18357
9Q-CWT	B727	18291
9Q-CWY	B747	21300
9Q-CZF	B737	17930
9Q-CZK	B707	17602
9Q-CZL	SE210	123
9Q-CZZ	SE210	105
9Q-DDD	B727	20419
9Q-FDZ	B707	19415
9Q-MNS	B707	19969
9Q-RDZ	B727	18934

Burundi

Reg	Type	Serial
9U-BTA	SE210	144

Singapore

Reg	Type	Serial
9V-BAS	COMET	6401
9V-BAT	COMET	6404
9V-BAU	COMET	6406
9V-BBA	B707	19737
9V-RBB	B707	19739
9V-BBC	B737	19769
9V-BBE	B737	19771
9V-BBH	COMET	6417
9V-BBJ	COMET	6414
9V-BCR	B727	20492
9V-BDC	B707	19530
9V-BEF	1-11	BAC.166
9V-BEH	DC-8	45902
9V-BEW	B707	19351
9V-BEX	B707	19352
9V-BEY	B707	19353
9V-BFB	B707	19738
9V-BFC	B707	19529
9V-BFD	B737	19768
9V-BFE	B737	19770
9V-BFF	B737	19772
9V-BFN	B707	18809
9V-BFW	B707	18808
9V-JEA	**B747**	**22579**
9V-JSA	**A320**	**2316**
9V-JSB	**A320**	**2356**
9V-JSC	**A320**	**2395**
9V-JSD	**A320**	**2401**
9V-JSE	A320	2423
(9V-JSF)	A320	2453
(9V-JSG)	A320	2457
9V-JSH	**A320**	**2604**
9V-SBA	**A319**	**1074**
9V-SBB	**A319**	**1098**
9V-SBC	**A319**	**1228**

Registration	Type	Serial
9V-SBD	A319	1698
9V-SBE	A319	2568
9V-SBF	A319	3104
9V-SDA	DC-10	46990
9V-SDB	DC-10	46993
9V-SDC	DC-10	46991
9V-SDD	DC-10	46995
9V-SDE	DC-10	46999
9V-SDF	DC-10	47817
9V-SDG	DC-10	47818
9V-SFA	B747	26563
9V-SFB	B747	26561
9V-SFC	B747	26560
9V-SFD	B747	26553
9V-SFE	B747	28263
9V-SFF	B747	28026
9V-SFG	B747	26558
9V-SFH	B747	28032
9V-SFI	B747	28027
9V-SFJ	B747	26559
9V-SFK	B747	28030
9V-SFL	B747	32897
9V-SFM	B747	32898
9V-SFN	B747	32899
9V-SFO	B747	32900
9V-SFP	B747	32902
9V-SFQ	B747	32901
9V-SGA	A340	492
9V-SGA	B727	21347
9V-SGB	A340	499
9V-SGB	B727	21348
9V-SGC	A340	478
9V-SGC	B727	21349
9V-SGD	A340	560
9V-SGD	B727	21458
9V-SGE	A340	563
9V-SGE	B727	21459
9V-SGF	B727	21460
9V-SGG	B727	21945
9V-SGH	B727	21946
9V-SGI	B727	21947
9V-SGJ	B727	21948
(9V-SGJ)	B777	28514
9V-SGK	B757	23125
9V-SGL	B757	23126
9V-SGM	B757	23127
9V-SGN	B757	23128
9V-SIA	B747	20712
9V-SIB	B747	20713
9V-SJA	A340	123
9V-SJB	A340	126
9V-SJC	A340	128
9V-SJD	A340	139
9V-SJE	A340	149
9V-SJF	A340	117
9V-SJG	A340	163
9V-SJH	A340	166
9V-SJI	A340	185
9V-SJJ	A340	190
9V-SJK	A340	202
9V-SJK	B777	33375
9V-SJL	A340	212
9V-SJM	A340	215
9V-SJN	A340	236
9V-SJO	A340	282
9V-SJP	A340	528
9V-SJQ	A340	554
9V-SKA	A380	003
9V-SKA	B747	23026
9V-SKB	A380	005
(9V-SKB)	B747	23027
9V-SKC	A380	006
(9V-SKC)	B747	23028
9V-SKD	A380	008
9V-SKD	B747	23029
9V-SKE	A380	010
(9V-SKE)	B747	23030
9V-SKF	A380	012
(9V-SKF)	B747	23031
9V-SKG	A380	019
(9V-SKG)	B747	23032
9V-SKH	B747	23033
9V-SKJ	B747	23243
9V-SKK	B747	23244
9V-SKL	B747	23245
9V-SKM	B747	23409
9V-SKN	B747	23410
9V-SKP	B747	23769
9V-SKQ	B747	24177
9V-SLA	A320	0872
9V-SLB	A320	0899
9V-SLC	A320	0969
9V-SLD	A320	1422
9V-SLE	A320	1561
9V-SLF	A320	2058
9V-SLG	A320	2252
9V-SLH	A320	2517
9V-SLI	A320	2775
9V-SLK	F.70	11536
9V-SLL	F.70	11561
9V-SMA	B747	24061
9V-SMB	B747	24062
9V-SMC	B747	24063
9V-SMD	B747	24064
9V-SME	B747	24065
9V-SMF	B747	24066
9V-SMG	B747	24226
9V-SMH	B747	24227
9V-SMI	B747	24975
(9V-SMJ)	B747	24975
9V-SMJ	B747	25068
(9V-SMK)	B747	25068
9V-SMK	B747	25127
(9V-SML)	B747	25127
9V-SML	B747	25128
(9V-SMM)	B747	25128
9V-SMM	B747	26547
9V-SMN	B747	26548
9V-SMO	B747	27066
9V-SMP	B747	27067
9V-SMQ	B747	27132
9V-SMR	B747	27133
9V-SMS	B747	27134
9V-SMT	B747	27137
9V-SMU	B747	27068
9V-SMV	B747	27069
9V-SMW	B747	27178
9V-SMY	B747	27217
9V-SMZ	B747	26549
9V-SPA	B747	26550
9V-SPB	B747	26551
9V-SPC	B747	27070
9V-SPD	B747	26552
9V-SPE	B747	26554
9V-SPF	B747	27071
9V-SPG	B747	26562
9V-SPH	B747	26555
9V-SPI	B747	28022
9V-SPJ	B747	26556
9V-SPK	B747	28023
9V-SPL	B747	26557
9V-SPM	B747	29950
9V-SPN	B747	28031
9V-SPO	B747	28028
9V-SPP	B747	28029
9V-SPQ	B747	28025
9V-SPR	B747	25702
9V-SPS	B747	25700
(9V-SQA)	B747	23033
9V-SQA	B777	28507
9V-SQB	B777	28508
9V-SQC	B747	20888
9V-SQC	B777	28509
9V-SQD	B747	21048
9V-SQD	B777	28510
9V-SQE	B747	21162
9V-SQE	B777	28511
9V-SQF	B747	21316
9V-SQF	B777	28512
9V-SQG	B747	21439
(9V-SQG)	B777	28513
9V-SQG	B777	28518
9V-SQH	B747	21683
9V-SQH	B777	28519
(9V-SQH)	B777	28998
9V-SQI	B747	21684
9V-SQI	B777	28530
(9V-SQI)	B777	28999
9V-SQJ	B747	21935
9V-SQJ	B777	30875
9V-SQK	B747	21936
9V-SQK	B777	33368
9V-SQL	B747	21937
9V-SQL	B777	33370
9V-SQM	B747	21938
9V-SQM	B777	33372
9V-SQN	B747	21939
9V-SQN	B777	33373
9V-SQO	B747	21940
9V-SQP	B747	21941
9V-SQQ	B747	21942
9V-SQR	B747	21943
9V-SQS	B747	21944
9V-SQT	B747	22150
(9V-SQT)	B747	23026
9V-SQU	B747	22151
(9V-SQU)	B747	23027
9V-SQV	B747	22245
(9V-SQV)	B747	23028
(9V-SQW)	B747	23029
(9V-SQX)	B747	23030
(9V-SQY)	B747	23031
9V-SQZ	B737	24021
(9V-SQZ)	B747	23032
9V-SRA	B777	28513
9V-SRB	B777	28998
9V-SRC	B777	28999
9V-SRD	B777	28514
9V-SRE	B777	28523
9V-SRF	B777	28521
9V-SRG	B777	28522
9V-SRH	B777	30866
9V-SRI	B777	30867
9V-SRJ	B777	28527
9V-SRK	B777	28529
9V-SRL	B777	32334
9V-SRM	B777	32320
9V-SRN	B777	32318
9V-SRO	B777	32321
9V-SRP	B777	33369
9V-SRQ	B777	33371
9V-STA	A300	117
9V-STA	A310	665
9V-STB	A300	121
9V-STB	A310	660
9V-STC	A300	126
9V-STC	A310	680
9V-STD	A300	169
9V-STD	A310	684
9V-STE	A300	174
9V-STE	A310	693
9V-STF	A300	222
9V-STF	A310	697
9V-STG	A300	268
9V-STH	A300	269
9V-STI	A310	347
9V-STJ	A310	350
9V-STK	A310	357
9V-STL	A310	363
9V-STM	A310	367
9V-STN	A310	372
9V-STO	A310	433
9V-STP	A310	443
9V-STQ	A310	493
9V-STR	A310	500
9V-STS	A310	501
9V-STT	A310	534
9V-STU	A310	548
9V-STV	A310	570
9V-STW	A310	589
9V-STY	A310	634
9V-STZ	A310	654
9V-SVA	B777	28524
9V-SVB	B777	28525
9V-SVC	B777	28526
9V-SVD	B777	30869
9V-SVE	B777	30870
9V-SVF	B777	30871
9V-SVG	B777	30872
9V-SVH	B777	28532
9V-SVI	B777	32316
9V-SVJ	B777	32335
9V-SVK	B777	28520
9V-SVL	B777	32336
9V-SVM	B777	30874
9V-SVN	B777	30873
9V-SVO	B777	28533
9V-SWA	B777	34568
9V-SWB	B777	33377
9V-SWD	B777	34569
9V-SWE	B777	34570
9V-SWF	B777	34571
9V-SWG	B777	34572
9V-SWH	B777	34573
9V-SWI	B777	34574
9V-SWJ	B777	34575
9V-SWK	B777	34576
9V-SWL	B777	34577
9V-SWM	B777	34578
9V-SWN	B777	34579
9V-SWO	B777	34580
9V-SWP	B777	34581
9V-SWQ	B777	34582
9V-SWR	B777	34583
(9V-SXA)	B727	21347
(9V-SXB)	B727	21348
(9V-SXC)	B727	21349
(9V-SXD)	B727	21458
(9V-SXE)	B727	21459
(9V-SXF)	B727	21460
9V-SYA	B777	28515
9V-SYB	B777	28516
9V-SYC	B777	28517
9V-SYD	B777	28534
9V-SYE	B777	28531
9V-SYF	B777	30868
9V-SYG	B777	28528
9V-SYH	B777	32317
9V-SYI	B777	32327
9V-SYJ	B777	33374
9V-SYL	B777	33376
9V-TAA	A320	2204
9V-TAB	A320	2195
9V-TAC	A320	2331
9V-TAD	A320	2340
9V-TAE	A320	2724
9V-TAF	A320	2728
9V-TAG	A320	2906
9V-TAH	A320	2952
9V-TAI	A320	2982
9V-TRA	B737	24679
9V-TRB	B737	24902
9V-TRC	B737	24570
9V-TRD	B737	25017
9V-TRE	B737	27457
9V-TRF	B737	28556
9V-TRY	MD80	49673
9V-VLA	A320	2156
9V-VLB	A320	2164
9V-VLC	A320	0739
9V-VLD	A320	0743
9V-VQX	A320	2322
9V-VQZ	A320	2292
9V-WGA	B727	21946

Rwanda

Registration	Type	Serial
9XR-CH	SE210	209
9XR-CV	AN7x	?
9XR-DU	TU154	91A-895
9XR-GY	YAK40	?
9XR-IS	B707	19335
9XR-JA	B707	19292
9XR-RA	1-11	011
9XR-RV	AN7x	?
9XR-SC	DC-8	46068
9XR-SD	DC-8	45956
9XR-SY	YAK40	?
9XR-VO	B707	19292

Trinidad & Tobago

Reg	Type	c/n
(9Y-)	B737	21339
(9Y-ANU)	737NG	28234
9Y-ANU	**737NG**	**28235**
9Y-BGI	**737NG**	**28232**
9Y-BWA	A321	0604
9Y-BWB	A321	0614
(9Y-BWC)	L1011	293A-1248
9Y-GEO	**737NG**	**28225**
9Y-GND	737NG	33419
9Y-JIL	A340	016
9Y-KIN	**737NG**	**28234**
9Y-POS	**737NG**	**28230**
(9Y-SLU)	737NG	28235
9Y-TAB	**737NG**	**28233**
9Y-TCA	B707	18043
9Y-TCO	B727	18794
9Y-TCP	B727	18795
9Y-TCQ	B727	18796
9Y-TDB	B707	18334
9Y-TDC	B707	18067
9Y-TDO	B707	17592
9Y-TDP	B707	17694
9Y-TDQ	B707	17695
9Y-TDR	B707	17693
9Y-TED	B707	19209
9Y-TEE	B707	19412
9Y-TEJ	B707	19631
9Y-TEK	B707	19632
9Y-TEX	B707	20027
9Y-TEZ	B707	20028
9Y-TFF	DC-9	47737
9Y-TFG	DC-9	47742
9Y-TFH	DC-9	47743
9Y-TFI	DC-9	47752
9Y-TGC	DC-9	47796
9Y-TGJ	L1011	193G-1179
9Y-TGN	L1011	193G-1191
9Y-TGP	DC-9	48122
9Y-THA	L1011	193G-1222
(9Y-THB)	L1011	193G-1233
9Y-THN	MD80	49390
9Y-THQ	MD80	49448
9Y-THR	MD80	49568
9Y-THT	MD80	49575
9Y-THU	MD80	49824
9Y-THV	MD80	49632
9Y-THW	MD80	49786
9Y-THX	MD80	49789
9Y-THY	MD80	49400
9Y-TJC	B737	21339
9Y-TJG	B737	21960
9Y-TJH	B737	22632
9Y-TJI	737NG	28209
9Y-TJN	**A340**	**093**

Commonwealth of Independent States

Reg	Type	c/n
17563	IL76	1053417563
17569	IL76	1033417569
19656	IL76	1053419656
42314	YAK42	22204245134
42317	YAK42	2202039
42319	YAK42	3402062
42330	YAK42	2505122
42342	YAK42	1706302
48110	YAK40	9230623
48112	YAK40	9211520
49858	TU134	73.49858
60142	TU134	73.60142
60475	TU134	60475
63957	TU134	63957
63976	TU134	63976
63982	**TU134**	**63982**
64003	TU204	..64003
64035	TU204	..64035
64121	TU134	64121
64615	TU134	64615
65014	TU134	46200
65025	TU134	48450
65030	TU134	48520
65039	TU134	49080
65044	TU134	49450
65075	TU134	49998
65077	TU134	60028
65098	**TU134**	**73550815**
65134	TU134	60647
65145	TU134	60985
65551	TU134	66212
65556	TU134	66372
65557	TU134	66380
65613	TU134	3352106
65684	TU134	62205
65702	TU134	63375
65705	TU134	63415
65708	TU134	63447
65709	TU134	63484
65711	TU134	63498
65713	TU134	63520
65714	TU134	63527
65718	TU134	63668
65720	TU134	62820
65731	TU134	1351401
65750	TU134	61042
65774	TU134	62519
65798	TU134	63179
65809	TU134	3352110
65832	TU134	17106
65893	TU134	5340120
65905	TU134	63965
65911	TU134	63972
65932	TU134	66405
65985	TU134	63468
71506	YAK40	9731255
72904	AN7x	72030425
72933	AN7x	72070698
72940	**AN7x**	**72080781**
72959	AN7x	72092858
72966	AN7x	72092847
72975	AN7x	72094888
72985	AN7x	47098973
76321	**IL76**	**0053457713**
76332	**IL76**	**0053462873**
76323	**IL76**	**0063466988**
76353	IL76	1023414454
76413	**IL76**	**1013407215**
76423	**IL76**	**0053457720**
76436	IL76	1023411368
76438	IL76	0083483513
76447	IL76	1023412389
76448	IL76	1023413443
76449	IL76	1023403086
76454	IL76	0063469074
76455	IL76	0073471125
76456	IL76	0073474208
76458	IL76	0013430888
76463	IL76	0013432960
76485	IL76	0063470088
76492	IL76	0043452549
76508	IL76	083413412
76517	IL76	093418560
76531	IL76	0023441181
76534	**IL76**	**0023442210**
76536	**IL76**	**0023442221**
76557	**IL76**	**0033446329**
76559	**IL76**	**0033446340**
76562	IL76	0033447365
76564	**IL76**	**0033448373**
76565	**IL76**	**0033448382**
76566	**IL76**	**0033448385**
76567	IL76	0033448390
76575	**IL76**	**0033449445**
76580	**IL76**	**0043450476**
76585	**IL76**	**0043451503**
76596	**IL76**	**0043453583**
76597	**IL76**	**0043453585**
76598	**IL76**	**0043453591**
76609	**IL76**	**0043453597**
76618	**IL76**	**0043455682**
76631	**IL76**	**0053458756**
76633	**IL76**	**0053459764**
76637	**IL76**	**0053460797**
76645	**IL76**	**0053461834**
76647	**IL76**	**0053461843**
76653	IL76	0053462875
76654	**IL76**	**0053462884**
76657	**IL76**	**0053463896**
76660	**IL76**	**0053463910**
76661	**IL76**	**0053463913**
76665	**IL76**	**0053464930**
76675	**IL76**	**0063466998**
76680	**IL76**	**0063467020**
76683	**IL76**	**0063468029**
76689	IL76	0063469066
76697	**IL76**	**0063470118**
76698	**IL76**	**0063471123**
76699	**IL76**	**0063471131**
76703	IL76	0063471147
76705	IL76	0063472158
76730	**IL76**	**0073476277**
76732	**IL76**	**0073476296**
76736	**IL76**	**0073476317**
76748	IL76	0073479386
76749	IL76	0073479392
76759	IL76	0083485558
76760	**IL76**	**0073479404**
76767	**IL76**	**0083487598**
76811	IL76	1013407223
76818	IL76	1013408264
76819	IL76	1013409274
76824	IL76	1023410327
76900	IL76	1053417563
76950	IL76	1063420697
78821	IL76	0093496914
78845	IL76	1003403095
82070	AN124	977305135912
85008	TU154	70M008
85050	TU154	73A-050
85104	TU154	75A-104
85147	TU154	76A-147
85158	TU154	76A-158
85163	TU154	76A-163
85168	TU154	76A-168
85177	TU154	76A-177
85188	TU154	76A-188
85192	TU154	77A-192
85199	TU154	77A-199
85249	TU154	77A-249
85274	TU154	78A-274
85285	TU154	78A-285
85294	TU154	78A-294
85313	TU154	78A-313
85329	TU154	79A-329
85332	TU154	79A-332
85345	TU154	79A-345
85359	TU154	79A-359
85391	TU154	80A-391
85393	TU154	80A-393
85394	TU154	80A-394
85397	TU154	80A-397
85398	TU154	80A-398
85430	TU154	80A-430
85438	TU154	80A-438
85464	TU154	80A-464
85492	TU154	81A-492
85496	TU154	81A-496
85507	TU154	81A-507
85518	TU154	81A-518
85533	TU154	82A-533
85537	TU154	82A-537
85548	TU154	82A-548
85549	TU154	82A-549
85561	TU154	82A-561
85575	TU154	83A-575
85578	TU154	83A-578
85600	TU154	84A-600
85601	TU154	84A-601
85624	TU154	87A-750
85651	TU154	88A-793
85653	TU154	88A-795
85675	TU154	90A-835
85686	TU154	90A-854
85698	TU154	91A-871
85700	TU154	91A-875
85701	TU154	91A-876
85708	TU154	91A-883
85711	TU154	91A-887
85715	TU154	91A-891
85717	TU154	91A-897
85734	TU154	92A-916
86012	IL86	51483201010
86016	IL86	51483202014
86028	**IL76**	**083415464**
86029	IL76	083415465
86030	IL76	093415475
86031	IL76	093415477
86083	IL86	51483206054
86451	IL62	4521152
86468	IL62	4749857
86527	IL62	4037758
86528	IL62	4038111
86529	IL62	4038625
86554	IL62	4053514
86573	IL62	4140536
86574	IL62	3344833
86575	IL62	1647928
86576	IL62	4546257
86577	IL62	2748552
86578	IL62	1951525
86579	IL62	2951636
86612	IL62	41804
86633	**IL76**	**073409256**
86648	**IL62**	**00605**
86666	**IL62**	**60201**
86711	IL62	4648414
86712	IL62	4648339
86854	IL76	0003425728
86900	IL76	0023435034
86915	**IL76**	**0023438116**
86918	IL76	0023438127
86922	IL76	0023440016
86923	IL76	0023441169
87200	**YAK40**	**9811956**
87218	YAK40	9440937
87228	YAK40	9841659
87229	YAK40	9841759
87230	YAK40	9541542
87237	YAK40	9530343
87243	YAK40	9531143
87257	YAK40	9311426
87278	YAK40	9311427
87297	YAK40	9321428
87337	YAK40	9510639
87413	YAK40	9420534
87460	YAK40	9431936
87466	YAK40	9430537
87478	YAK40	9440638
87533	YAK40	9541741
87569	YAK40	9220222
87643	YAK40	9140420
87644	YAK40	9140520
87662	**YAK40**	**9240625**
87807	YAK40	9231723
87812	YAK40	9230424
87817	YAK40	9230824
87918	YAK40	9730855
87946	YAK40	9611045
87964	YAK40	9820758
87968	YAK40	9841258
87972	YAK40	9921658
87995	YAK40	9541944
88174	YAK40	9621247
88187	YAK40	9620748
88199	YAK40	9630249
88203	YAK40	9630549
88211	YAK40	9631749
88237	YAK40	9640751
88290	YAK40	9840459
88294	YAK40	9331029
93926	TU134	1351204
94001	**TU334**	**01001**
94005	**TU334**	**01005**

Odds & Ends

Reg	Type	c/n
"18925"	B707	18925
"AB-HRS"	737NG	29251
		see A6-HRS
"B-4203"	A300	158
IS-76900	IL76	1053417563
		see RA-76900
"VR-VZA"	B707	20375
		see VR-BZA
"17696"	B707	17696
"26000"	B707	17720
"26000"	B707	18065
"28000"	B747	19727
MOLDOVA-74009	AN7x	47095898
ROSSIYA-64007	TU204	1264007

MILITARY INDEX

Algeria

7T-WIA	IL76	0083489674
7T-WIB	IL76	0093493803
7T-WIC	IL76	1003405154
7T-WID	IL76	1023414470
7T-WIE	IL76	1023414463
7T-WIF	IL76	?
7T-WIG	IL76	1023413435
7T-WIH	IL76	?
7T-WIL	IL76	0043454640
7T-WIN	IL76	0063469080
7T-WIP	IL76	1043419636
7T-WIQ	IL76	0053462879
7T-WIR	IL76	?
7T-WIT	IL76	?
7T-WIU	IL76	1023413423
7T-WIV	IL76	1043419649

Angola

SG-104	TU134	49830
T-450	YAK40	9820558
T-501	E145	14500981
T-700	AN7x	72060640
T-701	AN7x	72095907
T-702	AN7x	72093876
T-750	AN7x	?
T-902	IL76	1023409280

Argentina

5-T-10	F.28	11147
5-T-20	F.28	11145
5-T-21	F.28	11150
0740	F.28	11147
0741	F.28	11145
0742	F.28	11150
T-01	B757	25487
T-01	B707	21070
T-01	F.28	11028
T-02	F.28	11028
T-02	F.28	11048
T-02	F.28	11203
T-03	F.28	11028
T-03	F.28	11203
T-04	F.28	11028
T-04	F.28	11048
T-50	F.28	11048
T-50	F.28	11203
T-91	SE210	19
T-92	SE210	149
T-93	SE210	180
T-95	B707	19241
T-96	B707	19238
TC-51	F.28	11076
TC-52	F.28	11074
TC-53	F.28	11020
TC-54	F.28	11018
TC-55	F.28	11024
TC-91	B707	21070
TC-92	B707	20077
TC-93	B707	19962
TC-93	B707	20076
TC-94	B707	20076
VR-21	B707	19962

Australia

A12-124	1-11	BAC.124
A12-125	1-11	BAC.125
A20-103	B707	21103
A20-261	B707	21261
A20-623	B707	19623
A20-624	B707	19624
A20-627	B707	19627
A20-629	B707	19629
(A20-809)	B707	19809
A30-001	737NG	33474
A30-002	737NG	33542
A30-	737NG	33476
A30-	737NG	33477
A36-001	737NG	33986
A36-002	737NG	30829
A39-001	737NG	30790
A41-206	A330	747
A41-207	C-17	F.166/AUS1
	C-17	F.167/AUS2

Belgium

CA-01	A310	372
CA-02	A310	367
CB-01	B727	19402
CB-02	B727	19403
CE-01	E145	145449
CE-02	E145	145480
CE-03	E145	145526
CE-04	E145	145548

Benin

TY-24A	B727	20819

Brazil

FAB 2101	A319	2263
2401	B707	19840
2402	B707	19842
2403	B707	20008
2404	B707	19870
(FAB2405)	B707	19321
2520	E145	145023
2521	E145	145020
2522	E145	145027
2523	E145	145028
2524	E145	145034
2525	E145	145038
2550	E145	145350
2580	E145	145412
2581	E145	145462
6700	E145	145104
6701	E145	145122
6702	E145	145263
6703	E145	145365
6704	E145	145392
6750	E145	145140
6751	E145	145154
6752	E145	145257
VC92-2110	1-11	BAC.154
VC92-2111	1-11	BAC.118
VC95-2116	B737	21166
VC96-2115	B737	21165

Bolivia

FAB-...	146	E1081
FAB-098	146	E1076
FAB-100	146	E2080
FAB-101	146	E2041

Bulgaria

050	TU134	0350922
050	TU134	1351303
060	YAK40	9621547
LZ D 050	TU134	1351303

Canada

5301	COMET	06017
5302	COMET	06018
13701	B707	20315
13702	B707	20316
13703	B707	20317
13704	B707	20318
13705	B707	20319
15001	A310	446
15002	A310	482
15003	A310	425
15004	A310	444
15005	A310	441

Chile

01	B707	19000
901	B707	19402
901	B727	19196
902	B707	19443
903	B707	18926
904	B707	19000
904	B707	19374
905	B707	19000
921	B737	28866
922	B737	23524

China

18351	B707	18351
50054	TRDNT	2186
50056	TRDNT	2130
50256	TU124	5351808
50257	TU124	5351809

Colombia

1201	B707	19716
ARC-707	B707	20301
FAC001	F.28	11992
FAC0001	F.28	11992
FAC0001	737NG	29272
FAC0002	F.28	11992
FAC-1041	F.28	11162
FAC-1140	F.28	11165
FAC-1141	F.28	11162
FAC-1142	DC-9	45722
(FAC-1145)	B727	19303
FAC-1146	B727	19595
FAC-1147	B727	20303
FAC 1170	E145	145003
FAC 1171	E145	145774
FAC 1172	E145	145776
FAC 1173	E145	14500879
FAC 1176	E145	145165
FAC 1177	E145	145227
FAC 1180	E170	17000151
FAC-1246	B727	19595
FAC-1247	B727	20303

Cuba

12-41	YAK40	9631049
12-49	YAK40	9021260
12-50	YAK40	9021360
14-41	YAK40	9631049

Czech Republic

0260	YAK40	9940260
0420	TU154	80A-420
0601	TU154	84A-601
0723	YAK40	9230723
0823	YAK40	9230823
1003	TU154	00A-1003
1016	TU154	96A-1016
1257	YAK40	9821257
(1302)	TU104	86601302
(1303)	TU104	86601303
1407	TU134	1351407
2801	A319	2801
3085	A319	3085

East Germany

(115)	TU134	60108
(116)	TU134	60435
(117)	TU134	60612
(118)	TU134	62259
(119)	TU134	63260
(123)	TU134	49900
(144)	TU154	89A-799
(170)	TU134	3352102
(171)	TU134	3352106
(175)	TU134	4352205
(175)	TU134	9350904
176	IL62	4445827
176	TU134	4352206
(176)	TU134	63967
177	TU134	9350913
(178)	TU134	4352207
(178)	TU134	9350912
(179)	TU134	31218
180	TU134	1351304
181	TU134	35180
182	TU134	1351305
(183)	TU134	38040
(183)	TU134	63998
(183)	TU134	9350905
184	TU134	63952
(185)	TU134	40150
186	TU134	16155
(193)	TU134	66135
"494"	TU124	5351708
495 black	TU124	4351505
496 black	TU124	4351508

Ecuador

FAE078	B727	22078
FAE-112	F.28	11112
FAE220	F.28	11220
FAE228	F.28	11228
FAE273	B707	19273
FAE328	B727	20328
FAE560	B727	20560
FAE618	B727	21618
FAE620	B727	21620
FAE622	B727	21622
FAE691	B727	19691
FAE692	B727	19692
FAE788	B727	20788
FAE8033	B707	18033
FAE8036	B707	18036
FAE8037	B707	18037
FAE19255	B707	19265
FAE19277	B707	19277
FAE20033	B707	20033

Ethiopia

1601	YAK40	?

France

116/CE	SE210	116
141	SE210	141
1485	**A319**	**1485**
1556	**A319**	**1556**
158	SE210	158
193	SE210	193
201	SE210	201
201/36-CA	**B707**	**24115**
202/36-CB	**B707**	**24116**
203/36-CC	**B707**	**24117**
204/36-CD	**B707**	**24510**
234	SE210	234
240	SE210	240
251	SE210	251
264	SE210	264
418	**A310**	**418**
421	**A310**	**421**
422	**A310**	**422**
470/93-CA	**KC135**	**18679**
470/CA	KC135	18679
471/93-CB	**KC135**	**18680**
471/CB	KC135	18680
472/93-CC	**KC135**	**18681**
472/CC	KC135	18681
473/CD	KC135	18682
474/93-CE	**KC135**	**18683**
474/CE	KC135	18683
475/93-CF	**KC135**	**18684**
475/CF	KC135	18684
497/93-CM	**KC135**	**18480**
525/93-CN	**KC135**	**18508**
574/93-CO	**KC135**	**18557**
735/93-CG	**KC135**	**18695**
735/CG	KC135	18695
736/93-CH	**KC135**	**18696**
736/CH	KC135	18696
737/93-CI	**KC135**	**18697**
737/CI	KC135	18697
738/93-CJ	**KC135**	**18698**
738/CJ	KC135	18698
739/93-CK	**KC135**	**18699**
739/CK	KC135	18699
740/93-CL	**KC135**	**18700**
740/CL	KC135	18700
2801	**A319**	**2801**
3085	**A319**	**3085**
45570	DC-8	45570
45692	DC-8	45692
45819	DC-8	45819
45820	DC-8	45820
46013	DC-8	46013
46043	DC-8	46043
46130	DC-8	46130
F-RADA	**A310**	**421**
F-RADB	**A310**	**422**
F-RADC	**A310**	**418**
F-RAFA	DC-8	45820
F-RAFA	SE210	158
F-RAFB	DC-8	45692
F-RAFC	DC-8	45819
F-RAFD	DC-8	46043
F-RAFE	DC-8	45570
F-RAFF	DC-8	46130
F-RAFG	DC-8	46013
F-RAFG	SE210	141
F-RAFH	SE210	201
F-RBFA	**A319**	**1485**
F-RBFB	**A319**	**1556**
F-RBPR	SE210	240
F-RBPS	SE210	251
F-RBPT	SE210	264
(F-UKAS)	KC135	18499
F-UKCA	**KC135**	**18679**
F-UKCB	**KC135**	**18680**
F-UKCC	**KC135**	**18681**
F-UKCE	**KC135**	**18683**
F-UKCF	**KC135**	**18684**
F-UKCG	**KC135**	**18695**
F-UKCH	**KC135**	**18696**
F-UKCI	**KC135**	**18697**
F-UKCJ	**KC135**	**18698**
F-UKCK	**KC135**	**18699**
F-UKCL	**KC135**	**18700**
F-UKCM	**KC135**	**18480**
F-UKCN	**KC135**	**18508**
F-UKCO	**KC135**	**18557**
F-ZACE	SE210	116
F-ZACF	SE210	193
F-ZACQ	SE210	234
F-ZARK	DC-8	45570
F-ZBCA	**B707**	**24115**
F-ZBCB	**B707**	**24116**
F-ZBCC	**B707**	**24117**
F-ZBCD	**B707**	**24510**

Germany

10+01	B707	19997
10+02	B707	19998
10+03	B707	19999
10+04	B707	20000
10+21	**A310**	**498**
10+22	**A310**	**499**
10+23	**A310**	**503**
10+24	**A310**	**434**
10+25	**A310**	**484**
10+26	**A310**	**522**
10+27	**A310**	**523**
11+01	TU154	89A-799
11+02	TU154	89A-813
11+10	TU134	63967
11+11	TU134	63952
11+12	TU134	66135
11+20	IL62	3749224
11+21	IL62	3242432
11+22	IL62	4445827
17+01	VFW	G-014
17+02	VFW	G-018
17+03	VFW	G-019

Ghana

G-530	F.28	11125

Greece

145-209	**E145**	**145209**
374	**E145**	**145374**
135L484	**E145**	**145484**
671	**E145**	**145671**
729	**E145**	**145729**
757	**E145**	**145757**

Hungary

HA-926	TU134	12096
HA-927	TU134	17103

India

K-2370	B737	21498
K-2371	B737	21497
K-2899	**B707**	**19988**
K-2900	B707	19248
K-3187	B737	22860
K2412	**B737**	**23036**
K2413	**B737**	**23037**
K2661	IL76	0053458722
K2662	IL76	0053458725
K2663	IL76	0053458731
K2664	IL76	0053461849
K2665	IL76	0053462856
K2666	IL76	0053462857
K2878	IL76	0063465970
K2879	IL76	0063465973
K2901	IL76	0073478343
K2902	IL76	0073478353
K2999	IL76	0073480410
K3000	IL76	0073480419
K3012	**IL76**	**0083487614**
K3013	**IL76**	**0083488629**
K3014	**IL76**	**0093491750**
K3077	IL76	0093496892
K3078	IL76	0093496912
K3186	B737	20484
K3187	B737	20483
K3601	E145	14500867
K3602	E145	14500880
K3603	E145	14500910
K3604	E145	14500919
K5011	B737	22860
KW3553	IL76	?
RK3451	IL76	...3425855
RK3452	IL76	20.3425860
V642	TU124	6351901?
V643	TU124	6351902?
V644	TU124	6351903

Indonesia

A-2801	F.28	11042
A-2802	F.28	11113
A-2803	F.28	11117
A-7002	B707	21092
AI-7301	B737	22777
AI-7302	B737	22778
AI-7303	B737	22779
AI-7304	B737	21518

Iran

102	**B747**	**19678**
103	**B747**	**20080**
301	B707	20830
1001	**B707**	**21396**
1002	B727	19557
5-241	B707	20830
5-242	B707	20831
5-243	B707	20832
5-244	B707	20833
5-245	B707	20834
5-246	B707	20835
(5-247)	B707	21123
(5-248)	B707	21124
(5-249)	B707	21125
(5-250)	B707	21126
(5-251)	B707	21127
(5-252)	B707	21128
(5-253)	B707	21129
5-280	B747	19667
5-281	B747	19678
5-282	B747	20080
5-283	B747	19677
5-284	B747	20081
5-285	B747	19668
5-286	B747	20082
5-287	B747	19669
5-288	B747	20083
5-289	B747	19733
5-290	B747	19734
5-291	B747	19735
5-8101	**B747**	**19667**
5-8102	B747	19678
5-8103	B747	20080
5-8104	B747	19677
5-8105	**B747**	**20081**
5-8106	**B747**	**19668**
5-8107	B747	20082
5-8108	**B747**	**19669**
(5-8109)	B747	20083
5-8110	B747	19733
(5-8111)	B747	19734
5-8112	B747	19735
5-8113	B747	21486
5-8114	B747	21487
5-8115	B747	21507
5-8116	B747	21514
5-8117	B747	21668
5-8201	IL76	?
5-8203	IL76	?
5-8204	IL76	?
5-8205	IL76	?
5-8206	IL76	?
5-8207	IL76	?
5-8208	IL76	?
5-8210	IL76	?
5-8301	B707	20830
5-8302	B707	20831
5-8303	B707	20832
5-8304	B707	20833
5-8305	B707	20834
5-8306	B707	20835
5-8307	B707	21092
5-8308	B707	21124
5-8309	B707	21125
5-8310	B707	21126
5-8311	B707	21127
5-8312	B707	21128
5-8313	B707	21129
5-8314	B707	21475
15-22..	IL76	0063471155
15-2250	AN7x	470991021
15-2251	**AN7x**	**470991028**
15-2252	**AN7x**	**470991032**
15-2253	**AN7x**	**470991038**
15-2254	**AN7x**	**470991040**
15-2255	**AN7x**	**470991045**
15-2256	**AN7x**	**4701211048**
15-2257	**AN7x**	**4701211050**
15-2258	**AN7x**	**4701211053**
15-2259	**AN7x**	**4701211055**
15-2260	**AN7x**	**4701211058**
15-2261	**AN7x**	**4701211059**
15-2280	IL76	?
15-2282	IL76	?
15-2283	IL76	?
15-2284	IL76	?
15-2285	IL76	?
15-2289	IL76	?
15-2291	IL76	?

Iraq

634	TU124	5351609?
635	TU124	5351610?
2068	IL76	093418543
2803	IL76	093416506
4600	IL76	0013433984
4601	IL76	0013433999
4660	IL76	0013433996

Israel

001	B707	17612
004	B707	17668
006	B707	18012
008	B707	17667
009	B707	17610
010	B707	18013
1..	B707	17661
"103"	B707	17617
115	B707	17615
116	B707	17617
117	B707	17922
118	B707	18246
119	B707	17619
120	**B707**	**17921**
128	B707	18374
137	B707	18460

```
137     B707  17625      28-1001   C-1   8001      3507      B727  22412
140     B707  17625      28-1002   C-1   8002      3520      B737  23133
240     B707  17596      38-1003   C-1   8003      3540      DC-9  47087
242     B707  20110      48-1004   C-1   8004      4101      E145  145190
246     B707  20230      48-1005   C-1   8005      4111      E145  145694
248     B707  20429      58-1006   C-1   8006      4112      E145  145723
250     B707  20428      58-1007   C-1   8007      10506     SE210 211
255     B707  20629      58-1008   C-1   8008      10507     SE210 232
257     B707  19000      58-1009   C-1   8009      B-12001   B737  20127
258     B707  19291      58-1010   C-1   8010      TP-01     B727  19123
260     B707  20716      58-1011   C-1   8011      TP-01     B757  22690
264     B707  20721      58-1012   C-1   8012      TP-01     B757  22690
275     B707  21334      64-3501   B767  27385     TP-02     B727  19121
290     B707  21956      64-3502   B767  27391     TP-02     B737  24095
                         68-1013   C-1   8013      TP-03     B737  19772
4X-980  B707  21956      68-1014   C-1   8014      TP-03     B737  20127
4X-BYR  B707  20629      68-1015   C-1   8015      TP-03     B737  24361
4X-JYA  B707  18012      68-1016   C-1   8016      TP-04     B737  19772
4X-JYB  B707  17610      68-1017   C-1   8017      TP-05     B727  19123
4X-JYC  B707  19291      68-1018   C-1   8018      TP-0201   1-11  005
4X-JYD  B707  17667      68-1019   C-1   8019      TP-10501  B727  18912
4X-JYE  B707  17612      68-1020   C-1   8020      TP-10502  B727  19427
4X-JYG  B707  18013      74-3503   B767  28016     TP-10503  B727  18908
4X-JYH  B707  20721      74-3504   B767  28017     TP-10504  B727  18909
4X-JYH  B707  17668      78-1021   C-1   8021      TP-10505  B727  18911
4X-JYI  B707  17661      78-1022   C-1   8022
4X-JYI  B707  19000      78-1023   C-1   8023
4X-JYK  B707  18246      78-1024   C-1   8024      Morocco
4X-JYL  B707  18374      78-1025   C-1   8025
4X-JYM  B707  18460      78-1026   C-1   8026      CNA-NR    B707  21956
4X-JYN  B707  17619      88-1027   C-1   8027      CNA-NS    B707  18334
4X-JYN  B707  20716      88-1028   C-1   8028
4X-JYP  B707  17921      98-1029   C-1   8029      Mozambique
4X-JYQ  B707  20110
4X-JYS  B707  20230                                63457     TU134 63457
4X-JYT  B707  17625
4X-JYT  B707  17625      Kenya                      
4X-JYU  B707  20429                                NATO
4X-JYV  B707  17615      KAF308    F.70  11557
4X-JYV  B707  21334                                LX-N19996 B707  19996
4X-JYW  B707  17617      Korea                      LX-N19997 B707  19997
4X-JYX  B707  17922                                LX-N20000 B707  20000
4X-JYY  B707  20428      85101     B737  23152     LX-N20198 B707  20198
4X-JYZ  B707  17596                                LX-N20199 B707  20199
                                                   LX-N90442 B707  22855
                        Kuwait                     LX-N90443 B707  22838
Italy                                              LX-N90444 B707  22839
                        KAF-26    MD80  49809      LX-N90445 B707  22840
14-01   B707  20514      KAF 320   DC-9  47691      LX-N90446 B707  22841
14-02   B707  20298      KAF 321   DC-9  47690      LX-N90447 B707  22842
14-03   B707  19740                                LX-N90448 B707  22843
14-04   B707  20515                                LX-N90449 B707  22844
31-12   DC-9  47595      Libya                      LX-N90450 B707  22845
31-13   DC-9  47600                                LX-N90451 B707  22846
(MM.....) B707 21103     LAAF-072  AN7x  ?         LX-N90452 B707  22847
(MM.....) B707 21261     LAAF-722  AN7x  ?         LX-N90453 B707  22848
(MM.....) B707 21367     LAAF-723  AN7x  ?         LX-N90454 B707  22849
MM62012 DC-9  47595      LAAF-724  AN7x  ?         LX-N90455 B707  22850
MM62012 DC-9  47595      LAF110    IL76  ?         LX-N90456 B707  22851
MM62013 DC-9  47600      LAF118    IL76  ?         LX-N90457 B707  22852
MM62013 DC-9  47600                                LX-N90458 B707  22853
MM62148 B707  20514                                LX-N90459 B707  22854
MM62149 B707  20298      Malaysia
MM62150 B707  19740
MM62151 B707  20515      FM2101    F.28  11088     Netherlands
MM62173 A319  1002       FM2102    F.28  11089
MM62174 A319  1157       M28-01    F.28  11088     T-235     DC-10 46956
MM62209 A319  1795       M28-02    F.28  11089     T-253     DC-10 46986
MM62226 B767  33686      M47-01    CRJ   7140      T-255     DC-10 46987
MM62243 A319  2507       M53-01    737NG 29274     T-264     DC-10 46985
SM-12   DC-9  47595
SM-13   DC-9  47600      Mexico
                                                   New Zealand
                        1720      B727  22412
Japan                   3501      B727  18912      NZ7271    B727  19892
                        3503      B727  18908      NZ7272    B727  19895
08-1030 C-1   8030       3504      B727  18909      NZ7273    B727
18-1031 C-1   8031       3505      B727  22661      NZ7571    B757  26633
20-1101 B747  24730      3506      B727  22662      NZ7572    B757  26634
20-1102 B747  24731
```

North Korea

```
551     TU154 75A-129
552     TU154 76A-143
553     TU154 77A-191
885     IL62  3933913
889     IL62  2139.1.?
```

Oman

```
551     1-11  BAC.247
552     1-11  BAC.249
553     1-11  BAC.251
1001    1-11  BAC.247
1002    1-11  BAC.249
1003    1-11  BAC.251
```

Pakistan

```
65-18991  B707  18991
68-19635  B707  19635
68-19866  B707  19866
```

Panama

```
(FAP-400) B727  18894
FAP-501   B727  19815
```

Paraguay

```
FAP-01    B707  18957
```

Peru

```
369       AN7x  72096911
FAP-319   B707  19575
FAP-350   B737  19707
FAP 351   B737  23041
FAP 352   B737  23042
FAP 353   B737  19424
FAP 354   B737  20221
FAP 356   B737  27426
FAP 370   DC-8  46078
FAP 371   DC-8  45984
FAP 390   F.28  11100
PRP-001   B737  27426
```

Poland

```
031     YAK40  9331029
032     YAK40  9331129
034     YAK40  9331229
035     YAK40  9331329
036     YAK40  9510138
037     YAK40  9510238
038     YAK40  9441237
039     YAK40  9441137
040     YAK40  9541643
041     YAK40  9541843
042     YAK40  9541943
043     YAK40  9542043
044     YAK40  9840659
045     YAK40  9840759
046     YAK40  9021460
047     YAK40  9021560
048     YAK40  9021660
049     YAK40  9021760
101     TU134  3352005
101     TU134  73.49909
102     TU134  3352008
102     TU134  73.49985
102     TU154  90A-862
103     TU134  3351809
104     TU134  3351808
837     TU154  90A-837
862     TU154  90A-862
```

Portugal

| 8801 | B707 | 20514 |
| 8802 | B707 | 20515 |

Russia

01 red	YAK40	9530142
01 red	YAK40	9610446
22 red	TU124	7350610
33	AN7x	72093876
46 red	TU104	8350705
2207 red	AN7x	76096915

Saudi Arabia

1801	B707	23417
1802	B707	23418
1803	B707	23419
1804	B707	23420
1805	B707	23421
1811	B707	23422
1812	B707	23423
1813	B707	23424
1814	B707	23425
1815	B707	23426
1816	B707	23427
1817	B707	23428
1818	B707	23429
1901	B707	23428
1902	B707	24503
"17696"	B707	17696
SA-R-7	COMET	6461

Serbia

71501	YAK40	9120717
71502	YAK40	9120817
71503	YAK40	9222020
71504	YAK40	9231523
71505	YAK40	9630849

Singapore

750	KC135	18626
751	KC135	18232
752	KC135	17942
753	KC135	18633
59-1454	KC135	17942
63-8016	KC135	18633

Slovakia

| 0420 | TU154 | 80A-420 |
| 0823 | YAK40 | 9230823 |

South Africa

1415	B707	19522
1417	B707	19723
1419	B707	19917
1421	B707	20283
AF-615	B707	19522
AF-617	B707	19723
AF-619	B707	19917
AF-621	B707	20283
AF-623	B707	19706

Spain

45-10	B707	20060
45-11	B707	18757
45-12	B707	21367
45-13	B707	19164
47-01	B707	20060
401-01	DC-8	45814
401-30	DC-8	45814
401-07	DC-8	45658
408-21	B707	19164
T.15-1	DC-8	45814
T.15-2	DC-8	45658
T.17-1	B707	20060
T.17-2	B707	18757
T.17-3	B707	21367
T.22-1	A310	550
T.22-2	A310	551
TK.17-1	B707	20060
TM.17-4	B707	19164
TM.17-4	B707	19164

Sweden

| Fv85172 | SE210 | 172 |
| Fv85210 | SE210 | 210 |

Taiwan

2721	B727	19399
2722	B727	19520
2723	B727	20111
2724	B727	19818
3701	737NG	30139
B-10001	B737	28492

Thailand

22-222	B737	23059
33-333	B737	24480
55-555	B737	27906
44-444	A310	591
55-555	737NG	35478
99-999	B737	24866
60109	DC-8	46150
60110	DC-8	46129
60112	DC-8	45922
60201	B737	23059
60202	A310	591
60221	A319	1908
90409	B737	24866

Turkey

00325	KC135	18100
00326	KC135	18101
23512	KC135	18495
23539	KC135	18522
23563	KC135	18546
23567	KC135	18550
23568	KC135	18551
72609	KC135	17745
80110	KC135	17855
57-2609	KC135	17745
58-0110	KC135	17855
60-0325	KC135	18100
60-0326	KC135	18101
62-3539	KC135	18522
62-3563	KC135	18546
62-3567	KC135	18550
06-001	737NG	33962

Ukraine

02 red	AN7x	76097927
02 yellow	TU134	63960
UAF-63957	TU134	63957
72984	AN7x	76096926
72985	AN7x	76097927
76520	IL76	093420605
78820	IL76	0093496907
86639	IL76	073409235
551010	TU134	93551010

United Kingdom

7610M	COMET	06006
7905M	COMET	06037
7926M	COMET	06028
7927M	COMET	06029
7958M	COMET	06045
7971M	COMET	06035
8031M	COMET	06034
8296M	VC10	826
8351M	COMET	06022
8699M	VC10	854
8700M	VC10	856
8777M	VC10	825
8882M	COMET	6468
9164M	COMET	06030
(TS896)	ASHT	1395
(TS897)	ASHT	1396
(TS898)	ASHT	1397
(TS899)	ASHT	1398
(TS900)	ASHT	1399
(TS901)	ASHT	1400
WB490	ASHT	1395
WB491	ASHT	1396
WB492	ASHT	1397
WB493	ASHT	1398
WB494	ASHT	1399
WE670	ASHT	1400
XK655	COMET	06023
XK659	COMET	06025
XK663	COMET	06027
XK669	COMET	06024
XK670	COMET	06028
XK671	COMET	06029
XK695	COMET	06030
XK696	COMET	06031
XK697	COMET	06032
XK698	COMET	06034
XK699	COMET	06035
XK715	COMET	06037
XK716	COMET	06045
XM823	COMET	06022
XM829	COMET	06021
XN453	COMET	06026
XP915	COMET	06100
XR396	COMET	6467
XR396	COMET	6468
XR397	COMET	6469
XR398	COMET	6470
XR399	COMET	6471
XR806	VC10	826
XR807	VC10	827
XR808	VC10	828
XR810	VC10	830
XS235	COMET	6473
XV101	VC10	831
XV102	VC10	832
XV103	VC10	833
XV104	VC10	834
XV105	VC10	835
XV106	VC10	836
XV107	VC10	837
XV108	VC10	838
XV109	VC10	839
XV144	COMET	06033
XV147	COMET	6476
XV147	NIMR	6476
XV148	COMET	6477
XV148	NIMR	6477
XV226	NIMR	8001
XV227	NIMR	8002
XV228	NIMR	8003
XV229	NIMR	8004
XV230	NIMR	8005
XV231	NIMR	8006
XV232	NIMR	8007
XV233	NIMR	8008
XV234	NIMR	8009
XV235	NIMR	8010
XV236	NIMR	8011
XV237	NIMR	8012
XV238	NIMR	8013
XV239	NIMR	8014
XV240	NIMR	8015
XV241	NIMR	8016
XV242	NIMR	8017
XV243	NIMR	8018
XV244	NIMR	8019
XV245	NIMR	8020
XV246	NIMR	8021
XV247	NIMR	8022
XV248	NIMR	8023
XV249	NIMR	8024
XV250	NIMR	8025
XV251	NIMR	8026
XV252	NIMR	8027
XV253	NIMR	8028
XV254	NIMR	8029
XV255	NIMR	8030
XV256	NIMR	8031
XV257	NIMR	8032
XV258	NIMR	8033
XV259	NIMR	8034
XV260	NIMR	8035
XV261	NIMR	8036
XV262	NIMR	8037
XV263	NIMR	8038
XV814	COMET	6407
XW626	COMET	6419
XW664	NIMR	8039
XW665	NIMR	8040
XW666	NIMR	8041
XX105	1-11	008
XX914	VC10	825
XX919	1-11	091
XX944	COMET	6417
XZ280	NIMR	8042
XZ281	NIMR	8043
XZ282	NIMR	8044
XZ283	NIMR	8045
XZ284	NIMR	8046
XZ285	NIMR	8047
XZ286	NIMR	8048
XZ287	NIMR	8049
ZA140	VC10	814
7A141	VC10	809
ZA142	VC10	811
ZA143	VC10	813
ZA144	VC10	806
ZA147	VC10	882
ZA148	VC10	883
ZA149	VC10	884
ZA150	VC10	885
ZD230	VC10	851
ZD231	VC10	852
ZD232	VC10	854
ZD233	VC10	855
ZD234	VC10	856
ZD235	VC10	857
ZD236	VC10	858
ZD237	VC10	859
ZD238	VC10	860
ZD239	VC10	861
ZD240	VC10	862
ZD241	VC10	863
ZD242	VC10	866
ZD243	VC10	867
ZD493	VC10	812
ZD695	146	E1004
ZD696	146	E1005
ZD948	L1011	193V-1157
ZD949	L1011	193V-1159
ZD950	L1011	193V-1164
ZD951	L1011	193V-1165
ZD952	L1011	193V-1168

Reg	Type	c/n
ZD953	L1011	193V-1174
ZE432	1-11	BAC.250
ZE433	1-11	BAC.245
ZE700	146	E1021
ZE701	146	E1029
ZE702	146	E1124
ZE704	L1011	193Y-1186
ZE705	L1011	193Y-1188
ZE706	L1011	193Y-1177
ZH101	B707	24109
ZH102	B707	24110
ZH103	B707	24111
ZH104	B707	24112
ZH105	B707	24113
ZH106	B707	24114
ZH107	B707	24499
ZH763	1-11	BAC.263
ZJ514	NIMR	8026
ZJ515	NIMR	8033
ZJ516	NIMR	8022
ZJ517	NIMR	8017
ZJ518	NIMR	8009
ZJ519	NIMR	8046
ZJ520	NIMR	8008
ZJ521	NIMR	8002
ZJ522	NIMR	8020
ZJ523	NIMR	8003
ZJ524	NIMR	8018
ZJ525	NIMR	8028
ZZ171	C-17	UK.1
ZZ172	C-17	UK.2
ZZ173	C-17	UK.3
ZZ174	C-17	UK.4

United States of America

USAF

Serial	Type	Number
55-3118	KC135	17234
55-3119	KC135	17235
55-3120	KC135	17236
55-3121	KC135	17237
55-3122	KC135	17238
55-3123	KC135	17239
55-3124	KC135	17240
55-3125	KC135	17241
55-3126	KC135	17242
55-3127	KC135	17243
55-3128	KC135	17244
55-3129	KC135	17245
55-3130	KC135	17246
55-3131	KC135	17247
55-3132	KC135	17248
55-3133	KC135	17249
55-3134	KC135	17250
55-3135	KC135	17251
55-3136	KC135	17252
55-3137	KC135	17253
55-3138	KC135	17254
55-3139	KC135	17255
55-3140	KC135	17256
55-3141	KC135	17257
55-3142	KC135	17258
55-3143	KC135	17259
55-3144	KC135	17260
55-3145	KC135	17261
55-3146	KC135	17262
56-3591	KC135	17340
56-3592	KC135	17341
56-3593	KC135	17342
56-3594	KC135	17343
56-3595	KC135	17344
56-3596	KC135	17345
56-3597	KC135	17346
56-3598	KC135	17347
56-3599	KC135	17348
56-3600	KC135	17349
56-3601	KC135	17350
56-3602	KC135	17351

Serial	Type	Number
56-3603	KC135	17352
56-3604	KC135	17353
56-3605	KC135	17354
56-3606	KC135	17355
56-3607	KC135	17356
56-3608	KC135	17357
56-3609	KC135	17358
56-3610	KC135	17359
56-3611	KC135	17360
56-3612	KC135	17361
56-3613	KC135	17362
56-3614	KC135	17363
56-3615	KC135	17364
56-3616	KC135	17365
56-3617	KC135	17366
56-3618	KC135	17367
56-3619	KC135	17368
56-3620	KC135	17369
56-3621	KC135	17370
56-3622	KC135	17371
56-3623	KC135	17372
56-3624	KC135	17373
56-3625	KC135	17374
56-3626	KC135	17375
56-3627	KC135	17376
56-3628	KC135	17377
56-3629	KC135	17378
56-3630	KC135	17379
56-3631	KC135	17380
56-3632	KC135	17381
56-3633	KC135	17382
56-3634	KC135	17383
56-3635	KC135	17384
56-3636	KC135	17385
56-3637	KC135	17386
56-3638	KC135	17387
56-3639	KC135	17388
56-3640	KC135	17389
56-3641	KC135	17390
56-3642	KC135	17391
56-3643	KC135	17392
56-3644	KC135	17393
56-3645	KC135	17394
56-3646	KC135	17395
56-3647	KC135	17396
56-3648	KC135	17397
56-3649	KC135	17398
56-3650	KC135	17399
56-3651	KC135	17400
56-3652	KC135	17401
56-3653	KC135	17402
56-3654	KC135	17403
56-3655	KC135	17404
56-3656	KC135	17405
56-3657	KC135	17406
56-3658	KC135	17407
57-1418	KC135	17489
57-1419	KC135	17490
57-1420	KC135	17491
57-1421	KC135	17492
57-1422	KC135	17493
57-1423	KC135	17494
57-1424	KC135	17495
57-1425	KC135	17496
57-1426	KC135	17497
57-1427	KC135	17498
57-1428	KC135	17499
57-1429	KC135	17500
57-1430	KC135	17501
57-1431	KC135	17502
57-1432	KC135	17503
57-1433	KC135	17504
57-1434	KC135	17505
57-1435	KC135	17506
57-1436	KC135	17507
57-1437	KC135	17508
57-1438	KC135	17509
57-1439	KC135	17510
57-1440	KC135	17511
57-1441	KC135	17512

Serial	Type	Number
57-1442	KC135	17513
57-1443	KC135	17514
57-1444	KC135	17515
57-1445	KC135	17516
57-1446	KC135	17517
57-1447	KC135	17518
57-1448	KC135	17519
57-1449	KC135	17520
57-1450	KC135	17521
57-1451	KC135	17522
57-1452	KC135	17523
57-1453	KC135	17524
57-1454	KC135	17525
57-1455	KC135	17526
57-1456	KC135	17527
57-1457	KC135	17528
57-1458	KC135	17529
57-1459	KC135	17530
57-1460	KC135	17531
57-1461	KC135	17532
57-1462	KC135	17533
57-1463	KC135	17534
57-1464	KC135	17535
57-1465	KC135	17536
57-1466	KC135	17537
57-1467	KC135	17538
57-1468	KC135	17539
57-1469	KC135	17540
57-1470	KC135	17541
57-1471	KC135	17542
57-1472	KC135	17543
57-1473	KC135	17544
57-1474	KC135	17545
57-1475	KC135	17546
57-1476	KC135	17547
57-1477	KC135	17548
57-1478	KC135	17549
57-1479	KC135	17550
57-1480	KC135	17551
57-1481	KC135	17552
57-1482	KC135	17553
57-1483	KC135	17554
57-1484	KC135	17555
57-1485	KC135	17556
57-1486	KC135	17557
57-1487	KC135	17558
57-1488	KC135	17559
57-1489	KC135	17560
57-1490	KC135	17561
57-1491	KC135	17562
57-1492	KC135	17563
57-1493	KC135	17564
57-1494	KC135	17565
57-1495	KC135	17566
57-1496	KC135	17567
57-1497	KC135	17568
57-1498	KC135	17569
57-1499	KC135	17570
57-1500	KC135	17571
57-1501	KC135	17572
57-1502	KC135	17573
57-1503	KC135	17574
57-1504	KC135	17575
57-1505	KC135	17576
57-1506	KC135	17577
57-1507	KC135	17578
57-1508	KC135	17579
57-1509	KC135	17580
57-1510	KC135	17581
57-1511	KC135	17582
57-1512	KC135	17583
57-1513	KC135	17584
57-1514	KC135	17585
57-2589	KC135	17725
57-2590	KC135	17726
57-2591	KC135	17727
57-2592	KC135	17728
57-2593	KC135	17729
57-2594	KC135	17730
57-2595	KC135	17731

Serial	Type	Number
57-2596	KC135	17732
57-2597	KC135	17733
57-2598	KC135	17734
57-2599	KC135	17735
57-2600	KC135	17736
57-2601	KC135	17737
57-2602	KC135	17738
57-2603	KC135	17739
57-2604	KC135	17740
57-2605	KC135	17741
57-2606	KC135	17742
57-2607	KC135	17743
57-2608	KC135	17744
57-2609	KC135	17745
58-0001	KC135	17746
58-0002	KC135	17747
58-0003	KC135	17748
58-0004	KC135	17749
58-0005	KC135	17750
58-0006	KC135	17751
58-0007	KC135	17752
58-0008	KC135	17753
58-0009	KC135	17754
58-0010	KC135	17755
58-0011	KC135	17756
58-0012	KC135	17757
58-0013	KC135	17758
58-0014	KC135	17759
58-0015	KC135	17760
58-0016	KC135	17761
58-0017	KC135	17762
58-0018	KC135	17763
58-0019	KC135	17764
58-0020	KC135	17765
58-0021	KC135	17766
58-0022	KC135	17767
58-0023	KC135	17768
58-0024	KC135	17769
58-0025	KC135	17770
58-0026	KC135	17771
58-0027	KC135	17772
58-0028	KC135	17773
58-0029	KC135	17774
58-0030	KC135	17775
58-0031	KC135	17776
58-0032	KC135	17777
58-0033	KC135	17778
58-0034	KC135	17779
58-0035	KC135	17780
58-0036	KC135	17781
58-0037	KC135	17782
58-0038	KC135	17783
58-0039	KC135	17784
58-0040	KC135	17785
58-0041	KC135	17786
58-0042	KC135	17787
58-0043	KC135	17788
58-0044	KC135	17789
58-0045	KC135	17790
58-0046	KC135	17791
58-0047	KC135	17792
58-0048	KC135	17793
58-0049	KC135	17794
58-0050	KC135	17795
58-0051	KC135	17796
58-0052	KC135	17797
58-0053	KC135	17798
58-0054	KC135	17799
58-0055	KC135	17800
58-0056	KC135	17801
58-0057	KC135	17802
58-0058	KC135	17803
58-0059	KC135	17804
58-0060	KC135	17805
58-0061	KC135	17806
58-0062	KC135	17807
58-0063	KC135	17808
58-0064	KC135	17809
58-0065	KC135	17810
58-0066	KC135	17811

58-0067	KC135 17812	59-1456	KC135 17944	60-0324	KC135 18099	61-0286	KC135 18193		
58-0068	KC135 17813	59-1457	KC135 17945	60-0325	KC135 18100	61-0287	KC135 18194		
58-0069	KC135 17814	59-1458	KC135 17946	60-0326	KC135 18101	61-0288	KC135 18195		
58-0070	KC135 17815	59-1459	KC135 17947	60-0327	KC135 18102	61-0289	KC135 18196		
58-0071	KC135 17816	59-1460	KC135 17948	60-0328	KC135 18103	61-0290	KC135 18197		
58-0072	KC135 17817	59-1461	KC135 17949	60-0329	KC135 18104	61-0291	KC135 18198		
58-0073	KC135 17818	59-1462	KC135 17950	60-0330	KC135 18105	61-0292	KC135 18199		
58-0074	KC135 17819	59-1463	KC135 17951	60-0331	KC135 18106	61-0293	KC135 18200		
58-0075	KC135 17820	59-1464	KC135 17952	60-0332	KC135 18107	61-0294	KC135 18201		
58-0076	KC135 17821	59-1465	KC135 17953	60-0333	KC135 18108	61-0295	KC135 18202		
58-0077	KC135 17822	59-1466	KC135 17954	60-0334	KC135 18109	61-0296	KC135 18203		
58-0078	KC135 17823	59-1467	KC135 17955	60-0335	KC135 18110	61-0297	KC135 18204		
58-0079	KC135 17824	59-1468	KC135 17956	60-0336	KC135 18111	61-0298	KC135 18205		
58-0080	KC135 17825	59-1469	KC135 17957	60-0337	KC135 18112	61-0299	KC135 18206		
58-0081	KC135 17826	59-1470	KC135 17958	60-0338	KC135 18113	61-0300	KC135 18207		
58-0082	KC135 17827	59-1471	KC135 17959	60-0339	KC135 18114	61-0301	KC135 18208		
58-0083	KC135 17828	59-1472	KC135 17960	60-0340	KC135 18115	61-0302	KC135 18209		
58-0084	KC135 17829	59-1473	KC135 17961	60-0341	KC135 18116	61-0303	KC135 18210		
58-0085	KC135 17830	59-1474	KC135 17962	60-0342	KC135 18117	61-0304	KC135 18211		
58-0086	KC135 17831	59-1475	KC135 17963	60-0343	KC135 18118	61-0305	KC135 18212		
58-0087	KC135 17832	59-1476	KC135 17964	60-0344	KC135 18119	61-0306	KC135 18213		
58-0088	KC135 17833	59-1477	KC135 17965	60-0345	KC135 18120	61-0307	KC135 18214		
58-0089	KC135 17834	59-1478	KC135 17966	60-0346	KC135 18121	61-0308	KC135 18215		
58-0090	KC135 17835	59-1479	KC135 17967	60-0347	KC135 18122	61-0309	KC135 18216		
58-0091	KC135 17836	59-1480	KC135 17968	60-0348	KC135 18123	61-0310	KC135 18217		
58-0092	KC135 17837	59-1481	KC135 17969	60-0349	KC135 18124	61-0311	KC135 18218		
58-0093	KC135 17838	59-1482	KC135 17970	60-0350	KC135 18125	61-0312	KC135 18219		
58-0094	KC135 17839	59-1483	KC135 17971	60-0351	KC135 18126	61-0313	KC135 18220		
58-0095	KC135 17840	59-1484	KC135 17972	60-0352	KC135 18127	61-0314	KC135 18221		
58-0096	KC135 17841	59-1485	KC135 17973	60-0353	KC135 18128	61-0315	KC135 18222		
58-0097	KC135 17842	59-1486	KC135 17974	60-0354	KC135 18129	61-0316	KC135 18223		
58-0098	KC135 17843	59-1487	KC135 17975	60-0355	KC135 18130	61-0317	KC135 18224		
58-0099	KC135 17844	59-1488	KC135 17976	60-0356	KC135 18131	61-0318	KC135 18225		
58-0100	KC135 17845	59-1489	KC135 17977	60-0357	KC135 18132	61-0319	KC135 18226		
58-0101	KC135 17846	59-1490	KC135 17978	60-0358	KC135 18133	61-0320	KC135 18227		
58-0102	KC135 17847	59-1491	KC135 17979	60-0359	KC135 18134	61-0321	KC135 18228		
58-0103	KC135 17848	59-1492	KC135 17980	60-0360	KC135 18135	61-0322	KC135 18229		
58-0104	KC135 17849	59-1493	KC135 17981	60-0361	KC135 18136	61-0323	KC135 18230		
58-0105	KC135 17850	59-1494	KC135 17982	60-0362	KC135 18137	61-0324	KC135 18231		
58-0106	KC135 17851	59-1495	KC135 17983	60-0363	KC135 18138	61-0325	KC135 18232		
58-0107	KC135 17852	59-1496	KC135 17984	60-0364	KC135 18139	61-0326	KC135 18233		
58-0108	KC135 17853	59-1497	KC135 17985	60-0365	KC135 18140	61-0327	KC135 18234		
58-0109	KC135 17854	59-1498	KC135 17986	60-0366	KC135 18141	61-0328	KC135 18235		
58-0110	KC135 17855	59-1499	KC135 17987	60-0367	KC135 18142	61-0329	KC135 18236		
58-0111	KC135 17856	59-1500	KC135 17988	60-0368	KC135 18143	61-0330	KC135 18237		
58-0112	KC135 17857	59-1501	KC135 17989	60-0369	KC135 18144	61-0331	KC135 18238		
58-0113	KC135 17858	59-1502	KC135 17990	60-0370	KC135 18145	61-0332	KC135 18239		
58-0114	KC135 17859	59-1503	KC135 17991	60-0371	KC135 18146	61-2662	KC135 18292		
58-0115	KC135 17860	59-1504	KC135 17992	60-0372	KC135 18147	61-2663	KC135 18333		
58-0116	KC135 17861	59-1505	KC135 17993	60-0373	KC135 18148	61-2664	KC135 18340		
58-0117	KC135 17862	59-1506	KC135 17994	60-0374	KC135 18149	61-2665	KC135 18341		
58-0118	KC135 17863	59-1507	KC135 17995	60-0375	KC135 18150	61-2666	KC135 18342		
58-0119	KC135 17864	59-1508	KC135 17996	60-0376	KC135 18151	61-2667	KC135 18343		
58-0120	KC135 17865	59-1509	KC135 17997	60-0377	KC135 18152	61-2668	KC135 18344		
58-0121	KC135 17866	59-1510	KC135 17998	60-0378	KC135 18153	61-2669	KC135 18345		
58-0122	KC135 17867	59-1511	KC135 17999	61-0261	KC135 18168	61-2670	KC135 18346		
58-0123	KC135 17868	59-1512	KC135 18000	61-0262	KC135 18169	61-2671	KC135 18347		
58-0124	KC135 17869	59-1513	KC135 18001	61-0263	KC135 18170	61-2672	KC135 18348		
58-0125	KC135 17870	59-1514	KC135 18002	61-0264	KC135 18171	61-2673	KC135 18349		
58-0126	KC135 17871	59-1515	KC135 18003	61-0265	KC135 18172	61-2674	KC135 18350		
58-0127	KC135 17872	59-1516	KC135 18004	61-0266	KC135 18173	61-2775	C-141 6001		
58-0128	KC135 17873	59-1517	KC135 18005	61-0267	KC135 18174	61-2776	C-141 6002		
58-0129	KC135 17874	59-1518	KC135 18006	61-0268	KC135 18175	61-2777	C-141 6003		
58-0130	KC135 17875	59-1518	KC135 18006	61-0269	KC135 18176	61-2778	C-141 6004		
58-6970	B707 17925	59-1519	KC135 18007	61-0270	KC135 18177	61-2779	C-141 6005		
58-6971	B707 17926	59-1520	KC135 18008	61-0271	KC135 18178	62-3497	KC135 18480		
58-6972	B707 17927	59-1521	KC135 18009	61-0272	KC135 18179	62-3498	KC135 18481		
59-1443	KC135 17931	59-1522	KC135 18010	61-0273	KC135 18180	62-3499	KC135 18482		
59-1444	KC135 17932	59-1523	KC135 18011	61-0274	KC135 18181	62-3500	KC135 18483		
59-1445	KC135 17933	60-0313	KC135 18088	61-0275	KC135 18182	62-3501	KC135 18484		
59-1446	KC135 17934	60-0314	KC135 18089	61-0276	KC135 18183	62-3502	KC135 18485		
59-1447	KC135 17935	60-0315	KC135 18090	61-0277	KC135 18184	62-3503	KC135 18486		
59-1448	KC135 17936	60-0316	KC135 18091	61-0278	KC135 18185	62-3504	KC135 18487		
59-1449	KC135 17937	60-0317	KC135 18092	61-0279	KC135 18186	62-3505	KC135 18488		
59-1450	KC135 17938	60-0318	KC135 18093	61-0280	KC135 18187	62-3506	KC135 18489		
59-1451	KC135 17939	60-0319	KC135 18094	61-0281	KC135 18188	62-3507	KC135 18490		
59-1452	KC135 17940	60-0320	KC135 18095	61-0282	KC135 18189	62-3508	KC135 18491		
59-1453	KC135 17941	60-0321	KC135 18096	61-0283	KC135 18190	62-3509	KC135 18492		
59-1454	KC135 17942	60-0322	KC135 18097	61-0284	KC135 18191	62-3510	KC135 18493		
59-1455	KC135 17943	60-0323	KC135 18098	61-0285	KC135 18192	62-3511	KC135 18494		

62-3512	KC135 18495	62-4131	KC135 18471	63-8040	KC135 18657	64-0626	C-141 6039
62-3513	KC135 18496	62-4132	KC135 18472	63-8041	KC135 18658	64-0627	C-141 6040
62-3514	KC135 18497	62-4133	KC135 18473	63-8042	KC135 18659	64-0628	C-141 6041
62-3515	KC135 18498	62-4134	KC135 18474	63-8043	KC135 18660	64-0629	C-141 6042
62-3516	KC135 18499	62-4135	KC135 18475	63-8044	KC135 18661	64-0630	C-141 6043
62-3517	KC135 18500	62-4136	KC135 18476	63-8045	KC135 18662	64-0631	C-141 6044
62-3518	KC135 18501	62-4137	KC135 18477	63-8046	KC135 18663	64-0632	C-141 6045
62-3519	KC135 18502	62-4138	KC135 18478	63-8047	KC135 18664	64-0633	C-141 6046
62-3520	KC135 18503	62-4139	KC135 18479	63-8048	KC135 18665	64-0634	C-141 6047
62-3521	KC135 18504	62-6000	B707 18461	63-8049	KC135 18666	64-0635	C-141 6048
62-3522	KC135 18505	63-12735	KC135 18695	63-8050	KC135 18667	64-0636	C-141 6049
62-3523	KC135 18506	63-12736	KC135 18696	63-8051	KC135 18668	64-0637	C-141 6050
62-3524	KC135 18507	63-12737	KC135 18697	63-8052	KC135 18669	64-0638	C-141 6051
62-3525	KC135 18508	63-12738	KC135 18698	63-8053	KC135 18701	64-0639	C-141 6052
62-3526	KC135 18509	63-12739	KC135 18699	63-8054	KC135 18702	64-0640	C-141 6053
62-3527	KC135 18510	63-12740	KC135 18700	63-8055	KC135 18703	64-0641	C-141 6054
62-3528	KC135 18511	63-7976	KC135 18593	63-8056	KC135 18704	64-0642	C-141 6055
62-3529	KC135 18512	63-7977	KC135 18594	63-8057	KC135 18705	64-0643	C-141 6056
62-3530	KC135 18513	63-7978	KC135 18595	63-8058	KC135 18670	64-0644	C-141 6057
62-3531	KC135 18514	63-7979	KC135 18596	63-8059	KC135 18671	64-0645	C-141 6058
62-3532	KC135 18515	63-7980	KC135 18597	63-8060	KC135 18672	64-0646	C-141 6059
62-3533	KC135 18516	63-7981	KC135 18598	63-8061	KC135 18673	64-0647	C-141 6060
62-3534	KC135 18517	63-7982	KC135 18599	63-8075	C-141 6006	64-0648	C-141 6061
62-3535	KC135 18518	63-7983	KC135 18600	63-8076	C-141 6007	64-0649	C-141 6062
62-3536	KC135 18519	63-7984	KC135 18601	63-8077	C-141 6008	64-0650	C-141 6063
62-3537	KC135 18520	63-7985	KC135 18602	63-8078	C-141 6009	64-0651	C-141 6064
62-3538	KC135 18521	63-7986	KC135 18603	63-8079	C-141 6010	64-0652	C-141 6065
62-3539	KC135 18522	63-7987	KC135 18604	63-8080	C-141 6011	64-0653	C-141 6066
62-3540	KC135 18523	63-7988	KC135 18605	63-8081	C-141 6012	64-14828	KC135 18768
62-3541	KC135 18524	63-7989	KC135 18606	63-8082	C-141 6013	64-14829	KC135 18769
62-3542	KC135 18525	63-7990	KC135 18607	63-8083	C-141 6014	64-14830	KC135 18770
62-3543	KC135 18526	63-7991	KC135 18608	63-8084	C-141 6015	64-14831	KC135 18771
62-3544	KC135 18527	63-7992	KC135 18609	63-8085	C-141 6016	64-14832	KC135 18772
62-3545	KC135 18528	63-7993	KC135 18610	63-8086	C-141 6017	64-14833	KC135 18773
62-3546	KC135 18529	63-7994	KC135 18611	63-8087	C-141 6018	64-14834	KC135 18774
62-3547	KC135 18530	63-7995	KC135 18612	63-8088	C-141 6019	64-14835	KC135 18775
62-3548	KC135 18531	63-7996	KC135 18613	63-8089	C-141 6020	64-14836	KC135 18776
62-3549	KC135 18532	63-7997	KC135 18614	63-8090	C-141 6021	64-14837	KC135 18777
62-3550	KC135 18533	63-7998	KC135 18615	63-8470	KC135 18679	64-14838	KC135 18778
62-3551	KC135 18534	63-7999	KC135 18616	63-8471	KC135 18680	64-14839	KC135 18779
62-3552	KC135 18535	63-8000	KC135 18617	63-8472	KC135 18681	64-14840	KC135 18780
62-3553	KC135 18536	63-8001	KC135 18618	63-8473	KC135 18682	64-14841	KC135 18781
62-3554	KC135 18537	63-8002	KC135 18619	63-8474	KC135 18683	64-14842	KC135 18782
62-3555	KC135 18538	63-8003	KC135 18620	63-8475	KC135 18684	64-14843	KC135 18783
62-3556	KC135 18539	63-8004	KC135 18621	63-8871	KC135 18719	64-14844	KC135 18784
62-3557	KC135 18540	63-8005	KC135 18622	63-8872	KC135 18720	64-14845	KC135 18785
62-3558	KC135 18541	63-8006	KC135 18623	63-8873	KC135 18721	64-14846	KC135 18786
62-3559	KC135 18542	63-8007	KC135 18624	63-8874	KC135 18722	64-14847	KC135 18787
62-3560	KC135 18543	63-8008	KC135 18625	63-8875	KC135 18723	64-14848	KC135 18788
62-3561	KC135 18544	63-8009	KC135 18626	63-8876	KC135 18724	64-14849	KC135 18789
62-3562	KC135 18545	63-8010	KC135 18627	63-8877	KC135 18725	65-0216	C-141 6067
62-3563	KC135 18546	63-8011	KC135 18628	63-8878	KC135 18726	65-0217	C-141 6068
62-3564	KC135 18547	63-8012	KC135 18629	63-8879	KC135 18727	65-0218	C-141 6069
62-3565	KC135 18548	63-8013	KC135 18630	63-8880	KC135 18728	65-0219	C-141 6070
62-3566	KC135 18549	63-8014	KC135 18631	63-8881	KC135 18729	65-0220	C-141 6071
62-3567	KC135 18550	63-8015	KC135 18632	63-8882	KC135 18730	65-0221	C-141 6072
62-3568	KC135 18551	63-8016	KC135 18633	63-8883	KC135 18731	65-0222	C-141 6073
62-3569	KC135 18552	63-8017	KC135 18634	63-8884	KC135 18732	65-0223	C-141 6074
62-3570	KC135 18553	63-8018	KC135 18635	63-8885	KC135 18733	65-0224	C-141 6075
62-3571	KC135 18554	63-8019	KC135 18636	63-8886	KC135 18734	65-0225	C-141 6076
62-3572	KC135 18555	63-8020	KC135 18637	63-8887	KC135 18735	65-0226	C-141 6077
62-3573	KC135 18556	63-8021	KC135 18638	63-8888	KC135 18736	65-0227	C-141 6078
62-3574	KC135 18557	63-8022	KC135 18639	63-9792	KC135 18706	65-0228	C-141 6079
62-3575	KC135 18558	63-8023	KC135 18640	64-0609	C-141 6022	65-0229	C-141 6080
62-3576	KC135 18559	63-8024	KC135 18641	64-0610	C-141 6023	65-0230	C-141 6081
62-3577	KC135 18560	63-8025	KC135 18642	64-0611	C-141 6024	65-0231	C-141 6082
62-3578	KC135 18561	63-8026	KC135 18643	64-0612	C-141 6025	65-0232	C-141 6083
62-3579	KC135 18562	63-8027	KC135 18644	64-0613	C-141 6026	65-0233	C-141 6084
62-3580	KC135 18563	63-8028	KC135 18645	64-0614	C-141 6027	65-0234	C-141 6085
62-3581	KC135 18564	63-8029	KC135 18646	64-0615	C-141 6028	65-0235	C-141 6086
62-3582	KC135 18565	63-8030	KC135 18647	64-0616	C-141 6029	65-0236	C-141 6087
62-3583	KC135 18566	63-8031	KC135 18648	64-0617	C-141 6030	65-0237	C-141 6088
62-3584	KC135 18567	63-8032	KC135 18649	64-0618	C-141 6031	65-0238	C-141 6089
62-3585	KC135 18568	63-8033	KC135 18650	64-0619	C-141 6032	65-0239	C-141 6090
62-4125	KC135 18465	63-8034	KC135 18651	64-0620	C-141 6033	65-0240	C-141 6091
62-4126	KC135 18466	63-8035	KC135 18652	64-0621	C-141 6034	65-0241	C-141 6092
62-4127	KC135 18467	63-8036	KC135 18653	64-0622	C-141 6035	65-0242	C-141 6093
62-4128	KC135 18468	63-8037	KC135 18654	64-0623	C-141 6036	65-0243	C-141 6094
62-4129	KC135 18469	63-8038	KC135 18655	64-0624	C-141 6037	65-0244	C-141 6095
62-4130	KC135 18470	63-8039	KC135 18656	64-0625	C-141 6038	65-0245	C-141 6096

Serial	Type	C/n	Serial	Type	C/n	Serial	Type	C/n	Serial	Type	C/n
65-0246	C-141	6097	66-0152	C-141	6178	67-0001	C-141	6252	69-0006	C-5	500-0037
65-0247	C-141	6098	66-0153	C-141	6179	67-0002	C-141	6253	69-0007	C-5	500-0038
65-0248	C-141	6099	66-0154	C-141	6180	67-0003	C-141	6254	69-0008	C-5	500-0039
65-0249	C-141	6100	66-0155	C-141	6181	67-0004	C-141	6255	69-0009	C-5	500-0040
65-0250	C-141	6101	66-0156	C-141	6182	67-0005	C-141	6256	69-0010	C-5	500-0041
65-0251	C-141	6102	66-0157	C-141	6183	67-0006	C-141	6257	69-0011	C-5	500-0042
65-0252	C-141	6103	66-0158	C-141	6184	67-0007	C-141	6258	69-0012	C-5	500-0043
65-0253	C-141	6104	66-0159	C-141	6185	67-0008	C-141	6259	69-0013	C-5	500-0044
65-0254	C-141	6105	66-0160	C-141	6186	67-0009	C-141	6260	69-0014	C-5	500-0045
65-0255	C-141	6106	66-0161	C-141	6187	67-0010	C-141	6261	69-0015	C-5	500-0046
65-0256	C-141	6107	66-0162	C-141	6188	67-0011	C-141	6262	69-0016	C-5	500-0047
65-0257	C-141	6108	66-0163	C-141	6189	67-0012	C-141	6263	69-0017	C-5	500-0048
65-0258	C-141	6109	66-0164	C-141	6190	67-0013	C-141	6264	69-0018	C-5	500-0049
65-0259	C-141	6111	66-0165	C-141	6191	67-0014	C-141	6265	69-0019	C-5	500-0050
65-0260	C-141	6112	66-0166	C-141	6192	67-0015	C-141	6266	69-0020	C-5	500-0051
65-0261	C-141	6113	66-0167	C-141	6193	67-0016	C-141	6267	69-0021	C-5	500-0052
65-0262	C-141	6114	66-0168	C-141	6194	67-0017	C-141	6268	69-0022	C-5	500-0053
65-0263	C-141	6115	66-0169	C-141	6195	67-0018	C-141	6269	69-0023	C-5	500-0054
65-0264	C-141	6116	66-0170	C-141	6196	67-0019	C-141	6270	69-0024	C-5	500-0055
65-0265	C-141	6117	66-0171	C-141	6197	67-0020	C-141	6271	69-0025	C-5	500-0056
65-0266	C-141	6118	66-0172	C-141	6198	67-0021	C-141	6272	69-0026	C-5	500-0057
65-0267	C-141	6119	66-0173	C-141	6199	67-0022	C-141	6273	69-0027	C-5	500-0058
65-0268	C-141	6120	66-0174	C-141	6200	67-0023	C-141	6274	70-0445	C-5	500-0059
65-0269	C-141	6121	66-0175	C-141	6201	67-0024	C-141	6275	70-0446	C-5	500-0060
65-0270	C-141	6122	66-0176	C-141	6202	67-0025	C-141	6276	70-0447	C-5	500-0061
65-0271	C-141	6123	66-0177	C-141	6203	67-0026	C-141	6277	70-0448	C-5	500-0062
65-0272	C-141	6124	66-0178	C-141	6204	67-0027	C-141	6278	70-0449	C-5	500-0063
65-0273	C-141	6125	66-0179	C-141	6205	67-0028	C-141	6279	70-0450	C-5	500-0064
65-0274	C-141	6126	66-0180	C-141	6206	67-0029	C-141	6280	70-0451	C-5	500-0065
65-0275	C-141	6127	66-0181	C-141	6207	67-0030	C-141	6281	70-0452	C-5	500-0066
65-0276	C-141	6128	66-0182	C-141	6208	67-0031	C-141	6282	70-0453	C-5	500-0067
65-0277	C-141	6129	66-0183	C-141	6209	67-0164	C-141	6283	70-0454	C-5	500-0068
65-0278	C-141	6130	66-0184	C-141	6210	67-0165	C-141	6284	70-0455	C-5	500-0069
65-0279	C-141	6131	66-0185	C-141	6211	67-0166	C-141	6285	70-0456	C-5	500-0070
65-0280	C-141	6132	66-0186	C-141	6212	67-0167	C-5	500-0006	70-0457	C-5	500-0071
65-0281	C-141	6133	66-0187	C-141	6213	67-0168	C-5	500-0007	70-0458	C-5	500-0072
65-9397	C-141	6134	66-0188	C-141	6214	67-0169	C-5	500-0008	70-0459	C-5	500-0073
65-9398	C-141	6135	66-0189	C-141	6215	67-0170	C-5	500-0009	70-0460	C-5	500-0074
65-9399	C-141	6136	66-0190	C-141	6216	67-0171	C-5	500-0010	70-0461	C-5	500-0075
65-9400	C-141	6137	66-0191	C-141	6217	67-0172	C-5	500-0011	70-0462	C-5	500-0076
65-9401	C-141	6138	66-0192	C-141	6218	67-0173	C-5	500-0012	70-0463	C-5	500-0077
65-9402	C-141	6139	66-0193	C-141	6219	67-0174	C-5	500-0013	70-0464	C-5	500-0078
65-9403	C-141	6140	66-0194	C-141	6220	67-19417	B707	19417	70-0465	C-5	500-0079
65-9404	C-141	6141	66-0195	C-141	6221	67-22583	DC-9	47241	70-0466	C-5	500-0080
65-9405	C-141	6142	66-0196	C-141	6222	67-22584	DC-9	47242	70-0467	C-5	500-0081
65-9406	C-141	6143	66-0197	C-141	6223	67-22585	DC-9	47295	71-0874	DC-9	47467
65-9407	C-141	6144	66-0198	C-141	6224	67-22586	DC-9	47296	71-0875	DC-9	47471
65-9408	C-141	6145	66-0199	C-141	6225	67-30054	B707	19442	71-0876	DC-9	47475
65-9409	C-141	6146	66-0200	C-141	6226	68-0211	C-5	500-0014	71-0877	DC-9	47495
65-9410	C-141	6147	66-0201	C-141	6227	68-0212	C-5	500-0015	71-0878	DC-9	47536
65-9411	C-141	6148	66-0202	C-141	6228	68-0213	C-5	500-0016	71-0079	DC-9	47537
65-9412	C-141	6149	66-0203	C-141	6229	68-0214	C-5	500-0017	71-0880	DC-9	47538
65-9413	C-141	6150	66-0204	C-141	6230	68-0215	C-5	500-0018	71-0881	DC-9	47540
65-9414	C-141	6151	66-0205	C-141	6231	68-0216	C-5	500-0019	71-0882	DC-9	47541
66-0126	C-141	6152	66-0206	C-141	6232	68-0217	C-5	500-0020	71-1403	B737	20685
66-0127	C-141	6153	66-0207	C-141	6233	68-0218	C-5	500-0021	71-1404	B737	20686
66-0128	C-141	6154	66-0208	C-141	6234	68-0219	C-5	500-0022	71-1405	B737	20687
66-0129	C-141	6155	66-0209	C-141	6235	68-0220	C-5	500-0023	71-1406	B737	20688
66-0130	C-141	6156	66-30052	B707	18949	68-0221	C-5	500-0024	71-1406	B737	20688
66-0131	C-141	6157	66-7944	C-141	6236	68-0222	C-5	500-0025	71-1407	B707	20518
66-0132	C-141	6158	66-7945	C-141	6237	68-0223	C-5	500-0026	71-1408	B707	20519
66-0133	C-141	6159	66-7946	C-141	6238	68-0224	C-5	500-0027	71-1841	B707	20495
66-0134	C-141	6160	66-7947	C-141	6239	68-0225	C-5	500-0028	72-0282	B737	20689
66-0135	C-141	6161	66-7948	C-141	6240	68-0226	C-5	500-0029	72-0283	B737	20690
66-0136	C-141	6162	66-7949	C-141	6241	68-0227	C-5	500-0030	72-0284	B737	20691
66-0137	C-141	6163	66-7950	C-141	6242	68-0228	C-5	500-0031	72-0285	B737	20692
66-0138	C-141	6164	66-7951	C-141	6243	68-10958	DC-9	47366	72-0286	B737	20693
66-0139	C-141	6165	66-7952	C-141	6244	68-10959	DC-9	47367	72-0287	B737	20694
66-0140	C-141	6166	66-7953	C-141	6245	68-10960	DC-9	47448	72-0288	B737	20695
66-0141	C-141	6167	66-7954	C-141	6246	68-10961	DC-9	47449	72-1873	C-14	?
66-0142	C-141	6168	66-7955	C-141	6247	68-11174	B707	20016	72-1874	C-14	?
66-0143	C-141	6169	66-7956	C-141	6248	68-8932	DC-9	47297	72-1875	C-15	?
66-0144	C-141	6170	66-7957	C-141	6249	68-8933	DC-9	47298	72-1876	C-15	?
66-0145	C-141	6171	66-7958	C-141	6250	68-8934	DC-9	47299	72-7000	B707	20630
66-0146	C-141	6172	66-7959	C-141	6251	68-8935	DC-9	47300	73-1149	B737	20696
66-0147	C-141	6173	66-8303	C-5	500-0001	69-0001	C-5	500-0032	73-1150	B737	20697
66-0148	C-141	6174	66-8304	C-5	500-0002	69-0002	C-5	500-0033	73-1151	B737	20698
66-0149	C-141	6175	66-8305	C-5	500-0003	69-0003	C-5	500-0034	73-1152	B737	20699
66-0150	C-141	6176	66-8306	C-5	500-0004	69-0004	C-5	500-0035	73-1153	B737	20700
66-0151	C-141	6177	66-8307	C-5	500-0005	69-0005	C-5	500-0036	73-1154	B737	20701

73-1155	B737 20702	82-0069	B707 23420	86-0025	C-5 500-0111	94-0069	C-17 P.25
73-1156	B737 20703	82-0070	B707 23421	86-0026	C-5 500-0112	94-0070	C-17 P.26
73-1674	B707 21046	82-0071	B707 23422	86-0027	DC-10 48240	94-0285	B707 19442
73-1675	B707 21185	82-0072	B707 23423	86-0028	DC-10 48241	95-0102	C-17 P.27
73-1676	B747 20682	82-0073	B707 23424	86-0029	DC-10 48242	95-0103	C-17 P.28
73-1677	B747 20683	82-0074	B707 23425	86-0030	DC-10 48243	95-0104	C-17 P.29
73-1681	DC-9 47668	82-0075	B707 23426	86-0031	DC-10 48244	95-0105	C-17 P.30
73-1682	DC-9 47670	82-0076	B707 23427	86-0032	DC-10 48245	95-0106	C-17 P.31
73-1683	DC-9 47671	82-0190	DC-10 48212	86-0033	DC-10 48246	95-0107	C-17 P.32
74-0787	B747 20684	82-0191	DC-10 48213	86-0034	DC-10 48247	95-0121	B707 20016
75-0125	B747 20949	82-0192	DC-10 48214	86-0035	DC-10 48248	95-0122	B707 20495
75-0556	B707 21047	82-0193	DC-10 48215	86-0036	DC-10 48249	96-0001	C-17 P.33
75-0557	B707 21207	82-8000	B747 23824	86-0037	DC-10 48250	96-0002	C-17 P.34
75-0558	B707 21208	83-0008	B707 22836	86-0038	DC-10 48251	96-0003	C-17 P.35
75-0559	B707 21209	83-0009	B707 22837	86-0416	B707 19626	96-0004	C-17 P.36
75-0560	B707 21250	83-0075	DC-10 48216	86-0416	B707 19626	96-0005	C-17 P.37
76-1604	B707 21434	83-0076	DC-10 48217	86-0417	B707 19574	96-0006	C-17 P.38
76-1605	B707 21435	83-0077	DC-10 48218	(86-8800)	B747 23824	96-0007	C-17 P.39
76-1606	B707 21436	83-0078	DC-10 48219	(86-8900)	B747 23825	96-0008	C-17 P.40
76-1607	B707 21437	83-0079	DC-10 48220	87-0025	C-17 T.1	96-0042	B707 20319
77-0351	B707 21551	83-0080	DC-10 48221	87-0027	C-5 500-0113	96-0043	B707 20316
77-0352	B707 21552	83-0081	DC-10 48222	87-0028	C-5 500-0114	97-0041	C-17 P.41
77-0353	B707 21553	83-0082	DC-10 48223	87-0029	C-5 500-0115	97-0042	C-17 P.42
77-0354	B707 21554	83-0510	B707 23428	87-0030	C-5 500-0116	97-0043	C-17 P.43
77-0355	B707 21555	83-0511	B707 23429	87-0031	C-5 500-0117	97-0044	C-17 P.44
77-0356	B707 21556	83-1285	C-5 500-0082	87-0032	C-5 500-0118	97-0045	C-17 P.45
78-0576	B707 21752	83-4610	B727 18811	87-0033	C-5 500-0119	97-0046	C-17 P.46
78-0577	B707 21753	83-4612	B727 18813	87-0034	C-5 500-0120	97-0047	C-17 P.47
78-0578	B707 21754	83-4615	B727 18816	87-0035	C-5 500-0121	97-0048	C-17 P.48
79-0001	B707 21755	83-4616	B727 18817	87-0036	C-5 500-0122	97-0100	B707 19986
79-0002	B707 21756	83-4618	B727 21946	87-0037	C-5 500-0123	97-0200	B707 20317
79-0003	B707 21757	84-0059	C-5 500-0083	87-0038	C-5 500-0124	97-0201	B707 20318
79-0433	DC-10 48200	84-0060	C-5 500-0084	87-0039	C-5 500-0125	98-0001	B757 29025
79-0434	DC-10 48201	84-0061	C-5 500-0085	87-0040	C-5 500-0126	98-0002	B757 29026
79-0442	B707 22855	84-0062	C-5 500-0086	87-0041	C-5 500-0127	98-0049	C-17 P.49
79-0443	B707 22838	84-0185	DC-10 48224	87-0042	C-5 500-0128	98-0050	C-17 P.50
79-0444	B707 22839	84-0186	DC-10 48225	87-0043	C-5 500-0129	98-0051	C-17 P.51
79-0445	B707 22840	84-0187	DC-10 48226	87-0044	C-5 500-0130	98-0052	C-17 P.52
79-0446	B707 22841	84-0188	DC-10 48227	87-0045	C-5 500-0131	98-0053	C-17 P.53
79-0447	B707 22842	84-0189	DC-10 48228	87-0117	DC-10 48303	98-0054	C-17 P.54
79-0448	B707 22843	84-0190	DC-10 48229	87-0118	DC-10 48304	98-0055	C-17 P.55
79-0449	B707 22844	84-0191	DC-10 48230	87-0119	DC-10 48305	98-0056	C-17 P.56
79-0450	B707 22845	84-0192	DC-10 48231	87-0120	DC-10 48306	98-0057	C-17 P.57
79-0451	B707 22846	84-0193	B727 18362	87-0121	DC-10 48307	99-0003	B757 29027
79-0452	B707 22847	84-1398	B707 18713	87-0122	DC-10 48308	99-0004	B757 29028
79-0453	B707 22848	84-1399	B707 19566	87-0123	DC-10 48309	99-0006	B707 19998
79-0454	B707 22849	85-0001	C-5 500-0087	87-0124	DC-10 48310	99-0058	C-17 P.58
79-0455	B707 22850	85-0002	C-5 500-0088	88-0265	C-17 P.1	99-0059	C-17 P.59
79-0456	B707 22851	85-0003	C-5 500-0089	88-0266	C-17 P.2	99-0060	C-17 P.60
79-0457	B707 22852	85-0004	C-5 500-0090	88-0322	B707 24503	99-0061	C-17 P.61
79-0458	B707 22853	85-0005	C-5 500-0091	89-1189	C-17 P.3	99-0062	C-17 P.62
79-0459	B707 22854	85-0006	C-5 500-0092	89-1190	C-17 P.4	99-0063	C-17 P.63
79-1710	DC-10 48202	85-0007	C-5 500-0093	89-1191	C-17 P.5	99-0064	C-17 P.64
79-1711	DC-10 48203	85-0008	C-5 500-0094	89-1192	C-17 P.6	(99-0065)	C-17 P.65
79-1712	DC-10 48204	85-0009	C-5 500-0095	90-0175	B707 19621	(99-0066)	C-17 P.66
79-1713	DC-10 48205	85-0010	C-5 500-0096	90-0532	C-17 P.7	(99-0067)	C-17 P.67
79-1946	DC-10 48206	85-0027	DC-10 48232	90-0533	C-17 P.8	(99-0068)	C-17 P.68
79-1947	DC-10 48207	85-0028	DC-10 48233	90-0534	C-17 P.9	(99-0069)	C-17 P.69
79-1948	DC-10 48208	85-0029	DC-10 48234	90-0535	C-17 P.10	(99-0070)	C-17 P.70
79-1949	DC-10 48209	85-0030	DC-10 48235	92-0284	B707 19293	99-0165	C-17 P.65
79-1950	DC-10 48210	85-0031	DC-10 48236	92-3289	B707 19622	99-0166	C-17 P.66
79-1951	DC-10 48211	85-0032	DC-10 48237	92-3290	B707 19295	99-0167	C-17 P.67
80-0137	B707 22829	85-0033	DC-10 48238	92-3291	C-17 P.11	99-0168	C-17 P.68
80-0138	B707 22830	85-0034	DC-10 48239	92-3292	C-17 P.12	99-0169	C-17 P.69
80-0139	B707 22831	85-6973	B707 20043	92-3293	C-17 P.13	99-0170	C-17 P.70
81-0004	B707 22832	85-6974	B707 20297	92-3294	C-17 P.14	"99-0910"	DC-10 46524
81-0005	B707 22833	86-0011	C-5 500-0097	92-9000	B747 23825	99-6143	B757 25494
81-0891	B707 19518	86-0012	C-5 500-0098	(93-0011)	B707 18949		
81-0892	B707 19382	86-0013	C-5 500-0099	93-0597	B707 19294		
81-0893	B707 19384	86-0014	C-5 500-0100	93-0599	C-17 P.15	00-0001	B747 30201
81-0894	B707 19583	86-0015	C-5 500-0101	93-0600	C-17 P.16	00-0171	C-17 P.71
81-0895	B707 19381	86-0016	C-5 500-0102	93-0601	C-17 P.17	00-0172	C-17 P.72
81-0896	B707 19581	86-0017	C-5 500-0103	93-0602	C-17 P.18	00-0173	C-17 P.73
(81-0897)	B707 19236	86-0018	C-5 500-0104	93-0603	C-17 P.19	00-0174	C-17 P.74
81-0898	B707 19380	86-0019	C-5 500-0105	93-0604	C-17 P.20	00-0175	C-17 P.75
82-0006	B707 22834	86-0020	C-5 500-0106	93-1097	B707 19296	00-0176	C-17 P.76
82-0007	B707 22835	86-0021	C-5 500-0107	94-0065	C-17 P.21	00-0177	C-17 P.77
82-0066	B707 23417	86-0022	C-5 500-0108	94-0066	C-17 P.22	00-0178	C-17 P.78
82-0067	B707 23418	86-0023	C-5 500-0109	94-0067	C-17 P.23	00-0179	C-17 P.79
82-0068	B707 23419	86-0024	C-5 500-0110	94-0068	C-17 P.24	00-0180	C-17 P.80

00-0181	C-17	P.81
00-0182	C-17	P.82
00-0183	C-17	P.83
00-0184	C-17	P.84
00-0185	C-17	P.85
00-0201	C-17	UK.1
00-0202	C-17	UK.2
00-0203	C-17	UK.3
00-0204	C-17	UK.4
00-2000	B707	20043
00-9001	B757	25494
(01-0005)	737NG	33080
01-0015	737NG	32916
01-0040	737NG	29971
01-0041	737NG	33080
01-0186	C-17	P.86
01-0187	C-17	P.87
01-0188	C-17	P.88
01-0189	C-17	P.89
01-0190	C-17	P.90
01-0191	C-17	P.91
01-0192	C-17	P.92
01-0193	C-17	P.93
01-0194	C-17	P.94
01-0195	C-17	P.95
01-0196	C-17	P.96
01-0197	C-17	P.97
02-0042	737NG	33500
02-0201	737NG	30755
02-0202	737NG	30753
02-0203	737NG	33434
02-1098	C-17	P.98
02-1099	C-17	P.99
02-1100	C-17	P.100
02-1101	C-17	P.101
02-1102	C-17	P.102
02-1103	C-17	P.103
02-1104	C-17	P.104
02-1105	C-17	P.105
02-1106	C-17	P.106
02-1107	C-17	P.107
02-1108	C-17	P.108
02-1109	C-17	P.109
02-1110	C-17	P.110
02-1111	C-17	P.111
02-1112	C-17	P.112
02-4452	B757	25493
02-5001	B757	25494
03-3113	C-17	P.113
03-3114	C-17	P.114
03-3115	C-17	P.115
03-3116	C-17	P.116
03-3117	C-17	P.117
03-3118	C-17	P.118
03-3119	C-17	P.119
03-3120	C-17	P.120
03-3121	C-17	P.121
03-3122	C-17	P.122
03-3123	C-17	P.123
03-3124	C-17	P.124
03-3125	C-17	P.125
03-3126	C-17	P.126
03-3127	C-17	P.127
04-4128	C-17	P.128
04-4129	C-17	P.129
04-4130	C-17	P.130
04-4131	C-17	P.131
04-4132	C-17	P.132
04-4133	C-17	P.133
04-4134	C-17	P.134
04-4135	C-17	P.135
04-4136	C-17	P.136
04-4137	C-17	P.137
04-4138	C-17	P.138
(04-4139)	C-17	P.139
05-0730	737NG	34807
05-0932	737NG	34808
05-5139	C-17	P.139
05-5140	C-17	P.140
05-5141	C-17	P.141

05-5142	C-17	P.142
05-5143	C-17	P.143
05-5144	C-17	P.144
05-5145	C-17	P.145
05-5146	C-17	P.146
05-5147	C-17	P.147
05-5148	C-17	P.148
05-5149	C-17	P.149
05-5150	C-17	P.150
05-5151	C-17	P.151
05-5152	C-17	P.152
05-5153	C-17	P.153
06-0206	C-17	F.166/AUS1
06-6154	C-17	P.154
06-6155	C-17	P.155
06-6156	C-17	P.156
06-6157	C-17	P.157
06-6158	C-17	P.158
06-6159	C-17	P.159
06-6160	C-17	P.160
06-6161	C-17	P.161
06-6162	C-17	P.162
06-6163	C-17	P.163
06-6164	C-17	P.164
06-6165	C-17	P.165
06-6166	C-17	P.166
06-6167	C-17	P.167
06-6168	C-17	P.168
07-207	C-17	F.167/AUS2
07-7169	C-17	P.169
07-7170	C-17	P.170
07-7171	C-17	P.171
07-7172	C-17	P.172
07-7173	C-17	P.173
07-7174	C-17	P.174
07-7175	C-17	P.175
07-7176	C-17	P.176
07-7177	C-17	P.177
07-7178	C-17	P.178
07-7179	C-17	P.179
07-7180	C-17	P.180

Navy/Marines

159113	DC-9	47577
159114	DC-9	47584
159115	DC-9	47587
159116	DC-9	47580
159117	DC-9	47581
159118	DC-9	47585
159119	DC-9	47578
159120	DC-9	47586
160046	DC-9	47684
160047	DC-9	47687
160048	DC-9	47681
160049	DC-9	47698
160050	DC-9	47699
160051	DC-9	47700
160749	DC-9	47691
160750	DC-9	47690
161266	DC-9	48137
161529	DC-9	48165
161530	DC-9	48166
161572	CV880	22-7-3-55
162390	DC-9	47003
162391	DC-9	47004
162392	DC-9	47065
162393	DC-9	47325
162753	DC-9	47410
162754	DC-9	47476
162754	DC-9	47476
162782	B707	23430
162783	B707	23889
162784	B707	23890
163036	DC-9	47041
163037	DC-9	47221
163050	DC-8	45881
163208	DC-9	47639
163511	DC-9	47431
163512	DC-9	47474

163513	DC-9	47477
163918	B707	23891
163919	B707	23892
163920	B707	23893
164386	B707	23894
164387	B707	24500
164388	B707	24501
164404	B707	24502
164405	B707	24504
164406	B707	24505
164407	B707	24506
164408	B707	24507
164409	B707	24508
164410	B707	24509
164605	DC-9	47545
164606	DC-9	47496
164607	DC-9	47428
164608	DC-9	47565
165342	B707	18961
165343	B707	18962
165829	737NG	29979
165830	737NG	29980
165831	737NG	30200
165832	737NG	30781
165833	737NG	32597
165834	737NG	32598
165835	737NG	33826
165836	737NG	33836
166693	737NG	34304
177701	C-17	F.168/CA.1
553134	KC135	17250
563596	KC135	17345

Venezuela

0001	A319	1468
0001	B737	21167
0003	DC-9	47000
6944	B707	19760
8747	B707	18950
YV-03	DC-9	47000

Yugoslavia

73-601	B707	19177
7601	SE210	241
14301	B727	21080
14302	B727	21040
71501	YAK40	9120717
71502	YAK40	9120817
71504	YAK40	9231523
71505	YAK40	9630849
71506	YAK40	9731255
74101	SE210	241
74301	B727	21080
74302	B727	21040

Zaire

9T-MSS	B707	19969
9T-TDA	DC-8	45753

Zambia

AF605	YAK40	9532042
AF606	YAK40	9530843

Aircraft Codes
(Soviet Types)

1	AN7x	76092850
01 blue	AN7x	47098946
01 blue	TU134	60650
01 red	AN7x	76092850
01 red	AN7x	?

01 red	IL76	1003401024
01 red	TU124	?
01 red	TU134	0350001
01 red	TU134	60650
01 red	TU134	63550705
01 red	TU134	7350203
01 yellow	TU134	63957
2	AN7x	72090805
2	AN7x	72096912
2	AN7x	76092859
2	AN7x	76095899
02 black	AN7x	?
02 blue	TU134	62732
02 green	TU134	?
02 red	AN7x	76060645
02 red	AN7x	?
02 red	TU134	62732
02 red	TU134	64020
02 red	TU134	64140
002 black	AN7x	?
03 black	AN7x	?
03 blue	AN7x	?
03 blue	TU104	86601303
03 blue	TU134	63620
03 red	AN7x	72060610
03 red	AN7x	?
03 red	TU134	63620
03 red	TU134	?
03 yellow	TU134	63982
4	AN7x	76090808
04 black	TU134	?
04 Blue	AN7x	76090808
04 red	AN7x	?
05 red	IL76	1073423789
05 red	TU104	8350702
05 red	TU134	63875
05 red	TU134	63976
05 red	YAK40	9041015
06 red	IL76	?
06 yellow	AN7x	006
07 blue	TU134	73550795
07 red	AN7x	?
08 black	AN124	977305451600
08 red	TU124	3350004
08 red	TU134	?
09 black	AN124	977305495507
09 blue	AN7x	72093875
10 black	AN124	19530502127
10 black	TU134	63961
10 blue?	TU134	63961
10 red	IL76	0013430875
10 red	IL76	073409243
10 red	TU134	3350303
10 red	TU134	?
11	AN7x	72010949
11 red	AN7x	72010905
11 red	AN7x	72010949
11 red	TU124	3350103
11 red	TU134	64010
11 red	TU134	64148
11 red	TU134	64245
12 blue	TU134	64258
12 red	TU134	93551030
15 blue	AN7x	72092858
15 blue	AN7x	?
15 blue	TU124	?
15 red	IL76	073410311
15 red	TU134	64270
15 red	TU134	?
16 blue	AN7x	76096926
16 red	TU134	64073
16 red	TU134	?
17 blue	AN7x	76097927
17 blue	AN7x	?
17 red	TU134	64753
17 red	TU134	64753
18 blue	TU134	64800
18 red	TU134	64800
19 red	TU134	?

20 red	TU134	?
21	AN7x	72093868
21	TU124	1350303
21 black	AN124	977305283205
21 blue	TU134	64630
21 blue	TU134	93555016
21 red	IL76	043402041
21 red	TU134	64035
21 red	TU134	?
21 red?	TU134	64325
22	AN7x	76091825
22?	AN7x	76091830
22 blue	AN7x	76091825
22 red	TU134	64640
22 red	TU134	?
23 blue	TU134	?
23 red	TU134	64065
23 red	TU134	64350
24?	AN7x	72060610
24 blue	AN7x	76091830
24 red	TU134	?
25 red	TU134	13.63761
25 red	TU134	?
26	AN7x	76091827
26 red	TU134	64392
27 blue	AN7x	?
27 red	TU134	64400
27 red	TU134	?
28 red	TU134	?
28 yellow	TU124	7350606
30 blue	IL76	0093498959
30 red	IL76	0023436059
30 red	TU134	03551127
30 red	TU134	64845
31 blue	IL76	1003402040
31 blue	TU134	?
31 blue?	TU134	3350305
31 red	IL76	0053459777
31 red	TU134	93551050
31 red	TU134	?
32 blue	IL76	1003403068
32 red	IL76	0063466979
32 red	TU124	7350601
32 red	TU154	71A-015
33 blue	IL76	1013403097
33 red	IL76	0043454618
33 red	TU134	?
34 blue	IL76	1013404138
34 blue	TU134	83550970
34 red	IL76	0043449460
34 red	TU134	64182
34 red	TU134	?
35 blue	AN7x	?
35 blue	IL76	0043453559
35 blue	IL76	1013405188
35 red	IL76	0063473178
35 red?	TU134	63775
36 blue	IL76	1013405197
36 red	IL76	0073475260
36 red	TU134	?
37 red	IL76	0083476298
37 red	TU134	?
38 blue	TU134	83550968
38 red	IL76	0033447379
39 red	IL76	0053452537
39 red	TU134	?
40 blue	TU134	93550983
40 red	IL76	0073481457
40 red	TU124	?
40 red	TU134	63551120
40 Red	TU134	64820
041	YAK40	9541843
41 red	IL76	0083483499
41 red	TU134	?
042	YAK40	9541943
42 red	IL76	0093484538
42 red	TU134	64670
42 red	TU134	?
043	YAK40	9542043
43 blue	TU134	64152
43 red	IL76	0093479377
43 red	TU134	64678
43 red	TU134	?
44 red	IL76	0093486579
44 red	TU134	?
45 blue	TU124	?
45 red	IL76	0093493818
45 red	TU134	64700
45 red	TU134	?
46 red	IL76	0033443258
46 red	IL76	0053451498
46 red	TU134	?
47 red	IL76	0043453577
47 red	TU104	8350704
47 red	TU134	?
48 red	IL76	0063458738
48 red	TU104	86601302
48 red	TU134	64830
49	IL76	0063469057
50	TU124	4351601
50 black	TU124	3350603
50 blue	IL76	1003403079
50 blue	TU134	63979
50 red	IL76	1003496899
51 blue	IL76	1003403106
51 blue	TU134	3350305
51 red	IL76	1003488634
52	TU124	?
52 blue	IL76	1003403119
52 red	IL76	1013491739
52 red	TU134	93550999
53	IL76	0093497940
53 blue	IL76	1013407227
53 blue	TU124	?
53 red	TU124	5350402
55 blue	TU124	?
55 yellow	TU124	5350303
57	TU134	64775
57 red	TU134	73550752
59 red	AN7x	?
59 yellow	AN7x	?
60 blue	AN7x	?
63 blue	TU134	2350104
70	AN7x	72093872
70 red	AN7x	72093872
71 blue	TU134	?
72 blue	AN7x	?
72 red	TU134	64728
74 blue	TU134	53550550
74 blue	TU134	?
76 blue	TU134	3350302
77 blue	TU134	3350304
78 blue	TU134	3350401
80 blue	TU124	0350001
80 red	TU134	?
82 red	TU134	53550650
84 red	TU134	63550720
86 blue	TU134	53550580
87 blue	TU134	3350403
92 red	TU134	2350203
100 blue	TU134	?
100 red	TU134	?
101	TU154	90A-837
101 blue	TU134	63900
101 blue	TU134	?
0101 red	AN7x	72030470
121 blue	TU134	64121
602 black	IL76	033402031
616 black	IL76	063407185
626 black	IL76	063405135
629 black	IL76	063406148
632 black	IL76	073409251
634 black	IL76	063408214
635 black	IL76	063408217
644 black	IL76	043402046
645 black	IL76	043402049
680 black	TU134	49020
681 black	TU134	49760
713 Black	IL76	043403061
716 black	IL76	063406156
719 Black	IL76	073409263
722 black	IL76	073410276
725 black	IL76	073410285
728 black	IL76	073410322
762	IL76	0093486579
811 black	IL76	053404098
819 black	IL76	063407199
948	AN7x	72091815
949	AN7x	72091818
950	AN7x	72091819
976	AN7x	72094884
978	AN7x	72091815
993 black	TU134	63860
2323 blue	AN7x	72090810
5600 black	TU110	?
5812	IL76	?
5858 blue	AN7x	76094885
5959 blue	AN7x	76095895
06207	IL76	1013406207

HAVE YOU SEEN AIR-BRITAIN'S MAJOR AIRLINER TITLES?

DC-1, DC-2, DC-3
The First Seventy Years
by Jennifer Gradidge

This 2-volume A4 hardback is the ultimate history of this famous aircraft. It covers the development and operators of civil and military versions of the type worldwide, followed by the known histories of almost 11,000 individual examples built in the USA. In addition there are sections on Russian and Japanese production, turbo conversions and an invaluable cross-reference index. At 744 pages it contains some 140 colour photos and extensive black & white coverage.

ISBN: 0 85130 332 3
Air-Britain Members: £42.50; Non-Members: £63.75

THE LOCKHEED CONSTELLATION
by Peter J Marson

Fully updated A4 hardback now in 2 volumes with 560 pages, over 100 colour photos, nearly 70 colour line drawings and 500-plus black & white illustrations including advertising, timetables and other memorabilia. Full development and operational history of all civil and military versions of the Constellation series with detailed histories of all the 856 examples built.

ISBN: 9 780851 303666
Air-Britain Members: £29.95; Non-Members: £44.95

ALSO STILL AVAILABLE:

THE DH.106 COMET - An Illustrated History   368-page A4 extensively illustrated definitive history of the type. (Members £29.50, Non-Members £37.00)
SWINGTAIL - THE CL44 STORY   240 page A4 detailed history of the type and its operators worldwide. (Members £24.95, Non-Members £37.50)
THE CONVAIRLINERS STORY   Full histories of the civil and military versions of all the Convair propliners, 336 pages A4. (Members £22.50, Non-Members £27.00)

Air-Britain Sales - see page 943 for details.
Massive discounts for members on all Air-Britain books - see page 944.

AIR-BRITAIN'S ANNUALS -
STANDARD REFERENCES AND QR POCKET BOOKS

AIRLINE FLEETS and AFQR -
Market leaders for current fleets

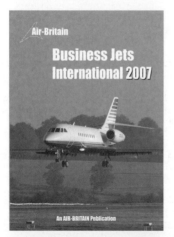

BJI - Complete production;
BizQR - All current registrations

Current UK Civil Registers - and
much more

For more details of these and other annual publications see opposite page

AIR-BRITAIN SALES

Companion volumes to this publication are also available by post-free mail order from

Air-Britain Sales Department (Dept JET07)
41 Penshurst Road, Leigh,
Tonbridge, Kent TN11 8HL

For a full list of current titles and details of how to order, visit our e-commerce site at www.air-britain.com
Visa / Mastercard / Delta / Switch accepted - please give full details of card number and expiry date.

ANNUAL PUBLICATIONS - 2007 NOW AVAILABLE, 2008 IN PREPARATION

AIRLINE FLEETS 2007   £19.00 (Members) £25.00 (Non-members)
Almost 3000 fleets listed by country with registrations, c/ns, line numbers, fleet numbers and names, plus numerous appendices including airliners in non-airline service, IATA and ICAO airline and base codes, operator index, etc. Now 792 pages A5 size hardback.

AIRLINE FLEETS QUICK REFERENCE 2007 £6.95 (Members) £7.95 (Non-members)
Pocket guide now includes airliners of over 19 seats of all major operators likely to be seen worldwide; regn, type, c/n, fleet numbers. Listed by country and airline. A5 size, 224 pages.

UK/IRELAND CIVIL REGISTERS 2007 £19.00 (Members) £25.00 (Non-members)
The 43rd annual edition of our longest-running title lists all current G- and EI- allocations, plus overseas-registered aircraft based in the UK, alphabetical index by type, military-civil marks de-code, full BGA and microlight details, museum aircraft etc. At around 600 pages this is the UK civil aircraft register bible.

UK and IRELAND QUICK REFERENCE 2007   £6.95 (Members) £7.95 (Non-members)
Basic easy-to-carry current registration and type listing, foreign aircraft based in UK and Ireland, current military serials of both countries, aircraft museums and base index. A5 size, 160 pages.

BUSINESS JETS & TURBOPROPS QUICK REFERENCE 2007   £6.95 (Members) £7.95 (Non-members)
Now expanded to include all purpose-built business jets and business turboprops, in both civil and military use, in registration or serial order by country. Easy-to-carry A5 size, 144 pages.

BUSINESS JETS INTERNATIONAL 2007   £18.00 (Members) £23.00 (Non-members)
Complete production listings of all business jet types in c/n order, giving full identities, fates and a comprehensive cross-reference index containing over 50,000 registrations. Available in hardback at approx 480 pages.

EUROPEAN REGISTERS HANDBOOK 2007   £21.00 (Members) £28.00 (Non-members)
Current civil registers of 42 European countries, all powered aircraft, balloons, gliders, microlights. Full previous identities and many extra permit and reservation details. Now in A4 softback format, 656 pages.

EUROPEAN REGISTERS QUICK REFERENCE 2007 £6.95 (Members) £7.95 (Non-members)
Contains the current civil and military listings of France, Switzerland, Austria and Monaco, including balloons, ulms and gliders in registration/type Quick-Reference A5 size softback format. Ideal for touring! ERQR 2006 covering Germany and the Benelux countries is still available at £5.95/£6.95.

MANY OTHER CIVIL and MILITARY AIRCRAFT PUBLICATIONS ARE AVAILABLE NOW, INCLUDING:

AVIATION MUSEUMS AND COLLECTIONS OF MAINLAND EUROPE £22.50 (Members) £28.00 (Non-members)
Revised and expanded with full details of location, detailed listings of exhibits, many photographs including colour sections and maps. 608 pages A5 hardback.

AVIATION MUSEUMS AND COLLECTIONS OF NORTH AMERICA £22.50 (Members) £28.00 (Non-members)
Companion volume to the above, includes 1,043 museums and collections in the USA and Canada. 640 pages A5 hardback with over 1200 illustrations.

Air-Britain also publishes a comprehensive range of military titles, please check for latest details of RAF Serial Registers, detailed RAF aircraft type "Files", Squadron Histories and Royal Navy Aircraft Histories.

IMPORTANT NOTE – Members receive substantial discounts on prices of all the above Air-Britain publications.
For details of membership see the following page or visit our website at http://www.air-britain.co.uk

AIR-BRITAIN MEMBERSHIP

Join on-line at www.air-britain.co.uk

If you are not currently a member of Air-Britain, the publishers of this book, you may be interested in what we have on offer to provide for your interest in aviation.

About Air-Britain

Formed over 50 years ago, we are the world's most progressive aviation society, and exist to bring together aviation enthusiasts with every type of interest. Our members include aircraft historians, aviation writers, spotters and pilots – and those who just have a fascination with aircraft and aviation. Air-Britain is a non-profit organisation, which is independently audited, and any financial surpluses are used to provide services to the ever-growing membership. Our current membership now stands at around 4,000 some 700 of whom live overseas.

Membership of Air-Britain

Membership is open to all. A basic membership fee is charged and every member receives a copy of the quarterly house magazine, Air-Britain Aviation World, and is entitled to use all the Air-Britain specialist services and to buy **Air-Britain publications at discounted prices**. A membership subscription includes the choice to add any or all of our other 3 magazines, News and/or Archive and/or Aeromilitaria. Air-Britain publishes 10-20 books per annum (around 70 titles in stock at any one time). Membership runs January - December each year, but new members have a choice of options periods to get their initial subscription started.

Air-Britain Aviation World is the quarterly 48-page house magazine containing not only news of Air-Britain activities, but also a wealth of features, often illustrated in colour, on many different aviation subjects, contemporary and historical, contributed by our members.

Air-Britain News is the world aviation news monthly, containing data on Aircraft Registrations worldwide, and news of Airlines and Airliners, Business Jets, Local Airfield News, Civil and Military Air Show Reports and International Military Aviation. Each issue averages 160 pages of lavishly–illustrated information for the dedicated enthusiast.

Air-Britain Archive is the quarterly 48-page specialist journal of civil aviation history. Packed with the results of historical research by Air-Britain specialists into aircraft types, overseas registers and previously unpublished photographs and facts about the rich heritage of civil aviation. Around 100 photographs per issue, some in colour.

Air-Britain Aeromilitaria is the quarterly 48-page unique source for meticulously researched details of military aviation history edited by the acclaimed authors of Air-Britain's military monographs, featuring British, Commonwealth, European and U.S. Military aviation articles. Illustrated in colour and black and white.

Other Benefits

Additional to the above, members have exclusive access to the Air-Britain e-mail Information Exchange Service (ab-ix) where they can exchange information and solve each other's queries, and to an on-line UK airfield residents database. Other benefits include numerous Branches, use of the Specialists' Information Service; Air-Britain trips and access to black and white and colour photograph libraries. During the summer we also host our own popular FLY-IN. Each autumn we host an Aircraft Recognition Contest.

Membership Subscription Rates – from £18 per annum

Membership subscription rates start from as little as £18 per annum (2008), and this amount provides a copy of 'Air-Britain Aviation World' quarterly as well as all the other benefits covered above. Subscriptions to include any or all of our other three magazines vary between £25 and £62 per annum (slightly higher to overseas).

*****Join now for two years 2008-2009 and save £5.00 off the total*****

Join on-line at <u>www.air-britain.co.uk</u> or, write to 'Air-Britain' at 1 Rose Cottages, 179 Penn Road, Hazlemere, High Wycombe, Bucks HP15 7NE, UK, or telephone/fax on 01394 450767 (+44 1394 450767) and ask for a membership pack containing the full details of subscription rates, samples of our magazines and a book list.